# EVERYMAN'S
# ENCYCLOPAEDIA

## IN TWELVE VOLUMES

VOLUME FIVE
DENNIS–FILEY

# EVERYMAN'S ENCYCLOPAEDIA

## VOLUME FIVE

### NEW AND REVISED EDITION

NEW YORK
E. P. DUTTON AND CO. INC.

# DENNIS—FILEY

# LIST OF ABBREVIATIONS

ac., acres.
A.D., after Christ.
agric., agricultural.
ambas., ambassador.
ann., annual.
arron., arrondissement.
A.-S., Anglo-Saxon.
A.V., Authorised Version.
*b.*, born.
B.C., before Christ.
Biog. Dic., Biographical Dictionary.
bor., borough.
bp., birthplace.
C., Centigrade.
*c. (circa)*, about.
cap., capital.
*cf.*, compare.
co., county.
com., commune.
cub. ft., cubic feet.
*d.*, died.
Dan., Danish.
dept., department.
dist., district.
div., division.
E., east ; eastern.
eccles., ecclesiastical.
ed., edition ; edited.
*e.g.*, for example.
Ency. Brit., Encyclopædia Britannica.
Eng., English.
estab., established.
*et seq.*, and the following.
F., Fahrenheit.
*fl.*, flourished.
fort. tn., fortified town.
Fr., French.
ft., feet.
Ger., German.
Gk., Greek.
gov., government.
Heb., Hebrew.
Hist., History.

*i.e.*, that is.
in., inches.
inhab., inhabitants.
Is., island, -s.
It., Italian.
Jour., journal.
Lat., Latin.
lat., latitude.
l. b., left bank.
long., longitude.
m., miles.
manuf., manufacture.
mrkt. tn., market town.
Mt., mts., mount, mountain, -s.
N., north ; northern.
N.T., New Testament.
O.T., Old Testament.
par., parish.
parl., parliamentary.
pop., population.
prin., principal.
prov., province.
pub., published.
*q.v.*, which see.
R., riv., river.
r. b., right bank.
Rom., Roman.
R.V., Revised Version.
S., south ; southern.
sev., several.
Sp., Spanish.
sp. gr., specific gravity.
sq. m., square miles.
temp., temperature.
ter., territory.
tn., town.
trans., translated.
trib., tributary.
U.S.A., United States of America.
vil., village.
vol., volume.
W., west ; western.
yds., yards.

# ENCYCLOPAEDIA

## D

**Dennis, Alfred L. P.,** b. May 21, 1874, in Beirut, Syria, where his parents, who were Americans, were temporarily sojourning. He graduated from Princeton, and afterwards studied at Columbia, Harvard and Heidelberg universities. He was Professor of History at Bowdoin College, 1901–4, and Associate Professor of History at the University of Chicago, 1904–5. He lectured on history at Harvard in 1905–6 and was Professor of History at the University of Wisconsin from 1906 to 1920, when he resigned to engage in research work. After the entrance of the U.S.A. in the Great War, he became a Captain on the Military Intelligence staff in 1918, and in the following year was Assistant Military Attaché at the American Embassy in London, afterwards reporting for duty with the Peace Conference in Versailles in 1919. Since 1923 he has been Professor of History and International Relations at Clark University. Among his books are: *Eastern Problems at the close of the Eighteenth Century,* 1900; *Anglo-Japanese Alliance,* 1923; *Foreign Policies of Soviet Russia,* 1924. His *Adventures in American Diplomacy,* published in 1928, covers the dramatic decade 1896–1906—one of the most perilous periods of American diplomacy. The author, with the aid of hitherto largely-unpublished State documents and private papers of Roosevelt, Olney, Hay, Root and other statesmen, here gives the inside story of the period when America was first called upon to aid in the solution of world questions.

**Dennis, John** (1657–1734), was the son of a saddler of London, where he was born. He was educated at Harrow and at Cambridge. He lived the improvident life of a literary adventurer, and was a political writer, a poet, a dramatist, and a critic. It is as the last he is principally known, not from his own works, but from having been preserved in the amber of Pope's *Essay on Criticism,* and *The Dunciad.*

**Denny,** a tn. of Scotland in the co. of Stirling, situated on the Carron. Iron and coal are obtained in the neighbourhood, and there are large foundries and iron-works, chemical works, and paper-mills. In the vicinity are the ruins of Torwood Castle and also of Herbertshire Castle, which was destroyed by fire in 1914, the Lady's Leap and Carron Glen The banks of the Carron were the scene of many of the most stirring and heroic deeds recorded in Scottish history. Pop. 9187.

**Denominations, The Three,** was composed of the three D. of dissenters —Presbyterians, Baptists, and Independents—living in or near London. They had the privilege of presenting an address to the sovereign at certain times, and in 1727 ' the General Body of Protestant Dissenting Ministers of the Three Denominations ' was organised.

**Denon, Dominique Vivant, Baron** (1747–1825), a Fr. artist and politician who went to Naples as a diplomat, and while there studied art. After the Revolution he attached himself to Bonaparte and went on an expedition to Egypt. While there he collected the materials for his book, *Voyage dans la Basse et la Haute Egypte pendant les campagnes du Général Bonaparte,* 1802. He also wrote *Monument des arts du dessin recueillis par le Baron Denon,* published in 1829 after his death.

**Denotation,** *see* CONNOTATION.

**Density.** ' Absolute D.,' a term used in physics to express the quantity or mass of matter contained in any unit of volume. ' Relative D,' or ' specific gravity,' is the comparison of the mass of the substance concerned with the mass of the same volume of some standard matter, which for liquids or solids is generally taken as water at its temperature of maximum D. (4° C., 39 F.) and at ordinary pressure; for gases the standard is hydrogen at ordinary temperature and pressure. Since in the metric system, which is usually employed, the unit of mass is the weight of a cubic centimetre of water at 4° C., the relative D. is the same as the absolute D. Since, however, 'weight' is proportional to 'mass,' the 'weight' may be substituted for the 'mass' without causing any material difference. The least dense substance known is 'lithium' (0·59°) if the D. of water be called unity; the densest is 'iridium' (22·4°); the D. of hydrogen is 0·0009. *See* SPECIFIC GRAVITY.

**Dent, John Charles** (1841–87), Canadian journalist and writer on historical subjects. Born at Kendal, Westmorland, he was taken to Ontario by his parents in infancy and was there educated at the public schools. After studying law, he was called to the Bar in 1865 and practised for a short period. He returned to England and for about a year contributed to the *Daily Telegraph*, then continued his journalistic work, first in Boston, then in Toronto. His published works include : *The Canadian Portrait Gallery*, 4 vols., 1880–81 ; *The Last Forty Years : Canada since the Union of 1841*, 2 vols., 1881 ; (in collaboration with Henry Scadding) *Toronto: Past and Present*, 1884 ; *The Story of the Upper Canadian Rebellion*, 2 vols., 1885. *See also* John King's *The Other Side of the 'Story'* . . . *of the Rebellion*, 1886.

**Dent, Joseph Malaby** (1849–1926), *b.* Darlington. Publisher. After some early training as a bookbinder in his native town, he went to London in 1867, where he worked at his craft for several years before setting up his own workshop. A book-lover from the first, he began then to experiment in a small way as a book producer and publisher. Having established himself in offices and a bindery in Great Eastern Street (remote from the ordinary London publishers' purlieus), in 1888 he put forth, in a most attractive format, some notable editions of Elia's *Essays* and other authors. He had already formed a friendship with some of the Toynbee Hall residents, attended lectures at that Whitechapel ''varsity,' and made excursions to France and Italy with them, which widened his ideas as a projector of fine illustrated books. In his quest for art he was a shrewd discoverer of talent in young artists, among these being Aubrey Beardsley, R. Anning Bell, and Arthur Rackham. The *Temple Shakespeare* appeared in 1894 and *The Temple Classics* in 1896, both under the editorship of Israel Gollancz ; and they were followed by pocket editions of favourite authors, which quickly gained for him a reputation as a London publisher of the first rank. In all these ventures he was hampered by lack of capital, as related in his *Memoirs*, which tells a moving story of his years of struggle. In 1897 the business was transferred to 29/30 Bedford Street, Covent Garden, and in 1912 he built Aldine House on the opposite

J. M. DENT

side of the same street. In the former building he planned the scheme which finally developed into 'Everyman's Library' (*q.v.*), the story of which venture he has told in some detail in his *Memoirs*. His idea was to build up a great 'City of Books' on democratic popular lines, and he always kept in view the type of reader who, like himself, had to gain his literary knowledge and information by reading volume after volume as time allowed.

Always zealous in the cause of education, he also produced many series of educational books, *e.g.* Dent's *Modern Language Series*, edited by Prof. Ripman, *The King's Treasuries of Literature*, edited by

Sir Arthur Quiller Couch, etc., which have proved their value by their wide circulation throughout the schools of the Empire. The conception of *Everyman's Encyclopaedia* and its realisation in its original form were also due to his enterprise. Throughout his career publishers and book-lovers and the great reading public in America appreciated and supported his many and varied enterprises. In Canada, too, he formed a growing connection by his repeated visits, and in 1912 a branch Aldine House was opened at Toronto.

**Dentalium,** or **Elephant's Tusk Shell,** one of the three genera of molluscs which form the class Scaphopoda. The shell is tusk-shaped and open at both ends, from the larger of which the long foot appears and is used in creeping movements. The mollusc has tentacles around its mouth, is lacking in eyes and heart, and lives in muddy sand at great depths of the sea.

**Dental Surgeon,** see DENTISTRY.

**Dentatus, Lucius Sicinius,** was a Roman tribune in the year 454. He fought against the Æqui and the Sabines, in which contests he was famous, and he is said to have had great prowess in warfare, while tradition assigns to him an enormous number of battles and wounds. He was put to death by his own soldiers in 450.

**Dentatus, M. Curius,** a Roman consul. After having been tribune to the people he became consul in 290 B.C., and during this consulship he gained victories over the Samnites and the Sabines, and in 275, when he was consul for the second time, he defeated Pyrrhus. In 274 he became consul for the third time.

**Dent-du-Midi,** a mt. summit, belonging to the Swiss Alps. It is situated in the prov. of Valais, and attains a height of 10,696 ft.

**Dentine,** and **Dentition,** see TEETH.

**Dentistry,** a department of medical science which treats of the care of the mouth, particularly of the teeth. The practice of D. has developed apart from medical practice generally, but the tendency in recent years is towards treating it as a specialised branch of the medical profession, and medical education and legislation have been directed to that end. The work that falls to the dentist is mainly comprised under the heads of Dental Surgery, Mechanical Dentistry, and Dental Prophylaxis, or the general prevention of teeth diseases. Dental surgery includes all measures for the treatment of unsound teeth and the correction of deformities and irregularities of the teeth; mechanical D. deals with the manufacture and adjustment of artificial substitutes for teeth; while the dentist is also often called upon to treat neuralgic pains associated with the teeth, and to inspect and cleanse teeth as a routine precautionary measure.

The art of D. has been practised from very early times. Egyptian skulls have been found with artificial teeth made of bone or wood fastened to the jaw by thread or wires. Herodotus mentions D. as a profession as far back as 500 B.C. The earlier operations were probably confined to extractions and the provision of rude substitutes, but in the 10th century Abulcasis describes the repairing of teeth by attaching artificial crowns to neighbouring sound teeth. As early as the time of Haroun al-Raschid (800 B.C.), decayed teeth were filled with gold. In the eighteenth century John Hunter practised the operation of transplanting teeth with considerable success, and in France M. Fauchard introduced the manufacture of porcelain substitutes. In the nineteenth century progress in dental science is particularly associated with the names of Blake, Fox, and Bell in England; Fonzi, Cuvier and Bertin in France; while many able scientists and practitioners made their appearance in America. The growing knowledge of the physiological relationships of the teeth with the rest of the human frame caused the medical fraternity to attach more importance to D. Hitherto it had been looked upon as a matter calling for manual dexterity rather than any special knowledge, and the practice had often been relegated to barbers and other empirical professors. When the medical profession more thoroughly realised the importance of dental treatment, two branches of the profession came to be distinguished: the old practical manipulators, who relied upon their strength and skill, and transmitted their knowledge by an apprenticeship system, and those who were regarded as specialised medical practitioners and based their art upon a more orthodox scientific knowledge. The necessity for preventing quackery led to the formation of associations, partly for mutual protection and partly to direct dental education. In 1840 the American Society of Dental Surgeons was established, and this was followed by other societies and the establishment of training institutions. In 1878 the profession was regularised in England by an Act which established a register of dentists, the conditions for registration being put in the hands of the Medical Council. Under this Act unqualified persons representing themselves as 'dentists' were liable to a penalty of £20. Nevertheless, practitioners of varying expertness, but without the protective L.D.S. or equivalent diploma, still continued to flourish, often by elaborate advertisement. The position was regularised by the Act of 1921, according to which all persons practising dentistry have to be registered. Those without recognised qualifications may call themselves 'dentists,' but the term 'dental surgeon' is strictly reserved to those who possess an L.D.S. or are otherwise professionally qualified. This long overdue legislation has greatly improved the status

forward teeth to the proper line during childhood.

*Diseased teeth.*—One of the commonest ailments to which civilised mankind is subjected is *dental caries*. It has been established that the disease is due to the action of bacteria (e.g. *Bacillus acidophilus odontolyticus*) which find a lodgment in the interstices of teeth and on the particles of starchy and carbohydrate food left in the mouth after mastication. The bacteria set up fermentation of these food particles and produce lactic acid, which dissolves the calcium phosphate of the teeth, tending to

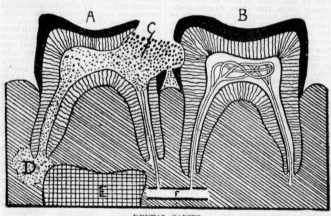

DENTAL CARIES

A, decayed tooth; B, tooth showing early decay (dentine laid bare near C; pulp healthy); C, fermenting food and germs (the pulp of A is infected, and a gum-boil is forming at D); E, germ of tooth of second set; F, artery in jaw.

of the profession. Registration is still supervised by the General Medical Council.

*Misplaced teeth.*—Considerable inconvenience may be suffered by the overlapping or other irregularity of healthy teeth. The abnormality of position results in imperfect or difficult mastication, renders proper cleaning impossible, and therefore opens the way to digestive and other disturbances. In some cases the best treatment is the removal of one of the back teeth, when the extra space will allow the others to take up their proper alignment. In other cases the best results are obtained by continuous pressure from rubber bands, springs, etc., while even such a simple device as sucking the thumb has proved effective in bringing

expose the softer portions of the tooth structure. Under ordinary circumstances, the exposure of the dental pulp leads to its disintegration, followed by the ultimate collapse of the tooth structure, and accompanied by inflammation and the characteristic pain of toothache. The measures taken by the dentist depend upon the extent of the disintegration, and the recent developments of his science tend to make preservation of the original structures the aim of treatment. Prevention is achieved by scrupulous cleanliness with regard to the teeth, but the dentist is usually only called in when the mischief has progressed to a considerable degree. A small operation called *scaling* is useful in preventing the accumulation of bacterial masses. This consists of removing the salivary calculus, or 'tartar,' by means of fine hooked instruments, by which the hardened deposits are loosened from the necks of the teeth.

*Filling.*—Where the tooth has been actually attacked, the operation aims at arresting the decay and repairing the structure by filling or stopping. The first part of the operation consists of excavating the decayed matter so as to leave a hole with healthy walls. This is effected by instruments of various patterns adapted for drilling, filing, etc., and frequently mounted upon a dental engine. This machine, which has manifold uses, is actuated either by foot-treadle or electric motor so as to give a rotary motion to the drills, brushes, and other instruments used; an excavating operation is by this means expeditiously and accurately carried out. The hole is then cleaned and dried, when it is ready for filling. The preservation of the soft dental pulp is effected by *capping*. This consists of treating the pulp with antiseptics and sedatives to allay irritation, and then fitting on a metal or celluloid cap lined with a sedative paste; the hole is then filled with cement and suitably covered. Where the pulp cannot easily be preserved, it is killed by removing it in sections or by treatment with arsenious acid. The cavity is then sterilised and filled. One of the oldest filling materials is gold, which was formerly forced in by hand pressure, but is now used in the form of foil which is first passed through a spirit flame to remove surface impurities and then hammered into place by blows from a mallet operated by the dental engine. Many other filling materials are used which are less expensive or less unsightly than gold. Amalgams of various composition, gutta-percha, and porcelain paste are commonly used. Porcelain has a good appearance for the outer part of a tooth, the filling being almost indistinguishable from the remainder of the tooth surface, after it has been polished by the dental engine. The operations of excavating and filling are facilitated by the use of a rubber dam, which prevents the salivary and other secretions from interfering with the operations.

*Extractions.*—The operation of extraction has been rendered safer by the introduction of new instruments and the increased knowledge of the anatomical relationships of the teeth. The well-equipped dentist has an instrument for every variety of tooth-form he is likely to meet with, and when the direction of the required movement is understood, no great force is necessary to remove the tooth. Extractions are rendered painless by the use of suitable anæsthetics. Nitrous oxide is that most commonly used, and is reliable and safe in its effects. It is usually supplied in the liquid form in cylinders, and is administered through a face-piece fitting over mouth and nostrils. A stop-cock enables oxygen to be administered as desired by the operator, so that no degree of asphyxiation need be present. Chloroform is used for longer operations, but is not so safe, and is followed by painful after-effects. Ether, administered by the open method, is much safer and in more general use to-day. In slight operations, spraying of ether or ethyl chloride is resorted to in order to numb the gum-tissues, but cocaine or eucaine injection is more largely practised. To localise the anæsthesia, admixture of a small quantity of adrenaline is made. Cocaine is effective in the majority of cases, but it has a poisonous effect and may lead to a sloughing of the poisoned tissues. In using cocaine, the dentist is always on guard against idiosyncratic reaction, which has on occasion proved fatal. To-day they are several synthetic substitutes equally effective and far less toxic.

*Artificial teeth.*—Single teeth are sometimes fitted on old stumps, or are fixed to neighbouring sound teeth by metal fastenings. Where a number of teeth have to be supplied, the dentist first makes a mould of the jaw and palate by fitting wax closely over it. From this a plaster model is made, from which two metallic dies are prepared, one made to fit into the other. A thin gold plate is then swaged between the male and female dies to the exact shape of the palate. To this base-plate porcelain teeth are fitted by means of platinum pins baked into the teeth and fused to gold stay-pieces, which in turn are fused to the base-plate. Where it is impossible to arrange for the support of the plate by fitting it to sound teeth, a vacuum chamber is made in the base-plate, which is exhausted by the wearer and serves to make the plate adhere to the palate. The use of vulcanised rubber has made the preparation of artificial sets easier and less expensive. A wax model is made of the jaw with the porcelain teeth fixed in position. The model is then enclosed in a plaster mould which is capable of being taken away in parts. While in the mould the wax is melted with boiling water and its place taken by the rubber prior to vulcanisation. After vulcanisation the teeth are firmly fixed and a proper adjustment can easily be made by a skilled operator.

Crown-work consists of capping the lower part of a tooth by a porcelain crown fixed by means of a platinum pin; sometimes a gold collar is used to effect the junction. A ' shell ' crown is prepared by fitting a gold cap filled with cement on the root end of a tooth. Bridge-work consists of supporting artificial crowns or ' dummies ' on neighbouring roots. The work requires exquisite accuracy of adjustment, but when well done is probably more efficient and less unsightly than any other method. Owing to the difficulty of making a fixed appliance cleanable and to the pathologist's distrust of devitalised teeth, bridge work is falling out of favour. The most important development in modern dental practice is undoubtedly the establishment of State interest and assistance in the problem of preserving the health of the nation's teeth. Dental officers have been appointed under the Ministry of Health, inspections of the teeth of children at elementary schools are carried out, and knowledge of oral hygiene has been widely disseminated. Useful work is also carried out by the various Infant Welfare Centres, and there is reason to hope that the general improvement of health consequent upon healthy teeth may soon be apparent to every member of the community. Parents in particular should all be made to realise that proper care of their children's teeth is a duty of primary importance. See C. N. Johnson, *Text-Book of Operative Dentistry* (2nd ed.), 1910; J. S. Marshall, *Principles and Practice of Operative Dentistry* (3rd ed.), 1909; H. H. Burchard, *Text-Book of Dental Pathology and Therapeutics* (3rd ed.), 1908.

**Denton:** (1) A suburb of Manchester, Lancashire, England. (2) Co. seat of D., co. Tex., N.W. of Dallas, raising cotton and grain and manufacturing pottery and bricks. The seat of the N. Texas College for women and of the College of Industrial Arts for women. Pop. 9587.

**D'Entrecasteaux,** a group of British is., situated in the Pacific Ocean, off the S.E. coast of New Guinea. They consist of three principal islands, separated by narrow channels, with a total area of 1083 sq. m. Their name is derived from the Fr. admiral, Bruni D'E.

**Denudation,** the wearing away of the surface of the earth, a process which is carried on by various agents. The effect of D. is seen in the various features of the earth's surface, as river valleys, gorges, and the shapes of cliffs and rocks. Water in various forms—rivers, streams, rain, frost, and glaciers—is the great cause of D., though some may be due to plants and animals. The rivers wear away their beds and make them wider with the continual flow of their water, and at the same time carry away particles of rock washed down by the rain or other agent, and so wear away the surface over which they flow, the amount of D. done by a river varying according to the region. Glaciers also are very powerful in this respect, owing to the debris which they carry along in their courses. Rain wears away the surface of the rocks considerably, both by actually beating on them and by chemical processes. Frost is instrumental in splitting the rocks to pieces, and in causing immense fissures in them, whereas the sea, with its continual action wears away the bases of cliffs, thus causing the overhanging rock to give way, and altering from time to time the shape of the coast-line. The general appearance of the land, therefore, is due to the various denuding agents in any particular locality, and although many hundreds of years may pass away before the change is perceptible, yet on examining the land it can be seen that it is always undergoing this D. *See* Lyell, *Principles of Geology.*

**Denver,** the cap. of Colorado, U.S.A., on the S. bank of S. Platte R., 15 m. from the E. base of the Rocky Mountains in a rolling plain. It is the largest city between the Missouri R. and the Pacific. The nearest large city to 20,000 square m. of gold and silver mines, and to 900,000 acres of oil shale, and the centre of what was once a waste, but is now a garden. Seventy-five years ago there were four people living on the site of D. To-day there are 287,861. Every street opens upon the mountains and every labourer can have his own garden. The city is the official gateway to twelve National Parks and thirty-two National Monuments. Among the peaks visible from D. are Pike's Peak, Mt. Evans, Gray's Peak, Long's Peak, and Torrey's Peak. The State Capitol of granite, with a dome covered with Colorado gold, cost 2½ million dollars. The State Historical Museum contains collections of relics of prehistoric, Indian and pioneering life. The City Park of 320 acres has a collection of Colorado animals, the University (with 3602 students) and the Carnegie Library (280,000 books). From a tower 330 ft. high on the Daniels and Fisher Store a bird's-eye view of D. can be obtained. It is 1 m. above the.

sea. The Union station was built in 1914. The municipal auditorium seats 12,000. The mint is one of the three coinage mints of the U.S.A. D. is a distributing centre of the automobile industry and has the largest cattle and sheep market in the W. The leading industries are meat-packing and mining machinery engineering. The pop. was 4759 in 1870, and 287,861 in 1930. In 1925 there were only sixteen days when no hours of sunshine were recorded.

**Denver and Rio Grande Railway.** This railway was built in 1871, and is one of the principal railways of the U.S.A., and the one to which Colorado owes a great deal of its progress in the past. This line, which is over 2500 m. long, crosses the Rocky Mts. and runs through some of the finest scenery in the U.S.A. Its route is S. between Denver and Española, which town is connected with Santa Fé by an extension of the line. At Ogden this railway joins the Union and Central, near Salt Lake City, thus forming a communication with Denver. There are also branches to Silverton and Durango, both in a W. direction.

**Deoband,** a tn. of India, in the United Provinces, with a celebrated Arab college, 45 m. N. of the city of Meerut. Pop. 18,000.

**Deodand** (*Deo* and *dandum*, to be given to God), the term used for anything which had caused the death of a human being, whether that death was brought about intentionally or accidentally, as by the law the thing was given over to the crown to be put to some good use, and thus ' given to God.' This practice was abolished in 1846.

**Deodar,** a native state of India, situated in Gujarat, Bombay. It has an area of about 440 sq. m., consisting of a hot sandy plain with no rivers. Pop. 19,700.

**Deodar,** or *Cedrus Deodara,* a species of Conifer, which occurs in the Himalayas. The plant is a beautiful evergreen tree, the leaves persisting for over a year, and the cone takes two or three years in ripening.

**Deodoriser** (Lat. *de,* away from ; *odor,* smell), a substance used for destroying harmful smells, chiefly those which arise from decomposing matter. Charcoal and quicklime are very powerful Ds. Disinfectants may be Ds. if they destroy smells as, for instance, zinc chloride.

**Deogarh,** a tn. of British India, in the presidency of Bengal, and the dist. of Sonthal Parganas. Twenty-two temples of Siva are found there ; it is a noted resort for pilgrims, and is on the E. India Railway. Pop. about 8500.

**Deols,** called also **Bourg-Dieu,** a tn. of France in the dept. of Indre, and lies N.E. of Châteauroux. It is noted for its mediæval abbey with its beautiful church now in ruins. Pop. 3040.

**Deoprayag,** *see* DEVAPRAYAGA.

**Deori,** a tn. of Sabbulpore dist., Central Provinces, British India. Pop. about 4000.

**Deoxidation,** *see* OXYGEN.

**Department** (Fr. *département*), a term used for a territorial division of France corresponding roughly to an Eng. county. Before the Revolution France was divided into thirty-four provinces, but in 1790 by a decree of the Assembly it was re-divided into eighty-three Ds. Under Napoleon the number was increased to 130, but in 1815 was reduced to eighty-six. They receive their names generally from a prominent river or mountain contained within their boundaries. Each D. is presided over by a prefect, and is divided into ' arrondissements,' each under a sub-prefect. The ' arrondissements ' are divided into ' cantons ' and the ' cantons ' into ' communes ' corresponding to an Eng. parish.

**Depauw University,** a co-educational institution of higher education founded by the Methodist Episcopal Church in 1837 in Greencastle, Indiana. As well as a college of liberal arts, there is a School of Music, and of military science and tactics. The courses include also, instruction in zoology, pedagogy, psychology, and comparative literature. There are some 1600 students. The Lucy Rowland Hall, a dormitory for women students, was opened in 1928.

**De Pere,** a city of Browne co., Wisconsin, U.S.A. It has foundries, machine shops and manufactures boats, paper, etc. Pop. 5521.

**Depew, Chauncey Mitchell** (1834–1928), a politician, attended Yale University, and was called to the Bar in 1858. His political career began in 1861 and in 1888, he was one of the candidates for the presidency. In 1899, and again from 1905 to 1911, he was U.S.A. senator (for New York). Besides being on six distinct occasions delegate at large to the National Republican Conventions to nominate the president, he was frequently chosen orator at centennial and other celebrations. Chairman of the board of directors for three railroads, including the New York Central and Hudson River Railroad Company.

**Depew,** a manufacturing village of Erie co., New York. Pop. 6536.

**Dephlegmator,** the section of a distilling apparatus which separates vapours of different boiling points the less volatile being condensed and returned to the still. The simplest form of D. is an elongated plain or bulbed tube emerging from the still in which condensation results from air-cooling, the surviving vapours roughly representing the more volatile constituents. The most effective D., however, consists of a column of bulbs so arranged that the condensed vapours are temporarily retained, while the vapours from the still pass through them. The result is that an exchange is continuously effected between the more volatile constituents of the condensed liquid and the less volatile constituents of the vapours arising from the still. If the heat is sufficiently regular, it is possible to tap distillates of different boiling points according to their distance from the source of heat. See S. Young, *Fractional Distillation*, 1903.

**Depilatories** (from Lat. *depilare*, ' to pull out the hair '), are chemical agents, such as calcium hydro-sulphide, or a mixture of pitch, resin, and lime, used for the removal of superfluous hair from the scalp, face, or other skin surface. Electrolysis is the modern and most effective D.

**Deploy,** a military expression, meaning literally ' to unfold.' A general is said to D. or spread out his troops when he so alters their formation as to present a wider front to the enemy, his object being to have as many weapons as possible on the front and fighting line.

**Deportation,** *see* TRANSPORTATION.

**Deportations (Belgium).** During the Great War one of Germany's measures which alienated much of the sympathetic feeling of certain neutrals towards her was her relapse to the barbaric practice of deporting the civil population of an enemy country occupied by the victor. This was carried out in Belgium, and the practice was adopted largely to secure what was in effect slave-labour. Not only the Belgian working class but even high officials suffered, *e.g.* the famous Burgomaster Max was deported to a Silesian fortress in September 1914. On Oct. 3, 1916, a decree was issued from German General Headquarters authorising Ger. military courts to deport, for the purpose of forced labour, any unemployed Belgians. The order raised a storm throughout many civilised countries, but it was put into execution, and thousands of men were compelled to work in Germany, thus releasing men for service in the field.

**Deposit,** in the law of bailments (borrowed from the Roman law), signifies a movable thing which a man puts in the hands of another to keep till it is asked back, nothing being given to the depositary for his custody of the thing. The benefit being entirely unilateral, the depositary is not liable for loss or deterioration, provided he is not guilty of dishonesty or gross negligence. If, however, he voluntarily undertook the custody of the thing, he would be answerable for loss or damage occasioned by merely slight neglect. Money is said to be on D. with a banker as opposed to money on current acount. The transaction is really a loan, repayable by the banker on demand with or without interest, according to agreement. In contracts for the sale of land D. means a sum customarily given in part-payment of the purchase-money as a guarantee of good faith.

**Deposition.** By the action of the various superficial or epigene agents of change (wind, sun, rain, running water, and frost), the rocks are disintegrated and the material is transported from place to place, finally forming the several deposits classified below. *Æolian deposits* are those deposits, showing no definite stratification, formed by the action of the wind. Examples of these are the sand dunes which occur on our coasts and the remarkable ' Loëss ' found in the valley of the Rhone and extending over the whole of Central Europe. *River deposits* occur in banks and terraces. The sediment carried by the river in suspension is laid down where the current is slackest along the river course. Thus, alluvial fans and cones are formed at the bases of hills where there is a sudden decrease in the gradient of the river. When a stream reaches a lake or the sea, its current is destroyed and the sediment in suspension is dropped, giving rise to deltas and ' lacustrine deposits.' The main types of river deposits are alluvial cones and fans, alluvial plains, deltas, and levees. *Glacial deposits* are occasionally of considerable thickness, as in terminal moraines (*see* GLACIERS). *Lacustrine deposits* may be mechanically formed, as when sediment is deposited from rivers, or may be chemically or organically formed. The chemically formed deposits are chiefly deposits of sodium chloride and carbonate and sulphate of lime, caused by supersaturation of the waters due to evaporation. The organically formed deposits are calcareous shells of freshwater molluscs, or may be the siliceous remains of diatomaceous plants. *Marine deposits* are of the greatest importance, and may be divided into two classes : (1) Shore or littoral deposits, and (2) deep sea deposits. The former consists of gravel, sand, or mud brought down by rivers or worn off the coasts by wave action, *i.e.* are made up of terrigenous or land derived material. The material brought down by rivers, if not directly deposited to form deltas, may be carried out and deposited on the sea bottom. The deposits thus formed may vary, alternately coarse and fine, according to the state of the river; but in the case of material formed by wave action, it is always arranged in order of coarseness, gravel nearest the coast, then sand, then fine mud and silt. These mechanical deposits are found fringing the land to a distance of from 100 to 200 m. out to sea, corresponding more or less with the 100 fathom submarine contour. On the outer edges of this fringe are found the blue, red, and green, and the volcanic muds. Beyond this depth we find the second class of marine deposits. These are chiefly organic, and are either calcareous or siliceous. The calcareous deposits are formed by the accumulation of coral polyps, giving rise to reefs and coral islands. The Globigerina ooze, which occurs throughout the Atlantic Ocean and in parts of the Indian and Pacific Oceans, consists of the calcareous shells of Foraminifera, which live at the surface of the water, but which after death sink and accumulate upon the ocean floor. Beyond a depth of about 2 m. this ooze is not found, since the shells are dissolved before they reach the bottom. On the ocean floor in the deeper parts, below 2½ m., are found the siliceous oozes, *i.e.* the radiolarian and diatomaceous oozes. The former is made up of the siliceous shells of Radiolaria, and is found in the E. Indian Ocean and in the Pacific. The latter, consisting of the siliceous frustules of diatoms, is found in a wide belt encircling the Southern Ocean. Red clay is a red-brown deposit, and consists of the insoluble residue of Foraminifera, manganese nodules, glauconite crystals, pumice, volcanic and meteoric dust, and phosphatic nodules. It is found in the deepest parts of the oceans below 2500 fathoms, and contains fossils such as the teeth of sharks and the ear bones of whales. The greater part of the floor of the Pacific Ocean is covered by the red clay, which is the most widely spread oceanic deposit. For classification of deep sea deposits see Sir John Murray's *Report of Challenger Expedition*, 1891.

**Deposition of Clergymen** is usually the result of immorality, matrimonial infidelity, or heresy. It involves the loss of benefice and Holy Orders, and is a weapon in the hands of the ecclesiastical courts of the Anglican and Scottish churches.

**Depositions.** In law Ds. are used to signify the written testimony of a witness in a judicial proceeding. Ds. before a magistrate are the sworn statements or affirmations of those who are cognisant of the facts relating to a crime for which some person has been arrested. These statements are committed by the magistrate's clerk to writing, and read over and signed by the witness making them and by the magistrate. Such Ds. are not evidence at the trial of the accused, but those of a witness who is dead or too ill to travel are evidence. Ds., whether in favour of or against the prisoner, may be taken before the committing magistrate in the presence of the prisoner and subsequently given in evidence at the trial. To perpetuate the testimony of persons whose death is apprehended, or who are dangerously ill, a magistrate has power to take their evidence down in writing and transmit it to the proper quarter to be read at the trial in the event of the deponent proving unable to appear. In all these cases the prisoner must be given an opportunity of cross-examining the deponent at the time the D. was taken. In civil courts, where the rule against hearsay evidence is much less strictly applied, Ds. were before the Judicature Acts the normal manner of producing evidence on the trial of a suit in Chancery. At the present day witnesses must be called, although affidavits are in constant use for the purpose of furnishing evidence upon minor issues of fact.

**Depot,** in the military sense, is the place where men, horses, and stores are mustered before distribution to the army, regiment, or corps which stands in need of them.

**Depreciation,** *see* BOOK-KEEPING.

**Depretis, Agostino** (1813–87), Italian statesman, early identified himself with the conspiracies of the followers of Mazzini, governor of Brescia in 1859, he accepted the following year the pro-dictatorship of Sicily, where his efforts to reconcile the divergent policies of Garibaldi and Cavour with regard to the political status of the island proved quite ineffectual. His premiership dates from 1881–87. Though his administration was marred by his 'transformist policy,' and his extravagance in finance, he was instrumental in enlarging the suffrage, creating the Triple Alliance, and removing the long-disputed grist tax.

**De Profundis** (Lat. 'Out of the depths'), the title and first words of Psalm cxxx., one of the seven penitential psalms. According to the Roman rite it forms part of the office for the burial of the dead.

**Deptford,** a metropolitan bor. of London, separated from Greenwich by the Ravensbourne, 3¾ m. E. of London Bridge. Part of St. Paul's parish lies in Surrey, whilst the whole of St. Nicholas' lies in Kent. The bor. consists only of the parish of Deptford St. Paul, that of Deptford St. Nicholas being included in Greenwich. Here are the Royal Victualling Yard, which supplies the Royal Navy, a hospital for master mariners and Goldsmiths' College. D. is a dist. of poor streets, but there is a park of eleven acres on the site of Sayes Court where Peter the Great stayed in 1698. D. is rich in historic memories. Here it was that Elizabeth knighted Drake on his return from his voyage round the world in the royal dockyard laid

AGOSTINO DEPRETIS

down by her father, and open until 1869. In a street brawl in D., Marlowe, the dramatist, met his death, and here lived Lord Howard, Evelyn, Admiral Benbow, and Grinling Gibbons, the sculptor. The acreage is 1562·7. Pop. 112,500.

**De Quincey, Thomas** (1785–1859), a man of letters, after an adventurous career as a youth, during which he cemented friendships with Wordsworth, Lamb, and other famous personages, and visited Scotland and the metropolis, found himself before he was thirty a victim of the opium habit. Settling at Kendal, he earned a living in 1819 as editor of the *Westmoreland Gazette*, a position he held for about two years. He then went to London, and was introduced by Lamb to the best literary society. He began to write for the *London Magazine*, and to this periodical contributed the *Confessions of an Opium-Eater*, 1821. He thenceforth wrote regularly for the monthlies, and be-

came a frequent contributor to *Blackwood's*, in which appeared his *Murder considered as one of the Fine Arts*. He published his novel *Klosterheim* in 1839, and his *Logic of Political Economy* five years later. De Q. is as happy when writing history as when writing literary criticism, as much at home when portraying his contemporaries of the Lake school as when engaged upon the story of his own life. He is so full of learning that he is always digressing. Even when his judgment is not sound, there is no doubt about the depth of his erudition. And with all this he is no dry-as-dust, no mere pedant, even when the subject-matter of his essay is caviare to the general, for he had studied life as well as books. One of his greatest merits is his splendid prose style. It is true that this is not always sustained, but when the spirit moved him there was no height to which he could not attain. Excellent when writing on such abstract subjects as *The Literature of Knowledge* and *The Literature of Power*, he could be pathetic, as in the episode of Ann of Oxford Street in the *Confessions*, or ironical, as in *Murder considered as one of the Fine Arts*. This last, if it lacks something of the strength of Swift's *Modest Proposal*, is free from its brutality. That this essay should be so successful is the more remarkable, because humour was by no means De Q's. strong point. That point was his imagination, the assistance of which he did not deny himself even when writing his autobiography. It was his imagination which inspired him to such essays as *The English Mail Coach*, and which enabled him to produce the dramatic ending of his essay on Joan of Arc, where he contrasted the death-visions of the Maid of Orleans and her judge, the Bishop of Beauvais. There are biographies published in 1881 by Masson and 'H. A. Page' (*i.e.* A. H. Japp), and an excellent appreciation by Sidney Low, introducing a volume of selection (1911).

**Dera Ghazi Khan,** or **Dera Ghazee Khan,** a dist. and tn. of the Punjab, British India, situated in the Derajat div. The area of the district is 5606 sq. m., and it is irrigated by government canals. The town of D. G. K. has manufactures of silk and cotton goods and ivory ornaments. Pop. 20,731.

**Dera Ismael Khan,** or **Dera Ismaeel Khan,** a dist. and tn. of the North West Frontier Province, British India. The district has an area of 9440 sq. m., and is very dry, being in parts almost desert. The town stands near the Indus, and has manufs. of cotton goods, scarves, and inlaid wood-work.  Pop. 39,341.

**De-rating,** or the scheme for the relief of rating embodied in the Local Government (De-Rating) Act of 1929, which was originally introduced by Mr. Winston Churchill in the Budget of 1928.  It is a measure of local government reform designed to give relief to industrial centres like Manchester, Birmingham, and the Potteries, and to agriculture by reducing or removing from industry the burden of rates.  Broadly, the Act ' de-rates ' or relieves agricultural land and buildings of the whole of the rate levied upon them at the date of the passing of the Act (May 10, 1929);  relieves productive industry of three-quarters of the previously existing rates;  spreads the rates burden over the whole country;  and substitutes for certain grants theretofore paid by the Exchequer to local authorities a lump sum which is distributed among the counties in proportion to their needs.  The contention of the Conservative Gov. which passed the Act was that under the Act the country as a whole would actually receive more money from the Exchequer grant than it would lose by the de-rating provisions;  that, by virtue of the method of distribution, the rates in many districts would be reduced, and only the wealthier residential localities might be faced with slightly higher rates—about twenty years thence;  and that the stimulus given to industry would so reduce the Poor Rate that there would be no rate increase anywhere in the country.  In any event, the Gov. guaranteed all local authorities against increase of rates (through the scheme) for at least five years from the passing of the Act.  The Act also considerably remodelled poor law administration by the abolition of the Boards of Guardians and the transfer of their powers to the councils of counties and county boroughs.  The advantages claimed for this change of administrative authority were that the burden of the poor rate would be more equally distributed by reason of the widening of the rating area from a single union to the whole county;  that wasteful expenditure would be prevented by the avoidance of overlapping;  and that medical and other treatment theretofore not obtainable by single unions owing to expense would be made available to the poor by the larger resources of the whole county.  The fund to be distributed to the county councils as from the abolition of the guardians was stated to be never likely to be less than £45,000,000 a year, an amount which, as to £24,000,000, represents the amount of loss suffered by the local authorities through the de-rating of industry;  as to £16,000,000, the equivalent of certain discontinued Treasury grants to local authorities;  together with an additional Treasury contribution of £5,000,000.  To cover possible fluctuations in the poundage local rates, further sums, to the minimum extent of £2,330,000 were to be found by the Treasury for a period of five years.  The year following the passing of the Act was one of world-wide commercial depression which still (1931) continues;  and this fact, combined with a change of government, makes it difficult to estimate the true value of the reform;  though undoubtedly the abolition of the Boards of Guardians has rendered poor law administration more economical and effective.

**Derayeh,** _see_ DARAIYEH.

**Derbend,** or **Derbent** (Persian ' iron gates '), a tn. in the Soviet state of Daghestan, Russia, on the western shore of the Caspian Sea, 153 m. N.W. of Baku, of Oriental appearance, the walls and citadel having been, possibly, built by Chosroes Anosharvan, Shah of Persia (531–579 A.D.), or by Alexander the Great to protect Persia against the northern tribes.  Has trade in fish, fruit and wine.  Pop. 23,110.

**Derby,** a parliamentary, municipal, and county bor., the co. tn. of Derbyshire, England, on the Derwent, 92 m. S.E. of Liverpool and 129 m. N.N.W. of London.  It possesses several fine churches, St. Peter's, in the Perpendicular style, with some Norman details;  St. Alkmund's, in Decorated style, rebuilt in 1846;  All Saints' (1509–27), one of the finest churches in the Midlands, with a Late Perpendicular tower.  Other buildings are the town-hall (1866), the grammar school (founded 1160), the free library and museum (presented by M. T. Bass, M.P.;  _d._ 1884), and the Roman Catholic Church of St. Mary, designed by Pugin.  D. is famous for its porcelain manufacture (1756–1814), recently revived.  It is the headquarters of the Midland section of the L.M.S. Railway, with vast storehouses and workshops and a large engine and carriage factory employing 10,000 men.  Other industries are silk, cotton, lace, hosiery, iron, lead, shot, fluor-spar or ' Blue John,' marble, paints, paper and motor cars.  D. is a suffragan bishopric in the diocese of Southwell, and returns two members to parliament.  There is an Art Gallery and a library, the latter containing over 40,000 books. There was a Roman settlement at Little Chester, a northern suburb of the town. It was captured by the Danes about 918, but was recovered by Ethelflæd, the Lady of the Mercians, after which it received the name of 'Deorby.' It was created a royal borough by Edward the Confessor, and first placed under a mayor in 1638. Richardson, the novelist, and Herbert Spencer were natives of D. The pop. was 32,741 in 1841, 52,606 twenty years later, and 129,796 in 1921. The boundaries of the bor. were extended in 1927.

**Derby,** a city of New Haven co., Connecticut, U.S.A., 10 m. W. of

EDWARD HENRY STANLEY 15TH EARL
OF DERBY

New Haven. It has an opera house and a public library. Among its manufs. are: pianos and organs, woollen goods, pins, keys, typewriters, and ammunition. Pop. 10,788.

**Derby, The Earls of.** The family of Stanley is of very considerable antiquity, and is very much older than the earldom. It was not until 1485 that *Thomas,* second *Baron Stanley* (1435–1504), was created Earl of Derby, presumably for having preserved a strict neutrality at Bosworth, and for having crowned the victor. *Edward Stanley,* third *Earl* (1508–72), took a prominent part in affairs military and political. He was a commissioner for the trial of Lady Jane Grey, and was a Privy Councillor under three sovereigns. *Henry*

*Stanley,* fourth *Earl* (1531–93), was a marked character in the reign of Elizabeth. He married in 1555 Margaret Clifford, granddaughter of Mary Tudor, sister of Henry VIII. He was a commissioner at the trial of Mary Queen of Scots (1586); two years later was sent on a mission to Spain, and on his return was appointed Lord High Steward. Many of the successors to the earldom distinguished themselves in one way or another; but none rose so high as *Edward George Geoffrey Smith,* fourteenth *Earl* (1799–1869). Entering Parliament in his twenty-third year, in the Whig interest, he was appointed by Canning in 1827 Under-Secretary for the Colonies, an office he retained under Goderich. In the Grey administration (1830) he became Chief Secretary for Ireland, in which capacity he did excellent work. He joined the Conservatives in 1835, and six years later accepted the Colonial Secretaryship under Peel. He it was who persuaded Peel not to offer Disraeli a post in his administration. In 1844 he went to the House of Lords as Lord Stanley. It was not until 1851 that he succeeded to the earldom. In the following year he formed a protectionist administration, in which, having overcome his dislike and distrust of Disraeli, he gave that statesman the office of Chancellor of the Exchequer. This administration held office only a few months; and Derby did not really enjoy the fruits of power until he again became Prime Minister in Feb. 1858, but his second ministry only lasted sixteen months. Derby became Prime Minister for the third and last time in 1866, but two years later ill-health compelled his resignation, and the once-despised Disraeli ruled in his stead. He was referred to by Lytton in *The New Timon* (1845) as 'frank, haughty, rash, the Rupert of debate'—which last phrase is often erroneously attributed to Disraeli, and on the whole it would be difficult to find a better description. He was not a great, or even a consistent statesman, and much of the credit that was given to him, especially in the reconstruction and reorganisation of the Conservative party after the fall of Peel, belonged of right to Disraeli. He was, however, a good man of business, and an excellent speaker. His eldest son, *Edward Henry Stanley,* fifteenth *Earl* (1826–1903), was also a statesman. Under-Secretary for Foreign Affairs in 1852, three years later he refused the Colonial Secretaryship under Palmerston, but accepted that office in his father's administration. In Derby's third ministry he became Foreign Secretary, and retained that position under Disraeli. He succeeded to the earldom in 1869, and became again Foreign Secretary under Disraeli (1874–78). He went over to the Liberal camp in 1880, and two years later become Colonial Secretary under Gladstone; but was opposed to Home Rule, and became leader of the Liberal Unionists in the House of Lords. Like his father, he was a good speaker, and it is to the credit of his sincerity that by leaving the Conservatives in 1880 he sacrificed his succession to the premiership. He *d.* in 1893, and was succeeded by his brother, *Frederick Arthur Stanley,* Baron Stanley of Preston (cr. Aug. 1886), *b.* 1841; who had been M.P. for Preston, for N. Lancashire, and

as Private Secretary to F.-M. Lord Roberts. Was Conservative M.P. for West Houghton div. of Lancs. 1892–1906, and held office as a Lord of the Treasury 1895–1900. From 1900 to 1903 he was Financial Secretary to the War Office and Postmaster-General 1903–5. During the Great War he rendered good service to the State as Director General of Recruiting 1915–16, and as Under-Secretary for War 1916–18. From 1922–24 he filled with distinction the post of British Ambassador to France. He is a great patron of the turf, having owned several classic winners. Lord D. was responsible for the Derby Scheme of recruitment during the Great War.

**Derby Day,** the second day of the

[*London, Midland & Scottish Rly.*

HATHERSAGE, DERBYSHIRE

for Blackpool, successively, from 1865 to 1886; a Lord of the Admiralty in 1868, Financial Secretary to the War Office 1874–77, to the Treasury 1877–78, Secretary of State for War 1878–80, Vice-President of committee of Council on Education 1885, Secretary of State for Colonies 1885–86, President of Board of Trade 1886–88, and Governor-General of Canada 1888–93. As sixteenth earl, he was Lord Mayor of Liverpool 1895–96, mayor of Preston 1901. He was at different times Chancellor of the Universities of Oxford and Liverpool, and, dying June 14, 1908, was succeeded by his eldest son, *Edward Geo. Villiers Stanley,* separately noticed as seventeenth earl.

**Derby, seventeenth Earl of,** Edward George Villiers Stanley, K.G., *b.* April 4, 1865, eldest son of sixteenth Earl and Lady Constance Villiers. Educated at Wellington College, and served in Grenadier Guards 1885–95. He was A.D.C. to Gov.-Gen. of Canada 1889–91. Saw service in S. African War as Chief Press Censor and then

Summer Meeting at Epsom in Surrey, falling sometimes in May, sometimes in June. The most important races are run on this day, especially the ' Derby race ' for the celebrated Derby stakes, instituted by the Earl of Derby in 1780. The subscription for the Derby is £50, the winner receiving a sum not less than £5000. The road from London to Epsom is covered on this day by a continuous stream of automobiles, coaches, carriages, vans, coster carts, etc. There is also a Derby run every Spring at Churchill Downs, the famous race track in Louisville Kentucky, U.S.A. The winner receives £10,000.

**Derbyshire,** a midland co., England, bounded by Yorkshire, Cheshire, Staffordshire, Leicestershire, and Nottinghamshire. The southern part of the county is very fertile, and produces cereals and root-crops, but the N. is very rugged and mountainous, and the Peak District provides some of the most picturesquely beautiful scenery in England. Here, in the southern spurs of the Pennine chain, rise the numerous rivers of the county, tributaries of the Mersey, the Don, and the Trent. After the Trent itself, which intersects the southern part of the county, the chief rivers are the Derwent, Wye, Dane, Goyt, Dove, and Rother. In the neighbourhood of Buxton and Matlock are valuable medicinal mineral springs. One of the chief industries of the county is coal-mining, chiefly in the eastern division; other minerals and metals worked are iron, lead, zinc, barytes, fluor-spar, and gypsum. Sandstone, marble, and pipe-clay for the potteries are also obtained. Sheep-farming is very extensive in the hilly district of the N., while the southern plains form a noted corn-growing and dairy-farming district. Other industries are porcelain, silk, cotton, hosiery, iron, woollen, lace, and elastic-web manufactures. The chief towns are Derby (the county town), Matlock, Buxton, Chesterfield, Glossop, Ilkeston, and Belper. D. contains numerous antiquities, but its only important historical association is with the retreat of Prince Charles Edward (1745). The chief places of interest are the ruined abbeys of Dale and Beauchief, the Saxon crypt of Repton, Haddon Hall, Hardwick Hall, and Chatsworth. The ' stone circle ' at Arbelow is the most important in England after Stonehenge. Since 1885 D. returns ten members to parliament, two for the borough of Derby and eight for the county. Area 1029 sq. m. Pop. 714,539.

**Derceto**, or **Dercetis**, the Gk. name for the Syrian goddess Atargatis, who is depicted as half woman and half fish. She is identified with Astarte, and the centre of her worship was Hierapolis.

**Derecske**, com. in Bihar co., Hungary. Pop. 9840.

**Dereham East**, a market town of England in co. Norfolk, 16 m. N.W. Norwich. There are iron foundries, malt-houses, coach works, and a boot factory. A monument has been erected to William Cowper, the poet, who took up his residence here in 1796, and is buried here. George Borrow was b. here in 1803. Pop. 2343.

**Derelict**, a term in English law, denoting any property which the owner has deserted or wilfully cast away. It is most commonly applied to a ship abandoned by the captain and crew. The first comers to a wreck can claim salvage from the crown or from the persons who have a right to unclaimed D. vessels. Land reclaimed from the sea is said to be D. (i.e. ' forsaken ' by the sea, from Lat. derelinquere), and belongs either to the owner of the adjoining lands, supposing it is given up gradually, or

to the crown in case of a sudden and considerable recession of the sea.

**Derg, Lough,** 4 m. N.W. of Pettigoe, co. Donegal, Irish Free State, is 3 m. long by 2½ m. broad, with an area of 24 sq. m. It has a beautiful aspect, in spite of its wild, dreary shores, being studded with many small islands. Saint's Isle has the remains of a ruined priory. Station Island was the reputed scene of St. Patrick's purgatory, and was long one of the most celebrated places of pilgrimage in Ireland It is still visited by many of the Irish from June 1 to Aug. 15.

**Derham, Rev. William** (1657–1735), an English philosopher and divine, b. at Stoulton, near Worcester. In 1896 he published the Artificial Clockmaker, and from 1711–12 he was Boyle lecturer. His other works are Physico-Theology, 1713 ; Astro-Theology, 1714 ; Christo-Theology, 1730 ; and A Defence of the Church's Right in Leasehold Estates, 1731.

**Dermatine**, a mineral compound with a specific gravity of 2·1, found in Waldheim, Saxony, and consisting of silica, magnesia, protoxide of iron and water. It is reniform, stalactitic, brittle, and resinous, its colour being blackish-green with yellow streaks.

**Dermestidæ**, a family of Coleoptera, contains numerous species of beetles which are harmless when adult, but in the larval stage do much damage to the collections of naturalists, and are particularly destructive to skins.

**Derna**, a coast tn. in the Italian Colony Cyrenaira. It is situated on a bay which is frequently inaccessible during spring and winter, in an oasis of date palms and bananas. After Bengasi it is the most important settlement in C. Pop. 10,000.

**Dernberg, Bernard.** The son of a Jewish family of Berlin. Many years before the Great War D. had been a very successful journalist, which profession he left for politics, where he was equally successful, but, realising that a Jew could not rise to eminence in Ger. politics, he retired in 1910. On the outbreak of the Great War he was sent by Germany to the U.S.A. to conduct a campaign of propaganda against England. Through the Press and his various activities he endeavoured to alienate American opinion from England by means of false news, but his callous and brutal defence of the sinking of the S.S. Lusitania so alienated American opinion that he was sent out of the country. He left on June 13, 1915, on a Norwegian ship for Germany.

**De Robeck, Admiral Sir John Michael** (1862–1928), second son of fourth Baron de Robeck, of Gowan Grange, Naas, Ireland. Entered the Royal Navy as a cadet 1875, Captain

1902, Rear-Admiral 1911, Vice-Admiral 1917, Admiral of the Fleet 1925. At the outbreak of the Great War was appointed to command of 9th Cruiser Squadron, and was engaged in the protection of commerce on the Finnisterre Station, where he captured the North-German Lloyd steamer *Schlesien*. He was appointed second-in-command of the fleet at the Dardanelles early in 1915, and succeeded to the Chief Command on March 16, 1915. At the end of 1916 he was appointed to command the 2nd Battle Squadron of the Grand Fleet, a position he retained to 1919, when he was appointed Commander-in-Chief of the Mediterranean Fleet. At the same time he was British High Commissioner at Constantinople pending the signature of Turkey to the Peace Treaty. In 1922 he was appointed Commander-in-Chief of the Atlantic Fleet and held that position until 1924.

**Déroulède, Paul** (1846–1914), a Fr. man of letters and politician, studied law from 1863 to 1869, and was called to the Bar in 1870. During the Franco-Prussian War, in which he served, he was taken prisoner at Sedan whilst trying to rescue his wounded brother (1870). His *Chants d'un Soldat*, published in 1872, attained unbounded popularity, so that in 1875 he was encouraged to bring out his *Nouveaux Chants d'un Soldat*. Gounod wrote the music for his patriotic hymn, *Vive la France*, which was sung at the exhibition of 1878. His name is especially associated with the *Ligue des Patriotes*, which he instituted in 1882. But when he tried to use the organisation to promote the cause of General Boulanger, he was obliged to retire from his presidency. The league was suppressed by government in 1889 as a political menace. Deputy for the first time in 1889, he became notorious for the violence of his anti-Dreyfus policy. Banished in 1900 for attempting to replace the Parliamentary Constitution by the Republican plebiscite, he was allowed to return to France in 1905.

PAUL DÉROULÈDE

**Derrick, Samuel** (1724–69), a writer, was first a linen-draper, then a play-actor, and finally succeeded Beau Nash as master of ceremonies at Bath and Tunbridge. Gross immorality brought to a miserable end his prodigal career, yet Boswell tells us that Dr. Johnson always spoke of him with kindly feeling. His literary performances, such as *Fortune, a Rhapsody*, etc., have deservedly sunk into complete oblivion.

**Derry, see** LONDONDERRY.

**Derry,** a tn. of Rockingham co., New Hampshire, 10 m. S.E. of Manchester. It is a summer resort and sends milk to Boston and has sundry manufactories. Pop. 5131.

**De Ruyter, Michael Adrianzoon** (1607–76), a Dutch naval commander, *b.* at Vlissingen, where there is a monument to him in the Jakobskerk. A captain in 1635, he was stationed some time in the E. Indies, and in 1647 sunk a detachment of Algerian ships off Sallee. In 1652 he succeeded in preserving his convoy of merchantmen in spite of the conflict with the Eng. fleet near Plymouth. During the war of 1652–54, De R. ably seconded Van Tromp, so that at the close of the struggle the Dutch leaders had at least held their own against Admiral Blake and Monk. During the second English war, De R. obtained a narrow victory, after a tough fight, over Monk in 1666, but was himself obliged to retreat to Dutch harbours before Ayscue a little later in the same year. But it was in 1667 that De R.'s daring brought him his highest glory, for with De Witt he sailed up the Medway as far as Chatham and there destroyed all the Eng. shipping. In 1659 he had aided Denmark by conquering the Swedish fleet. In 1671 he won some advantage over the combined English and Fr. fleets in Solebay, but in 1676, whilst engaging in a desperate encounter with the Fr. Admiral Duquesne, he received a mortal wound.

**Dervishes** (from a Persian word meaning ' seeking doors,' that is ' beggars '), are the same as the Arabian fakirs. In the earliest times the D. were the passionate disciples of some revered ' sheikh ' or master, learning from him words of wisdom, and fighting his battles against the unbelievers, but sometimes also deserting him to return to the world. Of the thirty-two orders of D. and the countless sub-orders, the best known is probably the Qualandarite, which figures in the *Arabian Nights* as the Calenders. This fraternity, the members of which are under an oath always to travel, is an offshoot of the Baktashite order, which flourishes in Albania and Turkey, and consists really of antinomians, like the

Rifaites or ' howling D.,' who in their ecstasy are held to be under the influence of divine inspiration, and can therefore commit the most horrible crimes with impunity. But their favourite actions at such periods are to cut themselves with knives, or to eat serpents, fiery coal or glass, or like the Mevlevis, founded by the pantheist Jelâl-ud-Din, to perform the most extravagant of dances. During their novitiate, candidates for admission to an order are almost invariably subjected to hypnotic influence from the sheikh. Attached to these orders are fellowships of lay brothers, not unlike the lodges of Freemasons. The theology is invariably some form of Sufi'ism which

navigable except in certain reaches near Matlock, for pleasure boats.

**Derwent Water,** a lake in the S.W. of Cumberland, England. At a height of 238 ft. above the sea level, it stretches for 3 m. to the S. of Keswick. An enlargement of D. W. which flows out towards the Irish Sea at the N. extremity, its greatest breadth is 1 m., the depth never exceeding 72 ft. Overlooked by Castle Head (530 ft.) and distant mountains at the foot, and engirt with abrupt rocky banks, it is noted for its wild beauty, and especially for the Floating Isle and the Lodore Falls near its head.

**Derwentwater, James Radcliffe, Earl of** (1689–1716), a leader in the

DERWENT WATER

embraces a belief in the sufi' hierarchy of saints. In spite of the wearisome sameness of their pious formulas and recitations, the D. are still held in the highest veneration among the people.

**Derwent :** (1) A riv. of Cumberland, rises near Bow Fell and Scafell, and flowing N. and N.E. to D. Water and Bassinthwaite, then W. through a narrow valley past Cockermouth, falls into the Solway Firth near Workington, a total length of about 34 m. The water is wonderfully clear, but the river is not navigable. (2) A riv. of Derbyshire, rises in Bleaklow Hill, N. of the Peak, and flowing through a narrow valley, where it receives the Noe and Wye, flows S. past Chatsworth, Matlock, and Belper into a low plain S. of Derby. From here it flows S.E. in a very winding course, to join the Trent, near Sawley, on the Leicestershire border, a total distance of about 60 m. The river is not

Jacobite rebellion of 1715, was captured and confined to the Tower after the rout at Preston. His youth, courtesy, bravery, and rank, as also the efforts of his friends, and his own appeal for the king's mercy were powerless to stay his execution, which took place in 1716 on Tower Hill.

**Derzhavin, Gabriel Romanovitch** (1743–1816), the greatest lyric poet of Russia in the age of Catherine, was b. at Kasan. In 1762 he entered the army as an engineer, and in 1791 Catherine appointed him Secretary of State, and in 1802 Minister of Justice. His best poetry was produced during the busiest part of his career, and is marked by sublimity and vigour of thought and expression. His most famous work is *Oda Bog,* or *The Address to the Deity.* His works have several times been reprinted and translated since the first collected edition in 1810.

**Desaguadero :** (1) A river of Peru and Bolivia, since 1904 part of the boundary of Bolivia. It is a sluggish stream, not navigable beyond Corocoro, draining Lake Titicaca and flowing S. for 184 m. with gradually lessening volume to Lake Pampa Aullaguas or Poopo. It gives its name to the valley district of the Andes, through which it flows. (2) A riv. in the W. of the Argentine, draining a depressed area of saline lakes and small streams, including Laguna Belvedero, and with apparently no outlet to the ocean. In its lower courses it is known as the Rio Salado.

**Desaix de Veygoux, Louis Charles Antoine** (1768–1800), a Fr. general, educated at the military school founded by the Marshal d'Effiat. Though he supported the revolutionists ; the fact that he belonged to the nobility and was popular with the soldiery led to his imprisonment and suspension from command for a short period. D. was present at the Battle of Lauterburg, played a commendable part in Moreau's skilful retreat through the Black Forest, drove back the Archduke Charles at Rastadt, and held the bridge of Kehl against his assailants. But the subjugation of Upper Egypt during Napoleon's campaign (1798–99) was the crowning distinction of his career. His high sense of equity and lovable disposition won from the natives the title of ' Just Sultan.' At the Battle of Marengo (1800), where he arrived just in time to turn the tide of victory in favour of Bonaparte, he received, by ill chance, a mortal wound.

**Desart, Sir Hamilton John Agmondesham Cuffe, fifth Earl of and seventh Baron,** also Viscount Castle Cuffe, of Desart, co. Kilkenny ; b. Aug. 30, 1848 ; second son of third earl. B.A., Cambridge. Called to Bar, 1872 ; solicitor to Treasury and Queen's (and King's) Proctor, 1894–1909. Director of Public Prosecutions, 1894–1908. Succeeded to peerage, 1898. British representative in various negotiations abroad. K.C.B., 1898. P.C., 1913. K.P., 1919.

**Desaugiers, Marc Antoine Madeleine** (1772–1827), a Fr. dramatist and song-writer ; fled from the terrors of the Revolution to San Domingo, where, however, during the great negro rebellion he was captured and within an ace of losing his life. On his return to France in 1797, a storm of popular applause at once greeted his operas and comedies, which were produced in rapid succession at the Théâtre des Variétés and the Vaudeville. A higher literary merit belongs to his drinking songs and lampoons, which he sang himself with consider-

able *éclat* in many Parisian salons. At his death he was acting as manager of the Vaudeville.

**Desbarres, Joseph Frederick Wallet** (1722–1824), an engineer, b. in England, of Huguenot parents. During the siege of Quebec he served as aide-de-camp to General Wolfe, and was in the act of reporting to Wolfe when the latter received his mortal wound. The engineering operations during the conquest of Canada, which followed, were under his charge, whilst from 1763 to 1773 he surveyed the shores of Nova Scotia. When he had made a number of charts of the N. American coast for Lord Howe, he accepted the lieutenant-governorship first of Cape Breton (1784–1804), and afterwards of Prince Edward Island (1805–13).

**Desborough, John** (1608–80), soldier and statesman, was b. at Eltisley, Cambs. In 1636 he married Jane, sister of Oliver Cromwell, on whose side he fought gallantly during the Civil War, and whom he upheld in Parliament. He stoutly opposed Cromwell's assumption of royalty, however, although he sat himself in Cromwell's House of Lords, and after the Protector's death he became a strong partisan of Fleetwood. Made a councillor of state by the Rump Parliament in 1659, he was later dismissed, and in 1660 and 1666 he was temporarily imprisoned in the Tower for intrigue. His death occurred at Hackney, London. Butler satirised him in *Hudibras* and the *Parable of the Lion and Fox.*

**Desborough, first Baron of Taplow ;** William Henry Grenfell, K.G., b. Oct. 30, 1855. Was educated at Harrow and Oxford. During his scholastic career he distinguished himself at sport, playing for the Harrow cricket eleven 1873–74 and representing Oxford in the three-mile relay race v. Cambridge in 1876. Lord D. rowed for Oxford in the University boat races 1877–78 and was president O.U.A.C. and O.U.B.C. He swam Niagara twice. Lord D. gave much time to public affairs and represented Salisbury in Parliament in 1880, 1885. He was returned M.P. for Hereford in 1892 but resigned. Was private secretary to Sir Wm. Harcourt when the latter was Chancellor of the Exchequer in 1885. From 1900–5 he represented the Wycombe division of Bucks in the Conservative interest. Lord D. was a member of Tariff Commission of 1904 and was president of the Central Association of Volunteer Regiments. He acted as chairman of committee appointed by the Home Office to inquire into the Police of England, Scotland and Wales.

**Descartes, René** (Latinised into

*Renatus Cartesius*) (1596–1650), a Fr. philosopher, *b.* at La Haye, in Touraine, and educated at the Jesuit school of La Flèche. In 1617 he went to Holland and entered the army of Prince Maurice of Orange. In 1619 he entered the service of Bavaria, and while in winter quarters at Neuberg on the Danube found time for the reflections which afterwards resulted in the *Discours de la Méthode*. In 1625 he settled in Paris, but went to the Netherlands in 1629, and lived there mainly until 1649. In 1650 he went to the Court of Sweden at the invitation of the Queen Christina, but he *d.* at Stockhom within a few months. In 1666 his body was removed to Paris, and

RENÉ DESCARTES

in 1819 transferred to St. Germain-des-Près. D. is generally considered the 'Father of Modern Philosophy.' Even in his school days he found it impossible to accept scholastic tradition and theological dogma as 'knowledge,' and his first step towards evolving a philosophical system was to discard all books. In 1637 appeared the *Discours de la Méthode*, in which he traces his mental development from his earliest years to the point when he refused to believe anything unless it were supported by incontrovertible and absolute proof. Starting with 'doubt' as the only sure test, he applied it to all that had hitherto passed as knowledge, and the only proposition which stood the test seemed the fact of his own existence. This he formulated as 'Cogito : ergo sum,' clearly describ-

ing the relation between consciousness and existence. From this he next concluded that 'Whatever is clearly and distinctly thought must be true,' whence he arrived at the idea of the existence of a 'Perfect Being,' because from the intuition of our own imperfection we evolve the idea of perfection, and if the idea of perfection is certain, then perfection must exist. The cardinal point in the philosophy of D. is the essential difference between spirit and matter, between thinking and extending substances, into one of which classes all things fall, and which can in no way exert any influence upon each other or partake of each other's attributes. The principles of the *Discours de la Méthode* are dealt with more fully in *Meditationes de Primâ Philosophia*, 1641, and *Principia Philosophiæ*, 1644. From philosophy he applied his principles to physics, and his celebrated theory of vortices, explaining the motions of the heavenly bodies, was only superseded by Newton's theory of gravitation. It was in mathematics that D. achieved the most lasting results ; he first recognised the real meaning of the negative roots of equations and founded 'Analytical Geometry,' the application of algebra to geometry. Besides his philosophical and mathematical treatises, D. was the author of *Traité des Passions de l'âme* for Queen Christina. *See* Millet, *Descartes, sa Vie, ses Travaux, ses Découvertes,* 1867–71 ; K. Fischer, *Descartes and his School* (Eng. trans.), 1887 ; *Descartes : his Life and Times,* and translations of the chief works by Miss E. S. Haldane, 1905–11 ; *Cambridge Modern History,* vol. iv., 1906, 'Descartes and Cartesianism.' *See also* INNATE IDEAS.

**Descent** (from Norman-Fr. *discent*), *see*—in heredity, DARWINISM ; in law, INHERITANCE ; in science, BIOLOGY.

**Deschamps, Eustache** (*c.* 1328–1415), a Fr. poet, led a life fascinating by its very variety and romance. One of the victims of the siege of Rheims and an eye-witness of the march against Chartres and the signing of the Treaty of Bretigny (1360), he cherished to his death a bitter hatred of the Eng. nation. Besides serving in the Flemish wars, he is said to have suffered imprisonment by the Saracens, and to have wandered through Syria and Egypt, besides visiting Italy and Hungary. Feasts, fighting, and tournaments formed daily occurrences in his life, and in his roamings from castle to castle, where he entertained lords and ladies with the singing of his songs, he must fully have satisfied his innate spirit of adventure. In

1360 he became vassal to Princess Isabella, and for some time he was *huissier d'armes* to King Charles V. Indeed, the list of honourable offices he held under nearly all contemporary princes attests his great popularity. The numerous virelays, satires, ballads rondeaux, and farces of this ' Roi de Laidure,' as he justly styled himself, which were unprinted till 1832, amply justify his claim to be recognised as the first lyric poet to write in modern French.

**Deschanel, Emile Auguste Etienne Martin** (1819–1904), a Fr. man of letters, was appointed to the Professorship of Rhetoric at Paris. He was obliged to leave France because of the vehemence with which he preached republican doctrines in his *Catholicisme et Socialisme* (1850). But in 1881 he was elected to the chair of modern languages in the Collège de France. Most of his publications as, for example, *Les Courtisanes Grecques,* 1854; *Etudes sur Aristophanes,* 1867; and *Le Romantisme des Classiques,* 1882, deal with the literature of the ancients.

**Des Chutes,** a riv. of U.S.A., which rises on the E. side of the Cascade Mts. Its course is chiefly N., and its length is about 320 m. It flows through a volcano district, intersecting Wasco co., and finally enters the Columbia R.

**Descriptive Geometry.** D. G. forms the theoretical basis of architectural and mechanical drawing. The architect has to represent by plans, elevations and cross-sections the building under construction in such a way that his drawings are not only intelligible to the contractor, but also so that the latter can deduce the actual dimensions of each part represented on the diagram. It is the business of D. G. to teach how such accurate representations can be made.

**Deseronto,** a small tn. of Ontario, Canada, situated on the Bay of Quinté, in Hastings co., about 30 m. S.W. of Kingston. Has trade in lumbering and fruit growing. Pop. 1847.

**Deserter,** or **Desertion,** the intentional abandonment of a post or obligation to which the offender is bound by legal or moral laws : (1) Desertion in the navy or army is being absent without leave when there is no intention to return, as distinguished from ' absence without leave ' from other causes. The practice of deserting from one regiment to another to avoid foreign service or aiding civil power is now designated 'fraudulent enlistment,' as distinguished from ' desertion.' Desertion when on active service is punishable with death in all European countries. All persons who attempt to induce desertion, or who harbour deserters, are liable to punishment. When desertion occurs at other times it is punished with a maximum of two years' imprisonment for the first offence, and a term of penal servitude, to be determined by the president of the court martial for all subsequent offences. All deserters must be tried by court martial, and when convicted forfeit all prior service and such advantages as may accrue to them from such service, as well as being liable to serve again for the full term of the forfeited service. (2) Desertion from the merchant service is punishable with forfeiture of pay, and as directed by the Merchant Shipping Act, 1894. (3) Desertion of wife or children. A deserted wife, by the law of England, may take proceedings against her husband for a maintenance order if she becomes chargeable to the parish. He may be charged as a rogue and vagabond under the Vagrancy Act, 1824. Under the Matrimonial Causes Act, 1857, she may obtain a judicial separation if the desertion has extended over two years. The Summary Jurisdiction (Married Women) Act of 1895 gives her the custody of any children there may be up to the age of sixteen, and provides that the husband shall pay a weekly sum, not exceeding £2, towards their maintenance. In such circumstances the wife may obtain an order to protect such property as she may herself acquire, or already possesses in her own right. In England desertion does not afford sufficient ground for a divorce, but in Scotland ' desertion, without sufficient cause ' for four years is sufficient ground for a decree of divorce. *See* DIVORCE and HUSBAND AND WIFE.

**Desert** (from Lat. *deserere,* to abandon), a geographical term for a barren and uninhabited district of large extent. The term is used to include the Tundras (*q.v.*), or frozen plains fringing the Arctic regions, the great ice-wastes of the Arctic and Antarctic continents, and sometimes the temporary wastes or steppes which are covered with vegetation only for a few months in the spring. The name is most usually restricted, however, to the hot, dry districts of the S. latitudes, where the temperatures are extreme, the rainfall very scanty, and evaporation very rapid. These hot D. occur in two belts encircling the earth ; in the N. hemisphere there stretch the Great Sahara, Libyan, and Nubian D., the D. of Arabia, Persia, Turkestan, and Gobi, and continued in the Great Basin of N. America. The S. ring less extensive and more broken, includes the Kalahari D. in Africa, the interior of Australia, and the Atacama D. in S. America. The essential characteristic of a D. is its lack of rain and the scarcity both of moisture on its surface and of watery vapour in the atmosphere which might decrease the excessive radiation. The temperatures are extreme, ranging from 120° F. in the daytime, with the sand itself at a temperature of 150° F., to below freezing-point at night. D. occur at all altitudes, from below sea-level to several thousand feet above it, and may be of a flat appearance broken only by driving waves of sand, and bounded by the sharp circle of the horizon, or a rocky plateau, hollowed and cut into valleys and ravines. Cloud bursts provide the greater part of the scanty rainfall, and sandstorms of terrific force and velocity are of frequent occurrence. The 'mirage' (q.v.) is a peculiar feature of great D., and is largely the cause of the tales of genii and evil spirits prevalent among D. peoples. Absolute lack of vegetation is rare, but the plants grow very scantily, and are specially adapted to D. conditions, being mainly of the spinifex family and the prickly variety of the cactus, whose glazed surface retains such moisture as it obtains from the soil. Animal life is similarly restricted, the camel being the only beast of burden able to withstand D. conditions. Where natural springs are found the surrounding land becomes a marvel of fertility, and an oasis (q.v.) settlement grows up, while the rivers, such as the Nile, are used for the irrigation of wide tracts, and the sinking of artesian wells is frequently practised in the Sahara. See SAHARA GOBI, KALAHARI; also Professor Walther's *Das Gesetz der Wüstenbildungen*, 1900.

**Desforges, Pierre Jean Baptiste Choudard** (1746–1806), a Fr. playwright, was the natural son of Dr. Petit. As an adapter and composer of plays, he joined a company of wandering players. With his actress-wife, he passed three years in St. Petersburg, where they drew large audiences. His adaptation of 'Tom Jones' (*Tom Jones à Londres*) was produced at the Comédie Italienne in 1782, his *Joconde*, which he wrote for the music of Louis Jadin, in 1790, and his *Les Epoux Divorcés* in 1790. But his first and most conspicuous success was a comedy *L'Epreuve Villageoise*, 1785, the music for which was composed by Grétry.

**Deshoulières, Madame,** *née* Antoinette Du Ligier de la Garde (1638–94), a Fr. poetess, elected member of the Ricovrati of Padua and the Academy of Artes, and considered by Voltaire the best of the women poets of France. She was a

prominent figure for her beauty and wit at the Court of Louis XIV., and was the centre of a circle of the most eminent literary men of her time. She spent her early married life at Brussels, and was imprisoned in the Château of Wilworden for eight months by the gov. (1657) on account of her efforts to secure her husband's pardon. She wrote odes, ballads, madrigals, and idylls, of which only a few of the last have lived. Complete editions of her *Œuvres* were published in 1695 and 1799.

**Desiccation** (Lat. *desiccare*, to dry up), the process of drying or removing water from a substance. This may be done by heating the substance and causing evaporation of the moisture, or by various chemical agents, such as calcium chloride, sulphuric acid, potassium hydrate, which are applied by means of a 'desiccator.' This is a closed vessel in which the substance to be dried is placed, together with the hygroscopic substance which is to dry it. Vacuum D. is a quicker process, and is caused by exhausting the air from the desiccator. Currents of dry air also act as desiccators. Certain organisms have the power of undergoing the process of D. and retaining sufficient latent life to enable them to recover, but the longer the period of D. has been, the longer they take to recover; hematodes, or 'paste-eels,' have been known to revive after nearly twenty years. Rotifers are said to recover after a long period of D., but it is generally considered that it is only the eggs which survive, that the fully developed organism is really dead. Bear-animalcules, or Tardigrades, are also said to survive. Among plants, seeds and spores seem able to resist any period of D.

**Design** (Lat. *designare*, to mark out), in the fine arts is the drawing or plan which is to act as a guide to the finished representation; the arrangement of the details which are to go to make the whole not only with regard to their artistic completeness, but also with regard to their appropriateness and general utility in the position which they are designed to occupy and the materials from which they are to be constructed. D. does not necessarily mean originality or novelty, far more frequently it is merely the development of old ideas to suit new conditions. In some arts, such as pottery and silver or goldsmiths' work, the form and material are an essential part of the D.; in such arts it is necessary, therefore, that the designer should know the processes, the qualities of the materials, and the practical use of the requisite tools, so that he is not only a designer, but also a practical craftsman.

**Design**, in law, *see* COPYRIGHT and TRADE MARKS.

**Design, Schools of**, which had been founded in 1837. The first school of design was opened under the auspices of the Council of the Government School of Design at Somerset House in 1837. It was the direct outcome of an awakened interest in industrial art, for it was realised that the training offered by the old-fashioned academies of art, which were still in bondage to the rigid theories of art teaching from the antique, in no way fitted the student for the work of practical design and decoration. On the re-organisation of the schools in 1852, the three main objects in view were : (1) The promotion of elementary knowledge of drawing and modelling ; (2) special instruction in the know-ledge and practice of ornamental art ; and (3) the practical application of such knowledge to the improvement of manufactures. In 1857 the Cen-tral or National Art Training Schools were removed to S. Kensington, where they have since remained. Similar S. of D. grew up in the large provincial towns. Thus as early as 1840 State grants were given to Man-chester, Birmingham, Glasgow, etc., to assist them in the erection of such schools. But in time it was found that these new schools also were a failure, as they became centres for training art teachers along stereo-typed lines and their students were drawn rather from the leisured classes than from would-be practical de-signers. Accordingly new technical schools were established throughout the country, where enamelling, metal repoussé, wood-carving, and other artistic handicrafts were taught, as well as drawing and the laws of orna-ment. Since the Education Act of 1902 the art schools in most towns have been taken out of the hands of private committees, and are now managed by the municipalities with moneys derived from the local rates. The Central Schools of Arts and Crafts in Southampton Row (established by the L.C.C. in 1896) may be taken as a type of the many modern establish-ments where art is taught in strict relation to industrial requirements.

**Desio**, a tn. of Italy, in the prov. of Lombardy, situated about 10 m. N. of Milan. Cultivates silk. It is the bp. of Pope Pius XI.

**Desirade**, an is. belonging to the Fr. W. Indies, situated 4 m. E. of Guadeloupe, and having an area of 10 sq. m. Fishing is the chief in-dustry. D. was the first is. discovered by Columbus on his second journey. Pop. 1480.

**Desire** is used in psychology of all instances where the subject is stirred to action not by percepts—that is, by signs of the presence of the objects of pleasure—but rather by imagination or ideas. D. in man corresponds to appetite in animals, and may be de-fined, according to Spinoza, as 'appetite with the consciousness of it.' But ' whether a man be conscious of his appetite or not, the appetite remains one and the same thing.' In ordinary speech it is customary to speak of the D. of tangible things as also of the D. of abstractions, such as of wealth or truth. The same object is not desirable at all times, the fact whether it is so or not depending on the contents of consciousness at the moment of its presentation to thought. When a new idea reaches the mind, movements necessary for its con-summation are often nascent. Now supposing there is some obstacle in the way of these movements or in-choate actions, then the ' desidera-tum,' or object desired, cannot be attained, and the mind of the subject is said to be in a state of D. or expectation, being intent on the desideratum. It is because con-centration of attention on the new idea or object of D. does not change that idea or object into a percept that D. continues to exist. Intensity of D. depends on the force of the impulse to action, and not on the degree of delight which is expected to follow the fulfilment of that D.

**Deslys, Gaby** (*c.* 1884–1920), Fr. music-hall comedienne and dancer, was well known in Paris before her first appearance in London—viz., at the Gaiety Theatre, Sept. 1906. Till 1915 she was a great favourite with the London public, alike for her great personal beauty and dainti-ness and for the dazzling nature of her costumes. Besides her principal business, she took part in light opera and farce ; and in 1915 she appeared at the Duke of York's Theatre as Rosy Rapture in Sir Jas. Barrie's play. She *d.* in Paris, Feb. 11, 1920. She left a life interest in her fortune of £400,000 to her mother and sister ; after their deaths it was to go to the poor of Marseilles.

**Desmids** (Gk. δεσμός, bond) con-stitute a large genus of fresh-water algæ which bear considerable re-semblance to diatoms, but differ from them in being bright green in colour and having the cell-wall composed of cellulose instead of silica.

**Des Moines** : (1) A river of Iowa, U.S.A. Rising in the S.W. of Minne-sota, it traverses Iowa with a south-easterly course and finally joins the Mississippi below Keokuk. Its drain-age area is some 14,650 sq. m., whilst its total length is 550 m. (2) Cap. of Iowa, U.S.A., at the mouth of the Raccoon R. on the Des Moines R., contains the Iowa State Capitol Building on a hill, with a fine view of the city; Fort Des Moines, the largest U.S. cavalry post; the City Hall; court house and coliseum; Des Moines University, belonging to the Baptist Bible Union of N. America, and the Drake University of the Disciples of Christ. There are 970 acs. of parks. The annual State Fair is attended by more than 400,000 persons. There is a large trade in corn and coal, also manufactures of meat products, clothing, furniture, agricultural implements and much printing of newspapers and journals. D. has the largest percentage of home ownership among the large American cities. It is under a commission form of government. The pop. has increased from 3965 in 1860 to 142,559 in 1930.

**Desmond, Earls of,** an Irish family who exercised considerable influence over the S.W. of Ireland. Beginning with Maurice Fitzgerald (*d.* 1356) the line came to an end in Gerald Fitzgerald, who was murdered finally in his retreat among the Kerry mountains, his place of hiding having been betrayed to the Eng. This Fitzgerald, the fifteenth of the title, had sacked Youghal and murdered the inhabitants as a direct challenge to Elizabeth's gov. Consequently he was proclaimed a traitor, and spent the last two years of his life wandering miserably from place to place.

**Desmoulins, Lucie Simplice Camille Benoist** (1760–94), a Fr. revolutionist and journalist, came into immediate notice after his excited harangue to the populace on July 12, 1789. ' To arms ! ' he cried ; ' this dismissal (*i.e.* that of Necker) is the tocsin of the St. Bartholomew of the patriots.' The mob, after hearing the address, rushed out in thousands to seize arms : two days afterwards the Bastille fell. Nevertheless a stuttering speech drove D. to write his inflammatory addresses. His pamphlets entitled *La Philosophie du Peuple Français,* 1788 ; *La France Libre,* 1789, and the series that subsequently appeared in *Les Révolutions de France et de Brabant* contain the germs of Socialism, whilst at the time their rapid dissemination caused the violent doctrines contained therein largely to control the trend of contemporary events. Associated first with Mirabeau, and on his death with Danton, D. was actually present with the infuriated people who stormed the Tuileries (Aug. 1792), and was largely responsible for the downfall and ruthless massacres of

the Girondists, for under the inspiration of the dictator, Robespierre (who had been his school friend), he had published his *Histoire des Brissotins,* which contained terrible denunciations of the Girondist leader, Brissot. After the Hebertistes had also been despatched, a revulsion against such wholesale carnage seized Camille, the result being the publication of *Le Vieux Cordelier* (1794). Herein he advocated a fresh policy,

DESMOULINS

this time one of forbearance and clemency, in which he was abetted by Danton and Lacroix, but his exuberant fancy and irresistible delight in Aristophanic humour had caused him to represent the great Robespierre in a ridiculous light. The latter, realising the extreme and personal danger of such an attack, suffered the Committee of Public Safety to condemn D. with the still nobler Danton to the guillotine in April 1794. A few days later Lucile Duplessis, his young and loving wife, in spite of her hold over the dictator, passed bravely in the tumbril to her death.

**Desna,** a riv., Russia, which rises in the prov. of Smolensk. It flows S.E. to Briansk, then S.W. until it joins the Dnieper. Its principal tribs. are the Seim and the Snov, and the river is navigable almost throughout its course of 550 m.

**Desor, Pierre Jean Edouard** (1811– 82), a Swiss geologist who climbed the Jungfrau in 1841. The results of his research into Jurassic echinoderms were published in his *Synopsis des Echinides Fossiles,* 1858, and *Echinologie Helvétique,* 1868–73, for the latter of which he collaborated with P. de Loriol. His *Aus Sahara,* 1865, contains his inquiry into the physical phenomena of that desert, whilst his investigations into the ancient lake habitations of Switzerland form a valuable contribution to palæontology.

**De Soto,** a tn. of Jefferson co. Missouri, U.S.A. It is situated on Joachim Creek, and has railroad shops, manufactories of plate glass, shoes and cloth. Pop. 5069.

**De Soto, Fernando** (1496–1542), a Spanish explorer, voyaged to Darien in 1519, under Davila, and joined the expedition of Nicaragua in 1527. During the conquest of Peru, in which he seconded Pizarro, he was so fortunate and came home with so much wealth (' an hundred and fourscore thousand ducats ') that the Emperor Charles V. suffered him to embark at his own expense on the subjugation of Florida. With a goodly company, De S. set out in 1539 from Tampa Bay in search of El Dorado. In 1541 he discovered the great Mississippi, and crossed over to the Washita R., but his companions were decimated by disease and continual skirmishes with the Indians, and all the clues as to the source of the treasure proved elusive. In 1542, therefore, De S. died of fever and disappointment, and the remnant of his expedition eventually reached Mexico. *See* Life by Cunninghame Graham (1904).

**Despard, Mrs. Charlotte French** (*b.* 1844), one of the principal leaders of the Women's Suffrage Movement; especially in its ' militant ' aspect. In the militant days she was twice imprisoned for actions in connection with this movement. Her reforming activities have been by no means confined to the Women's Movement. She laboured as a poor law guardian and a Socialist orator, and for a time lived at Nine Elms. She is as well known among the poor of Dublin, where she now resides. Though a sister to the late Earl Ypres, she was an extreme pacifist during the Great War. In 1919 she stood for Parliament at Battersea. Visited Russia, 1930.

**Despard, Edward Marcus** (1751–1803), an Irish conspirator, spent eighteen years in military service in the W. Indies, and later as superintendent of Yucatan. Recalled on trivial charges and found innocent even of these (1792), he was, notwithstanding, imprisoned for two years. He was finally beheaded because of his share in a plot to assassinate the king.

**D'Esperey, Franchet,** Fr. General who gained a considerable reputation during the Great War. A man of vigorous character and clear vision, he was well equipped for a military career, and soon came to the fore. After tne Battle of Charleroi (Aug. 1914) he was appointed to the command of the Fr. 5th Army, which, located on the right of the British Army, had decisively defeated the Gers. at Montmirail. In Sept. 1914, in co-operation with Foch, he brought to a standstill the Ger. counterattack from the valley of the Suippe which had an important bearing on their later movements on that front. In June 1918 he was appointed Commander-in-Chief of the Allied forces in Macedonia, and he at once infused his characteristic vigour into the operations on that front, which hitherto had been regarded as stagnant. He organised an offensive against the Bulgarians and in the autumn attacked and broke up their army as a fighting instrument. This success, which threatened Constantinople and hastened Turkey to conclude an armistice, undoubtedly influenced the general collapse of the Central Powers.

**Des Périers, Bonaventure** (*c.* 1500–44), a Fr. prose writer, was among the men of letters who enjoyed the patronage of Marguerite of Navarre, and is by many regarded as a joint author of the *Heptameron*, a work associated with Marguerite's name. The purity and animation of his style have won for him an assured place among the early masters of Fr. prose. In his dialogue entitled *Cymbalum Mundi,* he mocks at the religious views of the time whilst ostensibly poking fun at the superstitions of the ancients. His gift for story-telling is apparent in his *Nouvelles Récréations et Joyeux Devis* (published in 1558), as also his ability to write both in the humorous and romantic vein.

**Despotism,** in modern application, the oppressive and sometimes illegal rule of one man; the reverse of democracy. The name, like ' tyrant,' is of Gk. origin and had nothing of its present significance. The title ' Despot ' was given to the master of a household of slaves; then to the absolute ruler of Eastern countries with whom the Gks. came in contact. Later it came to be an honorary title given to princes in the Byzantine empire, and it is still employed in something of its old sense as a mode of addressing a bishop in the Gk. Church. The beginning of its present use was the employment, as in the case of Tyrant, of the word to describe a ruler who had no right to be the ruler although his actual method of government may have been excellent and beneficial.

**Despréaux,** *see* BOILEAU-DESPRÉAUX.

**Desquamation** refers to the shedding of the epithelium or surface skin, which takes place after certain diseases such as scarlet fever. It is likely that these epithelium scales are a source of infection; thus the patient is usually quarantined until the peeling of the skin is complete. A high temperature sometimes causes the skin to come off in large flakes.

**Dessalines, Jean Jacques** (1758–1806), *b.* in Guinea, Africa, and carried to Hayti as a slave. In the insurrection of 1791 he assumed the name of his master, a Fr. planter, and fought as a lieutenant under Toussaint l'Ouverture. After submitting to France he was made governor of the S. part of the is., but began the war anew, defeated the Fr. at the Battle of St. Marc, and after unspeakable cruelties drove them from the is., 1803. Hayti declared itself independent in 1804, and Dessalines was elected governor, and in the following year emperor under the title of Jean Jacques I. His tyranny and cruelty soon alienated his supporters, and in 1806, while trying to suppress a revolt, he was killed by Pétion and Christophe, the latter of whom succeeded him.

**Dessau,** the cap. of the former duchy now Free State of Anhalt, Germany, on the l. b. of the Mulde, 70 m. S.W. of Berlin. Among the

ARMS OF DESSAU

chief buildings are the former ducal Palace (1748), with a valuable library and picture gallery and standing in beautiful grounds; the town hall (1899–1900), several picture galleries, and the Schlosskirche. The fine W. wing of the Schloss dates from 1540. The town has monuments to 'Der alte Dessauer,' Leopold, Prince of Anhalt-Dessau (1676–1747), and to the philosopher, Moses Mendelssohn (*b.* here in 1729). It was also the birthplace in 1823 of Max Müller, the orientalist and philologist, who *d.* at Oxford, 1900. There are manufactures, aeroplane parts, machinery, chocolate, gas-cooking and heating apparatus and chemicals, and a good trade in corn and garden produce. Pop. 71,000.

**Dessuk,** a tn. of Egypt, on the Nile, 12 m. N.E. of Damanhur, has a Mohammedan high school with 290 students. About 7 m. N. are the ruins of the ancient Egyptian capital, Buto.

**De Staël,** *see* STAËL.

**Desterro,** *see* FLORIANOPOLIS.

**Desticker, Pierre-Henri** (1866–1928), Fr. general, *b.* at Avesnes, Nord. He was a major when the Great War broke out, but rose to the rank of General in 1918. On the General Staff, he served with Marshal Foch, when the latter presided over the Allied Military Committee at Versailles, and in 1924 he became Chief of Staff. In 1925 he was appointed by the League of Nations to be chairman of a Committee of investigation of Ger. armaments.

**Destinn, Emmy** (1878–1930), soprano; *b.* at Prague, daughter of Emmanuel Kittel. Began education as violinist under Lachner. Studied, 1892–98, under Maria Loewe-Destinn, whose surname she took. In 1898 engaged at Royal Opera, Berlin; in 1901 sang the part of Senta at Bayreuth. Appeared as Senta in *The Flying Dutchman,* and as Nedda in *Pagliacci,* at Covent Garden, 1904. Created heroine's part in *Madame Butterfly,* and Tatiana in *Eugène Onégin.* Other rôles : Aïda, Santuzza, Armide, Venus, Elsa, and Maddalena in *Andrea Chénier.* Published verses. Died, from a stroke, at Budéjovice, Bohemia.

**Destouches, Philippe** (1680–1754), a Fr. dramatist, *b.* at Tours. His real name was Néricault. In 1699 he became secretary to the Fr. ambassador in Switzerland, and wrote during the time *Le Curieux Impertinent,* 1710 ; *L'Ingrat,* 1712 ; *L'Irrésolu,* 1713 ; and *Le Médisant,* 1715. From 1716 to 1722 he was secretary to the embassy in London. On his return to France he was elected to the Academy, 1723, and subsequently produced *Le Philosophe Marié,* 1727, and his masterpiece, *Le Glorieux,* 1732, a picture of the struggle between the old nobility and the wealthy bourgeois. Like Molière, he wished to revive the comedy of character, but in style he rather followed Boileau ; his later comedies were spoilt by his carrying the moralising tendency to extremes.

**Destroyers,** *see* TORPEDO.

**Destructors** are furnaces employed for the destruction of refuse. The disposal of refuse from towns has presented a problem to the authorities from time immemorial, but with the concentration of population reached in modern civilisations the matter has become urgent. Such methods of disposal as dumping into the sea are clearly possible only in special circumstances, but the fact that much of the refuse consists of carbonaceous material (*e.g.* paper, straw, animal and vegetable remains, cinders, etc.) suggested the idea of destroying it by combustion. Destructor-furnaces are commonly erected in series, and, after the refuse has been collected, tins, cans, and bits of iron are withdrawn magnetically, fine dust is removed, and the residue then fed into the furnaces. High temperatures are necessary (about 2000°) for satisfactory destruction, and in some cases the heat evolved is used to produce steam and electricity. Destructors are comparatively expensive to construct and run, but the convenience and cleanliness are worth paying for. Many different types of destructors are in use, *e.g.* the Heenan type and the Horsfall and Sterling type, but for technical details professional journals and the literature of the manufacturing firms should be consulted. *See*, for example, the *Proceedings of the Institution of Civil Engineers*, passim.

**Desuetude**, a technical word in Scottish law, denoting the revocation of some law, simply through the practice of some usage, quite contrary to the terms of the law, which has received its sanction through a general consensus of opinion, and not through any legal enactment. Thus when a man was charged in 1887 with opening a pie and lemonade shop on Sunday he set up a plea of D. as regards the law of 1661 against Sabbath profanation. In this particular case the Act of 1661 was held not to have 'gone into D.' In the language of English jurisprudence, it is said that a statute never lapses 'by desuetude,' but can become inoperative only by repeal.

**Desvauxiaceæ**, a name formerly applied to monocotyledonous plants of the order Centrolepidaceæ. The species are small, sedge-like herbs of no known utility found in the southern hemisphere.

**Desvres**, a tn. in the Pas-de-Calais dept. of France, 10 m. E.S.E. of Boulogne. Pop. 1520.

**De Tabley, John Byrne Leicester Warren** (1835–95), poet, educated at Eton and Christ Church, Oxford. Between 1859 and 1865 he published seven volumes of verse, remarkable for their grace and refinement of feeling, but his *Philoctetes* (1866), which won the admiration of Gladstone and Browning, first gave full illustration to his fine classical culture. His careful drama entitled *The Soldier's Fortune* (1876) met with a cold reception; also published *Poems Dramatic and Lyrical* (1893), which proved that his poetical gifts had not been impaired by his life as a recluse. De T. was also an excellent amateur in botany and numismatics, and published a work on the flora of Cheshire.

**Detachment**, in its military sense, refers to a small number of infantry or cavalry despatched from the main army, regiment, brigade, company, or whatever division it may be, for the performance of some particular duty. In naval terminology the word is similarly used to denote the dismissal from the fleet or squadron of two or more vessels on a special service. A 'gun detachment' means the number of artillery soldiers told off to take care of a single gun.

**Detaille, Jean Baptiste Edouard** (1848–1912), Fr. painter, who was a pupil of Meissonier, his first picture exhibited in the Salon being 'A Corner of Meissonier's Studio' (1867). His finest pictures are undoubtedly his realistic paintings of military life, either of the scenes from contemporary wars, such as his 'En Reconnaissance' (1875), 'Le Régiment qui Passe' (1876), and his 'Salut aux Blessés' (1877), which represent episodes in

J. B. E. DETAILLE

the Franco-Prussian campaigns, or from the Napoleonic battles such as his 'Sortie de la Garrison de Hunigue en 1815,' and his representations of Napoleon in Egypt (1878), and of the engagement between Cossacks and the Imperial Guard in 1814 (1870). His best known portraits are of the Prince of Wales, Duke of Connaught, and Emperor of Russia (1898), whilst 'Le Rêve' (1888) and 'Les Victimes du Devoir' are two of his most famous pictures. In 1898 D. was elected a member of the Fr. Institute, and is the holder also of many foreign honours and decorations.

**Detective,** *see* POLICE.

**Detective Story, The,** was originated by the genius of the American, Edgar Allan Poe, whose *The Murders in the Rue Morgue* (1841) and *The Purloined Letter* have rarely, if ever, been surpassed in brilliance of analysis and invention. Poe was soon followed by the Fr. writer, Emile Gaboriau, whose *L'Affaire Lerouge* (1866) and *Le Dossier 113* (1867), etc., were eagerly read. Another of his countrymen, Boisgobey, proved in *Le Forçat Colonel* (1872) that he, too, was a master of detective writing. In England exciting works of this type have been composed by Fergus Hume,

Arthur Morrison, and, in particular, Sir Arthur Conan Doyle. Indeed, Sherlock Holmes, the astute detective, whose marvellous doings are narrated with such vraisemblance in the *Adventures, Memoirs*, etc., has become a household word in many quarters of the globe.

**Deterioration, Physical,** *see* PHYSICAL DETERIORATION.

**Determinants,** in mathematics, a system of symbols whereby many calculations are facilitated. Consider two homogeneous linear equations, $a_1x + b_1y = 0$; $a_2x + b_2y = 0$. By multiplying the first by $b_2$ and the second by $b_1$, and subtracting, we get $x(a_1b_2 - a_2b_1) = 0$, whence $a_1b_2 - a_2b_1 = 0$. This may be written $\begin{vmatrix} a_1a_2 \\ b_1b_2 \end{vmatrix} = 0$, and the expression on the left is called a D. of the second order, consisting of two rows and two columns. The value is not altered by changing rows into columns or *vice versâ*, thus $\begin{vmatrix} a_1b_1 \\ a_2b_2 \end{vmatrix} = a_1b_2 - a_2b_1$. Interchanging two rows or columns changes the sign; thus $\begin{vmatrix} a_2a_1 \\ b_2b_1 \end{vmatrix} = a_2b_1 - a_1b_2$. Consider three homogeneous linear equations, $a_1x + b_1y + c_1z = 0$; $a_2x + b_2y + c_2z = 0$; $a_3x + b_3y + c_3z = 0$. From the second and third we get by the rule of cross-multiplication $\frac{x}{b_2c_3 - b_3c_2} = \frac{y}{c_2a_3 - c_3a_2} = \frac{z}{a_2b_3 - a_3b_2}$. Substituting the proportional quantities for $x$, $y$, and $z$ in the first equation, we get $a_1(b_2c_3 - b_3c_2) + b_1(c_2a_3 - c_3a_2) + c_1(a_2b_3 - a_3b_2) = 0$, or $a_1\begin{vmatrix} b_2c_2 \\ b_3c_3 \end{vmatrix} + b_1\begin{vmatrix} c_2a_2 \\ c_3a_3 \end{vmatrix} + c_1\begin{vmatrix} a_2b_2 \\ a_3b_3 \end{vmatrix} = 0$. This may be written $\begin{vmatrix} a_1b_1c_1 \\ a_2b_2c_2 \\ a_3b_3c_3 \end{vmatrix} = 0$ and the expression on the left is known as a D. of the third order, consisting of three rows and three columns. It is to be noted that the coefficient of $a_1$, $b_1$, or $c_1$ is the D. of the second order obtained by omitting the row and the column containing that constituent in the D. of the third order. Some of the properties of D. are : if two adjacent columns or rows are interchanged, the sign of the D. is changed without other alteration in value ; if two rows or columns are identical the D. $= 0$ ; if each constituent in a row or column is multiplied by the same factor, the D. is multiplied by that factor. *See* Muir's *Theory of Determinants*.

**Determinism** (from Lat. *determinare*, to prescribe), the name applied to the doctrine that man's every action is directly dependent either on his environment or on his impulses and motives, the dependence being so mathematical that his behaviour could in every case be predicted were it possible to appreciate the exact nature and relative force of the external and internal impulses which drive him to behave as he does. It is therefore a doctrine in direct opposition to the doctrine of Free Will, taught in Christian ethics, and known to psychologists under the names of Indeterminism, Voluntarism, and Indifferentism, by which it is held that man has complete moral freedom to choose between different courses of action. ' Hard ' D. bears a very close resemblance to necessitarianism and the old fatalistic beliefs, whilst ' soft ' D. accounts for ' remorse ' by allowing that in some cases it is really open to a man to make a deliberate choice. The theory of evolution, by which man is regarded as a mere link in the ' chain of causal development,' as owing his motives, appetites, and aversions, and, indeed, his whole mental outlook largely to inherited tendency and environment, lends irrefutable support to the determinists.

**Detinue,** a term in law for the action brought for the recovery of goods, or their value, with damages for detaining them if they cannot be recovered, by the real owner of the goods against whoever is in actual possession of the same.

**Detmold,** cap. of the free state of Lippe, Germany, at the foot of the slopes of the Teutoburger Forest, 25 m. S. of Minden by rail. The chief buildings are the palace of the reigning princes (1550), a natural history museum, and a theatre. The industries are unimportant. There are many visitors in summer attracted by the beauty of the Teutoburger Wald. The poet F. Freiligrath (1810–76) and the dramatist Grabbe (1801–36) were both natives of D. On a hill about 3 m. S.W. of the town is a colossal statue of Arminius(Hermann), chief of the Cherusci, who defeated the Rom. general, Varus, here in 9 A.D. Pop. 15,300

**De Tocqueville,** *see* TOCQUEVILLE.

**Detonator,** a small supply of an easily-exploded substance used to discharge the main explosive constituent of a cartridge, shell, or mine. The substance commonly used for this purpose is fulminate of mercury, which in British service ammunition is mixed with potassium chlorate and antimony sulphide in proportions which depend on whether the D. is to be exploded by percussion or by a time fuse. The fulminate when exploded produces gases at a high temperature and pressure, conditions under which dynamite and other comparatively inert explosives are effectively discharged. The term D. is also applied to the small metal cases fixed on railway lines to serve as fog-signals. *See* SIGNALS.

**Detritus,** a geological term denoting gravel, sand, or other water-worn matter, and angular, or subangular débris, which have accumulated in consequence of the disintegration of rocks.

**Detroit,** the fourth largest city in the U.S.A., is in Michigan, on R. Detroit, 18 m. above Lake Erie and 284 m. E.N.E. of Chicago. It is built on the slope of the river bank, with wide tree-shaded avenues. Among the chief buildings are the City Hall (1868–71), the County Court House, the churches of St. John's Episcopal and First Congregational, the Rom. Catholic churches of St. Anne's and Sacred Heart of Mary, the Rom. Catholic College (1877) and dozens of huge sky-scrapers. D. is an important railway centre, and carries on an enormous commercial traffic by river and lakes. D. was established as a trading post in 1701 by a Fr. fur trader. In 1760 it was taken by the British and continued as a military post until it was surrendered to the U.S.A. in 1796. D. has been the home of the motor car since before Sir Thomas Lipton first steered a D. car among the London omnibuses and Queen Helena of Italy another past Trajan's column at Rome. The Ford Motor Co. was incorporated on June 16, 1903. The largest factories of automobile parts are at D., and all over the world space is conquered by D. products. D. is one of the chief centres of the manufacture of medical and pharmaceutical preparations, which began in 1856 in a single room 12 feet square. Other important industries are varnish, paints, oil, shipbuilding, railway works, lumber yards, machine shops, brick-making, tobacco, furniture, etc. The College of Medicine has 250 students. 60,000 children were enrolled in private and denominational schools in 1925. The University of D. was first so called in 1911. When the U.S.A. entered the Great War 296,677 men of D. were registered as available for service, many of them formed part of the famous Red Arrow Division nicknamed by the Fr. Les Terribles. On Dec. 15, 1925, the total deposits in D. banks were 692,237,000 dollars, of which 342,300,000 was in Savings Banks, the value of the goods manufactured the same year was 1599,000,000 dollars. The pop. was 79,577 in 1870, 466,000 in 1910, 993,680 in 1920, 1,568,662 in 1930, constituting it the fastest growing big city in the world.

**Detroit, University of,** an institution

for higher education conducted by Jesuit fathers under the auspices of the Rom. Catholic Church. Over 3000 students attend the various courses, which embrace arts and sciences, commerce and finance, civil engineering and law.

**Dettingen,** a vil., Bavaria, situated in Lower Franconia, on the Main, 8 m. N.W. of Aschaffenburg. It is noted for a victory which was won in 1743 by the British, Ger. and Austrian forces under George II. over the Fr., under Marshal Noailles. It was the last battle in which an English Monarch took part. Pop. 1480.

**Dettva,** or **Gyetva,** a market tn. of Hungary, situated about 18 m. E. of Altsohl. Pop. 7490.

**Deucalion,** in Gk. mythology, the son of Prometheus. When Zeus, in anger at the world's wickedness, resolved to destroy all mankind by a flood, D. built a boat which, after floating for nine days on the water, rested on the top of Parnassus. Having inquired of the oracle what they were to do next, they were ordered to throw stones behind them; those which D. threw became men, and those thrown by Pyrrha, his wife, became women. *See* Ovid, *Metam.* i.

**Deucher, Adolf** (1831–1912), Swiss statesman, *b.* at Thurgau, was by profession a doctor of medicine. Member of the National Council in 1867, he was elected to the Federal Council in 1883, and later became chief of the Departments of Commerce, Industries, and Agriculture. He was chosen president of the Confederation in 1886, 1897, 1903, and 1909. Died at Bern.

**Deule,** a riv. in the dept. Pas-de-Calais, N. France. It is a trib. of the Lys, which itself unites with the Scheldt in Belgium. Rising near Carency, if flows past Lille, where it fills the moat of the pentagonal citadel, and Quesnoy, joining the main river near Deulemont.

**Deus Nogueira Ramos, João de** (1830–96), a Portuguese poet, probably appeals to a greater number of his countrymen than any other native poet with the exception of Camoëns and Garrett. But for his ardent admirers, none of his poems would have reached the public, for he was indifferent to fame and a careless, spasmodic composer. Posterity will treasure above all his spontaneous and deeply emotional lyrical outpourings such as his *Rachel, Marina, Descalça,* and above all his exquisite *Ramo de Flores,* 1869. The *Campo de Flores,* 1893, is the best edition of his poems. By turns D.'s writing is imitative, idyllic, pessimistic, and devout, and notable for its intense purity and elemental simplicity.

**Deuteronomy,** the name of the fifth book of the Pentateuch, which from the seventeenth century onwards was one of the great battle-grounds of biblical criticism. Before that time, it was universally held to be of Mosaic authorship, but it is now often regarded as a gradual compilation, of which the greater part dates from the reign of Manasseh. An earlier form was discovered in the reign of Josiah, and exercised a great influence on that monarch. The work subdivides greatly. Chaps. i.–iv. and v.–xi. give two introductory exhortations, the former being largely historical. After this come a variety of exhortations and historical accounts interspersed with poems. The high moral tone of the book is shown by the fact that of a quotation from it Christ said : ' On these words hang all the law and the prophets,' and that from D. were taken all Christ's answers to the Tempter in the wilderness. The name of the book is taken from the Septuagint translation of the words ' this law ' in chap. xvii. 18. *See* Finn, *The Unity of the Pentateuch*, 1917.

**Deutsch, Felix** (1858–1928), Ger. industrial magnate, *b.* at Breslau. Together with Walter Rathenau, he was associated in the formation of the German Edison Co., which later, developed into the well-known ' A.E.G.' (Allgemeine Elektrizitats Gezellschaft) or General Electrical Co. of Germany. He succeeded Rathenau as president on the latter's assassination in 1922.

**Deutsch, Immanuel Oscar Menahem** (1829–73), a Ger. Hebrew scholar, studied Hebrew and Chaldee literature under his uncle, a rabbi, and in 1855 became an assistant in the library of the British Museum. His fame grew out of his brilliant article on ' The Talmud,' which appeared in the *Quarterly Review* of 1867. Besides contributing to Smith's biblical dictionaries, he wrote some 195 articles for *Chambers's Encyclopædia*, and was an authority on Phœnician antiquities.

**Deutschbrod,** or **Nemecky-Brod,** a tn. of Czecho-Slovakia, and the cap. of the dist. of that name. It is situated on the R. Sazawa, 60 m. S.E. of Prague. The manufactures are cloths machinery, and glass. Pop. 8990.

**Deutsche Bank** is one of the big banks in Germany. It was founded in 1870 with its chief office in Berlin. Its main purpose was to provide a ready assistance in all financial matters to Ger. commercial men. The D. B. did good service in Germany's rapid development in industry and commerce which took place during the last two decades of the nineteenth century and continued up to the outbreak of the Great War in 1914. In addition to the branches throughout the German Reich, it has others in Europe, particularly in the S.E. Its capital and reserves amount to over £110,000,000.

**Deutsch-Eylau,** *see* EYLAU-DEUTSCH.

**Deutsch-Krone,** a tn. of Prussian Germany, situated 15 m. N.W. of Schneidemuhl, between the lakes Radau and Arers. There is trade in wood and cattle. Pop. 10,580.

**Deutz,** a tn. of Prussian Germany, in the Rhine prov., situated on the r. b. of the Rhine, opposite Cologne, with which it was incorporated in 1888.

**Deutzia,** a genus of Saxifragaceæ, grows wild in the N. of India, China, and Japan. *D. scabra*, *D. gracilis*, and *D. crenata* are cultivated in Britain, and the first-named is remarkable for its silicious stellate hairs.

**Deuxponts,** *see* ZWEIBRÜCKEN.

**Deux Sèvres,** *see* SÈVRES-DEUX.

**Deva,** a tn. in Rumania. on the Maros, 82 m. E. by N. of Temesvar. It has picturesque ruins. Pop. 8700.

**De Valera, Eamon** (*b.* 1882). Irish patriot and politician. He gained great notoriety during the Irish revolution, which commenced at Easter, 1916. He was *b.* in New York City, his father being Spanish and his mother Irish. He was educated in Ireland at Blackrock College and the Royal University at Dublin. He gained several scholastic degrees and taught mathematics, Fr. and Latin in various colleges and educational establishments. Whilst engaged in his educational pursuits his political sympathies were being nurtured in the atmosphere of Sinn Fein, but though an enthusiast, he did not become a prominent Sinn Feiner until the 1916 Easter Revolution, during which he commanded a party of insurgents. He was taken prisoner and sentenced to death, but this was commuted to penal servitude for life. At the general amnesty in 1917 he was released, and again plunged into political affairs, becoming the directing head of the Sinn Fein movement. He gained great prestige on being elected member of parliament for East Clare and was elected president of the ' Irish Republic ' in Oct. 1917. He was re-arrested in May 1918 and confined in Lincoln prison, from which he escaped or was allowed to escape in Feb. 1919, to U.S.A. In 1921 he returned to Ireland, and was one of the negotiators of the treaty which brought the Irish Free State into being, although he repudiated the treaty. He revolted against the Irish Free State, and was captured in Aug. 1923, to be released in July 1924, when he again entered the political arena. In Aug. 1927 he took the oath of allegiance in Parliament, but the country was over-tired of upheavals, and his prestige has since declined markedly.

**Devanagri, or Nagari,** called also the 'town-script,' is that form of the Sanskrit alphabet which is in general use among Hindu scholars, and appears in all works on Sanskrit by Europeans. It was possibly introduced to India about 800 B.C. by traders from Mesopotamia. It is at least probable, in view of the similarity of certain letters, that there is some kinship between the Nagari and the Phœnician alphabet, which in its turn may have been derived from Egyptian hieroglyphics. The Indo-Aryan vernaculars, Gujarati, Rajasthani, and Bihari, are usually written in Nagari characters.

**Devaprayaga, or Deoprayag,** a vil., 2266 ft. above the sea-level, at the confluence of the Alaknanda and Bhagirathi, in the dist. of Garwhal, N.W. Provinces, India. The two rivers form the Ganges below Deoprayag. Here is the famous temple of Rama Chandra, the resort of Hindu pilgrims.

**Devavanja,** a tn. and com. of Hungary, 45 m. S.W. of Debreezea. Pop. 13,350.

**Development.** In music, whether referred to a phrase or more especially to a subject, denotes its fulfilment, or unfolding of all the qualities it contains by variation in harmony, rhythm, tonality, and by the building, as it were, of more or less elaborate structures upon the original melody. Signifies in geometry the unrolling of any conical or cylindrical surface, and in general the smoothing out into a plane surface of any curved one. In mathematics it always means the process by which one mathematical term is exchanged for another of equal value. D. may also be said to cover the whole subject of investigation in the science of embryology.

**Development and Road Improvement Funds Act, 1909,** provides for the appointment of Roads Boards with power to construct and maintain new roads and to make advances to County Councils and other highway authorities in respect of the construction of new roads and the improvement of existing roads. Every road constructed by the Board was to be a public highway. The powers are now merged in the Ministry of Transport. *See also* HIGHWAYS.

**Devenish,** an is. and par. of Ireland situated in Lough Erne, co. Fermanagh. The surface is hilly in parts, and boggy. The soil is very fertile, and good crops are raised. Lime-

stone and sandstone are quarried. Pop. 2990.

**Deventer,** an ancient tn. of Holland in Overyssel, situated on the Yssel, 8 m. N. of Zutphen, and 25 m. N. of Arnheim. It has exactly the appearance of a tn. of the Middle Ages. Part of the principal church dates from the twelfth century, the crypt of St. Lebuinus is supposed to date from 1040. The Weigh-house is a queer little edifice of 1528. There are many elegant and charming houses and iron foundries and carpet factories. D. was captured from the Spaniards by Prince Maurice of Orange. The artist Terburg, whose pictures are scattered all over Europe, lived at D. and died there in 1681. Pop. 34,960.

**Deventer, General Sir Jacob Louis Van** (1874–1922), S. African soldier, *b.* in Orange Free State. He came into prominence as one of General Smuts' lieutenants during the Boer War at the end of the nineteenth century, particularly in connection with the invasion of Cape Colony. He served on Botha's staff in the campaign in German S.W. Africa, 1914–15. Commanded a mounted brigade at the outset of the campaign against the Gers. in E. Africa and eventually commanded the whole force. After much hard fighting he drove his opponent, General Paul von Lettow-Vorbeck, into Portuguese territory.

**De Vere, Sir Aubrey** (1788–1846), an Irish poet, went to Harrow, where Byron and Peel were his schoolmates. A country gentleman, he lived a life of retirement, writing without any care for his public. He took a huge interest in public events, and was superior to the common prejudices of his class. His sonnets appeared first in 1842, and were spoken of by Wordsworth as 'the most perfect of our age.' *Julian, the Apostate,* was published in 1822, and several poems in the following year. When his distinguished son, Aubrey, printed a second edition of *Mary Tudor* (a play), in 1884, he prefixed it by a memoir of his father, the author.

**De Vere, Aubrey Thomas** (1814–1902), a poet, was the third son of Sir Aubrey de Vere, second baronet, of Curragh Chace, Adare, co. Limerick. In 1842 he published *The Waldenses, and other Poems,* which contained some exquisite lyrics, and in the following year he issued a companion volume, *The Search after Proserpine, and other Poems,* 1843. Besides poems, he wrote in prose concerning Ireland's wrongs, for while he held no brief for the disruption of the union he was an ardent sympathiser with the distress of the Irish folk. *English Misrule and Irish Misdeeds,* 1848, was the principal of these works, *Ireland and Proportional Representation*, 1885, the last. Not a great poet, yet at his best, especially when the theme was romantic, rose to a high level. He published his *Reminiscences* in 1897. Two years after his death Wilfred Ward issued a Memoir.

**Deveron**, or the **Blackwater**, a riv. of Scotland, which rises in the mts. of Cabrach at a height of 1850 ft It is at first merely a mountain torrent, but passing through Aberdeenshire and Banffshire, it gradually becomes broader and slower, until after a course of 60 m. it enters the sea at Banff. Salmon and trout abound in its waters.

**Devi**, or **Durga** (Sanskrit for ' inaccessible '), in Hindu mythology the daughter of Himavat (the Himalayas) and the wife of Siva. She is depicted with ten armed hands, a kindly face, and attendant lions to suggest the ferocity of her nature. Bloody sacrifices are offered her, whilst her birthday is annually celebrated at the great Bengalese festival in the sixth Hindu month.

**Deviation**, *see* COMPASS.

**Device**, *see* HERALDRY.

**Devil** (O. Eng. *deofol*, Lat. *diabolus*, from Gk. διάβολος, slanderer), in Christian theology the great spirit of evil who works in ceaseless antagonism to God. The word is also used for inferior evil spirits under his command. The general evolution of the idea of a single spirit of evil has already been shown in Demonology (*q.v.*), and its development in the O.T. and N.T. will here be shown. The idea appears first in the account of the fall given in Genesis. Here the temptation comes from the serpent, created by God, but most subtle of creatures, whose hostility to God is not clearly stated. The idea of subservience to God is also shown in such references as 1 Sam. xvi. 14, and 1 Kings xxii. 22, and the conception of Satan (Heb. ' the adversary ') is a development of the post-exilic period. Here, though his personality is made more distinct and his opposition to God and his servants is recognised, we still find him regarded as a minister of God. Thus, in Job ii. Satan appears among the sons of God, and asks God's permission to test the virtue of Job. It is this aspect of the tempter that is generally considered in later times. The dualistic idea, which considers Satan as the adversary of God, ruling over a separate kingdom of evil, is largely due to the contact of Jewish with Persian modes of thought In Tobit iii. Asmodeus appears as the equivalent of Satan, and in Wisdom ii. 24 is identified with the serpent who tempted Eve. The *Book of the Secret of Enoch* further relates the revolt of Satan and his fall from Heaven. In the N.T., the Jewish system is taken for granted. Satan is spoken of under a variety of names, the D. (Heb. ii. 14), the Enemy (Matt. xiii. 39), Beelzebub (Matt. x. 25), the Adversary (1 Pet. v. 8), and in Revelations as the Accuser of the Brethren (xii. 10), the Old Serpent (xx. 2), and the Great Dragon (xii. 9). Jesus distinctly recognises a kingdom of evil spirits, ruled by a prince, whom it is his work to overcome. The common conception in the early Church may be shown by a quotation from Harnack's *History of Dogma :* ' the present dominion of evil demons was just as generally presupposed as man's need of redemption, which was regarded as a result of that dominion.' The fathers generally held that Satan had dominion over this present world, though Christ had freed his servants from the Satanic power. Irenæus in the second century represents this freedom as being gained through Christ's payment of the ransom to Satan, and this idea gained ground, though it was definitely repudiated by Anselm among others. Present liberal Christian thought is inclined to neglect all consideration of the D., and to consider belief in Satan as an unessential part of the faith. For present views on the subject recourse should be had to the works of Kant. Schleiermacher, Dorner, Martensen, Ritschl, Kaftan, etc.

**Devil-fish**, an opprobrious name applied to various fishes, chiefly belonging to the Myliobatfdæ, or eagleray family. It is also applied to the octopus, which is, of course, not a fish, but a mollusc, and to the anglers (*q.v.*) or sea-devils which have the technical name of *Lophius piscatorius*. Sea-devils have flat and tesselated teeth, broad flat bodies and long, thin, whip-like tails; they are voracious and crush molluscs with their hard teeth. Species of the different genera attain great size.

**Deville**, *see* SAINTE-CLAIRE DEVILLE.

**Devil's Advocate**, *see* ADVOCATUS DIABOLI.

**Devil's Bridge** (Ger. *Teufelsbrücke*) : (1) A famous bridge over the Reuss in the canton of Uri, Switzerland, 1¼ m. from the spot where the St. Gothard Pass road comes out on to the Valley of Andermatt. Here the river, which is 4590 ft. above sea-level, forms a fine waterfall of 100 ft. (2) A hamlet in Cardiganshire, Wales, 10¼ m. E.S.E. of Aberystwith, and also a double bridge over the Mynach, which here runs at the bottom of a gorge, 114 ft. deep, making four falls from 16 ft. to

100 ft. within a mile. The upper bridge dates only from 1753, but the lower was built in the eleventh century by the monks of Strata Florida. *See* Borrow, *Wild Wales.*

**Devil's Coach-horse,** or **Black Cocktail,** the beetle known less graphically as *Ocypus olens.* This species, which is British, is about 1 inch in length, narrow in shape, active in habit, and usually carnivorous in diet.

**Devil's Dyke :** (1) An anct. earthwork extending from Wood Ditton to Reach in Cambridgeshire, England. It is 18 ft. high, and once formed a boundary between E. Anglia and Mercia. (2) A huge fissure, 4½ m. N.W. by N. of Brighton in Sussex, England. It has a railway station and is the object of excursions for tourists from Brighton, there being now a

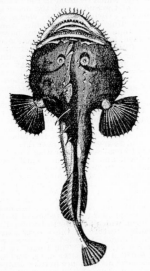

DEVIL-FISH (SEA-DEVIL)

cable way to take passengers across from one side of the chasm to the other.

**Devil's Island, French Guiana,** *see* Salut, Iles du.

**Devil's Lake,** a city in N. Dakota, co. seat of Ramsey, seat of the State school for the deaf. Near by is an important wild animal preserve. Pop. 5451.

**De Vinne, Theodore Low** (1828–1914), American printer and writer on typography, was *b.* at Stamford, Conn., on Dec. 25, 1828, and was early apprenticed to a printer. At twenty-one he was employed by Francis Hart of New York ; became junior partner in 1858, and after Hart's death in 1877 changed the name of the firm to Theo. L. De Vinne and Co. He was part-founder and president of the Grolier Club, whose early publications were produced by the De Vinne Press. His work was invariably of the highest quality, the *Century Dictionary* showing his artistry and care. His chief works are *The Invention of Printing* (1876), *The Practice of Typography* (1900–1904), *Notable Printers of Italy during the Fifteenth Century* (1910).

**Devizes,** a market tn. and municipal bor. of Wiltshire, England, near the Kennet and Avon Canal. The tn. owes its origin to a magnificent castle, of which very few fragments remain, built by Roger, Bishop of Salisbury, about 1132. Round the castle grew up a prosperous tn. which from the time of Henry VIII. till about 1820 was famous for its cloth, and from the time of Edward III. for its wool. The tn., besides its modern castle, contains a remarkable Gothic marketcross ; the partly Norman churches of St. John's and St. Mary's, a museum and a corn exchange. Its modern industries are the grain trade, tobacco, and snuff works, breweries, and the manufactures of silk and agricultural implements. Pop. (1921) 6022.

**Devlin, Joseph,** Irish nationalist ; *b.* 1872, Belfast. Educated there at Christian Bros. School. M.P., Kilkenny N., 1902–6 ; W. Belfast, 1906–18 ; Falls div. Belfast, 1918–22 ; Fermanagh and Tyrone since 1929. Member N. Ireland parliament : Co. Antrim and W. Belfast, 1921–25 ; W. Belfast, 1925–29 ; Central Belfast since.

**Devolution :** (1) The first war embarked on by Louis XIV. of France with the single object of extending the boundaries of his kingdom is known as the War of Devolution. When his father-in-law, Philip IV. of Spain, died, Louis, by introducing a civil right of inheritance into politics, claimed Flanders as the possession of his wife, Maria Theresa. (2) Also the name given to the schemes for the administration of Ireland, as enunciated by the Irish Reform Association, formed in 1903.

**Devon,** a riv. of Scotland, which rises in the Ochil Hills at a height of 1800 ft. It is noted for its beautiful scenery, which has been immortalised by Burns. There is a series of remarkable falls, below the Crook of Devon, known as the Devil's Mill, Caldron Linn, and Rumbling Bridge. Trout abound in the river, and after a course of 33 m., it falls into the Forth at Cambus.

**Devonian System,** in geology. The term was first used by Murchison for the greater part of the Paleozoic strata of Devonshire, instead of the older term ' Old Red Sandstone,' because the strata in Devonshire, while being otherwise identical with the ' Old Red Sandstone ' of Scotland, Hereford, and South Wales, and occupying the same position between the Silurian and Carboniferous periods, contain a much more copious and rich fossil fauna. The conditions under which the ' Old Red Sandstone ' and the ' Devonian ' strata were deposited are so very different, however, that later geologists do not use the terms synonymously. *See* OLD RED SANDSTONE.

**Devonport** (before 1824 called Plymouth Dock), until 1914 a parl., municipal, and county bor., situated on a peninsula formed by the Hamoaze and Stonehouse Pool at the head of Plymouth Sound, and forming with Plymouth and Stonehouse the ' Three Towns.' D. is one of the chief naval and military stations in the British Isles; it owes its origin to the dockyard established here by William III. in 1689. The naval establishments extend nearly 4 m. along the Hamoaze and include, besides the original dockyard, the Keyham steam yard and factory, the gunwharf, the Gov. House and Admiralty House on Mount Wise, the naval and military barracks and the Royal Naval Engineering College at Keyham. In 1896 fresh extensions were begun at the Keyham Yard, which were opened, under the name of Devonport North Yard, by the Prince of Wales in 1907. There is a powder magazine on Drake's Island at the entrance to the Hamoaze (estuary of the Tamar); Mount Edgcumbe on the N. side is guarded by forts, and the harbour is fortified and guarded by men-of-war. D. and Stonehouse were amalgamated with Plymouth in 1914, the three now forming the city of Plymouth, created such on Oct. 18, 1928. Pop. 81,678.

**Devonport, Sir Hudson Ewbanke Kearley, Bart.,** first ViscountandBaron, of Whittington, Bucks; *b.* Sept. 1, 1856, youngest son of George Ewbanke Kearley, of Tarrant Gunville, Dorset. Liberal M.P. for Devonport, 1892–1910. Parliamentary Secretary to the Board of Trade, 1905–9. Chairman, Port of London Authority, 1909–25. Food Controller, 1916–17. Formerly senior partner Kearley and Tonge. Baronet, July 22, 1908. P.C., Oct. 18, 1909. Ennobled, July 15, 1910; viscount June 22, 1917.

**Devonshire, Spencer Compton**

**Cavendish, eighth Duke of** (1833–1908), a statesman, was the eldest son of William Cavendish, second Earl of Burlington, and was known as Lord Cavendish until 1858, when his father succeeding to the dukedom of Devonshire, he bore the courtesy title of Marquis of Hartington. In 1857 he entered parliament, as a Palmerstonian Liberal, and in 1874, when Gladstone was badly beaten at the general election, resigned his leadership of the party, the Liberals chose Hartington in his stead. In 1880, on the defeat of Disraeli, he was invited to form an administration, but Gladstone having returned to the House to take up the matter of the ' Bulgarian atrocities,' he withdrew in favour of his old chief. In 1882 he went to the War Office, and was there during the period of disaster which resulted in the evacuation of, the Sudan and the death of Gordon. Owing to his views on Home Rule he declined office when Gladstone again came into power in 1886, and moved the rejection of the Bill, which shortly afterwards was thrown out on the second reading by a majority of ninety. At the general election which followed, the Conservatives and the Liberal-Unionists (as the seceders called themselves) were in a majority, and Lord Salisbury invited Hartington to form a Coalition Ministry, in which he would accept office. This Hartington declined to do, hoping that by some means the Liberals and the Liberal-Unionists might in the near future be able to coalesce. This wish was not fulfilled, and it was not until 1894 that the Duke of Devonshire (as he became in 1891) accepted office in a Conservative Gov. He then became President of the Council under Salisbury, and retained his office under Balfour. In 1904 he resigned, being opposed to the policy of tariff reform, which henceforth became the leading feature in the Conservative programme. He died at Cannes on March 24, 1908. ' The Duke,' as he was called in his later days, wielded an enormous influence in the country, and was one of the most popular figures in the kingdom. People were amused at his lethargic manner, and were delighted to believe the story that he yawned during his maiden speech in the House of Commons, and that thereupon Disraeli remarked to a neighbour, ' That young man will go far.' The duke was not a brilliant man, but he was, above all things, sound. In private life, he was also popular, and one of his most intimate friends was King Edward VII. In his early days he was fond of hunting, and all his life he was a notable follower of the turf, which was, perhaps his chief interest outside politics. There is a Biography by Bernard Holland, 1911.

**Devonshire, Sir Victor Christian William Cavendish, ninth Duke of,** K.G., P.C.,' etc., *b.* May 31, 1868; eldest son of third son of seventh duke. Educated Eton; and Trinity College, Cambridge. M.P. (Unionist), West Derbyshire, 1891–1908. Treasurer of Household, 1900–3; Financial Secretary to Treasury, 1903–5. Succeeded eighth duke, 1908. Chancellor, Univ. of Leeds, 1909. Mayor of Eastbourne, 1909–10. Civil Lord of Admiralty, 1915–16. Governor-General of Canada, 1916–21. Secretary of State for Colonies, 1922–24.

Plym. Besides its orchards, D. is rich in pastures, and is famous for its cattle and dairy produce. The climate is so mild that in some parts the vegetation is of a sub-tropical character, aloes and fig-trees, and even oranges growing in the open. The land is rich in minerals, the tin mines were long important, and copper, lead, iron, and manganese are all worked, as well as china and terra-cotta clays, granite, marble, limestone and sandstone. Fish abound round the coasts. Apart from the Gov. industries at Plymouth, the chief are the lace manufactures at Tiverton and Honiton, woollen goods and serges, boots and shoes, potteries, gloves,

NORTH OF HARTLAND QUAY, DEVONSHIRE

**Devonshire,** a S.W. co. of England, bounded by the Bristol Channel on the N., Cornwall on the W., the English Channel on the S., and Dorsetshire and Somersetshire on the E. It is the third co. in size in England, with an area of 2604 sq. m. The surface is hilly, with the rugged plateau of Dartmoor, broken into numerous rugged 'tors,' in the S.W.; Exmoor in the N.W., and Blackdown. On the lower slopes the soil is very fertile, especially in the district of 'South Hams' with its gardens and apple orchards. The coast-line of D. extends for about 150 m.; the N. coast is very rugged with cliffs 400–500 ft. high and great rocky inlets, of which the chief is Bideford Bay. On the S. coast are Bolt Tail and Start Point among others: and Tor Bay and Plymouth Sound, which is one of the finest harbours in the kingdom. The chief rivs. are the Tamar (59 m.), the Exe (54 m.), the Dart, the Teign, the Taw, the Torridge, and the

and paper-mills. Cider is made all over the county. Besides Plymouth, the chief towns are Torquay and Paignton, noted health resorts, Tiverton, Barnstaple, Tavistock, Brixham, Dartmouth, Teignmouth, and Princetown on Dartmoor, the great convict prison. Among the famous men born here were Drake and Raleigh, Hawkins, Davis, Sir Humphrey Gilbert, Sir Richard Grenville, Marlborough, Sir Joshua Reynolds, Coleridge, and Kingsley. D. is unsurpassed as a region for the holiday-maker. Scenery, history, antiquities including age-worn cromlechs and circles, a graciousness in its population a, mild climate, all combine to interest alike the literary man, the artist, the photographer, and the 'hiker.' The county returns seven members to Parliament. Pop. 709,488. *See* J. Prince, *Worthies of Devonshire,* 1701; Polwhele, *History of Devonshire,* 1797–1800; R. N. Worth, *History of Devonshire,* 1886;

Victoria County History, *Devonshire*, 1906.

**Devoy, John** (1842–1928) Irish patriot and journalist, *b.* in County Kildare, and educated in Dublin. Early a member of the Irish Republican Brotherhood, he was throughout his life a passionate protagonist of Irish independence. As a young man he joined the notorious Fenians, by whom he was deputed to seduce Irish soldiers from their allegiance to the Crown. He was arrested for this a year later and sentenced to fifteen years' imprisonment. After serving five years, he was liberated on condition that he spent the residue of his term in the U.S.A. In the U.S.A. he earned a living as a journalist, chiefly on Chicago papers, and later he edited the Irish-American paper, *The Gaelic American*, of New York.

**Devrient, Gustav Emil** (1803–72), an actor, was famous for his histrionic powers, his chief rôles being Hamlet (which he played in London and Dresden), Tasso, and Correggio.

**Devrient, Otto** (1838–94), a playwright and actor, won considerable recognition by his adaptation of Goethe's *Faust*, 1876. Other of his plays are *Tiberius Gracchus*, 1871, and *Gustav Adolf*, 1891.

**De Vries, Hugo,** Dutch botanist, *b.* at Haarlem in 1848, educated at Leyden and Heidelberg, and under Julius Sachs at Wurzburg. After holding various educational posts in Germany, he accepted the professorial chair of botany in Amsterdam, where he applied himself to the problems of evolution as they affect plant life. In his botanical research work he was much influenced by the Mendelian theories, and himself originated the theory of mutation. He made special use of the *Œnothera lamarckiana*, or evening primrose, which now grows profusely in Europe, though originally a native of America. *See* Essays in *Berichten der deutschen botanischen Gesellschaft*; and his principal work, *Die Mutationstheorie*, published in Leipzig, 1901. (*See also* BIOLOGY.)

**Dew** (Old Eng. *deaw*), the moisture found on the surface of the earth during the night and early morning, particularly after a hot day, and produced by condensation of the vapour of the atmosphere on contact with the earth cooled by radiation. The old theory, dating from the earliest times, was that D. fell from above; it was Dr. W. C. Wells, of London, in his *Essay on Dew*, 1814, who promulgated the above theory of radiation. He went on to say that for every definite pressure and temperature of the atmosphere there is a definite quantity of water-vapour which can be kept in suspension until it comes in contact with some cool substance, and is itself cooled below a certain temperature, when the vapour will condense. This point of temperature is called the ' dew-point.' In 1885 Aitken by experiments discovered that while undoubtedly some of the moisture called D. was the result of condensation of the atmosphere, the ' greater part ' is formed from moisture ' just risen from the earth or to the surface of plant leaves.' During the night, when evaporation ceases to a great extent, the vapour still rising from the ground is either condensed at once on its cold surface, or is trapped by the grass or plant-leaves which have cooled even faster than the surface of the ground. D. can be formed only under certain conditions; wind prevents the atmosphere from remaining sufficiently long in contact with the earth to cause condensation, and a cloudy sky prevents it by checking radiation. When the temperature of objects with which the vapour comes in contact falls below freezing point, the D. is condensed into a solid substance and is called 'hoar-frost.' The average annual deposit of D. near London is 1 to 1·5 in. *See* Dr. Charles Wells, *Essay on Dew*, 1818; J. Aitken, *On Dew.*

**Dewar, Arthur** (called **Lord Dewar**) (1860–1917), Scottish judge; *b.* at Perth; 4th surviving son of John Dewar, distiller. Educated at Academy of Perth and Edinburgh Univ.— graduated, 1882. Admitted to Bar, 1885 (took silk, 1904) Extra Advocate-Depute for Glasgow circuit, 1892–95. Liberal M.P., S. Edinburgh, 1899–1900, 1906–10. Solicitor-General for Scotland, 1909–10. Raised to bench of Court of Session, April 1910. Died in Edinburgh, June 14, 1917.

**Dewar, Sir James** (1842–1923), chemist and physicist, was *b.* at Kincardine-on-Forth, Sept. 20, 1842. He early developed a taste for music, and made violins. Educated at Dollar Academy and at Edinburgh Univ., where he assisted Lyon Playfair. Also studied at Ghent. Then became demonstrator of chemistry at Edinburgh, and lecturer in the Dick Veterinary College. In 1875 became Jacksonian Professor of Natural Experimental Philosophy at Cambridge, and in 1877 was made F.R.S. and Fullerian professor of chemistry at the Royal Institution, London. Among numerous other honours, he received the Rumford medal of the Royal Society in 1894, was the first holder of the Hodgkin's gold medal of the Smithsonian Institution, Washington, and the first British scientist to be awarded the Lavoisier medal of the Fr. Academy of Sciences (1904). He was co-inventor with Sir Frederic Abel of cordite, made valuable experiments in spectroscopy (from 1818 onwards), and investigated the physiological action of light; but his 'low temperature' discoveries form his most valuable contribution to science. (*See also* BEILBY; CARBONISATION.) He invented the thermos flask. Besides being the first to demonstrate before a public audience the liquefaction of oxygen and air, he invented an apparatus by which liquid oxygen by the pint can be produced, devised vacuum-jacketed vessels for the storage of liquid gases, first collected liquid hydrogen (in 1898), and finally (1899) succeeded in solidifying this gas as he had previously (1886) solidified oxygen. His experiments showing the gas-absorbing properties of cooled charcoal led, during the Great War, to the invention of antidotes to poison-gas. He was knighted in 1904; and *d.* at the Royal Institution, London, March 27, 1923.

**Dewas,** two native states and tn. of Central India, under British protection, and governed by the descendants of the two brothers, Punwar Mahrattas. The cap., D., is situated 20 m. N.E. of Indore. The state of the senior branch (749 sq. m.) has a pop. of 77,005; of the junior branch (419 sq. m.) one of 66,998.

**Dewberry,** or *Rubus cœsius*, is a species of Rosaceæ nearly related to *R. fruticosus*, the bramble. It receives its name from the fine waxy secretion which covers the black shining fruit and somewhat resembles dew. The fruit resembles the bramble in appearance, but is somewhat coarser and more acid, and the plant is also called the running briar or blackberry.

**D'Ewes, Sir Simonds** (1602–50), chronicler, was called to the Bar, but never practised. A Member of Parliament in 1640, he was expelled from the House when Pride's purge was applied. A conceited pedant, a Puritan, and a moderate Royalist, he collected a number of historical records, which proved invaluable to Selden, but he is best remembered by his autobiography and letters, published by Halliwell in 1845, which form an enlightening contemporary review of public events up to 1636.

**De Wet, Christian Rudolph** (1854–1922), Boer general and statesman, served in the first war (1880–81) between the Eng. and his countrymen as a field cornet. From 1885 to 1897 he was a member of the Orange Free State Volksraad, and when the S. African War broke out in 1899 he

became general and commander-in-chief of the Free State forces, fighting at first under Cronje in the W. He proved himself perhaps the most formidable of all the Boer leaders in guerrilla tactics. After capturing Sanna's Post, near Bloemfontein, and gaining soon afterwards the victory at Reddersburg, De W. showed himself a master in devising sudden manœuvres, falling unexpectedly on detached British columns, and destroying a number of weakly garrisoned outposts. In 1902, whilst the

DEWBERRY

negotiations for peace were in progress, he came to England with the other commandants, and in the same year published his narrative of the campaigns, the Eng. translation of which is entitled *Three Years' War*. In 1907 he was elected a member of the new Parliament of the Orange Free Colony and also Minister of Agriculture. In the Closer Union Convention of 1908–9 he was a delegate. An ardent Nationalist at heart, he chose the picturesque rôle of the Dutch patriot rather than wholeheartedly join the greater cause as a S. African. He gave expression to his views in 1912, when he joined General Hertzog, who was pursuing a separatist policy, and therefore seceded entirely from the S. African Party. He became an active member of the Nationalist Party, and the outbreak of the Great War gave him the opportunity of expressing his extreme views in an active form, for he headed a revolt against the Gov. He was captured by Botha in Dec. 1914 and brought to trial on charges of high treason, on many of which he was convicted. He was sentenced to six years' imprisonment and fined £20,000. After being in captivity for a year, he was released on giving an undertaking not to engage in political agitation. He *d.* at Bloemfontein on Feb. 3, 1922. In spite of his revolt, he seems to have been popular, owing to the prestige he had gained during the Boer War, on which, indeed, he relied too much in later years.

**De Wette, Wilhelm Martin Lebe-recht** (1780–1849), a Ger. theologian, came under the influence of Herder and later studied theology under Paulus. Professor of Theology at Heidelberg (1807–10), and Berlin University. His fearless and yet spiritual criticism of the Bible has earned for him a position aloof alike from such pure rationalists as Paulus and from the school of orthodox writers and super-naturalists. His chief works are : *Commentar über die Psalmen,* 1811 ; *Ueber Religion und Theologie,* 1815 ; and *Einleitung in das Neue Testament,* 1836.

**Dewey, George,** one of the greatest of American naval heroes, *b.* at Montpellier, Vermont, U.S.A., Dec. 26, 1837. Graduated at the American Naval Academy in 1858. He served with the Mediterranean Squadron until the outbreak of the Civil War, when he was made Commander-Lieutenant in charge of the sloop, *Mississippi.* He was in the fleet commanded by Admiral Farragut when the latter forced the passage between Fort St. Philips and Fort Jackson which guarded the entrance to the Mississippi some 70 m. below New Orleans. He also took part in the action by which Farragut captured that great southern city and port. After the war D. was made commander in 1872, and captain in 1884. In 1877 he was an instructor at the Naval Academy, and from 1893 to 1895 a member of the lighthouse board. He was made a Commodore in 1896, and when the Spanish-American War broke out, was in command of the fleet in Asiatic waters. At the time, his ship was off the Asiatic mainland, he received secret orders to proceed to the Philippines and engage the Spanish fleet. Manila Bay, where the Spanish ships were located, is one of the finest harbours in the far east. At its mouth are two small islands, rising 500 ft. out of the water. The Spaniards had these well fortified, and it seemed an extra hazardous undertaking to attempt to run the passage between these islands and attack the enemy. However, under the cover of darkness on the night of April 30, D. sailed his fleet through without being discovered. Dawn of the next day found him ready to engage the enemy. The Spanish ships had the protection of the guns of Cavite, a town near Manila. Moreover, the command of Admiral Montojo consisted of ten vessels, while D. had nine. However, the weight of metal was on the side of the Americans. The battle which ensued was short and decisive. In formation the American ships swung five times past the enemy, and gave him the full force of their broadsides. By early afternoon the Spanish fleet was a mass of smoking ruins, and hundreds of Spaniards were dead or wounded. Not a single American ship was disabled nor a single sailor killed. The news electrified the U.S.A., and D. became a popular hero. There followed a trying time while D. waited to co-operate with the army in the capture of Manila. A famous incident occurred when the Ger. fleet, under the command of Admiral Dietrichs, took up what was considered a menacing position. The Kaiser's sympathies were known to be with Spain. At the moment when the tension was at its acutest, the commander of the powerful British ship, the *Chichester,* put his vessel between the Gers. and the Americans. This simple friendly act, which proclaimed louder than words that blood is thicker than water, played an enormous part in developing kindlier feeling between Americans and Britons. Dewey and his fleet participated in the capture of Manila. After the war was over, D. returned to the U.S.A., to be given a regular Roman triumph. He was promoted Admiral, and Congress gave him a sword of honour. He served on the first Philippine commission in 1899, and in 1901 was president of the court of inquiry into the controversy arising out of the naval battle of Santiago. Admirals Sampson and Schley were in hot dispute, backed by partisans on both sides. At one time it seemed probable that the Democrats might nominate Dewey as their candidate for the Presidency, but nothing came of it. He *d.* Jan. 16, 1917.

**Dewey, John,** American philosopher; *b.* Oct. 20, 1859, at Burlington, Vt. ; son of Archibald S. Dewey. Educ. at Univ. of Vermont ; Ph.D., Johns Hopkins, 1884. Professor of Philosophy at Univ. of Minnesota, 1888–89 ; of Michigan, 1889–94 ; of

Chicago—where he was also director of the School of Education—1894–1904; and since then at Columbia Univ. He has been termed a pragmatist: but his is not the pragmatism of Wm. James; it is more like the *pragmaticism* of Peirce, and is more generally called Instrumentalism. In Sept. 1929 he presided at the inauguration of a League for Independent Political Action—intended to supply a new Labour Party in American politics. Works include:—*Psychology*, 1887; *Leibniz's New Essays*, 1888; *Critical Theory of Ethics*, 1894; *Study of Ethics*, 1894; *Psychology of Number*, 1894; *The School and Society*, 1899; *Studies in Logical Theory*, 1903; *How We Think*, 1909; *The Influence of Darwin on Philosophy*, etc., 1910; *German Philosophy and Politics*, 1915; *Democracy and Education*, 1916; *Reconstruction in Philosophy*, 1920; *Human Nature and Conduct*, 1922; *Experience and Nature*, 1925; *The Public and its Problems*, 1927; *The Quest for Certainty*, 1930.

**De Windt, Harry** (*b.* 1856), an explorer and journalist, acted as aide-de-camp to his brother-in-law, Rajah Brooke of Sarawak from 1876 to 1878. From 1887 to 1894 he divided his time between reaching France by land from Pekin, travelling on horseback to India, via Persia from Russia, and inspecting the mines and especially the prisons of Siberia. In 1895 he was chosen Eng. delegate at the Penal Congress in Paris. His effort to cross from New York to Paris by land, undertaken in 1896 for the *Pall Mall Gazette*, ended in wreckage on the Behring Straits, but in 1901–2 he successfully accomplished the journey the other way round (Paris to New York) for the *Daily Express*. Was special correspondent of the *Westminster Gazette* in 1906, in the Balkans and Russia, the sequel being the illuminating book entitled *Through Savage Europe*. Pub. *My Restless Life*, 1908; *A Woman in Black*, 1912; *Russia as I Know it*, 1916; as well as contributions to periodicals.

**De Winter, Jan Willem** (1750–1812), Dutch admiral, *b.* at Kamper. Entered navy at twelve. In 1787, fled to France. With Fr., re-entered Holland, 1795; entrusted with reorganisation of Dutch navy. Defeated by British Admiral Duncan at Camperdown, Oct. 11, 1797; prisoner in England till Dec. Dutch plenipotentiary, France, 1798–1802. Reappointed to command of Navy, subdued Tripolitan pirates. Marshal of France. Commander of sea and land forces of Holland under the Bonapartes. Died, Paris, June 2, 1812.

**De Witt, Cornelius** (1623–72), famous Dutch burgomaster and patriot, brother of John De W. (*q.v.*), *b.* at Dort, of which he became burgomaster at the age of twenty-seven. Also a member of the states of Holland and W. Friesland, in which capacity he accompanied De Ruyter on his naval expeditions. It was through his influence that his more famous brother became pensionary of Dordrecht. He supported his brother's policy with great ability and courage, notably when he sailed with De Ruyter after the proclamation of the 'perpetual edict'—of which he disapproved—abolishing the hereditary office of stadtholder. But after the defeat of the Dutch fleet the partisans of the House of Orange excited the hatred of the people against the two brothers, and Cornelius was arrested on a false charge of conspiring to poison the Prince of Orange. Killed at The Hague in 1672, after rendering great service to his country as its chief magistrate for some twenty years.

**De Witt, Jan** (1625–72), one of the most famous of Dutch statesmen, *b.* at Dort, the son of Jacob de W., a burgomaster of Dort and deputy to the States of Holland, from whom he inherited his republican principles and hatred of the House of Orange. In 1650 he was elected Pensioner of Dort, and opposed unsuccessfully the war against England. The disasters of the war made his pacific policy so popular that in 1653 he was elected Grand Pensionary of Holland for a period of five years, and was re-elected in 1658 and 1663. In the meantime William II., the Stadtholder, had died, leaving only an infant as heir, so that De W. was able to turn from his opposition to the family of Orange to international politics. In 1654 he negotiated a secret with Cromwell with a secret proviso that no member of the House of Orange should be made Stadtholder. On the accession of Charles II. to the throne of England the treaty of peace was rendered void, and in spite of De W.'s efforts for peace, war broke out again between the two countries in 1665. De W. conducted it with vigour and skill, and on the death of Admiral Opdam personally took command of the fleet, and by his diplomatic skill contrived the Treaty of Breda (1667) and the formation of the Triple Alliance between Holland, England, and Sweden (1668) to frustrate the designs of Louis XIV. in Holland. Louis, however, bribed Charles II. to desert the alliance, and in 1672 suddenly invaded the United Provinces. The action was too sudden to render preparation possible, and the people blamed De W., and appointed the young Prince of Orange commander of the forces. Jan De W. thereupon resigned his office of Pensionary. His brother, Cornelius, had been tried and acquitted on a charge of conspiring against William, and Jan De W. went to meet him on his release. An infuriated mob burst into the prison, probably at the instigation of their enemies, and murdered both brothers with the greatest barbarity.

**Dew Ponds,** found on the upper reaches of the chalk hills in the S. of England and in a few other localities. They are used as a source of water supply for cattle, and it was once thought that they were entirely dew-, not rain-fed. However, this theory is rather doubtful, though artificial D. P. or reservoirs are sometimes constructed, it being necessary to fill the basin with water at the start.

**Dewsbury,** a market tn., municipal and parl. bor. in the W. Riding of Yorkshire, England, on the R. Calder, 8 m. S.S.W. of Leeds, in the heart of the woollen district. Among the public buildings are the parish church of All Saints, with remains of early English architecture (rebuilt in the eighteenth century), town hall (1888), St. Augustine's Grammar School, a covered market, and a theatre. Coal is worked in the neighbourhood, and there are iron foundries, and machine, dyeing, and glass works. The chief manufactures are blankets, carpets, druggets, and worsted yarn. D. is a tn. of great antiquity, and, according to tradition, Paulinus preached Christianity to the heathen Saxons on the site of the parish church in A.D. 627. The fourteenth-century Court house of the Rectory Manor is used as a parish hall; Crow Nest Park is 73 acres in extent. Pop. 54,160.

**Dexter,** see HERALDRY.

**Dexter, Henry Martin** (1821–90), an American Congregationalist minister. He was pastor of a church in Manchester, New Hampshire (1844–49), and later at the Berkeley Street church in Boston (1849–67), but also found time to edit the *Congregationalist*, 1851–90, and the *Congregationalist Quarterly*, 1859–66. Furthermore, he was the author of many treatises, chiefly on Congregationalism (1865–85).

**Dextrine, or British Gum,** the soluble or gummy substance obtained from starch by the action of diastase or certain acids on starch, or by heating starch to 392° F. (200° C.). Both D. and starch are isomeric, and expressed by the formula $C_6H_{10}O_5$. D. receives its name from its power of turning polarised light to the right. Pure D. is an odourless, whitish substance. It does not reduce Fehling's solution. It is often used as a substitute for gum-arabic for stiffening materials, sizing papers, and thickening ink; also for postage stamps and adhesive labels.

**Dextrose,** also called glucose, grape-sugar, and diabetic sugar, a carbohydrate of the formula $C_6H_{12}O_6$. It occurs in honey, grapes, in the body fluids of the animal kingdom, and in the urine of diabetic patients. It forms about ·15 per cent. of normal arterial blood. The sugar of grapes consists largely of D. as the fruit ripens, but when quite ripe it becomes 'invert' sugar, that is, equal quantities of D. and lævulose. Pure D. crystallises in lumpy masses consisting of six-sided plates; it melts at 86° C., and loses its water of crystallisation at 110° C.; it is soluble in water, but only slightly soluble in alcohol. Invert sugar or saccharum is used in the brewing industry. It is prepared by treating cane sugar with dilute acid. The excess of acid is removed with chalk, and the product concentrated to a thick syrup. D. by itself is prepared from starch, which is treated with boiling acid. The product is first a mixture of dextrin and maltose and then becomes D. In Britain the starch used for the manufacture of D. is usually sago, rice, or maize; in Germany, potatoes; and in America, maize. D. is also used as the sweetening factor in jams, etc.

**Dey** (Turkish *dai*, a maternal uncle). The name was originally given to elderly men and taken by the janissaries as the title of their commanders, a commanding officer of the janissaries frequently becoming governor of the province in which he served. The name was given to all rulers of Algeria (before the Fr. conquest), and was extended to Tripoli, and to Tunisia in the form 'bey.'

**Dezhnev, or East Cape,** the most easterly point of Asia, situated at the entrance to Behring Strait in 190° E. A distance of about 56 m. separates it from Cape Prince of Wales on the American shore.

**Dhalac, Dahalac, or Dahlak,** a group of islands in the Red Sea, situated 30 m. E. of Massawa, belonging to Italy. They number three larger is., with numerous rocks. The chief, named Dhalac, was in Rom. times celebrated for its pearl fisheries. Pop. about 1900 of Abyssinian origin.

**Dhar,** a protected state in the prov. of Malwa, Central India. The tn. of D. is the cap., 35 m. S.W. of Indore. It contains several fine half-ruined mosques. Pop. 20,000.

**Dharma-shastra,** the title given to the whole code of Hindu law, but more especially to that collection of law received directly from a divine source by the sages of Manu, Tajna-walkya and others. It is divided into three parts: *Achara,* rules of conduct and practice; *Vyavahara,* the administration of justice; *Praya-schitta,* penance.

**Dharmsala,** a hill-station and sanatorium in the Kangra dist. of the Punjab, India. It stands on a spur of the Dhaola Dhar, and is surrounded by scenery of extreme beauty. The station was devastated by an earthquake in 1905, in which the barracks collapsed and buried a large number of the Gurkha garrison with their women and children. Pop. about 7000.

**Dharwar,** a dist. and tn. of British India in the Bombay Presidency. The dist. covers an area of 4536 sq. m. Cotton and wheat are the chief products, the former being of great importance. The capital is D., with manufactures of silk and cotton cloth. A college in arts and science was opened here in 1912; there are also training colleges for teachers of both sexes, and Anglican and R. C. churches. The District Jail is partly organised for juveniles on the Borstal System, the first of its kind in India, and there is a mental hospital. Pop. 34,750.

**Dhaulagiri,** or **Dhwalagiri,** a peak of the Himalaya Mts., once regarded as the loftiest, but now known to be the third in height. It is 26,826 ft. above the level of the sea, and is situated between Nepal and Tibet, in lat. 29° N. and long. 82° 30′ E.

**Dhole,** the wild dog of India. *See* DOG.

**Dholpore,** or **Dholpur,** a native state of Central India, in Rajputana, having an area of 1200 sq. m. The dist. is very fertile. The capital of the state, founded in the eleventh century, is also called Dholpur and is situated on the Chumbuh, 34 m. S. of Agra. The High School is housed in a building originally built as a mausoleum. In its vicinity, about 3 m. to the east, is an artificial lake upon whose banks are 114 temples. Population of state 230,188, of city 17,000.

**Dhow,** the regular Arab trading vessel of the Arabian Sea, and E. African coast; formerly used more particularly for the slave trade. It is generally from 150 to 200 tons burden, with a very long yard, and a single mast with a lateen sail. The language to which the word belongs is unknown.

**Dhrangadra,** a native state and tn. of India, in the Bombay Presidency, situated in the prov. of Gujarat. The cap. D., is about 74 m. W. of Ahmedabad. Pop. state 88,406, tn. 17,526.

**Dhuleep Singh** (1837–93), a maharajah of the Sikhs, son of Rujeet Singh, proclaimed in 1843. After repeated attacks on British territory, D. S. was defeated at the Battle of Gujarat in 1849 and deposed. He became a Christian, married a Ger. lady, and took up his abode in England. In 1882 he demanded money of the British Gov. The demand was refused, and he issued a proclamation to his former subjects and started for India. He was detained at Aden and publicly abjured Christianity, actually within the residency. In 1887 he returned to Europe and travelled through Russia, trying to find someone to take up his claim against England. In 1890 he was pardoned, but decided to remain in Paris, where he died.

A DHOW

**Dhulia,** a tn. of India, in the presidency of Bombay. It is the cap. of the Khandesh dist., and is situated 128 m. S.E. of Surat. There are textile manufactures and an extensive trade in cotton. Pop. 29,497.

**Diabase,** a group of rocks consisting of augite and triclinic felspar with iron oxides, to which are sometimes added apatite or olivine. Owing to the weathering of these rocks, the augite, which is black, speedily changes to chlorite and urath, which cause the rocks to assume a green colour, whence its old name of 'greenstone' is still sometimes used. The terms 'diabase' and 'dolerite' are used for different facies of the same set of rocks, the former being really a weathered form of the latter. Popular names for D. are 'trap,' 'toadstone,' and 'whin.' They form excellent stones for road-mending, and are found in the N. of England.

**Diabetes,** a metabolic disease, the chief symptom of which is an excessive discharge of urine. There are two distinct varieties: *diabetes mellitus* (*mel,* honey), in which the urine contains large quantities of sugar, and *diabetes insipidus,* which is charac terised by a chronic excess of ordinary urine. The tissues of a normal individual have a limited power of storing and utilising sugar, and if an excess of sugar is taken it quickly appears in the urine. Any condition which interferes with this power of the tissues may produce diabetic symptoms to a greater or less extent. The latest researches seem to point to defective functioning of the pancreas as the cause of chronic glycosuria, or *diabetes mellitus*. In some cases actual disease of the pancreas is reported, but in other cases D. exists with an apparently healthy pancreas, so that the causation of the disease is not yet satisfactorily established. Heredity is an important factor. Dwellers in cities are more liable than country folk, men more than women, Jews more than other races living under the same conditions. D. in individuals under middle age is a particularly serious condition, in older people it yields more readily to treatment, though cures are rare. The symptoms are continual thirst, deficiency in perspiration leading to a harsh and dry condition of the skin, skin eruptions, and discharges of urine up to as much as thirty pints *per diem*. On evaporating the urine, crystals of sugar are found. The disease is most dangerous from the possible complications. Wasting of the tissues occurs and phthisis or pneumonia may attack the patient; other possible by-effects are boils, gangrene, and cataract. Treatment by drugs is almost useless, though opium has sometimes a good effect. The most effective mode of combating the disease is a dietary which excludes all starchy foods and those containing sugar. Gluten bread, bran cakes, and almond biscuits should take the place of ordinary bread; green vegetables, fat of meat, and cream may be taken; but no sudden change should be made in the dietary, and carbohydrates should be resumed if there are any signs of drowsiness, as diabetic coma is an ever-present danger. *Diabetes insipidus*, or polyuria, has the same general effects on the system without the excretion of sugar characteristic of *diabetes mellitus*. It should be treated by a full diet and hygienic conditions. Valerian was usually administered before the discovery of insulin (*q.v.*). *See also* BANTING.

**Diablerets,** a noted mt., or secondary mt. group, of the Bernese Alps, Switzerland, situated between the De Vaud and Valais cantons. The highest point reaches 10,650 ft. It consists of four peaks, composed of limestone resting on soft shale beds, which easily become disintegrated, and fall, causing terrible catastrophes.

**Diadochi, Wars of the** (323–281 B.C.), arose over the problem of dividing Alexander's empire among the D. (or Successors)—former generals and companions of Alexander. The chief among them were Antigonus, whose ambition was to rule the whole empire, Antipater, regent of Macedonia, Lysimachus, Seleucus, satrap of Babylon, and Ptolemy of Egypt. After Antipater's death, his son, Cassander, murdered Alexander's widow, Roxane, and her infant son. Each of the D. then assumed the title of king, and the wars between them were resolved into a coalition of Seleucus, Ptolemy, Lysimachus, and Cassander against Antigonus and his son, Demetrius. Demetrius was successful in Greece, but Antigonus was finally defeated and killed at the Battle of Ipsus (301 B.C.). Later Cassander *d.*, and Demetrius became king of Macedonia. Lysimachus, king of Asia Minor, was betrayed into believing his son, Agathocles, a traitor, but by murdering him he involved himself in a war with Seleucus, and was defeated and killed at Coron (281 B.C.). Ptolemy had *d.* in 283, and Seleucis, the last of the D., relinquished his possessions, but was assassinated.

**Diadumenianus, Marcus Opilius Antonius,** a son of the Rom. emperor Macrinus, A.D. 217. His father bestowed the title of Cæsar on his son at Antioch in the following year. The father was defeated in A.D. 218 by Elagabalus, and the son, who was still a minor, was put to death. Owing to the bestowal of the title of Cæsar and his medals which bear it, M. O. A. Diadumenianus is sometimes reckoned among the emperors.

**Diageotropism,** *see* GEOTROPISM.

**Diaghilev, Serge Pavlovich** (1872–1929), producer of Russian ballet, was *b.* in Novgorod province. He studied law and music; and especially interested himself in old Russian art. In 1899 he founded *Mir Iskusstvo* (the World of Art) (*see* BAKST). D. held an unsuccessful exhibition of Russian painting and sculpture in Paris in 1906. In 1908 he was in Paris giving concerts and opera. In 1909 he was again in Paris with opera and ballet. The ballet made a sensation—especially *Scheherazade* by Bakst and Fokine, music by Rimsky-Korsakov, the production of which in London in 1911 revolutionised Eng. stage-dancing. Altogether, he produced over forty ballets and operas. Died at the Lido, Aug. 19, 1929.

**Diagnosis,** in medicine, is the method employed to identify a disease. It includes an enquiry into the past medical history of the patient and sometimes of his family, as well as an examination of his symptoms and general physical state. In addition, the practitioner will take into consideration any relevant knowledge of environment, habits of life and psychological characteristics. Information acquired in these ways is supplemented by physiological tests, X-ray examinations, chemical and bacteriological investigation of the blood, urine, etc., and of the results of measurements of blood pressure, heart action and the like, with suitable instruments. Correct diagnosis is a matter of the greatest general importance, since failure to identify a disease or to recognise it at an early stage may lead to very unfortunate results. Even before the rise of science in the last century and a half, diagnosis had been carried to a high degree of accuracy, but the modern physician has such an array of carefully collated material and a wealth of scientific information and appliances at his disposal, that he need not rely as much upon his own personal experience. In doubtful or difficult cases, recourse should at once be made to specialists, since proper treatment of a disease can obviously be made only when the disease has been definitely identified. Training in diagnostic method is a large and essential part of the medical student's course, and his success in his career depends largely upon his ability to effect accurate diagnosis. It should be mentioned that recognition of symptoms is a difficult problem, completely beyond the layman except in very simple instances. Self-treatment is consequently to be very much deprecated, as likely to cause more harm than good.

**Diagonal Scale,** a mathematical scale consisting of a set of parallel lines drawn on a ruler with other lines crossing them at right angles and at equal distances from each other. The extreme division of the equal divisions so formed is then further subdivided into a number of equal parts, and other lines drawn obliquely across the parallels through the points of intersection. With the aid of compasses, lines can be laid down by such a scale of any required length, down to the two-hundredth part of an inch.

**Diagoras,** of Melos, surnamed **the Atheist,** a Gk. poet and philosopher of the fifth century B.C., said to have been a pupil of Democritus of Abdera. He was accused of impiety, more especially of criticising the Eleusinian Mysteries, and in 411 B.C. was condemned to death in Athens (Aristophanes, *Clouds*, 425 B.C.). He fled

to Corinth, and probably *d.* there. Besides his work on the mysteries, he wrote lyrics and some philosophical treatises, none of which are extant.

**Diagram,** in mathematics is a figure serving to illustrate a definition or to aid in the proof of a proposition. In its more general sense it is a drawing to illustrate the structure of scientific apparatus, engines, machines, buildings, and so on, as opposed to a ' picture ' to which emotional significance or artistic value is attached. The value of a diagram lies in its power of conveying essential information at a glance; when the diagram is drawn to scale, this information may be quantitative as well as qualitative. Weather charts, temperature and pressure curves, road maps, etc., are very largely diagrammatic. An *indicator diagram* shows the effective work done by an engine. Constitutional formulæ in chemistry are conventionalised diagrams of what is believed to be the corresponding molecular structure. Biological diagrams bring out the features of biological importance in the objects drawn.

**Dial, The,** the literary organ of the Transcendental Club, of New England, U.S.A., in the formation of which Club Emerson took a leading part (*see* EMERSON). Sarah Margaret Fuller (*q.v.*) was the first and only editor (1840), with George Ripley as assistant editor. The D. was a paper for cultured readers, which discussed questions of theology, philosophy, music, art and letters; and its pages contained much verse. Among its best known contributors were Emerson, Thoreau, and Louisa Alcott. The public, however, disliked its peculiar and abstruse opinions, especially those in the *Orphic Sayings* of Louisa Alcott, and though Emerson succeeded in keeping the paper alive for a short while after Sarah Fuller relinquished the editorship, it ceased to exist in 1844.

**Dialect** (Gk. διάλεκτος, conversation, or manner of speaking). In its widest sense the name is applied to branch languages springing from a common root, as the Romance tongues, Fr. Italian, Spanish, sprang from a common Latin root. But the term is popularly used to express the divergence of some local form of speech from the generally accepted or ' literary ' form. It is quite wrong to speak of such local forms as ' corruptions ' of the accepted forms. The anct. Gk. tongue was divided into Attic, Doric, Ionic, and Æolic Ds. Modern Gk. is derived from the Attic form, in which the works of Thucydides were written, while Herodotus wrote in Ionic; no one will say that the tongue of Herodotus was a corruption of that of Thucydides. The origin of D. is not in corruption at all, but is the result of descent from a different form; in old England, as in old Greece, the country was inhabited by different races; the dispossessed Celts were driven into the mountains, while the Saxons, Jutes, and Angles spread over the land. From a variety of causes the D. which survives as modern literary Eng. is the Midland, that spoken by a branch of the Anglian tribes, but the D. forms the so-called ' corruptions ' of modern Eng., are not corruptions of the Midland Ds., but the direct descendants of the Celtic, the Saxon, the Northumbrian, and other forms of speech. Eng. itself, for that matter, is merely a D. of the Teutonic tongue, modified and enriched by Norman-French, Latin, and many later additions from classical and scientific sources. After the Anglo-Saxon settlement of Britain, the language of the country was roughly divided into six main forms of local speech, again divided into many small groups, which still prevail with characteristic variants from the accepted language, the Southern, Western, Eastern, Midland, Northern and Lowland Scotch. Modern provincial Eng. has been carefully studied, its origin, where possible, traced, and its locality recorded in the papers of the Eng. Dialect Society (1873–96). Upon these papers Professor Skeat, of Cambridge, has largely based his Eng. Dialect Dictionary, the first volume of which appeared in 1898. He was assisted by Professor Wright, of Oxford, who classified the various Ds. and obtained a unique collection of phonograph records to preserve the idiom, with its correct accent and intonation, of Eng. rustic speech in different localities. Sir James Murray has done a similar work for the Ds. of Lowland Scotland, in *Dialect of the Southern Counties of Scotland*, 1873. For further information, *see* Alexander Ellis, *Existing Phonology of English Dialects*, 1889; the works of Prince Louis-Lucien Bonaparte on Eng., Basque, Fr., and especially Italian Ds.; J. Winkler, *Dialektikor*, 1874, for Low German forms, and for hybrid Ds., Haldeman's *Pennsylvania Dutch*, 1872.

**Dialectic**, a term in logic generally applied to verbal fencing and abstract arguments without practical value, and frequently merely the clever statement of fallacies to make them pass for truth. The term was used in the Socratic philosophy to show the inadequacy of popular beliefs; Plato used it for the highest kind of thought connecting itself with the true nature or idea of things, while Aristotle limited it to a probable deduction from probable reasoning, as opposed to a scientific or demonstrative reasoning or proof. The Stoics divided logic into ' D.' and ' rhetoric,' and from their time D. is sometimes used as synonymous with logic. In modern philosophy the name has been used in several senses; Hegel uses it in its original Socratic sense, while Kant uses it in general for the doctrine of fallacies, for the uselessness of the attempt of reason to overcome the principles which govern phenomena.

**Diallage,** one of the pyroxene group of minerals characterised by its lamellar or foliated structure. The name formerly included ' bronzite,' from which it is very hard to distinguish it. Its colour is generally brown, but sometimes grey or green, and has a metallic lustre on surface of the broken crystals.

**Dialogue,** a conversation between two or more persons, reported in literary form and with a greater unity and continuity of subject than characterise an ordinary conversation. When joined to action the D. becomes a drama. It has always been a favourite mode with writers who, wishing to convince their readers of the truth of an argument, present both sides of a question in the mouths of two characters, and conduct the conversation in such a way that one is finally convinced of the correctness of the other. The D. is of Gk. origin, having been adopted by the Gk. philosophers as the best way of conducting their investigations and conveying their instructions to their pupils. The Ds. of Socrates took the form of question and answer, so that the master by means of questions led the pupil to originate himself the ideas which he, the master, wished to convey to him. The form of D. adopted by Plato was modelled on the Sicilian ' mimes,' little two-character plays which were popular before his time, none of which is extant. Plato simplified it to pure argumentative conversations, or philosophical dramas, and used the form for all his philosophical writings except the *Apologia*. One of the greatest masters of this form of literature was Lucian (second century A.D.), the title of whose most famous collection of Ds., *Of the Dead*, was borrowed by two great Fr. masters of the form, Fontenelle (1683), and Fénelon (1712) in their *Dialogues des Morts*. It has also been used by Erasmus in Latin; Wieland, Herder, and Lessing among the Germans; Petrach, Tasso, and Leopardi among the Italians. In England the most famous writers of non-dramatic D. are Berkeley in *Hylas and Philonous*, 1713, and Landor in his *Imaginary Conversations*, 1821–25.

**Dialysis**, the term in chemistry for the process discovered by Thomas Graham (1804–69), by which ' colloids,' such as silicic acid, can be separated from ' crystalline ' substances, such as salt or hydrochloric acid. He found that if a solution of a crystalline substance, salt for instance, were placed in a ' dialyser,' a vessel provided with a bottom made of parchment or animal membrane, and the dialyser placed in a larger vessel of water, the salt would permeate the parchment, whereas a similar solution of a ' colloid ' would not diffuse, remaining intact in the original solution. The process is performed more rapidly with an increase of temperature.

**Diamantina**, a river of Australia, also called Mueller's Creek, flowing from the high ground in the N. of Central Queensland in a south-westerly direction into S. Australia. In the dry seasons it dries up in the interior, but during the rains it flows into the N. end of Lake Eyre.

**Diamantina**, until 1838 **Tejuco**, a mining tn. in the state of Minas Geraes, Brazil, built on a steep hillside, 3760 ft. above sea level. It is the centre of a rich diamond district, and gold is mined in its neighbourhood. It has manufactures of cotton-weaving, cigars, and diamond-cutting. It is the seat of a bishopric, and is the centre of a large commercial district, famous for its wealth. Pop. of tn. 7750, of municipality 69,448.

**Diameter**, a term in geometry for the line which passes through the centre of a circle or a conic section, and which is terminated at either extreme by the curve.

**Diamond**, a form of crystallised carbon of very high value, which is usually regarded as the most precious of all stones. It is, however, not so valuable as the ruby. The D. is always found in crystals of the cubical system, and is found most frequently in the form of octahedrons, or rhombic dodecahedrons. The crystals are strongly striated and the cleavage is perfect. Contrary to general opinion, the D. is rather brittle and can be injured by the slightest fall. The stone has a lustre peculiarly its own, termed adamantine lustre. It has high refractive powers, the index for refraction being

2·4, and the angle of total reflection about 25°. The stone is highly phosphorescent, and will, after exposure to brilliant light, emit the rays to which it has been exposed and become self-luminous in the dark. Its specific gravity is just over 3·5, and its hardness is far greater than that of any other stone, and is indicated by 10 in the mineralogical scale. The chemical character of the D. was for a long time uncertain. During the seventeenth century it was held to be inflammable. Robert Boyle proved that when subjected to a high temperature part of it was dissipated, and finally, at the expense of Duke Cosmo of Tuscany, the Florentines proved that it was combustible. Lavoisier later showed that the product was carbonic acid gas, and finally, Tennant demonstrated that the amount of carbonic acid gas produced was equal to the oxygen consumed. The composition of the D. was therefore determined to be pure carbon in a crystallised form. Experiments have also been made as to the action of heat on Ds., and Gustaf Rose showed that under certain conditions Ds. when subjected to a great heat were gradually converted into graphite. For a long time India was regarded as the only D.-producing country, and it is certain that the Indian gem was the only stone known to the ancients. The chief D. districts of India are : the Golconda district in the Madras Presidency, the Sambulpur mines of the Central Provinces, and in Bundel-cund (*q.v.*). The D. production of India at the present time is not large. Brazil was not regarded as a great D.-producing country until 1727, when the Ds. were first noticed, having been used by the natives as counters in certain card games. These Ds. were, without reason, for a long time regarded as inferior to the stones of India. The principal D. mines are in the province of Minas Geraes, at Diamantina (*q.v.*). In Europe Ds. have been discovered, but in no great quantity. Australia has also produced somé, but these again are not of great importance. The most important D. fields are those of Kimberley, S. Africa, which were discovered quite by accident. Chief among the Kimberley mines are those of the De Beer, the Du Toit's Pan, and the Bultfontein companies. A number of the Ds. in existence at the present time have remarkable histories. The largest of all known Ds. is the Cullinan D. found near Pretoria early in 1905. It weighs 3032 carats, or more than three times the weight of any known diamond. It is at present in the British regalia. Another fine stone is the Orloff D. in the sceptre of the Russian regalia. It was purchased by Count Orloff for Catherine II. of Russia, and is supposed to have been the eye of an Indian idol. The Pitt D. holds the second place. It was brought back from India by the grandfather of the famous English statesman, Wm. Pitt, and sold by him to the Regent Orleans for £130,000. It is held to be the most perfect D. in the world. Amongst other famous stones may be mentioned the Florentine (133 carats), and the Koh-i-noor, the most famous of all the stones belonging to the for the necklace, bought it on credit. De Rohan, by the connivance of De Lamotte, was accorded an interview with the queen, personated by Demoiselle d'Oliva, in which she accorded him pardon for past offences and promised to pay for the necklace in instalments if he would act as security. Immediately on securing the necklace, De Lamotte and her husband disappeared and sold abroad the separate Ds. When the first instalment became due the jeweller obtained an interview with the queen and the whole truth was exposed. De Rohan and the girl Oliva were

DIAMOND SORTING

[*Canadian Pacific*]

British crown. This stone, which weighs 106·5 carats, has a long and romantic history, and came into the possession of the British Crown in 1850 after the annexation of the Punjab. The headquarters of the D.-cutting and polishing trade is at Amsterdam.

**Diamond Necklace,** a wonderful piece of jewellery made in Paris by the Court jewellers, Boehmer and Bassenge, in 1775, and intended for Madame du Barry, the favourite of Louis XV. Louis XV. died before the necklace was completed, and its price was beyond the reach of any purchaser (1,600,000 livres). Cardinal de Rohan, duped by an adventuress (calling herself Comtesse de Lamotte-Valois and pretending to be in the service of the queen) into believing that Marie Antoinette had expressed a desire

thrown into the Bastille, but acquitted after a sensational trial. De Lamotte and her husband were captured, the former branded as a thief, and the latter sent to the galleys for life. The question whether the queen and De Rohan were innocent in the matter and merely the dupes of De Lamotte was long debated, and resulted in an increased unpopularity for the queen. *See* Carlyle's *Miscellanies*, 'The Diamond Necklace,' 1837; Andrew Lang, *Historical Mysteries*, 1904; also Vizetelly's *Story of the Diamond Necklace*, 1880.

**Diana,** an anct. Italian goddess, identified by the Roms. with the Gk. Artemis, whose attributes she received. Her name is the feminine form of the Rom. Janus. She was the goddess of the moon and of light generally, and the protectress of slaves on account of the introduction of her worship into Rome by the plebeians, although, according to some accounts, Servius Tullius introduced the worship of D., and it was at first confined to the patricians. As the goddess of childbirth, she was worshipped as Lucina, and was regarded as the patroness of chastity, all her maidens being virgins. She is generally represented as the daughter of Jupiter and Latona, *b.* on the is. of Delos. She was sometimes called the Huntress, and represented with bow and arrows. Other names for her were Phœbe and Cynthia. There was a magnificent temple to her at Ephesus and a grove at Aricia. *See* ARTEMIS.

**Diane de France, Duchesse de Montmorency et d'Angoulême** (1538–1619), a natural daughter of Henry II. and Filippe Duc. She was twice married, first to Orazio Farnese, second son of the Duke of Parma, and then to François, Maréschal de Montmorency. She was formally legitimised in 1547. She was a wise and prudent woman, and had great influence with her brother Henry III., whom she succeeded in reconciling to Henry of Navarre. She directed the education of Henry of Navarre's son, afterwards Louis XIII., and then retired into great seclusion. *See* Brantôme, and J. de Thou, *Historia sui temporis.*

**Diane de Poitiers** (1499–1566), a beautiful Fr. woman. In 1515 she married Louis de Bréze, Grand Seneschal of Normandy. Left a widow in 1531, she gained the affections of the king's son. On his accession to the throne as Henry II., in 1547, she exercised almost unlimited power, and was created by him Duchesse de Valentinois. On the king's death she was expelled from court by Catherine de Medici (who took from her the beautiful Château de Chenonceaux) and *d.* at the Château d'Anet. *See* Capefigue, *Diane de Poitiers,* 1860; and Marie Hay, *Madame Dianne de Poytiers,* 1900.

**Dianthus,** a caryophyllaceous genus of beautiful plants which occur in temperate parts of Europe, Asia, S. Africa, and N. America. Most of them are perennial herbaceous plants, but a few are woody; they are distinguished from allied genera by the bracts under the calyx. *D. caryophyllus,* the clove-pink, a native of Britain, is a wild plant which has given rise to the cultivated carnation and the pink of the florists; *D. Libanotis,* the Syrian pink, has feathered petals; *D. barbatus,* the sweet-william, is a beautiful hardy herbaceous plant of S. Europe; *D. Chinensis* is a species cultivated in British gardens; while *D. deltoides, D. Armeria,* and *D. cæsius* grow wild.

**Diapason,** an anct. Gk. term for the musical interval of an actave. The name is given to the two foundation stops of an organ, the open and stopped D., and by the Fr. in 'diapason normal' as equivalent to 'pitch.'

**Diapensiaceæ,** a small natural order of dicotyledonous plants found in cold regions. *Diapensia lapponica* is a creeping plant of tufted habit found in the Alpine and Arctic regions.

**Diaper :** (1) In textile fabrics, the name given originally to a rich silken fabric with a pattern of the same colour embroidered on it. It is now restricted to linen or cotton material with a simple pattern woven

DIANE DE POITIERS

in it generally of a geometrical design. (2) In Gothic architecture, a small pattern of a conventional nature, generally geometrical, but sometimes floral in design, used for the surface decoration of stone. The idea was probably taken from the diapered pattern of Byzantine silks, and was also used in glass painting and illuminated manuscripts. There are good examples at Westminster Abbey and at Bayeux Cathedral.

**Diaphoretics,** measures taken to promote perspiration. The function of perspiration is to carry away waste products of metabolism through the skin and to keep the body cool. In some feverish conditions perspiration often ceases, so that the skin becomes dry and the internal temperature is not prevented from rising. It is advisable in some of these cases to promote perspiration by means of hot air, as in the Turkish bath; hot vapour, as in the Russian bath; by taking hot drinks or drugs such as opium and certain aromatics.

**Diaphragm,** a partition with a hole in it, which is used in landscape and portrait lenses as well as all optical instruments, such as the telescope, microscope, etc. It controls the rays of light, and throws up the image with greater clearness. The word comes from the Gk. διάφραγμα, partition.

**Diaphragm,** or **Midriff,** the partition which divides the thorax from the abdomen. It is in the form of a dome, the lower parts consisting of

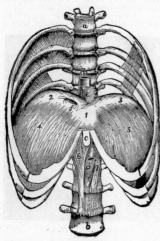

THE DIAPHRAGM

1, 2, 3, central tendon; 4, 5, muscular portion; 6, 7, crura; *a, d, e, f,* blood vessels and œsophagus (apertures for).

muscle and the centre of a tendon; it is concave towards the abdomen and convex towards the thorax, where the central tendon forms a floor for the heart. It arises in front from the posterior surface of the ensiform cartilage; at the side from cartilages connected with the lower six ribs; behind from the lumbar vertebræ. It has three large openings: one for the œsophagus and pneumogastric nerves, one for the aorta, thoracic duct, and large azygos vein, and one for the inferior vena cava. When the muscular fibres of the margin contract, the convexity of the D. is lessened and the size of the thorax is increased. Air flows in to fill up the additional space, and this, together with other

muscular movements, comprises the action of inspiration.

**Diarbekr :** cap. of the Turkish vilayet D. on a high mass of basalt rock on the r. b. of the Tigris, with a pop. of 97,997. Gold and silver filigree is made, and wool, mohair and copper ore are exported. D. is still surrounded with black basalt walls with four gates. It was fortified by Constantine in the fourth century, fell to Saladin in 1183, was conquered by Timoor in 1394 and by Sultan Selim I. in 1515. Three other vilayets were formed out of the V. of D. in 1923, Arghana, Mardin and Severek, leaving that of D. with a pop. of 193,000.

**Diarmid,** or **Diarmait,** the name given to three Irish kings: the first was ruler over Niú Neill, and his father was called Fergus MacCabeill. He was slain in 555 by Columcelle's kinsmen in revenge for his having hanged that individual. The second reigned from 658 to 665, whilst the third reigned over Leinster.

**Diarrhœa,** looseness of the bowels, resulting in copious ejections containing much fluid in which biliary secretions are often present. It is a symptom rather than a disease, and is specially characteristic of cholera, dysentery, and typhoid fever, and often accompanies liver disease, ulcerated bowel, and acute consumption. In other cases some temporary irritation of the intestines is the case, such as may be produced by improper or unfamiliar food, putrid or poisonous substances in food, or catarrh as the result of a chill. Generally speaking, D. should be regarded as the natural effort of the bowel to get rid of irritating substances, and this tendency should be encouraged by mild purgative measures, such as a dose of castor oil. D. is apt to continue after the predisposing cause has been removed, and as its effects are inconvenient and exhausting, astringents should be administered. During the acute phase of the attack, the patient should abstain from food and lie down as much as possible. Food of a light nature should then be taken; milk, arrowroot, toast, beef-juice, and white of an egg are suitable, while small doses of brandy form a useful stimulant. Opium is the most effective astringent, but its use is not always advisable; ipecacuanha, galls, iron and bismuth salts, chalk, and alum may be administered. Chronic D. is best combated by regulating diet. A patient with a constitutional tendency to looseness of bowel can tell from experience the diet which is suitable to his own case, and should avoid anything markedly different.

*Infantile diarrhœa* causes many deaths in the hot summer months. It may be avoided by strict attention to cleanliness. The milk should be sterilised and the bottle thoroughly cleaned after use. D. may also be caused by worms, tuberculosis, or teething. A tablespoonful of lime water to every three or four ounces of milk may cause it to be retained. In bad cases give four drops of brandy in a teaspoonful of warm water. Astringents should be given under the advice of a medical man.

**Diarthrosis,** the term in anatomy applied to joints which have the power of free movement, such as the socket joint of the hip, or the hinge joint of the elbow.

**Diary** (Lat. *diarium,* from *dies,* a day), the book in which a daily record of events or observations made by an individual is written. The 'Ephemeris' of the Gks., which was the original name of the ' diarium,' was originally a memoranda of military records, tables of the heavenly bodies, or of accounts ; it was not until after the Renaissance that the D. came to have any literary value. Since then it has often been of great value to the historian, not only in its supply of facts often unrecorded in historical chronicles, but as a picture of character and of the daily life of its writer's time. Among the most famous Ds. of English literature are those of John Evelyn (1620–1706) ; Samuel Pepys (1633–1703), perhaps the most valuable and minute record in existence ; Swift's *Journal to Stella* (1710–13) ; *John Wesley's Journal* (1703–91) ; *Fanny Burney's Diary* (pub. 1842–46). The D. of the Russian, Marie Bashkirtseff, created a great sensation in 1887, and that of Jules and Edmond de Goncourt in Paris in 1888.

**Diastase,** a species of ferment found in barley, oats, wheat, and potatoes after germination. It can be procured by placing a certain quantity of freshly germinated barley or ground malt in a mixture of three parts of water and one of alcohol, heated to 113° F. When obtained separately D. is a solid, white, tasteless substance, soluble in water and in weak alcohol. In solution at a temperature of 150° F., D. is powerful enough to break up starch, first into dextrin and then into sugar, particularly the variety called ' Maltose.'

**Diastole,** *see* HEART.

**Diastylis,** the typical genus of the Diastylidæ, a crustacean of the order Cumacea. *D. arenarius,* about one-fifth of an inch long, is found on the coasts of Georgia and Florida.

**Diathesis,** a condition of the body in which it is specially liable to certain diseases. The term is parti-

cularly applied to inherited or congenital predispositions which may, however, become observable only at a late period in life. In process of evolution, the human body has become a structure capable of adding to its substance by utilising food-material and of eliminating certain other substances, such as waste-products, bacterial and other poisons. While we can recognise certain sets of reactions as being typical of human bodily processes in general, it must not be forgotten that each individual has peculiarities of composition and structure. Certain constituents of various tissues may abound in a greater or less degree than the average, causing variations in chemical reactions which may appear inconsiderable taken separately, but in the sum of their effects may constitute a predisposition to being attacked by particular types of the agencies which threaten human health. Thus, there may be a constitutional lack of resisting power to the entrance of the tubercle bacillus. This condition is known as tuberculous D. As might be expected, D. is often determined by circumstances of heredity. The recognition of a D. is often important in connection with the treatment to be adopted for any morbid state, as it may indicate that certain remedial measures are best avoided in view of the patient's general condition. The tendency to some diseases may also be defeated by the adoption of a habit of life unfavourable to its development. The following are some of the chief types of D. : *Bilious* D., one in which there is imperfect elimination of bile as a chronic condition ; *calculous* D., a constitutional tendency to the formation of calculi or stones ; *cancerous* D., the imperfectly understood condition where cancers are liable to form ; *nervous,* or *psychopathic* D., an extreme sensibility of the nervous system, generally accompanied by a tendency to derangement ; *gouty, lithic, rheumatic,* or *uric acid* D., a constitutional tendency to the accumulation of uric acid and urates in the body fluids and consequent liability to gout, rheumatism, etc.

**Diatoms,** a group of algæ, also known as Diatomaceæ and commonly called by botanists Bacillarieæ. These wonderful minute plants are invisible to the naked eye, and were first discovered by Leeuwenhoek in 1702. Since then, no fewer than 10,000 species have been discovered. The D. exhibit a great variety of form, being either circular, disk-shaped, oval, or cuneate. They thrive best where they can obtain plenty of light and moisture, and are to be found mixed with other organisms on the surface of moist rocks.

**Diatonic,** a musical term derived from the Gk. use. In modern music it denotes the tones, intervals, and harmonies of the normal major or minor scale, as distinguished from the 'chromatic.'

**Diavolo, Fra** (1771–1806), an Italian brigand; nickname given to Michele Pezza, a famous Italian outlaw, formerly a monk, appointed by Cardinal Ruffo to help recover Naples, which was invaded by the French in 1799. Made one of the leaders of the 'bands of the Holy Faith'; these bands consisted of peasants, convicts, and brigands, and they succeeded in thwarting the enemy's plans. Upon the accession of Joseph Bonaparte to the throne of Naples, a price was placed upon D.'s head, and he was eventually captured by some Frenchmen and shot. Auber's celebrated opera *Fra Diavolo* has immortalised the name of the brigand.

**Diaz, Armando** (1861–1928), Italian soldier, *b.* at Naples, Dec. 5, 1861. Colonel in Tripoli war. Major-General, 1914. Director of Military Operations on outbreak of Great War. Lieut.-General, 1916; Duke of Aosta's third army. In 1917, commanded 23rd Corps on the Carso. After Caporetto, succeeded Cadorna as Chief of Staff. Victorious at Vittoria Veneto, Oct.–Nov. 1918. After Armistice, Inspector-General. Made Duca della Vittoria, 1921. Minister of War on establishment of Fascism. Resigned 1924 with new rank of marshal. Died in Milan, Feb. 29, 1928.

**Diaz (or Novaes, or Dias), Bartholomeu** (*c.* 1455–1500), a Portuguese navigator, famous chiefly for his discovery of the Cape of Good Hope. He resided at the court of King John II., where he came into contact with many scientific men. He was eager for adventures, and sent by the king on a further voyage of discovery along the W. African coast. On this journey he rounded the Cape of Good Hope and discovered Algoa Bay; he succeeded in finding 1260 miles of unexplored coast, but met with little recognition for his pains. Accompanied Vasco da Gama on one of his voyages.

**Diaz, General Felix,** nephew of Porfirio D. (*q.v.*), the Mexican general who by his seizure of the arsenal in Mexico city and week's bombardment of the palace in Feb. 1913, succeeded, in conjunction with General Huerta, in bringing about the downfall of President Maderó.

**Diaz, José de la Cruz Porfirio** (1830–1915), a President of the republic of Mexico, *b.* about Sept. 15, at Oaxaca, Mexico, sixth child and eldest surviving son of José de la Cruz Diaz, a labouring man, probably of mixed Spanish and aboriginal strain, who *d.* in 1833. Porfirio's mother was half-blood Indian. As a boy, he worked for a carpenter while not at school. At fifteen he was placed in the local seminary to train for the priesthood; but in 1849 he refused to take orders, entering the legal profession instead. Took part in the 'War of Reform' set on foot by Benito Juarez, a governor of Oaxaca. Also took part in resisting the invasion of the French and the Emperor Maximilian, and succeeded in entering Mexico City in 1867, when he resigned his command of the army and retired to his own native city. Disturbances soon arose in Mexico City, and at last D. was forced to come and set matters right. He entered Mexico City triumphantly in 1876, and was unanimously elected president, which post he held for eight terms; but in April 1911 he was deposed by the successful revolution of Maderó, who succeeded him in the presidency. He *d.* in Paris, July 2.

**Diaz de Gamez Gutierre,** a Spanish writer who lived in the earlier part of the fifteenth century. His principal work is *Victorial Cronica del Conde Buelna Don Pero Nino.*

**Diaz de la Peña, Narcisse Virgile** (1808–76), a French painter, *b.* at Bordeaux of Spanish parents. First began painting on porcelain in a studio at Sèvres; later he painted figures richly attired in Oriental garb. Became acquainted with Théodore Rousseau, who instructed him still further in his profession. He now learnt to subdue his colours, and began to excel in his forest scenes. He soon gained distinction for himself and exhibited at the Paris Salon. Among his masterpieces may be included 'La Fée aux Perles,' 'Sunset in the Forest,' and the 'Storm.'

**Diaz del Castillo, Bernal** (1498–1593), wrote a most faithful account of the conquest of Mexico under Hernando Cortes. Was himself one of the small band of faithful followers, and was consequently an eye-witness of the deeds of glory and brigandage narrated by him.

**Diazo-compounds,** a family of carbon compounds the first of which to be discovered was obtained by Peter Griess of Burton-on-Trent in 1858. They are characterised by the presence in them of the $-N_2-$ group of atoms (hence the name, from the Fr. *azote*, nitrogen). The constitution of this group is sometimes $-N=N-$ and sometimes $-N\equiv N$; in the latter case the compounds are known as *diazonium* compounds. Diazo-C. are most common in the aromatic (q.v.) sense, but aliphatic (q.v.) examples are known. Aromatic Diazo-C. are prepared by the action of nitrous acid upon cooled acidified solutions of primary amines. In the said state they are frequently very explosive, but this instability is less marked in solution, though even here they enter readily into numerous reactions and are therefore of great importance in synthetic chemistry. They are also used largely in the manufacture of drugs.

**Dibdin, Charles** (1745–1814), an actor and dramatist, but he is principally remembered to-day as a writer of sea-songs, the first of which, ' Blow high, blow low,' was introduced into *The Seraglio*. Many other songs were introduced into other plays and sketches long since forgotten. In all he wrote about six hundred sea-songs, and it is by the best of these he takes his place in English letters. Racy of the sea they are, with an excellent lilt, and some specimens of them will be found in all anthologies. He wrote his autobiography, and called it his *Professional Life*.

**Dibdin, Charles, the Younger** (1768–1833), a dramatist who produced his plays for the most part at Sadler's Wells, of which theatre he was proprietor. He was the illegitimate son of Charles D. (q.v.).

**Dibdin, Thomas John** (1771–1841), an illegitimate son of Charles D. (q.v.), and, like his father, a writer of plays and songs, of which he is said to have written about 200 and 2000 respectively. Few among his numerous works have lived; among the best known are : *The Cabinet* (an opera), *Past Ten O'Clock* (a farce), the pantomime of *Mother Goose*, *The High-mettled Racer*, an equestrian piece for Astley's. He published his *Reminiscences* in 1827. The collection of his father's sea-songs, prepared by order of the Admiralty, was published the year after his death.

**Dibdin, Thomas Frognall** (1776–1847), a nephew of Charles D. (q.v.), born at Calcutta; lost both parents when only four years old. He came over to England and was adopted by an uncle. Chiefly famous as a bibliographer. Amongst other works he wrote : *Introduction to the Knowledge of Editions of the Classics*, 1802; *Bibliotheca Spenceriania*, 1814–15; *Bibliomania*, 1809 ; *Reminiscences of a Literary Life*, 1836; and *Bibliographical Antiquarian*. The famous Roxburghe Book Club was founded by him, and Earl Spencer was elected first president.

**Dibon, or Dhibân**, a tn. in Transjordan, capital of the Moabites 840 B.C., off the shore of the Dead Sea, renowned for the discovery of the famous Moabite stone of King Mesha.

**Dibranchiata**, the order of molluscs. It includes all existing Cephalopoda except the pearly nautilus, and is subdivided into the Decapoda, with eight arms and two tentacles, *e.g.* cuttle fish ; and Octopoda, with eight arms only, *e.g.* the poulpe.

**Dibrugarh**, a tn. of British India situated in Eastern Bengal and Assam. It stands on the Dibru, and is the terminus of the Brahmaputra steamer navigation, and a railway terminus, and is one of the most attractive places in India. It is more like a colony than any other place in India on account of its large European population and the extent of their industrial enterprises. In the vicinity are petroleum springs and important coal mines. There are considerable tea plantations, and coal and tea are exported in large quantities. The town possesses several schools. Pop. 14,500.

**Dicæarchus**, an eminent Gk. peripatetic philosopher, the pupil of Aristotle and a friend of Theophrastus. He was *b.* at Messina in Sicily and flourished about 320 B.C. He wrote on history, geography, and philosophy, but only a few fragments of his works remain. The greatest of his writings were *Life in Greece*, discussing the moral, social, and political condition of the people, and *Lespiaci*, in which he tries to prove that the soul is mortal. The best edition of the fragments of his work is by Fuhr (1841).

**Dicast, or Dicastes**, the name given to those members who served on the jury courts in Athens. They attained to the zenith of their power after the fall of Areopagus in the time of Pericles, 460 B.C. Any citizen thirty years of age or upwards was entitled to assume the duties of the dicast, and the number of members varied from 1001 to 5001. The post was somewhat of a sinecure as the members were too much governed by party feeling and personal motives. They laid themselves open in consequence to the shafts of Aristophanes' satire in his comedy *The Wasps*.

**Dice** is the plural of the word ' die,' and comes from the Latin *dare*, to give. They are small ivory or bone cubes, the six sides of which are marked with black dots from one to six. These dots are so arranged that any two opposite sides on the cube always make up the number seven. Two D. are called a pair. They are used chiefly for gambling purposes, but they are also employed in backgammon and other games. D. boxes were made in ancient time of leather

Dicentra 50 Dick

or wood or some equally suitable material, and so constructed that no trickery could be resorted to in the throwing of the D. Palamades is said to have invented D. about the year 1244 B.C., but we have still earlier evidences of their use in Egyptian times. In the British Museum, in one of the cases in the Egyptian gallery, is to be seen an ivory astragal, which belonged to the Queen Hatesu, 1600 B.C. The astragal, or knuckle, or hucklebone, was the name given to the bone in the hind leg of cloven-footed animals such as the sheep, goat, or antelope. D. corresponding to ours have also been discovered at Thebes. The astragal undoubtedly corresponds to the hucklebone which was used in the old game of ' chance bone,' which was played by children in old British times. Again, this game of ' chance bone ' finds a striking parallel in the game of hazard played by means of two D., in which the player who first throws is called caster, while his opponent is called setter. This game with D. was declared to be illegal in the reign of George II. By 13 Geo. 2. c. 19, ' all games invented or to be invented with one or more die or disc ' were forbidden, backgammon or games on a backgammon board being sanctioned. The reason of this prohibition was not far to seek ; D. throwing had singular attractions for a certain class of swindlers, and it was a very common practice to use loaded D. This trick consisted in slightly weighting the sides of the D. bearing a small number. Gambling has existed among all nations in some form or another ; the Greeks and the Romans made use of the astragal or talus, and loaded D. have been unearthed in Pompeii. The use of D. in England can be traced back to earliest times, when the Britons inherited their passion for gambling from their conquerors the Romans and the northern nations.

**Dicentra,** a genus of Papaveraceæ in the sub-order Fumariaceæ, consists of fifteen species of N. American and Asiatic plants. Several are favourite ornamental herbs in Britain, especially *D. spectabilis* and *D. cucullaria,* or Dutchman's breeches.

**Dicey, Alber Venn** (1835–1922), English jurist, *b.* Feb. 4, at Claybrook. In 1854, entered Balliol College, Oxford, where he took first class in classics in 1858. Called to Bar in the Inner Temple, 1863. In 1890 he was elected Q.C. His principal contributions to literature are : *Introduction to the Study of the Law of the Constitution,* 1885 ; *England's Case against Home Rule,* 1886 ; and

lectures on the *Relation between Law and Public Opinion in England during the Nineteenth Century,* 1905 ; and (with Prof. Rait) *Thoughts on the Union between England and Scotland,* 1920. Died at Oxford, April 7.

**Dichotomy,** in botany, a system of branching in which the main axis at its apex divides into two, and each of these branches divide again at their apices into two, and so on. When the two branches are equally vigorous, the D. is said to be bifurcate ; if, however, at each division one branch becomes more strongly developed than the other two more forms of D. occur ; scorpioid, when the right and left branches alternately are the more vigorous and helicoid, when always the right or the left is the stronger branch. In the two latter systems the successive bifurcations appear to form an axis on which the weaker branches appear laterally.

**Dichroism,** a property possessed by some doubly refracting crystalline substances of appearing of different colours when viewed in polarised light, the difference of colour depending upon the direction in which the luminous vibrations take place. The D. of crystals can be observed or tested by means of a simple instrument called a dichroscope or ' dichroöscope.' It is simply a cleavage rhombohedron of Iceland spar with a weak magnifying lens. The crystal is held in a good light opposite one end of the instrument and on looking through it two images of the square hole are seen just touching each other. If the crystal is dichroic these will be of different colours and the colours will change if the dichroscope is rotated between the fingers. The most remarkable dichroic substances are the magnesian mica from Vesuvius, the tourmaline and ripidolite, also the sapphire and ruby. The phenomena of D. are best seen in crystals with two axes of double refraction, notably in iolite which crystallises in six or twelve sided prisms ; these prisms, when seen along the axis, are of a deep blue colour, but when viewed in a direction perpendicular to it, assume a yellowish brown colour. Tourmaline is another notable example, being blood-red when viewed along the axis, but yellowish-green when viewed at right angles to it.

**Dichroite,** *see* CORDIERITE.

**Dick, James** (1743–1828), noted for his generosity in contributing a large sum of money known as the Dick Bequest for the benefit of the parochial schoolmasters of Moray, Banff, and Aberdeen. He was *b.* at Forres in Morayshire, and at the age of nineteen went to the W. Indies, where he acquired a fortune, the chief portion of which he left ' to encourage active schoolmasters.' His bequest was reorganised in 1890, and placed under the management of thirteen governors.

**Dick, James** (1823–1902), *b.* at Kilmarnock, Ayrshire. He invented gutta-percha boots, and with his brother, Robert, set up a factory at Greenhead, Glasgow, for the purpose of making and soling boots and shoes. He also manufactured the balata belts which were used by the gold diggers in Johannesburg. He reaped a fortune, and gave a park to Glasgow and the Elmbank Institute to Kilmarnock, besides other benefactions.

**Dickens, Charles John Huffham** (1812–70), an English novelist, *b.* at Landport (Portsea), near Portsmouth (the house at which he was born was opened as a Dickens Museum in 1904). His father, John Dickens, a clerk in the navy pay office, was then stationed at Portsmouth, where he lived in very precarious circumstances. Charles was the second of eight sons. In 1816 the family moved to Chatham, remaining there for some five years. About particular details of these early periods of his life but little is known. In *David Copperfield*, however, the sketch of David's boyhood is in many points similar to his own, and Micawber is usually recognised as a sketch of his father. His education was of a most elementary nature, but, fortunately, his father possessed a small collection of the works of the old novelists, Smollett, Fielding, Goldsmith, and Defoe, together with *Don Quixote* and *Gil Blas*. The family fortunes soon began to decline. His father was careless and impecunious, and the family settled in a poor part of Camden Town. Then even the little education Charles had been getting came to an end, for his father's creditors refused to delay any longer, and consigned John D. to the Marshalsea Prison. His mother tried to support herself for a time by teaching children, and young Charles was sent to work in a blacking warehouse at Old Hungerford Stairs. The description of this period of his life is given in *David Copperfield* with a clearness and bitterness which showed how deeply these two years of humiliation affected the sensitive boy. He spent Sundays with his parents at the Marshalsea. These years, however, supplied him with much of that wealth of knowledge of low life, of the street, of the prison, and the poor, of which he was afterwards to make such marvellous use. In 1824 his father was enabled to pay his debts, and Charles spent another two years at school, a

private establishment at Hampstead, parodied as Salem House. In 1827 he entered the office of Mr. Blackmore, a solicitor, where he remained for over a year. His early ambition was still active, and his application great. He spent hours in reading at the British Museum and in mastering Gurney's shorthand. His natural powers of observation were also used to the best advantage, as his delightful sketches of legal dignitaries of all ranks clearly show. His father was still in difficulties, but Charles now managed to make his entry into journalism as a parliamentary reporter. It was in 1833 that he made his first appear-

CHARLES DICKENS

ance as a creative genius. In the *Monthly Magazine* for December of that year appeared the first of those sketches of contemporary manners, collected in 1836 under the title of *Sketches by Boz.* He also made some contributions to the *Evening Chronicle*. About this time the issue of sporting novels of a humorous character, embellished with plates far more important than the books, was popular. Messrs. Chapman & Hall were about to prepare a book of this kind dealing with the adventures of a club of Cockney sportsmen. Seymour, the famous rival of Cruikshank, had been engaged to provide the drawings, and D. was asked to write the letterpress. He pleaded his total ignorance of sport, and the plan was then changed to that of the Pickwick Club. On the suicide of Seymour, the sporting element was entirely dropped, and with ' Phiz ' (Hablot K. Browne) as illustrator, D. succeeded in making *The Posthumous Papers of the Pickwick Club* an immortal work. The introduction of Sam Weller marks the beginning of his success. From the advent of this character the monthly parts were awaited with feverish anxiety, and even the adverse *Quarterly Review* was compelled to admit that the whole reading world was discussing the Pickwickians. In 1837 the work appeared in book form, and in the same year the new novelist set to work on the grim satire of *Oliver Twist*. It may be noted that thus early in his career D. laid his hand to the ' novel with a purpose,' and that here, as always, he uses the method of gross caricature, making use of satire which ever remains too ludicrous to become ill-tempered, and which, however true the note of indignation may be, never loses sight of the humorous element. Here, too, appears the pathos, inclined to sentimentality, and the deep melodrama which was to be a stain, if an unavoidable one, on so much of his later work. At the beginning of 1838, while *Oliver* was not yet half finished, D. began the publication of *Nicholas Nickleby*, a picturesque story published on the same lines as *Pickwick*, and commenced writing *Barnaby Rudge*. Much of *Nicholas* is poor and melodramatic, but some of the sketches are only a little short of his highest work. Mrs. Nickleby, partly drawn from his own mother, is one of the best characters, and the sketches of Dotheboys Hall and the travelling theatre are also noteworthy. On the completion of this work D. started a weekly periodical to be known as *Master Humphrey's Clock*, where Pickwick and the Wellers are again brought to life. In this periodical began *The Old Curiosity Shop*. In spite of the highly complicated plot this is perhaps the richest mine of Dickensian characterisation. The humorous sketches of Dick Swiveller and his bizarre surroundings are unexcelled, but, in spite of Landor and Jeffrey, the overdrawn pathos of Little Nell is almost universally condemned by critics. *Barnaby Rudge* (1841), under the influence of Scott, appeared in the same publication. Here again the plot is complicated, and the work is also noteworthy as being, with the exception of *A Tale of Two Cities*, the only one in which D. dealt with the past. *Master Humphrey's Clock* then came to an end, and in Jan. 1842 D. started on his first American tour. He was received everywhere with acclamation, so that his visit became a veritable triumph. However, he deeply offended Transatlantic feeling by the publication of *American Notes* (1842), and on his return home he satirised American democracy far more freely and effectively in *Martin Chuzzlewit*

(1844), which is generally regarded as his greatest humorous work since Pickwick. It closes the great period of his observation and external caricature. Henceforward, almost all his good work is autobiographical. Here, however, his delineation of London, particularly at Todgers's, forms an incomparable work, with Pecksniff, Mrs. Gamp, Betsy Prig, and the Literary Ladies. Melodrama is again present with Jonas Chuzzlewit. In 1843 appeared *A Christmas Carol*, and the next two years were spent in a visit to Italy. At the beginning of 1846 he took up the editorship of the *Daily News*, but soon relinquished this uncongenial post, and returned to Switzerland, where he commenced *Dombey and Son*. This work, published in 1848, was a great success, and entirely re-established his fortunes. It marks, however, the beginning of his failing powers, and contains in the death of Little Paul the great monument of D.'s sentimentality. In 1849 appeared *David Copperfield*, favourite of D. and of most of his readers. The earlier portions are best, for here the autobiographical note is the stronger. In 1850 D. started a weekly paper, *Household Words*, designed to form a training ground for aspiring authors, which was later continued under the title of *All the Year Round*. In 1852 came *Bleak House*, where he satirises the Courts of Chancery. Though containing the figure of Harold Skimpole, drawn from Leigh Hunt, it is somewhat dull and uninteresting. Two years later came *Hard Times*, where D. violently opposes the industrial doctrines of the Manchester school. It is clearer and more connected than its predecessor, but does not rank high among his works. Between these two, in 1853, had been published the volume of *Christmas Stories*, containing ' The Christmas Carol,' ' The Chimes,' and other short works written at various times. To these must be put down almost the whole of the conventional idea of the secular or mid-Victorian Christmas, which is peculiarly English and Dickensian. It is important to notice that D. was the creator of this type, for he is generally associated with descriptions of Christmas in every mind. From 1855–57 *Little Dorrit* appeared, and here the loss of the old animal spirits and the spontaneous humour is grievously marked. By this time D. had finally taken up his residence at Gad's Hill in Kent, and an improvement is shown in *A Tale of Two Cities* (1859), which is genuine and powerful tragedy. It is the least characteristic of all his works, and is appreciated by many who do not relish his other books. Two years later comes *Great Expectations*, which Swinburne and many other critics have judged the best of his works. His own life again furnishes many of the incidents, but the most notable thing is the improvement in art. His mastery of the difficult art of sustaining an atmosphere is also shown in his next work, *Our Mutual Friend*, published in parts during 1864–65. In spite of brilliant effects of characterisation, as in the case of Silas Wegg, failing powers are shown here, and the work has never been a popular one. In 1867 D. made a second voyage to America under the pressure of pecuniary difficulties. He made an exhausting tour through the country, giving readings from his popular works. His effort was successful, and he returned home sufficiently reimbursed to set him at ease. He then retired to Gad's Hill, where he engaged himself on *The Mystery of Edwin Drood*, a work which he left unfinished. He d. at Gad's Hill on June 9, 1870. *See* Forster's *Life of Dickens*, 1872–74 ; *Letters*, edited by Miss Hogarth and Miss Dickens, 1880–82 ; Gissing's *Charles Dickens*, 1898 ; Fitzgerald's *History of Pickwick*, 1891, Kitton's *Novels of Charles Dickens*, 1897 ; Chesterton's *Life*, 1906 ; Payn's *Recollections*, 1894.

**Dickens Fellowship, The**, was founded in 1902 to encourage the study and discussion of Dickens' works, and to help to remedy those social evils which would have provided subjects for work for Dickens. It issues a monthly magazine entitled *The Dickensian*, the first editor of which was B. W. Matz, and his successor, Mr. Walter Dexter. Sir Henry F. Dickens, K.C., and Mrs. Kate Perugini, were both Life Presidents of the Fellowship ; while many eminent men and women of letters to-day are members of the society. The first offices were rented in Whitcomb Street, but after various moves, the Fellowship was finally established at 'The Dickens House,' 48 Doughty Street, W.C. 1, where once Dickens lived and wrote. The house was acquired by the Fellowship as a permanent Dickens Museum and Library, and as such presented to the nation ; it is vested in a trust in which the London County Council, the Corporation of London, and the D. F. all participate. The annual subscription of 10s. 6d. includes the quarterly *Dickensian*, and six monthly reunions for lectures and debates. The D. F. to-day consists of 69 branches, with approximately 12,000 members in large towns of the United Kingdom and also in the Dominions and the United States.

**Dickinson, Emily** (1830–74), American poetess ; *b.* on Dec. 10, 1830, at Amhurst, U.S.A., of an old-established Massachusetts family, of original Yorkshire stock. Her father, Edward Dickinson, a lawyer by profession, was of stern, jealous disposition, and remained an abiding influence in E. D.'s life until his death in 1874. She was, however, much in sympathy with him. She was educated at the Amhurst Academy and the Mount Holyoke Female Seminary, and in 1854 visited Washington and Philadelphia. Soon after this, however, she became a voluntary recluse, never, save on two occasions, setting foot beyond her garden gate, and her renunciation is commonly supposed to have been caused by her father's opposition to her marriage. Her lover is unknown, although legend has been busy with his name, but it is now almost certainly authenticated that he was George Gould, a theological student, who five years after Emily's renunciation married another, and in 1862 was ordained.

Having a sensitive mystical nature, E. D. composed her poetry in secret, and its existence was all but unsuspected. After her death, May 15, 1886, a collection of manuscripts was discovered by her sister Lavinia, and some unfortunately destroyed. The remainder were published in 1890 and were an immediate success. Her poems are short epigrammatic lyrics which may be grouped under such heads as Life, Love, Nature, Death. The verse has an exquisite and unusual music, her rhythms and hersensitivemanipulationofwordsare peculiar to herself, and these qualities are combined with a rare sensibility and an original mind. In her perception of life emotion was at once followed by a newness of thought. With Emerson, whom she resembled in method, E. D. ranks as one of the greatest American poets of the nineteenth century.

BIBLIOGRAPHY.—*Poems*, 1890, 1891; *Letters*, 1894 ; M. B. Bianchi, *The Life and Letters of Emily Dickinson*, 1924 ; *Complete Poems of Emily Dickinson*, 1928 ; *Further Poems*, 1929 ; J. Pollitt, *Emily Dickinson*, 1930 ; G. Taggard, *Life and Mind of Emily Dickinson*, 1930.

**Dickinson, Goldsworthy Lowes**, son of the late Lowes D., artist. He holds the position of fellow and lecturer at King's College, Cambridge, at the present time, and is also a lecturer at the London School of Economics and Political Science. His chief publications are : *The Development of Parliament in the Nineteenth Century ; The Meaning* *of Good; Religion and Immortality; Revolution and Reaction in Modern France.*

**Dickinson, Jacob McGavock** (1851–1928), American politician and lawyer, *b.* at Columbus. Served in the Confederate Army for a short period, and later studied law at Columbia, Leipzig and in Paris. After practising for over twenty years at Nashville, he became assistant Attorney General of the U.S.A. 1895–7. Later, he practised in Chicago and represented the U.S. gov. at the hearing of the Alaskan Boundary dispute. In politics, he was a democrat, but spoke in support of the Republican Taft in the presidential election campaign of 1908, becoming Secretary of War in Taft's Cabinet. Was vice-president of the American Society of International Law, and president of the American Bar Association.

**Dickinson, John** (1732–1808), an American statesman, *b.* in Talbot co., Indiana, studied law and entered Middle Temple, London, 1753. Returned to America, 1757, and practised law in Philadelphia, and was a member of the Pennsylvanian Assembly. He opposed the Declaration of Independence. He published a great number of pamphlets, the prime among which were the *Letters of a Farmer in Pennsylvania* (1767–68). He was very influential in state politics, but lost much of his influence through his opposition to the Declaration of Independence. He helped to found Dickinson College at Carlisle, Pennsylvania.

**Dicksee, Sir Francis Bernard** (1853–1928), President of the Royal Academy of Arts; *b.* Nov. 27, 1853, in London. Was educated at the Rev. Henslowe's school, London, and studied painting under his father and at the Royal Academy. Gained the gold medal of that institute for his 'Elijah confronting Ahab and Jezebel in Naboth's Vineyard,' 1876. He became A.R.A. in 1881; R.A. in 1891; and P.R.A. in Dec. 1924—when he was knighted. K.C.V.O., 1927. He belonged to the symbolic school of painters, and combined skilful draughtsmanship with subdued and tasteful colouring. Among his best works may be included 'Evangeline,' 'The Symbol,' 'Romeo and Juliet,' 'Funeral of a Viking,' 'The Magic Crystal,' 'Paolo and Francesca,' 'The Passing of Arthur,' 'La Belle Dame sans Merci,' and 'The Ideal.'

**Dickson City,** a city of Lackawanna co., Pennsylvania, U.S.A., situated on the Lackawanna about 3 m. N.E. of Scranton in the anthracite region. Pop. 12,395.

**Dicotyledons,** as distinguished from monocotyledons, constitute one of two large classes into which flowering plants are divided. One characteristic, from which the name is derived, is the presence of two (rarely more) cotyledons in the germinating seed. D. are subdivided into (1) Monochlamydeæ, the members of which have flowers with a sepaloid perianth or absent altogether, and often unisexual: to this belong the Urticaceæ, Amentaceæ, and other orders; (2) Polypetalæ, in which the flowers are hermaphrodite (*i.e.* contain both stamens and pistil), the perianth usually consists of calyx and corolla and the petals are free from one another; (3) Gamopetalæ, with hermaphrodite flowers, and petals joined.

**Dictamnus Fraxinella,** *see* DITTANY.

**Dictator** (Lat. *dictare,* to command), the title given to an official of the Roman republic whose earlier title was *Magister populi.* The office, as the earlier title suggests, was originally instituted in times of military crisis; the first D. was appointed in 501 B.C., according to Livy, on account of a crisis in the war with the Latins. It was a temporary revival of the power of the kings with some limitations. One of the conditions usually enforced was that a D. should previously have held the office of consul. He was to be nominated by a consul, although in later practice it was the senate who indicated the nominee. To emphasise his superiority over the consuls, the D. was preceded by twenty-four lictors, instead of twelve, bearing the *fasces.* In a later period the appointment of a D. was not only practised in times of military stress, but of constitutional crisis as well, and for criminal jurisdiction; this was the 'administrative' D., and he held his office for six months. Ds. appointed for minor purposes, to hold the elections, to conduct the games, and to preside at the festivals, were expected to resign their office as soon as they had completed their business. The other officers were not suspended when a D. was appointed; they simply became subordinate to him and continued their duties as his officials. In early times the D. had absolute power over the life and death of the citizens, but that power was limited by the *Lex Valeria* (300 B.C.). From the beginning his absolute power was checked by his being compelled to apply to the senate for money, and by having no authority outside Italy. Originally the office was confined to the patricians; C. Marcius Rutilus was the first plebeian elected in 356 B.C. The last regular D. elected was M. Junius Pera in 216 B.C. The office, as revived by Sulla in 82 B.C., was only similar in its bestowal of almost absolute power. He had himself elected ' for the establishment of the Republic,' and he held the office for three years. The dictatorship of Julius Cæsar was even less provisional and constitutional. In 48 B.C. he was appointed for one year, in 46 B.C. this period of office was extended for ten years, and in 45 B.C. for life. After his death the office was abolished by Marcus Antonius in 44 B.C. In later times the title and powers of Ds. have been seized by usurpers and the heads of revolutionary movements, notably in the S. American States, in Hayti. San Domingo, and Mexico. It might have been thought that the steady advance of democracy along constitutional lines in general, and the particularly marked advance throughout the nineteenth century, would have precluded the possibility of the reappearance of any individual in the shape of a D. to bless or burden mankind. Yet such is the uncertainty in human affairs and so often does history repeat itself, that Europe since the close of the Great War, up to the time of writing (1931), has seen the rise to power of two outstanding Ds. In Italy Mussolini (q.v.) became in 1919 an exponent and leader of Fascism. His followers were called Fascisti and they ardently denounced Bolshevism in all its guises. The Fascisti formed themselves into a political party which gradually became all-powerful in Italy. Towards the end of 1922 Mussolini as head of the Fascisti became head of the kings' gov. in Italy. Under constitutional forms he has really wielded the powers of D. In Spain, General Primo de Rivera, Marquis de Estella, issued on Sept. 12, 1923, a manifesto suspending the constitution and substituting a directorate of naval and military officers. This directorate lasted till Dec. 3, 1925, when it was dissolved and its place taken by a group of Ministers with Primo, virtually a D., at its head. He had already relinquished office when he d. suddenly in Paris, on March 16, 1930. It should be noted that in the case of Italy and Spain, Mussolini and Primo de Rivera both made strong and passionate and successful appeals to nationalist sentiment. Other if less striking modern dictatorships are those of Mustapha Kemal in Turkey; and of Alexander I. of Yugo-Slavia, who, in 1929, abolished the Constitution, dissolved the Skupshtina and assumed the executive power.

**Dicte,** a mt. in Candia or Crete, one of the largest islands in the Mediterranean. The mountains of this island are composed principally of freestone or marble.

**Dictionary,** properly and most usually, a book containing a list of the words of some language arranged in definite order, usually following the alphabet, together with explanations of these words. The term, however, has been generally applied to any work which professes to communicate information on an entire subject or entire branch of a subject, under words or heads arranged in alphabetical order. This alphabetical arrangement appears to be one distinctive mark of a D. ; but it is also necessary that there should be some explanation or interpretation added to the words so arranged. Thus an index, in which words or titles are merely put down in alphabetical order, with nothing more than a reference to some page or passage appended to each, is not a D. When the phrase is actually quoted instead of a reference being given, the work is called a concordance. Further, although the order and arrangement of a D. be arbitrary, the work must profess some unity and completeness of design. As has been said, it must profess to go over a whole subject, or field of knowledge, of greater or less extent. Thus a mere list of miscellaneous particulars, even with explanatory remarks or comments annexed, is not a D., but a catalogue. A collection of plays or of pamphlets might be arranged in the order of the alphabet, but it would not on that account make a D. The earliest D. of which any portions are extant is Δέξεις the 'Ομηρικαί, or Homeric Words, a lexicon to the works of Homer, written, according to Suidas, by Apollonius the sophist. Julius Pollux in the second century prepared an *Onomasticon* or Greek D., with the words arranged in order of meaning. The most famous Greek D., however, is that of Suidas (tenth century), giving an alphabetical list of words with details and illustrative quotations. It was first published at Milan in 1499. The first attempt at constructing a complete Arabic D. was made by Khalil ibn Ahmed of Oman about the middle of the eighth century, and his successors carried his work on till the end of the Middle Ages. Ds. of a kind are found in Sanskrit several centuries B.C., and special Ds. as well as literary compilations are also found in certain parts of the East. In Latin lexicography, the earliest works of importance are those by M. Terentius Varro and the compilation of Pompeius Testus entitled *De Significatione Verborum*. In the eleventh and following centuries, note should be made of the D. of Papias, and the *Catholicon* of Giovanni Balbi. In the sixteenth century appears the first polyglot D. of Colepino, which in its later editions included eleven languages. The great classical Ds. at the present days are :—Greek : Liddell and Scott's *Lexicon* (8th edition), 1897 ; Pape's *Wörterbuch der Griechischen Eigennamen ;* Thayer's *Greek-English Lexicon of the New Testament ;* Thayer's revision of Sophocles's *Lexicon of the Roman and Byzantine Periods ;* and Contopoulos' *Modern Greek-English and English-Greek Dictionary.* Latin : De Vit's edition of the *Totius Lexicon Latinitatis* (Prato), 1858–79 ; White and Riddle's *Latin-English and English-Latin Dictionary ;* ·Georges' *Deutsch-Lateinisches und Lateinisch-Deutsches Wörterbuch* (Leipzig, 4 vols.), 1880–85 ; and the great work commenced in 1900 by the German universities, the *Thesaurus Linguæ Latinæ* (Leipzig). For Mediæval Latin, recourse must be had to Du Cange's *Glossarium ad Scriptores Mediæ et Infimæ Latinitalis.* Ds. have sometimes been divided into three main classes or descriptions : (i.) Ds. of words ; (ii.) Ds. of facts ; (iii.) Ds. of things ; and although objections may be lodged against this method of distribution, it is sufficiently convenient for practical purposes. 1. *Dictionaries of words :* This, as we have seen, is the original application of the word D., and the sense in which it is commonly understood when it stands alone. In this sense the word corresponds to the Greek ' lexicon,' a word which seems to have been used by the Greeks in the modern sense. Some Ds. and vocabularies apply only to some particular author and work. The Λέξεις Ὁμηρικαί. already referred to, was of this kind, and the Greek classics have been well treated individually. Ds. of this kind usually confine themselves to the more difficult and unusual words, and are called *glossaries, e.g.* Tyrwhitt's *Glossary to Chaucer,* and the various Shakespearian glossaries. 2. *Dictionaries of facts :* This class comprehends Ds. of history, biography, mythology, geography, archæology, and all others that deal exclusively with things that have happened, or with facts that exist or have existed. Some of the old Greek lexicons were Ds. of facts as well as of words ; the lexicon of Suidas, for instance, is in the greater part made up of fragments of biography, history, and geography, and often contains large extracts from various writers both extant and lost. The work of Stephanus Byzantinus, known as Ἐθνικά or Περὶ Πόλεων, is chiefly a geographical and archæological D., and is the oldest compilation of that description that exists. Its meagre details under each head assimilate it in some respects to an imperfect gazetteer. In modern times the number of Ds. that have appeared, purporting to give a view of a more or less extensive field of facts, has been very great. Besides the various historical, biographical, and geographical Ds., general and particular, and the bibliographical Ds., there are Ds. of antiquities, of architecture, of heraldry, of painting, of music, of botany, of law, of legal decisions, of commerce, of medicine, of surgery, of miracles, of dates, and of almost every other department of human knowledge. 3. *Dictionaries of things :* This division comprehends Ds. of all the abstract sciences, the mixed or applied sciences, the departments of criticism and the fine arts, and the whole range of metaphysical and moral speculation. It is true that most of these subjects cannot be treated of without a reference to facts, but the facts here are not viewed simply as such, but either as subordinate to principles, or as modifying their operation. The remainder of this article will deal with the first class of Ds., and in these, in particular, much progress has been made during the century past. The present tendency towards completeness has led to the larger Ds. assimilating many of the peculiar features of the smaller ones. Ds. dealing with equivalent words in different languages are generally small, since they are intended for beginners and details are few. Similarly, for convenience of reference, Ds. of synonyms, homonyms, etc., are generally kept distinct from the large works. The improvement of these works of reference has been particularly full and rapid in Great Britain. Progress is first seen in the idea of the aim of the work, and this may be seen by comparison with the works of the seventeenth century. The aim of Johnson's D. (1755) was to provide a final authority as to what words were admissible among correct writers and what meanings they were to bear. The lexicographer constituted himself the supreme arbiter in such questions. This idea continued to dominate English lexicography until the time of Archbishop Trench, who was the first to apply sound philological principles to the subject and to emphasise the fact that the lexicographer must be, not the critic, but the historian of the language. The present conception of a dictionary, which is finding its greatest expression in the *New English Dictionary,* has this philological aim in view of giving a full account of *all* words used in English from the middle of the twelfth century, a point fixed as the starting point of New English. It gives a historical survey of the changes of meaning which words have undergone, with quotations from writers of all times. It definitely originated from the suggestion of Archbishop Trench that some such work should be undertaken by the Philological Society, and its full title is the *New English Dictionary on historical principles, founded mainly on materials collected by the Philological Society.* The work was commenced under the editorship of Herbert Coleridge, who was succeeded by Dr. F. J. Furnivall. The publication was not commenced, however, until 1884, when the work began to issue from the Oxford University Press under the editorship of Dr. (afterwards Sir) J. A. H. Murray. Great stress is laid on the etymological side of such a work, and in this department great accuracy has now been attained. The other department, that of quotation, was already recognised by Johnson, though its use apart from the historical method is by no means so great. Since the great value of quotation is to show the various shades of meaning which may be given to a word by different writers at different times, and since etymology now gives a short history of a word from its first use to its last, it follows that the ideal can only be completely realised in a work of vast size and with a vast initial expense. It has, in fact, only been attained in the D. we have just discussed. The great pioneers of philological science were the first to introduce etymology into Ds. The introduction dates from 1854, when Jacob and Wilhelm Grimm published the first volume of the *Deutsches Wörterbuch.* Its main application in France was in E. Littré's *Dictionnaire de la langue française,* 1863–72.

**Dictys Cretensis** (of Crete), a native of Cnossus who is reputed to have followed Idomeneus to the siege of Troy and to have written an account of it. Lucius Septimus in the fourth century published an *Ephemeris belli Trojani,* which purports to be a Latin translation of the Greek of Dictys. *See* edition by F. Meister, 1873; also G. Körting, *Dictys und Dares,* 1874, and N. E. Griffin, *Dares and Dictys,* 1907.

**Didactic Poetry** (Gk. διδάσκω = to teach) is poetry which openly expresses its intention of conveying knowledge or instruction. Aristotle considered that a didactic poem was no more than a treatise; but there are so many degrees of didacticism in poetry that while most didactic poems are very inferior as poetry some are great in spite of the didactic element, e.g. *Paradise Lost* is didactic in so far as it sets out with the dogmatic aim, ' to justify the ways of God to man.' The majority of notable Eng. didactic poems have a theological aim, e.g. the *Faerie Queene,* which is essentially a vindication of Protestantism and Puritanism; and much of the poetry of Cowper, who fancied that the vehicle of verse might bring many to listen to truths (as he held them) which they would be disinclined to have stated to them in simple prose, is directed to theological tenets. The same poet's *Tirocinum* or *Review of Schools,* is yet more obviously didactic, being written to 'recommend private tuition at home.' Shelley again, in his more didactic poems, e.g. *Rosalind and Helen,* teaches that all the world is evil and will continue evil until some unknown conqueror shall appear and reform all evil. Thus poetry of very varying merit may be in greater of less degree didactic; but in a more restricted sense D. P. is rather that in which the precepts or teaching are not merged in exalted flights of poetic imagination but are set out dogmatically, as e.g. Tusser's (q.v.) *Five Hundredth Poyntes of Good Husbandrie etc.* In ancient poetry, the *De Rerum Natura* of Lucretius (q.v.), a didactic poem on Epicurean philosophy, is the D. poem *par excellence*; and the *Georgics* of Virgil are also replete with precept, the Third Georgic containing practical precepts for farmers, and the Fourth giving much information about bees; but in both poets, though far more markedly in Virgil, the teacher is often dropped by the poet for the natural philosopher, speculating on the hidden reason of nature's operations. Bagehot, voicing the common opinion, thought that it was not the object of poetry 'to chill you with didactic icebergs,' but rather to select, idealise, purify and intensify the great features and peculiarities which make society as a whole ' remarkable and fancy-taking.' As poetry, D. P. is often commonplace, the matter not lending itself to the mode of expression which most appeals to the true poet, e.g. the precepts of the German Minnesänger, Walther von der Vogelweide (q.v.) and Wolfram von Eschenbach, are often, in spite of the excellent moral lessons inculcated, told satirically.

**Didelphia,** *see* MARSUPIALS.

**Didelphys,** *see* OPOSSUM.

**Diderot, Denys** (1713–84), a Fr. ' savant ' and author, *b.* at Langres in Champagne. He was educated at the Jesuit College at Langres and the College d'Harcourt at Paris. He was intended for the Church, but on his expressing a distaste for it he was placed with a procureur in Paris to study jurisprudence. Evincing an equal distaste for the law, and refusing to return to his father's home, he was left in Paris to live by his wits. He tried many occupations, but continued at none—only defying starvation with his pen. He wrote anything and everything, indices, catalogues, advertisments, sermons, and translations from English. His first important original work was *Pensées Philosophiques*, 1746, in which he set forth the doctrine of the band of freethinking philosophers who arose at this time of reaction against the

DENYS DIDEROT

tyranny of the Church; the doctrine which he summed up in his own dying words: 'The first step towards philosophy is incredulity.' For his next work, *Lettre sur les Aveugles*, he was imprisoned at Vincennes by order of the government. On his release D. collaborated with D'Alembert as editor of a *Universal Medical Dictionary*, a scheme which later grew into the *Encyclopédie, ou Dictionnaire Raisonné des Sciences, des Arts, et Métiers*. The work was enormous, and owing to the retirement of D'Alembert, D. was sole editor for the greater part of the time. The first volume was published in 1751, and the remaining sixteen, as well as eleven volumes of plates, in the years between 1751 and 1765. He embodied in his encyclopædia the philosophy which he had foreshadowed in the *Pensées Philosophiques*, the dreary, rebellious philosophy of Atheism and revolt, a reaction against Jesuit predominance in the Church and tyranny

on the throne, which he shared with his friend and great contemporary, J. J. Rousseau, and which was to lead to the Revolution. Among D.'s other works were the *Essay on Painting*, translated and praised by Goethe; *Lettres sur les Sourds et Muets*, 1751; *Pensées sur l'Interprétation de la Nature*, 1754; *Code de la Nature*, 1755; the tales of *Jacques le Fataliste* and *Le Neveu de Rameau*, the finest of his imaginative productions. *Les Bijoux Indiscrets*, an extreme example of the coarser style which he sometimes affected; *La Religieuse*, directed against convent life; *La Promenade du Sceptique; La Rêve d'Alembert; Lettres* to his mistress, Mdlle. Voland; and his last work, *Essai sur la Vie de Sénèque*. In his last years he sank into a state of extreme poverty. Catherine of Russia, to relieve him, bought his library, but appointed him custodian and paid him fifty years' salary in advance. In 1773 D. visited St. Petersburg to thank the empress and returned to Paris only twelve days before his death. Collections of D.'s works were published by Naigeon in fifteen volumes, 1798, reprinted in twenty-two volumes, 1821. *See also* Sainte-Beuve's *Portraits Littéraires* (3 vols.), 1844; *Studies* of D. by Rosenkranz. 1866, and Scherer, 1880; *Mémoires, Correspondance, et Ouvrages inédits de Diderot* (4 vols.), 1831; L. Ducros, *Diderot, l'Homme et l'Ecrivain*, 1894; and an essay on D. by Carlyle in *Miscellanies*, vols. xxvi.–xxx.

**Didius Julianus,** grandson of Salvius Julianus; reigned for only two months as emperor of Rome in the year 193 A.D. Distinguished in his earlier years for his industry and zeal. He won the throne of Rome through bidding the highest to the prætorian guards; the people would not brook this insult, and D. was eventually executed.

**Dido,** or **Elissa,** according to legend, was the daughter of Belus, King of Tyre, and the sister of Pygmalion, his successor. Pygmalion having murdered her husband, Acerbus or Sichæus (*see* Virgil), D. escaped with his treasures to Cyprus and thence to N. Africa, where she founded Carthage (Byrsa) on a piece of land bought from Iarbas, King of Libya. To escape from marriage with Iarbas, she built a funeral pyre and stabbed herself before her people. The version given by Virgil in the *Æneid*, that D. stabbed herself after her desertion by Æneas, the hero of Troy, is an anachronism, for three hundred years intervened between the legendary fall of Troy and the founding of Carthage.

**Didon, Henri** (1840–1900), a celebrated Fr. preacher belonging to the Dominican order. Was appointed to preach the funeral sermon over the Archbishop of Paris, who was murdered in 1871. His lectures on religion and science in Paris brought him into suspicion, and he was suspended, and had to seek retirement in Corsica. His most popular work is *Jésu-Christ*, published in 1890, and was the outcome of his visit to the Holy Land.

**Didot, François** (1689–1757), the founder of a family of famous Fr. printers. Started in trade as bookseller and printer in 1713, and noted for his collection of the travels of the Abbé Prévost in 20 vols. (1747). *François Ambroise* and *Pierre François* made significant improvements in the arts of type-founding and paper-making. *Henri D.*, son of Pierre François, was celebrated for his microscopic editions. *Pierre D.*, son of François Ambroise, noted for his Louvre editions of Virgil, Horace, and Racine. *Firmin D.*, his brother, distinguished as printer and type-founder; he also discovered the process of stereotyping, and published stereotyped editions of the classics at a very reasonable sum. Other printers of note are Ambroise Firmin and Hyacinthe, who worked together after their father's death. The former left a collection of MS. valued at two million francs.

**Didsbury**, a tn. of Lancashire, England, situated on the Mersey. It is about 5 m. S. of Manchester, and forms a residential suburb for many Manchester people. Pop. 14,928.

**Didymium**, a name given to a mixture of the two chemical elements *neo-didymium* and *praseo-dymium* before its dual nature had been ascertained.

**Didymotichon**, formerly called Demotika, a tn. of Thrace, Greece, near the R. Maritza and the Sofia–Constantinople rly. Pop. 8200.

**Didymus**, (c. 63 B.C.–A.D. 10), a celebrated grammarian and scholar; taught at Alexandria and then at Rome. Wrote many articles upon the Gk. poets and prose writers. His commentaries upon phrases and obscure words are most helpful to students and grammarians.

**Die**, *see* DROME.

**Dié, St.**, *see* VOSGES.

**Diebitsch-Zabalkanski Hans Friedrich Anton, Count von** (1785–1831), a celebrated Russian general. Made commander-in-chief of the Russian army, 1829. Chiefly famed for his passage of the Balkans, for which he received the titles of field-marshal and Count Zabalkanski.

**Dieburg**, a tn. of Germany, in the free state of Hesse, Germany, 8 m. N.E. of Darmstadt. Pop. 6200.

**Diedenhofen** (Fr. *Thionville*), a tn. of Germany, in Lorraine, situated on the Moselle, 20 m. N. of Metz by rail. It is of ancient origin, and strongly fortified. Imperial diets were held here in the eighth century ; in 1870 it surrendered to the Prussians. It has manufactures of wine, hosiery, and iron goods Brewing and tanning are also carried on. Pop. 10,000.

**Diefenbach, Lorenz** (1806–83), a German scholar, *b.* in Ostheim. Wrote an important work on Celtic origins called *Celtica*, 1839–40 ; compiled a famous Latin-German *Glossarium Latino-Germanicum Mediæ et Infimæ Ætatis*, a supplement to Du Cange's glossary ; also compiled a *Hoch-und-Niederdeutsches Wörterbuch*.

**Dieffenbach, Johann Friedrich** (1794–1847), a distinguished surgeon, *b.* at Königsberg in Prussia. First studied theology, then became a volunteer. Finally entered the medical profession, and became one of the most famous operators of the day; was appointed Professor of Medicine in the University of Berlin (1840); was particularly successful in the art of forming new noses, lips, etc.

**Die-hards.** A nickname in English politics which became current towards the end of 1918, when the Coalition Gov. under Mr. Lloyd George began to show signs of internal dissension, and to break up once more, as the electorate was already doing, into separate parties. Many Conservatives realising their own present strength, desired to return to the original party system. The proposal to set up an Irish Free State with a Parliament in Dublin, revived many old controversies, and the extreme section among the Conservatives became more urgent in their demands for separation. At first the leaders of this movement were few in number and small in influence, and they were called Die-hards almost in derision. But gradually their influence increased until at an important party meeting they found themselves to be in a majority of nearly three to one. The Coalition Gov. ceased to exist, and Mr. Lloyd George was succeeded in the Premiership by Mr. Bonar Law.

**Dielectric, or Insulator**, according to Faraday, is the name given to those substances through which electrostatic induction takes place. When one body attracts another, viz. a molecule of dust, the action which takes place is called induction, and the intervening medium in which the action occurs is called the D. There are two kinds of D., the one is gaseous and includes air and all gases, the other is solid and includes such substances as glass, silk, vulcanite, resin, mica, and gutta-percha. Brass and all metals are good conductors of electricity, while porcelain, marble, slate, and stoneware are such bad conductors that they are used for insulating telegraph and telephone supports, or the bases of switch-boards or stands, etc. In the same way the softer substances, silk, gutta-percha, and india-rubber, are used for insulating telegraph and telephone wires, or coils and wires in other electrical apparatus. The inductive effect of a given charge depends upon the D. surrounding the charged body, and the result obtained is called the specific inductive capacity. When hot, the power of a body is always diminished. Although air is a D., should an electric spark pass through it, its insulating power at once breaks down, and it ceases to act as a D. In the same way solid Ds. lose their solidity and become cracked, if touched by an electric spark.

**Diemen, Van,** *see* VAN DIEMEN.

**Diemen's Land, Van,** *see* TASMANIA.

**Diepenbeeck, Abraham van** (*d.* 1675), a Flemish painter, *b.* at Bois-le-Duc either in 1596 or 1607. He became a pupil of Rubens, and after-wards studied in Italy. His drawing is sometimes defective, and his work is, at its best, but an imitation of Rubens; a copy of Rubens' ' Descent from the Cross ' is D.'s finest work. He also illustrated Marolle's *Tableaux du Temple des Muses.*

**Dieppe,** a Fr. seaport, dept. Seine-Inférieure, standing on the Eng. Channel, 33 m. N. of Rouen. The tn. has a certain picturesqueness, with its high-roofed houses, and its streets running in lines parallel to the sea.

DIEPPE CASTLE

Its castle, now used as a barracks, and the Church of S. Jacques date from the fourteenth and fifteenth centuries. The chief manufactures are cotton goods, lace, tobacco, and machinery. Shipbuilding is also carried on, and there is a continuous service of steamers between this town

and Newhaven. The oyster culture and herring and mackerel fisheries are important. In 1927 800,000 tons of shipping entered and left the harbour, which can accommodate 200 ships besides fishing-boats. The tn. is fortified. It was a Pro-testant stronghold and lost its im-portance after the Revocation of the Edict of Nantes in 1685. Pop. 24,945.

**Dierx, Léon** (1838–1912), a Fr. poet, who is chiefly noted for the following works : *Poèmes et Poésies,* 1864 ; *Lèvres Closes,* 1867 ; *Poèmes d'un Vaincu,* 1871 ; *Poésies Complètes,* 1872. He also wrote a duologue called *La Rencontre.*

**Die-sinking,** used in the process of stamping an impression on coins or medals. The steel to be engraved for the die is at first carefully prepared and then subjected to a process which softens it. It is next given over to the engraver, who, by means of small hand implements of steel, cuts the design which he requires, and which must be a reversed one. When this is finished it has to be subjected to another process which makes it extremely hard. It is then ready for use, and is known as the matrix. As, however, the process of engraving is very expensive, it is seldom that the matrix is used for the actual stamp-ing process. Instead of this the im-pression is produced by considerable pressure in relief on a block of soft steel, which is known as the puncheon. The latter has to be hardened and it can then be used for conveying the design engraved on the matrix. Dies are also used in the manufacture of many other articles, as well as coins or medals. They are used in the manufacture of jewellery, such as clocks and watches, and also in stamping ornaments for curtain poles and articles of that sort. The art of engraving dies dates from very early times, and very many ancient Gk. coins, which have been stamped in this way, are still preserved.

**Dies Iræ** (' Day of Wrath '), a Latin hymn composed by Thomas of Celano, a friar belonging to the order of St. Francis. This hymn was in-serted by the Council of Trent in the mass for commemorating the souls of the faithful.

**Diest,** a tn. of Belgium, in the prov. of Brabant. It stands at the junction of the Demer and Bever. Marlborough took the tn. in 1705. There are numerous breweries. Pop. 8700.

**Diet** (Lat. *dies,* a day). This word originally applied to a session or sitting of a body of delegates or dignitaries, and the term was after-wards transferred to the bodies them-selves. The word applied to both legislative and ecclesiastical meetings, hence the phrase 'diet of worship.' Compare also the famous 'Diet of Worms' held in Luther's time. Now the word is applied to the assemblies held by the German parliament.

**Diet,** the food of an individual considered as a whole, particularly with regard to its efficiency in maintaining the nutrition of the body. A *dietary* is an organised system of taking food, the various constituents, their amounts, and time of eating being established beforehand. *Dietetics* is a branch of medical science which deals with the composition of various foods and their effect upon the body. A dietary may therefore be established as part of the treatment of some morbid condition. This is particularly important in such diseases as diabetes where some constituents of ordinary food are likely to have a harmful effect owing to the disturbed metabolism of the body. In institutions, such as prisons and workhouses, and in public services, such as the army and navy, dietaries are necessary if only to regulate the actions of the officials immediately concerned in the distribution of the food supply. In prisons and workhouses, the D. is dependent upon considerations of economy, efficiency, and discipline. The food must be sufficient in quantity and in its nature to satisfy the physical needs of the inmates, but at the same time a certain degree of austerity is considered desirable, so as to minimise the attraction which might be felt by individuals disinclined to work for food.

The constituents of food are usually classified as proteids, fats, carbohydrates, water, and salts. The proteids include such nitrogenous substances as form the body-tissues; the chief are albumin (in white of egg), myosin (in meat), casein (in milk), globulin and fibrin (in blood), and gluten (in flour). The fats include both animal fats and vegetable oils. Mineral oils, as petroleum emulsions, though useful as internal emollients, have no nutritive value. The carbohydrates are starches and sugars. The salts are sulphates, chlorides, phosphates, etc., occurring in animal and vegetable tissues, and usually supplemented by added sodium chloride, or common salt. The average man requires daily, 2700–2800 gms. of water, 30 gms. of salts, 70–150 gms. of proteids, 30–90 gms. of fats and 340–570 gms. of carbohydrates. The proteids are particularly concerned in building up the body during growth and in replacing waste. The fats and carbohydrates supply the energy for the carrying on

of vital processes. Energy, a form of heat, is measured in calories. Man needs 3000 calories a day, but feeding by the theoretic calory value of food presupposes perfect metabolism, whereas some foods are incompatible with others and should not be eaten together. 10 per cent. of food is waste. The relative proportions of fats, proteids, and carbohydrates in the D. are therefore capable of great variation, though proteids must never be withdrawn for long. Meat consists chiefly of muscle and fat. Muscle contains about 73 per cent. of water, 20 per cent. proteids and 8 per cent. of fats, and extractives. Of the proteid necessary each day 50 per cent., about $1\frac{3}{4}$ oz., should consist of 'complete' (animal) proteid, found in meat, eggs, milk, and cheese. Nuts also contain 'complete' proteid. A moderate proteid ration is beneficial to all except growing children and manual labourers. Meat-eating is popular for its stimulating rather than its nutritive value, and excess produces physical depression. Vegetable foods usually contain a large proportion of carbohydrates. Green vegetables are not as rich in starches as cereals, leguminous plants, and potatoes, but they effectively convey to the body necessary organic salts. Recent analyses of food have revealed chemical substances, called vitamins, each essential to life. Vitamin-$A$, an important growth factor, exists in cod-liver oil, fish roe, egg yolk, butter, and cream. Continued lack of Vitamin-$A$ causes blindness. Vitamin-$B$, anti-neuritic, is found in wholemeal wheat, rye, and maize, whole barley and whole rice, nuts, eggs, and yeast. A subsidiary vitamin, Vitamin-$B2$ or -$PP$, is found in these foods and in the lean of meat. Through lack of it people have died of a disease called pellagra, whereas lack of $B$ causes beri-beri. Vitamin-$C$, anti-scorbutic, exists in fresh fruit and vegetables. Cooking green vegetables with soda destroys $C$. Vitamin-$D$, anti-rachitic, is generally found in the same foods as $A$. Vitamin-$E$, necessary to fertility, is found in cod-liver oil and in various vegetable oils, also in whole wheat, oats, and lettuce.

*See* R. H. A. Plimmer, *Analyses and Energy Values of Foods*, 1921; and with V. G. Plimmer, *Food, Health, Vitamins*, 1928. V. H. Mottram, *Food and the Family*, 1925; Valentine Knaggs, *Things that Count in Diet*, 1928.

**Dietrich, Johann Wilhelm Ernst** (1712–74), a celebrated Ger. landscape and genre painter, *b.* at Weimar. First instructed in the art by his father, then studied under Alexander Thiele. His pictures were exhibited in the different European art galleries at Dresden, Paris, and London; and he secured the patronage of the kindly Count von Bruhl.

**Dietrich of Bern,** see THEODORIC THE GREAT.

**Dietrichson, Lorenz Henrik Segelcke** (*b.* 1834), a Norwegian art critic, *b.* at Bergen; gained distinction for himself by his brilliant lectures at Upsala on the modern literature of Denmark (1861). His principal contributions to literature are: *Det Sköna Verld,* 1872–79; *Fra Kunstens Verlden,* 1885; *Adolf Tidemand,* 1878–79; *Michelangelo,* 1880; *De Norske Stavkirker,* 1891–92.

**Dieulefit,** a small tn. of France, in the dept. of Drome, and famous in the sixteenth century as a resort of the Calvinists. Pop. 2590.

**Dieuze,** or **Duze,** a tn., in the dept. of Moselle, France. A mine near the tn., in activity since early times, still yields rock salt. D. also manufactures chemicals. Pop. about 2410.

**Diez,** or **Dietz,** a tn. of Prussia, in the prov. of Hesse-Nassau. The castle of the counts of Nassau-Dillenburg is now used as a gaol. Pop. 3460.

**Diez, Friedrich Christian** (1794–1876), a founder of Romance philology, *b.* at Giessen in Hesse-Darmstadt, Went to Bonn as a *privat-docent* in 1822; before this became acquainted with Goethe at Weimar in 1818, who urged him to make a study of Mediæval Provencal. Appointed Professor of Modern Literature in 1830 at the University of Bonn. His most important works are his *Grammatik der Romanischen Sprachen* and his *Etymologisches Wörterbuch der Romanischen Sprachen;* these two works may be said to have laid the foundation for the study of all the Romanic languages. An English translation of the introduction to the former work was made by Cayley in 1863. Other important contributions made by D. to literature, are: *Die Poesie der Troubadours,* 1826; *Leben und Werke der Troubadours,* 1829; he also issued various editions and translations of old Spanish romances and poems, and Portuguese court poetry

**Difference** and **Finite Differences,** in mathematics mean the excess of one quantity over another. This fundamental meaning of the term is almost lost in the higher parts of mathematics from the association of it with a methodised theory, derived from the consideration of the differences presented by successive quantities which follow a regular law. Summation of a series by the method of finite differences is a calculus of differences employed in problems involving interpolation or relating to annuities. By the operation of taking differences in this sense, we may find the rational integral function of the number of terms in a series or the general term of a series, when a certain number of the terms of the series are given. That is to say, the regular law of the series not being known by inspection, we proceed to take the first order of differences, viz. by subtracting each term from the term which immediately follows it and so forming a new series called the series of the first order of differences; then by repeating the process we get the series of the second order of differences, and so on until a series of regular or known form is arrived at, *e.g.* take the series −1, −3, 3, 23, 63, 129. . . and let $a_n$ denote the general term of the series, and $n$ the number of terms in the series. The successive orders of differences are:

$$-2, 6, 20, 40, 66$$
$$8, 14, 20, 26. . .$$
$$6, 6, 6$$

That is, the third order of differences gives equal terms, and $a_n$, the rational integral function of $n$, may be assumed $= v + x_n + y_n^2 + z_n^3$. Putting 1, 2, 3, 4 for $n$ in succession, we find $v = 3$, $x = -3$, $y = -2$, $z = 1$, and that the general term of the series is $3 - 3n - 2n^2 + n^3$.

**Differences,** a term used on the Stock Exchange to denote the amount of variation between the price at which it is agreed to buy or sell securities on a fixed day and the actual market price of the securities when that day arrives. Bargains for D. are not recognised by the rules of the Stock Exchange, being contrary to the law of wagering or betting contracts. It is not always easy to determine when an agreement with a broker is a mere betting contract or speculation on D., as in *bona fide* agreements the general practice is to carry over on every settling day and pay the D. only. The best test appears to be to ascertain whether each of the parties could in any event call upon the other to carry out his contract.

**Differentia,** a term in logic applied to the distinguishing characteristic which separates any two species of a genus. For example, the D. which separates the species man from the other species of the genus animal is the reasoning faculty.

**Differential Calculus,** see CALCULUS.

**Differential Equation.** An equation between two or more variables that contains one or more differential coefficients is called a D. E. The theory of D. E. deals with the solution of such equations, *i.e.* the elimination of the differential coefficients by integration *e.g.* $\frac{dy}{dx} = 3x$ is a D. E. and by integration with respect to the variable $x$ we obtain the equation $y = x^3 + A$, where A is any constant. The latter equation is called the solution of the D. E. D. Es. are of considerable importance in all branches of science; they may be divided into two classes, viz. (i) *Ordinary differential equation* which contains only one independent variable, *e.g.* $\frac{d^2x}{dt^2} = -\mu x$, where $x$ is the dependent and $t$ the independent variable. This D. E. is true of all types of simple harmonic motion of a particle in a straight line, $x$ is the distance of the particle from the centre about which it oscillates and $t$ is the time. The solution of this equation is $x = A \cos(\sqrt{\mu}t + a)$, where A and $a$ are constants determined by the particular conditions of the S.H.M. under consideration. Another famous ordinary differential equation is

$$LC\frac{d^2e}{dt^2} + RC\frac{de}{dt} + e = 0,$$

that is true for all cases of the discharge of a condenser of capacity C, through a circuit of resistance R, and self-inductance L. The solution of this equation determines the charge $e$ on the plates of the condenser in terms of the time $t$. This solution and its subsequent experimental verification forms the basis of modern wireless. (ii) *Partial differential equations* which contain two or more independent variables, *e.g.*

$$\frac{\partial^2 u}{\partial x^2} + \frac{\partial^2 u}{\partial y^2} + \frac{\partial^2 u}{\partial z^2} = 0,$$

where $u$ is the dependent, and $x$, $y$, $z$, the independent variables. This equation is extremely inportant in the theory of electricity and in the theory of gravitational attractions. The reader is referred to *A Treatise on Differential Equations* by A. R. Forsyth (Macmillan) for further information on the subject.

**Differential Forms.** A branch of mathematics that deals with the theory of transformations of co-ordinates; a knowledge of differential calculus and the theory of functions is required before dealing with the subject. D. F.s find important application in geometry, dynamics and physics, and in particular in Riemannian geometry and in Einstein's General Theory of Relativity.

**Differential Geometry.** The geometry of the more familiar curves such as the straight line, the circle, the plane, ellipse, etc., together with surfaces such as the sphere and the ellipsoid can be dealt with by the analytical methods of algebraical geometry. In general, however, the geometrical properties of curves and surfaces vary continuously from point to point and when we wish to investigate such properties it is necessary to employ the analytical methods of the differential calculus (*q.v.*) that is capable of dealing with infinitesimal and continuous variations. D. G. is the branch of geometry that deals with such problems, just as algebraical geometry deals with geometrical problems that may be solved by algebraic analysis.

**Differential Psychology,** the comparative study of psychological characters and the way in which they differ from individual to individual, from people to people, or from class to class, etc. The results of such study are not merely interesting from the theoretical point of view, but may have important sociological consequences; they are of especial value to teachers, employers of labour and government departments. Investigation is carried out partly by definite ' mental tests ' and partly by general observation of present and past racial development and history. There is, for instance, a steady increase in mental ability from childhood to early adult life, though striking peculiarities in intellectual reaction may occur at puberty. Noticeable psychological differences between girls and boys, and men and women, have been observed, while the influence of heredity and environment has been closely studied with the object of discovering their relative importance. Of the two, heredity would seem to be more potent than mere environment. As far as racial differences are concerned, Oriental peoples are credited with less general intelligence, particularly on the comprehensive or synthetic side, than Caucasians or whites, though the Oriental has a genius for detail and usually a good memory. Even between various white races, psychological differences have been detected, though how much is due in this case to differences of conditions, language and climate or conditions of life, is difficult to say.

**Differentiation** in biology, describes the gradual increase in complexity of an organism. In a simple unicellular organism, all the life functions are carried out by a single cell. In such a multicellular plant as the filamentous green Alga *spirogyra* all the cells are exactly similar, and each can, at necessity, lead an independent existence. As the evolutionary scale is ascended, however, we find first that special cells are set apart for special functions, and later that this differentiation results in the appearance of specialised multicellular organs and tissues. Roughly, it is true to say that those organisms that show the greatest degree of differentiation are the most highly evolved. The reverse process to differentiation is known as *dedifferentiation*, a good example of which is seen in cancer tissue.

**Diffraction**, in light, a modification which light undergoes in passing the edge of a body by which the rays appear to be bent and to invade the shadow. One of the strongest arguments used by Newton in his defence of the corpuscular theory of light transmission as opposed to the wave theory was that the latter did not explain shadows. If light from a small source is obstructed by an opaque body, it was said, a shadow with sharp outlines is produced, thus showing that light travels in straight lines. On the other hand, sound, which it was admitted travelled by waves, is only slightly affected by obstacles, as the impetus originated by the vibration makes its way round the edges of the obstacles. The argument fails because a small source of light does not produce a shadow with a well defined edge, and, on the other hand, sound may be cut off by an obstacle, if the obstacle be large enough. The difference is accounted for by the fact that sound waves are often several feet in length, and are therefore not affected by small obstacles, while the mean length of light waves is $\frac{1}{50000}$ of an inch. Suppose monochromatic light to proceed from a narrow slit towards a screen, and that an obstacle with a sharp edge be placed so that a portion of the light proceeding from the slit is cut off, it is found that, instead of there being a definite boundary line between illumination and darkness, a series of dark lines appears parallel to the edge of the geometrical shadow, becoming narrower and closer and more indistinct as they recede from the edge. At first these lines were explained by the interference of waves coming from the source with those reflected from the edge of the obstacle, but it was shown that the sharpness of the edge is immaterial. It was Fresnel who first proposed the theory of D., which states that each element of any wave-front proceeding from a given source acts as a source of vibration itself, and sends out secondary waves. When the wave front reaches an obstacle, some of these secondary sources are destroyed and the resulting effects on the screen are due to the interference of the waves from the remaining sources. Some of the waves reinforce each other, and some being in a different phase on account of the slight differences in distance of the screen from the point on the spherical wave-front, tend to counteract each other. The resultant effect is a series of bands merging into each other, alternately bright and dark. When the source is red light the bands are wide; when the source is violet the bands are narrow, owing to the shorter wave-length. When white light is used the bands are superposed, and a series of prismatic colours is produced. If light from a small source be allowed to pass through a narrow slit in an opaque screen, and then observed through a telescope behind the screen, a bright band of light will be seen, and on each side a series of alternately bright and dark bands gradually becoming less distinct as they recede from the middle band. If red light be used, the bands of illumination and of darkness will be broad; they will be narrower if green is used and so on. If white light is used, the colours are not exactly superposed, but a series of spectra will be seen, the violet being nearer the central band. If a grating composed of a parallel series of fine wires close together be used, the spectra will be seen with increased brilliance, and the closer such a grating can be made, the more brilliant will be the effect. D. effects by reflected light can be seen by cutting a series of fine grooves on a plane surface. The beautiful colours of mother of pearl are due to the striated nature of the surface and not to any absorptive powers inherent in the substance. Thus if a moulding of such a surface be taken in sealing-wax, the same colour effects are produced. D. spectra are preferable in many cases to prismatic spectra, as the nature of the material used is of no consequence, so that the bands of the spectrum take up their true position.

**Diffusion**, *see* CHEMISTRY and SOLUTIONS.

**Digamma** (Gk. δι and γάμμα) was the name given to the letter vau, which was sixth in the series of the ancient Gk. alphabet, found only in inscriptions. The name was given on account of the likeness which its form (*F*) was said to be to a double gamma. Its sound corresponded roughly to the sound of our letter ' W.' It had disappeared from Gk. by the time of the Homeric poems, but although not written its influence can be traced in them, as, judging from the metre, some of the words seem to have had a sound which was afterwards lost—thus ἔργον was Fέργον. This letter was introduced into the Latin language, where it lost its original sound and became *f*, F.

**Digby,** a co. and tn. of Nova Scotia, Canada, bordering on the Atlantic. The surface is varied with mountains, rivers, and lakes. Coal, copper, and silver are found. The cap., Digby, is a port, situated on Digby Neck, 45 m. S.E. of St. John, and is noted for its herring fishery. Pop. of co., 19,612, and of tn., 1230.

**Digby, Sir Everard** (1578–1606), was brought up a Protestant, and held office in Queen Elizabeth's household, but becoming a Catholic he embraced the cause of James I., by whom he was knighted. He was at the head of a party,whose design was to await news of the success of the ' Gunpowder Plot,' and then immediately to take arms. He was executed in St. Paul's Churchyard.

**Digby, Sir Henry** (1769–1843), a capable and distinguished English admiral. He captured (1799) a Spanish frigate, a French corvette, a privateer, and several other vessels, and at the battle of Trafalgar was in command of the *Africa*.

SIR KENELM DIGBY

**Digby, Sir Kenelm** (1603–55), a naval commander and writer. In 1627 he set out for Gibraltar on a privateering expedition, capturing several ships and gaining a victory over the French at Scanderoon. He spent the next few years in furthering Roman Catholic interests in England, and after being summoned before Parliament on account of his proposals to Charles I., was imprisoned and released on condition that he went to France. During his stay abroad

he carried on negotiations with the Pope, and after coming back to England in 1649 was compelled to go abroad again at once. On his next return in 1655 he was in close communication with Cromwell. Among the many books which he wrote are *Observations on the 22nd Stanza in the 9th Canto of the 2nd Book of Spenser's Faerie Queene*, 1643, and *Private Memoirs of Sir Kenelm Digby written by himself*, published 1827.

**Digby, William** (1849–1904), an English journalist and E. India agent and merchant. He advocated an extension of self-government among the natives of India and founded the Indian Political Agency for distributing information in England about the Indians. His works include *India for the Indian and for England ; Forty Years of Citizen Life in Ceylon*.

**Digest,** see CORPUS JURIS CIVILIS and JUSTINIANUS.

**Digestion,** the process by which food is assimilated and its nutrient constituents absorbed into the body-tissues. D. takes place in the alimentary canal, which starts at the mouth, continues as the pharynx, œsophagus, stomach, intestines, and rectum, and ends at the anus. In the mouth occur mastication and salivation. The purpose of mastication is to crush and grind the food into small particles. The saliva is poured into the mouth from three pairs of glands named parotid, submaxillary, and sublingual. The parotid gland secretes a clear saliva, the other two a sticky saliva containing mucin. The saliva effects the solution of such substances as salt and sugar and moistens the food so that it can be rolled by the tongue and palate into a soft bolus. Saliva also has an important chemical action, for by means of an enzyme called *ptyalin*, cooked starch in the food is converted into maltose, a kind of sugar. When the food is sufficiently masticated, it is pushed backwards by the tongue and urged rapidly into the gullet or œsophagus and thence into the stomach by a series of muscular movements. The stomach is entered by the cardiac orifice which relaxes to admit the food and then closes. The mucous membrane of the stomach is lined with columnar epithelium, in which are embedded little pits called the gastric glands. From these glands gastric juice pours when they are stimulated by the approach of food. The muscular coat of the stomach produces movements which tend to urge the food towards the intestine. The pylorus, or orifice leading from the stomach, only opens in response to an acid stimulus, and as the food received from the gullet is alkaline owing to the presence of salivary secretions, it remains in the stomach until thorough admixture with the gastric juice has rendered it acid. Gastric juice contains hydrochloric acid and an enzyme called *pepsin*, by which the proteins in the food are converted into peptones. The stomach proceeds to discharge its contents into the intestine about half-an-hour after the commencement of a meal, though it takes about three hours to empty itself. The

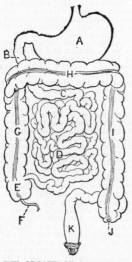

THE ORGANS OF DIGESTION

A, stomach; B, duodenum; C, jejunum; D, ileum; E, caecum; F, vermiform appendix; G, ascending colon; H, transverse colon; I, descending colon; J, sigmoid flexure; K, rectum.

intestine secretes a juice called *succus entericus* or intestinal juice; and two other secretions, pancreatic juice and bile, enter by their ducts, which open into the duodenum, or first part of the small intestine. Pancreatic juice contains three enzymes: *Trypsin*, which attacks proteins more powerfully than gastric juice, converting them into amino-acids; *Amylopsin*, which converts starch into maltose, thus taking over the function of salivary juice whose activity is stopped in the stomach; and *Lipase*, which splits the fats into glycerin and fatty acid. Bile by itself has no

digestive action, but it aids the action of lipase. The intestinal juice contains the following enzymes: *Enterokinase*, which is concerned in the production of trypsin; *Erepsin*, which aids trypsin in the breaking up of peptones; and enzymes which convert maltose and other sugars into glucose. Covering the surface of the mucous membrane of the small intestine are a large number of small prominences called villi. These increase the surface for absorption by which the products of D. of protein and carbohydrate diffuse into small blood-vessels lying immediately under the epithelium. The glycerin and fatty acid are carried into the central lacteal or lymphatic vessel, and are again united into small globules of fat. The amino-acids from the proteins are carried in the blood-stream to repair and build up the tissues; any excess is converted by the liver into urea, which is sent to the kidneys to be disposed of. The tiny globules of fat pass into the thoracic duct, whence they find their way into the blood-stream and ultimately into the tissues, where they produce heat by oxidation or are stored up in the form of adipose tissue. The sugar is temporarily stored in the liver as glycogen and given out as glucose when required. The small intestine is 22½ ft. long and the passage of the food occupies about four hours. It then travels more slowly through the 4 ft. of large intestine, taking from twelve to eighteen hours to reach the rectum. During this time water is absorbed and the waste residue is gradually compressed into a compact mass into the rectum and finally is expelled by the anus.

**Digges, Leonard** (*d.* 1571), an English mathematician, *b.* at Barham, Kent, and educated at University College, Oxford. He was the author of *A Book named Tectonicon, briefly showing the exact measuring and speedie reckoning all manner of Land, Squares, Timber, Stone, etc., 1556; A Geometricall Practise named Pantometria, 1571; An Arithmeticall Militaire Treatise named Stratioticos, 1579; and A Prognostication Everlasting, contayning Rules to judge the Weather, 1553-76*.

**Digges, Thomas** (*d.* 1595), a mathematician, was the son of Leonard D. In 1582 he began the repair of Dover Harbour, and two or three years later he was one of a party of explorers in the Antarctic with the special object of searching for the lands of the 'Cave of Cathaia.'

**Digit** (Lat. *digitus*, a finger), a word used to signify any symbol or number, from 0 to 9. Thus 4629 is a number of four Ds. Originally, the term was only applied to the actual numbers 1, 2 . . . 9, but by practice has come to signify the characters of the numbers.

**Digitalin,** a poisonous alkaloid, is obtained from *Digitalis purpurea,* the foxglove and kindred plants.

**Digitalis,** a genus of European and Asiatic Scrophulariaceæ, is known in Britain chiefly by *D. purpurea,* the stately purple foxglove of our woods. The leaves contain an active principle of a poisonous nature which has a strong effect on the action of the heart and is therefore valued in medicine. *D. grandiflora* is a cultivated species with yellow flowers; *D. lutea* grows in the woods of France and Germany, and *D. ferruginea,* with roundish rust-coloured flowers, in Asia and S.E. Europe.

**Digne,** a Fr. tn. and the cap. of the dept. Basses-Alpes. The tn. is situated on the R. Bléonne, and contains a cathedral and public library. It has hot springs. Pop. 6470.

**Dignities,** *see* TITLES.

**Digoin,** a tn. of France in the dept. of Saône-et-Loire, situated at the junction of the Loire with the Canal du Centre. There are manufactures of earthenware. Pop. 3400.

**Dijon,** a Fr. city, the cap. of the dept. Côte-d'Or, and originally the cap. of Burgundy. It is situated on the canal of Burgundy, where the Ouche and the Suzon join, and is a railway centre on the Paris–Lyons

ARMS OF DIJON

Railway. It is the seat of a bishop, a university tn., and possesses a library, natural history museum, an academy of art, botanical gardens, and a *lycée.* The commerce of D. is considerable, most of it consisting of the trading in Burgundy wines. Its manufactures are very varied, among them being wines, biscuits, preserves, mustard, oils, motor-cars, copper wares, hardware. D. is next to Paris

and Rouen in riches of works of art and especially in ancient and mediæval churches, some of which are St. Philibert, St. Bénigne, Notre Dame, St. Jean, St. Etienne (now the chamber of commerce). Notre Dame possesses the famous clock of Jaquemart, brought by Philip the Hardy from Courtrai in 1382. There are many richly adorned old houses; the splendid Palais de Justice and the Palace of the Dukes of Burgundy, in which is the Town Hall and the richest museum in Fr. outside Paris, the famous library is in the former Jesuit College. It was the magnificence and wealth of the Dukes of Burgundy that made the fortune of D., of which it was the capital from the twelfth century to 1477. St. Bernard, Bossuet, Charles the Bold and many other famous men were born here. Pop. 78,850.

**Dikoa,** or **Digoa,** North Cameroons, under the British mandate. An old tn. in a fertile plain. Pop. 15,000.

**Dilapidations, Ecclesiastical,** in English law, comes under the heading of waste. In Eng. the incumbent of a benefice is compelled to keep his residence and its outhouses in a proper state of repair, *i.e.* free from dilapidations. If he be rector or vicar he is further obliged to take charge of the fabric of the chancel, though he is not compelled to supply the ornaments or painting thereof. The holder of a benefice who fails to fulfil these obligations is liable for an action for dilapidations to be instituted by his successor, the money so recovered being applied to the repairs. On entering a benefice where the parsonage house, etc., are dilapidated, the new incumbent must carry out all repairs under the instruction of the bishop, issued on receipt of a complaint from the archdeacon, rural dean, or patron of the benefice. Each diocese has a surveyor of dilapidations, who reports on the condition of church property. In Scotland the heritors are under the obligation to repair manses, except in the case of 'free manses.'

**Dilemma,** a kind of argument which offers a choice between two alternatives, both equally disagreeable because both lead to the same conclusion. The two alternatives are called the 'horns' of the D., for if the adversary escapes the one he will be caught on the other. A classical example of D. is Aristotle's Athenian mother's advice to her son : ' Do not enter into public affairs; for if you say what is just, men will hate you ; and if you say what is unjust, the gods will hate you.' Dilemmatic arguments are very fallacious on account of defective foundation, the two alternatives seldom exhausting all the cases.

**Dilettanti, Society of,** a club founded about 1733 by a number of gentlemen for the purpose of social intercourse and for the study, as amateurs, of antique art. Funds having accumulated, the society sent out in 1834 an exploring party (under Chandler, Revett, and Pars), and later a second expedition, to collect details and make drawings of the most important monuments of antiquity. These expeditions brought back material for several volumes published by the society : *Ionian Antiquities; Specimens of Ancient Sculpture; Unedited Antiquities of Attica* ; and *Portfolio of Greek Architecture,* etc.

**Diligence,** the name given to a public conveyance of the nature of a stage coach. *See* COACH AND COACHING.

**Diligence :** (1) In Scots law : (*a*) A term nearly equivalent to *execution* in the Eng. law. It includes the various means by which the person may be seized and imprisoned or the property attached and disposed of, for the purpose of enforcing payment of a debt or performance of any civil obligation. (*b*) A warrant to enforce the attendance of a witness, or the production of writings. (2) In Eng. law the term Diligence may be used in the law of bailments to indicate the degree of care which a person to whom goods are entrusted must exercise in the custody of the goods to escape liability for loss or damage to them.

**Dilke, Charles Wentworth** (1789–1864), in early life devoted himself to the pursuit of letters. In 1814–16 he issued a continuation of Dodley's *Old Plays,* and became a regular contributor to the reviews. His connection with the *Athenæum* began in 1829, and in the following year he became editor and proprietor. Having made a success with this paper, he was offered the management of the *Daily News,* then in low water, and he directed the fortunes of that paper from 1846 for three years. Towards the end of that period he began to contribute to the *Athenæum* articles on Junius and Pope, which were in 1875 collected by his grandson.

His grandson, *Sir Charles Wentworth Dilke,* second Baronet (1843–1912), travelled much in his youth, and gave the world the benefit of what he had learnt in the colonies in *Greater Britain,* 1867. He entered parliament in the next year as a Radical. An effective speaker, and with much knowledge of the subjects upon which he delivered himself, he soon became a prominent figure in the House of Commons. In 1880 he was appointed Under-Secretary of Foreign Affairs, and he conducted very efficiently the business of his department until 1885, when Gladstone was forced to resign. A private matter, in which there is every reason to believe that he was sinned against rather than sinning, caused his temporary retirement into private life in 1886. He occupied his leisure in the composition of *Problems of Greater Britain* (1890), in some senses a sequel to his *Greater Britain*. Yielding to the entreaties of the friends who stood by him and believed in his innocence, he consented to be nominated as a parliamentary candidate for the Forest of Dean in 1892, and that constituency then and for the rest of his life returned him to Westminster. In the House of Commons he confined himself henceforth almost entirely to questions of foreign and imperial affairs, upon which he was a recognised authority. He never again held office, a loss that was less his than his country's.

**Dilke, Lady,** *née* **Emilia Frances Strong** (1840–1904), a writer on art, daughter of Major Strong of Oxford, wife first of Mark Pattison, then of Sir Charles Wentworth D. On the advice of Ruskin she became a student at the Art School, South Kensington, in 1859. She studied much in France, gathering material for her books, *The Renaissance of Art in France; Claude Lorraine* (written in Fr.) ; *French Painters; French Sculptors,* etc.

**Dill,** an aromatic umbelliferous plant, closely related to the parsnip. The fruit is employed medicinally as a carminative in the form of dill water, or *aqua Anethi,* and is also used as a condiment. The sowa D., or *Peucedanum Sowa* of Bengal, has a fruit which is often used in curries.

**Dillenaceæ,** an order of Dicotyledons, consists chiefly of tropical shrubs and trees, most of which bear yellow flowers and have leathery leaves. The bushes help to form the Australian scrub, the trees are found in woods in tropical India, the woods of Brazil have several kinds, usually of climbing or trailing habit. Typical genera are *Dillenia* and *Hibbertia,* the latter containing *H. volubilis,* a showy twiner with offensive-smelling flowers.

**Dillenius (Dillen), Johann Jakob** (1684–1747), a celebrated Ger. botanist who came to Eng. on the invitation of Sherard, and who finally settled in Oxford, becoming the first Sherardian Professor of Botany. He edited Ray's *Synopsis stirpium Britannicarum,* and wrote *Hortus Elthamensis, Historia Muscorum,* and many botanical papers.

**Dillingen :** (1) A tn. of Bavaria,

on the Danube, 24 m. N.W. of Augsburg. There are several churches
and monasteries and a thirteenth
century castle. Pop. 6100. (2) A tn.
in the Rhine, prov. of Ger. with large
iron works. Pop. 9620.

**Dillmann, Christian Friedrich
Auguste** (1823–94), a famous Ger.
orientalist and theologian, the first
authority on the Ethiopic languages.
He was *b.* in Würtemberg, and
studied under Heinrich Ewald at
Tübingen. During 1846–48 he visited
the libraries of Paris, London, and
Oxford, studying their Ethiopic MSS;
those of London and Oxford he cata-
logued. Chief works : Ger. translation of parts of the Ethiopic Bible,
*Grammatik der Æthopischen Sprache,
Ueber den Ursprung des Alt-testament-
lichen Religion.*

**Dillon, John** (1851–1927), an Irish
politician, M.P. for E. Mayo (1885–
1918); one of the leaders of 'Young
Ireland.' He first entered the House
of Commons in 1881 as member for
Tipperary ; he was then a supporter
of Parnell. In the same year he was
twice arrested for inciting to boy-
cotting. He was one of the pioneers
of the ' Plan of Campaign ' and the
Land League. After six months'
imprisonment in 1888 he went to
Australia and New Zealand collecting
funds for the National Party, then
was again imprisoned in 1891.
He declared against Parnell in 1891
and became leader of the United
Nationalist Party and chairman of
the Irish National Federation from
1896 till 1900—when John Redmond
became leader of the re-united party.
D. accompanied Redmond to Buckingham Palace in July 1914, on the
occasion of the conference on the
govt. of Ireland. When Redmond
died, D. succeeded him as leader.
His party was virtually extinguished
by Sinn Fein in Dec. 1918. He *d.* in
a London nursing home, Aug. 4.

**Diluent,** a medicinal agent which
dilutes the blood and the secretions
of organs. Water is the commonest
substance used for the purpose and
acts by increasing all the secretions,
especially those of the skin and
kidneys, thus aiding in the disposal
of waste products in the system. The
internal use of water in this way
forms part of the practice of *hydro-
pathy (q.v.).*

**Diluvial Formation,** *see* GEOLOGY.

**Dime** (Lat. *decima*, a tenth, through
Old Fr. *disme*), a small silver coin of
the U.S.A.; its value is 10 cents, or
$\frac{1}{10}$ of a dollar.

**Dimension,** in geometry, a direction
or mode in which extension may be
measured. A point, having no magnitude, has no D.; a line has one D.,
length ; a surface has two Ds., length

and breadth ; a solid has three Ds.,
length, breadth and thickness. The
motion of a point generates a line, the
motion of a line generates a plane or
surface, and the motion of a plane
generates a solid figure. Proceeding
to an analogous motion of a three-
dimensional solid, the concept of a
figure of four Ds. has been obtained,
and thus arises a branch of geometry
dealing with non-existent figures.

In algebra, terms formed by the
multiplication of a quantity by itself
are called ' squares,' and terms
generated by the product of three
similar factors are called ' cubes ' by
analogy from the geometrical concepts. Equations containing terms
of one degree or D. are called linear,
those containing terms of two degrees
or Ds. are called quadratic, and those
containing terms of three degrees or
Ds. are called cubic. It is to be
observed, however, that the symbol
$x^2$ does not represent a surface, or $x^3$
a volume, and in graphical representation the functions $x^2$, $x^3$ are
represented by lines ; $x^2$, in fact, represents a number merely, but if a preliminary statement be made that $x$
represents the number of units of
length in a certain straight line, then
obviously $x^2$ represents the number of
units of area in a square, each of
whose sides contains $x$ units of length.

In physics, symbols are used to
represent quantities measured in
terms of units of length, area,
volume, time, mass, velocity, force
etc. For the sake of brevity and
simplicity, such equations as $s = vt$
(space = velocity × time) are used.
The employment of such an expression does not mean, for instance, that
velocity is multiplied by time, if that
has any meaning at all, but that the
numerical measure of the space
traversed is obtainable by multiplying the numerical measure of the
velocity in terms of the unit of
velocity by the numerical measure of
the time taken in terms of the unit of
time. Of the units used in mechanics,
those of length, time, and mass are
fundamental, that is, we cannot
explain them by reference to anything else. The units of area, volume,
velocity, acceleration, force, etc., are
derived units ; that is, they can be
explained by reference to one or more
fundamental units. The quantities
used as fundamental units are chosen
arbitrarily. If we are speaking of
an interval of 2 hours, and use 1
hour as the unit of time, the interval
would be represented by the number
2 ; if 1 minute were the time-unit,
the interval would be represented by
the number 120, and so on. Suppose
[X], [Y], [Z] be three units in which
any physical quantity can be mea-

sured, and let $x$, $y$, $z$ be the numbers of those units which represent a certain amount of the quantity, then $x[X] = y[Y] = z[Z]$, whence $x : y : z = 1/[X] : 1/[Y] : 1/[Z]$ : that is to say, the number expressing the amount of any quantity is inversely proportional to the unit chosen for its measurement. Many writers use the centimetre as length-unit, the gramme as mass-unit, and the second as time-unit, but the foot as length-unit and pound as mass-unit are still often employed. If $m$ represents the number of grammes and $m$ the number of pounds in a given piece of matter, then $m[M] = m$ [M ], or $m = [M']m'/[M]$. The ratio $[M']/[M]$ is the number of grammes in a pound, or 453·59, and this ratio may be employed in transferring the measure of any mass from one system of units to the other.

The measure of density is indicated by the equation $d = m/v$, where $m$ represents the number of units of mass and $v$ represents the number of units of volume. If [L] be the unit of length, and a rectangular parallelepiped be supposed whose length is $l$[L], breadth $l'$[L], and height $l''$[L], its volume will be $ll'l''$[L]³. Now, if [V] be the unit of volume, and if there be $v$ units of volume in the parallelepiped, then $[V]v = ll'l''$[L]³. But $l$, $l'$, $l''$ and $v$ are mere numbers, therefore $v = ll'l''$, and $[V] = [L²]$. Now, returning to the equation for density, we get $[D]d = [M]m/[V]v$, or $[D]d = [M]m/[L]³l³$, whence $[D] = [M]/[L]³$. The ratio $[M]/[L]³$ is the Ds. of the unit of density in terms of the fundamental units of mass and length. Again, for velocity we have the equation $s = vt$. This means $s[L] = v[V]t[T]$, ∴ $v[V] = s[L]/t[T]$, where $v$, $s$, and $t$ are mere numbers and [V] is the unit of velocity. Therefore $[V] = [L]/[T] = [L][T]¹$. That is to say, the unit of velocity has D. 1 in length and D. –1 in time. Similarly from the equation $s = \frac{1}{2}ft²$ we obtain $s[L] = \frac{1}{2}f[F]t²[T]²$, where [F] is the unit of acceleration and $s$, $f$, $t²$ and $\frac{1}{2}$ are mere numbers. Therefore $[F] = [L]/[T]²$ or $[L][T]^{-2}$. The unit of acceleration has therefore D. 1 in length and D.–2 in time. The Ds. of other physical units may be similarly explained.

**Dimidiation** ( Lat. *dimidio*, to halve), the cutting of two coats of arms in half and joining the dexter half of the one to the sinister half of the other.

**Diminishing Return.** The law of diminishing return is one of the elementary laws of the science of political economy (*q.v.*). John Stuart Mill stated, perhaps exaggeratedly, of this law that it is the most important and in its different phases perhaps

the most commonly misapplied law in political economy. In respect of a piece of land (say an acre) the law states that after a certain point, other things remaining the same, the returns to successive applications of labour and capital will continuously diminish. The law applies of course to all other productive agents. Its peculiar value in the case of land arises from the fact that the quantity of land is limited and the better qualities still more limited; so that while capital and labour may go on increasing, land cannot so increase and any increase of the produce must be at an increasing cost, or in other words the return per unit diminishes. The law of diminishing return is of great value in its wider applications to the economic study of rent, population, value, incidence of taxation, etc. (*See* Nicholson's *Elements of Political Economy*.)

**Dimissory Letters** (Lat. *dimitto*, to dismiss), a letter in which a bishop consents to the ordination by another bishop of a candidate for holy orders of his diocese.

**Dimorphism** (Gk. δίς, twice, and μορφή, shape or form) : 1. A term applied in zoology and botany to the appearance of an organism in two different forms. The dimorphic organisms are fundamentally identical in structure and in origin. Thus, the bee is dimorphic in the female sex, the fertile queen and the barren worker presenting the two forms. The same phenomenon is seen in the ' nutritive ' and ' reproductive ' forms in colonies of hydroids. The two sexes present such widely different forms in some of the insects and crustaceans that they seem to belong to quite different genera—this is sexual D. Butterflies are subject to ' seasonal ' D. Among flowers, the varieties of the primrose offer good examples of dimorphic forms. 2. In the mineral kingdom a body is said to be dimorphous when it is capable of crystallising according to two different systems geometrically incompatible, the chemical composition of the dimorphic bodies being identical. Carbon, sulphur, phosphorus, carbonate of lime, and iodide of mercury are well-known examples. Carbon appears under one form as the diamond, and under another as graphite, with the following widely contrasting sets of properties : the *diamond* is colourless, transparent, has an adamantine lustre, is the hardest of all substances, a non-conductor of electricity, has a specific gravity of 3·52, and crystallises as octahedra ; *graphite* is grey, opaque, has a metallic lustre, is exceedingly soft, a good conductor of electricity, has a specific gravity of 2, and forms hexagonal crystals belonging to the rhomboidal system. Yet both have the same chemical composition, and both yield carbon dioxide when burned in oxygen; the diamond becomes graphite if heated in the electric arc. Red iodide of mercury when volatilised condenses into rhombic plates, which the slightest friction changes into octahedral crystals, the colour changing at the same time from yellow to a brilliant scarlet. Sulphur yields transparent amber-coloured octahedra under one treatment, prismatic crystals under another. The terms *trimorphism* and *polymorphism* indicate this phenomenon when the same organism or substance presents three or more different forms.

**Dimsdale, Thomas** (1712–1800), a Hertford physician, whose work as an inoculator brought him world-wide fame; his *Thoughts on General and Partial Inoculation* was translated into many languages. The Empress Catherine of Russia bestowed upon him a barony and a considerable pecuniary reward for the successful inoculation of herself and her son.

**Dinajpur,** a dist. and tn. of Bengal, British India. The area of the district, which is flat and fertile, is 4126 sq. m. with a pop. of 1,700,000. Rice and jute are the chief crops. The town of D. is 220 m. N. of Calcutta. Pop. 14,000.

**Dinan,** a French tn. of the dept. Côtes-du-Nord. It stands on the Rance, about 14 m. S. of St. Malo, being built on the summit of a hill, and at the spot where a high viaduct crosses the river. The town itself is picturesque, as some of its old walls and gates still remain. Its castle, which dates from the fourteenth century, is also well preserved. A great many of the old streets still exist, being characterised by their winding and narrow thoroughfares and their wooden houses. The churches of St. Malo and St. Sauveur are both of interest, the latter possessing an epitaph to the effect that it contains the heart of Bertrand du Guesclin. D. exports cattle, coal and wood. Pop. 10,160.

**Dinant,** a picturesquely situated tn. in the prov. of Namur, Belgium, on the Meuse, with 7100 inhabs. and tanneries. Manufs. of metal ware, called Dinanderies, spiced bread called ' couques de Dinant,' woollen goods, marble quarries, etc. It was sacked and destroyed by Charles the Bold in 1466, taken by the Fr. in 1554, and burnt and terrorised by the Gers. in 1914. On Aug. 15 of that year the Ger. advanced guards seized the citadel of D. and crossed to the left bank of the Meuse. Two hours later a Fr. brigade retook the town and drove the Gers. back across the river.

**Dinapur, Dinapore,** or **Danapur,** a tn. of Bengal, India, situated on the Ganges, 5 m. from Patna, to which it is joined. It is in two parts, Dinapur, and Dinapur Nizamat. Total pop. 30,877.

**Dinarchus** (Gk. Δείναρχος) (c. 361–291 B.C.), was the last of the ten Greek orators, and was b. at Corinth. He studied oratory at Athens under Theophrastus and Demetrius Phalereus. His fame as an orator began about 336 B.C., owing to the fact that the other Greek orators had died. The height of his power, however, was during the administration of Demetrius Phalereus (317–307 B.C.).

**Dinard,** a tn. and watering place on the N. coast of France, situated in the dept. of Ille-et-Vilaine. Pop. 8840.

**Dinaric Alps,** that part of the Alpine system which joins the Julian Alps with the Balkan range. The main chain lies N.W. to S.E., and divides Dalmatia from Bosnia and Herzegovina. It also separates the basin of the Save from the district drained by the Narenta, Kerka, and other rivers flowing into the Adriatic. The highest summits are under 7000 ft.

**Dindigul,** or **Dindigal,** a tn. of British India, situated in the presidency of Madras. It is about 30 m. from Madura, and has a citadel on an isolated rock, from the top of which Hyder Ali threw his prisoners. There are several tanneries, a large cotton ginning factory, and tobacco factory. Pop. 30,922.

**Dindings, The,** a group of islands situated off the W. coast of the Malay Peninsula, in lat. 4° 20′ N. and long. 100° 32′ E. They are about 70 m. in a S.S.E. direction from Penang. Poolo Dinding is covered with thick woods, and is noted for its great beauty.

**Dindorf, Karl Wilhelm** (1802–83), a distinguished German Hellenist and philologist, b. at Leipzig. He resigned a professorship at Leipzig University in order to give all his time to literary work, especially to the preparation (with his brother Ludwig and Hase), of a new edition of Stephanus's *Thesaurus Linguæ Græcæ,* the republishing of which (Paris, 1831–65), awakened tremendous interest. His philological researches into the text of the Greek classics, especially that of the dramatists, have contributed greatly to its accuracy and clearness. He edited a number of these classics, including an edition of Demosthenes (7 vols.), *Poetæ Scenici Græci*, and editions of Aristophanes, Sophocles, Euripides, Æschylus, and Homer.

**D'Indy, Paul,** *see* INDY.

**Dingaan,** *see* ZULUS.

**Dingaan's Day,** Dec. 16, the anniversary of the decisive defeat of Dingaan, a Zulu chief, by a small force of Boers under Pretorius in 1838. The cause of the conflict thus brought to a close was the massacring by the Zulus of a party of Boer settlers. The particular event in which this yearly celebration and public holiday originated is falling into oblivion, but on this day the anniversary of the proclamation of Boer independence in 1880 is celebrated, and it is looked upon as a day of thanksgiving for the spread of white civilisation in S. Africa.

**Dingelstedt, Franz Ferdinand, Freiherr von** (1814–81), a German poet, dramatist, and novelist. His *Lieder eines Kosmopolitischen Nachtwächters* caused a disagreeable sensation on account of the liberal principles expressed in them. He wrote a successful tragedy, *Das Haus der Barneveldt*, a society novel, *Die Amazone*, sketches of travel, and adapted Shakespeare and Molière to the German stage.

**Dingey,** or **Dinghy** (Mahratta *dingé*, the name of a small boat used in Calcutta, etc.), a small row-boat usually supplied to a ship as an extra boat for common uses.

**Dingle,** a par. and seaport of Ireland in co. Kerry. The tn. is situated on the N. side of D. Bay, 30 m. S.W. of Tralee. It is the most westerly town in the British Isles, and is sheltered by hills on three sides. The harbour is practically useless, but the fisheries are important, and the curing of mackerel employs many of the inhabitants. D. is said to have been founded by the Spaniards, who frequented the shores on account of its fisheries. Pop. 1884.

**Dingley Tariff.** The D. T. Act (named after the Chairman of Ways and Means Committee) was passed in 1897 in McKinley's first term. It embodied the Republican doctrine of high protection coupled with reciprocity. There were provisions for reciprocity arrangements with other countries which paved the way for possible reductions by a commercial treaty. The D. T. is now replaced by the Tariff Act, 1930.

**Dingo** (*Canis dingo*), the warrigal, or wild Australian dog. It is a strong, short-legged dog, sandy-coloured, and not unlike the European fox, being about 40 in. in length, its tail measuring an additional 11 in. It works havoc upon flocks and poultry, and

even after it has been tamed, seldom abandons its predatory habits. Its fossilised remains have been discovered with those of kangaroos and extinct Australian mammals. This has given rise to the opinion, held by Sir Frederick McCoy, Mr. Ogilvy, and others, that the D. must be an indigenous species of Australian fauna. But the existence in Java and India of a pariah dog, very similar in character to the D., has caused others to think that the D. was originally introduced into Australia by Caucasians from Ceylon or Malay.

**Dingwall,** a parl. bor. and tn. of Scotland, and cap. of the counties Ross-shire and Cromarty. It is situated on Cromarty Firth, 18 m. N.W. of Inverness. A small shipping trade is carried on, and there is a good harbour. The fisheries are important, and there is a corn market. Pop. 2651.

**Dinka,** *see* DENKA.

**Dinkar Rao, Sir** (1819–96), an Indian statesman, who was Prime Minister of the state of Gwalior, 1851–59. He held this office with great distinction, being indefatigable in his efforts to improve the condition of the people; he developed means of communication, reconstructed the revenue system, etc.

**Dinkelsbühl,** a tn. of Bavaria. It is situated on the R. Wörnitz, 40 m. N.W. of Donauwörth by rail. It is a mediæval tn. with completely preserved walls and towers of the fifteenth century, town-moat and gable houses, old town hall of 1300. St. George's church is one of the finest late Gothic in S. Germany. Pop. 5170.

**Dinoceras,** an extinct genus of amblypodous mammals, consists of huge, semiplantigrade animals, of which the fossil remains occur in N. America. In spite of the fact that the species rivalled the elephant in size, they possessed the smallest brain of any mammal. The limbs were heavy, and had well-developed bones; five short digits occurred on each foot. On the head there were three pairs of bony processes.

**Dinornis,** *see* MOA.

**Dinosaurs** are an order of fossil reptiles which are confined to the Mesozoic age. The crocodiles of the present age and the birds of the division Ratitæ are the nearest to them in general characteristics. The characteristics of these animals were somewhat varied. Some had very small fore-limbs, the hind-limbs being much longer, while some of them seem to have pursued the same method of locomotion as the kangaroo. Others again were provided with a long tail. The pelvis resembled that of birds in its structure, and the number of toes on the hind feet varied from five to three. The animals of this order were mostly land animals, and included both carnivorous and herbivorous species. Their size varied very much, some of them attaining enormous proportions—their length reaching 70 ft. or 80 ft. and their height 10 ft. or more, while others were quite small. D. lived during the Triassic, Jurassic, and Cretaceous periods, their remains being found in those

limbs and hollow bones and a bipedal means of locomotion. *See* Henry Neville Hutchinson, *Creatures of Other Days*, 1894; Othniel Charles Marsh, *Dinosaurs of North America*, 1896; and F. A. Lucas, *Animals of the Past*, 1901.

**Dinotherium,** an extinct genus of Proboscidea to which the living elephants belong, but differs from these animals in many features. The incisors were prolonged into long tusks on the lower jaw, but curved downward; the skull was more primitive, and the bulk much more vast. Examples of the D. have been found in the Miocene of Europe and Asia.

**Dinslaken,** a tn. of Rhenish Prussia, 25 m. N. of Dusseldorf, with coal mines and iron works. Pop. 25,080.

**Dinwiddie, Robert** (1690–1770), a lieutenant-governor of Virginia. He

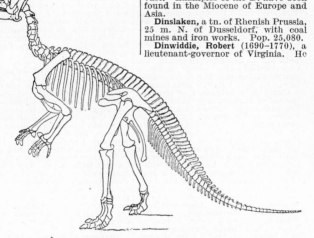

EUROPEAN CRETACEOUS BEAKED DINOSAUR

strata in Europe, Asia, Africa, America, and Australia. Dinosauria is subdivided into Sauropoda, Theropoda, and Predentata. Sauropoda : the species in this division are herbivorous and include some of the largest animals that have never existed, and some of the oldest of the D. Brontosaurus, Atlantosaurus, and Diplodocus are included in Sauropoda. Theropoda : the species in this subdivision have serrated teeth, hollow bones, and vertebral fore-limbs shorter than the hind-limbs, showing a tendency to an upright walking gait, most of them having moved like kangaroos. Predentata : these animals were herbivorous, either quadrupeds or bipeds, with a predentary bone on the end of the mandible. Under this subdivision are included Ornithopoda, having three-toed hind-

entered into conflict with the French, and against whom he sent Major George Washington. He was recalled on serious charges.

**Diocesan Court,** one of the ecclesiastical courts, a consistory. In every diocese of the Christian Church there is a D. C. presided over by the commissary or chancellor who acts as vicar-general for the bishop. Ecclesiastical cases arising within the diocese are here tried. Formerly their jurisdiction was much wider, but at the present day matrimonial, testamentary and even ecclesiastical cases, etc., being tried in other tribunals, the court is mostly concerned with points of order.

**Diocese** (Gk. διοίκησις, housekeeping, management, province), a district under the ecclesiastical jurisdiction and care of a bishop. In

D 2

Demosthenes the word is used for the treasury or finance department, in Cicero it is applied to the three districts of Cibyra, Apamea, and Synnada (added to Cilicia, 56–50 B.C.); D., from its original meaning 'administration,' coming to mean the part so administered. The term was primarily used in the civil administration of the Roman empire, Constantine the Great dividing it into thirteen Ds., which were subdivided into 120 provinces. These Ds. (of which Oriens was the largest, Britain the smallest) were governed by prætorian prefects, proconsuls, or vicars, the provinces by rectors or exarchs. The word in its present ecclesiastical signification was not in common use till about the ninth century, παροικία (parish) being the more usual term up to that time. Constantine (A.D. 306–337) made the ecclesiastical and political divisions correspond, the ecclesiastical Ds. being under a patriarch, the political under a prætorian prefect. Later D. came to mean a single metropolitanate or province instead of a group, and finally merely the sphere of jurisdiction of any bishop. In England an Act of Parliament is necessary to create fresh Ds. In 1836 the Ecclesiastical Commissioners Act created the Ds. of Ripon and Manchester. England and Wales have two ecclesiastical provinces, Canterbury and York, subdivided into thirty-three Ds. In the Catholic Church Ds. are erected by the Pope in consistory. See Cicero, *Epist. ad Fam.*, iii. 8, and xiii. 67; Arnold, *Roman Provincial Administration*; Hinschius, *Kirchenrecht*, ii. 38; Schiller, *Geschichte der Römischen Kaiserzeit*, ii. 1887; *New Engl. Dict.* iii. (Murray), 1897; Du Cange, *Glossarium*; Bingham, *Origines Ecclesiasticæ*, 1840.

**Diocletianus, Caius Valerius** (A.D. 245–313), Roman emperor, *b.* in Dalmatia, the son of obscure parents; entered the army and served with much success under Aurelian and Probus, later accompanying Carus on his Persian expedition, and at his death in 283 becoming commander of the Imperial Guards of Numerianus, son of Carus, who succeeded his father together with his brother Carinus. In the same year Numerianus was assassinated by Aper, and Diocletian was proclaimed emperor by the army of the East at Chalcedon, where he was then serving. Carinus had already been proclaimed in Italy, and a battle took place at Morgus in Mœsia in which Carinus, after nearly gaining the victory, was killed, and Diocletian remaining sole claimant. In 286 he assumed as his colleague in the empire Marcus Aurelius Maximianus, and gave him the title of Augustus. Maximianus took charge of European affairs, and Diocletian of the East. In 292 Galerius and Constantius Chlorus were also adopted as colleagues, and took up the government respectively of Thrace and Illyria (Galeius); and Gaul and Spain (Constantius), Diocletian superintending Asia and Egypt, and Maximianus Italy and Africa. Diocletian retained supreme command, and the arrangement resulted in great prosperity. In 297 a peace was concluded with Persia. In 303 Diocletian, under the influence of Galerius, issued a severe edict against the Christians, the persecution of whom has left a stain on his memory. After a long illness in 304, he abdicated in favour of Galerius in 305, and retired to Salona. He ranks high both as a general and a politician.

**Diodon**, *see* GLOBE FISH.

**Diodorus** (named **Diodorus Siculus**), a Greek historian, *b.* in Agyrium in Sicily, and lived in the time of Cæsar and Augustus. His idea was to write a history of all nations from the very early times to his own day. The work entitled *Bibliotheca Historica* consists of forty books in three sections, the first dealing with times previous to the Trojan War, the second ends with the death of Alexander the Great, and the third with Cæsar's Gallic wars. Only fifteen of these have come down to us. The work, however, is characterised by a want of order and critical power, though it is valuable as a collection of materials the sources of which are lost. On Babylon, for example, D. is as detailed as Herodotus, though less reliable.

**Diodorus of Tarsus**, a biblical commentator, native of Antioch. He was one of a succession of eminent men taught at Antioch by the aged Eusebius of Emisa, himself a pupil of Eusebius of Cæsarea. He became Bishop of Tarsus in A.D. 378. He commentated the books of the O.T. D. had great influence over Chrysostom and Theodore of Mopsuestia. *See* Harnack, *Diodor von Tarsus*, 1901.

**Diogenes** (*c.* 412–323 B.C.), was a Cynic philosopher of Sinope in Pontus. He was the son of Icesias, and on account of the latter's dishonest actions D. had to leave Sinope and take up his residence in Athens. After much persistence, in spite of constant harsh rebuffs, he became the pupil of Antisthenes, and laid down for himself an excessively austere rule of life, subjecting himself to every kind of self-mortification, and legend asserts that he lived in a tub, though the truth of this statement has been very much questioned. While on a voyage to Ægina, D. was seized and sold as a slave in Crete, and after being bought by Xeniades he became the tutor of his children. It was during this time that he is reported to have met Alexander the Great, causing the latter to remark that if he were not Alexander he would like to be Diogenes. The philosopher is said to have *d.* at Corinth on the same day as Alexander. His system of philosophy had a practical basis, and he ridiculed all men whose pursuits were not aimed at some practical end. *See* J. B. Mayor, *Sketch of Ancient Philosophy.*

**Diogenes Laërtius** was a Greek

DIOGENES
(From an old print)

author who lived probably towards the close of the second century A.D., though little is known about his exact date. He wrote the lives of the philosophers in ten books, which has been of great value to later writers on the subject. At the same time he made bad use of his information, as his work is not a methodical compilation nor is it an authority on philosophy, though it has preserved some interesting facts.

**Diogenes of Appolonia,** a Greek philosopher of the fifth century. He was a pupil of Anaximenes, whose doctrine, that air is the source of all being, he revived and propagated. According to this philosophy, all other substances are derived from air—which gives also life and soul to all things—by a process of condensation and rarefaction, in which mind and matter alike share.

**Diognetus, Epistle to,** a Greek

Christian work of the second or early third century of our era. In character it is an 'apologia,' propounding and answering questions as to the God and faith of the Christians. Its unknown author appears to have been familiar with the teaching of St. John and of St. Paul. *See* Lightfoot, *The Apostolic Fathers.*

**Diomede,** or **Diomedes,** son of Tydeus, a famous hero at the siege of Troy. After the death of Adrastus, whom he succeeded as King of Argos, he led eighty ships against Troy. Homer represents him as bold and enterprising, a favourite of Athene, with whose help he wounds Ares and Aphrodite. With Odysseus he undertakes many adventures, including the stealing of the palladium from the acropolis of Troy. He was worshipped as a hero in Greece and in parts of Italy.

**Diomede Islands,** a group of three small is., situated in Behring Strait, about half way between the two continents of America and Asia. The group consists of Ingaliuk and Imaklit Islands and Fairway Rock.

**Diomedea,** *see* ALBATROSS.

**Dionæa Muscipula,** the Venus' flytrap, a genus of Droseraceæ. The leaves form a small rosette on the ground, and are composed of a lower winged part and an upper expanded part fringed with teeth. Inside the upper part are numerous tiny digestive glands, and three long, delicate, hair-like organs. If one of these organs be touched by an insect the sides of the leaf collapse, the teeth interlace, and as the captive decomposes its products are absorbed by the plant.

**Dion Cassius, Cocceianus** (A.D. 155–*c.* 230), *b.* at Nicæa in Bithynia, and received a good classical education. In A.D. 180 he went to Rome, and when Pertinax became emperor, D. was made prætor, A.D. 193, which office he took up in the reign of Severus in A.D. 194. He was also made consul about the year A.D. 220, and again in A.D. 229, and after this he retired to Nicæa, where he spent the rest of his life. D. wrote several histories, among them one of Rome from the earliest times.

**Dion Chrysostomus** ('the golden-mouthed'), a celebrated Greek orator, born at Prusa in Bithynia, near the middle of the first century A.D. He received a good education and travelled considerably when young. After leaving Rome, owing to Domitian's hatred of philosophers, he is said to have visited Mysia, Thrace, and other places disguised as a beggar. He returned to Rome under Trajan, and after visiting Prusa went back to Rome, where he *d.* about A.D. 117. There is a good edition of his orations by Reiske.

**Dion of Syracuse,** a son of Hipparinus, and a native of Syracuse, *b.* at the beginning of the fifth century B.C. His sister married Dionysius the Elder, and he himself married her daughter. This Dionysius showed the greatest confidence in D., but his son, Dionysius the Younger, disliked him and refused to be guided by him, probably because their ways of living were so different, as D. was a man of stern life, whereas Dionysius was exceeding dissolute. He was therefore banished to Athens, but he succeeded in 357 B.C. in defeating Dionysius the Younger and in conquering Syracuse. The Syracusans, however, objected to his strict rule, and as the result of a conspiracy, he was murdered in his own house in 353 B.C.

**Dione,** one of the Titans, mother by Zeus of Aphrodite. Homer represents her on Olympus welcoming and consoling her daughter who has been wounded before Troy.

**Dionne, Narcisse Eutrope** (*b.* 1848), Canadian writer. Born at Saint-Denis de la Boutellerie, he was educated at Sainte-Anne's College, the Quebec Grand Seminary and Levis College, and obtained his medical degree at Laval University in 1872. After a short career as a physician, he adopted journalism as his profession, and his erudition and historical research into the early days of Quebec gained him the librarianship of the Quebec Legislature in 1892. Some of his publications are : *Jacques Cartier,* 1889 ; *Samuel Champlain, fondateur de Quebec,* 1891–1906 ; *Vie de C. F. Painchaud,* 1894 ; *John and Sebastian Cabot,* 1898 ; *Quebec et Nouvelle-France,* 1905–12 ; *Champlain,* 1905, revised 1926 ; *Les Ecclesiastiques et les Royalistes français réfugiés au Canade, 1791–1802,* 1905 ; *Galerie historique,* 8 vols., 1909–13 ; *Les Canadiens-Français,* 1914.

**Dionysia,** the festivals held in honour of Dionysus, the god of wine. These were Greek festivals, and the Attic ones were four in number, the Country Dionysia, the Lenæa, the Anthesteria, and the Great Dionysia. The first of these feasts was celebrated in the month of December, accompanied with processions and dramatic performances. The second was a city festival, celebrated during the next month. The Anthesteria lasted for three days, the ceremonies including a visit to the temple of Dionysus in Limnæ by the wife of the king, and a feast to dead souls, with a *libatim* to Hermes, and it was said that during this festival the

shades walked the earth. The Great Dionysia, the last of the four, consisted of a lyrical festival, followed by dramatic performances, and at the beginning of this festival the statue of the god was taken from the temple of the theatre. The Dionysia were great public holidays.

**Dionysius the Elder** (431 or 430–367 B.C.), a tyrant of Syracuse. Having by 405 B.C. constituted himself ruler of Syracuse, he made his position recure by a bodyguard of 1000 men,

DIONYSIUS AND FAUNUS

and by marrying the daughter of Hermocrates. In 397 B.C. he attacked the Carthaginians, and would have been defeated had they not been ravaged by a pestilence. After peace was made, D. turned his attention to the Greek cities, and finally succeeded in conquering Rhegium, which had always been hostile. From this time to 367 B.C. his power was absolute, having jurisdiction over most of Sicily, and indirectly over a large part of Italy. Although his rule was tyrannical, D. did much for the benefit of Syracuse, both in making it a magnificent city, and in encouraging literature.

**Dionysius the Younger,** a tyrant of Syracuse, succeeded his father, D. the Elder, in 367 B.C. Indolent in disposition, he rejected the counsel of Plato and followed the advice of dissolute people. He was compelled to leave Syracuse and went to Locri, which town he ruled as a tyrant for some years. He returned to Syracuse, but was again compelled to depart to Corinth, having surrendered to Timoleon, 343 B.C.

**Dionysius** (surnamed **Halicarnasseus**, from Halicarnassus, his birthplace), a Greek scholar of the reign of Augustus. He went to Rome about 30 B.C., where, after long and profound study, he wrote ' in the pursuit of truth and honesty,' a history of Rome, with the express purpose of reconciling his Greek compatriots to the yoke of their Roman conquerors. The work is still a valuable source of information.

**Dionysius of Colophon**, a Greek painter who lived about 500 B.C. He was a contemporary and rival of Polygnotus of Thasos, and was nicknamed ' Painter of Men ' (*Anthropographos*), because he aimed at portraying men as they really were, while Polygnotus gave his figures a touch of ideal or god-like beauty. He painted a portrait of Aristarchus carrying a figure of tragedy.

**Dionysius the Areopagite**, an almost legendary personage of whom little more is known for certain than that he was converted to Christianity by St. Paul at Athens (Acts xvii. 34), and that he was a member of the court of Areophagus. Eusebius says he became the first bishop of Athens. He is said to have suffered martyrdom under Diocletian, some say in Athens, others say in Paris at Montmartre, and these hold that he is the patron saint of France, ' Denys ' being the French form of Dionysius. Numerous writings on angelology, published in the fifth century, are ascribed to him.

**Dionysius Thrax**, or **the Thracian**, a distinguished Greek grammarian who lived about 100 B.C. He taught for some time in Rhodes and then had a school in Rome. He wrote the first scientific Greek grammar in existence, a work which was very popular, and highly valued in ancient times. His notes on the *Iliad* are included in the *Scholia Veterûm*.

**Dionysius of Byzantium**, a Greek poet of the second century. He wrote elegiac verses and an account of the navigation of the Bosphorus coast-line. Fragments of this work appear in various collections, *e.g.* in the *Geographi Minores* of Didot.

**Dionysius** (self-named in humility **Exiguus**, or ' the Little ') (*b. c.* 500 A.D.), a learned Greek theologian. He went to Rome and lived in a convent, where he made collections of the first fifty canons of the apostles, the canons of ten councils, and of thirty-eight decretals of the popes, all of which were recommended for use in 800 by Charlemagne. He introduced the method of counting the years from the birth of Christ instead of from the death.

**Dionysius** (surnamed **Periegetes**, or ' the describer of the earth '), a Greek poet who lived probably in the early days of the Roman empire. He wrote a *Descriptio Orbis Terrarum* in 1186 hexameter verses. His work, founded on that of the first scientific geographer, Eratosthenes, caused him to be considered by the later Greeks as the geographer *par excellence*. See Bernhardy's *Geographi Græci Minores*.

**Dionysius Cato**, the author of a work entitled *Dionysii Catonis Disticha de Moribus ad Filium*, which has been called a ' catechism of morals.' It consists of a preface, a series of injunctions such as *parentum ama, diligentiam adhibe*, etc., followed by 144 moral precepts. There has been much speculation as to the authorship and date of the work. It is frequently mentioned by Chaucer, and it seems to have been used as a school-book in the Middle Ages. See Ames, *Typographical Antiquities.*

**Dionysius**, *see* BACCHUS.

**Diophantine Equations**, so-called after Diophantus, a Gk. mathematician, who probably lived in the third century A.D. Diophantus published a book called *Arithmetica*, that included arithmetic and algebra. This book contains several problems that have been too difficult for any mathematician to solve. The type of problem may be illustrated by the following simple example. In how many ways can a Rugby team score nine points? If $x$ is the number of tries scored, $y$ the number of goals, $z$ the number of dropped goals, $p$ the number of penalty goals then $x + y + z + p = 9$. Such an equation is known as a D. E. In this case we can have $x = 3, y = 0, z = 0, p = 0$; $2, 0, 0, 1$; $1, 0, 0, 2$; $0, 0, 0, 3$; $0, 1, 1, 0$; *i.c.* five ways in all. The difficulty in solving such problems is that each one must be worked out *ab initio*, as there are no recognised algebraical principles that lead to their solution.

**Diophantus**, a Greek writer of Alexandria. His date is a matter of conjecture, some writers giving the fifth century, and others some time earlier. He was a writer on algebra, and his *Arithmetica*, of which six books are preserved, treats of numbers algebraically. There are one or two editions of D.'s work, and several paraphrases.

**Diopside** (Gk. δίς, twice, twofold, and ὄψις, appearance), a variety of pyroxene, containing no alumina. It is composed of silica (55·7), magnesia (18·5), and lime (25·8).

**Diopsis**, a dipterous insect given by most entomologists as the type of the family Diopsidæ in the group of *Muscidæ Acalyptratæ*.

**Dioptase**, or **Emerald Copper Ore**, a rare ore of copper found by analysis to consist roughly of 38 per cent. silica, 50 per cent. copper oxide, and 12 per cent. water. It occurs in beautiful green transparent or translucent crystals, similar in appearance to emeralds.

**Diopter** (Gk. διά, through, and ὁπτομαι, to see), the unit of refractive power of a lens, having a focal length of one metre. The ratio of one metre to its focal length is the expression of the numerical power of a lens in Ds. A lens of + 1 D. is a convex lens having a focal length of one metre, of + 2 Ds., a focal length of half a metre, etc. *See* LENS.

**Dioptrics**, that part of the science of optics which deals with the refraction of rays of light when passing through media such as glass and water. It treats particularly of the laws governing the refraction of light by lenses.

**Diorama**, *see* PANORAMA.

**Diorite**, a granitoid rock found in abundance in Germany and N. America, rarely in England, but frequently in the Scottish Highlands and Galloway. D. is composed essentially of felspar and one or more of the ferromagnesian minerals, such as hornblende, augite, biotite, or hypersthene. In colour it is greyish-white to almost black. Ds. from Guernsey are much valued as a road-metal in the S. of England.

**Dioscorea**, the chief genus of Dioscoreaceæ, is noted for its farinaceous tubers which are largely cultivated as food in the tropics and are known as *yams*.

**Dioscoreaceæ**, an order of monocotyledonous plants. They nearly all grow in the tropics, but *Tamus communis*, the black bryony, grows in Britain; many are nutritious and others are highly dangerous.

**Dioscorides Pedacius**, or **Pedanius**, a Greek physician (Διοσκορίδης). He is supposed to have been a native of Anazarba in Cilicia, and to have lived in the first or second century A.D. His chief work was a treatise on the *Materia Medica*.

**Dioscuri**, *see* CASTOR AND POLLUX.

**Dioscurides**, a gem engraver who lived about the time of Augustus, whose seal he engraved. He is one of the four engravers recorded by Pliny.

**Diosgyör**, a tn. of Hungary, situated in the prov. of Borsod. In the vicinity there are coal mines. Pop. 7250.

**Diosma**, a genus of rutaceous herbs, inhabiting the Cape of Good Hope. The plants are heath-like, with white or red flowers. *D. crenata* and *D. serratifolia* contain a volatile oil, and the leaves have an aromatic taste. By the Hottentots they have long been in use medicinally.

**Dip**, the angle which a magnetic needle makes with the horizon when the vertical plane, in which it moves, coincides with the magnetic meridian. The total magnetic force acting upon a magnetic needle may be resolved into two components, one acting horizontally and the other vertically. When the needle is suspended so as to move in a horizontal plane, as in the mariner's compass, the horizontal force tends to make it lie along the magnetic meridian, but the vertical force has an inconsiderable effect. When the needle is suspended so as to move in a vertical plane at right angles to the magnetic meridian, the horizontal force can only act in the direction of the axis of suspension, and therefore the needle is only affected by the vertical component, and so stands vertically. When, however, the horizontal component is free to act, the needle takes up a position at an angle to the horizon which increases as the position of the needle approaches the magnetic pole. The D. is subject to secular variation and in London has decreased from a maximum of 74° 42′ in 1723 to 67° 9′ in 1900.

**Diphtheria**, an acute infectious disease characterised by the formation on a mucous membrane, most commonly that of the pharynx, of a yellowish false membrane. The disease was first specifically described and named by P Brétonneau, of Tours, in 1826. In 1883 Klebs and Löffler identified the bacillus. The history of the micro-organism outside the human body is not well known. It appears to be ever present in a dormant state in the soil of all European and most American countries, and is often found in the throats of subjects who present none of the characteristic symptoms. Some individuals seem to be altogether immune, while others take the disease in a very mild form. It commonly attacks children with fatal results, and may occur in scattered cases or as a widespread epidemic. The early symptoms are a sore throat and a general feeling of uneasiness, such as might accompany a bad chill. A swelling of the glands of the neck and an inflamed condition of the tonsils next make their appearance; the temperature rises, and the beginning of the false membrane is seen in yellowish patches. These gradually spread and unite to form a firmly adherent membrane with the appearance of wet parchment. If removed, it leaves a raw ulcerated surface on which it speedily re-forms. When not checked, the exudation spreads upwards and downwards, invading the nasal passages and the lower respiratory passages. There is great pain and difficulty in swallowing, and the obstruction caused by the membrane may lead to death from asphyxia. At the same time, the effects of the bacterial poisons in the blood are to be noticed. The heart becomes weakened, albumin is present in the urine, and progressive anæmia is observed. The poison has a marked effect upon the nerve tissues, causing temporary and local paralysis, which may persist for some time after the other symptoms have been suppressed. The paralysis often affects the soft palate and pharynx, causing the food to be returned through the nostrils, or the eye may be affected, causing disturbances of vision. Recovery is a lengthy process, and the period of convalescence demands great care in consequence of the recrudescence of some of the early symptoms or of possible complications, to which the weakened state of the D. patient renders him liable. The anti-toxin mode of treatment overshadows all others; in fact, no other has been productive of good effects. The serum is obtained from a horse which has previously been inoculated with a mild culture of D. bacilli. The animal elaborates a substance which combats successfully the bacterial toxin and henceforth becomes immune from the poison. The serum withdrawn from the animal is injected subcutaneously into the D. patient, usually with the prompt cessation of the most exhausting symptoms. Injection of the serum is also recommended as a preventive measure for persons likely to come in contact with D. cases, and although a slight swelling of the joints has been observed in persons so inoculated, no permanent harm has ever been traced to the treatment. D. has not altogether shared in the general decline in the prevalence of zymotic diseases induced by superior sanitary conditions. There seems to be a periodic rise and fall in the numbers of cases recorded, and some attempt has been made to connect its prevalence with periods following upon a long drought, but without arriving at any satisfactory conclusion. There is no doubt, however, that when it does become virulent, it spreads with great rapidity by means of the contact of children in school.

**Diphthong** (Gk. δί, double; φθόγγος, sound), a compound sound, composed of two vowel sounds joined to form one sound distinct from either of the two original. There are four sounds in English which are pure Ds. These are $i = a + i$, as in the word aisle; $ū = i + u$, as in the word duke; $oi = au + i$, as in joist; and $ou = a + u$, as in south. Many vowels written as double ones in English are not Ds. in sound.

**Dipleidoscope** (Gk. διπλός, double, and σκοπέω, to see, view), an optical instrument for indicating the passage of the sun or of a star over the meridian, and used for the purpose of determining the correct time by transit observations. It consists of a triangular prism which has two silvered planes and one (in front) unsilvered; one of the silvered planes coincides with the plane of the meridian. The coincidence of the two images formed by a single and double refraction of the prism records the transit accurately if the adjustment is correct. Steinheil's ' transit prism ' grew out of the work of Bloxam, Dent, and Plössel on the D.

**Diplodactylus,** a genus of lacertilian reptiles, is closely related to the *Gecko* in the family Geckonidæ. A common example of these lizards is *D. vittatus*, and all the species are found in Australia.

**Diplodocus,** a genus of the dinosauria in the order Sauropoda. The species were enormous reptiles over 40 ft. in length, with an abnormally long neck and tail and small head, about one-thirtieth the size of the body. The vertebral column consisted of 15 cervicals, 11 dorsals, 4 sacrals, and at least 37 caudals. The high position of the external nases and the long tail indicate that it was probably aquatic, but the limbs are plantigrade and wholly terrestrial. The teeth are slender and cylindrical, arranged in descending order of size from the front of the mouth. *D. longus* and *D. carnegii* have been found in the Upper Jurassic of Wyoming. [*See* illustration overleaf.]

**Diplomacy,** the term applied to the art of conducting the affairs of one country with regard to those of another, owing to the intercourse which must take place between countries or states. This right of employing diplomatic agents belongs to those states only which have absolute power of their own and are not dependent on some other country. In England, nominally, the power to adjust relations with other countries rests with the king, but it is actually managed by others, the chief of whom is the Secretary of State for

Foreign Affairs. These officials may be either ambassadors, the actual representatives of the sovereign, envoys, or chargés d'affaires. When a man is in foreign territory, acting as a diplomatic agent for his country, he is judged by the laws of his own land, and only those laws can touch him. He has also a certain rank by reason of his commission, and ambassadors, as representatives of the sovereign, have an extremely high one. It has always been a in itself, and one which requires no little degree of skill in application to attain results of any permanent value. The deciphering of ancient writings is generally known in these days by the name of Palæography (*q.v.*), a science the importance of which is now so universally recognised that most civilised countries of the day have instituted chairs of palæography in various seats of learning. From this specialisation in one particular direction of the general

DIPLODOCI CARNEGII

custom, also, to adopt one language as a medium for diplomats—the one now used being French.

**Diplomatics** (Gk. δίπλωμα, (1) anything folded, or (2) a licence, from διπλόος, double), the science of diplomas or of ancient writings, literary and public documents, letters, decrees, charters, codicils, title-deeds, court-rolls, chartularies, etc.,which has for its object to decipher old writings, to ascertain their authenticity, their dates, signatures, and the general circumstances of their making. By the light of the internal evidence afforded by old public or private records, much may be inferred with respect to the customs and manners of former times, but although D. may be looked upon as a means to that end, it is also a science science of diplomas, it becomes necessary to distinguish the function of D. as being concerned to-day, not so much with deciphering as with preservation, co-ordination, and classification of old documents to facilitate the work of the palæographer, and with the particular duty of ascertaining their authenticity, not only from the internal evidence vouchsafed by the palæographer, but from any reliable external source of verification, and particularly from the form itself of any particular diploma or document. Sooner or later in the progress of civilisation it becomes necessary for a nation, not only to adopt set forms in documents, but to provide archives for those documents, for the custody of its public Acts. Yet it was not before the Middle Ages that the European nations as a whole attained to anything like the precision of the ancient Roms. in this respect. In England the preservation of both public and private documents was left rather to the discretion of those bodies or persons who were more personally affected by those documents than to officials—like the present keeper of the Public Record Office—whose duty lay towards the nation as a whole. Various courts from an early date kept records of decisions or grants made in such courts inscribed on the court rolls: the chancery very early kept a record of all royal grants in the shape of charters, privileges, and immunities, together with writs of process, and the chancery rolls from the beginning of the thirteenth century are both full and complete ; and there are also to be found countless deeds of conveyance of real property, not only in the Public Record Office, but in the archives of municipalities, private families, and in the British Museum. Preservation should be a state duty, carried out by expert palæographers able not only to decipher, but to classify for the benefit of future generations. Authenticity of documents, however, depends not only on preservation, but in the internal evidence furnished by the set forms in which such documents may be drawn. Hence it is that D. is a science which is largely concerned with the investigation of forms. In this direction it is curious to notice how far the ancient Roms. were in advance of mediæval Europe, and how remarkably deficient they were in the power to make use of their archives. In point of mere form, the Roms. would appear to have attained such precision and directness of statement that in the Middle Ages all the advancing nations employed the set styles of the Rom. documentary system. This may have been due partly to the fact that a great part of Europe inherited its legal system directly from the Rom. civil law, but it is more probably to be accounted for by the fact that the few who could write, and the still fewer who could compose a formal document, had acquired the necessary learning through the Church of the Holy Roman Empire. After the revival of learning and the passing of the dark ages, grants, charters, ordinances, proclamations, and all manner of official or public documents were composed in Latin, and whether avowed or not, there can be but little doubt that the Renaissance gave, not only the language, but the forms of the Romans to all manner of docu-

ments. The chancery in England was, in its inception, essentially ecclesiastical, and the makers of original writs (see CASE, ACTION UPON THE) were unquestionably scholars well acquainted with the Roman law. Diplomas in the particular sense of royal charters or grants of privileges all reveal, in the earlier stages of their history, a striking uniformity of style and arrangement—a style which in the title and preamble to a modern Act of Parliament in England has by no means disappeared. The French diplomas of the Carlovingian and Merovingian periods, much after the style of Roman lawyers, who were accustomed to mingle statements of the law with moral, religious, and philosophical reflections, generally began with an invocation, followed in order by the full name and style of the monarch, a preamble explaining shortly, or at considerable length, the motives, moral or religious, of the grant ; the subject-matter of the grant ; penalties against all who should infringe the privilege or immunity granted to the donee ; and the signature of the monarch, and, in Latin, the date of the grant. Later, an added security to authenticity was given by the use of seals. According to the late Edward Augustus Bond, the principal librarian to the British Museum, Acts emanating from royal authority prior to the thirteenth century are almost exclusively derived from ecclesiastical records. Those in England comprise charters of corporations, and, particularly, charters of foundation of monastic institutions. These, though drawn up in Latin, can hardly have been borrowed from Roman forms, inasmuch as the terms and conditions incorporated in the documents related to transactions and usages differing essentially from anything known to the Romans, at least of the classic period of the republic, when the preservation of tablets in the Roman archives was systematically observed. In the earliest periods, the Romans employed the term diploma to signify nothing more than a letter of licence to use public conveyances, the letter itself being inscribed on two leaves, or double tablets, hence the name. Subsequently the term embraced all public grants. Apart from the destruction of a great number of copies of brazen tablets by the burning of the capitol, and the deprecations of the invading Gauls, there is, according to Mommsen, no dearth of documents from the early Roman times. Writing was an art of high antiquity in ancient Rome, and there is sufficient proof of the existence of documents of the regal period. The sacred records of the Samnites, it is known, were inscribed on linen rolls, and there is evidence of the existence of written lists of the Roman magistrates, books of oracles, clan registers, and Alban and Roman calendars. No such documents are extant, but they were kept in the Roman archives and would have fulfilled the purpose of instructing future generations but for the deficiencies of Roman historians of the succeeding age. In England the mediæval historians were not slow to avail themselves of the information derivable from ancient charters. Much, however, has been lost of the history of Western Europe between the time of Charlemagne and the twelfth century. On the continent the science of D. would appear to have dated from the revival of learning in the Middle Ages, when, as a consequence of the recognised importance of documents in verifying facts and establishing the existence of rights, both public and private, the value of diplomas as evidence was defended by a Benedictine monk named Mabellon in a work entitled *De Re Diplomatica*. Such a work with its scientific analysis of the principles to be employed in investigating diplomas was of especial value at a time when the practice of forging diplomas and other documents was as constantly resorted to as it had been in the time of the forged capitularies of Benedict the Levite and the false decretals of the Pseudo-Isidore (*see* Pollock and Maitland's *History of English Law*), the latter being a collection of elaborate mosaics made up out of phrases from the Bible, the fathers, genuine canons, genuine decretals, and the West Goths Roman Law Book, the whole designed to establish the superhuman origin of ecclesiastical power and the sacro-sanctity of the persons and property of bishops. Palgrave, in commenting on forged Anglo-Saxon charters, points out, however, that when caligraphists attempted not merely to repeat the words, but to ' depicture ' the ancient charters, their real object in producing copies long after the conquest was to save the celebrated land-boc from impious and careless hands ; and that, as such imitations were easily detected by the skilled antiquary, he might be induced to condemn as a forgery that which was never intended to be anything but an innocent facsimile. The monks, too, were accustomed to falsifying charters of grants of land, and they were equally justified in many instances, inasmuch as their title rested on prescriptive possession. Having, therefore, no deeds or charters to prove a perfectly lawful ownership of church lands, they set to work to produce such charters in set form. There were, however, wholesale forgeries of papal bulls and church briefs at the end of the twelfth century in England, and a science which can lay claim to detecting ingenious forgeries in ancient records necessarily does much, not only to prevent the ignorant from delusion, and the deprivation of many of their private or public rights, but ensures a respect for ancient institutions which have been evolved from a long line of unimpeachable precedents.

*Authorities.* — Benjamin Thorpe, *Diplomatarium Anglicum Ævi Saxonici;* E. A. Bond, *Facsimiles of Ancient Charters in the British Museum*, 1873–78 ; G. F. Warner and H. J. Ellis, *Facsimiles of Royal and other Charters in the British Museum*, 1903.

**Diplomatic Service, British.** Great Britain like most other civilised nations is represented abroad in regard to its international interests by diplomatic agents and occasionally by consuls, though these latter are in general concerned exclusively with the interests of British subjects resident abroad. The former include *ambassadors* or officials permanently accredited to the court of some foreign state, and *chargés d'affaires.* A *chargé d'affaires* is either one who acts as deputy for an ambassador during the temporary absence of the latter, or one who is accredited as British representative to some foreign court of minor importance. Ambassadors are appointed by and derive their authority from sealed letters of credence (*see* CREDENTIALS) under the sign-manual addressed to the sovereign or president of the country to which they are accredited, and from instructions under the sign-manual to themselves personally. Consuls may represent Great Britain in its international relations only when expressly vested with diplomatic powers. Ambassadors are assisted by various other attendants known as attachés. These latter have to serve a probationary period, after which they become eligible for appointment as third secretaries. First and second secretaries constitute an intermediate class between third secretaries and councillors. Councillors in the D. S. are appointed to all embassies and to the legations at Peking, Teheran, and Cairo. All the members of the D. S. are expected to take their turn in whatever part of the world their services may be required, and every councillor, secretary, or attaché, whether married or unmarried, must be prepared to go to the post at which the requirements of the public service demand his presence and to which he may be appointed.  *See* Anson, *Law of the Constitution; Foreign Office List.*

**Dipnoi** (Gk.  δί,  twice ;  πνοή, breathing), or **Dipneusti,** a sub-class of fishes, is of great interest for its many peculiar features, some of which are typical of amphibians. The D. are all extinct but for three genera, the *Ceratodus* (*q.v.*), of Queensland, *Protopterus,* of Africa, and *Lepidosiren,* of America, but many fossils belonging to the group have been discovered, all either Palæozoic or Mesozoic.  The importance of the straight, and the general colour of the bird is brown, the throat and part of the breast being white.  It inhabits streams of Europe, Asia, and America, feeding on molluscs and insects, and is a good diver.  *C. aquaticus* and *C. albicollis* are British species.

**Diprotodon,** a genus of kangaroo found in fossil state in Australia ; it is characterised by a peculiarity of dentition.

**Dipsaceæ,** an order of dicotyledonous plants which is nearly allied to the Compositæ.  *Dipsacus sylvestris* is the common teazle found on waste ground in Britain, and *D.*

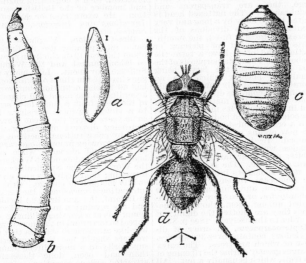

DIPTERA

*d,* Horn-fly (*Hæmatobia serrata*) Europe ; *b,* larva ; *c,* puparium magnified 8 times ; *a,* egg magnified 20 times

possession of a double-breathing apparatus is seen in Protopterus and Lepidosiren, both of which have gills as well as two lungs.  They are mudfishes which live in tropical swamps ; when the water is abundant they breathe by means of their gills, when it has dried up by means of their lungs. Ceratodus, however, lives in the deep pools of rivers, and it is not known definitely that the power of its single lung is ever tested.

**Dipper,** or **Water-Ousel,** the popular term for passeriform birds of the genus *Cinclus.*  Both wings and tail are short, the beak is fairly short and *fullonum* is the fuller's teazle which has hooked bracts, and the prickly fruit-heads are used in finishing woollen cloth.

**Dipsas,** a genus of Amblycephalidæ, are snakes which have much in common with the family Colubridæ.  The members of the genus are found in S. America and are harmless, though in appearance they resemble poisonous species.

**Dip-sector,** an astronomical reflecting instrument, similar to the sextant in principle, for ascertaining the dip of the horizon.  In 1803 Wollaston described in the Bakerian lecture a D. of his invention ; Troughton constructed these instruments.

**Dipsomania,** *see* ALCOHOLISM, DRUNKENNESS, INEBRIATES.

**Diptera** (Gk. δί, two ; πτερόν, wing), a large order of insects, of which over 40,000 species have been classified, but are not believed to nearly represent all of the species which are in existence. They are distinguished from other insects by the presence of one pair of wings, though in a few cases, *e.g.* the flea, these are absent or rudimentary, and the hind-wings are frequently represented by two pin-like, knobbed processes called halteres. The wings are never very large, they are transparent and membranous. The flattened head is united to the body by a long and very flexible neck, the divisions of the thorax are greatly fused, the mouthparts are adapted for piercing or suction, and often have a retractile proboscis. The metamorphosis of the flies is complete, the larva being usually a maggot which has no thoracic legs and only a minute head ; the organs it contains differ completely from those of the mature creature, and in undergoing its metamorphosis the contents of the body break down into a creamy substance from which the new organs of the adult are developed. It is usually only the females which have blood-sucking habits, and their larvæ are nearly always aquatic. The D. are divided by most zoologists into five groups, the Nemocera, Brachycera, Aschiza, Schizophora, and Pupipara, and the Aphaniptera, or fleas, are usually included among them, though sometimes they are allotted the dignity of an order to themselves. [See p. 83.]

**Dipterocarpaceæ,** an order of dicotyledons, contains over 300 species, most of which are trees. The calyx enlarges greatly during the ripening of the fruit, which is usually a nut. All the species produce such substances as resin and oil: *Dryobalanops camphora,* a kind of camphor, and *Dipterocarpus trinervis,* a resin which is made into plasters for ulcers in Java.

**Dipterus,** the oldest known fossil genus of dipnoid fish in the family Ctenodontidæ.

**Diptych,** two tablets made of carved ivory, etc., and united by leather hinges; their inner surface was covered with wax. The Romans wrote in them the names of the consuls and principal magistrates. They were also used in monasteries, to contain the names of the bishops and benefactors. The name is applied to pictures and bas-reliefs covered by two carved or painted shutters.

**Dipyre** (Gk. δί, two, and πῦρ, fire), a silicate of alumina and lime, which,

when subjected to heat, first becomes phosphorescent and then fuses : it occurs as a transparent, tetragonal mineral in the Pyrenees.

**Dirce,** the wife of Lycus, King of Thebes. She was dragged to death by a wild bull, to whose horns she had been bound by Amphion and Zethus, sons of Antiope, the divorced wife of Lycus.

**Dircks, Henry** (1806–73), a civil engineer and author, inventor of the optical delusion ' Pepper's Ghost.' As an apprentice in a mercantile firm he studied mechanics, chemistry, and literature, and later became a practical, then a consulting engineer, and member of the British Association. He wrote *Popular Education, Inventions and Inventors, Scientific Studies,* etc.

**Direct Action.** A phrase that came into popular use in England about the year 1910, chiefly in relation to labour unrest and the Women's Suffrage Movement. Like many slogans invented in times of agitation, it has no precise definition, but varies, according to the mood and character of the user, from a small local strike to a violent national uprising. For some years before the Great War, an increasing distrust of gaining their ends by constitutional methods was steadily growing among wage-earners at home and abroad; while such bodies as the Independent Workers of the World and the Syndicalists were increasing their activities and urging swifter methods of change. Growing international uneasiness, the tension in Ireland, the Agadir (*q.v.*) incident and the revolution in Portugal were symptoms of a growing willingness to appeal to force, and in the increasingly war-like atmosphere the plea that the workers should use their numerical superiority in a more direct manner than had been done theretofore attracted serious attention. During the same time the vigorous leaders in the cause of Women's Suffrage became increasingly contemptuous of lawful methods, and arrests of women law-breakers were of almost daily occurrence. The outbreak of the Great War temporarily checked the Direct Action movement, as women were enfranchised and the manhood of a citizen-army from instincts of national self-preservation found it less irksome to endure the bonds of ' discipline ' till after peace was declared. Bad trade and difficult times, however, following the War soon revived the popularity of direct action until the futility of the General Strike in 1926 somewhat damped the ardour of the extremists. *See* STRIKE, GENERAL.

**Direct and Retrograde,** terms used

n astronomy to indicate the apparent motions of a planet as seen from the earth. Its motion is said to be D. when it is progressing from right to left towards its eastern elongation, and R. when it is travelling towards its western elongation, apparently in the opposite direction.

**Direction,** a relative term. If two straight lines joining two pairs of points cut the celestial sphere at the same point, the D. of the two pairs of points is the same.

**Directoire Exécutif,** a body composed of five members, to whom the constitution of the year III. of the French Republic delegated the executive power (1795–99). It was succeeded by the consulat.

**Director,** in surgery, a grooved probe used to direct a bistoury, bullet-extractor, etc. The instrument directed slides along the groove.

**Director,** in law, see COMPANY, and PUBLIC PROSECUTOR.

**Directorium,** or Ordo, a list printed every year by authority of a Roman Catholic bishop ; it contains directions to ecclesiastics as to the office for each day.

**Directory,** an alphabetical list or index giving various kinds of information. Most useful is the Post Office Directory, compiled for districts ; the biggest is the London one, which contains information under the following headings : 1. *Court Directory :* Names of people occupying private houses, arranged alphabetically, but persons having any rank or title precede others of the same name. 2. *Official Directory :* Names of persons holding any government or law office. 3. *Street Directory :* Names of the principal streets of London, with their terminals and intersections with other streets named, and a selection of the inhabitants. 4. *Law Directory :* List of judges and official staff of all the courts and of the police force. 5. *Parliament Directory :* List of all peers of the United Kingdom, members of the House of Peers, members of the House of Commons and names and places for which they sit. 6. *Postal Directory :* All information connected with the transmission of letters, parcels, etc. 7. *City, Municipal, Parochial, and Clerical Directory :* Gives a large amount of miscellaneous information. 8. *Commercial Directory :* List of wharves, booking-offices, railway-carriers, etc. 9. *Banking Directory :* List of bankers, etc. 10. *Suburban Directory.* There are also various directories compiled by individuals, e.g. Perry's *Mercantile Guide,* Kelly's *Customs Tariffs,* Stubbs's *Manufacturers,* Macdonald's *English Directory and Gazetteer,* Crockford's *Clerical Directory, The Medical Directory, The Press Directory,* and *Who's Who.* All these are to be found at any good reference library.

**Directory** (1795–99), a body of five men, Barras, Carnot, Lépeaux, Latourneur, and Rewbell, to whom the executive of France was given in the year IV. after the defeat of the Terrorists. It was useless as a governing body and was suppressed by the Abbé Sieyès and Bonaparte.

**Directory of Public Worship,** a collection of rules for public worship drawn up by the Westminster Assembly of Divines in 1644. It was accepted by the General Assembly of the Church of Scotland and by the Scottish Parliament in Feb. 1645. It appears in vol. v. of *The History of the Puritans,* by Neal.

**Dirge** (Lat. imperative *dirige,* direct thou), the first word of the opening antiphon used in Rom. Catholic offices for the dead, thus the term is applied to a piece of music which is suitable for funeral ceremonies.

**Dirhem,** an Arabic silver coin equivalent to about 45 grs. The Fr. gramme is now called D. in Turkey. See DRACHMA.

**Dirigible Balloons,** see AERONAUTICS ; AIRSHIPS ; BALLOONS.

**Dirk,** the proper name for the dagger of the Highlander. It was worn either within the vest or with the pistol at the belt. The blade was some five inches long, and separated by a ' shoulder ' from the short, cylinder-shaped handle, which was usually of horn or wood, and was often richly carved.

**Dirt Beds,** see PURBECK BEDS, and GEOLOGY.

**Dis,** see HADES.

**Disability,** a term in law which is applied to a person who is not allowed to do a particular thing. This D. may be due to physical causes, as in the case of those mentally deficient, or to the fact that a person is under age, or to a point of law, as in the case of an alien.

**Disability Pensions,** see DISABLED MEN ; PENSIONS.

**Disabled Men.** The magnitude of the scale of operations of the Great War was reflected in the number of men disabled in them. All classes were affected and the resettlement of D. M. in civil life was a national problem which became especially acute after demobilisation. In 1915 the Appointments Board, under the Ministry of Labour, was constituted to place disabled officers and men of like standing. During the war and for some time after the Armistice disabled officers and men were given a course of training to fit them for civil employment in those cases where they could not follow their previous employment. To encourage employers to absorb the disabled the King's National Roll was inaugurated by Royal Proclamation in Aug. 1919. Those who engaged D. M. in the proportion of 5 per cent. of their total staff of employees were given a certificate and were entitled to use a special seal on their business stationery. In 1926 the number of employers on the roll was over 28,000. The roll is still in existence. Such organisations as the British Legion, St. Dunstan's Hospital for the Blind, etc., have done good work for D. M. War-disabled men, through the operation of the Joint Substitution Board, are still given preference over other applicants for work in Gov. Departments. In the U.S.A. interest in this problem was no less keen. Under an Act of 1917, provision was made for compensation to men and women disabled in the war. The welfare of this class is now largely under the ægis of such organisations as the American Legion (q.v.) and the Veterans' Bureau. In Belgium, welfare work was under the control of the Département des Secours, which made grants of money to the societies which were interested in the disabled.

**Disarmament,** see ARMAMENTS, LIMITATION OF.

**Discharge,** see BANKRUPT; ELECTRICITY; ABSCESS.

**Discharge, Arch of,** in architecture, an arch built in the masonry or brickwork above the lintel. Its object is to transfer the pressure from above to the points of stability on either side. It can generally be distinguished from the stone or brickwork in which it is built merely by the position of its stones. The earliest example is found in the Great Pyramid, consisting of two stones resting against each other above the lintels of the entrance. The A. of D. was used in Gk. and Rom. architecture.

**Discharge from the Army.** When a soldier has completed his legal term of service he can claim his discharge. He can also be discharged, at the discretion of the military authorities, before he has so completed his legal period, e.g. for medical unfitness, by purchase (the amount varies with circumstances), refusing to be vaccinated, misconduct, inefficiency, on conviction by civil power, for wife desertion, and other grounds. During a protracted war the army is augmented far beyond peace ' strength ' so that at its conclusion great reductions must take place, and those who are not required are, if enlisted as regulars, usually discharged ' on reduction of establishment,' being

granted compensation in proportion to their unexpired service. Reservists are also discharged from the reserve under somewhat similar rules to those which apply to serving soldiers. All men discharged from the army are given a Certificate of Service which contains certificates of transfer to the reserve, discharge and character.

**Disciples of Christ,** see CAMPBELL ALEXANDER.

**Disciplina Arcani** (Lat., ' discipline of the secret '), a term used in the seventeenth century to describe the system of reserve practised by the Christian Church during the first few centuries, by which the mysteries of the faith were concealed from unbelievers and the unbaptised. No trace of it is found till the end of the second century, and it began to die rapidly at the end of the sixth century. Strong traces of it remain in the Gk. liturgy. Baptism and the Eucharist were considered as the great Christian mysteries, and the latter was divided into a ' Liturgy of the Catechumens ' and a ' Liturgy of the Faithful.' The latter included the consecration and communion, and from it the unbaptised were excluded. See works, De Disciplina Arcani, by Scheistrate (Rome), 1685, and Tentzel (Leipzig), 1692.

**Discipline,** see ARMY, and MILITARY.

**Disco,** an is. on the W. coast of Greenland. It is 70 m. long and about 50 m. wide. Godhavn is a harbour in the S. of the is. There is much coal to be found.

**Discoboli,** or **Cyclopteridæ,** the family name of the acanthopterygious fishes known popularly as lumpsuckers from the frequent presence of a sucking disc formed from the united ventral fins. C. lumpus, the cock-and-hen paddle, and L. vulgaris, the sea-snail, are found on British coasts.

**Discoidea,** see ECHINODERMATA.

**Disconto Gesellschaft** is a Ger. finance co. which was founded in the middle of the nineteenth century. Its capital and reserves approximate to £10,000,000. Its headquarters are in Berlin, with branches throughout the Ger. reich and agencies all over the world, particularly in S. America. From its beginnings as a credit association it has developed along modern banking lines.

**Discount,** the amount of money deducted from a certain sum when that sum is paid before it is due. There is true or theoretical D., and commercial or banker's D. The former, which is practically not used at all, is the difference between the present worth of the bill and its face value or future worth. Thus the D. on £104 due one year hence at 4 per cent. per annum is £4. Tradesmen and bankers, however, adopt a different method of computation. They reckon the simple interest on the face value of the bill. Thus if a bill of £110 is due a year hence at 10 per cent., the banker deducts simple interest on £110 at the given rate, *i.e.* £11, instead of £10 as in true D. D. is also applied to stock if the actual purchasing value is below that of the nominal value ; thus if £100 stock can be bought for £95 cash, it is at D. of 5 per cent.

**Discovery,** a legal term denoting disclosure by a defendant in an action of certain facts, documents, or deeds, which the plaintiff obliged him on oath to discover to the court so as to make good his case. Similarly the defendant may call on the plaintiff for a ' discovery.'

**Discovery Committee,** a Colonial Office committee formed shortly after the Great War with the primary object of attempting to place the whaling industry on a scientific basis. Its other objects are to render service to navigation by conducting a hydrographic survey of the whaling areas, to inquire into the resources of whaling regions from the point of view of fisheries, and to add to scientific knowledge of the sea. For this work the royal research ship *Discovery I.* made investigations in the vicinity of the Falkland Islands between 1926 and 1927, the research ship *William Scoresby* carried out operations in the same period off the coast of S. Georgia, and the royal research ship *Discovery II.*, a new steel-built boat, sailed for the Falkland Islands in 1930. The chief investigations are directed to a study of the habits and haunts of whales, their rate and location of breeding, and related topics, with the view of securing data for regulating the industry. This had become an urgent matter owing to the increasing possibility of the extermination of the whale, and is of especial importance to the Falkland Island dependencies, where whaling is almost the sole industry and a lucrative one. Some fourteen companies—eleven Norwegian and three British—catch on an average some 12,000 whales during the season in these waters, a catch averaging about 60 per cent. of the world's supply, valued at nearly £4,500,000. It is therefore essential to determine the intensity with which the industry can be carried on without undue detriment to future supplies. The policy of the British Gov. is to restrain whaling to its present dimensions, while energetically searching for a basis for the determination of the maximum intensity of whaling desirable ; and this policy has been

carried out by the limitation of whaling licences and also by the institution of the *Discovery* investigations. This restriction is the more necessary in view of the success attending expansion of the industry, notably in the season 1927–28, through the taking of whales by catchers working from factory ships operating along the edge of the ice, instead of working from shore stations or from mother ships anchored in the shelter of land. The introduction of these new methods of whaling led to an immediate expansion of pelagic whaling, an expansion which soon absorbed increasing amounts of capital not only from Norway, but also from other countries. This expansion may have some bearing on the investigations of the D. C., as it is a less economic method of whaling and permits of indefinite extension of the grounds worked, even far outside territorial limits. As long as the pelagic whaler works outside territorial limits she is subject to no regulation except such as may be imposed by the Gov. of her own country ; but it is hoped to take steps to prohibit her from destroying cow whales with calves. The importance of the study of the distribution and migration of the whale lies in its bearing on the stock affected by whaling, and the cruises of the *Discovery I.*, extending from S. Africa to Cape Horn, and from Tristan da Cunha, have contributed to solving this question. Previously there were two views as to stock in the S.: one being that there is one vast circumpolar stock which, except in the course of N. migrations, occupies the whole Southern Ocean ; the other that the distribution is extremely irregular, whales being abundant only in certain areas. The *Discovery I.* found that distribution was governed largely by that of the small creatures on which the whale feeds, and that therefore if large tracts are found in which these creatures are scarce, no accumulation of whales can be expected. Direct evidence as to migration of whales is sought by marking whales with numbered darts, which, when returned from whaling stations, show the course travelled.

While the D. C. is primarily engaged in researches for definite economic ends, they consider it their duty to facilitate other scientific inquiries, inasmuch as experience has shown that most valuable results have ensued from researches undertaken with no other aim than the acquisition of knowledge. At the end of 1930 the D. C. reported that the Royal Research Ship *Discovery II.* had carried out a complete investigation and hydrographical survey of the S. Sandwich Islands, this being the first official visit made since the islands were declared British Territory by Letters Patent of July 21, 1908. Thus the ship has rounded off a chapter of Antarctic history associated with the historic names of Cook and Bellinghausen. Captain J. R. Stenhouse commanded the *Discovery I.*, Lieut.-Commander Irving the *William Scoresby*, and Commander Carey commands the *Discovery II.* The director of research for the D. C. is Dr. Stanley Kemp. (See *Annual Reports of the Discovery Investigations.*)

**Discus** (Gk. δίσκος, disc), a circular plate of stone (or metal), in ancient times from 8–12 in. in diameter, weighing 4–5 lb., used for hurling from a fixed mark to the greatest possible distance as a gymnastic

DISCOBOLUS

sport and exercise among the Gks. and Roms. Disc-throwing was included with jumping, foot-racing, spear-throwing, and wrestling in the *pentathlon* of the Olympic Games. The D. was held in the athlete's right hand, leaning against the forearm, and thrown like a quoit. Sometimes a kind of spherical quoit was used similarly, with a thong passed through a hole in it. A copy of Myron's famous ' Discobolus ' is in the British Museum (according to Gardiner the attitude is not strictly correct), and also in the Vatican and the Palace Lancellotti at Rome there are copies.

As played in modern times the D weighs about 4½ lb., and is thrown from a circle of 7 ft. *See Statius, Thebais,* 646–721.

**Discussion,** a term in Rom. law, and means the exhaustion of all lega means by the creditor to enforce payment from the principal debtor before taking proceedings against the person secondarily liable, *i.e.* the surety. In Scots law the term is also used in ' D. of heirs,' the proceedings against the heirs for debts contracted and left unpaid by the deceased.

**Diseases of Animals Act,** *see* Contagious Diseases (Animals) Acts.

**Disestablishment** is the annulling of the special recognition, status, and privileges which a particular religious communion has enjoyed by favour of the State. The tendency to terminate such relationship is on the increase. There is, at the same time, a growing feeling in some established churches that the attainment of spiritual freedom thus secured is well worth the cost. (Disendowment, a usual concomitant, is, however, separable in idea from Disestablishment.)

The dissociation of Church and State as a combination may be considered a British *religious* movement; while *politically* it is to some extent a ' liberty and equality ' concept of the Fr. Revolution. In France the Rom. Catholic Church was disestablished during the Revolution, reinstated by Napoleon in 1801 and the union was repudiated unilaterally by the State in 1906. In Great Britain the Church of England as established in Ireland, where the people were largely Rom. Catholics, was disestablished by a Bill of 1869 which came into force in 1871. The archbishops and bishops ceased to possess the right to seats in the House of Lords, and the rights of patronage were abolished. In the case of private patronage, compensation was made, and all offices which carried personal precedence with them were retained for life. Attempts to introduce a Welsh Disestablishment Bill began in 1895. The Liberal attempt in that year failed, but in 1909 another Bill was introduced as a result of the findings of the Royal Commission appointed in 1906. The Bill was finally passed by the Commons in the early part of 1913. In the following year it passed into law to come into operation in 1915, but the outbreak of the Great War led to the postponement of the measure, and it was not until 1920 that the Welsh Church was disestablished. In Scotland, where the people are mainly Presbyterian, the two great divisions of the Scottish Church—Established and Free (or United Free)—coalesced in 1929 on a unique basis, viz., complete independence of the State in all spiritual matters and internal government, along with a definitive transference of the anct. endowments to the United Church. In 1927, a movement of a voluntary nature took place in the Eng. Church in India that might be regarded as akin to disestablishment. But although the Indian Church separated in many official particulars, it still recognises Canterbury as the mother see. The new European republics, Germany, Portugal, Poland, Czechoslovakia, follow the example of the eldest republic, Switzerland, in adhering to Cavour's principle of a 'free church in a free state.' The Russian Soviets, not content to disestablish and disendow the Orthodox Church, are fiercely striving to extirpate all religions and religious ideas.

**Disfranchisement,** *see* ELECTIONS.

**Disinfectants,** agents used to neutralise the action of disease germs with the object of preventing the spread of infectious diseases. There are three classes of substances used to counteract bacterial action, whose functions overlap to some extent; they are antiseptics (*q.v.*), D., and deodorants. Antiseptics act by destroying the germs or neutralising their poisons; deodorants act by disguising the smell or changing the composition of noxious gaseous products without necessarily destroying germs; but D., which are usually applied to clothing, furniture, etc., must, in order to be effective, destroy all germs associated with the disease to be combated. The process of disinfection generally commences with the destruction of organic masses, as excreta and discharges, as soon as possible, and the burning of all inexpensive or much-soiled articles of clothing, and proceeds to subject all articles suspected of contamination to the action of some chemical or physical agent of a germicidal nature. When the articles are placed in a sealed room, an effective disinfecting agent is formalin, which has a particularly penetrative power, but has little action on colouring matter or metals other than iron. The fumes of burning sulphur were formerly much used, but the penetrative power is less than that of formalin, and there is some doubt as to the dry gas being an effective germicide, though vermin are readily destroyed by it. The application of considerable heat is the most effectual method of disinfection known. When applied in the form of hot air there is danger of scorching articles of clothing; but steam, at a temperature of about 120° C. and a

pressure of 5 lb., has no harmful effects on colours and fabrics. Public disinfecting stations have usually two chambers; the clothing, etc., is placed in a cage mounted on wheels so that it can be run from the steam chamber to the drying chamber, where the articles are handled by a different staff and conveyed in different wagons from those connected with the collection of contaminated articles. Liquid D. are used for cleansing articles in constant use in sick-rooms, for treating drains and sinks, etc. The manganates and permanganates of sodium and potassium, chloride of lime, carbolic acid, corrosive sublimate, etc., are used for this purpose. D. lose their power when much diluted, and the vapour of carbolic acid, though its odour gives a sense of security, has no particular germicidal effects.

*Disinfecting Stations.*—By various Acts of Parliament, notably the Public Health Act, 1875, it is incumbent upon sanitary authorities to cleanse and disinfect houses and their contents if they are likely to cause or spread disease. Bedding, clothes, and similar articles which are extremely likely to do this are removed to D. S. and disinfected at the public expense. If necessary they are totally destroyed, in which case compensation is given. The usual agent in D. S. is steam. Local authorities have power to disinfect persons also who through filth, disease, or vermin are a danger and a nuisance to the public.

**Disjunction,** in logic, the relation of the several terms of a disjunctive proposition, which is the statement of alternative possibilities. It is a matter of dispute among logicians whether the disjunctive form necessitates the mutual exclusiveness of the alternate predicates. A disjunctive judgment is one of the form ' A is either B or C,' when either the statement ' A is B ' or ' A is C ' must be true. *See* Welton's *Logic*, II. i. 209.

**Dislocation,** or **Luxation** (loosening), in surgery, the displacement of one bone from another with which it is articulated (commonly called ' putting out of joint '). Usually the result of an accident, but may be caused by disease or be congenital (occurring before birth). Displacements may be partial or complete. They are classified as ' simple ' when the skin is unbroken, ' compound ' when there is a wound. A complicated D. is a displacement of a bone, accompanied by severe local lesion of the soft parts or fracture of the bone. The process of righting a D. is called ' reduction.' Reduction of recent luxations is comparatively easy to doctors, but in old and long-neglected cases it involves an operation which may be followed by bad consequences for the patient. Since the introduction of anæsthetics treatment is much easier. Manipulation has, since 1870, largely replaced the method of traction or extension. Ds. are rare in infancy or old age. They usually take four to six weeks to heal. The shoulder is the joint most frequently dislocated, or the hip in the lower extremity.

**Dismal Swamp,** a large marsh about 500 sq. m. in extent in Virginia and N. Carolina, U.S.A. There are many trees growing there, mostly cypress and cedar trees. It is being gradually reclaimed, canals having been cut through it, the longest of which connects Chesapeake Bay and Albemarle Sound.

**Disna,** or **Dissna,** a tn. of Russia in the Gov. of Minsk, situated at the mouth of the Disna. Pop. 6800.

**Dison,** a tn. of Belgium in the prov. of Liége, with woollen manufactures. Pop. 10,650.

**Disorderly House,** *see* NUISANCE.

**Dispart,** in gunnery, the difference between the radius of the base ring at the breech of the gun and the ring at the swell of the muzzle. An allowance for D. is necessary in determining the beginning of the gradations on the tangent scale. The line which is drawn from the circumference of the base to that of the muzzle is known as the line of metal; the angle subtended by the D. at the base of the gun is equal to that which, in a vertical plane passing through the axis of the bore, would be contained between the latter and the line of metal. A special D. sight, raised in the centre of the gun between the trunnions, is used when the line of metal gives a large D.

**Dispensation,** in a wide sense, may be taken to mean the licence of a sovereign power exempting a particular person from any obligation imposed by the law. The Bill of Rights abrogated the assumption of this power by the crown of England, and though it survives in the shape of the prerogative of pardon and, more indirectly, in acts of indemnity, it is exercised in a strictly constitutional manner. In a narrower technical sense D. means the granting of a licence or the licence itself to do what is forbidden by a canon of the Church, or conversely, to omit something the power ot grant Ds. in the Rom. which is commanded. In the Rom. Catholic Church Ds. may be granted by the legislating authority or any superior authority: thus the Pope, his legates and those deputed by him may dispense from any merely ecclesiastical laws, but not from the divine or natural law, or in such a way as to injure the rights of third persons. A Rom. Catholic bishop may dispense from his own diocesan laws, or under a faculty from the Pope from universal laws of the Church. In England the Archbishop of Canterbury formerly had a considerable dispensing power, but it is now exercised chiefly in the shape of special licences for marriages. Bishops can still grant Ds. to clergymen from the law against holding pluralities and residence way from their parishes.

**Dispersion,** in optics, the decomposition of light into rays of different refrangibility. The light we receive from the sun is commonly called white light, but it can be shown that white light consists of various coloured rays. If a pencil of the sun's rays is allowed to pass through an aperture in the shutter of a dark chamber, it will form an image of the sun on a screen placed to receive it. If, however, a prism of flint glass be interposed horizontally, the ray appears to be spread out and is received on the screen as a series of colours at some distance from the position of the previous image. The explanation is that the light is refracted or bent on entering the glass and again on leaving it, and as some of the components of white light are more easily refrangible than others, they take up different positions on the screen. It is usual to distinguish seven colours: violet, indigo, blue, green, yellow, orange, and red, of which violet is the most refrangible and red the least. When prisms of different materials are used, spectra are formed of different lengths, but having the same colours and usually in the same order. When artificial light is thus dispersed through a prism, all the colours of the spectrum may not be seen; but the colours are found in the solar spectrum, and in the same order. If the artificial light is yellow, for instance, the dominant colour in the spectrum will be yellow; and such colours as blue, indigo, and violet may be very faint or missing altogether. If the light from the dispersing prism is caught on a concave mirror, so that the rays can be brought to a focus again, the combined rays will produce a light similar to that of the source, thus showing that the colours are simply components of the original light. The composition of white light can also be demonstrated by colouring a disc in sectors with the same colours in the same proportions as they appear in the solar spectrum, and then rotating the disc rapidly so that the retina retains the sensation of all the colours at the same time; the result is something approaching to white light.

*Anomalous dispersion.*—Some substances produce spectra in which the colours are seen in unusual positions. If a prism be made enclosing one of the aniline dyes it is found that the extent of refraction is greater for some of the colours of longer wavelength than for colours of shorter wave-length, so that the order of the colours is different from that in an ordinary spectrum. This shows that refrangibility does not necessarily depend upon wave-length, at any rate for substances with special absorptive properties.

**Displacement,** *see* TONNAGE.

**Displayed,** *see* HERALDRY.

**Disposal Board,** formed by the British Gov. shortly after the termination of hostilities in the Great War, in order to liquidate contracts for war supplies and to dispose of surplus war stores, of which there were vast quantities. Lord Inverforth, then Minister of Munitions, was chairman. The idea of evolving a permanent ' Ministry of Supply ' from the Ministry of Munitions was abandoned in 1921, when the latter Ministry was determined as such and its nucleus taken over by the D. B. By 1920 the greater part of the surplus stores had been sold, including some wool valued at £60,000,000, and large dumps of munitions, stores, etc., on the various war fronts. A large quantity of stores, like shells, were broken up for commercial purposes, having no value in their munition form. The total sum received was £350,000,000. After that time, the D. B. became the Disposal and Liquidation Commission under Sir Howard Frank, and existed merely to clear up the remainder of the work.

**Disposition,** in Scots law, is the name given to any writing by which the proprietor of a feu (fief or heritable estate in land), or of a personal right in any property heritable or movable, or of incorporeal heritable property (such as a reversionary right), makes over his property to another. Strictly, the transference of a personal right is specifically known as assignment, in contradistinction to D. Many changes have from time to time been made in the essentials of a form of D. Since the Conveyancing Act, 1874, the customary scheduled form, after the formal parts, assigns the rents and binds the person disposing to relieve the disponee of all feu-duties, casualties (*q.v.*), and public burdens, and to consent to the registration of the D. The creation of a new feu as opposed to transmission of a feu is by charter and not by D. The usual form of family settlements of heritable property in Scotland is by D.

**Disputation,** an exercise of argumentative skill very common in the old universities, a question being raised which some would attack and others defend. Among famous Ds. may be mentioned those between Knox and Kennedy (1562) and Laud and Fisher (1623).

**Disraeli, Benjamin,** *see* BEACONSFIELD.

**D'Israeli, Isaac** (1766–1848), a man of letters, at an early age determined, in spite of parental opposition, to become an author, and in the end, after a severe struggle, he had his way. His first work, a *Defence of Poetry,* in verse, was published in 1790, and in the following year he issued the well-known *Curiosities of Literature.* This was so successful that further volumes were issued by him at different periods of his life, in 1793, 1817, 1823, and 1834. *Calamities of Authors* saw the light in 1812–13, and *Quarrels of Authors* in 1814. Two years later he wrote an *Inquiry into the Literary and Political Character of James I.,* and between 1828 and 1830 he published his *Commentaries on the Life and Reign of Charles I.,* at once his most ambitious and his best work. In 1817, in consequence of a quarrel with the synagogue, D'I. withdrew from the congregation, and in that year he caused his children to be baptised. Many years later, in his *Genius of Judaism,* 1833, he wrote enthusiastically of the Jews in early days, but claimed for himself to have outgrown the superstitious practices still adhered to by his contemporaries. There is a sketch of his life, prefaced to the 1849 edition of the *Curiosities of Literature,* by his son, Benjamin, Earl of Beaconsfield.

**Diss,** a tn. of Norfolk, England, situated on the Waveney, 20 m. S.W. of Norwich. It was formerly noted for the manufacture of worsted and hemp cloth. There are malting works and breweries, also manufactures of brushes, etc. John Skelton, the author, was a native of the town. Pop. 3513.

**Dissection** (cutting apart) is used to represent those processes of separation of the parts of a body which are necessary to show their formation and their relationship to each other. It is, therefore, a branch of Anatomy (*q.v.*), and so one of the divisions of the science of Biology (*q.v.*). Although of great importance in all its branches, it is in connection with human anatomy that it has its greatest value. Democritus and, later, Hippocrates, are supposed to have had some knowledge of D., but Aristotle was the real founder of the art of D., although his work was almost certainly confined to the D. of animals. Erasistratus (250

B.C.) was probably the first to dissect human bodies, performing his work on the bodies of criminals. The progress, however, was slow, owing to the overwhelming prejudice which existed and still exists against the practice of dissecting human bodies. The consequent difficulty in obtaining subjects caused anatomists to have to rely, in the main, upon D. of lower qnimals, but in 1832 the Anatomy Act was passed, which provides that the bodies of unclaimed dead shall be handed over to the medical schools. The practice usually adopted is forcibly to inject a hot mixture of wax or paraffin and vermilion into one of the large blood vessels. Sometimes it is necessary to inject the same liquids into the veins and lymphatics. The body is then kept in preservatives until such times as it is required. In its deeper branches it becomes a most intricate subject, requiring special care and preparation. Under the microscope, by D. and differential staining, etc., it is possible to study the cellular structure of organs. Pathology depends to a great extent upon the study of Ds. of diseased subjects, while surgery and embryology are also deeply indebted to D. *See* ANATOMY, VIVISECTION.

**Disseisin,** *see* SEISIN.

**Dissenters,** *see* NONCONFORMITY.

**Dissepiment, or Septum,** the term applied in botany to the partitions in the inside of a fruit formed by the union of the sides of its constituent carpels. A false or spurious D. is sometimes formed by growths on the inner surface, *e.g.* in Astragalus.

**Dissociation,** in chemistry, is the term applied to the reversible decomposition of a substance by heat. Thus nitrogen peroxide has the formula $N_2O_4$ at ordinary temperatures, but on heating it splits up into molecules of $NO_2$; these recombine on cooling, forming $N_2O_4$ again : $N_2O_4 \rightleftharpoons 2NO_2$. To indicate the reversibility of the change the reversed arrows $\rightleftharpoons$ or $\leftarrow$ are used instead of the sign of equality $=$. At high temperatures, water-vapour dissociates into hydrogen and oxygen: $2H_2O = 2H_2O + O_2$. Similarly ammonium chloride vapour is found not to consist of $NH_4Cl$ molecules but of a mixture of ammonia, $NH_3$, and hydrochloric acid, HCl, dissociation having taken place : $NH_4Cl \rightleftharpoons NH_2 + HCl$. If dissociation results in the formation of an increased number of molecules, increase of pressure hinders D. If, however, there is no increase in the number of molecules, pressure is without effect, as, for example, in the action $2HI \rightleftharpoons H_2 + I_2$, the dissociation of hydrogen iodide.

Electrolytric D. refers to the splitting up of electrolytes into charged ions when dissolved in water or some other solvent. Thus sodium chloride, when dissolved in water, splits up reversibly into sodium ions (positively charged) and chlorine ions (negatively charged) : $NaCl \rightleftharpoons Na^+ + Cl^-$.

**Dissonance,** *see* MUSIC.

**Distaff,** a stick or staff, to which material for spinning, as cotton, flax, etc., was fixed, in the method of spinning by hand. The D. was held under the left arm, and the fibres, as they were drawn from it, were spirally twisted with the right hand. During the process of spinning, the thread was wound round a revolving reel.

**Distemper** (Fr. *détrempe*, It. *tempera*), originally any fluid medium for mixing with pigments, later restricted to glutinous substances, such as size, white or yolk of egg, gum-water, fig-tree sap, honey, etc. The pigments were ground up with these and water and applied to a smooth surface of dry plaster (not damp as in the case of frescoes), usually spread on wood or canvas. D. painting was known in Egypt, Babylon, and Nineveh very early, and used by the Greeks for interior decoration. Till replaced by the oils of the Van Eycks, it was the ordinary method of painting in the highest departments of art. In Italy its use continued till 1500, and early Flemish artists constantly employed it. When treated with oil-varnish such paintings are hard to distinguish from oils. They are precise in form and outline, and the rapid drying of the colours prevents blending of tints. It is still used for scene-painting and in preparing wall-paper. *See* Hamerton, *Graphic Arts*, 1882 ; Pereira, *Leitfaden für de Tempera malerei*, 1893.

**Distich,** *see* METRE.

**Distillation,** a process which consists of converting a solid or liquid substance into the gaseous form and afterwards condensing the vapours to a liquid form, in order to purify the substance or separate its components. The process was known to the ancients, who devised ingenious forms of apparatus. The essential parts of a distilling apparatus are a retort or still, in which the substance to be distilled is heated to vaporisation, a condenser, in which the vapours are cooled to a liquid form, and a receiver, in which the condensed liquid, or ' distillate,' is collected. The temperature at which a substance boils depends upon the pressure exerted upon it, and therefore it is necessary, in the case of liquids which decompose at a temperature below their boiling-point, to reduce the pressure so that they may boil at a suitable temperature. The simplest form of distilling apparatus consists of a glass retort communicating with a receiving flask by a straight tube gently sloping downwards and enclosed by a wider tube through which cold water is run, entering at the lowest point and leaving at the highest. To present a larger surface to the cooling action of the water, the condenser is often flattened or twisted into a spiral form, or ' worm.' A long, wide glass tube or air condenser may be used for liquids with high boiling points.

Another method sometimes employed is that of *Steam D.* Thus aniline, a liquid which boils at 184° C. under atmospheric pressure, if mixed with water and heated, distils off

DISTILLATION
(From a sixteenth century book)

together with water, when steam is passed through the mixture, and by condensing the mixed vapours, the two immiscible constituents aniline and water are obtained. This method is particularly useful for the purification of tarry and dirty preparations in which one of the components happens to be volatile in steam.

Fractional distillation is a process which aims at separating components of the original liquid which have different boiling-points. This is achieved by using a dephlegmating column (*see* DEPHLEGMATOR). In the distillation of coal tar, the dehydrated material is heated in a wrought-iron cylinder fitted with a thermometer, and the vapours are condensed in cast-iron cooling-pipes laid so as to have a continuous fall to the receivers. As the process continues,

the temperature rises and the less volatile substances are driven off until only the pitch remains as residue. The distillate is collected in fractions at different stages of the process, and such substances as ' first runnings,' ' light oil,' ' middle oil,' and ' heavy oil ' are differentiated. These are afterwards separately fractionated. The distillation of alcohol from a malt wort is an important stage in the preparation of whisky (*see* COFFEY'S STILL). The distillation of sea-water to procure water for drinking purposes is of importance in considering the equipment of ships, and all big liners carry apparatus for this purpose.

In large-scale operations two types of D. are employed, the continuous and the discontinuous. In the continuous method the liquid to be distilled is fed into the still at a constant rate as D. proceeds, and conditions are so arranged that the cooling of the vapours and the heating of the liquid in the still are carried out at as steady a rate as possible. By the continuous method, large amounts of material can be dealt with. In the discontinuous method, which is more suitable for small-scale operations, the distillation of a quantity of liquid is allowed to proceed until it is at an end. The process may then be repeated with fresh supplies of material. The method has the advantage that plant construction is simple, and costs are relatively low. (BIBLIOGRAPHY : Young, *Distillation Principles and Processes.*)

**Distinguished Conduct Medal** (D.C.M.), awarded to warrant officers, non-commissioned officers and men of the regular army.

**Distinguished Flying Cross** (D.F.C.), instituted in 1918 as a decoration for officers and warrant officers in the Royal Air Force for acts of gallantry when flying in active operations against the enemy. The Air Force Cross (A.F.C.), 1918, was instituted for bestowal to personnel as in the case of the D.F.C., but for acts of courage or devotion to duty when flying, although not in active operations against the enemy. The Disting. Flying Medal (D.F.M.), 1918, and the Air Force Medal (A.F.M.) were designed for warrant officers and non-commissioned officers for equivalent services as for the D.F.C. and A.F.C. respectively.

**Distinguished Service Cross** was instituted in 1914 in substitution for the Conspicuous Service Cross 1901 for bestowal on all officers of the navy below the rank of lieutenant-commander and on warrant officers.

**Distinguished Service Medal** was

instituted in 1914 for chief petty officers, men and boys of all branches of the Royal Navy and for non-commissioned officers and men of the Royal Marine artillery, and for all other personnel holding corresponding positions in the service afloat, for distinguished conduct in the Great War.

**Distinguished Service Order.** This order was instituted by royal warrant on Sept. 6, 1886. It is an order of military merit and was founded in order to recognise special services of officers in the army and navy. It has only one class, and holders of this order carry after their names the letters D.S.O. Its numbers are unlimited, and the companions of the order rank next in precedence after the companions of the fourth class of the Royal Victorian Order. The decoration itself consists of a white and gold cross with a red enamelled centre which bears the imperial crown surrounded by a laurel wreath. *See also* DECORATIONS.

**Distomum,** *see* LIVER-FLUKE.

**Distress,** the taking of goods or cattle out of the possession of a wrong-doer into the custody of the party injured, for the purpose of procuring satisfaction for the wrong committed. The most usual injury for which a D. may be taken is that of non-payment of rent. But the remedy may also be resorted to for the payment of taxes, rates, and duties, as well as to obtain compensation for damage done by cattle wandering over one's grounds. As between landlord and tenant a D. cannot lawfully be made after the tenant tenders to his landlord the full amount of the arrears. Various statutes and judicial decisions have resulted in the exemption of a large number of things from D. Some of these are *absolutely* privileged, *e.g.* fixtures; things in actual use; wearing apparel and bedding of the tenant, of his family, and the tools of his trade to the value of £5; machines used in cotton, woollen, and silk manufactures; goods delivered to the tenant in the way of his trade; and, in the case of tenants under the Agricultural Holdings Act, hired machinery and breeding stock. Some things, like the tools of a man's trade beyond £5 in value, are privileged only if there be other sufficient distrainable goods on the premises. By an Act passed in 1908 the goods of an under-tenant who pays a rent equal to the full annual value of the premises or part of the premises occupied by him are exempt from D. for the rent due from his lessor to the superior landlord; and by the same Act the goods of a lodger and those of any other person not being a tenant of the premises, or having any beneficial interest in any tenancy of the premises or any part thereof, are also exempt from D. in respect of the rent due from the tenant to his landlord. Goods comprised in a hire-purchase agreement (except in the case of machinery on an agricultural holding) or in a bill of sale belonging to the husband or wife of a tenant, are not exempt from D. No D. can be taken until the day following the day on which rent is made payable, and it must be taken between sunrise and sunset. No previous demand for the arrears is necessary in the absence of express agreement to that effect. Under the National Insurance Act, 1924, D. must be postponed in the case of a tenant who is an insured person where a doctor certifies that a D. would endanger his life. D. is usually levied through a certificated bailiff armed with a D. warrant. Goods distrained may be sold at the end of five days, and after notice to the tenant.

**Distribution,** *see* ECONOMICS.

**Distribution, Statutes of.** The first statute of distribution, which was passed in 1641, settles the disposition of an intestate's effects providing for the distribution of the residue after payment of debts among the next of kin. It applies only to personalty. The Act is in many respects declaratory of the previous rules and practice of the old ecclesiastical courts. These courts tried to force the administrator or 'best friend' of the intestate to distribute the residue among the next of kin, but were stopped by writs of prohibition from the common law (*q.v.*) courts. The result, until the passing of the statute, was that the administrator appropriated the residue to his own use. The result of the statutory provisions of this statute (22, 23 Car. II., c. 10) and the amending Act (1 Jac. II., c. 17) is that the widow (if any) of the intestate takes one-third where he also leaves children or descendants of children, the latter taking the remaining two-thirds. Where there are no children or descendants of children, the widow (if any) takes one-half and the crown one-half, but, under the Intestates' Estates Act, 1890, the widow takes the whole estate both real and personal if her husband dies without issue and the estate is under £500 in value; if it exceeds that value she is entitled not only to £500 rateably out of the realty and personalty before any distribution is made, but also to her one-half of the residue. The Act of 1890 applies only where a man dies without making a will, and not, as do the S. of D., to cases of partial intestacy also. Where the intestate dies leaving children and no descendants of any deceased child, the children take equally *per capita* (individually); if there are descendants of deceased children, the descendants take the share that would have gone to their parents; but where all the children are dead, leaving descendants, these latter take *per stirpes* (*i.e.* by representation). For example, if A and B, the children, and D, the child of B, all predeceased the intestate, leaving after the intestate's death C, the child of A, F and G, the children of D, and E the child of B—C takes one-half, E one-quarter, *i.e.* one-half the share B would have got, while F and G share the remaining one-quarter. Where there are no children or descendants of any child and no widow, the father takes the whole. If no widow, children or descendants of children, or father, the mother and brothers and sisters take equally, the descendants of a deceased brother or sister take their parent's share. If no brother or sister, or descendant of a brother or sister, the mother, if alive, takes the whole; and if the mother be dead, the brothers and sisters, or children of brothers and sisters, take the whole *per stirpes*. The children of deceased brothers and sisters take equally as next of kin with uncles and aunts where the mother and all the brothers and sisters are dead. If none of the above are living, nor nephews or nieces, the whole of the next of kin in the same degree of relationship from the intestate share equally, their descendants having no right of representation. The husband of a married woman is entitled to such of his wife's estate as is undisposed of. The earlier statute also provides that a child or other issue who has already received from the intestate in his lifetime an estate by settlement, or been advanced any sum by way of portion, is entitled to nothing unless he brings such estate or advancement into account as part satisfaction of his share. This does not apply to real estate devolving on the heir at law. The rights of a widow may likewise be altered by a prior settlement, whether ante-nuptial or post-nuptial, but she will not have to bring any sum or estate into account unless there is an express proviso to that effect. The S. of D. and the Intestates' Estates Act, 1890, extend to the whole of the United Kingdom.

**Distribution of Animals and Plants,** *see* GEOGRAPHICAL DISTRIBUTION.

**Distribution of Electricity,** *see* ELECTRICITY.

**Distribution of Terms** In formal logic, by 'distribution' of a term is simply meant 'taking it universally,'

or referring to all parts of it. In the 'opposition of propositions,' the 'universal negative' *distributes* its predicate, whereas the universal affirmative and particular affirmative do not. These distinctions are important, because the validity of any argument or syllogism will usually depend on the sufficient distribution of the terms occurring in it. In 'conversion of propositions,' *i.e.* in the transposition of subject and predicate, no term must be distributed in the Converse unless it was distributed in the Convertend, *e.g.* the converse of 'all metals are elements' is not 'all elements are metals,' but 'some elements are metals'; but that of 'no metals are compounds,' is 'no compounds are metals,' because, in this latter example, all the terms are distributed.

**Distributism.** The political faith of the Distributist League, whose chief protagonists are Mr. G. K. Chesterton (*q.v.*) and Mr. Hilaire Belloc (*q.v.*). The purpose of the League is the 'restoration of liberty by the distribution of property,' and the primary principles of D. are thus stated by Mr. Chesterton: '(1) That the only way to preserve liberty is to preserve property; that the individual and the family may be in some degree independent of oppressive systems, official or un-official; (2) that the only way to preserve property is to distribute it much more equally among the citizens; that all, or approximately all, may understand and defend it. This can only be done by breaking up the great plutocratic concentration of our time.' The policy of the League is to form nation-wide branches or groups for the discussion of the practical application of these principles, and, as immediate means to its ends, it advocates the destruction of the Press monopoly; increasing the areas of uncultivated lands available for small holdings; and the public audit of the secret party funds. The official organ of the league is *G. K's. Weekly*, and its offices, 2 Little Essex Street, Strand, London.

**Ditchfield, Peter Hampson** (1854–1930), English author; *b.* April 20, 1854, at Westhoughton, Lancashire; eldest son of Peter Ditchfield. English editor of *Magazine of Christian Art* (Philadelphia), 1907. His publications are numerous and varied, some being: *Our English Villages*, 1890; *Old English Sports and Customs*, 1891; *The Manor Houses of England*, 1910; *Cathedrals of Great Britain*; *Cottages and Village Life of Rural England*, 1912; *Oxfordshire*, 1912; *London Survivals*, 1914; *The*

*Village Church*, 1915 ; *The England of Shakespeare*, 1917 ; *By-Ways in Berkshire and Cotswolds*, 1920 ; *The Story of the City Companies of London*, 1926. Died at Barkham.

**Dithmarschen, or Ditmarsh, North and South**, a region in Germany, forming W. of Holstein, prov. of Schleswig-Holstein. It is low and marshy, giving rise to malarial fever, but has dykes to prevent inroads of the sea. Incorporated in Holstein, 1559 ; annexed to Prussia, 1866. Pop. 98,000. *See* Volkmar, *Geschichte des Landes Dithmarschen*, 1851 ; Nitzsch, *Das alte Dithmarschen*, 1862.

**Dithyrambus** (διθύραμβος), originally a surname of Dionysus (Bacchus) of uncertain etymology, later applied to a hymn sung in his honour to the accompaniment of flute or lyre, together with a dance around the altar. The subject was usually the birth and life of Dionysus, later other themes were added. The artistic choral or antistrophic form was supposed to have been developed out of the earlier passionate hymns for one or more singers by Arion at Corinth (or possibly Naxos, *c.* 620 B.C.). Out of the mournful dithyrambs rose the grand ancient Greek tragedy. At Athens there are yearly contests between dithyrambic choruses (usually fifty men, dressed as satyrs, representing Dionysus' companions) at the Greater and Lesser Dionysia, Panathenæa, and other great festivals. The prize was an ox, later a tripod. Though they flourished till after Aristotle's time, but few fragments remain. Pindar was said to have been trained by Lasus of Hermione. This lofty and vehement style of lyric poetry degenerated later into bombastic extravagance, and ' dithyramb ' was applied somewhat contemptuously to any lyric of unrestrained frenzy and excitement, such as might be written during intoxication. The nearest approaches to dithyrambic verse in English are Leigh Hunt's translation of Redi's *Baccho in Toscana*, c. 17 ; Dryden, *Alexander's Feast*, 1698 ; still better examples being the *Bacchic Songs of the Swedish Bellman*, 1791.

**Dittany**, the name applied to plants of various orders, the word being derived from a Cretan mountain on which they flourish. Both the D. of Crete, *Origanum dictamnus*, and the D. of the United States, *Cunila Mariana*, are members of the order Labiatæ, but the bastard common D., *Dictamnus albus*, also known as fraxinella, belongs to the Rutaceæ.

**Dittersbach, or Starsow**, a small tn. of Prussia, situated about 40 m. W. of Olmutz, with coal mines in the vicinity. Pop. 9000.

**Dittersdorf, Karl Dittersvon** (1739–95), Austrian composer and violinist, *b.* Neuhaus, studied under Ziegler and Bonno, and soon became one of the leading violinists of his time. In 1761–4 he was in the Court orchestra at Vienna. Contemporary with and of the same school as Mozart, his works were overshadowed by those of the latter composer. Wrote a score of operettas, mostly humorous, the best known of which are ' Doctor and Apotheker' (1756) ; ' Liebe im Narrenhaus ' (1757) ; ' Hieronymus Knicker ' (1757) ; oratorios, 'Isaak' (1767) and 'Esther' (1773). A number of his instrumental works have been republished in recent years. Also published *Die Grenzen d. Komisch u. Heroisch. in d. Musik* (' The limits of heroic-comedy in music ') and other essays. Memoirs : Krebs, 1900, and Riedinger, 1914.

**Ditton, Humphrey** (1675–1715), an English mathematician. He studied theology, and was a dissenting minister at Tonbridge for some years. He owed his election as mathematical master at Christ's Hospital to the influence of Sir Isaac Newton. William Whiston and he invented a method for discovering longitude which was approved by Sir Isaac Newton.

**Diu**, a Portuguese island at Gujerat, India. It is 7 m. long, and resembles a part of the coast to which it runs parallel. The town of D., situated at the E. end of the island, is surrounded by a wall, and is mostly in ruins. Formerly it was of considerable commercial importance. In 1535 it came into the possession of the Portuguese. It was occupied by the Arabs of Muscab in 1670 and retaken by the Portuguese in 1717, and is now of no importance. Pop. 13,000.

**Diuretics**, medicinal agents which stimulate an increased flow of urine. This is often desirable when from any cause the supply of urine is diminished, or when it is required to promote increased excretion to carry off morbid products circulating in the blood, or, as in dropsy, to aid in the removal of watery collections. Ordinary water, taken in large quantities, is an effective D. Digitalis and squill act by stimulating the heart movements and causing an increased blood pressure. Alcohol, turpentine, and cantharides stimulate the kidneys, but their irritating action renders their use inadvisable. Caffeine acts both as a cardiac stimulant and as a renal stimulant, and is a particularly effective diuretic.

**Divan** (Arabic, *dīwān*), a Persian word, common to many Oriental languages, meaning muster-roll, counting-house, register of payments (cf. Fr. *douane*, custom-house), council, court of justice, sofa. In the sense of a 'collection of poems' Goethe used it in his 'West-östolicher Diwan,' and the Persians spoke of the D. of Saadi or Hafiz. The Turkish D. is the great council or supreme judicial tribunal of the empire ('Divani humayun' at Constantinople). The word dates from the caliphate of Omar (A.D. 634–44). In the sense of low, cushioned seats or sofas, ranged against the walls as in Eastern reception-rooms, for which

DIVER
(*Colymbus glacialis*)

it was also commonly used, it became known in Europe in the eighteenth century. Ds. were especially fashionable about 1820–50. *See* Von Kremer, *Culturgeschichte des Orients*, i.

**Diver**, *see* DIVING.

**Divergency, Divergent** (in mathematics), *see* SERIES.

**Divers**, or *Colymbidæ*, the name of a family of water-birds which forms with *Podicipedidæ*, the grebes, the tribe Colymbiformes The species are all marine, with short tail-feathers and webbed feet. During the breeding period they live inland and the female lays two eggs which hatch into down-covered chicks. The Brit. species are the inconspicuous *C. septentrionalis*, or red-throated D.; *C. glacialis*, the great northern D.; *C.*

*Adamsi*, the white-billed northern D.; and *C. arcticus*, the black-throated D. The birds inhabit the temperate regions of both N. hemispheres.

**Dives**, the name of the rich man spoken of by Christ in His parable of the rich man and Lazarus in Luke xvi.

**Dives-sur-Mer**, a watering-place of North-Western France, in the dept. of Calvados, and situated on the Dives, 15 m. N.E. of Caen and 8 m. S.W. of Deauville. Formerly it was an important seaport, and it has houses of the fourteenth and fifteenth centuries. William the Conqueror sailed from here in 1066 for England. Pop. 4235.

**Dividend** (Lat. *dividendus*), literally a sum or quantity to be divided, especially applied in commerce to the annual or half-yearly interest payable on public funds or the National Debt, and on some other loans and debentures. The profits of joint-stock companies (banking, railway companies, and others), paid periodically to each stockholder or shareholder, are also called 'dividends.' They are usually fixed at a certain rate per cent. In the case of 'cumulative dividends' it is agreed that, if at any time they are not paid in full, the difference shall be added to the following payment. D. is also the term applied to the sum of money apportioned to creditors from the realised assets of a bankrupt's estate. It may mean either the whole sum divided or the proportion or share falling to each creditor. These Ds. are commonly reckoned at so much per pound of the claims (as 8s. in the £1).

**Dividing Range**, *see* AUSTRALIA.

**Divi-divi**, or *Cæsalpinia coriaria*, a species of Leguminosæ which occurs in S. America and the W. Indies. The pods are of economic importance, being used in tanning.

**Divination** (Lat. *divinatio*), the art of obtaining the knowledge of future things by some supernatural means, or by some system outside the ordinary bounds of reason. D. was generally regarded in the classical world as the revelation of the gods, though it was sometimes argued that divine revelation was not essential. Roughly, methods of D. may be divided into two classes, those in which some particular objects are made use of, as in the case of astrology and those in which the divine will is revealed directly to the human spirit, as in the case of dreams. Perhaps *astrology* would rank first among these methods. It pretends to tell, by the relations of the stars, the futures of states and individuals. It reached its highest stage about the seventeenth century. The system of D. by dreams (*oneiromancy*) is extremely ancient, and has been received by Christian, Pagan, and Jew. The dreams may be interpreted either literally or by contraries. The casting of lots (*sortilège*) was common in ancient times, and has survived now merely as an appeal to blind chance. A somewhat similar method is that of *bibliomancy*, by which a book is opened at hazard and some one or two lines selected at random. These lines are supposed capable of interpretation so as to give advice for the future. Of this kind were the *sortes virgilianæ*. In the case of *haruspication*, or the examination of entrails, the proceedings are far more elaborate, as the institution of the Rom. College of Augurs shows. The time and all the incidental circumstances must be propitious before a good result can be obtained. In the case of D. by *augury* and *omens* this is not so necessary. *Pyromancy* is a method of D. from the behaviour of fire, somewhat similar to the modern examination of tea leaves. *Crystallomancy* makes use of concentration of the mind induced by crystal gazing. *Cheiromancy* or *palmistry* pretends to tell the future of an individual by the lines of his hand, and has long been the prerogative of the gipsy race.

**Divine Right**, the principal insisted upon by James I. of Eng. and carried to extremes by the supporters of his son. The Stuarts set forth that they were the direct representatives of the Deity, and as such were to receive the obedience due to God's viceroy on earth. They themselves owed obedience to Him alone, and were relieved from all responsibilities towards their subjects. Charles I.'s claim to this D. R. was the direct cause of the royalist and parliamentary struggles of the seventeenth century. The idea did not really lose its hold until after the suppression of the rebellion of 1745 in Eng., and till the great Revolution in France. The doctrine was supported by Sir Robert Filmer in Eng., and in a modified degree by Bossuet in *Politique tirée de l'Ecriture Sainte*. It was opposed by Locke in his *Discourses on Civil Government*, and by J. J. Rousseau, *Contrat Social*. See Figgis, *The Divine Right of Kings*, and MacKinnon's *Growth and Decline of the French Monarchy*.

**Diving.** In Indian seas the art of D. has been practised from very early times. Before the introduction of mechanical aids, D. was the only means, of obtaining the pearls, sponges, and corals to be found in such oceans, and there is no doubt that great skill was shown by the natives. When all allowances are made, however, slightly over three minutes is the limit of time during which a naked diver can remain under water. Persons who habitually engage in D. suffer severely from the constant strain on the lungs. The attention of inventors was very early turned to the discovery of some means by which the diver could remain longer under water. The earliest invention was the D. bell, of which the principle is very simple. If an inverted jar be sunk in a vessel of water, the air contained therein excludes the water from the interior. Since air is compressible the water gradually rises up the sides of the jar as the depth of water increases; so that at a depth of 33 ft. the air would

[*Topical Press*

A RECENTLY DESIGNED STEEL
ARMOUR DIVING SUIT

Note the clamps at the diver's sides and the electric lights on his shoulders.

be compressed into half its original bulk. The D. bells of the first makers were strong, heavy vessels, generally formed of wood girded with iron hoops. The great drawback to these early forms of D. bells was that they had to be raised to the surface at frequent intervals for fresh supplies of air, and consequently their sphere of utility was very limited. Dr. Halley, the secretary of the Royal Society, communicated a paper to that society in 1720 proposing a plan to use two barrels of about 36 gallons each, with a hole in the bottom, and fitted with a leather hose to supply air. Though this marked an improvement, much time was still lost in sending fresh supplies of air vessels down. It was not, however, until

1778 that Smeaton devised a type of bell which contained all the elements of the present appliances. In repairing the shoeing of Hexham Bridge, Smeaton contrived a bell to which he attached a force-pump; this was the first time that the force-pump had been used for such a purpose. The modern D. bell is usually of a rectangular shape, and weighs about five tons. The air-supply pipe, connected with a force-pump, is screwed on to the top, which is supplied with windows of thick glass; the bell is fitted with seats inside, and is worked in water up to a depth of 35 ft. The invention of the D. dress was very gradual, and many persons contributed something to it, but Siebe did more than any other to improve it. In 1829 he invented the ' open ' D. dress, which consisted of a helmet and waterproof jacket. The air pumped in at the helmet was allowed to escape below the jacket, and hence it was called ' open.' The great drawback to this dress was that it obliged the diver to remain in an upright or gently stooping posture. Siebe accordingly invented the close dress in 1857, and this type is now in general use. It consists of a waterproof costume of strong twill and india-rubber, covering the whole body except the head and hands. The helmet is made of tinned copper, and fitted with three strong plate-glass windows in front. The middle eyepiece is made so that it can be unscrewed, in case the diver wishes to speak or rest without removing his helmet. The air is supplied from a pump by means of a vulcanised india-rubber pipe which is attached to an inlet valve in the back of the helmet ; the outlet valve is also fixed to the back. The escape valve is in some patterns regulated by the diver, but more commonly if an adjustable valve is desired, a self-righting pattern is used. A life line is attached to the diver's waist for signalling purposes. The boots of a diver are heavily weighted, with leaden soles, and weigh about 20 lb. each ; additional weights are attached to the shoulders when required. The Great War gave a strong impetus to D., as many of the ships that were sunk by submarines contained gold and other valuables estimated in some cases to be worth millions of pounds. Where these vessels lay upon a sea-bed that was not in very deep water and in places easily located the divers have been remarkably successful, sometimes recovering practically the whole of the lost treasure. The difficulties of the work were such that dependence on air from above was not desirable, and an apparatus was used that enabled the diver to re-purify the air by carrying oxygen, stored in bottles, which made him independent of outer supplies. Up till the War the lowest depth at which a diver had been able to work was about 200 feet, and even from this depth it was necessary to the ascend by slow and tedious stages, if he would avoid ill effects ; but recently Neufeldt and Fuhnke of Kiel, Ger., have invented a diving dress capable of standing the pressure of 25 atmospheres, in which divers have already worked at as great a depth as 515 feet, and for which it is claimed that their tasks can be carried on at as low a depth as 750 feet. The principle of this dress is that the terrible pressure of such depths comes on the shell in which the man works, and not upon the man himself. Within this envelope of steel and aluminium, the worker breathes easily the air that is renewed by oxygen, and when he ascends there is no need for him to wait for long periods below sea-level in order to prepare himself for lessened atmospheric pressure.

**Diving Bell,** see DIVING.

**Diving Rod** (known also as Virgula Divina, Baculus Divinatorius, Caduceus or Mercury's wand, Aaron's rod, etc.) is a forked branch usually of hazel or rowan, or sometimes artificially made, or a Y-shaped metallic rod (iron, brass, or copper), by means of which it was formerly supposed that water or minerals could be discovered beneath the earth's surface. The rod was suspended by its two prongs (often between the balls of the thumbs), and, held thus in front of the holder, was thought to twist or quiver suddenly when the exact spot was reached, bending down towards the concealed mine or spring. This superstition is very old ; Agricola, Sperlingius, and Kirchmayer all believed in the occult powers of the magic wand. Another use was to discover the authors of a crime, as used by Jacques Aymer in the case of murder and robbery at Lyons, 1692. Even at the close of the nineteenth century Cornish miners and even a few Eng. civic officials still clung to this superstition. It has at times been believed in, even by people possessing some scientific knowledge. See Bayle's *Dictionary* under 'Abaris'; *Gent. Mag.,* Nov. 1751 ; Cowley, *Pindaric Odes* ; Dr. Mayo, *On the Truth Contained in Popular Superstitions,* 1847, 1851 ; Chevreul, *De la Baguette Divinatoire,* 1854 ; Lang's *Custom and Myth,* 1884 ; Barrett in *Proc. Soc. Psychical Research,* 1897.

**Divinity,** see THEOLOGY.

**Division: (1)** A mode of finding how many times one number is contained in another. (2) A unit of the army which contains all branches of the service, and which is usually under the command of a general. The name is also applied to other sections of the army, but in general use its name implies as above. It may also be regarded as a section of the army which is capable of acting independently of the rest of the army. Its numbers, whilst theoretically fixed, differ very considerably under the conditions of active service. Three infantry Ds. are united together to form the chief basis of an army corps. An infantry D. consists roughly of 350 officers, 10,000 men, 2100 horses, 20 guns, and 400 wagons. The troops are provided with rations for three days and forage for the horses for two days. The name, as has been pointed out above, is given to other sections of the army. Two brigades of cavalry, or at home four, are called a cavalry D. The name is applied to a lieutenant's command in the artillery, and the garrison artilley of the whole country was grouped into divisions, which comprised regulars, special reserve, and territorials under the new territorial scheme. These divisions were formed in the military districts into which the whole of the country is divided. The term D. applies also to the navy. The fleet is divided up into two or more Ds., each of which in turn is divided into subdivisions. Each subdivision is commanded by a flag-officer.

**Division of Labour :** 1. In political economy a phrase used by Adam Smith, and since become current, to denote the separation of the aggregate labour necessary to produce any one complete manufacture into various distinct processes, and the assignment of each of the processes to a different labourer or body of labourers. D. of L. may be said historically to have begun with the specialisation of industry, or the earliest separation of different trades and employments from one another. The modern application of the term D. of L. to the specialisation of processes, as distinct from specialisation of industries, is no more than an extension of the same essential conditions. The effect of D. of L. is a proportional increase in production, the great increase of the quantity of work, which the same number of people are capable of performing, being by Adam Smith referred to three causes : (1) The increase of dexterity in every particular workman ; (2) the saving of time which would be lost by passing from one kind of work to another ; and (3) the invention of many labour-saving devices or machinery by reason of workmen becoming thoroughly familiarised with their own particular operations ; to which has been added (4) remuneration of different agents at different rates in lieu of paying for the easy and difficult labour at an equal rate, a result which would follow from all the work being done by one man. But there are many serious contervailing disadvantages : (1) Deadening of the faculties from their constant concentration on a single operation, involving as a corollary the inadaptability of the average workman to any other form of work; (2) the impairment of the physique of workmen, due partly to monotony of work, and partly to the herding together of great numbers of operatives in large industrial centres. But the passing of the Factory Acts, the collective action of trades unions in securing an amelioration of the conditions of labour, and, in a less degree, to private munificence of particular employers in the provision of healthful dwellings, has in a measure counteracted the physical drawbacks of D. of L. *See* Babbage, *The Economy of Machinery and Manufactures.* 2. In biology the physiological D. of L. in the organs of the same individual body, with an accompanying diversification of structure. In the protozoa, or most primitive animals, there is no D. of L., the individual being composed of one vital unit or cell, which consequently performs all the various functions of motion, nutrition, propagation, etc. In the second cardinal division of the animal kingdom, the metazoa or multicellular animals, the lowest forms contain at least two sets of cells, each adapted to the performance of distinct functions, and consequently there is at least a binary D. of L. Higher in the scale the subdivision becomes even greater, until all the essential functions are performed by different organs.

**Divorce,** the dissolution of the bonds of marriage by legal process. By Eng. law, prior to the Matrimonial Causes Act, 1857, the actual dissolution of the marriage tie, a D. *a vinculo matrimonii,* could only be obtained by Act of Parliament, and the courts could only grant a decree of judicial separation, *a mensa et thoro, i.e.* from board and bed, such as had formerly been granted by the ecclesiastical courts. Decrees of nullity, however, could be granted. The division of the Supreme Court of Justice, known as the Probate, Admiralty, and Divorce Court, has jurisdiction in all matrimonial matters, and can grant decrees in suits for D., judicial separation, nullity, and restitution of conjugal rights. The grounds on which a D. can be granted in Eng. law are : adultery on the part of the husband or wife ; on the part of the husband, adultery combined with cruelty, or with desertion for two years and over; adultery if with a woman whom he could not legally marry; adultery and bigamy; unnatural offences, and rape. Parties may legally marry again after a decree of D. is made absolute, *i.e.* six months after the decree nisi has been pronounced, if the king's proctor has not successfully intervened on the ground of collusion, etc. The parties may not marry if a decree for judicial separation only is granted. This may be granted for husband or wife on the ground of adultery, desertion, cruelty separately. Cruelty, in the eyes of the law, must involve danger to life, limb, or health, bodily or mental, or reasonable fear or danger of such. Desertion is wilful and persistent absenting from the wife's society against her wish. A petition for restitution of conjugal rights may be brought by a wife or husband if the other has withdrawn from cohabitation without proper cause. A disobedience to a decree for restitution amounts to desertion. The court *will* refuse a decree for ' connivance,' *i.e.* if adultery is known by the plaintiff and allowed to continue without attempt to stop it, ' condonation,' knowledge of the fact and forgiveness, or ' collusion,' an agreement not to oppose a D. without putting all the facts before the court, or where money passes to prevent the whole facts coming out, The court *may* refuse, on disclosure of the petitioner's adultery or cruelty, unreasonable desertion, misconduct, etc., leading to the adultery, delay in bringing the suit. A suit for nullity of marriage may be brought for impotence, which must be proved to have existed before marriage and to have continued ; where through fraud or doubt there has been absence of consent to the marriage ; where the marriage is within the prohibited degrees of affinity; a bigamous marriage, proof being given of a valid first marriage. Separation orders may be made (Summary Jurisdiction Act, 1895) by courts of summary jurisdiction after conviction of the husband for aggravated assault, for desertion, persistent cruelty, neglect of maintenance, resulting in living apart and (Licensing Act, 1902) habitual drunkenness. In Scotland, adultery or desertion for four years is a ground for divorce for either party, and a party may not marry the person with whom adultery

has been committed. In 1909 a Royal Commission was appointed to enquire into the law and its administration in regard to matrimonial causes, especially as to prohibitive costs, etc., as far as they affected the poorer classes. The report was issued in 1912 (*see* Report Cd. 6478). The principal recommendations of the Majority Report were : (1) The equality of both sexes in grounds for D.; (2) inclusion of insanity and epilepsy, and other special named causes, if unknown at marriage, as grounds for nullity; (3) powers of ordering a presumption of death, rendering a new marriage valid; (4) restriction by the court of publication of reports of matrimonial causes; (5) easier methods of suing *in forma pauperis*; (6) new grounds for D. to be desertion for three years, cruelty, incurable insanity lasting five years, habitual drunkenness for three years after separation order, commutation of a sentence of death to imprisonment. Legislative effect has been given to some of these recommendations. D. law and practice of Great Britain have been profoundly changed in the last decade, partly by Acts of Parliament pursuant to the removal of sex disqualification and partly through the operation of judicial decisions. The most revolutionary change was that effected by the Matrimonial Causes Act of 1923. Popularly known as the Entwhistle Act, which enabled a wife to obtain a decree of dissolution *a mensa et thoro* on the ground of adultery alone, thus placing the sexes on an equality in that respect. The Act was repealed and re-enacted in 1925 by the Judicature Consolidation Act, the effect of which legislation is to alter the procedure where the wife is the petitioner, by abolishing the necessity for petitioning in the first instance for the restitution of conjugal rights, a preliminary which involved a clumsy fiction. In 1926 an Act was passed to make unlawful the publication in newspapers of unwholesome details of divorce cases ; and under that Act only the following details may be reported : names, addresses and occupations of parties and witnesses ; concise statements of charges ; points of law ; and the judge's summing up. The effect of the Act has been to stifle reports for the most part, especially as points of law are of no interest to the great majority of newspapers. In regard to procedure, the Administration of Justice Act, 1920, provided a cheaper and more convenient method of obtaining D. in undefended cases, and also made special provision for those who petition as poor persons. As the chief difficulty of many persons in the provinces lay in taking proceedings a long way from their places of residence, a real hardship was thereby removed in a large number of cases. As to evidence, the *cause célèbre* of *Russell* v. *Russell* (1924) established that statements relative to access or non-access which are calculated to affect the legitimacy of issue are not admissible in evidence. This ruling has practically eliminated the chief evidence on which numerous decrees had previously been granted and opposes new difficulties to petitioners who may have been absent from their usual places of residence even for long periods. Another important judicial decision was that of Lord Merrivale in *A.* v. *A.* (1928) (45 *T. L. R.* 19) to the effect that the Court would refuse to sanction the practice of resorting to hotels to establish a *prima facie* case for dissolution of marriage. In *P.* v. *P.*, another case also decided in 1928, the same judge exercised his discretion in favour of a petitioner who was also a guilty party, it being held that the circumstances were such as to allow relief to be granted. Should this ruling be generally followed, numbers of persons living in unrecognised alliance would be free to marry.

So far as statistics are concerned, it is evident that the rate of D. has increased considerably in recent years. In 1929 the number of decrees made absolute was 4018, being an increase of more than 800 on the previous year, and the highest figure on record. A large number of these were childless unions, and an analysis of the figures suggests the stabilising influence of offspring. When, immediately after the Great War, the marriage rate rose to a remarkable degree, there were no doubt many imprudent marriages among them which helped to account for the increase of Ds. in 1920 and 1921; but the factor does not operate to explain the high rate of 1929, which is possibly explained by the extended facilities for obtaining D. Statistics also show that many divorced persons soon form other unons, and that these re-marriages of the divorced occur largely in the early twenties.

**Divorce in the U.S.A.** In the U.S.A. there is no federal law of D., nor any jurisdiction of the Federal Courts, the different states have their separate laws, and there are forty-eight different jurisdictions. S. Carolina provides no means of obtaining a legal D.; adultery, cruelty, or desertion are the grounds in practically all states. In thirty-nine states imprisonment is a ground, in thirty-eight drunkenness, in twenty-two neglect of maintenance. In some of the states other causes for divorce are insanity, venereal disease, addiction to drugs, and impotence. Restrictions on D. are greater in the Eastern states and lesser in the Western states. The rate is lowest in the Southern states of Louisiana, New Mexico, and Arizona, where Rom. Catholic influence is strong. Some of the states grant D. for comparatively trifling reasons, *e.g.* incompatibility. The prevalent opinion in Great Britain on the subject of D. in the U.S.A. is that the rates of D. to marriage is so high that American family life is in serious jeopardy. This opinion, largely based on the wide circulation given by the Press to all cases concerning American film 'stars,' is no doubt exaggerated; but as compared with the rate in Great Britain the American rate is certainly high : assuming approximately 343,000 marriages (1929) in Great Britain, and 4000 divorces, the rate per 1000 is 11·66 ; assuming 1,232,559 marriages in the U.S.A. (1929) and 201,475 divorces, the rate per 1000 is about 163. On the other hand, the rate varies considerably in the different states : *e.g.* while it doubled in Nevada in 1927, as compared with the year 1926, it declined by over 33½ per cent. in Vermont. These variations, however, merely corresponded to changes in the law, which in the former case reduced the period of residence necessary to secure a final decree and increased it in the latter state. In Nevada only three months' residence is required. Hence people of means flock there to secure their decrees. In Reno the famous 'divorce mill' of the state, 2103 decrees were granted in 1928. But at the same time 2977 marriages were celebrated. American statisticians are at pains to point out that marriages have greatly increased in the U.S.A., and that the divorce rate should be based not on the total population, but on persons of marriageable age, which, however, varies with individual opinion. Perhaps the best complexion that can be put on the statistics is that during the decade 1920–29 there were recorded 11,993,865 marriages to 1,760,701 divorces. For the U.S.A. as a whole, therefore, there were 6·1 marriages for every divorce reported.

**Diwan,** *see* DIVAN.

**Diwanieh,** or **Divanieh,** a tn. of Turkey in Asia, situated on the r. b. of the Euphrates, about 95 m. S.E. of Bagdad.

**Dix, John Adams** (1789 1879), an American general and statesman, *b.* at Boscawen, New Hampshire. From 1830–33 he was adjutant-general of New York, and from 1833–40 was Secretary of State and superintendent of schools for the state of New York. From 1845–49 he was a Democratic United States senator, and in 1861 he was Secretary of the Treasury. In 1861 he was appointed a major-general, and successively commanded the department of Maryland, 1861–62, Fortress Monroe, 1862–63, and the department of the East, 1863–65. In 1867 he was sent as minister to France, and in 1872 was elected Republican governor of New York, but was defeated two years later. He published *A Winter in Madeira and a Summer in Spain and Florence,* 1850. See *Memoirs,* by his son, Morgan Dix, 1883.

**Dixcove,** a British tn. on the W. African Gold Coast. It is situated N.E. of Cape Three Points. Pop. 1000.

**Dixie,** the name popularly applied to the S. states of the U.S.A. There are various explanations of the origin of the word. The S. states were those south of the Mason and Dixon line, and Dixie is supposed to be a corruption of Dixon. Another story has it that it came from the paper money printed in Louisiana before the Civil War. Owing to the number of people of Fr. lineage living in the state, the paper money had one side inscribed in Fr. Ten-dollar bills therefore had the Fr. word for ten, which is ' dix.' In popular nomenclature the bills became known as ' Dixies.' And Daniel Emmett gave it immortal currency in his famous song ' Away down South ' which to this day is the favourite tune in the S. states.

**Dixie, Lady Florence** (1857–1905), an Eng. author and explorer, the daughter of the Marquis of Queensberry, *b.* in London. In 1878–79 she explored the wastes of Patagonia, and acted as war correspondent of the *Morning Post* in the Boer War of 1880–81. It was mainly through her efforts that Cetewayo was released and sent back to Zululand. She was an ardent advocate of women's rights. In 1875 she married Sir Beaumont D. Among her writings are : *Songs of a Child* (3rd ed.), 1903 ; *Across Patagonia,* 1880 ; *In the Land of Misfortune,* 1882 ; and numerous poems,

**Dixie Highway,** an American road extending from Lakes Michigan and Huron to Florida and by a branch through Nashville, Tennessee. It is 1930 m. long in its W. and 2169 in its E. division. Dixie Overland Highway runs from Savannah,

Georgia, to San Diego, California, is 2660 m. in length and passes through Columbus, Meridian, Vicksburg, Dallas, El Paso and Phoenix.

**Dixmude** (Dixmuiden), a Belgian tn. in W. Flanders, 15 m. S. of Ostend. Has a trade in linen, chicory, butter, and cattle. Pop. (1927) 3075. During the Great War it was in the battle line almost throughout the operations on the Western Front. Situated on the R. . Yser, about midway between Ostend on the N. and Ypres on the S., its position exposed it to much bombardment and the tn. was practically destroyed. A Franco-Belgian force maintained hold on the tn. in 1914, after which the appropriate sluices were opened and a large flooded area kept the opponents apart. The Belgians entered the tn. again in Sept. 1918.

**Dixon :** (1) A city of Illinois, U.S.A. and the cap. of Lee co. It is situated about 97½ m. W. of Chicago. There are tanyards, and manufs. of boots and shoes ; there are also extensive flour mills. Pop. 9908. (2) Also the name of a strait on the W. coast of N. America, situated between Queen Charlotte Is. and the Prince of Wales Is. It is 100 m. long, and an average of 70 m. in breadth.

**Dixon, Charles** (*b.* 1858), an English naturalist. He has devoted special attention to the study of British birds, the migration of birds, and the geographical distribution of species. Among his publications are : *Rural Bird Life,* 1880 ; *Evolution without Natural Selection,* 1885 ; *Our Rarer Birds,* 1888 ; *The Migration of Birds,* 1892 ; *The Game Birds and Wild Fowl of the British Isles,* 1893 ; *The Nests and Eggs of British Birds,* 1893 (illustrated, 1894) ; *The Migration of British Birds,* 1895 ; *Story of the Birds,* 1900 ; *The Bird Life of London,* 1909.

**Dixon, George** (1820–98), an English educational reformer. From 1867–76 he was Liberal member of parliament for Birmingham, and from 1885–98 Liberal Unionist for the Edgbaston division. It was largely through his efforts that Birmingham secured Aston Hall and Park. He was practically the founder of the National Educational League (1868).

**Dixon, Henry Hall** (1822–70), an English sporting writer under the pen-name, ' The Druid,' *b.* in Cumberland and educated at Rugby and Trinity College, Cambridge. He practised for some time as a lawyer, but soon returned to sporting journalism, in which he had already won some repute. He began to write regularly for the *Sporting Magazine,* and published three novels in it,

*Post and Paddock*, 1856 ; *Silk and Scarlet*, 1859 ; *Scott and Sebright*, 1862. His other writings were : *Field and Fern*, 1865, an account of the herds and flocks of Scotland ; *Saddle and Sirloin*, 1870, of those of England ; and *The Law of the Farm*, 1858 (5th ed., 1892), a legal treatise. See Hon. Francis Lawley, *Life and Times of 'The Druid,'* 1895.

**Dixon, Richard Watson** (1833–1900), an English poet and churchman, *b.* in London, and educated at Birmingham and Pembroke College, Oxford, where he joined the ' Birmingham group ' of the Pre-Raphaelites, including Morris and Burne-Jones. He was ordained in 1858 and was successively vicar of Hayton, Cumberland, and Warksworth, and honorary canon of Carlisle. His first two books of verse, *Christ's Company* and *Historical Odes*, were published in 1861 and 1863 ; *Mano* in 1883, an historical poem in *terza rima*, which won the praise of Swinburne ; *Odes and Eclogues*, 1884 ; *Lyrical Poems*, 1886 ; and the *Story of Eudoria*, 1888. His prose works include a Life of his father, 1874, and *History of the Church of England*, 1878–1902. See Robert Bridges, *Selected Poems and Memoir*, 1909.

**Dixon, William Hepworth** (1821–79), English writer and traveller, born at West Ancoats, Manchester. He began his life as a clerk in his native city, but early resolved to take up literature. He gained some journalistic experience in Cheltenham, but in 1846 settled in London, where he contributed to the *Daily News* and the *Athenæum*. His series of papers in the *Daily News* on ' The Literature of the Lower Orders,' and ' London Prisons,' attracted great attention. In 1849 he published *John Howard and the Prison World of Europe*, which attained great popularity. In 1851 appeared *Life of William Penn*, in which he refuted the charges brought by Macaulay against the eminent Quaker. A visit to the United States in 1866 was followed by *New America* (1867) and *Spiritual Wives* (1868) ; in 1867 he was in Russia and wrote *Free Russia*. Other works : *The Switzers*, 1872 ; *The White Conquest*, 1875 ; *British Cyprus*, 1879 ; and *Royal Windsor*, 1879–80.

**Dizful**, a tn. of Persia in the prov. of Khuzistan. It is an important market and makes cotton goods. In the vicinity are the ruins of Susa. Pop. 30,000.

**Dizier, St.**, a tn. of France, in the dept. of Haute-Marne, on the R. Marne. It has important iron works. Pop. 14,782.

**Djarkora**, a tn. in Albania. Pop. about 25,000.

**Djemal Pasha**, Turkish politician and soldier, *b.* 1875 ; entered the Army and joined the Young Turk Movement (*see* ENVER BEY). Commanded a divison in Balkan War, and later became a Minister in the gov. During the Great War he held important posts in Syria and Palestine. In 1917 he returned to Constantinople and resumed his political activities. In 1918 the Young Turk gov. collapsed. Djemal fled to Europe, where he lived under an assumed name, and gradually disappeared from public life.

**Djezzar, Ahmed** (*c.* 1735–1804), surnamed ' The Butcher ' on account of his cruelty, *b.* at Bosnia and became the slave of Ali Bey in Egypt. He rose to be Governor of Cairo, and finally Pasha of Acre and Damascus, in which position, with the help and advice of Sir Sidney Smith, he successfully defended Acre for a month (1799) against Napoleon.

**Djibuti**, Fr. tn. and port in E. Africa, cap. of Fr. Somaliland and terminus of the railway to Addis-Ababa in Abyssinia, of which it is the outlet on the Indian ocean. Pop. 8300.

**Djidjelli**, a tn. of Algeria in the dept. of Constantine. Exports cork, wine and sardines. Pop. 9510.

**Djinn**, *see* JINN and DEMONOLOGY.

**Djokjokarta**, *see* JOKJOKARTA.

**Dmitrieff (Dimitriev) Radko.** A Bulgarian general who served with the Russian army during the Great War. He commanded the army which unsuccessfully besieged Przemysl during Sept.–Oct. 1914 ; his losses were very severe—70,000 casualties. At the Battle of Cracow (Nov. 1914) he showed great skill as a leader, and succeeded in driving back an Austro-Hungarian army. In the Battle of Dunajec-San (*q.v.*) in the spring of 1915 he commanded the Third Army, and suffered another heavy reverse at Gorlice-Tarnow, where an Austro-German force made a very wide break in his line and captured over 50,000 prisoners. He tried to hold up the enemy at the Lupkow Pass, but failed, and as a consequence Brussilov's (*q.v.*) army was also compelled to withdraw. After the Russian revolution he was massacred by the Communists at Piatigorsk.

**Dmitriev, Ivan Ivanovitch** (1760–1837), Russian statesman and poet, *b.* in Simbirsk. He served for some time in the army, but soon left it for the Civil Service. From 1810–14 he served as Minister of Justice under the Emperor Alexander. He occupied himself with literature during his leisure moments, and after his retirement in 1814. Among his poems are songs, odes, satires, tales, epistles, and his fables, partly translated from La Fontaine and Florian, are among the best in the language.

**Dmitrievsk,** a tn. of the Ukrainian Soviet Republic with coal mines and metal and chemical industries. Pop. (1926) 51,436.

**Dnepropetrovsk** (formerly Ekaterinoslav, *q.v.*), a tn. in the Ukrainian Socialist Soviet Republic with iron-smelting and metal industries. The civic buildings include a mining academy, an archæological museum and a library. Pop. 250,000.

**Dnieper,** or **Dnyepr,** third largest European river after Rs. Volga and Danube, rising on Valdai plateau in the government of Smolensk, flowing past Mohilev, Kiev, Ekaterinoslav, Kherson, and other important towns, entering the Black Sea at Dnieper-Liman (estuary or gulf), E. of Odessa. Its chief tributaries are Rs. Berezina, Pripet or Pripyat, Ingulets, and Teterev on the right bank, Rs. Sozh, Desua, Sula, Psiol, Vorskla, Orel, and Samara on the left. Steamers ply between Orsha and Ekaterinoslav, and Alexandrovsk and Kherson. The rapids (porogs) below Ekaterinoslav hinder navigation considerably. Length about 1400 m.; navigable from Dorogobuzh. Quantities of corn, timber, hemp, and other goods are shipped on the D. and its tributaries. It is connected with the Baltic by Rs. Dvina, Niemen, and Vistula, and their uniting canals Berezina, Oginski, and Dnieper-Bug. The ancient name was Borysthenes, later Danapris, Turkish Uzi; marked on mediæval maps as Eliel, Luosen, or Lerene. There are important fisheries in the estuary. At Kiev the river is ice-bound for about three months in the year, and there is a bridge across; at Smolensk the waters are frozen for about half the year. In summer the river is 35 ft. deep at Kiev, and often rises much higher, to over 50 ft., in the spring floods. The width varies from under 470 to 2300 yds. The D. played a large part in the making of Russia before the Mongolian invasions (thirteenth century), and later in the life of Little Russia. Near its mouth was the Milesian colony of Olbia, established for trading with the interior

**Dniester,** or **Dnyestr,** a river of Austria and Russia, rising in the Carpathians, Galicia, flowing into the Black Sea, 30 m. S.W. of Odessa. It separates Bessarabia from Podolia and Kherson, and in its course passes Sambor, Halicz, Khotin, Mohilev, Bendery, Akerman, and other important places. Its chief tributaries are Rs. Stryj, Reut, Botna, on the right bank, R. Sereth on the left. Navigation begins for steamers at Khotin; near Yempol, where it crosses the granite ridge of S. Russia, the rapids make navigation very dangerous. About 800 m. long; 180 to 350 yds. wide; 3 to 17 ft. deep. It ships much timber and corn, especially from Odessa. The ancient name was Tyras or Danastris, Turkish Turlia. Its mouth in the Black Sea is called Dniester Liman.

**Doak, William Nuckles,** *b.* Rural Retreat, Wythe Co., Virginia, U.S.A., Dec. 12, 1882. He was educated at the Southern Business College of Bristol, Va., and then started work as a trainman. He became General Chairman for the Brotherhood of Railway Trainmen in 1908, holding this post until 1916, when he became vice-president of the National Brotherhood of Railway Trainmen. He retained this position until 1928. He then became the editor and manager of the trainmen's weekly newspaper organ, and in 1930 was named by President Hoover to a seat in the Cabinet as Secretary of Labor.

**Doane, George Washington** (1799–1859), an American Episcopalian bishop, *b.* in Trenton, New Jersey U.S.A. Studied theology and was ordained priest. He helped to found St. Luke's Church in New York city. He was one of the editors of the *Episcopal Watchman.* In 1832 he was made Bishop of New Jersey. He published *Songs by the Way,* 1824.

**Dobb's Ferry,** a small tn. of New York, U.S.A., situated in Westchester co. The reputation of the tn. rests chiefly on its historical connection with Washington, Clinton, Rochambeau, and other leaders of the War of Revolution. It is now a residential suburb of New York City. Pop. 5741.

**Dobell, Sir Charles M.** (*b.* 1869), British soldier, joined Royal Welch Fusiliers, 1890, of which he was Colonel in 1926, Inspector-General of the W. African Frontier Force 1913–14. In the Great War he commanded the Allied Forces in the Cameroons (*q.v.*) (1914–16). Commanded, successively, W. and E. Egyptian Expeditionary Forces, 1916–17; commanded a division in Third Afghan War 1919; appointed to the Northern Command, India, 1920. Retired, 1923.

**Dobell, Sydney Thompson** (1824–74), English poet and critic, *b.* at Cranbrook, Kent. In 1836 his father, a wine merchant, removed to Cheltenham, with which Dobell was connected for the rest of his life. The influence of his grandfather, Samuel Thompson, brought him into contact with the 'Free-thinking Christians.' In 1850 under the *nom de plume* of 'Sydney Yendys' he published *The*

*Roman,* which met with great success. *Balder* appeared in 1854 ; *Sonnets on the Crimean War,* in which he was assisted by Alexander Smith in 1855 ; *England in Time of War* in 1856. D. belonged to what has been called ' the spasmodic ' school of poets. The undoubted charm of some of his lyrics and the value and originality of some of his thoughts are often marred by excess of metaphor and a general dreariness and nervelessness only relieved by bright ' spasmodic ' flashes. *See* J. Nichol, *Poetical Works of Dobell,* with Memoir, 1875, and the collection of his prose works under the title *Thoughts on Art, Philosophy, and Religion, being selections from Dobell's Unpublished Papers,* by the same writer, 1876 ; and Emily Jolly, *Life and Letters of Sydney Dobell,* 1878.

**Döbeln,** a tn. of Saxony, in the prov. of Leipzig, situated on an island formed by the Mulde and the Mühlgraben, 41 m. N.W. of Dresden by rail. It has iron foundries and manufs. of metal and wooden wares, chocolate and sugar. Pop. 22,560.

**Doberan,** or **Dobberan,** tn. and watering place in the grand-duchy of Mecklenburg-Schwerin, Germany, on a small river flowing into the Baltic, about 9 m. from Rostock. It has a Gothic church (1300–1368), a former Cistercian Abbey with many art treasures, and the tombs of numerous princes of Mecklenburg. It is much frequented on account of its radioactive steel springs. Pop. 5500.

**Döbereiner, Johann Wolfgang** (1780–1849), a German chemist, *b.* near Hof, in Bavaria. In 1810 he was appointed professor of chemistry, pharmacy, and technology at Jena, where he made the acquaintance of Goethe. He is chiefly famous for an invention known as ' Döbereiner's Lamp,' in which he demonstrated that spongy platinum in presence of oxygen can ignite hydrogen ; a process which has been used in many self-igniting coal-gas burners. He obtained the crystalline compound of alcohol with ammonia, and discovered furfurol. His works include treatises on pneumatic chemistry (1821–25), and the chemistry of fermentation (1822). He was one of the first to try to group elements according to their atomic weights, thus helping to prepare the way for Mendeléeff's Periodic System. He also discovered the catalytic effect of manganese dioxide upon the decomposition of potassium chlorate by heat.

**Döblin, Alfred,** physician by profession, literary man by avocation, *b.* Stettin, Germany, 1878. Of Jewish origin, he is considered one of the greatest of the present writers of his native land. From his twentieth to his thirty-fifth year he devoted himself to his profession of medicine. In 1915 he sprang into instant fame in Germany by his marvellous evocation of ancient life in China—*The Three Leaps of Wang-Lun.* The author had never been in China. It was said of him that so powerful was his imagination that ten Chinese poems translated into Ger. and a long visit to the ethnological museum of Berlin were enough to start him off on this long story. In 1920 appeared his romance *Wallenstein.* After writing a number of other novels as well as plays, he appeared as a modern epic poet in his *Manas* published in 1927 and dealing with India. His last novel *Berlin : Alexanderplatz,* published in 1930, had an enormous vogue. Unlike all his preceding work, this dealt with the criminal classes of Berlin and gave realistic pictures of thieves' quarters and their battles with the forces of law and order.

**Dobree, Peter Paul** (1782–1825), an English classical scholar and critic. At Trinity College, Cambridge, he became an intimate friend of Porson and in 1823 was appointed regius professor of Gk. After Porson's death D. was commissioned to edit the publication of his notes on Gk. authors, and brought out the *Plutus* of Aristophanes in 1820 and all Porson's *Aristophanica.* In 1822 he published the *Lexicon* of Photius, and left an edition of Demosthenes unfinished at his death.

**Dobrianka,** a tn. of Russia, about 50 m. N. of Tchernigov. Pop. 10,000.

**Dobritch,** the chief tn. of the Bulgarian dist. Dobrudja, situated 27 m. N. of Varna. It was formerly called Bagagik. The town has a fine mosque, and an important annual fair. Pop. 12,000.

**Dobrowsky, Josef** (1753–1829), a Slav philologist, *b.* at Gjermet, near Raab, in Hungary, of Bohemian parents. In 1792 he was commissioned by the Bohemian Scientific Society to travel all over Europe in search of the MSS. which had been scattered during the Thirty Years' War. Among his works are : *Scriptores Rerum Bohemicarum,* 1783–84, a history of Bohemian language and literature ; *Geschichte der böhmischen Sprache,* 1792, and *Institutiones Linguæ Slavicæ,* 1822. *See* Life by Palacky, 1833, in German.

**Dobrudja,** the English name for a dist. of Rumania, which is spelt by the French Dobroudja, by the Germans Dobrudscha, and by the Rumanians themselves Dobrugea. It is a low tract of Quaternary alluvium which stretches for a distance of 140 m. alongside the Black Sea. It rises in Sacar Bair to a height of 7765 ft., but the mean elevation of the district is only about 500 ft. During the Great War Rumania after declaring war on Austria-Hungary, Aug. 27, 1916, at once advanced into Transylvania on a front of 350 m. while holding the Dobrudja with a comparatively small force. Later, the Austrians, who had been taken by surprise, reinforced by Ger. troops, advanced under the Ger. field-marshal, Mackensen, into the Dobrudja on Sept. 4th, and Turtucain fell to them on Sept. 6. Ten days later Silistria was also taken and a new Russo-Rumanian defensive line was constructed between Rasova and Tuzia in the Dobrudja. The Rumanians continued to lose ground in their new sector until the second week in Nov. 1916, when they retook Hirsova. But this success was not consolidated, they were overwhelmed on other fronts, and fighting in the Dobrudja generally came to a standstill. It was prematurely agreed among the governments of the Central Empires and those of their allies that the eventual disposal of the D. should be in the hands of Germany and Bulgaria, the new understanding being that Bulgaria should regain what she asserted had been taken from her by the Western Powers after the last Balkan War; but as the ultimate victory was with the Entente, Rumania retained the territory.

**Dobson, Henry Austin** (1840–1921), entered the Board of Trade in 1856; became a first-class clerk in 1874, and principal clerk in 1884, which last position he retained until his retirement from the service seven years later. It was, however, as a man of letters rather than a government official that Austin D., as he usually subscribed himself, achieved fame. At an early age he came before the world as a poet; and he issued several books of verse : *Vignettes in Rhyme*, 1873 ; *Proverbs in Porcelain*, 1877 ; *Old World Idylls*, 1883 ; and *At the Sign of the Lyre*, 1887. His collected poems were published in 1897. One of the greatest living authorities on the Georgian period, D. wrote mainly on that era, his principal works being monographs on Fielding (1883), Steele (1886), Goldsmith (1888), Horace Walpole (1890), Hogarth (1891), Richardson (1902), Fanny Burney (1903), *Eighteenth Century Vignettes* (three series, 1892, 1894, 1896), and *At Prior Park* (1912). D. at Ealing, Sept. 2.

**Dobson, William** (1610–46), an Eng. portrait and historical painter; apprenticed as a boy to Peake, a picture-dealer. Van Dyck befriended him, and he became his pupil and imitator, succeeding him as court painter to Charles I. D. painted portraits of Charles I., the Prince of Wales, Prince Rupert, and several courtiers. Examples of D. in the National Portrait Gallery are : 'Francis Quarles,' 'Endymion Porter,' and others. There are also three at Hampton Court. 'The Decollation of St. John,' is one of his best historical works.

HENRY AUSTIN DOBSON

**Dobson, William Charles Thomas** (1817–98), an Eng. artist, *b.* at Hamburg. His paintings were mainly on historical and scriptural subjects, including 'Tobias and the Angel,' 1853 ; 'The Charity of Dorcas,' 1854 ; 'The Holy Innocents,' 1858 ; 'The Good Shepherd'; and 'St. Paul at Philippi,' 1873, in the Diploma Gallery.

**Docetæ,** or **Docetism** (Gk. δοκεῖν, to appear), a name given in the early church to a group of heretics who believed that during His residence on earth, Christ had no real but only an 'apparent' or phantom body. The doctrine originated in the Gk., Oriental, and Alexandrine theory that ' matter ' is essentially impure and imperfect, therefore the union of the divine spirit with matter was impossible. It appears in its most developed form among the Gnostics and Manichæans, and its believers were divided into three groups : those who held that the body of Christ was a real, earthly body, but had no essential connection with His divine nature; those who declared that His human body was a mere phantom, a delusion (Marcion, the Ophites, and Manichæans); and those who declared that it was an ethereal body, descended with Him from heaven (Valentinus, Basitides). The theory precludes the idea of the virgin birth and the Crucifixion, or holds them to be only ' phantoms.' The docetic doctrine appears among the Priscillianists and the Bogornils, and also among a small faction of the Anabaptists. See GNOSTICISM; also Dorner's *System of Christian Doctrine*, 1880, and Harnack's *History of Dogma*, 1894–99.

**Dochart,** a river and loch of Scotland. The river carries off the surplus waters of the loch, and flows in a N.E. direction for 13 m., finally entering Loch Tay at Killin. Salmon, pike, and trout are plentiful in the stream.

**Dock,** the common name of many perennial tap-rooted species of *Rumex*, a genus of Polygonaceæ, to which belongs also the sorrel. *R. cruspus*, the yellow dock, *R. obtusifolius*, and *R. Britannica*, the greater water-dock, are all species found in Britain as weeds, and the leaves are used by children as a cure for nettle stings.

**Dock,** in marine and river engineering, a space or structure in or upon which ships may be placed to discharge or load cargo, or to undergo repairs. There are two main classes of Ds., viz. the wet D., with which the tidal D. may be classed, and the dry D., with which we may consider the floating D.

*A wet dock* is a basin in a sheltered position, where vessels may lie alongside quays, which are fitted with proper appliances for taking on or discharging cargo. It adjoins the sea coast or a tidal river, and is closed with gates so that the water in it may be retained at a uniform level when the tide has gone down. Quays usually surround the D. as much as possible, as it is of importance to secure as large a quay area as possible. The disadvantage of the wet D. is that vessels are able to enter or leave it only at high tide when the water outside and inside is at the same level. This disadvantage is often minimised by locks which receive the vessel at the D. level, and then, by letting water out, drop it to the outside level. The depth given to a D. depends upon the depth of the channel by which it is approached. Of late years, owing to the great improvements made in the dredging system, the channels leading to most important ports have been deepened considerably, and in building a new D., the probability of any such improvement would be taken into account. The depth of channel available for vessels is reckoned from the high-water of the lowest neap tides. The period of time over which vessels can daily enter the D. depends upon the range of the tide. The approach channels to some of the S. Wales ports are inaccessible at low tide, for they are then nearly dry. It is in places where the range of tide is very great that the wet D. is used in preference to the tidal D. Liverpool, which possesses one of the finest D. systems in the world, is a case in point. Here the difference in level is over 30 ft., while in the Thames also it is some 20 ft. As a general rule it may be said that where the difference is more than 12 ft., wet Ds. are a necessity. The Liverpool D. system was developed greatly at the end of the nineteenth century, and the D. area is now some 1100 acres. The largest Ds. are the Canada (18 acres), the Langton (18½ acres), and the Alexandra (17¾ acres), with its branch Ds., area 44½ acres. The West Float Dock, with a water area of 52 acres, is the largest on the Birkenhead side of the river. The two principal London wet Ds. are the Royal Victoria and the Royal Albert. These two are built across a neck of land formed by a bend in the R. Thames and are connected by a channel. At the other end of each D. there is connection with the Thames. The channel leading from the Thames to the Royal Albert D. leads first into a small D. 350 ft. by 80 ft., then by locks into the main D., which is 6500 ft. long and 490 ft. wide. The water area is 84 acres, the quayage 5750 yds. The Royal Victoria D. is about 3000 ft. long and 1050 ft. wide. The water area is 74 acres, the quayage 8333 yds. The extent of quayage is greatly increased by the series of projecting jetties on the N. side of the D. Other important London Ds. are the London, St. Catherine's, Surrey Commercial, E. India, W. India, and Millwall. In France, the Havre Ds. deserve special mention.

*A tidal dock* is a basin similar to that described above, but open to the harbour waters, so that the level of the water in the D. rises and falls with the tide. Ds. of this kind are suitable where the difference between levels at high and low tide is small. This state of things prevails on the shores of the Mediterranean and the Atlantic coast of N. America, and as examples of such Ds. we may cite those at Marseilles, Genoa, and Naples in the Mediterranean, and the Atlantic Ds., Brooklyn, in the U.S.A.

Wet and tidal Ds. are usually constructed on low-lying land near the estuary of a river. The D. is here somewhat sheltered, and the excavation of the basin is facilitated by the lowness of the land. The river acts as an approach channel, and if, as in the case of the Albert and Victoria Ds., described above, a sharp bend in the river be utilised, upper and lower entrances are easily provided. In the Mediterranean ports, where the basins are actually in the sea, breakwaters, as at Marseilles, are built to act as shelters.

*Dry*, or *graving docks* are basins of particular shape, which can be shut up, and from which the water can be pumped so as to leave the vessel's hull dry for repairs, repainting, cleaning, etc. The dry D. has access to the sea from one end only, and this end is furnished with gates, or caissons, fitted with sluices, so that all the water may be drained away; but when it has access to a wet D. the water must of course be pumped out. The other end is generally shaped round in the form of a ship's bows. On the face the walls are stepped, the steps being known as 'altars.' The bottom is heavily paved, and slopes downwards from the centre so as to allow any water left in the D. to drain out. These Ds. were formerly constructed of timber in America, but they are now universally constructed, as formerly in Europe, of masonry, brickwork, or concrete. The 'altars' are lined with granite, blue-bricks, or specially strong concrete, and additional steps and means of access are provided for the men to ascend and descend. Along the centre line of the D. bottom are keel-blocks, upon which the ship settles as the water is pumped out. When brought into the D., which is of a length and depth sufficient to receive the largest vessels frequenting the port, it is placed carefully in position over the keel-blocks, and shored up with timber shores resting on the steps, which retain it in an upright position as it settles down. The largest London dry D., out of thirty-three, is the Tilbury, which is 846 ft. long, 70 ft. wide at the entrance, and 35 ft. deep. The size of the Canada D., Liverpool, is 925 ft. long, 94 ft. wide at entrance, and 31 ft. deep at high water.

*Floating docks* have been built in late years to serve the same purpose as graving Ds. They have certain very obvious advantages, but these are counterbalanced by grave disadvantages. The advantages plainly are : (1) that the D. can be built in the cheapest and best place, no matter how far distant this may be from the place at which the D. is needed. Thence, as in the case of the Bermuda floating D., it can be towed to its destination ; (2) it can be moved from one port to another, or from one part to another of the same port, as seems most convenient ; (3) it usually costs less to work than a dry D., where the cost of pumping out the water is apt to be very great. The disadvantages are : (1) that the durability is so much less, a floating D. cannot be expected to last for more than fifty years ; (2) the cost of maintenance is generally much higher ; (3) it cannot be used for such large vessels as can the regular graving D. A sheltered site, with a considerable depth of water, is necessary for a floating D. The first Bermuda D., already referred to, which was towed across the Atlantic in 1869, was of the obsolete U-shape. In these, gates or caissons were placed at each end so as to make the D. into a closed rectangle, thus decreasing the height to which the vessel had to be raised, and increasing the stability of the whole. The modern dry D., however, is of a somewhat simpler form. It consists of a number of pontoons or water-tight boxes, of which some form the bottom of the D. and others the two sides. The pontoons are divided into water-tight compartments, and for filling or emptying these compartments there is machinery in the side boxes. The machinery usually consists largely of steam-pumps. The lower boxes are at first filled with water so as to be well below sea-level. The vessel is then floated in, and carefully adjusted in position over the keel-blocks. The water is then pumped out from the water-tight compartments, and the bottom of the dock rises, lifting the vessel with it. Shores are at the same time placed between the hull and the side walls to retain the vessel in position. This continues until the hull of the vessel is well out of the water. The repairs are made, the D. is sunk, and the vessel floated out. Stability is ensured by making the displacement of that part of the deck below the bridge greater than that of the upper part of the D. plus the greatest vessel it could take. Floating Ds. are now almost all constructed of iron and steel, and are carefully overhauled at regular intervals. The difficulty of doing this has led to a notable improvement in form. Under the old system, the floating D. had itself to be brought into dry D. at regular intervals. Now, however, the floating docks are made self-docking. That is to say, they are constructed in three parts, so that if one of these requires cleaning it can be detached and dry docked on the other two parts as though it were itself a vessel.

*Dock entrances and locks.*—Access to a D. may be either by entrances or by a lock. The former, being so much the cheaper, is used when possible. Entrances consist of one or more pairs of gates at the opening of the D. These are fitted with sluices, closed by vertical sluice-gates, which are worked by hydraulic pressure. In the case of a dry D. opening on to the sea, these enable the water to be drained entirely away, and in this case they

the open channel, water is first passed through the sluices from the D. to the lock-chamber, so as to bring both to the same level. The gates between them are then opened, and the vessel passes into the lock-chamber. This pair of gates is then closed, and the other sluices are employed to bring the water in the lock-chamber down to the level of that outside. The outer gates are then opened and the vessel leaves by that entrance. The lock-chamber must be long enough to receive the largest vessels likely to

*[Cement Marketing Board*

TILBURY DOCKS

are supplemented by culverts in the side walls. In the case of a wet D. they serve to bring the water in the D. down to the level of that outside. These entrances are economical, not only in money but also in space, and it is much more easy for a vessel to pass through them. The disadvantage is that they are available for a comparatively short period of time daily, unless the difference between high and low water levels be very small. Locks, on the other hand, form a water-tight compartment *outside* the D. itself. At each end they are fitted with sluice-gates, as are the entrances. They are constructed on the same plan as the locks on canals and rivers, but the scale is much greater and more elaborate. When it is required to pass a vessel out from the D. into

need docking. The gates which close the entrances and locks are constructed either of wood or of iron, braced carefully so as to resist the pressure of the water. The leaves are constructed to meet absolutely truly in the centre, and the greatest care is also exercised to make the union of the heel-posts and side walls thoroughly watertight. Of woods, greenheart is the most suitable in salt water, as best resisting the action of the teredo. D. gates are sometimes made straight and sometimes segmental. Rollers are often placed along the floor to support the outer ends of the gates in very wide locks. Sliding or floating caissons sometimes take the place of gates.

*Recent Developments.*—During post-war years great attention has been given to the problem of approach and exit from Ds. at all states of the tide, in view of the enormous loss in earning power and the cost in interest and charges incurred by great liners and other shipping. The chief case in point is Liverpool, which has long been harassed by the bar that made her a closed port during many hours of the day and night. With the opening of the Gladstone D. in 1927 the disability is largely removed, for this D. can be entered at all states of the tide, the famous bar having been successfully pierced in circumstances that made a new record in the history of dredging. The Gladstone D. is about 60 acres in area, and has quays 3 m. in length. This D. is slightly exceeded in size by the King George V. D. (London), which was opened in 1921, and which constitutes a first step in a scheme to develop the R. Thames on both N. and S. banks so that greater ships can be brought near to the City. In the meantime there have been further developments at Tilbury. The Immingham D. near Grimsby, completed in 1912, has led to development of trade in the area served. The many natural advantages of Southampton for dealing with great ocean liners have been still further supplemented by additions of great lengths to D. sides. The speed and ease with which the largest ships in the world can berth and start in this port is one of its chief assets. Among other developments in D. construction during this period were the Esquimault D. at Victoria, Australia, opened in 1926, which has a length of 1150 ft.; a D. of about similar length opened in Durban, S. Africa, in 1925; while extensions at St. Johns, Canada, include a new D. opened in 1923, which is 1165 ft. long. In post-war years much public interest has centred on Singapore in view of the construction of its naval port; and the national and international questions involved have been of such a character as to overshadow mercantile aspects. Singapore is one of the greatest natural harbours in the world. In 1905 the British gov. acquired the Tanjong Ds., which it supplemented eight years later by the construction of the King's D. at a cost of £400,000. As this is now one of the largest and most convenient ports in the Eastern world, its development is regarded as extremely valuable to Eastern trade. See Rankine's Manual of Civil Engineering, 1907, for general principles of earthworks; L. F. Vernon Harcourt's Harbours and Docks, 1885; C. Colson's Docks and Dock Construction, 1894; Cunningham's Prin-

ciples and Practice of Dock Engineering, and De Cordemoy's Les ports modernes, 1900. Later authorities, C. Greene, Wharves and Piers, New York, 1917; R. S. MacElwee, Port Development, 1925; Brysson Cunningham, Dock Engineering, 1922; F. N. Du Plas-Taylor, Docks, Wharves and Piers, 1928. See also Report on Marine Structures by the U.S. National Research Council (1924).

**Dock Dues**, see TONNAGE DUES.

**Dock Warrants**, in England, are certificates given to the owners of goods warehoused in the docks. When goods are transferred the certificates are endorsed in favour of the purchaser, and thus become a warrant for the removal of goods. Under the Factor's Act of 1889, it is a 'document of title,' and any person lawfully in possession of it, although not the owner of the goods, by endorsement and delivery of it has the absolute right to all goods described in it. Warrants may be obtained for the whole or a part of the goods consigned. All D. W. require a three-penny stamp.

**Dockyards, Government** (in America called **Navy Yards**), in the fullest meaning of the term are the establishments where warships are built and repaired, supplied with stores, ammunition, and men, and put in a state of complete efficiency. As a fact, very few yards are so complete. In many of them there is no ship-building at all, while in many more although the frame of the ship is built in the gov. yard, the machinery and fittings are supplied from the workshops of some engineering firm. All British dockyards are under the Admiralty, and governed by officers under an admiral-superintendent at the larger yards, and the captain-superintendent at the smaller. All Admiralty instructions with regard to the building or commissioning of ships are directly conveyed to the superintendent, as well as to the officers more nearly concerned with the carrying out of the instructions. The chief Admiralty official is the Controller of the Navy (third Lord of the Board of Admiralty) and below him are the Director of Dockyards, the Director of Stores, and the Director of Naval Construction. The chief artisans of a dockyard comprise, besides the engineers, ship-wrights, platers, caulkers, joiners, smiths, sail-makers, rope-makers, and a large body of labourers. The scale of pay is determined bi-annually by a special board. The great dockyards of England are Portsmouth, Devonport, Chatham, Sheerness, and Pembroke Dock; of the empire, Malta, Gibraltar, Ascension, Bermuda,

Simonstown, Haulbowline (Ireland), Hong Kong, Sydney, and Wei-hei-wei. New docks, practically identical with those at Rosyth, were completed in Portsmouth just before the outbreak of the Great War. The docks at Rosyth under construction in 1910 were still far from complete when the War began, but were continued under great difficulties during the hostilities. The necessities of the Navy during the War brought a number of new bases into existence. Scapa Flow became the chief naval headquarters, while Immingham, Harwich and Dover were adapted as additional naval centres. Since the Armistice, Rosyth, Haulbowline, and Pembroke have ceased to be of importance, the two last having been closed. Since 1922 the plan to build naval yards and docks at Singapore has occupied a big place in political controversy. Construction, which was begun in 1923, was stopped when the Labour Party took office in 1924, and during the twelve months of the financial years the scheme was delayed, but was restarted by Mr. Baldwin's gov. of the following year. The project is estimated to cost £9,000,000. The principal dockyards of France are at Cherbourg, Brest, Lorient, Rochefort and Toulon; of Germany, at Wilhelmshaven and Kiel; of U.S.A., Portsmouth, Charlestown, Brooklyn, Washington, and Mare Is.; of Italy, Spezia, Naples, and Venice; of Russia, Leningrad, Kronstadt, Sevastopol, and Niko-laiev.

**Doctor** (Lat. for a teacher), one who is skilled or learned in any branch of knowledge, or whose attainments entitled him to express an authoritative opinion. As a title or degree it is granted by universities to those who have attained the highest qualification, and ranks above master; but the ranks vary, thus in divinity, law, music, etc., there are no masters, and the lower degree is bachelor; in other faculties such as arts, there are no Ds. In the fourteenth century the degree of D. was conferred in medicine, and in common parlance a ' D.' means a physician, or, quite generally, a qualified medical practitioner, whether he has taken the degree of D. in Medicine, M.D., or not. The first university degree of D. was granted at Bologna in the faculty of law, in the twelfth century. The faculties in which the degree is granted are too numerous to specify, and new faculties with the growth of specialisation tend to spring up. The universities are accustomed to grant honorary doctorates to members of other universities, and to those who have distinguished themselves in a particular branch of knowledge, or who are prominent generally, such as distinguished statesmen, military and naval officers, scientists, artists, writers, etc. Of these honorary degrees those of D.C.L., Doctor of Civil Law, at Oxford, and LL.D., Doctor of Laws, at Cambridge, are perhaps of the highest distinction.

**Doctors' Commons,** the name formerly given to a society of ecclesiastical lawyers in London, forming a distinct profession for the practice of civil and canon laws, and also to the buildings erected by them, 1567, on St. Bennet's Hill, St. Paul's Churchyard, under Harvey, Dean of the Arches. The houses (so called from the ' community of board ' of members of the college) were destroyed by the Fire, 1666, but restored in 1672. Advocates and thirty-four proctors (corresponding to attorneys and solicitors), all Oxford or Cambridge graduates duly admitted by the Archbishop of Canterbury, lived there, headed by a president (Dean of Arches for the time being). Incorporated by Royal Charter, 1768, but on establishment of the Divorce Court and Probate Court, the college was dissolved and the property sold, 1857, the various courts (Court of Arches, of Admiralty, of Delegates, Prerogative, Faculty, and Archdeacon's Court) being now open to the whole Bar. The buildings were demolished in 1867, but the old name still survives. In 1874 the Doctors' Commons Will Office was removed to Somerset House. See 20, 21 Vict. c. 77, etc.; Stow, Survey of London, 1598.

**Doctrinaire,** a theorist who pays no regard to practical considerations, generally a political ideologist. The term is of French origin, and was bestowed upon a group of politicians at the time of the Restoration (1815–30), who desired a constitution in France modelled according to historical principles and the monarchical system in England, and were opposed to absolutism as much as to revolutionary principles. The leaders were Royer-Collard, Guizot, and the Duc de Broglie.

**Doctrine,** see DOGMA.

**Dodd, William** (1729–77), man of letters, after distinguishing himself at Cambridge, and spending a short time in London as a man about town, took holy orders in 1751. He soon became a popular preacher, and attracted large congregations to the Magdalen House, of which he was chaplain from its inauguration in 1758. In 1763 he was appointed chaplain to the king, and soon after became tutor to Philip Stanhope, godson and heir to Lord Chesterfield. He became a noted person in Metropolitan society, but, living beyond his means, got into such straits that in 1777 he forged a bond for £4200 in the name of Lord Chesterfield. The forgery was discovered, and D. sent for trial, and condemned to death. Much influence was brought to bear upon the king to grant a pardon, but in vain. No less a literary personage than Dr. Johnson exerted himself on the prisoner's behalf. D. was hanged on June 27. Of D.'s many books, that best known is the volume of selections entitled *The Beauties of Shakespeare*, which has been reprinted many times. Besides some contemporary anonymous memoirs, there is a biography by Percy Fitzgerald (1865).

**Dodder,** the name applied to several

DODDER PARASITIC ON GORSE

(1) Parasite in flower; (2) Cluster of flowers enlarged; (3) Suckers (oblique section) penetrating vascular bundles.

*a,* main stem of Gorse host; *b,* branch spine; *c,* leaf spine; *d,* stem of Dodder, long internodes; *e,* tight coil of *d*; *f,* flowers of Dodder; *g.* sucker; *h,* vascular bundle of Gorse stem.

British species of Cuscuta, a parasitic genus of Convolvulaceæ. The plants twine round the branches of woody or other plants, strike minute suckers into their bark and thus obtain their necessary sustenance. *C. Europæa,* the common or greater D., attacks heath, furze, nettles, hops, and other plants. *C. epilinum* is the flax D., *C. trifolii* attacks clover, and *C. epithymum,* the lesser D., takes as host several low-growing plants.

**Doddridge, Philip** (1702–51), an English dissenting minister and writer. In 1729 D. opened at Northampton an academy for educating Nonconformist ministers He formed a society for distributing Bibles to the poor, and paved the way for foreign missions among Nonconformists. His chief works are : *Rise and Progress of Religion in the Soul,* 1750 ; *The Family Expositor,* 1739–56 ; *Course of Lectures* (published by Clarke), 1763 ; *Evidences of Christianity* (long used as a text-book at Cambridge), and hymns. See *Correspondence and Diary of P. Doddridge,* ed. by J. D. Humphreys, 1829–31.

**Dodecahedron,** in geometry, a solid enclosed by twelve plane faces, each solid angle being formed by three regular pentagons. In crystallography, a regular D. is an impossibility ; in the cubic system are the right rhombic D. and the pentagonal D., which has irregular faces.

**Dodecanese Islands.** These Ægean Islands which have been under Ital. rule since the Tripolitan War of 1911–12 formed a bone of contention between Greece, Italy, and Austria-Hungary during the bargaining in the Great War for alliances. Surrendered by Greece to Italy and Turkey in 1920. Pop. about 80,000. (*See* ÆGEAN SEA AND ISLANDS.)

**Dodecatheon,** a genus of plants belonging to the order Primulaceæ. They are hardy perennials, and easily cultivated in gardens with well-drained soil. The flowers, which somewhat resemble cyclamen, are variously coloured. *D. integrifolium* has clusters of handsome, rosy-crimson flowers, *D. Jeffreyi* is reddish purple, *D. Media* is pale lilac. Various hybrids derived from crossing *D. Media* with other species are popularly grown ; of these *D. M. lancifolium* has large leaves and red flowers with yellow markings. American cowslip is the popular name for the genus.

**Döderlein, Ludwig** (1791–1863), a German philologist, *b.* at Jena. Became director of the philological seminary of Erlangen in 1827. His principal works are : *Lateinische Synonymen und Etymologien,* 1826–38 ; *Lateinische Wortpildung,* 1838 ; *Handbuch der lateinischen Synonymik,* 1839, and *Homerisches Glossarium,* 1850–58 ; besides a valuable edition of the works of Tacitus, 1847, and Horace, 1856–60.

**Dodge, Mrs. Mary Elizabeth Mapes** (1838–1905), American authoress, *b.* in New York. For some years she assisted Harriet Beecher Stowe and Donald G. Mitchell in editing *Hearth and Home.* In 1873 she was appointed editress of *St. Nicholas.* Besides numerous contributions to periodicals, she wrote, *Irvington Stories,* 1864 ; *Hans Brinker or the Silver Skates,* 1865 ; *Rhymes and Jingles,* 1874 ; *Theophilus and Others,*

1876 ; *When Life was Young*, 1894; and the volumes of poems : *Along the Way*, 1879 ; and *Poems and Verses*, 1904.

**Dodge City**, in Kansas, U.S.A., seat of a Ford plant, with railway shops, flour mills, etc. Five m. E. is the State home for disabled volunteer soldiers. Pop. 10,059.

**Dodgson, Charles Lutwidge**, *see* CARROLL, LEWIS.

**Dodington, George Bubb, Lord Melcombe** (1691–1762), the son of Jeremias Bubb, an Irish apothecary. In 1720 he took the name of D. on inheriting a fine estate from his uncle. In 1715 he was elected to parliament, and was member for Bridgwater (1722–54). He was constantly changing sides, serving in succession Walpole, the Prince of Wales, the Duke of Argyle, and the Prince again. He was a patron of Young and Thomson, and wrote some poems himself, but he is only remembered through his posthumous *Diary* (1784), which reveals the intrigues of his time and his own egotism. He was created Lord Melcombe in 1761. *See* his *Diary* (1784), and Walpole's *Letters*.

DODO

**Dodo,** an extinct bird, in the family Dididæ, allied to the pigeon, was last known in 1681 in its living state. The bird was as large as a turkey, of unwieldy build, with short curly tailfeathers and rudimentary wings useless for flight ; the bill was blackish in colour, forming at the end a horny hook, and the aborted keel also indicated its flightless condition. *Didus ineptus* was the species in Mauritius, *D. borbonicus* in Réunion.

**Dodona** (Δωδώνη), an ancient tn. of Epirus, near the base of Mt. Tamarus (Tmarus) on Thesprotia's borders (*see* Strabo vii., Pliny ii.). Said to have been founded by Deucalion (Herodotus ii. 99), it was the seat of the oldest Greek oracle, dedicated to Zeus. The oracle divined by the flight of pigeons, dice,

the sound of a bronze bason, and the noise of the wind in the sacred oaks where the voice of Zeus was heard in the rustling of the leaves. The temple was destroyed during the war of the Aetolians and the Achæans 220 B.C. It was rebuilt a little later and in the second century A.D. games were celebrated there in honour of Zeus Naios. But Christianity soon transformed it into a church, and the bishops of Dodona sat at the Councils of the fifth and sixth centuries, at the end of which it ceased to exist. The remains were unearthed about 11 m. S.W. of Janina. The theatre is well preserved, and many valuable historical inscriptions were found.

**Dods, Marcus** (1834–1909,) a Scottish divine and theological scholar. In 1889 he was appointed professor of N.T. Exegesis in New College, Edinburgh, of which he became principal in 1907. Among his most important writings are : *Israel's Iron Age*, 1874 ; *Mohammed, Buddha, and Christ*, 1877 ; *On Genesis*, 1882 ; *The Gospel according to St. John*, 1897, in the Expositor's Greek Testament ; *The Bible, its Origin and Nature*, 1904. He also edited the English translation of Lange's *Life of Christ*, 1864, and *Augustine's Works*.

**Dodsley, Robert** (1703–64), author and bookseller, was in early life in domestic service as a footman. While so engaged he wrote occasional verses and received encouragement from his employer, the Hon. Mrs. Lowther, and later the active patronage of Defoe. He published *The Footman's Friendly Advice to his Brethren of the Livery*, 1731 ; *A Muse in Livery*, 1732, and other volumes ; and in 1835 his dramatic satire, *The Toy Shop*, was staged by Rich at Covent Garden Theatre. In the same year D., with capital supplied by Pope and other persons interested in him, set up as a bookseller at the sign of Talby's Head in Pall Mall. He continued throughout his life to write books and plays, but it is as a bookseller he is now best remembered. His first important venture as a publisher was in 1737 when he issued Pope's *First Epistle of the Second Book of Horace imitated*. In the following year he brought out Dr. Johnson's *London*. In 1759 the Ds.—for James had now joined his elder brother in the business—published Goldsmith's *Polite Learning*, and in the same year he retired into private life, with an ample competence and a host of friends. It was James D., who, after having refused a first version of *Tristram Shandy*, brought out Sterne's masterpiece, purchasing the copyright of the first two volumes for £250, and of the third and fourth volumes for £380. The biography of Robert D. has been written by Ralph Strauss.

**Dodsworth, Roger** (1585–1654), an English antiquary. He collected materials for a history of Yorkshire and an English baronage, and published, in collaboration with Sir William Dugdale, a *Monasticon Anglicanum*, 1655 and 1661. The MSS. he left to Lord Fairfax, who bequeathed them to the Bodleian Library at Oxford.

**Dodwell, Henry** (1642–1711), a theologian and chronologist. In 1688 he was elected Camden professor of history at Oxford, but was deprived of his post on refusing to take the oath of allegiance to William and Mary in 1691. His theological works are of far less value than those on chronology, among which are: *Annales Thucydides et Xenophontei*, 1702 ; *A Discourse Concerning Sanchoniathon's Phœnician History*, 1681 ; and *De Veteribus Grœcorum Romanorumque Cyclis*, 1701.

**Doe**, a female deer.

**Doe, John**, and **Roe, Richard**, *see* FICTION.

**Dog**, a term designating a quadruped of the domesticated variety, *Canis*, which may be extended to include wild Ds., jackals, foxes, wolves, etc.

*Its origin.*—Darwin believed the D. to be descended from two species of wolves, *Canis lupus* and *Canis latrans*, as well as from certain European, Indian, and African canine species, and from the jackal. The arguments in favour of the wolf origin are that the D. and wolf will interbreed with each other, and that the progeny thus obtained will again breed with either the D. or the wolf, whereas most hybrids are not fertile. On the other hand the domesticated D. is in one feature very different from the wild Canidæ. The pupil of its eye is round, whereas in the wolf the pupil is placed obliquely, and in the fox and jackal perpendicularly.

*Chief Characteristics.*—The dog is digitigrade, fissiped, with slender legs, the fore feet having five toes, the hind feet four, with non-retractile claws. The head is small, the muzzle pointed, but the shape of the head differs greatly in various species. The neck is short and thick-set. The teeth usually consist of six incisors, two canines and eight premolars in all, but the numbers vary. The upper jaw has four molars and the lower has six. The vertebræ of the tail vary in number, and some species have no tails. The tongue is smooth. The mammæ are sometimes four, sometimes five, on each side. The period of gestation is sixty-three days. There are four to eight, occasionally as many as twenty, pups in a litter. The young are born blind and remain so for about ten days. The average age of a D. is from ten to fourteen years, though some live to be twenty. The D. has a very acute sense of smell, and an extraordinarily keen intelligence. It has probably more highly developed mental qualities than any other animal. By nature it is carnivorous, and in its wild state will combine to hunt out its prey. It will feed on birds or fresh meat ; in cold countries it eats fish, and some kinds of Ds. will also eat crabs, reptiles, and insects. The Pariah D. of India feeds on carrion and offal, whereas the Chow-chow of China is a strict vegetarian. *See* V. W. F. Collier's *Dogs of China and Japan*, 1921.

*History.*—The dog was, apparently, the companion of man from the very earliest time. Canine remains have been found in the Danish kitchen-middens of the Neolithic period side by side with human remains. The Egyptians held Ds. in the greatest affection, almost veneration. The friezes of their temples were carved with figures of dogs, and many very early Egyptian monuments (dating from about 3000 B.C.) are decorated in like manner. The Jews, as we can see from the Old and New Testaments, regarded dogs with the utmost contempt, as unclean beasts. This feeling was perhaps the natural outcome of seeing the worship bestowed upon them by the neighbouring tribes of Egyptians and Syrians. Assyrian sculptures represent two forms, a greyhound and a mastiff, whereas the Egyptian represent a wolf-dog, greyhound, turnspit, and a kind of terrier. The Egyptians worshipped Sirius, a star, which they called ' D. Star,' because of its faithfulness in appearing at a certain season to warn them of the approaching overflow of the Nile. The Ethiopians went still further, and elected a dog to be their king, whose growlings or fawnings they received as directions of government. The Greeks used dogs in battle as well as in the chase. ' Ds. of war ' had spiked collars, and proved very valiant and dangerous fighters. Oppian, in his *Cynegetica*, is the earliest authority who mentions the use of dogs for hunting. The Greeks had formerly used nets to ensnare animals, but later pursued their prey with Ds. The Romans divided Ds. into three classifications : (1) *Canes venatici*, or hunting-Ds. ; (2) *Canes pastorales*, or sheep-Ds. ; (3) *Canes villatici*, or watch-Ds. The hunting-Ds. were further divided into *pugnaces*, who attacked the quarry, *nare sagaces*, who tracked it out, and *pedibus celeres*, who overtook it. Early Britain was renowned for its bloodhounds, which, according to Strabo, played an important part in the Gallic wars. During the Middle Ages, Ds. were used in England chiefly in sport. King John had a pack of otter hounds. Bull-Ds., then called Butchers' Hounds, were used for catching cattle, and in the popular sport of bull-baiting. Juliana Berners (fifteenth century) made out the following list of domestic Ds. : ' A Grehoun, a Bastard, a Mengrel, a Mastif, a Lemor, a Spanyel, Raches,

companions, Bran and Luath ; Cavall, ' King Arthur's hound of deepest mouth,' and Hodain, of the Tristrem and Ysold story. In Greek mythology we have Argus in the *Odyssey*, Ulysses' faithful D., who recognised his master after an absence of twenty years. Such another D. was Mæra, who, by his prolonged howling, directed Erigone to the spot where her father, Icarius, had been murdered. Mæra was placed among the stars by Zeus, where he was known as Procyon ('little dog') or *Icarius Canis*. Another faithful D. in story is the Dog of the Seven Sleepers, who accompanied his masters to the cave in which they were confined, and stood

SIBERIAN WILD DOG

Kenettys, Teroures, Butchers' Hounds, Dunghylle Dogges, Tryndeltaylles, Pryckeryd Currys, and small Ladyes' Poppees.' Ds. have taken a useful part in exploration, from the time of Columbus' discovery of America (1492) down to the Arctic expeditions of recent years. Among the most famous Ds. in history are the bloodhounds who attacked William Wallace of Scotland when fleeing from the English ; the mastiffs of the Knights of Rhode, who could smell out a heathen Turk in whatever disguise ; and the D. who woke up William the Silent on the eve of the attack at Mons to warn him of approaching danger.

*Dogs in literature.*—Ds. are present in the mythology and folklore of the earliest peoples. In this connection should be mentioned Fingal's favoured

on guard by their side for 300 years, without moving, eating, drinking, or sleeping. Mahomet admitted him into paradise under the name of Katmir. In folk-lore Ds. have often been credited with mysterious knowledge of spiritual things, and have sometimes been uncanny friends of such a magician as Cornelius Agrippa. It was a rabbinical superstition that Ds. howl at death. They were, too, depicted as terrible monsters, such as the snarling, many-headed Cerberus, who guarded the entrance to Hades on the further side of the Styx. Among the Ds. noted in English literature are Pope's Bounce, Byron's Boatswain, Scott's Maida, Dandie Dinmont in *Guy Mannering*, Mrs. Browning's Fluff, John Brown's *Rab and His Friends*, Gelder, the dog of Llewellyn. Consult

'The Dog in History and Folk-lore' in J. J. King's *Sketches and Studies, Descriptive and Historical*, 1874.

*Uses of dogs.*—The earliest races made a friend and companion of the D. No other animal shows such affection and gives such faithful service. Ds. have been and are used in the hunt, for coursing, and retrieving game. They are also valuable for collecting sheep and keeping the flock together, and are useful guards and watchers to keep off thieves. In the Arctic regions Ds. drag sleighs and other vehicles across the snow. They have frequently saved people from drowning, and from suffocation in snowdrifts. Barry, the famous St. Bernard, saved forty lives. Ds. may also be employed for tracking criminals, for scouting, and for ambulance work.

*Dog shows and clubs.*—The first club was formed by Lord Orford in 1776, at Marham Smeeth, near Swaffham. Though coursing meetings have been held since the time of Charles I., the first actual show took place in 1859 at Newcastle-on-Tyne, under the patronage of Mr. Pape and Mr. Shorthose. Sixty Ds. were exhibited, and the show was so popular that others were held in the same year at Birmingham and Edinburgh. Now that D.-breeding has become a lucrative business as many as 500 shows are held in the United Kingdom in one year. The Kennel Club was founded in 1873 by S. E. Shirley, who held the position of president till his death in 1904. This club has had an enormous influence in improving the condition of various breeds, and in promoting the welfare of Ds. in general. It has been instrumental in putting a stop to cropping of ears (1889), to mutilating the membrane of the mouth, and in some cases to docking the tail. It controls the different shows, and practically rules the canine world. Its own show is held in October at the Crystal Palace, while another famous Dog Show—Cruft's—is held annually at the Agricultural Hall, London. Other well-known clubs are the Ladies' Kennel Association, and the Westminster Kennel Club. Most breeds of Ds. have their own particular club, such as the London Bulldog Society, the Dandie Dinmont Terrier Club, the Gamekeepers' Association of the United Kingdom, the Pomeranian Club, etc. The chief foreign and colonial clubs are La Société Centrale (Paris), The Italian Kennel Club, The American Kennel Club, and the South African Kennel Club. A D. is valued by its points, so many marks being assigned to each. For example, a bloodhound is valued thus: Head, 20; ears and eyes, 15; legs and feet, 15; back and ribs, 10; chest and shoulders, 10; colour and coat, 7½; symmetry, 7½; flews, 5; neck, 5; stern, 5; total, 100. Ds. vary considerably in price, as much as £1500 having been paid for a collie, and 1000 guineas for a bulldog. A fox terrier has more than once fetched 500 guineas, and a pointer 200. Ladies' toy Ds. may be of great value, and have been sold for their weight in gold. The chief canine journals are *The Kennel Gazette* (1880), the monthly organ of the Kennel Club; *Our Dogs* (1895), published weekly in Manchester; and *The Field* (1853), a London weekly. Books of reference are: Rawdon B. Lee's *Modern Dogs*, 1897; Burges' *American Kennel and Sporting Dogs*, 1876 (New York); V. K. Shawls *Illustrated Book of the Dog*, 1889–91; Hugh Dalziel's *British Dogs*, 1887–96; J. H. Walsh's *Dogs of the British Islands*, 1886; Stonehenge's *The Dog* (revised by G. Armiage), 1896; Herbert Compton's *The Twentieth Century Dog*, 1904; Barton's *Non-Sporting Dogs*, 1905; Watson's *Book of the Dog*, 1905; W. H. Miller's *Complete Book of the Dog*, 1922; and *The American Hunting Dog*, 1926; T. Marples' *Show Dogs*, and *Prize Dogs*, 1926; and *The Kennel Encyclopædia*, edited by E. F. Barton, 1928.

*Classification.*—The various breeds of Ds. have increased greatly since the early part of the nineteenth century, owing to careful breeding—by crossing, selecting, and interbreeding, new varieties can be 'manufactured.' Many classifications have been made of Ds., though there is no generally accepted one. Cuvier recognised three main divisions—Mâtins, Spaniels, and Housedogs. Youatt enlarged this arrangement as follows: 1. Those with more or less elongated heads, with parietal bones widest at the base of the skull, gradually approaching each other as they ascend, and with the condyles of the lower jaw on a line with the upper molar teeth, *e.g.* the Irish Wolf-hound, Greyhound, etc. 2. Those with heads moderately elongated, and with the parietals diverging as they ascend thus enlarging the cerebral cavity, *e.g.* the St. Bernard, Newfoundland, Sheep-D., Spaniel, Setter, etc. 3. Those with more or less shortened muzzles, large frontal sinews, and elevated and diminished cranium, *e.g.* the Terrier, Bull-D., and many toy Ds. Fitzinger divided Ds. into 180 different classes. A very practical classification is that of Rawdon B. Lee (in *Modern Dogs*, 1897), into sporting and non-sporting Ds. These two great divisions have been defined by F. C. S. Pearce in the *Kennel Club Stud Book*, 1874, and were defined in further detail by that club in 1900, so that there might be no misunderstanding on the part of intending exhibitors.

*Breeds of Dogs.* The Kennel Club has registered sixty-two different varieties of Ds. But, with the free interbreeding of various types, many intermediate species occur, which account for the 185 types differentiated by naturalists. Numerous foreign Ds. have been imported into the United Kingdom during the last century, the Dachshund, the Schweisshund, and a breed of Mastiff, from Germany; the Chesapeake Bay D.,

or Cape Hunting D., is about the size of a wolf, and varies in colour, generally having large, irregular patches of black, yellow, and white. It is found in the region of the Cape and through the eastern belt of Africa as far as Kordofan. It runs in packs, and is semi-nocturnal, semi-diurnal. It is very swift-footed, and has three different and most curious cries. The Long-eared Cape D. or Fox (*Otocyon*, or *Megalotis lalandii*), stands about as high as a fox, and has a bushy tail about 2 ft. long. Its ears are very large and quite out of proportion to its head; they are held very erect. It has six more teeth than has the average D.

(2) *American wild dogs* include the

CRAB-EATING DOG

and the Boston Terrier from America; the Chow from China; the Japanese Spaniel from Japan; the Poodle from France, and many others. These, and British Ds. are dealt with in separate articles. O. E. M. Hollyer's *Dog-Keeping and Breeding*, 1926; R. E. Nicholas's *Principles of Dog-Breeding*, 1927; Robert Leighton *The Complete Book of the Dog*, 1922 (revised, 1927); C. J. Davies' *Theory and Practice of Breeding to Type*, 1928.

*Wild dogs.*—Among the wild Ds. may be included the Wolf (*Canis lupus*), the Fox (*genus Vulpes*), and the Jackal (*Canis anthus, Canis aureus*, etc.), which will be considered in special articles. Other wild Ds. may be divided into four groups, African, American, Asiatic, and Australian.

(1) *African wild dogs.*—Two types of wild D. occur in S. Africa. The Hyæna D. (*Canis* or *Lycaon pictus*),

Carasissi, or Crab-eating D. (*Canis Cancrivorus*) found in a region of S. America, extending from Orinoco to La Plata; the Bush D. (*Icticyon Venaticus*), found in Brazil and British Guiana; it is short-limbed, and varies in colour from red round the head and shoulders to black in its hind-quarters; the *Canis Azaræ* found in the region of the Andes; it is a solitary animal, that comes out at night to seek its prey, in colour, yellowish, or reddish-brown verging to black.

(3) *Asiatic wild dogs.*—The Pariah D. is very common in the East, where it moves about in bands, acting as scavenger and feeding on offal. The Dhole, also called Kolsun, and Buansuh (*Canis dukhunensis, Canis Primævus, Canis rutilans*) is found in various parts of India. It is rather larger than the jackal, and has a full, rather long tail. It hunts in packs of

about fifty, and is absolutely fearless in attack. Its habits are nocturnal, and it has a very keen scent. A similar kind of D. (*Canis Alpinus*) is found in the Himalayas and in parts of Tibet and Siberia. In general, the Dhole is untameable, though it has sometimes been employed for coursing and pig-sticking. The Racoon D. (*Canis procyonoides*) occurs in Northern China and Japan. It is so called (first by Mr. St. G. Mivart), because of its resemblance to the racoon. It has a pointed muzzle, a short and bushy tail, and short, round ears. Its body is arched and its legs stumpy. Its coat becomes thicker and longer in winter, and in colour is yellowish and brown.

(4) *Australian wild dog*, or *Dingo* (*Canis dingo*), is the only higher mammal found in that country. See separate article.

Wild Ds. can be and often have been tamed. In their natural state they hold ears and tail erect and do not bark. When tamed, they will fawn, crouch, wag their tails, and lavish affection upon the master in the manner of an ordinary domesticated D.

*Diseases of dogs.*—Distemper is an infectious catarrh of the mucous membranes in the eyes and nose. It generally occurs in Ds. between the ages of one and two years. The first signs are feverishness, loss of appetite and depression. Complications may ensue and the skin is sometimes attacked. Nourishing food, such as milk, bovril, eggs, minced meat, etc., and careful nursing are essential. The eyes should be frequently bathed in a solution of boracic acid, creolin and water. Rabies (hydrophobia) is contagious and may be transmitted by means of a bite. The disease has often been prevented from spreading by muzzling every D. within a certain area. Ds. suffering from mange or scabies should be shaved and then washed with anti-parasitic soap. Eczema, also known as surfeit, or blotch, is due to irregular and unwise over-feeding. The best treatment is to change the diet to a rational one, to keep the D. very clean and give it plenty of fresh air and exercise. Medicine must frequently be given internally, and the affected parts should be dressed. Consult J. Woodroffe Hill, *Management and Diseases of the Dog*, 1900; Friedberger and Fröhner, *Veterinary Pathology*, 1905; F. G. Hobday, *Canine and Feline Surgery*, 1906 (2nd edition); L. G. Neumann, *Treatise on the Parasites and Parasitic Diseases of the Domesticated Animals*, 1907 (new edition); L. Sewell's *Canine Distemper*, 1925; Dr. Georg Muller's and A. Glass's *Diseases of the Dog*, 1926; O. E. M. Hollyer's *Dog Ailments*, 1927; I. Alston's *The Care of the Dog in India*, 1927; D. E. Wilkinson's *Canine Nursing*, 1929.

*Law as to dogs.*—In the United Kingdom no person may keep a D., over six months old, without a licence. The licence is obtainable at any post office, costing 7s. 6d., and must be renewed annually. Ds. used solely for tending sheep and cattle, and for leading the blind, may be kept without a licence, certificates of exemption being obtainable from the commissioners of Inland Revenue. Any one found keeping a dog, not under these heads of exemption, without a licence, is liable to a penalty of £5. If a D. bites or attacks a person, on its second offence the owner is liable to an action of damages. The court may decide that such a D. should be killed. Dog-stealing, setting traps for Ds., injuring or killing Ds., etc., are offences punishable under criminal law statutes. Stray Ds., if not taken into homes for the purpose, may be adopted, sold, or killed by members of the police force. Consult Lupton, *The Law Relating to Dogs*, 1888.

*Glossary of technical terms.*—*Apple Head*, a head rounded on top. *Blaze*, a while mark or streak on the head. *Blue*, applied to shades of grey. *Brisket*, the front of the chest. *Brush*, the tail—usually applied to collies or sheep-Ds. *Butterfly nose*, a spotted nose. *Button ear*, where the tips of the ears fall over, covering the orifice. *Cat foot*, a rounded, high-knuckled foot. *Chops*, the pendulous underlip of a bull-D. *Cloddy*, stoutly built. *Cobby*, compactly built. *Couplings*, the part of the body between the shoulder blades and the hip joints. *Cow hocks*, hocks that turn in. *Dew claw*, extra claw. *Dewlap*, loose hanging skin under the throat. *Dish-faced*, when the nose is turned up and higher than the muzzle at the stop. *Dudley nose*, a yellowish nose. *Feather*, the hair on the legs and tail. *Flag*, the tail, usually of a setter. *Flews*, the hanging lips of a bloodhound and of some other breeds. *Forearm*, the part of the foreleg that extends from the elbow to pastern. *Frill*, long hair on the chest. *Hare foot*, a long narrow foot, carried forward, *Haw*, the red inside eyelid, showing in St. Bernards and bloodhounds. *Hucklebones*, the tops of the hip joints. *Leather*, the skin of the ear. *Occiput*, the bony lump at the back of the head. *Overshot*, the upper teeth projecting beyond the lower. *Pastern*, the part of the leg below the knee. *Pig eye*, small, sunken eye. *Pig jaw*, an exaggeration of overshot.

*Pily*, applied to a soft, woolly coat. *Roach back*, an arched back. *Rose ear*, where the tips turn back, showing the interior of the ear. *Septum*, the division between the nostrils. *Snipy*, with a too pointed muzzle. *Stifles*, the top joints of the hind legs. *Stop*, the indentation below the eyes. *Tupil ear*, an erect ear. *Undershot*, the lower teeth projecting beyond the upper.

**Dogbane**, or *Apocynum*, the name of a genus of Apocynaceæ which includes only three species. *A. cannabinum*, the Canadian hemp, and *A. androsæmifolium*, or fly-trap, both grow in N. America, and are used in medicine.

**Dog-cart**, originally a carriage fitted with a box under the seat for carrying

A.D. 697 to replace the former seven tribunes. At first their powers were largely undefined ; their attempts to make the office hereditary were checked (1032) by a declaration that the election of a D. Consort (son with father) was illegal. The privy councillors (*consiglieri ducali*) were appointed instead. In 1172 the Great Council of 470 members was formed as a check on the Ds. Sebastian Ziani, the first D. chosen from the candidates of this council, introduced the custom of wedding the Adriatic with a ring thrown from the ship *Bucentaur*. The office disappeared on the fall of the Venetian republic (1797). The Ds. of Genoa dated only from 1339. In 1528 restrictions were made on their power ; in 1797, on Fr. occupation

[*Canadian Pacific*

THE DOGE'S PALACE, VENICE

sportsmen's dogs ; now an ordinary open cart for driving, fitted with two transverse seats placed back to back, the hinder of these being so constructed that it can be shut up.

**Dog-days** (*Dies Caniculares*), the hottest period of the year, generally reckoned now from July 3 to Aug. 11. Various dates, from July 3 to Aug. 15, were assigned for the first of the D. by the Gks. and Roms. and various periods of duration from twenty to fifty-four days. They were generally associated with the influence of Sirius, ' the dog-star,' and according to Pliny, began with its heliacal rising on July 19 (New Style). They were regarded by the ancients as the hottest and most unhealthy period of the year, and as being the direct cause of madness among dogs.

**Doge** (Lat. *dux*, leader), a former title of the chief magistrate of Venice and Genoa ; the first Venetian D., Paolo Lucio Anafesto, being elected

of Genoa, the office disappeared, and after a short restoration vanished for good in 1804. In Amalfi Ds. existed from 897–1350. *See* Cecchetti, *Il Doge di Venezia*, 1864 ; Brown, *Venice*, 1893.

**Dog-fish**, the name given to any member of the Scyllidæ, a family of Elasmobranchs in the division Selachii. The species are marine, living in warm seas, and many fossil forms are found in the Jurassic and Cretaceous. There are two small spineless dorsal fins, a distinct spiracle, no nictitating membrane ; the mouth is inferior and the teeth are small. The females are oviparous and the egg cases are four-sided and large ; in habit the fishes are predacious. *Scyllium canicula* and *Sc. catulus*, the small-spotted and large-spotted dog, are Brit. species of small size ; *Stegostoma tigrinum*, the tiger-shark, attains a length of 15 ft. in the Indian Ocean *Pseudotriakis microdon* is a large shark found off the coast of N. America.

**Dogger** (Dutch *dogger-boat*, codfish boat), a vessel something like a ketch, with two masts, and of about 80 tons burden, used in the cod and herring fisheries in the N. Sea.

**Dogger Bank**, an extensive sand-bank in the N. Sea, between Eng. and Denmark. The average depth of the water above it is from 10 to 20 fathoms, but in some places there is only a depth of 6 fathoms. It is about 170 m. long by 65 m. broad, and is a famous fishing ground, probably obtaining its name from the Dutch *dogger*, a codfish boat. *See* Mather's *Nor'ard of the Dogger*, 1888. In 1781 the S. end of the bank was the scene of an indecisive battle between the Eng. and Dutch fleets under Admirals Hyde Parker and Zoutman. In 1904, during the Russo-Japanese War, a Russian fleet fired on the trawlers on the D. B., sinking one, injuring others, and killing two fishermen. The excuse given was that there were Japanese torpedo boats among the trawlers. A formal protest was made to the Russian government and a commission appointed, which decided against the Russian government, and ordered compensation to be made to the families of the victims. In the Great War the Battle of Dogger Bank was fought on Jan. 24, 1915, between Brit. and Ger. fleets, the former under the command of Admiral Sir David (later Earl) Beatty and the latter under Admiral Hipper. The Brit. Admiralty received information of Hipper's departure for the Dogger Bank on Jan. 23 and Beatty at once put to sea. He was joined on the following day by Commodore Tyrwhitt's squadron, of which the *Aurora* was the first ship of either squadron to engage the enemy. The sound of this preliminary engagement gave Admiral Beatty the intelligence he required and he disposed his fleet accordingly. His flagship was the *Lion*, which was repeatedly hit and had to drop out, so that the Admiral had to transfer his flag to a cruiser. As soon as Hipper saw Beatty's fleet he made for Heligoland and the battle developed into a chase. The Ger. warship *Blucher* was hit very early in the action and sank. The *Seydlitz* and *Derfflinger* were also badly hit. The result of the fight was to impose the greatest caution on the Ger. naval authorities. *See also* HELIGOLAND BIGHT.

**Doggett, Thomas** (*d.* 1721), an Eng. actor, *b.* in Dublin, and made his first appearance in D'Urfey's *Love for Money* in London, 1691. He was highly thought of, both for his acting and his personal character, and was associated with Cibber and others in the management of Drury Lane and the Haymarket. He is chiefly remembered, however, as the founder of the prize of ' D.'s Coat and Badge ' in 1715, in honour of King Geroge I.'s accession. The prize consisted of a red coat with a large silver badge on the arm, and was competed for by Thames watermen who had completed their apprenticeship within the twelve months prior to the race. The race took place on Aug. 1, and the course was from London Bridge to Chelsea. It is still held annually under modified conditions, and a list of the winners has been kept since 1791.

**Dog Licence,** *see* DOG.

**Dogma** (Gk. δόγμα, from δοκεῖν, to seem good or true), a term which has passed through many meanings, and is now chiefly used in theology, commonly in a disparaging sense. The D. of a Gr. assembly was merely its decree, or that which seemed right and proper. Originally an opinion stated as a positive assertion, the truth of which had already been proved, it came to be applied to a belief derived from authority, and especially to doctrines of the church, concerning which no questioning was allowed. From meaning the essential doctrines of Christianity as contained in the Scriptures or writings of the fathers, it came to be considered as equivalent to ' assertion without proof ' in English. In its continental use (Ger. *Dogmen*) it means ' doctrine,' with no censure implied, the science of Ds. having a separate professorship in the Protestant universities of Ger. Consult Shedd, *History of Christian Doctrine*, 1881 ; Farrar, *Lives of the Fathers*, 1889 ; Harnack, *History of Dogma*, 1895–96 ; Matthew Arnold, *Literature and Dogma*, 1873 ; Schmidt, *Dogmatik I.*, 1895 ; Wetzer and Welte, *Kirchenlexikon*, 1882–1901.

**Dogmatic Theology,** the systematic statement of Christian doctrine, considering each article of faith in connection with others with which it is in apparent relation. It deals, that is to say, with the actual abstract deposit of faith, and not with its relation to, and effect on, the life of the belief. Neither does it deal with doctrine from the point of view of history and development. The term is now of general use, though it did not become so until the seventeenth century. Previous titles for the subject among Protestant divines are *Thetic Theology* and *Positive Theology*. The earliest period of Christian doctrinal statement, comprised almost entirely of apologetics, may be said to end with Origen, who sketched out the main plan of the science. In the seventh century, it was brought to the highest level it has attained among the Gks. by John Damascene, and in the Middle Ages it developed greatly in the West. Important names are those of Anselm, Duns Scotus, and Thomas Aquinas. The period immediately following the Reformation produced many volumes of Protestant D. T., but since this time Protestants have shown a strong aversion to dogma, and the term has gradually been limited to apply to the authoritative beliefs of the Rom. Catholic Church.

**Dogs, Home for Lost and Starving,** this refuge was founded in 1860. It has two branches, viz. at 4, Battersea Park Road, London, S.W., and at Hackbridge, in Surrey. Every year thousands of dogs are rescued from the streets. Such homes now exist in all large cities.

**Dogs, Isle of, Poplar Marshes,** or **Millwall,** is situated on the l. b. of the Thames, opposite Greenwich. It has been suggested that the name received its origin from the lodging there of the king's hounds. The district is occupied largely by the W. India Docks.

**Dog's-tail Grass,** or *Cynosurus,* a genus of Gramineæ which is represented in Britain by two species. *C. cristatus,* the crested D. G. or goldseed, is valued as a pasture-grass on account of the fineness and closeness of its herbage.

**Dog's-tooth Violet,** or *Erythronium dens canis,* a species of Liliaceæ which grows in a mild climate, and in Britain is often used for borders. The bulb has a toothed appearance, and the flowers are violet-coloured; hence the name of the plant.

**Dogtooth Ornament,** in architecture, a moulding much used in mediæval building from Late Norman to Early Decorated, and cut in projecting teeth. It is thought that it was introduced from the East by the Crusaders; it first appeared in Europe about 1100. In later architecture the 'dogtooth' frequently becomes a four-leaved flower with the centre projecting, *e.g.* in Elgin Cathedral.

**Dog-watch,** a nautical term. The first D. is from 4 p.m. to 6 p.m., and the second from 6 p.m. to 8 p.m. *See* WATCH.

**Dog-whelk,** the popular name of *Nassa reticulata,* a Brit. gastropod mollusc; it is also applied to the near species of *Purpura lapillus,* the dog-periwinkle.

**Dohad,** a tn. of India, in the dist. of Panch Mahals, Bombay. Pop. 14,000.

**Doherty, Reginald Frank** (1874–

1910) and **Hugh Lawrence** (1876–1919), lawn-tennis champions, sons of Wm. D., were *b.* in London—R. F., Oct. 16, 1874; H. L., Oct. 8, 1876. For ten years, 1897–1906, they were, successively in singles, and jointly in doubles, supreme. They were defeated by Smith and Riseley at Wimbledon in 1906. R. F. *d.* in London Dec. 29, 1910. H. L. *d.,* after a long illness, at Broadstairs, Aug. 21, 1919.

**Dohrn, Anton** (1840–1908), Ger. zoologist. In 1870 he founded the great zoological station at Naples, which within ten years became one of of most noted schools and laboratories of natural science in the world, and was the model for many later ones. D.'s early studies were almost entirely concerned with insects, and his later with marine invertebrates. He is the author of many valuable natural science works, including *Ursprung der Wirbeltiere,* 1875; *Studien zur Urgeschichte des Wirbeltierkörpers,* 1882; and *Die Pantopoden des Golfs von Neapel,* 1881.

**Doiran, Battle of.** One of the surprises of the Great War was the Allied offensive on the Macedonian front in Sept. 1918. The new allied Commander-in-Chief, the Fr. General d'Esperey (*q.v.*) planned this attack immediately he assumed command. The Bulgarian army occupied strong positions on the heights to the west of Lake Doiran, from which they dominated their opponents. After a preparatory bombardment the Brit. forces attacked the 'P' Ridge on Sept. 18, whilst Gk. troops attacked Doiran Hill. After severe fighting General Sir George Milne, commanding the British and Gk. forces, gained Petite Couronne Doiran tn. and the lower slopes of Grande Couronne. On Sept. 21, on the Vardar front the Franco-Serbian offensive had reached the line Gradista–Boshava–Dragojil and the heights of Porta dominating the Vardar, thus turning the flank of the enemy on the Brit. front and cutting his communications. This forced the Bulgarians to retreat on the Doiran front. By Sept. 22 the Bulgarians were in full retreat in great disorder on a front of 100 m. On Sept. 26, a Bulgarian *parlementaire,* under a flag of truce, brought a proposal to conclude an armistice and on the 30th they accepted unconditional surrender. This collapse of Bulgaria exposed Turkey to attack on its W. flank and compelled it to cease offensive operations. The remaining forces of the Central Powers were now exposed to attack from the East, a factor which contributed to their decision to conclude an armistice.

**Doisig,** a tn. and com. of Rumania,

about 22 m. S.E. of Debreezin. Pop. 200.

**Doit,** or **Duyt,** a small Dutch copper coin, in value equal to half an Eng. farthing. It was also a small copper coin, equal to one Scots penny, or one twelfth of an Eng. penny, current in Scotland in the time of the Stuarts.

**Dol** (Dol-de-Bretagne), a Fr. tn. in dept. of Ille-et-Vilaine, 14 m. from St. Malo. The level, fertile district, Marais de Dol, is protected from the sea's inundations by a dyke, 22 m. long, built in the twelfth century. D. has a fine thirteenth century cathedral of granite, with good glass, sculptures, and two fine porches. In 1793 the Vendeans defeated the republicans here. Pop. 4565.

**Dolabella, Publius Cornelius,** a Rom. general and the husband of Cicero's daughter, Tullio; *b.* about 70 B.C., and one of the most notorious profligates of his age. He took the side of Cæsar in the civil wars, and fought for him at Pharsalia, and accompanied him to Africa and Spain. On Cæsar's death (44 B.C.) he seized the consulship and allied himself with Brutus and the conspirators, until he changed sides again when Antony offered him a higher bribe, the province of Syria. On his way there he plundered various cities in Greece and Asia, and murdered C. Trebonius, the proconsul of Asia, who refused to allow him to enter Smyrna. Cassius was sent to supersede him, and besieged him in Laodicea. To avoid capture D. ordered one of his soldiers to kill him. *See* Cicero's *Letters.*

**Dolce, Lodovico** (1508–68), an It. author and scholar, *b.* at Venice of a noble family. The circumstances of his life are not known, but he lived at Venice for the greater part, and it is believed in a state of poverty. His work consisted chiefly of translations from the classics and of plays based on the classics. Of his translations the chief were Homer's *Odyssey, The Battle of the Frogs and Mice,* Virgil and Ovid, and a Sp. translation of Ariosto. He wrote four tragedies from Euripides, two from Seneca, and comedies from Plautus; and he also edited the works of Petrarch, Boccaccio, and Dante.

**Dolci** (Dolce), **Carlo,** or **Carlino** (1616–86), a Florentine painter chiefly of religious subjects, pupil of Jacopo Vignali. He painted also portraits of the Imperial family at the Emperor's court. Among his best works are : Christ on Mount Olivet '; 'Holy Family '; ' Madonna and Child ' (Pitti Gallery, Florence); ' St. John the Evangelist ' (Berlin Gallery); ' Poesy,' and 'St. Apollonia ' (Corsini Palace, Rome); ' St. Cecilia,' and ' The Daughter of Herodias ' (Dresden); ' St. Andrew ' (Pitti Palace); ' Ecco Homo ' (Munich); ' Adoration of the Magi ' (Glasgow); ' La Madonna colle Stelle '; ' Pentitent Magdalen ' (Munich); ' St. Veronica ' (Dulwich); his own portrait (1674, Uffizi, Florence); portrait of Cardinal Ghisi (Alexander VII.).

**Dolcigno** (in Albania), *see* DULCIGNO.

**Doldrums,** *see* WIND.

**Dole.** A colloquial rather than official term which came into general use in Great Britain during the years that followed the end of the Great War. The unemployment insurance scheme, which came into operation during 1912, had been largely free from any suggestion of unearned charity, although the nation contributed a percentage of the money required to operate the scheme (*see* LABOUR EXCHANGE: UNEMPLOYMENT. In 1919 the return of large numbers of ex-soldiers and sailors from the theatres of war upset the conditions of the labour market and necessarily many of these men remained unemployed for different lengths of time. In order to meet this difficulty the gov. provided for an out-of-work donation to be paid to ex-service workers. This allowance varied from 20s. to 29s. for men and from 15s. to 25s. for women. It was to this donation that the word ' dole ' was at first more particularly attached. In 1920, the difficulty and cost of having two separate systems of allowances for unemployment in operation side by side led to a new Act, which repealed all previous legislation and placed all unemployed persons on the same level. Contributions from employers, employed and the gov. were increased and powers were granted to borrow money up to £30,000,000 for the difficult period. The word ' dole ' had, by that time, become the common synonym for unemployment pay, and is still so used. Its contemptuous connotation is naturally resented by the honest seeker of work and by those whose contributions justly entitle them to relief when they fall out of work. On the other hand, there have been and are many abuses of the system, and undoubtedly considerable numbers of people draw unemployment pay who are not entitled to it. The actuarial basis of unemployment insurance is that at a constant average unemployment census not greatly in excess of a million persons, no additional charge should fall on the Exchequer; but the excess of unemployment in 1930–1 was far beyond this total.

**Dole, Nathan Haskell** (b. 1852), an American author, b. at Chelsea, Massachusetts. Graduated at Harvard (1874). Edited the *Rubaiyat* of Omar Khayyam, 1896; *Collected Works of Tolstoi*, 1899; *The International Library of Famous Literature*, 1897. Wrote Lives of Tolstoi, 1911, Francis William Bird, 1897.

**Dôle,** or **Dole,** a Fr. tn., cap. of arron. in the dept. of Jura, on R. Doubs, 30 m. from Dijon. Anciently Dola Sequanorum, it faces the heights of the forest of Chaux, on a vine-clad slope. The Gothic church Notre-Dame belongs to the sixteenth century, and contains a beautiful chapel. In the seventeenth century was built the façade of the Jesuit church, now a chapel of the public college, and the Hôtel-Dieu with its watch-towers. There are also a fine library, Palais de Justice (fourteenth-century convent), barracks, and the Tower of Vergy (now a prison). Many houses are in the style of Sp. renaissance. There are iron and copper foundries; manufactures of tiles, pottery, chemical products, soap, and candles: there are also mills, and trade in grain and meal. D. belonged to the Duchy of Burgundy until 1479, when Louis XI's army took it and burned it. Later through the marriage of Marie of Burgundy to the Archduke Maximilian it became an Austrian possession, but after being taken by Louis XIV in 1668 and 1674, it was ceded to Fr. in 1678 by the Treaty of Nimeguen. The winding streets are still lined with houses of the long ago. Pop. 18,090. It was the bp. of Pasteur.

**Dolerite,** a coarse-grained basaltic rock used for road mending and kerbstones. It consists of augite and plagioclase felspar with the addition of olivine in some varieties, and of quartz in others. Variable quantities of hornblende, apatite, and biotite are often present.

**Dolet, Etienne** (1509–46), a Fr. scholar of the Renaissance, b. at Orleans. He studied at the University of Paris and in various It. cities, finally settling in Toulouse about 1530, where he became orator in the university. For promulgating the humanistic views he had imbibed in Italy, he suffered imprisonment, and in 1534 removed to Lyons. He set up a printing-press in 1542, and was on several occasions arrested for publishing heretical works. In 1544 he was imprisoned on a charge of heresy and was burned in the Place Maubert, 1546. Consult his Life by Christie (1880), and Galtier (1908).

**Dolgelly,** an urban dist. of N. Wales, and the cap. of Merionethshire. It is situated at the base of Cader Idris, on the Aran and Wnion, 230 m. from London. In the neighbourhood is the Parliament House, in which it is said Owen Glendower held a parliament in 1404. It is the focus of some of the sweetest glens in the kingdom. Pop. 2014.

**Dolgorouki, Catherine Michailowna, Princess,** the favourite of Alexander II., Emperor of Russia, to whom she was married (1880), after the death of his first wife Marie. She had been maid of honour to the empress from 1867–73. After her husband's death she went abroad, and at Geneva in 1882 published *Alexandre II.; Détails inédits sur sa Vie intime et sa Mort*, under the name of 'Victor Laferté.'

**Dolichocephalic,** *see* ANTHROPOLOGY.

**Dolina,** a tn. in Poland, possessing salt industry and salt springs. Pop. 8353.

**Doll,** a figure in the shape of a human being, used as a child's toy. Various derivations have been suggested, of which 'idol' is the most probable. Others are Norse *daul,* woman, and the name 'Dorothy.' Ds. date from very anct. times, and were common in Greece, Rome, and Egypt. Early primitive people delighted in rude images carved out of wood or bone. To the negro a D. has a magical significance, and may be regarded variously as a Mascot, a votive offering, or an idol. Wooden Ds. were introduced into England from the Netherlands, and were called Flanders babies, or simply 'children's babies.' Since then the manufacture of Ds. has greatly advanced, and the stiff wooden D. has been superseded by the stuffed sawdust D., with composition or wax head. Its features became more and more realistic. Hair was substituted for painted ringlets, joints were made; wire mechanism was introduced so that the D. could squeak or shut its eyes at pleasure.

**Dollar,** a tn. in Clackmannanshire, Scotland, 6 m. N.E. of Alloa. It has an academy, founded in 1818, and endowed by Captain John M'Nab (1732–1802). It has a bleaching industry. An object of interest is the ruin of Castle Campbell. Pop. 1954.

**Dollar** (derived from the Ger. *thaler*), applied especially to the unit of the monetary system of the U.S.A. and Canada. Brought into common use in America about 1794, since the Act of 1837, the silver coin has contained 371·25 grains of silver, 41·25 of alloy, total weight being 412¼ grains. Before this time the weight was 416 grains. Under the Act of 1873 trade Ds. of 420 grains (378 grains silver, 42 alloy) were coined for the purpose of export to

China and other Asiatic regions, not legal tender at home. There are paper as well as silver Ds. The D. mark $ is written before the number, a sign whose derivation is much disputed. A D. contains 100 cents (*s. 2d.*). Silver half and quarter Ds., and dimes (10 cents), are also issued; nickel half-dimes and copper cents. A gold coin of similar value 25·8 grains in weight; 23·22 grains of old, 2·58 of alloy) was used from 849–90. Though declared the standard of value in the U.S.A. in 1900, no fresh coins have been issued. Other coins of nearly corresponding value are the rigsdaler of Denmark, riksdaler of Sweden, peso (8 reales) of Spain and the Spanish-American colonies, peso of Mexico and Central and S. American republics (69·8 to 96·5 cents), Arabian piastre, yen of Japan, sol of Peru, sucre of Ecuador, etc. Our double florin (first struck 1887, now rarely seen) about equals a D. By 600 the word was common in England for the Ger. thaler, a silver coin of varying value, current from the sixteenth century, and was especially used later for that worth, 3 marks 2s. 11d.). Sometimes used roughly as a slang term for crown (5s.). For compounds *see* Murray's *New English Dictionary*, iii.

**Döllinger, Johann Joseph Ignaz von** 1799–1890), an eminent Ger. Catholic theologian *b*. at Bamberg in Bavaria. He was educated at the gymnasium and university at Würzburg, and in 1822 was ordained priest. After lecturing for three years in the Lyceum at Aschaffenburg (1823–26), D. was appointed to the chair of ecclesiastical history and law at Munich. During the early part of his career it has generally been assumed that he was an ardent champion of Ultramontanism in Germany, though even as a young man his views were by no means narrow. He was a friend of the leaders of the Oxford Tractarian movement—Pusey, Hope Scott, Manning, and others—and wrote vehemently against Protestantism in *Die Reformation*, 1846, and *Luther*, 1851. His visit to Rome (1857) worked a great alteration in his opinions. In 1861 he delivered certain lectures at Munich in which he declared his belief that the progress of the Rom. Catholic Church did not depend on the temporal sovereignty of the Pope. He answered his assailants in *Kirche und Kirchen*, 1861; and *Die Papstfabeln des Mittelalters*, 1863. In 1864 Pius IX. issued his *Syllabus* condemning certain current philosophic systems, which was replied to anonymously by the publication of *Janus*, written by D. in collaboration with Huber and Friedrich. When in 1870 the Vatican Council defined the doctrine of papal infallibility, D. headed a protest, and in 1871 addressed his famous letter to the archbishop of Munich, in which he refused to accept the doctrine. He was excommunicated, but several of the leading universities of Europe expressed themselves in his favour by conferring on him honorary degrees. During the latter years of his life he endeavoured to bring about a union of the Christian churches which do not belong to the Roman Communion. He was elected a president of the Munich Academy in 1873. His later publications include *Geschichte des Konzils von Trent*, 1876; and *Studies in European History* (Eng. translation), 1890. *See* Life by Friedrich (3 vols.), 1899–1901.

**Dollond, John** (1706–61), a distinguished London optician, by trade a silk weaver. He studied mathematics, astronomy, and optics, and was also a good linguist. In 1752 he became a practical optician in partnership with his son, Peter, founding the well-known firm of Dollond & Co., Ltd., in St. Paul's Churchyard. In 1758 his treatise on the dispersion of light, published in *Philosophical Transactions*, won him the Copley medal from the Royal Society. Its result was his invention of the achromatic telescope.

**Dolman** (Turkish *dōlāmān*), originally a long, loose garment with narrow sleeves. It was worn usually by the Turks, and was the name of the uniform jacket worn by hussars.

**Dolmen** (Celtic *daul*, table; *maen*, stone), a modern archæological term

KITS COITY HOUSE

applied to the megalithic framework of prehistoric sepulchral structures, which were formerly called cromlechs. On the Continent the term is used to describe the whole structure with the cairn or covering mound. There are numerous Ds. in France, the Grotte aux Fées at Mettray, near Tours, and La Pierre Turquaise in Seine-et-Oise being very fine specimens. In England the word is usually applied only to the stone props with accompanying stone roofs, such as Kits Coity House, near Aylesford in Kent. There are over 700 Ds. in Ireland. *See* Borlase's *Dolmens of Ireland*, 1897.

**Dolo**, a tn. in the prov. of Venice, from which it is 12 m. distant, in Italy. Pop. 8700.

**Dolomieu, Déodat-Guy-Sylvain-Trancrède Gratet de** (1750–1801), a famous Fr. geologist and mineralogist of Dolomieu, Isère, France. Early a member of the Order of

calcite. The crystals are usually white in colour, and have curved faces, some varieties being almost spherical. The term D. is also applied to rocks containing that mineral Such rocks are common to every geological formation both in the Old World and in the New. They seldom contain fossils and are often found in the neighbourhood of rock salt and gypsum. Many of the D. rocks of Britain are esteemed as building stone. The Houses of Parliament were built with D. from Bolsover, in Derbyshire; other localities are Nottinghamshire (Mansfield stone) and Durham. Ds. are common in the Alps and a district in the S. Tyrolese Alps

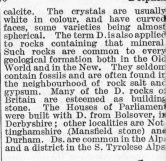

DOLPHIN

Malta, he killed a knight of his galley in a duel (1768), but the death-sentence was revoked by the grand master, and nine months' imprisonment substituted. D. soon left the army to study science, visiting Etna, Vesuvius, the Apennines, Lipari Is. and Calabria. In 1783 he published *Voyage aux îles de Lipari* ; in 1784, studies an earthquakes; and in 1785 appeared memoirs on basalt, the mineral 'dolomite' (named after him, 1791); *Pierres Figurées de Florence* ; and *Constitution Physique de l'Egypte*. Professor of Geology at the School of Mines, 1796 ; Daubenton's successor at Natural History Museum, 1800. In 1798 on the scientific staff that accompanied Bonaparte's expedition to Egypt. Returning for his health, 1799, he was imprisoned at Taranto, and only released after the battle of Marengo, 1801. Other works are : *Mémoires sur les îles Ponces . . .*, 1788 ; *Dernier voyage dans les Alpes*, 1802 ; *Philosophie Mineralogique*, 1802 (partly written in prison). *See* Thomson, *Annals of Philosophy*, xii., 1808.

**Dolomite**, a common mineral crystallising in rhombohedra and consisting of carbonates of calcium and magnesium. It has a hardness of 3½ to 4, and a specific gravity of 2·8, and is therefore harder and heavier than

much favoured by tourists, is known by that name.

**Dolomites, The**, a mountainous dist. in the S. Tyrolese Alps. It is chiefly composed of magnesian lime stone, where the peaks rise in most fantastic forms and shapes, and are streaked by veins of wonderful vivid colourings. The D. region lies be tween the Brenner Railway from Franzensgeste to Trent, and the road over the Monte Croce Pass from In nichen in the Drave Valley by way of the Sexten glen, and the Piave valley to Belluno and Feltre. The highest peak is the Marmolata, 10,971 ft., but other much more typical peaks are the Sorapiss, the Cimon della Pala, the Langkogel, the Pelmo Drei Zinnen, and Rosengarten.

**Dolon-Nor**, or **Lama-Miao**, a tn. of Mongolia. It is situated 165 m. N. of Peking, and is noted for the manu of brass and iron idols, vases, bells etc. It is a centre of trade for E Mongolia. There are numerous ruin and Buddhist temples in the neigh bourhood. Pop. 30,000.

**Dolores**, a tn. of Buenos Ayres in the Argentine Republic. It is 127 m from the city of Buenos Ayres by rai Pop. 14,600. (2) A tn. in Uruguay S. America. Pop. 8000.

**Dolphin**, a popular name given to many cetaceans, but applied parti ularly to members of the genus *Delphinus*, which belongs to the amily Delphinidæ. There are four known species of these mammals, all of which have a long and distinct beak, numerous teeth—forty to sixty in number—and sickle-shaped fins; in length they are not usually more than 10 ft.; in habit they are gregarious, and the diet consists chiefly of herrings. *D. delphis*, the common D., is found in the Mediterranean and N. Atlantic; *D. tursio* is sometimes found off British coasts. Other members of the same family, but of different genera, are called Ds., and two well-known species are *Sotalis sinensis*, the Chinese white D., and *Grampus riscus*, Risso's D. In anct. times the D. was sacred to Apollo, and has since been used as a symbol. The fishes known as Ds. are members of the family Coryphænidæ (*see* CORY-PHÆNA).

**Dom,** the highest peak of the Alpine group of the Mischabelhörner, which rises between the valleys of Saas and Zermatt. The D. is 14,942 ft. in altitude; it was first ascended by the Rev. J. L. Davies in 1858.

**Domat,** or **Daumat, Jean** (1625–96), a Fr. jurist, was the author of *Lois Civiles dans leur Ordre Naturel Suivies du Droit Publique*, 1689. This work, which earned for D. a pension of 2000 from Louis XIV., is still regarded as a valuable and authoritative treatise on the science of law, all law being considered a development from principles of ethics. When Pascal *d.*, D. took care of his private manuscripts.

**Dombasle,** a small tn. of France, in the dept. of Meurthe-et-Moselle, situated about 10 m. S.E. of Nancy. It has the most important works in France for the manufacture of soda and its chemical products.

**Dombes,** the name of a former dist. of France, which now forms a part of the dept. of Ain. Numerous small lakes are found, which rest on a substratum of clay that was artificially made in the ninth and tenth centuries. Owing to the unhealthiness of the district, two-thirds of the marshes have been reclaimed.

**Dombrowski, Jan Henryk** (1755–1818), a Polish general, from 1792–94 took part in the Polish campaigns against Russia and Prussia, gaining distinction during the siege of Warsaw under Kosciusko. In the Italian campaign he was conspicuous for his bravery at the Trebbia (1799). With the divisions of Poles he had organised for Napoleon in 1806, he commanded in the Polish campaign of 1809, and during the fatal march on Moscow in 1812 was wounded whilst crossing the Beresina. For his reorganisation of

the Polish forces he was appointed cavalry-general in the new kingdom of Poland (1815).

[*Canadian Pacific*

THE FIVE DOMES OF ST MARK'S, VENICE

THE DOME OF LES INVALIDES, PARIS

**Dome** (It. *duomo*), applied since the Renaissance strictly to the outer part of a circular or polygonal roof (of which the ' cupola ' is the inner part), rising above the rest of the building. It was known to the Assyrians and Persians, and used to a certain extent among some Gk. tribes. It formed a very favourite feature of Renaissance church architecture. Each vertical section forms a semicircular or pointed arch. The Roms. really developed the D. as an architectural ornament, though it is often spoken of as a product of the East, owing to its frequent use in mosques. In Italy ' dome ' often had the wider meaning of cathedral or chief church (*domus*, or house of God). Cf. Ger. *dom* or *domkirche*, cathedral. Ds. are much used in the Mohammedan architecture of Turkey and India, notable examples being Santa Sofia, Con-

first patron, and employed him in his palace. D. helped Annibale Carracci at the Farnese, and painted ' The Death of Adonis ' from his own designs. He painted frescoes for Cardinals Borghese, Farnese, and Aldobrandini. He ought to be judged chiefly by his frescoes, and is undoubtedly one of the finest of all Italian painters (*see* Landon, *Vie et Œuvres des Peintres les plus Célèbres*, 1803–34). Some of the best are the series at the Basilian Abbey of Grottaferrata. His famous oil painting, ' The Last Communion of St. Jerome,' was judged by Poussin next best in Rome to Raphael's ' The Transfiguration.' In 1617 he returned to Bologna disgusted by the jealousy of rivals, but was in Rome again in 1621. In

AN EXCERPT FROM THE 'DOMESDAY BOOK'

stantinople (A.D. 538), supported on four arches by means of ' pendentives '; Taj Mahal, Agra. The most noted in modern Rome are the Pantheon (probably of Trajan's time, A.D. 98–117); St. Peter's (139 ft. in diameter, 330 ft. high). St. Mark's, Venice, has five Ds. The Invalides and Panthéon of Paris are famous, also the Capitol at Washington, America. In London, St. Paul's Cathedral and the Albert Hall are the best examples. *See* Isabelle, *Les Edifices Circulaires et les Dômes*, 1855 ; Choisy, *L'Art de bâtir chez les Romains*, 1873 ; *L'Art de bâtir chez les Byzantins*, 1883.

**Domenichino, Domenico Zampieri** (1581–1641), an Italian painter of the Bolognese school, pupil of Calvært and the Carracci. A friend of Albani, he visited with him Parma, Modena, and Reggio, to study Correggio and Parmigiano, later joining him at Rome. Cardinal Agucchi was his

1630 he went to Naples to decorate the Capella del Tesoro. His fame roused much envy among the established painters there, and it was suspected that he was poisoned. Among his works are : ' The Flagellation of St. Andrew ' (1608), frescoes of the lives of St. Nilus and St. Bartholomew (1609–10), frescoes of St. Cecilia (St. Luigi de' Francesi, Rome), ' The Four Evangelists ' (S. Andrea della Valle), ' Diana and her Nymphs,' ' The Sybil of Cumæ ' (Borghese Palace), ' The Repose of Venus,' ' Diana and Actæon ' (Pitti, Florence), ' The Angel and Tobias,' ' St. George and the Dragon ' (landscapes, National Gallery, London), ' Moses and the Burning Bush,' ' Combat of Hercules and Acheloüs,' ' The Triumph of Love ' (Louvre), ' St. John in a Vision,' ' Time Trampling on Youth.' His portrait of Cardinal Colonna was highly praised.

**Domesday Book,** or **Doomsday**

**Book,** a valuation survey of England made by William the Conqueror. The survey was begun in 1085 and completed in 1087. The book records the owners of the land, the nature of its cultivation, the number of its inhabitants, and their respective classes —freemen, villeins, and serfs. The compilation of the book was a marvellous enterprise, admirably planned and of inestimable value both in times of peace and of war. It made taxation on a sound basis possible, besides being a census roll and a record of estate valuations. To the historian the book is priceless. The survey was called the D. B. because in the eyes of the people it was like the great reckoning of doomsday. See Round's *Domesday Studies,* 1888 ; and Maitland's *Domesday and Beyond,* 1897.

**Domestication of Animals,** the process by which man has changed certain species of animals to suit his own needs. This change can only be rendered effective if carried on for successive generations, as the term domestication implies permanent changes in certain characteristics, and also in the structure in many cases, these changes being brought about by alteration of their environment and a system of breeding. This includes also the protection and provision of food for some animals and the special control exercised over them which prevents their leading an absolutely wild life. It is necessary in the case of the animals that they should be able and willing to adapt themselves to this control, and that they should be fertile though under control or living under different conditions. The process by which domestication is produced consists principally in selecting certain species which possess the most desirable qualities and in causing them to breed only with other desirable species, at the same time, in all probability, altering their food and surroundings. This leads to changes in their outward form, in some cases not very noticeable, in others very marked, as the difference in feathers, hair, colouring, and, deeper-seated still, those of structure. Among domestic animals there may be mentioned a number or birds, as fowls, ducks, geese, and many others. Dogs, cats, and several other animals among mammals are also domesticated. While certain kinds of insects and fishes have certainly been altered by man, if they cannot lay claim to the title of domesticated animals. See Charles Darwin, *The Variation of Animals and Plants under Domestication,* 1868 ; and Nathaniel Southgate Shaler, *Domesticated Animals, their*

*Relation to Man and his Advancement in Civilisation,* 1896.

**Domestic Economy** (from Gk. οἰκονομία, management, which is made up of οἶκος, house, and νέμειν, to manage) is the only expression in which the original sense of house management survives. To-day it is used both of the thrifty control of the home from a financial point of view and more generally of the science which teaches household duties and control.

**Domestic Relations, Law of,** means in U.S.A. that group of rules which defines the rights and obligations of the parties to the relations of husband and wife, parent and child, guardian and ward, and master and servant. The rights of the husband to the society of his wife, of the father to the presence and services of his children, of the guardian to the custody of his ward, of the master to the labour of his servant, as against all, and the corresponding obligation to compensate all persons who had suffered actionable wrongs through his failure to maintain and properly control them, constituted the greater portion of this law until within the past three or four generations. Social development has, however, given to this branch of law, as to most others, a wider field and more numerous details, and the internal rights and duties of the parties to the relation toward one another have thus obtained some legal recognition. The appointment of guardians by the courts or by the wills of deceased persons under the supervision of the Courts, the establishment of the relation of master and servant by specific contracts, the emancipation of the personality of the wife from its entire submergence in that of the husband, have been among the causes of this change, and account for many of the differences which appear between the statements of the law contained in the certain treatises and those of the present day. (William C. Robinson, *Elements of American Jurisprudence* (Boston) 1900 ; James Schouler, *Law of the Domestic Relations* (Boston), 1900.)

**Domestic Servants** are those employed to perform the so-called menial work of a household. The greater majority of them are women, though page boys, footmen, and butlers, etc., are indispensable in all large establishments. A mistress may dismiss a maid at once for dishonesty, immorality, hopeless incapacity, or flagrant disobedience, and is not obliged to give a character if she judges the maid unworthy of one. Servants are usually paid by the quarter or the month, a month's notice being required on either side for the termination of a contract. They are entitled to a month's wages if summarily dismissed. D. S. are included in the Employers' Liability Act, and under the Workman's Compensation Act of 1925 can claim compensation for injuries arising during their employment, provided that gross negligence or other wilful misconduct on their part has not caused the injury. If the servant loses his life, his dependants are entitled to a sum equal to three years' earnings or £200, whichever sum is larger, but not exceeding in any case £300 ; if he leaves no dependants, a sum not exceeding £15 must be allowed by the employer for medical and funeral expenses. If the servant is totally or partially disabled, his master must pay him a sum not exceeding 30s. a week till death or recovery. A licence, for which 15s. must be paid annually, is needed for each male D. S. Dismissal without just cause shown entitles the servant to normal and also to board wages until the expiration of the half year. All D. S. must insure against sickness under the National Insurance Act of 1924, the conditions being the same for them as for other workers. Statistics show a decrease in the number of D. S. proportionate to the population, both in the British Isles and the U.S.A., where the domestic problem threatens to become very serious. The decrease in the number of servants in the British Isles may be explained partly by the influx of women into factories and business offices and partly by their emigration to Canada and Australia, where their scarcity leads to the offer of high wages. The census returns of 1921 showed that 371,682 men-servants were employed throughout Great Britain in that year, and 1,844,574 women, giving a total of 2,216,256. Since the War various organisations for the absorption of ex-soldiers into domestic service have been formed, and more recently even for unemployed miners, with satisfactory results. The shortage of women servants in 1930 proved so acute that Miss Margaret Bondfield, Minister of Labour, suggested that unemployed girls and women refusing to enter D. S. should be deprived of the dole. A Domestic Servants' Benevolent Institution was established under the patronage of the Duke of Connaught and the presidency of the Earl of Bathurst, in 1846, to give relief and maintenance to members in old age or permanent sickness, or infirmity, by granting them pensions; and also to give relief in cases of urgent temporary distress. Offices, 4 Deni-

son House, 296 Vauxhall Bridge Road, London.

**Domett, Alfred** (1811–87), a British colonial statesman and poet, contributed a number of poems to *Blackwood's Magazine*, his ' Christmas Hymn ' being widely read. During the ten leisured years he spent in London he enjoyed an intimacy with Robert Browning, who made him the subject of his verses ' Waring.' Became Premier of New Zealand in 1862. *Ranolf and Amolia* (1872) and *Flotsam and Jetsam* (1877) are two collections of his poems.

**Domett, Sir William** (1754–1828), an Eng. admiral, *b.* in Devonshire. He was present in the fight off Ushant (1778), in the *Chesapeake* under Arbuthnot (1781), and in the battle of the Saintes (1782). In Howe's battle (1794) he commanded the flagship *Royal George*, and in 1795 he was present in the action off L'Orient. Four years later he fought in Basque road, and at Copenhagen he served as flag-captain under Sir Hyde Parker (1801).

**Domfront,** a tn. in the dept. of Orne, France. Owes its origin to a hermit Saint Front, of the sixth century. It is perched on a hill and has kept fourteen towers, and the high wall which enclosed it in the eleventh century, the dungeon of its castle, old granite houses, and a beautiful church. It suffered much from war and was besieged in 1574. Pop. 4010.

**Domicile,** according to Rom. law, the place ' where a person has his family abode and chief business premises, whence he does not depart unless business affairs compel him, and on leaving which he considers himself a sojourner, and on returning to which he considers himself at home ' (Cod. 10, lit. 40, 1, etc.). The D. of the parents is the D. of the child, and the latter changes with the D. of the parent during the child's minority. An illegitimate child takes the D. of the mother. Should the father die during the minority of a child, the child's D. is the last D. of the father. A woman when she marries takes the D. of her husband. A new D. is acquired by residence and intention of adoption. When a man has two or more places of residence, his D. is that residence which he selects as his home and which is the centre of his affairs. D. is therefore of three types : (1) D. of origin, depending on the D. of the parents at the time of birth ; (2) D. of choice, which is voluntarily acquired by a party ; (3) D. by law, *e.g.* the D. which a wife acquires by marriage.

As in England, so in the U.S.A., the law of domicile has not yet been usted by political nationality as a test of private law. But though the U.S.A. has not yet adopted this world-wide test, the law of D. is not of the great importance it is in England, because questions of capacity are generally referred not to any personal law, but to the *lex loci contractus*. See LEX LOCI.

**Dominic, St. (Dominic de Guzman)** 1170–1221), was *b.* at Calahorra, a small tn. in the diocese of Osma in Old Castile, Spain. As a young priest he resigned a canonry to take up missionary work among the Albigenses in the S. of France. Subsequently he founded his order of mendicant friars, adding to the Rule of St. Augustine his own constitutions. Pope Innocent III. recognised and sanctioned the order in 1215. The régime of the order was most severe, enjoining silence, poverty, and fasting. The friars were called Dominicans from their founder ; Preaching Friars from their zeal in persuasion ; Black Friars from the colour of their dress ; and in France, Jacobins, from their original headquarters in the Rue St. Jacques at Paris. For women desirous of following the same Rule the "Second Order" was formed ; and a confraternity of men and women in the world but governing their lives by the same principles was called the "Third Order." The order numbered some famous divines, *e.g.* Thomas Aquinas. The Dominican Order have always upheld Aquinas's theological system (Thomism), their chief opponents in this being the Franciscans and later the Jesuits. The Order furnished examining judges and often the presidents of the Spanish, Roman and Portuguese Inquisitions. St. Dominic was canonised by Pope Gregory IX. in 1235. *See* Jessopp's *The Coming of the Friars*, 1888 ; and Herklers' *Francis and Dominic*, 1901.

A DOMINICAN MONK

**Dominica,** the largest of the Leeward Islands, British W. Indies, is 29 m. long and 15 m. broad, area 305 sq. m., of volcanic formation and very mountainous, with a healthy climate and a rainfall of 80 in. in parts and over 250 in. in others. Sugar has ceased to be an article of export, and the main industry is the cultivation of limes and the manufacture of their products. There are about 100 pure Caribs still living on the island. Pop. 41,671. Roseau (6803) is the cap.

**Dominical Letters,** the letter used to denote the Sundays throughout one year. The seven letters, A B C D E F G, are used in succession to denote the first seven days of the year, from Jan. 1 to 7, and then in rotation the next seven days, and so on. Thus, if Jan. 3 be a Sunday, it is evident that the D. L. for the year is C, as the number of letters and of the days of the week is the same. Leap year has two D. L., one for the days preceding Feb. 29 and the other for the rest of the year. The intercalary day is marked by the same letter as the day preceding it, thus effecting the change on the following Sunday. D. L. displaced the nundinal letters in the Rom. calendar : rules and tables for finding them are given in prayer books.

**Dominican Republic,** *see* SANTO DOMINGO.

**Dominion Steamship Line, The,** amalgamated with the American and Atlantic Transport Companies and the White Star Line to form the Morgan combination (so called because it was established by an American syndicate under Mr. J. Pierpont Morgan). This combination became in 1902 the 'International Mercantile Marine Company,' with a capital of $120,000,000. Messrs. Harland and Wolff of Belfast, who constructed the excellent passenger steamers for this line, also largely control its management. As part of the White Star Co., the name of the Dominion line was gradually changed to ' The White Star Dominion Line,' and subsequently to the ' White Star Canadian Service.' In 1928 The Oceanic Steam Navigation Co. purchased the White Star and its associated lines from the International Mercantile Marine Co., so that once against this important organisation became a British Co. The capital is now £9,000,000.

**Dominis de, Marcus Antonius** (1566–1624), an Italian theologian and natural philosopher, *b.* at Arba in Dalmatia. While preparing for his novitiate in the Jesuit order, he taught rhetoric, mathematics, and physics. It was during this period that he wrote his *De Radiis Visus et Lucis in Vitris Perspectivis et Iride*. He became bishop of Segni and afterwards of Spalatro, but being implicated in the disputes between Rome and Venice, having quarrelled with the pope and exhibited, moreover, certain Protestant leanings, he was obliged to resign his see. He was subsequently received in 1616 by James I. of England. As dean of Windsor he wrote *De Republica Ecclesiastica*. He afterwards expressed a desire to return to the Catholic Church, but some letters he possessed belied his conversion, and he was imprisoned under the Inquisition at St. Angelo, where he *d.* in a few months. His chief merit rests on his discoveries with regard to the refraction of light in the rainbow.

**Dominium**, a term in Rom. law which has been adopted into most European codes. It signifies complete and lawful right to and in an object, being distinct from the usufruct which is merely the right arising from actual possession.

**Domino**, originally the hood or cape with which officiating priests protected themselves in cold weather. In Venice and other parts of Italy the D. was worn at masquerades and fancy-dress balls by people not otherwise dressed in character. It was a wide-sleeved enveloping cloak with a half-mask. The word D. is popularly used as synonym for mask.

**Dominoes** (probably so called from the resemblance of the black backs of the pieces to the mask known as the domino), a game, partly of chance, partly of skill, played by any number of players, from two upwards. Twenty-eight oblong pieces of ivory, bone, or wood, white on the face, are required. The white face is divided into two parts by a line, and, except in the case of the double-blank, there are dots on one side or both sides of this line from the number of which the piece takes its name. Thus there is the double-six, with six dots on either side, the six-five, the six-four, etc.; the double-five, five-four, etc., ending with six-blank, five-blank, etc. Sometimes sets are also used ranging up to double-nine and double-twelve. The *block* and *draw* games are played as follows: The pieces, called also cards, are shuffled on the table face downwards, and each player draws the number of cards required, usually seven. The remainder of the pieces form the *stock*. The leader then plays, or, technically speaking, *poses* a D., generally the highest he has; the second player must then pose one from his own set so that one of its numbers shall be the same as one of those on the D. first posed. Thus, if double-six were first posed, he can follow with any D. which has six on one side. By some rules, however, if a player pose a double he may play a second card if possible. If a player cannot match he 'passes,'

and the first player (supposing the number be two) plays again. If the 'draw' game is being played, however, a player who cannot match may draw on the stock until he gets a card that does match, provided always that two cards be left in the stock. If a player play out all his pieces he cries 'Domino' and wins the hand, scoring a number of points equivalent to the number of *pips* on his opponent's remaining cards. If neither can play any further, each counts the number of pips on his remaining D., and each then scores the number of his opponent's pips. Fresh hands are then dealt until one player reaches 100. Double cards are laid crosswise (*à cheval*). This is the commonest system of playing D. in England, but the *matador* is the commoner form on the Continent and is perhaps the more scientific. The object here is not to match the end number, but to make that number up to seven. See *The Handbook of Games*, vol. i., published in Bohn's Library (Bell).

**Domitianus, Titus Flavius**, the youngest son of the Emperor Vespasian, who succeeded his brother Titus as emperor in the year A.D. 81. Though Tacitus (*Hist.* iv. 51, 68) alludes to the immoral practices of his youth, he commenced his reign with an earnest attempt to stem the tide of immorality at Rome. He reorganised the government of the provinces and erected some fine buildings at Rome. During his reign the conquest of Britain was effected by Agricola. The vices that disgraced his youth, however, grew malignant towards the end of his reign. He exiled Epictetus and other philosophers from Rome. In A.D. 93 a persecution of the Christians and Jews took place with cruel massacres. A conspiracy was formed against the emperor in A.D. 96, and he was put to death by his officers in his own chamber.

**Domodossola**, a tn. in Italy in the prov. of, and 55 m. N.W. of the tn. of Novara. It is 25 m. S.E. of the head of the Simplon Pass. Pop.7600.

**Domremy-la-Pucelle**, a vil. of France, in the dept. of Vosges. It is situated on the l. b. of the Meuse, about 7½ m. N. of Neufchâteau, and 30 m. S.W. of Nancy. It is historically interesting as being the birthplace of Joan of Arc, 1412. The house in which she lived is preserved, and over the door are the arms of France, together with the following inscription: 'Vive Labeur; vive le roi Louys.' Opposite the house is an immense bust of the heroine, and there are several monuments erected to her memory. Pop. 280.

**Don,** called by the ancients the Tanais, a river of S. Russia, rises in Lake Ivanski in Tula, and flows in a S.S.E. direction through Ryazan, Tambov, Voronej, and the territory of the Don Cossacks (*q.v.*), but repelled by the mountains. Situated to the W. of the Volga, it turns in a S.W. direction and enters the Sea of Azov. A canal planned by Peter the Great connects the D. and the Volga. The river is 1156 m. long and is navigable up to Zadonsk. In spring the river overflows its banks and covers the adjoining territory with unhealthy swamps. The fisheries on the river are extremely valuable.

**Dona Francisca,** or **Joinville,** situated in the prov. of Santa Catharina, S. Brazil. It is to the W. of the town of São Francisca, and about 80 m. N. of Florianopolis. Pop. 25,000.

**Donaghadee,** a tn., Ireland, in co. Down, situated on the Irish Channel, near Belfast Lough. It is the nearest port to Britain. The harbour is small, and accommodation scanty, but a shipping trade in dairy produce and cattle is carried on. Pop. 4879.

**Donaghmore,** the name of numerous places in Ireland, situated in counties Cork, Down, Meath, Tyrone, Wicklow, Queen's county, Limerick, Kildare, Kilkenny, etc

**Donaldson, James** (1751–1830), a bookseller and philanthropist, acquired a fortune by carrying on his father's business, which consisted in issuing cheap reprints of works out of copyright. The hospital for poor children in Edinburgh, which was built in 1842–51, was the result of his bequest of £240,000.

**Donaldson, Sir James** (1831–1915), a Scottish classical scholar. In 1890 he became vice-chancellor and principal of the university of St. Andrews. His classical works include a *Modern Greek Grammar* (1853) and a discussion of the position of women in Greece and Rome (1907), but his most important work, first published in 1864–66, and again in 1874 as *The Apostolical Fathers*, is a valuable contribution to the history of the early church. Died at St. Andrews.

**Donaldson, John William** (1811–61), a philologist. His *New Cratylus* (1839) and *Varronianus* (1844) are the earliest attempts outside Germany to apply to Greek and Latin the principles of comparative philology. Also he recast Buckham's *Theatre of the Greeks,* but his most ingenious literary effort was an attempt to rescue from the Hebrew Pentateuch the scattered Book of Jashar (1854), an attempt which proved very distasteful to the contemporary theologians.

**Donash ben Labrath,** a Jewish poet and grammarian of the tenth century, *b.* at Bagdad. Not only was he one of the first to treat grammar scientifically, but he also wrote the earliest known specimen of metre in Jewish language, his verse being an imitation from the Arabic.

**Donatello,** or **Donato di Nicoldo di Betto Bardi** (1386–1466), a famous sculptor, *b.* at Florence. His father a wool merchant, came to Rome at the age of seventeen with his friend Brunelleschi, where the two youths, besides carrying on the trade of goldsmith, devoted themselves to the study of architecture. After some years, both men returned to Florence rich in ideas and inspiration. D. is celebrated for his marble and bronze statues, which are beautifully executed, and which reveal the nobility and force of those works of antiquity which formed his constant study and delight. He combines the good points of the Renaissance together with his own original way of treating his subject. The Renaissance betokened the revival of the Classic as opposed to the Gothic in the history of architecture, and Brunelleschi, D.'s life-long friend, was the inaugurator of this new movement. D.'s patron was Cosmo de'. Medici, who well rewarded him for his industry. The sculptor was correspondingly generous towards his friends. His principal works are the marble statues of St. Peter and St. Mark in the church of San Michele at Florence ; a bronze statue of David at Florence, another bronze figure of the equestrian Gattemalata in a public place at Padua. Other sculptural works are the statues on Giotto's belfry, decorative work on the pulpit of St. Lorenzo, and figures in the baptistery at Florence. *See*

ST. JOHN THE BAPTIST
(*by Donatello*)

Vasari's Lives; Lord Balcarres' *Donatello*.

**Donati, Giovanni Battista** (1826–73), an Italian astronomer. From 1854–64 he discovered six comets, the finest, which appeared in 1858, bearing his name. By subjecting the light of a comet to the spectrum analysis, he was able to describe its gaseous composition.

**Donatio Mortis Causa,** a gift made in prospect of death. This practice is derived from Roman law, and is thus defined in the *Institutes* (ii. tit. 7) : ' A gift made under an apprehension of death, as when a thing is given on condition that, if the donor die, the donee shall have it, but that it shall be returned if the donor shall survive the danger he apprehends or repents of his donation or if the donee die before the donor.' Actual transfer is necessary, but where the nature of the goods makes this impossible the transfer of a symbol of ownership (*e.g.* a key) is permitted.

**Donatists,** a powerful sect which arose in the Christian Church in N. Africa at the commencement of the fourth century. There had long been two parties in Carthage : a moderate party, headed, until his death in 311, by the bishop Mensurius; and a strong fanatical party, headed by Lucilla, a wealthy widow. This latter party carried on in a more developed form the African tradition of severity towards *traditores*. In 311 Mensurius died, and, in order to be beforehand with the rigorists, the moderate party hastily elected Cæcilian as bishop, without awaiting the arrival of the Numidian bishops, and secured his consecration by Felix, Bishop of Aptunga. Secundus, Bishop of Tigisis, treated this act as illegal, and convened a synod of seventy bishops at Carthage, which excommunicated Cæcilian. The lector Marjorinus was elected in his stead, and on the death of Marjorinus in 315, Donatus the Great, from whom the sect is named, took his place. Both parties had, before this time, appealed to the Emperor Constantine, and his decisions had been in favour of orthodoxy. General synods at Arles (314) and Milan (316) also pronounced against the D., but the schism spread, and there were soon rival bishops throughout N. Africa. The D. excommunicated the rest of the Church, baptising again all Catholics who seceded to them. The orthodox reaction against this practice gave rise to the theory of a sacramental character imparted in baptism, confirmation and order. Finding them proof against persuasion, Constantine ignored them, but they were subjected to severe persecution under Constans.

In 411, a great disputation, attended by 286 Catholic and 279 D. bishops, was held at Carthage, and decision again given for the orthodox. The sect died out before the seventh century. See *Histories* of Möller, Neander, Völter, etc., and the work of Optatus of Milevi.

**Donative,** *see* ADVOWSON.

**Donatus, Ælius,** a grammarian who lived in the middle of the fourth century A.D. He wrote a grammar and a commentary on Virgil and Terence. St. Jerome studied grammar under him. The commentary on Virgil ascribed to him is now supposed to be spurious.

**Donauwörth,** a tn. and river port of Germany, in the prov. of Schwaben, Bavaria. It is situated on the l. b. of the Danube, at its junction with the Wörnitz, 25 m. N.N.W. of Augsburg. At one time it was a free imperial city, and it contains several old buildings of interest, including a Benedictine abbey. It was stormed by Gustavus Adolphus and taken by King Ferdinand during the Thirty Years' War. Flax and hemp, hops and fruit are cultivated. There are manufs. of heavy iron goods, machinery, etc., and there is some considerable trade carried on by the Danube. Pop. 4860.

**Donawitz,** a tn. of Austria, in the prov. of Styria, situated 2 m. N. of Leoben. In it there are iron foundries. Pop. 18,120.

**Don Benito,** a tn. of Spain in the prov. of Badajoz, 57 m. N.E. by E. of the city of that name, and 25 m. N.E. of Merida. There are manufactures of hats and oil presses. A trade is carried on in corn, fruit, and wine. Pop. 19,000.

**Don Carlos,** *see* CARLOS.

**Doncaster,** a market tn. and county bor., 37 m. S.W. of York. It is situated on the W. bank of the Don. The ' Town Moor ' racecourse dates from 1703, and the ' Sandall Mile ' course was made in 1892. Both belong to the municipality, and the profits derived therefrom have reduced the rates of D. to practically nil. St. George's, the parish church, was built in 1855 to replace the old church burnt in 1853. A tower 170 ft. in height is the only remaining portion of the ancient building. The modern church is very beautiful and impressive. The locomotive works of the L.N.E. Railway are situated at D., and employ a large proportion of the population. Agricultural implements are also manufactured, and there is a large trade in grain and wool. Cartwright's first power-loom was set up in this town. Pop. 54,064.

**Don Cossacks, Territory of the,** a country of S. Russia bounded on the

N. by the provinces of Voronesh and Saratov, on the S. by Caucasia and the Sea of Azov, on the E. by Astrakan, and on the W. by Ekaterinoslav and Voronesh. The country consists mainly of steppes, without trees or shrubs, but rich in pasturage. The steppes contain numerous mounds and tumuli of ancient origin, supposed to be the tombs of the Scythians. Many of these tombs have been found to contain relics of ancient civilisation of great value. The country is watered by the Don and other smaller rivers, of which the chief is the Moloschna. The principal lake is the Bolskoi. The climate is on the whole good ; the heat in summer is tempered by plentiful rainfall, and the cold in winter is dry. The N. and E. of the country is inhabited by the Don Cossacks (see COSSACKS). Wheat is the principal produce. Oats, barley, and maize are also grown in considerable quantities. Merino wool is also a produce of importance. The vineyards of the territory were also of increasing importance before the Great War. The Cossack horse is of small and ungainly proportions, but is sturdy and enduring. The western division of the province is one of the richest portions of the country. The fisheries in the Don and the Sea of Azov are valuable, and fish, caviar, and isinglass are exported in large quantities. The chief towns are Old Tscherkask, New Tscherkask, and Perdjansk. The area of the territory is 63,537 sq. m., and the pop. 2,575,818.

**Donegal,** a co. of Ireland in the prov. of Ulster, is bounded by the Atlantic Ocean and the counties of Londonderry, Tyrone, Fermanagh, and Leitrim. The coast-line is very irregular, being broken by Lough Swilly, Sheep Haven, Boylagh Bay, Gweebarra Bay, and Donegal Bay. The coast is fringed by many islands, of which the chief are Inistrahul, Tory Is., and Aran Isles. The surface of the country is mountainous. These mountains include eight summits of which Mt. Errigal (2466 ft.) is the highest. Adjoining Malin Beg Head in the W. of Donegal Bay there is a sea cliff 1964 ft. in height. The chief rivers are the Foyle, the Finn, the Swilly, the Erne, the Gweebarra, the Gweedore and the Owenea. The county also possesses many lakes, of which the principal are Loch Derg, Loch Deele, Loch Gartan, Loch Eask, and Loch Glen. The climate of D. is inclement. Rude winds prevail, rendering great tracts of the county barren. The mould in some regions consists of light clay, suitable for crops of potatoes, oats, and barley. Agricultural implements are for the most part primitive. The breeding of cattle and sheep is the most profitable occupation of the inhabitants. The fisheries of the coast support the great majority of the inhabitants. The country women occupy their time with the embroidery of linen, lace, and muslin. Linen and tweed (Donegal tweed) are also manufactured in the county. Of the historical remains the most interesting is the Grianan of Aileach, the palace of the kings of N. Ireland from most ancient times. There are also interesting relics of St. Columba and the famous Purgatory of St. Patrick situated on an island in Loch Derg. Area 1,190,268 acres. Pop. 168,537.

**Donelson Fort,** a camp at Dover, Tennessee, U.S.A. It was built in the time of the Civil War by the Confederates for the purpose of guarding the Lower Cumberland R., and it consisted of two lines of entrenchments on the land side, and water batteries. It was taken by the Federals in 1862, the prisoners numbering nearly 15,000, which was considerably over two-thirds of the original army.

**Doneraile,** a small tn. of Ireland, in co. Cork, situated on the Awbeg, about 5 m. N.E. by N. of Mallow. Pop. 830.

**Donetz,** the name of a great coal dist. of Russia, which forms part of the prov. of Ekaterinoslav. It extends over much of the Donetz plateau, which is one of the highest portions of the Russian interior. The actual coalfield has an area of about 16,000 sq. m., and produces excellent anthracite and steam coal ; iron is also extensively mined. Geologically, the coals are not found until the close of the Lower Carboniferous period. The R. Donetz ('little Don'), which gives its name to the above district, is a river of S. Russia which flows generally S. for 280 m., receiving on the right the Oudai. It then turns to the W. at Oskal, forms the boundary of the Donetz plateau, and finally flows into the Don, after a course of 680 m. During high water the river affords access to the government of Kharkov.

**Dongen,** a tn. and com. of the Netherlands, situated in the prov. of N. Brabant. Pop. 7200.

**Dongola,** a prov. of the Sudan, stretching between lat. 70° 50′ and 19° 40′ N. It consists of a long, narrow plain, situated in the valley of the Nile, and includes both banks of that river, while to the E. lies the Nubian desert, and to the W. is the Libyan desert. From 1820 to the Mahdi insurrection of '85 it was Egyptian. General Kitchener took it in 1896. New D., the cap. of the prov., is situated on the W. bank of the Nile. It is the chief centre of trade ;

also a military depot. Old D., a decayed town, is 75 m. S.S.E. of New D. The Nubian race are the principal inhabitants of the province, and the pop. of the capital is about 15,000.

**Doni, Antonio Francesco** (1513–74), an Italian priest, was a native of Florence. In Venice he settled down as a printer and writer, publishing many original works, distinguished rather by their curious conceits and eccentric style than for real worth. *La Morale Filosofia*, and the *Marmi*, both published in 1552, are his best known works. In the former, for which he was largely indebted to Firenzuola, he makes his moral teaching palatable by sugaring it with allegories, legends, and fables, whilst in the latter he freely reviles the vices, and especially the superstitions, of the age.

**Donizetti, Gaetano** (1797–1848), an Italian musical composer, studied music in his native place, Bergamo, and later at Bologna. For some time (until 1822) he served in the army. The opera which made his name was *Anna Bolena*, produced in 1830 at Milan. Altogether he composed sixty-four operas. His *Lucia di Lammermoor*, produced at Naples in 1835, roused quite a *furor* and gained him a professorship of counterpoint in that city. His closing years were saddened by signs of lunacy brought on, it is said, by intemperance. Considering that his rivals were Rossini and Bellini, D.'s contemporary popularity is a remarkable tribute to his talents. *La Fille du Régiment* (1840) is his most popular work, but the finest probably is *La Favorita*, produced, curiously enough, in the same year. D. combined the gift of writing pleasant melodies and composition, peculiarly suited to the voice, with extreme facility, vigour, and some sense of humour, as shown in *Don Pasquale* (1843).

**Don Juan**, a famous figure in legend, whose prototype is found in the Spanish play (published in 1630), entitled *El Burlador de Sevilla y convidado*, and attributed to Tirso de Molina. Like the Faust of northern legend, D. J. sacrifices everything to self-gratification, but with this fundamental difference that, whereas for Faust self-gratification means intellectual supremacy, for D. J. it is the consummation of all, even the lowest, sensual pleasures. The following is a bare outline of the story, though different versions are found in all European countries, and even so far afield as Iceland, D. J., of the noble family Tenorio, is an abandoned profligate who lived in the days of Peter the Cruel at Seville. When Ulloa thwarts D. J. in his machinations to seduce his daughter, he is promptly stabbed by the dissolute lover. An arrant disbeliever, D. J. mockingly challenges a stone image of his victim to a banquet in his tomb. The outraged Ulloa accepts and thereupon carries his murderer off to the very hell at which he has so exultingly scoffed. This quaint story has been immortalised by Mozart's magnificent music to Da Ponte's libretto. Hence came the inspiration for Mérimée's novel *Les Ames du purgatoire*, Dumas' *Don Juan de Marana*, and Balzac's *Elixir d'une longue vie*. Henry Purcell, however, who used Shadwell's obscene play, *The Libertine* (1676), was the first to write a musical setting, whilst Gluck's ballet music is still played. Goldoni, Molière, Espronceda, Flaubert, Landau, and Heyse have all coloured the legend according to their own fancy, but of all later writers Zorrilla, whose *Don Juan Tenorio* has come to be regarded as a national work, may justly claim the distinction of having cast the story into its most popular form.

**Don-nai, Donaii or Dongnai,** a riv. of Lower French Cochin-China, rising at an altitude of 5000 ft. It receives the Saigon and others, and after a course of 250 m. enters the China Sea in the N. E. of the Mekong delta, which communicates with the river by several channels.

**Donnay, Maurice Charles,** Fr. playwright and author, *b.* Oct. 12, 1859, in Paris. His first work for the stage was a Gk. shadow-play, *Phryné*, 1891. In 1892 he adapted the *Lysistrata* of Aristophanes. He was elected to the Academy in 1907. Among his other plays are : *Amants*, 1895 ; *Douloureuse*, 1897 ; *L'Affranchie*, 1898 ; *Le Torrent*, 1898 ; *La Bascule*, 1901 ; *L'Autre Danger*, 1902 ; *Le Retour de Jérusalem* (a satire on Max Nordau), 1903 ; *Paraître*, 1906 ; *La Patronne*, 1908 ; *Ménage de Moliere*, 1912 ; *Les Éclaireuses*, 1913 ; *L'Impromptu du Paquetage*, 1916 ; *Le Théâtre aux Armées*, 1916 ; *La Chasse à l'Homme*, 1920 ; *Le Roi Candaule*, 1920 ; *Un Homme léger*, 1925 ; *La Reprise*, 1925 ; *L'Ascension de Virginie*, 1929. He has also collaborated. Of his nondramatic works *Alfred de Musset* appeared in 1914.

**Donne, John** (1573–1631), an English poet, is quaintly enough the hero of a truly romantic love-story. This is strange because the very glow of his spiritual life, combined with his melancholy and fantastic humours, would seem to leave small room for romance. Both at Oxford and Cambridge he proved an excellent scholar, but his religion, Roman Catholicism, forbade his taking the oath necessary for a degree. His life-long intimacy with Sir Henry Wotton dates from his Oxford days. At seventeen he began to study law at Lincoln's Inn, and it was at this time that he became a Protestant, finding himself after careful scrutiny more in sympathy with the Anglican than the Roman standpoint. After a year spent in Italy and Spain, he became Lord Elsinore's secretary, fell in love with his patron's niece, whom he secretly married, and thus lost his position. D. was imprisoned by his father-in-law, but finally won back his freedom and his wife after a protracted lawsuit which ran away with nearly the whole of his property. Whilst with Sir Robert Drury in Paris, he saw the phantom of his beloved wife carrying a dead infant

JOHN DONNE
(in his shroud)

in her arms; twelve days later he heard that his wife had at that very time been delivered of a still-born child. With the accession of King James his fortune changed. So delighted was the king with D.'s polemic against Catholicism (*Pseudo Martyr*), that he insisted on the author taking holy orders and appointed him his chaplain-in-ordinary. Other honours followed, and at his death, which was hastened by consumption, he was vicar of St. Dunstan's and dean of St. Paul's, The famous angler, Sir Izaak Walton, has left a delightful life of the pious D. In the pulpit he was, according to his biographer, 'always preaching to himself like an angel from a cloud, but in none.' As a poet, Mr. Saintsbury justly praises 'the magical illumination of obscure and shadowy thoughts with the lightning of fancy,'

whilst Dryden's verdict that he was 'the greatest wit though not the best poet of our nation' is not amiss. But it would be difficult to find a better appreciation than that contained in Ben Jonson's prophetic remarks, that he was 'the first poet in the world in some things,' but that he would perish 'for not being understood.' The very daintiness of his fancy and wealth of erotic fervour are obscured from the ordinary gaze by a host of fantastical conceits, of 'quips and cranks' expressive of far-fetched, if ingenious, imaginings and of wanton deformities, both of wit and metre. Life by Gosse, 1899.

**Donnelly, Ignatius** (1831–1901), an American author, *b.* in Philadelphia. Representative in Congress (1863–69); nominated for vice-president twice, but not elected. He was interested in the Bacon–Shakespeare controversy, and wrote *Great Cryptogram*, 1887; and *Cipher in Shakespeare's Plays*, 1900, an attempt to prove that Francis Bacon was the real author of Shakespeare's plays. He also wrote a book called *Atlantis* to prove that there once existed in the Atlantic a land which was the Atlantis of the ancients.

**Donnybrook**, an old vil. of Ireland, in the co. of Dublin. It now forms a western suburb of the city of Dublin. It is historically interesting. King John established yearly fairs, which were held towards the end of August. These became notorious for the riotous disorder practised, and were eventually discontinued in 1855.

**Donoghue, Stephen** (*b.* 1885), a famous Eng. jockey. Rode Derby winner on four occasions. His portrait was in the Royal Academy in 1925.

**Donop, General Sir Stanley Brenton von** (1860), British soldier. Appointed Master-General of the Ordnance in 1913. It was during his administration that so much criticism was levelled at the War Office on account of the shortage in munitions during the earlier years of the Great War. The deficiency, however, was probably due entirely to industrial troubles, and General Donop rendered most valuable services as Master-General of Ordnance throughout his tenure of office from 1913 to 1916. Before the war he was Professor of Artillery at the Royal Military Academy, Woolwich, and Superintendent of Experiments at Shoeburyness, and later Director of Artillery at the War Office (1911–13).

**Donora**, a tn. of Westmoreland co., Pennsylvania, U.S.A., with manufactures of steel, nails, chemicals, etc. Pop. 13,905.

**Donovan, Edward** (1768–1837), an

F 2

English natural historian and botanist, was a fellow of the Linnean Society. The results of his strenuous labours were published in his *Natural History of British Insects*, 1792–1813, and his natural histories of British birds, 1799–1819; British fishes, 1802–8; and British shells, 1800–4, etc.

**Donzy**, a tn. in the dept. of Nièvre, France, 26 m. N. of Nevers. Cardinal Mazarin founded factories here in 1659, and there are Roman ruins. Pop. 2500.

**Doo, George Thomas,** (1800–86), an English line engraver,' had the misfortune to live in a time when his art was no longer appreciated. He tried portrait paintings in oils, but art-lovers will remember him rather as a fine engraver, remarkable for his faithfulness to the original, his free animated style, and his sensitive lines. His plates of ' Knox Preaching,' after Wilkie, and his ' Italian Pilgrims,' after Eastlake, are admirable; but his best are those after Correggio's 'Ecce Homo,' and Raphael's ' Messiah ' and ' Infant Christ bearing the Cross.'

**Dooley, Mr.,** *see* DUNNE, FINLEY PETER.

**Doom,** or **Doum,** the popular name of *Hyphœne thebaica*, a palm-tree of Upper Egypt, clumps of which occur near Thebes. The fruit is about the size of an orange, reddish in colour, and has a spongy, tasteless, but nutritious rind.

**Doomsday Book,** *see* DOMESDAY BOOK.

**Doon,** a loch and riv. of Scotland, in the co. of Ayrshire. The loch is 3 m. S. of Dalmellington; it is 6 m. long and one mile wide, being nearly 700 ft. above the level of the sea. There are several small islands, and it is enclosed by mountains. The R. Doon flows through the loch, emptying itself in the Firth of Clyde, 3 m. from Ayr. Trout and char abound in both loch and river. The poet Burns immortalised the R. Doon.

**Doones, The,** were a tribe who lived in Exmoor, Devonshire, England. Very probably these people were descendants of the ancient savage Britons. Their chief home was at Badgworthy, and they lived by plunder. In Blackmore's book, *Lorna Doone,* published in 1869, the tribe figures largely. They were so dreaded that they were practically rooted out in the seventeenth century by the people of Devon.

**Door,** in architecture, the filling, usually solid, of a doorway, so constructed that it may easily be opened or shut. The D. and doorway have always been regarded as one of the features of a building upon which

architectural ornament should be lavished, and they have generally been made of an imposing nature. In the Egyptian and Assyrian systems

NORMAN DOORWAY
*(Essendine Chapel, Rutland)*

the doorway was made of great size and was flanked with colossal statues. In the Gk. and Roman temples size was also aimed at, but when, as

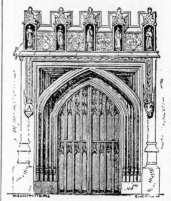

PERPENDICULAR DOORWAY
*(Magdalen College, Oxford)*

in the case of Gk. architecture, the flat lintel was used, it was impossible to span a very large space. The introduction of the arch opened the way to many improvements, and doorways were now generally spanned by this method. All the later architectural systems derived from the Roman inherited this tradition. In Romanesque architecture the arch is semicircular, ornamented with heavy engravings, the arched head being frequently filled in with a flat stone, so as to make the D. opening rectangular. Among the Gothic styles, it is in France especially that the doorway receives magnificent treatment. The triple portal of Rheims Cathedral is perhaps the most superb of all. The Ds. themselves are usually constructed of timber adorned with iron-work, though metal was occasionally used.

**Doornik,** Flemish name for Tournai.

**Doppler, Christian Johann** (1803–1853), a celebrated Austrian scientist chiefly remembered for ' Doppler's principle.' This states (*a*) that the pitch of a sound is changed if the object emitting it is moving relatively to the observer, and (*b*) that the light emitted by a moving star is changed in colour as perceived by a relatively stationary observer. Doppler's principle has proved of great value in physics and astronomy.

**Dorado,**' the sword-fish,' a southern constellation, discovered by Bayer in 1603, situated in the southern hemisphere between Pictor and Hydrus, and cut nearly in half by a line joining $\alpha$ Argus and $\alpha$ Eridani. Alpha Doradûs is a white star of 3·5 magnitude, with a peculiar spectrum. The S. pole of the ecliptic lies near $\epsilon$ Doradûs, a star of the fifth magnitude.

**Doran, John** (1807–78), a miscellaneous writer, became at an early age a man of letters. In 1869 he was editor of the *Athenæum,* and, later, of *Notes and Queries.* His works were as diversified as his tastes, and his books, always well-informed, are usually instructive as well as readable. He wrote an admirable memoir of Edward Young, 1853 (enlarged 1854), and in 1855 published *The Queens of England of the House of Hanover,* a collection of biographies in which fiction is sometimes allowed to show its head. His most ambitious work is *Their Majesties' Servants,* an account of the English stage. Other books : *Table Traits, Habits and Men, The History of Court Fools, A Lady of the Last Century* (Mrs. Montagu), and *Memories of our Great Towns.*

**Dorat, Claude Joseph** (1734–80), a French author and poet. He left the career of advocate to devote himself to literature, imitated Voltaire, and contributed largely to *l'Almanach des Muses.* He wrote comedies, fables, madrigals, romances, and dramas, but had no very real talent, being merely a ' boudoir poet '

of considerable popularity in his own time. Among his plays are : *Zulica,* 1760 ; *Adélaïde de Hongrie.* His *Réponse d'Abélard à Héloïse* gained immediate popularity. Among his poems may be mentioned : *Sélim et Sélima, Le Mois de Mai, Les Tourterelles. Le Tartuffe Littéraire,* 1777, was an attack on La Harpe and Palissot. Consult Desnoireterre, *Le Chevalier Dorat,* 1887 ; Cohen, *Guide de l'Amateur de Livres du XVIIIᵉ Siècle,* 1876, 1887.

**Dor-beetle,** or *Geotrupes stercorarius,* a species of Scarabæidæ frequently found in England, where it is sometimes called the buzzard clock. It is a dung-beetle, not quite an inch in length, and in colour it is a metallic black. In summer evenings it flies about at dusk with a curious droning sound.

**Dorcas Society,** the name given to working parties of ladies, where they make garments for charity. The name is derived from Dorcas (mentioned in the Acts), who made coats for the widows.

**Dorchester:** (1) A parl. and municipal bor., cap. of Dorsetshire, England, situated 140 m. S.W. of London. The town is very picturesquely situated. The boulevards, built on the site of the Roman wall, surround about three-fourths of the town and make a delightful promenade. The town was an important military station of the Romans and was called Durnovaria or Durinum ; Maiden Castle, a Roman camp, is situated to the S. of the town. The Roman amphitheatre at Maumbury is the most finely preserved Roman structure in the kingdom. Since 1868 D. returns one member to parliament (previous to 1868, two). There is a Grammar School founded in 1569, but now rebuilt, an almshouse built in 1616, and a museum with the fore-paddle of a Pliosaurus, 7 ft. long. Thomas Hardy, the poet and novelist, was *b.* 3 m. from Dorchester at Upper Bockhampton, and he designed the house at Max Gate, Fordington, in which he resided, looking down upon the roofs of Dorchester. Max Gate took its name from an old turnpike gate. Pop. 9550. (2) A par. and vil. co. Oxford, England, 9 m E. by S. of Oxford. In A.D. 634 St. Birinus, the apostle of the West Saxons, here baptised Cynegils, King of the W. Saxons, to whom King Oswald of Northumbria was godfather. Birinus founded a bishopric at D. which lasted for 450 years, until Remigius (1067–1092) transferred it to Lincoln. The Abbey Church is a very remarkable building with many interesting tombs. There is a missionary college for twenty-six students, a Rom. camp, and an ancient British earthwork. Many Rom. coins have been found. Pop. 959. (3) A district of Boston, U.S.A., contains two of the oldest houses in New England and a burying ground dated 1634. It was founded by 140 colonists from Dorsetshire, England, encouraged thereto by Rev. John White, of Trinity par., Dorchester. (*See* W. D. Orcutt: *Good Old Dorchester.*)

**Dordogne,** a dept. in S. France, comprising almost wholly the basin of the D. The surface of the department is hilly and is well wooded, and the valleys are remarkably beautiful and prolific. Vineyards abound on the gentle slopes of the hills, where the vines are trained on the branches

richest and most important trading town of Holland and a member of the Hanseatic League. It still retains many quaint thoroughfares and gabled houses. The original residence of the counts of Holland, it witnessed in 1572 the declaration of independence of the United Provinces, and in 1618–19 the famous synod which anathematised Arminius' heresies. Pop. 55,200.

**Doré, Louis Auguste Gustave** (1833-83), a book illustrator, drew first for the *Journal Pour Rire*, 1848, and later for the *Journal Pour Tous*. His drawings show genius for grotesque and humorous illustration as also fertility of invention and preference for the fantastic. Among the works he illustrated were: Balzac's *Contes*

DORDRECHT

of the elm and walnut trees. Chestnut trees are abundant; the yield of chestnuts is immense and contributes largely to the food-supply of the inhabitants of the country, and provides provender for hogs. Wheat, peas, beans, and maize are also grown. The choice truffles de Périgord are a product of the soil. Iron, coal, and manganese mines are worked, and there are many important foundries. The capital of the department is Périgueux. The area is 3561 sq. m., and the pop. 392,490.

**Dordrecht** (popularly called **Dort**), a seaport on the Merwede, 12½ m. S.E. of Rotterdam by rail, in the prov. of S. Holland. Intersected by a number of canals which greatly facilitate communications, it is engaged in many industries, such as shipbuilding and engineering, and also manufactures. But Rotterdam has diverted a great part of the traffic which made it the

*Drolatiques,* 1855; Dante's *Inferno* 1863; *Purgatorio and Paradiso,* 1865-1866; *The Bible* and *Paradise Lost,* 1866; Tennyson's *Idylls,* 1867-68; La Fontaine's *Fables,* 1867, and Rabelais' work. As a sculptor he is remembered for his statue of Dumas, in Paris, whilst he was ambitious for fame as an historical and religious painter. In the Luxembourg hangs his 'Tobit and the Angel,' whilst the Doré Gallery in London was long decorated with his huge canvases depicting 'Christ leaving the Prætorium,' 1867–72, etc. Life by Jerrold.

**Dorema,** a genus of Umbelliferæ, *D. ammoniacum* is found in dry plains and gravelly soil, exposed to the burning sun in Persia; it yields the gum ammoniacum used in medicine.

**Dore Monts,** a volcanic mt. group of France, belonging to the Auvergne system, and situated in the dept. of Puy-de-Dôme. The chief heights of all are in this group, and include the Puy-de-Sancy, which has an elevation of over 6000 ft.

**Doria, Andrea** (1466-1560), a Genoese nobleman, who, like his ancestors, entered on a military career. First served under various Italian princes on different expeditions; he next entered the service of the French king, and eventually became high admiral of the Levant. Later on, resigned his command of the fleet, as he feared for the safety of Genoa, which was threatened by the French. In 1528 D. expelled the French from the garrison of Genoa, and refusing a sovereignty, ruled the city on republican lines. He was very active in his attacks against sea pirates, and was called 'Father and Liberator of his Country.'

**Dorians,** are, like the Ionians and the Æolians, one of the chief peoples in historic Greece. In Hellenic times the whole of the Peloponnese, except Ellis and Achæa, Doris in Northern Greece, together with Megara and Ægina, the islands of Crete, Rhodes, Cnidus, Melos, Thera, etc., and the southern shores of Sicily, colonised from Corinth, etc., were inhabited by D. Legend says that Dorus, son of Hellen, the founder of the race, settled in Doris before 1100 B.C. Archæologists conclude that about 1100 B.C. rude D. invaders overthrew the Achæan civilisation described in Homer, which in its turn had supplanted the Mycenean. Compared with the Ionians, the D. were hardier, rougher, simpler, more conservative, and aristocratic—a truth to be appreciated alike in their stern and majestic architecture, their archaic all-hallowed dialect (retained in the choruses of Attic drama), and the customs and constitution, for instance, of Sparta, where the Helots were jealously kept in their servile condition, and where the rigid martial discipline of Lycurgus prevailed.

**Doric Dialect, The,** was spoken in Hellenic times in every region where Dorians (*q.v.*) settled. The broad features which distinguish it from Ionic are *-μες* for *-μεν* in first person plural; *-αε* and *-αη* for *ῇ*; *κά* for *ἄν*, and *-σεω*, *-σιω*, and *-σῶ* as ending for the first person of the future. The Dorians invariably claimed a greater antiquity for their dialect than Ionic, a fact which probably accounts for the archaic Doric, which appears as an anachronism in Attic drama. Pindar wrote in Doric.

**Doric Order,** the earliest and most characteristic type of architecture produced by the Gks. The Doric column is a massive fluted pillar imposing in its severity and absence of adornment; base and mouldings are absent from the foot of the column; the capital is plain and composed of merely an echinus, abacus, and triglyphed frieze.

**Dorigny, Sir Nicholas** (1657-1746), a French engraver. From 1711 to 1719 he worked for Queen Anne at Hampton Court, engraving the cartoons of Raphael. Heaviness of outline, hard contrasts, and excess of vigour mar most of his reproductions of Italian paintings, but his 'Transfiguration' after Raphael is good.

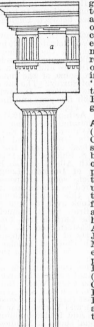

DORIC COLUMN

**Dorion, Sir Antoine Aimé** (1816–91), a Canadian statesman. He became leader of the Liberal party, and was the first to enunciate clearly the principle of federation as applicable to his country. As Minister of Justice in the Mackenzie government, he passed the Electoral Law (1874), and the Controverted Elections Act. In 1874 he was appointed justice of the province of Ontario.

**Doris, or Archidoris,** an important tenus of nudibranchiate mollusc, is typical of the family Dorididæ. The species are usually a white, brown, or yellow colour, whence they are called sea-lemons, but they often take to themselves the colour of their surroundings. *D. pilosa* and *D. tuberculata* are well-known members of the genus.

**Doris,** in ancient geography a mountainous dist. of Central Greece. It was surrounded by Phocis, Locris, Ætolia, and Malis, and it contained the sources of the Cephissus. The Dorians claimed this territory as their home. It is now included in the government of Phocis.

**Dorislaus, Isaac** (1595-1649), an Anglo-Dutch lawyer, attended Leyden University, and held for a short time a lectureship in history at Cambridge. During the Bishops' War (1640), and again in the parliamentarian army (1642), he acted as judge-advocate, whilst he helped to draw up the charge of high treason against the king. Royalist conspirators assassinated D. at The Hague, where he had gone on a diplomatic mission to bring about an alliance between England and Holland.

**Dorking,** a market tn. in Surrey, England, 6 m. W. of Reigate and 29 m. S.W. of London, on the Southern Railway. It is picturesquely situated on the North Downs and within a small radius are some of the most beautiful spots of Surrey. The town is famous for its poultry. D. fowls are noted for their fine eggs and fine quality of flesh. Pop. 8058.

**Dorman, Sir Arthur** (1848–1931), British constructional steel manufacturer, *b.* at Ashford, Kent. Educated at Christ's Hospital and in Paris. Apprenticed to an ironmaking firm in S. Shields. In 1876 he founded, with Albert de Lande Long, the firm of Dorman, Long, a venture which soon prospered and was registered as a company in 1889. In 1923, this constructional steel company took over the undertakings of Bell Bros., Sir B. Samuelson and Co., the Carlton Iron Co., and the North-Eastern Steel Co. In 1929 the interests of the company were fused with those of Bolckow Vaughan and Co., the capital of the two undertakings amounting to about £20,000,000, this being one of the most important mergers in Great Britain since the Great War. Dorman, Long & Co. own coal and ironstone mines, blast furnaces and coke ovens in Durham and Yorkshire, iron and steel works and bridge-building and constructional shops at Middlesbrough, and constructional works in London, together with a structural engineering business in Melbourne and Sydney. Sir Arthur Dorman was knighted in 1918 and received a baronetcy in 1923.

**Dormer,** or **Dormer Window,** of which the Hôtel de Ville in Rouen furnishes a splendid illustration, is a little window set in a gable jutting out from a sloping roof. After 1350 dormers appear in Gothic domestic architecture.

**Dormitory** (from Lat. *dormitorium,* a sleeping place) was the name given to the sleeping quarters of monks. In most monasteries the Ds. were on the ground floor, giving easy communications with the church, though sometimes they formed the upper story of the cloisters. Sometimes they were long halls, but more often a series of cells or cubicles. To-day

the name is applied to large bedrooms in schools, etc.

**Dormont,** a residential borough of Pittsburgh, Pennsylvania, U.S.A. Pop. 6455.

**Dormouse,** the name given to members of the rodent family Gliridæ, consists of small, arboreal animals living in the Old World. The eyes and ears are large, the tail is long and hairy, and the intestine has no cæcum. The animals are squirrel-like in habit and diet, but they are nocturnal.

DORMOUSE

*Muscardinus avellanarius,* the common D., is found all over Europe, and is remarkable for its winter sleep, the period of time during which it hibernates being about six months. *Myoxus glis,* the fat or squirrel D., is an allied European species.

**Dorn, Johann Albrecht, Bernhard** (1805–81), a German orientalist. In 1843 became head of the Imperial Library, St. Petersburg. His catalogue of the oriental MSS. in that library was published in 1852. His publications include a *History of the Afghans,* 1836; and *A Chrestomathy of the Pushtu,* 1847, both written in English; and *Muhammedanische Quellen zur Geschichte der südlichen Küstenländer des Kaspischen Meeres,* 1850–58.

**Dornbirn,** a tn. of Austria, in the prov. of Vorarlberg. It is situated on the r. b. of the Dornberner Ach, near Lake Constance. It is an important centre of industry, and the most densely populated town in Vorarlberg. There are iron-works, cotton factories, dye-works, etc. Pop. 14,390.

**Dornburg,** a tn. of Thuringia in Germany. It is situated on the l. b. of the Saale, 14 m. E. of Weimar. It possesses three castles. The Altes Schloss was frequently used as a residence by the Emperors Otto II. and III. The Neues Schloss was built in the Italian style of architecture, in 1748. Goethe visited here as a guest. The third castle is a modern palace. Pop. of town, 930.

**Dornoch,** a par., royal, and police burgh, seaport, and cap. of the co. of Sutherlandshire, Scotland. The tn. is situated on the N. of Dornoch Firth, 14 m. E. of Bonar Bridge, and 8 m. S.E. by S. of Mound Station. In pre-Reformation times it was the see of a bishop, and Gilbert de Moravia, who *d.* in 1245, and was the last on the calendar of Scottish saints, built a cathedral, which was restored in 1837 by the Second Duke of Sutherland. The last execution for witchcraft in N. Britain took place here in 1722. Skibo Castle, about 4 m. from D., belongs now to Mrs. Andrew Carnegie. The golf links in the vicinity of D. are very fine, and these, together with its bracing climate and bathing and boating facilities, have made the tn. renowned as a holiday resort. Pop. of par., 2475 ; tn., 768.

**Dorohoi,** or **Dorogoi,** a tn. of Rumania. There is considerable trade in dairy and farm produce, also timber. A noted annual fair is held in June. Pop. 16,000.

**Doronicum,** or **Leopard's Bane,** a genus of bright orange composite plants found in Europe.

**Dorpat,** a tn. in Esthonia, now known as Tartu-Dorpat, and formerly Russian, with the official name of Yuriev. Picturesquely situated. It has a university founded in 1862, which formerly served all the Russian Baltic provs., but it was reorganised during the Great War as the Voronezh Univ., solely for Esthonia. In the Great War, D. fell to the Ger. in 1918. Pop. about 40,000.

**D'Orsay, Alfred Guillaume Gabriel, Count** (1801–52), the second son of General Count D'O., served in the Fr. army until 1822, when, after a tour of the continent with the Earl and Countess of Blessington, he came to Eng. Though married to a daughter of Lord Blessington by his first wife, D'O. was on very intimate terms with Lady Blessington, and was always to be found at Gore House. Exceptionally handsome, the most admired man of the day, he was a leader of the dandies, though he never had the sway of Beau Brummell. During his twenty years' residence in this country he executed a series of admirable drawings of his most noted contemporaries. In 1849 he went to Paris, where he *d.* three years later. There is a biography of D'O. by W. Teignmouth Shore.

**Dorset, Charles Sackville, Earl of Middlesex,** sixth **Earl of Dorset** (1638–1706), the son of Richard Sackville, fifth earl, and grandson of the first earl of Middlesex. In Charles II.'s first parliament he was M.P. for E. Grinstead, and in 1665 joined an expedition against the Dutch. The early part of his career, however, was spent in pleasure and dissipation. He had no prominent place at court during the reign of James II., but was reinstated on the accession of William III. The only work by which he is remembered is his poem, *To All You Ladies now on Land.*

**Dorset, Thomas Sackville,** first **Earl of** (1536–1608), *b.* at Buckhurst. He collaborated with Thomas Norton in the writing of the first tragedy in blank verse, *Gorboduc,* founded on the Senecan model, and noteworthy on account of its pureness of style. About the year 1567 Sackville was

THOMAS SACKVILLE, EARL OF DORSET

created Lord Buckhurst and shortly after that entered the diplomatic service in France. He was made a K.G. in 1598, and ten years later was appointed Lord High Treasurer, which office he held till his death. He also wrote the *Induction to the Mirror for Magistrates,* 1563.

**Dorsetshire,** a maritime co. on the S.W. of Eng., between Devonshire and Hampshire, the cap. being Dorchester. Open downs, affording excellent sheep pasturage, are the salient features of its undulating surface. To the E. the beautiful coast-line is broken by Poole Harbour, to the S. of which lies the peninsula known as the Isle of Purbeck. Chesil Bank, which ends in Portland Bill, is a remarkable stretch of shingle connecting the Isle of Portland with the mainland at Portland Roads, where a harbour of refuge has been constructed with the help of huge breakwaters. The principal streams are the Stour, flowing S.E. into Hants, and the Frome and Piddle, which enter Poole Harbour. Agriculture is the chief industry, the country being noted for its excellent dairy produce, whilst the industry second in importance is quarrying. The white freestones of Portland are well-known to builders, and the coarse marbles and white pipeclay of Purbeck are also in great demand. Gillingham and Sherborne in the N. are on the Southern main line, branch lines serving Dorchester (9554), Swanage, Weymouth (24,570), and Portland (12,434), etc. Weymouth and Portland Island are on the Great Western Railway. Bridport, Lyme Regis, Swanage, Weymouth, and Poole (43,661) are the chief seaports. The fine ruins of Corfe Castle and Wimborne Minster, Milton Abbey and the abbey church of Sherborne, possess considerable antiquarian interest, and remains of immense reptiles have been unearthed at Lyme Regis. The total acreage of the county is 632,270 ; pop., 228,258.

**Dorsetshire Regiment, The,** formerly the 39th and 54th Foot. The 39th was raised in 1702, and after service in Europe went to India in 1754, being the first King's Regiment to serve in that country, a fact which is still commemorated in its motto ' Primus in India.' The 54th was raised in 1755. Towards the end of the eighteenth century William Cobbett was Regimental Sergeant-major of the 54th. The Dorsetshire Regiment has a long roll of battle honours, and its battalions served on many fronts during the Great War. The 2nd Battalion was with General Townshend at Kut-el-Amara, and was taken prisoner at the capitulation ; another 2nd Battalion was raised to take its place.

**Dorsten,** a tn. of Prussia, in Westphalia, situated on the Lippe, 35 m. S.W. of Munster. Pop. 8490.

**Dorstfeld,** a small tn. of Prussia, in the prov. of Westphalia. It is situated 2 m. N.W. of Dortmund, and there are collieries in the vicinity. Pop. 4500.

**Dort,** *see* DORDRECHT.

**Dortmund,** the most important tn. in Westphalia, Ger., with 325,000 inhabs., is the centre of a great mining dist., with numerous foundries. There are extensive beds of iron ore. It was a free, fortified Hanseatic tn., but the site of the walls is now occupied by promenades. The Reinoldi Kirche is of the thirteenth century and the Marien K. of the twelfth and the Propstei K. of 1331–1354. The Municipal Museum contains prehistoric, Rom. and Westphalian collections.

**Dortmund-Weser-Ems** Canal, a canal of Ger. which unites the Westphalian coalfield to the seaports of the North Sea. Between 1892 and 1899 Ems was canalised for 43 m., and this was the nucleus of the present canal, which is 169 m. long ; 108 m. of which were excavated. The canal has a width of 98½ ft. at the surface, 59 ft. at the bottom, and a depth of 8 ft. 2 in. The cost was about 3¾ million pounds.

**Dory,** or **John Dory,** the *Zeus faber,* a species of Zeidæ allied to the halibut and other flat-fishes. It is a marine fish found in temperate seas of the Old World, and is valued highly as a food. The body is laterally compressed and about 1½ ft. in length, and the general appearance is very unprepossessing. During the breeding season it utters curious sonorous noises.

**Dôsah** (Arabic, treading), a religious ceremony performed by the dervishes of the Sa'di order in Cairo. The chief, or sheikh, of the order rode on horseback, allowing his horse to tread upon the bodies of the dervishes who were lying down, and who were said to be unhurt by the hoofs of the animal. The ceremony was done away with in 1884.

**Dos Hermanas,** a tn. of Andalusia, Spain. Manufactures olive oil and textiles. Pop. 10,000.

**Dossi, Dosso** and **Battista,** brothers, and painters of the It. school. Battista D. (*d. c.* 1548), who worked with his brother, was the landscape painter, while Giovanni di Nicolo di Lutero (*c.* 1479–1542) (as his real name was) painted the figures. Both these brothers seem to have been pupils of Lorenzo Costa, and they also spent some time in Venice together, and probably also in Rome. These painters, whose work is notable for its beautiful colouring and originality, are mentioned by Ariosto in his *Orlando Furioso.* Many of their paintings are in the gallery at Ferrara and in the palace there, as they were employed by the duke. Among their works are : ' St. John at Patmos,' ' Circe,' and ' The Hours of the Day,' the latter in the Ferrara Palace.

**Doss-megen-ora Mountains,** the highest points in the Boro-khoro Mts. of the Tian Shan group of Central Asia. They rise to a height of 20,000 ft.

**Dost Mohammed** (*c.* 1798–1863), the brother of the vizier of Mahmud Shah. For a time he had complete power in Kabul, but was eventually compelled by the Brit. to surrender. *See* AFGHANISTAN.

**Dostoievsky, Fedor Mikhailovitch** (1822–81), one of the giants of Russian literature and one of the greatest novelists of all time, *b.* Nov. 11, at Moscow, son of a military surgeon. He had a troubled childhood, due to epilepsy, of which he was a sufferer all his life, and which had much to do with the mysticism, mingled with religious ecstasy and humanitarian pity and pardon for the lowly and the outcast, which was to mark his great works. He went to the St. Petersburg engineering school and made good progress, but had already shown that his love for writing was greater than his desire to be an army officer. In 1846 his first work *Poor Folk*, appeared, and gave him considerable celebrity in his own country. In 1849 he was arrested for alleged association with a revolutionary band. He was sentenced to

FEDOR M. DOSTOIEVSKY

death, and endured a horrible moment expecting to be shot, but he was reprieved and sent to Siberia, where he spent four years of misery. His confinement among criminals and political outcasts was to furnish him with boundless material for his later works. After serving a certain time in the army, he wrote *Memoirs of a House of the Dead*, which was drawn from his own life. This appeared 1861-2. In a momentary period of comparative affluence he spent some time travelling in Europe, but was incurably Slav and gladly returned to his own country. Turgeniev was the brightest star in the Russian galaxy then, and also had a great reputation abroad. Dostoievsky never forgave him for being too Europeanised. In 1866 he wrote one of his greatest works, *Crime and Punishment*, filled with the peculiar Russian pity for the outcast, even

the murderer. All the rest of his life he struggled with his epileptic ailment and with spells of grinding poverty. Like Balzac, he sat at his writing-table penning immortal novels in the endeavour to keep the wolf from the door. At one time he wrote that he had a notion to hang himself. He could neither pay his debts, he said, nor travel. Some of his other notable novels are *The Idiot, The Possessed* and *The Brothers Karamazoff*, his last major work. Dostoievsky understood Russia and the Russians as few writers of his country have done. Nietzsche, not given to praise, said he was the only man who had taught him something of psychology. He was less touched by European influences than any other great Russian writer and appreciation of him has not only increased abroad, but has largely influenced all the writing of his country since his death. Despite their enormous length, his major novels have been translated into all modern languages. See *F. Dostoievsky : a critical study,* by J. M. Murray, 1916, and in French *Dostoievsky* by André Gide.

**Dot,** in music, is a mark which is placed after a note and increases its duration by one half. When the D. is placed over the note it indicates a short staccato tone.

**Dothan,** a city of Henry co., Alabama, U.S.A., about 120 m. S.E. of Montgomery. It has iron-works and cotton mills and many diverse manufactures. Pop. 16,046.

**Dotterel,** or *Eudromias morinellus,* a limicoline bird of the plover family, or Charadriidæ. Its home is N. Europe and Asia, but in Britain, *e.g.* in the Lake District and the Scottish mountains, it is approaching extinction owing to the custom of shooting the birds during the breeding season to ensure the delicacy of their flesh. The general colour is ashy-brown, with white and black markings, and the three eggs which are laid in hollows of the ground, are pale green with brown marks.

**Dou, Dow,** or **Douw, Gerard** (1613-c. 1675), a Dutch painter, *b.* at Leyden, and at an early age became a pupil of Rembrandt, from whom he acquired the art of beautiful colouring. He soon, however, gave up portrait painting and devoted his time to scenes of everyday life. His pictures number in all about two hundred, ' The Woman with the Dropsy,' in the Louvre, being his masterpiece. Other well-known ones are ' The Poulterer's Shop,' portrait of himself, and ' The Evening School.'

**Douai,** a tn. in the dept. du Nord, France, 15 m. E.N.E. of Arras, on the Scarpe and the Canal de la Sensée, is an industrial tn. with iron-works, and refineries, breweries and trading in coal and corn. It possesses old houses, a belfry of the fourteenth to fifteenth centuries, the remains of an abbey, now the courts of justice, a museum and libraries. The Academy was transferred to Lille in 1889. In the fourteenth to fifteenth centuries D. was famous for its tapestries. The Douai Bible, the authorised Eng. version for Catholics, was issued here. Pop. 34,130.

**Douarnenez,** a fishing tn. of Western France, in the dept. of Finistère, and the arron. of Quimper. The sardine and mackerel fisheries are important. Other industries are boat-building, net- and rope-making. Pop. 12,260.

**Douaumont,** Fr. village, and the name of the first of the outlying permanent forts of Verdun. It was attacked by the Gers. in the Great War on Feb. 25, 1916, the Branden-burger troops losing a great number of men. This supreme assault, witnessed by the Kaiser from a distant hill, captured the fort on that day, the fort itself being then in ruins ; but the D. hill, nearly 400 metres high, was still held. General Pétain arrived at the fall and re-organised the demoralised defence. For many days a great battle raged round the ruins of the fort and the village of D., and by March 1 the Ger. defence of the position had given way before the Fr. counter-attack. Large reinforcements reached the Fr., and the vital defences of Verdun remained intact (*see,* further, under VERDUN). Later in March and in April ruined D. changed hands several times, the Ger. Crown Prince striving to capture Pepper Ridge in order to turn the D. position, but the repulse by the Fr. at that hill finally deter-mined the failure of the Ger. blow at Verdun. In Oct. of the same year General Nivelle recovered both Fort D. and Vaux village in a furious attack on the E. bank of the Meuse.

**Double-Base,** or **Bass** (music), *see* VIOLIN.

**Double Entry,** *see* BOOK-KEEPING.

**Double-Flowers** are a product of cultivation, in which the stamens and pistil have been replaced by petals, and the plant is therefore incapable of producing seed. No plant in the wild state is found double, but the cultivated form which is most popu-lar is often the double one, *e.g.* rose.

**Double Refraction,** the name applied by physicists to the splitting up of a ray of light incident on a crystal of calcite into two refracted rays. The phenomenon was first described by Erasmus Bartholinus in 1669, who was led to its discovery by observing that when objects were viewed through certain transparent crystals of Iceland spar two images of each object were seen. If a pencil mark is made on a sheet of white paper and a crystal of calcite is placed upon it, two images of the pencil mark are seen. On rotating the crystal, one image remains stationary while the other revolves in a circle about it. The stationary image is called the ordinary image, while the moving image, which is always displaced in the direction of the shorter axis of the rhombic face of the crystal, is called the extraordinary image. When a beam of light falls obliquely on a crystal of calcite the two rays into which it divides are called the ordinary ray and the extraordinary ray. The ordinary ray obeys the laws of refraction in the usual way, but the extraordinary ray departs from the plane of incidence, and the ratio of the angles of incidence and refraction which it makes with the face of the crystal is not constant. The two re-fracted rays are found to be polarised in perpendicular planes.

**Doublings,** a term used in heraldry, and is applied to the linings of state robes, or mantles, or to mantlings.

**Doubling the Cube,** a problem which originated in early Gk. times, and was one of the three great problems studied by the early mathematicians. Hippocrates, Archytas, and others solved the prob-lem, though its solution could not be obtained by simple geometry, but necessitated a more advanced know-ledge. There are various traditions as to how the question arose, one of them being an attempt of the Delians to double a cubical altar, so that it is sometimes known as the Delian problem.

**Doubloon** (Sp. *doblon,* double), a gold piece, once coined in Sp. and Sp. America, worth two pistoles. Up to 1848 its value was £3 4s. 8d., but the ' Doblon de Isabel,' which entered the currency in that year, was worth £1 0s. 8d. only.

**Doubs,** an Eastern frontier prov. of Fr., once part of the duchy of Burgundy and later of Franche-Comté, served by the Paris–Lyon and the Dôle–Switzerland railways. Bounded on the N. by Belfort and Haute Saône, on the E. and S.E. by Switzerland, and on the S.W. and W. by Switzerland, it falls naturally into three zones. The plain region be-tween the Ognon (on the W.) and the Doubs is the most fertile, producing wheat, oats, and other cereals, besides vegetables, hemp, fruits, and vines in abundance. The second region, mostly given to pasturage and forests, covers the central districts, whilst the third is very mountainous, being crossed by four parallel chains of the Jura in the direction N.E. to S.W. Mont d'Or (4800 ft.) in the easternmost ridge is the highest peak. The chief exports are watches (manufactured at Besançon, the cap., and Morteau), hardware (at Hérimoncourt and Valentigney),iron (from foundries at Audincourt), live-stock, vegetables, and wine. Building-stone and rock salt are the only noteworthy minerals. Besançon, Pontarlier, Baume-les-Dames, and Montbéliard are the four arrondissements. The total pop. was 296,600 in 1926, the area being 2030 sq. m.

**Douce, Francis** (1757–1834), an Eng. antiquary, published his curious *Illustrations of Shakespeare* in 1807, and his *Dance of Death* in 1833. A contributor to the *Archæologia* and *Gentleman's Magazine*, he bequeathed at his death a valuable collection of books, illuminated manuscripts,coins, etc., to the Bodleian Library.

**Douglas**, the cap. of the Isle of Man, and a popular seaside resort, situated 80 m. N.W. of Liverpool and 62 m. W.N.W. of Fleetwood, with both of which it is in regular steamer communication. D. has grown up round a splendid bay in the E. of the island, at the confluence of the Awin-Dhov and Awin-Glass. A fine esplanade encircles the bay from Derby Castle on the N. to Douglas Head on the S., N. of which lies the harbour. D. is served by steamers crossing in the season to Barrow, Dublin, Belfast, and Glasgow; by trams, and by the Isle of Man Railway, connecting it with Peel, Castletown, and Port Erin. It has public buildings (including the House of Keys), a free library and a great number of attractions for its visitors, who exceed half a million from Easter to Oct. Pop. 25,000.

**Douglas**, a city of Arizona, U.S.A. with copper and lead smelters. Pop. 9828.

**Douglas**, the name of a Scottish family. *William of Douglas* is the first one of this family of whom anything definite is known, and of him there are records between the years 1175 and 1213. He was succeeded by his son, *Sir Archibald*, who d. about the middle of the thirteenth century. *Sir William of Douglas* (d. 1298) (' le Hardi ') was the grandson of the former. He rose against Edward I. in 1297, for which he was imprisoned and d. in the Tower the following year. *Sir James of Douglas* (1286–1330), known as the 'Good' Sir James, was his son, and bore the title lord of Douglas. During the life of Robert Bruce, D. was his firm supporter, sharing the command at

Bannockburn, and being successful in many border raids, till his name the ' Black D.' roused terror among the people. After many deeds of daring, he set out in 1330, according to Bruce's request, to carry the heart of the latter to Palestine, and was killed on the way. *William D.*, his son, d. at the battle of Halidon Hill, and *William D.*, first earl (1327–84), became owner of the estates through his uncle Hugh, and was made Earl of Douglas about 1358, and became Earl of Mar by his marriage. His son, *James, Earl of Douglas and Mar* (d. 1388), succeeded him, and was slain at the battle of Otterburn. As there was no direct heir to the estates, *Archibald D.* (c. 1328–c. 1400), a natural son of Good Sir James, became the third earl. He in his turn was succeeded by his son *Archibald* (c. 1369–1424), who was made a prisoner at the battle of Homildon Hill and at Shrewsbury. He afterwards became Duke of Touraine, and was killed at the battle of Verneuil. His successor was his son *Archibald*, fifth earl (c. 1391–1439). *William*, his son and heir, was murdered with his brother in Edinburgh Castle, 1440, by order of Sir William Crichton. The estates then passed to *James D.*, their great-uncle, known as the 'Gross.' His son *William*, eighth earl (c. 1425–52), was murdered by James II. in Stirling Castle, and *James* (1426–88), his brother, became the ninth earl. He proceeded at once to war with James on account of the murder of his brother, but had to surrender. His brothers identified themselves with his cause, but were defeated by the Earl of Angus, another branch of the D. family who were coming into prominence. The lands of the D. branch were given over to the fourth Earl of Angus, known as the ' Red D.' *Archibald*, fifth Earl of Angus (c. 1449–1514), called ' Bell-the-Cat,' was succeeded by *Archibald* (c. 1489–1557), his grandson, who married Margaret, sister of Henry VIII., King of Eng., and their daughter Margaret was the mother of Lord Darnley, father of James VI. This Earl of Angus was for a time extremely powerful in Scotland, but was eventually compelled by James V. to relinquish that power. His successors were *David*, seventh earl, and *Archibald*, eighth earl, the estates then passing to another branch, *William D. of Glenbervie*, ninth earl. In 1633 his grandson *William* (1589–1660), the eleventh earl, was made Marquis of Douglas, and his son became the third Duke of Hamilton by his marriage. *James D.*, second marquis (c. 1646–1700), and grandson of the first marquis, was succeeded by his son *Archibald* (1694–1761), first Duke of Douglas, but as he had no heirs the title died with him. About the year 1760 one of the twin sons of Lady Jane D., sister of the duke, became the heir to the estates in spite of his right having formerly been disputed, and in 1790 became Baron D. of Douglas, being raised to the peerage. He was succeeded in turn by his three sons, and when the fourth Baron D. *d.*, the earls of Home became the next heirs. The Dukes of Hamilton, Buccleuch, and Queensberry, as well as the Earls of Morton and Wemyss, are members of this family. *See* David Hume of Godscroft, *History of the House of Douglas and Angus*, and Sir William Fraser, *The Douglas Book*.

**Douglas, Sir Andrew Snape** (1761–97), a British naval officer. In 1781 he commanded the *Chatham* and captured over fifty Fr. vessels. He was appointed flag-captain of Lord Howe's flag-ship the *Queen Charlotte*, and was dangerously wounded on the ' glorious first of June,' 1794. He recovered sufficiently to take part in the victory off L'Orient in the following year, but *d.* two years later.

**Douglas, Sir Charles** (*d.* 1789), a rear-admiral. Made commander in 1759, he was sent out to defend Quebec in 1776, and was present at the battle of Ushant in 1778.

**Douglas, David** (1798–1834), a traveller and botanist, was *b.* at Scone. He was originally a gardener, but in 1823 went to the U.S.A. on a commission for the Royal Horticultural Society, and on his second journey to America about two years later he made several discoveries of plants, among them the spruce named after him.

**Douglas, Gawin** or **Gavin** (*c.* 1474–1522), a Scottish poet and bishop, was a son of Archibald, ' Bell the Cat,' fifth Earl of Angus. Educated at St. Andrews for the priesthood, he became provost of St. Giles, Edinburgh, in 1501, and finally bishop of Dunkeld in 1516. But as he had disobeyed the statute which forbade any one accepting preferment through the pope's bull, he underwent a term of imprisonment before taking up office. Although his nephew married the widowed queen of James IV., D. failed to rise so high in the church as he had hoped. When the regent Albany was trying to negotiate for the queen a divorce from Angus, D. made futile efforts to interest Henry VIII. in his kinsman's favour. D. wrote two allegorical poems, *The Palace of Truth*, and *King Hart*, both of which illustrate the writer's indebtedness to Chaucer, but his chief literary work was his translation of the *Æneid*, the first version of a Latin classic published in Britain (*c.* 1513).

**Douglas, Sir George Brisbane Scott** (*b.* 1856), a Scottish author, *b.* at Gibraltar, was educated at Cambridge. Among his works are : *The Fireside Tragedy*, 1887 ; *A History of the Border Counties, Roxburgh, Selkirk, Peebles*, 1899 ; *The New Border Tales*, 1896 ; *Poems of a Country Gentleman*, 1897.

**Douglas, J. W. H. T.** (*d.* 1930), an Eng. cricketer and one-time captain of the Eng. test team, and of the M.C.C. team in S. Africa. He was captain of Essex county team for many years. Drowned at sea.

**Douglas, Sir Robert** (1694–1770), a Scottish genealogist. His chief work was a *Peerage of Scotland*, which was published in 1764. He also wrote a *Baronage of Scotland*, and in 1813 another edition of the *Peerage* was published, improved by John Wood.

**Douglas, Stephen Arnold** (1813–61), one of the greatest American statesmen and orators of his time, *b.* Brandon, Vermont, April 23. Son of a doctor, he studied law and settled in the state of Illinois, and soon became a leader in the Democratic party. In 1836 he entered the state legislature ; in 1840 he became its secretary, and in 1843 he was elected Congressman. Four years later he was elected to the U.S. Senate, and remained there until his death. He had hardly taken his seat in the Senate than he was marked out as one of its leaders. In fact, to the end, he was the chief of the Democrats of the N., and, on account of his small stature, was known to the people as the ' Little Giant.' He came into nation-wide prominence when he presented a Bill to organise into a territory the vast W. section of country which was the N. part of the Louisiana purchase. The U.S.A. was steadily heading for the inevitable conflict between the S. slave states and the N., which was gradually coming round to abolition. In 1850 Utah and New Mexico were ordered to be organised as territories without any decision for or against slavery. This was to be left to a decision by the people themselves. Douglas now proposed that the same principle be applied to the vast territory covered by his Bill of 1854, and later introduced another Bill for the repeal of the Missouri compromise, in which it was enacted that slavery was to be forbidden in all the territory now under consideration. Never before in the history of the country were the debates so keen and so heated. Douglas spoke to a packed Senate all night long, and his Bills finally passed and were signed by the President. This made him a hero in the S. slave-holding states, but he was bitterly denounced in the N. He was said to have betrayed his section of the country. A woman sent him thirty pieces of silver— Judas' price. Great play was made with his middle name—'Arnold '— and it was recalled that the greatest military traitor the colonies had, when they were fighting for their independence, was named Benedict Arnold. Douglas was hissed off the stage when he sought to speak in his city of Chicago. But in 1858 he again came to the fore. President Buchanan sent to Congress a Bill to make a state of Kansas. The constitution, which had been framed, virtually made of Kansas a slave state. The people of the territory had asked for a chance to vote on this constitution and had been denied. Douglas, true to his theory that the people should always be allowed to decide, vigorously opposed the Bill and helped defeat it. Once more he was a hero in the N. and damned in the S. His second term in the Senate was expiring. He again ran as a Democrat. The new-born Republican party nominated Abraham Lincoln, who challenged Douglas to a series of debates. It was a daring thing to do, as Douglas was considered the greatest speaker of his day. The debates drew enormous crowds and were followed with breathless interest by the nation. Douglas and Lincoln had both risen from poverty; they had sat in the same legislature; they had paid court to the same young woman; they had been personal, but not political friends. There was a piquant contrast in their personalities. Douglas was small and compactly built; Lincoln was tall and angular; Douglas had a voice of pleasing music; Lincoln had a rather high drawl; Douglas had a nation-wide reputation as the undisputed leader in the Senate; Lincoln was comparatively unknown. Douglas was elected Senator for the third time, but the great debates, in which the slavery question had come up inevitably, had made of Lincoln a national figure too. The Republicans nominated him for the Presidency in 1860. The N. Democrats were anxious to fulfil Douglas's life's dream and ambition—the Presidency. The Democratic convention met at Charleston, S. Carolina. The Southerners insisted on a platform committing the party to slavery. Douglas refused to run on such a platform. The southerners finally seceded from the convention. Later two were held, one by the men from the N. at Baltimore, the southerners holding theirs at Richmond. The N. Democrats nominated Douglas. The southerners nominated John C. Breckinridge. Lincoln was easily elected. Civil war was now certain. Much depended upon the attitude Douglas would take. The Democrats of the N. looked to him for leadership, and he gave it to them. If the S. slave-holders thought Douglas would oppose Lincoln and divide the N. in the coming conflict, they were bitterly disappointed. In the Senate Douglas superbly defended Lincoln's inaugural address. He did more. He went to the White House and pledged Lincoln his support. In the last great speech of his life, which he made at Columbus, Ohio, on his way to Washington, Douglas declared that the union must be preserved at all costs. The N. now closed ranks to fight the S. Douglas *d.* in Chicago, June 3.

**Douglas, Sir William Fettes** (1822–91), a Scottish painter, *b.* in Edinburgh. From 1877–82 he was curator of the National Gallery of Scotland, and in 1882 he became president of the Royal Scottish Academy. His pictures are characterised by their perfection of detail and colouring, among his best being : ' The Alchemist,' ' The Rosicrucians,' and ' A Fishing Village.'

**Douglass, Frederick** (1817–95), an American journalist and orator. He was *b.* at Tuckahoe in Maryland, and was at first brought up as a slave for his father, who was a whit man, had married a negro slave. In 1838 he managed to free himself by escaping from a shipyard in Baltimore, and he then assumed the name of D. instead of Bailey, his original one. After living at New York and then New Bedford, he was appointed a lecturer by the Anti-Slavery Society on account of his eloquence. He published *Frederick Douglass's Paper* on the abolition of slavery, and in addition he filled some important offices, among them marshal for the district of Columbia and minister to Hayti.

**Douglass, Sir James Nicholas** (1826–98), an engineer, *b.* in London. After being apprenticed and holding one or two posts as an engineer, he became in 1862 chief engineer to Trinity House, his chief work being the designing of the new Eddystone Lighthouse of 1878.

**Doukhobors,** *see* DUKHOBORS.

**Doullens,** a Fr. tn. in the dept. of Somme. It stands on the Authie to the N. of Amiens, and has a fine sixteenth century church. Pop. 5805.

**Doulton, Sir Henry** (1820–97), an

Eng. pottery manufacturer, *b.* in London. He was at first employed under his father, and afterwards opened at Lambeth the pottery works bearing his name, which are the largest in the world. He is noted especially for reviving art in connection with the design and manufacture of pottery.

**Doumer, Paul** (*b.* 1857), Fr. statesman, and President of the Fr. Republic. Unsuccessful at the Presidential elections of 1906, he was elected President in 1931.

**Doumergue, Emile** (*b.* 1844), Fr. theologian, *b.* Nîmes. Studied theology in Geneva, Montauban, and in Germany. Then made a special study of Calvinism and published a series of volumes on Calvin, among which are *L'Art et le sentiment dans l'œuvre de Calvin; La Piété réformée d'après Calvin; Calvin le fondateur des libertés modernes.*

**Doumergue, Gaston** (*b.* 1863), Fr. statesman, and President of the Fr. Republic 1924 to 1931 ; *b.* at Aigues-Vives, and son of a farmer. Educated at the lycée, Nîmes. Practised as a barrister and became magistrate first

*[Topical Press*

GASTON DOUMERGUE

in Cochin China, and then in Algiers. Deputy for Gard 1893, Secretary of the Chamber of Deputies, 1895–6 ; Colonial Minister, 1902, 1905 ; Vice-President of the Chamber, 1905–6 ; Minister of Commerce, Industry and Labour, 1906–8 ; of Education, 1908–10 ; and Premier in 1913. On the outbreak of war, he was Colonial

Minister in Viviani's Cabinet. He has the distinction of being the first Protestant President of the Republic.

**Doune,** a Scottish vil. situated in the co. of Perthshire, on the Teith. It lies to the N.W. of Stirling and contains the well-preserved ruins of its castle, built in mediæval times. The old bridge was erected by the tailor of Princess Margaret of England, afterwards queen of James IV. Pop. 868.

**Dour,** a com. of Belgium in the prov. of Hainaut, 10 m. S.W. of Mons. There are coal-mines in the vicinity. Gen. Allenby's cavalry was hotly engaged here Aug.. 24, 1914. Pop. 12,500.

**Doura,** a ruined tn. on the banks of the Euphrates, founded 300 B.C., but abandoned after the destruction of Palmyra in A.D. 273. The British troops discovered here in 1920 paintings of the second and third centuries, and excavations were made by the Fr. Académie des Inscriptions, which revealed the plan of the fortress, the streets, the temple of the Palmyrian gods, frescoes, sculptures and inscriptions

**Doura,** or **Durra,** the flour from a kind of millet seed yielded by different varieties of *Andropogon sorghum,* which is a coarse kind of grass much cultivated in Asia, Africa, and S. Europe. Indian durra makes inferior bread, but is used as a substitute for rice. The leaves and stalks of this variety before the plant flowers are poisonous to cattle. The name durra is often wrongly used to represent the genus *Sorghum,* but, correctly speaking, it applies only to the flour.

**Douro** (anct. Durius), the third largest riv. of the Iberian Peninsula (about 485 m. long), drains an area of some 37,500 sq. m. Rising in the Pico de Urbion (7389 ft.), S. of the Sierra de la Demanda, the D. crosses the Castilian plateau in a W. direction, then from 3 m. E. of Paradella to Barca d'Alva runs S.W., being for 65 m. the boundary between Spain and Portugal, and finally reaches the Atlantic at São Joao da Foz, 3 m. below Oporto, having traversed Portugal with a W. course. The tributaries on the right bank are the Pisuerga, Valderaduey, and Esla (in Spain), and the Sabor, Túa, and Tamega (in Portugal), and from the left the Spanish Adaja, Tormen Yeltes, and the Portuguese Agueda, Côa, and Paiva. A sand-bar at the mouth, rapids and swift inundations render the lower courses useless for navigation. Toro and Zamora are on its right bank.

**Douroucouli,** the popular name for S. American monkeys of the genus *Nyctipithecus* in the family Cebidæ.

The incisors in the lower jaw project forwards, and the eyes of the monkeys are large, both of which features give them a lemurine appearance. They are unlike many of their allies in having the long tail non-prehensile.

**Dove,** a riv. of England, rising in Axe Edge, Derbyshire, 4 m. from Buxton. It forms the S.W. border of that county, and is noted for its beauty. Trout abound in its waters, and for this reason it was well known to Izaak Walton. The river flows into the Trent near Burton.

**Dove.** In very early times the D. was used in pictures to represent the Holy Ghost, and is often seen in pictures which deal with the various periods of Christ's life, especially in those of the Annunciation and His baptism. It was used also as the form of the pyx, and was sometimes placed on fonts. When represented with three pairs of wings it typified the church.

**Dove,** *see* PIGEON.

**Dove, Heinrich Wilhelm** (1803–79), a Ger. scientist, *b.* at Liegnitz. He was Professor of Natural Philosophy in Berlin, and did much for science, especially in electricity and meteorology, being head of the Royal Meteorological Institute. It was he who detected forged banknotes by means of the stereoscope. Among his works are *Distribution of Heat on the Surface of the Globe.*

**Dovedale,** a picturesque dell on the borders of Staffordshire and Derbyshire, England, extending from Thorpe Cloud to Dove Holes. The scenery is a charming combination of wood, rocks, and water.

**Dover,** the chief of the five Cinque Ports, a market tn., and a watering-place in the co. of Kent, England. It is situated in a breach between high chalk cliffs on the N.W. side of D. Strait. It is separated from Cape Grisnez (21 m.) on the opposite side of the English Channel, by an hour's journey on quick steamers, and lies 66 m. to the E.S.E. of London. The dominant feature of the town is its castle, with an altitude of 375 ft. above sea-level, which includes in its grounds a Rom. lighthouse, the anct. cruciform church of St. Mary-in-Castro, a massive Norman keep now used as a bomb magazine, and barracks for 200 men. The prospect from the keep includes, on a clear day, the Fr. coast from Boulogne to Gravelines, and the cliffs from Folkestone to Ramsgate, together with the many elaborate fortifications which honeycomb the D. cliffs on either side. D. College has been built round the fine remains of the twelfth century St. Martin's priory. The Admiralty Pier (begun in 1847)

and the Prince of Wales Pier (begun in 1893), the former of which has an overhead railway, enclose many acres of sheltered waters. In 1896 the construction of an artificial naval harbour, with an area of 610 acres, was commenced, and also that of three great enclosing breakwaters of concrete, the combined length of which are over 1⅞ m. There are two docks, the Granville and the Wellington, the latter of which was widened for large Channel steamers in 1888. D. has shipbuilding, rope- and sail-making industries, besides her fisheries and traffic in dairy produce with France. The Dover–Calais route to the Continent is popular, as it has the shortest sea crossing. There is a pilot station with seventy-five pilots and the largest and fastest life-boat in the world. The boundaries were extended in 1921. Pop. (1921) 39,985.

**Dover :** (1) The oldest (1623) city in the Strafford co. of New Hampshire, U.S.A., on the Cochecho R., 68 m. N. by E. of Boston. It has cotton and woollen mills, besides print works. The University of New Hampshire is at Durham 5 m. S.W. Pop. 13,573. (2) The cap. of Delaware, U.S.A., and co. tn. of Kent co. on Jones' Creek and the Philadelphia, Baltimore, and Washington Railway, 48 m. S. of Wilmington. Besides being the centre of a fruit district, D. has factories for canning fruit, etc. Pop. 4800 (3) A tn. of Morris co., New Jersey, U.S.A., with iron mines and manufactures. Pop. 10,031. (4) A city of Tuscarawas co., Ohio, with iron ore and coal and manufactures. Pop. 9716.

**Dover Patrol.** On the outbreak of the Great War the D. P. formed part of the E. Coast Naval Command, under the command of Admiral Ballard. Its duties were to prevent Ger. ships forcing their way into the English Channel, and to inspect neutrals for contraband (*q.v.*). Soon after the War commenced it was made a separate command under Admiral Hood (*q.v.*), (who was subsequently killed at the Battle of Jutland). Later on, ' drifters,' *i.e.*, vessels equipped with drift nets in order to catch submarines, and trawlers to sweep for mines were added to the Patrol. Eventually it consisted of twenty-four distinct classes of fighting vessels. Admiral Bacon was in command from 1915 to 1917, being succeeded by Admiral Evans of Antarctic fame. The work of the D. P. was very varied. Besides safeguarding the transport of troops to France, the Patrol was engaged offensively against the Gers. on the Belgian coast, and against their bases at

Zeebrugge and Ostend; and in all, twenty-eight bombardments were carried out. Mines and mine net barrages were laid along the Belgian coast, a procedure which stopped enemy mine-laying in the Channel. Over five million troops were transported to France without a single casualty. (The record of the D. P. is well told by Admiral Sir R. Bacon in his *The Dover Patrol, 1915–1917*.)

**Dover, Strait of** (the anct. *Frelum Gallicum* and the Fr. *Pas de Calais*), the narrow channel separating France and England, and joining the English Channel with the North Sea. It is about 22 m. in length, and at its narrowest part, from Dover Pier to Calais, its breadth does not exceed 21 m. It extends from Dungeness and Cape Grisnez in a N.E. direction to S. Foreland and Calais. The greatest depth is not quite 180 ft. The geological formation of the channel bed points to the fact that at one time England joined the continent. The tides of the North Sea and the English Channel meet in the D. S.

**Dovercourt**, a watering-place of Essex, England, situated at the mouth of the Stour estuary, S. of Harwich. There are two lighthouses guarding the entrance into Harwich Harbour and also marking the position of a sandbank. Good bathing is to be obtained at D. Pop. 7694.

**Dover's Powder**, a prescription of Dr. Dover (1660–1742). It is regarded as a medicine of great value, and acts as a sudorific. The ingredients are : one part each of powdered opium and powdered ipecacuanha root, together with eight parts of sulphate of potash. From five to ten grains constitute an ordinary dose.

**Dovrefjeld**, forms part of the mountainous tableland of Norway, being marked off by the valleys of the Sundal, Laagen, and Rauma, and by the fjords off Nordmöre. Precipitous, irregular spurs, attaining an elevation of 6000 ft., shut in the Rauma valley (well known to tourists as the Ramsdal), but Snehaetten, a magnificent snow field, is the highest peak (7615 ft.).

**Dow, Lorenzo** (1777–1834), an American Methodist preacher, *b.* at Coventry, Connecticut. Was sent as a missionary to the Catholics in Ireland, and both in England and America attracted great audiences: helped to found the Primitive Methodist Society in England. He was a strenuous opponent of the Rom. Catholics.

**Dow, Neal** (1804–97), an American temperance reformer, *b.* at Port-

land, Maine; educated as a Quaker : he was a strong prohibitionist, and drafted the Maine prohibitory law of 1851. He served as brigadier-general during the Civil War. In 1880 he was candidate of the National Prohibition Party for President.

**Dowager** (from Fr. *douairière*), meant originally a widow with a dower. First used in England of Catherine of Aragon, widow of Prince Arthur, it is now applied to all widows of high rank to distinguish them from their sons' wives.

**Dowaziac**, a city and summer resort of Cass co., S.W. Michigan. Manufs. furnaces. Pop. (1920) 5440.

**Dowden, Edward** (1843–1913), native of Cork, where he began his education, afterwards proceeding to Trinity College, Dublin. He held first the post of Professor of Oratory

EDWARD DOWDEN

at that university, and afterwards that of Professor of Literature. He was a great authority on Shakespeare and an able critic, his chief works being *The French Revolution and English Literature* (lectures), 1897 ; *New Studies in Literature*, 1895 ; *Life of Percy Bysshe Shelley*, 1886 ; *Goethe in Italy*, 1886. He also edited or wrote introductions to the following : *The International Shakespeare*, 1884 ; *The Sonnets of Shakespeare*, 1881; *Shakespeare's Scenes and Characters*, 1876 ; *Romeo and Juliet* (The Arden Shakespeare), 1899 ; *Essays, Modern and Elizabethan*, 1910, etc.

**Dowie, John Alexander** (1847–1907), *b.* in Edinburgh, was for a time a student at Edinburgh University.

He afterwards went to S. Australia, where his parents were living, as the minister of a Congregational church. Later on he claimed the power of being able to heal people by means of prayer, and organised the ' Christian Catholic Church in Zion,' he himself being the overseer, and at the beginning of 1900 he settled with his followers on the shores of Lake Michigan in Zion City. In 1903 and 1904 he visited England, where he did not meet with much encouragement, and in 1906 his prestige over his followers was lost after the revolt of Zion City. D. was popularly known by the title of ' Doctor,' and he himself claimed to be Elijah.

**Dowlais**, see MERTHYR-TYDFIL.

**Dowlas**, a coarse kind of unbleached linen. Exceedingly strong; it was used by workmen for their aprons and sometimes for their shirts. It is not used so much, however, in the present day.

**Down**, a maritime co. with a coastline of 67 m., in N. Ireland, having an acreage of 611,927. Belfast Lough, Dundrum and Carlingford Bays are spacious inlets along the indented shores, but the largest is Strangford Lough, whose waters are studded with 260 islets. Slieve Donard reaches the highest altitude (2796 ft.) in the Morne Mountains to the S. The Bann, the Lagan, and the Annacloy are the chief rivers, whilst the Newry Canal a›ong the W. gives increased facilities for communication. Oats, potatoes, wheat, turnips, and flax are widely cultivated, whilst pigs and cattle are reared. Linen, hosiery, woollens, leather, cattle, butter, and corn are the principal exports. The county town is Downpatrick. Round towers, stone cairns, raths and abbeys are among the antiquities of interest. Two members represent Down in Parliament. Pop. 204,303.

**Downham**, a mrkt. tn. and urban district of England, in the co. of Norfolk. It is situated on the Ouse, 11 m. S.W. of King's Lynn and has a large flour mill, malt houses and a brewery. Pop. 2342.

**Downing College, Cambridge**, founded in the year 1800 by money which had been left in 1717 by Sir George Downing for that purpose, and its charter was sealed in the same year, making it part of the University of Cambridge. The college must consist of a master, two professors (one of laws of England, and one of medicine), and a certain number of fellows and scholars. There are scholarships which may be competed for by those who are not members of the university. Some of these are foundation scholarships, and others are minor ones of less value, and those obtaining them may afterwards compete for foundation ones.

**Downing, Sir George** (c. 1623–1684), Eng. soldier and politician, son of Emmanuel D., of the Inner Temple and later of Massachusetts. Educated partly in England and partly at Harvard College. Went to England about 1645, and became a scoutmaster-general in Cromwell's Scottish Army, and a teller of the Exchequer. Was deputed by Cromwell, after the war, to make a settlement with Scotland. Represented Edinburgh in Parliament, and later represented England at The Hague, being one of the foremost advisers on foreign policy during the Protectorate, under both Oliver and Richard Cromwell, his greatest mission of that time being to try to bring about a union of all the European Protestant Powers. Always a zealot for the old Constitution, he was active, on the accession of Charles II., in endeavouring to arrest the regicides who had sought refuge on the Continent. He received large grants from the king for his services, but though an able man, he was crafty, avaricious and treacherous. He is often mentioned in Pepys' Diary.

**Downing Street**, a street of Westminster, London, leading into Whitehall. Its name is derived from Sir George Downing, a celebrated politician, who lived in the reign of Charles II., and was Secretary to the Treasury in 1667. The Foreign Office and also the Colonial Office are here, as well as the official residences of the Prime Minister and the Chancellor of the Exchequer : numbers 10 and 11 respectively.

**Downpatrick**, the cap. of co. Down, Ireland, 28 m. S.S.E. of Belfast (by the Belfast and County Down Railway), is a town of extreme antiquity, situated close to the S.W. fringe of Strangford Lough. Though St. Patrick founded the see in 440, the present cathedral (Protestant) is not older than 1790. Ships of 100 tons come up as far as Quoile quay, about a mile from the town. The dun or rath of Keltar, extending over an area of 10 acres, is one of the best in Ireland. Its race meetings attract visitors, and Rom. Catholics seek its holy wells. Brewing, tanning, soap and linen making are the chief industries; cattle, pigs, corn, and potatoes the chief exports. Pop. 3200.

**Downs, North and South**, two ranges of rounded chalk hills, situated in the S. and S.E. of England, the enclosed valley being called the Weald. They have their beginning in Hampshire, by Salisbury Plain. The N. D.

lie in Surrey and Kent, ending in the S. Foreland. The highest points reach over 800 ft. above sea-level. The S. D. cross Sussex, and terminate in Beachy Head. The highest points reach 860 ft. above sea-level. The sheep reared on the Downs are celebrated.

**Downton,** a par. formerly a market tn. of England in the co. of Wiltshire, situated on the Avon, 6 m. S.E. of Salisbury. D. is of anct. origin, having been important in Anglo-Saxon times. The 'Moot' and earthworks of that period still remain. It sent two members to Parliament until 1832. Cerdic, the Saxon, gained a victory here in 519. Pop. 1906.

**Doxology** (Gk. δοξολογία, praise-giving), an ascription of praise to God. The name is given to the short ascriptions given at the end of some of the N. T. epistles, and occurring sometimes in the middle of an argument (*e.g.* the ends of Rom. and 2 Pet., and in Rom. ii. 36). The title is, however, more particularly applied to (1) the ascription, 'Glory be to the Father and to the Son, etc.,' repeated in the Anglican and Rom. churches, principally at the end of psalms and canticles. This is known as the Lesser D.; (2) the Trisagion or Tersanctus taken from Isaiah vi. 3; (3) the concluding part of the Lord's Prayer, 'For Thine is the Kingdom, etc.'; (4) the Greater D., known also as the *Gloria in Excelsis*, which occurs at the beginning of the Rom. Mass and the end of the Eng. Communion Rite.

**Doyen, Eugène Louis** (1859–1916), Fr. surgeon, *b.* at Rheims. He made many innovations in surgery and gynæcology; and he claimed to have discovered the cancer microbe, but his claim was not substantiated. His modifications of surgical instruments have been widely adopted. His works include: *Traité de la chirurgie de l'estomac,* 1895; *Atlas de bactériologie,* 1897; *Traitement de Cancer,* 1904; *Le Malade et le Médecin,* 1906; *Traité de Thérapeutique chirurgicale et de Technique opératoire,* 1907; *Le Cancer,* 1909. He *d.* on or about Nov. 21.

**Doyle, Sir Arthur Conan** (1859–1930), Eng. author, eldest son of Charles D. the artist; also nephew of Richard D. of *Punch*, and grandson of the famous John D. (' H. B.'). He studied medicine, and took his degree at Edinburgh; afterwards practising at Southsea, until his success as a writer induced him to devote himself entirely to letters. During the S. African War, however, he went out as senior physician of the Langman Field Hospital. His first book, *A Study in Scarlet,* in which ' Sherlock

Holmes ' made his first appearance, was published in 1887. He published many stories of different kinds: historical novels such as *The White Company,* 1890; *The Exploits of Brigadier Gerard,* 1896; *Uncle Bernac,* 1897; and the excellent picture of the Georgian rakehelly set, *Rodney Stone,* 1896. But fame came to him through the creation of ' Sherlock Homes,' the wonderful inductive detective, whose adventures thrilled the entire world, which followed his adventures with breathless interest. Undoubtedly suggested by the ' Dupin ' of Edgar Allan Poe, Holmes was a mere caricature of that excellent conception: he captivated, not by real astuteness, but by mannerisms and by a portrait that was an afterthought of the illustrator —whether suggested by D. or not; and it is more than suspected that his creator held him in derision. D. wrote also for the stage; and his dramatic version of a story of his own, *A Story of Waterloo,* gave Sir Henry Irving one of his most popular successes. The latter part of D.'s career was largely expended on psychic research; and, after the inevitable ' war-books,' came *The Wanderings of a Spiritualist,* 1921; and *History of Spiritualism,* in 2 vols., 1926. The hero he found it so difficult to kill made his last appearance in *The Case Book of Sherlock Holmes,* 1927. Sir Arthur was finally successful in his long effort to obtain the release of the unjustly condemned Oscar Slater; and he *d.* at Crowborough, Sussex, July 7.

**Doyle, Sir Francis Hastings Charles** (1810–88), poet and professor of poetry at Oxford from 1867–77. His chief works are: *Miscellaneous Verses,* 1841; *Two Destinies,* 1844; *Return of the Guards,* 1866; *Reminiscences and Opinions,* 1886.

**Doyle, James William Edmund** (1822–92), was the son of John D. His chief work was the publication of the *Official Baronage of England,* 1886.

**Doyle, Richard** (1824–83), caricaturist, was the second son of John D., also famous as a caricaturist. At the age of fifteen he published *The Eglington Tournament, or, The Days of Chivalry Revived,* In 1843, when *Punch* was two years old, he became a regular contributor, and much of his best work appeared in it, notably ' Manners and Customs of ye Englyshe,' until in 1850 he retired, owing to the paper's attacks on papal aggression. He illustrated many books, among others Thackeray's *Rebecca and Rowena* and *The Newcomes,* Locker's *London Lyrics* and the *Bon Gaultier Ballads.* As an artist he was at his best in fantastic designs, for his fancy was unbounded, and in dainty elf-like designs such as those, by him, which still decorate the cover of *Punch*.

**D'Oyly Carte, Richard** (1844–1901), was for some time a concert and lecture agent, but at the age of thirty-one he became a theatrical manager, and it was in that capacity he became known to the world. In March 1875 he produced at the Royalty Theatre, London, *Trial by Jury*, the first of the series of comic operas written by Sir W. S. Gilbert and composed by Sir Arthur Sullivan. At the Opera Comique he brought out *The Sorcerer* and *H.M.S. Pinafore*, and followed these with *The Pirates of Penzance* and *Patience*. All these were successful, and the triumvirate netted, it is said, £60,000 a year. D. invested his share of the profits in the erection of the Savoy Theatre, where he put on the other Gilbert and Sullivan plays, nearly all of which had a long run. D. in 1891, opened the building now known as the Palace Theatre as the English Opera House, but here he met with his first and only check. The venture was a failure, and the building was disposed of to a syndicate for music-hall purposes.

**Dozy, Reinhart Pieter Anne** (1820–83), was an orientalist. He was *b.* at Leyden, and was a student at the university there, eventually being appointed professor of history at the same university. He wrote many books, among them : *Histoire des Musulmans d'Espagne jusqu'à la conquête de l'Andalousie par les Almoravides*, 1861 ; *Historia Abbadidarum*, etc., 1852 ; *Het Islamsone*, 1863 ; *Recherches sur l'Histoire politique et la Littérature de l'Espagne pendant le Moyen Age*, 1849 ; *De Israëliten te Mekka*, 1864 ; and was also the editor of other works written in Arabic.

**Draba**, a genus of Cruciferæ, is native to N. temperatures and flourishes in N. America ; the few Brit. species are known in Britain as whitlow grass.

**Dracæna**, a genus of Liliaceæ, comprehends forty species found in warm parts of the Old World. It was established by Linnæus and named from one of the species yielding the resinous exudation known as dragon's blood. *D. terminalis* is regarded as a symbol of truth and of peace in the Eastern Archipelago ; sugar and an intoxicating drink are obtained from the roots in the islands of the Pacific. *D. draco*, the dragon-tree, which yields the red gum-resin, had a celebrated representative in Teneriffe. This tree, which was blown down in 1868, was 45 ft. in diameter, 70 ft.

in height, and was supposed to be about 6000 years old.

**Drachenfels**, a mountain peak in Ger. belonging to the Siebengebirge range. It is situated on the right or eastern bank of the Rhine, 10 m. S.E. of Bonn, and close to Konigswinter. Rising to a height of 1055 ft., it is noted as being the steepest mountain of the whole group. The Drachenhohle, or the dragon's cave, is in the slopes,

DRACÆNA DRACO

(The Dragon-tree)

around which is woven the story of the dragon that was slain by Siegfried. The peak is ascended by a mountain railway.

**Drachenstein Mountains**, a chain of mountains in the S.W. of Cape Colony, S. Africa. They extend N. and S. to a distance of 25 m. eastward of Cape Town.

**Drachm**, or **Dram**, *see* WEIGHTS AND MEASURES.

**Drachma** was, in ancient Greece, a silver coin, equal in value to one-hundredth part of a mina and a six-hundredth part of a talent. Until Solon's day a D. was worth a little over a shilling, but the Attic D. was equivalent to about 9¾d. in Eng. currency. The obol was equal to one-sixth of a D. In Athens the principal coin in use was the tetradrachmon, worth four drachmæ, having the head of Pallas engraved on one side, and the owl on the other. As a weight measure, 100 drachmæ were again equal to 1 mina (almost a lb.). The Gk. D. in modern currency,

*Left:* a double drachma of Aegina. *Right:* a Parthian silver drachma of Arsaces VI.

supposed to be of the same value as a Fr. franc, is really worth about 8½d. It is divided into 100 lepta.

**Drachmann, Holger Henrik Her-holdt** (1846–1908), a Danish writer. He travelled in most of the countries of Europe and made a special study of life among sailors and fishermen, the descriptions of which make his books famous. Among poems he wrote: *Daempe der Melodier*, 1875; *Ranker og Roser*, 1879; as well as stories such as, *Den Nellige Ild*, 1899; novels, among them being *Forskrevet*, 1890, and dramas like *Völund Soned*, 1894; and *Brav-Karl et Skuespil*, 1897.

**Dracina, Draconin,** *see* DRAGON'S BLOOD.

**Draco** (seventh century B.C.), an Athenian statesman and lawgiver. He was the first codifier of the laws of Athens. Before his time the laws were unwritten and were ad-ministered by the Eupatridæ. Tradi-tion has always connected his name with a severity which has become proverbial in the word 'draconian.' Demades, the orator, declared that D.'s laws were 'written in blood,' for nearly every law-breaker suffered the penalty of death. It is now generally agreed by scholars that the constitution assigned by Aris-totle (*Athen. Polit.*) is not authentic. *See also* ATHENS and GREECE: *History*.

**Draco, or Flying Dragon,** a genus of lizards, belongs to the family Agamidæ. The species are brilliantly coloured and are unable to change their hues; in habit they are entirely terrestrial, and in diet insectivorous; their harmlessness makes them suit-able for pets. Their great peculiarity lies in the wing-like membranes, which extend from their sides, can be opened and shut at their owners' will, and serve as a parachute when they leap from one branch to another. *D. volans*, a Malayan lizard,

is the best-known species; in length it is about 5 in., with another 5 in. for the long, thin tail.

**Draco** ('the dragon'), a constella-tion in the northern hemisphere. A star in Draconis was used by Bradley in his discovery of the aberration of light. It is situated almost in the solstitial colure, and so the minor axis of the lesser aberra-tional eclipse lies in the meridian at its transit.

**Dracontium,** *see* DRAGON.

**Dracut,** a tn. of Middlesex co., Massachusetts, U.S.A. Pop. 6912.

**Dra-el-Mizan,** a tn. of Algeria in the arron. of Tizi-Ouzon, with marble quarries and cork manufs. Pop. 6740.

**Draft,** an order written by the drawer to authorise the payment of a sum of money by some other person acting as an agent. These Ds. are used in commerce between firms and in municipal affairs by corporations.

**Draga, Queen,** *see* ALEXANDER OBRENOVICH.

**Dragashani, or Dragasani,** a Ru-manian tn. situated in Wallachia, near the Aluta R. Pop. 12,000.

**Drago Doctrine,** the principle that force may not be used by one power to collect money owing to its citizens by another power. It appears to have originated in 1902 when Britain, Ger. and Italy blockaded the ports of Venezuela for that purpose, Dr. L. F. Drago, a well-known Argentine jurist, maintaining that their action was contrary to international law. Most of the S. American republics supported the doctrine, which has ever since been known as the D. D.

**Dragomans** (Fr. *dragoman*, It. *dragomanno*, Arabic *tarjuman*), the men in the East who act as inter-preters. They act as guides, and in addition to that they make all the arrangements for their travellers, some of them being employed at the ambassadors' courts.

**Dragomiroff, Michael Ivanovich** (1830–1925), Rus. soldier. Served in the Austro-Prussian War of 1866, the Russo-Turkish War of 1877, and was so severely wounded in the latter that he had to retire. His services, however, as a writer on tactics, strategy and military reorganisation were as valuable as his leadership, and in the War with Japan, in 1904, he was on the Rus. headquarters staff.

**Dragon** (Gk. δράκων, the seeing one, from δέρκομαι, to see; Lat. *draco*, Fr. *dragon*), in the mythology of almost all the nations, is typical of the power of evil which has to be overcome, hence the great work of the heroes of the nations was to kill the D. The conception of its shape seems to have varied slightly, but in its essential principles it was snake-like, probably having wings and being able to breathe out fire from its mouth. With this idea of the snake's representing the power of evil is connected that of the N.T., in which the serpent is typical of sin, as the D. held a similar place in the sacred writings of the Hebrews. In the Gk. mythology, the hydra, or monster with nine heads, was slain by Hercules, while others among the heroes also slew Ds. In the same way the heroes of the stories of northern mythology made their great feat the slaying of the D., among them being the god Thor, Siegfried, whose story is related in the *Niebelungenlied*, and Beowulf, the hero of the poem of that name. This idea is found in later Gk. Romances and in the mediæval stories of King Arthur and Tristram.

**Dragon**, the popular name of several species of lizards, and is particularly applied to members of the American genus *Dracæna* and the Malayan genus *Draco* (*q.v.*).

**Dragon**, in botany, is the name applied to plants in the araceous genus *Dracontium*. The stem is usually mottled, and the flowers have a gaping mouth. Green Dragon is a herb found in S. America. The corn contains a sap used locally in medicine. The term 'dragon plants' is applied to the two species of *Dracunculus* which flourish round the Mediterranean. The name of dragon-wort is given to two distinct herbs, *Artenisia dracunculus*, a species of Compositæ, and *Polygonum bistorta*, a species of Polygonaceæ. The plant known as the dragon-tree is *Dracæna draco*, a liliaceous tree from which exudes the resin called dragon's blood. Dragon-Root occurs in hot countries and is believed to be fertilised by snails; the tuber is used in medicine. Dragon's Head, or *Dracocephalum*, a genus of the Labiætæ which receives its name from the appearance of the corolla.

**Dragonet**, or *Callionymus*, a genus of small fishes living in the sea, the males have the fin-rays produced into filaments. *C. draco* is known as the skulpin.

**Dragon-fly**, the name of a number of insects now considered to belong to the order Odonata, though some writers still call the family Libellulidæ. They are sometimes called 'devil's darning needles' and 'horse-stingers,' but are at the same time harmless except to the insects which form their food. They are characterised by a very freely moving head, large eyes; an overhanging upper lip enabling them to catch their prey; small antennæ; two pairs of wings equal in size, the main nervures having a longitudinal direction crossed by a number of nervules; an elongated abdomen and slender legs. In the early stages of their life they live close to the water—the eggs being deposited in or near the water, and there is no stage of quiescence between the larva and the nymph. During the larva stage the 'mask,' a modification of the lip, enables them to obtain their prey. The number of species is about 2000, distributed over the globe, but principally in tropical regions, a few, however, being natives of Britain. They are exceedingly voracious and very active, some species having a brilliant and beautiful colouring. *See* William Forsell Kirby, *A Synonymic Catalogue of Neuroptera Odonata*, 1890; William John Lucas, *British Dragon-flies, Odonata*, 1900.

**Dragonnades**, *see* CAMISARDS.

**Dragon's Blood**, a name applied in ancient pharmacology to the resin derived from a number of plants, chief of which are the *Calamus draco*, an E. Indian palm, *Dracæna draco* of the Canary Is., and the *Croton draco* of Mexico. D. B. is an opaque, brittle substance, reddish-brown in colour, soluble in alcohol and fixed and volatile oils, giving off benzoic acid when heated, and obtained by melting the resinous exudation of the fruits in the sun, or boiling it in water. Regarded once as a valuable medicine, because of its astringent properties, it is now used for colouring lacquers, varnish, and Chinese writing papers, and also for dentifrices.

**Dragon's Mouth** and **Snapdragon**, the popular names for flowers of the genus *Antirrhinum*, and order Scrophulariaceæ. The corolla is personate, and when pinched between the fingers the mouth opens and then closes with a snap.

**Dragoon** (Fr. *dragon*), originally applied to a cavalry soldier, trained to fight on foot. He received his name from his weapon, a 'dragon' or short musket, so called from the dragon's head worked on the muzzle, which was first carried by the horsemen of Marshal Brissac in 1600. Accustomed to fight with the infantry, they were organised into companies, their officers bearing infantry titles. Ds. were naturally at a disadvantage, as regards armament and horsemanship, compared with the *bona fide* cavalry regiments. Since the campaigns of Frederick the Great, the term D. has been used of medium cavalry. In police and in all kinds of guerilla warfare, Ds. have been employed, because they combine efficiency with economy. When Louis XIV. proceeded against the Protestants, he was said to 'dragoon' or 'dragonnade' them. The Scots Greys (established in 1683) is the oldest D. regiment in the British army. *See also* ROYAL DRAGOONS; SCOTS GREYS.

**Dragoon Guards.** Prior to the Great War there were seven regiments of D. G.: the 1st (King's), 2nd (Queen's Bays), 3rd (Prince of Wales's), 4th (Royal Irish), 5th (Princess Charlotte of Wales's), 6th (Carabiniers), and 7th (Princess Royal's). After the war, the progress made in mechanisation (*q.v.*), combined with the need for economy, resulted in the amalgamation of many of the old cavalry regiments. To-day the 1st and 2nd survive in their pre-war style, but the remainder, as amalgamated, are the 3rd D. G. (being the 3rd and 6th amalgamated); the 4/7th D. G. (being the amalgamated 4th and 7th D. G.), and the 5/6th D. G. (being the 5th D. G. amalgamated with the 6th Dragoons).

All the old regiments of D. G., except the 7th, were raised at the time of the Monmouth rebellion of 1685. The 1st (King's) acquired their title 'King's' in 1746. They fought, as did most of the other regiments of D. G., in Marlborough's campaigns; also in the S. African War; and at Ypres and Loos in the Great War. The Queen's Bays fought at the Battle of the Boyne as the 3rd Regiment of Horse, and their present name was given in the time of the Seven Years' War. They fought at Mons, Le Cateau (*q.v.*) in the Great War, notably in co-operation with the celebrated 'L' Battery, R. Horse Artillery at Néry, and at Gheluvelt, in 1914, and at various times in the other Ypres battles. The 3rd D. G., the old-time 4th Regiment of Horse, fought under Marlborough as 'Wood's Horse' and received their title, 'Prince of Wales's,' in 1768. Besides taking part in Marlborough's campaigns, they fought in the Peninsular battles; and, in the Great War, at Hollebeke, Klein Zillebeke, and Gheluvelt in the First Battle of Ypres, and in 1915 took part in combined cavalry operations in the second Battle of Ypres. The Royal Irish D. G., raised in 1697 as 'Arran's Cuirassiers,' received their present name in 1788, and fought with distinction at Balaclava and other Crimean battles, and at Tel-el-Kebir. In the Great War they are credited officially with being the first Brit. troops to come into contact with the Gers., charging and routing a column of Uhlans at Jemappes on Aug. 20, 1914. They also fought at Mons, and at various places in the Ypres sector. The 5th D. G. were the former 2nd Green Irish Horse of

1717; they also fought in Marlborough's battles, and in those of Wellington. In the Great War they were at Le Cateau, Néry and Ypres. The Carabiniers, formerly the 8th Regiment of Horse, became the 3rd Irish Horse in the '45 rebellion and the 'Carabiniers' in 1788. Besides taking part in Marlborough's campaigns, they fought in the Afghan War of 1789 and at Paardeberg in the S. African War. Like other regiments of cavalry, their fighting in the Great War was mainly in the capacity of infantry in 1914, notably at Gheluvelt. The 7th D. G. were raised in 1689 by the first Duke of Devonshire to support the Protestant cause during the Revolution. At the Battle of the Boyne they fought as Schomberg's Horse. After Marlborough's battles, their commanding officer was the famous Jean Louis Lord Ligonier (*q.v.*). Their other battles prior to the Great War included Dettingen and Tel-el-Kebir. In the Great War they were at the Battle of the Somme, 1916, being especially prominent in the stiff fighting around Bazentin and Longueval.

**Draguignan,** a tn. of France in the dept. of Var, and the cap. of the dept. It has a mild climate and is charmingly situated on the R. Nartuby, 50 m. N.E. of Toulon. Pop. 9440.

**Drain (Sewers),** *see* SEWAGE.

**Draining, Drainage,** the process of rendering a mass of substance free from moisture. Drainage is often associated with the carrying away of sewage matter in artificial channels (*see* SEWAGE), and with reclaiming land by enclosing it with dykes and carrying off the water by special channels. In the practice of agriculture, however, the term is most often used to designate the removal of excess of water, which would otherwise become stagnant, in from a clayey soil. Such D. was practised by the Roms., who kept their lands dry by open trenches or drains in which a porous channel was maintained by a layer of stones or twigs. The use of covered drains was revived in Eng. by Joseph Elkington about 1763, who showed that land could be freed from stagnant water by tapping the obstructing clay by deep drains in suitable directions. In 1823, James Smith of Deanston introduced the parallel system which is the basis of all methods now in use. When the slope of the field, or of any section of it, is determined, and a suitable outlet for the water obtained, a main receiving drain is constructed along the lowest part of the ground, and a series of parallel drains made so as to fall towards the main drain. Smith suggested that each trench should be 30 in. deep; at the present day they are usually cut to a depth of 3 to 4 ft., the width at the bottom being just sufficient to receive the line of porous cylinders which carry off the water. Formerly these were connected by collars, but if well laid there is no necessity for that method of joining. The distances between the parallel drains may be from 10 to 40 ft., according to the extent to which water is imprisoned.

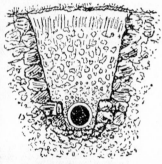

SECTION OF A DRAIN

The effect of D. land is greatly to increase its agricultural value. In a marshy soil, aquatic plants and mosses thrive and prevent the proper development of grass or corn. The temperature tends to be low from the constant evaporation, and crops are, therefore, liable to fail in bad seasons. Tillage is difficult on account of the toughness of the soil. The excess of moisture prevents the passage of air through the soil, thus starving the roots. Sheep and cattle are much more liable to disease. When the land is drained these disadvantages disappear. By this means many districts in the low-lying parts of the E. of England have been converted into good arable and pasture land. The Land Drainage Act, 1930, was passed to promote schemes of land drainage, but such schemes are awaiting the formation of catchment authorities under the Act.

**Drake, Sir Francis** (1540–96), a navigator. One of the most popular figures in England's naval annals, and his praises have been sung from his own day until ours. In his youth D. was apprenticed to the sea. In 1565 he sailed with Captain John Lovell to the Spanish Main, and his capacity for handling a vessel became so well known that two years later he was selected to command the *Judith* in that ill-fated expedition of Sir John Hawkins, which was defeated with great loss off San Juan de Lua. Between 1570 and 1573 he made three voyages to the W. Indies, during which he sacked Portobello and Vera Cruz, and accumulated a considerable fortune. It was in 1577 that he set out for the R. Plate on a buccaneering expedition, and he made his way through the Straits of Magellan, sailed through the Indian Archipelago, rounded the Cape of Good Hope, and returned to England, having thus completed the circumnavigation of the globe, the first Englishman to have done so. To his vessel, the *Golden Hinde*, came Queen Elizabeth on April 4, 1581, and there knighted the intrepid sailor. Four years later he was given the command of a fleet, and committed many assaults on the Spanish fleet and the Spanish coast towns. He was urgent in his advice that every effort should be made to destroy the Spanish fleet in its own waters, but other counsels prevailed with the government. So it came about that in 1588 the Spanish Armada sailed for England, and D., having the chance of his life, seized it, and defeated the Armada off Gravelines, pursuing it and destroying several vessels, as the fleet sailed northwards up the coast to Scotland. Still vigorous, D. now carried the war again into the enemy's country, and laid waste many towns and destroyed

SIR FRANCIS DRAKE

many ships and vast stores, thus putting an end for many years to come to any fears of a further armada being sent. In 1594 he was sent with a fleet to the W. Indies, and it was whilst on this expedition that he died at Portobello. He was buried at sea, the proper cemetery for a brave and brilliant seaman. The best biography is by Barrow (1843).

**Drake, Friedrich Johann Heinrich** (1805–82), a German sculptor, *b.* at Pyrmont. His chief works are : ' A Dying Warrior crowned with Victory,' ' The Eight Provinces of Prussia,' as well as statues of Schinkel, Rauch, Frederick William III., and William I., also those of Bismarck, Moltke, Ranke, and Raumer.

**Drake, Joseph Rodman** (1795–1820), an American poet *b.* in New York City ; graduated in medicine in 1816. Went to Europe in 1818 and wrote for the *New York Evening Post* satirical verses since republished and very popular. He died of consumption. His chief poems were *The American Flag* (1819) and *The Culprit Fay* (1816).

**Drake, Nathan** (1766–1836), an English essayist and doctor, *b.* at York. His best-known book is *Shakespeare and His Times*, 1817.

**Drake, Samuel Gardener** (1798– 1875), an antiquarian, *b.* in Pittsfield, New Hampshire. When he was thirty years old, he went to Boston and there established a shop for the sale of antiquarian books. Among other works he wrote : *The Book of the Indians of North America, Comprising Details in the Lives of about Five Hundred Chiefs and Others*, etc., 1833 ; and *History and Antiquities of Boston, the Capital of Massachusetts*, 1857.

**Drakenberg Mountains, or Dragon Mountains,** a chain of mountains, situated in S.E. Africa and lying parallel to the coast, between Cape Colony and the Vaal R. The seaward slopes are steep and precipitous, while landwards the slopes are more gradual and form part of the tableland. That portion of the chain, between Natal and Basutoland, contains the highest points, Champagne Castle, Mont-aux-Sources, and Giant's Castle, each being considerably over 10,000 ft. in altitude, and all within 60 m. of each other. The principal heights along the Transvaal, Natal, and Orange Free State frontiers are Malani, Inkwelo, Tintwa Majuba, and Drakenberg. The southern part of the chain forms the watershed between the rivers flowing westward to the Atlantic and those flowing E. and S. to the Indian Ocean. The Orange R. and the Tugela rise in Mont-aux-Sources. Van Reinen's Pass and Laing's Nek are the chief passes crossing the range.

**Drakenborch, Arnold** (1684–1748), a Dutch scholar, *b.* at Utrecht. He studied under Burmann at Utrecht. His chief work was an edition of Livy, 1738–46 ; he also edited *Silius Italicus*, 1717

**Drama,** a tn. of Macedonia, Greece celebrated for its tobacco. Has an active trade and fertile surroundings. Pop. about 14,000.

**Drama** (from the Gk. δράω, to be doing), a form of literary art for the direct representation of human actions and characters, through individual impersonation, before an audience. In literary history the D. is classified as a branch of poetry, though many plays have been written in prose. Both the epic, or narrative, and the lyric, expressing individual emotion, are applied in D., where the facts of a story are developed in interchange of speech and action. This latter distinguishes the D. from simple dialogue ; the illusion of reality is rendered plausible by the scene-painter and the stage-manager ; altogether they express objectively every emotion by word, gesture, or play of feature. The division of a play in acts and scenes originates in the subject-matter of the D. itself ; the invention of the drop-curtain and scene-shifting has created mechanical accessories. All these divisions mark the different stages of the development of the plot, show the complications leading to the climax, and finally solve the problem by the ' catastrophe.' The famous doctrine of the ' unities ' is hardly more than a formulation of the inevitable stage-restrictions. Their origin may be traced to Aristotle's remarks on tragedy, but as conventions of the theatre they were definitely accepted by the classical French dramatists, foremost among them being Racine and Corneille. The ' dramatic unities ' are three : of place, of time, and of action. Place precludes any extensive change of scene ; time is limited to the space of one day for the development of events ; action requires that all the events shall converge on a simple plot. Shakespeare, Lessing, and the French romanticists recognise as fundamental only the last of the three. Upon the Greek stage, the model for the classicists, there was no curtain and very little possibility for change of scene, consequently, unity of place was practically inevitable. Unity of time was necessary from the habitual presence of the chorus on the stage. Unity of action is simply an application of the principle on which is based every work of art. Sometimes a secondary plot is created by the author to enhance subsidiary characters of the play, mostly for the purpose of enhancing, by contrast, the effectiveness of the main action. The classic departments of the D. are tragedy and comedy ; tragedy has a sad ending, comedy ends happily. But there are other differences. Tragedy deals seriously with serious themes, with the sufferings of humanity, and with fatality. Comedy exploits the follies and absurdities of the ridiculous and the base. Tragedy entertains through the excitement to pity and sympathy, comedy through the excitement to mirth. Satirical purposes may dictate the choice of the object of ridicule. Under-plots in tragedy introduce a comic element as a counterpoise to tragic emotions and heighten the impressiveness of the latter (see the grave-digging scene in *Hamlet*). Modern plays, however, contain much more diversity of plots than the ancient, and many of them are neither tragedy nor comedy, neither fish nor flesh. Of the different kinds of D., the so-called historical or romantic are sufficiently defined by their names; *melodrama*, of Italian origin, is a broadly treated mixture of tragedy and comedy, appealing to the lesser critical emotions; the French *drame*, described variously as *tragédie bourgeoise*, or *comédie larmoyante*, represents life with little imitation as to form. Comedy has developed in not a few varieties, from the 'comedy of manners' of the eighteenth century to farce, burlesque, and vaudeville. Pantomime and ballet are ancient offshoots of the regular D., perhaps parts of its origin. Mimicry is fundamental to the acted D., an inevitable part of human nature, and doubtless common to all people. The dramatic dialogue of the Book of Job and the dramatic lyrics in the Canticles may be the primitive form of dramatic tendency, but the regular dramatic history begins in Greece.

*Greek drama*, both tragedy and comedy, was the consequence of the worship of Dionysus or Bacchus. At the Dionysian festivals in Attica, the followers of the wine-god were impersonated by choruses of men half-clad in goat-skins (τράγος, a goat, and τραγῳδία, goat-song, whence probably derives the word tragedy), singing dithyrambic songs in honour of the god as they danced about the altar; thus, about 600 B.C. the Corinthian poet, Arion, led a cyclic chorus of fifty. Half a century later appeared Thespis of Attica, whose innovation was the introduction of an actor to fill the intervals of singing with stories, mimicry, and short dialogues with the leader of the chorus. Soon after the more serious performances were limited to the sadder parts of Dionysus' story and of other mythological tales. Pisistratus established at Athens the *Lenæa* festival, for which, as somewhat later, at the *Great Dionysia*, prize dramatic contests were included, and the development of tragedy was continued by Chœrilus, Phrynichus, and other playwrights. The fifth century B.C. produced the greatest tragic writers of the Athenian stage: Æschylus, who enlarged the dramatic possibilities by making the number of actors two; Sophocles added a third. The original chorus of fifty was divided into four of twelve each (increased to fifteen by Sophocles), and plays were presented in groups of four called tetralogies, in one of which in each tetralogy the original satyric form was maintained. The other three, called trilogy, formed a consecutive series upon a single legend. A tragedy generally was made up of a series of 'episodes,' separated by lyrics sung by the chorus, introduced by the 'prologue' and terminated by the 'exode.' The actors were trained by the author, and to 'teach' a D. was equivalent to producing it. The expenses of the production were borne by a chosen citizen, called the *choregus*, who thus participated in the contest. The Athenian tragedy was a sort of serious religious function. Aristotle in his *Poetics* defines its motive as 'to purify the passions of fear and pity through the exalted exercise of them.' Characterisations of the 'great tragic trio' of Athens have been innumerable from the times of Aristophanes. With Æschylus, the idea of *Nemesis* (divine vengeance) is an overwhelming mystery; with Sophocles it is a part of the moral law of life; with Euripides it becomes a source of human sadness. Under this trinity, tragedy in Attica became the means of expressing the deepest religious thoughts; their successors, Ion, Achæus, Agathon, and others, were insignificant, as none of their works have come down to us. Later, most of the lyrical element was lost through the dropping of the chorus; from being an Athenian institution, tragedy spread to other Greek towns, and its special relation to the worship of Dionysus disappeared. However, the earlier works were continually reproduced; we find them performed under the Ptolemies at Alexandria. Greek comedy developed parallel with tragedy; it originated with the crude songs of the more rustic Dionysian festivals, which led naturally to a dramatic composition of a gay character. It is said to have been introduced into Attica early in the sixth century B.C. by Susarion and Megara, but before it was encouraged at Athens it developed elsewhere, particularly among the Dorians in Sicily, where flourished Epicharmus and Sophron, the inventor of mimes.

Athenian comedy is commonly divided in the three periods of Old, Middle and New Comedy. Aristophanes was the great master of the first; Cratinus, Crates, and Eupolis were his contemporaries. It was constructed on similar lines to tragedy, but with a chorus of twenty-four and an additional element, the *parabasis*, in which the audience was directly addressed; it dealt frankly in personalities, was largely political and did

the types then created, the gullible old man, the dissipated son, the impudent servant, serve still in our days. This latest Greek comedy is chiefly known to us through the adaptations of the Roman comedians Plautus and Terence.

*Roman drama.*—The Romans who had but few dramatic gifts naturally preferred comedy to tragedy. Comic elements are to be found in the *saturæ* of the early Latin

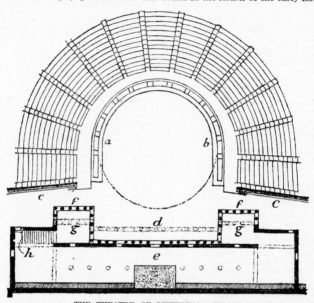

THE THEATRE OF LYKURGOS, ATHENS

*ab*, orchestra; *cc*, parodoi; *d*, proskenion; *e*, skene; *ff*, paraskenia; *gg*, Hellenistic paraskenia; *h*, staircase.

not hesitate to caricature the leading men of the day. At the period of middle comedy the freedom of speech was somewhat limited, and the butt of the comedian's ridicule were the follies and foibles of whole classes rather than those of individuals. The chorus was dropped. The new comedy, at the beginning of the third century B.C., had brought the aforementioned tendency to a full development. Political questions were neglected, and writers like Menander and Philemon devoted themselves to the exhibition of ridiculous complications of the social life of a decadent society. Some of

towns. It is generally assumed that the Romans borrowed their first idea of a play during a period of national despondency (364 B.C., Livy vii. 2) from the Etruscans, from whom came their word *histrio*, an actor. The rude farces known as *fabulæ Atellanæ* were effusions of sportive humour, and came from the Oscans. Mimes they took from Magna Græca; and their literary D. was practically an imitation of the Greek. The D. was one of the earliest branches of literature cultivated by the Roms. Both comedies and tragedies were written by Livius Andronicus, Nævius, and Ennius;

tragedies by Pacuvius and Attius, none of which have come down to us. Nævius is celebrated for having got into trouble by ridiculing prominent people in imitation of the old comedy of Athens. What is left to us of Rom. comedy belongs to the works of Plautus and Terence, of the class called *palliatæ*; closely adhering to the Greek models, as distinct from the so-called *togatæ*, which had Rom. subjects. Plautus, once a poor labourer, has a degree of rough vigour and broad jocularity, while Terence, a Carthaginian slave, is more refined and delicate in his wit and characterisation. The works of both are based on Menander and Philemon, but one change of form is to be particularly noted; the prologue ceased to be the first act of the play, and became what it has since remained, a detached explanation. Tragedy, more as literature than for stage production, was cultivated by writers of the Augustan age and later. Of all these attempts naught remains except the rhetorical Ds. attributed to Seneca, though certainly not all to this philosopher. One of them, *Octavia*, is of the class called *prætextæ*, treating historical Rom. subjects; the remainder are all from Gk. mythology. With the decadence of the Rom. empire, all 'legitimate' D. declined, and the stage was held by dancers and pantomimes, some of whom became great popular favourites. Cicero testifies to the excellence of Roscius, the most celebrated of Rom. actors.

*Indian drama* was long said to have been derived from the Gks., but is now generally thought to be of independent origin. Like the Gk., it arose from religious ceremonies, along with the dances and songs of popular festivals. However, the Hindu D. is not tragic, and makes far more of romantic love than does that of the Gks. Kalidasa, the greatest literary genius of India, commonly assigned to the first century B.C., is by recent criticism placed several centuries later. The best period of Sanskrit D. was from about the fourth to the ninth century A.D. A peculiar feature of Indian plays is the use of different dialects for different characters. Gods, heroes, and men of high standing speak Sanskrit; women and men of low position speak Prakrit in various forms. The best known Sanskrit play is Kalidasa's *Sakuntala*, a heroic love D. of poetical beauty. Another five-act play of Kalidasa's is *Micramorvasi* (The Hero and the Nymph). Among other Hindu dramatists deserve to be mentioned Bhavabhuti, a Brahman of Southern India in the eighth century; two of his three plays concern the adventures of Rama, the hero of the epic of *Ramayana*, on which several of the later Indian Ds. are founded. Other noted plays are: *Mricchakatika* (the Toy Cart), a D. of social life, in ten acts, credited to King Sudraka, of the sixth century; and *Ratnavali* (the Pearl Necklace), a romantic play, supposed to have been written by King Sriharsha, of the seventh century. The Mohammedan invasion killed the D. in India, and, though Sanskrit plays have been written in modern times, they are rarely acted.

*Chinese drama.*—Of all the other Oriental races, the only one which has a sort of dramatic literature is the Chinese, and their D., in spite of the antiquity of the other Chinese literature, is comparatively modern. There are reasons for attributing its origin to the Tartars, though it has commonly been considered an evolution from the native songs and dances. In the eighth century A.D. a sort of academy of music, known as the 'Pear Garden,' was founded by an emperor of the F'ang dynasty. D. proper did not develop till about the thirteenth century; the most famous of Chinese plays is called *Pi Pa Chi* (Story of the Guitar) of a somewhat later period. There are many printed collections of plays, but they differ materially from their acted versions. The avowed aims of the Chinese D. are of the most elevated, the glorification of all the virtues. Generally the plays are rather arid and conventional; as acted, they include much interpolated matter, which may account for the low esteem in which actors are held. Chinese plays are broadly classified, not as tragedies or comedies, but as 'civil' or 'military.' The latter include combats and all sorts of violent deeds. The former are quieter and deal with the more ordinary aspects of social life, with a tendency to the comic. There is little attempt at realism or stage setting. Women's parts are taken by men. Whole series of plays are commonly performed without intermission, which has led to statements as to the extraordinary length of Chinese plays. *See also* CHINA; *Chinese Literature.*

*Japanese drama.*—The origins of Japanese D. were both social and religious. First written references to Japanese D. occur in the *Ko-ji-ki*, a Record of Ancient Matters, A.D. 712, where an account of *Kagura*, God-Music, is given. *Kagura* may have been originally music and dance either between, or in the presence of, gods. It is still played before *Shinto* shrines, and chants, rhythmic accompaniments to the movements of labour, such as the song for driving in stones, seem to have been incorporated into the *Kagura*. Field dances, *Tamae*, and Field music, *Dengaku*, are of ancient origin; while other dramatic forms of social origin are *Saibara*, songs probably sung when the people were about to carry tribute to their rulers, and *Azuma mae*, songs of the Eastern provinces. The *Matsuri* (processions of cars) are still popular in Japan.

*Dengaku* included six forms of D.— *Shiba* (Lawn), *Dai* (Great), *Sho* (Small), *Maiko* (Dancing girls), *Maru* (Village) and *Kachi* (Walking, probably on horseback)—and, with other dance D. such as *Ennen*, became formalised with the growth of Buddhism and developed into the *Noh* plays ('noh' meaning accomplishment), which are extremely conventionalised. *Noh* of *Sarugaku*

A COVENTRY MIRACLE PLAY

(monkey-music) was originally comic, but lost its comic nature under the influence of the priests. In *Noh* there are two or more actors, the play is in verse and is chanted, the players are often masked and all movement is formalised. By the end of the fifteenth century four types of *Noh* plays were in existence—*Shinto noh*, which deals with mythological subjects; *Shugen noh*, commemorating customs; *Yurei* and *Serei noh*, in which ghosts and spirits occur, and *Genzai mono noh* dealing with things of life to illustrate a moral truth. As the literary preservation of *Noh* plays was under the care of Buddhist priests all comic element in them

disappeared. The comic plays were extempore, and became incorporated in *Kyogen*. Kyogen means easy speech, and is realistic, non-literary social comedy. It is in prose, and is performed as interludes in the long programmes of Noh plays.

*Mediæval drama.*—During the Middle Ages the church, practical as ever, undertook to replace the pagan shows by a Christianised equivalent, which seems to have arisen naturally out of the responsive chants and narrations of biblical events with which the congregations were both instructed and entertained. Later these entertainments took the form of regular liturgical D., which developed into the *miracle-plays*, *mysteries*, and *passion-plays*, which at Oberammergau and elsewhere have come down to our own days. With a similar purpose arose also the *moralities*, which mostly were performed by wandering churchmen. Out of these beginnings, varied occasionally by secular tendencies, modern D. may be said to have developed till the Renaissance came with a new impulse.

*Italian drama.*—In Italy, where the revival of the classical D. was earliest, the religious D. came to a full development before it was superseded by the modern dramatic form. The *Rappresentazione Sacra*, mostly in connection with the festivities in honour of Saint John the Baptist, were responsible for two works of great merit, *Abramo e Isacco* (1449) by Feo Belcari, and *San Giovanni e San Paulo* by Lorenzo de' Medici. At the beginning of the sixteenth century Plautean comedy was revived in the writings of Cardinal Bibbiena, Ariosto, and Machiavelli, and some erratic attempts, like that of Poliziano, but the modern Italian D. was born when Aristino produced a rather dull and conventional tragedy in blank verse, *Sofonisba*. Torquato Tasso's *Aminta* (1573) set the fashion of pastoral plays. At the end of the same century Giambattista della Porta wrote his familiar and sometimes farcical comedies of a pleasant originality. The romantic D., originated in Spain, found favour in Italy, and the reaction against the domination of the classic school became effective. Borghini, Michelangelo Buonarotti (a nephew of the great artist), with his comedies *Fancia* (1612) and *Fiera* (1618), and others, supported the movement. At the same period Rinuccini and his followers, by uniting music to the romantic D., created what was called the *melodrama*. Consequently tragedy and comedy were rapidly superseded by the *musica opera*, which, a century ater, was brought to a literary level by Zeno, and perfected to the utmost by Metastasio, who with his *Didone Abbandonata* (first produced in Rome 1723) completely fascinated the Italian public. His long series of works culminated in the triumph of his *Atilio Regolo* (1750). Maffin produced his *Merope* (1713) with the definite purpose of restoring classic tragedy. But French dramatic art soon began to influence the Italian stage, especially through the efforts of the actor-playwright Riccoboni. The eighteenth century produced Italy's three greatest dramatists: Goldoni, Gozzi, and Alfieri. Goldoni left his native Venice in 1761 for Paris; he is called the 'Italian Molière,' and may be called the master of Italian regular literary comedy. Gozzi, his great rival, pursued quite a different style; he transformed the popular *Commedia dell' arte* ('Comedy of Masks') into a literary shape which for some time enjoyed immense success. Alfieri was of quite another metal. He was bold and passionate, a follower of the classic school and observer of the unities, and helped to revive the national spirit by such tragedies as *Filippo II.*, *Saul*, and *La Congiura de' Pazzi*. His successors, Monti, Nicolini, Manzoni, Silvio Pellico, and Cossa relaxed their adherence to classic forms. In the nineteenth century Italy was influenced by Shakespearian methods, in consequence of which her dramatists affected to give prominence to the historical D. Some exceptionally good works were successfully performed by the great Italian actors, Modena, Salvini, Rossi, and Madame Ristari. In recent years the poet Gabriele d'Annunzio has gained some reputation as a playwright, principally by such of his works as he wrote specially for the great actress, Eleonora Duse. Luigi Pirandello (*b.* 1867) is one of the greatest twentieth century dramatists. His drama is metaphysical, and is influenced by the theory of relativity. There is nothing absolute about his plays and the characters in them are always concerned with their real, though hidden, personalities. Although the problems of his plays may be considered as abstractions, the characters are so possessed with these abstractions that the problems become human, and the characters lose nothing of their reality. The language of the plays is exact and unembellished, and his whole dramatic treatment is objective, but his dramas hold the spectator throughout, and possess something of the quality of poetry. *Henry IV.* and *Six Characters in Search of an Author* are two of his best plays, most of which have been translated into Eng.

*Spanish drama.*—Spain may well be considered as the birthplace of the romantic D. Santillana, Lope de Rueda, called the patriarch of the Spanish stage, and Naharro were the beginners; Cervantes, Lope de Vega, and Calderon became the perfectioners, the masters of Spanish dramatic literature. It is not generally known that Cervantes, of Don Quixote fame, is also the author of *La Numancia*, a serious tragedy of literary worth and dignity. Of his lesser contemporaries Cueva, Virues, and Argensula may be mentioned. Lope de Vega, the most prolific of dramatists of all times and nations, set all literary laws at defiance. He wrote with the most prodigious facility and with dramatic vigour. The number of his plays is said to exceed 1800, and won immense popularity, to which he often sacrificed some of his better qualities. Contemporaries of him were Ruiz de Arlacón, and Tirso de Molina (Gabriel Fellez), in whose *Burlador de Sevilla*, *ó el convidado di pietra*, was first introduced the figure of Don Juan. Calderon was greater than Lope de Vega. He was the greatest of Spanish dramatists and one of the great dramatists of the world. He is lyrical and animated by the highest sentiments. His ideals were devotion to the king, to the church, and to personal 'honour.' Some of his best works are the religious plays called *autos sacramentales*, in which the mystery of the Eucharist was dramatically set forth. With his death in 1681 the brilliant period of the Spanish theatre was practically closed. His contemporary, Moreto, wrote numerous fine comedies, mostly of the 'cloak and sword' sort, for which the Spanish stage is proverbial. José Echegaray (1842–1916) wrote more than sixty plays, many of which have as their theme a conflict between two forces. His best play is *El Gran Galeoto*. He attempted to deviate in his plays from the so-called 'punto de honor,' on which Spanish drama had centred hitherto. In 1904 Echegaray divided the Nobel Prize with Frédéric Mistral, but the younger Spanish dramatists, the 'generation of '98,' revolted against the past theatre of Spain and expressed their grievances in a manifesto against Echegaray. Benito Perez-Galdos (*q.v.*) (1845–1920), a contemporary of Echegaray, was exempt from the criticism of the 'generation of '98.' His plays usually express some attitude of revolt, and are written regardless of stage technique, but the characterisation is good. One of the most famous of the 'generation of '98' is Jacinto Benavente (b. 1866), whose work is prolific and varied. His plays form the link between the old and new D. of Spain, and contain the varied thought of all the most important European dramatists of the nineteenth century. Among twentieth century dramatists Gregoria Martínez Sierra and the brothers Quintero may be mentioned.

*French drama.*—France, accepting the 'unities' as the first essentials in the D., revived the classical D., which appeals strongly to the logical temper of the national genius. In the *mystères, moralités, soties, farces,* romantic or anti-classic tendencies were manifest, but no great advance in proper dramatic achievement was made. The first regular five-act tragedy was written by Jodelle for the court of Henri II. He wrote some more plays, not without merit, but nothing remarkable was done till Corneille appeared under Louis XIII., when the star of Richelieu was shining brightly. He had to humour the Court by humouring the Academy, and to please the Academy he had to observe the rules of Aristotle. He had already produced several plays of classical elegance and dignity, when, attracted by its romantic tendencies, he wrote his masterpiece, *The Cid.* All Paris rang with the praises of this work, but the Academy held aloof, Corneille had to return to the classical limitations, and was rewarded with a seat in the Academy. It was more than came to his contemporary, the great Molière, who insisted on remaining an actor, a résolve which the dignified academicians could by no means tolerate. Molière's name is doubtless in all the essentials of pure comedy the foremost name in the history of the stage. Like Shakespeare he borrowed much from the Italians, the Spaniards, and the Latins, but he made his theatre truly French in wit, expression, and characterisation. Racine was the great tragedian of the times of Louis XIV. He was not tempted, like Corneille, to overstep the academic proprieties. He was perhaps the most tender and the most elegant of French writers, and it may be truly said that his *Athalie*, his masterpiece, has never been surpassed in noble elegance and severe grandeur. The brilliant and erratic Voltaire astonished Europe with the audacity and power of his romantic tragedies. Could he have been able to temper the intolerant iconoclasm of his fight against superstition he would have ranked as a dramatist with Corneille and Racine. In the nineteenth century, the D. of France was much more prolific than

that of any other nation. Alfred de Vigny, Scribe, and Legouvé, Alexander Dumas père and Victor Hugo, the leaders of the 'romantic movement,' Alfred de Musset, Emile Augier, Dumas fils, Octave Feuillet, Victorien Sardou, Edmond Rostand, the reviver of poetical plays, Jean Richepin, François Coppée all produced meritorious dramatic works. Writers who composed their plays on the 'marital triangle,' giving great attention to construction, are P. Hervieu (*q.v.*) (1857–1915), praised for his literary style, Maurice Donnay (b. 1860), and Henry Bataille (1872–1922). Other twentieth-century dramatists who specialise in sex drama, often with applied psychology, are Henry Lavedan (b. 1859), Jules Lemaître (1853–1914), and Georges de Porto-Riche (b. 1849), while the plays of Alfred Capus (*q.v.*) (1858–1922) are sceptical in the extreme. Henry Bernstein (*q.v.*) (b. 1876) is a popular dramatist whose plays are almost melodrama. Eugène Brieux (*q.v.*) (b. 1858), with other of his contemporaries, François de Curel (1854–1928) and Henri Becque (1857–99), had his plays first produced at the Théâtre Libre, which was founded by Antoine in 1890. Brieux is known in Europe for the controversial subjects of his plays, but his dramatic ability is great and his language is incisive. Sacha Guitry (b. 1885) is another twentieth-century dramatist, but his fame is more in connection with his acting and elocution. Since the Great War French D. has developed European importance in the works of H.-K. Lenormand, Jean-Jacques Bernard, Jean Sarment, Jules Romains, and Paul Géraldy, and experiment has taken the place of tradition.

*German, Austrian, and Czecho-slovakian drama.*—German drama dates practically from Lessing, Goethe and Schiller. Its origin is similar to that of all cultured nations, and up to the middle of the eighteenth century the German stage was little more than a feeble reflex of Fr. influence. Lessing, both by his works and critiques, was the reformer, not to say the inaugurator, of Ger. dramatic art. His tragic plays, *Miss Sarah Sampson* and *Emilia Galotti*, and his comedy *Minna von Barnhelm*, opened a new era for the German D., while in his *Hamburgische Dramaturgie* he attacked Fr. classicism and praised Shakespeare. Goethe, one of the world's greatest geniuses, does not rank as high as a dramatist. His *Faust* is doubtless one of the greatest modern compositions; but his chief purpose is self-cultivation, and in the prologue, his last and most famous production, he explains why, although writing in dramatic form, he cannot accommodate himself to the exigencies of a popular theatre. Schiller is the dramatic poet proper of Germany. Goethe's genius was fuller and more complete, but Schiller compensated by the intensity of his powers. Of his contemporaries there deserve to be remembered Heinrich von Kleist, Körner, Effland (actor, manager and author), of his successors Grillparzer, Grabbe, Otto Ludwig, Hebbel, Halm, Mosenthal, Gottschall, Auzengruber. Hauptmann (1862–1913) is an important dramatist of the late nineteenth century. His plays are naturalistic and poetic and, with those of Sudermann, were performed by the Free Stage Society, founded in Berlin in 1889. Sudermann's greatest play is *Magda*. A contemporary of his, Frank Wedekind (1864–1918), wrote plays which refuse to be classified. *The Awakening of Spring* is one of his best known plays: his dialogue is brilliant and his influence on post-war dramatists great. If Wedekind may be called a writer of expressionistic drama, two important twentieth-century dramatists may be classed with him, Georg Kaiser (*b.* 1878) and Ernst Toller (*b.* 1893). Max Reinhardt (*b.* 1873) is important in the history of the theatre, and his designs for productions are world famous. Arthur Schnitzler (*b.* 1872) is an important Austrian dramatist, his best play being *The Green Cockatoo*, and Hugo von Hofmannsthal (*b.* 1874) is a tragic poet of profound influence, while Czechoslovakia has two expressionistic dramatists, the brothers Capek, whose best-known play is *R.U.R.*

*Scandinavian and Flemish drama.* —The Flemish D. is hardly more than an imitation of Fr. romantic plays. Nothing remarkable has been produced in Holland save for the work of Hermann Heijermans (1864–1924) or in Flemish Belgium. Fr. Belgium is the motherland of the poet Maeterlinck, whose plays are of a rather extreme type of some of the features of the symbolist movement. The Scandinavian countries have in recent times developed a D. of importance. The Norwegians, Björnson and, first and foremost, Ibsen (1828–1906), have become very distinctive figures in the D. of psychological and social problems. Ibsen's influence on European drama is immeasurable. *Hedda Gabler*, *Peer Gynt*, *The Pillars of Society*, *A Doll's House* and *The Wild Duck* are some of his best-known plays. Contemporaries and followers of him are Gunnar Heiberg, Vetle Visle, Gabriel Finne, Anders Stilloff, and Knut Hamsun. A. Strindberg, the Swede (1844–1912), a powerful but somewhat discursive dramatist, is an antidote to Ibsen's feminism. In Denmark, Oehlenschlaeger in the first half, Molbech in the second half of the nineteenth century have both been successful with their dramatic work. A far wider influence, however, belonged to Edward Brandes, both dramatist and critic. Early twentieth-century dramatists are Otto Benson, Fru Emma Dad, Gustav Esmann, Sven Lange, Gustav Wied, Hans Wiers-Jennsen, and Hjalmar Bergström.

*Russian drama* is of very recent development. It is said that in earlier days Russian religious plays have been performed. The first Russian theatre was established in 1756 in St. Petersburg, and its manager, Sumarokoff, and Kinaznin, and other forgotten authors, wrote plays for it in the Fr. style. Catharine II. herself elaborated satirical comedies, and at her time Ozieroff was a writer of tragedies of repute. In the nineteenth century we have Griboyedoff, the author of *Goreet Nama* (The Misfortune of being too clever); Gogol, whose comedy *Revizor* (The Inspector) has become known all over the world; Pushkin, whose *Boris Godunoff* shows Shakespearian influence; Ostrowski, whose plays are realistic and deal with the emotions of the people; Alexander Tolstoy, whose dramas are founded on stories of the Russian Kings; and Count Leo Tolstoy (*q.v.*), whose plays follow no traditions, but contain great character studies. Early twentieth-century dramatists are Maxim Gorki (*q.v.*), whose greatest play is *The Lowest Depths*, and Leonid Andreyev (*q.v.*), whose plays are written in excellent prose. Both these authors belong to the period of the first Revolution. Anton Tchekoff (*q.v.*), one of the greatest twentieth-century dramatists, wrote plays for the Moscow Art Theatre. These plays are naturalistic artistically, needing simple yet sensitive acting. A later twentieth-century writer is Evreinov, much of whose work is based on his own theory of 'mono-drama.' Since the Revolution, 1917, a new theatre has been built up in Soviet Russia, which has reflected the various phases of the republic. Lack of money made simplification of production necessary, and out of this grew geometrical construction in scenery. The stage has been used considerably for propaganda, which at its best has proved a dynamic expression of social life. Plays for the mass of the people have been produced by Maierhold and by the Proletcult Theatre, while plays and pageants are performed by the masses in the open air. In the provinces there are Little Theatres and Strolling Players. Other theatres are the experimental State Theatres and State Circus, Jewish Theatres, and the Moscow Art Studios.

*English drama*, as in other coun-

Eng. comedy is (1531 or thereabouts) *Ralph Roister Doister*, by Nicholas Udall, a learned master of Eton. A few years later Sackville and Norton produced their dull tragedy in blank verse, *Gorboduc, or Ferrex and Porrex*. Thereafter dramatic production was rapid, but mostly worth-

INTERIOR OF ELIZABETHAN THEATRE (THE SWAN)

tries, had its origin in the religious plays, written and performed by churchmen, who understood how to spice their miracle plays and mysteries with grotesque amusement, and it was not until the middle of the sixteenth century, as elsewhere, under the influence of the Renaissance, that the Eng. D. freed itself from these anct. fetters. The earliest known

less; authors were Bishop Still, Kyd, Lodge, Lyly, Peele, Green, and Nash. The first dramatist of real merit was Christopher Marlowe, the great predecessor of Shakespeare, whose best tragedies are *Doctor Faustus* and *Edward II*. But the great luminary of Eng. D.—it may well be said of all the world's D.—is Shakespeare (*see* SHAKESPEARE). Among dramatists, the worthiest of his contemporaries are Ben Jonson, and Beaumont and Fletcher. Jonson wrote comedies and tragedies, stood more under the influence of the classics, but withal became famous with his light and graceful masques, which were the court's favourite entertainment. Beaumont and Fletcher worked in collaboration, and stand next to Shakespeare in romantic D. Dekker, Massinger, Ford, Webster, Chapman, and Shirley were authors of older Eng. dramas, when this kind of literature was abruptly and sharply terminated by the Puritan Revolution. With the Restoration, Fr. influence became apparent. *Display* mastered the *play*, and lavish staging over-ranked the value of the work. Lee and the unfortunate Otway wrote tragedies. Shadwell and licentious Wycherley produced comedies, Vanbrugh, Congreve, and Farquhar brilliantly depicted society under a veil of immorality and indecency even more marked than that of some of Shakespeare's immediate predecessors. Then came Gay, Mrs. Centlivre, and the actor-playwright Colley Cibber, who was not lacking in dramatic spirit and invention. Famous, in another way, became Addison's tragedy *Cato*, a solemn literary work, written in blank verse. Lille, Moore, Garrick the actor, Goldsmith, the Colmans, and Cumberland nearly all wrote in prose. They produced agreeable comedies; but, except Goldsmith's *She Stoops to Conquer*, hardly any of their works had a lasting success. Sheridan, who gave the impulse to what the Fr. call *Comédie de Salon*, and whose *School for Scandal* is the best Eng. specimen of it, has long acquired a lasting place in the history of the Eng. D. Sheridan's immediate successors, Holcroft, 'Monk' Lewis, Maturin, Mrs. Inchbald, and others are insignificant. Later Joanna Baillie, Coleridge, Byron, Shelley, and Henry Taylor wrote free book-dramas little suited for theatrical production. Then came in more recent times the dramatic poetry of Tennyson, Browning, and Swinburne. Plays of scenic power were written by Sheridan, Knowles and Bulwer-Lytton, and during the Victorian era many mediocrities flooded the Eng. stage with their wares. Their names are Talfourd, Jerrold, Shirley Brooks, Tom Taylor, F. W. Robertson, H. J. Byron, Sydney Grundy, and *tutte quanti*. A sort of speciality was created by W. S. Gilbert in 'the libretti' he wrote for Arthur Sullivan's operas. Late nineteenth-century dramatists were H. A. Jones (1851–1929), A. W. Pinero (*b.* 1855),

and Oscar Wilde (1854–1900), who wrote comedies of wit. Bernard Shaw (*b.* 1856), with his plays that followed his dramatic criticism, brought new life to the Eng. theatre. His plays are controversial and witty, and have received world-wide recognition. *Arms and the Man*, one of his earliest plays, was produced by the Independent Theatre that was founded by Grein in 1891. Other twentieth-century dramatists are John Galsworthy (*b.* 1867), whose plays are statements of social problems, J. M. Barrie (*b.* 1860), who introduces an element of phantasy, the Poet Laureate, John Masefield (*b.* 1875), Somerset Maugham (*b.* 1874), Frederick Lonsdale (*b.* 1881), Clemence Dane, and Harley Granville Barker (*b.* 1877), whose most important work is in stage production. Repertory theatres that have been formed in the provinces have produced such dramatists as Stanley Houghton (1881–1913) and Allan Monkhouse (*b.* 1858), while verse drama has been written by Stephen Phillips (1867–1915), Thomas Hardy (1840–1928), Robert Bridges (1844–1930), Laurence Binyon (*b.* 1869), Laurence Housman (*b.* 1865), and Gordon Bottomley (*b.* 1874). One of the few important post-war Eng. dramatists is Noel Coward (*b.* 1899), who writes satirical comedies.

In 1899 the Irish Literary Theatre was established by Edward Martyn, George Moore, and W. B. Yeats, later to be joined by Lady Gregory and 'A. E.' In 1904 this theatre became the Irish National Theatre, when it was financed by Miss Horniman as the Abbey Theatre. Two types of plays have been produced—literary plays and folk plays. Irish dramatists who have written for this theatre are J. M. Synge, the greatest (1871–1909), W. B. Yeats (*b.* 1865), Lady Gregory (*b.* 1859), Sean O'Casey (*b.* 1884), and Lennox Robinson (*b.* 1886). Other Irish dramatists are Lord Dunsany (*b.* 1878) and St. John Ervine (*b.* 1883).

*American D.* is a recent development. Up to about thirty-five years ago Fr. and Eng. influence prevailed. With the advent of such popular melodrama as the *Old Homestead* of Denman Thompson, and such essentially indigenous farces of low life as those semi-improvised works of Harrigan and Hart, native originality first began to reveal itself. Probably James A. Herne, actor and stage manager, gave the greatest impetus to American D. with his realistic play of New England rural life, *Shore Acres* (1892), and his late pieces *Griffith Davenport* (1898) and *Sag Harbour* (1900). In their direct-

G 2

ness, sincere representation of human nature and absence of all psychological finesse, lay their popularity—a popularity re-echoed by the modern *Mrs. Wiggs of the Cabbage Patch.* Perhaps the most successful of modern American dramatists was Clyde Fitch, whose social Ds., modelled on Fr. contemporary work, put him in the very front rank. His best-known plays are *The Climbers* (1900), and *The Truth* (1906). Other successful modern American Ds. are *The Easiest Way* (1909) by Eugene Walter; *The Great Divide* (1907) by William Vaughan Moody; *Jeanne d'Arc* (1906), a poetical play by Percy MacKaye, and *Salvation Nell*, a striking slum theme by Edward Sheldon. The plays of these authors and also of Augustus Thomas, whose dialogue is excellent, Charles Rann Kennedy, and J. M. Paterson, are serious in intent and are written on European models, but perhaps it is not so much from these plays as from those aiming at a box-office success that a truly American D. will develop. Plays of this latter type, such as those by George Ade and George Cohan, depend for their success on being up to date with current American opinion. America's greatest dramatist, however, whose work is most alive with new possibilities, is Eugene O'Neill, a realist writer who also uses the expressionism technique, as in *The Hairy Ape.* Another Expressionist playwright is Elmer Rice, although in his best play, *Street Scene,* he abandons expressionism.

*The Theatre, Actors, and Acting.*— The modern European theatre is thought to have taken its shape from the circular Gk. theatre, built on the side of a hill. But it may equally well have developed from the rough platforms and benches set up in the inn-yard for the use of a company of strolling players, or even from the arrangement of a bear-pit. The Gk. actors performed on a raised platform in the valley, wearing masks and high-soled buskins, while the chorus moved before them on the dancing-floor or orchestra. The Rom. theatre imitated the Gk., but the acting profession deteriorated and became the occupation of slaves. With Christianity and the decline of the Rom. theatre into gladiatorial shows, the theatre fell into disuse, but was revived in the Middle Ages by the church for the festival services of Christmas and Easter in which the priests were the actors. Out of the acted versions of the Christmas and Easter stories grew long cycles of plays, the Mystery Plays. These were Bible stories, and were acted by the Town Guilds on a number of wagons, representing Heaven, Hell, the Ark, etc. In England the first theatre was built in 1576. The Elizabethan stage protruded into the audience, but in the Restoration period the stage became more like a three-sided room with a smaller protrusion called the 'apron.' A later development was the picture-frame stage. Scenery, although used in Italy, does not appear in England until the eighteenth century, but stage properties were in common use. In the nineteenth century there was an extensive use of scenery, but in the twentieth century there is a tendency towards simplification on the stage, curtains or a series of geometrical blocks, with elaborate lighting effects, being used. No woman played on the mediæval stage, but companies of boy actors were favoured in Elizabethan times. Adrienne Lecouvreur (1692–1730) was the first famous tragic actress, while Richard Burbage (1567–1619) and his contemporary, Edward Alleyn, are the first actors of whom we have much knowledge. Other famous actors and actresses through the centuries, many of whom had parts written for them, are : Mrs. Bracegirdle, Nell Gwyn, Betterton, and Harris in Restoration times, followed later by David Garrick, Mrs. Siddons, Mrs. Jordan, and Mrs. Woffington. In the nineteenth century the actor-manager came into existence with such men as Kemble, Kean, Macready, Henry Irving, and Beerbohm Tree. Talma was a celebrated Fr. actress of the time of Napoleon. In the twentieth century the Fr. actor Sacha Guitry became as famous as his father, Lucien, and among Eng. actresses Sybil Thorndike has excelled in tragedy and Edith Evans in comedy, while Gerald du Maurier represents a return from the declamatory style of Henry Irving to a more naturalistic form of acting. It was not until 1760 that there was any attempt at historical accuracy in costume upon the Eng. stage (*See* under COSTUME DESIGN, THEATRICAL.)

*Bibliography.*—Consult Aristotle's *Poetics* (ed. by S. H. Butcher), 1895 ; J. W. Donaldson, *The Theatre of the Greeks* (7th ed.), 1860 ; J. Dryden, *Essay on Dramatic Poesy* (ed. by W. P. Ker), 1900 ; W. L. Courtney, *The Idea of Tragedy in Ancient and Modern Drama,* 1900 ; E. K. Chambers, *The Mediæval Stage,* 1903 ; A. W. Pollard, *English Miracle Plays, Moralities, and Interludes* (3rd ed.), 1898 ; J. P. Collier, *History of English Dramatic Poetry,* 1879 ; A. W. Ward, *History of English Dramatic Literature to the Death of Queen Anne,* 1899 ; J. A. Symond, *Shakspere's Predecessors,*

1884; W. C. Hazlitt, *The English Drama, 1543–1664*, 1869; L. N. Chase, *The English Heroic Play*, 1905; Davenport Adams, *A Dictionary of the Drama* (vol. i.), 1904; J. L. Klein, *Geschichte des Dramas* (13 vols.), 1865–68; Viollet-le-Duc, *Ancien Théâtre français* (10 vols.), 1854–57; Parfait, *Histoire du Théâtre français* (15 vols.), 1745–49; Ashley Dukes, *Modern Dramatists*, 1911, also *The Younger Drama*, 1923, and *Drama*, 1926; J. M. Brown, *Theatre of To-day*, 1927; T. H. Dickinson, *An Outline of Contemporary Drama*, 1927; H. K. Moderwell, *The Theatre of To-day*, 1927; A. Nicoll, *Development of the Theatre*, 1927; J. Palmer, *Studies in the Contemporary Theatre*, 1927; B. H. Clark, *A Study of Modern Drama*, 1928; H. Carter, *New Spirit of the Russian Theatre*, 1929; also K. Macgowan and R. E. Jones, *Continental Stagecraft*, 1923.

**Dramburg,** a tn. in the prov. of Pomerania, Prussia, with cloth manufactures. Pop. 6400.

**Drammen,** a seaport of Norway, 33 m. S.W. of Oslo by rail, at the head of Dramsfiord, through which the broad Dramselv empties its waters into Oslo Fiord. Timber, floated down from the upland forests, and wood pulp are the staple exports, saw-milling and the manufacture of paper, and shipbuilding and cotton spinning being the other active industries. It has much trade with England and Holland. The town had a population of 25,700 in 1927.

**Drane, Augusta Theodosia** (1823–94), an Eng. writer. Having been influenced by Tractarian teaching at Torquay, she became a Rom. Catholic (1850). In 1852 she joined the third order of St. Dominic, and was prioress of Stone Convent, Staffordshire, 1872–81. Her essay questioning the morality of Tractarianism was attributed to Newman. Other works are : *The History of St. Dominic*, 1857, 1891; *The Knights of St. John*, 1858; *Three Chancellors*, 1859; *Life of St. Catherine of Siena*, 1880; *Songs in the Night*, 1876 (verse). See *Memoir of Mother Francis Raphael* (ed. by Wilberforce), 1895.

**Drang Nach Osten,** the expressive phrase given to the Ger. pre-war policy of forcing a way to a foothold in the East through the Balkans. In the Great War they had by 1916 so far translated the dream into a reality as to secure uninterrupted and unthreatened communication and commerce with Constantinople, over the two main arteries of Asiatic Turkey, and also with the cities of Damascus, Mecca, Jerusalem and Bagdad. (*See also* BAGDAD; BAGDAD RAILWAY.)

**Drant, Thomas** (*d. c.* 1578), an Eng. divine; the first Eng. metrical translator of Horace. He won fame by his sermons before the court at Windsor (1569), and to the congregation at St. Mary Spital, London (1570). He wrote verses in Eng., Latin, and Gk. (1564), his works including : *Medicinable Morall . . .,* 1566; *Sylva*, 1576; and a translation of Horace's *Epistles, Satires, and Ars Poetica*, 1567. See Ritson, *Bibliog. Poetica*.

**Draper, Mrs. Elizabeth** (1744–78), is best remembered for her association with Sterne, an association which there is no doubt never went beyond sentimental flirtation. The daughter of May Sclater and an Anglo-Indian official, she married at the age of fourteen Daniel D. of the East India Company's service, a man much older than herself. Coming to England in 1776 for her health she met Sterne, and was flattered by the attention of the great man. When she returned to India, he wrote regularly to her, and began the *Journal to Eliza*, which, owing to Sterne's death early in 1778, never reached her. In 1772 she left her husband, returned to England, and settled at Bristol. She was buried in Bristol Cathedral. The full story of her life is told, and her letters are printed, in the *Life of Sterne*, by Lewis Melville, 1911.

**Draper, John William** (1811–82), an Eng. chemist and historical and scientific writer. He emigrated to America, 1833; accepting the chair of chemistry in New York University in 1839. Professor D. gave special study to the chemical action of light, spectrum analysis, and the chemistry and physics of living organisms. His works include : *Text-Book of Chemistry*, 1846; *Text-Book of Natural Philosophy*, 1847; *Human Physiology . . .,* 1856; *The History of the Intellectual Development of Europe*, 1863; *History of the American Civil War*, 1867–68; *History of the Conflict between Religion and Science*, 1874. D. made great improvements in the art of photography, and did much to perfect Daguerre's process, 1839. Consult Barker, *Biog. Memoirs of the Nat. Acad. of Science*, ii., iii., 1886–88; *Dict. Nat. Biog.*

**Draught** (from A.-S. *dragan*, to draw), a current of air, in particular one which is induced or artificially forced to support combustion. *Natural* D. is produced by a chimney, through which the heated gases rise by reason of their lesser density, thus inducing a current of cool air through the fire. *Forced* D. may be produced by driving air at more than atmospheric pressure through the fire by means of fans. In locomotive boilers the D. is increased by turning the exhaust steam into the chimney, thus increasing the velocity of the current of air.

**Draughts**, generally conjectured to be one of the most anct. of table games. A game of this kind was known to the Gks. and Roms., and various monuments represent the anct. Egyptians as engaged in a similar amusement. It became common in Europe during the sixteenth century. The game is played by two persons on a board similar to that used for chess, *i.e.* a square board containing sixty-four squares, checkered in black and white alternately. Each player has twelve ' men ' in the form of circular discs, one set being black and the other white. These men are arranged on the three rows directly before each player. They may be placed either on the black or the white squares, but the extreme left hand square on the board before each must always be occupied. Lots are cast to decide which colour each player shall have, and black plays first. The players then change colours after each game. The men move diagonally, one square at a time, so that play continues entirely on squares of one colour. If a man comes next to a man of the opposite side he is unable to move past unless there be a vacant square on the other side of his adversary's man, in which case he must jump over this man and occupy the vacant square, removing his enemy's man from the board. If, after taking a man in this way, it is possible for him to jump another man, taking this one also, he must do so in the same move. In the rare event of a player neglecting to take when the opportunity is given him, his adversary may either take the piece with which the capture would have been made (a proceeding known as ' huffing '), or compel him to revoke his last move and perform the capture. He may also, if he wish, allow the move to stand. If a player gets one of his men into his adversary's back line, this man becomes a ' king,' and is ' crowned ' by having another man of the same colour put on top of him. The king may move either backwards or forwards, whereas the ordinary men can move only forwards, but this is the only privilege he has. He captures in the same way as ordinary men, except for this one difference. If a player touches a piece, he must move it if possible. The game is won by a player removing all his adversary's men from the board or by his placing them in such a position that they cannot move. *See* J. Sturges's *Guide to the Game of Draughts*, 1800 (new edition, 1899); A. Anderson's *Game of Draughts* (revised by R. McCulloch), 1888; and works by Drummond, Hoffmann, Gould, etc.

**Drave** (Ger. *Drau*), a riv. of Austria and an important trib. of the Danube from the right. Rising in the Tyrol at an altitude of over 4000 ft., it flows 449 m. before its final confluence with the main river at Alma, 13 m. E. of Esseg. With an E. or S.E. course it traverses Carinthia, Styria, and Hungary, which it enters near Friedau, forming from this city onward the boundary between the last-named province and Croatia-Slavonia. It was through the long valley of the D. that the Huns and Slavs reached the Alps. Of the many affluents the largest is the Mur on the left. Steamers can go up only as far as Bárcs (95 m.).

**Dravidians** (Sanskrit *Drāvida*, or *Drāmida*), the name of a large group of Indian peoples (non-Aryans) and their family of languages. Their main territory lies chiefly in S. India, extending upwards from the peninsula N. to the Arabian Sea, about 100 m. below Goa, thence along the W. Ghat to Kolhapur, N.E. through Hyderabad, and E. to the Bay of Bengal. It includes also N. Ceylon, and scattered tribes are found in other parts (*see* Cust and Constable's linguistic and racial maps). The more important languages in the D. group are Telugu, Tamil, Kanarese, Malayālam, Tulu, and those of ruder tribes, such as Gōndi, Kōta, Kurux, Kui, and Rajmahal. The tribes of the N. have gradually become Hinduised, and their language has been considerably modified by the Aryan forms of speech. The Brāhūis of Baluchistan, however, still speak a D. dialect. The D. languages seem to have formed a quite distinct group, independent of the Aryan or Indo-Germanic. There are about a dozen different tongues comprised in the group, differing from each other radically and not merely in dialect forms, and yet derived from a common D. source. Tamil, Malayālam, Kanarese, and Telugu are the chief literary languages. Inflections are expressed by ' agglutination,' or affixing particles to primary roots or bases, but these additions do not blend with the roots as in the case of inflectional languages. Nouns are of two classes, high-caste and casteless (for rational and irrational beings respectively); gender being distinguished only in the former. A peculiarity is the double form for the first person plural of the personal pronoun, for including or excluding the person addressed. There are no relative pronouns, relative participles being used instead. A separate negative conjugation, usually with only one tense, exists for verbs. D. tongues were spoken by some 57,497,980 people according to the census of 1901. The D. were probably the aborigines of the Deccan. They are among the most primitive of Indian types, the Tōdas of the Nīlgiri Hills representing a very low stage of civilisation. They are mostly very dark-skinned, with wavy, black hair (not woolly), and are possibly descendants of the Negritos of

A DRAWBRIDGE FROM THE INTERIOR OF A MEDIÆVAL CASTLE

Malaysia. Their religion consists partly in nature-worship, partly in creeds adopted from more civilised tribes. See Caldwell, *A Comparative Grammar of the Dravidian Languages* . . ., 1856 (2nd ed. 1875); Müller, *Grundriss der Sprachwissenschaft*, iii., 1884; 'Munda and Dravidian Languages' in Grierson's *Linguistic Survey of India*, iv. 1906; Reclus, *Primitive Folk*, 1890; Risley, *Tribes and Castes of Bengal*, 1891; Kingscote, *Folklore of S. India*, 1890; Sweet, *History of Language*, 1900; Keane's 'Race and Speech' in *East and West*, 1905; Hultzsch, *S. Indian Inscriptions, Tamil and Sanscrit*, 1809–95.

**Drawback**, *see* CUSTOMS DUTIES.

**Drawbridge**, in anct. times an invariable adjunct of a castle. It was a bridge hinged at one end and free at the other, so that it could be drawn up or let down as required. The original form was the lifting D., used to span the moat of a castle; this form is used now to provide a passage over canals, etc. The swing-bridge is a D. which revolves in a horizontal direction.

**Drawing**, the expression in line of the form of objects. When a beginner is learning the art, he is given copies to imitate in which the lines are already marked, so that they can be copied exactly as they stand. D. from natural objects, however, is far more difficult, since the appearance of these is not regulated solely by outline. Far more important is the effect of light and shade. The ability to recognise this and the power to express the effect in line must be possessed by any one wishing to draw. Similarly, it is necessary to remember that distance diminishes both the natural size and also the distinctness of objects. The sharply-pointed pencil is first used to draw with, though it is not necessarily retained later. The most beautiful effects in line D. are to be produced by the process known as etching. Here there is not the confusion of line which often appears, and each line contributes its full quota to the general effect. Wood-cuts also give much variety of tone. The method of Flaxman, exemplified in his illustrations of Dante, etc., are severe and classical in form. He gives little more than the outline of the object, and is very sparing of extra ornament. In painting, the principle of nature is more closely followed, masses being again used to represent masses. There are also special departments of D., which have their own regulations and procedure. Many of these necessitate the use of somewhat complicated aids to perform them correctly. Such are architectural and mechanical D. Architectural D. is employed to give, either on the same or a reduced scale, the plans or sections of details and of buildings. In the designing, say, of a house, three sets of Ds. are made. The first shows the plans of the different floors, the second shows sections, that is the appearance the house would present if it were cut vertically and one part removed. The third shows the various elevations, that is, the external appearance of the house from the various sides. These are drawn on a very reduced scale, one-eighth of an inch, perhaps, on the plan representing a foot. The strictest accuracy is observed and perspective is not employed, the whole being brought to one plane. Ds. of details, such, for example, as sections of mouldings are generally drawn natural size. Mechanical or engineering D. is used to show the construction of engines, ships, motors, and mechanical devices of all kinds.

**Drayton, Michael** (1563–1631), was at one time ' a proper goodly page,' and seems to have settled in London about 1590, but biographical details are curiously lacking. In his *Idea, The Shepherd's Garland*, of 1593, he sang his love sorrows, but his first poem of length and importance (1596) appeared as *The Barons' War* in the revised edition of 1603. Written in *ottava rima*, it is a rather tedious narrative of episodes in the Wars of the Roses, but its inequalities and rudeness of style disappear in his *England's Heroical Epistles* (1597), historical poems written on the model of Ovid's *Heroides*, and containing

MICHAEL DRAYTON

some of his very finest lines. Few read with pleasure his ponderous *Polyolbion* (1613–22), which he himself aptly describes as a ' Herculean toil.' For he undertook to describe everything of antiquarian or topographical interest throughout Great Britain. This vast work, barren and wearisome in the extreme, at least demonstrates the utter unsuitability of the Fr. classical metre (couplets of Alexandrines) as a vehicle for Eng. verse. Yet D. could write a poem of the grace and charm of his *Nimphidia* (1627), which is the inspiration of many of Herrick's lyrics ; a spirited patriotic song, like the famous *Ballad of Agincourt* (1605), and one splendid sonnet, ' Since there's

no help, come let us kiss and part,' which Rossetti proclaimed ' almost the best in the language, if not quite.'

**Drayton-in-Hales,** *see* MARKET DRAYTON.

**Dreadnought,** a Brit. battleship, 490 ft. long, of 17,950 tons, with speed of 21 knots. The first of this since famous class was launched and completed at Plymouth (1906), the designs having been accepted in 1905. A marked improvement on former types was shown in this vessel, her speed and fuel endurance being much greater. For armament she had ten 12-inch guns, twenty-seven 12-pounder quick-firing anti-torpedo-boat guns, and five submerged torpedo-tubes. The steam turbine system of propulsion was adopted for the first time on a battleship in the case of the D. ; there was a coal-stowage of 2700 tons, and oil-fuel could also be carried. The total cost was about £1,813,100. Other nations quickly followed Great Britain's example and began producing rival vessels, and improvements are constantly being made.

**Dreaming,** may be defined as the manifestation of a conscious process during sleep. During sleep conscious activity is, under ordinary circumstances, entirely in a state of suspense ; the sensory nerves no longer perform their usually active duties, the action of the heart becomes slower, the brain is at rest, and during this period gets rid of the waste tissue and is restored to fresh activity. Our faculties, however, need not all be in an equal state of inactivity; it is possible to perform a number of quite ordinary actions whilst in a state of sleep, *e.g.* soldiers have often marched for some considerable distance whilst, to all intents and purposes, in a deep sleep. We dream, then, principally because the suspension of mental activity is not complete. It has been held that sleep is never so profound as to be dreamless, but this is a theory which cannot be proved. On the other hand, it has been held that we dream only during those periods of falling asleep and awakening during which our mental activities are in a semi-conscious state. This, again, is a theory which cannot be actually proved, but which it is possible to obtain some evidence against, since it is well known that manifestation of dreaming has been noticed in cases where the subject was in a deep sleep. Further, in many cases sleepers suddenly awakened have aroused themselves with difficulty from a dream. That all our powers of judgment are inactive during a dream cannot be held as true, since on occasion we find that we desire to prolong a dream of peculiar happiness, whilst we can arouse ourselves from one which terrifies us by its horror. Dreams whilst resembling in many ways the process of conscious activity, on the other hand differ characteristically from the experiences of our waking life. Time, space, and order are not to be found during our dreams. We annihilate space, we keep no record of time, we live in a disordered world during our dreams. Further, a dream in almost all cases exaggerates. Also the events which occur to us during these periods leave a great impression on our mind for the time being, although we may on awakening remember little or nothing of the experiences undergone during sleep. That the activities of the day, or the immediate time preceding, have influence on our dreams is undoubted. Incidents trivially passed over during our waking experience form often the basis of a dream, details forgotten in the routine of the day will occur time and time again during sleep. Problems in mathematics have been solved, legal decisions given, and even sermons have been produced during sleep, whilst we may here quote the famous example of Coleridge's *Kubla Khan* as a poem which was composed during sleep and which was written immediately on awakening. Experiments have been made in order to test the effect of the senses in dreams, and it has been proved that certain effects experienced by the senses during sleep result in the causing of dreams which can easily be related to the immediate cause. Certain drugs, such as opium, and hashish, have peculiar effect upon the character of dreams, whilst the physical state of the body can often give peculiar effect also to the dreams. That peculiar form of dream, which we usually call by the name nightmare, or 'anxiety dream,' may be due to the presence of undigested food in the stomach, other uncomfortable dreams may be caused by inability to breathe properly, or by an uncomfortable position in sleeping. The state of the brain is also an important factor in the causing of dreams. An over-active brain will give rise to a number of rapid dreams, whilst when the brain is depressed the result is usually a series of depressing and horrible dreams. The effect of dreams varies with the character of the dream and of the dreamer. Many of our dreams are forgotten before the dreamer awakens, some are remembered for a short time, and a few, emphasised by their horror or their happiness,

remain for years after the actual dream, sometimes forming even the basis of other dreams. Dreams are in some cases not only thought out but actually acted by the dreamer; cases of this kind, such as sleep-walking, the performance of acts during sleep which the sleeper has no recollection of after wakening, sleep-talking, are all phenomena of this state of mind. In many cases the dreamer performs acts which he would regard with horror during his waking hours, and undergoes experiences calmly which he would, in full possession of mental activity, dread. Amongst the ancient people dreams were regarded as of divine origin, the interpretation of dreams took an active part in the life of the nation, and the 'seer' was regarded with awe by the people of the nation. The whole matter of the interpretation of dreams was put on a scientific basis in the twentieth century by the work of Sigmund Freud (*q.v.*) and his followers. The dream is regarded by Freud and the psychoanalysts of all schools as the best clue to the contents of the 'unconscious' mind, the correct diagnosis of the latter being the first step in mental therapeutics. Consult: S. Freud, *An Interpretation of Dreams*, and J. Dunn's *An Experiment with Time* (a non-psychoanalytic explanation of dreaming). *See* PSYCHOANALYSIS.

**Drebbel, Cornelius van** (1572–1634), claimed, erroneously, to have been the joint-inventor with Santorio of the thermometer, but was famous among his credulous contemporaries rather for his empirical inventions, such as a boat for rowing under water, in which the passenger could read without artificial light, than for his real discoveries. A pensioner of Emperor Rudolph II. and tutor to Ferdinand II.'s son, he owed his release from imprisonment in Austria (in consequence of a revolution) to James I. of Eng. In this country he passed the rest of his life. Besides his water thermometer, D. discovered a bright scarlet dye, afterwards used with effect in the Gobelins manufactories, and devised improvements in the microscope and telescope.

**Dredging Machines** are machines for cleaning and deepening the entrances to and channels of rivers, canals, docks, and harbours, by removing the mud or rock from the sea bottom. There are several kinds of dredgers, which can be divided into three main classes : (1) *The grab dredger;* (2) *the bucket-ladder dredger;* and (3) *the suction dredger.*

(1) *The grab dredger* is used only where the amount of mud is small, or where time is of not too great im-

portance. It consists of a pair of heavy iron jaws hinged together at the top, and slung by chains over a crane, which is usually mounted on a float, although it may be worked sometimes from the shore. The 'grab' is lowered to the sea bottom with the jaws held open by means of side chains. As the hoisting chain is slackened so under its own weight the 'grab' sinks into the mud. The side chains being then slackened and the hoisting chain drawn upwards, the two jaws close together and so bring up a quantity of mud with them. By means of the crane, then, the 'grab' is hauled up and swung so that the mud may be discharged into a barge; the jaws being opened again by means of the side chains.

the chains on one side are hauled in while the others are slackened. So the D. M. is gradually drawn right across the bank to be cut. When this has been done, then the D. M. is hauled a little further forward, and the process repeated by hauling in the chains on the other side, so that the machine is drawn back across the bank. As the buckets are turned over by the top tumbler they naturally discharge the mud into a shoot. Usually this shoot projects over the side, and so the mud is discharged into 'hopper' barges, fitted with trapdoors on the bottom held up by chains, which on being suddenly released drop the cargo. Sometimes the D. M. are built with a hopper well, so that they carry their own mud and deposit it.

DREDGING FOR GOLD IN THE YUKON

*Canadian Pacific*

(2) *The bucket-ladder machine* consists of a long ladder, one end of which is fixed high above the deck. The other end projects downwards through a well in the float, and being held by a chain which runs around a 'topping lift' which enables the ladder to be lowered or raised to the depth required. This ladder is usually placed in the centre of the float, although there are *double ladder machines*, the two ladders being side by side, and *side ladder machines*, in which the ladders project over the sides of the float so that they may be used close to dock-walls, etc. In all cases, however, an endless chain of buckets passes round the ladder which is fitted with tumblers at each end. The top tumbler is moved by a system of steam gearing, so causing the buckets to rotate. Meanwhile the machine is moored by bow and stem cables with further cables over both bows and quarters, and as the buckets revolve so cutting mud up from the bottom,

They are then known as hopper dredgers. It is evident, however, that such hopper dredgers lose time when compared with the others, for they have to proceed to the 'dumping ground,' whereas the ordinary dredger is continually dredging and filling other 'hopper' barges. Not only that but a deal of time is wasted in picking up the moorings each time, and this is not always an easy matter.

(3) *The suction dredger* is fitted with a centrifugal pump, with a flexible suction pipe, which is dropped to the sea bottom. Through this the sand or mud is pumped up and discharged either into other barges or into its own hopper well, if it is provided with one.

**Dred Scott Case, The,** a most important decision of the U.S.A. Supreme Court, handed down in 1857, and one of the contributing causes of the Civil War.

D. S. was a Missouri slave, taken

by his owner in 1834 into Illinois (where slavery was prohibited), and later into Minnesota (then part of the Louisiana Purchase). D. S. had married and had two children while on free soil, but he and his family were later taken back to Missouri.

In 1848 he sued for his freedom on the ground that his residence in a free state had given him the standing of a freeman. The Supreme Court of Missouri held that on return to Missouri the status of slavery re-attached to him and that he had no standing in court, but the U.S.A. Circuit Court before whom the case came in 1850 decided that as a citizen of Missouri D. S. had standing in court, but that he was still a slave.

The case was argued before the Supreme Court of U.S.A. in '55 and '56, and the decision (not unanimous) that D. S. was not a citizen, that the Constitution guaranteed security in private property and that value of such property in a slave could not be constitutionally invalidated in any state, even by the Federal government, roused the most intense feeling throughout the country and made it clear that slavery would not be abolished along constitutional lines. Chief Justice Taney had not only remanded Scott to slavery, but had gone out of his way to proclaim the Missouri compromise void and denied the right of Congress to make slaves or their descendants citizens. He practically said that the negro had no rights that white men were bound to respect.

**Dreiser, Theodore,** American novelist and playwright, *b.* Aug. 27, 1871, at Terre Haute, Ind., twelfth child of poverty-stricken and piously Catholic parents of Ger. descent. Educated at common schools, and at Indiana University. He was on the staff of the Chicago *Daily Globe*, 1892 ; dramatic editor and travelling correspondent of the St. Louis *Republic*, 1893–94 ; editor of *Smith's Magazine*, 1905–6 ; managing editor of *Broadway Magazine*, 1906–7 ; editor-in-chief of Butterick publications, 1907–10. His first novel was *Sister Carrie*, 1900, which was suppressed and denounced as immoral because in it unchastity underwent no punishment. His next was *Jennie Gerhardt*, 1911. Then came *The Financier*, 1912 ; and *The Titan*, 1914—two parts of a trilogy intended to portray the career of the late Charles Tyson Yerkes, the traction millionaire. Other works : *A Traveller at Forty*, 1913 ; *The Genius*, 1915 ; *Plays of the Natural and Supernatural*, 1916 ; *A Hoosier Holiday*, 1916 ; *Free and other Stories*, 1918 ; *Twelve Men*, 1919 ; *The Hand of the Potter* (tragedy),

1919 ; *Hey Rub-a-Dub-Dub* (essays and philosophy), 1920 ; *Book About Myself*, 1922 ; *The Colour of a Great City*, 1923 ; *An American Tragedy*, 1925 ; *Moods* (verse), 1926 ; *Chains* (lesser novels and stories), 1927. The charge of immorality was merely a piece of ' cornstockery.' A more serious ground of indictment in D.'s writings is heavy-handedness and over-elaboration. *An American Tragedy* is a long and powerful story of a boy brought up in a sloppily religious family, who ends in the electrocution chair on account of a murder never committed but only half-planned.

**Dresden,** the cap. of the Free State of Saxony, Ger., 111 m. S. of Berlin by rail and 70 m. E.S.E. of Leipzig, in the pleasant valley of the Elbe. On the left and southern bank lie Friedrichstadt and Altstadt (the old town), from which, however, most of the picturesque mediæval houses have been swept away. These quarters are connected with Neustadt and Antonstadt by a spacious new bridge, which has replaced the beautiful Augustusbrücke (1727–31), demolished, unfortunately, in 1906. The river is also spanned by the Carola, Albert, Marien, Losehwitz and railway bridges. The industrial quarters have greatly increased of late owing to the coal mining in the dist. of which it is the cap. In 1927 there were 7988 undertakings with 172,217 workpeople (the cigarette industry is the oldest), the making of chocolate, photographic apparatus, machines, stone ware, glass, lead, chemical preparations. The technical high school has 2862 students. The national library has 682,000 volumes. D. is known chiefly to the world as a repository of fine art. Its famous collection of pictures, including Raphael's priceless ' Madonna di San Sisto,' Correggio's ' La Notte ' and ' Mary Magdalene,' ' The Adoration ' of Paul Veronese, Titian's ' Tribute Money,' and paintings by Rembrandt, Van Dyck, and Rubens, was begun by Augustus I., but its true founder was Augustus III., who in 1745 bought the unique Modena Gallery, containing 2400 pictures by Italian and Flemish masters. Thus there is every justification for Herder's reference to D. as the ' German Florence.' It was from D. that rococo art spread in the eighteenth century, the Rom. Catholic Hofkirche (1739–51), and the Zwinger (1711–22), which now houses sculptural, zoological, and mineral collections, being excellent illustrations of this style. The unique collection of porcelain (over 15,000 examples), as well as the Historical Museum, may be seen in the Johanneum. In the Japanese palace (1715) are accommodated the national library and the collection of classical sculptures and antiquities. Besides the handsome royal palace (1530–35) in the Ger. Renaissance style, other noteworthy buildings are the magnificent Hoftheater (1871–78), designed by Semper, the domed and lanterned Frauenkirche (1726–34), the twinspired Sophienkirche (1351–57, and later), and a second royal theatre. D. is further remarkable for its fine squares, its statues, including the Rietschel monument by Schilling on the Brühl Terrace, and its public pleasure gardens, especially the Grosser Garten. Its excellent Conservatoire of Music and the splendid orchestra in the court theatre, with which have once been associated such master-musicians as Weber and Wagner, serve as further attractions for the numerous foreigners who constantly visit D., whilst in the summer time pleasure steamers conduct them to delightful places along the river's banks. In 1270 Henry the Illustrious chose D. as his capital, and its prosperity increased rapidly when in 1485 Saxony fell to the Albertine line. But again and again the city has been devastated by fire and sword, as during the Seven Years' War (1756–63), and Napoleon's campaign of 1813, when he here won his last great victory at the cost of 15,000 dead and wounded and 12,000 prisoners to the allies and a loss of 10,000 to the Fr. In 1849, from May 3 to 6, there was desperate street fighting and the old opera house was burnt down. It was occupied for a time by the Prussians in 1866. It has now the largest garrison in Germany. It is the headquarters of the Lutheran Church in Saxony. The pop. in 1925 was 619,157, of whom 540,053 were Protestants, 35,160 Catholics and 5120 Jews.

**Dresdner Bank,** one of the largest and most influential banks in Germany, arose out of the private banking establishment of Michael Kaspel of Dresden in 1872. Its original share capital was 9·6 million marks. This was gradually increased, and in 1889, through the amalgamation of the Niedersischische Bank, a further 20 million marks accrued to the capital. In 1881 a branch establishment was founded in Berlin—now the head office—and in 1892 another in Hamburg. In 1895 other offices were established in London and in Bremen, and the next five years saw branches in Nürnberg, Fürth, Hannover, Detmold, Bücheburg, Mannheim, Chemnitz, Lübeck, and Altona. The Dresdner Bank now has up-to-date establishments throughout Ger-

many and agencies in several neighbouring countries.

**Dressmaking.** The name dress is usually applied to any outer, complete feminine garment except a coat and skirt; it is sometimes restricted to a bodice and skirt made up apart as distinguished from a robe or gown, which is generally made in one garment, reaching from neck to bottom hem. The pattern of dresses depends entirely on the prevailing fashion, but the general characteristics of dresses suitable for different occasions are, as a rule, very similar. Morning or walking dresses are short, made of some firm and durable material for winter wear, or cotton for summer, and are more often the work of tailors than of dressmakers; afternoon dresses are generally made of some rich material—velvet, satin, silk—while evening dresses are cut low in the neck, without sleeves, and are of soft, light materials. The present (1931) skirts for morning wear have lengthened from the knee length of 1930 to midway between knee and ankle, and for afternoon and evening wear to ankle length, but older women sometimes prefer a train, thus giving them height. The general procedure in D. is practically the same whatever the prevailing fashion may be. The class of dress once decided upon and the material selected, the dressmaker proceeds to cut out a lining of cotton fabrics, moirette, or silk, to fit the figure of the client. The linings must be soft and pliable, and at the same time firm and not too stretchy in texture, and should be the same colour as the material. The width of materials varies, the average width of cotton fabrics being from 27 to 36 in., of woollen materials from 42 to 54 in. (so-called double width), while that of silks and velvets is from 18 to 27 in. The amount of material used depends entirely upon the style of the dress; the present fashion for morning frocks requires from three to four yds., while afternoon and evening frocks require from five to six yds. The making of bodices and skirts is generally in the hands of two quite separate bodies of workers in large establishments. The pattern is first drafted out according to an accepted set of rules in D., and particular care must be taken to ensure accurate balance as well as the correct measurements. Fit and style depend largely upon correct balancing, which varies with the carriage of the figure, the set of the shoulders, and the curve of the waist line, largely dependent upon the manner of life of the wearer and the style of corsets worn. Thus even if the measurements are taken accurately, if the dress is made for a well-set-up woman whereas the destined wearer is very round-shouldered, the result will be that the bodice is dragged at the back and the skirt considerably shorter behind than in front. For a round figure only one half of the pattern is required, as the two sides of the garment can be cut alike. In the case of one shoulder being higher than the other, or any one-sided deformity, it is wisest to cut the two sides separately. When the pattern is partially tacked together it should be tried on the client and the necessary alterations made. Throughout D., both in the cutting of the pattern and of the material, it is imperative that an ample margin be left, any superfluous turnings being cut off when the garment nears completion. The cutting of the primary pattern to fit the client is frequently omitted if the skill of the dressmaker is sufficient to cut the lining accurately at once. But when a primary pattern has been accurately fitted on the client, it should next be placed upon the lining, which has been previously doubled and laid on a flat surface. Care must be taken that the middle of the length of each piece is on the straight-length thread of the material so that all the seams may fall slightly on the bias. The outline is then marked through, being either pierced with a stiletto or by a special piercing wheel, as well as indications of the special style, yoke, vest, or any ornament. When the lining has been cut from the pattern, the material itself is cut in a similar way from the lining with allowance for draping or folds. Where the style of the garment involves tucking, the tucks should be made before the material is cut. Each piece of material being laid quite flat over its separate piece of lining, the two are then tacked together and the double material, lining and stuff, tacked to the similar pieces which form the other side. When the back and fronts are attached at the back and under the arms the bodice should be tried on and any necessary alterations made, it being generally possible to effect such alterations at the shoulder side seams by putting the tacking stitches a little forward or back as may be required. Boning the bodice is rarely practised, but where bones are required they should be inserted at this stage. During the process of trying on, indications of necessary alterations are generally made on one side only, and by means of pins or coloured cottons, to save the client the fatigue of standing. The garment is then taken back to the work-room and similar alterations made on the other side. The seams are then closed, machined, and neatened, either by being scalloped out, or by oversewing, or by a binding of thin silk. The sleeves, which are cut and made up separately, are fitted on to the client at the same time as the bodice, and should now be fitted into the arm-holes, and where there are gathers they should be carefully arranged to give ease to the movements of the arms. The quality of the work and the style of the garment depend upon the class of dressmaker and upon the price paid. Most firms have stock-sized dress models to fit the garments upon, and many clients have their dress stands made exactly to their own shape and measurements, and so avoid the fatigue of trying on the garment until it is completed. Fashions change as often as the seasons. The skirt of a quarter of a century ago was cut in 'gores,' tight round the hips and flowing out at the feet; that gave place to the full skirt gauged at the waist, which in time was ousted by the 'directoire,' 'tube,' and 'hobble' styles. These were followed by the skirt cut in four pieces, a front piece, two side pieces and a 'panel' back to give the appearance of straight lines, which in turn have given place to the present fashion, in which, generally, the straight lines are maintained and a freedom of movement is given by pleats in the front of the skirts. Bodices or blouses are fairly close fitting and without trimmings and with loose, wide-fitting collars. Front pieces are slightly 'gored,' *i.e.* narrowed from the bottom up to the top on both sides, with the centre falling straight with the selvedge threads; they should never be cut with a join down the centre. The side pieces are cut narrow and slightly gored at the bottom; they fall better if one side is cut on the straight or selvedge edge, and one on the cross, the straight side of each being nearest the front. The back piece is cut very similarly to the front, and is joined on to the side pieces to give a 'panel' effect. An average walking skirt measures about 2 yards round the bottom. The measure required for the length of the skirt will be different for the front, for the sides, where allowance must be made for the curve of the hips, and for the back; it is best to take the measurements for each separately. Skirts are generally finished off at the waist with elastic, a hem being made to take elastic ¾ in. wide. Alternately a placket hole is provided by making an opening of about 10 in. in length under a pleat. Skirts are at present too tight fitting to permit of pockets. The more elaborate draped skirts are generally made to be joined in one garment with the bodice, and so come under the heading of gown or robe. Habit skirts are usually only made by tailors, as are most sports skirts, which are made shorter and fuller than the ordinary skirt for walking. Apart from good work, which is always essential in good D., success depends upon 'style,' and 'style' is the art of catching and adapting the prevailing fashion to suit individual figures, to bring out all the best lines and cover any deformities or discrepancies in the figure without sacrificing the smartness of the garment. In big firms the usual term of apprenticeship for learners is two years, after which the learner serves for some months as an 'improver' before she is rated as a regular hand. Where the 'branch' system is in force, the learners serve in groups as fitters and cutters, as bodice hands and skirt hands, and have thoroughly to master their particular branch. Private dressmakers generally keep assistants to do the stitching and finishing, but do the cutting and fitting themselves, handing the cut and fitted lining and material on to one of the hands with the design and, perhaps, a few words of instruction, after which she is supposed to be able to complete it. In a humbler class of the trade the dressmaker only keeps one or two apprentices, and does all except the actual stitching and finishing herself. Sometimes the dressmaker provides the material and all the necessary items, and charges for the completed garment, but many clients like to provide their own materials and have them made up at a fixed charge. Besides regular dressmakers, there are a number of visiting workers, who come to their clients' houses and either make or renovate at a charge of so much for the day, irrespective of the amount of work done. Women the world over still look to Paris for their inspiration in all matters of dress, although the importance of London is slowly but surely gaining a hold upon other countries. Vienna also ranks very high in the scale of fashion. Numerous periodicals are published which give the latest modes from the world's fashion centres, and for many years it has been the custom of the home dressmaker to copy and adapt these models for her own use. A great drawback in home-dressmaking is that, unless she is prepared to take a thorough course of instruction in the art, the amateur needlewoman will find that there is practically always a lack of finish in her own productions which betrays their origin. For the women with

leisure or inclination to take a course in dressmaking, or for those who are adopting it as a career, every facility is now offered in the numerous Domestic Science schools throughout the kingdom, in the polytechnics and technical schools of London and the provinces, in women's institutes, and other educational centres. The 'professional touch' can be acquired only when all the details of a dress are properly finished. The novice must learn first how to make her own patterns, how to cut out the material to best advantage from her patterns, and finally how to make up the material into a fashionable and well-fitting garment. Various stitches must be mastered, from the preliminary tailor's or ordinary tacking to the finished embroidery stitches. Seams, hems, and bindings are all given a variety of treatment, according to their sphere of utility; the making of buttonholes, pleats, tucks, cordings, pipings, and facings are all essential subjects in dressmaking. The neat fitting of a collar, the insertion of sleeves, and even the right method of dealing with the almost obsolete pocket are all part of the dressmaker's lore, requiring skill and care. Fashions change so swiftly in modern times that works on all but the veriest elements of dressmaking quickly become out of date. A few books, however, which would be of service to the beginner in dressmaking are *Constructive Pattern Making*, by Gertrude Fearnside (Pitman), 1930; *Clothing for Women*, by Laura I. Baldt (J. B. Lippincott Co.), 1929; *Ladies' Garments: how to Cut and Make Them*, by the Editor of the *Ladies' Tailor* (John Williamson Co., Ltd.), 1928. Prevailing fashions can be noted in the current issues of numerous periodicals for women, such as *Vogue*, *Coming Fashions*, and *Weldon's Dressmaker*.

**Dreux**, once the chief city of the Gallic tribe, the Durocasses, now the capital of an arrondissement in the dept. of Eure-et-Loire, N.W. France, on the Blaise, 27 m. N.N.W. of Chartres by rail. Though it possesses the ruins of a mediæval castle, once owned by the counts of D., its chief pride is the exquisite chapel built in 1816 within the castle precincts by the mother of Louis-Philippe, containing fine stained glass and sculptured tombs belonging to the Orleans family. Its sixteenth century Gothic hôtel de ville and a magnificent church of St. Peter with a twelfth century choir and fifteenth century nave help to make D. famous. Pop. 10,910.

**Drevet, Pierre** (1664–1739), Fr. engraver, studied under Germain Audran at Lyons, and then under

Gerard Audran at Paris. In 1696 he became engraver to the king, and an Academician (1707). His best portraits include those of Louis XIV., Cardinal Fleury, the Dauphin, Robert de Cotte, and Boileau.

**Drevet, Pierre Imbert** (1697–1739), son and pupil of above, surpassing his father. He was admitted to the Academy, 1729. His portrait of Bossuet after Rigaud (1723) is considered his masterpiece. Other works are portraits of Lecouvreur, Bernard, Cardinal Dubois, and Pucelle. 'La présentation au temple' is the best of his historical subjects. His engravings are mostly after Coypel, Boullongne, Restout, and Rigaud. See Firmin-Didot, Les Drevet, 1876.

**Drew, Samuel** (1765–1833), Eng. writer, known as the 'Cornish metaphysician.' After a wild youth he joined the Wesleyan Methodists (c. 1785), and became a local preacher. He early won fame by his Remarks on Paine's 'Age of Reason,' 1799, followed by Essay on the Immateriality and Immortality of the Soul, 1802. He edited the Imperial Magazine from 1819. See Life by his son, 1834; Autobiographical sketch prefixed to Essay on the Identity . . . of the Body, 1809; Polwhele, Biog. Sketches of Cornwall, i.

**Drexel, Anthony J.** (1826–93), American banker, and son of the founder of Drexel & Co., now Drexel Morgan & Co., b. at Philadelphia. He became owner of the Philadelphia Ledger in 1864. Founded the Drexel Institute of Art, Science, and Industry, Philadelphia. His son Anthony D. (b. 1864) succeeded him in the business. Noted as a yachtsman. His yacht Marguerite was sold to the King of the Belgians and renamed Alberta.

**Dreyfus Affair, The,** the result of the anti-Semitic feeling in France, of which the real culprits in this case (Henry and Esterhazy) availed themselves in order to hide their own delinquencies. Captain Alfred D. was the son of a rich Jewish manufacturer in Paris. He entered the army, became an artillery captain, and was attached to the general staff. In 1894 he was arrested, accused of delivering documents to the Ger. Gov. He was tried by court-martial sitting in secret, was found guilty and condemned. He was degraded and transported to Cayenne, Ile du Diable. His condemnation roused throughout the whole of France a great wave of anti-Semitism, and the majority of the French nation were prepared to believe anything evil of the Jews. But his conviction had only strengthened in the minds of his relatives the fact that he was innocent, and the

military party in France, by their mere attempts to establish the truth of the conviction, convicted themselves of conspiracy. The publication of the bordereau which D. was supposed to have sent to the attaché of another Power proved to his friends that it was a forgery. But still they held back; they desired full proof before they proceeded further. Colonel Picquart convinced himself that the sentence was unjust, and was sent to the hinterland of Tunis. In 1897 Captain Esterhazy was accused of being the real author by Captain D.'s brother. Esterhazy was tried by court-martial and acquitted. The next person to take up cudgels on behalf of D. was Zola. To Zola as to all the Dreyfusards it had become apparent that the military staff would not allow justice to be done. Zola in an open letter to the president announced this fact in plain hard language. He was tried for libel, convicted, and fled the country. In 1898 the case was taken up by Clemenceau, and one of the documents was found to have been forged. Henry, the chief of the Intelligence Department, was placed under arrest, and immediately afterwards cut his throat, having confessed that he had fabricated the document. The struggle was now against the army, and for a short time the republic itself was in danger. M. Brisson's cabinet, however, transferred the case to the Court of Cassation, and another court-martial was held at Rennes, where D. was again convicted, but obviously his conviction was merely the last struggle of the military party, since extenuating circumstances were admitted and the sentence reduced. This was followed almost immediately by a free pardon. The only common-sense conclusion which could be reached was that Esterhazy and Henry were the real culprits, and that the army was too obstinate to admit an obvious fact. The proceedings against D. were finally quashed in 1906, and he was again restored to the army, being given the rank of major. Probably the republic has never been in such great danger since as it was in the days when the heat of the anti-Jewish feeling almost made the army supreme.

**Dreyse, Johann Nikolaus von** (1787–1867), a Ger. locksmith and inventor; worked in a musket factory in Paris (1809–14), and on his return founded an ironware factory in Sömmerda. He manufactured percussion caps under a patent (1824), and invented improved firearms, notably the muzzle-loading needle-gun (1827), and the breech-loading one (1836).

Adopted by the Prussian army (1840), its superiority was shown in the war with Austria (1866). The modern repeating rifle has replaced it. See *D. und die Gesch. des Zündnadelgewehrs,* 1866; Von Loebell, *Das Zündnadelgewehr . . .,* 1867.

**Driffield, Great,** a market tn. of Buckrose div., E. Riding, Yorkshire, England, in the wolds, 19 m. from Scarborough. It communicates with Hull by the Driffield navigation and R. Hull. There are mills and manufs. of cotton-seed and linseed. Pop. 5975.

**Drift,** *see* GEOLOGY.

[*Topical Press*]

JOHN DRINKWATER

**Drill,** the *Papio* (or *Cynocephalus*) *eucophœus,* is a baboon of the same genus as the mandrill, but it differs from this hideous creature in the absence of bright colours on its muzzle and nose. It is a ferocious inhabitant of W. Africa.

**Drill,** *see* BORING.

**Drin, River,** *see* ALBANIA.

**Drinkwater, John** (*b.* 1882), Eng. poet and dramatist, educated at Oxford High School and Birmingham Univ. Was for twelve years a clerk in an insurance office. Assisted in founding the Pilgrim Players, which later became the Birmingham Repertory Theatre under Sir Barry Jackson. His first poems were *Men and Hours,* published in 1911, and his first play, a one-act play in verse, 1911. Then followed topical plays on war, *Rebellion,* in verse, 1914, and *Swords and Ploughshares,* 1914. But his greatest success was *Abraham Lincoln,* a play produced in 1919. His *Oliver Cromwell* followed in 1921, but did not attract such attention as the earlier play. Produced a dramatic version of Hardy's *Mayor of Casterbridge* in 1926. Has also written a number of essays, including a striking study of his friend, Rupert Brooke (*q.v.*).

**Driver, Samuel Rolles** (1846–1914), an Eng. divine and Hebrew scholar. After a brilliant career at Oxford, he became Regius Professor of Hebrew, and canon of Christ Church, 1883. His publications include: *Introduction to the Literature of the Old Testament,* 1897; Commentaries and notes on Leviticus (1894–98), Deuteronomy (1902), Samuel(1890), Minor Prophets (1905), Genesis (1909); *Modern Research as Illustrating the Bible,* 1909; *Hebrew and English Lexicon of Old Testament* (with Brown and Briggs, new ed.), 1906. D. was a member of the O.T. Revision Committee, 1876–84. Died at Oxford.

**Driving** (of animals). Many animals are used for traction in various parts of the globe, but the most common are the horse, the mule, the ass, and the ox; in very cold climates the reindeer and the dog are also utilised. Ever since man possessed domesticated animals he has made use of them in this manner; an element of sport has also been associated with D. from very early times. Thus the Roms. were very fond of chariot races, as also were the Gks. The custom of D. for pleasure, without racing, is of modern development; such a pleasure would have been impossible before Macadam and Telford made such a revolution in the art of road-making. Spring carriages and level roads were a necessary corollary, but when these existed there sprang up a great number of D. clubs, of which the Bensington Driving Club, founded in 1807, was the pioneer. The most usual method of D. is with one horse; when two horses are driven, they are either abreast (the customary way) or in tandem; four horses are driven in two pairs, the foremost pair being the 'leaders,' the other the 'wheelers.' Practice is essential before a good driver can be made, but the quality known as 'good hands' is to a large extent innate and instinctive. The reins are held in the left hand between the thumb and forefinger and second and third fingers. The left hand should be held on a level with the bottom of the driver's waistcoat, at a little distance from the body. The upper arm should hang freely against the side, the forearm should make a right angle with the elbow joint, and be held horizontally across the front of the body. The wrist should be slightly bent inwards with the back of the hand facing the horses. When the reins are thus held an experienced driver will ' feel ' the horse's mouth without irritating or checking it. The D. of a tandem or a four-in-hand is a more difficult matter, as two pairs of reins have to be manipulated. The reins are held in the following manner: those of the leaders are separated by the forefinger ; those of the wheelers by the middle finger. Thus between the forefinger and middle finger are the reins of the off leader and the near wheeler. The reins are first of all gathered together in the right hand, in the same position as they will be in the left, before the driver mounts to his seat. In starting a four-in-hand it is essential that the leaders and wheelers should start simultaneously, and when started, the driver should, by adjusting their length with his right hand, ensure that he has each horse under perfect control. When rounding corners a ' loop ' of one or two inches of the leaders' reins is taken up by the right hand and placed under the left thumb. It is absolutely necessary that a driver who has any pretensions to skill should be able to handle his whip to perfection. He should be able to strike with the thong any horse he wishes, with what amount of severity he likes. When the leaders need the whip the wheelers should not be disturbed ; a first-class driver can ' touch up ' the off leader under the swinging-bars (under which the thong should always pass) without agitating the wheelers at all. In tandem D. skill with the whip is even more necessary, as a well-directed cut with the whip will check the leader as a rule if he should try to turn right round. Four-in-hand D. is not so difficult as tandem, as although there is more weight on the hands, there is much more control over the leader.

**Drocourt–Quéant Switch,** in the Great War a key position of the famous Hindenburg Line. It was the British objective in the Battle of Arras of April 1917, but was not taken. In Sept. 1918, after extremely bitter fighting, the ' switch,' as the position was called, was taken by storm by the troops of General (later Lord) Horne together with many towns and villages.

**Droeshout, Marten (Martin)** (*fl.* 1620–51), an engraver of the seventeenth century, probably of Dutch extraction. He settled in England, working chiefly for booksellers and engraving portraits. His most famous production is the engraved portrait of Shakespeare, prefixed to the first folio edition (1623) of his plays. This was probably copied from the original painting made by D.'s uncle, which was discovered in 1892, and placed in the Shakespeare Memorial Gallery at Stratford-on-Avon. Other portraits were of Villiers, Duke of Buckingham, the Marquis of Hamilton, Dr. Donne, John Fox, and Sir Thomas Overbury. *See* Redgrave, *Dictionary of Artists;* Nagler, *Monogrammisten,* iii., iv ; Lee, *Life of Shakespeare* (new ed.), 1909.

**Drogheda** (anct. Droicheadatha, ' the bridge of the ford '), a seaport, market tn. and municipal bor. (till 1885 a parl. bor.) on either bank of the Boyne, 4 m. from its mouth in the Irish Sea, on the Great Northern main line, 31¼ m. from Dublin, in the counties of Meath and Louth, Irish Free State. The depth of water alongside the N. quay is 21 ft. at highest and 14 ft. at lowest tide. Considerable agricultural produce is shipped to Liverpool and Glasgow, and the salmon fishery in the Boyne has its centre here. Recently the former flourishing linen and damask industries have been revived, and there are manufactories of various articles including soap, leather, beer, and flour. The St. Lawrence Gateway still remains of the anct. walls, and there are relics of the Augustinian abbey (1206) and the Dominican monastery (1224). When Cromwell captured the town in 1649, most of the garrison were butchered. In 1690, after the famous Battle of the Boyne, D. surrendered to William III. Pop. 12,200.

**Drohobycz,** a tn. of Poland with 26,735 inhabs., centre of the petroleum region of S. Poland. The Austrians defeated the Russians here in 1915.

**Droit Administratif.** That system of law which in France gives an overriding authority to the state tribunals over the ordinary law. It exists also in other European states, but is not so marked a feature as in France. There is no precise equivalent in our language ; but it is defined in general terms by the Fr. authorities as ' the body of rules which regulate the relations of the Administration or of the Administrative authority towards private citizens.' D. A. is in fact that portion of Fr. law which determines : the position and liabilities of all state officials ; the civil rights and liabilities of private individuals in their dealings with officials as the representatives of the state; and the procedure by which those rights and liabilities are enforced. The modern D. A. of France has grown up and assumed its existing form during the nineteenth century, being the outcome of more than a century of revolutionary and constitutional conflict. The essential characteristics of D. A. are: the rights of the state are determined by special rules, *i.e.* as opposed to the ordinary law; the ordinary law courts have no jurisdiction in matters concerning the state, and administrative litigation is thus determined by the Administrative Courts; the co-existence of judicial courts and administrative courts results in a conflict of jurisdiction in which the latter courts prevail; and state officials are protected against the ordinary law. Dicey, *Law of the Constitution*; Jèze, *Les Principes généraux de Droit Administratif* (1904); Seissier, *La Responsabilité de la Puissance Publique*, 1906.

**Droits of Admiralty,** *see* ADMIR-ALTY, DROITS OF.

**Droitwich,** a market tn. and municipal bor., on a canal connected with the Severn, and also on branch lines of both the Great Western and L.M.S. Railways, 6 m. N.N.E. of Worcester, in Worcestershire, England. It is famous for its brine springs or 'wyches,' which are mentioned in the Domesday Book. Pop. 4588.

**Drôme,** a dept. in the S.E. of France, bounded on the N. and N.E. by Isère, on the E. by Hautes-Alpes, on the S.E. by Basses-Alpes, and the S. by Vaucluse, and on the W. by the Rhone. Its total area is 2533 sq. m. Between the Rhone and Isère lies the fertile and hilly district known as the Viennois, and including the region of the Valloire, called the 'golden valley.' The natural division through which flow the upper courses of the D., Roubion, Jabron, etc., is quite mountainous, the highest peak having an altitude of 7890 ft. The main crops are wheat, potatoes, and oats. Fruit, including olives, figs, and walnuts, wine, cheese, live stock, and silk obtained from silkworms fed on native mulberries, are the staple exports, whilst the principal import is coal. Native minerals supply many potteries and porcelain manufactories. Besides Valence, the capital, the chief cities are Die and Nyons, which all give their names to arrondissements, and Montélimar, Crest, and Romans. Pop. 263,750.

**Dromedary,** or *Camelus dromedarius*, the species of camel which is distinguished by its solitary hump, *C. bactrianus* having two. It is a large ruminant which occurs in Arabia and is never found wild; the hump is adipose, and the body is covered with hair. *See* CAMEL.

**Dromia,** a genus of crabs in the family Dromiidæ, has well-defined orbits into which the eyes can be retracted, the fourth and fifth pairs of trunk-legs are small and are held dorsally, and the carapace is shaggy. *D. vulgaris* is found on British and Mediterranean shores.

**Dromore,** a par. and tn. of N.W. co. Down, Ireland, on R. Lagan, 15 m. from Belfast. The present cathedral was erected after the destruction of the town in the insurrection of 1641, and has the tombs of Jeremy Taylor (1613–67) and other bishops. Linen is manufactured. Pop. 2365.

**Drone,** *see* BEE.

**Dronfield,** a par. and tn. of England in the co. of Derbyshire, 6 m. from Chesterfield, and 6 m. S. of Sheffield. It is situated on the R. Drone, in the midst of collieries. Iron and steel goods are manufactured. Pop. 4435.

**Drontheim,** *see* TRONDHJEM.

**Drop-Forging,** or die-forging, a process which has replaced the old drophammer used in swaging, die-work, striking up sheet metal, etc. Many of the operations performed at the smith's anvil can be more quickly and better done by such a machine as the die-forge. A white-hot mass of metal is placed in the die, and the blows of the hammer force it into the same shape as the die; the metal goes into the die as a shapeless mass, so that when hammered some of it is squeezed out of the side of the die and, if this is not checked, would prevent the die from closing, and so spoil the stamping. To obviate this possibility, the metal is placed on a die of the same shape as the object, but pierced right through; when hit by the hammer the forging is forced through the die, thus leaving the stripped fin or metal behind, and the forging is then proceeded with. In the manufacture of automobiles and other machines having many small parts the forgings are stamped so accurately that very little metal is wasted by machining in the shops, thereby saving both time and money.

**Dropsy,** a shortened form of *hydropsy*, an accumulation of serous fluid in the tissues or cavities of the body. Serum is the colourless liquid constituent of blood, and under normal conditions is exuded through the walls of the blood capillaries in order to build up the tissues; a part of the exuded fluid is returned to the blood-stream by the veins and some by the lymphatics. When from any cause serum is exuded in abnormal quantity or is not absorbed to a sufficient extent, collections of fluid are apt to form. D. is therefore not a disease itself so much as a symptom of disease. Half of the cases of general D. are due to heart disease, and many are due to kidney disorders. Other causes may be weakening of the walls of the capillaries, by which exudation is increased, or, in the case of local D., any obstruction of a vein which causes increased blood pressure. *Œdema* is D. of the superficial tissues, limited in area ; *Anasarca* is the term applied to other Ds. of the subcutaneous tissues. *Ascites* is an accumulation of serum in the abdominal cavity, generally due to diseases of the liver and spleen. *Hydrocephalus*, or water on the brain, is an accumulation in the brain-cavities. *Hydrothorax* is a D. in the pleural cavities, characterised by a large proportion of albumen in the fluid. *Hydropericardium* is an accumulation in the membranous sac enclosing the heart. The treatment of D. involves the employment of purgatives, diaphoretics, and diuretics, in order to promote increased excretion. In severe cases tapping is resorted to, when a small drainage tube may be inserted to draw off the fluid.

**Drosera**, a genus of Droseraceæ, comprises nearly one hundred beautiful insectivorous plants, growing in boggy places in all parts of the world. In Britain there are three species, *D. longifolia*, a common bog-plant; *D. anglica*, found chiefly in Ireland ; and *D. rotundifolia*, the common or round-leaved sundew. The latter is an acrid and caustic plant used in Italy in making the liquor called Rossoli.

**Droste-Hülshoff**, Annette Elizabeth, Freün (Countess) von (1797–1848), a Ger. poetess, a writer chiefly of lyric and narrative verse. Her *Gedichte* appeared in 1844, *Das geistliche Jahr . . .* about 1850 (religious poems). In 1860 L. Schücking issued her *Letzte Gaben*, with the short story ' Die Judenbuche.' The *Gesammelten Schriften* appeared in 1878–79. See Life by Schücking (1871), Hüffer (1887), Wormstall (1897), Busse (1903), Reuter (1905); Zottmann, *Deutschland grösste Dichterin*, 1897 ; Medwin's translations.

**Drouais**, a family of Fr. artists, the third being the most famous :

*Hubert* (1699–1767) was intimate with Nattier, Van Loo, and Oudry. His portraits include those of the painter Christophe, and of the sculptor Robert le Lorrain.

*François Hubert* (1727–75), son of above, painted children's portraits, and did much work in Louis XV.'s reign. Examples are portraits of Mme. de Pompadour, Mme. du Barry, Mme. Clotilde, Marie Antoinette. His ' Child playing with a Cat ' (1768) is characteristic.

*Jean Germain* (1763–88), son of above, pupil of David and Brenet. He won the Academy prize (1874) with ' Christ et la Cananéenne.' While in Rome he painted ' Marius à Minturnes,' ' Philoctetes . . .,' and ' A Wounded Gladiator.' See Chaussard, *Notice sur Drouais.*

**Drouet, Jean Baptiste** (1763–1824), a Fr. revolutionist, instrumental in causing the arrest of Louis XVI. at Varennes (1791). As a member of the convention (1792), he joined the extreme party, voting for the death of Louis and the overthrow of the Girondists. D. was a member of the Council of Five Hundred, 1795. He became sub-prefect of Sainte-Menehould under Bonaparte, and received from him the cross of the Légion d'Honneur, 1807. Obliged to quit France on the second restoration, he returned to Mâcon later, living under the assumed name of Merger. See Lenôtre, *Le Drame de Varennes*, 1905 ; Thiers, *History of the French Revolution.*

**Drought**, or **Drouth** (A.-S. *drugaŏ*, from *drugian*, to dry), a dryness, want of rain or water. The term is especially applied to such lack of rain and moisture as affects the earth and its fertility, preventing the growth of plants. ' Periods of more than fourteen consecutive days without measurable rain ' were fixed by Symons (1838–1900) as the exact time that must elapse without rain to cause an ' absolute drought.' See Symons' *British Rainfall*, published annually since about 1863, and his *Meteorological Magazine.* Countries liable to D. have much need of irrigation. The cholera year of 1854 was very dry, and famine and disease are often caused by D. Between 1891 and 1901 the number of sheep in New South Wales and Queensland declined considerably through D. The Sahara and Kalahari deserts of Africa, the Gobi desert of Central Asia, Great Salt Lake district in N. America, and certain regions of India and China suffer from D. nearly all the year round. The regions which suffer from almost continual D. are often shut off by high mountain ranges from the influence of winds carrying moisture.

**Drowning.** The cause of death by D. is asphyxiation, and the entrance of water into the lungs. After death the skin of a drowned person presents the appearance known as ' goose skin,' or *cutis anserina*, the face is exceedingly pale, a frothy liquid is found in the lungs and air passages, and water in the stomach. Complete insensibility supervenes in from one to two minutes, and death in about five minutes, though persons have been known to recover who have been immersed for a considerable length of time. There are four methods which are in use for the restoration of persons apparently drowned. Dr. W. Hawes was instrumental in founding the Royal Humane Society (*q.v.*), which has been the means of rendering the principles head, grasps his arms by the elbow and draws them up simultaneously till they are in a line with the body. He then carries the arms down to the side, without a pause, making them overlap the chest a little, on which they are firmly pressed. This is repeated at the rate of fifteen times a minute. In Howard's method the

DROWNING

*Top:* Sylvester's method of restoration. *Bottom:* Howard's method.

of live-saving widely known. The earliest method, that of Marshall Hall, which dates from 1856, consisted briefly in raising and lowering the patient from his side to a position on his face and *vice versâ* at the rate of fifteen times a minute. The method recommended by the Royal Humane Society is that of Dr. Sylvester, which is briefly as follows. The operator stands or kneels behind the patient's body is first of all placed face downwards with a roll under the stomach. After being pulled over the roll, the patient is turned over, and the arms placed above the body with the hands near the head. The operator kneels over the body, places both hands on the lower part of the patient's chest, with the thumbs just under the lowest ribs. The operator then presses forward steadily, raising the ribs and bending himself forward, after which he throws himself slightly backward, repeating this about fifteen times a minute. This method is easier than the Sylvester, and can be practised when the patient's arms are hurt; care must be taken that undue pressure is not exercised. The latest method, which was proved by experiments on dogs to be the most efficacious, is the Schafer method. The patient is laid face downwards and the operator kneels over him, with his hands flat upon the lower part of his back. He throws the weight of his body forward, so putting pressure on the chest of the patient, and then leans back again, and so on at the rate of fifteen times a minute. In all these methods the operator should continue for as long as there is any hope, for an hour or more if necessary. When the patient is coming round, teaspoonfuls of hot water, brandy, etc., should be administered, and hot-water bottles applied. In olden times D. was a capital punishment; it was abolished in Eng. about 1620, in Scot. in 1685, in Switzerland 1652, in Austria 1776, and in Ireland 1777. For methods of rescuing persons who are D., *see* SWIMMING.

**Droylsden**, a par. and tn. of Lancashire, Eng., 4 m. from Manchester. The manufs. of cottons and chemicals are important, and it has print-fields and dye-works. Pop. 13,877.

**Droysen, Johann Gustav** (1808–84), a Ger. historian. He took part in the Schleswig-Holstein dispute with Denmark, upholding the Ger. claims. His works include: *Geschichte der Preussischen Politik*, 1855–85 ; *Grundzüge der Historik*, 1876. *See* Duncker's *Leben*, 1885 ; Dahlmann-Waitz, *Quellenkunde der deutschen Gesch.*, 1906 ; Kruger, *Outlines of the Principles of History* (trans. by Andrews), 1893.

**Drugget** (Fr. *droguet*), a common felt or coarse woollen fabric, often printed on one surface. The heavier kinds are chiefly used for covering carpets (hence called 'crumb-cloths'), as a substitute for carpets, or as a lining or border. The lighter kind is used for table-covers. A strong dress-fabric of this name was formerly used largely for petticoats and workmen's aprons.

**Druids**, a caste of priests among the Celtic inhabitants of ancient Gaul and Britain, about whom a considerable body of tradition has descended, no doubt largely modified and coloured by legend, especially in the case of the Irish D. Etymologists differ as to the derivation of the name itself ; the long accepted connection with the Gk. δρῦς, oak, is now doubted.

The Welsh and Breton *derwydd* and *drouiz* are not original forms. The Latin form *druida* points to a Gaulish *druids*, Irish *drui*, which has been analysed into *dru-vid*, very learned, knowing. Cæsar gives the first circumstantial account of the D. ; he tells us that all nobles and men of dignity in Gaul were among the D. ; that they were the law-givers and priests ; that the caste was not hereditary ; the chief D. was elected ; they had the power of inflicting heavy punishment for disobedience to their de-

DRUIDS
(from a bas-relief found at Autun)

crees. They had a written language, believed in the immortality of the soul, and were learned in astrology and the natural sciences. It appears that Cæsar may have over-estimated their powers. Britain was the headquarters of the D., and but a yearly meeting was held in Gaul ; the Gaulish novices came for training to Britain. Human sacrifices seem generally to be attributed to them, and they studied divination by the flight of birds and by the dying con vulsions of their victims. The oak tree was sacred and all its fruits, hence, too, mistletoe ; religious ceremonies were performed in oak-groves. Pliny writes of them as practisers of medicine and sorcery, and of their cutting the mistletoe, robed in white, with golden sickles, and of the sacrifice of white bulls. Strabo tells of their golden collars and armlets ; he describes them as bards and soothsayers. Tacitus gives us an account of their last stand, A.D. 61, on the island of Mona (Anglesey), when the British D. were exterminated and their sacred groves cut down, and the suppression of the D., which had been the object of Rome since Augustus, was accomplished both in Gaul and at any rate in Eng. and Wales. The later history is confined to the Irish D. Ancient Irish literature has many tales concerning them, much overlaid with legends and with the traditions of the early Christian struggle with the supporters of pagan rites. Thus it is that the Irish accounts attribute to them sorcery and witchcraft. They are found with power of changing the weather; the archdruid appears as a leaping juggler, tossing swords and balls in the air; when a famine occurred, the D. ordered the son of a sinless married couple to be sacrificed and his blood mixed with the soil; a D. by enchantment causes the death of King Cormac; they appear also as bards and poets. The legends of the struggle of the D. against St. Patrick and St. Columba are also interesting. *See* D'Arbois de Jubainville, *Les Druides et les dieux Celtiques*, 1906; P. W. Joyce, *Social History of Ancient Ireland*, 1903.

**Druids, Ancient Order of,** an affiliated friendly society, or 'order,' founded in London in 1781. In fancied imitation of the ancient Druids, the members cultivated a masonic ritual and called their lodges 'Groves.' There are also orders of the same name in Ger. and the U.S.A. which were founded in 1872 and 1839 respectively. A feature of this and similar orders, which in America are known as fraternal societies, is the large amount distributed by way of sick benefits. *See also* FRIENDLY SOCIETIES.

**Drum,** a musical instrument of percussion. Although it is said to have been introduced into Europe about the time of the Crusades, nevertheless, instruments which strongly resemble it were known during the early days of the Rom. empire. Obviously one of the most primitive of musical instruments, it forms almost exclusively the sole musical instrument of savage peoples. The tom-tom, a form of D. played with the fingers, is the chief music of many primitive tribes, and this instrument is also known. to have existed in Egypt considerably more than 1000 years before Christ. There are three varieties of Ds.: (1) The common or side-D., (2) the bass-D., and (3) the kettle-D. The side-D. is, as its name implies, worn at the side of the player, and is played upon the upper side with two sticks.

It is found nowadays almost exclusively as an accompaniment to fife bands. The bass-D. is almost entirely a military instrument, being very similar in construction to the side D., but larger. It is played with two sticks, both sides being used. The bass-D. has within recent years been introduced into large orchestral music by the more modern composers. The only instrument of real musical value, however, is the kettle-D. This instrument is composed of a shell or kettle of copper or brass, over the mouth of which is drawn tightly a parchment cover attached to an iron ring. By means of screws it is possible to tune this D. within narrow limits. In a full orchestra two are usually found, one with a compass from F to C, and the other from B♭ to F on the bass stave. The music is invariably written in the key of C. The kettle-D. is carried by the cavalry, this being the only use made of it in military circles.

**Drum of the Ear,** *see* TYMPANUM and EAR.

**Drumcliff,** a par. of N.E. Sligo co., Ireland, on D. Bay, 4 m. from Sligo. It has a carved Celtic cross and a round tower. Pop. 5053.

**Drumclog** (Gaelic, 'ridge of stone'), a moorland tract of Lanarkshire, Scot., 17 m. from Lanark. An obelisk commemorates the defeat of Claverhouse by the Covenanters, or Cameronians (1679), near London Hill. *See* Scott's *Old Mortality* for a description of the battle.

**Drumlins,** or **Drumlings** (from *druim*, ridge), in geology, smoothly-rounded, oval hills of compact, unstratified, glacial drift or boulder-clay, apparently deposited and piled up beneath the Pleistocene ice-sheets. They are usually about ½ m. long, 100 to 200 ft. high, the longer axis always lying parallel to the former local glacial motion. They occur in America in Massachusetts, round Boston harbour, W. New York, S.E. Wisconsin, and the lake region, and in the parts of Europe and Asia lying N. of the terminal moraine of the Continental glacier. A good example exists between Belfast and Lisburn. See *Journ. Roy. Geol. Soc. Dublin*, i., 1833; Garwood's papers on geology, *Quart. Journ. Geol. Soc.*, 65.

**Drum-major,** since 1878 called the sergeant-drummer, the first or chief drummer in a regimental band, the officer who leads a drum-corps or band, directing its movements, and regulating the pace when on the march. He attends to the bugle calls and teaches the under-drummers. The D. ranks with the sergeants of the line. His official designation, from 1881, was sergeant-drummer or sergeant-piper (as the case might be), the reversion to the old name being made by the War Office in 1928. The rank is over two centuries old and is to be traced as far back as 1632, in which year it is mentioned by a music writer named Cruso; and seven years later there was a D.-M. on the strength of the Royal Scots and a few years later, on that of the Coldstream Guards.

Drummond, George (1687–1766), a public-spirited Scottish officer. He fought against the Pretender at Sheriffmuir (1715). He was Lord Provost of Edinburgh for the first time in 1725, being chosen six times in all. D. was energetic in resisting the rebels of the '45 outbreak, joining Cope after the surrender of Edinburgh. He helped to found the Edinburgh Royal Infirmary, erected the Royal Exchange, 1753, and laid the foundation-stone of the North Bridge, 1763. See *Scots Mag.*, lxiv., 1802; Grant's *University of Edinburgh* . . ., 1884; Wodrow, *Analecta*, iii.; Ramsay's *Poems*, i. 375, 1800.

Drummond, Henry (1786–1860), an Eng. politician and writer, for some time a partner in Drummond's Bank, Charing Cross. D. founded the chair of political economy at Oxford (1825). He was also one of the founders of the Catholic Apostolic or Irvingite Church. He wrote *Condition of the Agricultural Classes*, 1842; and *History of Noble British Families*, 1846.

Drummond, Henry (1851–97), a Scottish scientist and theologian. He travelled widely; *Tropical Africa*, 1888, and *Travel Sketches in Our New Protectorate*, 1890, being the resulting works. His *Natural Law in the Spiritual World*, 1883, and *The Ascent of Man*, 1894, were attempts to reconcile evangelical Christianity and evolution, and were more remarkable for rhetoric than for logic. See Life by Smith (1899), Lennox (1901), Simpson (1901).

Drummond, James (1816–77), a Scottish historical and genre painter, studied under Allan in the School of Design. His first exhibit in the Scottish Royal Academy was ' Waiting for an Answer,' 1834. He became a R.A. (1852), and curator of the Scottish National Gallery (1868). Among his best works are ' The Vacant Chair,' 1837; ' The Porteous Mob,' ' The Covenanters in Greyfriars Churchyard,' ' Peace,' ' War.' See Redgrave's *Dict. of Artists; Art Journal*, 1877.

Drummond, James (1835–1918), an Eng. Unitarian theologian, edu-

cated at Trinity College, Dublin. He became a colleague of Gaskell at Manchester (1859–69), and then professor of theology at Manchester New College, London (1869), succeeding Martineau as principal (1885–1906), and moving with the college to Oxford (1889). His works include *Introduction to the Study of Theology*, 1884; *Via, Veritas, Vita*, 1894; *The Pauline Benediction*, 1897; *Life and Letters of Dr. Martineau* (with Upton), 1902; *Character and Authorship of the Fourth Gospel*, 1904; *Paul: his Life and Teaching*, 1911. Died at Oxford.

Drummond, Hon. Sir James Eric, first Secretary-General of the League of Nations; b. Aug. 17, 1876; second son of tenth Viscount Strathallan; half-brother and heir-presumptive to the fifteenth Earl of Perth. Educated at Bedford Grammar School and Eton. Entered British Foreign Office, April 1900. Private secretary to Under-Secretary of State for Foreign Affairs, 1906–8 and 1908–10. Précis-writer to Foreign Secretary, 1908 and 1910–11. One of Mr. Asquith's private secretaries, 1912–15. Private secretary to Foreign Secretary, 1915–19. As from April 28, 1919, head of the secretariat of the League.

Drummond, Thomas (1797–1840), inventor and administrator, entered the Royal Engineers in 1815, but in 1820 accepted Colonel Colby's offer to join him in an ordnance survey of Great Britain. It was in 1825 near Belfast that he first tested the power of his lime-light apparatus (Drummond light), being able to see it at a distance of 67 m., and four years later he adapted it for use in lighthouses. D. also invented an improved ' heliostat,' a mirror especially designed to facilitate the turning of rays of light in a certain direction. Appointed superintendent of the boundary commission in 1831, he became Under-Secretary for Ireland in 1835, when he discharged his duties so as to win universal respect. See also HELIOGRAPH.

Drummond, William (1585–1649), of Hawthornden, Scottish poet, obtained his M.A. degree at Edinburgh University, studied law and literature in Bourges and Paris, and spent the greater part of his life at his ' sweet and solitary seat ' of Hawthornden, dividing his life between poetry, royalist pamphlets, and melancholy. It was with bitter resentment that he signed the abhorred Covenant in 1639. D. has been called the Scottish Petrarch because of his passionate sonnets inspired by the early death of his first love, Mary Cunningham, yet he is in no sense a national poet, for his inspiration and much of his sensuousness are drawn from Spenser, and his poems prove him to have been well acquainted with the works of Sidney and many It. poets. His *Cypress Grove* (1623), a musical poem on death, best preserves the quiet gloom of D.'s mind, and is free from extravagant conceits

WILLIAM DRUMMOND

which sometimes mar his verse. Other of his works are a prose *History of the Five Jameses*, 1655, and *Forth Feasting*, 1617. See Life by Masson.

**Drummond, Sir William** (c. 1770–1828), a Brit. diplomatist and writer, head of the Ds. of Logie-Almond. He was sent as envoy to Naples and Sicily (1801), and again in 1806, and to Turkey (Ottoman Porte), 1803. His works include the blank-verse poem *Odin*, 1817; *A Review of the Governments of Sparta and Athens*, 1795; translations of Persius, 1798; *Œdipus Judaicus* (issued privately), 1811, asserting the allegorical nature of parts of the O.T. See *Quarterly Rev.*, ix.; *Edinburgh Rev.*, Oct. 1805; *Gent. Mag.*, ii., 1828.

**Drummond, William Hamilton**, (1778–1865), an Irish poet and Unitarian minister. He wrote poems, *The Battle of Trafalgar . . .*, 1806; *The Giant's Causeway*, 1811; *The Pleasures of Benevolence*, 1835; *Ancient Irish Minstrelsy*, 1852, and Eng. metrical translation of Irish ballads in Hardimans' *Irish Minstrelsy;* polemical works, such as *The Doctrine of the Trinity*, 1827; *Original Sin*, 1832; and biographies of Michael Servetus, 1848; A. H. Rowan, 1840, and others. See Porter's 'Memoir' in *Sermons*, 1867; Mrs. Campbell's MS. *In Memoriam.*

**Drumright,** a city on an oil and gas field of Oklahoma. Pop. 4922.

**Drunkenness, or Inebriety,** may vary from a state of hilarity, mental excitement or exaltation to complete coma or unconsciousness, ending possibly in death. Again it may be an occasional lapse or an habitual and chronic state of alcoholism. It may be the cause of foolish and disorderly behaviour, or of deep-seated fatal diseases, or of insanity. It may lead to a fine for a condition of helplessness in the streets, or to a long term of imprisonment or capital punishment for a brutal assault or a murder. Medically or physiologically D. is a condition of intoxication or poisoning due to the consumption of an excessive amount of alcohol, either in rapidly taken doses, or spread habitually over a period of time, with a cumulative effect. The outward signs of alcoholic intoxication, the thickness of speech, blurred or double vision, inability to maintain equilibrium, etc., are due to paralysis of various parts of the nervous system. Pathologically it includes acute alcoholism, in various stages leading to complete coma, delirium tremens, and chronic alcoholism, with its most usual results of various profound nervous disorders, impaired digestive powers, cirrhosis of the liver, etc. A proof of the effect of alcohol on the nervous system is found in the fact that in post-mortem examinations traces of it may be found in the cerebrospinal fluid when it has disappeared in every other organ. Viewed racially, it may at once be recognised that D. is far more prevalent among the races of northern, damp, and cold climates than in the S. Scandinavia, N. Russia, and Scotland are in marked contrast to Italy, Spain, Portugal and Southern France. Further, in connection with this, are the beverages commonly consumed, the lighter wine with the more ardent spirit. The comparison of national drink bills, based on consumption per head, is usually fallacious; it is the kind of alcohol taken, *i.e.* whether light wines or beers or ardent spirits, and the manner of consumption, *i.e.* as part of the daily diet or crowded into a few hours, that makes the difference as far as the national health is concerned. The interrelation of hereditary alcoholism is not thoroughly worked out. To some the result of past alcoholism should tend to an immunisation, racially if not individually. Insanity produces a weakness of resisting power to surroundings encouraging intoxication and D., and that again reacts on an unstable nervous diathesis which may result in insanity.

In the eyes of the law, D. does not affect a man's civil capacity ; he may make contracts, wills, marriages, etc., as long as he is capable of knowing what he is doing and no undue advantage is taken of his state. So, too, as regards criminal responsibility, but in those crimes where a criminal intention is essential, his state may be taken into consideration. *See* further under CRIMINAL LAW. As an offence in itself, the law looks first to the effect : it is not an offence to be drunk *per se*, but only if it be accompanied by disorderly conduct in a public place or leads to a breach of the peace ; or it is an offence to be drunk and incapable in a public place, or drunk in a licensed house, or when in charge of a vehicle of any kind or the like. Stringent laws regulate the offence of selling drink knowingly to drunken persons or to known inebriates, or of permitting drunken persons to remain on licensed premises. Finally, the law takes into account habitual drunkards in the technical phrase, inebriates. They may be voluntarily committed to licensed houses for a maximum period of two years, which can be extended on application. Further, habitual drunkards or inebriates, after conviction for an offence punishable by imprisonment, if the offence was committed when drunk, may be committed to a State or Certified Inebriate Reformatory.

**Drury, Dru** (1725–1803), an English naturalist. His cabinet collections of home and foreign insects were much prized, and his writings did much for the advancement of entomology. Linnæus, J. E. Smith, Kirby, and others thought very highly of D. His chief works are *Illustrations of Natural History*, 1770–82 ; *Directions for Collecting Insects in Foreign Countries*, 1800 ; *Thoughts on the Precious Metals* . . .,¡ 1801 ; *Exotic Entomology* (edited by Westwood with ' Memoir '), 1837. Moses Harris did the many plates and figures accompanying these works. *See* C. H. Smith, ' Life ' in the *Naturalists' Library*, i., 1843 ; *Gent. Mag.*, lxxiv. (1), 1804.

**Drury, Robert** (*b.* 1687), an English sailor, wrecked off the coast of Androy, S. Madagascar (1702). He was kept there as a slave and endured many hardships for fifteen years, finally returning to England and becoming porter at the India House. He died between 1729 and 1743. *See* his *Madagascar, or Journal during Fifteen Years' Captivity* . . ., 1729.

**Drury, William Price**, son of a naval officer, educated at Brentwood School, Essex, and Plymouth High School. Saw a considerable amount of service at sea on China and Mediterranean stations and elsewhere. From 1900 to 1901 he was a member of the Naval Intelligence Department. He is the author of *The Flag Lieutenant*, the successful play produced at the Playhouse in 1908, and has also published several stories.

**Drury Lane Theatre**, a famous London playhouse in Covent Garden, one of the oldest existing in London, deriving its name from the old Cockpit or Phœnix Theatre (*c.* 1616), actually in Drury Lane, where Killigrew acted, before granted a patent by Charles II. (1663) for opening a new one. This was known as the Theatre Royal, and opened by Killigrew and his company called the ' King's Servants.' A fire destroyed this first house (1672), and it was rebuilt by Wren (1674). In 1682 the ' Duke's Servants ' under Davenant joined Killigrew, and both companies played together at Drury Lane. There was a secession under Betterton to Lincoln's Inn Fields (1694), and by 1709 the theatre was closed. Collier took over the management in 1710, Lacey in 1744, soon being joined by Garrick. Among noted actors who performed here in the eighteenth century were Colley Cibber, Doggett, Wilks, Quin, Macklin, Pritchard, Kitty Clive, ' Peg ' Woffington, and Mrs. Siddons. Garrick was manager from 1746–76, opening with Dr. Johnson's prologue (1747), and the triumphs of himself and his company renewed the prosperity of the theatre. In 1784 Kemble made his first London appearance as Hamlet, becoming manager in 1788. The house was pulled down in 1791, reopened by Sheridan (1794), but again burnt down in 1809. The present house, built by Wyatt, was opened in 1812, with a prologue by Lord Byron. The committee's advertisement for this prologue gave rise to the *Rejected Addresses* of J. and H. Smith. The interior was rebuilt in 1822, the present seating capacity being about 2500. Kean and Macready won fame here in the early nineteenth century. Pantomimes, spectacular pieces, and melodrama, such as *Ben Hur*, 1902 ; *The Whip*, 1909 ; *The Hope*, 1911 ; *Everywoman*, 1913, are now mostly produced. *See* Stirling, *Old Drury Lane*, 1881 ; Pepys' *Diary*, 1663 ; Doran, *In and About Drury Lane*, 1881.

**Druses (Druzes)** an anct. race and religious sect of Syria, of much-disputed origin. They are variously said to be Arabs from the Yemen ; of Chinese stock ; and descended from the Kurds with whom Esarhaddon repeopled Samaria after the second captivity of Israel. They are also regarded as Iranians. Their numbers are impossible to estimate with any degree of accuracy, and they have been assessed at 70,000 and 200,000. They live chiefly in the mountain regions of Lebanon and Anti-Lebanon and in the district of Hauran. They call themselves 'Muwahhidin' (Unitarians), but are known to others as 'D.,' a name probably derived from Ismail Darazi or Durzi (confessor of Hakim), their first apostle in Syria. He was forced to flee for refuge to Lebanon, 1016, after preaching publicly the divine incarnation in Hakim, one of the seven cardinal beliefs of the sect. Others connect the name 'D.' with various Arabic words. Hamzé, a Persian disciple of Hakim, gave the Druse faith its settled form. They mingle teachings of the Pentateuch, the Christian gospels, the Koran, and the Sufi allegories, and believe in one God. They hold that the Deity has on no fewer than ten occasions been made manifest in human form, the last occasion being in the person of Hakim, the Nero-like Fatimite Caliph of Egypt (966–1021). One tenet of their faith is that the number of souls is definite, and that when one man dies his spirit assumes another fleshly cloak and lives a life conditioned by classes of Akals (Initiated) and Djahils (Uninitiated). Both classes look forward, as a prelude to the end of the world, to an Armageddon between Islam and Christendom, and celebrate their religion in mysteries. A most fanatical and warlike people, they have revolted against all their rulers—the Turks, the Egyptians, and in late years the Fr. They yet discourage proselytism and Mohammed is not accepted by them as an incarnation of the Deity. In the seventeenth century Emir Fakr-ed-din Maan II., a noted Druse leader and the most famous figure in the history of the race, annexed Beirut and Sidon, and menaced Damascus. He intrigued with the Christians, and was executed by the Turks (1635). In the eighteenth century the Turks and D. revolted against Egypt, and the famous Emir Beshir was exiled to Malta, dying at Constantinople, 1851. From 1840 to 1860 there was endless bitter strife between the D. and the Maronite Christians. After the Maronite Massacres of 1860, the Fr. interfered (1861) and in 1864 the European Commissioners drew up a new constitution for Lebanon under a Christian governor chosen by the Porte, Daoud Pasha being the first. He founded an educational establishment at Abey. There was a fierce revolt in 1925 against the Fr., who hold the mandate for Syria under the League of Nations, and the revolt was crushed

with extreme severity. But it is generally conceded that the D. were goaded into rebellion by the reactionary policy of General Sarrail (*q.v.*), who at the time was High Commissioner in Syria. Sarrail failed to appreciate the character of the D., and his high-handed proceedings and tactless conduct led to his recall in 1925, when he was succeeded by Jouvenel. The revolt was led by El Attrash, the Sultan, who, with some few thousand followers, established himself in the Rom. fortress of Azrak, an oasis in Wadi Sirhan, and, with this as his headquarters, led raids across the frontier into Fr. administered Hauran. The Fr. military courts thereupon condemned him, and most of his adherents to death, and this sentence still hangs over their heads. After the Emir Abdullah of Transjordan had signed a treaty of extradition with Syria, an ultimatum was sent to the D. to leave the fort within a day, and this was made effective through the co-operation of British aeroplanes and armoured cars. The D. fled to Haditah, some 80 m. distant, where they now dwell in a city of tents by some deserted wells, through the clemency of Ibn Sa'oud, King of Najd. In the old days the D. were famous silk manufacturers, and they still carry on the trade, chiefly at Shimian; but the nomad section of the people under Attrash eke out a hazardous existence by gathering salt from the basalt gravel of Haditah. A little corn also is raised by those still in Syria. Deirel-Kamar is their chief city, but Baklin (near by) later became their headquarters. Kunarvat is the chief town of the Hauran district. *See* Silvestre de Sacy, *Exposé de la religion des Druses*, 1838 ; Wolff, *Die Drusen und ihre Vorläufer*, 1842 ; Earl of Carnarvon, *Druses of the Lebanon*, 1860 ; Churchill, *The Druzes and Maronites under Turkish Rule*, *1840–60*, 1862 ; Guy, *La Nation Druse*, 1864 ; Oliphant, *Haife*, 1887 ; Bell, *The Desert and the Sonn*, 1907 ; J. F. Scheltma, *The Lebanon in Turmoil*, 1921. B. H. Springett, *Secret Sects of Syria and the Lebanon*, 1922 ; L. Stein, *Syria*, 1925.

**Drusus, Nero Claudius (Germanicus)** (38–9 B.C.), a Rom. general, was the adopted son of the Emperor Augustus and the younger brother of Tiberius. Horace, in one of his odes, has celebrated D.'s campaign against the Rhæti and Vindelici, who threatened the Gallic frontiers, but historically D. is remembered for the subjugation of Germany by his victories over the Usipetes, Sugambri, Chatti, and Suebi, and by the fact that he was the first Rom. general to reach the Elbe. Had not an accident caused his death in early manhood, it seems likely that his winning manners, strategical genius and brilliant success, which had combined to win him an extraordinary popularity, would have enabled him, had he chosen, to overthrow the empire.

**Drusus Cæsar** (c. 15 B.C.–A.D. 23), son of the Emperor Tiberius and Vipsania Agrippina, after being twice consul, and winning victories in Pannonia and Germania, was given the tribunician authority by his father, a sign that one day he would inherit the empire. But he died early in life, being slowly poisoned by the ambitious Sejanus, who had also seduced Livia, his wife.

**Dryads,** in Gk. mythology, the nymphs of the trees. Each δρῦς (oak, tree) was the home of its own particular D., whose life was bound up with that of her tree (Hamadryad, ἅμα).

**Dryas,** of the order Rosaceæ, consists of two species of Arctic plants. D. octopetala, the mountain avens, grows in Alpine districts of Europe, on Scottish and Irish mountains, and in Yorkshire. The plant is procumbent, with simple leaves, a woody stem, and white flowers ; after fertilisation the style grows feathery, and the fruit is oval and long-tailed. D. depressa has been found in Ireland.

**Dryburgh** (Dárach-bruach, bank of oaks) **Abbey,** a beautiful monastic ruin in S.W. Berwickshire, Scotland, on R. Tweed, 4 m. from Melrose. It was founded about 1150, probably by David I. Burned by Edward II. (1322), it was partly restored by Robert the Bruce. Under Richard II. it suffered again (1385), and was reduced to ruins by Bowes and Latoun (1544), and by the Earl of Hertford's expedition (1545). The style is mainly Early English and Transitional Norman. St. Mary's aisle in the N. transept has the tomb of Scott (1771–1832), and of J. G. Lockhart. The yew near the chapter-house is at least as old as the abbey itself.

**Dry-cleaning,** an operation for cleaning textile and similar materials and fabrics, and articles made of them (e.g. garments, curtains, etc.) without the use of water. It depends on the fact that oils and grease are soluble in certain organic liquids, such as petrol, acetylene tetrachloride, carbon tetrachloride, alcohol and acetone, and that when the greasy substance has been thus removed the residual particles of dirt may be eliminated by brushing, by the use of vacuum extractors, or by other mechanical means. The great advantage of D. C. is that it does not spoil the shape of the articles cleaned, and very rarely affects their colour in any way. Modern dry-cleaning plants operate on a large scale, and economy is effected by recovering the solvents after use. In early days, the process of D. C. was attended with serious risks of fire, owing to the inflammable nature of the solvents employed, but the advance of chemical research has provided the dry-cleaner with excellent non-inflammable liquids ; these are quickly replacing the solvents formerly employed. For home use, light petroleum, or ' petroleum ether,' is a good general solvent, but it very readily takes fire, so that it must be employed with caution.

**Dryden, John** (1631–1700), an English poet, b. at Aldwinkle, Northamptonshire, on Aug. 9. He was descended on both sides from ancient families, which had at this time strong leanings towards the Puritans and against the monarchy. He was educated at Westminster School under the famous Dr. Busby, and later proceeded from there to Trinity College, Cambridge. In 1649 had appeared his first contribution to poetry in the shape of a poem commemorative of the death of Lord Hastings. In 1654 he took his bachelor's degree, and in the same year his father died, leaving him property worth about £60 a year. He seems to have remained at Cambridge during the following three years, although this is not quite certain. In 1657, at any rate, he seems to have taken up his residence in London, where, in all probability, he lived under the protection of his cousin, Sir Gilbert Pickering. In the following year appeared his stanzas commemorative of the death of the protector. In 1660 he published Astræa Redux in honour of the Restoration, and followed this up by a panegyric in honour of King Charles' coronation in the following year. Without attempting any disguise, he proclaimed frankly that he was endeavouring to obtain as much money as he could, and in the preface to four of his plays he owned that he would force his genius to perform that which the humour of the public demanded. The taste of the public was not overchoice, and yet D., in his first attempt to satisfy that public taste, overstepped even the wide limits of the decency of the Restoration age. In fact, this general criticism may be made of all his plays, that in an age when decency was at a discount, he successfully managed, by the virulency of his indecencies, to overstep the limits of the time in almost every case.

This is not altogether to be wondered at, since he was forcing his genius to perform something for which it was totally unsuited. The *Wild Gallant* (1663) was a failure, but D. learnt from his lack of success, and the *Rival Ladies*, produced in the same year, was more of a success. In the same year he collaborated with Sir Robert Howard in the composition of *The Indian Queen*, which proved a great success, and in the same year he married the Lady Elizabeth Howard. In 1665 appeared from D.'s pen alone *The Indian Emperor*, which was also a great success. Probably in 1666 appeared his poem *Annus Mirabilis*, which commemorated the Dutch War and the Great Fire in the heroic stanzas of the Cromwellian ode. Between the appearance of this poem and 1681,

JOHN DRYDEN

D. appears to have confined himself entirely to stage plays. He wrote many during this period, and these plays may be divided into two distinct classes : the one following the general tendency of the day and attempting to make up by their ribaldry for their want of genius ; the other, dramas founded upon striking incidents in the history and mythology of the world. In the former, for reasons already given, he was almost uniformly unsuccessful, in the latter his success was really popular. He was at this time under contract to Shelley's Theatre to write three plays a year, receiving in return about £400 per annum. He failed to fulfil the conditions, producing only about ten plays during the ten years during which he was under contract. Amongst the plays which he produced at this time (not all under the contract conditions) are : *Secret Love,*

*Sir Martin Marall, An Evening's Love, Ladies à la Mode, Marriage à la Mode, Love in a Nunnery, Tyrannic Love, The Conquest of Granada.* The extravagant boasting of the preface to the *Conquest of Granada* was the cause of the production of the *Rehearsal,* a play written in burlesque principally by the Duke of Buckingham. In 1670 D. had become poet laureate. In 1674 he attempted to turn *Paradise Lost* into rhymed couplets, having, it is said, the permission of Milton ' to tag his verses.' *Aurungzebe* was the last of his rhymed plays, and was published in 1675. In 1678 appeared *All for Love,* a version of the story of Antony and Cleopatra, but written from an entirely different point of view from that of Shakespeare. A comparison of the two plays leaves us entirely convinced that Shakespearian drama was the highest form, but it gives us also a very much greater opinion of D. than can be obtained from any of his other plays. Other plays which D. wrote subsequently to this are : *Œdipus, The Duke of Guise, Troilus and Cressida, The Spanish Friar, Albion and Albanius, Amphitryon, King Arthur, Cleomenes,* and *Love Triumphant.* D., after abandoning the rhymed couplet, adopted satire as the instrument of his genius, and published in 1681 *Absalom and Achitophel,* after having been mistaken for the author of a previous satire. This satire was written from the court point of view, probably with the idea of gaining favour for himself, and was certainly immensely popular. Edition after edition sold rapidly, and certain it was that D.'s satire was appreciated. He had not the faculty of delicate satire, but the blows which he struck were hard. His next satire was the *Medal,* a poem written in savage commemoration of the medal struck when Shaftesbury was acquitted. He attacked and attempted to demolish Shadwell under the title of Mac-Flecknoe. In 1682 appeared *Religio Laici,* which attacked the Papists and still more bitterly urged on the persecution of the Nonconformists. On the accession of James II. in 1685, D. became a Catholic. By many his conversion has been held to be the result of sincere conviction, while, on the other hand, the majority hold that it was merely another example of his time-serving characteristics. Be that as it may, he wrote a poem, *The Hind and the Panther,* in which he strongly advocated the faith of his new religion. The Revolution of 1688 found him still unchanged, and as a result of his Catholicism he lost his office of poet laureate, and had to fall back upon his pen for his living. In 1693 appeared some translations of Ovid and Homer, and almost immediately afterwards he set to work on a complete translation of Virgil, which appeared in 1697. This was followed by the famous second ode on *St. Cecilia's Day*. His last work, published a few months before his death, was the *Fables*, principally founded on the stories of Boccaccio and Chaucer. During the later part of his life he had been dependent on the translations for his daily bread, and he also seems to have received presents from his friends. Although deprived of his position as laureate, he still continued to be recognised as the greatest living poet, and he lived without fear of molestation from the government and respected by all. He *d.* May 1700. By his conversion he became the literary parent of the greatest poet of the succeeding age, Pope. His genius is undoubted, and showed itself principally in his ability to imitate and to excel those whom he imitated. He had no great originality, yet his position as one of the greatest of our poets remains. He established little, yet he excelled all. Lives by Scott and Saintsbury.

**Dry Farming.** In those areas where the rainfall is limited it is necessary to adopt special measures in order to secure the fullest benefit from all natural sources of irrigation. Experience has shown that the twofold problem of trapping all the rain that falls and of securing that it shall not easily trickle away is best met by treating the upper surface and the lower soil in two different ways. The surface soil is broken up and treated in a manner that makes it specially permeable by moisture so that as much as possible of any rainfall shall be immediately absorbed; while the lower soil is kept in a clogged and clay-like condition that retains the water thus secured.

**Drying Machines,** devices for drying textile materials. Those for drying printed calicoes or long webs of similar fabrics usually consist of a series of revolving metal cylinders heated from within by steam. The machine commonly used in bleaching or laundry-works is formed of two drums or cylinders open at the top. The articles to be dried are placed in the inner one, which is made to revolve at high speed. The moisture is forced out by this centrifugal action through the perforated sides of the inner into the outer drum, whence it is drained off by means of a pipe. Open-air or hot-chamber drying usually completes the process. The ordinary 'wringer' or 'mangle' has two rollers mounted parallel one above the other, with an adjustment by means

of which the distance between them can be varied. The Blackman air-propeller is used for drying wool by drawing heated air through it. Slightly different apparatus is used in paper manufacture.

**Dryopes,** an aboriginal Gk. tribe who first settled round Mt. Œta, in the dist. called after them ' Dryopis,' extending N. to R. Spercheius. *See* Herod., i., viii.; Strabo, ix.; Paus. vi., v.

**Dryophis** (Gk. δρῦς, a tree ; ὄφις, snake), the generic name of the whip-snakes, non-venomous reptiles, native to tropical America, W. Africa, and India.

**Dry Rot,** a species of decay which attacks timber in certain instances. The chief fungi responsible for the destruction are ' Merulius lacrymans,' ' Polyporus destructor,' and ' Polyporus hybridus.' Stagnation of warm, humid air, insufficient drying of the timber, and the felling of trees in the spring, when the sap is full, are all likely to lead to D. R. It has often been decreed that timber should be felled in winter only, so as to prevent sap fermentation. Submerging wood in water ' seasons ' it by dissolving, or at least changing its putrescible material; whilst in modern times timber is preserved by being creosoted, burnettised (treated with zinc chloride), or kyanised (treated with corrosive sublimate).

**Dual Alliance,** a secret defensive alliance made between Russia and France in 1892 and nullified by the Russian Revolution of 1917.

**Duala,** tn. and harbour in Fr. Cameroons. W. Africa, the most important port of C. for palm oil products. Has a hospital, schools, three missions, shipyard and railway workshops. There are 400 white inhabitants. In the Great War it was captured by the British forces on Sept. 26, 1914. Pop. (estimated) 22,000.

**Dualism** (Lat. *duo*, two), a philosophical term applied to any theory which rests on two co-existent and different principles. It is the opposite of Monism. The earliest dualist was Plato, who held that good truly exists, but in combination with evil, which is non-existent. Aristotle believed form and matter to lie at the bottom of all things. Descartes, arguing from his proposition ' Cogito, ergo sum,' maintained the absolute D. of consciousness or thinking (*res cogitans*), and extension (*res extensa*). In theology, D. assumes the separate existence of two underlying principles, good and evil, as in the doctrine of Zoroaster which postulates two contending deities, Ormuzd and Ahriman. In Christianity arises the difficulty of reconciling the omnipotence and perfect goodness of God with the existence of evil and pain.

**Dual Number,** a grammatical term denoting a form of a noun, pronoun, or verb, employed with regard to two things. Thus in Gk. the dual form of γίγας, giant, is γίγαντε, and the plural γίγαντες. The D. N. existed in Sanskrit, Arabic, and Hebrew, but in Latin we only find it in two words, *duo* two, and *ambo* both. The D. N. is rare in the Teutonic languages. In Old English the dual forms exist in the declension of *ic*, I, and *du*, thou, only. They are, of the former, nom. *wit*, acc. *uncit*, *unc*, gen. *uncer*, dat. *unc*. of the latter, nom. *git*, acc. *incit*, *inc*, gen. *incer*, dat. *inc*. In Gothic, they are found in the declension of *ik*, I, and *pu*, thou, and in the verbs. For example, the second person imperative of *sōkjan*, to seek, has three numbers: sing. *sōkei*, dual *sōkjats*, plur. *sōkeiþ*.

**Du Barry, Marie Jeanne Gomard de Vaubernier, Comtesse** (1746–93), a mistress of Louis XV., *b.* at Vancouleurs, Meuse. She entered a milliner's shop in Paris at the age of sixteen, and became the mistress of the dissolute Jean, Comte du Barry, through whom she met Louis XV. Her beauty and wit attracted the attention of the old king, who before long made her his official mistress at court, after her merely formal marriage with Jean's brother Guillaume. After Louis' death in 1774 she was obliged to live in retirement at Luciennes, and on the outbreak of the revolution she came to England to raise money (1792), but was arrested and beheaded on her return (1793). *See* Life by Vatel (1882–83), and R. Douglas (1896).

**Dubbo,** a tn. in Lincoln co., New South Wales, Australia, situated on the Macquarie R. Coal and copper are found in the neighbourhood, and the town has flourishing manufs. Pop. 5032.

**Du Bellay,** *see* BELLAY, JOACHIM DU.

**Dubica,** a fortified tn. on the r. b. of the R. Unna, Croatia, Yugo-Slavia. There were terrible battles here between Turks and Austrians in 1788. Pop. about 5700.

**Dublin,** the capital of the Irish Free State, in the prov. of Leinster and co. of Dublin, and is built on both sides of the Liffey, where it enters D. Bay in the Irish Sea. It is distant 334½ m. W.N.W. of London via the Holyhead route, and 138 m. W. of Liverpool. Quays faced with granite, 2½ m. long, run along the two banks of the river, which is spanned at D. by four iron, including a swivel, and six stone bridges. The Dublin Port and Docks Board (instituted in 1898) has made considerable improvements in the harbour. Thus vessels drawing up to 23 ft. may be admitted into the great Alexander basin and alongside the quays even at low water, and there are also docks in connection with the Royal and Grand Canals, which pursue courses N. and S., respectively, of the city, both finally meeting the Shannon. Water is supplied through the Vartry water-works, which control a recently enlarged reservoir at Roundwood, some 20 miles south of the city. D. is in direct communication with all Ireland, for the following railways have termini there: the Great Northern (in Amiens Street); the Midland Great Western (Broadstone terminus); the Great Southern and Western (Kingsbridge), and the Dublin and South-eastern (Harcourt Street and Westland Row). The various railway systems are connected by a local loop line (the City of Dublin Junction). Electric trams thread through all the main streets, connecting them with the various suburbs. Steam packets keep D. in constant communication with Belfast, Glasgow, Liverpool, Cork, Heysham, Bristol, Plymouth, Southampton and Havre. The London Midland and Scottish Railway controls the direct route to London, via Holyhead. The woollen, cotton, silk, and linen industries are quite unimportant to-day, but D. poplins are still prized. Whisky and porter (from the Guinness brewery, etc.) are the staple products, whilst much of the agricultural produce of Ireland passes out through D. The exports and re-exports in the year ending in Sept. 1930 amounted to £47,406,958, the imports for the same year being £57,891,726. There are two Anglican cathedrals, that of Holy Trinity, or Christ Church, founded by the Danish king Sigtryg in 1038, and that of St. Patrick, erected originally in 1190. The architecture of the former is Transitional Norman and Early English. In the latter will be found monuments in memory of Dean Swift and 'Stella.' The Rom. Catholic cathedral is in Marlborough Street. In front of Trinity College (founded in 1591), which constitutes Dublin University, are two fine statues of Burke and Goldsmith. A magnetic observatory is in the gardens of the college. The Catholic university (1854) is built on St. Stephen's Green. Between the two universities are many important buildings, including the Royal Dublin Society (1683), whose object is to promote agriculture, etc., the Science and Arts Museum (of Irish Antiquities), the National Library, the Museum of Natural History, and the

National Gallery of Ireland (1853). Most of D. Castle, which, in spite of its height and excellent position, is quite unimposing, dates from the sixteenth century or later. What was formerly the House of Parliament is now the Bank of Ireland. This structure, begun in 1729, was completely remodelled in 1803. Of the many charitable institutions may be mentioned Simpson's Hospital for the blind, gouty, etc.; Swift's Asylum for lunatics (1745); the Blue Coat School (1670), and many special hospitals. Phœnix Park, comprising 1753 acres, lies to the W. of the city, and again in the rebellion of 1922. On Easter Monday, in 1916, the General Post Office in Sackville Street, now O'Connell Street, was seized by the rebel forces, who made it their headquarters. It suffered accordingly, being ultimately reduced by bombardment and fire to a mere shell. The S. side of the street also was destroyed by fire. Shops were looted, rebel snipers fired from the roofs and the city was put under martial law. Before the buildings destroyed at this period had been completely reconstructed, the rising of June 1922 took place. Sackville Street again

THE NEW DUBLIN—O'CONNELL STREET

[*Topical Press*

and has in its grounds the Hibernian Military School; the Wellington Monument; the 'Fifteen Acres'—a natural amphitheatre used as a racecourse and review ground—a magazine; a zoological garden, and the former viceregal, chief and undersecretaries' lodges. There are also various technical schools, an academy of music, and a gallery of modern art in the city. The suburbs besides Phœnix Park are Kilmainham (to the S.); Chapelizod and Lucan (to the W.); Clondalkin, Glasnevin, Finglas, and Clontarf (to the N.), and to the S. Rathmines, a favourite residential quarter. The name 'Dubh-linn,' signifies 'Black Pool.' Christianity was first introduced by St. Patrick in 450. Thorkel I. (832) was the first Danish king of Dublin, though Norsemen had appeared earlier. The Normans finally dispossessed the Danes in 1171. The city of D. suffered severely during the Easter rising of 1916 suffered greatly, for those opposed to the treaty with Great Britain occupied houses on the N. side of it, which, being subjected to a heavy bombardment, were destroyed by fire. The Customs House was set on fire and destroyed in May 1922 by the Irish Republican army, and the Four Courts building was also ruined. O'Connell Street is now reconstructed and a handsome new Customs House has been erected. The Four Courts building, however, had not been completed by 1930, and the Law Courts were still housed in Dublin Castle. The Free State gov. made the College of Science in Merrion Square its gov. building, and Leinster House and the Dublin Museum adjoining were used as parliament buildings. Pop. (1926) 316,693.

**Dublin,** a city, co. seat of Laurens co., Georgia, U.S.A., with cottonseed oil mills, wood-working industries, etc. Pop. 6681.

**Dublin Fusiliers, The Royal,** formerly the 102nd and 103rd Foot. Both regiments had their origin in independent companies of Foot raised in India by the East India Co. during the seventeenth century: they were regimented about the middle of the eighteenth century. The 102nd were previously the Royal Madras Fusiliers and the 103rd the Royal Bombay Fusiliers. They were given their numbers on being transferred to the Crown after the Indian Mutiny. In 1881 they were linked to form, respectively, the 1st and 2nd Battalions the Royal Dublin Fusiliers, which was disbanded in 1922. A distinguished member of the Madras regiment was Ensign Clive (later Lord Clive) the victor of Plassey. Both regiments took a leading part in all the Indian campaigns, and gained great distinction during the Indian Mutiny, 'Neil's Bluecaps' and the 'Old Toughs,' as they were called, always being to the fore. In the S. African War they were especially conspicuous at Wagon Hill, near Ladysmith; indeed it was largely in commemoration of the bravery of the D. F. and other Irish regiments in the S. African War that the Irish Guards were raised. During the Great War the regiment raised eleven battalions, which served in France, Flanders, Gallipoli, Egypt and Palestine.

**Dubno,** a tn. in Volhynia, Russia, 140 m. W. by N. of Zhitomir. The fortress of D. was captured from the Austrian garrison in the Great War in the general advance on the Pripet and Sereth by General Brussilov (*q.v.*) in 1916. Pop. 9100.

**Dubois,** a bor. of Clearfield co., Pennsylvania, U.S.A. It is an important manufacturing town, with iron works, machine shops, and coal mines. Pop. 11,595.

**Dubois, François Clément Théodore** (1837–1924), a Fr. musical composer, *b.* at Rosnay, Marne. He studied at the Paris Conservatoire, winning the Grand Prix de Rome with his cantata, *Atala*, 1861. He was *maître de chapelle* of the church of St. Clotilde 1863–68, and then he accepted the same position in the church of Madeleine, of which he became organist in 1877. He became professor of harmony at the Conservatoire (1871); professor of composition (1891); and director, in succession to Ambrose Thomas (1896). His sacred music includes *Les Sept Paroles du Christ*, 1867; for the theatre he has written *La Farandole*, 1883, and *Xavière*, 1895; for the orchestra *Hylas*, 1890, and *Notre Dame de la Mer*, 1897, besides numerous other works. Died in Paris June 11.

**Dubois, Guillaume** (1656–1723), a French cardinal and statesman, *b.* at Brive, in Limousin. In 1687 he was appointed tutor to the young Duke of Chartres (afterwards Regent Duke of Orleans), and contrived to win royal favour by arranging a marriage in 1692 between his pupil and Mademoiselle de Blois, the legitimised daughter of Louis XIV. He became an ambassador in London, and on his return (1701) secretary to his former pupil, and councillor of state (1715). By this time he had acquired tremendous influence over the regent, and practically held the reins of power in his own hands. He negotiated the Triple and Quadruple Alliances (1717, 1718) and forced Philip V. of Spain to dismiss Alberoni. D. secured for himself the archbishopric of Cambrai (1719) and the cardinal's hat (1721). *See* Life by Wiesener (1891) and *Mémoires secrets*, edited by de Sevelinges, 1815.

**Dubois, Jacques,** *see* SYLVIUS, JACQUES DUBOIS.

**Dubois, Paul** (1829–1905), a Fr. sculptor, first studied law, then entered Toussaint's studio (1856). 'Saint Jean Enfant,' 1860; 'Saint Jean-Baptiste' (bronze), 1863; 'Narcisse au Bain,' 1867, were among his earlier works. 'Le Chanteur florentin,' exhibited 1865; 'Le Connétable de Montmorency,' 1886; and the equestrian statue of 'Jeanne d'Arc,' 1895, are some of his finest productions. The beautiful 'Tombeau du Général Lamoricière' in Nantes Cathedral is one of his best-known works. After 1873 D. became known as a portrait-painter, 'Mes Enfants' being exhibited in 1876. He painted in Henner's manner, and produced busts of Henner, Dr. Parrot, Baudry, and others. He became director of L'Ecole des Beaux-Arts, 1878. *See* Brownell, *French Art*, 1892.

**Du Bois-Reymond, Emil** (1818–96), a German physiologist and scientific historian, studied at Berlin and Bonn. He was professor at the London Royal Institute for three years, with Faraday as his patron, and succeeded Müller in the chair of physiology at Berlin (1858). His researches in animal electricity and the functions of the nerves are especially famous, and he may be said to have created experimental physiology. Among his works are: *Untersuchungen über tierische Elektrizität*, 1848–84; *Ueber tierische Bewegung*, 1851; *Vorlesungen über die Physik des organischen Stolfwechsels*, 1900. *See* Engelmann's *Gedächtnisrede*, 1898.

**Dubovka,** a tn. of Stalingrad gov., Russia, an important port on the Volga, with fishing, fruit and wine industries. Pop. 16,530.

**Dubréka,** or **Doubréka,** a station of French Guinea, W. Africa, under direct Fr. gov. since 1882. It has much trade with the interior, and good coffee plantations.

**Dubuque,** a city and port of Iowa, U.S.A., co. seat of Dubuque co., situated on the Mississippi. It is the seat of an Episc. and Rom. Cath. bishop. The town is the oldest in the state, being now a manufacturing centre, with saw-works, wagon and boiler-making, tobacco, etc. The lead deposits which are now abandoned were formerly worked by the Indians. Pop. 41,679.

**Du Camp, Maxime** (1822–94), a Fr. poet and man of letters, son of Théodore (d. 1824). He travelled widely in the East and Europe. One of the founders and directors of the *Revue de Paris* (1851). His works include : *Les Convulsions de Paris,* 1878–79 ; *Le Crépuscule,* 1893 ; *Mémoires d'un suicidé* (novel), 1853 ; *Les Chants modernes,* 1855; *Les Convictions,* 1858 (poems).

**Du Cane, Sir Edmund Frederick** (1830–1903), an English soldier and prison reformer ; second lieutenant of R.E. (1848). From 1851–56 he organised convict labour in Swan R. colony (W. Australia), was director of convict prisons (1863), succeeding Henderson as chairman of the board (1869), and inspector of military prisons. D. reorganised the county and borough prisons, which were brought under government control (1878) owing to his efforts, and produced the first ' Black Book ' list, 1877. He retired from the army as major-general (1887). He contributed to periodicals, and wrote *The Punishment and Prevention of Crime,* 1885. See *Biography,* 1883 ; Porter, *History of the R.E.,* 1889.

**Du Cange, Charles Dufresne, Sieur** (1610–88), a Fr. scholar and historian, educated at the Jesuit College of Amiens, later studying law at Orleans. His most famous work is *Glossarium ad scriptores mediæ et Infimæ Latinitatis,* 1678 (completed later by Carpentier, Henschel, Faure, 1884–87), followed by a similar *Glossarium . . . Græcitatis,* 1688. He edited many Byzantine historians. Paulus Silentiarius, 1670 ; Zonaras, 1687 ; *Chronicon Paschale,* 1688. Other works were *Hist. de l'empire de Constantinople sous les empereurs français,* 1657 ; *Historia Byzantina,* 1680 ; *Les Familles d'Outre-Mer,* 1669. See Life by Hardouin, 1849, Fougère, 1852 ; Dufresne d'Aubigny, *Mémoires historiques . . . de Du Cange;* *Nouvelle Biog. Générale.*

**Ducat,** a gold coin, which came into currency about A.D. 1100, and seems to have been named from a word in the inscription which the Apulian coins of 1140 bore : ' Sit tibi, Christe, datus, quem tu regis, iste ducatus ' (Lord, thou rulest this duchy ; to thee be it dedicated !). The D. which Venice struck in 1280–84 later became known as the zecchino or sequin. Introduced in the fourteenth century to Hungary and Bohemia, and adopted in 1559 by the imperial diet of Germany into the monetary system of the empire, its currency later extended all over W. Europe. The value was about 9s. 4d., but Ds. varied in weight and amount of alloy. Italian silver Ds. were worth 3s. 4d.

**Duccio** (c. 1260–c. 1340), son of Buoninsegna, and Italian painter, was the first of the Sienese painters to abandon the Byzantine style of painting, and may justly be regarded as the founder of the Sienese school. It was he who began the decoration of the pavement of the Sienese cathedral with figures in 'chiaroscuro,' and the famous altar-piece he executed for this cathedral between 1308 and 1311 is the only unquestioned work of his still remaining. Painted on both sides, this huge picture (14 ft. by 7 ft.) represents on the one face the ' Virgin and Child,' and on the other twenty-seven episodes from the life of Christ. D. worked also for churches in Florence, Pisa, Lucca, and Pistoja, painting often on gold grounds and left his glorious invention of ' chiaroscuro ' pictures in marble as a legacy to the Lorenzetti and his other disciples.

**Du Chaillu, Paul Belloni** (1835–1903), an African explorer and author, of Fr. Huguenot parentage, educated in Paris. He early went to the Gabun country, Africa, where his father was a trader. After spending some years in America, he undertook a botanic and zoologic expedition to the Ogowé basin (1855–59). His descriptions of the Abongo pygmies and gorillas (of which he was the first to secure specimens) of the interior in *Explorations and Adventures in Equatorial Africa,* 1861, were discredited by many as mere exaggerations. Later investigations, however, proved the truth of his natural history discoveries. In 1863–65 he visited Ashango Land, and the Ngunye Falls, the resulting work being *A Journey to Ashango Land,* 1867. Du C. explored N. Europe (1872–3), and travelled in Russia (1898–1902). Other works are : *Lost in the Jungle,* 1869 ; *The Country of the Dwarfs,* 1870 ; *The Land of the Midnight Sun,* 1881 ; *The Viking Age,* 1889, and *Ivor the Viking,* 1893, attempts at proving the Scandinavian origin of the British ; *The World of the Great*

*Forest*, 1900. See *Proc. Zool. Soc.*, i., 1905.

**Duchange, Gaspard** (1662–1756), a clever Fr. etcher and engraver, *b.* at Paris. He was a pupil of Jean Audran, and became one of the most noted engravers of his period. The ' Io,' ' Danaë,' and ' Leda of Correggio ' are three of his most celebrated works.

**Duchesne, Père,** *see* HÉBERT, JACQUES RENÉ.

**Duchy of Lancaster,** *see* LANCASTER, HOUSE AND DUCHY OF.

**Ducis, Jean François** (1733–1816), a Fr. dramatic poet, chiefly noted for his adaptations of Shakespeare's plays for the Fr. stage. He succeeded Voltaire in the Fr. Academy, 1779. D. paved the way for Lemercier and the Romantic school. His *Collected Works* appeared in 1827. *See* Leroy, *Etude* . . ., 1832 ; Campenon, *Mémoires* . . ., 1824 ; Villemain, *Cours de Littérature* ; Lacroix, *Hist. de l'influence de Shakespeare*, 1856 ; Jusserand, *Shakespeare en France*, 1898.

**Duck,** the name given to birds of the family Anatidæ, which contains also both swans and geese ; it should properly be applied to the female, the male bird being a drake, but it is frequently used to include both sexes. The species are aquatic and have short webbed feet and scaly legs ; the bill is broad, depressed and rounded at the tip. There is a great variety exhibited in the coloration of the fifty odd species, and many are very handsome birds. They inhabit N. regions of the world, and as they frequent lakes and seas, their diet consists of such creatures as fish, frogs, and worms. *A. boscas*, the wild duck or mallard, is the species from which all domesticated Ds. have taken their origin. (For various forms of D. see special articles.)

**Duckbill,** or **Duckmole,** *see* ORNITHORHYNCHUS.

**Ducking-stool,** a strongly made wooden arm-chair, fixed to the end of a long wooden beam, in which offenders, such as scolding wives, shrews, and sometimes quarrelsome married couples, were seated, fastened in by iron bands, and immersed in water, the beam being placed at the edge of the pond, or river, and working on the see-saw principle. In many districts dishonest bakers and brewers were punished by this ducking system. The earliest record of it is at the beginning of the seventeenth century, and it was in use in England as late as the nineteenth century, the last recorded cases being a Mrs. Gamble at Plymouth in 1808, Jenny Pipes, 1809, and Sarah Leeke, 1817, of Leominster, though the latter

sentence could not be carried out as there was no water in the pond at the time.

**Duckweed,** the British name for the native species of *Lemna*, the chief genus of Lemnaceæ. The plants are perennials, and are found swimming freely in ponds and tanks. The British species are known as *L. minor*, *L. gibba, L. trisulca*, and *L. polyrhiza.*

**Duckworth, Sir John Thomas** (1748–1817), an Eng. admiral, served in N. America, and the W. Indies. In 1794 he won distinction in Howe's great victory over the Fr. off Ushant. In 1800 he became rear-admiral ; commander-in-chief at Jamaica, 1802. D. defeated the Fr. off Saint Domingo (1806). He was sent to dictate terms to the Porte (1807), and failing in his

A DUCKING-STOOL

mission retreated from the Turks, forcing the passage of the Dardanelles. From 1810–13 he was governor of Newfoundland, and knighted, 1813. See *Naval Chron.*, xviii. ; Ralfe, *Naval Biog.*, ii.

**Duclaux, Madame Agnes Mary Frances,** *née* Robinson (*b.* 1857), an Eng. poetess and novelist. She married Prof. James Darmesteter, and, after his death, Prof. Duclaux, 1901. Her works include *Arden* (a novel), and *Life of Emily Brontë*, 1883 ; *An Italian Garden, A Book of Songs*, 1886 ; *The Crowned Hippolytus* (from Euripides), *with New Poems*, 1881 ; *Collected Poems*, 1902 ; *The Return to Nature*, 1904 ; *Life of Emile Duclaux*, 1907 ; *The French Ideal*, 1911 ; *Madame de Sévigné*, 1914 ; *A Short History of France*, 1918 ; *Life of Victor Hugo*, 1920 ; *La Pensée de Robert Browning*, 1922 ; *Life of Racine*, 1925 ; *A Portrait of Pascal*, 1927.

**Duclos, Charles Pinot** (1704–1772), a Fr. author, *b.* at Dinan, Brittany, and was sent at an early age to study at Paris. His first publication of importance was his *History of Louis XI.*; when the post of historiographer of France became vacant by the retirement of Voltaire, D. was appointed to take his place.

**Ducrow, Andrew** (1793–1842), an equestrian performer, son of a professional ' strong man,' known as ' the Flemish Hercules.' By 1808 he was chief equestrian and rope-dancer at Astley's Amphitheatre. After touring abroad (1814), he appeared at Covent Garden (1823), and Drury Lane (1824 and later). See Genest, *English Stage*, ix.

**Ductility,** the property of some metals, such as gold, silver, copper, iron, etc., which renders them capable of being extended by hammering or drawing, without breaking. Glass also possesses the property when in a semi-molten state, and quartz, when in an intensely hot state, can be drawn out into such thin fibres as to be invisible. Wollaston showed that by forming a platinum core inside a silver wire, afterwards drawing out the silver wire, he could, by dissolving the silver coating, obtain a finer platinum wire than he could otherwise have done by drawing out the platinum directly. The wire was so fine that it could only be seen when an electric current was sent through it and made it glow.

**Ductless Glands.** The function of a gland is the secretion of an individual product, which in most cases passes out by means of a duct; in the case of the ductless glands, however, the secretion passes into the blood by means of capillaries or lymphatic vessels. Examples of ductless glands are the thyroid, parathyroid, thymus, spleen and adrenals. The thyroid gland in the embryonic condition is connected with the pharynx, but by degrees this sac becomes divided from it until at length it is a distinct body. When the internal secretion of the thyroid becomes excessive, it may result in goitre, and when insufficient it may produce cretinism. (*See also* BIO-CHEMISTRY.)

**Duddingston,** a par., vil., and loch in Edinburgh. The vil. is noted as having been the headquarters of Prince Charles before the battle of Prestonpans. The lock lies at the base of Arthur's Seat. Pop. par. 4570.

**Duddon,** a riv. of England, which rises in the Wrynose, on the borders of Cumberland and Lancashire. At Broughton it widens out into an estuary of over 2 m. wide, eventually losing itself in the Irish Sea. Salmon and trout are found above the mouth.

**Duderstadt,** a tn. of Hanover, Prussia, with two beautiful four teenth-century Gothic churches, fif-teenth- to sixteenth-century town-hall and many other old buildings. Pop. 6500.

**Dudevant, Madame,** *see* SAND, GEORGE.

**Dudley,** a market tn. and municipal co., and parl. bor., 18 m. W.N.W. of Birmingham on the Great Western and London Midland and Scottish railways, in a detached part of Worcestershire, England. The D. canal communicates with the Birmingham canal and the R. Severn. Its active industries of iron- and brass-founding, engineering, glass- and brick-making have sprung up because D. is the centre of a great coal-mining district. Abundant limestone and fire-clay are found. There are ruins of an eighth-century castle, a free grammar school, a training college, and fossils of great geological interest. There are extensive caverns under the castle and the scanty ruins of a priory. The new town-hall is a war memorial. Pop. 55,894.

**Dudley, Dud** (1599–1684), an Eng. ironmaster, the originator of the use of pit coal for fuel in place of wood, thereby causing a change in iron-making.

**Dudley, Sir Edmund,** *see under* EMPSON.

**Dudley, Sir Henry Bate** (1745–1824), an Eng. journalist, *b.* at Fenny Compton, Warwickshire. On completing his education he took orders and succeeded his father in the living of North Fambridge, spending most of his time, however, in London, and leading a life of pleasure. He was one of the first editors of the *Morning Post*, established 1772, his contributions frequently leading him into quarrels, and earning for him the nickname of the ' Fighting Parson.' D. also founded the *Morning Herald*, the *Courrier de l'Europe*, and the *English Chronicle*.

**Dudley, Thomas** (1576–1658), a British colonial governor of Massachusetts, *b.* at Northampton, England. In 1630 he sailed to America with Governor John Winthrop, to settle in New England, D. himself being appointed deputy-governor. D. had great influence in Massachusetts, and was governor four times ; he was one of the earliest promoters of Harvard College. He had little religious tolerance, being a stern Puritan. His son, *Joseph Dudley* (1647–1720), colonial governor of Massachusetts, was *b.* in Roxbury, Massachusetts, and graduated at Harvard College, 1665. He was sent to London to prevent the revocation of the Charter of Massachusetts by Charles II. He secretly used his influence against his mission, to his own advancement. His whole rule was unpopular and his actions dishonourable.

**Dudley Limestone,** *see* WENLOCK BEDS.

**Dudweiler,** a tn. of Germany in the Prussian prov. of Rhineland, situated

on the Sulzbach, 4 m. N.E. of Saar-
brücken. There are coal mines, iron
works, and manufs. of fire-proof
bricks. Pop. 23,550.

**Duel** and **Duelling** (Lat. *duellum*,
from *duo*, two), in modern significance an arranged combat between
two persons to avenge an insult,
reflection upon the honour, or to
settle matters of private dispute for
which the law provides no remedy or
such as is not deemed satisfactory.
The person aggrieved is the challenger, and the preliminaries and all
the arrangements of the combat are
settled by the ' seconds,' the supporters of each party. The choice of
weapons lies with the challenged
party. The combat of two single
persons to decide great questions
dates back to prehistoric times ; the
tales of Hector and Achilles, of David

ORDEAL COMBAT OR DUEL
(Royal MS.)

and Goliath indicated the practice,
but the D. proper must be traced to
a Teutonic institution, the judicial
combat of ' wager of battle,' a form of
legal trial of questions in dispute,
which was regarded as an appeal to
God to decide the justice of the
quarrel or dispute. The custom
spread over N.W. Europe and in 516
the Burgundian King Gundobald
legalised the judicial D. Duelling was
condemned by Pope Nicholas I (858–
67) and by many succeeding Popes.
The judicial combat was only formally
abolished by Act of Parliament in
1818, after the case of Thornton *v.*
Ashford. In 1385 a judicial combat
in the presence of Charles VI. of
France between one Jacques Legris
and Jean Caronge led to the defeat
of the former and the subsequent
discovery of the real guilty party, a
blow to the popular belief in the justice of the D. from which it did not

recover. Duelling thus came to its
present form as a means of settling
private quarrels, especially among
the gently born or the military
classes ; it was most prevalent in
France, especially from the time of
Francis I. It had grown to such
an extent and so many men of noble
birth were slain that in 1626 Richelieu
confiscated the property of duellists
and banished them from France.
Stronger measures were required
and beheading was resorted to. In
Great Britain, duelling did not become fashionable till the Restoration.
The historic fatal D. between Lord
Mohun and the Duke of Hamilton is
familiar from Thackeray's *Esmond*.
In the eyes of the law, a challenge to
a D. is a breach of the peace, a fatal
result is a homicide, whether murder
or manslaughter, and the seconds are
accessories. Many historic Ds. have
been fought, as those between Pitt
and Tierney, Canning and Lord
Castlereagh, O'Connell and D'Esterre,
the Duke of Wellington and Lord
Winchilsea. In 1840 Lord Cardigan
wounded Captain Tuckett, was tried
by the House of Lords and acquitted.
At the present day duelling still occurs
in France, but with rarely fatal or
serious results. In Germany, apart
from the fencing bouts (*Mensur*) of
the various student corps or clubs at
the universities, the D. is a matter
of serious importance for military
officers. Forbidden by law, an officer
who refuses a challenge, after a
decision of a court of honour, must
still fight or leave the army.

**Duet** (from It. *duetto*, and Lat. *duo*,
two), in music denotes a composition
designed for two singers or two
players. The term is not properly
applied to a composition performed
by one instrumentalist and one singer,
for it is likely that the former will play
a subordinate part (*i.e.* an accompaniment). Ds. may be written for
similar or different instruments.

**Dufaure, Jules Armand Stanislaus**
(1798–1881), a Fr. statesman.
Under the premiership of Guizot he
became Councillor of State (1836) and
Minister of Public Works (1839). In
1876 he was made Premier, a position
which he resigned in 1879 at the
termination of MacMahon's presidency. *See* Life by Picot (1883).

**Duff,** or **Wilson Islands,** a group of
eleven small islands in the Pacific
Ocean, lying to the N.E. of Santa
Cruz.

**Duff, Alexander** (1806–78) a Scottish missionary, *b.* near Pitlochry,
Perthshire, and ordained first missionary to India, 1829. Established
schools and colleges in India in which
religious teaching was combined with
science, literature, and other branches

of Western learning. He first encountered some opposition, but this soon died down, and he was upheld by government officials. D. was one of the founders of the University of Calcutta, and helped to start the *Calcutta Review* in 1844, editing it till 1849. *See* Life by G. Smith.

**Duff, James Grant** (1789–1858), an historian, *b.* at Banff, Scotland. In 1818 he was appointed to the important post of resident of Sattara, the centre of the Mahratta confederacy. His *History of the Mahrattas* was written on his return to Scotland.

**Duff, John Wight**, a professor and author, *b.* at Dundee in 1866. From 1891–93 he was assistant Professor of Greek at Aberdeen, and from 1893–98 Professor of Classics and English at Newcastle. A celebrated scholar, he has published *A Literary History of Rome*, 1909, 1927 ; *Writers of Rome*, 1923 ; besides various articles in journals and magazines, consisting of reviews, papers on Gk. travel, translations from Latin, etc.

**Duffel**, a Belgian commune, situated to the S.E. of Antwerp, on the Nethe. It was bombarded by the Gers. in 1914. Pop. about 10,000.

**Dufferin, Hélène Selena Sheridan, Lady** (1807–67), a song-writer, granddaughter of Richard Brinsley Sheridan, and mother of the Marquis of D. and Ava. Her songs and verses were published anonymously, the chief being *The Charming Woman* and the *Irish Emigrant*. See *Memoir* written by her son, 1894.

**Dufferin and Ava, Frederick Temple Hamilton-Temple Blackwood, first Marquis of** (1826–1902), a British diplomatist, *b.* at Florence. In 1860 was appointed British commissioner in Syria, where his ability and judgment were warmly recognised. From 1872–78 was Governor-General of Canada, and during this period inspired the several provinces with the true spirit of confederation and with the idea of a great nation within the empire. In 1879 became British ambassador at St. Petersburg, afterwards filling the same position at Constantinople, Rome, and Paris. From 1884–88 he was Viceroy of India. In 1897 he was induced by Whitaker-Wright to accept the chairmanship of the London and Globe Finance Corporation, and on learning that it was in difficulties, courageously explained the position to a meeting of shareholders, his own honour being unimpeached. This disaster, together with the death of his eldest son, wounded in the S. African War, embittered his last years. *See* Life by Sir A. Lyall, 1905.

**Duffield**, a small tn. and par. in Derbyshire, England, situated on the R. Derwent. It is 4½ m. N.W. of the town of Derby. Pop. 2200.

**Dufftown**, a vil. in Banffshire, N.B., founded by James Duff, Earl of Fife, in 1817. Popular resort for invalids. Has distilleries and limeworks. Pop. 1500.

**Duffy, Sir Charles Gavan** (1816–1903), at an early age drifted into journalism. Going to Dublin to study for the Bar, he founded in 1842 the *Nation*, which from the first became the organ of Young Ireland. In season and out D. therein demanded the cleavage of the union, and sought to band his countrymen together to re-establish, by force if necessary, the Irish Parliament. For preaching open rebellion D. was arrested in 1848, but the juries disagreeing, he was discharged. He revived the newspaper after his release, but the cause of Irish unity at that time seeming hopeless, in 1855 he abandoned the struggle. He went to Australia, entered the Victorian Parliament, and, after holding minor offices, in 1871 became Prime Minister for a short time, and later Speaker of the House of Assembly. He wrote several books on Ireland, and issued a volume of interesting *Conversations with Carlyle*.

**Dufourspitze**, the highest peak of Mont Rosa in the central zone of the Middle Alps. Has an altitude of 15,215 ft.

**Dufrénoy, Pierre Armand Petit** (1792–1857), a noted Fr. mineralogist and geologist, became Professor of Mineralogy and director of the Ecole des Mines, and Professor of Geology at the Ecole des Ponts et Chaussées. In conjunction with Elie de Beaumont, with whom he travelled through France, England, and Spain, D. published, *Voyage métallurgique en Angleterre*, *Mémoires pour servir à une Description géologique de la France*, and *Explication de la Carte géologique de la France* (3 vols.), 1873.

**Dufresne, Charles**, *see* DU CANGE.

**Dugdale, Sir William** (1605–85), garter king-of-arms, at an early age showed a love for antiquarian research. Through friendly influences he was in 1638 appointed a pursuivant-extraordinary, and in the following year rouge croix pursuivant with rooms in the Heralds' College and a salary of £200 a year. During the Civil War he went from library to library quietly amassing material for the important works upon which he was engaged, viz. the *Monasticon Anglicanum*, the first volume of which appeared in 1655, and the third and last eighteen years later ; the *Antiquities of Warwickshire*, 1658 ; and *The Baronage of England*, 1675–76.

D. is not always to be relied upon for accuracy, but beyond all question he rendered valuable service to students of antiquarianism. His autobiography was first published in 1713, but the edition to consult is that of 1827, to which is added his diary and correspondence.

**Dugong, or Halicore,** a genus of the mammalian order Sirenia, or sea-cows. The few species are aquatic, usually marine, and in diet they are herbivorous; the existing forms are found in the Red Sea, Indian Ocean, and near Australia. They bear some resemblance to whales, *e.g.* in the notched tail, the reduced nasal bones, lack of posterior limbs, and in the short neck, but in most of their characteristics they are quite unlike these mammals. The D. attains a length of eight feet, and it is said to have originated the idea of the mermaid, for the female has two mammæ, holds its young to its breast by means of one of its nailless flippers, and often raises its head out of the water. The teeth of this animal are five or six molars on each jaw, two incisors on the upper and four on the lower jaw.

**Duguay-Trouin, René** (1673–1736), a famous Fr. sea-captain, *b.* at St. Malo. Originally intended for the church, he abandoned the idea, and went to sea in 1689 on the outbreak of the war with England and Holland. He displayed great courage and made brilliant captures of both Eng. and Dutch ships. In 1697 he entered the Fr. navy as commander, distinguishing himself in the War of the Spanish Succession, his most famous action being the capture of Rio de Janeiro in 1711. He subsequently served with the army, attaining the rank of lieutenant-general. *See* his *Mémoires*, 1742, and Lives by La Landelle and Poulain.

**Du Guesclin,** *see* GUESCLIN, BERTRAND DU.

**Dühring, Eugen Karl** (1833–1901), a Ger. political economist and philosophical writer, *b.* at Berlin. His doctrine is in many points akin to that of Comte and Feuerbach, and in economics he is a disciple of the American writer, H. C. Carey. He teaches an ethical communism in political economy and attacks the Darwinian principle of the struggle for existence. His chief works are: *Kapital und Arbeit, Kritische Geschichte der Philosophie,* and *Der Ersetz der Religion durch Vollkommeneres. See* H. Druskowitz, *Eugen Dührung,* 1888, and Life by Döll, 1892.

**Duikerbok, or** *Cephalophus,* a genus of small African antelopes (*q.v.*) with crested heads, large muzzles, and short, conical horns in the males only.

**Duilius, Gaius,** a famous Rom. general, who defeated the Carthaginians in a great sea fight (260 B.C.). By using grappling irons, he deprived the enemy of their advantage in naval tactics.

**Duirinish,** a parish in the N.W. of the island of Skye, in Inverness-shire, Scotland, 18 m. long by 15 m. wide, area 80,067 acres, pop. 2621. Lady Grange, a Jacobite heroine, was buried near a pillar called 'Trying Stone of Trumpan.' Dunvegan Castle is the seat of the Macleods of Macleod. This par. was celebrated for its pipers. The hills called 'Macleod's Tables' rise from the peninsula of D.

**Duisburg,** on the r. b. of the Lower Rhine, Germany, combined in 1905 with Ruhrort and Meiderich to form one community (pop. 272,200) in the vicinity of the Ruhr coal-field, which has favoured the growth of iron and machine-building industries. The chemical, tobacco, and textile industries are also represented. The combined harbours form the largest river port in Europe, and export coal and wrought iron. In 1860 D. and Ruhrort had together 22,000 inhabs. The tn. was occupied by Fr. troops from March 1921 till Aug. 1925.

**Dujardin, Félix** (1801–60), a Fr. naturalist, wrote a *Natural History of Infusorial Animalcules* (1841), and a *Manual of the Microscope* (1843), in the use of which he was eminently successful. D. was the first to classify the Foraminifera with the Rhizopoda and to investigate satisfactorily the nature of protoplasm.

**Duke** (Fr. *duc,* Lat. *dux,* a leader), first came into use as a formal title when Constantine called military governors of provinces either counts or Ds., to distinguish them from the administrators of justice and finance. Under the Franks the Ds., who often ruled several provinces, became very powerful, whilst the counts, who had once been the most distinguished of the provincial commanders or Ds., now became their lieutenants. Thus the E. Frankish empire was split up into the dukedoms of Swabia, Saxony, Bavaria, Franconia, and Lorraine, and similarly the W. into the duchies of Aquitaine, Burgundy, Gascony, Normandy, and the Ile de France. Although with the strengthening of monarchies the substantial powers of the Ds. waned, the latter still rank next to princes of royal blood. The Black Prince was the first Eng. D., being granted by his father the duchy of Cornwall (1337), whilst the first Scottish king to confer the title was Robert III., who made his two sons Ds. of Rothesay and Albany respectively (1398).

**D. C. L. I.** (Duke of Cornwall's

Light Infantry) formerly the 32nd and 46th Regiments, which were linked together in 1881 to form the D. C. L. I. The 32nd were formed in 1702 as Marines, and were present at capture of Gibraltar in 1704. Served in Spain in 1705 under Lords Peterborough and Galway. Fought at Dettingen (1743) and Fontenoy (1745). Under Moore it fought at Corunna, and under Wellington during several battles of the Peninsular Campaign. For its distinguished conduct during the Indian Mutiny it was made into a Light Infantry regiment. The 46th were raised in 1741, and served for many years in America and W. Indies, India and Crimea Campaign, also Egyptian Campaign of 1882, Nile 1884–5, and S. Africa 1899–1902. Raised fifteen battalions for Great War, which served in France, Flanders, Macedonia, Palestine and Aden.

**Duke of York's Monument,** erected by public subscription to the second son of George III., 1830–33. The monument keeps guard over the space of ground where George IV. built Carlton House in his regent days. It is at the end of Waterloo Place on the steps leading into St. James's Park. Made of Scottish granite, the column (designed by Wyatt) is 124 ft. high. It is surmounted by a bronze statue of the duke, 14 ft. high, executed by Westmacott. A staircase leads to the gallery, from which a fine view of the West End of London and Surrey hills can be obtained, but of recent years it is no longer used.

**Duke of York's School, Chelsea,** called also the **Royal Military Asylum,** was founded in 1801 by Frederick Duke of York (1763–1827) for soldiers' sons. In 1909 it was removed to Dover.

**Duke of York's Theatre,** in St. Martin's Lane. It was opened in 1892 as the 'Trafalgar,' but later received its present name. Among the more notable plays first staged here were Pinero's *Letty;* Barrie's *Peter Pan* and *What Every Woman Knows;* Galsworthy's *Justice;* the farce *Brewster's Millions;* and the detective drama *Arsène Lupin.*

**Duker, Carl Andreas** (1670–1752), a Ger. classical scholar, studied under Perizonius at Franeker and subsequently brought out the second edition of Perizonius' *Origines Babylonicæ et Ægyptiacæ* (1736). D.'s *magnum opus* was his edition of *Thucydides,* 1731.

**Dukeries,** *see* WORKSOP.

**Duke Town,** *see* CALABAR.

**Duke University,** a co-educational institution for higher education estab. in Durham, N. Carolina, in 1924, and named after James B. Duke, from whose endowment fund the cost of its establishment was defrayed. The premises have recently been considerably expanded by the addition of a science building, a chapel, library, dormitories, etc. It is attended by about 1500 students annually, and has endowment funds of over 20 million dollars. A feature of the University is its medical school.

**Dukhobors, or Doukhobors,** are a Christian community of nonconformist Russian peasants. Their name means 'spirit fighters,' and was applied to them by the Orthodox priests with the implication that they warred against the Spirit of God, but a review of their doctrine and practice shows that they make an earnest endeavour to realise something of the Gospel conception of love and universal brotherhood. Equality, peace, and loving-kindness are their ideals, and although they assemble for public worship, they counsel silent prayer and attach small weight to outward ceremony. Alexander I. banished them to Tauris, and Nicholas I. drove them from their new homes to Transcaucasia (1840–50). Their refusal to obey the law afforded a pretext for this persecution. In this barren region they nevertheless prospered, by dint of sober living and dogged perseverance. In 1895 they burnt their arms to show their disapproval of compulsory military service, and were subjected to the barbarous tyrannies of the Cossack soldiers. Eventually through the offices of Tolstoy and the Society of Friends in England, some 8000 were despatched as emigrants to Canada (1898–99), where they have been given territory in Saskatchewan.

**Dukinfield,** a municipal bor. of Cheshire, England, 6 m. E. of Manchester. It is situated in the centre of a colliery and manufacturing district. There are cotton and calico printing mills, iron foundries, and brick and tile works. Pop. 19,493.

**Dulac, Edmund,** illustrator; *b.* Oct. 22, 1882, at Toulouse. As 'Edmond' D., educated at Toulouse University, and unwillingly studied law for two years; for three years attended drawing and painting classes at Toulouse art school, and for three weeks at Julian's in Paris. Illustrated books since 1905. Exhibited portraits at Paris salon, 1904–5. Has exhibited portraits annually at Leicester Galleries, London, since 1907. In 1912 he became 'Edmund' D., a naturalised British subject. Illustrations published include: *The Brontë Novels,* 1905; *Arabian Nights,* 1907; Shakespeare's *Tempest,* 1908;

*Rubáiyát of Omar Khayyám*, 1909; *The Sleeping Beauty and other Tales*, 1910; Poe's *The Bells and other Poems*, 1911; *Edmund Dulac's Fairy Book*, 1916; Hawthorne's *Tanglewood Tales*, 1918; weekly cartoons in *The Outlook*, 1919: *The Kingdom of the Pearl*. 1920.

**Dulcigno**, a tn. and port of Montenegro, situated on the Adriatic Sea, 12 m. S.E. of Antivari. It is built on a rocky cape, and enclosed by forests and hills, which combine to give it a most picturesque appearance. D. was ceded to Montenegro by Turkey in 1880 in consequence of a naval demonstration under Admiral Seymour. In 1919, with Montenegro it became Yugo-Slavian. The old quarter is walled and has a mediæval castle. Pop. 3074.

**Dulcimer**, one of the oldest musical instruments, being found in Assyrian mural decorations. The different notes are obtained by striking wires, stretched with tuning pegs across a horizontal sound-chest, with two cork-headed hammers. It is the prototype of the modern piano.

**Duleepsinhji, Kumar Shri,** Indo-Eng. cricketer, *b.* June 13, 1905; nephew of the famous cricketer of a former generation, K. S. Ranjitsinhji, now Maharaja of Nawanagar. Educ. at Cheltenham and Cambridge. At Fenner's in 1927 made record undergraduate score of 254 not out against Middlesex. Played as ' twelfth man ' in tests in Eng. against Australia, 1930; and made 173 in first innings of second match, thus beating record of ' Ranji ' against Australia.

**Dülken**, a tn. of Ger., in the Prussian Rhine prov., 11 m. S.W. of Crefeld, and 20 m. W of Düsseldorf. It has manufactures of silk, velvet, and cotton, and there are important iron works. Pop. 15,220.

**Dulmen**, a tn. of Prussia, in the prov. of Westphalia, 17 m. S.W. of Munster. There are iron mines and blast furnaces in the neighbourhood. Pop. 8850.

**Dulong, Pierre Louis** (1785–1838). Fr. physicist and surgeon. Pupil of Berthollet and Thenard. Early distinguished for the discovery of chloride of nitrogen, in the preparation of which he lost an eye and two fingers. Collaborated with Berzelius in the analysis of water by the method of passing a current of dry hydrogen over red-hot copper oxide. But it is rather as a physicist that he acquired fame, particularly by his experiments in the theory of heat, to which he applied himself constantly from 1818. He also evolved the air manometer for measuring the density of gases and the cathetometer for measuring

small differences of level of different liquids in tubes.

**Dulse**, the popular name given to two species of edible seaweed, *Rhodymenia palmata* and *Iridœa edulis*.

**Duluth**, an important lake port of Minnesota, U.S.A., situated on steep and picturesque slopes at the W. end of Lake Superior. It is second only to New York in commercial tonnage handled. It exports iron ore, wheat, butter and eggs, automobiles, and coal from the rich agricultural and iron-mining regions of the N.W. The Minnesota Steel Co. mills are here. Hydroelectric power contributes to the manufacture of steel and the milling of flour. The city, which is governed by commission, has 442 acs. of parks and 21 m. of scenic drives. Pop. (1870) 3131; (1930) 101,463.

**Dulverton**, a par. and tn. of W. Somersetshire, Eng., 21 m. W. of Taunton. It is a fishing and hunting resort, and is the headquarters of the W. Somerset Yeomanry. Pop. 1298.

**Dulwich**, a suburb of London, in the metropolitan bor. of Camberwell. The D. College, one of the important Eng. public schools, was founded by Edward Alleyn in 1606, and was formally opened in 1619 in the presence of the Lord Chancellor Bacon and numerous other eminent men. In documents signed by Edward Alleyn in 1626, immediately prior to his decease, it was intended that the school should educate eighty boys, twelve of whom were to be poor scholars. The remainder should be the children of D. residents, and ' towne or foreign schollers,' who would pay a fee appointed by the master and wardens. The college now comprises an Upper Dulwich College and a Lower Alleyn's School. There is a valuable collection of pictures which was bequeathed by Sir P. F. Bourgeois, R.A., in 1811. It contains several Murillos and valuable pictures from the Dutch school.

**Duma, The,** or **Gosudarstvennaya Duma,** the Russ. national parliament. It formed the Lower House, the Upper being the Council of the Empire. It was created in 1905, when Czar Nicholas II. granted his celebrated constitution. The first D., in which a Radical party, known as Constitutional Democrats, preponderated, was opened in 1906, and dissolved in two months. Its members had no experience of parliamentary procedure, and expected at once to carry such drastic reforms as the expropriation of the landlords and universal suffrage. The second was convened on March 5, 1907, and only lived till June 16, 1907. The temper of the House was again highly progressive and socialistic. It clamoured for the abolition of the field courts-martial and refused to be put off with the leisurely reforms proposed by Stolypin, Minister of the Interior. An excuse for the dissolution was found in the implication of certain Socialist members in what was called a treasonable plot to suborn the army. The third D., which was convoked in Nov. 1907, sat till 1912. This was elected in accordance with an imperial *ukaz*, which, contrary to the famous Oct. manifesto of 1905, had tampered with the electoral law in such a way as to secure a majority for the moderate party, known as Octobrists, and the reactionary Right. In its early sessions, however, this parliament paved the way for a class of peasant proprietors by partially sweeping away the communal ownership of land, and also passed measures dictated by a spirit of religious toleration. The mode of election was extremely elaborate, having been carefully designed to give every advantage to the Russian as opposed to the foreign and subject populations, and also to the wealthy, conservative and property-owning, as opposed to the peasant, democratic and labouring classes. Seven great cities, including St. Petersburg and Moscow, elected direct representatives, but elsewhere the more complex system of electing members, through electoral colleges, was in operation. The Russian revolution in 1917 and the establishment of the Soviet system of government, under the practical dictatorship of Lenin and Trotsky, brought a dramatic close to the history of the Fourth Duma. (*See* RUSSIAN REVOLUTION.)

**Dumaguete**, the cap. tn. of the prov. of Negros Oriental, island of Negros, Philippine Is., on the Tañon Strait. It lies in a fertile agricultural district, and is an important commercial centre and the seat of the Sillman Institute. Pop. 16,336.

**Dumangas**, a city in the prov. of Iloilo, Panay, Philippine Islands. In 1903 it was annexed to Barotac Nuevo. Pop. 12,428.

**Dumanjug**, a tn. in the prov. of Cebú, island of Cebú, Philippine Is., on the W. coast at the mouth of the D. river. Pop. 23,671.

**Dumas, Alexandre, père** (1803–70), while serving as a clerk to the Duc d'Orléans, devoted his leisure to play-writing. His success was immediate, for the vaudeville, *La Chasse et l'Amour*, which he wrote in collaboration with two friends, was produced at the Ambigu Comique in the

autumn of 1825. Thus encouraged, he composed plays, writing comedy, drama, tragedy, in prose and in verse, with equal facility, until the production of *Madame de Chamblay* in 1868. Some of the plays were good; others were absurdly bombastic; some, such as *Kean*, frankly (and unconsciously) ridiculous; but whatever their merits or demerits, the author's knowledge of the stage was generally equal to making them successful for the moment. It is, however, unnecessary to devote any space to the consideration of these works, for it is not D. the playwright

ALEXANDRE DUMAS (PÈRE)

who is now remembered, but D. the novelist. In fiction his first effort was *Souvenirs d'Anthony* (1835), a collection of short stories, and this was followed by *Isabel de Bavière*, and *Acté* (1839). The most famous of all his books is the *Mousquetaires* series—*Les Trois Mousquetaires* (8 vols.), 1844; *Vingt Ans Après* (10 vols.), 1845; and *Le Vicomte de Bragelonne* (26 vols.), 1848–50. The two other principal series are: (1) *Joseph Balsamo*, 1846–48; *Le Collier de la Reine*, 1850; *Ange Pitou*, 1853; and *La Comtesse de Charny*, 1853–55; (2) *La Reine Margot*, 1845; *La Dame de Monsoreau*, 1846, and *Les Quarante-Cinq*, 1848; *Le Comte de Monte Cristo* appeared in twelve volumes in 1845. In the novels mentioned D. is at his best. ' I seem to see myself set on a pedestal which trembles as if it were founded on the sands,' the great man said one day towards the end of his life in a moment of despondency to his son.

He need have had no fear as to the foundations on which his reputation rests. ' These sands, your uncounted volumes, are all of gold, and make a foundation more solid than the rock,' wrote Andrew Lang. Thackeray again and again expressed his fervent admiration of his great contemporary. ' All the forenoon I read with intense delight a novel called *Le Vicomte de Bragelonne*,' he wrote to Mrs. Brookfield, ' a continuation of the famous *Mousquetaires*, and just as interesting, keeping one panting from volume to volume, longing for more.' ' D. is wonderful. He is better than Walter Scott,' he said on another occasion. *Les Trois Mousquetaires* is one of the world's masterpieces. Its faults are obvious, but who cares about these in face of the overpowering merits of the book? Exaggeration, bombast, historical blunders, what are these to the wonderful high spirits, the miraculous adventures, hair-breadth escapes, splendid fights, indomitable courage, never-failing resource of the heroes of Dumas? D'Artagnan, Athos, Porthos, and Aramis, Milady, Chicot, and the rest, have taken their place in the world's portrait gallery. D. was epic in his writings. He conceived largely, and executed his conception on the grand scale, and limned his characters with a broad brush. For the rest he let them reveal themselves as the story proceeds, never halting to indulge in psychological studies. Yet these are living human beings, not only the outstanding figures on the vast canvases, but those who occupy minor positions. The innkeeper is as clearly defined as the cardinal ; the captain of the King's Guard no more alive than the executioner of Lille. His very dialogue caught the infection of his scenes, and is as tense and brilliant and as witty as the repartee is glittering. It is sometimes asserted that much of the credit of these wonderful books is due to D.'s collaborators, but to take credit away from Dumas to give to Maquet and the rest is absurd. No doubt his collaborators did their work well as Dumas' henchmen ; but what is the value of the work that they did alone when the master-hand was withdrawn? Dumas wrote his own *Mémoires* so far as 1832 (22 vols., 1852–54), but they cannot be regarded as a very trustworthy guide. There are biographies by Blaze de Bury (Paris, 1885) and Davidson (London, 1902).

**Dumas, Alexandre** (1824–95), natural son of the novelist, and one of the most distinguished Fr. dramatists of his century, was *b.* at Paris.

His whole career presents a strange contrast to that of his father, and the same may be said of his literary productions. His father shows the riotous prodigality and lavish, brilliant fancy of the romanticists, while he himself is Parisian in his minuteness and delicacy of work. He shows, too, after the preliminary period in which he sowed his wild oats, a moral force and earnestness that make his plays almost social sermons. He was early legitimised, and after a course of training at the Institution Goubaux and the Collège Bourbon, he led a wild life for some years, accumulating a vast stock of debts. To pay these off, he seriously took up his father's profession, and his true literary experience begins with the publication of *L◆Dame aux Camélias* in 1848. Not only does this novel treat the common romantic theme of the courtesan brought back to virtue by honest love, it also furnishes some autobiographical notes. His succeeding novels, though all readable, are commonplace. The dramatisations of *La Dame aux Camélias* and *Diane de Lys*, played at last in 1852 and 1853 respectively, mark an epoch in his own career and in that of the Fr. stage. Henceforward, though he did not give up the novel, his best work was given to the drama, and his success was great. Almost all his sixteen plays are masterpieces of construction and style. Each of them on its appearance gave rise to lively discussion, which he treats in his celebrated Prefaces. He soon became wealthy and honoured. In 1874 he was made a member of the Institute, and continued his work till his death at Marly-le-Roi. He left unfinished *La Troublante* and *La Route de Thèbes*. Other important plays of his are : *Le Demi-Monde*, 1855 ; *La Question d'Argent*, 1857 ; *Les Idées de Madame Aubray*, 1867 ; *Une Visite de Noces*, 1871 ; *Denise*, 1885.

**Dumas, Jean Baptiste André** (1800–84), a Fr. chemist, studied chemistry in Geneva, and was carrying on original research before he was twenty-one. In 1823 he migrated to Paris, and henceforward made that metropolis his home. In 1824 he founded the *Annales des Sciences Naturelles*. As a professor of his science at the Sorbonne and elsewhere, he always succeeded in gathering round him an eager band of students. Under the Second empire he served for a time as master of the mint (1868). His idea of substitution (' metalepsis '), which he supported by proving the similarity in properties between acetic acid and trichloracetic acid (where chlorine has replaced the original hydrogen), assisted largely in the correction of the atomic theory, whilst he also discovered ingenious methods of ascertaining the amount of nitrogen in organic compounds, and of estimating the densities of gases.

**Du Maurier, George Louis Palmella Busson** (1834–96), a Brit. artist and writer, was the son of a Fr. émigré and an Eng. mother. In 1851 he was studying chemistry at University College, London, and after living in Paris and Antwerp, where he lost the sight of one eye, settled down in London (1860). His drawings appeared in *Once a Week* and *Cornhill Magazine*, but it is as a *Punch* artist that he lives. In its pages he drew pretty women, spruce nursemaids, happy children, and proud fathers just as they ought to appear in ' good society.' It was his finished and graceful style which suggested to Mark Lemon the analogy between Du Maurier and the ' romantic tenor.' His impossible novels, including *Trilby*, 1894, share the charm and wit of his illustration.

**Dumba, Konstantin Theodor,** Austrian statesman; *b.* June 17, 1856, in Vienna. Graduated there in law, 1878. Entered Foreign Office, 1879. Became ambassador to U.S.A., April 24, 1913. In Sept. 1915 the British gov. discovered he was attempting to stop supplies of war material from America by means of strikes. President Wilson insisted on his recall; he left America Oct. 5. Appointed to Upper House of Reichsrath, May 1917. Made a vice-president of the International Union of League of Nations Societies at Prague, Oct. 1928.

**Dumbarton,** the co. tn. of Dumbartonshire, Scotland. It lies on the R. Leven, near its confluence with the Clyde, and is about 14½ m. N.W. of Glasgow. After Clydebank, it is by far the most important shipbuilding centre in the shire, and, besides extensive engineering works, has brass and iron foundries and saw mills. The fortress and castle on the basaltic Rock of D. (240 ft.) is rich in historical interest. William Wallace was confined within its ugly walls in 1305, and in 1571 it was captured, after a brilliant assault, by Crawford, who fought for King James. Formerly the capital of Strathclyde, it was christened Dunbreatan (' fort of the Britons ') by the Gaels. Pop. 23,150.

**Dumbartonshire,** a co. of western Scotland, bounded on the N., E., and S.E. respectively by the shires of Perth, Stirling and Lanark, on the S. by the Clyde, and on the W. by Loch Long, a beautiful salt-water inlet, and Argyllshire. Ben Vorlich (3092 ft.) and Ben Vane (3004 ft.), and at least ten peaks over 2000 ft. high, crown the highlands in the W. and N.W., whilst in the S. rise the Kilpatrick Hills. The chief rivers are the Clyde, with its affluent, the Leven, and the Kelvin; the principal glens of the hilly regions, Glens Sloy, Douglas, Luss, and Fruin are named after the streams, which water their bed. The splendid scenery of Loch Lomond attracts many visitors each year, and Garelochhead, near the Gareloch, is also a favourite tourist centre. The neighbourhood of so large a market as Glasgow has led to the establishment of large dairy farms, and the successful adoption of highly intensive cultivation. Clydebank (46,506 inhabitants) is busily engaged in shipbuilding, and Alexandria (10,359), Renton, and Bonhill in bleaching, Turkey-red dyeing, and printing cottons and other fabrics. Coal is mined in Kirkintilloch (11,689). Pop. 150,801.

**Dumb Cane,** or *Dieffenbach Seguine*, a species of Dieffenbachia. The plant occurs in tropical America, and has an acrid juice, which paralyses the power of speech in one who chews the stem. The natives made use of this in the torturing of slaves.

**Dumbness.** By the ancients, D. was thought to be, not the natural result of deafness, but the consequence of some brain trouble, or incapacity of the vocal organs, and by some was imagined to be possessed by an evil spirit. Pedro Ponce de Leon (1520–84), a Spaniard, was the first instructor of the deaf and dumb, teaching many of them to speak, read, and write. There are three principal methods in the instruction of the deaf and dumb: the oral, the sign, and manual, and the combined method. The oral method instructs by and through speech; the pupils learn to pronounce the elemental sounds of the language, and to read from the lips. The second method is by a language of signs, and the third combines speech, lip-reading, writing, and signs. *See* DEAF AND DUMB.

**Dum-Dum,** or **Dam-Dama,** a tn. of Brit. India, in the presidency of Bengal, and the dist. of the Twenty-four Parganas, 6 m. from Fort William. For seventy years, until 1853, it was the headquarters of the Bengal artillery, and it was regarded as the ' Woolwich ' of India. The Dum-Dum bullets were manufactured here. The town is noted for the fact that the mutiny of 1857 originated here.

**Dumfries,** the co. tn. of Dumfriesshire, Scotland. It lies on the Nith, 8½ m. from its mouth in Solway

Firth, and is connected by three bridges with Maxwelltown, its suburb, which, as it is situated on the right bank, belongs to Kirkcudbrightshire. The town is engaged in the manufacturing of tweeds and hosiery. Robert Burns, who lived here from 1791 till his death (1796), lies buried in St. Michael's Church (1746), and the site of the Franciscan monastery, where Bruce murdered the Red Comyn, is now partly covered by the Gothic Greyfriars Church (1867). The stately Carlaverock Castle, to which Edward I. laid siege in 1300, is 8 m. from the city, and is still in excellent preservation. Pop. 19,014.

**Dumfriesshire**, a border co. of Scotland, bounded on the N. by the counties of Lanark, Peebles, and Selkirk; on the E. by Roxburghshire; on the S. and S.E. by Solway Firth and Cumberland; and on the W. by the shires of Ayr and Kirkcudbright. The chief highlands, including White Coomb (2695 ft.) and the Lowther Hills (2377 ft.), lie N. The valleys of the three main rivers, the Nith, the Annan, and the Esk, all of which empty into the Solway, separate the N. of the shire from the S. Railways ascend Nithsdale, Annandale, and Eskdale, as far as Langholm. Loch Skene (1750 ft. above sea-level) in the N. gives rise to the beautiful waterfall called Grey Mare's Tail. The rural population is engaged in cattle and sheep rearing, and beyond Dumfries, Annan (3928 inhabitants), Langholm, and Lockerbie are the only towns of importance. Area 1072 sq. m.; pop. 75,370.

**Dümichen, Johannes** (1833–94), a Ger. Egyptologist. His series of learned works on Egypt, including *Geographische Inschriften altägyptischer Denkmäler* (4 vols.), 1865–85, was the fruits of extensive travel and original research, especially into inscriptions.

**Dumont, François** (1688–1726), Fr. sculptor, *b.* in Paris and *d.* at Lille. He studied under his father, and first gained distinction with a figure of David, and of a Titan. Afterwards executed a number of monuments and works for churches. Died as the result of a fall while erecting the tomb of the Duke of Melun. His son Edmé executed the well-known statue of Milon of Crotona testing his strength, which is in the Louvre.

**Dumont, François** (1751–1851), Fr. miniature-painter. Executed portraits of Louis XVI. and his queen, and Charles X. Many of his best works are in the Louvre.

**Dumont, Pierre Etienne Louis** (1759–1829), a Fr. political writer. His *Souvenirs sur Mirabeau*, 1832, are of peculiar interest, both because the author was a personal friend of the Fr. statesman—he is said to have composed some of Mirabeau's speeches—and because they give the impression which the Great Revolution made upon a discerning eye-witness. D. was instrumental in restoring freedom to his native city, Geneva, and has earned the gratitude of posterity for his able editorship of the *Traités de Legislation* and other works of Jeremy Bentham, the jurist.

**Dumont d'Urville, Jules Sebastian César** (1790–1842), a Fr. navigator, was an accomplished linguist and had also studied entomology and botany. It was he who discovered and recognised the priceless Venus of Melos (Milo). The find occurred during a hydrographic survey of the Mediterranean in 1820. In 1830 he was in charge of the ship which took Charles X. to England. In 1838 he sailed for the Antarctic and discovered Joinville Island, Louis Philippe Land, and later (1840) Adélie Land. An island off New Guinea, which he visited during his second voyage of circumnavigation (1826–29), bears his name, D'Urville.

GENERAL DUMOURIEZ

**Dumouriez, Charles François** (1739–1823), a celebrated Fr. general, was *b.* at Cambrai. In 1757 he entered the Fr. army and fought under his father, a commissary royal, during the Seven Years' War. He was afterwards sent as an envoy to Poland and Sweden, but while engaged in the latter country he fell into disgrace, and, being recalled, was imprisoned in the Bastille. On the succession of Louis XVI. he was released, and was soon made commandant of Cherbourg, where he did much to improve the naval affairs. On the outbreak of the revolution, he took the popular side, ultimately becoming connected with the Girondins, by whose influence he was made Minister of Foreign Affairs. He resigned this post to receive command of the army in the N., and carried on a successful campaign against the Duke of Brunswick. It was by his exertions that the latter was defeated at the battle of Valmy, and France was saved from the dangers of invasion. Later in the same year he pressed into the Austrian Netherlands and won the victory of Jemappes. In 1793 his career of conquest came to an end. He had attempted to make arrangements for the restoration of the monarchy, and he was charged with treason. Four commissioners were sent to arrest him, but he captured them and took refuge with the Austrians. He was not able to remain here long, and wandered throughout Europe with a price on his head, settling finally in England, where he d. at Great Marlow. Of his numerous publications the most important is his *Mémoires*, 1796.

**Dumping.** In its restricted business meaning D. refers to the method of disposing of superfluous stock at a low price in some place where its sale shall not affect the regular business. Thus: a firm trading in easily recognised goods in the S. of England finding it desirable to sell a quantity of them quickly might offer them to a few substantial buyers in the N. of England. In the same way, a manufacturer, hard pressed for money, might dispose of his stock to a distant buyer at or below cost. Similarly, should his trade be confined to eight or nine months in the year, rather than allow his factory to remain idle during the other three or four, he might manufacture goods for a market that would not injure his own trade, at prices that allow no profit. D. is also a method adopted by the more heartless kind of Trust or Ring, and has frequently been used to force a competitor to come to terms or to drive him out of trade. The method used is to copy the competitor's best lines and to offer them to his customers at prices he cannot afford to accept. Like many commercial terms D. has been seized on as a convenient political word, and here its significance largely depends on the party outlook of the man who uses it. Naturally business men whose trade is affected by the sale of cheap goods from other countries do not hesitate to make use of the term to describe the commodities that under-sell their own productions.

Among the most fruitful causes of discussion as to what constitutes D. since the Great War have been: (1) The heavy selling of goods by Germany during her periods of inflation, which was a natural consequence of the rush of the Ger. people for more stable paper money than their own marks; (2) the return of Russia to international trading, with consequent heavy selling of oil and flour in British home markets; and (3) the more trivial but spectacular selling of American superfluous magazines and publications in this country.

**Dumráon,** a tn., 64½ m. W. of Patna, dist. of Sháhábád, Bengal, British India. Pop. less than 19,000.

**Dun,** a Celtic and Teutonic root, meaning 'hill,' and connected with the Anglo-Saxon *tun*, from which 'town' is derived. Cf. also Eng. 'downs' and Fr. *dunes*. Various forms of it occur in place names like *Donegal, Dunedin*, and *Dumfries*. In early times the word was used in Ireland and Scotland of forts with ramparts. Such 'duns' are found at Dunecht and Tap o' Noth in Aberdeenshire, and in many Irish villages.

**Dünaburg,** *see* DVINSK.

**Duna-Földvar,** a tn., 33½ m. S.E. of Stuhlweissenburg, on the r. b. of the Danube, Hungary, with mills, tiles, pottery, hemp, and food industries. Pop. 11,730.

**Dunajec-San, Battles of.** The Rs. Dunajec and San both run N. from the Carpathians in Galicia. During the Great War their direction, and the fact that Tarnow is situated on the former and Przemysl on the latter, brought them into prominence. In their advance the Russians swept over these areas in Sept. 1914, and reached Tarnow. The fact that the Russians had been reinforcing their Carpathian front at the expense of the Tarnow area decided the Central Powers to attempt a break-through at that place, which had it succeeded, would have 'rolled up' the Russian forces on the Carpathians (*q.v.*). The Ger. withdrew a number of divisions from the Western front, and these, together with an Austro-Hungarian force, the whole under the command of General von Mackensen, were concentrated in Galicia for the operation. The attack opened on May 2, 1915, and, owing to the intense preparatory bombardment, the Russians gave way almost everywhere, and the lower Dunajec was crossed during the same day. Great pressure was brought systematically against various parts of the sector, and although the Russians withstood it bravely, the tactical combinations of their opponents were too much for them. Tarnow, in fact, was not evacuated until May 5, and only after a desperate struggle. The Russians were attacked again on May 8, and by the night of May 12 the Central Powers were threatening their positions on the San, particularly Przemysl. By May 24 the struggle for the fortress had begun, and although a powerful counter-attack was launched by the Russians, it failed, and by the first week of June they were forced back from the San.

**Dunbar,** a seaport of Haddington-shire, Scotland. It is 29¼ m. E.N.E. of Edinburgh by the L. & N.E. Railway, and has two harbours, both fairly accessible, at the entrance of the Firth of Forth. The castle and Grey Friars monastery, which dates back to 1218, are both picturesque ruins. The former was captured by Edward I. (1296), and offered refuge to Edward II. after Bannockburn (1314), to the unfortunate Duke of Albany (1479), and twice to Mary, Queen of Scots. The golf links and the slight rainfall attract many visitors in summer-time, and close by is the scene of the battle of Dunbar (1650). Pop. 3839.

**Dunbar, Earls of :** *Cospatrick* was created first Earl of Dunbar by his kinsman, Malcolm III., and in 1072 received from him the grant of the town of Dunbar with the surrounding lands of Lothian.

*Patrick* (1284–1368), the tenth Earl, sheltered Edward II. in 1314 after the battle of Bannockburn at Dunbar Castle. He married ' Black Agnes ' the sister of the Randolph who led the centre of the Scottish forces at that same battle. ' Black Agnes ' herself is famous for her defence of Dunbar Castle against the Eng. under Salisbury in 1337, when she successfully held the castle for five months.

*George*, the eleventh Earl, was deprived of his title and estates by James I. of Scotland in 1434. In 1605 the title was revived in favour of George, third son of Alexander Home of Manderston, who took a leading part in the re-establishment of episcopacy in Scotland.

**Dunbar, William** (*c.* 1465–*c.* 1530), the greatest of the old Scottish poets, is generally supposed to have been *b.* in E. Lothian and educated at St. Andrews. Practically nothing is known of his early life, and little of his later. He early entered the order of the Friars Minor (Franciscan), but gave this up in disgust. Thereafter he appears to have been employed by James IV. in some court and political business. His chief poems are *The Thrissil and the Rois* (The Thistle and the Rose), in which he celebrates James's marriage with Margaret Tudor (1503); *The Dance of the Seven*

*Deadly Sins,* an allegory ; and various lyrics, of which the most notable is *The Lament for the Makaris* (poets) (*c.* 1507). In all these there is true poetry. In his allegorical poems, D. follows Chaucer in his setting, and is thus more or less imitative and conventional : in his satirical pieces and lyrics he takes a bolder flight and shows his native power. His comic poems are somewhat gross. The date and circumstances of his death are uncertain, some holding that he fell at Flodden, others that he was alive so late as 1530. Other works are *The Merle* and *The Nightingale,* and the *Flijting* of D. and Kennedy. D. is described by Sir E. Gosse as ' the

ADAM, FIRST VISCOUNT DUNCAN

largest figure in Eng. literature between Chaucer and Spenser.' He has strength, swiftness, humour, and pathos, and his descriptive touch is vivid and full of colour.

**Dunblane,** a market tn., on Allan Water 14 m. S.S.W. of Crieff, in W. Perthshire, Scotland. Woollen goods are manufactured, but the chief interest of the town is historic. The cathedral, which was rebuilt in 1240 by Bishop Clemens, is in the Early Pointed style, and its W. window won high praise from Ruskin. Pop. about 4000.

**Duncan, Adam,** first **Viscount** (1731–1804), an Eng. admiral, *b.* at Lundie in Forfarshire. He received his earliest education at Dundee, and in 1746 was placed under Captain Haldane in the frigate *Shoreham.* Assisted in the attack on Goree, a Fr. settlement in W. Africa. In 1795 he hoisted his flag as commander-in-chief of the North Sea, and began harassing the Dutch. On Oct. 11, 1797, he gained a decisive victory over the Dutch, and in recognition of his services he was created Viscount Duncan of Camperdown and Baron of Lundie, and also was granted a pension of £3000 to himself and two next heirs to the title.

**Duncan, Andrew, the Elder** (1744–1828), a Scottish physician, *b.* at Pinkerton, near St. Andrews. From 1774–76 he lectured on medicine at the university of Edinburgh. In 1790 he was appointed president of the Edinburgh College of Physicians and Professor of Physiology. In 1776 he founded a public dispensary, and in 1807 a lunatic asylum at Morningside, Edinburgh. His chief writings were *Medical and Philosophical Commentaries*, a quarterly journal of medicine (1773–95), continued as *Annals of Medicine* until 1804, when his son took over the work of editor and issued the *Edinburgh Medical and Surgical Journal*. He also wrote several medical treatises. *See* Autobiographical Fragment in his *Miscellaneous Poems by A. D.*, 1818.

**Duncan, Andrew, the Younger** (1773–1832), a Scottish physician, son of the preceding, *b.* at Edinburgh. In 1807 he was appointed first professor of medical jurisprudence in Edinburgh. From 1819–21 he was joint professor of physiology with his father, and from 1821–32 he was professor of *materia medica*. His chief literary work was for the *Edinburgh Medical and Surgical Journal* and an improved version of Lewis' *Edinburgh New Dispensary*, 1803.

**Duncan, Henry** (1774–1846), founder of savings banks, *b.* at Lochrutton, Kircudbrightshire. He was intended for a commercial life, but left it for the church, and in 1798 was ordained minister of Ruthwell in Dumfriesshire. He was remarkable for the breadth of his views and the diversity of his interests. He was captain of a company of volunteers, an ardent antiquarian and geologist, the publisher of a popular series of tracts entitled *The Cottage Fireside*, the editor of *The Dumfries and Galloway Courier*, and the author of *The Sacred Philosophy of the Seasons*, 1836. His most important labours were connected with the establishment of savings banks, the first being instituted at Ruthwell in 1810, and later, through his efforts, all over the country. *See* Life by his son (1848).

**Duncan, Isadora** (1878–1927), American dancer and pioneer in the revival of Gk. classical poses and dances with flowing draperies; *b.* in San Francisco, she had appeared on the New York stage before emigrating with her family to England. In 1901 she appeared in Paris, and at the Théâtre Sarah-Bernhardt in 1903.

Possessing a slender, well-proportioned figure, she reproduced with much success the unconscious grace of the figures depicted on the old Gk. vases. She also won a reputation by her ' interpretations ' of music by means of dancing, and, in London in 1921, created a stir by her interpretation of a Chopin programme designed as a musical history of Poland. Her life was, however, marred by tragedy : in 1913 her two children, with their nurse, were drowned in the Seine at Neuilly as the result of a motor accident ; and in 1927 she herself was strangled by her own scarf while motoring. In 1921 she married the young Russian poet Serge Yessenin, whom she divorced two years later, and who was suspected in America in 1922 of being an agent of the Soviet, probably because it was known that her school of dancing in Moscow was opened at the request of Lenin. Her memoirs, *My Life*, were published in 1927.

**Duncan, John** (1796–1870), a theologian and Semitic scholar, *b.* at Aberdeen. In 1840 he was sent by the Scottish society for the conversion of the Jews, as missionary to Pesth, Hungary, where he made many notable converts, including the Rev. Dr. Edersheim. In 1843 he was recalled as Professor of Oriental languages in the New College (Free Church), Edinburgh. He wrote very little, but many of his ideas and sayings are recorded by Professor Knight of St. Andrews in *Colloquia Peripatetica*, 1870. *See* Life, by David Brown, D.D., and *Recollections of John Duncan, LL.D.*, by A. Moody Stuart, 1872.

**Duncan, John** (1794–1881), a Scottish weaver and botanist, *b.* at Stonehaven, Kincardineshire. In the intervals of his occupation as a weaver he studied Culpeper's *British Herbal*, and began a collection of British herbs with the help of a gardener named Black ; he also taught himself astronomy and some Latin and Gk. His manner of life was of the simplest, and he only once went as far as Edinburgh. He presented his herbarium to the Aberdeen University in 1880. *See* Life, by W. Jolly, 1883.

**Duncan, Robert Kennedy** (1868–1914), American chemist ; *b.* Nov. 1, 1868, at Brantford, Ontario, Canada ; son of Robert Augustus D. He graduated at Toronto in 1892, and then studied at Clark and Columbia Univs., U.S.A. Instructor in physics and chemistry : Auburn (N.Y.) Acad. High School, 1893–95 ; Dr. Julius Sach's Collegiate Inst., New York, 1895–98 ; the Hill School, Pottstown,

Pa., 1898 – 1901. Professor of Chemistry at Washington and Jefferson College, 1901-6. He visited Europe in 1903-4 and 1907. Was sent abroad by *McClure's Magazine*, 1901, to study radioactivity; by A. S. Barnes & Co., 1903, for materials for *The New Knowledge*; and by *Harper's Magazine*, 1905-6, to study relations of modern chemistry to industry. From 1906 he was Professor of Industrial Chemistry at the Univ. of Kansas; and from 1910 director of industrial research—taking, at the same time, the same positions in Pittsburgh University. He discovered and patented : a new process for manufacturing phosphorus ; a new low-melting glass ; and processes for decorating glass. Initiated in 1907, at Univ. of Kansas, a scheme of industrial fellowships, which has since grown to remarkable proportions there and at Pittsburgh. Publications : *The New Knowledge*, 1905 ; *The Chemistry of Commerce*, 1907 ; *Some Chemical Problems of To-Day*, 1911. Died Feb. 18.

Duncan, Thomas (1807–45), a Scottish painter, *b.* at Kinclaven, Perthshire. He began to exhibit at the Scottish Academy in 1828, and won so great a reputation that in 1830 he was elected a member of the Royal Scottish Academy and in 1843 an associate of the Royal Academy, London. His principal pictures represent scenes from Scottish history, and are remarkable alike for their skill in colouring and for the faithful portraiture of Scottish character. There are fine specimens of his work in the National Gallery of Scotland, including portraits of himself, Lady Stuart of Allanbank, and Lord Colonsay. His illustrations from literature include ' Jeanie Deans on her Journey to London ' (1831) and ' The Woefu' Heart ' (1841), from *Auld Robin Gray*. His chief historical pictures are : ' Prince Charles Edward entering Edinburgh ' (1840), ' Prince Charlie Asleep after Culloden ' (1843), ' The Martyrdom of John Brown of Priesthill, 1685 ' (1844), now at Glasgow.

Duncan de Cérisantis, Mark (*d.* 1648), a writer of Latin verse. He entered the service of Sweden, and was Swedish ambassador to France in 1645, but renounced his position and his Protestantism and went to Rome. In 1647 he met the Duc de Guise, and accompanied him to Naples as secretary. He *d.* of a wound received in an engagement with the Spaniards while aiding Guise in his attempt to'take Sicily from Spain. His fame as a Latin versifier was great ; the most celebrated of his poems being the *Carmen Gratulatorium*, on the marriage of Charles I. of England and Henrietta Maria. See *Mémoires du Duc de Guise*, 1668.

Duncansby Head, a promontory (210 ft.) forming the N.E. extremity of Caithness, Scotland, 18½ m. N. of Wick and 1¾ E. of John o' Groat's house.

Dunciad, The, a celebrated satire published in 1728 in three books, to which a fourth was added in 1742, in which Alexander Pope takes revenge for the hostility of his critics by holding them up to ridicule as members of the court of Dullness.

Duncker, Maximilian Wolfgang (1811–86), a Ger. historian. In 1857 he accepted the post of Professor of History at Tübingen, but was recalled to Berlin in 1859, becoming counsellor to the Crown Prince in 1861, and director of the State archives from 1867 to 1874. His high place among Ger. historians depends chiefly on his *Geschichte des Alterthums*, 1852–57 (5th edition, 1878–86 ; Eng. translation by E. Abbott, 1877–82). He also published *Origines Germanicæ*, 1840 ; *Die Krisis der Reformation*, 1845 ; *Zur Geschichte der Deutschen Reichsversammlung*, 1849 ; and *Feudalität und Aristokratie*, 1858.

Dundalk, cap of co. Louth, Irish Free State. It is situated on the R. Castleton, near its entrance into D. Bay, 12 m. S.W. of Newry. It is a railway centre for the Great Northern (Ireland) Railway, and there are important works belonging to the railway. There is also a daily service of steamers to Liverpool. A considerable trade in dairy and agricultural produce and live stock is carried on ; there are also mills for flax-spinning, breweries, and distilleries. The fisheries are important, especially the salmon-fishing industry. Pop. 14,010.

Dundas, a tn. of Wentworth co., Ontario, Canada, at the head of Burlington Bay, Lake Ontario. It has large mills worked by water, and manufactures leather, paper, flour, machinery, and tools and textiles. Pop. 4978.

Dundas, a group of about 500 coral islands (also called Juba Is.), off the E. coast of Africa, in lat. 1° S. They possess only one safe harbour.

Dundas, a baronial castle, 1¾ m. S.W. of Queensferry on the S. bank of the Firth of Forth, Scotland. It dates from the eleventh century, and was the seat of the family of Dundas until 1875.

Dundas, Sir David (1735–1820), British general and writer on tactics, *b.* in Edinburgh. He entered the army in 1752, and was aide-de-camp to General Elliott in 1760-1, in the campaigns in Germany. Every year he was present at the manœuvres of the Fr., Prussian and Austrian armies, and in 1788 published the results of his observations of their tactics in *The Principles of Military Movements, chiefly applicable to Infantry*. His *Rules and Regulations for the Formation, Field Exercises, and Movements of his Majesty's Forces* (1792) were published as the official orders for the army, and were followed by *Rules and Regulations for the Cavalry* (1792). It was under these rules and regulations that the battles of Moore and Wellington were fought. He was made governor of Chelsea Hospital in 1804, and commander-in-chief of the army from 1809–11.

**Dundas, Henry,** first **Viscount Melville** (1742–1811), a member of a distinguished legal family, was educated at Edinburgh University. At the age of twenty-four he was appointed Solicitor-General for Scotland. In 1774 he became a member of parliament, and in the next year was made Lord-Advocate. He was a regular attendant at Westminster, where he vigorously opposed any concession being made to the American colonies while they were in arms against the Mother Country, and in 1778 he supported a motion for the repeal of the Massachusetts charter. His advance was as rapid as it was steady. Later he was Home Secretary in Pitt's administration, and in 1794 Secretary for War, with William Windham as Secretary-at-War. He was in 1802 created Viscount Melville, and two years after returned to office with Pitt as First Lord of the Admiralty. Charged with malversation in 1806, he was impeached, but acquitted on all charges, and his name, which had been struck off the roll of privy councillors, was restored. He never again held office, and in 1809 declined the earldom that Perceval offered him. An able man, and a ready speaker, he stands in the political history of his times as the intimate and trusted adviser of William Pitt. There is no biography of him.

**Dundee,** a royal parl. and municipal bor. and seaport in Scotland, situated on the N. shore of the Firth of Tay in 56° 27′ N. lat., 2° 56′ W. long. The town stands on a gentle slope, rising from the water's edge to the hill known as Dundee Law (571 ft.). The estuary opposite the town is nearly two miles wide, and its shipping is important enough to make it the second port of Scotland. The town is well built, and underwent much improvement in the course of the last century. It possesses many fine buildings, among which are the Town Hall, in Rom. Ionic style, and the Albert Institute, which includes a free library, museum, etc. This institute, in the fifteenth-century Gothic, was designed by Sir Gilbert Scott. Other important edifices are the Royal Exchange, St. Paul's Church, University College, Kinnaird Hall, and the Technical Institute. There are several fine parks, chief of which are the Baxter Park, 37 acres in extent, and the still larger park on the hill of Balgay. The chief industry of D. consists in the manufacture of coarse linen fabrics such as sailcloth. There are also manufactures of cordage, fine linen, jute, confectionery, and marmalade. Some ship-building is carried on, and mill-wright work, and there are marine engine works. There are also extensive saw-mills. On Dec. 28, 1879, part of the bridge over the Tay here and the train passing over it were blown into the river, with the loss of over seventy lives. There are thirteen Trade Guilds, about 100 spinning mills, D. being one of the chief centres of the linen and jute trade. There are manufactures of machinery, steam-engines, boilers. D. has steadily increased in population, at the rate of about 20,000 in ten years. It was once strongly fortified, and suffered greatly from war at various times. On account of the prominent part taken by its citizens in forwarding the work of the Reformation it is often given the title of 'The Scottish Geneva.' Pop. 168,315.

**Dundee, John Graham of Claverhouse, Viscount** (c. 1649–89), Scottish soldier. He served as a volunteer in the Fr. army, and in the Dutch army under the Prince of Orange, where he obtained a cornetcy in 1674 for saving the life of the prince at the battle of Seneffe. In 1677 he returned to England and obtained a captaincy in the regiment of the Marquis of Montrose, charged with enforcing the penal laws against the Scottish Covenanters. Graham's attempt to disperse an armed force of Covenanters at Drumclog ended in his defeat, and was the signal for a serious and general rising. He was more successful at Bothwell Bridge (1679), and afterwards made a tour through the south-western counties in search of rebels, routing a company at Aird's Moss and killing the leader, Cameron. In 1682–84 he suppresssd the Covenanters of Dumfries, Annandale, Kirkcudbright, Ayr, and Lanark with the severity enjoined by the government, killing, robbing, and starving them when they would not submit. In 1688 he was appointed second in command of the Scottish army, and was ordered South with his forces to protect the Stuart throne and oppose the landing of William of Orange. In the same year James II. created him Viscount Dundee. After James II.'s flight to France D. returned to Scotland and was indefatigable in supporting the Stuart cause. In July 1689 he organised a rising in the Highlands, and completely routed the forces of Mackay, but was killed in the moment of victory at Killiecrankie. *See* Mark Napier, *Memorials and Letters of Graham of Claverhouse*, 1859–62 ; C. S. Terry, *John Graham of Claverhouse*, 1905 ; and Ian Maclaren's *Graham of*

JOHN GRAHAM, VISCOUNT DUNDEE

*Claverhouse*, 1908 ; also Scott's *Old Mortality*, and *Redgauntlet*.

**Dundonald,** a kirk town in the par. of D., Ayrshire, Scotland. D. Castle, erected in the twelfth century, where Robert II., the first Stewart sovereign, died in 1390, and Old Auchans Castle are ruins. Pop. 1646.

**Dundonald, Douglas Mackinnon Baillie Hamilton Cochrane,** twelfth **Earl of** (*b.* 1852), British soldier. He entered the 2nd Life Guards in 1870 ; served in the Nile expedition from 1884–85, and in Stewart's march to the relief of Khartoum, and fought at the battles of Abu-Klea and Goubat. In the Boer War he was present at the battle of Colenso, and at the head of the Second Cavalry Brigade was the first to enter Ladysmith at the raising of the siege by Sir Redvers Buller (Feb. 28, 1900). Commander of the British forces in Canada 1902–4 but recalled by the Secretary of State for War in consequence of his public criticism of one of the ministers. Served overseas in Great War. Special ambassador to Peruvian centenary, 1921.

**Dundonald, Thomas Cochrane,** tenth **Earl of** (1775–1860), British

admiral, *b.* at Annsfield in Lanarkshire. He entered the navy in 1793, and in 1801, as commander of the *Speedy*, he captured, with singular audacity, the Spanish frigate, *El Gamo*, off the coast of Spain. In 1806 he returned as member for Honiton, and made his mark as a Radical in the House of Commons by denouncing abuses in the navy. In 1809 he was engaged in an attack on the Fr. squadron in the Basque Roads, and inflicted immense damage. Through his criticism of Admiral Gambier's action in the engagement, however, he fell into disfavour at the Admiralty, which was increased by his speeches in the House. In 1814 he was accused of a share in a notorious fraud on the Stock Exchange, and in spite of lack of proof of his complicity was ordered to be dismissed the service, sentenced to a year's imprisonment, and fined £1000. From 1818–22 he commanded the Chilian navy and distinguished himself by the capture of the *Esmeralda*. From 1823–25 he was in the service of Brazil, and helped that country to establish its independence. In 1827 he became an admiral in the Gk. navy and fought against the Turks. In 1832 he secured his restoration to his place in the British navy and to the Order of the Bath in 1847. He wrote *The Autobiography of a Seaman*, 1860–61. *See* Life by his son, and J. B. Atlay's *The Trial of Lord Cochrane before Lord Ellenborough*, 1897.

**Dundrennan,** a vil. in the parish of Rerwick, co. of Kirkcudbright, Scotland, 5 m. S.E. of Kirkcudbright, with the ruins of an ancient Cistercian abbey (1142).

**Dune,** a mound or ridge of loose sand heaped up by the wind on the seashore or occasionally on the shore of an inland lake and on the banks of a river. The name is also used for the wide stretches of sand in an inland district of low rainfall. Among the minerals which occur among sand deposits, quartz is by far the most common and of the longest duration, as it is comparatively hard, has practically no cleavage, is insoluble in water, and does not readily decompose, while the other grains decompose comparatively rapidly. In general, the sand grains which form the Ds. are rounded, due to mutual attrition during transport; the greater the distance travelled the smoother and rounder the grains. The wind which heaps up the Ds. seldom carries even the smallest grains in suspension, but rolls them along the ground, sometimes with a movement as smooth as flowing liquid, and sometimes with a skipping motion. A D.

has a gentle windward slope and a steep leeward descent; the rolling grains being driven up a gentle incline and falling steeply into the hollow below. Moving sands are in many places altering the surface of the land; the continuous blowing of a steady wind in one direction frequently covering fertile tracts with this arid deposit, moving at the rate of from 60 to 70 ft. per annum. The average height of coastal sand Ds. is from 200 to 300 ft., but in the crescent-shaped sand Ds. of the Sahara they sometimes rise to a height of 600 ft. in a wide belt of sand called 'Igidi' or 'Gidi,' from the Berber word for Ds., and are separated by depressions, sometimes below sea-level, called ' Juf.' Little can be done to arrest the progress of moving sand Ds., but they can be fixed to a certain extent by planting *Carex arenaria*, and similar plants with long creeping roots. *See* Schirmer's *Le Sahara*, 1893, and ' Sand Dunes of the Libyan Desert ' in *Geog. Journal* for April 1910.

**Dunedin**, cap. of the dist. of Otago, New Zealand, at the head of Otago Harbour, 15 m. from the sea. It is surrounded by steep forest-clad hills. The harbour is accessible to vessels drawing 19 ft. right up to D., but Port Chalmers, 9 m. N.E. by rail, receives most of the shipping. Among the buildings are the bank of New Zealand, town hall, Athenæum and museum, the university with schools of arts, medicine, and mineralogy, the First Church, Knox Church, and Roman Catholic cathedral. There are manufactures of woollens, and meat is frozen in large quantities. In 1861 the discovery of gold in the neighbourhood led to a great rush of settlers. In 1925 the exports amounted to nearly six million pounds sterling and the imports to three and a half million. On Nov. 17, 1925, the New Zealand and S. Seas International Exhibition was opened at D. in the presence of 45,786 people by the Governor-General, who read a message from H.M. the King wishing all possible success to it. 83,935 visitors attended the closing ceremony on May 1, 1926. Pop. 85,000.

**Dunedin and Stenton, Andrew Graham Murray, first Viscount and Baron**; a Scottish lawyer and statesman, *b.* at Edinburgh, Nov. 21, 1849; son of Thos. Graham Murray, of Stenton, Fordie, and Locholly, Perthshire, writer to the signet and sheriff of Aberdeen. He was called to the Scottish Bar in 1874, sheriff of Perthshire, 1890–1; Solicitor-General for Scotland, 1891–2, 1895–6; Lord-Advocate of Scotland, 1896–1903;

Secretary for Scotland, 1903–5 ; Lord Justice General and Lord President of the Court of Session, Scotland, 1905–13. Since then lord of appeal in ordinary. Conservative M.P. for Buteshire, 1891–1905; raised to the peerage in 1905; viscount, 1926. Appointed to War Compensation Roy. Commission, Aug. 1915 ; Chairman, Roy. Commission on Honours, Aug. 1922; Memb. of judicial committee of privy council on Irish boundary, July 1924.

**Dunfermline** (Gaelic for ' the fort on the crooked linn '), a tn. 3 m. from the Firth of Forth and 16 m. N.W. of Edinburgh, in Fifeshire, Scotland. It is fed by the L. & N.E. Railway. Since 1718 the town has been busily engaged in the linen industry, and it now has dye and bleach works, iron foundries and distilleries. The fine Norman nave, which is all that the Reformers spared in their assault on the abbey (1560), now forms the vestibule of the modern parish church. Malcolm Canmore and Margaret, who were married in D. (1070), were buried in the abbey, which for over two centuries afterwards was the recognised place of royal sepulture. St. Margaret, whose tomb may still be seen, Ralph Erskine, and Sir Noel Paton, are some of D.'s worthies, but of all her sons, her greatest benefactor is Andrew Carnegie, who presented the town with Pittencrieff Park and Glen, and a free library, besides an annual income of £25,000. Pop. 25,250.

**Dunfermline, Sir Alexander Seton, first Earl of** (c. 1555–1622), a Scottish statesman. He studied at the Jesuit College, Rome, but gave up this proposed admittance to the priesthood, and studied law in France, being called to the Scottish Bar in 1577. He became judge in 1593, Lord President of the Court of Session in 1598, Baron Fyvie in 1597, and Chancellor in 1640–8. He was appointed guardian of Prince Charles, afterwards Charles I., and helped to arrange the union between England and Scotland. He was created Earl of Dunfermline in 1606.

**Dungannon**, a tn. of northern Ireland in the co. of Tyrone, 10 m. S.W. of Cookstown. It was the home of the kings of Ulster. There are manufs. of linen goods, earthenware, firebricks, and tiles, also a trade in corn and flax. Pop. 3830.

**Dungarpur**, a protected state of Rajputana, Central India, with a cap. of the same name. Under British protection since 1818. Area 1447 sq. m. Pop. 189,272. Capital, Dungarpur; pop. 7327.

**Dungarvan**, an urban dist. and seaport tn. of Irish Free State, in co.

**Waterford.** It is situated on the bay of D. There are fisheries and a trade in dairy and agricultural produce. The legend runs that the town was spared by Cromwell because a woman drank his health at the gateway. Pop. 5200.

**Dungeness :** (1) A low headland on the S. coast of Kent, England, 10½ m. S.E. of Rye, with a lighthouse, coast-guard station, and a small fort. Lloyd's signalling station is near. (2) Port at the entrance to the Hitchenbrook Channel, Cardwell co., Queensland, Australia, 60 m. N.W. of Townsville.

**Dungeon,** or **Donjon** (Late Lat. *domnionem* from *dominus*, a lord), the principal tower or the keep (*q.v.*) of a Norman castle. The modern use of the word ' dungeon ' for a prison is derived from the position of the Norman prison in the ground story of the ' donjon.'

**Dungiven,** a market tn., Ireland, in the co. of Londonderry. Near it are the remains of an Augustinian abbey founded in 1100. The quartz crystals known as ' Dungiven diamonds ' are found near here. Pop. 638.

**Dunglas,** a promontory on the Clyde, Scotland, 2½ m. E.S.E. of Dumbarton. It is a rocky headland, supposed to have been the site of a Roman station, and the end of the wall of Antoninus. It has ruins of the castle of the Colquhouns of Luss, and a monument to Henry Bell (1767–1830), the pioneer of steam navigation in Britain.

**Dunkeld,** a tn. of Scotland, in the co. of Perthshire. It stands on the N. bank of the R. Tay, 15¾ m. by rail from Perth. A bridge of seven arches (which was opened in 1838) here spans the river. The tn. is said to have derived its name from a Culdee church, founded in 815 by Constantin, King of the Picts. Opposite D. is Little D., famed for its waterfalls. The cathedral contains a recumbent figure in armour of the Wolf of Badenoch. The most celebrated Bishop was Gawain Douglas, translator of Virgil. The choir is still used as the parish church. Pop. 1049.

**Dunkers, Dunkards,** or **Tunkers,** also called ' Dippers,' and by themselves ' The Brethren,' a sect of German Baptists founded in Germany in 1708 by Andrew Mack, of Swartzenau. Persecutions began almost at once, and the Dunkers fled to Holland, and from thence, between 1719 and 1729, emigrated to the United States, settling first in Pennsylvania round Philadelphia. They now number over 100,000, have many converts in Canada, and support missions in Europe, India, and Asia Minor. Their creed is strictly evangelical, and they enforce baptism by immersion, and only for adults. They resemble the Quakers in the plainness of their dress, in the avoidance of war and litigation, and in the refusal to take oaths.

**Dunkirk** (Fr. Dunkerque), the fifth port of France, on the Straits of Dover, has communication with the whole world, but especially with Tilbury and Hull in England, Antwerp, Germany, the Atlantic and the Mediterranean, and by canals with the whole of E. France. It imports iron, wool, cotton, textiles, phosphates and nickel, and exports provisions and manufactured goods. It manufactures goods of hemp and jute and iron, and refines petroleum. The pirates or privateers of Dunkirk preyed on Eng. commerce until in 1713 the Treaty of Utrecht provided that the port should be filled up and it remained so until 1783. It was in the possession of England from 1658 to 1662, when Charles II. sold it to Louis XIV. It was vainly besieged by the English in 1793. Jean Bart was born here in 1651. During the Great War D. became a base for British aircraft and seaplanes, mainly to deal with Ger. air raids over England. The base was established in 1914, and gradually expanded with the needs of the war. During the latter part of 1915 offensive raids against the Germans were made successfully by the D. station, the success of which led to its prompt development and expansion as a base. Working in close co-operation with the aircraft on the Western Front, it achieved notable successes, both in fighting and bombing. On May 25, 1917, a Ger. flying squadron raided S.E. England, and although the entire squadron escaped from England, one raider was brought down at sea by one of the D. station. Although it was one of their objectives, the Gers. never reached D., having been brought to a standstill at Nieuport, 20 m. to the E. The words ' ville héroique sert d'exemple à toute la nation' were added to the arms of the town in 1917. Pop. 34,748.

**Dunkirk,** a city of Chautauqua co., New York, U.S.A., on Lake Erie, and 48 m. S.W. of Buffalo by rail. It has a good harbour and lake traffic, and has railway repair works, and manufs. locomotives, motors, agricultural implements and other iron goods. Pop. 17,802.

**Dunlap, William** (1766–1839), an American painter and dramatist, *b.* at New Jersey. He was a pupil of Sir Benjamin West and painted ' Christ Rejected ' (1821) and ' Calvary '

(1828), after the manner of similar pictures of his master's. He wrote a number of plays, including *The Father*, 1789; *Leicester*, 1807; *The Archers*, 1796; and also a *History of the American Theatre*, 1832; and *History of the Rise and Progress of the Arts of Design in the United States*, 1834.

**Dunlin, Oxbird,** or *Tringa Alpina*, a species of Charadriidæ which inhabits the northern parts of both the Old and the New World, and frequents flat coasts and tidal rivers of Britain. The colours of this sandpiper are reddish black, white, and grey, and both bill and feet are black: in winter the plumage is grey and white. In habit it is gregarious.

**Dunlop,** a par., Ayrshire, Scotland, 8 m. N.N.W. of Kilmarnock, famous for its cheese. Pop. 1335.

**Dunlop, Alexander Colquhoun Stirling Murray** (1798–1870), a Scottish writer, lawyer, and politician, *b.* at Greenock. He devoted himself disinterestedly to the cause of social reform and to the work of the church of Scotland. He was joint editor of *Shaw and Dunlop's Reports* (from 1822), and among his other writings are *Legislation for the Poor in Scotland*, and *Legislation for Parish*.

**Dunlop, Frances Anne Wallace** (1730–1815), a friend and correspondent of Robert Burns, whose acquaintance she made as a result of her admiration for *The Cottar's Saturday Night*, 1786. He wrote to her frequently and was in the habit of enclosing poems in his letters, among those which he sent to her are *Auld Lang Syne*, and *Farewell, thou fair day*. He named his second son Francis Wallace after her. *See* Burns' *Works*, 1901 (new edition), and *Correspondence of Burns with Mrs. Dunlop*, 1898 (edited by William Wallace).

**Dunlop, John Colin** (1785–1842), a Scottish man of letters. He is noted for his *History of Fiction*, 1814, which still is recognised as the best work on the subject. He also wrote *A History of Roman Literature*, 1823–28, and *Memoirs of Spain during the Reigns of Philip IV. and Charles II.*, 1834.

**Dunlop Rubber Company.** Received its present name in 1900, being previously registered in 1896 as Byrne Bros. India Rubber Co. Its authorised capital is £20,000,000, and the present chairman is the Rt. Hon. Sir Eric Geddes. The company owns *inter alia* the capital of 'Dunlop' manufacturing companies in France, Germany, Japan and other countries, and of 'Dunlop' trading companies in most of the chief countries of the world. It also controls the Dunlop Tire and Rubber Corporation, of New York, which was incorporated in 1919 as Dunlop (America) Ltd. This corporation has tyre manufacturing plant in Buffalo and spinning mills in Utica, New York State.

**Dunmanway,** a market tn., Ireland, co. Cork, 30 m. W. thereof. It manufs. flannels, blankets, tweeds, and friezes, and has flax mills and tanneries. Pop. 1619.

**Dunmore :** (1) A vil. and wateringplace of Ireland, on Waterford Harbour, in co. Waterford, and 8½ m. S.E. of the city of that name. Pop. 422. (2) A small market tn. in co. Galway, Ireland, 7½ m. N.N.E. of Tuam. Pop. 577. (3) A banking post-borough in Lackawanna co., Pennsylvania, U.S.A., on the Erie and Lackawanna railroads, adjoining Scranton. The town was incorporated in 1862. It is an important centre for anthracite coal, iron, and brick, and has flourishing silk industries. Pop. 22,627.

**Dunmow :** (1) Great D., a small market tn. in Essex, on the Chelmer, 10 m. W. of Braintree. It is supposed to have been the Roman Cæsaromagus. Pop. 2506. (2) Little D., 2 m. distant from the above, possesses some interesting remains of an Augustinian priory, founded in 1104. The D. Flitch of Bacon was instituted in 1244 by Robert de Fitzwalter as a prize to any married couple who 'will go to the priory, and kneeling on two sharp-pointed stones, will swear that they have not quarrelled nor repented of their marriage within a year and a day after its celebration.' The first recorded award was made in 1445, and successful claimants still continue to come forward. Consult W. Andrews, *History of the Dunmow Flitch*, 1877. Pop. 318.

THE DUNMOW FLITCH CHAIR

(in which winners of the flitch were carried)

**Dunmurry,** a vil., co. Antrim, Ireland, on the Glenwater, 4½ m. S. by W. of Belfast. Has linen manufs. Pop. 1462.

**Dunn, James Nicol** (1856–1919), Scottish journalist. Educated for the law, but gave up legal studies for journalism, in which sphere he began contribution to the magazines and weekly newspapers. Joined the staff of the *Dundee Advertiser* as a reporter and later acted as special correspondent to the *Scotsman*. While with this paper he assisted in producing *Art and Literature* and *Pen and Pencil*. Afterwards managing editor of the *Scots' Observer* (subsequently re-named *National Observer*), a paper which long maintained a very high level of literary excellence. To him belongs the credit of bringing out such writers as George Steevens and W. E. Henley. In 1894 he was news editor of the *Pall Mall Gazette* and in 1895 edited *Black and White*, which periodical under his direction flourished considerably. His best days, however, were from 1897 to 1905, during which period he was editor of the *Morning Post*, in which capacity he enjoyed great popularity among the writers and artists of the London Press. His later appointments were the editorship of the *Manchester Courier* (1905–1910) and of the *Johannesburg Star* (1911–14), and the London editorship of the *Glasgow Evening News* (1914–1919).

**Dunn, Samuel** (*d.* 1794), an Eng. mathematician. He wrote on astronomical subjects and is chiefly noted as the inventor of the 'universal planispheres or terrestrial and celestial globes in plano.' Author of *The New Atlas of the Mundane System*, 1774, *The Navigator's Guide to the Oriental or Indian Seas*, 1775, etc.

**Dunnage,** a name given to the loose logs of wood that are placed between the cargo in the hold of a ship to keep it steady.

**Dunne, Finley Peter** (*b.* 1867), an American humorist, *b.* in Chicago. He became a newspaper reporter in 1885 ; city editor of the *Chicago Times*, 1891–2 ; joined the staff of the *Chicago Evening Post* and *Times Herald*, 1892–7 ; and was appointed editor of the *Chicago Journal*, 1897–1900. He is well known as the creator of 'Mr. Dooley,' the incomparable Irish-American philosopher of Archey Road. The sayings of this gentleman on social and political questions first appeared in the *Chicago Journal*, and were collected in 1898 under the title of *Mr. Dooley in Peace and in War*. This was followed by *Mr. Dooley in the Hearts of his Countrymen*, 1898 ; *Mr. Dooley's Philosophy*, 1900 ; *Mr. Dooley's Opinions*, 1901 ; *Observations by Mr. Dooley*, 1902 ; *Dissertations by Mr. Dooley*, 1906 ; *Mr. Dooley Says*, 1910.

**Dunnet Head,** the most N. point on the mainland of Great Britain. It is a rocky peninsula in Caithness-shire, Scotland, 346 ft. high, with a lighthouse on its summit, and the small fishing village of Dunnet on the S.W. of the bay.

**Dunning, John,** *see* ASHBURTON, LORD.

**Dunnose,** a rocky headland on the S.E. coast of the Isle of Wight.

**Dunnville,** a banking vil. and port of entry in Haldimand co., Ontario Canada ; on the Grand R. and the Grand Trunk Railway, 40 m. S.S.E of Hamilton. It is an important agricultural district, and the town has lumber interests. Pop. 3224.

**Dunois,** a former ter. of France, in the prov. of Orléannais, comprising the present depts. of Eure-et-Loir; Loir-et-Cher, and Loiret.

**Dunois, Jean, Count of** (1402–68), a Fr. soldier, commonly known as the 'Bastard of Orleans,' being the natural son of Louis, Duke of Orleans. He fought at Beaugé (1421) and Verneuil (1424), and defeated the Eng. at Montargis (1427). He held Orleans till the arrival of Joan of Arc in 1428, and in the following year with her won the battle of Patay. He laid siege to Chartres and Lagny in 1432, and drove the Eng. from Paris in 1436, and from many cities in Guienne. He joined the league of revolted nobles in 1464; for which act Louis temporarily deprived him of his estates.

**Dunolly,** a tn. of Gladstone co., Victoria, Australia, 30 m. W.N.W. of Castlemaine. Pop. 853.

**Dunoon,** a popular watering-place in Argyllshire, Scotland, on the Firth of Clyde, 7½ m. W. of Greenock. The ruins of a castle remain which was formerly the seat of the Stewarts. It was the site of hanging of thirty-six Lamonts by the Campbells in 1643. The town is pleasant and well built, with a steamboat pier and esplanade, etc. Pop. 13,659.

**Dunraven and Mount-Earl, Windham Thomas Wyndham-Quin,** fourth **Earl of** (1841–1926), an Eng. politician, *b.* Feb. 12 at Adare Abbey. During the Franco-Prussian War and at the siege of Paris he acted as war correspondent to the *Daily Telegraph*. In 1902 he was Chairman of the Irish Land Conference, and became President of the Irish Reform Association. He strongly advocated the policy known as 'devolution,' which was denounced by the gov., with the result that the Chief Secretary of Ireland, Mr. Wyndham, resigned from office in 1905. Lord D. was a keen yachtsman, and twice tried, without success, for the America Cup, in 1893 and 1895. His publications include : *The Great Divide, the Upper Yellowstone*, 1874 ; *The Irish Question*, 1880 ; *Self-Instruction in the Theory and Practice of Navigation*, 1900 ; and *The Legacy of Past Years*, 1911. Died in London, June 14.

**Dunrossness,** a peninsula in the S. of Shetland mainland, which terminates in Sumburgh Head. The par. includes part of Pomona and Fair Is. Picts Castle is a cylindrical structure 158 ft. in circumference at the base and 40 ft. high. Pop. 3280.

**Duns, or Dunse,** a police bor. of Berwickshire, Scotland, 30 m. W. of Berwick-on-Tweed. It has a corn exchange and a town hall. Duns Scotus and Thomas Boston were natives. In 1699 General Leslie, with his army of Covenanters, encamped on Duns Law, a high mound rising some 700 ft. Pop. 2069.

**Dunsany, Edward John Moreton Drax Plunkett,** eighteenth Baron, Irish playwright; b. July 24, 1878; eldest son of seventeenth baron. Educated at Eton and Royal Military College, Sandhurst. Formerly Lieut. Coldstream Guards; Captain Royal Inniskilling Fusiliers. Succeeded to barony, 1899. Fought in the S. African War 1899–1900, at Battles of Belmont, Graspan, Modder R., and Magersfontein ; and in Great War (wounded). Unsuccessfully contested W. Wilts. as a Conservative, Jan. 1906. In 1909 his first play, *The Glittering Gate,* was produced at the Abbey Theatre, Dublin. The play shows a dead burglar and a dead murderer, before the gate of heaven, which they have to force open to gain admission to find nothing inside. In 1911 came *King Agrimenes*; also— probably his best play—*The Gods of the Mountain,* wherein a company of beggars, with an artful genius to lead them, impose themselves upon a city as gods—with the result that they are punished by becoming real green-jade gods, pure and immovable. Other plays of his are : *The Golden Doom,* 1912 ; *A Night at an Inn,* 1916 ; *The Tents of the Arabs,* 1917 ; *The Laughter of the Gods,* 1919 ; *If,* 1921 ; *Alexander, and Three Small Plays,* 1925 ; *Mr. Faithful,* 1927. These plays are intellectual dreams. They deal in mythology ; but it is a mythology of the author's own. He has also published some volumes of tales.

**Dunscore,** a vil., Scotland, in co. Dumfries, 10 m. N.W. of the town of that name. It is chiefly noted for the fact that Burns once lived there. Pop. 1036.

**Dunsinane,** one of the Sidlaw Hills in Perthshire, Scotland. It has an elevation of 1012 ft., and is situated 8½ m. N.E. of Perth. On its summit are the remains of ' Macbeth's Castle,' where Siward, Earl of Northumbria, is supposed to have defeated Macbeth in 1054. *See* Shakespeare's *Macbeth,* V. i. 92.

**Dunsink,** a hill 4 m. N.W. of Dublin, on which is the observatory of Trinity College.

**Duns Scotus, Johannes** (1265 or 1274–1308), a mediæval philosopher. His birthplace is uncertain, Duns in Berwickshire, Dunstane in Northumberland, and Dunum (Down) in N. Ireland, all claiming that honour. It is supposed that he became a Franciscan and studied and lectured (about 1301) at Oxford. In 1304 he moved to Paris, and three years later the doctor's degree was conferred upon him by the university, and he was appointed regent of the theological school. In 1308 he was despatched to Cologne to found a university, and d. there a few months after his arrival. D. S. acquired the title ' Doctor Subtilis ' on account of his dialectical ingenuity and wit. In philosophy he revived nominalism in a mitigated form and denied the real distinction between essence and existence. In theology he strongly upheld the doctrine of the Immaculate Conception, which was opposed by the Dominicans, called Thomists, because they were followers of Thomas Aquinas. Scotus also preached that no one could attain to a pure knowledge of theology by reason alone, that revelation must give part of that knowledge. During the Revival of Learning, the Scotists, we are told, ' raged in every pulpit,' and thus ' Dunsmen ' gave the word ' dunce,' meaning a dullard, or ignoramus. Scotus wrote commentaries on the Bible and on Aristotle, and the *Sentences* of Peter Lombard, called *Opus Oxoniense,* or *Anglicanum.* A complete edition of his works was published in thirteen volumes by Luke Wadding in Lyons, 1639. Consult W. J. Townsend, *The Great Schoolmen,* 1881 ; C. Frassen, *Scotus Academicus* (new ed.), 1900 ; and R. Seeberg, *Die Theologie des J. Duns Scotus,* 1900.

**Dunstable,** a tn. 36½ m. N.W. of London, in the S. of Bedfordshire. It is connected by branches with the London Mid. and Scottish and L. & N.E. main lines. Since the eighteenth century it has been chiefly engaged in the manufacture of straw hats. D. is linked with history, because its Augustinian priory, founded by Henry I. in the early twelfth century, was the scene of the first miracle play performed in Eng. ; because Cranmer here annulled Catherine of Aragon's marriage (1533), and because until 1643 it possessed an Eleanor Cross. The church of St. Peter and St. Paul is a remnant of the old priory. Pop. 8894.

**Dunstaffnage,** a ruined castle in Argyllshire, Scotland, on Loch Etive, 2½ m. N.E. of Oban. According to tradition it was the royal seat of the Dalriadan kings. It was captured by Robert the Bruce in

1308, and became the stronghold of the Campbells and Macdougals. It formed an Eng. military station during the risings of 1715 and 1745, and for a while the prison of Flora Macdonald in 1746. In 1910 the Duke of Argyll disputed the ownership, but the case was decided in favour of A. J. Campbell, hereditary captain of D.

**Dunstan, Saint** (c. 925–988), an Eng. archbishop and statesman, *b.* at or near Glastonbury, in Somersetshire, of noble parents. After receiving a careful education, he was taken by his uncle, Aldhelm, to Athelstan's court. He did not remain here, however, but retired to

ST. DUNSTAN
(Cotton MS.)

a hermitage near Glastonbury, where he devoted himself to a life of prayer and austerity. In 940, on the accession of Edmund, D. was called from his retirement and made Abbot of Glastonbury, and he rebuilt and restored the abbey. The next king, Edred, gave D. almost unlimited power, and the prelate used this to introduce the Benedictine order into Eng. and strictly enforce ecclesiastical discipline. For a time D. lost his influence, but it was soon regained, and in 959 he was made Archbishop of Canterbury. He maintained almost absolute power during the reigns of Edgar and Edmund, but his credit and influence declined after the murder of the latter prince. He retired to Canterbury, where he died.

**Dunstan, Sir Wyndham Rowland** (b. 1861), an Eng. scientist. In 1885 was appointed lecturer in chemistry at Oxford. He subsequently held the posts of professor of chemistry to the Pharmaceutical Society (1886) and was later director of the scientific department of the Imperial Institute His publications include: British Cotton Cultivation, 1904 and 1908 Agriculture in Asia Minor, 1908 and Cotton Cultivation of the World 1910.

**Dunstanborough Castle** is situate on the Northumbrian coast, 8 m N.E. of Alnwick. The cliffs are basaltic in structure, and the quart crystals found in the neighbourhood are called Dunstanborough diamonds

**Dunsterville, Major-General L. C** (b. 1865), a Brit. soldier, entered R Sussex R. 1884, reaching rank o Major-General in 1918. He transferred to the Indian Staff Corps i 1887, and held various important staff appointments. Served in the Waziristan 1894–5, N.W. Frontie (India) 1897–8, China 1900, and Grea War campaigns. Commanded Dunster Force, expedition to Baku, which was detached from Mesopotamia Expeditionary Force from Jan. to Sept. 1918. D. was Kipling's origina of ' Stalkey.' He wrote Adventure of Dunster Force.

**Duntocher**, a tn., Scotland, co Dumbarton, 8 m. N.W. of Glasgow Manufactures farm tools. Pop. 3250

**Dunton, John** (1650–1733), a Eng. bookseller, b. at Graffham who started a business at the Sig of the Raven, near the Royal Ex change. He published a number o political pamphlets and squibs on the Whig side, and an interesting auto biography, Life and Errors of John Dunton, 1705.

**Dunwich**, a par. and vil. of Eng in E. Suffolk. It is situated on the coast 4½ m. S.W. of Southwold. It is now merely a small watering-place owing to the disastrous action of the sea, which has been undermining the tn. since the fourteenth century. It is, however, historically interesting. King Sigeberht built there a palace for himself and a church for Bishop Felix. It was formerly the cap. o E. Anglia and from 673 to 870 the head of a bishop's see. In the reign of Edward III. the sea destroyed 400 houses. It sent two members to Parliament from 1296 to 1832. The corporation was not abolished until 1886, although the pop. was only 189 in 1920. There was a monastery at D. until the sea swallowed it up. Pop. 156.

**Duodecimals**, a system of arithmetical notation where the local value of a digit increases by powers of twelve as it moves to the left, instead of by powers of ten as in the ordinary or decimal notation. Two extra symbols are required, one to denote 10 and one to denote 11. The advantages of such a system, if universally adopted, arise from the fact that 12 splits up into the small factors 2.2.3. *D. arithmetic*, as practised by surveyors, is a system by which the calculation of square measure and cubic measure is reduced to operations in the powers of 12. The table for square measure is 12 sq. in. = 1 superficial prime; 12 superficial primes = 1 sq. ft. That for cubic measure is 12 cub. in. = 1 solid second; 12 solid seconds = 1 solid prime; 12 solid primes = 1 cub. ft.

**Duodenal Ulcer,** *see* ULCER.

**Duodenum,** *see* DIGESTION and INTESTINES.

**Dupanloup, Félix Antoine Philibert** (1802–78), Bishop of Orleans, *b.* at St. Félix, near Chambéry. Ordained a priest in 1825, he became a vicar of the Madeleine, Paris, and for a time tutor to the Orleans princes. Later he founded the famous academy at St. Hyacinthe. In 1849 he was appointed Bishop of Orleans. His educational doctrines had a farreaching influence, and he wrote many books on the subject to propagate his theories. Among these are : *Méthode Générale du Catéchisme*, 1841 ; *De l'Education*, 1850 ; *De la Haute Education Intellectuelle*, 1855, and *L'Enfant*, 1869. D. was a leader of the moderate Catholics, and his writings on ecclesiastical and religious subjects include *La Souveraineté Pontificale*, 1860 ; *Le Mariage Chrétien*, 1869 ; and *Histoire de Notre Seigneur Jésus Christ*, 1870. The *Journal Intime de Mgr. Dupanloup* was edited by Branchereau in 1902. *See* Life by F. Lagrange (Eng. translation by Lady Herbert, 1885).

**Duperrey, Louis Isidore** (1786–1865), a Fr. navigator, *b.* in Paris. He accompanied Freycinet on his voyage of exploration in the N. Pacific (1817–20), and on his return to France he was given the command of the *Coquille*. In 1822–25 he explored parts of Australia and New Guinea, and on his return published *Voyage autour du Monde* (1826–30).

**Dupin, André Marie Jean Jacques** (1783–1865), a Fr. statesman and advocate, *b.* at Varzy in Nièvre. In 1811 he was appointed on the commission charged with the codification of the laws of the empire, and in 1815 he sat for a few months in the Chamber of Deputies on the side of the Liberal Opposition. He was president of the Chamber eight times between 1832 and 1848, resigning in 1848 on account of his failure to secure the crown for the young Count of Paris. The emperor restored him to his former office in 1857. D.'s writings are numerous and include : *Principia Juris Civilis* (5 vols.), 1806 *Mémoires et Plaidoyers de 1860 au 1er Janvier 1830* (20 vols.) ; and *Mémoires ou Souvenirs du Barreau* (4 vols.), 1855–57. Consult Ortolan, *Notice sur Dupin*, 1840.

**Dupleix, Joseph François** (1697–1763), Governor-General of Fr. India, *b.* at Landrecies, dept. Nord, France. In 1715 he sailed for India on one of the vessels of the French East India Company, and in 1720 was elected a member of the counci at Pondichéry. In 1742 he was ap pointed governor-general over all French India. When war broke out between France and Eng. in 1744, D. strove to obtain the ascendency of France in India by making overtures to the native princes. He laid siege to Fort St. David (1747), and spread his troops over the Carnatic. He attempted the subjugation of the S. of India, and at one time was proclaimed its viceroy by the natives. His plans were, however, defeated by Clive, until he was summarily recalled by the Fr. government in 1754, and was never rewarded for the undoubted services he rendered to his country. Consult Tibulle Hamont, *Dupleix, d'après sa correspondance inédite*, 1881 ; H. Castonnet, *Dupleix, ses expéditions et ses projets*, 1888 ; G. B. Malleson, *Dupleix*, (in the Rulers of India series), 1890 ; and the Lives by E. Guérin, 1908, and Colonel J. Biddulph, 1910.

**Duplex Querela** (Lat. twofold complaint), a process in ecclesiastical causes, consisting of an appeal from an authority to one above it, as from a bishop to an archbishop, and from an archbishop to the crown in council.

**Duplicate Ratio,** the proportion or ratio which the squares of any numbers bear in relation to that of the radical quantities. If any number of quantities be continued proportionals, the ratio of the first to the third will be a duplicate ratio of that of the first and second.

**Dupnitza,** a tn. of Bulgaria, 22 m. S. of Sofia. It grows tobacco and there are springs. Pop. 13,750.

**Duponceau, Pierre Etienne** (1760–1844), a Fr.-American writer and scholar, *b.* at Saint-Martin-de-Ré, France. He became secretary to Baron Steuben, whom he accompanied to America in 1777, and fought for the Americans in the War of Independence. He retired from the American army on grounds of health in 1781, and became translator and correspondent to Robert Livingston, then Secretary for Foreign Affairs. Subsequently devoted much time to philology. His works include :

*English Phonology,* 1818; and *Mémoire sur le système grammatical des langages de quelques nations indiennes de l' Amérique du Nord,* 1838.

**Du Pont de Nemours, Pierre Samuel** (1739–1817), Fr. statesman, *b.* at Paris, negotiated with the Eng. Commissioner for the recognition of the Independence of the U.S.A. Went to U.S.A. in 1799, where he was employed by Jefferson. His family settled in U.S.A., where they established at Powder Mill in Delaware, and many of the descendants were distinguished men.

**Dupont, Pierre** (1821–70), a Fr. poet, *b.* at Lyons. He was the son of a blacksmith, but, being left an orphan at five, he was brought up by a village priest. In 1839 he went to Paris, and three years later a song of his received a prize from the Academy. His best-known songs are : *La Chanson du blé, La Vache blanche,* and *Le Braconnier.* They were collected under *Chants et Chansons,* 1852–54, and *Chants et Poésies* (7th ed.), 1862. Consult Déchant, *Biographie de Pierre Dupont,* 1871, and Ch. Lenient, *Poésie patriotique en France,* 1889.

**Düppel,** or **Dyböl,** a vil. Schleswig-Holstein, Prussia, on the peninsula of Sundewitt, 15 m. N.E. of Flensburg. It was the site of a struggle between the Danes and Gers. in 1848–49, and was bombarded by the Prussians in 1864.

**Dupré, Giovanni** (1817–1869), Tuscan sculptor, of humble Fr. origin, *b.* at Siena. As a boy he was put to hard manual toil, but was early fortunate in obtaining the help of the Rom. priesthood, who gave him the means of studying sculpture. Some busts of cardinals shown in Rome made a sensation. These were followed by a figure of 'Abel,' of exquisite sentiment, which was shown at the Paris Salon in 1855. His other best works were the 'Triumph of the Cross;' a superb figure of 'Cain'; 'Picta'; and the bust of Mme. Dora D'Istria. Died in poverty.

**Dupré, Jules** (1811–89), a Fr. painter, *b.* at Nantes. He was the son of a porcelain manufacturer, and worked first in his father's, and later in his uncle's china factory. D. belonged to the romantic school of landscape painters, and painted nature best in her tempestuous moods. On his visit to Eng. in 1831 he learnt much from Constable's pictures. D.'s best-known works are: 'The Forest of Fontainebleau,' 'Morning and Evening.' His 'Crossing the Bridge' is in the Wallace Collection, London.

**Dupuis, Charles François** (1742–1809), a Fr. writer, politician, and advocate. A member of the National

Convention, he was appointed a commissioner of public instruction. His abridgment of his own *Origine de tous les cultes,* 1795, helped to foster the anti-clerical spirit among his countrymen.

**Dupuy de Lôme, Stanislas Charles Henri Laurent** (1816–85), a Fr. naval architect, *b.* at Ploëmeur near L'Orient. He studied at the Ecole Polytechnique and in Eng. He designed the first Fr. war steamer, the *Napoléon* (1848–52), and invented methods of changing sailing men-of-war into steamers. During the siege of Paris he planned a steering balloon, but the siege was over before it was put to any use. He was appointed Inspecteur-Général du Matériel de la Marine in 1866, was elected a member of the Academy of Sciences in 1866, and a senator for life in 1877.

**Dupuytren, Guillaume, Baron** (1777–1835), a Fr. surgeon, had a struggle with poverty until, in 1801, he received a coveted anatomical appointment in Paris. His connection with the Hôtel-Dieu dates from 1808, and in 1815 he became chief surgeon. He was an indefatigable student, especially of morbid anatomy, enjoyed a high reputation for the skill with which he performed a number of difficult operations, and throughout his life was lecturing to crowded halls of students. His *Treatise on Artificial Anus* is one of many.

**Duquesne,** a banking post-borough of Allegheny co., Pennsylvania, U.S.A., 10 m. S.E. of Pittsburg, on the Monongahela R., and on the Pennsylvania Railroad. It has steel works and blasting furnaces. Pop. 21,396.

**Duquesne, Abraham, Marquis** (1610–88), a Fr. admiral, *b.* at Dieppe. He first joined the merchant service, and took part in the defeat of the Spaniards at the capture of the Lerins Is. (1637). He also fought at Guetaria (1638), Corunna (1639), Tarragona (1641), and Barcelona (1643). In 1676 he defeated the combined fleets of Spain and Holland off Stromboli, for which victory he was promoted to the rank of marquis by Louis XIV. He also bombarded Algiers (1682–83) and Genoa (1684), and did much service to his country by reorganising the Fr. fleet. Consult Jal, *Abraham Duquesne et la Marine de son Temps,* 1873.

**Duquesne, Fort,** a Fr. fort and trading-post built in 1754 on the site where Pittsburg now stands. The Brit. expedition against it under Braddock was repulsed in 1755, but in 1758 General Forbes captured it from the Fr., and in the following year began the building of Pittsburg and Fort Pitt, in honour of William Pitt, then Prime Minister in Eng.

**Duquesnoy, François** (1594–1646), a Flemish sculptor, commonly known as François Flamand. He chiefly excelled in modelling children. He executed groups of children for the high altar at St. Peter's, Rome; a ' Concert of Cherubim ' in the church of the Holy Apostles, Naples; ' St. Susanna,' in the Loretto church at Rome; and ' St. Andrew,' in the basilica of St. Peter's. D. *d.* at Livorno, and was supposed to have been poisoned by his brother.

**Duramen,** in botany, is the heart-wood, or older internal portion of the secondary wood, as distinguished from the outer sap-wood (*alburnam*).

**Durance,** a riv. of France, which rises near Mont Genèvre. Its course is chiefly S.W. until it reaches Pertuis, when it turns N.W. It passes through Hautes-Alpes and Basses-Alpes. About 3 m. S.W. of Avignon it joins the Rhone. Its total length is 218 m., and the chief feeders are the Buech and Verdon.

**Durand, Alice Marie Céleste** (1842–1902), a Fr. novelist who used the pseudonym ' Henry Gréville.' She was *b.* in Paris, but lived for many years in St. Petersburg, where her husband was professor of law. She made a tour in the U.S.A. in 1886, giving lectures on Fr. and Russian literature. Her novels are sensational in character, and include *Dosia*,1876 ; *Frankler*, 1877 ; and *Sonia*, 1877.

**Durand, Jean Nicolas Louis** (1760–1834), professor of architecture at the École Polytechnique. He came of a poor family, but rapidly rose to a high position. He became draughts-man to the king's architect, Boulée, and in 1780 won the great prize at the Académie Royale d'Architecture. He executed some designs for public buildings at the request of the National Convention, and was ap-pointed to the professorship above named. He published *Recueil et Parallèle des Édifices de tous Genres,* 1800, which consists of eighty-six plates, to illustrate Legrand's text-book of architecture. He also wrote *Précis des Leçons d'Architecture* and *Partie Graphique des Cours d'Architecture.*

**Durango,** (1) a state of Mexico, 38,009 sq. m. in area, with a pop. of 370,294. Is very mountainous. The rugged peaks of the Sierra Madre cross the W. Grizzly bears, wolves, deer and wild turkeys entertain the traveller. Cotton is indigenous. Columbus saw Indians clothed with it in 1502. The Toltecs believed that the god of the air had taught them its use, and it is still one of the great

staples of D. Corn, tobacco, fruits and sugar cane are also produced and cattle-breeding is carried on. The iron mountain is almost unique, and is nearly a mile in length. There are also rich gold, silver and copper mines. (2) Cap. of the state, 6207 ft. above sea-level, has an almost matchless climate, and the region round it is an open-air sana-torium. The cathedral is 250 ft. long by 153 ft. high. The cotton mills are important. Men and women promenade in the evening separately, going in opposite directions. There is a Bull Ring, as in other Mexican tns. Pop. 40,000.

**Duránis, or Durránis,** the dominant race of Afghans, comprising the Zirak and the Panjpai. They inhabit the northern slopes of the Safed Koh.

**Durant,** a banking post-tn. in Bryan co., Oklahoma, U.S.A., 19 m. N.E. of Denison. It is an agri-cultural centre, and has cotton and cotton-seed oil industries. The tn. received a charter in 1904. Pop. 7340.

**Durante, Ser,** a poet of Tuscany who flourished in the early part of the thirteenth century and made an adaptation of the *Roman de la Rose.* Consult G. Massatinti, *Inventario dei MSS. Italiani delle Biblioteche di Francia* (vol. iii.), 1888.

**Durazno,** the name of a dept. and city of Uruguay, S. America. Vast numbers of sheep are pastured in the district. The tn. is on the main line from Montevideo to Rivera, and is situated on the Yi R. Area of the dept. 5525 sq. m. Pop. 65,000, tn. 13,500.

**Durazzo** (ancient *Epidamnus* and *Dyrrachium*), a port on the bay of Durazzo, some 49 m. S. of Scutari, in Albania. Epidamnus was founded in the seventh century by settlers from Corinth and Corcyra. The Roms., who seized it early in the fourth century B.C., preferred to call the place Dyrrachium. It was a favourite harbour in which to disembark Rom. troops sailing eastward, and it was here that Pompey gained a short-lived triumph over Cæsar, be-fore his defeat at Philippi (48 B.C.). It was destroyed by an earthquake in A.D. 345, and was besieged and taken in 481, 1082 and 1185. Be-longed to Venice from 1392–1501, and then to the Turks. It was the cap. of Albania during the Great War. A sand bar now blocks the harbour, though olive oil and grain are still exported. From it the retreating Serbs were shipped to safety in 1915 by Fr. vessels. Pop. 4800.

**Durban,** the port and largest city of the colony of Natal, S. Africa. It lies on a landlocked tidal bay and is the

I

only harbour of any importance between Delagoa Bay and E. London. The inner basin covers about 7 sq. m. with 3 m. of quays. It is the clearing-house for all the coast products, such as sugar, tea, coffee and fibre, and there are various local industries. D. has become a sea-side resort, and many thousand visitors live there during the winter, when the climate resembles that of the S. of France. The tn. and suburbs are very beautiful, especially that on the Berea, a range of hills with fine views, on which there are four public parks. Fruit is very plentiful, including the orange, mango, pineapple, guava, shaddock, etc. There are an Art Gallery, a museum, a handsome Town Hall, etc., erected at a cost of £352,000, new Law Courts, a Market House which cost £57,000, Botanic Gardens. The Victoria Embankment along the Bay side has a memorial to Vasco da Gama, who discovered Natal on Christmas Day, 1497. Pop. 156,000, of whom 56,840 are white living in the city, and 17,046 in the suburbs, 55,610 coloured and 57,505 Asiatics.

**Durbar** (from Persian *darbár*, meaning 'court' or 'audience'), the executive council of a native province of India and formerly used in this sense by Indian chieftains, who discussed state administration and other business in D. To-day the word is most commonly applied to such ceremonial gatherings or festivals as Lord Lytton held at Delhi in 1877, for the purpose of proclaiming Queen Victoria Empress of India. Delhi was the scene of similar state functions in 1903 and 1912, when Edward VII. and George V. were respectively proclaimed emperor.

**Düren**, a tn. on the Roer, 18½ m. E. of Aix-la-Chapelle, in the Prussian Rhine prov., Ger. It is a railway centre with a Gothic church of thirteenth to fourteenth century, the Gewandhaus of 1450, Kornhaus of 1588, a museum, manufactures of paper, metal goods, cloth, carpets, glass and chemicals. Pop. 37,180.

**Dürer, Albrecht (Albert Duerer)** (1471–1528), a famous Ger. painter and engraver of Nuremberg, son of a goldsmith. Founder of the Ger. school of painting, he was also considered the inventor of the art of etching and of printing woodcuts in two colours. His copper-plate engravings are especially famous, and he ranks higher as a designer of woodcuts than as a painter. In 1486 he became a pupil of the great painter Michael Wohlgemuth. From 1490–94 he went on a tour probably through Ger., visiting Strasburg, Colmar, Basle, and Venice, where Mantegna's

works impressed him greatly. On his return he married Agnes Frey, but their union is thought to have been an unhappy one. For a time he probably worked in Wohlgemuth's studio, but by 1497 had one of his own. D. went to Venice, 1505–7, where he painted 'The Martyrdom of St. Bartholomew.' In 1512 he became court painter to Maximilian I., and painted for him 'The Virgin with many Angels.' He was deputy for Nuremberg at the Augsburg Diet, 1518, and painted Maximilian's por-

DÜRER

From a drawing by himself at the age of 13

trait there. In 1521–2 D. and his wife visited the Netherlands (*see* Lange and Fuhse, *Dürer's Schriftlicher Nachlass*, 1893) and won the patronage of Charles V. He favoured the doctrines of the Reformation and was a friend of Luther. The mural decorations of Nuremberg City Hall— 'The Calumny of Apelles' and 'The Triumph of Maximilian'—were designed by D. Among his most famous engravings are: 'Adam and Eve,' 1504; 'The Nativity'; 'The Great Horse' and 'The Little Horse,' 1505; 'Melancholia' and 'St. Jerome in his Study,' 1514; 'The Knight, Death, and the Devil,' 1513; 'The Prodigal Son,' 1503. Noted woodcuts are: 'The Apocalypse' (sixteen subjects, including the Revelation of St. John), 1498; 'The Greater Passion' (twelve subjects); 'The Lesser Passion' (thirty-seven subjects). Among his best pictures are: 'The Feast of the Rosary,' 1506 (now in Strahow monastery, near Prague); 'Martyrdom of the 10,000 Christians,' 1508 (Vienna Gallery); 'Adoration of the Magi,' 1504 (Uffizi, Florence); 'Adam and Eve' (Florence); 'Adoration of the Trinity,' 1511 (Imperial Gallery, Vienna); 'The Four Apostles,' 1526 (now in Munich Gallery); 'Crucifixion,' 1511. Among his portraits are those of Raphael, Melanchthon, Erasmus. The series of engravings known as 'The Passion in Copper,' was done between 1508 and 1513. All D.'s work is marked by exuberant imagination, sublimity, and correctness of design, but some critics lament the lack of It. training. D. wrote on geometry and perspective, on mensuration (1525), on fortification (1527); *Von menschlicher Proportion* appear-

misdemeanour. The constraint may also consist of imprisonment.

**D'Urfey, Thomas** (1653–1723), a poet and dramatist, perhaps better known as 'Tom Durfey,' from childhood was addicted to the use of the pen. At the age of twenty-three he had the pleasure of witnessing the production at the King's Theatre of his play, *The Siege of Memphis*, a tragedy that did not score any great success. He was happier in attracting the popular favour with the many comedies that followed his first effort. He wrote a great number of songs, which caught the public ear and were

**DURHAM CATHEDRAL**
(The Galilee Chapel showing the Tomb of Bede)

ing in 1528. Consult Campe, *Reliquien von A. Dürer*, 1828; Sandrart, *Deutsche Academie*, 1675–79; Vasari, *Vite de' piu eccellenti Pittori*, etc., 1878–82; Eastlake, *Five Great Painters*, 1883; *L'Art*, xiv., 1878; Heller, *Das Leben und die Werke Durers*, 1827–31; Michiel, *Etudes sur l'Allemagne*; Schefer, *An Artist's Married Life*; Naglar, *Dürer und seine Kunst*, 1837; *Edinburgh Review*, July 1861; Zucker, *Dürer*, 1900.

**Duress** (from Lat. *duritia*, harshness), a law expression for 'constraint.' It is open to a defendant to advance a plea of D. if he has been driven by menace (*per minas*) of death or bodily harm to commit some act which would normally constitute a crime or

sung all over the kingdom. These he published from time to time. He issued also: *Tales, Tragical and Comical*, 1704, and *Tales, Moral and Comical*, 1706, as well as other works. A noted wit, his presence was sought in all companies, and among his admirers was Charles II.

**Durham** : (1) A maritime co., with an area of 637,672 acres, in the N.E. of Eng., bounded on the N. by Northumberland, on the E. by the North Sea, on the S. by Yorkshire, and westward by Westmorland and Cumberland. To the W. of a line drawn from Barnard Castle to Consett are highlands belonging to the Pennine Range, which rise to 2300 ft. ; this district is mostly barren moorland. Loamy soil lies about the principal rivers, the Tyne, Tees, and Wear. About a half of the county is given over to pasturage, but oats and barley are grown. Sunderland (151,159 inhabitants) is the port for the valuable coalfield and, like Stockton-on-Tees (52,154) and West Hartlepool (63,932), has a thriving shipbuilding trade. The lead mines of Teesdale and the limestone quarries are a source of wealth. There are numerous iron foundries and glass, earthenware, and chemical works. Pop. 1,478,506. (2) The co. tn. of D., Eng., lies 12 m. to the S. of Newcastle. Both the cathedral and castle are magnificently situated on a tall, rocky peninsula almost encircled by the Wear. About 995 Bishop Aldune brought the bones of St. Cuthbert here from Ripon, the site being then called Dunholme (Hill Island). In 1093 Bishop William Carileph began the Norman structure, which still forms the main body of the cathedral, as a last resting-place for the saint's relics. It is a stately pile, and with its massive Norman nave, Early Eng. chapel, and Perpendicular tower, forms one of the chief architectural glories of the country. The crypt chapel of the castle dates back to its foundation by William the Conqueror in 1072, whilst Framwellgate and another bridge over the Wear were built originally in the thirteenth century. Pop. 17,329. (3) The co. seat of D. co. N. Carolina, U.S.A., 25 m. N.W. of Raleigh, with a great trade in tobacco and manufacture of cigars and cigarettes, with one of the largest factories in the world. It has also large cotton and hosiery mills. It is the seat of Duke University, the North Carolina college for negroes and the Lincoln hospital for negroes. Pop. 52,037.

**Durham, John George Lambton, Earl of** (1792–1840), eldest son of W. H. Lambton of Lambton Castle, and M.P. for Durham. An Eng. stateman, educated at Eton, and afterwards served in the 10th Hussars. At the early age of twenty, he married Miss Harriet Cholmondely, by whom he had three daughters. At the death of his wife in 1815, he married the following year Lady Louisa Elizabeth, a daughter of Earl Grey. In 1828 he was raised to the peerage, taking the title of Baron D. In 1830 he became a member of the cabinet as Lord Privy Seal. The liberality and ultimate success of the Reform Bill are said to be chiefly due to him. He was sent to Russia in 1835 as ambassador, and remained there two years, when he was then sent to Canada as Governor-General, 1838. The country at that time was full of unrest, and though D. successfully quelled all discontent he found he was not supported by the gov. as he had expected to be ; he consequently, without either being recalled or resigning, returned to Eng. the same year, thus ending his public career.

**Durham Light Infantry**, formerly 68th and 106th regiments, linked in 1881 to form Durham Light Infantry. 68th formed in 1756 as 2nd Battalion, 23rd Regiment, but became 68th in 1758. Served mainly in France, West Indies and Gibraltar and joined Wellington's army in Peninsula in 1811. Later, served in N. America, Crimean War and Maori War in New Zealand (1846). The 106th Regiment was raised in India by the East India Co. in 1826 as 2nd Bombay European Regiment. Served in Scinde and Aden and in 1857 in Persian Expedition, and during the Indian Mutiny. After the mutiny it was transferred to the British establishment as 106th Regiment and came to Eng. in 1871. Fought in Egyptian Campaign of 1884–5. The Durham Light Infantry served in South African Campaign of 1899–1902 and was in the Ladysmith relief column. During the Great War it raised some thirty-seven battalions which served in France, Flanders, Italy, Macedonia, Egypt, N.W. Frontier of India, and Archangel. The regiment also served in the Third Afghan War in 1919 against the ex-king Ammanullah (q.v.).

**Durham University**, opened in 1833. Archdeacon Thorp (d. 1862), who was largely responsible for the scheme for its erection drawn up by the chapter in 1831, was appointed the first warden. University College and Bishop Hatfield's Hall, which was especially designed to give facilities for a university career to poorer students, are the chief residential establishments. Degrees are granted in music (since 1889) and hygiene, besides in all the ordinary branches of learning. Women have been admitted as graduates since 1895. As early as 1300 there was a hall in Oxford reserved for Durham students.

**Durio**, a genus of Bombacaceæ, is indigenous to the Malay Archipelago. D. zibethinus is a large and lofty tree with smallish, alternate leaves, and yields the fruit known as durian. The durian is remarkable for the delicacy and richness of its flavour and the offensiveness of its odour, which has been compared with that of decaying onions.

**Dürkheim**, a grape-cure health resort with mineral springs, 6 m. S.W. of Mannheim, at the foot of the Hardt

Mts., in the Bavarian Palatinate, Ger. Pop. 7220.

**Durlach,** a tn., Ger., in the Free State of Baden, 2½ m. from Carlsruhe by rail. In 1565 a castle was built there, now in use as a barracks. The manufs. are brushes, tobacco, beer, sewing-machines, bicycles, dental instruments, organ building. Pop. 18,000.

**Dürnstein,** or **Dürrenstein,** a vil. beautifully situated on the l. b. of the Danube, 43 m. W.N.W. of Vienna, in Lower Austria. Close by are the ruins of the fortress in which Richard the Lion Heart was imprisoned (1192). Pop. 570.

**Durra,** or *Sorghum vulgare,* is a grass resembling Indian corn, much used for food in Africa, Asia, and India. The stem produces sugar, and the grain is fermented and made into alcoholic drinks. It is highly valued as a forage crop, as pasturage for sheep and all stock, and also as poultry food. When eaten green, sorghum has caused the death of animals, by reason of prussic acid found in the leaves.

**Dursley,** a tn., Gloucestershire, Eng., 5 m. S.W. of Gloucester. It was once famous for cloth manufacture, but now its industry consists in the manufacture of pins and agricultural tools, incubators, and cream-separators. The reformer Fox, Bishop of Hereford, was b. here in 1496. Pop. 2800.

**Duruy, Jean Victor** (1811–94), a Fr. historian and statesman, sprang from the working-class. He passed with eminent distinction through the Ecole Normale Supérieure, where he learnt from Michelet, and having assisted the emperor, Napoleon III., in his *Vie de César,* was appointed, in 1863, Minister of Education. During his six years in office he modernised the curricula of lycées and colleges, instituted secondary education for girls, and founded the 'conférences publiques.' His *Histoire des Romains* (7 vols.), 1879–85, is a splendid monument to his fame.

**Duse, Eleanora** (1858–1924), It. actress; b. Oct. 3, at Vigevano; only child of Alessandro Vincenzo D.—a Venetian actor (the son of the famous actor, Luigi D.). She was on the stage from childhood, and toured continually. During her first season of success at Naples, with *Les Fourchambault* by Augier, she was deserted by her lover, Martino Cafiero; and the boy to whom she gave birth at Turin lived but a few days. In 1881, at Florence, she married Tebaldo Checchi, a fellow-actor. They played in Rossi's company; and, at the Carignono Theatre, Turin, she scored a success (immediately after a Bernhardt season) with *La Princesse de Baghdad* by Dumas *fils.* After a success at Rome she returned with her husband to Turin, where a daughter was b. The company visited S. America; and at Rio de Janeiro she separated from her husband on account of her passion for Flavio Andò, a young actor who had joined them. Checchi soon afterwards d. in a consular post at Lisbon, and left her a legacy. On return to Europe the company was disbanded; and she formed a new one, with Andò as its head. She was much influenced by the poet-musician Arrigo Boito, whom she had first met in 1881. She began to tire of the old-fashioned Dumas plays, and came under the influence of Ibsen. She created the part of Santuzza in *Cavalleria Rusticana;* visited Russia; then (Feb. 1892) Vienna; then Berlin. In 1893 she visited U.S.A. and London; in 1895–6, Scandinavia and Russia. She rivalled Bernhardt in Paris in 1897. Her favourite resorts were Venice and neighbouring Chioggia—where her great-grandfather had been a fisherman; but, if she can be said to have had any home, it was at Asolo. After her relations with Andò had cooled, she was associated with D'Annunzio (*q.v.*) in an attempt to revive classicism in the It. theatre. Their association began in 1897, cooled about 1899, ended 1902. Many of his plays were written 'round' her. She played in such different rôles as Juliet, Francesca da Rimini, Marguerite, Camille, Fernande, Magda, Paula Tanqueray, and Ellida in Ibsen's *Lady from the Sea.* She would have nothing to do with make-up—relying on her natural liveliness of feature, voice, and gesture. Her early vehemence was toned down by the D'Annunzio influence—too much so, except for 'classical' enthusiasts. She made another visit to America in 1902; and retired from the stage in 1909. Owing to war losses, she returned to it in 1921, and repeated her triumphs in Italy, London, and America. She d. of influenza at Pittsburgh, Pa., April 21.

**Dussek, Johann Ladislaus** (1761–1812), a Bohemian pianist and composer, was a choir boy at the convent of Iglau, attended a Jesuit college and afterwards took his degree in philosophy at the University of Prague. For some time he supported himself as organist, and having made a name at Amsterdam as a pianist of remarkable virtuosity and delicacy of touch, he became professor of music to the stadtholder at The Hague. Whether he played in Berlin, St. Petersburg,

Milan, or London, he invariably attracted large audiences. His attempt to found a music-publishing business in London was a complete fiasco, and he was obliged to take refuge from his creditors in Hamburg. From 1809 till his death he directed the concerts of Prince Talleyrand in Paris. But he undermined his constitution by drinking heavily, in a vain effort to rouse himself from the excessive languor to which his obesity had reduced him. He wrote many pianoforte sonatas, trios, and quartets, etc., which have true melodic charm.

**Düsseldorf,** on the r. b. of the Rhine in the Rhenish-Westphalian industrial district of Ger. Has 432,000 inhab. and important iron and steel works. Industries include cotton spinning and weaving, paper, silk, dyes. chemicals, furniture. The traffic in the harbour is considerable. The Academy of Art was founded here by the Elector Charles Theodore in 1767. It is housed in an imposing Renaissance edifice of 1881, and contains Flemish and It. seventeenth- to eighteenth-century paintings and 14,000 drawings. The municipal Picture Gallery of modern D. painters is in the Kunst Halle. There is also a Museum of Industrial Art and a library of 90,000 volumes. The Lambert church is of the thirteenth century and the Town Hall of 1570–3. D. was occupied by the Fr. from Mar. 1921 till Aug. 1925. An asylum for homeless children has been carried on in a former Trappist monastery since 1819. The extensive Rhenish metal ware and machine factory, formerly engaged in the production of heavy guns, now turns out locomotives and railway carriages. The poet Heine was *b*. at 53 Bolker St., D., in 1797.

**Dust,** small particles of earth, etc., which are moved by the slightest air-currents. Even in a room which has been kept spotlessly clean the existence of D. can be demonstrated when a strong beam of sunlight enters by a window. The D. of the atmosphere consists of tiny fragments of minerals, organic matter, carbon, and ash from burning substances, volcanic D., salt from sea-spray, and D. formed by the disintegration of meteors on their way through the atmosphere. D. was formerly considered an unavoidable nuisance, but J. Aitken, in 1880, demonstrated that it combined with its disadvantages several useful functions. When air containing water vapour is cooled to the point of saturation, the water vapour does not condense at once unless there is some solid substance for it to condense upon.

Under suitable conditions of temperature the D. particles in the atmosphere become nuclei or centres for the condensation of water. These minute globules form clouds, mists, and fogs, and on coalescing form drops of rain. Aitken devised an instrument for counting the D. particles in a known volume of air. The results show that D. is more abundant than was suspected, the number of particles varying from 100 per c.c. in very clear air to about 100,000 per c.c. in the air of large cities. Many modifications of the sun's light are due to D. Without it we should have no twilight, no blue sky, no gorgeous sunsets, and none of the chiaroscuro effects which make scenery charming.

**Dutch Antilles,** *see* WEST INDIES.

**Dutch East India Company.** This famous company was founded by Charter, dated March 20, in 1602, by the union of a number of smaller trading companies and was given by the Dutch gov. the monopoly of the trade between the Strait of Magellan and the Cape of Good Hope, together with the right to enter into treaties and alliances in the name of the States-General and to set up factories. Like its Eng. counterpart, it was also empowered to build forts and to employ its own troops. In 1619 the company founded Batavia on the site of a native town, and some three decades later was in possession of most of the chief commercial centres throughout the Indian Archipelago, such as Sumatra, Java, Ceylon and Borneo, besides itself owning thriving colonies in S. Africa. It was not dissolved until 1798, when its possessions were assigned to the Dutch Gov. Consult François Valentyn, *Beschryving van oud en nieuw Oost Indien* (Amsterdam—1724).

**Dutch East Indies, The** (*Nederlandsch Indie*), situated between 95° and 141° E. long. and 6° N. and 11° S. lat., form the Asiatic possessions of Holland. They include Java and Madura; the island of Sumatra; the E., S., and W. of Borneo; Bali and Lombok; the Celebes; the Moluccas; Timor Archipelago; New Guinea to 141° E. long.; Banca; Riau-Lingga Archipelago, and Billiton. They are controlled by a governor-general, who is assisted by a council of five. In 1918 a national council, or Volksraad, was formed, to act in an advisory capacity; of its members—European, native, and foreign Oriental—some were elected, some appointed by the gov. A further step towards self-government was made in 1925, when this Volksraad was made, in conjunction with the Governor-General, the legislature for all matters of internal policy. The bulk of the native pop. is Mohammedan in religion, but the islands enjoy complete religious toleration. There are many public schools, both primary and secondary, also private schools and training schools, Dutch being the language of instruction. In 1928 there were some 4558 m. of railway, chiefly in Java and Sumatra. Batavia, in Java, is the capital. Rice, maize, cotton, sugar, coffee, cinchona, rubber, tea, potatoes, cassava, groundnuts, soya beans, and tobacco are cultivated, sugar, rubber, tea, tobacco, and cinchona being the chief exports. Both tin and coal are mined, and increasing quantities of mineral oil are obtained annually. In 1928 the value of the exports was about £132,490,000 as compared with £85,851,500 for the imports. The expenditure in 1930 was about £5,800,000 in excess of the revenue. There is a colonial army for defence, about five-sixths of which are composed of native troops, and also a flying corps. The total area is 788,000 sq. m., and the population in 1927 was approximately 52,824,569. Java is the most densely populated of the islands, being in some districts over-populated, and efforts are being made to persuade the Javanese to emigrate to S. Sumatra and other more sparsely peopled parts. The Dutch E. India Co., founded in 1602, ruled the islands from that date until 1798, when the company was dissolved.

**Dutch Guiana,** or **Surinam,** a possession of Holland, on the N. coast of S. America, has an area of 46,060 sq. m. It is bounded on the N. by the Atlantic Ocean; on the E. by the R. Maroni (on the other side of which lies French Guiana); on the S. by impenetrable forests, reaching to the Tumuc Humac Mts.; and on the W. by the Corentyn (beyond which lies British Guiana). The savannahs, drained by the upper reaches of the Maroni and the Nickeri, are inhabited by Indians, who hunt, fish, and cultivate manioc and cassava. The sugar, cacao, rice, maize, banana, and coffee plantations lie along the lower courses of the Surinam and Saramacca, and also in the low-lying coastal regions, and the chief settlements are among these plantations. Balata or gum, used for insulating wire, is a valuable product. Paramaribo (46,929 inhabitants), the capital, is situated at the mouth of the Surinam. A railroad connects Paramaribo with the goldfields of the Upper Surinam and Maroni. The bush negroes, who number some 10,000 and speak a debased form

of English, are the descendants of escaped slaves. The settlements are inhabited by Javanese, Chinese, coolies, negroes, and about 2000 whites. The total population, exclusive of the 9000 Indians who dwell in the almost unexplored hinterland to the S., is estimated at 140,000, of whom 45,550 live in Paramaribo. There are 30,024 Moravian Brethren, 25,219 Roman Catholics, 35,592 Mohammedans, and 10,985 Lutherans and members of the Reformed Church. There are also 23,689 Hindus. The colony is ruled by a governor, assisted by an executive council of four beside himself; these are all nominees of the

R. C. DUTT

queen. There is a legislative assembly of 16 members called the States, which is re-elected every sixth year. In 1927 the expenditure for the year was £590,000 and the local revenue £382,000. Exports and imports are of the annual average value of £850,000, Holland being the chief customer, and the prin. exports are balata, sugar, rice, maize and coffee.

**Dutch New Guinea,** see NEW GUINEA.

**Dutens, Joseph Michel** (1765–1848), a French engineer, was appointed chief engineer of the department of Léman in 1805, and assisted in constructing the railway viâ the Simplon Pass. His *Mémoires sur les Travaux publics de l'Angleterre* (1819) was the fruits of his appointment to study the inland navigation of that country.

**Du Toit's Pan,** see DIAMOND.

**Dutt, Romesh Chunder** (1848–1909), an Indian writer and civil servant, was a native of Calcutta, and was educated at Presidency College before he came to England and studied at University College, London. Having passed with the highest distinction into the Indian Civil Service (1871), he was appointed divisional commissioner in 1894 and 1895, being the first native to receive so high a post. In 1897 he retired from the service, and from 1904 to 1906 acted as revenue minister of the Baroda state. He wrote on the economic history of his country from 1757 until 1900, translated Sanskrit writings into English verse, including the *Rama-yana* and the *Maha-Bharata*, and published many novels in his native Bengali. *See* Life by J. N. Gupta.

**Dutt, Toru** or **Tarulata** (1856–77), a Hindu author, was a Christian girl of Calcutta, who, like Marie Bashkirtseff, developed in her girlhood a literary genius which showed small sign of immaturity. For over three years (1869–73) she was abroad in France and England. Her *Sheaf Gleaned in French Fields* (1876) contains English versions of French poems, and she also translated into English passages from the Sanskrit *Vishnupurana.* Gosse has edited her *Ancient Ballads and Legends of Hindustan,* 1882.

**Dutt, William Alfred** (*b.* 1870), an author and journalist, *b.* in Norfolk. He was educated at Bungay Grammar School. It was on the staff of the *Eastern Daily Press* that he received most of his journalistic training, and he was assistant editor of the literary department of the National Press Agency. He has published the following works : *George Borrow in East Anglia, The Norfolk Broads, The Norfolk and Suffolk Coast,* and *The King's Homeland.*

**Duty,** *see* EXCISE and CUSTOMS DUTIES.

**Dutyea,** an anthracite mining bor. of Luzerne co., Pennsylvania, U.S.A. Pop. (1920) 7776.

**Duumviri,** a name applied in the republic of Rome to a magistracy of two : 1. *Duoviri Sacrorum* were the first two men to whom was entrusted the charge of the Sibylline books. 2. *Duoviri navales,* were specially elected for the purpose of equipping or recruiting the navy. 3. *Duoviri Jure Dicundo* were men with the highest judiciary powers in municipal towns. 4. *Duoviri Æde Dedicandæ* were elected for the purpose of dedicating a temple. 5. *Duoviri Perduellionis* tried those accused of treason. The office was created by Tullus Hostilius, but was afterwards abolished.

**Duval, Claude** (1643–70), a highwayman, was a native of Normandy, and came over to England as servant

to the Duke of Richmond. Eventually he was hanged for his crimes, but his epitaph in Covent Garden church duly records his gallantries :

' Here lies Du Vall : Reader, if male
    thou art,
Look to thy purse : if female to thy
    heart.'

**Duveyrier, Henri** (1840–92), a French traveller, studied Arabic, and from 1859 to 1862 explored the Sahara, and lived for several months with the Tuareg, whose manners and speech he described in his *Exploration du Sahara : les Touareg du Nord,* 1864. He also interested himself in the ' shats ' of Algeria and Tunis. In 1881 he published *La Tunisie.*

**Dux,** a manufacturing tn. at the southern base of the Erzebirge, 4½ m. S.W. by W. of Teplitz in Czechoslovakia. There are lignite mines close by. Pop. 12,620.

**Duxbury,** a city of Plymouth co., Massachusetts, U.S.A., on Duxbury Bay, 24 m. E.N.E. of Taunton. The cable line laid across the Atlantic in 1869 from Brest, France, terminates here. In 1872 an imposing monument was erected on Captain's Hill to Miles Standish, one of the first settlers here in 1631. The house of his son Alex S., built in 1666, is still standing. Pop. 1696.

**Dvina,** or **Dwina :** (1) The Northern or Syevernaya D. It waters the governments of Vologda and Archangel, drains an area of 136,000 sq. m., is 760 m. long, including the Sukhona, and is free from ice for six months of the year. Its source is traced from the confluence of the Sukhona and Jug, and after traversing a broad flat country it enters the Gulf of Archangel in the White Sea by three mouths. The chief affluents are the Vychegda (625 m. long) and the Pinega on the right, and the Vaga on the left. Considerable merchandise is shipped down this waterway. During the Great War, the D. R. was an effective barrier against Ger. offensives projected to envelop the Russian right flank. The Gers. did not make any very serious attempt to break through at this point until the summer of 1915. They were supported by their fleet, which, however, was defeated by the Russian fleet, supported by British submarines. General von Below, who was in supreme command of the Ger. forces in this region, endeavoured to offset the naval defeat with a victory on land, and to this end he organised offensives against Lennewaden and Friedrichstadt, from which the Russians withdrew after destroying the bridges. Another offensive was directed against Jacobstadt, where the railway crosses the D. But here the Russians fought stubbornly and brought the offensive to a standstill by the end of the first week in Sept. Beyond a small Russian offensive in Feb. 1916, which had for its object the prevention of Ger. troops being sent further S., the region was quiet until the following June, when a Ger. offensive failed. In July 1916 a Russian counter-offensive overwhelmed the Gers. to a depth of 10 m. In 1919 it was the centre of operations by the forces of General Ironside against the Bolsheviki, where troops, together with those of General Maynard at Murmansk, were evacuated in the spring of the same year by the N. Russian Relief Force under General Rawlinson. (2) The Western D. or the Düna. It rises in the government of Tver on Valdai Plateau, has a basin of 33,000 sq. m., is about 600 m. long, and is provided with excellent canal connections which augment its commercial importance. Vitebsk, Riga, Dünaburg, etc., are situated on its banks. After receiving many tributaries, it empties itself into the Gulf of Riga.

**Dvinsk**, a tn. of Latvia, cap. of the prov. of Latgalia, on the Düna, with trade in flax, hemp and wood. There was much fighting here between the Gers. and Russians in Sept. 1915. Pop. 40,640.

**Dvořák, Anton** (1841–1904), a Bohemian musical composer, b. of humble parents at Nelahozeves, Sept. 8. Destined at first for the calling of a butcher, but his remarkable talent for music so attracted the attention of his first teacher that he was sent to the organ school of the Gesellschaft der Kirchenmusik in 1857. Joined the orchestral band of the Bohemian Interimstheater at Prague in 1862, and eleven years later became organist of the church of St. Adalbert in that town. During this time he wrote many songs, overtures and symphonies, and in 1874 produced his opera, *König und Kohler*, which was not a success, composed diligently in this period when he was, for a time, under the strong influence of Wagner. His first success came in 1873, his *Hymnus* with text by Halek being well received by the Bohemian public. Then, through the influence of Brahms, Vienna became interested in his work, and after the publication, in Vienna, of his *Moravian Duets* and particularly his *Slav Dances* (1878), his fame spread into most countries. He was appointed director of the National Conservatory of Music in New York (1892–95), and in 1901 director of the Prague Conservatory. The most successful of his choral works produced in England was *Stabat Mater* (1883). Visited England several times up to 1887, conducting *The Spectre's Bride*, the *Requiem* and *St. Ludmila*. After his appointment in New York, the melody and rhythmic structure of his work show the influence of negro folk-music. In his later years he somewhat eschewed symphony and chamber music for opera and symphonic poem. D. had great creative power; 'intellectual control' is subordinated to elemental expression. Often a certain melancholy and religious fervour characterise his work, which shows a very wide range. He is often compared with Smetana, for both represent in modern Czech music the typically national-classical generation. (*Dict. of Modern Music and Musicians*, 1924 (DENT).) Other well-known works of his are the cantata, *The Spectre's Bride*, 1885; the oratorio, *St. Ludmila, Slawische Tänze*, a composition for two pianos, and the symphonies in D. minor, E minor, F, and G. Consult W. H. Hadon's *Studies in Modern Music* (1908).

**Dwarf** (from A.-S. *dweorg*), an individual considerably below normal size. The causes of dwarfism are somewhat obscure; in most cases heredity plays an unimportant part and the general diminutiveness of all the structures is not readily explainable by any known defect in the nutritional conditions of the embryo. A distinction should be drawn between pygmies, where small stature is normal to the race, and individuals who fall considerably short of the size of their parents. True Ds. should further be distinguished from rickety Ds., where the deficiency is not general, but can be attributed to a more or less local condition. Such cases usually exhibit a bent spine and misshapen lower limbs, while the head and other structures may be of normal size, the effect of the whole being a certain measure of grotesqueness. Even true Ds. are found to possess heads and chests large in proportion, though many famous Ds. are said to have presented in miniature the proportions of a well-built normal man. While giants are often constitutionally feeble, the dwarf condition is not usually accompanied by other physical and mental defects, except that very diminutive individuals are not uncommonly sterile, even when mated with individuals of similar proportions. Ds. are usually robust, free from disease, long-lived, and of ordinary or even superior mental endowment.

*Famous dwarfs.*—Owing to their

dainty appearance and lively intelligence, Ds. have often been the favourite attendants of persons of high position, and history records many instances of the high value set upon diminutive persons by wealthy European and Oriental monarchs. The Egyptian Pharaohs undoubtedly used members of the dwarf tribes of equatorial Africa as court attendants. It is also recorded that Ptolemy Philadelphus had as tutor the poet Philetas of Cos, who was said to be so small that he had to wear leaden weights to avoid being blown away. Julia, niece of Augustus, had two Ds., Coropas and Andromeda, each of whom was 2 ft. in height. Mary I. of England had a page named John Jarvis who was 2 ft. high. A fair amount of information is obtainable concerning the life of Jeffery Hudson, who was born of normal parents in 1619 at Oakham in Rutlandshire. At nine years of age he was 18 in. high and well proportioned in every way. He was introduced to Charles I. and his queen in a pie which was brought to the dinner table, and was adopted into the service of the royal family. He became a soldier in the Royalist cause, and is said to have fought two duels, one with a turkey-cock and one with a full-sized antagonist, whom he shot dead. At thirty years of age he was 3 ft. 9 in. high, having grown, so he announced, during his imprisonment by Turkish pirates, who ill-treated him. He d. in 1682 at the age of sixty-three. Queen Henrietta Maria had two other Ds., Richard and Anne Gibson, who were married at the instance of the queen and had children of normal size. Of continental Ds., the chief are Bébé, the favourite of Stanislas, King of Poland, who was 2 ft. 9 in. high, and Richebourg, who was only 1 ft. 11 in. high; he d. in 1858 at the age of ninety. In the nineteenth century many Ds. were publicly exhibited in England. The Pole, Borulwaski, was 3 ft. 3 in. high when full grown; he d. in 1837 at the age of ninety-eight. Charles Stratton, popularly known as General Tom Thumb, was exhibited in London in 1844 and 1857. He was 2 ft. 7 in. high, and married another D., Lavinia Warren, in 1863; he d. in 1883. Other exhibited Ds. were: Don Francisco Hidalgo, 2 ft. 5 in.; Jan Hannema, 2 ft. 4 in., the so-called Aztecs, who appeared in 1853; and the Chinese D., Che-mah, who measured 2 ft. 1 in.

*The Dwarf in Mythology.*—The folk tales of most countries include accounts of diminutive people, usually with super-human attributes. It has been suggested that such accounts have their origin in the existence of pygmy races in Europe in the Neolithic period, but the widespread nature of the fairy legend hardly needs such explanation. The fairy is by no means always pictured as of diminutive size. The true fairy, or invisible spirit, is probably a little person simply in order to explain the difficulty of seeing him. It is otherwise, however, with the D. of Teutonic legend. These are people of grotesque appearance, often malicious and of marvellous cunning in the working of metals. They possess in an exaggerated form the characteristics of many individuals of stunted growth; a disinclination for human society, great strength of arm and hand, shrewdness above the ordinary, a tendency to revenge for fancied slights, but a capacity for great devotion where their affections are engaged. Ds. amongst the ignorant and superstitious have been credited with supernatural powers, especially those individuals who are deformed.

*Dwarf Races.*—The existence of races of people with an average height of about 4 ft. had been asserted by travellers from very early times. Two great divisions are now recognised: the Negrillos of Equatorial Africa and the Negritos of Asia and Oceania. The Ds. of Africa inhabit regions between lat. 3° N. and 3° S. The chief branches are the Akkas of the Upper Nile and Niam Niam, the Bambute of the Ituri forest, and the Batua to the S. of the Congo. In Asia the chief tribes are the Aëtes of the Philippine Is., the Mincopis of the Andaman Is., and the Karons of New Guinea. These pygmies are in general brachycephalic, with crisp hair, flattened noses, and long upper lips; they are prognathous in profile, and reddish-brown in colour. They are usually nomadic, make temporary huts of woven branches, and live by hunting rather than agriculture. Their religious ideas are very scanty, many tribes believe in no possibility of existence after death. They have some artistic capabilities as a rule, are able to make remarkably faithful sketches with the rudest of material, and have a talent for mimicry. Their tribal organisation is not very complex, and they frequently have no chieftains. There are two theories as to their origin: one is that they represent a survival of a primitive type, and the other that they are a result of degeneration caused by peculiar local conditions.

**Dwarfing Trees,** an art introduced some centuries ago by the Japanese. The tiny trees have all the appearance and characteristics in miniature of the same species growing freely in the open; they sometimes live as long as 250 years. They are best grown from seed, and the treatment consists of frequent pruning of shoot and root, twisting and bending of the branches, insufficient nourishment, the use of small pots so as to confine the roots and anything which can paralyse vitality without actually killing the plant.

**Dwarka,** a maritime tn., Guzerat, British India, in the W. of the Kathiawar Peninsula, Bombay. By the seashore stands the great temple of Krishna, with a pyramid 140 ft. in height, which is annually visited by 10,000 pilgrims. Pop. about 5000.

**Dwight, Timothy William** (1752–1817), an American author and divine, graduated at Yale College, 1769. During the War of Independence he served as an army chaplain, and wrote *Columbia,* a fine battle song. His books show a great diversity of interest. Southey believed that posterity would best esteem his *Travels in New England and New York* (4 vols.), 1821–22, because of the light they throw on contemporary social and economic conditions, but his sermons, entitled *Theology Explained and Defended* (5 vols.), 1819, enjoyed for many years a conspicuous popularity.

**Dwina,** *see* DVINA.

**Dwygyfylchi,** a par., N. Wales, in Carnarvonshire, 3 m. from Conway. Pop. 4483.

**Dyaks,** or **Dayaks,** certain semi-barbarous tribes inhabiting Borneo. They belong to the same race as the Malays, and are probably the aborigines of the island. They are slightly built, and in colour lighter than a typical Malay. They are very strenuous and persistent workers and have a cheerful disposition. Their chief industries are weaving and spinning, dyeing, manufacturing iron and steel implements. Their former practice of head-hunting is now hardly known. In warfare their chief weapons are the blowpipe and a long spear or a curved sword. They are estimated to number nearly two and a half millions. *See* Carl Bode's *Head-hunters of Borneo* (1882).

**Dyas,** *see* PERMIAN.

**Dyce, Alexander** (1798–1869), an eminent English critic and scholar, *b.* at Edinburgh, and educated at the Edinburgh High School, and graduated at Exeter College, Oxford. He entered holy orders, but in 1825 settled in London and devoted his time to literature. His first publication was *Select Translations from Quintus Smyrnæus,* 1821. He is famous for his annotated editions of the early dramatists and poets, which include Peele, 1828–39; Webster, 1830; Greene, 1831; Middleton, 1840; Beaumont and Fletcher, 1843–46; and

Marlowe, 1850. His scholarly edition of Shakespeare, published in 9 vols. (1857), has not been surpassed. D. also edited the poems of Shakespeare, Pope, Akenside, and Beattie, and the critical and theological works of Richard Bentley. With Collier, Halliwell, and Wright, he founded the Percy Society, and for the Shakespeare Society published two early plays which he had discovered, namely, *Timon* and *Sir Thomas More.* His *Recollections of the Table-Talk of Samuel Rogers* (1856) must also be mentioned. He attacked Payne Collier's edition¹ of Shakespeare in *Remarks on Collier's and Knight's Editions of Shakespeare* (1844), and *Strictures on Collier's New Edition of Shakespeare* (1859), which cost him his friendship with his fellow writer. D. left his valuable library, which contained many rare books, to the South Kensington Museum. In the *Catalogue,* published in 1875, is a 'Biographical Sketch,' by John Forster.

**Dyce, William** (1806–64), a British artist, *b.* at Aberdeen. His most famous scriptural paintings were a 'Madonna and Child,' and 'Joash shooting the Arrow of Deliverance'; some of his classical pictures also are of great merit, but his finest and best-known works are the Arthurian frescoes in the robing-room of the House of Lords.

**Dye Trade.** The history of the trade in dyestuffs goes back to the middle of last century, when an Eng. chemist, in collaboration with a scientist of Ger. extraction, but living in England, discovered for the first time the secret of making dyes from coal tar. Eng. people were slow to see the importance of the discovery, and as a result of far-sighted action on the part of the Gers. there was developed in Germany an immense dye-making industry, enabling the Ger. firms to obtain practically a monopoly of the dye trade of the world. When the Great War broke out the Gers. had ready to hand factories fully equipped for the production of high explosives of all kinds in great quantities. On the other hand Great Britain and her allies were put in a position of the gravest possible embarrassment and danger owing to the absence of such factories. After the Armistice the British Gov., as the result of a series of resolutions passed by the Allies in Paris, took steps to prohibit the import of dyestuffs under the Customs Act, 1876. It was decided in the Courts that the prohibition was illegal, and accordingly the Import Regulation Act of 1920 was passed, setting up a Committee for the issue of licences for the importation of dyestuffs. Unfortunately there was an interval of nearly a year between the decision of the Courts and the operation of the Act, and the Gers. availed themselves of that opportunity to pour into Great Britain enormous quantities of dyes of all kinds. The result was that for over two years after the Act became effective the dye-makers of this country were struggling against an overwhelming burden of foreign competition. During the past ten years, however, they have made very remarkable strides indeed—so remarkable that an unsuccessful effort was made by the Labour Gov. in 1930 to bring an end to the Act of 1920 (generally known as the Dyestuffs Act), the assumption being that the British dye-makers had done so extraordinarily well that they were in no further need of protection. To-day (1931), of the dyestuffs used in Great Britain 93 per cent. are produced in that country and the whole of the intermediates are home-made. All that is left to the foreign producer is 7 per cent., consisting very largely of comparatively small quantities of dyes of a novel or particularly complex type, because British dye-makers have wisely concentrated on the production of dyes for which there is the greatest demand. Before the War the production of dyes in Great Britain was about 9,000,000 lb. avoirdupois; to-day (1931) it is 55,000,000 lb., and exports, which were 4,000,000 lb. before the War, are now 15,000,000 lb. When the Act came into operation at the end of 1920 the price of dyestuffs was 4s. 4d. per lb.; the pre-war price was 1s. per lb. To-day the average price of British dyes is 1s. 5d. per lb. The British dye-makers claimed that this Act must be continued for a time unless the country is prepared to run the risk of seeing a great deal of the work which had been done thrown away and the development of the industry suddenly arrested, and this view prevailed in the House of Lords where the Government was defeated. Both in Germany and the U.S.A. there are substantial dye-making industries sheltered by high protective tariffs, securing for the dye-makers a monopoly of their own market. This has been very effective in the U.S.A. where the tariff Act of 1930 levies a duty of 7 cents per pound plus 40 per cent. ad valorem on American selling price of similar competitive articles. The result is that in the last year reported the U.S.A. produced 111,421,505 lb. of dyes, 13,244,676 lb.

of colour lakes, 5,000,000 lb. of coal tar medical products, 1,599,430 lb of coal tar perfumes and 2,292,450 lb of perfumes.

**Dyer, Sir Edward** (d. 1607), a poet and courtier, b. at Sharpham Park, Dorset. After studying at Oxford he travelled awhile, and then entered the court of Elizabeth, who employed him on several embassies. He, Sir Philip Sidney, and Fulke Greville were intimate friends from boyhood, Sidney himself writing of their having ' one mind in bodies three.' D. and Greville were chief pall-bearers at Sir Philip's funeral. Spenser speaks highly of D. as a poet, but only one of his songs is now generally remembered, *My Mind to me a Kingdom is.*

**Dyer, George** (1755–1841), an English author, b. in London, educated at Christ's Hospital and Cambridge. Besides writing a *History of Cambridge University* and other volumes, he assisted in the preparation of Valpy's edition of the classics (141 volumes), ruining his eyesight in the work. His friend Charles Lamb speaks of him very tenderly in his essays, *Oxford in the Vacation,* and *Amicus Redivivus.*

**Dyer, John** (c. 1700–58), a British poet, spent some months sketching and painting in S. Wales. *Grongar Hill* (1726), which describes his native scenery of Towy, secured instant renown. The impressions of his tour in Italy are expressed in his *Ruins of Rome* (1740), which is more readable to-day than his didactic epic on sheep and wool, entitled *The Fleece* (1757).

**Dyer, Reginald Edward Harry** (1864–1927), British brigadier-general, b. Oct. 9, at Simla, India; son of Edwd. Dyer, brewer. Educated at Middleton Coll., co. Cork. Commissioned in W. Surrey Regt., 1885. Transferred to 25th Panjabis of Indian army; served in Burma campaign, 1886–7; in Hazara expedition, 1888; relief of Chitral, 1895; Waziristan blockade, 1901–2; Zakka Khel expedition, 1908. In Great War, commanded 45th infantry brigade on E. Persia border; received C.B. Brigade-Commander at Jalandhar, 1919; sent by Viceroy in April, to Amritsar, where rebellion was strongest. Here he pursued a policy of terrorism (see AMRITSAR). Particulars became known but gradually; D. was appointed in May to command on frontier. An inquiry at Lahore, Nov. 1919, at which D. gave evidence, resulted in his being directed to resign. He afterwards dabbled in science, and was inventor of a range-finder. Wrote *The Raiders of the Sarhad,* 1921. Died at

St. Martin's, Long Ashton, Bristol, July 23.

**Dyer, Thomas Henry** (1804–88), an English historian and antiquarian, *b.* in London. Chief historical works, *Life of Calvin*, 1850; *History of Modern Europe*, 1861–4, and several volumes on Roman history, which have been severely handled by critics. His antiquarian books on Pompeii and Athens have met with greater approval.

**Dyer, Sir William Turner Thiselton-** (1843–1928), English botanist, *b.* July 28, at Westminster. Professor of natural history at R.A.C., Cirencester, 1868; professor of botany, Royal College of Science, Ireland, 1870; assistant director at Kew Gardens, 1875; and director, 1885–1905. He also acted as British Commissioner at several great exhibitions —Melbourne, Paris, and St. Louis. He edited the Eng. edition of Sachs's *Text-book of Botany*, also *Flora Capensis*, and *Flora of South Africa*. Was vice-president of the Royal Society (1896–97), and was made K.C.M.G. in 1899. Died at Witcombe, Glos.

**Dyersburg,** a city of N.W. Tennessee, co. seat Dyer co., with flour and saw mills, cotton gins and textile mills, etc. Pop. 8733.

**Dyes and Dyeing,** the art of colouring fabrics, textile or otherwise, in such a way that the colour is evenly distributed and is difficult to remove. D. is in common use with wool, silk and leather, which are animal in origin, and with cotton, jute, linen, etc., which come from the vegetable world. It is an old art practised by Eastern peoples from time immemorial. Thus there is mention in the Book of Exodus of 'blue and purple and scarlet,' and it is believed that the Tyrian dyes were discovered by the Phœnicians as far back as 1000 B.C. It is this purple, which was manufactured at Tyre, Tarsus, and Alexandria, that is constantly referred to, not only in the O.T., when the prophets speak of the purple-dyed vestments of the priests, but in the works of Homer, Strabo, and Herodotus, and indeed the one D. process described at any length by the natural historian, Pliny, is that of obtaining these same Tyrian dyes. Thus from the account of Pliny certain shell fish have been made by moderns to yield the royal colour over again. Other evidence that D. was one of the primitive arts is offered by blue and fawn, and reddish pieces of mummy cloth discovered by Egyptologists, whilst coloured church vestments that are still preserved clearly show that D. was practised with considerable success in the so-called dark twelfth and thirteenth centuries.

*Cotton and linen* are composed of fibres essentially of cellulose, which are susceptible to strong acids and alkalis, but dilute alkalis and weak acid solutions have little effect.

*Wool* contains sulphur and has basic properties. Alkalis and strong acids tend to destroy it.

*Silk* resembles wool in some ways, but is more resistant to acids and alkalis.

*Jute* contains cellulose and a tannin combined.

*Artificial silk* is of two kinds : rayon (including viscose, decomposed nitrocellulose and cupramonium types), which is essentially cellulose, and a cellulose acetate type, which is no longer composed of cellulose, but of the compound cellulose acetate. This type of altered cotton has presented many difficulties to the dyer, as it shows differences from cotton and from rayon.

*Unions,* e.g. fabrics made of more than one of the above.

The prime necessities of a good dye are, of course, that it is both permanent and even—two qualities which it is by no means easy to obtain. Thus, the simplest process affords hardly any safe dyes. This method may be briefly described as submersion of the fabric to be dyed in a bath of the colouring matter. Hardly any natural dyes are effective when so used, but good results are obtained by bringing certain artificial dyes, such as sulphindigotic acid and picric acid, which were once popular, or modern aniline dyes, into contact with wool and silk. The pigments are in some way absorbed by the fibre, and the solution is robbed of its colour. It has been found by experience that temperature has a great deal to do with the goodness of the dye. The next process is similar to the first, except that the reduction of an insoluble colouring matter to a soluble state forms to it an indispensable prelude. Thus, arnotto and indigo are applicable in this way if, that is, they have first been acted upon by solvents, whilst the pink pigment of safflower is set free by the action of an alkali.

Cotton possesses no affinity for native colouring matters. It is therefore necessary to introduce what are known as 'mordants' to prepare the material for the reception of the dye. An example will best illustrate the function of a mordant. It is required, let us say, to obtain black calico with the aid of the natural dye, logwood. First of all the calico is steeped in a hot aqueous solution of sulphate of iron. As the acid of this salt is not volatile, the cloth is passed through lime water, the effect of which is to precipitate the mordant, in this case, hydroxide of iron, which enters into some kind of intimate combination with the calico. If the calico is now put into a hot logwood decoction, it will, within half an hour or so, assume a dense black colour. (A great many substances are now employed as mordants, the chief of which are the salts of tin, iron, aluminium, copper, and chromium. Stannous chloride, or muriate of tin, is one of the most popular.) What has really happened is that the colouring principle (logwood) has lost its solubility and entered into combination with the iron hydroxide, the resulting compound being precipitated and in some manner infused into the fibre. The precipitate so formed is technically called a lake of the logwood, or the iron hydroxide. If the 'lake' were first made and then the calico put into a bath of it, there would be no D. at all, as the precipitate would simply rest on the surface of the fibre and would enter into no sort of intimate union at all.

There are two classes of mordants, the acid and the basic. *Acid mordants* include bodies such as tannin and oil mordants, *e.g.* that made by the action of strong sulphuric acid on olive oil. They are used largely for the fixation of basic dyes on cotton, the process being carried out either in a moderately cold solution or up to about 70° C. A *feebly* acid substance is usually added to slow down the dyeing process and obtain even shades.

*Basic mordants* include the hydroxides of metals such as iron, chromium, tin, and aluminium, all of which are insoluble in water. They are used in conjunction with acid dyes. Wool is capable of splitting up some salts of these metals and precipitating the corresponding hydroxides. Cotton, however, is unable to do this, and therefore a salt of the required metal with a very weak acid such as acetic acid is decomposed by the action of water (hydrolysis) to give the metal hydroxide. Or sometimes a fixing agent is used to perform the precipitation of a basic substance.

Before proceeding to a classification of dyestuffs, there are a few other points to which it is necessary to draw the reader's attention. 'Adjective' dyes are those where a mordant is used, whilst the other and more direct dyes are often spoken of as 'substantive.' Mordants may be introduced in three ways: (1) By the 'mordanting and

D.' method, the material is first mordanted and the D. is a separate and subsequent operation; (2) the material may first be dyed and afterwards mordanted, the two operations being performed in a reverse order. This is called the 'D. and saddening' method, and is largely employed with acid mordant dyes. As the colour is clearly fixed in the first bath and only developed in the second, this process does not commend itself for the matching of patterns; and (3) the two operations of D. and mordanting may be performed together by what is called the 'single bath' method.

*Classification of dyestuffs.*—For convenience of discussion and clearness of arrangement, it is usual to divide dyestuffs into three broad groups: (a) Organic natural dyestuffs; (b) mineral dyestuffs; and (c) organic synthetic dyestuffs, which include nitro-, azo-, and azine-compounds; sulphurised dyestuffs, and quinone and triphenylmethane derivatives.

(a) *Organic natural dyestuffs.*— One of the oldest of these is indigo. This is obtained from the *Indigo tinctoria*, a plant much cultivated in India. For twelve hours the leaves are steeped in a water vat, and are then transferred to a second vat and agitated. The result of this is that the soluble indigo-white, formed in the first vat, is oxidised by means of the oxygen in the air to indigo, which falls down as a blue sediment. The contents of the vat are then boiled and repeatedly strained, after which the indigo is compressed into slabs, from which are obtained the well-known cubes of commerce. Natural indigo, like so many other native dyes, is now being rejected for an equally effective synthetic preparation. Yarn and piece goods especially are dyed with indigo. Textile fibres readily absorb the soluble indigo-white referred to above, which is obtained from the commercial product by the action of a reducing agent. Exposure to air re-oxidises the dye so that the cotton or other stuff is dyed to the requisite blue. Indigo is freely used in combination to produce other shades. Logwood is derived from a tree indigenous to Central America, the scientific name for which is *Hæmatoxylon campechianum*. It is invaluable in the production of black or blackish wool and cotton, the shade depending on the particular mordant. Thus, with salts of iron it produces dark greys and black; with dichromates, various blues and black; with aluminium salts, purple; and with different copper salts, dull blends of green and blue. If a very fast black is wanted for cotton, it is usual to employ iron-tannate as the mordant. This is fixed on to the fibre by first working the cotton in a decoction of sumac or some other tannin compound and then dipping it into a bath of the soluble iron salt. The cloth is now ready for immersion in logwood, provided, that is, it has been first thoroughly well washed. Cochineal, which is obtained from a small insect, the *Coccus cacti*, is especially suitable for animal fibres, and can be made to impart some fine scarlets and crimsons to woollen fabrics. Various reds and reddish-browns are still produced in wool-D. from sanderswood, barwood, and camwood, which are procured from W. African species of *Baphia* and *Pterocarpus*. Different shades of yellow are procurable from fustic, which comes from the *Morus tinctoria*, a species of mulberry tree, and also from weld, which comes from a wild mignonette (*Reseda luteola*); Persian berries, derived from the Rhamni of the Levant, and from the Quercitron bark, which is the inner bark of a N. American oak (*Quercus tinctoria*).

(b) *Mineral dyestuffs.*—These have been largely replaced by coal-tar dyestuffs. The colours obtainable are Prussian blue, manganese brown, chrome yellow, and iron buff. The first is procured on cotton by treating it first with prussiate of potash and then with salts of iron, whilst on wool the prussiates must be decomposed with mineral acids. The brown is produced from potassium permanganate. Animal fibres boiled in a solution of this salt become impregnated with it, and the permanganate thus absorbed is easily reduced to the insoluble manganic hydroxide, which is also brown. If cotton is to be dyed brown, it must be mordanted with manganous chloride. After the D. operation, it must be passed through a hot solution of sodium hydrate so as to get a precipitation of manganous hydroxide. This salt is readily oxidised to the brown manganic hydroxide, the common practice being to pass the cotton into a cold and dilute solution of bleaching powder. Ferric hydroxide gives iron buff, and yellow and orange may be obtained in cotton D. by fixing lead sulphate or lead oxide on to the fibre, and then submitting the fibre to a solution of bichromate of potash.

(c) *Organic synthetic dyestuffs.*— A remarkably wide range of colours is producible from such dyestuffs, and as they are easy to manipulate and effect often a cheaper and faster dye than the natural dyestuffs, they are popular with manufacturers and are rapidly superseding the former class altogether. Generally speaking, the colour depends on the chemical group to which the dye belongs. It will be convenient to classify these colouring matters :

(1) *Nitro-dyestuffs.*—These are applicable to animal fibres, which are dyed in a bath slightly acidified with sulphuric acid. The chief members of this section are aurentia, picric acid, Victoria- palatine- and naphthaline-orange, and naphthol-yellow.

(2) *The di- and tri-phenylmethane group.*—Methyl violet, magenta, malachite green, and auramine, and indeed most of the basic dyes, belong to this class. If sulphonated, these bodies become acid dyes and give such colours as acid violet, acid magenta, guinea-green, etc. Wool is dyed most of these colours in a neutral bath. The dye-bath is at first cold, but the temperature is gradually raised to boiling point so that practically the whole of the bath is exhausted. Cotton fabrics should first be mordanted with tannic acid and fixed in tartar emetic. The chief objection to this class is that they are fugitive to light.

(3) *The azo-group.*—Members of this class may be sub-divided into monazo- disazo- trisazo-, etc., dyes according to the number of their azo-groups, and they may be still further split up into oxyazo- (OH), and amino-azo- ($NH_2$) dyes. In this group are counted nearly all the direct dyes, and their application is quite straightforward. Acid or neutral baths may be used. One means of overcoming the tendency of these colours to fade on exposure to light is to treat the fabric after D. with a hot solution of chromium fluoride, or copper sulphate. Under this heading fall the benzidine colours.

(4) *Anthracene-derived dyes.*—Alizarin (synthesised in 1868 by Graebe and Liebermann) is the oldest of these. Others are, anthrapurpurin, flavopurpurin, anthracene blue, alizarin brown, alizarin green, alizarin indigo blue, alizarin black. In recent times several vat dyes have been made. These vat dyes, like indigo, are insoluble in water, but can be obtained as the leuco-compounds when reduced. These are soluble in alkalis, and if the fabric to be dyed is steeped in an alkaline solution of the leuco-compound, the latter is taken up. Subsequent oxidation brings out the coloured material required.

Indanthrene (in various shades of green, yellow, etc.), the Algol colours, (yellow, red, etc.) and anthraflavone are examples. The trade name for the common method of obtaining some alizarin colours is the sulphated oil process. The stuff to be dyed is impregnated with alizarin oil, and then dried. After being mordanted with aluminium acetate, it is dyed, steamed and finished. Alizarin gives splendid Turkey-reds on cotton. These dyestuffs give stable colours.

(5) *Aniline black.*—The composition of this colour is still a vexed question. It is produced by the oxidation of aniline. There are, broadly speaking, three stages in the oxidation. Emeraldine is produced if the oxidation is limited; nigraniline is the second product and gives a violet-black; the third and final product is ungreenable black, which is remarkably stable.

(6) *The phthaleïn group of colouring matters.*—This includes gallein, erythrosin, and the eosins. The dyes produced are wonderfully bright but fugitive to light.

(7) *The synthetic indigo group.*— The synthetic production of indigo on a manufacturing scale was made possible by the researches of Baeyer (1880) and Heumann (1890). Indigo itself is a vat dye. Other dyes are the cibia colours (containing bromine) thioindigo colours (containing sulphur), etc.

(8) *The sulphide dyes.*—These have been largely developed of late years. They are insoluble in water, but are soluble in sodium sulphide. Frequently the dye is reduced to a leuco-compound, which is then taken up by the fabric, when subsequent oxidation brings out the colour. They are largely used for D. artificial silk, but are not so good for wool. They give excellent fast colours. Vidal black is a typical example.

(9) Other classes of dyes are azine, oxazine, thiazine, thiazole, acridine, nitrose, quinoline, cyanine D.

*Theory of Dyeing.*—It is probable that the process, as applied to wool and silk, results in chemical action, but it is idle to make even this tentative assertion in the case of cotton and other vegetable stuffs. Writers on the subject uphold either the mechanical or chemical hypothesis. According to the first the colouring matter is absorbed into the fibres of the material; variation in size of dye molecules and in the pores of different fibres accounts for the fact that the same dye will not colour all fabrics equally well; furthermore, heat and the action of certain chemicals are held to expand the pores. The following facts support the chemical combination theory: not only colouring matters, but also textile fibres are all either acid, or acid and basic in character, and the fibres can absorb and retain acids, alkalies, and certain salts.

**Dygasinski, Adolph** (1839–1902), considered one of the greatest modern Polish writers, *b.* at Niegoslawice. At the commencement of his career he was a school teacher, and afterwards a journalist. He gave himself up to a literary career, beginning in 1882, and soon distinguished himself by his representations of the life, moods and, so to speak, thoughts of the living creatures. He did not make them apes of man nor seek to put the soul of man into the skins of the animals. Rather they felt as we would imagine animals feel. He *d.* in 1902, and it was only after this that there appeared his masterpiece, *Les Noces de la Vie*, as the title is given in Fr. In this there are two themes: above, the drama of the divine elements; below, the idylls and dramas of their humble subjects. The four seasons of the year are represented in a beautiful love story. There is the sun, sublime lover, who embraces and fecundates, and the Earth, his passionate sweetheart, mother of all living things. Many of these creatures are presented in most vivid manner, particularly the feathered songsters and the way in which their lives are affected by the changes in the seasons.

**Dyk, Victor,** one of the leading men of letters, as well as politicians, of Czechoslovakia, was *b.* in 1877. After his earliest efforts in literature, he distinguished himself from his contemporaries, who affected to take no interest in the political future of Bohemia, by playing an extreme nationalist rôle like that of Maurice Barrès in France. During twenty years he kept before his countrymen the idea of a free, self-governed Bohemia. He wrote in one of his poems:

' Cursed be the land which bears cowards and the mother who gives them birth.'

Even during the Great War he continued to defend his ideals, and was imprisoned in Vienna. From his cell he sent forth a poem famous in modern Czech annals, *The Earth Speaks*, in which there are prophetic lines.

When Czechoslovakia became a free nation, he was a member of the Legislative Assembly, then of the House of Representatives and, finally, of the Senate, where he still sits. Among his books are *Force of Life*, 1898; *Vanities*, 1900;

*Satires and Sarcasms*, 1905 ; *Windows*, 1921 ; *The New Wave*, 1930.

**Dyke, Sir William Hart** (*b.* 1837), an English politician ; *b.* in Kent. He was chief Opposition whip, under Disraeli (1868–74), and Patronage Secretary to the Treasury (1874–80), but his chief work was done as vice-president of the committee of council on education (1887–92), when he carried through the Free Education Act, did away with ' Payment by Results,' and introduced a system of technical education.

**Dykes** are wall-like masses of igneous rock which fill up more or less vertical fissures in the earth's crust, and are so called from the Scottish word for wall. The two main characteristics of D. are : (1) They are bounded by more or less parallel surfaces and are of nearly constant width ; (2) they are generally vertical at the time of intrusion. They commonly occur on the sites of old

*d.* Igneous rock forcing its way in overlying stratified rocks. When this solidifies in the cracks igneous dykes are formed.
*b.* A dome of lava solidified before coming to surface—a laccolith.

volcanoes, and the manner of their formation can be observed in the active volcanoes such as Vesuvius and Etna. Volcanic cones are fissured either by the hydrostatic pressure of the column of lava in the pipe, or by explosions due to the pressure of dissolved vapours and gases acting on the walls and roof of the funnel. Into the rents and fissures so formed the lava rises, forming D., veins, and horizontal sheets or sills. If the lava is extremely fluid, it ascends rapidly in the cracks and fissures and, cooling quickly on the outside but more slowly in the centre, forms D. with a vitreous edge and a crystalline interior. When, however, the lava is most viscous, it may solidify before reaching the top of the fissure, leaving a cavity which in time becomes filled with fragmental material by the crumbling of the walls, thus giving rise to ' Agglomerate D.' Since D. are of deep-seated origin, they are only exposed to observation as

the result of erosion. If the sedimentary strata, into which they have been injected, are more easily weathered than the igneous material of the D., the latter stand up as vast walls, while where the igneous rock is more easily denuded the course of the D. is represented by a trench. As a general rule, D. run in straight lines, but may occasionally be zig-zag. They vary in thickness from a few inches to 20 or 30 yds., and may be any length from a few feet up to 100 m. The Cleveland D. of the N. of England is 60 m. in length, and some of the Scottish D. are even longer. As well as forming a net-work in fissure eruption regions, as in Scotland, Iceland, and the Faroe Islands, D. occur in the neighbourhood of large plutonic intrusions, such as granite bosses. These D. are finer grained than the granite from which they come, and may merge into mica porphyries, granophyres, and quartz-felsites. Where D. are intruded in the sedimentary strata, whether through fissures or along joint planes, the adjacent rocks are to some extent affected by the extremely high temperature of the igneous material. The rocks may occasionally be recrystallised, sandstones being altered to semi-crystalline quartzites, and limestones converted into crystalline marbles ; more often, however, they are only baked or indurated, as when soft clays are metamorphosed to flinty shales, Lydian-stone, or porcellanite (*see* METAMORPHISM). Regarded petrographically, D. belong to the phase ' Minor Intrusions ' (sometimes called the dyke-phase), the third phase in the regular cycle of igneous activity, and according to their distribution and arrangement may be referred to two types : (1) D. in plateau regions ; (2) D. in mountain districts. The former are characterised by a regional parallelism, whilst the latter are more often grouped about certain centres and tend to a radiate arrangement. *See* IGNEOUS ROCKS, VOLCANOES, etc.

**Dykes, John Bacchus** (1823–76), a church composer ; graduated at Cambridge, and became minor canon and precentor of Durham in 1849, Mus. Doc. in 1861, and vicar of St. Oswalds, Durham, 1862. As joint-editor of *Hymns Ancient and Modern*, he wrote for that compilation some of its best-known tunes, *e.g.* ' Jesu, lover of my soul ' ; several of his anthems and services also have attained great popularity.

**Dykh-Tau**, the third highest mountain in the Caucasus, 17,190 ft. ; it belongs to the Elburz group.

**Dymoke**, an English family holding

the right of hereditary championship to the crown. Their representative formerly had to appear at the coronation banquet and challenged all comers to dispute the king's title. This office is held by tenure of 'grand serjeantry' in connection with the manor of Scrivelsby, Lincolnshire, which passed to Sir John D. (fourteenth century) by his marriage with the heiress of the Marmions.

**Dynamical Units,** see UNITS.

**Dynamics** (Gk. δύναμις, strength, force), the science of motion, a branch of mechanics devoted to all problems of motion, as opposed to *Statics* that deals with problems of bodies in equilibrium or at rest. D. depends on three laws, called Newton's laws of motion. These state (1) Every body continues in a state of rest, or of uniform motion in a straight line, except in so far as it may be compelled by impressed force to change that state; (2) change of motion (momentum) is directly proportional to the impressed force, and takes place in the direction in which the force acts; (3) to every action there is always an equal and opposite reaction, viz. if a body A exerts a force on a body B, then simultaneously the body B exerts an equal and opposite force on the body A. On these three laws depend all our knowledge of motion of terrestrial and heavenly bodies. Einstein's theory of Relativity has shown that in certain very special problems the system of mechanics based on Newton's laws fails to account for the quantitative results obtained. The science of D. was begun by Galileo at the end of the sixteenth century, when he studied the motion of falling bodies and disproved the Aristotelian idea that the speed of a falling body depended on its weight. Galileo, Huyghens, and especially Newton, laid the foundations of the subject, which was further developed by continental mathematicians in the eighteenth century, and subsequently by numerous other mathematicians and scientists. The reader will find Loney's *Treatise on Elementary Dynamics* a suitable introduction to the subject, leading to more advanced text-books such as Ramsey's *Dynamics*, and Lamb's *Higher Mechanics*.

**Dynamite,** an explosive consisting of some absorbent material impregnated with nitro-glycerin. Nitroglycerin, which was discovered by Sobrero in 1846, is produced by dropping glycerin into a mixture of strong nitric acid and strong sulphuric acid, and is itself a powerful though dangerous and unreliable explosive. In 1863 A. Nobel commenced experiments with absorbent substances with a view to arriving at a solid or plastic explosive with nitro-glycerin as its active constituent. He was only moderately successful until he applied the method of causing explosion by detonation with fulminate of mercury. He finally fixed on a siliceous earth known as kieselguhr as the absorbent best suited for the purpose. Kieselguhr or guhr is composed of the fossilised remains of diatoms, and consists of silica to the extent of about 95 per cent. It is found in Austria, Australia, Germany, Norway, and Scotland. It has the advantages of being itself inert and non-combustible, and of being capable of absorbing three times its weight of nitro-glycerine. In actual manufacture the nitro-glycerin is produced by mixing three parts of nitric acid of sp. gr. 1·5 with five parts of sulphuric acid of sp. gr. 1·84; the mixture is cooled and the nitroglycerin is introduced in a thin stream by means of compressed air. The kieselguhr is prepared by calcination at low red heat in which moisture and organic substances are removed. The guhr is usually pink at this stage, owing to the presence of iron. (If not, red ochre is added.) Magnesium carbonate or calcium carbonate up to 2 per cent. is then ground in. (These carbonates serve to neutralise any acid subsequently formed if the nitro-glycerin decomposes during the lapse of time before the dynamite is used.) The well-ground mixture is then sifted through a 30-mesh sieve. The guhr is weighed out into lined rubber bags, and three parts of nitro-glycerin are added for every part of guhr, and the mixture is thoroughly completed by hand, after which the product is compressed into cartridge form by means of a special D. pump in which all precautions are taken to avoid friction. The D. is then wrapped in waterproof paper. D. is a greasy plastic solid of sp. gr. 1·59 to 1·65. It burns quietly when ignited, but may be exploded by a fairly vigorous percussion. It explodes with great rapidity, requires very little tamping, and has great shattering power if simply laid upon the ground. This has given rise to the saying that 'dynamite explodes downwards,' as a hole is torn in the ground even when it is unconfined in other directions. It loses only one-sixth of its power under water, so is well adapted for subaqueous operations. It freezes at 40° F., and when frozen is difficult to explode. The operation of thawing D. is attended with some danger, and should only be performed when the rise of temperature can be carefully regulated. D. is used chiefly for blasting. Its shattering power is too great for quarry work generally, but for breaking up huge boulders and roots of trees, and for destroying obstacles to navigation under water, its efficacy is unrivalled. The rapidity of explosion renders its use as a propellant in guns impossible, though it is used as a shell explosive in the pneumatic guns of the U.S.A. military and naval services. There are many modifications of the D. made with kieselguhr. One of these is blasting gelatine, where the nitroglycerin is incorporated with collodion cotton, forming a gelatinous plastic material which is quite unaffected by

converted into heat due to friction. Therefore there is never a complete conversion of the mechanical energy into electrical energy. Some of the original energy is lost, and therefore a D. is judged by its *efficiency*, which is *the ratio of the developed electrical energy to the total mechanical energy supplied to the machine.* There is a variety of causes besides friction which reduce this efficiency, most of which are due to electro-magnetic phenomena. Friction can be minimised by good design and workmanship, and careful lubrication, but these other causes require careful study in order that they may be minimised, although usually the loss due to these causes can be localised in the same manner as that due to

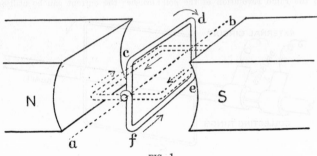

FIG. 1

damp. In order to prevent D. from freezing, the addition of such compounds as monochlorodinitroglycerin or glycerin dinitrate has been suggested.

**Dynamo.** A brief study of electricity is sufficient to show that when a conductor is moved in a magnetic field transversely to the lines of force traversing that field, an electromotive force (E.M.F.) is developed, which sets up an electric current in the conductor. Those machines which in this manner transform mechanical energy into electric energy are known as Ds. Now any D. must consist of at least two parts : the *field magnets*, for creating the magnetic field, and the *armatures*, or conductors ; and one or other of these must be in a state of motion, so that the lines of force may be cut, or rather so that the number of lines of force passing through the conductor may continually vary. It is the mechanical energy which is expended in causing this motion which is converted into electrical energy, but, as in all machines which have moving parts, some fraction of the energy is

friction, since they also tend to develop heat energy.

*Alternate current machines.*—Starting with the simplest type of D., viz. alternate current machines, and taking the simplest form of this type (Fig. 1), we can trace the gradual development of the highly efficient practical machine. Since an E.M.F. is only induced in a conductor when the lines of force in a field are being cut by the conductor, it is evident that, to obtain constant succession of currents, either the conductor or the field must be continually in motion. Fig. 1 shows the case of a fixed field and a moving conductor. We will suppose that by the aid of two large permanent bar-magnets we have obtained a strong, fairly uniform field, *i.e.* one in which the lines of force are nearly straight, parallel, and equidistant. In this field a wire bent into a rectangular coil is placed at right angles to the lines of force. Twisted through a right angle it takes up the position shown by the dotted lines ; in which position it can be seen that no lines of force are cut by the coil, whereas in its original position as many lines of force as possible are cut. As the coil turns on the axis (*ab*) it is thus evident that the number of lines cut by the limbs (*cd* and *ef*) vary from a maximum to zero, so setting up an E.M.F. in the wire. From the article on ELECTRICITY it will be seen that currents will then be set up in opposite directions in these two limbs in the directions shown. The side limbs do not have a current induced in them because they slide through the limbs of force, and do not cut them, their use being solely to complete the electric circuit. As the coil turns through another 90°, *cd* becomes the bottom limb and *ef* the top one ; so a current will be induced in *ef* from back to front, and in *cd* from front to back. So the rapid revolution of the coil

we speak of the frequency being, say, 100 per second, we mean that the current reaches from zero to a positive maximum, back to zero, then to a negative maximum, and so to zero again, 100 times per second. Now a rectangular coil of the shape shown in Fig. 1 would do no work, for the current would merely flow around the coil and waste its energy in heating it. So some apparatus must be added to lead the currents off to an external circuit. Fig. 2 shows one manner of doing this. The rectangular coil is mounted on a spindle, and its ends connected to two separate rings placed on it as shown. Then by means of springs or brushes pressing against the rings, contact is made ; and by means of wires attached to the brushes the current can be utilised.

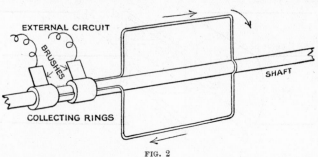

EXTERNAL CIRCUIT

BRUSHES

SHAFT

COLLECTING RINGS

FIG. 2

results in an *alternating current.* For one half of the revolution the currents flow through the wires as shown, but in the other half of the revolution the direction alters in each horizontal limb. The reversal of the current takes place as the coil passes the points at which it cuts the greatest number of lines of force, *i.e.* when the plane of the coil is at right angles to them or when the coil is in a vertical position (Fig. 1). Since as the horizontal limbs turn from top and bottom, the current is reversed, and since at that moment these limbs are moving almost parallel with the lines of force, the induced E.M.F. then is zero. As the coil moves to the horizontal position, it cuts the lines of force almost at right angles, so that it is then that the E.M.F. has its maximum value. From this it follows that as the coil turns so the current alternates, and according to the number of revolutions that the coil makes, so we can find the 'rate of the alternation of the current,' or as it is more generally termed, its *frequency* or *periodicity.* So when

This roughly gives the principles attached to the working of an alternator, but it is evident that many improvements must be made to obtain an E.M.F. of practical value. In the first place it is necessary to obtain a strong magnetic field. In small machines permanent magnets are used, and the horseshoe type is found to be convenient. It is bored out or fitted with soft iron cheeks, in such a manner that the coil may just revolve between them. Then again, it is essential to get as many of the lines of force as possible to pass through the coils. By using a soft iron core, and winding the rectangle round it, the lines are concentrated and the number passing through the coil increased. This method, as shown in Fig. 3, was first introduced by Siemens in 1856, and is known as the simple shuttle wound armature. The area of the rectangle should be as great as possible, and it is further advantageous to wind the wire into a coil, so increasing the number of turns in the wire. As is shown in Fig. 3, the armature, consisting of a great length of silk-covered copper wire, is wound in the slots cut in the armature core. Usually this is about twice as long as its diameter. It is driven by machinery and fitted, as in Fig. 2, with the apparatus for leading the current off. The E.M.F. of such a machine cannot be increased indefinitely by increasing the number of turns in the coil. In the first place the conditions are such that self-induction of the armature is very liable to occur. This effect is always possible with rapidly alternating currents, and as it increases as the square of the number of turns in the coil, the number of these is evidently limited. Therefore it is the strength of the field and the *length* of the active limbs of the coil that are increased. Now the shuttle wound

FIG. 3

armature has many faults, as is natural in early designs. After rotating for a while the core becomes warm, even when the coil is removed. Thus some of the energy supplied is being converted into heat and wasted. Whenever a mass of metal is so moved in a magnetic field, *eddy* or *Foucalt* currents are set up at right angles to the lines of force, and to the direction of movement of the mass. So in the shuttle armature they move lengthways along and around the core. These currents, following the general law, tend to stop the motion of the core, and so power has to be utilised in moving the armature, which should be available for conversion into electricity. The E.M.F. of these currents are not high, but they generate great heat, owing to the great mass and low resistance of the core. To prevent this the core is laminated, *i.e.* built up of discs instead of one solid piece, and these discs are insulated from one another either by varnish or some similar means. So the core is discontinuous in the direction of the eddy currents and continuous in the direction of the lines of force. Again, although the E.M.F. varies as the rate at which the lines of force are cut, yet it is not practicable to increase the speed of revolution beyond certain limits, because of the eddy currents

already mentioned, the electro-magnetic reaction of the current in the armature upon the magnetic field, and the self-induction of the armature. The current induced in the coil converts the armature into an electro-magnet. In the case shown in Fig. 1, a N. pole would be developed in the end of the armature, near the S. pole of the field magnet, and vice versa. This tends to retard the motion of the coil. So the greater the speed of rotation of the coil the greater is this tendency to retard the motion, and the magnetic field is distorted and the E.M.F. is prevented from rising in proportion to the speed. Further, as the lines of force due to the current passing through the coil are increased as the current increases, its permeability may be lowered, so that fewer lines of force due to the field may pass. Thus the eddy currents through, and the self-induction of, the core becomes more marked with the increase of speed, with the consequence that a deal of energy is wasted.

We have already examined two of the methods of obtaining an increase in the E.M.F., viz. : (1) By increasing the speed of revolution, and (2) by increasing the number of turns in the coil. Another two methods are possible, viz. (3) by increasing the area of the coils, or by making the core greater, and so causing the coil to cut a larger number of lines of force ; (4) by increasing the strength of the field. Of these four methods the last is the best. One great advantage which it possesses is that a very strong field is developed in comparison with that induced in the armature, and so the distortion in the field is lessened. To do this now powerful electro-magnets are used, but in the older machines permanent magnets were employed. Sometimes a distinction is drawn between these machines having electro-magnets for producing the field and those having steel magnets, and the latter are then called *magneto-electric* machines.

*De Meritens' magneto machine* was one of the earliest of the latter type, and it is still extensively used in lighthouses. In principle it is similar to the elementary machine already considered, viz. currents are generated in coils rotating so as to cut lines of force due to permanent magnets. But several magnets are used, and a corresponding number of coils glide past the poles of these in turn, instead of rotating in one field only. The armature consists of sixteen coils fixed on a wheel of brass or some nonmagnetic material. Each flat core of soft iron, consisting of eighty pieces of sheet iron one millimetre thick, has about 1½ lb. of insulated copper wire wound round it, and is insulated from the adjacent coils by thin strips of copper. The field is developed by eight laminated magnets placed horizontally round the armature ring, the armatures therefore alternately passing N. and S. poles. Thus each coil passes sixteen alternate poles in each revolution, and by connecting up the coils in series, the total E.M.F. is sixteen times that developed in one coil, and the current alternates eight times as fast as it would were there only one magnet employed and the armature rotated at the same speed.

*Kapp alternator.* Now the field developed by permanent magnets is limited, because the number of lines of force which can be urged through steel are low compared with the number that can be forced through soft iron. So machines which have the field developed by electro-magnets are smaller than those in which steel magnets are used. The lines of force are produced by a current passing through a coil, and it used to be the practice to use small Ds.—*exciters*—which supplied its own field magnet coils with current and also gave a continuous current. The alternating machine designed by Kapp follows naturally after the De Meritens. In this machine the field is produced by two crowns of short cylindrical electro-magnets. In a typical example there are twenty-eight magnets consisting of copper wire wound round wrought-iron cores about 4 in. in diameter. These jut out, as it were, from two rings or wheels, forming two crowns, each containing fourteen magnets. The wire is wound so that the polarity of adjacent magnets is opposite, while opposing pole faces are similar in polarity. The armature is built up by winding thin iron on a cast-iron ring, the layers being insulated with varnish. This armature is divided into fourteen coils wound over the core ring. The current is generated in a manner similar to that in which it is produced in the De Meritens machine, except that the lines of force enter and leave the armature on both sides of the flat ring. The armature wires are connected to brass rings and collected by copper brushes. Since the E.M.F. is high, it is usual to have the collector rings on opposite sides of the armature, so that there is no danger of touching both brushes at the same time.

*Siemens alternating-current dynamo.* —The field coils in this machine are similar to those in the Kapp machine, except that the opposing faces are of opposite polarity. The armature consists of coils wound so that alternate ones are opposite in direction; these are pear-shaped and are wound round wooden cores fitted to a wheel; and there are an equal number of armature coils and fields.

*Mordey alternating machine.*—In this machine we have two complete departures from the machines described previously : (1) The armature is fixed and the field magnet rotates; (2) the lines of force in the various fields projected through the armature coils are all in the same direction, all those on one side being of N. and on the side of S. seeking polarity. The space between opposing pole faces is kept small in order to reduce resistance and to keep the field from spreading. The armature consists of coils of copper ribbon wound on flat pear-shaped cores of wood, the different layers being insulated from one another, and the whole is bound together. The broad ends of these cores are clamped between German silver plates against ebonite insulators and bolted to the inner side of a large ring. The ends of adjacent coils are connected by conductors through porcelain insulators. Since none of the iron supports come between the poles of the field magnets, eddy currents are only produced in a small degree, the high resistance of German silver also tending to minimise these. The field magnet consists of one coil wound round a short iron cylinder. This is surrounded by a massive iron casting which roughly consists of a number of claws curving inwards from each end of the cylinder until they almost touch. In the space between them the armatures just fit, so that there is just room for the coil and its big casting to revolve around them. These great claws of course constitute magnets, all on one side being S. poles and all on the other N. poles.

*Inductor alternators.*—So far we have described machines in which either the armature or the field coils revolve, but there is a type of machine in which neither field magnet coils nor armature coils move, but in which the lines of force are cut by moving masses of iron in such a way that alternately good and bad circuits are set up through the field magnet and armature coils. These machines possess great advantages. The moving mass is only a mass of iron which, if balanced properly, offers no mechanical difficulties to rotating at a very high speed, and since the coils are stationary, reliable connection with the external circuit is very easy. One of the earliest *inductor alternators* consists in an outer iron ring, which has pole pieces projecting inwards wound alternately with field magnet and armature coils. Inside these are a number of laminated pieces of iron carried on a non-magnetic framework, and this inner portion revolves. At one moment one of these portions just covers the one pole face and the adjacent armature core. At that moment a large number of lines are passing through it, but as it moves on the air space increases, decreasing the number of lines, while lines of force in an opposite direction begin to thread through the iron from the N. pole which it is approaching. So the number of lines of force is continually varying, and an alternating current set up. One of the best known of such machines is the Fynn alternator.

*Direct current machines.*—There is a great deal of work which alternators are unable to do, notably the charging of secondary batteries and the electro-deposition of metals. In these and other cases the current must flow in one direction only. In nearly all cases the current generated in the armature alternates, but it is possible so to arrange that the current shall flow in one direction in the external circuit, by means of *commutation*, and the apparatus used for this purpose is styled a *commutator* (*q.v.*). Again, when this has been done, it is possible to use up current developed by that machine to magnetise its own field magnets. At the beginning of this article it was pointed out that the direction of the current alters at the end of each half revolution. If, therefore, at the end of each half revolution the position of the two brushes were interchanged, then the current would always be flowing in the same direction in the external circuit. Instead of changing the brushes the rings are modified. Instead of the two rings shown in Fig. 2, one ring is used, which is split lengthways into two halves. Each end of the rotating coil is fixed to one of these halves, and the brushes press on the insulating divisions between the sections at the moment that the coil is vertical, *i.e.* when the reversal takes place. It is evident then that the brushes take off a series of short current always in the same direction. If the number of sections in the ring be increased and the same number of segments be made in the armature, as in Fig. 4, then the variations in the E.M.F. are considerably reduced, so that a continuous direct current which is uniform in strength is obtained. Gramme, in 1870, was the first to utilise this principle, and Fig. 4 gives an approximate illustration of the action of a Gramme armature. An armature of that type would, however, be of little utility in a modern machine, as it would be liable to fly to pieces. A modern type of armature consists of flat rings of charcoal insulated from each other by paper, all being mounted on a steel shaft; the armature conductor consists of cotton-covered copper wire lying round the core. In each of seventy-six sections there would be two turns, so that the commutator would consist of seventy-six copper segments, insulated from each other with mica, and the whole is bound together in three places with several turns of wire in order to prevent bulging. The brushes are not placed vertically over one another. They are so placed that every division between the segments of the armature passes a brush just when the coil connected to those segments is idle.

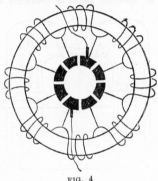

FIG. 4

This always happens when the coil is at right angles to the lines of force, but the field is distorted when a current is established, since the armature becomes a magnet itself. So the brushes have to be adjusted, and their new position is known as their lead, and the angle through which they are moved as the angle of lead. Practically the best position is found by adjusting them while the machine is running until no sparking takes place.

*Drum armature* is really a development of the shuttle-wound armature, and consists of a cylindrical core at one end of which is a commutator. From one segment of this a coil proceeds lengthways round the drum, and is connected then to the next segment to the one to which the other end of the coil starts. The second coil starts where the first terminates and so on. There are many disadvantages which obviously arise from the crossing of these wires, one of which evidently is the difficulty of replacing a faulty coil, while its great advantage is that the conductors cut all the lines of force passing through the armature core. When the current is obtained from an entirely separate source—a primary battery or an auxiliary D.—the machine is termed a *separately-excited* D. Fig. 5 shows one of these, where the pole pieces of a massive horseshoe electro-magnet are magnetised by coils wound in the direction shown, the armature revolving between the pole faces. Some of the lines of force will not pass through the armature, but will escape as shown. These machines possess certain advantages in that the exciting current is independent of the E.M.F. developed by the machine itself, but the difficulty arises of providing a

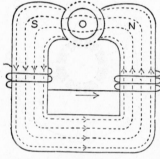

FIG. 5

separate source of current for the field magnet coils.

Ds. which are self-exciting may be classified according as the current for the field magnets is supplied. Thus if the ends of the coil (Fig. 5) shown were connected to the brushes on the armature, a circuit would evidently be made and the current would flow around the iron shoe, so creating a field. Now if this outer wire running from one of the brushes around to one end of the coil included the external resistance, then the D. would be connected up in *series*. Serious difficulties arise if such a system be put under varying loads—where the amount of current used varies—so this system is only used where currents of constant strength are required. Taking Fig. 5 again, it would be possible to run the ends of the field magnet coil to the brushes and also lead off the external circuit from the brushes at the same time. This would give a *shunt* D. Ds. connected up in this manner are less affected by changes in the external circuit, but

even this type is not self-regulating under all changes. Now a D. may be expected to maintain (1) a constant current through the external circuit, or (2) a constant potential difference at the ends of the circuit. It is impossible to construct a machine to fulfil both these conditions, so some automatic method must be used. This is done by combining in one machine the series and the shunt methods of winding. When this is done *compound winding* has been utilised. There are many machines of the direct current type which utilise the Gramme ring or the drum armature, among which may be mentioned the Kapp, the Edison-Hopkinson, and the Manchester Ds. Fig. 6 illustrates a D. which is said to be *multipolar*. The field magnet coils are wound round cores projecting inwards, each pole face covering rather less than a quarter of the armature surface. As shown, the poles are alternate and the lines of force flow in the direction shown. Two well-known machines of this type are the Kapp and the Fynn multipolar dynamos.

Cross magnetisation due to the armature can be neutralised to a certain extent by a proper amount of advanced field being provided by using interpoles or commutating poles. These are small field magnets between the main poles which are connected in series with the armature; the interpoles produce a cross-field which neutralises cross-magnetisation of the armature so that the magnetic neutral axis of the machine is coincident with the geometric neutral axis. Armature magnetisation varies with the current, but these fields, being in series with the armature, also provide a field proportional to the current. Interpoles also produce a field which acts on the short-circuited coil and has the effect of checking the old current and setting up the new in the short time available. In a dynamo, an interpole has the same polarity as that of the next pole ahead, and in a motor the next pole behind; and by this method sparkless running at all loads is obtainable with fixed brushes; in the case of a motor, since the brushes are on the geometric neutral axis, rotation in either direction can be obtained with fixed brushes.

Owing to the losses being converted into heat, the temperature of a dynamo will rise above that of the surrounding air till ultimately a steady temperature is reached, when the machine dissipates heat at the same rate at which it is produced. This final temperature is limited by the temperature which the insulation used is capable of withstanding before losing its mechanical and insulating properties. The rating of a dynamo is the output assigned to it by the maker, together with the associated conditions on the rating plate. Final temperature of the windings is limited to 80° C., and commutator to 85° C.

There are of course many other Ds., each having some distinctive feature, but a study of the types shown will give an insight into the principles underlying the generating of electricity. The general modern trend is to simplify the construction and make it more uniform. As an example, commutators to-day are generally made of hard drawn copper, and insulated where necessary, as in closed

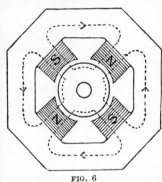

FIG. 6

coil machines, with mica. Then, whereas at first brushes were made of brass or copper strips, then of copper gauze, and later of a mixture of copper and carbon, they are now usually made simply of carbon. *See* ELECTRICITY.

*See* Slingo and Brooker, *Electrical Engineering ;* S. P. Thompson, *Dynamo Electric Machines ;* Carus-Wilson, *Electro-Dynamics.*

**Dynamometer,** any instrument used for the measurement of force or power developed in machinery. It is often termed a brake or absorption D., so called because it absorbs energy from the machine due to a frictional resistance. The instrument measures this absorption, and so affords a method of obtaining the rate at which the machine is doing work on the brake. As a transmission D., it transmits the power measured without any absorption of energy other than that due to the friction of the machine, and which by construction can be reduced to a minimum.

**Dyne,** the dynamical absolute unit of force in the centimetre-gramme-second (C.G.S.) system. It is defined as the force which, applied to a mass of one gramme, will produce in it an acceleration of one centimetre per second. The practical unit of force is the megadyne, *i.e.* 1,000,000 dynes.

**Dyrrhachium,** *see* DURAZZO.

**Dysart,** a royal burgh and seaport, near Kirkcaldy, Fifeshire, Scotland ; the earldom dates from 1643. There are coal mines near and the tn. weaves textiles and exports coal. The castle of Ravenscraig is ruinous. Pop. 4593.

**Dysentery** (Gk. δυσ-, difficult; ἔντερον, intestine), an infectious inflammatory disease of the large intestine, characterised by the formation of ulcers and the consequent evacuation of blood and shreds of tissue. The disease was at one time common in temperate climates, but is now practically restricted to the tropics, particularly where sanitary arrangements are imperfect. There are two main types : *amœbic* D., caused by the presence of a protozoan, *Amœba dysenteriæ*, and *bacillary* D. Two distinct bacilli have been identified as associated with dysenteric symptoms ; that discovered by Shiga in Japan and that discovered by Flexner in the Philippine Islands.

*Symptoms.*—The onset of the disease is accompanied by general illness and diarrhœa. The desire to evacuate is particularly distressing and the discharge is often scanty in amount. The evacuations are at first slimy, then blood-streaked, and if the disease is not checked, ultimately consist almost wholly of blood and shreds from the lining of the large intestine. The ulceration commences about the solitary glands of the colon, and gradually spreads until the greater part of the organ is affected. Occasionally the ulcers perforate the intestine, and death is likely to result from hæmorrhage or peritonitis. Febrile symptoms become intensified, it is difficult to satisfy thirst, and the patient becomes greatly exhausted. Gangrenous matter may appear in the evacuations. If recovery takes place, convalescence is protracted, and the disease may persist in a chronic form for years, as the injury to the tissues of the colon is usually extensive.

*Treatment.*—Owing to the great mortality produced by the disease when epidemic or endemic, preventive measures are of great importance. The diet should be carefully regulated, no intemperance either in eating or drinking should be permitted, and unripe fruit should be avoided. The most efficacious remedy at the onset of the disease is a good dose of castor oil accompanied by laudanum. Afterwards, ipecacuanha or large doses of salines should be administered. The pain may be alleviated by opium administered every two or three hours. Opium in warm water and antiseptic solutions may be injected into the bowel, but frequently the passage is so inflamed and irritated that such treatment becomes impossible. Enemata of quinine have been found particularly efficacious in amœbic D. The variety caused by the bacillus of Shiga is best combated by the specific anti-toxin. In some cases of D. recourse is had to appendicostomy, when the appendix is brought to the surface and used as an entrance for irrigating fluids.

**Dysmenorrhœa,** see MENSTRUATION.

**Dysodil,** a yellow, greyish, or greenish mineral substance found in Sicily. It is bituminous, and burns vividly, with a disagreeable smell. It is laminated in structure, and often contains fossil fishes and plants.

**Dyson, Sir Frank Watson,** Astronomer-Royal, Greenwich Observatory since 1910 ; b. Jan. 8, 1868, at Ashby-de-la-Zouch ; son of Rev. Watson D., Baptist minister. He was educated at Bradford Grammar School ; and at Trinity College, Cambridge—where he had a distinguished career, being Second Wrangler and Smith's Prizeman, also winning the Isaac Newton studentship. He was chief assistant at the Royal Observatory, Greenwich, 1894–1905, and secretary to the Royal Astronomical Society, 1899–1905 ; in the latter year he was appointed Astronomer Royal for Scotland. He became F.R.S. in 1901, and has contributed many mathematical and astronomical papers to the society's *Transactions,* and other scientific journals, and besides official publications, has written *Astronomy:* a handy manual, 1910. Knighted 1915.

**Dyspepsia** (Gk. δυσ-, badly ; πέπτειν, to digest), a functional derangement of the digestive processes. It is simply another name for indigestion, which may be due to general weakness in the organism owing to other disease, or may be caused by the imperfect carrying out of digestion owing to unsuitable habits of life. By far the commonest cause of D. is improper feeding, either as regards quantity and quality, or as to the manner in which the food is assimilated. The general tendency is to eat too much and too hurriedly. In the first case the stomach and intestines are overworked, and in the second they are given unsuitable material to work upon owing to insufficient mastication. Other causes are the taking of large quantities of liquid during meals, thus diluting the secretions of the digestive tract, and the excessive use of stimulants, including alcohol tea, coffee, and aromatic substances D. may be traced to causes not directly connected with food. Diseases of the teeth, liver, and pancreas catarrh of the stomach, poverty of the secretions owing to deficient blood supply are all possible precursors of difficult digestion. One of the characteristic symptoms of incipient consumption is a particularly intractable indigestion. Any derangement of the nervous system, such as is caused by worry, mental anxiety, or excitement, is liable to interfere with proper digestion.

The *symptoms* of D. include flatulence, eructations, heartburn, and the characteristic furred, pallid, or pimple tongue. Discomfort is felt in some part of the digestive tract ; diarrhœa is likely if the condition be temporary, whilst constipation is characteristic of a more chronic form of D. Other organs suffer impairment of function ; vision becomes cloudy or weak, the muscles lose their power to some extent, and there is a general feeling of unfitness for effort. Perhaps the greatest suffering is due to mental symptoms ; the dyspeptic finds it difficult to take an optimistic view of things, and is a prey to irritable impulses and gloomy foreboding.

*Treatment.*—In the first place, D. may be avoided by bestowing some attention to diet. Faulty teeth should be repaired or replaced, a habit of thorough mastication must be formed, food must be taken regularly and in reasonable quantity, and fluid should be taken separately from the more solid constituents of food, and should preferably be plain water. There are many systems of diet advocated as preventive of D. Probably all of them prove beneficial in some cases or other, but the individual can generally hit upon a system which suits his own peculiar tastes and habits of life. The great secret is temperance. An established dyspeptic need not necessarily have recourse to drugs. He should take regular exercise, devote plenty of time to meals, avoid all food which his experience shows him to be unsuitable, and fight against a habit of constipation. When drugs are recommended, the particular circumstances must be borne in mind. A transitory attack may be met with a purgative. If stimulants are required, whisky, quassia, and gentian tonics are usually recommended. Bismuth has a soothing effect on the nerves of the gastric region. If acid is deficient in the gastric juice, dilute hydrochloric acid may be taken, and other constituents of the secretions replenished with pepsin or rennet. Where the presence of gaseous products causes discomfort, charcoal in the form of biscuits has an easing effect.

**Dysprosium,** a metal belonging to the 'rare earth' family. It was discovered in 1886 by Lecoq de Boisbaudran. Its symbol is Dy, its atomic number 66, and its atomic weight 161·2 (H = 1) or 162·5 (O = 16). Dysprosium oxide is a white solid. D. occurs naturally in the minerals euxenite, fergusonite, xenotime, polycrose and gadolinite, etc. Chemically it is related to erbium, holmium and thulium.

**Dytiscidæ,** or true water-beetles, are coleopterous insects with bare eleven-segmented antennæ, and hind legs capable of swimming only. The perfect insect is purely aquatic, though it can fly from one pond to another, the larva is also aquatic, but before changing into a pupa it comes to earth and buries itself, and the pupa is wholly terrestrial. The beetle can live for several hours in a submerged state, but is obliged to come to the surface for air ; this it stores up in air-tubes under its elytra, or wing-cases, which fit tightly to its body. It is an active creature, carnivorous of habit, and after fixing itself upon its prey it sucks the juices from it swiftly and fiercely. The males are frequently found attached to the females by suckers on their fore-feet. There are nearly 2000 species of this family already known inhabiting waters of cooler parts of the world, and among the chief genera are Dytiscus, Cybister, and Hydroporus.

**Dzherzhinsky, Felix Edmundovich** (1877–1926), Russian revolutionary of Polish birth ; *b.* at Wilna. Joined Social Democratic Party in 1895. Between 1897 and 1902 he was sent to Siberia three times, and three times escaped. Took part in revolution of 1905 and was banished ; returning to Warsaw in 1912, was imprisoned until released by the revolution of March 1917. He organised the secret police or Cheka— later known as the Ogpu. In 1921 he became Commissar of Transport. In 1924 he was head of the supreme Economic Council. Died suddenly in Moscow, July 20, 1926.

**Dzhizak,** or **Djizzak,** a tn. in prov. of Samarkhand, Russian Turkestan, on the Samarkhand–Tashkent Railway. Pop. 15,000.

**Dzungaria,** *see* ZUNGARIA.

# E

**E,** the second vowel, and the fifth letter of the alphabet, and the most frequently used of all the letters. Its long and natural sound in English, as in *here, me,* agrees with the sound of *i* in the French and Italian languages. It has a short sound, as in *met, men ;* and the sound of *a,* open or long, as in *prey, vein.* As a final letter it is usually silent, as in *cheese.* As a numeral, E stands for 250, and in the calendar is the fifth of the dominical letters.

**E,** in music, is the third note in the natural scale of C. Its major key has four sharps.

**Ea,** one of the twelve great gods of the Assyro-Babylonians, god of the ocean and subterranean springs, called Oannes by Berosus (third century B.C.). E. was father of Merodach. Eridu (modern Abu Shahrein) was especially sacred to him, as also his Euphrates.

**Eadie, John** (1810–76), a Scottish theologian. From 1843 to the end of his life he was professor and lecturer of biblical literature in the United Secession Divinity Hall. He possessed wide learning and much power of exposition. His chief works are : *Biblical Cyclopœdia,* 1849 ; *Ecclesiastical Encyclopœdia,* 1861 ; editions of Cruden's *Concordance,* 1839, and the *Family Bible,* 1851.

**Eadmer (or Edmer) of Canterbury** (*c.* 1064–1124), an English historian and monk, an intimate friend of Anselm. He was nominated Bishop of St. Andrews in 1120, but as there was controversy between Canterbury and York for jurisdiction over the see, while the Scottish king maintained his independence of either, E. returned and resigned the position. His chief works : *Historia Novorum, 1060–1122* (first printed 1623), and *Vita Anselmi* (published 1551) are both in the Benedictine edition of Anselm's *Works,* 1721. Rule's edition in the Rolls series appeared in 1884. E.'s Lives of Dunstan, Bregwin, and Oswald are in Wharton's *Anglia Sacra,* ii., 1691. *See* Grub, *Ecclesiastical History of Scotland,* 1861 ; Ragey's *Eadmer,* 1892.

**Eads, James Buchanan** (1820–87), an American engineer and inventor, granted a government contract (1861) for constructing a fleet of iron-clads for use on the Mississippi. With these, the capture of Fort Henry was effected during the Civil War. E. constructed the steel arch bridge at St. Louis (1867–74), and undertook to deepen the Mississippi's channel by means of jetties. He also planned a ship-railway across Tehuantepec isthmus, but it was not carried out. *See* How, *J. B. Eads,* 1900.

**Eagle,** a term employed in speaking of many species of Falconidæ in the sub-family Aquilinæ. They occur in all parts of the world, usually building eyries in forests or on mountains, and all are fierce and powerful birds

GOLDEN EAGLE

of prey. The species known to mythology and art belonged to the genus *Aquila,* but the individual is not known. *A. chrysaëtus,* the golden E., is a large and fiercely predaceous bird rarely found in Britain ; *A. nœvia,* the spotted or screaming E., occurs in N. Europe. The sea-Es. are represented by the genera *Haliaëtus* and *Thalassaëtus ;* the hawk-Es. by *Spizaëtus* and *Limnaëtus ;* the fishing

Es. by *Pandion ;* the harrier-Es. by *Circaëtus.* See under separate headings for descriptions of species.

**Eagle :** (1) A gold coin of U.S.A., worth 10 dollars or over £2. The double E. is a gold $20 piece, and there are half and quarter Es. The bird represented is the *Haliaëtus leucocephalus* (bald or white-headed E.). (2) The military standard of the Romans and earlier nations. The Persians, in the time of Cyrus the Younger (fourth century B.C.), carried an E. on a spear as their standard. The Roman E. was of silver, bronze, or gold, with wings extended. It was carried on the top of a spear, with a cross-bar supporting it. Some held thunderbolts in their talons. Napoleon's armies had a similar standard (1804). As an armorial bearing the Imperial E. was adopted by the Holy Roman empire (800), and later by Austria, France, Germany, Russia, and the U.S.A.

**Eaglehawk,** a municipal bor. of Bendigo co., Victoria, Australia, 4 m. from Bendigo, and 105 m. from Melbourne ; noted for fine gold mines. Pop. 4719.

**Eagle-hawk,** *see* HAWK-EAGLE.

**Eagle-owl,** or **Bubo,** a genus of the family Strigidæ, which is represented in all parts of the world but Australia.

**Eagle Pass.,** a tn. of S.W. Texas on the Rio Grande, in an agricultural and coal-producing district. Pop. 5059.

**Eagle-wood, Aloe-wood,** or **Agila-wood,** the inner part of the trunk of *Aquilaria ovata,* and *A. Agallochum,* forest trees belonging to the natural order Aquilariaceæ, growing in tropical Asia. These trees contain a very fragrant substance, dark in colour, and besides being much used for medicinal purposes, the wood is much sought after for fumigation, also as incense in religious ceremonies. Its fragrance remains for many years.

**Eakins,Thomas**(1844–1916), American painter ; *b.* July 25, 1844, at Philadelphia, Pa. ; son of Benjamin E. Graduated at high school ; studied art in Paris under J. L. Gérôme at the Ecole des Beaux Arts, also under Léon Bonnat. Also worked in the studio of Dumont, sculptor. In America, he was professor and lecturer on anatomy and painting in various schools of art. Painted many pictures of early American domestic life, studies of American sports and negroes ; also large composition portraits—such as ' Dr. Gross in his clinic ' (now in Jefferson Medical Coll., Philadelphia), and ' Dr. Agnew in his clinic.' Assisted his pupil Samuel Murray to model the colossal figures of the Prophets on the Witherspoon Build-

ing, Philadelphia ; modelled two reliefs on the Trenton battle monument, also the horses ridden by Grant and Lincoln on the Soldiers' and Sailors' Monument at Brooklyn. Painted the Crucifixion in Overbrook Seminary ; portrait of Cardinal Martinelli ; and many other portraits —being best known as a portrait painter. National Academician, 1902. Died in Philadelphia, June 25.

**Ealdelm,** or **Aldhelm** (*c.* 640–709), a Saxon ecclesiastic and scholar, educated at Canterbury. He became Abbot of Malmesbury (676), and Bishop of Sherborne (705). The Church of St. Lawrence at Bradford, Wiltshire, alone remains of his buildings. He wrote treatises and verse in Latin and English, some of which survive. The best known are : *De laude virginitatis* (prose) and *De laude virginum* (poetry). *See* Giles, *Patres Eccles. Angl.,* 1844 ; Migne, *Patrologia Latina,* lxxix., 1844–64.

**Ealing,** a parl. bor. and suburb of London, 9 m. W. of St. Paul's Cathedral. The ancient village, now the centre of the town, lies S. of the high road to Uxbridge. Pop. 67,753.

**Eames, Emma** (*b.* 1867), an American prima donna, *b.* at Shanghai, China ; studied at Boston, Massachusetts, and Paris. Made her début at Covent Garden in 1891. Has sung during the seasons in Europe and America since then.

**Ear.** The E., the organ of hearing, is divisible into three parts : (*a*) the external ; (*b*) the middle ; (*c*) the internal. The most important portion is the internal E. or *labyrinth,* the other two can be considered merely as accessories to this, their function being the collection and transmission of the sound waves so that the sentient portion of the organ may be affected. The parts will be described from the exterior inwards. The external E. consists of two parts, the *pinna* and the *meatus.* The former is a broad, peculiarly shaped, and for the most part, cartilaginous plate, concave on the whole, but thrown into various elevations and hollows to which distinct names have been given, the largest and deepest hollow being the *concha,* which surrounds the entrance to the meatus. The variety of contour is to ensure that the sound waves collected within the rim of the pinna are reflected into the external auditory canal, somewhat similar to the action of the Whispering Gallery of St. Paul's. The meatus, about 1¼ in. in length, has an outer cartilaginous portion with many fine hairs and a large number of sebaceous glands which secrete *cerumen* or E. wax. The innermost half of the tube enters the temporal bone which encloses the middle and internal E. The meatus is first directed upwards and then, narrowing in diameter, surmounts a convexity in the floor of the osseous part to dip downwards and widen again to its termination at the obliquely placed *membrana tympani.* The middle E., *tympanum* or *drum,* is a narrow, irregular cavity varying in width from ⅛ in. to $\frac{1}{12}$ in. between the tympanic membrane and the outer bony wall of the labyrinth. Its enclosed air is in direct communication with the pharynx by means of the *Eustachian tube.* This arrangement ensures that the cavity is kept supplied with renewed air at the same pressure as that of the external E. It contains a chain of small bones which convey the vibrations across

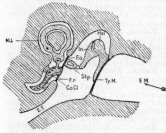

DIAGRAM ILLUSTRATING THE RE-
LATIVE POSITIONS OF DIFFERENT
PARTS OF THE EAR (after Huxley).

E.M., external auditory meatus; Ty.M., tympanic membrane; Mal., malleus; In., incus; Stp., stapes; F.o., fenestra ovalis; F.r., fenestra rotunda; E.T., eustachian tube; M.L., membranous labyrinth, only one canal and its ampulla being shown; Sc.V., Sc.T., scalæ vestibula and tympani; Co.Cl., cochlear canal (the cochlea is supposed partly unrolled); *** sites of auditory epithelium.

the cavity to the middle E. The membrana tympani is an ellipsoidal disc about 0·37 in. by 0·33 in., and about $\frac{1}{250}$ in. thick. To its inner surface is attached the handle of the first bone (the *malleus,* see diagram), the rounded head of which fits into a corresponding hollow in the second bone (*incus*), and this in its turn articulates with the *stapes,* which fits into the *fenestra ovalis* of the internal E. The *fenestra rotunda* separates the scala tympani from the middle E. The complicated ligament and muscle attachments of the chain of bones ensure an exact reproduction at the fenestra ovalis of the highly

complex movement of the tympanic membrane. The internal E. is contained in the petrous portion of the temporal bone and consists of a complex cavity, the *osseous labyrinth,* hollowed out of the bone and containing the *membranous labyrinth.* The former is incompletely divided into three parts, viz. the *vestibule,* the *semicircular canals,* and the *cochlea ;* the membranous labyrinth is smaller, and the space between the two is occupied by *perilymph,* while *endolymph* is contained in the inner labyrinth. The vestibule forms the central chamber of the labyrinth and communicates in front, by means of a large opening, with the cochlea, and behind, by means of five smaller openings, with the semicircular canals ; its outer wall is penetrated by the fenestra ovalis mentioned above. The semicircular canals are three tubes differing from one another in direction, length, and position with regard to the vestibule ; they are arranged in three planes mutually at right angles, and whatever may be their function in hearing they are certainly of the greatest importance in the guidance of co-ordinated movement so that bodily equilibrium may be maintained. Each canal is about $\frac{2}{50}$ in. wide, but each is dilated at one end forming an *ampulla* about $\frac{1}{10}$ in. in diameter, and on each ampulla is a crest or ridge (*crista acustica*) projecting into the cavity of the canal and consisting of *auditory epithelium,* which contains distributed filaments of the auditory nerve. The cochlea appears in the form of a blunt cone about ¼ in. in height and the same in breadth at the base. It consists of a gradually tapering spiral tube of 2½ turns and some 1½ in. in length, the inner wall of which is formed by a central column, or *modiolus,* from which projects a spiral lamina along the whole extent of the cochlea. The membranous labyrinth consists of structures lined throughout by epithelium, and at certain parts receives branches of the auditory nerve. In the vestibule and canals the structures have a general resemblance in form to the complicated cavity in which they are contained. They do not, however, lie loose within the osseous labyrinth, but along the convex border of the canals, and at the places of entrance of the nerves into the vestibule and ampullæ they are fixed to its walls. In the cochlea the membranous structures complete the septum and enclose an intermediate cavity. In the osseous vestibule there are two membranous sacs : (*a*) the *utricle,* connected with the canals, and (*b*) the *saccule,* connected with the cochlea ; these sacs are only in indirect communication with one another. Both contain small masses of calcareous particles (*otoliths*) which are set in movement by vibrations, and they also contain patches of auditory epithelium with nerve filaments. The cavity of the osseous cochlea is divided into three distinct parts : *scala vestibule, scala tympani,* and *canalis cochleæ,* by means of two membranes : (*a*) the *basilar,* and (*b*) the more delicate *membrane of Reissner,* the oblique direction of which latter causes the smallest portion, the cochlear canal, to have a triangular section ; this is in communication with the saccule and contains endolymph, whereas the other two scalæ contain perilymph. The cochlear canal is highly complicated, and only a brief description is possible here. The most important structure of the floor of the cochlear canal, that is, on the basilar membrane, is the so-called *organ of Corti,* which consists of *rods of Corti.* There is an inner row and an outer row all along the spiral, each row containing several thousand rods, flanking the rods are rows of cells (several thousands in each row), each cell bearing short *hairs* on its free surface, and the auditory nerves passing through the lamina spiralis reach the cochlear tube along the whole length of the spiral and end in filaments which are lost in the organ of Corti, but are probably connected with the *hair cells.* It is thought that the cochlea distinguishes pitch and timbre in notes. What takes place in hearing may be summarised thus : The vibrations set up by a sounding body are conducted by the accessory apparatus to the perilymph through the membranous sac, thence to the endolymph. The vibrations in time reach those particular places containing auditory epithelium, and set the auditory hairs or the otoliths in movement, and so excite the delicate filaments below, which causes impulses to pass along the auditory nerve to the brain.

The *diseases of the ear* are particularly numerous, and briefly include : the blockage of the auditory canal by wax and other products ; inflammation of the lining membranes ; displacement, fracture, or thickening of the tympanic membrane ; the impeding of the movement of the ossicles by exuded liquid ; ' running ear,' pointing to an accumulation of decaying matter in close proximity to the brain, is particularly serious. In all cases of aural disease skilled treatment is essential.

**Earheart, Amelia** (*b.* 1898), American social service worker and airwoman, *b.* in Atchison, Kansas.

Was the first woman to fly the N. Atlantic, flying as a passenger from Newfoundland to Burry Port, Wales, in 1928. She served with the Red Cross during the Great War and now directs a social service centre in Boston.

**Earl,** a title of British nobility, between a marquis and a viscount. It was during the Norman period that this title first became hereditary, and for some time they were called counts, and their wives in the present day are called countesses. The title of earl was the highest hereditary dignity until the reign of Edward III., who created his eldest son ' Duke ' of Cornwall, 1337. The eldest son of an E. bears the title of ' viscount,' while the younger sons are ' honourables.'

**Earl, Maud,** an animal painter, *b.* in London. She studied in her father's studio, and made her first exhibit in the Royal Academy in 1885. She has painted the portraits of all the principal dogs of Great Britain and the Continent, including those of King Edward VII. and Queen Alexandra. Some of her works are : ' A Cry for Help,' ' The Dog of War,' ' The Dogs of Death,' ' Their Last Trail,' ' I hear a Voice,' ' The Absent-minded Beggar,' ' British Hounds and Gun-Dogs,' ' His Majesty King Edward's Terrier, Cæsar.'

**Earle, John** (1824–1903), an English philologist and clergyman, professor of Anglo-Saxon at Oxford, 1849–54 ; re-elected, 1876. He became rector of Swanswick in 1857, prebendary of Wells (1871), and rural dean of Bath (1873–77). His works include : *Two of the Saxon Chronicles Parallel,* 1865 ; *A Book for the Beginner in Anglo-Saxon ; The Philology of the English Tongue,* 1866 ; *Anglo-Saxon Literature,* 1884 ; *English Prose,* 1890 ; *The Psalter of 1539,* 1894 ; *A Simple Grammar of English now in Use,* 1898 ; *The Alfred Jewel,* 1901. See *Times,* Feb. 2, 1903 ; *Oxford Mag.,* Feb. 11, 1903 ; *Men and Women of the Time,* 1899.

**Earle, William** (1833–85), an English soldier, served in the Crimea. He became military secretary to Northbrook, viceroy of India (1872–76), commander of the garrison of Alexandria during Wolseley's campaign (1882–84), and led a column of the Gordon rescue expedition (1884). While leading his detachment against the Arabs at Kirbekan, he was killed. A memorial statue was erected in Liverpool. See *Times,* Feb. 16, 1887 ; Brackenbury, *The River Column.*

**Earlestown,** an eccles. par. of S. Lancashire, England, 5 m. from Warrington. The London Midland and Scottish Railway Co. have a large establishment for building wagons and there is a sugar refinery near. Pop. 10,077.

**Earl Marshal of England.** The king's marshal (A.-S *mearh* and *sceale*, groom) became early one of the chief officers of state, and, under the Norman and Plantagenet kings, judge in the Courts of Chivalry. Since 1672 the office has been hereditary in the family of Howard (Dukes of Norfolk). The earl marshal is now head of the Heralds' College in England, regulates all matters connected with armorial bearings, standards, etc., and controls the arrangements for state functions, such as royal processions, drawing-rooms, balls. In Scotland a similar dignity was hereditary in the family of Keith from the fourteenth century till 1716.

**Earlom, Richard** (1743–1822), an English mezzotint engraver, a pupil of Cipriani. He was the first artist to make use of the point in mezzotint work. He engraved plates after Rembrandt, Vandyck, Correggio, and others; the six after Hogarth's ' Mariage à la Mode' are well known. ' Fruit and Flowers,' after J. van Huysum, made his reputation, and ' Bathsheba leading Abishag to David' won much praise. His patron, Boydell, published the ' Liber Veritatis,' 1777, with a series of prints from the originals of Claude Lorrain.

**Earl's Court,** part of the metropolitan bor. of Kensington, London, England, on the District Railway and Piccadilly Tube. The E. C. Exhibition is held annually near by.

**Earlston, Ercildoune,** or **Erceldoune,** a par. and market tn. of Berwickshire, Scotland, on Leader Water, 4 m. from Melrose. Tweeds, ginghams and other textiles are manufactured, and there are dye-works. Ruins of an ancient tower remain, the traditional abode of Thomas the Rhymer (thirteenth century). Pop. 1643.

**Early Closing.** The movement for reducing the working hours of shop assistants was inaugurated in 1842, since which year the compulsory weekly half-holiday, the introduction of ' summer time,' and other reforms, have appreciably improved their conditions. The provisions of the Shops (Early Closing) Act, 1920–21, were permanently adopted in 1928. The Act states that for only one day weekly may a shop remain open until nine o'clock, and on the remaining evenings it must close no later than eight, customers inside the doors before closing time or anyone requiring some article urgently in case of illness may be served. Table-waters, sweets, chocolates, tobacco and smokers' requisites may be obtained until 9.30 on most evenings, and until ten on the ' late day.' Exemptions are given in respect of exhibitions, seasons such as Christmas, while special provisions are made for holiday resorts and sea-fishing centres. The occupier of a shop breaking the law is liable to a maximum fine of £5 for a first offence, and £20 for any subsequent offence. The President of the Early Closing Association is Winston Churchill, and its Secretary, Albert Larking, C.B.E.; the head offices are 34–40 Ludgate Hill, London.

**Early, Jubal Anderson** (1816–94), an American Confederate general, practised law from 1838–61. He served in the Florida War (1837–38), and in Mexico (1847–48). In the Civil War he commanded a brigade at Bull Run (1862), and distinguished himself at Williamsburg, Antietam, Fredericksburg, Chancellorsville, and Gettysburg, commanding part of Lee's army. After some successes in the Shenandoah Valley, he was defeated by Sheridan (1864), and by Custer at Waynesborough (1865). He wrote *A Memoir of the Last Year of the War for Independence in the Confederate States*, 1867. See Pond, *The Shenandoah Valley in 1864*, 1883; *Battles and Leaders of the Civil War*, iv. (Johnson and Buel's edition, 1887).

**Early English Text Society,** founded in England by Furnivall, 1864, in connection with the Philological Society, as were also the Chaucer and Ballad Societies of 1868, and the Wyclif Society of 1882. For these societies he has edited many works, such as *Saint Graal* in English verse by Lonelich, 1440 (1861–63); Walter Map's *Quest del Saint Graal*, 1864; *The English Conquest of Ireland, 1165–85,* from Giraldus Cambrensis, 1896. The aim is to increase a general knowledge of Old English writers.

**Earn,** a loch of Perthshire, Scotland, about 6¼ m. long by ¾ m. broad, and about 300 ft. deep. Ben Voirlich is a lofty mountain near by, and Ardvarlich House (S.) is the ' Darnlinvarach ' of Scott's *Legend of Montrose.* The river issues from the loch, flows E. through the well-wooded valley of Strathearn, past Comrie, Crieff, and Bridge of E., a watering-place near the saline springs of Pitcaithly. The E. finally joins the Tay near Abernethy (about 6 m. from Perth).

**Earnest** (Scottish *arles*), a trifling sum of money or token given to ' bind the bargain ' of a sale or agreement, marking the assent of both parties to a contract. A practice of great antiquity, it is still sometimes observed in England and Scotland. It is not quite the same as part payment, for in the case of E. proper, or ' dead E.,' no allowance is made later for the value of the token given beforehand by the purchaser. *See* Erskine's *Institutions ;* Sale of Goods Act, 1893 ; Fry in ' Howe *v.* Smith ' (27 Ch. D. 89, 1884) ; Statute of Frauds (29 Car. II., c. 3).

**Ear-ring,** strictly a ring worn as an ornament suspended from the lobe of the ear, which is pierced for the purpose. The custom of wearing Es. has existed among the Orientals from the earliest times. It was common to both sexes among the Asiatic races (Persians, Babylonians) and Carthaginians, but reserved for women only among the Greeks and Romans. In Elizabethan times in England, Es. were still worn by men, and sailors sometimes continue the custom. This form of jewellery is not now so universal in Europe as formerly. The two chief kinds are a jewelled stud fitting closely to the lobe, or a drop or pendant hanging from a gold loop.

**Ear-shell,** *see* HALIOTIS.

**Earth** (A.-S. *eorthe*), the planet on which we live. The term is also used to denote the solid portion of the globe, in particular the uppermost layer, consisting of disintegrated rock and organic particles loosely bound together, otherwise known as soil. The early chemists recognised four elements : fire, air, water, and E., of which all other substances were thought to be mixtures or modifications. In modern chemistry the term persists as applied to certain metallic oxides. The older chemists gave the name E. to non-metallic substances which were insoluble in water and were not affected by high temperatures. As many of them had an alkaline reaction they were known as alkaline Es., but subsequent investigations have shown that each such E. is a compound of a metal and oxygen. The term alkaline E. is now restricted to lime, strontia, and baryta, these being oxides of calcium, strontium, and barium. There is another extensive group of oxides known as the rare Es. They occur in several rare minerals found in Scandinavia, Siberia, Greenland, and N. America, and are employed in the manufacture of mantles for incandescent gas lamps. The chief metals of the rare Es. are scandium, yttrium, lanthanum, didymium, terbium, and erbium.

*The Earth as planet.*—The E. is a member of a group of bodies distinguished from other bodies in the universe by their motion around one member of the group, the sun. The central body, or sun, is the only

member of the group, as far as we know, which shines by its own light. The other bodies consist of planets which move in elliptical orbits about the sun, and satellites which revolve around certain of the planets. The planets, in order of nearness to the sun, are Mercury, Venus, the Earth with its satellite the moon, Mars, with two satellites; then come a vast number of minor planets or asteroids, and outside of these the larger planets, Jupiter, Saturn, Uranus, and Neptune, with seven, ten, four, and one satellite respectively. The path of the E.'s motion round the sun, that is of its *revolution,* is an ellipse of which the sun forms one focus. The mean distance of the E. from the sun is about 93,000,000 m., and the eccentricity of the orbit is about 3,250,000 m. The plane of the orbit is called the ecliptic, and it is inclined to the E.'s equatorial plane at an angle of 23½°. The time which the E. takes to make a complete circuit is known as the solar year, and measures 365 days 5 hrs. 48 mins. 46 secs. The E. has another movement, rotating about its own axis, thus causing points on the E.'s surface to have periods of sunlight alternating with periods of darkness. Owing to the inclination of the E.'s axis to the plane of the ecliptic, some places are presented to the rays of the sun more directly than others; this causes the phenomena of the seasons. Also places in high latitudes are presented for longer periods to the sun's rays according to the position of the E. in its orbit; this accounts for the variations in the lengths of day and night in those latitudes. The E. is nearly spherical in shape. The ancients believed it to be a flat disc, and the belief persisted in the popular mind for many centuries. Pythagoras, however, asserted that the E. was spherical, and his view was strongly supported by Aristotle, who employed many of the arguments current to-day. The horizon becomes wider as the position of a spectator becomes more elevated, the E. always throws a circular shadow on the moon when it is in eclipse, and the lower part of a receding object is the first to disappear. The E. is, however, not a perfect sphere. In the seventeenth century Jean Richer observed that a clock which kept perfect time in Paris lost about 2½ minutes a day at Cayenne, and the pendulum had to be shortened in order to correct the error. Newton explained the occurrence by showing that the attraction due to gravity was less at the equator than in more northerly latitudes owing to an increased distance from the E.'s centre of gravity. This conclusion received confirmation by experiments with delicate spring balances, which registered less weight for a given mass in equatorial than in regions of higher latitudes. It was also observed that the length of a degree of latitude is greater towards the poles than near the equator. The degree is readily indicated with great accuracy by astronomical methods, and its length being determined by careful E. measurement showed beyond doubt

puted as about 5·5, the density of pure water at 4° C. being taken as unit. The planet E. is a great magnet. If a magnetic needle is placed upon a pivot so as to oscillate freely it takes up a position which is approximately N. and S. The N. and S. poles of the E. considered as a magnet are some distance from the poles of the rotatory axis and are liable to secular variation of position.

*Origin and history of the Earth.*—No

GREAT NEBULA IN ORION

that the E. is flattened at the poles. The amount of the flattening is not great, the extent by which the polar diameter is less than the mean equatorial diameter being about $\frac{1}{298}$ of its length. The equatorial section of the E. is also slightly elliptical. The approximate length of the polar diameter is 7899 miles, and the mean length of the equatorial diameter is about 7926 miles, giving a difference of 27 miles approximately. The mass of the E. is given by the most recent researches as 6,000,000,000,000,000,000,000 tons. The mean density of the earth is com-

theory of the origin of the E. has been generally satisfactory. The nebular hypothesis, which appears to be most in favour, states that the solar system was at one time a great mass of vapour, in which a central nucleus was gradually formed. This nucleus, which is represented by our sun, cast off the less central portions of the mass, which cooled down to form the present planets. The satellites were thrown off from the planets in the same way as the planets separated from the parent sun. There is certainly abundant evidence that the E. was at one time at a much higher temperature than to-day. The gradual rise of temperature on descending towards the E.'s interior suggests that the innermost regions are still at an enormously high temperature. The existence of volcanoes which pour out molten rock and hot gases is taken by some as sufficient evidence that the interior is still in a fluid condition, and that the crust is a solidified envelope of comparatively little depth. Physical facts are, however, rather against the likelihood of a permanent gaseous or molten interior, and some scientists have gone as far as to say that the amount of radium in the E. indicated by the discoveries fairly near the surface is sufficient to account for almost any degree of temperature. Attempts have been made to compute from geological, physical, and other data the length of the period during which the E. has been in a solid state. Lord Kelvin based his hypotheses on arguments derived from consideration of three kinds of data. By judging the rate of the loss of heat from this planet, he placed the limits of not less than 20,000,000 years and not more than 400,000,000 years, as the length of time from the first superficial solidification of the E. to its present condition. From estimating the amount of retardation of the E.'s rotation due to tidal friction, he judged that the E. became consolidated not much more than 100,000,000 years ago. Thirdly, by calculating the probable age of the sun's heat, he brought down his estimate of the age of the E. to about 20,000,000 years. Geologists, however, are disinclined to accept any period less than 100,000,000 years as sufficient for the elaboration of the present structure of the E. It is indisputable that many millions of years probably thirty or forty, must have elapsed while the great sedimentary rocks were being deposited. With respect to the larger features of the E.'s surface, it is likely that two different kinds of movement are responsible. Where the contraction of the E. has caused a lessening of the support below the surface, there has been a subsidence of great areas. In the second place, where the rigid crust has been able to contract into a smaller space, great ridges and folds have been formed, showing marked continuity and parallelism. The subsidences which caused the ocean appear to have taken place at different ages. The Atlantic Ocean probably dates from middle Cainozoic times; the Indian Ocean may be older, and the Pacific, whether a subsidence of great antiquity or not, has certainly suffered great modifications in com-

paratively recent times. Akin to the general discussion of the age of the E. is speculation concerning its future. The gradual loss of energy which has diminished the speed of rotation of the E. and caused its cooling and condensation is still going on. The constant operation of tidal friction will cause it to rotate more and more slowly, and the gradual cooling of the sun itself, if not fed by meteors from outer space, will inevitably diminish the amount of energy in the system. A time will come, many millions of years distant, when the members of the solar system will return to their ancient nucleus, and by the force of their impact will establish a nebula of sufficient energy to proceed upon another cycle of planet formation.

*Structure of the Earth.*—The E. consists of an outer gaseous envelope, the *atmosphere*, a middle layer of water, the *hydrosphere*, occupying the hollows in the surface of the globe, and a central core of solid material, the *lithosphere*. In the course of its solidification, the lithosphere developed ridges, which are represented by the great mountain ranges, and subsidences, which are represented by the great oceans. The progressive cooling had its consequence in stresses in various parts of the surface of the lithosphere which took effect in various movements, sudden occasionally, but long sustained for the most part, and so the general shape of the E. was and is constantly changing; in places the land is gradually lifted above the sea, while other lands are gradually submerged, only to reappear in a later age. There are other agencies at work tending to change the form of the E. The disintegrating forces of frost and water action gradually wear down the older rocks, while the deposition of the débris, mixed with relics of organised life, builds up layers of sedimentary rock. The oldest sedimentary rocks, known as Archæan, contain no traces of life. The sedimentary rocks containing fossils are divided into four great groups : the *Palæozoic*, containing such formations as the Cambrian, the Old Red Sandstone and the Coal Measures; the *Mesozoic*, containing the great chalk layers; *Tertiary*, containing friable rocks rich in fossils; and the *Quaternary*, consisting of sands, gravels, and clays of recent formation. The study of the crust of the E. is the aim of the science of *Geology*. In *Geography*, the surface of the E. is considered; its division into continent and ocean, the features of the land masses, mountains, rivers, plateaus, plains, etc., the distribution of life on the globe, the manner in which the various sections of the human race have grouped themselves, the nature of their governments, their industries, their cities and towns, roads of communication, commerce and markets. *Astronomy* deals with the E. as a planet, its movements, and the methods of accurately measuring them. The measuring of the surface of the E. is the concern of *Geodesy*. The constitution of the various rocks is dealt with in *Mineralogy* and *Chemistry*. The constitution and phenomena of the atmosphere are the business of *Meteorology*. The hydrosphere is studied under the name of *Oceanography*.

**Earth-closet,** *see* SEWAGE.

**Earth Currents.** The discovery of E. C. was made after the introduction of telegraphy. They arise from a variety of causes, viz. (i.) electro-chemical action in mineral deposits, (ii.) electric waves such as wireless waves, (iii.) electric railways, etc., and (iv.) telegraph lines are traversed by E. C., and were discovered by C. V. Walker and W. H. Barlow in England, and the latter E. C. are the most noteworthy. If two metal plates are sunk in the earth at some distance from each other, and then connected by a wire, E. C. flow from one plate to the other, and may be detected by a delicate galvanometer placed in the circuit. The potential difference between the plates may be as much as 20 millivolts per kilometre distance between them. This P.D. varies daily, and indeed may cause serious interference with the transmission of messages. The lines running from N.E. to S.W. in England are the principal sufferers from E. Cs. Within recent years prospectors for mineral deposits have made use of E. Cs. set up in a wire joining two plates embedded in the earth. The presence of such mineral deposits decreases the electrical resistance of the return earth circuit and by shifting the plates it is possible to locate the deposits by the large increase in the E. Cs. traversing the circuit.

**Earthenware,** *see* POTTERY.

**Earth-house,** or **Yird-house,** the usual name throughout Scotland for archaic underground buildings, also known as 'Picts' dwellings,' 'weems,' 'coves' or 'caves.' Examples remain in the British Isles (especially in N.E. Scotland), in Nebraska, Kansas, and the western states of N. America, where they are called 'dug-outs'; in Austria, Germany (*see* Tacitus, *Germ.*, xvi.), and other parts of Europe, and in Armenia and Egypt. Aristotle, Xenophon, and Strabo gave descriptions of structures of the kind, which are evidently of very ancient origin, though it cannot be definitely settled by whom they were first built. They are perhaps of Celtic origin in the British Isles. Very similar are the adobe dwellings in California and the dome-shaped snow-huts of the eskimos. Es. existed also in Asia and in Japan, especially in Korea and the N. An E. usually consists of a single irregular chamber of unhewn stones, the side-walls gradually converging towards the top till only a space of from 4 to 5 ft. remains to be spanned by rough flag-stones. A passage or gallery (8–10 ft. deep) leads to the room, getting wider and higher as it proceeds from the entrance. The roof was often only 1 ft. below the surface, and the whole was covered in by earth, sometimes raised very slightly in a mound above the level of the surrounding district. In later times there were often two or three rooms connected with each other. A few such houses were dug out of hard soil or chalk, and had no stone-work. Various implements of flint, bone, or metal are the chief remains found in them. Clovamoor (near Alford), Aberdeenshire, and Crichton (Midlothian) possess specimens belonging to post-Roman times. *See* Martin, *Description of the Western Islands,* 1703 ; Anderson, *Scotland in Pagan Times : the Iron Age,* 1883 ; Karner, *Künstliche Höhlen aus alter Zeit,* 1903.

**Earth-nut,** the name applied popularly to the tuberous roots of several umbelliferous plants, but especially to those of *Bunium bulbocastanum* and *B. flexuosum,* also known as earth chestnuts.

**Earth-pillar,** a pillar of earth or soft rock capped by a large boulder or some harder material, such as sandstone or limestone. These columns are formed by the action of rain on a mass of soft, stony clay, and the washing away of softer substances beneath cracks formed in the cap of rock. They occur in the moraines of glaciers, boulder-clay, and similar formations, and are from 30–100 ft. high. Examples are found in the 'bad lands' of western N. America, in the 'Garden of the Gods,' in Colorado, and at Botzen (Tyrol). There are also specimens at Foch-abers in Scotland and elsewhere.

**Earthquake,** a trembling or shaking of the earth. The intensity of the phenomena associated with seismic disturbances may vary from a slight tremor only perceptible with the aid of delicate instruments to a great convulsion accompanied by considerable changes in the surface structure of the earth, with consequent destruction of much life and property. Great Es. may or may not be heralded by preliminary tremors. These are followed by a shock or a series of great shocks extending over a few minutes, during which buildings are cracked and huge fissures appear in the earth. This is the period of greatest destruction, unless the advent of a huge sea-wave carrying with it large masses from the shore makes the havoc more complete. After the main shocks comes a series of minor disturbances, which may extend for many weeks or even years, gradually diminishing in intensity and frequency. In many cases observers have testified to the existence of sound-rumblings unconnected with any visible displacement of E., gradually increasing to a maximum and then decreasing to silence.

a vertical shock being sustained. Further away from the epifocus the shocks are more oblique in their direction. Much good work in the determination of the seat of disturbance in Es. was done by Robert Mallet (1810–81), who derived his conclusions from the direction of cracks in damaged buildings. Proceeding from the assumption that the direction of the fracture was in general at right angles to the direction of the wave, he obtained a series of directions, the intersection of which would give the position of the centre of disturbance. Other methods of determining the depth of the focus have since been elaborated, notably that employed by Major Dutton in connection with the Charleston E. of 1886. This depends

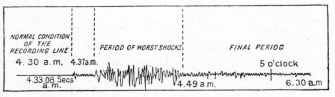

SEISMOMETER RECORD OF THE MESSINA EARTHQUAKE (1908)

The *nature* of E. movements has been studied by the aid of self-recording instruments called *seismometers* (*q.v.*). The movements consist of series of waves, which appear to be of two distinct types. The first type consists of waves of elastic compression proceeding from a centre of disturbance in much the same way as waves of sound are propagated in air by a vibrating body. The centre of disturbance is some point, or rather assemblage of points, at some distance below the surface of the earth's crust, and from this the waves proceed in all directions, thus giving the form of a series of spherical or spheroidal shells with a common centre or focus. The amplitude of the wave is the distance which each particle moves from its mean position ; the period is the time required to complete each oscillation The greater the amplitude and the less the period, the more violent are the effects at the surface of the earth. Other waves exist which move in a direction transverse to the direction of propagation of the waves of elastic compression. These are due to a change of shape in the medium in which the waves are propagated. The point of the surface immediately above the focus is called the epifocus, and it is here that the effects of the wave are most immediately felt,

upon the determination of an ' index-circle.' Over a great area surrounding the scene of the E. isoseismic lines were drawn connecting those points where the vibration felt was observed to be equal in intensity. The ' index-circle ' was defined as the curve joining the points where the intensity suddenly diminished. Theoretical considerations showed that the focal depth was obtained by multiplying the radius of the index-circle by the square root of three. Such determinations are made with difficulty, because, although the waves are theoretically propagated in spherical or ellipsoidal form from the focus, the heterogeneous nature of the structure of the earth's crust causes many disturbances of direction, the waves being refracted and reflected by masses of varying density and elasticity in the medium.

The *cause* of Es. may be broadly explained by reference to the contraction of the outer crust of the earth due to the cooling of the planet. The crust itself possesses a certain amount of rigidity, but the contraction of the interior occasions differences in the amount and distribution of the support afforded to the crust by the underlying structures. Hence there occur subsidences accompanied by the fracture of strata, or folding movements generally bearing some relation to the direction of folds on the earth's surface. Thus the greater proportion of observed Es. appear to take place in regions where there is a sudden slope towards a great depression, as on the Pacific coast. Generally speaking, the more violent manifestation of E. action may be located on two great circles, the one encircling the Pacific Ocean, and the other following the great depression of which the Mediterranean forms a part.

The *effects* of Es. are immediate and permanent. The immediate effects include the widespread destruction of life and property, often exceeding in extent the effects of the most disastrous wars. The more permanent effects are due to changes effected or induced in the surface of the earth's crust. Thus the elevation or depression of an area by only a few feet may lead to great changes in the drainage system of the country, with consequent far-reaching effects on its economic condition. Though occasionally a displacement may lay bare some hitherto hidden source of mineral wealth, the general consequences to a country of its position in an E. belt are fraught with danger to its economic prospects and the moral condition of its inhabitants. It is perhaps for this reason that Japan has been for some years the foremost of all countries in the world in its encouraging attitude towards seismological research.

*Notable earthquakes.*—Among Es. of particularly disastrous effects are the following : Lisbon (1755), when from 30,000 to 40,000 lives were lost ; the greater part of the city was wrecked, fire broke out, and a tidal wave swept over the quays and destroyed the shipping ; property was destroyed to the value of £20,000,000 ; Calabria (1783), when 60,000 lives were lost ; Aleppo (1822), 20,000 lives lost ; Naples (1857), 12,000 lives lost ; Peru (1868), 25,000 lives lost ; Krakatoa, where the E. was accompanied by a volcanic disturbance by which the island was completely destroyed ; Charleston (1886), where almost every building was damaged ; India (1896), when Assam was devastated ; Mont Pelée (1902), 20,000 lives lost ; India (1905), where a disturbance spread from Kangra over an area of 1,500,000 sq. m., causing the loss of 20,000 lives ; California (1906), when a large portion of San Francisco was destroyed ; Valparaiso (1906), 2500 lives lost ; Messina (1908), when Messina, Reggio, and many villages were totally destroyed, with a loss of life estimated at 77,283. Japan suffered its worst disaster on Sept.1,

1923, when an E. followed by a tidal wave and fire destroyed the capital city, Tokyo, one of the world's largest cities, and Yokohama, the chief port. Casualties were 246,540, of whom 103,733 were injured, 99,331 killed, and 43,476 missing and probably all killed ; 447,128 houses were destroyed by fire, and 128,266 by collapse ; total loss 5,500,000 *yen.* On July 23, 1930, the region near Naples had one of its worst Es. ; 2142 persons were killed and 4551 were injured. In March 1931 Nicaragua had an E. which destroyed the capital city of Manaquao, hundreds of persons being killed and injured.

See J. Milne, *Seismology,* 1898, and *Earthquakes,* 1898 ; C. E. Dutton, *Earthquakes in the Light of the New Seismology,* 1904 ; C. Davison, *A Study of Recent Earthquakes,* 1905.

**Earth-shine,** the light reflected from the earth's sunlit surface to the moon, causing the dark parts of her surface to become slightly luminous (with a reddish tinge) for a few days before and after new moon. The appearance popularly described as ' the old moon in the new moon's arms ' (the whole surface being visible in ashy-coloured light) is a result of the E.

**Earthworks,** Military, *see* FORTIFICATION.

**Earthworms** belong to a division of Annelids called Oligochæta. They are found in all parts of the world, though naturally they do not thrive in arid tracts ; and their effect upon the fertility and drainage of the soil can hardly be calculated. Burrowing into the ground, they cast up the earth they have swallowed, and so pursue a constant and thorough system of ploughing. Though eyeless, they evade the light and only come out of their burrows at dusk, often

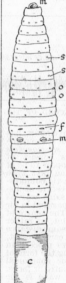

EARTHWORM
Ventral surface of anterior end showing *m.* mouth ; *s,* setæ ; *o,* openings of sperm-storing sacs ; *f,* openings of female reproductive organs ; *m,* openings of male reproductive organs.

remaining, even then, with their tails in the holes and their bodies working round and round. The British E. are confined to the Lumbricidæ, and are usually about 6 in. long, with a pointed head, rounded body, and slightly flattened tail. The *Allolobophora*, which are largely distributed over England and Ireland, are also found in the Arctic regions, and are the only E. capable of burrowing through snow and ice; *Lumbricus terrestris*, the common E., and *L. fœtidus*, the dunghill worm, represent another genus; and *Allurus*, the remaining genus, are equally at home on earth or in water. Some tropical species of E. reach a gigantic size, those found in Central Africa, Australia, and Ceylon growing to a length of 3 to 6 ft.

**Ear-trumpet**, *see* AUDIPHONE.

**Earwig**, the name given to certain species of Forficulidæ. *Foficula auricularia*, the common E. is found all over Europe, and is regarded by horticulturists as a great pest, as it feeds on young shoots, the petals of flowers, and the flesh of soft, ripe fruit. The name arises from a popular but erroneous idea that this insect will crawl into the ear and remain. The E. is gregarious and nocturnal, and makes its home under stones, beneath the bark of trees, or in almost any dark hole or crevice. The larvæ, when hatched, cluster round their mother, whom they closely resemble, except for the lack of wings.

**Easdale**, a small island on the W. coast of Argyllshire, Scotland, in the Firth of Lorn. It is 1½ sq. m. in area, and is noted for its primary slate quarries, belonging to the Earl of Breadalbane.

**Easements** form one of the class of rights called incorporeal hereditaments (*q.v.*) (and *see also* GRANT). E. consist of those rights in the nature of privileges or conveniences without profit which one or more persons have in, or over, the land (*q.v.*) of another, as *e.g.* a right of way or a watercourse (*see* LAND LAWS). E. are usually annexed or appurtenant to the ownership of a particular piece of land (the dominant tenement), and are said to be *affirmative* if the owner of the *servient* tenement must *allow* the owner of the *dominant* tenement to *do* something, as *e.g.* to use a right of way across his land; *negative* if he must *refrain from doing* something, as blocking up the 'ancient lights' of the other. E. consist chiefly of rights of way, watercourse, and light (*see* LAND LAWS), but any right over the land of another which is not 'capricious,' *e.g.* a right to increased lateral support for land weighted with buildings, and a right to access

of air for one's chimney or window is an E. A right to light may be defeated by blocking access to light, unless the right arose by express grant or by prescriptive title or user of twenty years. E. arise either by (1) custom, *e.g.* where villagers have been accustomed for a number of years to use a pathway over a piece of land; (2) grant; (3) prescription, either at common law, *i.e.* where the right has been enjoyed from the time of legal memory (accession of Richard I.); or under the Prescription Act, 1832, which makes an uninterrupted user for twenty to forty years respectively, *prima facie* evidence (*q.v.*) of the right to a way or watercourse, and twenty years as uninterrupted user conclusive of a right to light; (4) necessity, *i.e.* where absolutely necessary to the reasonable enjoyment of a tenement, *e.g.* if A sells B a piece of land entirely surrounded by other land of A's, a right of way in B is necessarily implied over the surrounding land. E. are lost by non-user for twenty years, by express release, or, of course, by reason of the dominant and servient tenements falling into the possession of the same person.

**East**, the quarter of the horizon where the sun rises, when in the equinoctial. From very early times the E. has been clothed in a certain sacred mystery, and it was the custom of many of the pagans to build their altars in the eastern part of the temples, so that they could offer their sacrifices towards the rising sun. Hence arose the custom of turning towards the E. for prayer, also the practice of laying the dead with their feet toward the E.

**East, Sir Alfred** (1849–1913), English painter and etcher; *b.* Dec. 15, 1849, at Kettering; studied art in the Glasgow School of Art, and later at the Ecole des Beaux-Arts in Paris, where he received lessons from Bouguereau. A.R.A., 1899. In 1906, the year when he published his *Landscape Painting in Oil Colour*, he was chosen president of the Royal Society of British Artists. His pictures are widely distributed, and may be seen in the galleries of Birmingham, Chicago, Budapest, and Venice. As a painter of landscape, he evinced a rare gift for so arranging his lines and masses as to produce, almost invariably, a charming and well-balanced composition. 'The White Carnival' (Brussels), 'Autumn' (Manchester), and 'Passing Storm' (the Luxembourg), display this and other merits. Knighted, 1910. Elected R.A., July, 1913. Died in London, Sept. 28.

**East Africa, German**, *see* AFRICA, GERMAN EAST, CAMPAIGN IN (GREAT

WAR) ; RUANDA ; and TANGANYIKA TERRITORY.

**East Africa, Portuguese,** *see* PORTUGUESE EAST AFRICA.

**East Africa Protectorate,** *see* KENYA COLONY AND PROTECTORATE; UGANDA PROTECTORATE ; and ZANZIBAR.

**East Anglia,** *see* ANGLIA, E.

**Eastbourne,** a mun. and county bor. and favourite seaside resort, 64 m. S.S.E. of London, in Sussex, England. Formerly the site of the present town was occupied by the three hamlets of East-Borne, South-Borne, and Sea-Houses, the antiquity of which is attested by the mention of Borne in the Domesday Book. The interesting parish church of East-Borne belongs to the Transitional Norman period, and dates back to the twelfth century. The modern city, with its miles of terraced promenade, its spacious, tree-lined streets, pavilioned pier, theatre, golf links, and handsome public structures, owes much to the seventh Duke of Devonshire, whose name is commemorated in Devonshire Park, a fine public pleasure-ground. The boundaries of the borough were extended in 1911 and 1927. Pop. 62,030.

**East Cape** (Asia), *see* DEZHNEV, CAPE.

**East Chicago,** a city of Lake co., Indiana, U.S.A., on Lake Michigan, with a port importing coal, iron ore, and limestone, and exporting gasolene and steel products. There are important steel works, oil refineries, etc. Pop. 54,784.

**East Cleveland,** a city of Cuyahoga co., Ohio, U.S.A., a suburb of Cleveland. Pop. (1900) 2757, (1910) 9179, (1920) 27,292, (1930) 39,667.

**East Conemaugh,** a bor. of Cambria co., Pennsylvania, U.S.A., 3 m. N.E. of Johnstown. Pop. (1920) 4979.

**Easter,** a religious festival of great antiquity observed among Christians, in commemoration of the resurrection of Christ, occurring about the time of the vernal equinox. The English name E. and the German Ostern are said to be derived from the name of the feast of the Teutonic goddess Ostera, celebrated by the ancient Saxons early in the spring. When Christianity was introduced some definite way of fixing a date for E., upon which many other festivals of the church depended, became necessary. There was much difference of opinion, and the Eastern churches commemorated our Lord's death on the fourteenth day of the moon after the spring equinox, and kept E. two days later ; while the Western churches kept E. on the Sunday following the fourteenth day of the moon. The sect known as Quartodecimans com-

memorated only the death of Christ, on the same day as that of the Jewish Passover. The Eastern Church adhered to this, but the Church of Rome soon rejected it, saying that Christ's resurrection took place on the first day of the week after the Passover, and ought in that case to be kept on a certain Sunday. In A.D. 325 the Council of Nicæa was held, and there it was settled that E. should be held on the first Sunday after the fourteenth day of the moon that occurred next after the vernal equinox, and that should the fourteenth day of the moon fall on the day of the equinox, the following Sunday was to be E. Sunday. Also it was decided that, in finding E., the vernal equinox should be considered to fall every year on Mar. 21. It was later directed that this calculation should be made according to the tables of Victorius of Aquitaine, which he introduced in A.D. 457. As Britain was now no longer a part of the Roman empire, this sixth century order regulating E. had no effect at first on the British church, which continued its calculation on the method originally approved of. But after more than a century of controversy the matter was ultimately settled at the synod which was held at Whitby, Yorkshire, in 664 ; and after this date the British clergy conformed to the general practice of the Western church. Sir. J. G. Frazer observed that ' at Rome the sacred fire in the temple of Vesta was kindled anew every year on the 1st of March, which used to be the beginning of the Roman year,' and from this old custom bonfires are still lit by the priest on E. Eve in many parts of Europe, especially Germany. The E. fire of Germany corresponds to the Beltane fire of Celtic Europe, which has the same ceremonies and beliefs, namely, that wherever the light of the fire reached, the fields would be fruitful and the inhabitants safe from sickness and danger. Games were also in use to celebrate E., such as dramatic performances, dances, songs, etc., and special cakes were made, of which custom the present-day ' hot-cross buns ' and ' simnel cakes ' are remainders.

**Easter Island,** or Rapanui, a lonely island, with an area of 46 sq. m., in the Pacific, situated in 27° 8′ S. lat., and 109° 26′ W. long. Since 1888 it has belonged to the Chilians, who use it as a convict station. It was so called because admiral Roggeveen discovered it on Easter Day in 1722. In shape the island is triangular, and the three corners are each marked by volcanic heights. So far the Polynesian natives only take advantage of the fertile soil to grow potatoes, sugar-cane, and bananas, but a French house of Tahiti has introduced cattle-grazing. The spacious stone dwellings, the huge carved images of grey trachytic lava, and the broad platforms of massive, uncemented masonry, which are found on the island, are an enigma to archæologists, who are at a loss to account for their presence on shores so remote from the known centres of early civilisation. Since the Peruvians deported the natives to work guano (1863), the number of these latter has dwindled to a hundred.

**Eastern Church,** see GREEK CHURCH.

**Eastern Empire,** see BYZANTINE EMPIRE.

**Eastern Question, The,** an expression which derives its origin from the problems connected with the existence of a portion of the Ottoman Empire in Europe. The main aspects of the problem are the struggles of the Christian populations in Turkey to regain their lands and rights and the efforts of Russia to obtain free entry into the Mediterranean Sea through Turkish territory. Connected with the latter aspect is the attitude of other European Powers, who had no desire to see Russia gain a strategic advantage which might in the event of war be turned against the countries bordering the Mediterranean Sea. There was also a strong desire in Greece to regain Constantinople, which had been captured by the Turks in 1453. The question became one of first-class importance to European statesmen in 1807, but the Congress of Vienna failed to make Turkey comply with its terms; from which circumstance Russia gained considerable prestige in view of the fact that she had contended that the question was a purely local one, and this failure appeared to confirm that view.

In 1850 France raised the question with Turkey regarding the right to protect Catholics in Turkey and the guardianship of the holy places in Palestine. France considered that she still had these rights, but the matter was contested by Russia, who made a similar claim. No agreement was reached, and the Crimean War resulted.

The Serbians had for ages borne much from the Turks, but in 1862 they drove them from Belgrade, a success which, however, only served to intensify the difficulties among the Christians of Herzegovina. This eventually forced them to revolt against Turkish rule in 1875. Afraid of the intervention of the Great European Powers, Turkey made a show of granting certain measures of reform, but as these were proved to be worthless (and in view of the Moslem massacre of the French and German Consuls at Salonica in May 1875), the Berlin Note was sent to the Porte requiring it to give guarantees for the execution of the reforms. As, however, Great Britain did not assent to the Note, Turkey believing she had the moral support of the British gov., took no action. Bulgaria also revolted against Turkey in 1875, but this was quelled by wholesale massacre. In 1877 Russia, Servia, and Rumania declared war on Turkey, the battles round Plevna being the most notable of this campaign. The allies swept on to Adrianople, and by Feb. 1878 were in sight of Constantinople, when the British gov., alarmed at their success and apprehensive of its consequences, sent a fleet to defend Constantinople. The war was brought to a close by the Treaty of Berlin, under which Turkey lost much territory.

The E. Q. became acute again in 1895, when Turkey embarked on a career of massacre of the Armenians in spite of strong representations from Great Britain and France.

No finality to this question appears possible, and the record of wars in the Balkans and about the Danube would appear to support this view. Just before the Great War the Balkan War (*q.v.*) of 1912–13 brought about certain territorial adjustments which irritated most countries concerned and were one of the contributory causes of the Great War.

**Eastern Rumelia,** see BULGARIA.

**East Flanders,** a prov. of Belgium, with Antwerp to the E., Brabant to the S.E., and W. Flanders to the S.W. It includes the basin of the Scheldt, and under skilful cultivation yields excellent crops, especially in the Waes district, which was once barren marsh. The chief towns are Ghent, the capital (pop. 165,149), Alost, and St. Nicolas. The area is 1249 sq. m. Pop. (1928) estimated 1,134,291.

**East Friesland** (*Ost Friesland*) now forms part of the dist. of Aurich in the prov. of Hanover, Prussia. It is bounded on the N. by the North Sea, and W. and E. by Holland and Oldenburg, respectively. Like W. Friesland it is flat and low, but the waste lands have been reclaimed and the Frisians live by agriculture as well as by fishing.

**East Ham,** a municipal bor. of S. Essex, England. It adjoins West Ham, and is included in greater London. Pop. 143,304.

**East Hampton,** a township of Suffolk co., New York, U.S.A., in the

K 2

S.E. of Long Island. It is a favourite summer resort and much frequented by artists and tourists during the season. Silverware is manufactured here. E. H. has many old churches and educational establishments. Pop. 1934.

**Easthampton**, a tn. of Hampshire co., Mass., with manufs. of textiles, rubber, thread, and fireproof doors. Pop. 11,323.

**East India Company**, a company founded for the purposes of trading with India and the E. Indies. It received its original charter at the hands of Queen Elizabeth in 1600, and this charter, at first granted for fifteen years, was subsequently granted for ever by James I. Companies for similar purposes had been already formed in the great maritime nations of Europe. It was in fact the monopoly of trade by the Dutch E. I. C. which led to the foundation of the English E. I. C. in the year already mentioned. The first governor of the company was Sir Thomas Smythe, and the company early established a trade, not only with the stations which it founded on the coasts of India, but with the Far East as well. The early ventures (usually private ones) of the company were entirely successful, and huge profits were realised. The competition of the English aroused the anger and jealousy of the Dutch and led to many outbreaks of quarrels between them. These culminated in the massacre of Ambogna, when the Dutch captured and ill-treated a number of English traders. The indignity was never forgotten, but for the time the English traders confined their attentions to the mainland of India, leaving the islands to the Dutch. The trade with India led to the building of fine merchant vessels, and the palm of mercantile shipping must be given to the E. I. C. up to the nineteenth century. During the seventeenth century the company began to spread and to gain territory. It built fortresses, raised troops, and gained general recognition, but still in quite a small way. This monopoly was interrupted by the advent of a number of interlopers who, feeling that they had equal rights with the company to trade, did so. The company appealed against the interlopers, but it was held that except by special Act of Parliament all British subjects had the right to trade with India (1694). In 1698 one may say a new E. I. C. sprang into being, when by loan of £2,000,000 to the state, the company was reorganised and reinstituted. Quarrels between the rival companies continued down to the reign of Queen Anne, and the

Gov. only renewed privileges to the original company after obtaining large grants of money. The company still remained merely a trading concern, and its authority, as stated in the charter of Queen Elizabeth, still held good. But during the eighteenth century the rivalry of France and England extended to India, and gradually the company rose, after the victories of Clive, to the position of a ruling power. The company still held unchecked power over its servants and soldiers, until the Regulating Act, 1773, created a governor-general, appointed by the company, but approved of by the crown. A council of four was also created, together with a court of judicature. Pitt's India Bill (1784) created a Board of Control and gave the political, financial, and military control into the hands of the Gov. Indian policy was no longer a matter for the company but for the Gov. Gradually the monopolies of the company were taken away, and the company in this way ceased to be a trading company at all, but merely an administrative body. Finally, after the disaster of the Mutiny (1857), the entire administration of India passed into the hands of the crown (August 1858).

**East India United Service Club**, established in London, 1848. The club-house is at 16 St. James's Square, London.

**East Indies** is opposed in the broadest sense to W. Indies, the name given by early explorers to islands in the Atlantic which they believed to be off the coast of India. It thus includes India and many groups of islands in the Pacific. But the name is commonly used of the Malay Archipelago, and especially of the Dutch E. Indies (*q.v.*). This archipelago is the largest cluster of islands in the world. It lies to the S.E. of Asia, and to the N. and N.W. of Australia, between 95° and 141° E. long., and 6° and 11° S. lat. Borneo—which is larger than the British Isles—the Philippines, Java, Sumatra, and Bali must once have formed part of the Asiatic continent : the shallows about them—nowhere are the surrounding seas deeper than 250 feet—indicate that they are summits of submerged hills. The investigations of botanists and zoologists all go to prove that the more easterly islands are closely associated with Australia. It is a curious fact that of the two adjacent volcanic islands of Bali and Lombok, separated by a narrow but very deep channel, Bali is entirely Asiatic in fauna and flora, Lombok markedly Australasian. In other cases the Asiatic and Australasian characteristics merge in the central islands and only become marked in those near the continents. Tin, malachite, copper, petroleum, and precious stones are the chief source of mineral wealth. There are many volcanoes, and the soil, as might be expected, is very fertile, yielding sugar, coffee, rice, maize, tea, coconuts, plantains, and spices in plenty. The land is, however, covered, for the most part, in unexploited forest. Java, the most developed of the islands, shows what riches could be produced were they all as systematically cultivated. Their natural resources are immense. Most of the islands belong to the Dutch, the chief being Java, Madura, and Sumatra, and parts of Borneo, Timor, and New Guinea. In 1898 the Philippines were ceded by Spain to the U.S.A.; Portugal holds a part of Timor; N. Borneo is a British possession, as is Papua, the south-eastern part of New Guinea. The north-eastern part of that island was formerly a German possession, but now constitutes, with the Bismarck Archipelago, the Mandated Territory of New Guinea. The native population includes Papuans or Melanesians and Malays.

**East Indies, Dutch,** *see* DUTCH EAST INDIES.

**Eastlake, Sir Charles Lock** (1793–1865), an English painter, was for some time a pupil of Haydon, a fellow Devonian. He once saw Napoleon, a captive on the *Bellerophon*, in the harbour of his native Plymouth, and later executed a fine life-sized portrait of the emperor largely from sketches made on that occasion. From 1817–30 he lived chiefly in Rome, and became R.A. in 1830. In 1850 he was president of the Royal Academy, and having been appointed director of the National Gallery in 1855, he exerted his influence towards improving the Italian schools. In his best work, such as ' Christ lamenting over Jerusalem,' 1843 ; ' Pilgrims arriving in sight of Rome,' 1828 ; and ' Byron's Dream,' 1834, it is grace and finish which impress.

**Eastland,** a city of Texas co., seat of E. Co. Centre of oil producing region. Pop. 4648.

**East Lancashire Regiment,** formerly 30th and 59th regiments, linked in 1881 to form E. Lancs. Regiment. The 30th was raised in 1702 as Marines, and served at the capture of Gibraltar, 1704 ; thence in W. Indies, America, and in fleet against Fr. coast. In 1782 it was named ' The Cambridgeshire Regt.,' served under Abercromby in Egypt 1801, and went through Peninsular Campaign with Wellington. It was in the Crimean War, and later went to Canada. The 59th was raised in 1755, and served in the American War of Independence. In 1782 it was called the ' 2nd Nottinghamshire Regt.,' and afterwards took part in Moore's retreat on Corunna, the Peninsular Campaign and the B. of Waterloo. It then served in Gibraltar, West Indies, China and Afghanistan. The East Lancashire Regiment served in South African Campaign : raised seventeen battalions during Great War, which served in France, Flanders, Macedonia, Gallipoli, Egypt, and Mesopotamia.

**Eastleigh** and **Bishopstoke** are two towns in Hampshire, England, on the Southern Railway. The railway company's rolling stock works are here. Eastleigh is 2 m. and Bishopstoke 5 m. N.N.E. of Southampton. Pop. of Eastleigh and Bishopstoke (1911) 15,247.

**East Liverpool,** a city of Columbiana co., Ohio, U.S.A., on the Ohio R., 44 m. W.N.W. of Pittsburg by rail. Pottery and earthenware are its chief manufs. Pop. 23,329.

**East London,** a seaport of S.E. Cape Colony, 543 m. by sea from Cape Town, and 253 m. from Durban, 665 m. from Johannesburg and 1222 m. from Buluwayo. With a white pop. of 23,010 (1926) and 14,800 coloured (1921). It is the principal wool port of the S. African Union. Its pier is 1289 ft. in length with promenade deck. There are several colleges and many schools, and a fine new Post Office, City Hall, and Public Library. Queen's Park is one of the largest in South Africa and the Esplanade one of the finest. The beautiful scenery and excellent bathing make it a popular seaside resort.

**East Lothian,** *see* HADDINGTONSHIRE.

**East Main,** the former name of the portion of Labrador peninsula (Hudson Bay Territories) bounded N. by Hudson Strait, W. by Hudson Bay, S. by Quebec. It is now the Ungava district of the Dominion of Canada, with a scanty Indian population.

**East Moline,** a city of Rock Island co., Illinois, U.S.A., on the Mississippi R., with important manufactures. Pop. 10,107.

**Easton :** (1) Cap. of Northampton co., Pennsylvania, U.S.A., on Delaware R., above the rapids, at the confluence of Lehigh R., about 60 m. from Philadelphia. It is on various railways, and connected with New Jersey and South E. by bridges. The fine public buildings include Lafayette College (Presbyterian, 1826). There are important and various manufactures, including steel, cement, slate, silk, doors, pianos, fire-escapes, furniture, pumps, dental supplies and machinery. The bell rung to summon the people to hear the Declaration of Independence still hangs in the court house. Pop. 34,468. *See* Condit, *History of Easton,* 1889. (2) A tn. of Bristol co., Massachusetts, U.S.A., 9 m. from Taunton. There are iron foundries and manufs. of automobiles, shovels, and wire goods. Pop. 5298.

**East Orange,** a city of Essex co., New Jersey, U.S.A., adjoining Newark, 12 m. from New York, of which it forms a suburb. It has wide, well shaded streets and many attractive houses. There are electrical works and manufs. of pharmaceutical supplies. Pop. 68,020. *See* Whittemore, *The Founders and Builders of the Oranges,* 1896.

**East Palestine,** a city of Columbiana co., Ohio, U.S.A., manufactures automobile tyres, china wares, etc. Pop. 5215.

**East Pittsburg,** a bor. of Allegheny co., Pennsylvania, U.S.A., 12 m. S.E. of Pittsburg. Manufs. electrical apparatus. Pop. 6214.

**East Point, Georgia,** a suburb of Atlanta. Pop. 9512.

**Eastport,** a city and port of entry of Washington co., Maine, U.S.A., on Moose Island in Passamaquoddy Bay. It is on the U.S. eastern frontier; Fort Sullivan defends the harbour. Fishing and lumber trade are the chief industries, and it has sardine canning establishments. Pop. 3466.

**East Providence,** a tn. and post vil. of Providence co., Rhode Island, U.S.A., separated from Providence by the Seekonk (Blackstone) R., on Narragansett Bay. It is a summer resort. Oysters are shipped and there are chemical, paper, and electric works, and a bleachery. Pop. 29,995.

**East Prussia,** the detached eastern-most prov. of the Free State of Prussia, area 15,043 sq. m. Pop. (1925) 2,270,283, cap. Königsberg. Oats, rye, potatoes and flax are grown and horses and cattle bred, there is much fishing and amber is found in some localities. A large part of the prov. is forest, moor and bog, and wolves and lynxes still survive.

**East River,** a strait connecting New York Harbour with Long Island Sound, E. of New York City, U.S.A. It is 15 m. long, ½ to 3½ m. wide. With its N. arm (Harlem R.) and Spuyten Duyvil Creek it is connected with Hudson R. It separates the boroughs of Manhattan and the Bronx (W. and N.) from those of Brooklyn and Queens (E. and S.). Among its islands are Blackwell's, Randall's, Ward's, and Riker's. The channel at Hell Gate (between Ward's and Long Island) has been made navigable by blasting the rock. Brooklyn, Williamsburg, and two other suspension bridges span the East River.

**East Saginaw,** *see* SAGINAW.

**East St. Louis,** a city of St. Clair co., Illinois, U.S.A., on Mississippi R., opposite St. Louis, connected with it by steel bridges. It is an important railway terminus, has large stock-yards, mule and horse markets, mills, railway car construction, and the manuf. of iron and steel products, food preparations, baking powder, glass, paints and refined petroleum. Pop. 74,347.

**Eastwood,** a par. and urban dist. of Nottinghamshire, England, about 8½ m. from Nottingham, with coal mines. Pop. 5074.

**Eaton, Arthur Wentworth Hamilton,** Canadian writer; *b.* Dec. 10, 1849, in Kentville, Nova Scotia; eldest child of Wm. E., schoolmaster and school-inspector. He graduated from Harvard in 1880, entered the episcopal ministry, and was rector of St. Andrew's Church, Chestnut Hill, Mass., 1885–87. He is the author of : *The Heart of the Creeds;* *Historical Religion in the Light of Modern Thought,* 1888 ; *Acadian Legends and Lyrics,* 1889 ; *Tales of a Garrison Town* (with C. L. Betts), 1892 ; *College Requirements in English,* 1900 ; *Poems of the Christian Year,* 1905 ; *The Lotus of the Nile and other Poems,* 1907 ; *The History of King's County, Nova Scotia, Heart of the Acadian Land,* 1910 ; *The Famous Mather Byles,* 1914 ; *The Eaton Family of Nova Scotia,* 1929.

**Eaton, Dorman Bridgman** (1823–1899), American lawyer, *b.* June 27, 1823, at Hardwick, Vt. Grad., university of Vt., 1848 ; Harvard law school, 1850. Admitted same year to New York Bar. In Europe 1866 and 1870–73. Appointed to first Civil Service Commission, 1873 ; twice afterwards appointed to similar position. Once seriously assaulted for his opposition to Boss Tweed. Wrote : *Should Judges be Elected ?* 1873 ; *Civil Service in Great Britain,* 1880 ; *The Spoils System and Civil Service Reform,* 1882 ; *Problems of Police Legislation,* 1895 ; *The Government of Municipalities,* 1899. Died in New York, Dec. 23, 1899.

**Eaton, Long,** a tn. and par. of Derbyshire, England, 7 m. from Nottingham. Net lace is manufactured, and railway carriages are built here. Pop. 19,503.

**Eaton, Margaret O'Neill** (1796–

1879), ' Peggy O'Neill ' ; daughter
of Wm. O'Neill, who kept a tavern
in Washington, D.C. About 1823
she married John B. Timberlake,
purser in navy, who committed
suicide in 1828 in the Mediterranean.
In Jan. 1829 she married John
Henry Eaton—appointed Secretary
of War that year. It was reported
that she had had relations with Eaton
while Timberlake lived. Wives of
Cabinet Ministers refused to recognise
her. President Jackson on this
account reconstructed his Cabinet ;
favouring Van Buren, who was
friendly towards Mrs. Eaton. She
was popular in Madrid society when
her husband was ambassador in
Spain 1836–40. Her husband dying
in 1856, she next year married
Antonio Buchignam, an Italian,
aged about twenty. He squandered
her money, and was separated from
her. She d. in Washington, Nov. 8,
1879.

**Eaton, Theophilus** (c. 1590–1658),
an English colonial governor, son
of an English clergyman. Educated
in Coventry, where he formed an
enduring friendship with John Davenport, the Puritan divine, through
whom, later, he was influenced to
settle in New England. Prior to
migrating he had a successful mercantile career under the East Land
Company who made him their
' Deputy governor ' or representative
in Northern Europe. Following the
religious persecutions in England, he
accompanied Davenport to Holland
and thence went to America and
interested himself in settlement. He
became governor of New Haven, and
was active in procuring the charter
for Massachusetts in 1629. His
administration was, however, embittered by the disputes between
English and Dutch colonists.

**Eaton, William** (1764–1811), an
American soldier, b. at Woodstock,
Connecticut, graduated at Dartmouth College, 1790. Appointed consul at Tunis, 1797. Organised American expedition to re-establish Ahmet
Karamanli at Tripoli.

**Eau Claire**, a city of N.W. Wisconsin, co. seat of Eau Claire co., with
many manufactures, a state teachers'
college, tuberculosis hospital, and
hospital for the insane and a municipal auditorium seating 2000 ; 300
acs. of parks, boating and fishing.
Pop. 26,287.

**Eau Créole**, a fine French liqueur
made in Martinique by distilling the
flowers of the W. Indian wild apricot
or mammee apple (*Mammea Americana*) with pure spirit of wine.

**Eau de Cologne**, a celebrated perfume, probably invented by Johann
Maria Farina (1685–1766), who came

from N. Italy and settled in Cologne
(1709). Some forty firms at Cologne
bearing the name of Farina claim to
possess the original recipe for its
manufacture. The main ingredients
are pure distilled alcohol and various
essential aromatic oils (neroli, orange,
rosemary, citron, bergamot), so
blended as to yield a refreshing odour.
It relieves headaches, and is very
occasionally taken as a stimulant.

**Eau de Javelle**, one of the earliest
bleaching solutions obtained, so
called because first made at Javelle,
near Paris. It is a poisonous solution of hypochlorite of potash, used
as an antiseptic and to remove stains
from muslin, linen, and white marble.
It is usually adulterated with bi-
carbonate of potash.

**Eaux-Bonnes**, a health resort of
Basses-Pyrénées, France, about 3 m.
from Laruns. There are seven warm
medicinal springs used for drinking,
especially in cases of diseases of the
respiratory organs and rheumatism.
It was a favourite resort of the
Empress Eugénie. Pop. 460.

**Eaux-Chaudes, or Aigues-Chaudes,**
a com. and watering-place of Basses-
Pyrénées, France, 3 m. from Eaux-
Bonnes. It is in the gorge of the Gave
d'Ossau, at the foot of the Pic du
Midi d'Ossau (about 9500 ft.). Its
warm sulphur springs are much
used for bathing. Pop. 750.

**Eavesdrip, or Eavesdropping**, literally the dripping of water from the
eaves of a building. The term is
chiefly used in connection with the
Anglo-Saxon custom preventing any
one from erecting a house at the extremity of his estate, lest the eavesdrip should injure his neighbour's
land. This custom corresponded to
the ' stillicidium ' or urban servitude
of the Romans. The right to permit
rain-water to fall from one's roof upon
a neighbour's ground is in the nature
of an easement. In a derivative sense,
eavesdropping means loitering about
to overhear private matter with
intent to repeat it.

**Ebbsfleet**, a hamlet on the Isle of
Thanet, Kent, England, about ½ m.
from Pegwell Bay. The Saxons are
supposed to have landed here under
Hengist in 449. It was also the land-
ing-place of St. Augustine (597).

**Ebbw Vale**, an urban district in
co. Monmouth, England, containing
the works and collieries of the E. V.
Steel, Iron and Coal Co., with a
pop. of (1921) 30,624.

**Ebel, Johann Gottfried** (1764–1830),
a writer, b. in Prussia, but in 1801
became a naturalised Swiss. His
life was devoted to popularising the
history, geology, and topographical
details of Switzerland. Until the
publication of Murray his *Anleitung*

*auf die nützliche und genussvollste Art in der Schweitz zu reisen*, 1793, was by far the best guide-book to Switzerland.

**Ebeling, Christopher Daniel** (1741–1817), a German man of letters, was professor of history and Greek at the gymnasium of Hamburg and chief librarian in that city for over twenty years, he lavished his best years on a voluminous *Geography and History of the United States of North America*, a work which earned for him the public thanks of Congress.

**Ebenaceæ**, a natural order of tropical Dicotyledons, consisting of about 300 trees and shrubs. The inflorescence is solitary or cymose, and the flowers are usually dioecious.

**Ebenezer** (Heb., ' stone of help '), the name of the monument which Samuel raised to God after the victory of the Israelites over the Philistines (*see* 1 Sam. vii. 12). The site is not exactly known, but is thought to be near modern Deir Aban.

**Eberhard I. im Bart** (1445–96), Duke of Würtemberg, succeeded his elder brother, Louis II. Duke of Würtemberg-Urach, in 1457. He lived a careless, dissolute life till 1468, when he went on a pilgrimage to Rome, and on his return proved himself to be a capable ruler. In 1482, by the treaty of Münsingen, he brought about the reunion of Stuttgart and Urach, and granted to Würtemberg its first constitution in 1492. He was raised to the rank of duke by Maximilian I. in 1495. He founded the University of Tübingen (1476), and was a patron to scholars. *See* Life by Rösslin, 1793, and Bossert, 1884.

**Eberhard, Christian August Gottlob** (1769–1845), a German writer, who is now only remembered by his *Hannchen und die Küchlein*, 1822, a long narrative poem, and *Der Erste Mensch und die Erde*, 1828, an epic poem on the creation written in hexameters.

**Eberhard, Johann Augustus** (1739–1809), a German philosophical and theological writer, *b.* at Halberstadt. His first work, *Neue Apologie des Socrates*, 1772, advocated a broader theological outlook towards those who have not accepted the tenets of Christianity. His principal works are : *Amyntor eine Geschichte in Briefen*, 1782 ; *Versuch einer allgemeinen Deutschen Synonymik*, 1795–1802 ; and *Handbuch der Æsthetik*, 1803–5. *See* study by F. Nicolai, 1810.

**Ebers, Georg Moritz** (1837–98), a German Egyptologist and novelist, *b.* in Berlin. He became lecturer of Egyptian at Jena (1865), and professor at Leipzig (1870). The famous Papyrus Ebers, which he discovered

during his travels, was published in 1874. He also wrote *Ægypten und die Bücher Moses*, 1868 ; and *Ægypten in Wort und Bild*, a descriptive work. In 1876 he resigned his professorship through ill-health, and began a series of instructive historical novels with the object of popularising Egyptian lore. The chief of these are : *Uarda*, 1877 ; *Der Kaiser*, 1881 ; *Serapis*, 1885 ; *Kleopatra*, 1894. Many of his tales have been translated into English. His *Gesammelte Werke* were published in twenty-five volumes (1893–95). Consult his *Die Geschichte Meines Lebens*, 1893, and a study by Gosche, 1887.

FRIEDRICH EBERT

**Ebersbach**, a tn. in Saxony, 14 m. S.S.E. of Bautzen, with one of the finest organs in Saxony. Pop. 9460.

**Eberswalde**, a tn. of Prussia, 28 m. N.E. of Berlin, has a fourteenth-century church, remains of town walls, school of forestry, iron foundries, rope works, etc. In 1913 one of the largest treasures of prehistoric gold objects in Germany was discovered here (1050–850 B.C.) and presented to the State Museum for pre-history at Berlin. Pop. 29,570.

**Ebert, Friedrich** (1871–1925), first President of the German republic ; *b.* Feb. 4, 1871, at Heidelberg ; son of a poor Catholic tailor. He was apprenticed to a saddler in his native city at the age of fourteen. He became a travelling journeyman saddler, and helped to found a saddlers' union. Married and settled in Bremen. In 1894 he became editor of the Bremen *Bürgerzeitung*, a socialist paper which he gave up to become secretary of the Bremen branch of the party. For a while he kept an inn. He unsuccessfully contested the Hanover dist., 1905. In 1912 he was elected for Eberfeld-Barmen—a seat his party had lost in 1907, and in the following year was elected President of the party in succession to Bebel. He supported the gov's. demand for war-credits in 1914, in view of the Russian danger. He lost two sons in the war. He was at the Socialist Peace Conference at Stockholm, 1917. When the overthrow of Kaiserism was seen to be inevitable in 1918, and when Prince Max of Baden called in the Socialists to share the gov., E. was in favour of a limited monarchy. When Scheidemann had proclaimed the republic, Prince Max commissioned E., as Chancellor, to form a gov. He was violently attacked by minority Socialists, for insisting on constitutional procedure ; and in Jan. 1919 he made a display of force against them in Berlin. On Feb. 10 the National Assembly at Weimar made him President. He reaffirmed his socialism—which, in his case, was coupled with agnosticism. After the Kapp ' putsch ' had been defeated, E. put forward, in June 1920, a request that the Presidency should be regulated according to the Constitution, which required popular election. He renewed this request in 1921 ; but the Reichstag passed a resolution permitting him to retain office till 1925. He was much overworked, and *d.* in West Charlottenburg sanatorium, Feb. 28, 1925. He was of very striking appearance—not much above middle height, stout, bull-necked, with prominent eyes and angular eyebrows ; an impetuous speaker, yet always sticking to common-sense.

**Ebert, John Arnold** (1723–95), a German poet. As a translator, whether the work were Young's *Night Thoughts* or Greek epigrams, he was eminently successful, but in his own poetry his deficiency in original force is at once apparent. His compositions include drinking songs, lyrics, epistles, and some much-admired epigrams. A representative of the school of Saxe, he faintly recalls Horace and Anacreon in his pictures of rural scenes and praise of simple pleasures.

**Ebert, Karl Egon** (1801–82), a Bohemian poet, *b.* at Prague. He held for many years the librarianship of Donaueschingen, and wrote many dramatic and lyrical pieces, which were collected in seven volumes in 1877.

**Ebingen,** a tn. of Würtemberg, Germany, on the Schmiecha, a trib. of the Danube, 21 m. S. of Tübingen, with textile manufs. Pop. 12,130.

**Ebionites** (Hebrew *ebion*, poor man), a name probably applied at first to all Christians, later used particularly of an ultra-Jewish party who, though Christians, remained outside the Catholic Church. Their gospel was a form of that known as the Gospel according to the Hebrews ; they strictly adhered to all the customs and ordinances of Mosaic law, thus regarding Paul as an apostate whose epistles they rejected ; and some of them did not believe in the miraculous birth of Jesus Christ. The chief authorities as to their early history are Irenæus, Hippolytus, Origen, and Justin. Those who lived E. of the Jordan held Essene doctrines, which gave rise to the ' Clementine ' literature.

**Eblis,** or **Iblis,** of Moslem demonology, a fallen angel (Azazil), who attained the characteristics of the devil, and became chief of the Jinn.

**Ebner-Eschenbach, Marie Freifrau von** (1830–1916), an Austrian novelist, *b.* at Zdislavič in Moravia ; the daughter of Count Dubsky. Her first literary work was a drama *Maria Stuart in Schottland*. She is best known for her witty and lifelike presentations of country and town life in Austria. Her principal works of fiction are : *Die Prinzessin von Banalien*, 1872 ; *Zwei Comtessen*, 1885 ; *Aus Spätherbsttagen*, 1901, *Agave*, 1903 ; and *Meine Kinderjahre*, 1906. In 1900 the university of Vienna conferred upon her an honorary degree of doctor of philosophy. *See* Life by Bettelheim, 1900, and Necker, 1900.

**Ebonite,** *see* RUBBER.

**Ebony** (Gk. ἔβενος, Lat. *ebenum*), an extremely hard wood of various species of the genus *Diospyros* (order Ebenaceæ), the genus of the Date Plum and allied genera. The best quality is deep black in colour, consists of heart wood only, and is very durable. It is yielded by *D. Ebenum*, a tree that flourishes in S. India and Ceylon. Various kinds of E. are procured from *D. tomentosa* in Bengal, *Brya ebenus* in the W. Indies, *D. dendo* in Angola, and *Dalbergia melanoxylon* in Senegal.

**Eboracum,** *see* YORK.

**Ebro** (Lat. *Hiberus*), a river of Spain which rises at Fuentibre in the prov. of Santander and flows into the Mediterranean Sea. Its chief tributaries are the Ega, Aragon, Gallego, and Segre on the left, and the Jalon, Martin, Guadaloupe, and Matarraña on the right. The principal cities on its banks are Logroño, Calahorra, Tudela, Saragossa, Mora, and Tortosa. It is navigable for small vessels from Logroño, but navigation is difficult, for the river is blocked with sand and its course obstructed by many rapids. Length, 470 m.; area of basin, 32,000 sq. m.

**Ebullition** (boiling of fluids), *see* FLUID.

**Ecbatana,** or **Agbatana** (Hebrew *Achmetha*), the cap. of ancient Media, founded according to Herodotus by Deioces (about 700 B.C.). It was captured by Cyrus (549 B.C.), and became the seat of government and the favourite summer residence of Persian and Parthian kings. It was surrounded by seven walls, within which lay the royal castle, built of cedar and cypress wood, covered with gold and silver. The city was plundered by Alexander the Great and Seleucus I. The modern Hamadan is built on its site.

**Ecce Homo** (Lat., ' Behold the Man '), the title given to pictures representing Christ crowned with thorns. One, by Correggio, hangs in the National Gallery, London, and one of the best known of such pictures is a Titian of 1543, which is to be seen in the Imperial Gallery at Vienna.

**Eccentric,** a contrivance for taking an alternating rectilinear motion from a revolving shaft, and consists of a disc connected eccentrically with regard to the shaft, which in rotating carries the disc with it in a circular movement, thereby actuating a connecting rod and giving it a regular to and fro motion. The distance between the centre of the shaft and that of the disc is called the ' throw,' and is one half of the resultant rectilinear motion.

**Eccentric Club,** a social club (founded in 1890), 11 Ryder St., London, S.W. 1. Drama and the arts are discussed especially. The entrance fee is 10 guineas, annual subscription 5 and 3 guineas.

**Eccentricity,** *see* CONIC SECTIONS.

**Ecchymosis,** or **Bruise,** a discoloration of the surface of the skin, caused by an effusion of blood below. It occurs as a result from a blow or violence of some kind, but sometimes it is met with in diseases of the blood and blood-vessels. A fresh E. has the appearance of a group of pin-pricks.

**Ecclefechan,** a vil. of Dumfriesshire, Scotland, 5 m. N. of Annan, a mile from a station on the L.M.S. Railway. Thomas Carlyle, who was born and buried here, introduces it into *Sartor Resartus* under the name ' Entepfuhl.' Pop. 680.

**Eccles,** a municipal bor. of Lancashire, England, and a suburb of Manchester. It was incorporated in 1892. There are engineering works, cotton mills, and manufs. of ginghams and fustian goods. E. cakes take their name from the neighbourhood, where they are largely made. Pop. 44,327.

**Ecclesfield,** a civil and eccles. parish partly included in the borough of Sheffield. There are large collieries and iron and steel works, and manufs. of cutlery and nails. Pop. of civil par. 22,944, of ecclesiastical, 4980.

**Ecclesia** (Gk. ἐκκλησία, from ἐκ, out, and καλεῖν, to call), the name given to the general assembly of all freemen of the state in Athens. After the reforms of Cleisthenes, it was known as the E. when it met for political purposes, and ' Hellaea ' when it had judicial business in hand. It is not thought that the E. had any definite form before the time of Solon, though some such institution was doubtless in existence. The reforms of Solon are not known exactly, but there is no doubt as to their general effect, which was to give the Thetes, the lowest class, a voice in the E., and the power of criticising and exercising some check over the actions of the Eupatrids, the governing class. All citizens of Athens over eighteen years of age were eligible to appear in the E., save those who had for any reason suffered loss of civil rights. The meetings were of three kinds, ordinary, extraordinary, and those convened by special messengers; the last were held only when the attendance of the country members was desired. The proceedings were opened by various religious formalities, and if the omens were unpropitious, or the weather was bad, no meeting was held. The voting was as a rule by show of hands, or, on special occasions by ballot. The practice of payment for attendance was instituted some time in the fourth century B.C. The E. was the sovereign power in Athens throughout the time of her greatness, though being an untrained body it could not initiate laws; this was done by a committee of the Boule. In 308 B.C. Demetrius of Phalerum curtailed the power of the E. by instituting Guardians, who could prevent it from voting on an illegal motion. As a governing body the E. perished when Athens became a *civitas libera* of Rome.

**Ecclesiastes** (' the Preacher '). This is one of the O.T. books (Heb. *qôbeloth*, Gk. ἐκκλησιάστης), the fourth of the five Megilloth in the ordinary Hebrew Bible. The Greek title, from which the English is derived, means ' a member of assembly '; the Hebrew has occasioned some discussion, as it only appears in this book, and seems to mean the ' herald ' who summons an assembly. On the whole, Luther's translation, followed by the English version, is fairly satisfactory, the purpose of the book is hortatory, and the form of the word implies an assembly; the translation *der prediger* (' the Preacher ') combines the two ideas.

*Scope and contents.*—The literary form is that adopted by Browning in *The Ring and the Book*, a monologue which conceals a real dialogue. In matter it is the narrative of a series of speculations and spiritual experiments of the ' highest good.' It is proved that if the individual makes it his aim to attain merely and solely his own personal happiness, whatever the sphere be in which he makes the attempt, the result is ' Vanity of vanities, all is vanity.' The epilogue is the necessary conclusion of the whole matter. ' Fear God and keep his commandments, for this is the whole duty of man '; not pleasure, but duty, is man to make his purpose of life.

*Language.*—The Hebrew of E. is unlike that of any other portion of the O.T. No other book has so large a proportion of words, phrases, and senses of words peculiar to itself. In its vocabulary and many of its constructions, it is related to the ' Mishna.' We need only remark on the preference for the short relative, the rare use of the ' vav,' ' conversive,' and avoidance of the sign of the accusative. At the same time it must be observed that most of the linguistic peculiarities have anologues in classic Hebrew.

*Date and Authorship.*—No one without violence to facts can maintain the Solomonic authorship. The author assumes the name of Solomon as Browning speaks as ' Abt Vogler ' or ' Fra Lippo-Lippi.'

*Canonicity.*—It formed part of the Alexandrian Canon when the younger Siracides went to Egypt. In the time of Josephus it was in the Canon of Judea. The Talmudic stories about the Council at Jabne are of historic value.

*Versions.*—The LXX. is slavishly close to the Hebrew. The Peshitta is much freer. The Targum is very diffuse, but supplies the Jewish interpretation which is very interesting. The Vulgate is fairly accurate.

*Commentaries.*—The full list up to 1860 is given in Ginsburg's *Coheleth*. Since then there have been commentaries by Wright, Bulloch, Zockler.

**Ecclesiastical Commissioners,** a body appointed in 1835 as a perpetual corporation to examine into the temporal affairs of the Church of England. They made five reports, recommending alterations in the number of bishoprics, and the appropriation of part of the revenues of charters and collegiate bodies to parochial purposes. Some of their recommendations have been adopted since that time. E. C. were also appointed for Ireland to receive and apply the incomes of the suppressed bishoprics in that kingdom under an Act passed in 1833. The E. C. are composed of certain bishops and other church dignitaries, together with certain laymen. They exist now to administer church property, to create new ecclesiastical parishes, and to sanction repairs and improvements in churches or church buildings. When an incumbent dies or resigns they are the body to settle any questions of dilapidations that may arise. One of the chief aspects of their general power of administering church property lies in the direction of enhancing the value of the smaller livings so as to provide the worst paid clergy with more substantial incomes. In this work they have been assisted by the efforts of other societies, lay and clerical, and by the organisation of funds outside, like the ' Bishop of London's Fund.' A scheme for the administration of a pension fund for facilitating the retirement of aged or infirm clergy holding poor benefices was framed in 1907 and enlarged in 1915.

**Ecclesiastical Courts** are courts in which the canon law is administered and causes ecclesiastical determined. Formerly these courts had a wide criminal and civil jurisdiction over laymen as well as clergymen, embracing among civil matters divorce, probate, and suits for tithes, and among criminal, blasphemy (*q.v.*), apostasy from Christianity, and brawling within the precincts of a church. Gradually the common law courts have usurped almost the whole of this jurisdiction so far as laymen are concerned, while as to clergymen, the jurisdiction of a more purely civil and temporal character exists only to provide spiritual sanctions in the shape of suspension or deprivation. Their jurisdiction in practice, if not in theory, is for the most part over purely spiritual causes, *i.e.* in matters of church discipline and the correction of offences of a spiritual kind. The principal E. C. are : (1) The Bishops' Consistory Court, presided over by the bishop's chancellor (*q.v.*), which can try clergy for uncleanliness and wickedness of life, but not for doctrinal offences. Some authorities believe it can still try laymen guilty of heresy or incest. Since the passing of the Incest Act, 1908, made the offence of incest a crime cognisable by the ordinary courts, it may be assumed that jurisdiction of the consistory courts over laymen is obsolete, although theoretically it can punish laymen by refusing them the Sacrament and prohibiting them from entering a church for such offences as the above, and for brawling. In exercising quasi-criminal jurisdiction the chancellor is assisted by five assessors who act as judges of fact. (*See also* CLERGY DISCIPLINE ACT, 1892.) The bishop can veto the prosecution of a clergyman for uncleanliness and wickedness of life; the civil jurisdiction of the court relates principally to the grant of faculties for alterations in churches, questions of repairs to church fabric, and with disputed rights to pews. (2) The Court of Arches, presided over by the Dean of Arches. This court hears ecclesiastical appeals from the consistory courts of the bishops of the province of Canterbury, and has jurisdiction over the thirteen peculiar parishes in the diocese of London. It also has the transferred jurisdiction of the old provincial court of the Archbishop of Canterbury. The court tries also doctrinal offences and practices under the Public Worship Regulation Act, 1874. (3) The Provincial Court of the Province of York, which hears appeals from the consistory courts in the diocese. (4) The Court of the Archbishop, presided over by the archbishop or his vicar-general, which has jurisdiction to try bishops for ecclesiastical offences. The Court of the Bishop sitting in person, the Provincial Court of the Archbishop of Canterbury, and the Court of the Archdeacon are obsolete. The judicial committee of the Privy Council is the supreme court of appeal in all matters ecclesiastical.

**Ecclesiastical Law,** the law administered by the ecclesiastical courts (*q.v.*), the principles of which are derived mainly from the canon law and civil law (*q.v.*). In England E. L. never gained that ascendancy over the municipal law of the state which characterised countries where the traditions of the Holy Roman empire were so deep-rooted as to subordinate the state to the papal see. The revival of the study of Roman law, or the new learning as it is called, in the eleventh century, at the time Irnerius lectured at Bologna, had no permanent effect on England; it ' found a small, homogeneous, well-conquered, much governed kingdom, a strong legislative kingship. It taught us much, and then there was healthy resistance to foreign dogma ' (Professor Maitland). The assimilation in part of the principles of canon and civil law may be said to have been due to the fear of the church that the revival of learning of the eleventh

century would crush the monarchy of theology over the intellectual world : and the church to save itself vivified its teaching in law much in the same manner as the fathers imported some of the philosophy of Aristotle into the Bible. E. L. in England was always useful in overcoming the inelasticity of the common law, the principles of which for centuries allowed of no testamentary disposition of lands, and at a time when personal property was of little importance. E. L. governed also wills of personalty, through the jurisdiction of the lord-ordinary. E. L. also prevailed in all kinds of matrimonial causes. But although many of the principles of E. L. are still retained in probate, divorce, and matrimonial causes, the jurisdiction of the ecclesiastical courts in these matters has passed to the High Court. *See also* ECCLESIASTICAL COURTS.

**Ecclesiastical Titles Act,** an Act passed in 1851 to prohibit the assumption by any unauthorised person of a title from any place in the United Kingdom, whether or not such place were the seat of an archbishopric, bishopric, or deanery, and declaring null and void all acts done by them, or gifts made to them under such titles. The Act was the legislative expression of the hatred of papistry, which was so rife during that period. The immediate cause of the Act was the Oxford Movement led by the celebrated Mr. (afterwards Cardinal) Newman, whose followers, the so-called Tractarians, endeavoured to prove that the doctrines of the Church of England were essentially similar to those prevalent in the primitive Catholic Church. The people, as a whole, took this revival of religious energy to be no more than a reconciliation with Rome, and the prevalent excitement consequent on the secessions from the Established Church to the Church of Rome led to Lord John Russell securing the passing of the E. T. A., which, however, through the weakness of its provisions, remained nugatory. It was repealed in 1867. In this connection we may note that the Statute Book still contains an Act passed in 1829 which prohibits the assumption by any persons other than the person authorised by law, of the name, style, or title of an archbishop, bishop, or dean of the Church of England.

**Ecclesiasticus** (' the wisdom of Jesus, the Son of Sirac '), the church book, an apocryphal (deuterocanonical) work to which this name was given by the Roman Church. The Greek name is ' the wisdom of Jesus, Son of Sirach,' or, more briefly, ' wisdom of Sirach.' The original name is said to have been ' Proverbs ' in Hebrew, though it was known to the Rabbis under the name ' Book of Ben Sira.' The original was in late Hebrew, and only a few verses are preserved by the Jewish oral tradition in a very mutilated condition, but if its prologue may be trusted, the Greek translation was made by a descendant of the author and, it is thought, from an autograph copy. This is the only case in Biblical literature in which the family tradition of a book has been preserved.

*Authorship.*—The statement of the translator fixes the date of the author approximately as being in the third century B.C. Josephus makes mention of it, but he can never be taken with safety as a guide to historical facts, and a date about 200 B.C. is generally accepted as the date of this work.

*Contents.*—The Book of Ben Sira is upon much the same lines as the Biblical Books of Psalms, Proverbs, and Ecclesiastes, and as such contains hymns, prayers, rules of conduct, and speculations on a variety of subjects. It would seem that the book was at first intended for the author's family, as the precepts are often addressed ' my son, my children.'

*Relation to canonical books.*—The author appears to have a thorough knowledge of the O.T. books, and quotes very freely from them, and although he omits the names of Daniel, Ezra, and Esther from his list of Hebrew heroes, some of his phrases seem to be taken from the Book of Daniel. He appears to have been unacquainted with the Chronicles.

*Language and style.*—Late Hebrew with the rabbinical terminology well developed.

*History of the text.*—Josephus' silence about the work is attributed to the supposed antipathy of the author to the Maccabæan and Herodian dynasties. The original text existed as late as the fourth century A.D., because Jerome claims to have seen it. It is supposed to have been destroyed by the Jews owing to the similarity of the sayings of Jesus of Sirach and Jesus of Nazareth. Many attempts have been made to restore the original, but up till now none have been successful.

**Ecclesiology** (from Gk. ἐκκλησιά, a church, and λόγος, a discourse), the science and study of church archæology, architecture, and decoration. It also comprises church history, as revealed by these.

**Eccremocarpus,** a genus of Bignoniaceæ, contains three species of handsome Peruvian plants. *E. scaber*

is climbing and half-shrubby in habit; it grows in thickets and hedges of its native country, and will live in the open air in the milder parts of England.

**Echegaray, José** (1832–1916), a Sp. politician and dramatist. In 1858 he became a professor of mathematics and published several valuable scientific works. It was not till he was forty years of age that he turned his attention to the writing of dramas and comedies. His works, which were issued under the *nom de plume* of Jorge Hayaseca, satirise the vices of society, and were very popular. Among his works may be mentioned : *La Esposa del vengador*, 1874 ; *En el pilar yen la cruz*, 1878 ; *Muerte en los labros*, 1880, etc.

**Echelon** (Fr. ladder), a military term used of a regiment, the formation of whose troops resembles a ladder ; that is, the divisions march in parallel lines, not exactly behind each other, but each to the right or left, of the preceding one.

**Echidna, or Spiny Ant-eater,** the name given to two species of mammals in the order Monotremata ; these are *Echidna aculeata*, or common E., and *Proëchidna bruinii*, or three-toed E. The former, which has five toes on each foot, all clawed, inhabits Australia, Tasmania, and New Guinea, while the latter is found only in N.W. New Guinea. Both are fossorail and mainly nocturnal animals, frequenting rocky districts and subsisting chiefly on ants. The upper surface of the head and body is covered with a mixture of stiff hairs and short thick spines. It has a long, slender, beak-like snout, with the elongated, cylindrical tongue common to all ant-eaters.

**Echigo,** a prov. of Japan, which is principally notable from the fact that it yields the greatest part of the petroleum obtained in Japan. The wells date back to A.D. 615.

**Echinidæ, or Echinoidæ** (Gk. ἐχῖνος, a hedgehog), the sea-urchins, form a class of Echinodermata. They live off rocky coasts and move by means of their spines and their tube-feet. The spines also serve as organs of protection, and some sea-urchins have a poison-gland attached. Some species cover themselves with bits of rock and seaweed, and so move about unobserved ; others bore their way into holes and remain there. The common *Strongylocentrotus* is a boring urchin, and when the waves wash into the hole it sets its spines against the rock and retains a rigid position. *Echinarachnius*, the shield urchin, *Brissopsis*, the heart urchin, and *Diadema*, which is said to be covered with compound eyes, are other well-known genera. Palæo-Echinoidea, the fossil forms, appear in the Lower Silurian rocks.

**Echinocactus,** a genus of Cactaceæ, contains about two hundred species, most of which are natives of Mexico and the W. Indies, but a few occur in Brazil. Many of the flowers are large and conspicuous for their beauty.

**Echinococcus,** the name given to certain Cestoda in the cystic or bladder-worm stage. *E. polymorphus,* or *E. veterinorum,* is found in sheep, in domestic animals, and occasionally in man; in its mature or tapeworm stage it infests dogs. See TAPE-WORM and BLAD-DERWORM.

ECHINOCOCCUS
*E. veterinorum*

**Echinococcus Disease,** see HYDATID DISEASE.

**Echinodermata** (Gk. ἐχῖνος, hedge-hog, and δέρμα, skin), the name given to the great branch of invertebrate animals which includes Holothuroi-dea, the sea-cucumbers; Echinoidea, the sea-urchins; and Asteroidea; the star-fishes, etc. They are exclusively marine, and feed chiefly on small animals; their great characteristic is the water-vascular system, which is connected with the tube feet, and provides the means of progression and respiration. Many of the E. have the power of casting off and regenerating different parts of their bodies. The Echinoidea are predominantly globular, but a few are discoid. The body is enclosed in a shell of polygonal plates, accurately arranged in double rows, and covered with knobs or spines, and small stalked outgrowths, pedicellariæ, some provided with two, others with three, blades, between which they seize any foreign particles or small animals and remove them, so keeping the shell clean. There is a complicated masticating apparatus, formed by the five teeth and fifteen other pieces, and known as Aristotle's lantern. The animals move generally with the mouth directed towards the ground. There are two orders: 1. Palæechinoidea, comprised solely of extinct and fossil forms, the oldest members being found in the Upper Cambrian. 2. Euechinoidea, including all living and some extinct species. The Asteroidea is typified by *Asterias rubens,* the common five-rayed star-fish, whose native haunt is the floor of the ocean at great depth, but which is often seen in shore pools at low tide. Allied to this class are the Ophiuroidea, or brittle-stars, whose

arms, however, branch out more abruptly from the central part. Like the *Echinoidea,* the *Asteroidea* have outgrowths of spines and pedicellariæ. At the end of each arm there is a bright red spot, the 'eye,' which is sensitive to light. Starfishes feed on bivalves, flattening the tube feet on the two halves of the shell and then widening the arms of the star so that a steady pull on the muscle is exerted. The water-vascular system communicates with the exterior by a short canal, the stone canal, and an opening, the madreporite, which in *Echinoidea* and *Asteroidea* is represented by a porous plate. The Holothurians differ at first sight from other E., as they have a plump, cylindrical body and a soft, leathery skin, in which is embedded a series of calcareous plates. Holothurians are generally sedentary. They live on the sea floor, and can crawl by means of their tube feet. These are not developed in species which burrow

ECHINODERMATA
Left: *Holothurian.* Right: *Asteroidea.*

in the mud. The Crinoidea, feather-stars or sea-lilies, grow together in great masses, and are mostly fixed to the sea-bottom, or rock surface, by a jointed stalk. The feather-star swims by movements of its 'arms' and alights by means of small leg-like outgrowths on them. Most E. lay small eggs in the sea, and these develop into larvæ of various types. E. in the colder seas retain the eggs in the body-cavity, or swallow them and keep them in the stomach until they develop. In a few cases, after their release, the young are protected by the mother, and lie in depressions or among the spines on her body. The Blastoidea and Cystidea, extinct classes of E. are found in the Lower and Upper Silurian and some Cystides in the Cambrian rocks.

**Echinolampas** (Gk. ἐχῖνος, a hedge-hog, and λάμπη, a torch), the generic name of certain species of echino-derms in the family Cassidulidæ. They are heart-urchins, with the anus on the under-surface.

**Echinophora,** a genus of umbel-liferous plants, is to be found in the Mediterranean. *E. spinosa,* the sea-parsnip, is an inhabitant of sandy sea-shores, and has pinnate spinose leaves.

**Echinorhynchus,** the name given to a genus of parasitic worms belonging to the Nematoda, and grouped under a special class, Acanthocephala.

**Echinus,** *see* SEA-URCHINS.

**Echites,** the name of a genus of Apocynaceæ. The species are bushy plants with large and brilliantly coloured flowers, and came originally from India.

**Echium** (botany), *see* VIPER'S BUGLOSS.

**Echmiadsin,** meaning in Armenian, 'the only begotten Son came down.' A celebrated monastery in the Armenian Soviet Republic. Since 1441 the seat of the Armenian 'Catholicos' and the religious centre of the Armenian Church. The monastery con-

ECHITES

sists of three walled enclosures, each with a cathedral. The oldest is the principal cathedral, dating from the year 305; the most famous from an architectural point of view is that of St. Ripsimi, built in 618. Near by is an archæological and ethnographic museum. A motor road leads to Erivan. E. was long under Persian rule, but was ceded to Russia in 1828.

**Echo,** in Gk. mythology, was a nymph who repelled the advances of Pan; the god, in revenge, caused the shepherds to tear her to pieces till only her voice remained. Another version, related by Ovid, is that E. was a nymph whom Zeus employed to talk to Hera in order to prevent her from discovering his amours. Hera, discovering the ruse, changed E. into a person who could only repeat the last words of somebody else's speech. E. then fell in love with Narcissus, and pined away in despair till only her voice remained.

**Echo,** an imitative sound produced by the waves of sound when reflected from something denser than the aerial medium. Sound obeys the same laws as light, and is reflected at the same angle as it strikes the reflecting object. Since the velocity of sound is 1125 ft. per second, an observer situated at a distance of 562 ft. from a reflecting surface at right angles would hear the E. in one second, and would hear as many words as would last for that space of time. Various natural peculiarities of configuration have made the Es. in many different parts of the world famous.

**Echo de Paris,** a daily newspaper of Paris. It was founded in the year 1884 by Aurelian School. The paper was managed with skill, and numbered among its contributors many men of versatility, wit, and talent. At the time of the Dreyfus affair it was noteworthy as espousing the cause of the Army. Among the best known of its editors have been Jules Lemaître and Quesnay de Beaurepaire.

**Echternach,** a tn. of the Grand Duchy of Luxemburg. It stands on the R. Sure, about 20 m. N.E. of the city of Luxemburg. The inhabitants are chiefly engaged in the manuf. of damask, linen, porcelain. It is famous for the annual procession on Whit-Tuesday, in gratitude for the ending of the penitential dance mania which raged in this neighbourhood in the eight century. The many participants under the leadership of the priests and numerous musicians jump backwards two steps for every one they advance. There is a famous abbey here, founded by the Anglo-Saxon Willibrord, Bishop of Utrecht, and a thirteenth-century parish church. Pop. 4500.

**Echuca,** a tn. of Victoria, Australia, situated on the Campaspe and Murray rivers, 156 m. N. of Melbourne. A bridge 1905 ft. long connects E. with Moama on the New South Wales side of the Murray. It trades in wool, wine, red-gum, timber, etc. Pop. 3745.

**Ecija,** or **Ezija,** a tn. of Spain, in the prov. of Seville. It is situated on the l. b. of the R. Genil, or Jenil, a feeder of the Guadalquivir. The district is extremely fertile, and the corn crops are good. Fruit is also cultivated, and wine is one of the chief products. A small amount of cotton is also grown. The manufs. are woollens, flannel, silk, linen, leather, and shoes. The climate is very hot, and this has earned for the town the nickname of the 'frying pan of Andalusia.' Pop. 29,930.

**Eck, Johann Maier von** (1486–1543), a Ger. scholar and theologian, *b.* at

Eck. He excelled in controversy, and attacked Luther's thesis on indulgences, and defended the Catholic doctrines in the celebrated congress of Leipzig in 1519. Thenceforward he was one of the bitterest opponents of the Reformation; in 1525 his exposition of Catholic dogma appeared in answer to *Lieux theologiques* of Melancthon, and was very successful. He took a prominent part in the congresses at Baden and Augsburg, and in 1530 sent a refutation of the Protestant confession to Charles V. In 1537 he published a Ger. New Testament, and took part in the meetings at Worms in 1540 and Ratisbon in 1541.

Eck, Loch, a loch of Scotland, situated in Argyllshire. It is about 6 m. long and enclosed by mountains. Salmon and fresh-water herrings abound.

Eckart, *see* ECKHART, MEISTER.

Eckermann, Johann Peter (1792–1854), a Ger. writer, and a friend of Goethe, who is known principally through his *Conversations with Goethe*, 1837, translated into Eng. by Margaret Fuller, 1889.

Eckersberg, Carl Christoffer Wilhelm (1783–1853), a Danish historical, marine, and portrait painter, *b.* at Varnäs, Schleswig. He became a pupil of Abildgaard and afterwards of David, and later, Thorwaldsen. It has been stated by his native admirers and critics, that he first 'created a Danish colour.' His landscape scenes are clear and definite and the outlines natural, while his figures are conventional.

Eckhart, Johannes, very generally styled Meister (1260–1329), a Ger. mystic, and one of the first of speculative thinkers, *b.* probably at Strassburg or Saxony. Very little is known concerning his life. He entered the Dominican order, and studied and taught in Paris. After being made prior at Erfort, he was vicar of his order at Thuringia. He was made vicar-general of Bohemia in 1307, and a few years later he preached at Frankfurt, Cologne, and Strassburg. His reputation for learning was very high, and he assisted in a controversy between Pope Boniface VIII. and Philip of France. In 1327 his enemies caused him to be summoned at Cologne before the Inquisition on a charge of heresy, where he partly recanted. Two years later he was again accused, and extracts from his works condemned, but he died before the bill against him was published. His sermons and tractates written in Ger. and Latin are all that remain of his works. In his teaching he was an Aristotelian. He began with his doctrine of the Divine nature, following it by the relationship of God and man. His style was curt and abounded in symbolic expressions.

Eckhel, Joseph Hilary (1737–98), a famous numismatist, *b.* at Enzersfeld, Austria, who, in 1773 was made professor of antiquities and numismatics at the Vienna University. His chief work is *Doctrina Numorum Veterum*, 1792–98.

Eckington, a par. and tn. of Derbyshire, England. The tn. is situated 7 m. S.E. of Sheffield, There are saw-mills, and manufs. of agricultural implements. Pop. 12,624.

Eckmühl, or Eggmuhl a vil. of Bavaria, situated on the Laber, 15 m. S. of Ratisbon. It is noted as the scene of a battle fought there in 1809 between the Archduke of Austria and Napoleon I., in which the former was defeated. Pop. 420.

Eclampsia (from the Gk. word ἐκλάμπειν, 'to call aloud'), a term applied to a form of epileptiform convulsions occurring in pregnant women, with an associated condition extremely dangerous to the child, and not free from danger to the mother. It is due to changes in the kidney, which can be detected only by chemical examination of the urine. E. is a haunting dread before and during confinement, as suddenly a woman, in apparently perfect health, may be seized with convulsive attacks which may end fatally. E. is prevented by checking the longings of pregnancy, leading a quiet healthy life, and giving careful attention to hygiene.

Eclecticism (Gk. ἐκλέγω, I select), in philosophy is the principle of selecting and adopting views from various systems of philosophy, and uniting them into one composite system of thought. Among the earliest eclectics must be numbered Cicero, the Peripatetics, and the Neoplatonists. The eclectic system of philosophy has gained great popularity in France, owing to the teaching of Victor Cousin, Adolphe Garnia, and others. Cousin asserted that ' Each system is not false, but incomplete, and in reuniting all incomplete systems we should have a complete philosophy, adequate to the totality of consciousness.'

Eclipse, *see* OCCULTATION, MOON, SUN, STARS, and SAROS.

Eclipse Stakes, The, *see* RACE MEETINGS.

Ecliptic, The, the path which the sun takes in its apparent yearly journey from west to east among the fixed stars. This path lies through the middle of the constellations known as the Signs of the Zodiac (*q.v.*). Of course the E. is only the apparent path of the sun, for the earth revolves around the sun. If it were possible to view the earth from the sun, it would be found that the earth's orbit lay along the E. The E. lies at an angle to the equinoctial of 23° 28′ at the time of the sun's greatest declination, and cuts the equinoctial at two opposite points, called the 'equinoxes,' at about March 21 and September 23.

**Eclogite, Eklogite,** or **Disthene Rock,** a rock formation, crystalline in character, and composed of smaragdite and red garnet. Occasionally felspar, quartz, iron ores, etc., form a part of this exceedingly beautiful rock. It is not found in any great abundance, but it is seen among the Alpine mountains, the Fichtelgebirge range, at Baden, etc. The garnets in E. are frequently surrounded by a covering of bright green hornblende.

**Eclogue,** the name given to a short pastoral poem in verse. The derivation of the word is obscure, the most common one being from ἐκλέγειν, to choose, E. thus being selected poem ; another derivation is from αἴξ, a goat, and λόγος, speech, the word thus being a dialogue of shepherds. In the first form, dialogue was not indispensable to an E. ; it was owing to the grammarians, who reserved the term E. to the bucolica of Virgil, which were in the form of dialogues, that E. came to mean only a poem in such a form. The first poet to write Es. was Theocritus, of whose works in this form there are about thirty extant ; they are written in the Doric dialect, and mostly in hexameters. Then Virgil wrote his Es., which he purposely called bucolica in order to challenge comparison with Theocritus. Other writers of Es. in Latin were Calpurnius Siculus and Nemesianus. In the sixteenth and seventeenth centuries the writing of Es. was again practised ; Alexander Barclay (1514) was the initiator of the fashion. The most successful of the Eng. writers of Es. was Spenser, whose *Shepheard's Calendar*, of 1579, was much admired. From this period until the time of Pope, Es. were produced at intervals. Among the collections published may be mentioned Drayton's *The Shepheard's Garland, The Shepheard's Pipe*, by Browne, Wither, Brooke, and Davies. Pope and Ambrose Phillips published volumes of Es. in 1709, but both were outclassed by the *Shepherd's Week*, 1714, of Gay. Since then Es. have not been written, save by John Davidson in *Fleet Street Eclogues*. The treatment of most of these Es. is akin to pastoral, and for a fuller description of peculiarities of form, etc., see the article on PASTORAL POETRY. Of foreign Es. those in Fr. of J. R. de Segrais (1624–1701) are noteworthy, and those in Spanish of Garcilaso de la Vega (1503–36). In fact, the latter's *Se dulce lamentar de los pastores* is one of the finest poems of its kind, whether ancient or modern.

**Ecology** (Gk. οἶκος, house or abode, λόγος, discourse) is the study of the organism as a whole in relation to its environment. Since land plants are stationary, the study of plant E. is much easier, and consequently much more advanced, than that of animal E. On the other hand, plants and animals are so closely interdependent that investigation of the E. of one group involves that of the other.

There are two main subdivisions of E. (1) Autecology, concerned with the separate environmental factors and their effect on individuals. (2) Synecology, dealing with the combined effects of these factors on plant and animal communities.

The chief environmental factors governing the distribution of plants and animals are temperature, humidity, climate, soil, the intensity of light, the nature of the food, and interaction with other plants and animals. The individual effect of each separate factor is studied in the laboratory ; the combined effects are seen out of doors, in woods, fields, swamps, lakes, seas, and other habitats.

Generally speaking, animal communities are determined by plant communities—that is, by plants growing together and forming groups with a certain individuality. Any particular type of community is described as an association, and the general appearance of a plant association is determined by dominant species, *e.g.* the pine tree is the dominant species of a pine-wood association : in a mixed wood, oak and beech may be co-dominants. Associations having only one dominant species are called consociations.

Plant associations show stratification ; in a wood, trees constitute the uppermost strata, bushy undergrowth the next, herbs the third, and mosses and liverworts the fourth. Beneath these are soil algæ, fungi, and various bacteria, and Protozoa, which by effecting changes in the soil affect the plants growing in it. Further change is effected by the constant addition of humus to the soil, and as a result of such changes the character of the plant community gradually alters, other organisms better adapted to the changed soil gradually replacing the earlier ones. This process is termed ecological succession, and is concomitant with an ecological succession of animals. By studying the changing conditions as the level of Lake Michigan falls. Shelford has been able to predict, with regard to beetles of the genus *Cicindella*, the succession that will be determined by further fall in level.

Since within limits animals can choose their habitat, behaviour is an additional factor of animal ecology.

Animals form strata in a different manner from plants. The bottom stratum may be regarded as composed of animals forming food for those of the next stratum, and so on, until at the top are animals which have no enemies or are able to defeat them by virtue of size or skill. Thus spiders eat flies; small birds eat spiders; larger birds eat smaller birds. In this way animals form food chains, those forming the first link being far more numerous than those of the last. The first link consists obviously of herbivores capable of reproducing in enormous numbers, while the animals of the last link have limited means of reproduction and reduce competition between themselves by sharing out food areas.

Other important factors in animal E. are the size of food and the status of the animal in the community, and interesting problems are presented by the phenomena of symbiosis and the specialisations of parasites.

The extensive field of E. provides interesting material for the amateur who makes careful observations and keeps accurate records.

**Economic Association, American.** Founded in 1885 at Saratoga, N. York, to provide economic research and to publish literature on economic subjects. It has a membership of over 3500 persons, including college professors, politicians, business men, lawyers, and various other persons interested in the economic aspects of political and social questions. In the series of volumes issued between 1885 and 1910 are contained excellent monographs on contemporary economic topics which afford the best possible history of economic thought in the U.S.A. Its quarterly, *The American Economic Review*, which was first published in 1911, is an accepted guide in such matters as banking, accounting, foreign commerce, labour problems, agriculture, markets, etc.

**Economic Blockade,** *see* BLOCKADE; DECLARATION OF LONDON.

**Economics,** a term by which the anct. Gks. used to signify the art of prudent and systematic household management, with particular reference to income and expenditure, and to the labour and satisfaction of the wants of the members of the household. Political economy, in our days generally described as E., signifies the art of directing carefully the pro-

duction and consumption, the incomes and expenditures of the state and its subjects. It was not commonly conceived as a neutral science till the nineteenth century, when it became the science of wealth and exchangeable values. In the theoretical treatment of the matter some economists proposed to limit the term ' political economy ' to the narrow science of wealth; but in about the middle of the nineteenth century, the Historical school (Roscher and others) maintained that the subject of the study was not wealth, but man's relation to wealth; that it was part of general social science and could not be detached from ethics and politics. Economical investigation may be divided into four stages. The first to describe, classify, define, and enumerate economic events. The second to analyse and interpret these events, to reveal cause and effect, to discover uniformities and sequences. The third to arrive at conclusions about economic progress, and to determine the theory of such progress by an interpretation of approximate aims and ideals. The fourth stage is to discuss and find means to attain these aims and ideals. Corresponding to the first stage are Economic History, Economic Methodology, and Economic Statistics; to the second, Economic Theory; to the third, Ethics of Political Economy; to the fourth, Applied Political Economy (not Art of Political Economy as often wrongly applied). Economic Theory, sometimes called E., Social E., etc., is usually subdivided into inductive and deductive theory, the latter being also called hypothetical, abstract, or speculative. Some writers (H. von Scheel, Laveleye, and most of the Gers.) use the term ' political economy ' to cover all. The leading Eng. economists of the present time use it to cover all except ethics and applied political economy. Following Adam Smith, and popular interpretations of the term, political economy may be defined as the ordered knowledge of the social phenomena arising out of man's activity in the acquisition and use use of wealth. Wealth means things possessing value of some kind which usually cost labour, which satisfy human wants, and exist in quantities below the demand, so that each unit of them possesses distinct importance to man. The history of economic thought begins with the anct. Gks., who confided everything to the power of the state, which resulted in subordination of the individual to the state, and consequently to the subordination of E. to ethics and politics. The Gk. philosophers condemned interest-taking, and vere prejudiced against trade and commerce. The Roms. followed the Gks.' ideas, and made also important studies on particular economic problems, but failed to establish a dominant system of economical thought. Christianity strengthened in general the prevalent Aristotelian system of economic philosophy, its condemnation of usury and the pursuit of wealth in trade, its assertion of the superiority of agriculture, and its support of the social system of status. Christianity thus strengthened the Christian of E. to ethics, but subject the subjection of E. to weaken. The early fathers, in their politics, tion of avarice and their condemn of fraternal love, some exultation expressions which, taken times useves, imply an utter con- by themseof private property and demnationy of communism among an advoca, but this was only an the faithfuivate property was early ideal, and pb a necessity resulting recognised a of man. The effect of from the fallwever, appears in the this ideal, hcrine, that the main-accepted doc poor was not a matter tenance of they, but an obligation. of philanthroptitude towards wealth The scripturalaatic statement of the led to an emphty of agriculture and moral superiori trade and commerce handiwork overning a livelihood, and as a means of ea seemed almost unani-the early writeref that what the seller mous in the bel, the buyer necessarily made by trade increasing temporal lost. With thehurch and the great power of the of commerce which development reventh century, came marked the e of harmonising the the necessity the church with the doctrines of irements of commerce, obvious requncessions were made by and many conists. Thomas Aquinas the later can ncedes that it is lawful (1226–74) coa simple livelihood, or in to trade for pply a country with the order to suarticles which it does not necessary or when the profits of the produce devoted to some honourable rade ose, such as the assistance of the poor, but that, save in exceptional circumstances, a seller is bound to reveal a fault in an article, and that it is not permissible to sell an article for more than its worth. The fundamental axiom, in accordance with which all these conclusions are reached, is that every commodity has a fixed and objective value, which can readily be ascertained, and which determines its just price. The distinctively ethical standpoint of the canonists is shown in the prohibition of usury, which was based upon Scriptural injunctions against it, and upon Aristotle's argument, that money

being barren, it would be extortion to charge for its use. As the growing commerce of the Middle Ages made the need of borrowing capital more and more imperative, the canonical theory had to be stretched so as to accommodate many ingenious forms of contract for what was practically, though not nominally, usury. In the latter half of the fifteenth century the Franciscans themselves instituted the Monts-de-piété, or charitable banks, for lending money to the poor at a small rate of interest to defray expenses of management. Ethical considerations dominated mediæval economic theory; political necessities that of the early modern period. The new national governments had to

ADAM SMITH

secure greater revenue. It was necessary to levy revenue in a liquid form, to wit, in ready money, which is most easily transformed into armies, navies, and other necessities for a national power, and therefore it was imperative to find or create some more productive sources of revenue than the then backward agriculture. These necessities led to the application of a mercantile system. The restrictive regulations, discriminating laws, and state interference which Adam Smith and his immediate successors described as the essential features of mercantilism have been, in a sense, incidental. State interference was a minor consideration, as it was not the problem at issue. Moreover, the mercantile system resulted not in a loss, but in a net gain of individual freedom. Contemporaneously with the imposition of those external restrictions which mark the mercantile economy went a rapid and extensive abolition of internal restrictions, which had been far more numerous, brutal, and destructive than the new external regulations which succeeded them. The economic and political unit had merely increased in size. Mercantilism was the most important phenomenon of economic thought in the sixteenth and seventeenth centuries, but it constituted nothing more than a part of a widespread and eager investigation of concrete economic facts. These studies became materials for Adam Smith's work. Money, banking, the rise of prices, population, poor relief, etc., were extensively discussed in brochures and monographs. The maintenance of the poor was a constant subject of pamphlet and tract; Sir Thomas More, in his communistic *Utopia*, gives striking evidence that the problem of poverty occupied the attention of the best thinkers of the time. True, economic study had been separated from ethics and theology, but men like Bodin, Grotius, Pufendorf, Hobbes, and Locke developed E. into an essential part of a general political philosophy. After the narrow favouritism of commerce and industry by mercantilism, a reaction in favour of agriculture became a necessity. Mercantilism was enthusiastic about nationalism; as a natural consequence the favour for agriculture had to ally itself with the broad principles of natural law and liberty expounded in the works of Grotius, Pufendorf, and Locke, and the favour of agriculture and industrial liberty found expression in the doctrines of the so-called physiocrats, the originator of which may be considered Quesnay (1756). The fundamental creed of the physiocrats was the subjection of economic and politic phenomena to ' natural law,' which, as interpreted by them, gave rise to the familiar political doctrine of radical individualism, and a certain materialistic conception of wealth which somehow explains their peculiar economic theories. Adam Smith found that the physiocrats treated not only of political economy, ' but of every other branch of the system of civil government,' and that their political and economic theories were indissolubly fused in their general doctrine of a beneficent law of industrial freedom, according to which the largest production and most just distribution of wealth would be best secured by permitting each individual to ' pursue his own interest in his own way,' so long as he did not infringe on the liberty of others. This theory has been perpetuated and popularised by Adam Smith, and has influenced subsequent thinkers more than any other economic doctrine ever formulated. The

physiocrats exposed the common error of confusing wealth with the precious metals, but they themselves fell into the error of confusing wealth with material objects, by identifying the production of wealth with the production of raw materials, whereby they concluded that manufactures and commerce, which merely change the position or form of raw materials, are barren and unproductive, though useful and desirable w strictly subordinated to agricul that the value added to raw ma e; in the process of trade and ind ials equivalent merely to the ry is production, while agriculturost of a net surplus over and above yields of production. Quesnay the cost the large agricultural emploonsiders the real producer of wealtyer to be agricultural labourer. not the being thus the sole sour Agriculture revenue, simplicity, ee of national justice demand that theonomy, and by a single direct tax lstate revenue rent. Accordingly the levied upon were the first who sta physiocrats making theory of surt the epoch- the theory also that thus value, and dustry contains a cer product of in- to the co-operation of ain value, due which is in excess of natural factors, muneration required he minimum re- and sacrifice of induto elicit the toil constitutes, on this try, and which factory source of account, a satis- Smith, whose Wea xation. Adam appeared in 1776, m th of Nations sidered as the greatest well be con- His influence hastened of economists. he popularised and free trade, and systematic study of w dignified the most important service alth; but his ing political economy fro was in divorc- partly from politics. m ethics, and clearly in the deline such appears lectures, divided into foltion of his Natural Theology; II. ur parts : I. cluded in his *Theory of* Ethics (in- ments); III. Justice an Moral Senti- dence; IV. Political Econ Jurispru- has been accused of treatin my. He merely a wealth-producing anim an as whom altruistic motives are wil in absent; but in his *Theory of Moral Sentiments* the motives of duty and sympathy are fully recognised, and the desire for wealth is treated as only one of the worthier objects of ambition. Further, in the *Wealth of Nations* he opposes piecework as calculated to excite the labourer to over-exertion, and voices the necessity for rest, diversion, and even ' dissipation.' His whole attitude is essentially this : ' Assuming that the object of the study is to increase the national wealth, this object will be most effectually secured by perfect industrial liberty.' On the other hand e did not succeed in separating politics from E., because his ultimate purpose was to prove the supreme efficacy of the doctrine of *laissez-faire*. Before being able to lay down maxims for the increase of wealth, he had to inquire how wealth was actually produced and distributed. It was his passionless analysis of production, value, and distribution which had the greatest effect upon the economists who followed him, and led to the attempt to formulate a non-partisan science of political economy, which should pass no ethical or political judgments. It must not be forgotten that Adam Smith was not always consistent in the development of his theories. Sometimes he advocates ' perfect industrial liberty,' yet he does not hesitate to recommend the regulations of banking by the state. The same inconsistency, which was in reality due to breadth of thought, is visible in his method of investigation. Withal the fact remains that with economists immediately following him the science itself became increasingly theoretical, deductive, and abstract. His most potent single quality was ' universalism.' His work dealt with the wealth of nations, not of a single one; his confidence in the existence of a natural law of universal application became a creed. As an economist he is immortal. Before dealing with the men who continued, and completed, the work of Adam Smith—that is, with the Ger. Historical and the Austrian school of E.—it may be useful to review the so-called Classical school, and the subsequent development of Eng. political economy. The Classical school had as its leaders, in the early part of the nineteenth century, a group of thoughtful writers including Bentham, Malthus, J. B. Say, Ricardo, McCulloch, James Mill, and others, who have been variously designated as the Classical, Orthodox, Ricardian, or Eng. school. Their general system of thought is harmonious, but they differed upon points of economic doctrine. They are deductive in method, pessimistic in tone, utilitarian and materialistic in assumptions, and cosmopolitan in the sense that their ultimate scientific ideal was the discovery of universal economic laws applicable at all times and to all nations. The ethical framework of classical economy is due to Jeremy Bentham (1748–1832) through his formulation and continuous propagation of utilitarian philosophy. Utilitarianism was skilfully originated by Smith and the physiocrats as an application to the ethic of individualism, which is self-interest. Bentham put it that ' To obtain the greatest portion of happiness for himself is the object of every rational being.' The materialism, pessimism, and mechanism of the Classical school seem to be intensified in Malthus's famous *Essay on the Principle of Population*. His favouritism of the historical method of research had little effect, while his famous theory that population tends to increase faster than food became the very backbone of classical economy, and modified almost every department of human thought. David Ricardo (1772–1823), in his theory of distribution, made the most important use of the Malthusian proposition. He held that

JEREMY BENTHAM

as a country grew and population increased, society would be forced to resort to poorer and poorer soils to obtain its supply of food, the law of diminishing returns would set in, and as the margin of cultivation was forced down, an increasing share of the product of industry would go to the landlord in the shape of economic rent—the difference between the natural productivity of the better land and the worst land in cultivation. Excluding rent, the division of the remainder of the product between the labourer and the capitalist was determined by a corollary of the Malthusian principle—the ' iron law of wages.' He held, further, that in the long run wages would tend to equal the price of food, necessaries, and conveniences required for the maintenance of the labourer and his family in their accustomed style of living. Profits, naturally, consisted of the product, less rent and wages, and were to be the ' leavings of wages.' T is makes clear Ricardo's theory of 'progress.' Time passing and the country settling, rent would absorb a larger share of the absolute and relative produce; wages would increase relatively, but remain constant in amount, with a tendency, however, to decrease as rents rose; but profits would necessarily decrease both absolutely and relatively. This theory of distribution is fully developed as an integral part of his famous cost-of-production theory of value, and may be summed up 'that commodities will tend to exchange in quantities proportional to the respective expenses of producing them.' When Ricardo said at times that all the expenses of production could be resolved into the toil and sacrifice of labour, he supplied the socialists with their celebrated labour theory of value, according to which labour is the sole cause of value, and consequently is entitled to the whole produce of industry, and Henry George with his doctrine that progress means poverty as long as private ownership of land is legal. But, as a final result, Ricardo's theory shifted the centre of economic interest from the land-owning classes to the capitalist class—from fat into the fire. The most influential of Eng. economists, between Ricardo and the younger, and greater, Mill, was N. W. Senior (1790–1864). He propounded the abstinence theory of interest; and formulated the famous doctrine of the wages fund (neglected by Smith, Ricardo, and others), 'that the average rate of wages is the quotient secured by dividing the number of workmen into the fund of capital set aside by the capitalists for the employment of labour.' With the exception of the Malthusian principle, this doctrine may have contributed more than anything else to make political economy the 'dismal science.' Senior also exposes the extent to which the monopoly element enters into ordinary economic life. He declares that under perfect competition prices of commodities would accurately measure 'the aggregate amount of the labour and abstinence necessary to continue their production.' But he also points out repeatedly that different advantage of any kind in production gives rise to a monopolistic rent, which includes all income obtained without a proportionate sacrifice of labour or abstinence. John Stuart Mill (1806–73) was a thorough reformer, and typifies the transition in England from the Classical to the Modern school of economic thought. He was first entirely under the influence of Ricardo, but in later years he followed Auguste Comte and the socialistic tendencies of his time.

Fettered by the Ricardian E., but moved by the warm desire to find some means to improve the condition of the masses, which he conceived through observations in his maturer years, his mind struggled hard to find a compromise between the two systems. The outcome of this mental battle appeared in 1848 under the title, *Principles of Political Economy, with Some of their Applications to Social Philosophy*. This book was not very logical in its conception, but it was so brilliantly written, so fully alive with the desire to improve the condition of the masses, that it became widely popular, and exercised an enormous influence upon the subsequent development of Eng. economic thought. The modifications of the old doctrines which Mill introduced exercised, probably, a greater influence than the old theories which he incorporated in his *Principles*. He preserved the old doctrine of rent and profits, and advocated *laissez-faire* as a general principle of political expediency, but made so many exceptions that at times they seem more important than the rule. He also endorsed the doctrine of the wage fund, a theory which he abandoned in his later years, when he recommended 'views of the taxation, and regulation of inheritance and bequest which break down large fortunes and bring about a wider diffusion of property.' Since 1850 Eng. economic thought has been deeply affected by the reaction against the classical system. The logical successors of Ricardo and Senior were Cairnes, Bagehot, Fawcett, and, perhaps, Professor Marshall. All of them have been defenders of the Orthodox school, though they have recognised and expounded its limitations as a theoretical science. Most pronounced was Fawcett, as an extreme partisan of the deductive type of economic theory, Thorold Rogers, Cliffe Leslie, Arnold Toynbee, Ashley, and Cunningham were historical economists who have more or less endorsed the general views of the Historical school (see below). A psychological school of political economy was founded by Jevons. His most distinguished disciples are Professor Edgeworth of Oxford and Professor Smart of Glasgow. They all, especially Jevons and Edgeworth, made important contributions in every branch of the science, particularly in statistics. The contemporary Eng. economists have ceased to be pedantic adherents to established doctrines, as well as those of other countries, and make the most of all schools or methods, be they deductive, historical, psychological, statistical, or mathematical. The reaction against the school of classical economy began earlier in U.S.A. than in Germany, where it came to perfection. The first to stir into the old nest of hornets were Alexander Hamilton, Daniel Raymond, Friedrich List, and some others. Raymond was the first to advance a distinctively American system of political economy, which he exposed in his *Thoughts on Political Economy*, 1820. He holds, unlike Adam Smith, that wealth is not an aggregation of exchange values, but the capacity or opportunity to acquire the necessaries and conveniences of life by labour. In his opinion the Eng. political economy, and the laws of wealth given by Adam Smith, were a study on exchange values, of private economy, as opposed to national economy, and untrue of a nation conceived as a unity. He maintained that the interests of one class do not always coincide with the interests of the nation as a whole, and that national wealth in its true sense will be most rapidly increased by developing all the national powers to their widest possible extent. He is clearly as opposed to the doctrine of *laissez-faire*, as in favour of protection. The second period of American E. belongs to the most influential of the earlier American economists, to Henry C. Carey (1793–1879). He was the most ardent apostle of protection, the staunchest opponent of Ricardo, and may be considered as the originator of the present economical system of the U.S.A. He flatly denied the Malthusian principle and the law of diminishing returns, and drew his lessons from American experience alone. His teachings were applicable exclusively to the America of his time, but he clearly showed that the fundamental premises of classical economy were not universally applicable. His principle doctrine is that of association. The increase of wealth and of the mastery of man over nature, and the development of the nation's powers, he holds dependent on increasing association between agriculture and manufactures. The younger generation of American economists have been largely trained in Germany, and have mainly accepted the positive doctrines of the Ger. Historical school. Henry George and Francis A. Walker have exerted a world-wide influence upon economic thought. These Americans are more practical than the great Eng. economists, because their investigation aims to test and supplement deductive reasoning by a bold perusal of statistics, law, and history; because they make criticism give way to construction. The general development of economic thought since 1850 is to be

considered as a series of reactions against the dominant doctrines of the classical system. The earliest and most virulent protests against classical economy came from the socialists. The antagonism between the two systems is irreconcilable. The rise of modern socialism may be dated from William Godwin's *Inquiry concerning Political Justice*, 1793. Godwin inclined personally to anarchy, but was otherwise moved, like all early socialists, by intense hatred of orthodox political economy. Through Karl Marx socialism acquired a positive theory which has been largely adopted by the socialists of our day. Logically this 'scientific socialism' derives from Ricardo's theory of value and distribution. Ethically interpreted, the claim of scientific socialism is that, as labour is the sole cause of value, the labourer is entitled to the whole produce of industry. They assert that capitalism is but a temporary stage in industrial evolution, and that it must inevitably give way to collective production. Marx's theory of value has met with but little favour, but his doctrine, that the underlying causes of social currents, such as religion, literature, and art, are economic in character (he calls this doctrine the 'materialistic conception of history '), has dominantly influenced economic science, particularly in Germany. Auguste Comte (1798–1857) is the father of modern sociology. His influence was immense. He was the first to protest against the Ricardians' aim at an abstract science of rigid precision, universal in application, raised above the limitations of particular epochs and national boundaries, an aim by which were neglected history, custom, law, and ethics; their ideas were as if the existing stage of economic development was permanent. Comte was the precursor of the Ger. Historical school, which undertook the most influential reaction against classical economy, and is usually dated from Lorenz von Stein's *Der Socialismus und Communismus des heutigen Frankreichs*, 1842, and, perhaps more justly, from Wilhelm Roscher's *Grundriss zu Vorlesungen über die Staatswirtschaft nach geschichtlicher Methode*, 1843. Bruno Hildebrand and Karl Knies, both contemporaries, must be associated with Roscher and Stein in the introduction of this method, which not only has entirely transformed economic science in Germany, but also has deeply affected it all over the world. Roscher and his disciples may be said to have annihilated the classical economists. Their positive doctrines maintain the propositions that E. is a social or political science which can be profitably pursued only in connection with the other sciences of political or social life, particularly administration, law, and history. Thus a universal political economy was superseded by an historical national economy. The work of this Historical school of Germany must be treated as the most important thought in the second half of the nineteenth century. It was simply the application to economic investigation of a method which Grimm, Savigny, Eichhorn, Bopp, and other Ger. investigators had applied to philology, history, and jurisprudence a whole generation before. The nationalistic spirit of the school was the result of irresistible political forces, and was first expressed in Friedrich Lish's economical publications (1789–1846). Germany was in the process of developing into a great empire, and such a period in the life of a nation is always attended with protective legislation, intended to make the new state industrially, as well as politically, independent and homogeneous. The German economists succeeding Roscher and his disciples made predominant use of the inductive method and adhered closely to actual economic phenomena; they studied specially the effect of legal institutions, custom, law, and ethics upon economic events; they held an intermediate attitude between extreme protection and extreme free trade; and they had discriminating sympathy for the claims of socialism. Generally they prefer state initiative to that of individuals for the solution of the problem of poverty, and have thus earned the nick-name of *Katheder-Socialisten* (socialists of the professorial chairs), or State Socialists, as contrasted with the Social Democrats, whose programme they refused to endorse. The theory of the marginal utility of value, which constitutes the essence of reaction within the limits of classical economy itself, has been most thoroughly developed and most widely applied by a group of Austrian economists, as the leaders of which may be considered Menger, Wieser, Sax, and Boehm von Bawerk. They are commonly called the Austrian School of E., though their theory itself was propounded almost simultaneously in 1871 by Professor Jevons in England, and Professor Menger in Austria, and is now used by a large majority of economists of all nations. The disciples of this school hold that the utility, or power, of satisfying want possessed by a commodity decreases per unit as the amount consumed increases, and the value itself expresses the utility of the last or marginal increment of the

commodity supplied for consumption. Thereby they have doubtless transformed economic theory; the former unit of real value—*i.e.* the pain and sacrifice of labour—has made room for a unit of utility; the cost of production theory of exchange has been replaced by a wider conception which holds that value determines the expenses of production, rather than the expenses of production-value, that capital receives its value from the finished product, and not *vice versa*. The tendency of this theory has been to shift the centre of gravity in E. from the capitalist to the consumer, and to block the movement to confine political economy to a study of exchange-value. It has certainly clarified the general conceptions of wealth and exchange, very similarly as the theory of evolution has clarified the general conception of progress. Political economy is closely related to all branches of human science. Comte, H. von Scheel, and Ingram hold that because of the intimate and inseparable connection between all forms of social activity, the study of economic phenomena cannot be separated from the general study of sociology; Senior, Mill, and Cairnes, find that political economy is an absolutely independent science, dealing with the phenomena of wealth alone. Nowadays both these opinions are considered to be erroneous. While it is now admitted that political economy is a social science, the bewildering complexity of social phenomena, together with the slow progress of society, conceived as the general science of human association, has deeply strengthened the conviction, borne out in other departments of scientific investigation, that specialisation and the isolation of phenomena are indispensable. These decisive arguments apply to all three relationships, but principally to the relationship between ethics and political economy. Substantial unanimity exists upon the following points : (1) that ethics and E. are, for purposes of investigation at least, two distinct sciences of not great extension; (2) in applied political economy account must be taken of ethical requirements, as no economist could maintain that in actual life men are freed ' from the ordinary obligations of justice and humanity ' ; (3) in so far as economical activity is affected by ethical forces, economic science has to take account of these forces. Another essential part of economic science is economic progress. The law of economic growth is, probably, the most powerful factor in determining economic evolution : what ought to be done is dependent upon what can be done.

n certain matters such as taxation, ust and reasonable public prices, etc., like railway rates, for instance, the economist is not only compelled to pass judgment on what is just and reasonable, but he discovers on investigation that economic considerations are the most important factors in determining his judgment. The broad zone between ethics and E. may be of little importance for the science of ethics, but for economic purposes it wants a thorough clearing. It is wrong to assert that the science of political economy should refrain from

*[Topical Press*

**PROFESSOR J. M. KEYNES.**

passing ethical judgments. It is logical to conclude that certain minor divisions of political economy may be investigated ' without passing ethical judgments,' but illogical to conclude that the whole science may be so investigated and formulated. Considering the relation of E. to laws and politics, and looking on the progress of the past or the conditions of the present, we find the economic success or failure of many laws and policies which are still in force or under active consideration, and which will be endorsed or repudiated largely upon economical grounds. Political economy depends certainly more upon his-

tory than any other science. We may not go so far as the extremists of the Historical school, who hold that until a larger store of historical results is accumulated, it is of little use to attempt broad theoretical generalisations. Thereby they confine E. for the present to the philosophy of economic history. Dr. Keynes classifies the functions of economic history in connection with economic theory, as follows : ' First, to illustrate and test conclusions not themselves resting on historical evidence; secondly, to teach the limits of the actual applicability of economic doctrines; thirdly, to afford a basis for the direct attainment of economic truths of a theoretical nature.' Psychology is the alpha and omega of political economy. Any study beginning with human effort, and ending with the satisfaction of all human wants, begins and ends with psychology. ' The satisfaction afforded by commodities decreases per unit as the amount consumed increases,' which is an analysis of the theory of value, is purely psychological. But E. deal with man in society, psychology with man as an individual. Economists employ diverse methods to come to their conclusions. Predominating are the deductive and the inductive methods. In England, through the economic theory prevalent from Ricardo to Cairnes, the postulates of the deductive science were very much simplified. Ricardo, as well as Adam Smith, liked to draw his premises from an imaginary primitive industry. The postulates assumed by different economists must vary widely in different branches of the science, and it would be impossible to enumerate them all. Generally it is assumed that men desire, and know how to obtain, the maximum satisfaction with the minimum effort; that certain industries incline to increasing rather than to diminishing returns; that the satisfaction afforded by a commodity decreases per unit as the amount consumed increases; that existing laws, public opinion, and ethical standards in general remain constant. The intermediate is most appropriately called deductive, because with it are employed the familiar processes of deductive logic. But withal, results obtained from artificially simplified premises of ordinary deductive theory are of a doubtful value. If the postulates be absolutely true and the deduction faultless, the conclusions express abstract tendencies which will be modified in real life by the action of secondary forces not taken into account in the premises, which, however, is the case of pure theory in all sciences. But if the premises practically cover the predominant forces in any economical domain, they may yield results capable of explaining actual economic conditions, and afford a basis to provision. Cliffe Leslie and others of the Historical school have characterised the conclusions of Eng. theory as inapplicable either to the explanation of existing conditions, or the solution of practical problems. Such antipathy to deductive theory is justified in no way. Given the necessity of the study of the past, it cannot be denied that the present and the future furnish the ultimate and principal problems of political economy. Many of these problems are new; to solve them factors at work must be isolated, their effects separately calculated, and an estimation tried of the net results. This process is necessarily and largely deductive, and a practical science ought not to be attacked, as it is by the historical method, for the employment of methods indispensable for the solution of practical problems. The verification by observation is in practice exceedingly difficult: when Mill attempted to apply Ricardo's theories, he quickly found out that there is limitation to all methods. The inductive method is ' to observe the effects of a cause coming singly in action while all other forces remain unaltered.' There are two inductive processes: the method of difference, and the method of agreement. In the method of difference circumstances are compared with exactly similar ones, minus one factor. The chief instrument of the method of difference is the experiment, and, in E., the observation of extraordinary instances in which the conditions of an experiment are closely approximated by some fortuitous or extraordinary event. In theory the method of difference requires that the collateral or surrounding circumstances shall be identical. Such condition seldom arises even approximately, and instances enough may be cited in which the method has been abused. The method of difference is entirely satisfactory where the conditions are perfect, but otherwise it is always narrow and restricted. It shows what a given cause can produce in certain set circumstances, but it tells nothing of what will happen in another set of circumstances. The method of agreement is used to generalise, and to establish uniformities: it is somewhat speculative. In examining the movements of the export, and the movement of the marriage rate, the finding that a rise in exports *per capita* regularly corresponds with a rise in the marriage rate, leads to the safe acceptance of this connection as an economic uniformity. Theoretically this method requires to exhaust every possible combination of circumstances before concluding that its results have become a standard economic law. I little is to be done without the deductive method, it seldom convinces The above cited case of the export and the marriage rate is a proof of it Both rises are evidently the results o a single cause—active business, etc Brisk trade, high wages, constant employment, etc., stimulate marriage and usually conduce to increased ex ports. But there may be a commercial prosperity without an augmentation of exports. Would thus marriage rise or not rise, irrespective of exports' The difficulty of induction in E. is the complexity of economic phenomena For example, the five-and-twenty years preceding the repeal of the Corn Laws in England were far less prosperous than the twenty-five year which succeeded the repeal. Can i be concluded therefrom that free trade would be advantageous to every country of the world ? On the other hand, when the creation of great modern European monarchies was accompanied by protective tariffs colonisation schemes, etc., were the extremists of the German Historical school justified in demanding that the German empire should start with protective tariffs, colonisation schemes and the policy of the mailed fist Methods cannot be applied to every case; they should be used wherever possible. Consult Adam Smith' *Wealth of Nations;* Malthus's *Essay on the Principle of Population ;* Johr Stuart Mill's *Principles ;* Marshall' *Elements of the Economics of Industry* J. A. Hobson's *Economics of Distri bution* and *The Social Problem ;* H Sidgwick's *Principles ;* J. Ruskin' *Unto this Last ;* Karl Marx, *Capita* (3 vols.); Henry George's *Progress and Poverty ;* G. B. Shaw's *Fabian Essays* and *The Impossibilities of Anarchism* Böhm-Bawerk's *Capital ;* Sir L. G Chiozza-Money's *Riches and Poverty* F. A. Walker's *Political Economy* R. Griffen's *Economic Enquiries.*

**War-time Economics.** The outbreak of the Great War necessitated special regulations and arrangements for dealing with finance. So successful were many of these in achieving the immediate purposes for which they were brought into being, that the study of economics became popular, and, as might be expected many pseudo-economists propounded new theories as remarkable as they were unsound. Broadly, most of these opinions centred on the notion that economic laws can be asserted and maintained by the arbitrary acts of govs. and bankers. It took many years to break down some fallacies while others, even at the time of writing (1931), still appear to dominate many minds. The stern necessity of withdrawing gold from circulation, and the substitution of paper currencies, were the immediate causes of these heresies. It was discovered that the issue of paper money, in slowly or rapidly increasing quantities, constituted a national treasure chest in itself, as it writes down, not only the old liabilities, but also the recent ones as rapidly as the currency is inflated. During the War this power was used at different rates of speed by different countries, in some cases gaining a momentum that led to national bankruptcies during the years after the Armistice. As inflation temporarily stimulates trade by creating an eager demand for goods, and seems to create prosperity, these movements received popular support. The policy of Great Britain in deflating the currency was much criticised, it being held by many that the British gov. would have acted more wisely to follow the example of France, namely, to adhere to the gold standard, but with a smaller gold sovereign as the unit. France having reduced the value of her old franc to about one fifth, it has been suggested that Britain should have reduced her sovereign to about one half. Britain's policy of deflation, while in progress, naturally embarrassed trade but re-established her financial credit. Throughout the War and the years that followed the gold standard remained the unchallenged measure by which all other commodities were valued. As paper could be changed for paper anywhere, and a ten-dollar bill could be changed for gold in New York, gold remained the real test of values from 1914 to 1930, powerful enough throughout the whole period to write down the worth of all paper issues, in the markets of the world, as swiftly as they were inflated, and almost as rapidly to reduce their purchasing power in the places of issue. The gold standard, however, could not operate with absolute precision while the free circulation of gold was hampered and great nations were endeavouring to manage without the use of gold because its value in other commodities could only be approximately estimated. During 1930 it became apparent that the trade of the world had increased at a more rapid rate than the stocks of gold, and in consequence the average prices of other commodities had been too high. As the world-wide demand for gold increased, these prices slumped at a rate that caused grave anxieties in banking and trading circles. War-time experience and its aftermath did not so much re-establish gold as the standard of value as emphasise the futility of trying to find a substitute. None the less, it has been found that a nation which uses the powers of inflation cautiously and, by means of high tariffs cuts itself off from international trade, can persist in its policy over an amazing length of years before it is ultimately forced to deflate or become insolvent. Gov. control of the means of wealth creation was another subject around which there was much controversy during the period under review, and in many countries, including Great Britain, practical proposals for taking over mines, railways and other undertakings became party and gov. policies. By far the greatest movement in this way took place in Russia, where, under the Soviet system, all industry appears to have become nationalised. This vast experiment still continues at the time of writing, and is a subject upon which only a future historian can adequately comment, although indications are not wanting that a return to some form of capitalism if not already in operation is inevitable. As a summary of the whole period, it may be stated categorically that the War has confirmed rather than destroyed orthodox economics.

**Economics and Political Science, The London School of,** a school which provides special courses of training, for men and women, for examinations in economics and political science, also in commerce and industry. Established in 1895, it is suited for business men, civil and municipal servants, journalists, etc. In connection with the British Library of Political Science, courses of lectures are provided on the methods of investigation, etc., and studentships of a value of from £25 to £200 are awarded. Preparation is also given for the B.Sc. and D.Sc. degrees in Economics of the London University. The School of Sociology and Social Economics has been merged in the above school. The average annual number of regular, as opposed to occasional students, is 1000, occasional numbering about 1400 (1930). Inter-collegiate students, who are nearly all regular students of other colleges, number nearly 500. The increase in recent years of regular students reflects a growing recognition of the importance of the studies in the school.

An increase in the women students in 1930 was largely due to the institution of a new course in Mental Health, designed particularly for training workers to deal with backward children. To meet this growth, etc., many additional professors, readers, and lecturers have recently been appointed and a new building is in course of erection. New departures include the establishment in 1930 of a Chair of Imperial Economic Relations, a Research Chair of Social Biology; and, furthermore, the school has become the organising centre for a comprehensive co-ordinated history of prices, covering Britain, France, Germany, Austria, Spain, and America; the funds for which work were provided by a special grant from the Rockefeller Foundation, and the work is carried out under the supervision of an international scientific committee of which the director of the school is chairman. Another new feature is the department of Business Administration Research and Training, the scheme of which supplements the general Commercial Degree. A standing committee has been set up to co-ordinate the school's activities with those of the Royal Institute of International Affairs and to act as a centre of communication with similar committees in other countries. The school is situated in Houghton St., Aldwych, W.C.

**Economist, The**, a London weekly journal, founded in 1843 'to discuss financial questions in their wider social and commercial aspect.' James Wilson was the founder and editor of it from its inception until 1877, when he was succeeded by Walter Bagehot. *The E.* has always been a force in politics; it was a strong advocate for the repeal of the Corn Laws, and later was opposed to indiscriminate laudation and extension of the railways. General commercial information for the current week is also to be found in *The E.*

**Economus**, or **Ecnomus**, a hilly cape on the S. coast of Sicily, situated between Agrigentum and Camarina. It was the site of a battle fought in 311 B.C., when the Syracusan Agathocles suffered defeat at the hands of the Carthaginians.

**Economy**, a township of Beaver co., Pennsylvania, U.S.A., on the Ohio R., 17 m. N.W. of Pittsburgh. Until 1904 it was owned by a communist sect, the Harmony Society. It came to an end owing to the celibacy of the communists. Pop. 1138. *See* RAPP, GEORG.

**Ecrins, Barre des** or **Pointe des**, the termination of the Dauphine Alps. Until 1862 it was regarded as belonging to Mont Pelvoux, but F. F. Tuckett in that year established its separate existence. It reaches a height of 13,463 ft.

**Ecstasy**, or **Trance** (from the Gk. ἔκστασις, meaning 'to put out of place'), a term which is used to describe a morbid state of mind, or a condition, when the mind, having temporarily lost all self control, is ruled by one idea, object, or emotion. Hysteria and catalepsy are similar forms of the disease, if such it can be called. It often accompanies religious mania, and the patient may lie as in a trance, or be convulsed in movement.

**Ethyma**, an anct. Gk. medical term applied to a condition of the skin, which at various times and in various languages has had different meanings. It is best understood as an angry-looking sore, the origin of which is due to infection at the start, or later when the surface is broken, as in *impetigo contagiosa.*

**Ectropion**, a curving outwards of the eyelids, resulting from chronic, long-continued irritation. This produces an unsightly condition, which comes under the category of 'bleareyed.'

**Ecuador** (so called because the equator crosses it), a republic of S. America, bounded on the S.E. and S. by Peru, on the N. and N.E. by Colombia, and on the W. by the Pacific. The boundaries between E. and the neighbouring countries are not definitely settled; the question has been referred to arbitration. The country is triangular in shape, and may be divided into three sections, the narrow, low-lying coast-land, the mountain region, and the vast plains to the E. These districts may be called the Cis-Andine, Inter-Andine, and Trans-Andine respectively. The principal peaks of the Andes which are situated in E. are Chimborazo (20,702 ft.), Cotocachi (16,301 ft.), Cayambe (19,186 ft.), Antisana (18,864 ft.), Cotopaxi (19,498 ft.), Iliniza (17,405 ft.) and six others with an altitude of over 16,000 ft. The principal port of the country is Guayaquil, the capital and seat of Quito; and Cuenca and Riobamba are important cities. The chief rivers are the Esmeraldas, the numerous streams that combine to form the Guayaquil; these flow to the Pacific. Trans-Andine E. is watered by the upper waters of many tributaries of the Amazon. The fauna includes deer, tapirs, peccaries, parrots, humming-birds, and numerous reptiles; the condor, which inhabits the slopes of the Andes, is the most remarkable bird. The climate of the country is hot and unhealthy save in the valleys of the middle region, where it is cool and salubrious. Vast areas of the country are clad in virgin forest, rich in rubber, cinchona, dyewoods, and other valuable timbers. Most of this forest area lies in the Amazon basin, but the Pacific slopes of the

Andes up to an altitude of 5000 ft. are also forest clad. In the coastal regions and lower river valleys tropical farming is carried on, and cocoa, coffee, cotton, tobacco, sugar, and rice are grown; among the foot-hills and mountain valleys is land suitable for grazing and dairy-farming and the cultivation of potatoes, cereals, and temperate fruits and vegetables. The output of cocoa, E.'s staple produce, is declining owing to competition, but it is still the most important export; coffee, ivory-nuts, wild rubber, rice and fruits are other vegetable exports. Panama hats are another article of trade. Petroleum is the chief mineral; considerable quantities of gold are found, and silver, copper, lead, iron and coal are known to exist; sulphur is another important mineral product. Communications are bad, roads being very poor; there are river transport in some districts and some 700 m. of railroad. There is no state religion, and toleration prevails; education is fairly well provided for, though methods need improvement. There are univer-sities at Quito, Guayaquil and Cuenca, and a law college at Loja. The gov. is in the hands of a president, a council of state, a senate, and a chamber of deputies. There are two senators for every province, and a deputy for every 50,000 inhabitants elected by universal suffrage; the president is elected for four years. No privileges of rank or race are recog-nised. The country has recently revised its economic arrangements, having accepted as laws the recommendations of an American Financial Mission which visited E. in 1926. This has led to a new customs tariff, a new monetary law, re-introducing the gold standard, and a new banking law, a Central Bank being established in 1927. The area of E. cannot be definitely given, owing to its boun-dary disputes, and estimates vary between 109,978 sq. m. and 220,502 sq. m. The Galapagos Islands add 2868 sq. m. The Incas of Peru conquered this area towards the end of the fifteenth century, and were in their turn conquered by the Spaniards under Pizarro. For 200 years the country remained part of the Spanish state of Peru; then, in 1822, a revolutionary war gave it inde-pendence, it becoming a part of the republic of Colombia. In 1830 there was a civil war in this newly-created republic, and the presidency of Quito became the republic of Ecuador. The population, which is estimated at between 1½ and 2 million, is com-posed chiefly of aboriginal Indians, descendants of the Spanish con-querors and people of mixed blood. Spanish is the language of the country.

**Ecumenical,** see OECUMENICAL.

**Eczema,** see SKIN—*Diseases.*

**Edam,** one of the so-called Dead Cities of the Zuyder Zee, Holland, but still very much alive, with a large Gothic fourteenth-century church, a museum in a house in the likeness of a ship built by a sixteenth-century sea-captain, and a bell tower with a very musical chime. The country round is noted for its cheese, to which the tn. gives its name. Pop. 7960.

**Edda** ('great grandmother'), the name of two anct. Icelandic works, which are authorities for Northern mythology. The first, or the 'Elder Edda,' was compiled during the thir-teenth century. It was discovered about 1643 by Brynjolf Sveinsson, who attributed it erroneously to Sæmund Sigfusson, an Icelandic clergyman (1056–1133). The poems in the compilation date from the ninth, tenth, and eleventh centuries. They are thirty-three in number, and consist of epic tales of the Scandi-navian gods and goddesses, and nar-ratives of Scandinavian popular heroes. The verse of the pieces is all typical alliterative Scandinavian poetry; two forms are employed. The first part of the book is written in epic metre, or kridhuháttr, the verses in this part are divided into strophes of eight lines. The second part is written in godhahattr or didactic metre, and in strophes of six lines. The other compilation of poems, or 'Younger Edda,' was discovered in 1628 by Arngrim Jonsson, and arranged by Snorri Sturluson. The actual date of com-position is about 1150. This book may be divided into five portions; it is the principal authority on Northern mythology and poetry. The first part is the preface or Formali; this is of a comparatively modern nature, and gives an account of the begin-ning of the world, etc., on orthodox Christian lines. The second part is entitled Gylfaginning, the delusion of Gylfi, and is a kind of prose synopsis of Northern mythology. The third part is a continuation of the second; it is entitled Bragaræður, 'the say-ings of Brag,' which consist of further legends of deities. The fourth part is called Skaldskaparmal or Art of Poetry and is a treatise on Scaldic poetry and versification. The last part consists of three poems in honour of Haakon, King of Norway (d. 1263), with a running technical commentary, and is entitled Hattatal, a system of prosody.

**Eddington, Sir Arthur Stanley** (b. 1882). Plumian Professor of Astronomy and director of the

Observatory at Cambridge, an astronomer of world-wide reputation, chiefly because of his contribution to the theory of stellar evolution, the motions of stars, and the theory of relativity ; *b.* at Kendal, Dec. 28, 1882, he was educated at Owens College, Manchester, and Trinity College, Cambridge, where he was Senior Wrangler in 1904 and Smith's Prizeman in 1907. He was made a Fellow of his college in 1907, and after seven years' work (1906–13) as chief assistant at the Royal Observatory at Greenwich he was appointed professor in Cambridge, and subsequently elected a Fellow of the Royal Society in 1914. Within recent years he has been the recipient of many honours both from British and foreign scientific bodies, and he was knighted in 1930. He has made many contributions to contemporary literature on astronomy. His two books, *Space, Time and Gravitation* (C.U.P. 1920) and *Stars and Atoms* (Clarendon Press 1927), are written in a fascinating and lucid style for the educated layman. His philosophic views have exerted much influence upon modern thought.

**Eddoes** (E. Indian species of Araceæ), *see* COCCO.

**Eddy,** *see* WHIRLPOOL.

**Eddy (Mrs.), Mary Baker** (1821–1910), discoverer and founder of Christian Science and author of its text-book, *Science and Health, with Key to the Scriptures,* and other works on Christian Science. Mrs. E., whose maiden name was Mary Baker, was *b.* to Congregational parents of Puritan ancestry at Bow, New Hampshire, U.S.A., July 16. She was thrice married. After a frail youth and middle age, most of which time she devoted to study, writing, and experimenting in the various systems of therapeutics in order to discover if possible the cause and cure of disease, Mrs. Eddy, who was a profound student of the Bible, as the result of the instantaneous healing of the effects of an accident considered fatal, discovered in 1866 what she declared to be the divine principle underlying Jesus' works. On this discovery she founded her healing system and named it Christian Science. In 1875 she published *Science and Health, with Key to the Scriptures :* founded the first Christian Science Church, in Boston, Massachusetts, in 1879 ; established successively the Massachusetts Metaphysical College in 1881, *The Christian Science Journal* (monthly), *Sentinel* (weekly), *Herold* (monthly in German), and *Monitor* (daily). She *d.* Dec. 3, 1910. The most thorough authorised biography of Mrs. E. is that by Sibyl Wilbur,

*Life of Mary Baker Eddy.* In it the reader will find details of Mrs. E.'s early life ; of her struggles to gain a hearing for her ideas and her book and to protect them and herself from persistent attacks made from various sources—pulpit, Press, and medical—which involved wholesale misrepresentation of both ; of her final triumph in which she saw her church grow, prosper, and become a power. Mrs. Eddy left the bulk of her estate, valued at $2,000,000, in trust for the extension and promotion of Christian Science as taught by her. Suits were brought against the executors of her will by a son and adopted son of Mrs. Eddy, but these were finally withdrawn. *See also* CHRISTIAN SCIENCE.

**Eddystone Lighthouse,** the name given to a light in the Eng. Channel erected to mark a group of rocks which lie in the fairway from the Start to the Lizard, and are visible only at ebb-tide. The lighthouse is situated about 9 m. from the Cornish coast, and 14 m. S.S.W. of Plymouth. The present structure is the fourth which has been erected. The first was in the form of a wooden polygon 100 ft. in height with a stone base ; it was built by Henry Winstanley in 1696 and carried away by the storm of 1703. The second was also of wood on a stone base ; it was erected by Mr. Rudyerd in 1706, was 92 ft. high, and was burned down in 1755. The third edifice was designed by Mr. Smeaton, and was built of blocks of Portland oolite encased in granite and dove-tailed together. It was 26¾ ft. at the base, 15 ft. at the top, and 85 ft. in height. The rock on which it was built was undermined, so the structure was taken down and re-erected on Plymouth Hoe ; the first floor was left on its site. The present lighthouse was designed by Sir J. N. Douglas and completed in 1882 ; its lamp has a dioptric apparatus and gives a light equal to 159,600 candles. The light gives a double flash every half minute and can be seen for 17½ m., being 133 ft. above the water.

**Edelinck, Gerard** (1649–1707), a Fr. engraver, *b.* at Anvers. He was a pupil of Poilly. Louis XIV. entrusted to him the execution of several important works. He was the first engraver to change the material on which he engraved according to the object represented, so giving tone and colour to the engraving. Among his works, which number over 300, his 'Holy Family,' after Raphael, is one of the best known.

**Edelweiss,** or *Leontopodium alpinum,* a well-known species of Compositæ which occurs in its wild state in Switzerland, but can be cultivated in Britain. The dense involucre consists of outer female florets and inner male florets, and these are surrounded by hairy bracts.

**Eden**, a river of England, which rises among the Pennines, on the borders of Westmorland and Yorkshire. It flows in a N.W. direction, through Appleby, Edenhall, and Carlisle. After a distance of 65 m., it forms a wide estuary at Rockcliffe, in the upper part of the Solway Firth.

**Eden, Garden of** (Heb. ' delight '), the first home of man, and the district in which the Garden of Paradise was situated. There has been much discussion regarding the exact site of Eden, and many futile efforts have been made to reconcile the mythical geography of Genesis with modern knowledge. Recent discoveries, how-

**Eden, George,** see AUCKLAND, G. E., EARL OF.

**Eden, William,** see AUCKLAND, W. E., LORD.

**Edenhall,** a vil. and mansion in Cumberland, England. The village is situated on the R. Eden, about 3½ m. N.E. of Penrith. The mansion is the family seat of the Musgraves. There is a spring in the grounds named St. Cuthbert's Well, around which a pretty legend is told, connected with an anct. goblet, called the ' Luck of Eden Hall.'

**Edentata,** an order of mammiferous animals characterised by the absence of teeth in the front of the jaws and by the simple structure of their cheekteeth, which are composed solely of ivory and cement, without any trace

EL QURNAH

(*See* GARDEN OF EDEN)

ever, have shown that *Edin* was the Sumerian name for the plain of Babylon, and at the S. end of it was the city of Eridu, and near it a beautiful garden containing the Tree of Life. The accepted modern location appears to be El Qurnah, in Iraq. It would seem, from all accounts, that the Garden was in Eden, and the river with its four heads, spoken of in Genesis, must have been the Persian Gulf, which the Babylonians regarded as a river. The idea of the ' tree of life ' situated in the Garden of Eden would appear to have existed in the *Vedas*, in which, the first man is represented as leading men to the garden of immortality where he dwelt in fellowship with the gods. It may also be traced in Babylonian and Assyrian monuments ; but the idea of the primæval state of man, as in the biblical account of Paradise, is of a more religious and ethical nature than any of the earlier forms. See the commentaries on Genesis and Delitzsch's *Wo Lag das Paradies,* 1881.

of enamel. They are of a low degree of organisation, although many of them are specialised for particular modes of life. All Edentates are either aboreal or terrestrial, and several of the carnivorous forms are burrowing animals. The typical forms of this order are the sloths, ant-eaters and armadillos.

**Edenton,** a city of N. Carolina, U.S.A., co. seat of Chowan co. with many historic associations. On Oct. 24, 1774, fifty-one ladies at the ' Edenton Tea Party ' signed resolutions that they would not use tea or anything manufactured in England until the tax on tea should be repealed. The royal governors lived here. During the eighteenth century the N. Carolina Legislative Assembly met here, and many important statesmen lived near E. Pop. 3563, of whom one half are negroes.

**Edessa:** (1) an anct. city of Turkey in Asia, and is the modern Urfa. In 137 B.C. the capital of an independent kingdom, it was made tributary to Rome ; later it was a seat of Christian learning between the fourth and fifth centuries. From 1097 until 1144 the Crusaders held it, and it was destroyed in 1147 by the Turks, into whose possession eventually it came. The modern town is surrounded by walls and a moat and has an anct. citadel, and is in the centre of a wheat industry. Pop. probably about 40,000. (2) A splendidly situated tn. of Greece, cap. of the prov. of Pellis on the railway from Salonika to Monastir, with 13,120 inhabs.

**Edfu,** a tn. of Upper Egypt, situated on the W. bank of the Nile, in lat. 24° 59' N. It is the anct. Apollinopolis Magna, and is noted for its remarkable sandstone temple of E., which is the most complete Egyptian temple existing. It was begun by Ptolemy XIII. in 57 B.C. and took over 180 years to complete. It is approached by two great pylons of great antiquarian interest. The town of E. stands 484 m. S.S.E. of Cairo, and has manufs. of earthenware.

**Edgar,** or **Eadgar** (c. 942–975), surnamed ' The Peaceable,' an Anglo-Saxon king, succeeded at the age of seventeen to the kingdoms of Mercia and Northumbria, but enlarged his dominions by degrees until he ruled over all Britain. In spite of the warlike propensities of his neighbours he lived in peace, hence his title of ' The Peaceable.' During his reign wolves were largely destroyed in England. He was a man of unbridled passions when once aroused; he snatched Wilfreda from her convent by force, and later killed Athelwalda, the husband of Elfrida, because he stood in the way of his desires.

**Edgar Atheling** (*fl.* 1066–1107), the grand-nephew of Edward the Confessor. In spite of being the heir-presumptive, he was thought by the witenagemot to be too young on the death of Edward. They accordingly chose Harold, Earl of Godwin, to succeed; Harold was slain at the battle of Hastings, and E. was thereupon chosen king by the citizens of London. As soon as William the Conqueror appeared on the scene, however, E. placed the crown in his hands, and retired into obscurity, from which he emerged only to place one of his nephews on the throne of Scotland.

**Edgcumbe, Sir Edward Robert Pearce** (1851–1929), an Eng. politician, traveller, and writer. Was pioneer of the small holdings movement. His works include : *Zephyrus, or Travels in Brazil and on R. Plata,* 1887 ; *Bastiat's Popular Fallacies ; Sir J. Reynolds,* 1901.

**Edgehill,** a hilly ridge in Warwickshire, 7 m. from Banbury. It is noted as the scene of the first battle of the Civil War in 1642. A huge figure of a horse is cut out on the hillside, and the spot is called the ' Vale of the Red Horse.'

**Edgeworth, Henry Essex** (1745–1807), known as ' Abbé Edgeworth,' *b.* at Edgeworthstown, where his father was rector. In 1748 the latter was converted to Catholicism and went to Toulouse. E. entered the priesthood, and when he was ordained took the surname of De Firmont. He was made confessor to the Princess Elizabeth in 1791, and in 1793 to her brother, Louis XVI., whom he attended to the scaffold. In 1796 he went to England, and was made chaplain to Louis XVIII., who was in exile there. He *d.* at Milan of a fever caught whilst attending the Fr. prisoners.

**Edgeworth, Maria** (1767–1849), a novelist, was the daughter of Richard Lovell E., an author of some note in his day, by the first of his four wives. She does not seem to have had any precocious call to letters, but in 1782 she translated Madame de Genlis' *Adèle et Théodore.* In London, where her early years were spent, she mixed with her equals ; in Ireland, where she spent the next years, she acquired a considerable knowledge of the habits and ways of thinking of the peasantry ; and her acquaintance with these sections of society was useful to her when she began to write fiction. Novels, however, were not her earliest literary output. Her first publication was *Letters to Literary Ladies,* 1795 ; her second, *The Parent's Assistant,* 1796. It was not until 1800 that she published anonymously *Castle Rackrent.* Her *Popular Tales* appeared in 1804, and then came a succession of books, *Leonora,* 1806 ; *Tales from Fashionable Life* (two series), 1809, 1812 ; *Patronage,* 1814 ; *Harrington,* 1817 ; *Ormond,* 1817 ; and *Helen,* 1834. She was a friend of Walter Scott, who much admired her Irish characters, and declared that it was after reading her books he set himself to do for the Scots what she had done for the Irish. Her works on education had a considerable vogue, and the popularity of her children's stories endures to this day. There is a biography by Helen Zimmern, 1883.

**Edgren,** or **Edgren-Leffler, Anna Carlotta** (1849–92), a Swedish authoress, *b.* at Stockholm. She married Judge E. in 1872 ; he did not share her advanced views, and she obtained a divorce in 1889. In the following year she married Pasquale del Pezzo, Duc di Cajanello. She published her first volume of stories in 1869, entitled *By Chance* ; later she wrote plays, of which the chief are *The Struggle for Happiness* (1887) and

*How One Does Good* (1895), etc. All her works reflect her keen observation and her modern views; her dramatic method may be said to lie between Ibsen and Strindberg.

**Edgware**, a vil. of Middlesex, England, 11 m. N.W. of London. A portion of the old Watling Street crosses the parish, and it is said that Handel composed his *Harmonious Black-smith* one rainy day in a forge which once stood in the village. Pop. 1516.

**Edict of Nantes**, an edict signed by Henry IV. of France on April 1598. It allowed the Huguenots free exercise of their religion, gave them definite rights of public worship, threw open to them all the offices of state, and established a Protestant chamber in the Paris Parliament, and joint chambers in the local govs. This measure did much to promote the concord and prosperity of France, but unfortunately, in Oct. 1685, Louis XIV. formally revoked it. As a consequence religious rivalry was again stirred up, riots took place, and 400,000 of the most intelligent and industrious section of the community had to flee the country. They settled down in Protestant countries, many in Holland and Great Britain, and were an acquisition to whatever country they went.

**Edicta** (Lat. *edicta*), were proclamations made by all the higher magistrates at Rome, such as the prætors, tribunes, curule ædiles, censors, etc. All these had the *jus edicendi*, and made known on their entry into office certain rules which they proposed to follow in administration. Since they had the *juris dictio*, the prætors in particular developed new legal principles in their edicts, and the latter played an important part in the evolution of the Rom. law.

**Edictal Citation**, a term of Scots law used to describe a citation where personal service of the summons is impossible, as in the case of a non-resident debtor. Originally a proclamation was made, and an edict or order of the court was posted up in a public place. Now, however, a copy of the summons with a schedule of the citation attached is sent to the keeper of E. Cs. at the Edinburgh General Register House.

**Edinburgh**, the capital of Scotland, and one of the most ancient as it is one of the finest cities in the United Kingdom. It is situated within 2 m. of the S. shore of the Firth of Forth, 390 m. N. of London, and 105 m. from Aberdeen. Three eminences which run from E. to W. form the site of the city, which is surrounded on all sides, save the N., by hills. The steep ridge descending from the castle rock to Holyrood constituted the ancient city, and on it the High Street is built. To the N. of this ridge was formerly the Nor' Loch; this is now drained. The New Town lies on the ground which rises beyond the valley of the Nor' Loch. As viewed from the Calton Hill, the following is a bird's-eye view of the city. On the right may be seen the New Town, with its wide streets and stately houses stretching down towards the shore. Princes Street, nearly a mile long, lies opposite; whilst the serried masses of houses forming the Old Town stretch on the left as far as the castle. There are still further streets on the S. towards the Braid Hills, and on the E. to Arthur's Seat; whilst the northward view from the Calton Hill includes Leith, the Firth of Forth, and the hills of Fifeshire. The Nor' Loch, or rather the hollow which formerly was the Nor' Loch, separates the New Town from the Old Town. The former occupies a ridge which is broader and not so steep as that which forms the site of the Old Town. The slopes on both sides of the hollow are laid out as public gardens. This quarter of the city has many attractions, though, of course, it does not possess the historical character and interest of the older portion of the town. The streets and squares are well planned, and the buildings, most of which are built of a handsome white freestone which is quarried in the vicinity, are magnificent. The extensive pleasure grounds in this quarter of the city are another attraction. The most noteworthy streets in the New Town are Princes Street, George Street, and Queen Street, which all run parallel to each other, eastward and westward. At the W. end of Princes Street are the Caledonian Railway Hotel and Station, St. Cuthbert's Church, and St. John's Episcopal Church; at the E. end are the L.N.E. Railway Hotel and Waverley Station, one of the largest in Great Britain, the General Post Office, and the Register House. Calton Hill forms the eastern extremity of the street; this is a rocky eminence studded with monuments, including the Nelson Column and the unfinished National Monument. Salisbury Crags, a huge belt of precipitous rock nearly 580 ft. in height, rises beyond the eastern extremity of the city; whilst behind this is Arthur's Seat, a conical hill, 822 ft. high, with a narrow rocky summit. On the slopes of the Calton Hill are situated the Royal High School, the Burns' Monument, and the county prison (now closed). George Street, which is bounded by St. Andrew Square and Charlotte Square, has many fine statues and houses with literary associations. Queen Street contains the National Portrait Gallery and Antiquarian Museum, presented by J. R. Findlay; charming views of Fife may be obtained from its cross streets. The Water of Leith at Canonmills and Stockbridge forms the boundary of the New Town; many famous buildings and places are situated in this neighbourhood, including Donaldson's Hospital, Fettes College, and Stewart's College. The principal street in the Old Town is that built on the steep ridge which extends from the castle rock to Holyrood. This old street is more than a mile in length, and is called, at different points, Canongate, Netherbow, High Street, Lawnmarket, and Castle Hill, the whole being often termed ' the

Many other historic sites are situated in the High Street, including Burns' lodgings, Riddell's Close, Ramsay Lodge, Flesh-market Close, Old Fish-market Close, and World's End Close. Past the Netherbow the street is called the Canongate; at one time all the nobility of E. lived here, and the Moray House and the Huntly House still remain. The Old Canongate Tolbooth and the Canongate church may also be seen in the Canongate; the closes off this street are as historically interesting as those of the High Street, though at the present time it is hard to realise its former splendour. The closes are numerous narrow lanes which descend laterally

EDINBURGH CASTLE BEFORE 1573

Royal Mile.' The aspect of this backbone of Old E. is quite in keeping with its traditions; the houses are all very ancient and very lofty. The High Street opens into Parliament Square on the right hand side, going E.; the latter contains the old Parliament House and St. Giles' church, a large and ancient edifice in the later Gothic style of architecture, which was renovated in 1830. The ancient cross of E. which was removed in 1756, but in 1885 was restored at Gladstone's expense, now stands hear the E. end of the church. The site of the Netherbow port, one of the ancient gates of the city, is a little further on, adjoining the house in which John Knox lived. The grave in which Knox is buried is situated in the graveyard near Parliament Close, to the rear of St. Giles'.

in regular rows from the main street; they are not as a rule more than six feet wide at the entrance, and those which admit of the passage of a carriage are called ' wynds.' The old street called the Cowgate runs to the S. of and parallel with the High Street, and opens at the W. end into the Grassmarket. ' The Palaces of the Cowgate ' was a common term in olden times, as the palaces belonging to the princes of the land were there; it is now noted mainly for old-clothes shops. George IV. Bridge and South Bridge cross the Cowgate at a height of two or three stories; the university is the chief ornament of the latter, whilst the Carnegie Free Library stands on the former. The castle of E. is one of the most interesting of the public buildings. The fortress contains accommodation for 2000 soldiers. The old piece of ordnance called 'Mons Meg,' built of malleable iron casks, stands on a small flagged area which occupies the summit of the castle. The earliest portion of the castle, the old Parliament Hall, was restored in 1888–89; the room in which Queen Mary gave birth to James VI. is situated at the E. end of the S.E. side of the castle. Holyrood Palace, standing at the lower end of the street leading to the castle, does not date in any part from earlier than 1528, whilst the greater portion of it was built in the time of Charles II. The apartments occupied by the hapless Queen Mary are in the N.W. angle of the building. The ruins of the chapel belonging to the Abbey of Holyrood, founded by David I. in 1128, adjoin the chapel of the Holyrood Palace on the N. side. The Parliament House, the building in which the Scottish Parliament met before the Union, is a magnificent hall, with a lofty roof, and contains various marble statues of celebrities. The Advocates' Library, the largest library in Scotland, and the Signet Library are adjoining buildings to the Parliament House. Among the other noteworthy public buildings of E. are the Royal Institution, the National Gallery, the Scottish National Portrait Gallery, the Surgeons' Hall, the General Post Office, the Museum of Science and Art, the Theatre Royal, the Tron Church, the Bank of Scotland, the High School, the Royal Astronomical Observatory, etc., etc. The monument to Sir Walter Scott, situated on the S. side of Princes Street, and designed by G. M. Kemp, is the finest in the city. It represents a marble sitting figure, and is in the form of an elaborate Gothic cross 200 ft. in height. Other monuments in the city are to Burns, Hume, Allan Ramsay, James Watt, Livingstone, William Pitt, Dugald Stewart, Playfair, etc. The Scottish National War Memorial was opened by the Prince of Wales on July 14, 1927. The actual memorial, which reposes in a Shrine in a noble structure on the apex of the rock on the site of the old barracks, consists of books containing the names of over 100,000 Scots who fell in the Great War. The E. Cenotaph or Stone of Remembrance was unveiled by Prince Henry the same year. The manufactures of E. cannot be called either numerous or important. The chief is ale brewing, for which it has been noted for more than 200 years. Only a few publishing houses still make E. their headquarters, but there is still much book-making. Several new magazines of a high standard have been started at E.; the *Edinburgh Review*, *Blackwood's Magazine*, and *Chambers's Journal* were all started there. The educational side of E. is the most important; in addition to the University (for which see separate article) it has many schools. Amongst them may be mentioned the College for educating theological students of the United Free Church, the Edinburgh High School, Edinburgh Academy, Fettes College (an endowed high school), the training colleges for teachers. The Heriot Trust and the Merchant Company are represented by such institutions as the Heriot-Watt College, the Heriot Technical School, George Watson's College, and the Queen Street and George Square colleges for ladies. The city returns five members to Parliament, has an area of 11,416 acres, and a pop. of 420,264. The origin of E. is involved in obscurity, like most towns whose history extends for a long way into the past. The most probable account of the origin of the name E. is that it was derived from the Northumbrian King Eadwine; it had obtained the name Eadwinesburg or Edwinesburg as early as the beginning of the seventeenth century. After this time very little is known of the history of E. until the reign of Malcolm Canmore (the son of Duncan in *Macbeth*), when Donald Banc besieged Edinburgh Castle after Malcolm's death. In the year 1128, E. is called by David I. 'his burgh of Edinburgh'; David lived more at E. than his predecessors had done, and this custom was followed by his descendants. By the Treaty of Falaise, in the reign of William the Lion, E. was ceded to England, but was restored as part of Ermengarde de Beaumont's dowry when she married William. Though E. had been frequently used as a royal residence, it was by no means the capital of the country yet. Bruce held a parliament at Holyrood in 1327, and his last parliament was held in E. in the following year, but the chief importance of the town was from a military point of view. E. was held by the Eng. for several years, but with the outbreak of war between England and France in 1338, the Scots gained their lost ground. A new era began for E. with the accession of James I. E. may be called the capital of the Stuarts; it shared the vicissitudes of that dynasty, and sank into comparative unimportance when they deserted it. It was not a walled town until the middle of the fifteenth century. The first printing press was erected in the beginning of the sixteenth century; in the succeeding reign E. was recognised as the undisputed capital of the country. At an early period of the Reformation E. was converted to the Protestant faith;

and in succeeding ages the great majority of its inhabitants adopted the Calvinistic creed and adhered rigidly to the Presbyterian form of worship, in spite of various forms of persecution. The Union of England and Scotland aroused great excitement in E., and attempts were made to intimidate the members of the Scottish Parliament who were favourable to the Act of Union, but the Act was eventually passed without bloodshed. An unsuccessful attempt was made by the Jacobites to surprise the castle in the rebellion of 1715. In 1745 the Jacobites were more successful, and were masters of the town from Sept. 15 to Oct. 31, but could not reduce the castle. The Porteous affair of 1736 was a remarkable occurrence; the populace took the power into their own hands and lynched the captain of the guard, Porteous, who had fired on the crowd and killed six persons. The city was ordered to pay £2000 to the widow of Porteous; the ringleaders were never discovered. In 1779 the mob burnt one Catholic church and plundered another during the parliamentary discussions on the subject of Catholic claims. The societies which were formed in E. about the time of the Fr. Revolution in sympathy with the principles prevailing in France were put down with great severity when they came to the notice of the gov. George IV. visited E. in 1822, and won great popularity by wearing the Highland dress. He was the first sovereign to visit the city since 1650. Holyrood was granted as a residence to the exiled King of France, Charles X., in 1830, and in 1842 Queen Victoria and Prince Albert visited the city.

**Edinburgh, Alfred Ernest Albert, Duke of,** see ALFRED, ERNEST ALBERT.

**Edinburgh Review, The,** a Whig quarterly, founded in 1802 by Francis Jeffrey, Sydney Smith, F. Horner, and Brougham. Sydney Smith gives the following account of its beginning : ' I proposed that we should set up a Review. This was acceded to with acclamation. I was appointed editor, and remained long enough in Edinburgh to edit the first number of the Review. The motto I proposed for the Review was : " *Tenui Musam meditamur avenâ* " (We cultivate literature on a little oatmeal). But this was too near the truth to be admitted ; so we took our present grave motto from Publius Syrus (" *Judex damnatur cum nocens absolvitur* "), of whom none of us had, I am sure, read a single line.' It was the earliest of the great reviews, and has had a far-reaching influence on literature and politics. Sydney Smith

was the first editor, and he was followed by Jeffrey (1803-29), Macvey Napier (1829-47), Professor Empson (1847-52), Sir George Cornewall Lewis (1852-55), and Henry Reeve (1855-95). Its early literary criticisms were amazingly savage, notably in the case of Wordsworth and Southey, and gave rise to Byron's satire, *English Bards and Scotch Reviewers.* Ceased publication in 1929.

**Edinburgh University,** the youngest of the Scottish universities, having been founded in 1582 by a charter granted by King James VI. of Scotland. In 1621 an Act of the Scottish Parliament ratified the charter and granted the university all the privileges and immunities which were enjoyed by the other universities in the kingdom ; this Act was confirmed at the time of the Union. In 1858 the University Court and a body of curators were created, and various regulations were made for the governance and discipline. The university is a corporation, consisting of the chancellor, the lord rector, the principal, the professors, graduates, and undergraduates. Its government is in the hands of the University Court, the Senatus Academicus, and the General Council. The lord rector is elected by the undergraduates, the principal is the resident head of the college and president of the Senatus Academicus for life. The Senatus Academicus is composed of the Principal and the whole body of Professors, as well as a certain number of Readers and Senior Lecturers. There are six Faculties at the University : Arts, Science, Divinity, Law, Medicine, and Music ; the Arts and Medical courses having the greatest number of students, Music the least. Among the principal Univ. buildings are the Old College, dating from 1789 ; the Univ. New Building (School of Medicine) built between 1878 and 1883 ; the M'Ewan Hall (1888-1897); the King's Buildings (Chemistry) begun in 1919 and completed in 1924 ; the departments of Agriculture, Forestry and Entomology, erected in 1914 ; and the Engineering Dept., open for occupation in 1931. There are also dissecting rooms and 28 laboratories, mainly medical ; the Royal Botanical Garden, a Natural History Museum, Anatomical Museum, and about a dozen smaller specialised museums. The Library contains about 350,000 printed volumes and 8000 MSS., many of which are of great value. The separate Theological Library has 10,000 volumes, and there are about a dozen departmental libraries. Numerous bursaries and scholarships are given, many being restricted to students bearing a particular Scottish surname or residing in a certain locality. The Univ. unites with St. Andrews, Glasgow, and Aberdeen as one constituency to send three members to Parliament. The Rector, elected in October or November for matriculated students, holds office for three years. The Rt. Hon. Winston Churchill was elected Rector for the period 1929–32.

**Edinburghshire**, or **Midlothian**, a co. of Scotland, bounded on the N. by the Firth of Forth, on the W. by Linlithgowshire, on the E. by Haddingtonshire and Berwickshire, and on the S. by Lanarkshire, Peeblesshire, and Selkirkshire. In the southeastern and south-western parts of the county are the Moorfoot Hills and the Pentland Hills, the latter of which extend to within 4 m. of Edinburgh ; the chief summits are Scald Law (1898 ft.) and Carnethy (1881 ft.). Of the rivers, the Gala flows S. to the Tweed, and the Tyne, after a course of only 7 m. in the county, flows into Haddingtonshire ; the N. and S. Esk rivers, and the Water of Leith, all flow into the Firth of Forth. Half of the country consists of arable and pasture land ; the most fertile part of the country is the lowlands which stretch to the Forth. Many large farms are worked here on up-to-date methods, and dairy farming is extensively carried on in the hillier districts. The chief crops are oats, barley, turnips, and potatoes ; horse-breeding is also a considerable industry. Coal is mined in the north-eastern and south-eastern parts, iron-stone is found at Lasswade and Penicuik, and other minerals are limestone and freestone. The chief industry is paper-making, and the ales of the county have long been famous. Other manufs. are whisky and gunpowder, whilst the fisheries are valuable. The chief towns of the county are Edinburgh, Leith, Dalkeith, Musselburgh, and Portobello. Area 234,339 acres. Midlothian and Co. Peebles send two members to Parliament. Pop. 506,378.

**Edison, Thomas Alva** (b. 1847), an American inventor, is of Dutch origin on his father's and Scottish on his mother's side. Beginning life, at the age of twelve, as a newsboy on the Grand Trunk line running to Detroit, he owes all his distinction and advancement to his own faculties. After printing and circulating the *Grand Trunk Herald*, the first newspaper to be issued from a railway train, he gladly assimilated the principles of telegraphy from a friendly stationmaster. From 1871 he was superintendent to the New York Gold and Stock Company, till in 1876 he set up his own works at Menlo Park, New Jersey. Here his extraordinary inventive genius had full scope. The following is a mere catalogue of some of the more important of his 1,000 patents : The duplex, quadruplex, etc., system of telegraphic transmission, the printing telegraph for gold and stock quotations, a microtasimeter (for detection of small changes in temperature), the aerophone, the megaphone, the phonograph, the incandescent light, the kinetoscope, and the carbon telephone transmitter. It was an observation made by E. in one of his experiments, which led to the invention of the thermionic valve, used in radio-telegraphy and radiotelephony. This valve, so essential to radio-telegraphy, was at first known as the " Edison effect." E. also invented a system of wireless telegraphy to and from moving railway trains. He is also credited with the invention of motion pictures and the alkaline storage battery. During the Great War he designed and operated benzol plants and plants for carbolic acid. Has received innumerable honours from all nations. The reader is referred to Dickson's absorbing *Life and Inventions of Edison*, 1894.

**Edmonton** : (1) a northern suburb of London, 10 m. N.N.E. of Liverpool Street Station, situated in the Enfield parliamentary division of Middlesex. Charles Lamb is buried here, and the poets Keats and Cowper resided in the neighbourhood. The parish church is an anct. structure, containing several interesting monumental brasses and tablets. Pop. 66,809. (2) Cap. of Alberta, Canada, on the North Saskatchewan R., an important railway centre with large railway car shops. It is served by twelve branch railways. Market for Central and N. Alberta, N. British Columbia, and N.W. Territories. The principal industries are meat-packing, coal-mining (1½ million tons per annum), lumbering, building supplies, garment making, manufacture of metal goods, biscuits, chemicals, boats, flour, butter and cheese, etc. The Edmonton City Dairy is the largest in Canada. E. is a great shipping point for live stock, and for thousands of bushels of registered seed grain. It is the seat of the provincial university, and of many colleges. It is surrounded by numerous beautiful lakes and summer resorts. Pop. (1921) 58,820.

**Edmund, St.** (840–870), King of E. Anglia. He succeeded to the throne when quite a boy. In 870 E. had a fierce battle with the Danes, but was beaten and killed upon the field of action. The date of his canonisation is unknown, but his shrine was famous in every part of England, and his saintly reputation extended all over Europe.

**Edmund (Rich), St.** (1175–1240), an English ecclesiastic, *b.* at Abingdon, near Oxford; he studied at this university, and later in Paris. In 1233 he was elected Archbishop of Canterbury at the suggestion of Gregory IX., and at once leapt into prominence by the outspoken way in which he rebuked Henry III. for encouraging foreign favourites; the king appealed to Rome for a legate who at once opposed and thwarted E. at every point. In 1240 he withdrew to Soissy, where he died the same year. His canonisation took place in 1247.

**Edmund I.** (*d.* 946), King of the the south. Soon afterwards E. died.

**Edmunds, George Franklin** (1828–1919), an American senator, lawyer, and political leader. He was a member of the Vermont House of Representatives, and a member, as a Republican, of the United States Senate. In 1883–85 Edmunds was President *pro tem.* of the Senate. He was the author of the Act for the suppression of polygamy in Utah, and of the anti-trust law of 1890. Resigned 1891. He was well known as a constitutional lawyer. Died in California.

**Edom** (Heb. 'red,' Gk. 'Ἰδουμαία), an extent of country to the S. of Palestine, some 100 m. long by 20 m. wide extending southwards from the Dead

[*Courtesy of Canadian Government*

PARLIAMENT BUILDINGS, EDMONTON

English. He succeeded to the throne in 940, but had already played a prominent part in the battles of the previous reign. E. had many battles with Anlaf, King of Northumbria, but a reconciliation was brought about by Odo of Canterbury, and Wolfstan of York. In 945 E. ravaged Strathclyde. He was killed by a robber, who had been previously banished from the court. E. was buried at Glastonbury Abbey.

**Edmund II. (Ironside)** (980–1016) King of the Anglo-Saxons. He attempted to resist Canute (Cnut) when the latter invaded England, but was obliged eventually to submit. On the death of Athelred the citizens of London chose E., and the witan elected Canute (Cnut) as their king. Fierce warfare proceeded between the two rivals, until E. was at last persuaded to accept a reconciliation. He and Canute swore friendship, agreeing to divide the kingdom, Canute taking the north and E. Sea to the Gulf of Akabah. Its name is probably derived from the ruddy colour of the sandstone rocks, and its name appears thus under an Assyrian form in a tablet of the second century B.C. It was originally inhabited by the cave-dwelling Horites, but it later came into the possession of Esau, who received the surname of Edom, the derivation of the name being made from the red pottage given him by Jacob (Gen. xxv. 29 ff.). The Esauites did not entirely drive out the conquered race, but intermarried with them to a certain extent (Deut. ii. 12 and Gen. xxxvi. 20–21). The relations between the Israelites and Edomites were generally hostile, and the O.T. tradition dates the commencement of this hostility from the time when the Edomites refused the Hebrews a passage through their country to the land of Canaan (Num. xx. 14 ff.). Under David and Solomon the Hebrews brought their ancient foes into apparent submission, but there were frequent re-bellions. The Edomites remained subject to Judah until the reign of Jehoram, when they made a successful rising. But they were again sub-dued by Amaziah and Uzziah. They regained their freedom after the fall of Judah, and waged war somewhat unsuccessfully with Judas Maccabæus. They were later completely subdued by John Hyrcanus at the end of the second century B.C. From about 300 B.C. the eastern part had been in the hands of the Nabathæans. After the Rom. Conquest, E., Judea, Sam-aria, and Galilee were united as a pro-curatorship under Antipater the Idu-mean, founder of the Herodian dynasty. The religion of the country was polytheistic. Chief towns : Selah (later Petra), Maon, Punon, and Bozrah (now Buseirah).

**Edoni,** a Thracian tribe showing remarkable skill in music, literature, and the working of gold and silver. They inhabited the region from Olympus to the Pangæan district.

**Edred** (d. 955), King of the Anglo-Saxons. The youngest son of Edward the Elder, he succeeded to the throne in 946. In revenge for the incon-stancy of the Northumbrians, who after tendering him their submission shortly afterwards broke their pledges and acknowledged Eric Bloodaxe, the Norwegian, for their king, Edward ravaged the whole country and enforced compensation. His pub-lic policy was greatly influenced by St. Dunstan with whom he was on terms of intimacy.

**Edriophthalma** (Gk. ἕδρα, seat, and ὀφθαλμός, the eye) is the name given to a group of crustaceans with sessile eyes, sometimes called the Arthrostraca. They are widely dis-tributed individuals of large size, being found especially in the Arctic seas. The group is divided into three orders : Anisopoda, which contains *Cyamus balænarum,* the whale-louse ; Isopoda, containing several parasitic genera, both terrestrial and aquatic, as *Cymothoa,* which breeds on fishes, and *Oniscus* and *Porcellio,* the wood-lice ; and Amphipoda, containing *Gammarus pulex,* the common fresh-water shrimp, and *Talitrus* and *Orchestia,* two genera popularly called ' beach fleas.'

**Edrisi, or Idrisi, Abu Abdallah Mohammed El-** (1099–1170), an Arabian geographer, who under the patronage of Roger II. of Sicily wrote of a description of the ' in-habited earth ' from observations, and not merely from books. Emis-saries were sent into various countries to obtain information which E. inserted in the new geography, en-titled *The Rogerian Treatise.* This

contained a full description of the world as far as it was known at that time. Little is known of the life of E., but for being a courtier of a Christian prince he was regarded by strict Moslems as a disgrace to his race.

**Education.** The term E. in the widest application may be held to include the whole process of develop-ment through which a human being passes from infancy to maturity, gradually adapting himself to his physical and social environment ; but the more definite sense in which the term is ordinarily employed is restricted to those influences which are *designedly* brought to bear upon the younger by the adult portion of the community for the purpose of maintaining and, if possible, of rais-ing the level of culture attained, and it is to this sense of ' schooling ' that we must confine ourselves in the short scope of this article. In searching for the origin of E. amongst the primal races of mankind, it is difficult to discern at what stage the parental instinct to train the young in self-preservation may be said to have emerged into a conception of formal E. Amongst the earliest stages of mankind, the training given to the young was of a purely incidental character : manners and customs were at first acquired by a process of imitation rather than by any con-sciously designed instruction. With the development of religious or rather superstitious ideas and the consequent rise of a priesthood it was natural that the priests should arro-gate to themselves the E. of the young that, by instilling superstition into the young mind at its most receptive period, and moulding it while still in a plastic condition, the dominance of the priesthood might be maintained in succeeding generations. Provision would have to be made also for in-struction in the secrets of the craft to be given to a select few in order to secure the succession of the office. There are in almost every tribal group special ceremonies of social com-memoration and celebration, and in connection with these there are initia-tion rites for admission of younger members of the group attaining a certain age into fuller social member-ship, and these rites evidently fulfil an educational as well as a religious purpose. As the arts of life, civil and military, became more complex, pro-vision was made for them and with the invention of letters, requiring a special training for the mastery of the symbols, and encouraging the accu-mulation of knowledge far wider than provided by the immediate environ-ment, schools as formal institutions came into existence.

In the limited scope of this article the consideration of the school as the most important factor in the process of E. must necessarily be our chief concern. Nevertheless, the importance of home life in the upbringing of the child must not be entirely overlooked. The infant school and kindergarten are of value only in so far as they afford the natural surroundings of a good home to those children whose parents cannot or will not perform their natural duties in these respects.

Before proceeding to outline the systems of E. in vogue at the present time, a brief survey of E. in past ages is necessary, in order to understand the foundations on which modern systems are laid. The Jews always held E. in great esteem, and it is probable that instruction in the arts of reading and writing was generally given at a very early period. Moral training and the care of the body were considered of paramount importance. The priestly tribe of Levi had special professional schools, but there is no evidence of schools being established for the people until after the captivity, E. being regarded as a family affair, and the father undertaking the duties of teacher. Among the Spartans the E. given aimed simply at the development of soldier citizens, trained to the utmost physical effectiveness, and in such moral and intellectual virtues as would make for the perpetuation of Sparta as a military power. Gymnastics formed the greater part of the training, while music (μυσική, including reading, writing, and easy arithmetic) represented the intellectual side of the curriculum. The art of stealing was also taught as a training in resourcefulness and judgment; the Spartans believing that any disregard for the rights of others which might result would be outbalanced by the intensely moral and social character of their educational system as a whole. Schools were organised by the state on a more or less barrack system, and E. began at a comparatively early age. In the *Republic* and *Laws* of Plato will be found a representation of the ideal of E. at Athens, and of the importance given to dialectic and music (including a wider range of studies than among the Spartans) as a training for the logical and æsthetic faculties, and to gymnastic exercises for the body. The moral influence of gymnastics on the mind was also recognised. There was, however, practically no regulation by the state of schools for boys until they reached the age of seventeen years, when they entered the *ephebea*. The

younger boys were sent by their parents, in charge of slaves, to professional teachers, who were of three kinds : the *grammatistes* who taught reading, writing, and arithmetic; the *citharistes* who taught singing and playing on musical instruments; and the *pædotribes* who trained the boys in wrestling, boxing, running, jumping, etc. The latter training was left till the age of fourteen, but instruction in μυσική began at about seven years of age. During the early period of the Rom. Republic E. was left entirely to the parents. The boy was taught to read, to reverence the gods, and honour the state, and was trained in hardihood of body. With the influence of Gk. culture schools began to spring up under professional teachers who were for the most part Gks. In these the young boy was instructed in the three Rs. by a master known as *literator*. On attaining the age of twelve or thirteen he was sent to another master, *literatus*, under whom he studied grammar (including the form and content of literature), poetry, history, philosophy and Gk. Schools of rhetoric were also established, restricting themselves to training in oratory, the value of which is insisted upon by Quintilian and Cicero. In Quintilian's *Institutio Oratoria* we are given a discussion of the whole of E. from the cradle upwards, from which it would appear that the E. given by the *literatus* was much as in Eng. grammar schools up to the eighteenth century.

With the rise of Christianity schools were instituted for instructing the young in the Christian faith; the method of teaching was entirely catechetical, and among the early Christians no attention was paid to the cultural studies of the pagan schools. This was due to their antagonism to the literature of the period, which was naturally saturated with paganism. As men of culture were attracted to the Christian church, however, the question of adapting pagan culture to Christianity caused serious discussion. St. Augustine and St. Jerome contended that the study of literature and rhetoric was good so long as kept subservient to Christian life. The contentions which raged fiercely over this question had, temporarily, a very disastrous effect on E. As Christianity grew the old pagan schools gradually disappeared and their place was taken by schools whose object was of a purely religious nature. These were mainly connected with monasteries, and prepared young men for the monastic life. The chief monasteries generally had, however, external schools for pupils not proposing to enter the order, as well as the internal schools for novices. By degrees the curriculum was widened to include the seven liberal arts, relics of the old Rom. E., known as the *Trivium*—grammar, didactic, and rhetoric (including the study of law)—and the *Quadrivium*—geometry (which corresponded rather more to physical geography than what is now understood by the term geometry), arithmetic, music, and astronomy. In addition to this clerical training a form of E. adapted to the needs of court and castle life was developed amongst the knightly classes. The profession of arms became a highly organised career, and the page underwent a prolonged training in the arts of riding, hawking, shooting with the bow, swimming, etc., before attaining to knighthood. At a lower level, with the development of city life and trade guilds the boys were trained to commercial life by serving an apprenticeship in the arts of the counting house and the workshop. During the latter part of the eighth century the famous palace school (or *Palatine Academy*) was established by Alcuin (735–804) under the patronage of Charlemagne. This school generally accompanied the court. Alcuin's favourite method of instruction was dialogue, especially dialogue in allegorical character. The curriculum consisted of the *trivial* and *quadrivial* studies, but a more liberal interpretation was given than in the monastic schools of the time. Alcuin also supervised the work of the monastic schools throughout the Carolingian empire. His educational writings include treatises on grammar, orthography, rhetoric, and dialectic. During the eleventh and twelfth centuries contact with Eastern civilisation, consequent on the wars of the Crusades, and with the highly civilised Moors in Spain, produced an intellectual revival which took expression in the formation of many universities, and a great increase in the numbers of and attendance at the monastic and grammar schools. The desire for E. penetrated even to the lowest classes of the people, and elementary A B C schools came into existence, generally presided over by the parish priest, to give instruction to the children of the poor in reading, writing, and easy arithmetic. The difficulties of travel and communication and the scarcity of books confined the organised machinery of culture for adults to special centres, and universities arose in Italy, France, and England, not by deliberate foundation, but by the gathering, at selected spots, of men of learning from all countries. The most famous of these were the university of Paris, the chief centre for philosophy and theology, which formed the model on which the universities of Oxford and Cambridge were organised, the university at Salerno, at which the study of law took first place, and the university of Bologna, for the study of medicine. The need for acquiring a definite status induced most universities to apply to the Pope or the Emperor for recognition, though a few of the greater universities did not find it necessary to do this. Charters were granted by Henry III. to the two English universities, Cambridge in 1231 and Oxford in 1248. The Ger. universities were of later founda-

ERASMUS

tion, and were mostly established by civic authority; Prague was established in 1348, and Vienna in 1365, and obtained charters from the Emperor later. Though universities were intended mainly for more advanced E. of men, the distinction between them and grammar schools was not everywhere clearly marked, and young boys frequently attended.

As has already been noted, the rise of the Christian church and the barbarian invasion of the Dark Ages had led to a break in the study of classical literature. The ascetic religion of the Middle Ages was naturally inimical to a literature which was the work of pagans and told of heathen myths; which also encouraged interest in romance, in beauty of form, and secular subjects with which the mediæval church was out of sympathy. Hence, although great attention was paid to logic, scholastic theology, and law, the church discouraged the study of literature as such, and the time given to it, together with free-thinking philosophy and classical philology, was looked upon as being wasted, and better spent on religious subjects. This contempt for the most elementary rules of literature was forcibly expressed by Gregory the Great when he wrote : ' The place of prepositions and the cases of nouns I utterly despise, since I deem it unfit to confine the words of the celestial oracle within the rules of Donatus.' The literature studied, therefore, was very limited. Gk. and Hebrew were practically unknown languages in Western Europe, and the literature, when read at all, was read in translations into Latin, which language had degenerated in the hands of monkish writers into a very debased dialect. The Renaissance, however, essentially a movement of revolt against established authority and the assertion of individual liberty, led to a free and unfettered study of all that appealed to the intellect of man. The movement originating in Italy, which consisted in going back to the ancients and reviving the free study of all classical writers, both Latin and Gk., assimilating their reasoning, and making a philological study of their language, is termed the *Revival of Learning.* Such literature was styled *literæ humaniores* and those who advocated its study were called *Humanists.* In E. the Humanists were pioneers to whom we still owe a debt of gratitude. Vittorino da Feltre (1378–1446) was perhaps the most famous of the early Italian humanist schoolmasters. His ideal was the patriotic and well-equipped citizen rather than the self-contained scholar, and with him, at least, scholarship was no excuse for aloofness from the common duties and sympathies of life. Another great humanist of the period was Guarino da Verona (1370–1460), who worked under the patronage of the Estes at Ferrara. Classics naturally formed the foundation of the curriculum in the humanist schools. In addition to their value in stimulating literary taste and culture, they provided a disciplinary training much more than at the present day. The grammatical rules had to be acquired from careful observation of the literature read, there being no formal grammars, and plain texts provided a more valuable intellectual study than the modern text-book in which all difficulties are eliminated by the aid of notes. The classics were also looked upon as providing practical text-books, such as Cæsar for war,

Virgil for agriculture, etc. But in addition to the classics, the curriculum embraced mathematics, astronomy, history (Gk. and Rom.), music, natural philosophy, and natural history. Great attention was paid to elocution and conversation, and stress was also laid on the training of the memory. Regular exercise and a healthy life formed part of Vittorino's method, and he discouraged work in the hours of play. Except, however, as producing hardihood, games seem to have been scarcely regarded as developing character. The later humanist theories of E., which the schools con-

MELANCTHON

tinued to follow generally for two or three centuries, were taken mainly from Erasmus (1467–1536) and Melancthon (1497–1560). To Erasmus Humanism, which in the eyes of the Italians was an end in itself, was only the means to the propagation of the truth. Melancthon was a great supporter of the claim of the classics to impart a culture not otherwise attainable, and was also the author of several school text-books. The Latin *gymnasien,* founded at Strasburg by Melancthon's friend Sturm (1507–89), became the model which the grammar schools of Protestant Europe strove to copy. In this school practically the whole of the time was given to acquiring a mastery of the Latin language. In England Humanism did not spread so quickly until it was adopted by the universities, where it encountered less opposition than in Ger. St. Paul's School, founded in 1512 by Dean Colet, provided for a distinctively Humanistic E. In Catholic countries the church retained entire control of E., and the Society of Jesus, founded in 1540 by Ignatius Loyola, established many schools which were extremely successful. The curriculum in these Jesuit schools was purely Humanistic, and a particular feature was the attention paid to the individual character of each pupil.

While Latin was accepted as the medium of learning and so long as new branches of knowledge were not discovered, the schools remained in harmony with the culture of the day; but during the seventeenth century the difference between the needs of life and the E. furnished by the grammar and other classical schools grew gradually wider, and many schools owing to the rapidly decreasing numbers in attendance fell into decay. Indeed, in England many of the old grammar schools degenerated into elementary schools of a very poor and inefficient character, and at the beginning of the eighteenth century organised E. was at a very low level. But there was no lack of educational theorists and writers. Comenius (1592–1671), the author of *The Great Didactic; the whole Art of Teaching all Things to all Men*, and a number of text-books on original lines, takes first place amongst the realists, of whom Pestalozzi and Froebel were latter-day disciples. The realists maintain that things not words must provide the organon of E., and that the child must be brought into contact with the concrete before proceeding to the abstract. John Locke (1632–1704) on the other hand is to be classed among the naturalists who hold that the duty of the teacher is to treat the child as an individual who is being prepared for life by living. He does not, however, appear to concern himself with any but the children of the wealthy, for he declares roundly in favour of a home E., under a private tutor, as opposed to that given in public schools. During the eighteenth century E. became more and more to be looked upon as the property of the select few. The individualistic rationalism of Voltaire (1694–1778) and the Encyclopædists, derived from Locke, resulted in an extreme of selfishness among the aristocratic classes, an example of which may be seen in Lord Chesterfield's *Letters to his Son*. In 1762 appeared Jean Jacques Rousseau's famous *Emile*, the underlying motif of which is an appeal for a return to nature. The book gives an account of a boy's upbringing from infancy to marriage. With small faith in the

family under the conditions of modern civilisation, Rousseau (1712–78) begins by assuming that Emile is an orphan, and that his tutor is charged with parental responsibilities. According to Rousseau the essence of life lies in the gratification of desires and impulses of the moment. He would abolish all moral training, and free the child to the reactions of the physical world upon his activities. With all its violent paradoxes *Emile* exercised a wonderful influence on E. Rousseau also made a special plea for child-study. At this time Pestalozzi (1746–1827) was a young student at

J. J. ROUSSEAU

Zurich. Though by method a realist, he drew his inspiration from Rousseau, and this early influence is traceable in his ardent belief that an important factor in E. had hitherto been insufficiently considered—the child himself. In spite, however, of his belief in the value of psychology, Pestalozzi made little use of it in his own teaching, in which, indeed, he was thoroughly unmethodical and unpractical. Froebel (1782–1852), however, succeeded in constructing a complete and consistent system for Pestalozzi's scheme. ' The boy,' says Froebel in his *Education of Man*, 'has not become a boy, nor has the youth become a youth, by reaching a certain age, but only by having lived through childhood, and further on, through boyhood, true to the requirements of his mind, his feelings, and his body.' The duty of the teacher consists in clearing the way for nature to do her proper work : to stimulate and direct the child's self activity, without in any way interfering with it. To this end he devised his scheme of gifts and occupations. Froebel's ideas as regards young children, though his native land has never given him due recognition, have been largely accepted outside his own country. The same principle of self E. underlies the Montessori system, which has created widespread interest in recent times. Dottoressa Montessori, who is the first woman to whom the degree of Doctor of Medicine was granted by the university of Rome, was for some time (1898–1900) directress of the Scuola Ortofrenica (mind-straightening school) at Rome for feeble-minded children, and the results obtained by her system were so successful that the 'idiots,' as she calls them, were able to compete with normal children of

PESTALOZZI

their own age. In 1907 Dottoressa Montessori applied her educational theories to the training of normal children with such success that several schools on her method were started in Rome and Milan. The curriculum of a Montessori school includes in the order given : (1) The training of the senses and of speech; (2) control of the limbs and of the movements of the body; (3) writing and reading; (4) arithmetic. One of the greatest influences at work in E. at the present time is that of Johann Friedrich Herbart (1776–1841) the pupil of Fichte and successor of Kant. The most important of the pedagogical applications of Herbart's opinions are the recognition of the value of apperception, the concentration of studies, and the 'formal steps.' Great importance is attached by Herbartians to what are called the 'Five Formal Steps,' the successive stages in every

lesson given in what they consider the only right way : (1) preparation, (2) presentation, (3) association, (4) formulation, (5) application.

The relation between the state and the individual in the matter of E. has long been a favourite theme of discussion and controversy. It is, however, now generally recognised that the state has the duty of providing and the right of prescribing E. for all its children. Even Adam Smith and John Stuart Mill, the apostles of 'natural liberty' and *laissez-faire*, admitted the exception of E. Adam Smith was in favour of state-controlled elementary E., though he hardly disguised his disapproval of state interference in higher E. Mill, on the other hand, advocated that the state should provide for both elementary and higher E., and that elementary E. should be made compulsory. England for long lagged behind most of the other great civilised nations in this respect, and it was not until 1880 that elementary E. was made compulsory, but secondary E. was left practically untouched by the state until 1902.

The various stages of growth from infancy to maturity require, and have created in most modern civilised states, a graduated system of schools adapted to the needs of each particular period. As has already been asserted, for the sub-primary stage, *i.e.* during the first six years, the child's proper place is the home, but the complexity of modern life, especially in congested areas, where the mother has to go out to work, has made the kindergarten and infant school indispensable institutions as places of refuge for children whose parents are unable to fulfil their proper parental functions. In England children are permitted, though not now encouraged, to go to school at three years of age; in France there are the *écoles maternelles*, and in America the work of the kindergarten has received the serious attention of many able teachers and educationists. In Ger., on the other hand, no official cognisance is taken of children under six years of age. It is generally accepted at the present time, however, that neither at home nor at school should there be during this period any question of formal instruction. The next stage in school life covers the period between the ages of six or seven and thirteen or fourteen. In nearly all civilised countries compulsory attendance for children between these ages is now enforced. Corresponding to the 'elementary school' of Eng. there is the *Volkschule* of Ger., the *école primaire élémentaire* of France, and the 'common school' of the U.S.A. In these schools the E. given is designed to meet the needs of the poorer classes of the community, who are unable to extend the period of E. for their children. The higher elementary schools of Eng., the *Höhere Bürgerschule* of Ger., the *école primaire supérieure* of Fr., are designed to continue for one or two years the work of the primary school in a practical direction. Parallel to the public elementary schools there are also in Eng. private preparatory schools of various types, generally designed in order to secure continuity in the course of study for pupils proposing to proceed to secondary schools. These together with the preparatory and junior forms of secondary schools provide primary E. for the children of more well-to-do parents. The secondary school provides for the E. of boys and girls from the primary stage to an age varying from sixteen to nineteen, and may be divided into two classes : the first-grade schools, at which pupils remain until the age of eighteen or nineteen, many of them then proceeding to a university; and the second-grade schools, at which the pupils usually leave at sixteen or seventeen. In addition to the ordinary type of secondary school, there has come into existence a new type of school, offering a special training for vocational needs; in Eng. there are the technical and agricultural schools; in Ger. the *Gewerbe Schule;* and in America the industrial schools.

GERMANY.—In Germany state intervention in E. began at the time of the Reformation, and towards the end of the sixteenth century two states, Saxony and Würtemberg, had organised fairly complete educational systems in connection with the church. The Thirty Years' War had a disastrous effect on E., but in the eighteenth century the state system was revived in the two states above mentioned, and their example was followed by Hanover and Prussia. As early as 1717 a law was in force in Prussia requiring all children to attend school wherever schools were accessible, and a nominal fee for instruction was fixed. Twenty years later a grant for the establishment of schools was made by the state. In 1806, when Prussia lay at the feet of Napoleon, the control of E. was all that was left to that state by her conqueror, and in response to Fichte's appeal in his *Address to the German Nation,* a thorough system of national E. was founded by von Stein in 1807. A state leaving examination was instituted, and by 1834 candidates for the civil service

and the learned professions were required to pass this exam. In 1850 a law was passed making elementary E. free, and the teaching profession a branch of the civil service. The basis of Ger. elementary E. in its present form is the Prussian Code of Regulations of 1854, as modified by the Falk Laws of 1872. The classification of scholars is according to age. Attendance is compulsory on all children between the ages of six and fourteen, and if at the latter age the pupil has not attained a certain standard, he is bound to continue his education for two or three years either at the day school or at an evening or Sunday school. The secondary schools, with the exception

STEIN

of the Realschulen in Berlin, are organised almost entirely independently of the ordinary elementary schools, without any dovetailing of curriculum, and in such a way that clever boys have generally to leave the elementary school at nine years of age in order to enter the secondary school at the beginning of its quite different curriculum. There are two types of secondary schools, the *gymnasien* or classical schools, and the *real-gymnasien* or modern school. These again are divided into schools with a nine years' course and schools with a six years' course. That national culture should form the basis of E. was strongly insisted upon by the Ger. Emperor at the Berlin Conference of 1890.

FRANCE.—In France, as in most Catholic countries, state intervention was longer delayed. Elementary E. was practically non-existent before the Revolution, and the higher schools formed a bone of contention between the church and the gov. The Revolution, however, made a clean sweep, and a strongly centralised system of E. was established. There is now a very complete system of E. under the control of the Minister of Public Instruction. All schools, *primaire*, *secondaire*, and *supérieure*, are examined by the state. The system of elementary E. in force was organised in 1886. Public elementary instruction is free, and attendance is compulsory on all children from six to thirteen years of age. Teachers, in all but the largest towns, are state servants. Religious instruction in state schools has been abolished and replaced by moral instruction according to official curricula. In addition to the *écoles primaires élémentaires*, there is a very efficient system of higher elementary schools, *écoles primaires supérieures*, admission to which is accorded only to those who have obtained the elementary school leaving certificate. Secondary E. is carried on at the *lycées*, which are largely subsidised by the state, and *collèges* which are generally maintained by local authorities and are of a second-grade character. In 1902 the scheme of studies was reorganised. The course extends for seven years, divided into two periods of four and three years. The first period provides two kinds of curricula : (1) Latin, obligatory, and Gk., optional; (2) No Latin. At the end of the first period a state *certificat d'étude secondaire du premier degré* is granted. The second period provides a choice of four courses : (1) With Latin and Gk.; (2) Latin and modern languages; (3) Latin and science (these three continuing course 1 of the first period), and (4) Modern languages and science, continuing course 2 of the first period. There are also many technical schools and universities.

In *Denmark, Norway, Sweden, Austria, Switzerland, Holland*, and *Belgium*, elementary E. is free and compulsory. *Switzerland* has an admirably organised system, and the management of the schools is in the hands of each canton. Primary schools and secondary schools are provided in every district, and there are also numerous technical schools and several universities.

UNITED STATES.—E. in America is under popular control, and there is very great local freedom. Each state, and many of the large cities, has its own system, and provides its own schools and teachers. Compulsory attendance is in force in most states. The schools are divided into three kinds; primary for children from six to ten; grammar schools for those between ten and fourteen (these are grouped together as ' common schools ') and high schools from fourteen to eighteen. In all states E. in the first two grades is free, and some states provide free E. in the high schools also. The curriculum is very similar to that of Eng. schools, but more attention is paid to history and citizenship, and in the high schools physical science and modern languages receive more attention than in secondary schools of the same type in Eng. The length of the school year varies considerably in the different states, and is generally longer than in Eng. because the school term is nine continuous months with none of the long holiday breaks that are customary in England. The main holiday is for the three summer months, due to the great heat of that period. An interesting plan has recently been adopted by the city of Cleveland, in which city the public elementary schools are kept open through the summer vacation, and backward children are required to attend for four quarters of the year instead of three to make up their deficiencies. School buildings generally in the U.S.A. are fitted up extremely well with the most up-to-date educational appliances. Normal schools for the training of teachers are provided by many states, but there is no national standard of qualifications, each state granting its own diplomas, and special training in normal schools is not necessarily indispensable to obtain these. Many of the states have their own tax-supported state universities which are free to the youth of the states.

ENGLAND.—In contrast to the complete systems which have been conceived and established during comparatively recent times in other countries, the educational system in vogue in Eng. is the result of growth and adaptation, and also particularly of sectarian rivalry to obtain control of the young.

*Secondary Education.*—Even before the Reformation it seems probable that there was a fairly complete system of endowed schools, and although the majority were connected with ecclesiastical orders, such as the monastic schools, chantry schools, and choristers' schools, there is reason to believe that there existed also many schools supported by secular foundations. At the Reformation the dissolution of monasteries reduced the number of schools very considerably, many of the schools attached to these institutions perishing irretrievably, though a few lingered on though deprived of their endowments. In 1548 all the endowed schools in Eng., other than the cathedral schools, were threatened, and the vast majority destroyed by the Act for the dissolution of colleges and chantries. But the spirit of the Reformation unquestionably inspired a considerable amount of individual educational effort, and many schools were founded, and in many instances the old foundations were renewed. The Act of Uniformity (1662) and the Five Mile Act (1665), prohibiting all teaching in public or private schools, except by Church of Eng. men, had the effect of creating large numbers of private schools, as it was held in the courts that the law could only be enforced in the case of endowed grammar schools. No dissenter, however, was allowed to be a master or a member of the governing body of an endowed school, and even a dissenting pupil had to go to church and learn the catechism. The endowed schools, therefore, were under the sole control of the church, with the result that at the end of the eighteenth century they were in a worse condition than at any time in their history. The heavily endowed schools, which were supported by the aristocracy, alone flourished. For many years many schools existed—without scholars, or with two or three only: many were definitely converted into elementary schools (Grammar Schools Act, 1840), and poor ones at that. Some improvement was made after the report of Lord Brougham's commission, but the Public Schools Commission Report of 1863, and the Schools Inquiry Report of 1868, showed a lamentable condition of affairs. The Endowed Schools Act of 1869 remedied this state of affairs very considerably by the removal of religious disabilities and by widening the curriculum. At the same time many of the old foundations were used to establish girls' high schools. The affairs of the larger public schools were fairly efficiently dealt with by the Public Schools Act of 1868. The Schools Inquiry Commission also submitted proposals for the general administrative organisation of a system of secondary E. But these proposals were not included in the Act. In 1874 the control of the endowed secondary schools was transferred to the Charity Commissioners. In 1889 the Technical Instruction Act gave powers to county, borough, and urban district councils to levy a rate not exceeding a penny in the £ in aid of technical or manual instruction,

and in 1890 technical instruction was mentioned as one of the purposes to which contributions paid to local authorities in respect of the beer and spirit duties might be applied. A liberal interpretation of technical instruction allowed of the inclusion of mathematical and physical science and modern languages under that heading. The Department of Science and Art, formed in 1851 to supervise and administer grants to the science and art classes, which were being established all over the country, was also aiding secondary E. by grants towards mathematical, scientific, and even literary studies. In 1899 the Department of Science and Art was united to the E. department, which then became the Board of Education with a president and parliamentary secretary, and the powers of the Charity Commissioners in regard to educational endowments were transferred to this new board, but it was not until 1902 that any real steps towards organising secondary E. were taken. The Act of 1902 provided the local authorities with power 'to take such steps as seem desirable, after consultation with the Board of Education, to supply or aid the supply of E. other than elementary, and to promote the general co-ordination of all forms of E.' For this purpose the application of the money received by the Local Education Authority under the Local Taxation (Customs and Excise) Act of 1890 (popularly known as 'whisky money'), hitherto optional was made compulsory, and power was given to levy a rate. By the Education Act of 1918, the limit of the rate to 2d. in the £ was repealed, which Act also provided that the state's contribution should not be less than one-half of the approved expenditure of the local Education Authority. A council must not require any particular form of religious instruction or observance, but facilities may be given at the request of parents for any particular religious instruction to be given at such times and under such conditions as the council thinks desirable, not, however, at the council's expense. Since the Act has been in force, great progress has been made in secondary E. Before then no public provision for secondary E. as such had been made, though indirect financial aid had been given under The Technical Instruction Act. In 1907 greatly increased grants were placed at the disposal of the Board of Education for the purpose of secondary E. In order to qualify for the higher grant which was then offered, schools are required to provide 25 per cent. of free places for scholars from public elementary schools. This percentage is now (1931) sometimes increased, and experience in the past decade has shown that the system makes for efficiency and for a higher standard of education. A secondary school, as defined by the Board, is a school which offers to each of its pupils a progressive course of instruction (with the requisite organisation, curriculum, teaching staff, and equipment) in the subjects necessary to a good general E. on lines suitable for pupils of an age-range at least as wide as from twelve to seventeen, and with at least more than twenty pupils over twelve years of age. The number of secondary schools recognised as efficient by the Board of Education in 1912 included 862 schools in receipt of grants, and 96 schools dispensing with the grant. In 1928 the number of secondary schools in receipt of grants was over 1300; while the number of free-place pupils, now annually about 130,000, is only about 33,000 below the total number of pupils in the secondary schools recognised as efficient in 1912. The amount of the grant has been increased from £5 each pupil over 12 years of age to £7; while in addition, there are special grants in respect of advanced courses. Official inspection is an essential condition of the grant and this inspection extends to all the activities of the school.

*Technical Education.*—As has already been seen, technical E., since 1851, was greatly assisted by the Science and Art Department, which instituted examinations in the various branches of technology, but it was not until 1878, with the foundation of the City and Guilds of London Institute for the Advancement of Technical Education, that it was organised to a large extent. This institute extended the examinations and established many schools and the great Royal College of Technology since incorporated in the Imperial College of Science and Technology. The Technical Instruction Act of 1889, giving local authorities permission to raise a penny rate for the purpose and the allocation of 'whisky money' to the extent of three quarters of a million to technical instruction, resulted in the establishment of flourishing institutions devoted to this form of E. all over the country.

*Examinations.*—The confused and elaborate system of external examination which has gradually grown up to provide a test for the relative efficiency of E. in Eng. secondary schools is the result of state neglect in this as in other departments of

secondary E. The Department of Science and Art, founded in 1851, instituted examinations, which were, however, of too specialised a character to affect many schools other than the science schools which that department established. In 1853 a chartered association of schoolmasters, the College of Preceptors, began to examine pupils in Latin, Fr., Eng., history, geography, mathematics, drawing or one science subject, and Gk., and laid the foundation of much useful effort. In 1857 Sir Thomas Acland and Dr. Temple held an examination at Exeter, which proved so successful in its results that in the same year the university of Oxford appointed delegates to conduct similar examinations on a permanent footing in the future. Thus were instituted the Oxford Local Examinations, and the following year Cambridge University followed suit. Both universities issue junior, senior, and honour certificates, open to candidates of all ages (with the exception of honours certificates, which is restricted) and, since 1870, to both sexes. The example of the older has since been followed by the newer universities. The more important secondary schools, however, demanded a more specially directed effort on the part of the universities, and in 1870 the Headmasters' Conference appointed a committee to confer with the older universities upon the institution of leaving examinations corresponding to the *Abiturienten-examen*, provided by the state in Ger. This resulted in 1873 in the formation of a joint board granting upon examination certificates exempting pupils from the first or matriculation examination of the universities. In 1878 this examination was extended to girls' schools, and in 1883 a lower certificate for younger candidates was instituted. This examination has perhaps more than any other agency stimulated and raised the efficiency of Eng. Public schools. The Northern Universities have also adopted a similar plan of an exemption certificate. The University of London, founded in 1846, has also provided by its matriculation examination a recognised certificate, which serves as a preliminary qualification for many professions. The university has also done excellent work in the inspection of schools.

*Elementary Education.*—Prior to the Reformation what little E. for the poor existed in Eng. was oral instruction in the doctrine and duties of the Faith, given by the parish priest. The conception of elementary E. adapted to the needs of the masses of the people was unfamiliar, E. being regarded as a privilege of the select few. With the rise of industrialism, however, during the seventeenth century, the need for some form of elementary E. became very apparent, and a universal system of elementary schools was advocated by Hoole and Petty. In 1699 Dr. Bray founded the Society for Promoting Christian Knowledge, and by 1741 nearly 2000 charity schools had been established throughout the country by the agency of this society. Many schools of the same type, but with a different religious bias, were founded by dissenters. These schools were expressly intended for the poor, and teachers were forbidden to take money from the children's friends. Girls were admitted as well as boys, being instructed in reading, sewing, knitting, etc., while the boys were taught to read and write and the elementary rules of arithmetic. The qualifications of the teachers, however, left very much to be desired, and an objectionable feature of the schools was the definitely charitable character presented, the children wearing a special uniform, which had the effect of producing a servile spirit and of pauperising the parents. In 1784 Sunday-schools were founded by Robert Raikes, which for many years provided all the E., both religious and secular, which many children received. In addition there were numerous private 'schools,' kept by dames who received and 'minded' the children for a small weekly fee. The beginning of the nineteenth century saw the rise of voluntary societies for the E. of the poorer classes, chief among them being the British and Foreign Schools Society and the National Society for Promoting the Education of the Poor in the Principles of the Established Church. In 1802 Joseph Lancaster, a Quaker, published a pamphlet in which the wretched condition of the schools existing for the children of the poor is described; in this pamphlet he tells how he founded his school in the Borough Road in 1798, and invented the monitorial system, by which the older boys, under his supervision, were organised to teach the rest. The E. given, though essentially of a religious character, was unsectarian. About the same time Dr. Andrew Bell had been led to adopt the same methods of employing pupils to instruct one another in a school in Madras. The religious instruction given in Dr. Bell's school was of a definitely Church of England character, and therein lay the main difference between the two systems. From these institutions were founded the

Royal Lancasterian Society (1808), later known as the British and Foreign School Society, and the National Society (1811). The National Society had ampler funds at their disposal, and their schools were soon spread all over the country. The first real step towards state intervention in E. was not taken until 1883. In 1816 a committee of the House of Commons, presided over by Brougham, had been appointed to inquire into the E. of the poorer classes of London, and reported strongly on the necessity for providing means of E. Nothing, however, was done until 1833, when a grant of £20,000 towards school buildings was made by the House of Commons and placed in the hands of the British and National societies for distribution. The grants, however, made no provision for either the maintenance, instruction in, or inspection of, schools. In 1835 Lord Brougham brought forward a series of resolutions on the necessity for parliamentary encouragement of the foundation of schools and the provision of training colleges for teachers. In 1839 a committee of Council on Education, presided over by the Lord President and four other ministers, was formed to administer parliamentary grants for the purpose of elementary E. in Eng. and Wales. In 1840 the right of inspection of schools was made a necessary condition towards qualifying for a grant, but it was agreed that all Church of Eng. schools should be inspected by clergymen approved by the Archbishop of Canterbury, while the British Schools should be visited by laymen approved by the Society. In the same year a training college for teachers was established at Battersea, to which in 1842 grants were obtained from parliament. This college was taken over by the National Society in 1843, and has continued a successful career ever since. The Borough Road Training College was established about the same time by the British and Foreign Society, which extended and adapted Lancaster's old school for this purpose. In 1842 an attempt was made in connection with the Factory Regulations Act to provide schools for the poor out of the local rates, but a provision that the religious teaching should be in accordance with the Church of England raised such opposition amongst the Nonconformists that the attempt was defeated. In 1853 the Council on Education was formed into the Education Department with a staff of officials and clerks, and in 1856 a vice-president of the Council was appointed, who should be responsible to the

House of Commons for the distribution of grants, which had until then been dispensed on the responsibility of a departmental committee. By 1858 the E. grant had grown to £663,400, and the rapid increase resulted in a Royal Commission being appointed to inquire into the state of E. The report issued in 1861 recommended: (1) That the system of direct personal payments to teachers and pupil teachers should be abolished, and all grants should be paid to school managers, who should be left free to make their own contracts; (2) that grants should be made dependent upon efficiency to be tested by a searching examination of all children in aided schools; (3) that part of the grant should be furnished out of the local rates. In 1862 Robert Lowe, then vice-president of the Council, introduced the famous 'Revised Code,' which made 'payment by results' the basis on which grants were to be made, the test being an examination in reading, writing, and arithmetic. It also abolished the personal relations between the teacher and the department, so far as the annual grant was concerned, but did not adopt the suggestion of a local rate. The year 1870 marked a revolution in the elementary educational system of this country. In that year Mr. Forster, the vice-president of the Council, carried an Act, providing that in any district where, within a certain period, sufficient school accommodation was not provided, a school board, under the control of the Education Department, was to be formed with power to raise money from local rates for the purpose of supplying such school accommodation. In boroughs the school boards were elected by the parliamentary electorate; in parishes by all who paid rates. These boards were empowered to make attendance compulsory, but this was not insisted upon. The Act also provided that in all public elementary schools whatever religious teaching was given should be imparted either at the beginning or end of the school session, and that an unbroken period of two hours in each session should be given to secular instruction : in all schools provided or maintained by public school boards religious instruction was to be entirely undenominational in character. In 1876 the power to enforce compulsory attendance became general and the leaving age was raised from thirteen to fourteen, unless the child passed the examination standard for exemption before that age. In 1880 an Act was passed making it compulsory on school authorities to enforce attendance.

By the code of 1882 the curriculum of the infant school was enlarged by the inclusion of object lessons and kindergarten occupations; while in the senior schools the grants for such subjects as English history, geography and elementary science were graduated according to the quality of the instruction given. The general efficiency of the school, as well as the number of passes obtained in examination, was also taken into account in awarding the grant. In 1886 a Royal Commission was appointed to inquire into the working of the Education Act, and issued in 1888 two reports. The higher standard of efficiency in elementary schools, which had resulted from the establishment of school boards, had made the financial position of many voluntary schools untenable in spite of liberal aid from gov., and the majority recommended that voluntary schools should be enabled to draw subsidies from the local rates, but a strong minority protested against such a course and the suggestion was not carried out. The commission also recommended that the method of individual examination should be superseded by a general test of the quality of instruction given, and effect to this recommendation was given in the Code of 1890, when the grant was based upon the average attendance. The following year elementary E. was made free to all children between the ages of three and fourteen. In 1900 the system of making grants for individual subjects was abolished (except in the case of domestic and manual instruction), and a block 'grant' per head was instituted. The annual examination was also abolished in favour of inspection without notice. By the Act of 1902 all elementary schools were placed under the local authority; in urban districts with a population exceeding 20,000 the urban council is the local authority for E.; in boroughs of more than 10,000, it is the borough council; and elsewhere the county council is the authority. The council is required to appoint an E. committee in accordance with a scheme approved by the Board of Education. The chief duties of the councils as E. authorities relate to (1) the management of schools; (2) the appointment and direction of teachers; (3) financial control over educational machinery. Each school is required to have a board of managers not exceeding six in number, four of whom are appointed by the E. committee of the council, and two by the minor local E. authority (where such exists) in the case of 'provided' schools, i.e. schools taken over from the old school boards; in the case of 'non-provided' schools four of the managers are appointed under the trust deed of the school and two by the E. authority. In 1906 and 1907 power was given to local authorities to provide for the feeding of necessitous children in Eng. and Wales and for the medical inspection of all children in elementary schools.

In 1913, Lord Haldane, the Lord Chancellor, foreshadowed a 'colossal scheme of national E.' The broad outlines of the gov. proposal were, roughly, to lengthen the period of elementary E., and abolish the half-time system under fourteen years of age; to widen the curriculum, especially in regard to manual and technical instruction; to extend medical treatment and the provision of school meals to necessitous children; to increase the number of free places in secondary schools, and provide for every elementary school child whose capacity justifies it the chance of further E.; to increase the number of civic universities of the type of Liverpool, Leeds, etc.; and to raise the number and status of teachers in both primary and secondary schools. Lord Haldane also laid stress on the necessity for improving the status and qualifications of teachers. He also hinted at a settlement of the religious difficulty.

The Education Act, 1918, frequently called the H. A. L. Fisher Act, repealed in 1921, and re-enacted as part of the Consolidation Act of that year, made several important changes in the educational system of Great Britain. The Act, as shown by its preamble, aims at 'the establishment of a national system of education for all persons capable of profiting thereby'; and local authorities, called upon to prepare suitable schemes under the Act, are advised to consult parents and other persons locally concerned in order that the most convenient arrangements may be made. The Act also gives local authorities power to establish Nursery Schools for children from the ages of two to five. The most revolutionary part of the measure was the change in the age for compulsory school attendance. This was not only raised from twelve to fourteen years, but powers were granted to local authorities to extend this age to fifteen in those places where such an extension would seem desirable. Part-time attendances were entirely abolished, and in order to carry this into effect the Act declared that 'no child should be employed in a factory unless legally so employed.' Provision was made

for the establishment of central schools for more intelligent children with the evident intention that there should be a possible avenue for the really brilliant scholar from the humblest position to the university. Local authorities are also encouraged to provide means by which suitable children could be transferred and prepared for higher education, and with this object in view the Act removes the limit on contributions from the rates for all education other than elementary. The Act establishes the principle that education should not cease before the age of eighteen, and provision is made for the establishment of schools for young persons between the ages of fourteen and eighteen, the compulsory hours of attendances to be not less than thirty-two in the year. The Act also urges on authorities the importance of physical training and gymnastics as well as adequate medical supervision. Special provisions are also contained in the Act for the supply and training of teachers. On the whole the Act had worked well, but the trade depression of 1923 affected the cases of young persons over the age of fourteen where local authorities were financially unable to provide facilities contemplated by the Act. The passage of this Act synchronised with much discussion on the payments and pensions of teachers and in 1920 many changes were made under a National Scheme which improved the outlook of teachers in all state-aided schools, the Burnham Scale of Pay, as the new rates were called from the fact that Lord Burnham (q.v.) was chairman of the Scheme. This scale increased the pay and pensions of teachers at a time when salaries and wages were higher in most other occupations than they have been at any period since. The scheme has worked out well as a whole and certainly gives the teacher an enhanced status. The duty of preparing older children for work in technical occupations has received increasing attention by the Educational authorities. Such schools as Sibford School in Oxfordshire where technical education forms a large part of the curriculum have influenced both elementary and advanced education (see TECHNICAL EDUCATION). The post-war period gave a great impetus to university training both in the modern universities and in the two historic seats of learning, Oxford and Cambridge. Broadly speaking, this new enthusiasm was practically all centred in scientific and practical studies. Great extensions took place in Liverpool, Bristol, Leeds and Manchester, while such cities as Southampton, Reading, Nottingham and Exeter made definite movements toward securing their own Charters. In any educational review of the post-war period it is important to recognise the great influence of the commercial world upon higher education. The war, in developing towards its close into a struggle of chemists and scientists, impressed the heads of business and trading concerns with the belief that commerce would derive most benefits in the future from the more specialised education of those of its men and women employees who held key positions. Although the enthusiasm for this new faith has somewhat cooled in the years of trade depression from 1923 onward the zeal for higher education has survived among the greater commercial and banking houses, many of whom insist on a matriculation 'pass' for entering to the office staff, and prefer applicants with university degrees for higher posts. (*See also* ADULT EDUCATION.)

WALES.—Until recent years Wales was included with Eng. for the purposes of educational administration, but the remarkable national revival witnessed towards the end of the nineteenth century led to a demand for a national system of higher E., and the Welsh Intermediate Education Act of 1889 provided for the establishment of joint E. committees, nominated by the county council and the lord president of the council in every county in Wales, which for this purpose was held to include Monmouthshire. These committees had power to raise money by a halfpenny county rate, to which was added a treasury grant not exceeding the amount raised, for the purpose of establishing intermediate and technical schools. These E. committees were superseded by the local E. authorities established by the Education Act of 1902. The revised regulations relating to secondary schools were applied to Wales in 1908. The system of E. beyond elementary is much the same as in Eng., though the schools are under earlier statutory provision, and are called 'Intermediate' in many cases. There is a Central Welsh Board for Secondary E. A Welsh department of the Board of Education was established in 1907, with a permanent secretary and a chief inspector.

IRELAND.—In Ireland state intervention in E. began with the foundation of schools by the Elizabethan gov. in pursuance of their Anglicising policy. Until 1802 there was a great lack of local effort in E.,

but in that year the Catholic Society of the Christian Brothers was instituted, which continues its great educational efforts. In 1811 also was founded the Kildare Place Society, which attempted to provide schools upon a compromise between the Catholic and Protestant religions. Both societies received grants from the Treasury in aid of E. until 1833, when a national system of elementary schools was established under a board of commissioners, among whose powers were those of aiding in the erection of schools, appointing inspectors, and awarding grants to teachers, and of providing a training college, and of issuing text-books. In 1861 special provision was made that the membership of the board should be equally divided amongst Catholics and Protestants. The schools are now almost entirely definitely denominational, either Catholic or Protestant. In the Irish Free State primary E. is directed by the state. Secondary education is in private hands, and is for the most part conducted by Religious Orders. School attendance is compulsory for children from six to fourteen years. State grants to Irish University institutions were transferred from the Treasury to the Irish state governments (Free State and N. Irish) as from April, 1922. In N. Ireland there are some 1900 public elementary schools, and about seventy-two preparatory, intermediate, and secondary schools recognised by the Ministry of Education. There are also 135 Centres of Technical Instruction.

SCOTLAND.—E. has always received marked attention in Scotland. Even as early as 1494 freeholders were required by a statute of King James IV. to send their heirs to school to acquire 'perfect Latin.' In 1560 the Church Assembly decreed, under the influence of John Knox, that every church in 'any town of repute' should have attached to it a Latin school, and in every parish of country districts there should be a teacher of 'first rudiments.' In large towns, moreover, there was to be a college for 'logic, rhetoric, and the tongues.' In 1696 parish schools in connection with the Established Church of Scotland were set up by parliamentary statute, and a tax was levied upon landowners for their support. The burgh schools or academies were also established in most towns, and came under the control of the municipal authorities. In 1839 the system of inspection and annual grants to schools was established in Eng., and applied to Scotland. Until 1872 educational legislation extended to both countries alike, though slight modifications and allowances were made in the actual working of the schemes in Scotland. In 1872 the Scottish Education Act made the provision of school boards universal and the property and control of the existing schools, burgh and parish, were transferred to them. Compulsory attendance for all children from five to thirteen was enforced. The age has since been raised to fourteen. The Act also distinguished between three types of school, the elementary school, the higher grade school, and the higher class school, all of which have primary departments. Powers were also given to school boards to provide meals and medical attendance, defray cost of conveyance in outlying parts, etc., and the Act enabled them to make bye-laws requiring attendance at continuation classes up to seventeen years of age. In 1885 the Scottish and Eng. Education Departments were separated, and the former has since had its own committee and secretary. In 1888 a state system of leaving certificate was introduced into the higher class schools, and was soon extended to all schools doing higher work. There is also a qualifying examination for transition from primary grade to the intermediate course provided by the higher grade and higher class schools, and the supplementary course provided by the elementary school, and an intermediate certificate for transition from the intermediate to the post-intermediate course of the higher class school.

There are now about 2900 primary schools with accommodation for about 865,000 pupils. For E. beyond elementary, there are preparatory and secondary departments under the same Commissioners and local authorities as the elementary schools. There are over 200 preparatory departments with some 75,000 pupils on the register and 250 secondary departments with 78,000 pupils. The authorities make a point of securing honours graduates as far as possible. All teachers are certificated.

BIBLIOGRAPHY.—For the history of E., Mahaffy's *Old Greek Education;* Laurie's *Pre-Christian Education;* A. S. Wilkins's *Roman Education;* Compayre's *History of Pedagogy;* Quick's *Educational Reformers;* Davidson's *History of Education;* Oscar Browning's *Educational Theories;* Prof. Adams' *Evolution of Educational Theory.*

Shuttleworth's *Four Periods of Public Education;* Leach's *English Schools at the Reformation;* Rigg's *National Education and Public Elementary Schools,* and Montmorency's *Progress of Education in England,* deal particularly with the history of Eng. E., and the Report of the Schools Inquiry Commission of 1867, and the Report of the Select Committee. April 1887, are also useful for this purpose, as is Norwood and Hope's *Higher Education of Boys in England.* On the theory and practice of E., Laurie's *Studies in the History of Educational Opinion from the Renaissance;* Raymont's *Principles of Education;* Thring's *Theory and Practice of Teaching;* Fitch's *Educational Aims and Methods;* James's *Talks to Teachers on Psychology and some of Life's Ideals;* Sully's *Handbook of Psychology,* and Magnus' *Educational Aims and Efforts.* In the Ger. language Stürm, Fichte, Herder, Richter, von Raumer, Beneke, Grube, Herbart, Hegel, Kant, and Ziller have contributed much valuable thought, and in Fr. there is Rousseau's *Emile;* Brunn's *Manuel de Pédagogie;* Jacolot's *Enseignement Universel,* and Charbonneau's *Cours Théorique.* Amongst American writers on E. we have Henry Barnard, Prof. Payne, Prof. W. James, Elmer Brown, Horace Mann, Miss Peabody, Prof. O'Shea, Dr. James Russell, and Dr. J. W. A. Young amongst many others. An excellent account of Pestalozzi's life and work is to be found in Holman's *Pestalozzi,* while in Adams's *Herbartian Psychology* and Hayward's *Critics of Herbartianism* will be found an exposition of Herbartian theories. Sully's *Studies in Childhood* and Mumford's *Dawn of Character* are intensely interesting studies of child life ; Prof. Findlay's *The School* is an admirable little book on organisation ; and lastly all phases of educational history and theory are dealt with in *The Teachers' Cyclopædia of Education* (7 vols.).

**Education, Agricultural.** By the terms of the Technical Institutions Act of 1889, agricultural subjects were directly included as subjects to which grants could be made and 'whisky money' applied, while manual instruction was defined as comprehending instruction in 'processes of agriculture.' A Board of Agriculture was also created the same year with powers to distribute a parliamentary grant of £5000 for the promotion of A. E., and to undertake the inspection of any schools other than elementary, in which instruction is given connected in any way with agriculture or forestry. Such education was not at first taken up as earnestly in England as in Wales and Scotland, but the Modern University movement on one hand and the activities of County Councils on the other presently laid the foundations of a widespread national movement in England, while in Ireland such pioneers as Sir Horace Plunkett placed the subject high among new national interests. In the higher education for agriculture, degrees are granted by many universities, which necessitate a course of almost three years, and the training is highly scientific. A more technical education is provided by County Councils in special agricultural schools, while, in addition to these, there is a custom which has developed since the Great War of practical education on the actual farms by students, who pay a premium and under a system analogous to apprenticeship for longer or shorter terms. Some of the educational schools, especially those connected with the Universities, are advisory centres to give assistance to agriculturists within their areas, and as such receive grants that become of service for educational purposes. Agricultural Research is greatly linked up with A. E., as analyses of soils, effects of chemicals on crops and local insect life, form some of the bases of inquiry and teaching. Although England was far behind other nations and her sister countries until quite recently, the energy and enterprise that have been displayed in her colleges in the scientific part of this training have given her agricultural diplomas a high reputation throughout the world. The chief agricultural schools in Great Britain are the Royal Agricultural College, Cirencester ; the Agricultural College, Aspatria, Cumberland ; the Dauntsey Agricultural School, West Lavington, Wilts ; the Adams Agricultural College, Newport, Salop ; the South-Eastern Agricultural College, Wye, Kent ; Uckfield College, Sussex ; Holmes Chapel School, Cheshire ; the agricultural department of the University College, Reading ; the Armstrong College, Newcastle, and the Harris Institute, Preston. Agricultural departments are also attached to the universities of Cambridge, Leeds, Edinburgh, Glasgow, and Aberdeen, and the university colleges of Aberystwith and Bangor.

**Education, Technical,** see TECHNICAL EDUCATION.

**Education, University,** see UNIVERSITIES.

**Edward the Confessor** (1004-10 to 1066), apparently the second son of Ethelred the Unready and his wife Emma of Normandy. The greater part of his early life was spent in exile, since, on the death of his father, the throne of England passed into the hands of a Danish dynasty. His mother married Canute (Cnut) after the death of Ethelred the Unready, and by him had two sons, Harold and Hardicnut. In 1041 Hardicnut invited Edward from the Norman to the English court, an invitation which carried with it recognition of his claim to the English throne. In 1042 Hardicnut died, and E., not without some opposition, was elected king of England. His reign was one long story of England struggling against the influence of Normandy. His long exile in Normandy had made him more Norman than Saxon, and the atmosphere of his court was almost entirely Norman. The most prominent English family, the Godwins, struggled against this, but recognition of the Saxon point of view meant recognition of the unspoken claim of Harold, Godwin's son, to the throne of England. E.'s reign is chiefly noted for the rule of the Godwins and the visit of William the Bastard of Normandy, to whom E. is alleged to have promised the crown. E. was more priest than king. He was a man of ability, but was unable to use that ability in the right direction. He died in 1066, on Jan. 6, after practically nominating Harold to the English throne. He was canonised, with the title of Confessor, in 1161 by Pope Alexander III. Had he lived within the shadow of the cloisters his life might easily have been of value and service, but as a king-monk he was entirely out of place.

**Edward I., the Elder** (d. 924), King of the West Saxons. E. was the second son of Alfred the Great ; he succeeded his father in 899. After a succession of battles with the Danes, E. was chosen as ' father and lord ' by the Scottish, Northumbrian, and Welsh kings.

**Edward II., the Martyr** (926-978), King of the English, whose short reign was mostly marked by the anti-monastic reaction. His assassination at Corfe Castle in Dorchester was probably arranged by his step-mother, Ælfthyth, who was anxious to place her own son, Æthelred, upon the throne. Shortly after his death he was popularly esteemed to be both a saint and a martyr.

**Edward I.,** King of England, and eldest son of Henry III., was b. in June 1239 at Westminster. He was married in 1254 to Eleanor of Castile, and on the occasion of his marriage was invested with the baronetcies of Gascony and Wales. It was in Gascony that he first received that training as a warrior which was to stand him in such good stead later on. During the baronial troubles of his father's reign, his attitude may best be defined as defending the royal claims and prerogatives, whilst at the same time realising the justice of the claims of Simon de Montfort, and later incorporating them with his own views. He was at an early age distinguished as a warrior and a general, and took a prominent part in the Baronial Wars. He was responsible for the overthrow of the Royalist forces at Lewes, since by the wild charge which swept his sworn enemies, the Londoners, from the field, he so weakened the Royalist force that on his return from the pursuit he found his father's forces defeated, and surrendered himself a prisoner. He escaped from prison in 1265, and defeated Simon de Montfort at the battle of Evesham (1265). After the Dictum of Kenilworth had practically ended the civil strife, it is almost safe to say that E.'s reign begins, since he is influential enough to be able to prohibit the misrule of the earlier days of his father's reign. In 1270 he set out on a crusade, and returning to Europe in 1272, after a narrow escape from death at the hands of an assassin, he learnt of his father's death. The principle of primogeniture may be said to have been safely established by his recognition as King of England during his absence. E. was regarded by his subjects as their first truly English king, and certainly his policy was thoroughly English, even though his speech and ideals were not. He was a tall, good-looking man, and has been described by at least one authority as ' every inch a king.' His reign is important from every point of view. He instituted, or caused to be instituted, numerous legal and social reforms. He adopted an ideal and essentially insular home policy. He carried out to the best of his ability a foreign policy which redounded to the honour and glory of England. He was crowned in Aug. 1274, having spent the intervening two years in settling affairs in Italy, France, and Gascony. His first trouble at home came from Wales, and he was able to commence his policy of creating a ' united Great Britain ' by annexing Wales after the second Welsh War, which ended in the overthrow and death of the last Llewellyn (1282). The Statute of Rhuddlan made Wales an English possession. Between 1284 and 1290 the time was occupied with the initiation of new legislation. E. was determined to be king not only in name but in reality, and his legislation tended towards that end, incorporating perhaps also to a certain extent the ideal of ' what touches all should be approved of all.' The chief measures that may be mentioned are : The abolition of the office of Justiciar, leading to the organisation of the three common law courts, the Assize of Winchester (a nation in arms at the disposal of the

king), the Statute of *Mortmain*, and *Quia Emptores* (a means of preventing subinfeudation). It is perhaps merely coincidence that all the great legislative reforms should cease with the death of Badnell, the chancellor, and that by far the most stormy period of E.'s reign should follow that death. The next great trouble of the reign was the interference of E. in Scottish affairs. In 1286 Alexander III. had died, leaving as his heir the Maid of Norway, his granddaughter, who was only six years of age. In pursuance of his ideal of a united Great Britain, E. planned a marriage between the Maid and his son, Edward of Carnarvon. The marriage was accepted in Scotland, but in 1290 the Maid died, and the affairs of Scotland became chaotic. E. as arbitrator at Nottingham chose John Baliol as king of Scotland, out of a dozen claimants, the most prominent of whom was Robert Bruce. Baliol did homage to E. as his overlord, but the Scottish people, resenting keenly the attitude of E., forced Baliol into open rebellion, and E. invaded Scotland. By the end of 1296 he had reduced Scotland, and at Brechin had forced Baliol to surrender the crown. He appointed his own regents for Scotland and departed southward, taking with him the famous Stone of Destiny. In 1297 Scotland, led by the hero Wallace, was again in rebellion. Northern England was harried, and at Stirling Surrey and Cressingham were totally defeated. E. hurried back, and in 1298 overthrew Wallace at Falkirk. The struggle still continued, but E. may be said to have been master of Scotland between 1298 and 1306. In the meantime affairs at home and abroad had not been going well. In 1295 was called the Model Parliament. In 1297 and 1298 came his troubles with the clergy under Winchelsea, and the barons under Boyd and Bohun. The taxation of the period was excessive, and strong though E. was, the barons and the people wrung from him the *Confirmatio Cartarum* and the *De Tallagio non Concedendo*. In 1299 he had married the sister of the King of France. In 1305 Wallace was captured and executed, and in the following year Bruce murdered Comyn, and seized the crown of Scotland. E. hurried northward, but he was failing fast in health, and in July 1307 he died at Burgh-on-Sands. He ordered his body to be borne before the army until Scotland was conquered, but his graceless son sent it down to Westminster for burial. On his tomb is inscribed *Edwardus Primus Malleus Scotorum hic est.* He may best be described as a man of stern character, jealous of his honour and of the honour of his country, true to his word when it suited his end, and only then. When it was necessary, E. did not hesitate to break his pledged oath, and his motto, *Pactum serva*, may be almost regarded as a fine ideal which the spirit of the age made it impossible for him to attain. *See* Lives by E. Jenks and R. B. Seeley.

**Edward II.**, King of England, was *b.* in April 1284, and was the first of the English crown princes to bear the title of Prince of Wales. He succeeded his father in July 1307, and disobeyed the last command to continue the war with Scotland. Weak

EDWARD II.
(From the tomb at Gloucester Cathedral)

and incapable, his reign is one long record of his struggle with the barons. His favouritism of Piers Gaveston was most unpopular, and the honours showered upon the favourite cost Gaveston his life. The barons, forming a committee, drew up the Ordinances which E. was forced to accept (1318). Two important constitutional points were settled in this reign : (1) That grants of aid should be preceded by redress of grievances ; (2) that the consent of parliament consisted not only of the consent of the barons but of the people as well. In 1326 Isabella, the queen, who had been in France with her son (Edward), returned, landed at Orwell, and marched against the king. The Despensers, favourites for the moment, were captured and executed, and the king was deposed. In 1327 he was

murdered in Berkeley Castle. Outside England, E. had shown his weakness in the total defeat of the English army at Bannockburn in 1314, a victory which was followed up by the capture of Berwick, and resulted in the practical independence of Scotland. *See* H. Baker's *Chronicle ;* Stubb's *Chronicle ; Originalia Rolls.*

**Edward III.**, son of Edward II., *b.* in 1312 and crowned in 1327. In 1328 he married Philippa of Hainault. During the early years of his reign Isabella and Mortimer retained the real power, until in 1330 he banished his mother and executed Mortimer. He then made peace with France in order to turn his attention to Scotland, where in the early years of his reign (1330–36) he fought three campaigns, in which he defeated the Scots and forced Edward Baliol to do homage to him. After each campaign, however, the Scots rallied, and E.'s attacks on Scotland were stopped by the outbreak of war with France. His formal claim to the throne of France in right of his mother was correctly regarded as a pretext. The war was essentially a commercial war, and was fought by Edward because he desired to retain the Flemish woollen trade, and also because he was deeply imbued with the ideals of chivalry and regarded himself as a warrior king. He also probably adopted the style of King of France in order to obtain the allegiance of the Flemings. The war opened with the battle of Sluys (1340), a naval victory for England. The next few years were not so successful, but in 1346 was fought the battle of Crécy, which resulted in the overthrow of the French army and the vindication of the tactics of the English and the downfall of feudalism on the Continent. In the following year Calais fell into the hands of the English, and in the previous year the battle of Neville's Cross had delivered David, King of Scotland, a prisoner to the English queen. The outbreak of the Black Death in England in 1349 put an end to the war for some time, and resulted also in the changing of the labour market in England. The relationship between the lords of the manor and the inhabitants changed, and although the Statute of Labourers tried to fix wages, it was found to be really unworkable. In 1355 war was renewed, and Edward the Black Prince won a great victory at Poitiers. The French king, John, became prisoner and was taken to England. In 1360 the Treaty of Bretigny was signed, and E. gave up his pretensions to the French throne and received Aquitaine and Ponthieu as a sovereign prince. The Scottish king had been released in 1357 on the pay-nent of ransom, and the French king in 1360. The latter, however, finding t impossible to raise the ransom, returned to England, and died there a prisoner in 1364. War again broke out in 1369, and dragged on not very successfully until 1377. In that year Edward the Black Prince died early in June, to be followed by his father towards the end of the month. The latter years of his reign had been years of decadence. E. had fallen under the influence of Alice Perrers, his mistress, and the power had passed largely into the hands of John, Duke of Gloucester, who was not altogether enlightened or unscrupulous. But the reign had been distinguished for the setting up of a sound commerce and for the beginning of the revolt against the Roman Church. The Church had been shown to be lax, too wealthy, and too idle; the Lollards increased the activity of the churchmen and gave them the necessary spur which was to carry them to 1530. The Statute of Præmunire showed the setting of the current towards separation from the Roman Church. The greatest change, however, was the change in the relationship of labourer and master. *See* Lives by W. Longman, W. Warburton, and J. Mackinnon.

**Edward IV.** (1442–83), son of Richard, Duke of York, and Cicely Neville, *b.* at Rouen on April 28. He bore in his youth the title of Earl of March, and spent the greater part of his early life on the Marches. He took part in the first unsuccessful struggles of the Yorkists, and retired to Calais, from whence he returned with the other Yorkists in 1459. He was on the Marches of Wales when he heard of the overthrow of his father at Wakefield. He marched towards London, winning on the way the battle of Mortimer's Cross, where he routed Gaspar Tudor, and then, by threatening London, prevented the victorious Lancastrians from entering, and himself entered it in March 1461. He was proclaimed king, and immediately marched north again where in March he established his position by the great victory of Towton. He owed his position more to his relatives the Nevilles and especially to Warwick, the king-maker, and at first showed his gratitude by practically allowing Warwick to rule the country. He showed, however, that he was essentially ungrateful by twice flouting Warwick's policy of foreign marriages, especially was this seen when he disclosed his marriage to Dame Rivers when Warwick had advocated and practically arranged a marriage with a French princess. Still matters did not come to a head

until Warwick, acting in conjunction with Clarence, imprisoned E. in his castle at Middleham. He escaped, and Warwick retired to France, only to appear in the next year with an army which forced E. into exile in Burgundy. After some little difficulty he received assistance from Charles of Burgundy and returned, defeating Warwick at Barnet and Margaret of Anjou at Tewkesbury (1471). He was still troubled by the intrigues of Clarence, who was murdered in 1478. E. *d.* on April 9, and was buried at Windsor. In character he was reckless and dissolute, yet not devoid of ability. After the Lancastrian struggles he was strengthened by the wealth which he obtained by confiscation and by his recognition of the fact that England needed a breathing space after her century of war. He was autocratic, and may be styled the first of the new monarchy kings. He was a typical product of the Renaissance period; tyrannic in rule, but a patron of learning and of the new discoveries. He was a great patron of Caxton. *See* J. Bruce (Camden Society), 1838; W. Habington's *History.*

**Edward V.** (1470–83), the elder son of Edward IV. His uncle, Richard, Duke of Gloucester, was appointed regent for him. With feigned reluctance Richard accepted the crown of England for himself. The king and his brother were at this time living in the Tower, and when an attempt was concerted to release them the news spread that they were dead. The manner of their death only became known some twenty years later, when it was established practically beyond doubt that they had been smothered in the Tower by order of their uncle, Richard VI. *See* Lives by Grant, Sir C. R. Markham, and Strickland.

**Edward VI.** (1537–53), the only son of Henry VIII., and the only child of Henry by his third wife, Jane Seymour, who *d.* twelve days after his birth. He was given a sound and careful education, but from his birth it was recognised that he would probably not live long. He was never created Prince of Wales, but bore the title Duke of Cornwall from his birth. He succeeded his father when not quite ten years of age, and as was natural, the power of government was exercised by his regents, first, the Duke of Somerset, and second by the Duke of Northumberland. He was practically a nonentity during his short reign, the famous Acts assigned to him being the work of his regents. He was brought up in the Protestant faith, and gave promise of becoming a fanatic. He left a will when he died which was obviously the work of

Northumberland. By it he set aside the will of his father and left the throne to Lady Jane Grey and her heirs male. Lady Jane Grey had but recently been married to the eldest son of Northumberland. Edward *d.* in July and was buried in Henry VIII. Chapel. *See* Lives by Sir C. R. Markham, J. G. Nicholls, and Strickland.

**Edward VII.** (1841–1910), Albert Edward, King of Great Britain and Ireland and of the British dominions beyond the seas, Emperor of India, was the eldest son and second child of Queen Victoria and Prince Albert, and was *b.* at Buckingham Palace on Nov. 9. In the December following he was created Earl of Chester and Prince of Wales. He was educated under private tutors, and in 1859 went to the University of Edinburgh. From here he went first to Christ

EDWARD VI.

(After Holbein)

Church, Oxford, and later to Clare College, Cambridge. In 1858 he had been made a Knight of the Garter, and a colonel in the army. In the following year, travelling under his first formal incognito, he visited Italy and Spain, and in the following year travelled through Canada and the U.S.A. He had already impressed the people whom he had met with his good-fellowship and his charm, but his early life was passed under many restrictions, restrictions which did not lessen in severity after the death of his father the Prince Consort. He returned from America, having left there a very favourable impression, to continue his university course, after which in 1861 he went to Ireland to the Curragh, where he joined his regiment the 10th Hussars. In the

September of the same year he met for the first time the Princess Alexandra of Denmark who was ultimately to become his wife. The year 1861, however, was a sad one for the prince, early in the year his maternal grandmother *d.*, and on Dec. 13, the prince, hastily summoned from Cambridge, was present at the death of his father. In 1862 he went under the guidance of Stanley, for a tour through the Holy Land, and early in 1863 was admitted a member of the Privy Council and took his seat in the Lords as Duke of Cornwall. On March 10, in the same year, he married the Princess Alexandra. He was granted an income of £40,000 a year in addition to the revenue of the Duchy of Cornwall, and Sandringham was purchased for him, whilst Marlborough House became his town residence. In 1864 his eldest son, Prince Albert Victor (Duke of Clarence), was *b.*, 1865, Prince George Frederick Ernest Albert (George V.), Princess Victoria Louise, 1867, Princess Victoria, 1868, Princess Maud (Queen of Norway), 1869. After his marriage the Prince of Wales played an important part in the social life of the nation. The death of the Prince Consort had been an overwhelming blow to the queen, and for many years following it she lived in practical retirement. The prince, however, fulfilled his duties admirably; he was always ready to help forward charitable movements, and he played an important part in the linking together of the empire by his various foreign tours and visits. He had already visited France, and had formed a lasting friendship for that country, a friendship which did not waver in spite of many political incidents. Amongst his more important visits may be mentioned, Egypt, 1869 ; Ireland, 1871 ; Russia, 1874 : India, 1875 ; Ireland, 1885. In 1871 he was struck down with typhoid fever, and for a time his life was despaired of, but gradually he recovered, and in Feb. 1872 a public thanksgiving was held at St. Paul's. In 1892 his eldest son, Prince Albert Victor, on the eve of his marriage to the Princess May Victoria of Teck, *d.* after a very brief illness. In the following year the marriage of his son, Prince George, took place, his bride being the Princess May Victoria of Teck. In 1894 a son was *b.* to the Duke of York, Prince Edward of Wales. In 1897 the Prince of Wales took a leading part in the arrangements and the actual events of the Queen's Diamond Jubilee. In the following year whilst paying a private visit to the late Baron Ferdinand de Rothschild he broke his knee-cap, an accident from which, however, he entirely recovered. Whilst passing through Brussels in the next year he was fired at by a youth named Sipido, but fortunately no injury was done. Early in 1901, his mother, Queen Victoria, d., and the prince succeeded with the title of Edward VII. In May 1902 the war in S. Africa was brought to an end. The personal popularity of the king was seen from the very beginning of his reign. He took an active part in the political and social life of his people ; but he refrained

[*Topical Press*

EDWARD VII.

always from showing any marked political bias. He was continually visiting in various parts of the country, and he undoubtedly kept well in touch with the opinions of his people. He was thoroughly constitutional, and though much has been written to the contrary, his outlook on foreign policy was evidently capable and statesmanlike. In spite of his continual visits to various parts of the country, he always spent at least three months of every year abroad, and he was always extremely popular abroad. The early part of his reign was clouded by his illness just before his coronation, but he

recovered and was crowned on Aug. 19, 1902. In 1905 the Conservative government resigned and was succeeded by a Liberal one. The year 1909 was one of grave political crisis, the budget of Lloyd George, Chancellor of the Exchequer, created unprecedented excitement in the country and was rejected by the House of Lords. The government dissolved, but the Liberals were again returned to power, this time with the abolition of the veto of the House of Lords as the foremost plank of their platform. The speech from the throne containing the words, ' in the opinion of my ministers,' was the formal speech of the Prime Minister, and had *not* been altered in any way by the king. The king supported his ministers in their demands, as by the constitution he was bound to. Early in 1910 the king was taken ill, but recovered, but again on May 5 he was reported to be suffering from bronchitis, and on the following day he died of heart failure. In spite of his lack of political training, and on that point there is no contradiction, E. won for himself speedily the affections of his people. Whether he was great as a foreign statesman, or whether his policy was but the policy of his ministers, by his subjects he was unanimously hailed as Edward the Peacemaker. *See* Lives by Sir Sidney Lee, Sir E. Dicey and Estcott ; also *Dictionary of National Biography.*

**Edward, the Black Prince,** *see* BLACK PRINCE.

**Edwardes, Sir Herbert Benjamin** (1819–68), Anglo-Indian official and soldier, *b.* at Frodesley, Shropshire. In 1842 he was a second-lieutenant in the First Bengal Fusiliers ; 1847 he began the civil administration of Banu, which he successfully accomplished. In the following year he led an expedition to Multan and routed the Sikhs at Kinyeri and Sadusam. In 1850 he came to England and brought out his book, *A Year on the Punjab Frontier.* In 1851 he returned to India ; 1853 he became commissioner of the Peshawar frontier where he was successful in bringing about a reconciliation with Afghanistan.

**Edwardesabad,** a tn. in British India, also called Banu and Dhulipnagar. It lies in the valley of the Kuram R., and forms the base for all punitive expeditions to the Tochi Valley and Waziri frontier. Pop. 22,261.

**Edward Nyanza,** formerly **Albert Edward Nyanza,** a lake of Central Africa, and one of the Nile's western reservoirs. It was discovered by Stanley in 1889, when he succeeded in tracing the Semliki—the one and only outlet of the lake—to its source, and by him named Albert Edward after the Prince of Wales, who became Edward VII. It was agreed by the Anglo-German Boundary Commission of 1902–4 that it lay within the sphere of influence of the Congo Free State. The total length of the lake, which is oval in form and scarcely at all indented, is 44 m., the breadth never exceeding 32 m. Lake Dweru, which is connected by a narrow stream with the north-eastern extremity of E. N., was discovered by Stanley as early as 1875. This smaller sheet of water is formed chiefly by the Mpango, which flows from the eastern ridges of the Ruwenzori range, whose southern slopes form in the distance a splendid background to the northern fringes of the larger lake. E. N., which is fed by the Ruchuru—a headstream of the Nile—is wreathed during the dry seasons by dense mists. But when the rains come, these roll away, disclosing to view the splendid amphitheatre of hills to W. and N. Vegetation is scarce.

**Edwards, Amelia Ann Blandford** (1831–92), English novelist and Egyptologist, was a Londoner by birth. She published over fifteen novels, the best of which are usually admitted to be *My Brother's Wife*, 1855; *Debenham's Vow*, 1870, and *Lord Brackenbury*, 1880. Her lectures on Egypt appeared in print under the title of *Pharaohs, Fellahs, and Explorers*, 1891, but her most universally appreciated book was one of travel entitled *A Thousand Miles up the Nile*, 1877. In 1882 she founded and was long an honorary secretary of the Egyptian Exploration Fund.

**Edwards, Henri Milne-**, *see* MILNE-EDWARDS, HENRI.

**Edwards, John Passmore** (1823–1911), a newspaper proprietor, a man of humble origin, became a journalist and a lecturer on temperance and the corn laws. Coming to London in 1845, he was one of the promoters of the Early Closing Association, and was active in his advocacy of a peace society. Five years later he began to found newspapers, but it was not until 1862, when he purchased the *Building News*, that he began to prosper in his affairs. In 1876 he acquired the *Echo*, the first halfpenny newspaper, which, though it had been eight years in existence, was in low water. The *Echo* and the *Weekly Times* were the foundation of the great fortune he made. The bulk of this fortune was distributed in his lifetime in gifts of free libraries and institutions in various parts of England. In his life-

time he was much honoured as a philanthropist, and he was offered a knighthood by Queen Victoria and again by Edward VII., but on both occasions he declined the distinction. In 1905 he printed privately an autobiography, entitled *A Few Footprints*.

**Edwards, Jonathan** (1703–58), an American divine, was the son of a clergyman, and was himself ordained in 1727. For nearly twenty-four years (1727–50) he was associated as minister with Northampton, Massachusetts. Here he successfully piloted his people through the great wave of Revivalism, which swept his parish among so many others after the preaching of George Whitefield. But his vigorous crusade against the circulation of immoral literature and, above all, his insistence on admitting none but true converts to the Holy Communion, forced him to give up his pastorate. His *Freedom of the Will*, 1754, has established him as one of America's foremost metaphysicians, whilst his spiritual nobility shines out in his *True Nature of Christian Virtue*, in spite of the cloud of a somewhat austere Calvinism.

**Edwards, Jonathan** (1745–1801), an American divine, was the second son of the above, and the acumen and clear mental vision displayed in his *Dissertation concerning Liberty and Necessity*, 1797, proves him to have been almost his father's equal in intellectual force. Educated at the college of New Jersey, he was pastor from 1769 to 1795 in White Haven, Connecticut, and at his death was president of the new Schenectady College, New York.

**Edwards, Richard** (1523–66), an English musician and playwright. He was appointed a gentleman of the Chapel Royal, and master of the children. In the Christmas of 1564 he produced a play which was acted by his choir boys, and later his *Palamon and Arcite* was played before Queen Elizabeth. In his day E. was highly esteemed. He is supposed to have written his poem, *The Soul's Knell*, when he was dying.

**Edwardsville:** (1) a tn. in Luzerne co., Pennsylvania, U.S.A., on the Susquehanna R. Its chief industries are mining and brewing. Pop. 8847, of whom nearly half are Welsh. (2) a city in Illinois, U.S.A., 18 m. N.E. of Saint Louis, with coal mines and manufactures, and nearby the co-operative village of Leclaire. Pop. 6235.

**Edwin, Ædwine,** or **Edwine** (585–633), King of Northumbria, and the son of Ella of Deira. E. was favourably disposed towards Christianity. On the day of the birth of his daughter, his life was attempted by his enemy Cwichelm, King of Wessex. E. vowed that, should he conquer his enemy, he would abstain from worshipping the gods of his race. He was killed by Cadwallon of Wales at Hatfield.

**Eeckhout, Gerbrand van Den** (1621–74), *b.* at Amsterdam; he was a pupil of Rembrandt. His chief subjects are biblical, and of these his small pictures are the best. Some of his pictures are : ' Tobit,' in the Brunswick Gallery; ' The Woman taken in Adultery,' at Amsterdam; ' Simeon in the Temple,' at Dresden; ' Christ among the Doctors,' at Munich.

**Eeckhout, Jacob Joseph** (1793–1861), a painter of historical pictures and portraits, *b.* at Antwerp. He imitated Rembrandt, and is considered one of the most famous painters of the Dutch school. His best works are : ' The Death of William the Silent,' ' Peter the Great at Zaandam,' ' The Departure of the Recruits of Scheveningen,' ' Collec-

EEL

tion de Portraits d'Artistes modernes, nés dans le Royaume des Pays-Bas,' 1822.

**Eecloo**, a tn. in Belgium, 11 m. N. of Ghent. The chief manufs. are cotton, linen, and wool. Pop. 14,150.

**Eel.** The *anguilla*, or fresh-water Es. belong to the family Murænidæ, a group of soft-rayed osseous fishes, distinguished by the presence of an opening to the air-bladder, and the absence of the pelvic fins. The name is also applied, popularly and scientifically, to other genera, notably the *Conger*, which is usually larger than the true E., and lives in the sea. The fresh-water E. only migrates to the sea to spawn, and this happens but once in its life. It is characterised by an elongated form of body, by the rudimentary scales buried in the skin, and by the rounded tail-fin confluent with the median fins. There are no accessory breathing organs; the stomach has a blind appendage; the vent is generally situated far back, but may be near the pectoral fins ; and the ovaries have no ducts. In the skeleton the pectoral arch is unconnected with the skull and attached to one of the earlier vertebræ. The true Es., congers and murænas, or large marine Es., are marked by a normal structure of the upper jaw, which is

formed in front by the premaxillæ, and laterally by the toothed maxillæ. All the family of Murænidæ are predatory and voracious, and feed on almost any animal food they can obtain, living or dead, the conger being especially fond of squid, the fresh-water E. devouring carrion of all kinds.

**Eel-pout,** *see* BURBOT.

**Effendi,** a Turkish title of respect corresponding to the English ' sir.' It follows the personal name, and is generally given to physicians or members of the learned professions when they have no higher title.

**Effervescence.** The extent to which gases are soluble in water depends upon pressure and temperature. When the temperature is low and the pressure great, the gas is more soluble, consequently when the temperature is raised or the pressure lowered, the gas escapes in small bubbles. This phenomenon is called E. The term effervescence is also applied to the tumultuous upheaval of any liquid by a gas produced in it, giving it the appearance of boiling (Latin, *fervere*, to boil). The similar phenomenon *frothing* is often a nuisance during distillation; it may be partly or wholly prevented by adding bits of broken unglazed earthenware to the liquid undergoing distillation.

**Efficiency.** In any method of transmitting energy from point to point, or of transforming one kind of energy into another, some of it is dissipated or become useless. The ratio of the energy available at the end of the process of the total energy supplied is called the E. of the process. Thus, in transmitting mechanical energy by means of shafting, some of it is used in overcoming friction of bearings, etc. The numerical value of the Es. of machines varies very widely. In a simple machine, such as a pulley, the E. may be as high as 80 per cent., and in a screw jack, as used on motor cars, as low as 36 per cent. It must be remembered, however, that the loss of E. is compensated by the fact that the friction prevents the screw jack running backwards when left free. In transmitting electrical energy, some of it is used up in the wires or cables which carry the current. As this loss is proportional to the current, it is advisable to transmit energy at high voltage when the current will be low. In processes for transforming energy from one kind to another, the Es. show wide variations, and the object of most improvements in 'transformers' or engines is to increase the E. A locomotive engine may transform less than 10 per cent. of the heat of the coal burned into available mechanical energy. But in transforming mechanical energy into electrical energy, or *vice versa*, the Es. are usually greater, as much as 92 per cent. of the energy supplied being available for use after transformation. The term E. is sometimes used in speaking of electric lamps, where it expresses the candle power per unit of electrical energy supplied.

**Efflorescence**, in chemistry, is the term applied to the crumbling to powder of crystals, caused by the loss of water originally present in them. It occurs whenever the vapour pressure of the water in the crystal is greater than that of the moisture in the surrounding air. Glauber's salt and ordinary washing-soda are good examples of efflorescent substances. The converse of E. is deliquescence (*q.v.*).

**Effusion of Gases**, *see* GAS and GASES.

**Eft.** The terms E. and newt are applied to almost all species of lizards found in the British Islands. *See* NEWT.

**Ega de Queiroz, José Maria** (1845–1900), Portuguese author, *b.* either at Villa do Conde or at Provoa do Varzim; son of a retired judge. Educ. at Univ. of Coimbra. Collaborated in *As Farpas* (satirical sketches), 1871. Consul at Havana, Newcastle, Bristol (1876), and Paris (consul-general 1888). Died in Paris. Publications include the novels: *O crime do Padro Amaro*, 1874 (re-written, 1880); *O primo Basilio*, 1877; *A Reliquia*, 1886; *Os Maias*, 1888. His short stories are particularly admired. *The Sweet Miracle* has been translated into both English and Irish. He is considered the greatest modern Portuguese writer and is certainly the only one whose books have been considered worthy of translation into many languages. *The Crime of Father Amaro*, his masterpiece, recently created great interest in its German translation.

**Egan, Pierce, the Elder** (1772–1849), an author, is now principally re-membered for his *Life in London*, 1821, which, illustrated by George and Isaac Cruikshank, presented a general survey of life in the metropolis. This book is further interesting in that it was the first work of fiction to be published in monthly parts. Its popularity was so great that in 1828 E. issued a sequel, *Finish to the Adventures of Tom, Jerry, and Logic*. E.'s other works included *Boxiana, or Sketches of Modern Pugilism*, 1818–24; and *The Life of an Actor*, 1824. In 1824, also, he founded *Pierce Egan's Life in London and Sporting Guide*, a weekly newspaper that afterwards merged into *Bell's Life in London*. His son, Pierce Egan, the Younger (1814–80), was the author of many novels, none of which, however, have survived to the present day.

**Egbert**, King of Wessex from 802 to 836, when he *d.* He was commonly called Egbert the Great, was the son of Ethelmund, and a direct descendant of Cedric. In his youth he was driven from England and sought refuge at the court of Charles the Great. The first nine years of his reign were a period of peace, but he then attacked Cornwall and Devon, and reduced them to submission in 813. In 823 he defeated Beornwulf, King of Mercia, and soon after Kent and Essex submitted to his rule. Northumbria acknowledged E.'s supremacy in 829, and in 830 Wales was reduced to submission. E. was then made bretwalda, being the eighth Saxon king to receive that dignity. The last years of his reign were marked by invasions of the Danes, but they were defeated at Hengistdune in 835.

**Egede, Hans** (1686–1758), a Norwegian missionary. He studied theology at Copenhagen University, and was appointed pastor at Vaagen in 1707. In 1721 he went to Greenland, where he remained for fifteen years, working zealously among the people. On the death of his wife, in 1736, he returned to Copenhagen, but continued his work for the Greenland mission, of which he became bishop in 1740. He wrote a book on the natural history of Greenland.

**Eger**, a tn. and also a riv. of Czecho-Slovakia. The tn., situated on the R. Eger, at the base of a spur of the Fichtelgebirge, is close to the Bohemian borders, and was an important fortress until 1809. It is the cap. of the Egerland, Bohemia, inhabited by Gers. It is an important railway centre, with many high-gabled houses. Wallenstein was murdered in the town-hall, which is now a museum, on Feb. 25, 1634, by an Irishman. Schiller lived in the

'Schiller haus' in 1791. Wallenstein's generals were murdered in the Kaiserburg built by Frederick Barbarossa. The Gothic church of St. Nicholas dates from 1230 to 1270, and two others from the thirteenth century. The manufactures include textiles, bicycles, agricultural machines, earthenware, meal, beer, and a substitute for coffee. Pop. 27,520, of whom 23,130 are Gers. The R. Eger rises in the Fichtelgebirge at a height of more than 2300 ft. Its general direction is easterly. There are numerous cataracts and an abundance of fish. After flowing 190 m., it joins the Elbe about 30 m. N.W. of Prague.

**Egerdir :** (1) A tn. of Turkey in Asia, situated on Lake E., in the vilayet of Konieh, or Konia, 84 m. to the W. of that city. The ruins of Antioch, in Pisidia, are in the vicinity. It exports opium, skins and leather to Singapore. Pop. 24,000. (2) Lake E., a lake of Konieh, Asia Minor, situated in lat. 38° N., between the Taurus range and the Sultan Dagh. It is about 30 m. long, and drains S. into the Mediterranean.

**Egeria,** in Roman legend, was a nymph. She was the wife of Numa, and was worshipped both in Rome and Aricia as the goddess of childbirth. She was connected with the Camenæ (water nymphs), who were worshipped in Italy before the Muses.

**Egerton, Gen. Sir Charles** (b. 1848). He entered the army in 1867, became a colonel in 1895, and served in the Afghan War, 1879–80 ; Black Mt. expedition, 1888 ; Dongola expedition, 1897–98. He was made a general in 1906, and retired the following year. Was awarded the D.S.O. (1891) for valour in the Miranzai expeditions, where he was severely wounded.

**Egerton, Francis,** see BRIDGEWATER.

**Egerton, Admiral Sir George le Clerc** (b. 1852). He entered the navy in 1866, and served with distinction in the Arctic expedition in 1875. In 1893 he was made a captain and from that year till 1897 he saw a good deal of active service, and was mentioned in several despatches. He became naval A.D.C. to His Majesty in 1905, and K.C.B. in 1910. Was Second Sea Lord of the Admiralty 1911–12. Full Admiral, March 1913. Commander-in-Chief, Plymouth, 1913–16.

**Egg** (Old Eng. *aeg ;* Ger. *Ei ;* Swedish *ægg,* probably also Gk. ᾠόν), the female reproductive cell which develops into a new individual. In all but parthenogenetic animals, this process only takes place after fertilisation by the male gamete. When the word is used in this sense, it is directly parallel to the Latin word *ovum,* and applies to the intra-maternal as well as the extra-maternal existence of the cell. In common speech the word only applies to the extra-maternal *ovum.* Es. vary very greatly in size. In all cases the essential embryo is very small, but variations occur in the amount of yolk present, and in the thickness and structure of the surrounding parts.

*Eggs of birds.*—Birds lay on the whole the largest Es. The Es. of the extinct *Æpyorius* have a cubic content of over two gallons. The ostrich lays the largest Es. of any extant bird. One weighs about as much as twelve

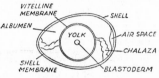

THE EGG OF A HEN

hens' Es. At the other end of the scale is the E. of the humming bird which only weighs a few grains. The shell of a bird's E. is mainly composed of carbonate of lime. It is often coloured, the colouring being specific to the particular variety of bird. Seven different pigments have been separated from the colouring of Es. Their origin is still obscure, but they are probably derived from the hæmoglobin in the blood, and may be in some way similar to bile-pigments. The significance of the colour of Es. is difficult to understand. It probably depends upon the environment of the nest. Thus snakes and such birds as deposit their Es. in holes and in domed nests lay white Es. In such cases coloured Es. would be invisible, and they would be in danger of being broken by the mother. Es. which are laid in open nests, or on the bare ground, are coloured to imitate their surroundings. The brilliant Es. are always found in nests with elaborate protective devices, or in ones that are carefully hidden.

*Eggs of mammals.*—Only two mammals are oviparous : the *Echidna* or *spiny ant-eater,* and the *Ornithorhynchus,* or *duck-billed platypus.* The *Echidna* carries her Es. in a pouch such as the kangaroo has.

*Eggs of reptiles.*—These are always white or yellowish. They are smaller than birds' Es., but yet possess a good deal of yolk. The shell is nearly always membranous, but in tortoises, turtles, and crocodiles it is calcareous like a bird's. A few lizards and snakes are viviparous.

*Eggs of fishes* differ greatly in size and appearance, and some extraordinary varieties are known. Most fishes lay enormous numbers of Es. The sturgeon lays 7,000,000 Es., the turbot over 14,000,000. The number always depends on the risk of destruction, and this rule applies to all animals. For further particulars, *see* BIRD, POULTRY, REPRODUCTION.

**Egg, Isle of,** *see* EIGG.

**Egger-Moths** belong to the Lasiocampidæ, and are well known in Great Britain. They are of large size, covered with scales, and possess a highly developed hind-wing. The length across the wings may vary, as in the genus *Suana*, from 1½ to 4½ in. The walls of the cocoons have sometimes a smooth, shell-like appearance, hence the name.

**Eggishorn,** or **Eggeschhorn,** a mt. of the Alps in Switzerland, situated in the canton of Valais, near the head of the Rhone valley, and on the southern slope of the Bernese Oberland. It rises to an altitude of 9625 ft.

**Eggleston, Edward** (1837–1902), *b.* in Vevay, Indiana. He was pastor of the Church of Christian Endeavour, Brooklyn, from 1874–79. After this date he devoted his time to literature. His works afford a picture of the life, manners, and dialect of the Central West, and his *Hoosier Schoolmaster* was so popular that it was translated into French, German, and Danish. Among his works are : *Mr. Blake's Walking-Stick,* for children ; *The Graysons,* a novel.

**Egham,** a par. and vil. of Surrey, England, situated on the Thames, 8 m. from Windsor, and 20 m. from London. The par. adjoins Berkshire, and has an acreage of 7786. The Royal Holloway College for women, with 200 students, is here, and was opened by Queen Victoria in 1886. In the neighbourhood is the historic Runnymede. Pop. 13,753.

**Egin,** or **Ekim,** a tn. of Asiatic Turkey, in Armenia, situated on the Euphrates. It is built in a picturesque manner in a kind of elevated basin surrounded by steep rocks. The houses are stone built, and the streets resemble stone ladders. Wine, silk and fruit are produced and wax, hides and carpets exported. Pop. 22,975.

**Egina,** *see* ÆGINA.

**Eginhardt,** or **Eginhard,** *see* EINHARD.

**Eglantine,** the old English name for *Rosa Eglanteria,* the sweet-briar rose. It is misapplied in the lines from *L'Allegro :*

‘ Through the sweet briar, or the vine, Or the twisted eglantine.’

**Eglinton and Winton, Archibald William Montgomerie, Earl of** (1812–61), *b.* at Palermo. He was descended from the famous family of Montgomerie, which dates back to about 1150. In 1859 he was made Earl of Winton, and was twice Lord-Lieutenant of Ireland. He took a great interest in racing, and won the St. Leger in 1842, and the Derby in 1849. He is also famous for the tournament which took place at Eglinton Castle in 1839, and in which Prince Louis Napoleon took part. This is described by Disraeli in *Endymion.*

[*Canadian Pacific*

MOUNT EGMONT

**Egmont, Lamoral, Count of, Prince of Gavre** (1522–68), *b.* in Hainault. He served as a soldier under Charles V. at Algiers in 1541, and in 1546 was made a knight of the Golden Fleece. In 1554 he went as ambassador to England to arrange a marriage between Philip and Mary, which was afterwards solemnised at Winchester in his presence. For his successes at St. Quentin in 1557, and at Gravelines in 1558 (where he was in charge of the cavalry), he was made governor of Flanders and Artois, and in this position he took up the cause of the Netherlands, who were opposed to the Catholic policy of Philip. In consequence of this, in 1568, he was accused of treason and beheaded at Brussels.

**Egmont, Mount,** an extinct volcano of New Zealand, in the S.W. portion of N. Island, in lat. 39° 15′ S. and long. 174° 13′ E. It is about 18 m. S. of New Plymouth, and is exceedingly beautiful in form. Perpetual snows cover its summit, which reaches a height of 8280 ft.

**Ego,** a term used in philosophy, denotes the individual considered abstractly and not in connection with the world and other persons. It is used in two senses, which are termed by Kant ' pure ' and ' empirical '; the latter term signifies the self in a more concrete sense and includes some part of experience, *i.e.* an object, while the former, the ' pure ego,' is the conscious subject only, and denotes that everything is referred to a self which experiences it.

**Egoism** (Lat. *ego*, I), a term used in ethics, and generally signifies a system in which the happiness of the individual is the main object in view. Another form of the word ' egotism,' in direct contrast to ' altruism,' means selfishness. The ethical doctrines consider that the self consists of an individual and those things in which he is interested, the self being all-important in the application of moral principles, the egoist, seeking the ideal for himself, standing in direct contrast to the altruist, who seeks it for others. But the distinction between altruism and E. is complicated, seeing that the two are often combined, *e.g.* Christian ethics enjoin duty to self and duty to others, while a truly egoistic system can very rarely be carried out. Indeed those who have studied human character assert that men in general are egoistic, seeing that they aim at the gratification of their personal aims and desires.

**Egorievsk,** *see* YEGORIEVSK

**Egremont:** (1) A tn. of Cumberland, England, situated on the Eden, 6 m. from Whitehaven. E. Castle, built in the twelfth century, is now in ruins. Pop. 6584. (2) A par. and tn. of Cheshire, England, on the Mersey. The town is almost opposite Liverpool, and is a steamboat station. Pop. 13,179.

**Egret,** a term applied to several species of white herons with long tufts of feathers on the head or neck. The great white E., or the European white heron, is *Herodias* (or *Ardea*) *alba*; and the little E. is *Garzetta* (or *Ardea*) *garzetta*, a native of Europe,

Africa, and Asia, which is occasionally to be met with in Britain. *See* HERON.

**Egripos,** *see* EUPŒA.

**Egypt,** a country forming the N.E. shoulder of Africa, bounded on the N. by the Mediterranean, S. by the Anglo-Egyptian Sudan, E. by the Red Sea, and W. by Tripoli and the Sahara. The western frontier cannot be very clearly defined; the line properly taken is from the Gulf of Sollum, skirting the oasis of Siwa in the Libyan desert and following S. to Wadi-Halfa, so that the oases of the Libyan desert are included. The N.E. frontier is a direct line from Taba, the head of the Gulf of Akaba, following up the boundary of Palestine to the Mediterranean Sea, the peninsula of Sinai being included in the dominions of Egypt. The area is 400,000 sq. m.; a large part of this is desert. The country is divided into Upper and Lower Egypt; Upper Egypt, or *Es-Said*, the happy or fortunate, being the Nile valley, and Lower Egypt, or *Er-Rif*, the fertile, being the delta. The chief features of Egypt are the R. Nile and the desert. Without the Nile Egypt would never have existed. The river, with its rich deposit of alluvial soil carried down from the highlands of Abyssinia and given to the land annually during the overflow, has transformed the desert into the fertile strip of valley and the delta. E. and W. of this cultivated land lies the waste of deserts with occasional oases. The delta is a fan-shaped plain, formed of a deep layer of mud and grey sand, lying on the yellow quartz sands, gravel and clay, which were laid there in prehistoric times by the sea. It is an extraordinarily fertile stretch of land, watered by the two branches of the Nile, the Rosetta and the Damietta, and intersected with canals. The valley of Upper Egypt is narrow, and the fringe of mountains on either side are of no great height, so that the landscape varies but little and might appear to be monotonous but for the rich and wonderful colouring of all the scenery, the vivid green of the fields, the rich red-brown of the river, the bright yellow of the rocks, with overhead a deep blue sky and brilliant sunshine. The coast-line of Egypt covers about 600 m., and except at the delta is rock-bound, possessing no harbours worthy of mention. The delta coast-line is low and forms two bays, one being the Bay of Aboukir. The source of the Nile (*q.v.*) is Victoria Nyanza (Lake Victoria), discovered by Speke, 1858. The river flows into Egypt proper N. of the second cataract, a little S.

of Wadi-Halfa. The Blue Nile, which rises in Lake Sana, joins the Nile at Khartum; this stream brings down an immense quantity of red mud. The tributary Atbara joins 200 m. below Khartum. The cataracts are six in number (*see* NILE). The important feature of the river is its annual inundation. At the end of May the river is at its lowest level; it rises gradually in June and continues rising until the middle of Sept.; it then remains stationary from two to three weeks, rising again until the end of Oct.; it is then at its highest level and commences gradually to fall, until by May it is once more at its lowest. The river rises from 21 to 28 ft.; when it did not reach this level the crops failed, and when it exceeded it the land was overflowed and ruin faced the people. Nowhere in the world is there such a large population depending solely on the produce of the soil. As the climate is exceedingly dry, the annual rainfall averaging about 1·50, irrigation became as early as the second Dynasty (about 4514 B.C.) an object of national importance. All through the ages can be marked the tireless persistence and mechanical ingenuity employed in the problems of irrigation. During the nineteenth century, Mehemet Ali Pasha began a gigantic system of canals and locks and weirs. A French engineer of great ability, Mougel Bey, was employed to carry out this difficult task; his great barrage across the Nile, at the apex of the delta, is still a very impressive work; unfortunately the system was a failure. Later, British engineers undertook the management of irrigation, and in 1902 the Nile dam, at the head of the first cataract above Assuan, was completed. It had been planned to raise the dam to such a height that the beautiful temples on the islet of Philæ would have been submerged; for five years they were spared, but in 1907 the dam was raised, and during several months of the year the ruins are no longer visible. The chief lakes of Egypt, from W. to E., are Mareotis, Edku, Burlus, and Menzala; these lie only a few miles from the coast and are shallow and brackish. The seven famous natron lakes lie in a valley in the desert, 80 m. W.N.W. of Cairo. In the province of the Fayum is the Birket-el-Kerum, 30 m. long and 5 m. wide, forming the remains of the Lake Moeris, which Herodotus believed to have been artificially constructed. Certainly Amenemhat III. completed what his fathers had begun by building a vast embankment and reclaiming an area of 40 sq. m., also carrying out a scheme of irrigation

in connection with this great *natural* reservoir. The climate is extremely dry. E. lies in an almost rainless area. The days are warm and the nights are cool. Jan. is the coolest month. On the coast rain falls during the winter months, but snow is unknown. In Sinai, snow occasionally falls during the winter, and heavy storms of rain occur which flood the rocky ravines and drown both men and beasts; these, however, are only occasional and irregular. One interesting feature of the climate is the continuous N. wind, which blows throughout the year, and the sailing boats are thus able to ascend the Nile against the strong current. During the spring the *Kamsin* occurs, a hot, dry S. wind laden with sand, forming a yellow stifling fog almost obscuring the sun; it lasts from one to three days. There are five large oases or fertile places in the western desert, Siwa, Baharia, Kharga, Dakla, and Farafra. These have been occupied since 1600 B.C. Kharga possesses a temple of Ammon, built by Darius I., and also other interesting ruins of the time of the Ptolemies. Siwa contains the oracle temple of Jupiter Ammon, consulted by Alexander the Great. The town is built on the rocks and has the appearance of a fortress. It was used for many years as a place of banishment for criminals.

*Minerals.*—Gold and precious stones were formerly found and mined in the hills by the Red Sea. The Moslem conquest caused the abandoning of this industry. The turquoise mines of Sinai are still productive. The first Dynasty of Egyptian kings, about 4777 to 4514 B.C., possessed these mines and had them worked, and from that time down, through all the centuries, the turquoises from Sinai have been famous. There are emerald mines at Jebel Zubara. Salt is obtained from Lake Mareotis in large quantities; alum is found in the western oases; carbonate of soda is taken from the natron lakes; hæmatite iron is obtained in considerable quantities from Sinai and the Red Sea hills. Porphyry quarries once existed, with granite quarries, at Jebel-el-Fatira, and during the Rom. occupation were extensively worked. Gold-mining began once more in 1905 at Um Rus and Um Garaiat.

*The flora* of E. is not of a great or large variety. There are no forests or woods, and all available land is used for agricultural purposes. Date palms grow wherever they are allowed, together with the sunt tree and tamarisk, the mimosa, the eucalyptus and the cypress, also some few others. The rose grows freely, and the violet and many kinds of daisies and poppies.

Jasmine is largely grown, being much loved by the Arab and Egyptian. The famous papyrus is not now grown in E., and the lotus flower (a water lily) blooms no longer on the Nile, though found in the delta and cultivated in various private gardens.

*Fauna.*—The camel and the ass are the common domestic animals of E. The camel is not indigenous, but was introduced at an early period. Horses are few and of very inferior type. There are not a great variety of wild animals; the hyena, jackal, and fox are numerous, and wild boars are still found in the delta. Wild cats and

or peasant, the Arabs or Bedouins, Nubians, and foreigners (205,998). The fellah (Arabic for ploughman) forms the bulk of the peasantry. They are chiefly Mohammedan in faith, though the Copts (*q.v.*), also natives of E., have kept their Christian belief. The fellah is a hard-working and industrious person, of big build, with a fine oval face, smooth black hair (the head is usually shaved), and well-formed features. The women are often of great beauty, both in form and feature, though they lose their youth early. The Copts are racially the purest descendants of the ancient

[*Canadian Pacific*

THE GREAT PYRAMID AND SPHINX

hares abound, and snakes and reptiles of various kinds are exceedingly numerous. The crocodile and the hippopotamus, once famous and sacred, no longer dwell by the Nile in E. The bird life is rich; vultures, eagles, hawks, and buzzards are found in quantities, and water fowl in large varieties, but the sacred ibis has gone. The five most familiar animals and flowers, usually associated with ancient E., are no longer common, *i.e.* the crocodile and hippopotamus, the papyrus and the lotus, and the sacred ibis; the sixth most familiar object, the beetle (the scarabæus), still flourishes in many varieties.

*The population* of E. is (census 1927) 14,168,756, consisting of the fellahin

Egyptians. The colouring of the fellah varies from a fair yellowish shade in Lower Egypt to a deeper tone in Middle Egypt, and in Upper Egypt the majority are a deep bronze. The Arab portion of the pop. is of two classes: the Arabic-speaking tribes who come from the deserts, and the Hamitic tribes who speak a language of their own, probably descended from the Blemmyes, preserving many non-Islamic religious practices and regarding the serpent as sacred. The Nubians are chiefly mixed with Arab blood. The foreigners are mainly Gks., Turks, Italians, British, Fr., Syrians, Levantines, and Persians. The chief towns of E. are Cairo (*q.v.*), the capital, on the E.

M 2

bank of the Nile, built by the Arabs at the head of the delta about 12 m. from the division of the river, pop. 1,059,824, Port Said (*q.v.*), pop. 104,603; Alexandria (*q.v.*), chief seaport, pop. 570,314; Damietta (*q.v.*), pop. 34,812; Rosetta (*q.v.*), pop. 23,048; Suez (*q.v.*), S. entrance to canal, pop. 40,523. In the interior of the delta are a few flourishing towns; the chief is Tanta, pop. 90,014. The chief town in Upper E. is the capital of the province of the Fayum, Medinet-el-Fayum, pop. 52,372. Many of the modern towns are built upon the sites of ancient cities referred to later in the section on antiquities. The great industry of E. is agriculture. About 4,000,000 acres are under perennial irrigation, and from these, two to three crops can be annually harvested; the land under basin-irrigation covers 1,750,000 acres, and only one crop can be grown in the year. Cotton, rice, and sugar are the main summer crops, and maize, millet, wheat, barley, and flax form the winter crops. Although modern iron ploughs and other agricultural machines have been introduced, the native wooden plough is still largely used. In the Fayum there are fields of roses, grown for rosewater and perfumes; saffron, indigo, and henna are also grown. The cotton industry is increasing every year. the average for 1897 to 1905 was £E14,000,000; over 1924 to 1928 £E45,777,088. The common fruits are the date, fig. orange, citron, grape, banana, peach, and apricot. In smaller quantities melons are grown and mulberries, also olives. The date is the most valuable of all the fruits, forming one of the chief foods of the people.

The *currency* is based on a gold standard. The Egyptian pound equals £1 0*s*. 6*d*. sterling, divided into 100 piastres. There are silver piastres, value 20, 10, 5, and 2, and nickel pieces of 1, $\frac{1}{2}$, $\frac{1}{3}$, and $\frac{1}{10}$ of a piastre, and in bronze $\frac{1}{20}$ and $\frac{1}{40}$. For purposes of local government the chief towns constitute governorships, and the remaining country is divided into fourteen provinces, further divided into districts. The towns with governorships are Cairo, Alexandria, Port Said, Suez Canal, Damietta, Suez, and El Arish. The provinces in Lower E. are: Behera, including the oasis of Siwa, Gharbia, Menufia, Dakahlia, Kaliubia, and Sharkia. In Upper E., Giza, Beni-Suef, Fayum, Minia, Assiut, Girga, Kena, and Assuan. For the Anglo-Egyptian Sudan, under a governor-general, appointed by the Khedive with British approval, *see* SUDAN. There are four judicial systems; two apply to Egyptian subjects only, one is applicable to

foreigners only, and the fourth can be used for both. Foreigners are almost exempt from jurisdiction in the native courts, but criminal jurisdiction is exercised by the consuls of the fifteen powers who possess this right by treaty.

*Education* is being greatly developed. The government primary schools give a four years' course, preparing the scholars for admission to minor government posts, the agricultural college, etc. The secondary schools admit to government posts and to the three colleges at Cairo, of law, medicine, and engineering. The police force, which is administered by the Ministry of the Interior, embraces city and provincial police. The city police muster 306 officers (75 Europeans), 476 European constables and 6585 men, and the strength of the provincial police is returned at 369 officers and 6162 men.

*The Egyptian army.*—The fellah, as a soldier, is useless without capable officers; when under good control he is excellent. The ancient conquests have been attributed mainly to mercenaries. For centuries foreign legions were employed, and Mehemet Ali was the first to use conscription among the fellahs. The system employed was so much loathed and dreaded that the peasants mutilated themselves rather than become soldiers. They blinded themselves in one eye or cut off the fingers on their right hand, but even this did not save them, one-eyed battalions were formed and the men with injured hands were taught to shoot from the left shoulder. It was not until 1883 that a fair system was arranged. In 1885 an equitable law was made and greatly improved upon in 1900. Service in the Egyptian Army is nominally compulsory for all Egyptian subjects, the age limits being nineteen to twenty-seven, each year's recruits being chosen by ballot. There are certain exceptions which include professors, students, civil servants, etc. Exemption from army service may be purchased for £E20 if paid before the ballot. The defence of Egypt is under British control, and the British garrison, which is under the command of a general officer, consists of three cavalry regiments, two companies of engineers, seven infantry battalions and one armoured car company.

*Finance.*—In 1929–30 the revenue was £E38,950,000 and the expenditure £E47,410,000. The total exports amounted to £E51,751,994 and the total imports to £E56,089 in 1929. On April 1, 1929, the public debt was returned at £90,288,200 (pounds sterling).

*Exploration.*—The exploration,

which has been carried on for so many years by Egyptologists, met with a wonderful find on Nov. 4, 1922, when an Englishman, Howard Carter (*q.v.*), discovered the tomb of Tutankhamen in Thebes. The tomb was opened by Carter and the Earl of Carnarvon (*q.v.*) on Nov. 26. Despite the fact that the tomb had been rifled some time after the king's burial, the contents were found practically undamaged and in a wonderful state of preservation. The discovery must be ranked as the most important that has yet rewarded the efforts of explorers (*see* TUTANKHAMEN). But though so far (1931) this find has dwarfed all others before or since, many others, valuable to the archæologist and historian, have been made in the past few years. In 1925 great interest centred on Sakkara, where the work begun in 1924 by the Department of Antiquities in investigating the area surrounding the Step Pyramid, the oldest stone building in the world (3rd dynasty), reaped its reward in the bringing to light of a temple built to commemorate the thirty-year jubilee of King Zoser. There were found near the temple a colonnade 85 yards in length, which seems to have formed the main entrance to the pyramid enclosure. This colonnade comprises forty-eight columns of white limestone, arranged in pairs, and all were originally 5 metres high and 1 m. in diameter. The shafts are not fluted, like those found shortly before, but are carved to imitate a bundle of reeds. The E. and W. ends of the colonnade have curious imitation doors carved in the masonry of the walls, having the appearance of doors swung open. In a bay space between the columns were found the heads in diorite representing foreign prisoners, and in the style of the so-called Hyksos statues, and now regarded as belonging to the middle kingdom. The colonnade is the work of Imhotep, the first known architect, who was subsequently canonised and worshipped as the patron saint of wise men and scribes. On the wall near by was found the record of a tourist eleven centuries B.C., who stated, in a fair round hand, that he had taken a holiday to see the wonders of Sakkara, after having spent several years in campaigns, of which he was the sole survivor of his troop. In 1925 also was found at Deir el Bagara, near Thebes, among other things, Queen Hatshepsut's statues. Karnak excavations in 1926 disclosed a temple to Pharaoh Akhenaton, thus supplementing the work begun the previous year when two

enormous statues of Pharaoh Akhenaton were discovered. The area being cleared in 1926, six more similar statues, having the same grotesque facial and bodily characteristics as the first two, were unearthed. The temple was found behind the statues, and though the existence of the temple had been recorded by historians it had not up to 1926 been found. The statues evidently formed the courtyard to the temple, and were in good condition. Other finds of 1926 included a bronze statuette of a singing girl unearthed in the remains of Fustat and an ancient plough found at Thebes. The most notable discovery in 1927 was that of the secret tomb of Queen Hetepheres, mother of Pharaoh Khufu (Cheops) by the Boston–Harvard Expedition at Giza ; but the mummy itself was not found, having evidently been destroyed by robbers. What was found was an alabaster canopic box on a wooden tray with a perforated pottery bowl covering the box. The box had four rectangular compartments, each containing a mass of organic matter, probably the Queen's viscera removed at the time of mummification, and the theory is that the officials, dreading the wrath of Pharaoh Khufu if the violation of the mummy were discovered, conceived the plan of reclosing the sarcophagus as it originally was, before acquainting Pharaoh of the robbery of the gold and other ornaments. The Vienna Academy of Science also made finds of tombs near the Giza pyramids, including a group of statuary of Senab, wife and children. The Fayum oasis has also proved a fertile hunting field for the archæologist, Dr. Johnston, the Oxford University librarian, conducting excavations there just before the Great War and discovering numerous interesting articles including women's vanity bags and children's toys by no means dissimilar to those of to-day. Excavation work has been continued there almost without a break for many years and as recently as 1930 some interesting Roman remains were found at Tebtunis. The study of Philistine tombs and Israelitish culture has been furthered by various discoveries in 1929 at Tel-el-Amarna, one of genuine human interest being that of a child's toy thousands of years old, representing a monkey in a chariot drawn by monkeys, which was found by the Egyptian Exploration Society, which body also found there a number of tools, ornaments and weights.

HISTORY.—The origin of the Egyptians is still a matter of dispute. It is quite probable that they were Semitic, though they appear to belong to the Berber type or N.E. Africans; they certainly possessed many characteristics of the fair-skinned Libyans; they have no real negroid trace about them, though probably there is a strain from intermarrying; thus it is likely that they may have been a fair-skinned indigenous race, mixed also with people of Asiatic origin, and a certain amount of negro blood. The earliest types, as pictured by themselves on monuments, show men of fine build with no trace of the negroid type: the males are painted red-brown and the females a light yellowish tint. The earliest prehistoric remains are at Thebes, viz. so-called palæolithic flints, rudely chipped, but these may have been produced by natural forces. On the desert implements of quite clearly defined form have been discovered. The Neolithic remains are found in considerable quantities and in interesting forms and varieties, though their age is doubtful; the province of the Fayum is very rich in these relics. The Egyptians appear to have learnt the use of metals very early : copper and bronze instruments of a very early date have been found. Apparently iron was not familiar, or at least not freely worked or used in E., although countries such as Syria sent it to them as tribute yearly. In the British Museum (Case A, first Egyptian room) is the body of a man whose grave was discovered on the western bank of the Nile in Upper Egypt; he belonged to the later Neolithic age, a relic of remote antiquity. He was buried on his left side with the knees drawn up nearly to the chin; the hair and skin are fair, the fingers long and slender; by the side of the body were flint knives and black and red and buff pottery, pointing to the belief in the existence of a future life even in that prehistoric period. The first really historical king is Mena (Menes of the Gks.); he was king of the ancient empire, a Thinite from the city of This; he founded the kingdom of white-walled Memphis. Mena is the first king of the First Dynasty, i.e. the family or line of kings governing successively. Manetho, the Egyptian priest historian, who lived in the reign of the early Ptolemies, first divided the kings of E. into dynasties, naming and numbering them; unfortunately only fragments remain of his valuable history. Manetho's list of kings and dates is scarcely trustworthy. Very few people are agreed as to the actual dates, there being a slight discrepancy of 2000 years between the leading authorities in the date of the first

Dynasty, some persons placing it as far back as 5869 B.C., others as late as 3315 B.C. The following table of Egyptian kings, with dates, is a rough attempt to place them correctly and give some idea of about the time they existed.

*The Old Kingdom.*—*First Dynasty* (from the city of This): Menes, or Mena, 4400 B.C.; Teta, or Atet, 4366; Ateth and Ata, of whom nothing is known; Hesepti, or Semti, 4266; Semen-Ptah, or Semsu, 4200. *Second Dynasty* (from the city of This): Neter-bau, or Kha-Sekhemui, 4133; Ka-ka-u (?), 4100 (Ra-Neb may be the same); Hetep-Sekhemui (?); Ba-en-Neter (?), 4066. Names have been found of kings of this dynasty of whom at present very little has been discovered, such as Uatchnes, Senta, Nefertkara, Neferkaseker. Hetchefar, Bebi, or Tchatchai. *Third Dynasty* (from Memphis): Neb-ka, 3900; Zeser, or Ter-sa, 3866. Other names appear as kings of this dynasty but details are wanting. Hen-Nekht, Tcheser-Teta, Setches, and Nefer-ka-Ra-Huni. The dates of these kings have not been settled yet. *Fourth Dynasty* (from Memphis): Sneferu, 3766; Khufu, or Cheops, 3733; Khaf-Ra, or Chephren, 3666; Men-kau-Ra, or Mykerinos, 3633. Other kings are identified with this dynasty, Tet-f-Ra, placed between Khufu and Khaf-Ra, Shepseskaf probably succeeded Men-kau-Ra. *Fifth Dynasty* (from Elephantine): Us-Kaf, or User-kaf, 3566; Sahu-Ra, 3533; User-en-Ra-An, 3433; Tat-ka-Ra, or Assa, 3366. Other kings of this dynasty are, Kahaa, Nefer-ari-ka-Ra, Shep-ses-ka-Ra, Kha-nefer-Ra, Mem-kau-Heru, and Unas, 3333. *Sixth Dynasty* (from Memphis): Teta, 3300; Pepi I., or Ra-Meri, 3233; Queen Men-ka-Ra, or Nitocris, 3066. Other kings of this dynasty are : Userka-Ra, Mer-en-Ra, Nefer-ka-Ra, or Pepi II., and Mer-en-Ra Tchefau (?) Em-sa-F. *Seventh Dynasty* (from Memphis) : very little is known of this dynasty at present; it appears to have possessed seventy kings in as many days. *Eighth Dynasty* (from Memphis): apparently had twenty-seven kings, of whom we have discovered nothing. *Ninth and Tenth Dynasties* appear to have had nineteen kings each, of whom we know nothing. *Eleventh Dynasty* (the Old Theban).

*The Middle Kingdom.*—Antefa, 2600 or 2700. Many names belong to this dynasty, but up to the present time very little has been discovered about them, many of them end with the name of Menthu-hetep. Sanhk-ka-Ra (c. 2500) appears to have arranged the first voyage to the land of Punt. *Twelfth Dynasty* (from Thebes): Amenemhat I., 2466; Usert-

sen I., 2433: Amenemhat II., 2400;
Usertsen II., 2370 or 2366; Usertsen III., 2340 or 2333; Amenemhat
III., 2300; Amenemhat IV., 2265;
Queen Sebek-Neferut-Ra, 2255. *The
thirteenth, fourteenth, fifteenth, sixteenth, and seventeenth Dynasties* are
exceedingly difficult to make clear,
as so very little is known. The thirteenth Dynasty apparently reigned
at Thebes, and Sebekhotep I. was its
first king.

*The Hyksos*, the shepherd kings,
probably nomad Semites, invaded E.
and established themselves, driving
the Fourteenth Dynasty to Xois. The
fifteenth is purely a Hyksos dynasty;
some of their names were Salatis,
Beon, Apachnas, Apophis, Yannas,
and Asses. The Seventeenth Dynasty
saw the end of the Hyksos.

*The New Empire.—Eighteenth Dyn-
asty* (from Thebes): Aahmes I., or
Amasis I., 1635; Amenhotep I. (?);
Tehutimes I., or Thothmes (Teth-
mosis) I., 1590, ? 1550; Tehutimes II.,
or Thothmes II., 1565 (?); Queen
Hatshepsu, 1552; Tehutimes III., or
Thothmes III., 1530; Amenhotep II.,
1500; Tehutimes IV., or Thothmes
IV., 1470. Amenhotep III. (the
Memnon of the Gks.), 1455, ? 1450;
Amenhotep IV., or Khun-Aton, or
Akhnaton, 1420 (?); Saa-Nekht (?),
1400; Tut-ankh-Amen (?), 1390; Ai
(?), 1380; Hor-em-heb, 1368 (?).
*Nineteenth Dynasty* (from Thebes):
Rameses I., 1365, ? 1370; Seti I.,
1355; Rameses II. (the Sesostris of
the Gks.), 1345 (?); Meneptah, or
Merenptah, 1285; Seti II., or Merenp-
tah, 1250; *Twentieth Dynasty* (from
Thebes): Set-Nekht, 1235; Arsu, or
Ariser, probably a Syrian conqueror;
Rameses III., 1225. After this successive Rameses continue to twelve,
the thirteenth prince of the name was
murdered or died, and Her-Hor, the
priest, succeeded. *Twenty-first Dynasty :* E. was divided at this period.
*Kings of Tanis :* Smendes, Pasebkhanut I., Amen-en-Apt, Sa Amen,
Pasebkhanut II. *Kings of Thebes :*
Her-Hor or Her-Heru, Piankhi, Painetchem I., Painetchem II., Masaberth,
Men-Kheper-Ra, Painetchem III.
*Twenty-second Dynasty* (from Bubas-
tis): Shashanq I., or Shishak, 945,
? 950; Uasarken, or Osorken I. (?);
Thekeleth I. (?); Osorken II. and
others (?). *Twenty-third Dynasty*
(from Tanis): Peta-Bast (?), 766;
Osorken III.; Piankhi, king of N.
Sudan, was reigning at the same time.
*Twenty-fourth Dynasty* (from Sais):
Bakenrenef (the Bocchoris of the
Gks.) (?). Other kings are ascribed
to this dynasty, of whom nothing is
known. *Twenty-fifth Dynasty* (from
Nubia): Shabaka, or So, 700 (?).
Other kings are named, but their

history is still obscure. *Twenty-sixth
Dynasty* (from Sais) : Psamthek I., or
Psammetichus, 666 (?); Neku II.,
610, ? 612; Psamthek II., 594; Uah-
Ab-Ra, or Hophra, or Apries, 589;
Aahmes II., or Amasis II., 570 (?);
Psamthek III., 526 (?). *Twenty-
seventh Dynasty* (from Persia) : Cam-
byses, 527; Darius I., 521; Xerxes
I., 486. There are other kings of this
dynasty, some Persian, some Libyan,
some native princes; see historical
record below. *Twenty-eighth Dynasty*
(from Sais) : Amen-rut, a native
prince, 405 (?), 399 (?). *Twenty-ninth
Dynasty :* five kings of small importance. *Thirtieth Dynasty* (?) : Nekht-
Heru-Hebt, 378 (?). Some few others,
unknown, belonging to this dynasty.
*Thirty-first Dynasty :* Ochus, or
Artaxerxes III., 340 (?), 358 (?);
Alexander the Great, 332.

*The Ptolemaic Period*, 304. There
are thirteen Ptolemies, followed by
Cleopatra and her son, Ptolemy XIV.

*The Rom. Period*, 30 B.C.

*The Moslem Conquest*, A.D. 639.

This table of dynasties gives a
small idea of the rulers of E., and
below is a short record of the most
important events of the best known
periods, but it must be remembered
that every year the search of the
archæologist is rewarded with fresh
facts coming to light which may alter
the time and even the name of the
chief actors in many of these events.
The first dynastic king of E. was
Mena, or Menes of the Gks. According to tradition he founded Memphis;
he also united the N. and S. kingdoms.
The name of Aha has been identified
with Menes. He resided at Abydos
as well as at Memphis. His tomb
was discovered at Abydos, a large
brick-lined pit with props to support
an inner lining of wood. Tradition
asserts that he was slain by a hippopotamus. The great interest which
centres round this king and his whole
dynasty is the remarkable stage of
civilisation the country had reached.
The furniture of inlaid ivory and
ebony, the carved alabaster vessels,
and the copper work, also the wonderful skill of the gold-workers, examples
of which have been discovered, prove
how far advanced the Egyptians were
already at the early date of about
4400 B.C. Hieroglyphic writing was
coming then into common use, and a
state religion and priestly organisation
were fully regulated and established.
During the third Dynasty, Tcheser
(or Zoser) built the great step pyramid
at Sakkarah. The great Sphinx of
Gizeh may have been built during
this dynasty, though some authorities
attribute it to the fourth. It is interesting here to state that when the
king became (as Menes) ruler of Upper

4400
B.C.

3866
B.C.

and Lower E. the red crown of the delta was worn outside the white helmet of the kingdom of the valley; this curious headdress of royalty has become familiar to all who see the various statues in museums. The *urœus* worn by kings was the model of the African cobra or asp whose name ' Ouro ' signifies king. It was represented with the body erect and the hood expanded. The fourth dynasty kings were the great builders of pyramids (*q.v.*) (and see illustration on p. 329). The first King Sneferu finally established the peninsula of Sinai as part of the Egyptian

3766 B.C.

GREEN SLATE ' PALETTE ' OF NARMER, A KING OF THE FIRST DYNASTY

dominion, with its rich copper and turquoise mines. Cheops or Khufu built the Great Pyramid. His reign seems to have been marked by the great oppression of his people. Tradition says the temples were closed and all labour ceased, so that all persons could be employed to build the Great Pyramid. Khaf-Ra, the Chephren of the Gks., built the Second Great Pyramid: he also appears to have been an oppressor of his people. The Third Great Pyramid was built by Men-kau-Ra. Many legends attach themselves to this king; he appears to have been beloved by his people; the temples were re-opened and the people returned to labour at their proper occupations. During the Fifth

3733 B.C.

3633 B.C.

Dynasty few great monuments were built. The Palermo Stele or Stone, engraved with various events and the names of some pre-dynastic kings, belongs to this period, also the papyrus of accounts and the Proverbs of Ptah-hotep. Some traditions place in the Sixth Dynasty Queen Men-ka-Ra, the Nitocris of Herodotus, round whom have gathered many legends. Some of the pyramids at Sakkara were built during this dynasty, also the red granite Sphinx of Tanis. The city of white walls received its later name of Memphis at this time. Herkuf, a prince of Elephantine, who led many successful caravan expeditions, brought from the land of Punt by way of the Red Sea a dancing dwarf to please the boy king, Pepi II., whose letter of boyish delight to Herkuf is fully engraved on the façade of the latter's tomb. During the Eleventh Dynasty Sankh-ka-Ra despatched a successful expedition to the land of Punt, bringing back spices and scented gums, much prized by the Egyptians for the purpose of embalming. The Twelfth Dynasty established the power of Thebes after a period of anarchy. The monuments of this period are numerous and of splendid design and workmanship. The great temple of Amen at Thebes was built, and the papyrus of Amenemhat I., containing the famous instructions to his son, belongs to this dynasty These kings were great irrigators, and Amenemhat III. completed the great work of Lake Moeris; he also built the labyrinth at Hawara. Art, sculpture, architecture, and trade flourished during his reign; many interesting buildings and statues belong to this period, also very beautiful jewellery. The following period of the thirteenth, fourteenth, fifteenth, sixteenth, and seventeenth Dynasties is a time of doubt and confusion. Three or four hundred years seem the probable time of the whole of these dynasties, and the Fifteenth Dynasty seems to mark the arrival of the Hyksos, or shepherd kings, who invaded Egypt and apparently conquered her without a blow. Manetho in his history describes them as the foreign Phœnician kings. Josephus calls them the children of Israel. It is fairly certain these people were Asiatic, possibly a nomadic tribe from the Syrian desert, but this matter is still obscure, and the problem remains unsolved. The bitter hatred of the Egyptians for these invaders roused them at last to a more martial spirit, and the final and complete expulsion of the Hyksos opened one of the most glorious periods of Egyptian history. Relics of the Hyksos are very scarce. They were termed Barbarians by the Egyptians, and Josephus quotes from Manetho, ' We had formerly a king whose name was Timaios. In his time it came to pass, I know not how, that God was displeased with us, and there came up from the East in a strange manner men of ignoble race, who had the confidence to invade our country and easily subdued it by their power without a battle.' Probably the horse and the war-chariot were introduced into E. by the Hyksos. The princes of Thebes who were vassals of the Hyksos at last revolted. One named Seqenen-Ra III., who was married to an Egyptian princess of pure blood, determined to throw off the yoke of the Barbarian. The Hyksos king ordered him to worship their god Sutekh; he refused, and the war of independence began. Seqenen-Ra appears to have been a determined man of great courage; when his mummy was discovered at Deir-el-Bahri, and subsequently unrolled at Cairo, the skull was hacked and split, the lower jaw-bone was broken and there were other large wounds; obviously he had died fighting for his country's freedom. His son, Ka-mes, continued the bitter struggle, and at last Aahmes, or Amasis, I. captured the stronghold of the Hyksos at Avaris and expelled the Barbarians. Aahmes became the founder of the Eighteenth Dynasty. This king rebuilt the temples and the cities ruined by the Hyksos, and at last established law and order. He was a great soldier, and fought successfully in Syria and in Nubia. Once more E. became a strong rich country. Amenhotep I., his son and successor, founded the great brotherhood of the Priests of Amen. Thothmes I., or Tehutimes I., followed Amenhotep; this great warrior king subdued Cush, or Nubia, fixed the boundary of his kingdom at the fourth cataract, and carried his armies victoriously to the Euphrates. He built on to the Theban temple of Ammon or Amen at Karnak (q.v.), which gradually became the greatest temple in the world. He was the first king to be buried in the valley of the tombs of the kings of Thebes. Thothmes II., who succeeded, married his half sister, Hatshepset; after her husband's death she became sole queen of E. Thothmes III., her nephew, was nominally king also. Hatshepset was a woman of great force of character, and her father's military genius appears to have descended to her, and in her capable hands many warlike expeditions were successfully carried out. She was a great builder, among her works being the famous temple of Deir-el-Bahri. Her design was to make a paradise for

the god Amen, and a large expedition to Punt was organised to obtain the necessary incense trees and spices. A fleet was sent off and reached Punt in safety, returning laden with ivory, gold, ebony, myrrh, dog-headed apes, leopard-skins, and thirty-one incense trees whose roots were properly balled up with earth. These trees were planted on the terraces of the temple for the pleasure of the god. This famous queen usually dressed herself as a man, but allowed herself to be described as a woman in her inscriptions. On her death Thothmes III. became sole king; one of his first acts was to deface the late queen's monuments and replace her name either by his own or his father's. He seems to have been filled with rage and hate at the very thought of her, regarding her as a usurper of his rights. Afraid of her during her life, his only revenge at her death was an act of vandalism utterly unworthy of the great warrior king he afterwards became. Thothmes III. built an enormous number of temples both at Memphis, Abydos, Denderah, Coptos, etc., his greatest work being the colonnade at Karnak; he also set up several magnificent obelisks. His conquests had made the country exceedingly rich. His campaigns in the revolted Syria, in Libya, and Ethiopia were splendidly successful; he secured the Phœnician ports, and Crete, Cyprus, and the Ægean Isles sent annual tribute to him. This great king died at a very great age; his mummy was wrapped in a fine linen sheet inscribed with the 154th chapter from the Book of the Dead. After the unimportant reigns of two kings followed Amenhotep III., the Memnon of the Gks., one of the richest kings E. ever saw. The country was now at the height of her greatest splendour and prosperity; his wife, Thiy, was a very beautiful and remarkable woman. It is not yet perfectly certain whether she was a Syrian by birth, but she certainly seems to have been of foreign extraction. Her father, Yuaa, may have been a Syrian, and her mother, Thuaa, an Egyptian. Amenhotep's buildings were very extensive. Among them are the Apis chapels at Sakkarah, the temple to the Theban Triad at Luxor, one of the greatest monuments of Thebes. He also built a famous palace on the W. bank of the river, under the Theban hills, with a large pleasure lake for his beloved queen, Thiy; it must have been a place of great beauty. The excavations there have brought to light a dim idea of this age of wealth and luxury; among other things of interest found in the palace were bath-rooms, eight in number, properly drained. The two great Colossi known to the Gks. as the Colossi of Memnon were carved for Amenhotep; they represent himself seated, and look out over the W. plain of Thebes; one was famous from a sound which was said to issue from it at dawn. There they still sit, gazing with sightless eyes across the plain, in memory of a great king dead over 3000 years ago. Amenhotep was succeeded by his son Amenhotep IV. He was only a child at his father's death, and his mother, Thiy, took over the control of the state. Her own ideas of religion may have influenced her son; though she was too wise actually to break with the powerful priests of Amen, it is certain she worshipped Aton or the one God. Amenhotep IV. stands out for us as a most significant individual in human history. This boy, so delicate and probably an epileptic, formed in his mind and soul a true monotheistic religion and taught it to his people. He was an idealist, and this new religion of his swept away the ancient superstitions and the great multitude of gods with their ceremonies and traditions; in their place he preached simplicity, honesty, and purity, a code of morality hardly exceeded by the later teaching of Christianity. His god was not a person, he was an essence, the source of life and eternal love. In the face of the ancient traditions of E. and in a land utterly priest-ridden, this boy-king set up his beautiful and wonderful faith. He called it 'The heat-which-is-in-Aton,' and symbolised it by the sun, the giver of joy and energy. He changed his name from Amenhotep to Akhnaton, so that the word Amen might not be connected with it. He married only one wife and strove to teach his people the sanctity of marriage. He built the city of Tel-el-Amarna purely for the worship of Aton. Egyptian art now underwent a great change; Akhnaton wished to be represented really and not conventionally, and his monumental pictures are utterly different in style from the previous Egyptian art. On the death of his mother he broke finally with the powerful priesthood of Amen, and retired to his beautiful city of Khu-aton or Tel-el-Amarna. Here he developed his great creed, and lived entirely in a world of ideals and dreams. One of the hymns he wrote to Aton is of exceeding beauty, and is strangely similar to Psalm civ. (*see* A. E. P. Weigall, *The Life and Times of Akhnaton*, 1920). The king having practically retired from his kingdom, the inevitable happened. Whilst he was preaching love and peace, red war knocked at the outposts of his empire; in vain his governors sent

for help, one by one the hard won victories of his fathers were forgotten, and enemies and plunderers began to show themselves unafraid. Thus the great empire of E., greatest in the world during his father's reign, crumbled to pieces, while he dreamed beautiful dreams in Tel-el-Amarna. Syria revolted and intrigued with the advancing Hittites. He had no son to succeed him, and he died at the early age of thirty-five. The kings who followed him were of no importance until Hor-em-heb became the Pharaoh. This man was a practical soldier and a worshipper of Amen. Akhnaton was regarded as a criminal heretic by him, and wherever the name Aton occurred it was effaced. When Akhnaton's mummy was discovered it was found that his name had been erased from both coffin and wrappings; this being nameless, the priests of Amen felt satisfied, because to the Egyptian the nameless soul was homeless and a wandering shadow without rest throughout eternity. One of the great discoveries belonging to this reign were the tablets of Tel-el-Amarna; they were found in the city ruins, they are nearly all written in Semitic dialect and in the cuneiform character, They consist chiefly of letters from Amenhotep to various royal persons and from foreign kings to Thiy and Amenhotep, and are of the greatest value and interest for the history of Palestine and N. Syria at this period. Rameses I. was the founder of the Nineteenth Dynasty, he was probably a distant relation to Hor-em-heb: his two years were spent in severe fighting. His son, Seti I., succeeded him. Seti was a soldier; and his great campaigns against Palestine, Syria, Libya, and the Sudan were successful, and he returned home laden with spoils. He continued the building of temples, and added seventy-nine columns to the hall of columns at Karnak. He re-opened the copper mines of Sinai, and built many good roads. He commenced a beautiful temple at Abydos, but died before it was finished. He was succeeded by Rameses II., the Sesostris of the Gks., who had been associated with his father on the throne for some years. He is frequently called 'the Great,' but he must rank below his father in the eyes of history. He was a vigorous and able king, but possessed of the most amazing vanity and ambition. His pride, his cruelty, and his appalling extravagance sapped the strength of E. The various wars undertaken by Rameses were successful, and the commemoration of his victories was lavishly carved on every temple. The Kheta (Hittites), whose ever-increasing power was a menace to the empire, were not conquered by him, but a treaty was arranged by which each country was sworn not to molest the other's territory. Rameses built the rock-hewn temple of Abu-Simbel, the temple of Bet-al-Wali, and the Ramesseum at Thebes, with many others. All over the land his name is found carved in many buildings that he did not build, for he placed his name on these that the people to come might believe he was the greatest king of E. His harem was enormous, and he was the father of nearly

RAMESES II. IN HIS CHARIOT AT THE BATTLE OF KADESH

a hundred sons and fifty-nine daughters, yet none survived worthy of his name. He lived to a great age, and his oppressive rule left E. impoverished and suffering from an incurable decline. The gathering hosts of the enemy waited at the gates to force them open. E. never again took her place as the strongest nation. Mer-en-Ptah, the thirteenth son, succeeded him ; the elder son who should have become king died before his father; this prince, called Kha-em-uast, was reported to be a magician and filled with learning. Mer-en-Ptah is supposed to be the Pharaoh of the Exodus. He was nearly sixty when he came to the throne. Among

the records of his victories is a reference to the conquest of the Israelites in Palestine, proving that there were people of that name already living in Palestine. His reign was full of wars against the encroaching enemies. The great Libyan War, in which he was victorious, once more saved E. from being overwhelmed. He appears to have been an excellent general, though an old man at the time of his great victories. His mummy was discovered in the tomb of Amenhotep II., and when unrolled showed the placid face of a stout old man with the high-bred aristocratic features of his fathers, difficult to associate with the Pharaoh who hardened his heart. After his death comes a period of misery and trouble; the country fell into a state of anarchy, and the kings following were of little importance. The founder of the Twentieth Dynasty was Rameses III. His father Setenkhot appears to have driven a Syrian invader from the throne and restored the monarchy. Rameses once more established a certain amount of order, and drove out his enemies. His greatest victory was over the confederation of people from Cyprus, Crete, Philistia, and the N. shores of the Mediterranean combined with the Libyans. They divided their forces and attacked E. by land and sea. Rameses, however, outwitted them, and won the famous naval battle near Pelusium and overthrew the land league with much slaughter, thus winning a great double victory. This king was evidently a man of some ability; his life-work was to restore the prosperity of his country. He kept two large fleets for trading purposes, one in the Red Sea and one in the Mediterranean, and greatly increased the declining commerce of E. After his death several kings followed of small importance, all named Rameses. The last, Rameses XII., was utterly priest-ridden, and the country had become poor and oppressed. On his death Her-Hor, the high priest of Amen, seized the throne and probably murdered the young prince, Rameses, a lad of great promise, who is heard of no more; so pathetically ends the great line of kings begun some two centuries before. After the accession of Her-Hor, E. became divided, with two kings ruling at the same time, one in Upper and one in Lower E.; great confusion followed, and not until the founder of the Twenty-second Dynasty came to the throne was there any king of importance. This king was Shashanq I., the Shishak of the Book of Kings; he invaded Palestine and sacked Jerusalem. He filled all the chief posts in the gov. with members of the royal family, so that presently E. became a land of petty kings. In the reign of Shashanq III., Piankhi, the king of N. Sudan, invaded E. and conquered her. The Twenty-fourth Dynasty from Sais contains the King Bakenrenef, or Bocchoris of the Gks.; he was supposed to be a great law-giver. Shabaka, the Ethiopian, who succeeded him, is said to have defeated Bocchoris and burnt him alive, an appalling crime in the eyes of the Egyptians. At the end of this Ethiopian dynasty, Thebes was sacked by the Assyrians. Psamthek I. from Sais is the first king of the Twenty-sixth Dynasty; he restored Thebes and established a certain amount of order. Nekau, who succeeded him, led an army against Syria, and on the way slew Josiah, King of Judah, but was defeated by Nebuchadnezzar II. His son Psammetichus II. found time during his short reign to repair the temples. His son, Haa-ab-Ra, the Pharaoh Hophra of the Bible and the Apries of the Gks., succeeded him on the throne. This king made an expedition to Syria purposing to assist Zedekiah, King of Judah, but failed to arrive in time, and Jerusalem fell into the hands of Nebuchadnezzar II. The remnant of the people who escaped fled to E. carrying Jeremiah, the prophet, with them. Haa-ab-Ra was dethroned by his own people, and Aahmes, or Amasis II., who was a general in the army, became king. Haa-ab-Ra was slain by an arrow while watching a fight from his galley, though some say he was strangled by order of Aahmes. The son of Aahmes was Psammetichus III., who reigned only six months. The Persian king, Cambyses, now invaded E. and conquered her. Tradition says that Psammetichus was forced by Cambyses to drink bullock's blood in sight of the people so that he died; in any case he was practically murdered, and E. became a Persian province. This closes the history of the Pharaohs; the fate of the once glorious land of E. now lay in the hands of the half-insane and wholly cruel King of Persia, who heaped misery and insults on his victims. From the various legends and records concerning him, the man appears to us only as an inhuman brute. Having married two of his sisters, he took the younger to E. with him and slew her for grieving over the death of her brother, Smerdis, whom he had previously murdered. He desecrated the temples of E., and the Egyptians believed his increasing fits of madness were due to a curse because he wounded the sacred calf 'the Apis.'

His successor, Darius I., appears to have been a less oppressive ruler, and more inclined to conciliate the native population. He encouraged the Egyptian priesthood, restored their temples and built fresh ones. The full titles of the Pharaohs were adopted by him and his successors, but the hatred smouldering in the heart of the Egyptian for E.'s conquerors could not appreciate these things. The country now was not strong enough to combine in a national revolt. In 486 B.C. they rose against Xerxes, who speedily crushed the rebellion. Later on Amyrtæus of Sais revolted successfully against Darius II., and for perhaps sixty years E. was once more independent. Nectanebus II. was the last native king of E. Artaxerxes III., or Ochus, the Persian, subdued E. finally with great brutality. Her condition now became so miserable that Alexander the Great was welcomed as a deliverer. After the victory of Issus, Alexander travelled to Memphis and from there marched to the oasis of Siwa to worship at the oracle of Jupiter Ammon. He also founded the port of Alexandria. In the division of his conquests, E. fell to the share of one of his generals, Ptolemy, son of Lagus, who founded the Ptolemaic Dynasty. Under the rule of the Ptolemies, in spite of heavy taxation, E. once more prospered. Ptolemy I., or Soter I., commenced the famous library and museum at Alexandria. He wrote a history of Alexander's campaigns, and he introduced the worship of Serapis. Ptolemy II., Philadelphus, built the lighthouse at Alexandria known as Pharos, regarded as one of the seven wonders of the world. The splendour of his court was famous. Manetho the priest wrote his history of E. during this reign. Ptolemy III., Euergetes II., left more monuments than his fathers, among them the temple of Edfu, finished by Ptolemy IX. Ptolemy IV. was merely a debauchee, and the decline of the Ptolemaic kingdom began during his misrule. In the reign of Ptolemy V., who came to the throne at five years old, E. suffered from a series of incompetent regents. When the child grew to manhood his chief pleasure seemed to lie in athletic games and hunting. During his reign the suppression of native rebellions was remarkable for their cruelty and tyranny. While Ptolemy V. was quite a child, the chief priests met in council at Memphis and passed a decree ordering that special honours be paid to this king. This decree was duly carried out and inscribed on stone steles. The Rosetta stone, now in the British Museum, which was dug up by M. Boussard in 1798, is one of these steles. Its name is derived from the place where it was found. It is of especial interest and value, because it was inscribed in hieroglyphic, demotic, and Gk., and consequently helped materially to decipher the hieroglyphics. Ptolemy VI., Philometer, reigned jointly with his brother Ptolemy VII., Euergetes II., nicknamed Physkon. The infant son of Philometer, Ptolemy VIII., was murdered, and Ptolemy IX., his uncle and murderer, seized the throne and married the mother of the little king. Ptolemy IX. was a man utterly vile in his habits and himself. During his reign he finished the temple of Edfu and repaired many other temples both in E. and Nubia. Ptolemy X. was murdered by the people, and an illegitimate son of Soter II. was chosen as Ptolemy XI.; he was called Auletes, the flute-player. Rome supported this man, and after he was driven out by popular hatred, restored him. On his death he left the kingdom to his eldest son, aged ten, Ptolemy Dionysus, who was married to his beautiful and famous sister Cleopatra, when she was barely seventeen years old. These two children ruled jointly under the care of the Roman Senate. The great Pompey was appointed their guardian. Pompey was murdered off Pelusium by order of the boy-king, who had succeeded in banishing his beautiful and trouble-some sister. Cleopatra had with-drawn to Syria to make preparations to recover her rights by force; thence she went to Rome and encountered Julius Cæsar. One legend asserts that at her command she was wrapt up in a bundle of rugs and skins and sent as a present to Cæsar; her singular beauty and charm overcame his scruples and he resolved to place her on the throne of E. It is certain that he undertook the war for the purpose of reinstating Cleopatra. In 48 B.C. he landed in E., having defeated Ptolemy, who perished in the naval battle off Alexandria. Cleopatra was replaced on the throne to rule with her younger brother, Ptolemy XIII.; the child died soon afterwards; tradition says he was poisoned by Cleopatra's order. She then lived openly as Cæsar's mistress, but after his assassination she went no more to Rome, and her son, whom she asserted to be Cæsar's child, called Cæsarion, was associated with her on the throne as Ptolemy XIV. The Rom. triumvir, Mark Antony (q.v.), succeeded Cæsar in her affections; the story of their love is well known; it was the ruin of both Antony and E. When Octavianus sailed to E.

he murdered the little Ptolemy XIV., Mark Antony died by his own hand, and Cleopatra, knowing her kingdom lost, and refusing to become a Rom. captive, died, according to tradition, by applying an asp to her breast. Thus ended the reign of the Ptolemies, and E. now became a Rom. province. The Ptolemies left many beautiful monuments behind them, among them those on the island of Philæ. The last native king of E., Nectane-bus, built a temple to Isis there, which Ptolemy Philadelphus reconstructed. The unfinished kiosk, known as 'Pharaoh's bed,' is one of the most beautiful ruins on the island; the temple of Ptolemy (Euergetes I). is also famous for its beauty. As a Rom. province, 30 B.C., E. was under the rule of a prefect. The first prefect was Cornelius Gallus; he appears to have made a treaty with the Queen of Nubia at Philæ. This queen, Amen-taret or Candace, broke the treaty five years later, marched from her city of Meroe and invaded E. The Roms. defeated her and marched to Napata, which they sacked, and Can-dace was forced to retire and submit. During the reign of Claudius the valuable Indian trade was secured for E. Most of the Rom. emperors from Tiberius onwards adopted Egyptian names and titles in E. Hadrian twice visited E., and founded Antinoe. Græco-Rom. buildings of this period are numerous. Under Marcus Aure-lius the suppression of a serious re-bellion caused lasting damage to the prosperity of the country. One Rom. general called Avidius Cassius struggled to make himself Emperor of E., but he was slain by his own troops. When Christianity first began in E. is not quite certain, but pro-bably very early; many Egyptians adopted it as the hope of a future life coincided with their own views. It must always be remembered that the Egyptians thought more of the future life than the present, and that from the earliest times they were a deeply religious race; it was obvious therefore that having adopted Chris-tianity they would do so thoroughly, and under Severus they suffered severe persecutions which merely added to their zeal, and they soon made Alexandria a centre of Christian learning. During the rule of Caracalla (A.D. 211) all the men who could possibly bear arms as soldiers were massacred in Alexandria, because of some real or fancied insult to Cara-calla. Under the rule of Decius the Christians again suffered terrible per-secutions. In A.D. 270 Zenobia, the famous Queen of Palmyra, invaded E., and Athenodorus, her son, governed E. jointly during the reign of Claudius.

When Aurelian became emperor he perceived the dangerous policy of the great Palmyrene queen, as her son was already having coins struck bearing the imperial title. Aurelian drove the Palmyrenes from E. His army was led by Probus, and E. was ruled by Rome again. Probus became governor of E., and under his rule repelled the great tribes of Blemmyes who came from the E. Sudan and who were dominating the whole of the Thebaid. Under Diocletian the country was still troubled by them, and a formidable revolt broke out led by Achilleus, who called himself into churches. The temple of Serapis was the scene of a disgraceful and bloody conflict between the Christian mob and the remnants of the pagans; finally it was converted into a church for the use of the Christians. This was the real death-blow to Paganism; the Christians showed as little mercy as their brother pagans in asserting the supremacy of their belief. During the reign of Justinian, while the army was concentrated in quelling an invasion of the Blemmyes, Chosroes, the Persian, invaded E. and conquered her easily, holding her for ten years. Heraclius defeated the Persian

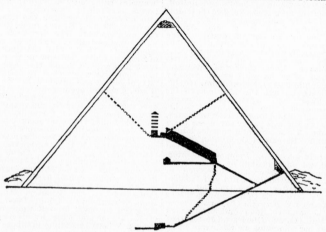

A SECTION OF THE GREAT PYRAMID, SHOWING THE POSITIONS OF THE
PASSAGES AND CHAMBERS OR TOMBS

the Emperor Domitianus. Diocletian came to E. and captured Alexandria, and Achilleus was slain. The Blemmyes retired to the Sudan, and an arrangement was made to pay them a fixed annual sum on the understanding that they ceased from raiding Rom. territory. A temple was built at Elephantine where both sides could swear to observe this covenant. ' Pompey's Pillar ' was erected during Diocletian's rule to commemorate part of the corn tribute being paid to the Alexandrians. The Christians at this period were again persecuted with savage cruelty and they fled to the deserts in large numbers, building and hiding in obscure monasteries. In 378 Theodosius the Great proclaimed Christianity to be the religion of his empire. E. at once turned her attention to converting the temples of the ancient gods of her country and won back the country for a little while, but one stronger than he was rapidly gathering forces on her borders to take and possess her finally. E., weakened by her long internal struggles and utterly impoverished by the years of misrule, now fell an easy prey to Amr-Ibn-al-Asi, the general of the Khalifa Omar, and the once great E. became a province of the newly-founded Arab empire. See below, *Moslem Conquest*.

*Religion and Antiquities.*—The ancient religion of the early Egyptians is exceedingly difficult to disentangle or explain. The multitude of tribal gods and the enormous number of various legends and beliefs belonging to each separate god of one district makes it impossible, except at great length, to show how all were subject to and fulfilled their various functions under the one supreme head. The names of many gods and goddesses have been lost, but a total of about 2200 have been discovered. The Egyptian never had any real uniformity of religion, but always the chief god reigned supreme, the others merely fulfilling their allotted parts. We cannot, with absolute truth, describe their ancient religion as monotheistic, but the one supreme being *was* their real and *only* God, and the multitude of others were but attendants and symbols. The most familiar gods from the ancient records are first Thoth, who was the heart of Nu, Nu being a god who floated in vast waters and Thoth the heart or idea of Nu who created the universe. The sun, Ra, sprang into being from the endless waste of waters and thereafter ruled the heavens. Osiris (whose name must not be spoken) and Isis, his beloved sister and wife, were the children of Ra, also Set, the wicked one, and Nephthys, his wife and sister. The legends of Osiris and the cult of that same god are as old as dynastic E. (probably older). Osiris was the good god-man who, for love of this world, suffered, died, and rose again to rule in Heaven. He was to the Egyptian the proof of the resurrection, and their great hope of eternal life. The description of his kingdom. ' The fields of peace, the pleasant pools of peace,' prove how readily acceptable such a creed was to the hard-worked Egyptian who lived in abject poverty, depending entirely on the Nile for his hard-won crops. Isis, the most famous goddess of E., the wife and sister of Osiris, had many beautiful legends attached to her name. One of the stories of her love for Osiris and the finding of his body may be briefly told : Set, the wicked one, the god of evil, killed Osiris and divided his body into fourteen pieces; Isis wandered over the earth until all the parts of her husband's body were found. During her wanderings, Horus, her divine son, was born. The holy child, under the instructions of his devoted mother, performed certain ceremonies over his father's burial, and assisted in raising him from the dead; from that time on Osiris became the king of Amenti, the under-world, the land of hopes and dreams. The worship of the gentle mother Isis increased gradually, spreading at last to Rome and Greece. She became the goddess of the under-world of love, of magic, and of healing. As the goddess of magic, a legend of the new kingdom describes how she discovered the hidden, all-powerful name of Ra, which no one knew (names always bore a large part in Egyptian ceremonies). To the Egyptian she was

always the great gentleness, the pure in heart, and the devoted wife and mother. Her worship withstood longer than any other the overwhelming tide of Christianity, and there is much in common between the two doctrines. Thoth was usually represented as the scribe of the gods; he it was who weighed the hearts of the dead men and women in the court of Osiris; by his side always waited a half-animal monster known as Am-mit, the eater of the dead, patiently waiting to devour the heart that would not balance against the feather. Among the other better-known gods and goddesses are Ptah of Memphis, who assisted in the creation, the Hephæstus of the Gks.; Maat, the goddess of truth ; Hathor, the lovable, represented with a head-dress of the horns of a cow and the solar disc between them; the old god Bes of the Sudan; Hapi, the Nile god; Anubis, the jackal god, son of Set; Nut, the goddess of the sky; Bast, the goddess of Bubastis, to whom cats were sacred; and many others. Later, many foreign gods crept in and were either worshipped separately or associated with the gods of E.; such were Hap, the Apis Bull, and Serapis, and the great god Ammon or Amen of Thebes, who became associated with Ra of Memphis as Amen-Ra. Amen-Ra became a very powerful god; his worship reached its zenith during the Eighteenth Dynasty. The great priesthood of Thebes associated Ra-Harmachis of Memphis with him because of their desire to absorb all the lesser gods, Amenhotep IV., or Akhnaton, who formed his own creed apart from all previous Egyptian teaching, was as a child dedicated to Ra of Memphis; thus at the beginning of his new religion his god Aton was associated with Ra. Aton has been identified later with the Syrian-Asiatic Adonis (*cf.* Hebrew *adonai*, Lord !). The worship of Serapis was introduced by Ptolemy Soter, Serapis being identified with Userhapi the Osiris-Apis. A Gk. statue of this god was placed in the Serapeum of Alexandria, the destruction of which place by the Christians has already been referred to. The dead Apis, or sacred bull, was embalmed and buried at Memphis. Sacred amulets were popular with the Egyptians, and were supposed to possess magical properties. The best known are the *scarab* or beetle, symbol of the god Khepera, who was one of the creators; the girdle of Isis, symbol of protection; the *anhk*, symbol of life; the *shen*, or circle, which became the cartouche of the kings, meaning protection from Ra; and many others. Sacred figures were used to bury with the dead, known as *Ushabti* figures; these came to life in the other world and performed all the hard work for the person who was buried with them. The god Thoth, who was the scribe of the other world, invented writing. Hieroglyphics were used until the Rom. period, then demotic writing took their place. The hieroglyphics were purely pictorial; they were used for monumental purposes, but for ordinary use on papyrus the hieratic writing soon came into use. The key to their decipherment, the Rossetta stone, has been referred to above. Writing materials consisted of papyrus, a reed-pen, and ink. The papyrus used was the stem of the plant which grew in the marshes by the Nile; the strips of the stem were arranged in a sheet perpendicularly and another sheet placed horizontally, the two sheets being then gummed together and dried. The Coptic writing consisted of the Gk. alphabet and several signs. Of the large amount of literature which has been saved, the greatest part is religious. ' The Book of the coming forth by Day,' or ' The Book of the Dead,' is a series of formulas collected by the priests of Heliopolis about 3300 B.C. ' The Book of Breathings ' contains a number of prayers. Others are ' The Book of the Lamentations of Isis and Nephthys,' and ' The Book of Traversing Eternity,' an account of a journey through the other world. There are many other curious and interesting books of litanies, hymns, and prayers, etc. Some of the hymns are very fine. Among the literature not religious may be mentioned the ' Precepts of Ptah-hotep,' ' The Instructions of Amen-em-hat I.,' ' The maxims of Ani,' and a ' Hymn to the praise of Learning.' There are many stories of marvellous adventure, and some interesting scientific works on astronomy and geometry. The Turin Papyrus is a chronological list of 300 kings, with the length of their reigns; the tablets of Abydos were lists made for Seti I. There are various medical works of great interest, but although learned physicians existed, magic was mixed up with medicine and probably believed in more than drugs. A good deal of poetry must have been written; many songs and verses have been saved, among them the love-songs from the Harris Papyrus. The manners and customs of ancient E. are exceedingly interesting. Women enjoyed great freedom; unlike the women of other Eastern countries they went unveiled, and met men friends on equal terms. The legal wife passed in and out of the house as she chose, and when she became a mother

her influence greatly increased. The descent of a house was traced through the mother, not the father. Brothers were allowed to marry sisters, and uncles their nieces. Kings and nobles were allowed several wives and concubines, but only one was the legal mistress of the house, whom it was almost impossible to divorce; all the wives were free and respected and appear to have lived happily together without jealousy. The poorer class women worked very hard, and being married frequently at fourteen and fifteen and often having large families they naturally aged very rapidly. but all enjoyed common right and freedom and held a much better position than the other Eastern countries gave to their women. The children had many toys; several have lasted long enough for us to see them, such as dolls, balls, animals with movable limbs, ninepins, and many others. A certain amount of education was given at various schools, and colleges for the students of magic and religion existed, learning being always held in high repute. The people ate their meals with their fingers and used the flat bread-cakes to wipe them on. Beer was the common drink of the country and made in several ways; date-wine was also largely drunk. Dancing men and women were popular and greatly amused the people, also tumblers and contortionists. The harp, the drum. and the sistrum were favourite musical instruments. The furniture of royal and noble houses was very rich and beautiful, inlaid ebony and ivory being much used. From the earliest time the Egyptian was an excellent potter. Vessels of a great variety of shape and size were always in use. The making of glass was an ancient art in which the workers excelled, porcelain was much used, and many beautiful coloured vases, figures, beads, etc., have been discovered; the colouring of their porcelain was often exceedingly vivid and lovely; the beautiful rich turquoise blue, with which most people are familiar, and brilliant greens and purples delighted them. Jewellers excelled in their art at a very early date; some extremely early specimens of exquisite design have been discovered, such as the gold bracelet of the wife of a king of the First Dynasty. The weaving of fine linen was always a flourishing trade; apparently each temple possessed its staff of linen weavers. Their currency appears to have been ring money of gold and copper, and later of iron, also bags of gold dust, representing a certain fixed value. A distinct class of the people were employed as embalmers of the dead, who had certain restrictions and privileges. For the methods of embalming, see MUMMY. The clothes worn by the Egyptians were very simple for a long period; a loin cloth and a belt for the men and a short tight petticoat for the women, made of linen, wool being unclean. The children went naked, both rich and poor. Later the men wore a skirt reaching to the knees, with a curious triangular front which stood out as though starched. The women's skirts became longer and were held up by braces over the shoulders, leaving the upper part of the body bare. The people of the Eighteenth Dynasty wore more elaborate clothes; cloaks and tunics became fashionable with fringes and embroideries. Sandals were made for the feet and elaborate wigs for the heads. The men all shaved their heads, the young boys retaining a long plaited lock on the side of the head until they came to manhood. The women plaited up their own hair with strings of beads, and wore decorated bandlets. Both sexes wore a quantity of jewellery and frequently carried fans and mirrors.

*Moslem Conquest.*—In A.D. 639 Omar I., the second Caliph, sent an army of 4000 men, under the command of Amr, to take E. They marched through Syria to Pelusium, which fell easily, then on to the Fayum, and defeated the Roms. at Heliopolis, A.D. 640. It is probable that Cyrus, the governor of E., may, for reasons of his own, have assisted in betraying the country to the Moslems. It is certain the Copts helped the enemy, and E. was conquered with very little difficulty. The pagan population embraced the faith of Islam, but the Copts remained Christians. The Arabic language rapidly spread and gradually superseded Egyptian. Now began a history of bloodshed, cruelty, tyranny and treachery that it would be difficult to exceed. For about the first 100 years the Christians were tolerated, and then a series of terrible persecutions commenced. Heavy taxation began and steadily increased. A series of ineffectual revolts occurred, but the unhappy people had suffered so long that they were utterly incapable of a properly organised struggle for freedom and their futile efforts were instantly crushed with great cruelty. In 832 the Copts raised a more serious revolt, and Motasin, the feudal lord, failed to suppress them with an army of 4000 Turks. The Caliph Mamun came to E. to assist and the Copts were defeated. All the men who were caught were massacred horribly and the women and children sold as slaves. This finally subdued the Coptic nation. In A.D. 868 E. was given in fief to a Turkish general called Bayikbeg, the son of a slave, who had risen in the Caliph's service; from this time onwards various Arabs, Turks, and Syrians succeeded in obtaining the throne of E.; many of them were murdered, and the struggles of different persons to obtain power, together with heavy taxation, reduced the country to an utterly wretched condition. In 1164 the Franks invaded E. and joined a usurper called Shawar; they were defeated by Shirguh and his nephew, the famous Saladin (*q.v.*). Saladin took the title of Sultan, and during his rule E. recovered a little. His son Othman succeeded him, and another period of disputes and disasters convulsed the country. The Mameluke Dynasty began after the death of the Sultan Nagm-al-din, who had purchased vast numbers of slaves and turned them into soldiers; these were called the Bari Mamelukes. In 1515 war began with Selim I., the Ottoman Sultan, who defeated the Mamelukes and incorporated E. with the Ottoman empire; the country then became a Turkish province.

*Modern History.*—From this time until the Fr. expedition in 1798, the gov. suffered constant changes; several rulers were murdered, with continual bloodshed, cruelty, and internal revolts. The Fr. expedition was presumably to suppress the Mamelukes and restore the authority of the Sublime Porte, but it was the beginning of that dream of Oriental conquest that always possessed Napoleon. Napoleon landed, and, after taking Alexandria, defeated the army of Murad Bey and Ibrahim Bey at the battle of the Pyramids. He then established a municipal council at Cairo, and the Fr. exercised dictatorial power. The Fr. fleet was destroyed by Nelson and the Eng. in the great battle of the Nile in 1798. Napoleon went off on an expedition to Syria, leaving Fr. governors at Cairo, Alexandria, and Upper E. The Sublime Porte sent a double expedition to recover E. by force. The Fr. general, Kléber, defeated the Turks, and a certain amount of order was restored. Kléber was assassinated, and General (Baron) de Menou succeeded in command. His declaration of a Fr. protectorate over E. convulsed the country again. In 1801 the Eng., commanded by Sir Ralph Abercromby, landed at Aboukir and invested Alexandria. General Menou attacked them, but he was defeated. Sir Ralph Abercromby *d.* from his wounds received in the battle. The combined British and Turkish armies under General J. Hely Hutchinson and Yusuf Pasha marched to Cairo, and the Fr. general, Belliard, finding himself overwhelmed, agreed to evacuate Cairo and leave E. with his troops. General Menou at Alexandria was compelled to accept the same conditions, and both left for France, thus terminating the Fr. occupation of E. Troubles arose almost at once. The Turks treacherously tried to exterminate the Mamelukes. General Hely Hutchin-

rule was abominable and the half-starved and ruined people of Cairo waited in misery for a deliverer. Three thousand Kurdish troops were sent from Syria to Cairo to strengthen Khorshid, but they behaved with such brutal ferocity that Mehemet Ali returned, and was hailed by the people as their leader and saviour. A furious and bloody struggle took place between the forces of the two Pashas. Khorshid was recalled to Turkey, and Mehemet Ali

[D. McLeish]

THE GREAT TEMPLE OF DIER-EL-BAHRI IN THE VALLEY OF THE TOMBS
OF THE KINGS AT THEBES

son took measures at once against the Turks, who submitted and gave up their prisoners. Mohammed Khosrev was the first Turkish governor after the Fr. occupation. The Turks and Mamelukes continued to fight, and the Albanian soldiers rebelled against the Turks successfully, and Mahommed Khosrev fled. Tahir Pasha, the leader of the Albanians, seized the gov., but was assassinated twenty-three days afterwards. Mehemet Ali, an Albanian commander, allied himself to the Mamelukes: this was the beginning of further terrible struggles; one faction of the Albanians placed Ahmed Pasha Khorshid in the seat of gov. His

made himself governor of E. The Beys (Mamelukes) disputed his authority; Mehemet Ali arranged and carried out successfully a treacherous and horrible massacre of the Mamelukes. In 1807 a British fleet arrived under the command of General Mackenzie Fraser. The troops entered Rosetta without opposition, but were trapped in the narrow streets, every roof and window rained fire on them from the hidden garrison, 185 Eng. were killed and 281 were wounded. A series of disasters followed. Mehemet Ali marched to Cairo, having allied himself to his enemies, the Beys, for the purpose of driving out the Eng. The Eng. were defeated and obliged to retire. Mehemet Ali then proceeded to massacre the remaining Beys, and finally remained the sole undisputed possessor of E. He recognised the suzerainty of the Sultan, and complied with the command of the Porte to send an army against the Wahabis (q.v.). He returned to Cairo on the day of the battle of Waterloo. Mehemet Ali now turned his attention to Egyptian domestic affairs; he created for himself a monopoly of the industries of the country, and by nationalising the land became the proprietor of all the cultivated soil of E. He started and encouraged the cotton-growing industry in the delta, which was perhaps the best thing he ever did. He ordered the new canal between the Nile and Alexandria to be dug, which was done with forced labour and under such wretched conditions that 20,000 fellahin died before it was completed. The country was still heavily taxed; all the necessities of life were four times the price they formerly had been; the land became utterly impoverished; and the finances were in hopeless chaos. In 1838 a commerical treaty with Turkey was arranged which destroyed the monopolies, and matters grew a shade better. Mehemet Ali reorganised his army, and the fellahin and negroes replaced Turks and Albanians. The Sultan appointed him governor of Crete, and in 1824 a fleet of sixty Egyptian vessels sailed to Suda Bay to assist the Sultan against the Gk. insurgents. The European powers intervened and Mehemet Ali withdrew to E. In 1833, the Sultan appointed Mehemet Pasha of Syria and the district of Adana, so that Mehemet now became the sole ruler of a large empire, while he was only responsible for a small tribute to the Sultan. In 1841 the powers again intervened: Mehemet was becoming too strong and too aggressive; he was compelled to submit to certain restrictions. He died in 1849 at the age of eighty. This remarkable man had achieved a great deal during his long and stormy career. His history bears the records of many treacherous deeds and violent scenes of bloodshed, but he was, in spite of all, a wonderful, strong, and interesting character. Among the really good things he accomplished for E. was the fostering of the cotton industry in the delta and the conquest of the Sudan. His son Ibrahim being dead, Abbas I., Mehemet's grandson, ruled. During his reign the railway from Alexandria to Cairo was commenced at the suggestion of the British gov. Abbas was murdered by his own slaves after only six years' rule. He was succeeded by Said, the fourth

son of Mehemet. During his rule Ferdinand de Lesseps obtained the concession (1856) for the construction of the Suez Canal (q.v.). The Eng. secured the right to start the Telegraph Company and established the Bank of E. The national debt was commenced under Said: he died in 1863. Ismail, who succeeded him, did a great deal to reorganise the gov., and made many improvements, but his extravagance landed him in bankruptcy; he sold his shares in the Suez Canal to the British gov., thereby paving the way for the international control of the Khedive's affairs. He was compelled to submit to a constitutional ministry, which he soon found means of getting rid of. Ismail was immediately deposed by the Sultan, and his son, Tewfik, succeeded him as Khedive. In 1879 the Eng. and Fr. re-established the constitution; Major Baring (Lord Cromer) and M. de Blignières represented the two countries. A movement now began among the Arab troops to remove the foreigners; it was led by a fellah officer, calling himself Ahmed Arabi. This man was promoted and made Under-Secretary for War, and then member of the cabinet. Arabi possessed a gift of a rough kind of eloquence, which appealed to the people; it is probable that the man was sincere at heart himself and an unconscious tool in stronger and more unscrupulous hands. At the instigation of an Arabic faction, a massacre took place in Alexandria, 1882, and, fearing a serious revolt, the British and Fr. fleets arrived. The forts were bombarded, but the nationalist movement prepared to resist with great determination. The British gov. decided to employ military force. The Fr. declined to share the responsibility and Eng. acted alone. Troops were landed under the command of Sir Garnet Wolseley, and the revolt was crushed at the battle of Tel-el-Kebir. The Khedive returned to Cairo, and a fresh ministry was formed. Arabi was sentenced to death, but his life was spared and he was banished. The task of restoring the country to order fell to Lord Dufferin, the High Commissioner; he laid down lines for the reorganising of the administrative parts of the gov., and the practical carrying out of this general scheme was undertaken by Sir Evelyn Baring (Lord Cromer), who was appointed Consul-General in 1884. The Sudan now claimed the immediate attention of the country. A religious rebellion had broken out led by a fanatic calling himself a Mahdi of Islam. Colonel William Hicks Pasha had been sent with 10,000 men to suppress the revolt, but was utterly defeated in a great battle at Obeid, 1883. The Khedive wished to make another attempt to regain his lost province, but Sir Evelyn Baring insisted that there being neither men nor money, the Sudan must wait. The Mahdi was now master of the chief part of the Sudan, though Khartum (q.v.) still held out, and some other places. General Valentine Baker, with an army of 2500 mixed troops, was sent by the Khedive to relieve Sinkat and Tokar; they were defeated with great loss. Suakin was in grave danger now. A British force of 4400 was sent and concentrated at Suakin. Sinkat fell, and Tokar surrendered to the Mahdi. General Gordon and Colonel J. D. Stewart, who had been sent by the British gov. to Khartum to discover the best method of evacuation, were now entirely cut off from help and besieged in Khartum, and the problem was how to extricate them. There was a long delay, caused by various reasons. General Gordon was only provisioned for five months; the siege began on March 18, 1884, and held out till January 1885. Sir Charles Wilson, arriving on January 28, found Khartum in the hands of the enemy and General Gordon murdered two days before. Khartum had fallen, Gordon was murdered, the relief expedition had come too late. Lord Wolseley's Nile expedition, though failing in its ultimate purpose, experienced some severe fighting, and won the battles of Abu Klea and Metemmeh, etc. The British troops were withdrawn in June, and the Mahdi died before the rearguard had left Dongola. During this time Sir Evelyn Baring was fighting the internal difficulties of E., the question of finance being the hardest to overcome. The Convention of London (1885) enabled E. to raise a loan of £9,000,000; of this, when the indemnities and debts were paid, £1,000,000 remained over, and this was invested in irrigation and largely helped to save the country from bankruptcy. In 1892 the Khedive Tewfik died, and his son Abbas Hilmi succeeded. He was quite a young man and at first failed to comprehend the need of understanding his position as Khedive under the protection of Britain. He secretly encouraged an anti-British agitation, but at last realising his own danger, he submitted without further trouble. During this time the Khalifa Abdullah-el-Taaisha succeeded the Mahdi and ruled the Sudan. His intention was to conquer E., and though delayed at first by trouble with Abyssinia and various massacres of Egyptians, he arranged his campaign

and placed Wad-en-Nefumi, the Dervish Amir (who had defeated Hicks Pasha), in command of the army that was to conquer E. Another large portion of the army under Osman Digna, once a slave-dealer of Suakin, and now one of the greatest generals under the Khalifa, was engaged in fighting the Abyssinians. Osman Digna was defeated with great slaughter and fled to Kassala. In 1886 Colonel Kitchener seized Osman Digna's stronghold and a large store of ammunition; Osman himself escaped. Kitchener became Governor of Suakin in the same year and Sirdar of the Egyptian Army in 1890. It was not until 1898 that the power of the Khalifa was broken. The great battle of Omdurman was the destruction of the Khalifa's rule. His army was 40,000 strong. Kitchener marched to Omdurman, driving the enemy back as he went. Among the many deeds of gallantry that occurred must be mentioned the famous charge of the 21st Lancers. They were surprised by 2000 Dervishes but cut their way through with heavy loss. During the battle over 10,000 Dervishes were killed and as many wounded; 5000 were taken prisoner. The black flag of the Khalifa was captured and sent to Queen Victoria. The result of this victory was the extinction of Mahdiism and the recovery of the Sudan for E. The Khalifa fled. On the Sirdar's return he encountered the Fr. expedition at Fashoda under Captain Marchand. Matters were diplomatically arranged, though the crisis became very acute. Captain Marchand returned to France. The Khalifa was killed in an encounter in 1899, and his son surrendered. Osman Digna was captured at Yebel Wariba in 1900. Meanwhile the country of E. continued to increase in prosperity. In 1907 Lord Cromer resigned, having completed his great work of creating from the ruins of hopeless misrule and ignorant tyranny a country that was steadily progressing and prospering. Sir Eldon Gorst succeeded him. The Anglo-Fr. Agreement of 1904 put an end to the foreign complications attendant on the somewhat anomalous position of Great Britain; it recognised the protection and occupation of E. by Great Britain as a *fait accompli*. It was further of inestimable importance in freeing the country from the financial embarrassments imposed on her by the foreign bondholders through the Caisse de la Dette, and to this freedom the increasing prosperity of the country must be regarded as mainly due. Trouble arose with Turkey over a boundary question on

he Eastern frontier in 1906, but this
vas adjusted, and the Nationalist
novement then became the chief
ause of political anxiety. This
ulminated in the murder of Butros
Pasha, the Coptic prime minister, in
910, by one Wardani, who, after a
ong trial, was executed in the follow-
ng year. The resignation of Sir
Eldon Gorst in 1911 owing to ill-
health was followed by the appointment of Lord Kitchener as British
Agent and Consul-General. Kit-
hener's administration was marked
by great personal prestige, and the
policy of his predecessor was to a
ertain extent reversed. The cry of
Egypt for the Egyptians ' was not
quite so insistent, and any measure
of independence which Egyptian
ministers had previously enjoyed was
quietly but firmly withdrawn. The
British officials were again ensconcing
themselves in administrative posts, and
strange as it may seem, these actions
eemed to pass without demur on the
part of the Egyptians. During the
years of the British occupation there
had been little or no social intercourse
between the Egyptians and the
members of that vastly different
race who were administering and
virtually ruling their land for them.
Indeed the social barriers had been
well defined; but it was part of
Kitchener's policy to alter this and
to foster social intercourse between
the British and the Egyptians. The
Great War interrupted Kitchener's
activities in E. and on Aug. 6, 1914, he
became Secretary of State for War.
Great Britain declared war on Turkey
on Nov. 5. This was followed on
Dec. 18 by Great Britain declaring
E to be a British Protectorate.
Next day the Khedive was deposed
and his uncle, Hussein Kamil, was
proclaimed Sultan of E. Sir Henry
MacMahon, who had rendered poli-
tical service in India, but was with-
out experience of E., was made High
Commissioner. In 1916 Sir Henry
MacMahon was succeeded in the
High Commissionership by Sir R.
Wingate, Governor of the Sudan and
Sirdar. On Oct. 9, 1917, the Sultan
Hussein Kamil (or Kamel, q.v.) died,
and was succeeded by his brother
Ahmed Fuad. After his accession
(Oct. 30) an armistice between Turkey
and the Allies was proclaimed, to be
followed on Nov. 11 by the armistice
between the Allies and Germany. (For
the campaign in Egypt, see EGYPT,
GREAT WAR CAMPAIGN IN.) It is not
surprising that the wave of self-
determination that had risen, as a
direct consequence of the Great War,
among the smaller races in Europe,
was not without its effect on the
political situation in E. The Nation-

alists were becoming extremely res-
tive, and by skilful propaganda were
adding daily to their numbers and
enhancing the self-assertiveness of
their adherents. They were led by
Saad Zaglul Pasha, an able man of
humble origin and a former Minister
of Education and Minister of Justice,
who within a couple of days from the
signing of the Armistice led a deputa-
tion to the High Commissioner asking
that permission might be granted to
send an Egyptian delegation to
London to discuss Egyptian affairs.
The request received the backing of
Sir R. Wingate, but was refused in
somewhat curt terms by the Foreign
Office. A carefully worded reply by
Zaglul, in which the request was
renewed, was also rejected against
the advice of the High Commissioner.
This refusal determined Zaglul, and
early in 1919 he announced the
Nationalist programme at a public
meeting. This programme demanded
no less than complete independence
for E. It is difficult to understand
the policy of the British gov. at this
juncture. It had acted against the
advice of its own High Commissioner,
Sir R. Wingate, who on account of
advice he had tendered was recalled.
The next stroke was the banishment
of Zaglul with three other prominent
Nationalists to Malta, and this was
the occasion of rioting and strikes.
Property was destroyed, Eng. offices
were wrecked and a state of general
lawlessness prevailed. The British
troops were called out, and several
rioters were shot. The rioting spread,
and on March 18 at Deirut a train was
attacked, and two British officers, an
official and five soldiers were murdered. For these murders about
thirty people paid the extreme penalty
on April 9. General Allenby (q.v.),
who had been appointed Special
High Commissioner, succeeded in
restoring order, and Zaglul and his
fellow-exiles were allowed to return to
E. Acting on the recommendation
of General Allenby, the British gov.
proclaimed the end of the British
Protectorate, and E. was recognised
as an independent sovereign state
(Feb. 28, 1922). This proclamation
was subsequently ratified by the
British Parliament, which reserved
the four following points for a later
settlement : (1) Security of communications between various parts
of the Empire; (2) defence of E.
against foreign attack; (3) protection
of European interests ; (4) the Sudan.
The Sultan Ahmed Fuad became
King Fuad I. (q.v.). On April 19,
1923, the Constitution of the Kingdom
of E. as an hereditary constitutional
monarchy was proclaimed. The constitution settled the succession, de-

clared the gov. to be representative, and established equal legal, civil, and political rights for all Egyptians. Religious and personal liberty is guaranteed, and compulsory free elementary education for both sexes is provided in gov. schools. Islam is declared to be the state religion, and Arabic the official language. Parliament consists of two houses, the Senate and the Chamber of Deputies. The king nominates two-fifths of the members of the Senate, and the remainder are elected by universal suffrage, one senator to every 180,000 inhabitants. The king also nominates the President of the Senate. The Chamber of Deputies is between his Prime Minister, Abd-el-Khalig Sarwat Pasha, and Sir Austen Chamberlain, the British Foreign Secretary, took place in respect of a draft treaty between the two countries. The main points of the treaty offered by the British gov. as a result of the negotiations were : E. to become a member of the League of Nations ; British troops to remain in E. for another ten years, when a fresh agreement would be made ; Great Britain to be represented in E. by an Ambassador who was to take precedence in the diplomatic corps ; the organisation of the Egyptian army and the existing administration of the Sudan to

[D. McLeish

THE WONDERFUL AVENUE OF SPHINXES AT THE ENTRANCE OF THE
TEMPLE OF KARNAK

elected by universal suffrage, one member to 60,000 electors. The term is for five years, and each member receives an allowance of £E600 per annum. The first election under the new constitution took place in Nov. 1923, and resulted in a large majority for the Nationalist party. Zaglul became Prime Minister, and the first demands put forward by his party were for the complete independence of E., the withdrawal of British troops and the return of the Sudan. On Nov. 19, 1924, General Sir Lee Stack, governor-general of the Sudan, was assassinated by Egyptian Nationalists at Cairo. The British gov. insisted on the withdrawal of detachments of Egyptian troops from the Sudan. In Oct. 1925 Lord Lloyd was appointed High Commissioner by the Baldwin gov. and held office till his recall by the Labour gov. in 1929. In midsummer 1927 King Fuad visited England and conversations remain unaltered. The treaty was rejected by the Nationalists, to the leadership of whom Mustafa en-Nahhas Pasha had succeeded on the death of Zaglul Pasha on Aug. 28, 1927. The Ministry of Sarwat resigned on the rejection of the treaty terms and Mustafa en-Nahhas became Prime Minister. His term of office was brief, the ministry being dismissed on June 24, 1928. Muhammed Mahmud Pasha was appointed Prime Minister three days later, but, on July 19, Parliament was dissolved by royal decree and parliamentary gov. was suspended. In May 1929 an agreement between Great Britain and E. was concluded in respect of the rights of E. and the Sudan in the waters of the Nile and the regulation of irrigation works. In 1930 another attempt was made by the British (Labour) gov., with Arthur Henderson as foreign secretary, to settle the outstanding differences between the two countries, but the question of the final settlement of the Sudan proved a stumbling-block, and no treaty was concluded. England of course is naturally nervous about the adequate defence of the Suez Canal, which forms such an important link in the chain of communications of the British Empire.

BIBLIOGRAPHY.—*Ancient :* The histories of W. H. Flinders Petrie, E. A. Wallis-Budge, J. H. Breasted, and G. Maspero should be consulted ; Garstang's *Short History* ; A. Erman, *Life in Ancient Egypt* ; the *Guides to the various Egyptian Rooms in the British Museum,* by E. A. Wallis-Budge, are an admirable source of knowledge ; the article ' Egypt ' in the *Ency. Brit.* is a storehouse of the latest expert knowledge, with full bibliographies to all the different sections. *Moslem :* A. J. Butler, *The Arab Conquest of Egypt,* 1901 ; Lane's *Modern Egyptians* gives a clear picture of the early nineteenth century. *Modern :* Lord Cromer's *Modern Egypt,* 1908, and the *Annual Reports.* See *Egypt,* by George Young, 1927.

**Egypt Exploration Fund** was founded in 1883 by Miss Amelia Edwards, who was greatly interested in Egyptian antiquities, and who was one of its first secretaries. Indeed, she gave up her other literary work to devote her time to writing about Egypt, her work being published under the title *Pharaohs, Fellahs, and Explorers.* The object of the society is to collect all the information possible which has reference to the history and nature of the sites excavated. The society publishes annual reports, which are beautifully illustrated. Some of the distinguished men who have worked for it are Professor Flinders Petrie, Professor Gardner, and Doctors Grenfell and Hunt.

**Egypt, Great War Campaign in.** Although Turkey was not in a state of war with Great Britain until Nov. 5, 1914, she had been under Ger. influence for some years before the Great War broke out, and an alliance actually existed between the two countries. The Central Powers had regarded Egypt as the ' throat of England,' and to Turkey had been allotted the task of throttling England, when such a task was considered strategically necessary. In Oct. 1914 Germany's fortunes were at a low ebb : she had lost the Battle of the Marne, Russia had overrun E. Prussia, the Austrians had suffered heavily at Lemberg, and reinforcements to British arms were moving freely from India and the Dominions. The time had therefore arrived for Turkey to come into the arena of

war and play her allotted rôle. The pre-war British garrison was required in France, and in Sept. 1914 the 42nd (E. Lancs.) Territorial Division was sent out to replace it. Troops from India, Australia and New Zealand also arrived, and by the end of 1914 about 70,000 troops were concentrated in E.

Early in Nov. 1914 a Turkish force under Jemal Pasha advanced through the Sinai peninsula, against the Suez Canal. Jemal's Chief of Staff was Colonel Kress von Kressenstein, a Bavarian officer of great ability and energy. They advanced in three columns, and arrived at the canal on Jan. 25, 1915. Their strength was about 12,000–15,000 men. They raided Kubri, 7 m. N. of Suez, on Jan 27, and Kantara on Jan 28. On the night of Feb. 2–3 a general attack was made between Serapeum and Tussum, but was repulsed by gun-fire. The Turks succeeded in throwing three pontoons across the canal, but all the Turks in them became casualties. At 9.30 a.m. on Feb. 3 the enemy brought up reinforcements and made another but equally unsuccessful attempt, and withdrew at 1.30 p.m., leaving sixty dead and 300 prisoners with the British.

The next operations were against the Senussi (a Mohammedan nonconformist sect founded in 1835), which occupied the W. desert, with centres at Kufra and Siwa. The sect had many adherents in E. and was susceptible to Turkish propaganda. The Kaiser sent Sayed Ahmed, their leader, arms and munitions by submarines, which were landed on the coast of Tripoli. In Nov. 1915 they captured the crew of H.M.S. *Tara,* which had been torpedoed near Sollum, and committed other hostile acts against the British. This led General Sir John Maxwell, the British Commander-in-Chief in this theatre, to take offensive action against them. Actions were fought at Hazalin and at Agadir in Dec. 1915 and March 1916, respectively, in which the Senussi lost heavily. An armoured car detachment under the command of the Duke of Westminster found forty survivors of the *Tara* in a distant camp and rescued them.

When the Gallipoli Peninsula was evacuated the British troops went to E., and the whole of the garrison was reorganised under General Sir Archibald Murray. The total force amounted to thirteen divisions, six of which were sent to other theatres of war. A line to the E. of the Suez Canal was occupied, where a much-advertised Turkish advance was awaited. They were under the command of Kress von Kressenstein, and numbered about 18,000 men. By the middle of July 1916 they were in touch with the British outposts. On the night Aug 3–4 they attacked Romani, but, being heavily counter-attacked, fell back in disorder, having suffered 9000 casualties, 4000 being prisoners. The British followed up this success and drove the Turks out of E., the Sinai Peninsula and eventually out of Palestine.

**Egyptian Bean,** the name sometimes given to the bean-like fruits of *Nelumbium speciosum*, the sacred Lotus, now found only in Asia and Australia. The seeds are eaten in some parts of India, and are believed to be the *beans* which Pythagoras forbade his disciples to consume.

**Ehrenbourg, Ilya Grigorievitch,** *b.* in 1891, is one of the best novelists and poets of the young generation of Russians. He spent a good many years of his youth abroad, but returned in time to live in Russia the four stormy years after the 1917 revolution. Outside his own country, he is best known in Germany, where many of his books have been translated. There is an acrimonious tone about most of them which stamps him as a pamphleteer rather than romancer. His best novel is *Julio Jurenito,* which seeks to give a picture of most of Europe after the Great War. His most successful book of short stories gives the true facts connected with thirteen pipes in his collection and the lives of those who once owned them. One of his most beautiful poems is *The Sons of Our Sons,* in which he tells how future generations will think the war period was all blood and horror, whereas the truth was that flowers still bloomed, birds still sang, the sun still gilded the trees, and the sons of men still rejoiced in these lovely things.

**Ehrenbreitstein,** until 1919 'the Gibraltar of the Rhine,' a tn. of Prussia, situated on the Rhine opposite Coblenz. The fortress is famous, and is situated on an almost inaccessible rock, 400 ft. high. The sides are steep except on the S., where the approach is winding and strongly defended. It was conquered in 1631 by the Fr., in 1637 by the Imperialists, and again in 1799 by the Fr. The castle is anct. and the site was a Rom. fort. In the eleventh century, a noble named Erembert held it, from whom it derived its name. In the twelfth century Archbishop Hillin of Trier had possession of it. When the Allied troops of occupation were stationed on the Rhine after the Great War

American soldiers occupied th fortress and the American flag flev over it.

**Ehrlich, Paul** (*b.* 1853), Ger. chemist *b.* in Silesia. His first notable dis covery was of 'tri-acid stain.' A the Koch Institute, Berlin, his stan dardisation of anti-toxins won fo him the appointment as head of th Institute for Experimental Thera peutics, Frankfort-on-Main. His chie discovery was of Salvarsan as a remedy for various diseases.

**Eibar,** a tn. of Spain in the prov of Guipuzcoa, noted for its damas cened ' E. work.' Pop. 11,880.

**Eibenstock,** a tn. of Germany, i the kingdom of Saxony, situated o the R. Mulde. It is a centre of th tambour embroidery. Pop. 9230.

**Eichendorff, Joseph, Freiherr vo** (1788–1857), a Ger. poet, *b.* a Lubowitz. He was a famous membe of the Ger. Romantic school. Hi chief work of romance is *Aus den Leben eines Taugenichts*; and hi chief dramas are : *Ezzelin vor Romano ; Der letzte Held von Marien burg ; Die Freier.* He is best known however, as a lyric poet ; indeed, h is the greatest lyricist of the Ger Romantics. His language is simple and musical ; some of his poems hav been set to music both by Schumani and Schubert. Two of his best lyric are *Nachts* and *Waldesgespräch.*

**Eichhorn, Hermann von** (1848– 1918), Ger. soldier, *b.* at Breslau Won the Iron Cross in the Franco Ger. War of 1871. In the Great Wa he served throughout on the Russiar front. He came into prominence a one of Hindenburg's chief lieutenant in the E. Prussian campaign, in whicl he took a notable part in the seconc battle of the Mazurian Lakes (Feb 1915). As commander of the Tentl Army he directed the operations against the Niemen, and was in command of the forces which capturec the important stronghold of Kovno ir Aug. 1915, whereby the Russians were compelled to abandon Brest-Litovsk and the whole of Poland. In 1918 he was made field-marshal and Ger commandant in the Ukraine. Bombed in the streets of Kieff by social revo lutionists, he *d.* of his injuries in July 1918.

**Eichhorn, Johann Gottfried** (1752– 1827), a Ger. historian. In 1788 he was made professor at Göttingen where he lectured both on orienta languages and on political economy. He is important as being the first to subject the books of the Bible to the ordinary methods of literary criticism.

**Eichstätt,** or **Eichstädt,** formerly **Eistet,** a tn. of Bavaria, in Franconia. It is situated on the Altmühl, in a eep valley, 38 m. S. of Nuremberg. he cathedral was begun in the leventh century. Other noteworthy uildings are the Schutzengel (proecting angel) church (1640), the hurch of the Capuchin monastery, ith an imitation of the Holy epulchre at Jerusalem, etc. The wn owes its origin to the grave of t. Walpurgis, and St. Willibald, an nglo-Saxon missionary, to which ilgrimages were made from A.D. 870. op. 8010.

**Eider,** a riv. of Prussian Germany, hich rises to the S. of Kiel. It rosses Schleswig-Holstein, forming boundary between those two divions. Its direction is first N. and hen generally W., but it has an xceedingly winding course, and after owing 117 m. it enters the North ea at Tönning. The E. is navigable s far as Rendsburg, a distance of 0 m., and from this place a canal onnects it with the Baltic Sea.

**Eider-Duck,** the popular name of a pecies of *Somateria,* included in the ub-family Fuligulinæ of the duck amily Anatidæ. They inhabit N. egions and are to be found on the oasts of the Atlantic and Pacific. he commonest species, *S. mollisima,* is occasionally found in Britain n the breeding season. The bill nd feet are olive green, and the own is much valued in commerce or stuffing quilts and cushions. )ther well-known species are *S. pectabilis,* the king E., which furishes most of the down exported rom Greenland ; *S.* (or *Heniconetta) telleri,* known as Steller's E. ; *S.* (or *Irctonetta) Fischeri,* the spectacled E.

**Eidograph** (Gk. εἶδος, form ; γράφειν, vrite). This is a machine which is ften used instead of a pantagraph, nd is employed for copying drawngs, maps, and plans on the same cale, or for enlarging or reducing hem in any proportion.

**Eifel, The,** a volcanic plateau of Rhenish Prussia, stretching from the rontier of Belgium to the Rhine and he Moselle. The heights reach from 4500 to a little more than 2000 ft., nd the surface is generally undulatng, with ridges and well-wooded valleys. The plateau is composed principally of Devonian rocks and imestone, with numerous fossils.

**Eiffel, Alexandre Gustave** (1832– 1923), Fr. engineer, *b.* Dec. 15, at Dijon. Studied at the Ecole Cenrale for three years. His first vork was the construction of the ron bridge over the Garonne at Bordeaux, where he worked his caissons ' with compressed air. The pridge over the Douro at Oporto, the viaduct of Garabit, as well as other metal bridges, are also his work ; and

it was he who designed the immense locks for the Panama Canal. His best-known work is the E. Tower, on the completion of which in 1889 he was made an officer of the Legion of Honour. In 1907 he pub. *Recherches experimentales sur la Résistance de l'air, executées à la Tour Eiffel.* Later, he made experiments in aeronautics, on which he pub. two books and also a report in 1919, and, in 1920, *L'Hélice Aérienne.* Died in Paris, Dec. 28.

**Eiffel Tower,** stands in the Champ de Mars, Paris. It consists of three stories, and the platform of the sum-

THE EIFFEL TOWER

mit is 985 ft. above the ground. Almost 7500 tons of iron were consumed in its construction, and the cost of its erection was about £250,000.

**Eiger Mountain,** a mountain of Switzerland, in the Bernese Oberland, situated about 4 m. from the Jungfrau. Its height is over 13,000 ft.

**Eigg, or Egg Island,** an island belonging to the Hebrides, W. Scotland, situated 5 m. S.W. of Skye. It has an area of 12 sq. m. The S. extremity, called the Scaur of Eigg, is a remarkable basaltic cliff, reaching 1346 ft. in height. In one of the caves 200 of the Macdonalds were suffocated by the Macleods. Pop. 197.

**Eight Hours Labour Law,** an Act passed by Congress in 1912 limiting the hours of daily service of labourers and mechanics employed upon work done for the United States or for any Territory or for the District of Columbia to eight hours. Violations of this law are met with a penalty.

**Eight, Piece of,** the popular name given to an old Spanish silver coin. It was divided into eight silver reals, hence the term P. of E. Other names for it were piastre or dollar. (*See* PIASTRE and DOLLAR.) Its value was about 4*s.*

**Eighty Club.** A political Liberal club, which was established in London in 1880, the title corresponding to the date.

**Eikon Basilike** (Εἰκών Βασιλική) (*The Pourtraiture of His Sacred Majestie in his Solitudes and Sufferings*). This work was published immediately after the death of Charles I., and being written in the first person was ascribed to Charles himself. Indeed, his words about his treatment of Strafford confirm that belief. Dr. John Gauden said he started the work about 1647, and submitted it to Charles, but those in favour of Charles' authorship say that he wrote the first six chapters before 1645, *i.e.* before the battle of Naseby. The general verdict, however, is against Charles.

**Eildon Hills** are three high hills situated in Melrose, Roxburgh, Scotland. The central peak rises to an elevation of 1385 ft., and commands a most magnificent view of the surrounding country. The remains of a Rom. camp are to be seen on one of the hills, and several legends are told concerning them. The poet Thomas the Rhymer is associated with them, and Scott remarked that, standing on the Eildons, he could point out forty-three places famous in war and verse.

**Eileithyaspolis,** the Gk. name of Nekhab, a city of anct. Egypt, which stood on the Nile about 40 m. from Luxor or Thebes. In anct. Egypt, E. or Nekhab, now represented by the ruins of El Kab, was the capital of Upper Egypt. In the midst of every town was the temple of the local god, and the vulture-goddess of El Kab, called Nechbet (Nekhbi, Nekhebi), was the goddess E. of the Gks. The city contains the ruins of the following temples : that of Rameses II. dedicated to Ra, another built by Euergetes II. and dedicated to Nekhab (E.), and a third by Amenophis III. which is dedicated to the local deities. Some rock-tombs have also been excavated, some of which date back to the thirteenth century. The remains are now very scanty because all the stones worth taking were appropriated for the building of sugar factories under the Khedives Mehemet Ali and Ismail Pasha.

**Eilenburg,** a tn. of Prussian Saxony. It has manufactures of agricultural implements, calico, and cloth; there are also breweries and chemical works. E. possesses an

anct. castle, known as Ilburg. Po 18,000.

**Eilendorf,** a tn. of the Prussia Rhine prov., situated about 3 m from Aix-la-Chapelle. Pop. 11,570.

**Eilithyia** (Εἰλείθυια), called al Ilithyia, was the impersonation of th pains of childbirth, and was there fore worshipped as the goddess wh assisted women in labour. But seeir that all moon-goddesses had influen over birth, she is identified at tim with Artemis, Hera, and Aphrodit According to the Cretan legend, I was *b.* at Cnossus, and from the her worship spread over Delos an Attica. Another legend says she wa *b.* in Crete, but came to Delos t assist Leto. She is at times co nected with the Fates, who also hav control over childbirth.

**Eimeo,** or **Aimeo,** called by th Fr. Moorea, the most important the Fr. Society Islands in the Pacif Ocean, is situated about 15 m. N. Tahiti. Its area is about 50 sq. m. its surface is hilly and the valleys ai well cultivated. The London Mi sionary Society was established o this island.

**Einbeck,** a tn. of Hanover, Ge many, 50 m. S. of Hanover. Th picturesque old inner tn. is stī partially enclosed by its former fort fications, and contains the fourteentl century Alexander church, thirteentl century Market church, fifteenth century New town church, the six teenth-century town hall and fir mediæval houses. From the end c the fourteenth century its beer ha brought it prosperity. It also make carpets, engraving tools, weavin machinery and bicycle parts, an has saw mills and horsehair spinnin works. Pop. 9600.

**Einfischthal,** the Ger. name, mor correctly spelt Eivischthal, of Va D'Anniviers, an Alpine glen in th Swiss canton of Valais. It is summer resort, and its chief village i Sierre.

**Einhard,** or **Eginhard** (*c.* 770–840) the biographer of Charlemagne, *b.* i E. Franconia. Owing to his extra ordinary ability he came under th notice of Charlemagne at an earl age. His artistic skill gained for hin the name of 'Bezaleel,' and th basilica of Aix-la-Chapelle, as wel as other buildings, have been attri buted to him. He became ver friendly with the emperor, and whe he died, Louis, his son and successor appointed E. tutor to his own sor Lothair. His best work is *Vit Caroli Magni,* which is a splendic biography of Charlemagne and i perhaps the finest historical bio graphy of the Middle Ages. Of hi other works, the most importan are : *Epistolæ*, and *Annales Franco-rum*.

**Einsiedeln,** a tn. in canton Schwyz, Switzerland, the most famous pilgrim-resort in Switzerland, with a Bene-dictine Abbey, founded about 948 on the site of the cell of St. Meinrad, who was murdered in 861. It was dowered with land by two emperors, and became an independent prin-cipality of the Holy Roman Empire. The church (1719–35) is 446 ft. long, and is one of the most noble works of the baroque period. In the Gnaden-Kapelle is the ' Black Virgin,' a richly decked miracle-working image in wood. The Abbey Library com-prises 100,000 volumes, and 1300 MSS., some of the eighth to the twelfth centuries. The celebrated chemist Paracelsus was born here in 1493. Pop. 8500.

[*Topical Press*

ALBERT EINSTEIN

**Einstein, Albert,** propounder of the doctrine of Relativity (*q.v.*), was *b.* March 14, 1879, at Ulm in Würtem-berg ; son of Hermann E., a Jew, described as owner of electro-technical works. The family removed to Munich during the childhood of Albert, who was slow in learning to speak, shy, and unsociable, with a taste for music. His early education was Jewish at home, Catholic at school. When older, he attended the Luitpold Gymnasium at Munich. In 1894 the family removed to Milan, and Albert began wandering tours in N. Italy. He wandered into Switzer-land, and at Aargau studied mathe-matics and physics at the canton

school. With a view to school-mastering, he began studying at Zürich Technical School at the age of seventeen, and remained there four years. He afterwards acted as tutor at Schaffhausen and Bern. In 1901 he was naturalised a Swiss citizen ; and he was engaged as a technical ex-pert in the Patent Office at Bern, 1902–5. In 1903 he married a S. Slavonic student, from whom he was afterwards divorced. In 1905 he published, in the *Annalen der Physik*, papers on the production and transformation of light, the Brownian movements, molecular dimensions, and the electrodynamics of moving bodies. The last-named brought him under the notice of Max Planck. In 1909 he became professor extra-ordinary at Zürich of Theoretical Physics ; in 1911 professor ordinary at Prague. In the autumn of 1912 he returned to Zürich as professor at the Polytechnic. Early in 1914 he was appointed director of the Kaiser Wilhelm Physical Institute at Berlin, in which city he has ever since resided. His second marriage was with a cousin of the same surname. By 1916 he had published *Die Grundlage der allgemeinen Relativitäts-theorie* ; followed in a few years by *Über die spezielle und die allgemeine Relativitätstheorie*—the (largely un-read) Bible of the Relativists. He staked his doctrine on certain phenomena being observable at the solar eclipse of May 29, 1919 ; and, as these were said to have been observed thereat, his doctrine was immediately declared confirmed. In 1921 he was lionised by philosophers and astronomers in U.S.A. and Eng-land. His doctrine, falling in with the reaction toward mysticism, owes none of its success to any lucidity or persuasiveness on E.'s part. His exponents prefer their own expres-sions and illustrations, especially in the matter of the relativity of simul-taneity. It has been epigrammati-cally said of E. that he takes a formula and calls it a theory.

**Eisenach,** a tn. in the Free State of Thuringia, Germany, is beautifully situated on the edge of the Thuringian forest. The mineral waters from Creuzburg attract many invalids (8500 in 1927). There are several churches of the early thirteenth century, the town hall (1508, rebuilt 1638) and the castle of the former grand duke in which is now a picture gallery. In the Karls Platz in the centre of the tn. stands a statue of Martin Luther, who attended the Latin school in the tn. from 1498 to 1501. The manufactures are dyes, agricultural machines, electrical articles. There are many educational establishments and museums, one on the Wartburg, where Martin Luther, too, passed some years in this town, and the chapel in which he preached is still in existence. The town dates back to about 1065, and was founded by the Landgrave of Thuringia; later it passed into the hands of a Saxon family, and finally in 1741 it became the property of the duchy of Saxe-Weimar. It contains the Klemda, a castle built about 1260, a ducal palace, built in 1742, a town hall, and the late Gothic Georgenkirche. It is still famous for its pottery. Pop. 43,390.

**Eisenberg** : (1) a tn. in the prov. of Hessen Nassau, Prussia, with 21,530 inhabs. (2) A tn. in Thuringia, Germany, with a pop. of 11,220 and the castle of Christiansburg, which is used as the town hall. Sausages, porcelain, and pianos are made.

**Eisenerz,** a tn. in the Austrian prov. of Styria, in the Erzberg Mts., which is famous for its iron mines. Pop. 8670.

**Eisenstadt,** a tn., Austria, situated 26 m. from Vienna. Pop. 3260.

**Eisleben,** a tn. of Prussia, 24 m. from Halle, the b. p. of Martin Luther. The house in which he was *b.* has been a museum since 1917. Both that and the house in which he died are in the Altstadt or old town. The churches include the Andreaskirche, with the pulpit in which Luther preached, the fifteenth-century church of Peter and Paul, with the chapel in which he was baptised, the Nicholas Church, 1426, and the Anna Church, 1514. The town-hall is of the date 1519–30. Besides the mining of copper and silver, there is a trade in seeds. Pop. 23,700, mostly Protestant.

**Eisner, Kurt** (1868–1919), Bavarian journalist and statesman of Jewish descent. Wrote voluminously on art, the drama and sociology. Won a high reputation at the Berlin Gymnasium in philosophy and Germanic studies, and early in life wrote an excellent treatise on Nietzsche. Wrote for the *Frankfurter Zeitung* in 1892 onwards, and for his socialist opinions was sentenced to a term of 9 months' imprisonment in 1897. Subsequently co-operated with Wilhelm Liebknecht in the editorship of *Vorwärts.* Was on the staff of the *Fränkische Post,* 1905, and the *Münchner Post* in 1910. Organised a bloodless democratic revolution in Bavaria towards the close of the Great War, becoming Premier after the abdication of King Ludwig, but was murdered by Spartacist soldiers early in 1919. Highly talented, very courageous and energetic, he certainly assisted to bring about the collapse of Germany's effort by means of strikes which his able pen and abler speeches never ceased to foment. His last work, *Die Neue Zeit,* comprises speeches and a Volkslied on the Bavarian Republic. Years previously he had assisted the first revolution, the story of which he tells in his history of the Königsberg treason trials. He prophesied the World War in his Morocco treatise, *The Sultan of the World War.*

**Eisteddfod** (plur. eisteddfodau), a congress of Welsh bards, was instituted in order to encourage the composition and preservation of national poetry and music. Its origin dates back to very early times, and an E. was held at Caerwys, in Flintshire, about the beginning of the twelfth century. It was first sanctioned in England after the annexation of Wales, and there are records of eisteddfodau having been held in the reigns of Edward III., Henry VI., Henry VIII., and Elizabeth. The festival then seems to have been discontinued, but was again revived in 1789. Its celebration generally occupies three or four days, and a president and conductor are appointed for each day. There are competitions in poetry, music, singing both choral and solo, as well as singing with the harp. The third day is the chair day, when the fortunate winner is proclaimed.

**Ejectments,** *see* RECOVERY OF LAND.

**Ejectors,** *see* PUMPS.

**Ekaterinburg,** or **Yekaterinburg,** a city in the gov. of Perm, Russia, on the Asiatic side of the Urals, about 860 ft. above sea-level. It has two cathedrals, a monastery, and a mint for copper coinage. It is the chief mining town of the Ural Mts., and has a laboratory for the assay of gold. Its manufs. are machinery, soap, and candles. There are also establishments for polishing precious stones, and trade is carried on in cattle, cereals, iron and woollen goods. Pop. about 56,500.

**Ekaterinodar** (Russia), *see* YEKATERINODAR.

**Ekaterinodar Nikolskaya,** *see* YEKATERINO NIKOLSK.

**Ekaterinoslav,** or **Yekaterinoslav** (now called Dnepropotrovsk) : (1) a gov. of Ukrainia, bounded on the N. by the govs. of Poltava and Kharkov, on the E. by the territory of the Don Cossacks, on the S. by the sea of Azov and Taurida, and on the W. by Kherson. Its area is 24,477 sq. m. and its pop. about 3,500,000. Its surface is mostly steppe and its soil is the fertile black earth which yields large grain returns. The chief iron deposits of Ukrainia are found in the W. part of the gov., and considerable and varied manufacturing is carried on. (2) City in Ukrainia and cap. of gov. of same name situated on the Dnieper. It is one of the greatest Ukrainian centres for iron working. It has also manufactories of agricultural machines, tobacco, soap, and tanneries and potteries. Pop. about 220,000.

**Ekhmim, or Ikhmim,** see AKHMIM.

**Ekron,** a city of the Philistines on the borders of Judah and Dan, where Beelzebub was worshipped. It was the place from which the Ark of the Covenant, which had been captured by the Askalonites, was returned to Israel. At a later period it became part of the territory ruled by the Maccabees. Its present inhabs. number about 1200, and in its neighbourhood is a Jewish agricultural settlement founded by Baron Rothschild.

**Elabuga,** a tn. of Russia, situated on the Kama R. It has flour mills and exports corn. In 1858 the celebrated ' Ananiynskiy Mogilnik ' (burial-place) was discovered 3 m. from this town.

**Elæagnus,** see OLEASTER.

**Elæocarpus,** a genus of Elæocarpaceæ. *E. serratus* bears an olive-like fruit used by the natives of India as an ingredient of their curries; *E. cyaneus* has white flowers and is one of the most ornamental of Australian plants.

**Elæococca** (Gk. ἐλαία, the olive tree, and κόκκος, a berry), a genus of Euphorbiaceæ. The seeds yield valuable oil. *E. verrucosa* of Japan produces seeds supplying oil for burning, and *E. vernicia* of China furnishes oil used for painting.

**Elæodendron,** a genus of Celastraceæ, occurs in all tropical countries, and is divided into thirty species. *E. glaucum* is a small tree about 14 ft. in height; it is a native of Ceylon and Coromandel and has been introduced into Britain as Ceylon tea. *E. Roxburghii* grows in the mountains of India, and *E. orientale* is found in Madagascar.

**Elæolite,** a crystalline plutonic rock composed largely of nepheline and alkali felspar. It resembles granite in appearance, and is of a pale grey or pink colour; green is also found. It does not contain quartz, but is rich in many other minerals which contain alkalis.

**Elagabalus, or Heliogabalus,** Emperor of Rome (A.D. 218–222), was *b.* at Emesa, A.D. 205, and was then called Varius Avitus Bassianus. When very young, however, he became priest of E., the sun-god, and so obtained this name. In A.D. 218 E. was proclaimed emperor as the successor of Caracalla, and was successful in overcoming Macrinus, who had murdered Caracalla and had occupied

the throne for a short time. His reign, which lasted over three years, was characterised by the most unheard-of excesses, and he was eventually murdered by the prætorians.

**Elam,** the anct. name for that part of the land which lies E. of the lower course of the R. Tigris. Susiana (from the name of Susa, its principal city) was the name given in classical history to the S. portion of this land, the modern name of which is Khuzistan. This portion was called by the Gks. Elymais.

**Elan,** a riv. of Wales. It flows through Cardiganshire and Radnorshire, joining the Wye S. of Rhayader. A dam has been constructed on this river for the purpose of forming a reservoir which supplies the city of Birmingham with water.

**Eland,** the popular name of a genus of large and almost exclusively African antelopes, characterised by the general absence of horns in the females and by those of the male being devoid of rings, angulated in front, and usually spirally twisted. Both sexes have a large dewlap, and the crowns of the upper molar teeth are low and broad. The common E., *Orias canna*, formerly ranged over the greater part of S., E., and Central Africa, but is now extinct in the S. of the continent. Its complete extirpation is probably only a matter of time, the animal being frequently slaughtered for its hide. The magnificent species known as the Derbian E., *O. derbianus*, replaces the common species on the W. coast in the districts of Angola and Senegambia.

**Elanet, or Elanus,** a genus of Falconidæ closely allied to the kites, found in all the continents. *E. cærulus*, the black-winged kite, is common to Africa and Asia, and is occasionally seen in Europe. *E. scriptus* belongs to Australia; *E. dispar*, the black-shouldered hawk, occurs in America. All are birds of prey and some will eat even insects.

**Elaps,** see CORAL SNAKES.

**El Arish,** a tn. at the mouth of the Wady, E. A. forming the frontier between Egypt and Palestine. It was occupied by the British advanced guard on Dec. 20, 1916.

**Elasmobranch.** The Elasmobranchii are an order of fishes marked by the cartilaginous nature of the bones and by the absence of sutures in the cranium. Such are the shark, ray, sturgeon, skate, etc., and a number of more or less allied extinct forms. They appear in the Upper Silurian epoch, and as they are the oldest fishes with which we are acquainted, it is probable they may have been the stock from which all fishes were derived. A Japanese shark, *Chlamysdoselachus*, is said to be the oldest living fish. All the existing members of the order are carnivorous, but whereas the tropical shark is highly predaceous, some of the largest species have very small teeth and feed on molluscs and other invertebrates. The Elasmobranchii are marine fishes, but many ascend tidal rivers.

**Elasmosaurus** (Gk. ἐλασμός, metal plate, σαῦρος, lizard), a gigantic fossil reptile belonging to the Elasmauridæ, and allied to the Plesiosauridæ. It is found in the Upper Cretaceous rocks in Kansas, and its computed length is 45 ft.

**Elasticity.** A substance is said to be elastic when, on being left free, it recovers wholly or partially from a deformation. A very general proof of compressibility and of E. of bulk is afforded by the fact that the great majority of bodies are capable of transmitting sound-waves, for the propagation of sound consists essentially in the handing on by resilience, from layer to layer of the medium, of a state of compression or dilatation. All ordinary sounds are propagated in air; the rate of passage of sound has been measured in the waters of the Lake of Geneva and elsewhere, and it is a matter of common observation that sound can be transmitted through solid bodies, such as a wall or a floor. The one kind of deformation which can be experienced by a fluid, i.e. a gas or a liquid, is change of bulk. This change of bulk can only be brought about by a pressure acting equally in all directions. The E. in these cases is the ratio of the change of pressure to the change of volume per unit volume. A change of volume of a gas is accompanied by an evolution or an absorption of heat, which is usually shown by a rise or a fall of temperature. It is sufficient to state here that there will be two values for the E. of a gas, according as the change takes place without loss or gain of heat or without change of temperature. In the latter case, the E. is numerically equal to the pressure, if the gas obeys Boyle's law. The ratio of the E. when heat is neither gained nor lost to the E. at constant temperature, is equal to the ratio of the specific heat of the gas at constant pressure to the specific heat at constant volume. The change of volume which can be produced in a liquid by pressure is very small, being about five parts per 100,000 for one atmosphere change of pressure. The E., according to the above definition, is, therefore, very high. When we pass to the consideration of solids, we are met with another kind of E., the E. of form. The processes of manufacturing many

articles show clearly that it is possible to bring about changes of form from which the body does not recover on removal of the forces. The moulding of clay in pottery work, and the forging, stamping, and wire drawing of materials are familiar instances of such effects. On the other hand, the recovery of form and shape is used, very frequently, in such cases as hair-springs of watches, spring balances, carriage springs, buffers, and so on. These examples show clearly that there is an elastic limit within which bodies will recover their form and shape, and beyond which they will be permanently changed. Two terms, strain and stress, which are frequently used in E., may be defined as follows : Any alteration in form or bulk of a body is called a strain, and the combination of forces producing a strain is called a stress. The resistance which a solid offers to a pure change of form is measured by its rigidity, and if for this change the body is truly elastic, the rigidity is measured by the ratio of the deforming stress to the resulting strain. A pure twist applied to a rod or wire involves no change of volume. The resistance which such a rod offers to a change of form depends on its rigidity and form, and is independent of its compressibility. But in most cases, where a body is strained by a particular form of stress, the ratio of the stress to the strain involves both the rigidity and the compressibility. Thus, when a wire is stretched by applying a tension parallel to its length, it increases in length but diminishes in volume. If the ratio of the stretching force per unit area of cross section to the increase in length per unit length be called E, then $\frac{1}{E} = \frac{1}{9k} + \frac{1}{3n}$ (where $k$ = bulk, modulus = ratio of a hydrostatic pressure to the change in volume per unit volume of the solid produced by that pressure, and $n$ = the rigidity), and the ratio $\frac{\text{lateral contraction}}{\text{elongation}} = \sigma$ (or Poisson's ratio) is equal to $\frac{3k - 2n}{6k + 2n}$. Thus the quantity E, which is called Young's modulus, is not an independent quantity. Young's modulus is of importance in engineering, for it determines not only the contraction which will be produced in a pillar by a given load, but also the resistance which a beam or a bar offers to bending (see STRENGTH OF MATERIALS). It has already been stated that there is a certain limit of strain called the elastic limit, beyond which a permanent strain or set will be produced in a body. The limits of perfect E.

are very low—if they exist at all—for glasses and other hard, brittle solids ; but metallic substances, such as copper, iron, platinum, brass, and steel, are very nearly perfectly elastic as regards distortion, provided the distortion is not too great. The

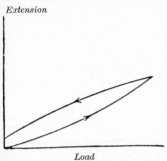

*Extension*

*Load*

FIG. 1

exact value of these limits is somewhat indefinite, for a small stress acting for a long time will produce a permanent change of form, which could only be produced in a short time by a very much larger stress. But within the elastic limit, and with stresses applied for a short time, experiment

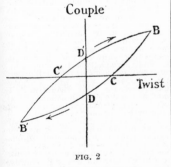

Couple

B

D'

C'

C          Twist

D

B'

FIG. 2

shows that the stresses are proportional to the strains. This relation was stated in 1678 by Robert Hooke, in the form *Ut tensio, sic vis.* Applying Hooke's law to the case of a stretched wire, it follows that the extension is proportional to the stretching force over a considerable range of values. Even within the elastic limit, Hooke's law is not accurately true, although the diverg-

ences are not great. It will be seen from Fig. 1 that the extension produced in a wire by a given load depends on the way in which the given load is obtained, whether by increasing or decreasing a former load. It is also seen that the wire is slightly longer at the end of the experiment than it was at the beginning. Similarly, if a rod is subjected to torsion, the twist produced by a given couple will depend on the previous treatment of the rod. When a cyclic state has been established, the relation between the couple and the twist is that shown in Fig. 2. It is seen that the twist lags behind the couple. Thus, as we pass from B to B¹, the couple vanishes at C, but the twist does not vanish till we reach D. The lagging of the effect (in this case the twist) behind the cause (the couple) has been called hysteresis by Ewing. The area enclosed by the curve B¹D¹BDB¹ is proportional to the energy dissipated in each cycle.

**Elastin** and **Elastic Fibre,** *see* TISSUE.

**Elatea** (the modern **Drachmani**) was in anct. times the largest tn. in Phocis, Greece. It was not far from Cephisus, whilst one of the chief passes from Thessaly to Bœotia was near at hand. Once it was famous for a temple to Æsculapius, and ruins of one dedicated to Athena Cranæa were unearthed here in 1883. In the course of his subjugation of Greece, Philip of Macedon captured the city in 338 B.C.

**Elater Beetle,** *see* CLICK BEETLES.

**Elateridæ**, the name given to a family of Coleoptera commonly known as click-beetles, glow-worms, fireflies (*q.v.*), etc.

**Elaterin** (Gk. ἐλατήρ, a driver), the active principle of elaterium. It is a chemical substance, its formula being $C_{20}H_{28}O_5$. It is extracted, by means of boiling alcohol, from the juice of *Ecballium agreste* in the form of colourless hexagonal crystals which are insoluble in water. Elaterium is a vegetable extract obtained from *Ecballium elaterium*, a perennial tropical plant. It is very bitter, and a powerful purgative. It is also used as a remedy for dropsy and cardiac diseases.

**Elaterite** (Gk. ἐλατήρ, a driver), an elastic bitumen. It is blackish-brown in colour, translucent, and is found in soft, sticky masses in Derbyshire, near Edinburgh, and in Fifeshire. It is sometimes called mineral caoutchouc, and is very much like india-rubber.

**Elatinaceæ**, a dicotyledonous order, contains about thirty shrubby or herbaceous species found in marshy places and under water in tropical and temperate parts of the globe. *E. hydropiper*, the water-pepper, grows under water in France and sometimes in Britain.

**Elba** (known as Αἰθαλία to the Gks., and ' Ilva ' to the Roms.), an island, 18 m. long, in the Mediterranean Sea, lying some 6 m. from the mainland of Italy, and forming part of the province of Livorno, from which it is separated by the Gulf of Piombino. Monte Capane, its highest peak, attains an altitude of 2925 ft., but the whole island is mountainous. Mining is the chief industry, the mines near Rio Inferiore yielding excellent hematite and other iron ore. Marble, lead, sulphur, and alabaster are also exported. Olives, the vine, and wheat are grown, but agriculture is backward. Porto Ferrajo is the cap. E. is best known as the realm which the deposed Emperor Napoleon ruled from May 3, 1814, until Feb. 26, 1815. Pop. 29,490.

**Elbasan**, a tn. of Albania, on the r. b. of the R. Shkumbi, with numerous mosques, in a fertile plain. Olives and maize are cultivated. Pop. about 16,000, of whom 85 per cent. are Mohammedans. E. was captured by the Serbs during the Balkan wars but was returned to A.

**Elbe** (the ' Albis ' of the Latins and the ' Labe ' of the Czechs), the riv. next in importance to the Rhine in the Ger. Empire. The area of its drainage basin is estimated at 56,000 sq. m., whilst its total length is 525 m. Ocean vessels can sail up as far as Hamburg (84 m. from the mouth), and the river is navigable for a distance of 525 m., that is up to the confluence of the Moldau, at Melnik. It is distributed chiefly over Bohemia (190 m.), Saxony (77 m.), Prussia (350 m.), and Hamburg (108 m.). The E. rises, at an altitude of 4600 ft., on the S. slopes of the Riesengebirge in Bohemia. At first it flows S., then N. and N.W. Above Brandeis it is joined by the Iser, whilst at Melnik the Moldau more than doubles its volume. At Leitmeritz the Eger reddens its waters, and soon, after piercing the basaltic Mittelgebirge and passing the beautiful Saxon ' Alps ' of the Elbsandsteingebirge, it oversteps the Bohemian frontier, flows past Dresden and Meissen, and begins, in a N.W. direction, its long course over the N. Ger. plain. Leaving behind on its banks the towns of Torgau, Wittenburg, Magdeburg, Hamburg, and Altona, and swollen with the waters of the Mulde and Saale from the left, and the Havel and Elde from the right, it finally reaches the North Sea at Cuxhaven. The two streams, the Norder and Süder E., which separate above Hamburg, are reunited at Blankenese. At Kolin the width is 100 ft., at Dresden 960

ft., whilst near the estuary it varies from 4 m. to 9 m. Since 1871 rapid improvements, including harbours, docks, etc., and numerous canals, have been made in the E. navigation, although inundations continue at times to retard its progress. The E., Reek, Rüdersdorfer-Gewässer, Rheinsberger, and Sacrow–Paretzer Canals have effectually joined up the E. and Oder systems, whilst the Elbe–Trave Canal (42 m.) of 1900 has opened up direct communication between Lübeck and the E. A great deal of timber is floated down the river, and the goods traffic, which is greater than on any other Ger. river, is carried on by steamers and barges, which are partly hauled by the towing chain fastened in the river bed between Hamburg and Aussig. Passenger boats are mostly confined to Saxony and Bohemia. The many international changes resulting from the Great War, and especially the recognition of Czecho-Slovakia as a separate nation, have given a new political importance to the Elbe, which, according to the Treaty of Versailles, is now declared to be an international river from its union with the Voltava, under a committee on which Germany, Czecho-Slovakia, Britain, France, Italy and Belgium are represented. This gives Czecho-Slovakia access to the North Sea and the Baltic, and the gov. is now making arrangements to canalise the upper reaches of the riv. in order to connect it with the Oder and the Danube, and thus to gain a waterway to the Black Sea. Commercially, however, the E. has lost much of its heavier traffic of recent years, owing to the amalgamations of Ger. railways. At one time competing railway lines found it useful to give facilities to traders who used the riv. ports, or by partly using riv. transport, were able to give quotations for long distances, but now, as the united railways cover the whole area, transfer of goods during transport is no longer necessary.

**Elberfeld**, an important industrial centre of Germany. It is in the Prussian Rhine province and adjoins Barmen, with which it is now really merged. For 9 m. along either bank of the Wupper, on which E. stands, there stretches an endless line of factories, warehouses, etc. It is the chief centre in Germany of textile manufactures and haberdashery. It produces carpets, tailors' articles, hats and caps, machines, enamel work, lead wares, tools, and paperdyes, and fine chemicals, rubber goods, wall papers and stained glass. E. contains many benevolent institutions. The municipal museum of fine and applied arts is in the old

town hall; the new one has a tower
243 ft. nigh. The tn. is surrounded
by grounds and promenades. There
are Zoological Gardens. Pop. E.
165,100; B. 184,900.

**Elberton,** a tn. of Elbert co., 100 m.
E. by N. of Atlanta, Georgia, U.S.A.
It produces cotton, grain, peaches,
alfalfa, and manufactures cotton
drills, cotton-seed oil and artificial
silk. Pop. (1920) 6475.

**Elbeuf,** or **Elbœuf,** an important
woollen manufacturing tn., 14 m. S.
by W. of Rouen by rail, on the l. b.
of the Seine, in the dept. Seine-Inférieure, France. Pop. 18,730 (a decrease of over 3000 on that of 1872).

**Elbing,** an important seaport on
the navigable Elbing R., 72 m. S.W.
of Königsberg by rail, in W. Prussia.
The Kraffohl Canal connects the E.
with the Nogat arm of the Vistula,
whilst the river joins Lake Drausen
with the Frisches Haff, which is 5 m.
to the N. Founded in the thirteenth
century by settlers from Bremen and
Lübeck, the old inner tn. possesses
numerous gable houses of the fifteenth
to the eighteenth century, the Protestant Mary church begun in 1246, the
Holy Ghost church of the thirteenth
century, with the Holy Ghost hospital, the St. George's Chapel (fourteenth century), and remains of
the old fortifications. In the newer
quarters important industries are
located—shipbuilding, locomotive
machines and turbines, automobiles,
motor ploughs, tractors, etc.; 3000
workers are engaged in the manufacture of cigars, parts for flying machines and ot er articles, including
chocolate and organs. Pop. 68,000.

**Elbogen** (Czech Loket), a picturesquely situated tn. in N.W.
Bohemia, Czecho-Slovakia, near
Karlsbad. Has a large porcelain
factory and a fine old castle, which
was vainly besieged by the Hussites
in 1427. Pop. 3840.

El ow, see RM.

**Elbruz,** or **Elbrooz,** the highest
mountain in the Caucasus range, its
W. peak attaining an elevation of
18,470 ft. The other summit, which
was reached for the first time in
1868 by Freshfield, is 18,347 ft.
above sea-level. It is an extinct
volcano, whose glaciers cover 46 sq.
m. The Baksan glacier extends down
to a distance of 7350 ft. above the sea.

**Elburz Mountains,** a lofty range in
the N. of Persia, trending from
within 20 m. to 50 m. of the Caspian
Sea, right across to N.E. Khorassan,
thus covering a distance of some 650
m. The E. M. may conveniently
be considered in three sections.
The first reaches with a N. to S.
direction for 120 m. from Lenkoran,
being known as the Talish range.

Several peaks attain an elevation of
10,000 ft. The second section
stretches for 240 m. with a direction
N.W. to S.E. from near Resht to a
point beyond Mt. Demavend, the
crowning summit of the whole chain
(19,400 ft.) which rises E. of Teheran.
There are great heights in the Talikan
range, N.W. of Teheran, whilst between Talikan and Demavend are
over seven ranges with an average
elevation of some 12,800 ft. The
Safid Rud, by whose banks passes
the great trade route between the
Caspian and inner Persia, and the
Herhaz, cut their way through this
section. The chief ranges of the
third section (290 m. long) strike
S.W. to N.E. and extend as far as
N. Afghanistan, rising often over
10,000 ft. above sea-level. The N.
slopes form the main watershed.
Here are plentiful forests and natural
vegetation, and in the valleys fertile
lands, gardens, and orchards. Endless stretches of barren ridges and
arid wastes disfigure the scenery S.
of the watershed.

**El Capitan,** a granite peak, 3300 ft.
high, in the Yosemite valley, on the
W. slope of the Sierra Nevada, in
California, U.S.A.

**El Centro,** a city of S. California,
co. seat of Imperial co., in the midst
of Imperial Valley, which irrigation
has transformed from desert into
fertile farmland. Some crop is harvested every month. Pop. 8434.

**Elche,** a tn. S.W. of Alicante,
on the railway joining Alicante and
Murcia. The surrounding grove of
almost 100,000 date-palms provides all
Spain with leaves for Palm Sunday and
absorbs all the summer waters of the
R. Vinalapo. It has a fine and lofty
domed church, and the only mystery
play in Spain is performed on Aug. 13
and 14 each year. Pop. 33,187.

**Elchingen,** or **Oberelchingen,** a vil.
5 m. N.E. of Ulm., close to the
Danube in Bavaria, Germany. Marshal Ney became Duke of E. because
in 1805 he here defeated the Austrians.

**Elcho Challenge Shield,** see BISLEY.

**Elder.** The Old Testament E. was
only the successor of what had
existed in all anct. countries, and
in all primitive communities where
age was always looked up to with
respect and called upon to rule and
judge. Moses chose seventy Es. to
assist and share with him the burden
of responsibility in the Wilderness,
and from this evolved the Sanhedrin,
the court that condemned Jesus
Christ. New Testament E. or bishop,
which in Gk. means the same, is an
ordained office-bearer in the church.
The session of a Presbyterian
church is composed of Es., preaching
and ruling. The preaching E. is the

minister, who is ordained and inducted by the Presbytery and is the moderator of the congregational session. The ruling Es. are elected for life by the congregation, and are ordained and inducted by the moderator of the session. In some American branches of the Presbyterian Church the Es. are only elected for a certain number of years. The session has the spiritual government of the congregation in its hands, and only through it can members of the congregation appeal to a higher court of the church. When John Knox set up the Presbyterian government in Scotland he meant the ruling Es. to be salaried office-bearers and thought that they should be elected annually. However, the alienation of the church funds from ecclesiastical to secular holders prevented his idea from being carried into effect. An E. should, in the words of Timothy (1 Tim. iii. 2), ' be blameless, the husband of one wife, vigilant, sober, of good behaviour, given to hospitality, apt to teach.' The courts of the Presbyterian Church are entirely made up of Es., preaching and ruling, e.g. the congregational session, one preaching E. and one ruling E. for about every twenty members. Presbytery and Synod, generally one preaching and one ruling E. from each congregation. General Assembly, a certain number of each from each Presbytery within its government. Thus the Presbyterian Church claims apostolic authority for its church government.

**Elder,** or *Sambucus,* a genus of the natural order Caprifoliaceæ. The species are widely-distributed, deciduous shrubs. *S. nigra,* the common elder, or the bourtree of Scotland, is found in many parts of Europe. It grows quickly, in almost any kind of soil, to a height of about 20 ft. The wood of the stem is hard and when polished is used for making fishing-rods, toys, and combs. The flowers contain oil, and the berries are used for making wine. It was formerly highly valued for its medicinal properties and used as a cathartic. There are several horticultural varieties, the most beautiful being the *S. racemosa,* the scarlet berried E.

**Elderberry Wine,** made by fermenting elderberries, which usually ripen in the early autumn. It was an old household cure for coughs, and is now often used for the adulteration of port wine. The *Sambucus canadensis,* a species very common in Canada and the U.S.A., produces a prolific crop of berries, and a great quantity of wine is made therefrom.

**Eldon, John Scott,** first **Earl of** (1751–1838), Lord Chancellor, almost blighted his prospects by making a runaway marriage as soon as he had won his fellowship at University College, Oxford. However, he was called to the Bar in 1776, and from that time success smiled on him. He entered Parliament, became Solicitor-General in 1788, Attorney-General in 1793, Chief Justice of the Court of Common Pleas (1799), and finally Lord Chancellor for many long years. His only politics were a lively hatred of the Rom. Catholics, and he was a poor speaker, a tedious but sound judge, and a victim to parsimony. But he was graced with a winning disposition, and he had a big share in establishing modern equity as a coherent body of principles no longer measurable by ' the length of the Chancellor's foot.'

**El Dorado :** (1) means in Spanish ' The Golden,' and was the name given to a fabulous city long believed to exist somewhere in the interior of S. America. It was the imaginary goal of countless futile expeditions, such as those of Orellana (1540), Philip von Hutten (1541–45), who told how once he had caught a glimpse of the gleaming city, and Ximenez de Quesada (1569). The purely legendary Manoa, with roofs and walls of precious stones, to which Martinez said he had been taken, long occupied a conspicuous place on the map, till Humboldt proved it to be a fiction. But though E. D. was swept from the atlas, it has secured a high niche in literature as the goal of happiness after which humanity never wearies of striving. (2) A city of Saline co., Illinois, U.S.A., a trade centre with a pop. of 4482. (3) A city in the oil-fields of S. E. Kansas, U.S.A., co. seat of Butler co. Pop. 10,311. Centre of a farming and oil-producing region. (4) A city of S. Arkansas, co. seat of Union co., chief tn. in the pioneer oil-field of the state. Pop. 16,421.

**Eleatic School, The,** a school of Gk. philosophy which flourished from 570–450 B.C., so-called because its leaders were natives of the Gk. colony, Elea, in Lower Italy. Parmenides may not have been its founder, but he at least, with Zeno, became identified to a peculiar and especial degree with its salient principles. After the death of its great exponents, the Eleatics gave themselves over to futile verbal debates, whilst their serious contributions to mental science formed the basis of Plato's metaphysics. Parmenides and his adherents dilated on the unity of being and all phenomena, and on the paradoxical conception that ' the All is One,' and argued that this truth is hidden from the masses because their senses mislead and confuse them. Thought alone can attain to this conception by soaring high above the domain of the false and sensuous seemings.

**Elecampane**, or *Inula Helenium*, a composite plant with aromatic and bitter leaves and root.

**Election** (in divinity), see PRE-DESTINATION.

**Election, Equitable Doctrine of,** in law, the act or right of choosing between two inconsistent alternate rights or benefits. It arises chiefly in cases of wills, but sometimes also in the case of a deed or other instrument. A person who accepts a benefit under a deed or will is obliged to conform with all its provisions. Thus, if A bequeaths B's property $x$ to C, and A's property $y$ to B, B must ‘make his election’ between accepting his own $x$ or A's $y$. See *Ency. of Laws of England*, v.; Watson, *Practical Compendium of Equity*.

**Elections :** PARLIAMENTARY.—*The election writ—Polling districts.*—The authorisation for the issue of the E. writs by the Clerk to the Crown is the royal proclamation after a dissolution of parliament; but where only a by-E. is to take place by reason of the death of a member, or the vacating of his seat in any other way, the writ is drawn up by the Clerk of the Crown in Chancery on the authority of the Speaker's warrant. The writs for a general E. are always prepared in the Crown Office, and ready for issue in the event of a sudden dissolution before the normal term of five years. They are sent to the returning officers of the constituencies, who, in county areas are the sheriffs, and in urban areas the mayor or chairman of the borough council. The Postmaster-General, after giving his receipt, sends them at once, as registered letters, to local postmasters, who remit them to the returning officers. A book is kept by the Postmaster-General for entering all particulars, and this book is open for inspection. Formerly notice had to be given within specified statutory periods of the day fixed for nominating candidates, but nomination day is now the same in all constituencies, the eighth day after the date of the Royal Proclamation. On that day the returning officer in each constituency attends at the municipal buildings or court house, within certain fixed hours, generally from 10 a.m. till noon, to receive nomination papers. Under the Ballot Act, 1872, each candidate must be nominated by a separate nomination paper, and the returning officer must supply a form of nomination paper to any registered elector requiring the same during the allotted

two hours. The candidate must be sufficiently described in the paper and otherwise accord with the necessary formalities, its sufficiency being a matter for the decision of the returning officer who may reject it for non-compliance. His decision is final where he allows, but not where he disallows, an objection ; an appeal being taken on a petition. The first schedule to the above Act requires that each nomination paper be signed by a proposer and seconder, both registered electors, and contain also the names and addresses of eight other electors in support of the nomination. Public notice must be given of withdrawals. If within one hour after the time appointed for the poll the number of nominated candidates does not exceed the vacancies, they are to be elected. The polling districts are fixed by the local authorities, but the returning officer fixes the polling stations. The Corrupt and Illegal Practices Act, 1883, provides that a polling station shall be assigned by the returning officer to each district in such manner that, so far as is reasonably practicable, every elector shall have his polling place within a distance not exceeding three miles from his residence. The returning officer must also select presiding officers for the different stations and a suitable staff of clerks. The returning officer's expenses are paid by the Treasury.

In the case of a by-E., proper notices must be given within the statutory periods of the day fixed for nomination, and also of the polling date. The actual dates within the statutory periods are determined on by the returning officer. In the case of a county or district borough E., the day of E. is fixed by the returning officer not later than the ninth day after the date on which he receives the writ, with a clear three days' interval between the day on which he gives notice and the polling day ; in the case of a borough, not later than the fourth day, with a clear two days' interval. In county or district boroughs polling must take place not less than two nor more than six days after nomination ; in boroughs not more than three days after nomination.

*Qualifications and Disqualifications for Membership.*—Membership of the House of Commons is remarkably free and unrestricted. The somewhat anomalous position is that a pauper, landless, homeless and without a vote, may be elected, while only a man of position and property, at least to the extent of being a householder of six months' standing and a ratepayer either directly or indirectly, may vote. The property

N 2

qualifications which formerly made candidature the privilege of the well-to-do were abolished in 1858, though the law had notoriously been evaded years before that date by fictitious transfers of land. With the removal of the necessity for any property qualification and the abolition of any incapacity by reason of religious creed, there are now no general grounds of ineligibility beyond the exclusion of aliens who have not been naturalised. The candidate must be either a natural born British person or a naturalised foreigner. Colonists and native Indians are eligible. A candidate must be at least twenty-one years of age, though the production of a birth certificate is not required. Such disqualifications as exist are all put upon some special incapacity, either inherent, as in the case of infancy or lunacy, or acquired, whether by reason of some moral or social defect, *e.g.* criminality, corruption, insolvency; or by reason of the holding of some office deemed incompatible with E. as a member for parliament. Those disqualified by reason of office include judges of the Supreme Court of Judicature, county court judges, recorders as regards their own boroughs, London stipendiary magistrates, sheriffs as regards their counties, the commissioner of metropolitan police, bankruptcy officials, barristers appointed to try municipal E. petitions, and governors of Indian dependencies or colonies; those disqualified for other special grounds include infants, lunatics and idiots, felons who have neither served their term of imprisonment nor have been pardoned, and persons convicted of treason; pensioners at the pleasure of the crown, except civil service, army, or diplomatic pensioners; holders of any gov. contract other than company directors; clergymen of the Church of England, of the Church of Scotland, and Rom. Catholic priests (members of dissenting churches are, however, qualified); civil servants on the permanent staff of a gov. department are ineligible (commissioned officers of the Army, Navy and Air Force are qualified, but Army officers become M.P. only at the sacrifice of half their pay. Returning officers may not stand for the places where they are commanded by writ to hold an E. Eng. peers and peers of Great Britain and the United Kingdom, being hereditary members of the House of Lords, are disqualified (it is the succession to a peerage and not the receipt of the writ of summons which is held to disqualify); Scottish peers are also precluded, including those outside the sixteen

representative peers of Scotland; the Irish peerage is not disqualified, for by the Act of Union an Irish peer, providing he is not one of the 28 representative peers elected by the Irish peerage to sit in the House of Lords, may be returned for any constituency in Eng. or Scotland but not for an Irish constituency. An adjudicated bankrupt is disqualified until the adjudication is annulled or until he gets his discharge. A person once convicted of personally committing bribery or personation is for ever disqualified for the constituency in respect of which he was guilty of such corrupt conduct, and he is debarred from sitting for any other constituency for seven years. A candidate who has innocently, through his agents, committed the offences of personation, bribery, treating, or undue influence, is debarred for seven years, unless exonerated by the E. judges.

*The Parliamentary Franchise.*— The preparation of the register of voters, first provided for by the Reform Act of 1832, is the duty of the 'registration officers,' and is discharged under the Representation of the People Act, 1918, at the public expense, half being defrayed out of the local rates and half by the Treasury. The 'registration officers' are, in borough divisions, the town clerk, and in county divisions, the clerk of the county council. The rate book is the basis upon which the registration officer draws up the list of voters. The franchise no longer rests on a property or occupation qualification so far as men are concerned, the Act of 1918 having substituted what is practically adult suffrage.and mere residential qualification, though the minimum age for a female voter was thirty against twenty-one for a male. The Representation of the People Act (Equal Franchise), 1928, assimilated the franchise for men and women (both for the Parliamentary and Local Government Es.). The qualifications for registration as a Parliamentary elector are that the person is twenty-one years of age and not subject to any legal incapacity; and has the requisite residential qualification, *or* the requisite business premises qualification, *or* is the husband or wife of a person having a business premises qualification. 'Residence' is the actual inhabitancy of premises, *i.e.* the place where he has his home and sleeps. The residence must have been during the whole of the qualifying period, *i.e.* three months in the constituency or in another constituency in the same Parliamentary borough or Parliamentary county;

if not, it is essential that the residence should have been successive from a Parliamentary borough or Parliamentary county contiguous to that borough or county. The Administrative County of London is treated as a Parliamentary borough, ' Business premises ' means land or other premises of at least £10 yearly value; the premises must be occupied for the purpose of the business, profession or trade of the person to be registered. By the Act of 1928 a person may not vote at a general election for more than one constituency for which he or she is registered by virtue of a residential qualification, or for more than one constituency for which he or she is registered by virtue of other qualifications of any kind. This means, in effect, that the person may, if qualified, lawfully vote twice at a general election, but one vote must be in respect of a residential qualification, and each vote must be recorded in a different constituency.

A person of full age, and not subject to any legal incapacity, who has received a degree is entitled to registration as an elector for a University constituency; a woman who has passed the final examination and fulfilled the conditions required of women by a University which did not at the time the examination was passed admit women to degrees is also qualified.

The voters' lists, as first compiled from the rate books, are supplemented by a house to house inquiry to ascertain the names of householders whose rates are paid through the landlord and the persons qualified as wives or lodgers. Under the Act of 1928, each parliamentary borough and parliamentary county is an ' electoral registration area.' It is the duty of the registration officer to compile a register for all persons entitled to vote whether as parliamentary or as local gov. electors in his area, and he must comply with any directions by the Secretary of State as to the arrangements for carrying out the registration. Separate lists are prepared for absent voters, the ballot papers being sent to the voters, who mark them and remit them with a declaration of identity. Voting by proxy is permitted in the case of naval and military voters in distant areas, and merchant seamen, pilots and fishermen at sea. A copy of the electoral lists can always be inspected at the office of the registration officer, and generally at the chief post office and other convenient places in the area. Claims and objections may be made by notice as directed. Appeals from a decision

of a registration officer lie to the County Court; a further appeal on any point of law lies to the Court of Appeal, whose decision is final. Persons disqualified from voting closely approximate to those who are ineligible as members of parliament. They include : aliens (unless naturalised); idiots, lunatics, felons (but not misdemeanants), peers, persons employed for reward at E., and persons convicted of corrupt and illegal practices.

*The poll.*—All polls at a General E. are held on one day. The presiding officer of each polling station must be at his station before 8 a.m. on polling day. He must then remove from the room all but authorised persons. It is advisable always to have adequate police support at hand. Voters may enter to record their votes at 8 a.m. Polling terminates at 8 p.m. A voter must present himself at his right station, and to ensure this the register is consulted. The actual recording of his vote takes place in a booth screened from observation. Voting is effected by marking a cross in the space opposite the chosen name. Where a voter gives as his name that of a person who has already voted he gets a special ballot paper which he does not place in the ballot box but hands to the presiding officer, who does not count it, but enters it on the ' tendered votes list.' Ballot papers may be marked for blind voters, voters physically incapable of recording a vote, or unable to read, or Jews who object to voting in the prescribed manner. At the close of the poll the presiding officer must deliver the ballot boxes and the various E. documents, including unused or spoilt ballot papers, made up in separate packets, to the returning officer. The returning officer then opens the boxes and counts the papers in the presence of the candidates or their agents, afterwards mixing all the papers together. The actual counting of the votes must be in the presence of the agents, the returning officer rejecting papers invalid for want of an official, or any mark, for uncertainty, or by reason of the voter having voted for more candidates than he is entitled to vote for. The returning officer cannot vote at the E., but should there be a tie between the candidates he may, if a registered elector, give a casting vote; but his casting vote is operative only if exercised on the declaration of the poll. Every candidate must deposit the sum of £150 with the returning officer, the sum being forfeited if the number of votes polled by him or her does not exceed one-eighth of the total number polled, and returned in any other case. The counted and rejected papers, after the ballot paper account of the returning officer has been verified in the presence of the candidates or their agents, are then sealed in separate packets and sent to the Clerk of the Crown, together with all the other E. documents. It is in case there should be a demand for a scrutiny and recount of the voting papers in any constituency, or a petition presented to declare the E. null and void under the Corrupt Practices Act, that all the documents are stored in the Crown office cellars for a year and a day before they are destroyed. The writs are kept by the Clerk of the Crown until the dissolution of Parliament, when they are sent to the Public Record Office, where they are preserved.

*Corrupt and Illegal Practices at Elections.*—The offences coming under the category of corrupt practices are personation, bribery, treating, and undue influence. Personation consists in applying for a ballot paper in the name of another, or after having once voted. The punishment is imprisonment with or without hard labour up to two years. Bribery (*see* at greater length under BRIBERY) as an E. offence has a very comprehensive connotation. The element of corruptness is consistent with honesty of motive; the essential element is the intention to influence the mind of the person voting. By the Corrupt Practices Prevention Act, 1854, bribery consists in any gift or promise of a gift, directly or indirectly, to a voter, whether in the shape of money or any other valuable consideration, or of a promise of employment. It is bribery to pay money to another to be used in bribery, or to repay money known to have been so used. It is not bribery to pay money on account of legal expenses *bona fide* incurred at an E. By the Representation of the People Act, 1867, it is bribery corruptly to pay a person's rates to enable him to be registered as a voter and to influence his mind at any future E. It is sometimes difficult, by the light of the numerous decisions on the point, to say what is and what is not bribery, *e.g.* paying a voter's travelling expenses to the polling station after he has promised his vote is, but general payments to curry favour, without aiming at a particular vote or votes, are not bribery. Gifts after an E. may be bribery if before the E. something was said or done to raise the voter's hopes. Treating, which is really a specialised form of bribery, consists in providing or pay-

ing for meat, drink, or other entertainment so as to influence an elector, the latter being also guilty of treating if he corruptly accepts. The punishment for both bribery and treating is imprisonment up to twelve months with or without hard labour, or a fine not exceeding £200. Undue influence, by the Corrupt and Illegal Practices Act, 1883, consists in the use of force, fraud, or threats to impede a person in the free exercise of his vote. To dismiss one's employees on the eve of an E. may well amount to undue influence; so, too, giving a tenant notice to quit. But in every case a corrupt motive must be proved.

*Illegal Practices* comprise a great number of heterogeneous acts made illegal by the Corrupt and Illegal Practices Act, 1883; the element of corrupt intention is by no means essential. All such practices are misdemeanours, punishable summarily by a fine up to £100. Acts deemed to be illegal practices comprise the following: Expenditure by a candidate or his agent on his E. beyond a certain amount, which varies according to the number of the electorate, the scale providing for a maximum of 7d. for each elector in a county constituency and 5d. in a borough; paying or contracting to pay for the conveyance of electors to and from the poll; payments to electors for the use of any house, land, or premises for the exhibition of bills or notices; payments on account of any committee-room in excess of the statutory limit which is one for every 2000 electors, with an additional room for an incomplete part of 2000 electors. It is not an illegal practice to make a fair business payment to an elector who is also an advertising agent. No person, unless authorised by the election agent of a candidate, may incur any expense by holding meetings or issuing advertisements or circulars to promote the election of any candidate. Other illegal practices are payments for bands of music, flags, and cockades; corruptly inducing a person to withdraw his candidature, or falsely publishing the withdrawal of a candidate; using as a committee-room any elementary school, or any club (other than a political club of a permanent character) where intoxicants or refreshments are sold; employing canvassers for hire; procuring a vote of a person not entitled to vote; voting with knowledge that one is not entitled to vote; employing at an E. more than the statutory number of persons for remuneration; publishing false statements of fact in regard to the personal character or conduct of a candidate without belief in their truth; and, by the Public Mutiny Act, 1908, creating a disturbance at a meeting held for the purpose of supporting the candidature of a particular person. Under the most recent Representation of the People Bill (1931), considerable importance is attached to the use of motor-cars at elections, the general view being that, if a fair vote is to be obtained, it is not desirable that one party should have more cars at its disposal than another. The method proposed is that only those cars should be used for taking voters to the poll which are registered with the returning officer, and these, in accordance with the directions of the Secretary of State, will be allotted by the returning officer to work in various districts and carry voters irrespective of their party allegiance.

*Election Petitions.*—These are only triable before two judges chosen, in Eng. from the Divisional Court, and in Scotland from the Court of Session. Any rejected candidate, or nominee for candidature, or elector, may present a petition. A candidate declared elected by the returning officer, but whose return is questioned by petition, takes the oath and his seat in the House of Commons and serves in the usual course until the report of the judges is delivered to the Speaker and by him communicated to the House. It is in the discretion of the judges at the close of the trial to give or withhold a certificate of indemnity against further legal proceedings, civil or criminal, and all witnesses who speak the truth are entitled to such a certificate. The judges then certify to the Speaker of the House of Commons the result of their findings, which may be either that the E was void, or that someone was duly returned.

Local Government.—The qualifications for the local gov. franchise as provided by the Representation of the People Act, 1928, are the same for men and women. A person is entitled to be registered as an elector who is twenty-one years of age and not subject to any legal incapacity; and (i.) is on the last day of the qualifying period occupying as owner or tenant land or premises in the electoral area, and (ii.) has throughout the qualifying period occupied as owner or tenant any land or premises in that area; if the area is neither an administrative county nor a county borough, then in any administrative county or county borough in which the area is situate; or (iii.) is the husband or wife of a person who is entitled to be registered in respect of premises in which both the person entitled and the husband or wife reside. There is, in addition, a ' service ' qualification for the local gov. franchise: a person who inhabits any dwelling-house by virtue of any office, service or employment is deemed to occupy the dwelling-house as a tenant and is thereby entitled to be registered provided the dwelling house is not also inhabited by the employer. These qualifications apply to all local gov. Es., whether borough, county council, district council or parish council.

*Borough Elections.*—In the case of all cities and tns. to which the Municipal Corporations Act, 1835, applies, and in all towns or districts incorporated since Dec. 31, 1882, to which the provisions of the Municipal Corporation Acts are extended by charter, the right to elect tn. councillors is regulated by the Municipal Corporations Act, 1882, and the County Electors Act, 1888, as amended by the Representation of the People (Equal Franchise) Act, 1928 (*see also* under Borough; Burgesses). In the case of the metropolitan boroughs, the right to elect councillors is in the parochial electors of the parishes and places comprised in the respective borough electoral areas. The parochial electors of a parish are the persons whose names are on either the local gov. or the parliamentary register for the particular parish. London city is outside the cities to which the Municipal Corporations Acts apply. The tn. councillors of a municipal borough, *i.e.* boroughs subject to the Municipal Corporations Act, 1882, as amended by subsequent Acts, were formerly elected by the enrolled burgesses (*q.v.*), but registration as an elector is now sufficient. A person to be entitled to vote as a burgess must in any given year and during the whole of the then last preceding twelve months have been in occupation, joint or several, of any house, warehouse, counting-house, shop, or other building in the borough, and during the whole of such twelve months have resided either in the borough or within 7 m. thereof (except the time not exceeding four months that he may have allowed his house to be occupied as a furnished dwelling-house). Non-payment of rates is no longer a disqualification; nor is the receipt of poor relief.

*Qualifications of Borough Councillors and Aldermen.*—To be eligible as a councillor or alderman a person (1) must be entitled to be enrolled as a burgess, or (2) being so entitled in all respects save as to residence, must reside beyond 7 but within

15 m. of the borough, and in any case either (a) possessed of real or personal property to the value of £1000, or, in the case of a borough having more than four wards, £500; or (b) in the case of a four-ward borough rated on an annual value of £30, and in the case of a smaller borough, £15. But a person qualified as an elector and resident in the borough requires no property qualification. Women may be elected councillors or aldermen, but may not act as justices of the peace *ex officio* (*see also* under BOROUGH). E. are conducted in accordance with the Ballot Act, 1872, with the necessary modifications. Aldermen are eligible from councillors or persons qualified to be councillors, and are elected by the council. They serve for three years, one-third retiring annually (*see also* under BOROUGH).

*City of London.*—The lord mayor, sheriffs, chamberlains, and minor public officials of the city are elected in Common Hall by the freemen and liverymen of the city. Aldermen, common councilmen, and ward officers are elected at wardmotes by £10 freemen occupiers, ordinary £10 occupiers, and all other persons registered as parliamentary or local gov. voters for the city, and persons who but for the fact of non-residence would be entitled to be registered as parliamentary voters in respect of occupation.

*Metropolitan Boroughs.*—Parochial electors consist of parliamentary and county electors. If a person has occupied in immediate succession during the twelve months immediately preceding the 15th day of July different premises in the administrative county which would qualify him as a county elector, he is entitled in respect of the occupation thereof to be registered as a county elector in the parish or township in which the last occupied premises are situate.

*Municipal Elections in Scottish Burghs* (*q.v.*).—Persons qualified under the Representation of the People Acts, 1832, 1867, and 1884, qualified to exercise the parliamentary vote, are also qualified to vote at elections of town councillors. Women are not disqualified by sex. Any occupier or inhabitant occupier, male or female, whose occupancy of lands or premises would qualify him for the parliamentary franchise, is eligible as a councillor. The provisions of the Ballot Act, 1872, extend to Scottish municipal elections. Councillors hold office for three years, one-third retiring annually.

COUNTY COUNCIL.—For the persons qualified as county councillors or aldermen of counties, *see* under COUNTY COUNCIL. The Local Government Act, 1888, which created county councils, regulates E. in connection therewith. The manner of conducting a county council E. is as nearly as possible assimilated by the Local Government Act, 1888, to that of municipal elections. The county council appoints the returning officer, who may exercise his powers by deputy. The election of Scottish county councillors is regulated by the Local Government (Scotland) Act, 1889. The constitution of a Scottish differs somewhat from an Eng. county council; there are no aldermen, and all councillors, instead of one-half, retire triennially. The chairman is elected by the councillors, who themselves must be county electors in the particular county.

DISTRICT COUNCILS.—The E. of district councillors is regulated by the rules contained in the Urban District Councils Election Order and Rural District Councils Election Order issued by the Local Government Board in 1898. The provisions of the two orders are as far as possible the same. Notice of an E. must be given by the returning officer—who is the clerk of the council or his deputy—not later than the second Friday in March, or, if the first Monday in April is Easter Monday, not later than the first Friday in March. The returning officer must provide nomination papers free of charge to any parochial elector applying for them, and, in rural districts, to the overseers also. The nomination papers must state whether the candidate is qualified as a parochial elector and so be signed by two parochial electors of the district or ward, or, in a rural district, of the parish or other electoral area, as proposer and seconder. Nomination papers must be sent to the returning officer and received by him not later than twelve o'clock noon on the Thursday following the day on which notice of E. was given. The returning officer's decision on the validity of a nomination paper, which must be notified to the candidate not later than the following Friday, is final. A candidate may withdraw on giving notice in writing to the returning officer. The day of E. will be the first Monday in April or, if that is Easter Monday, the last Monday in March, unless the county council fix another day. Public notice of the poll must be given by the returning officer five clear days at least before the E. If there are no valid nominations there will be no poll, and the retiring councillors will stand re-elected. If the nominations are less in number than the vacancies those retiring councillors who were highest at the poll at which they were elected will be deemed re-elected in order to fill up the deficiency. Each candidate may appoint an agent to represent him at the counting of the votes. In an equality of votes the returning officer has a casting vote; the deputy, if he counted the votes and is a parochial elector, would be entitled to give the casting vote, but would not be entitled to any other or second vote. When a casual vacancy arises a person is elected to hold office until the time when the councillor whose place he takes would ordinarily have gone out of office. Casual vacancies arise either on death, resignation, subsequent disqualification, or non-acceptance of office after E. No E. need be held to fill a casual vacancy if it occur within six months before the ordinary day of retirement from the office in which the vacancy occurs, the vacancy being filled at the next ordinary E. The provisions of the Municipal Corporations Act, 1882, relating to corrupt practices and E. petitions, have been adapted by the Elections Order, 1898, with necessary modifications, to district council E. In Scotland, parish councils take the place of district councils. Elections in Scotland are regulated by the Local Government (Scotland) Act, 1894. The manner of conducting the E., which are held in the burghal and landward parishes, is closely assimilated to that of the municipal and county councils respectively. Parish councillors are eligible from the parochial electors, and any person qualified as a county council or municipal elector is qualified to vote at a parish council election. Councillors hold office for three years.

UNITED STATES OF AMERICA : *Presidential Election.*—By the Federal Constitution each state is to appoint, in such manner as its legislature may direct, a number of electors equal to the whole number of senators and representatives to which the state is entitled in Congress. These electors then vote for the President and Vice-President. Theoretically, the people at large have no direct voice in the E., and the electors, or electoral college, have an unfettered freedom of choice, which freedom was formerly in fact exercised. As a fact the party system has long ago ensured that the persons nominated at the great National Party Conventions for the offices of President and Vice-President shall ultimately be voted for by the members of the electoral college. The electors themselves are polled for, by a direct vote of the citizens on a ' general ticket,'

like the Fr. *scrutin de liste,* but the candidates for the office of elector are all nominated beforehand by Party Associations, with the result that as soon as the polling for electors is over, the choice of the new President and Vice-President follows as a matter of course. By the Constitution Congress may determine the time of choosing the electors and the polling day, which must be the same throughout the states. The E. is held every fourth year, and at the present day electors are chosen in the different states on the Tuesday following the first Monday in November. The electors thereafter meet in their state capitals to record their votes on the second Monday in January next following their appointment. Their certificates of choice are sent to Washington and opened and counted in the presence of both Houses of Congress on the second Wednesday in February. (For qualifications of the President *see* under CONSTITUTION.) No senator or representative or person holding an office of trust or profit under the U.S.A. is eligible as an elector. If there be no majority of votes for President, the House of Representatives chooses one from the three names highest on the list, each state having one vote; if no majority for Vice-President, the Senate chooses one from the two names highest on the list. *Election of Senators.*—The Senate consists of two members from each state elected by popular vote for a term of six years. Candidates for the office of senator must be over thirty years of age, have been citizens of the U.S.A. for nine years, and be residents of the state for which they are elected. *Election of Representatives.*—The 435 members of the House of Representatives are elected every second year according to the electoral laws of the several states. They must be citizens over twenty-one years of age and have lived in the country at least seven years The forty-eight individual states, through their legislatures, have the power to prescribe the qualifications that entitle a citizen to vote. Thus the time of residence required in a state before being allowed to vote in that commonwealth varies from two years to three months. There are further qualifications as to length of residence in the county, the city and the ward. Before any citizen votes, he must register for this purpose on a day set aside for the business, and is subject to challenge by representatives of the various political parties if they do not think he is eligible. Many states prescribe that, in order to be a voter, the citizen must be able to read the constitution and write his name. Many southern states, to avoid allowing negroes to vote, specify that the voter must have paid a poll tax or be a property owner of a certain amount or be able to explain the constitution, or all three.

Electorate, in a political community, denotes the whole body of persons entitled to the right of electing the chief magistrate or other representatives to the communal assembly. The idea of election in one form or another is as old as the institution of the earliest units of the state. In England and other Teutonic lands the families enlarged into clans, occupying each its original common territory, early developed into the territorial unit of the *mark* or *township*. The township, then, was the lowest territorial division and political unit of a tribe, and possessed its own assembly and peculiar political organisation. This unit, which in other countries is the commune, in England becomes either the *municipal corporation* or *parish*. It is doubtless true that the feudal system and the manorial system changed the primitive community of the mark or township, holding its common land by its own right, into a body of tenants, holding their land of a feudal baron; but their essential character as political units was never really lost, and it may be said that the whole electoral system of England (apart from the representation of the classes in the counties), modified admittedly in the course of time, grew out of the principle of representation as evolved in the burghs or towns of the Middle Ages. Their adaptability to this end was due partly to the fact that even before the Conquest they possessed a complete political organisation, partly to the wealth that accrued to them from the grant of the charters of incorporation. Before the Conquest and immediately after many of them passed into the absolute ownership of the overlord; but the necessities of the latter soon led to the corporators gaining a measure of independence through the commutation of the feudal exactions for a fixed rent (*firma burgi*). Other territorial divisions such as the shire and the hundred co-existed with the town or burgh, but in most cases the latter, especially after acquiring charters, were for all judicial and administrative purposes independent of those divisions. The folk-moot of the shire and the moot of the hundred were no doubt assemblies consisting of local representatives, but they met almost exclusively for the purposes of bringing criminals to justice or assess-

ing the freeholders to the royal revenue, and from compulsion of natural circumstances could never have acquired the integral civic existence of the towns. These, on the other hand, soon developed a strong organisation for administrative as well as merely judicial purposes, and, through the institution of merchant and craft gilds fostered by the crown, rapidly acquired considerable accession of wealth both from their exclusive privileges of buying and selling free from exorbitant tolls and from the revenue accruing from corporate property. The gilds all tended to become the governing body of the town, and still further developed their privileges of self-government and self-assessment. The result was that they became close corporations, election to which was a thing to be coveted, and the representation of which in parliament an object no less desirable. Parallel with the development of the borough franchise, the county representation was evolved through the elective principle of the old county court (*q.v.*). In pre-Norman times the freeholders assembled in the county court or shire-moot for fiscal and judicial purposes, and to the moot also came burgesses and the reeves from the towns. Later the town representatives seceded, having through the grant of charters gained a right to send out their own representatives to bargain with the exchequer officials. The county freeholders continued to elect knights, who either assembled in the county court or were summoned by the sheriff to some central point for the same purposes, or to be consulted about a grant. When this representation for purposes of assessment became a representation for deliberative purposes too, election to parliament in the modern sense was begun. At first it seems that towns did not appreciate the honour of sending members to parliament, and the representation, such as it was, was chiefly the county representation of the classes. Many Acts were passed in the beginning of the fifteenth century to regulate the franchise in the counties, and in 1430 an Act was passed to restrict the right of voting for knights to persons possessing freeholds in the shire to the value of forty shillings a year, and all copyholders and villeins were disfranchised. The forty-shilling freeholders remained the only county voters till the Reform Bill of 1832. In the intervening centuries, however, the boroughs, grown wealthy, began to realise the value of the right of election. Control over the royal expenditure meant the power to secure the redress of grievances. There was, however, always this difference between the county representatives and those of the boroughs : the crown could increase or diminish the number of boroughs represented—a power based on the doctrine that borough privileges were gifts of the crown, and that their status was historically that of the royal demesne ; the number of shire knights, on the other hand, could not be altered. From this fact and the subsequent association of the knights with the burgesses as representatives of the people instead of the classes, the representation of the third estate of the realm was saved from the extinction that the corresponding bodies encountered abroad. But the institution of the representation of the third estate of the realm was as yet a far cry from even the most modified democratic ideal. The boroughs rapidly became corrupt, the franchise passing into the hands of a close body of corporators who frequently sold the borough seats to the king's ministers. By the beginning of the nineteenth century the borough had practically ceased to represent public opinion at all. From the time of the Reform Bill in 1832, which abolished the 'rotten' boroughs, there has been a series of Acts extending or limiting the franchise in one direction or another, and, until recently (1918-31), leaving the general system of the English E. in a somewhat bewildering condition. In 1884 the franchise conferred in 1867 on householders and lodgers in boroughs was extended to similar persons in the counties. A year later the E. in England underwent a fundamental alteration, the whole country being divided into numerous county and borough constituencies, each county being subdivided into two or more constituencies, and each constituency returning one member, the idea being to create equal electoral districts. The principle of division adopted by the Redistribution of Seats Act, 1885, was eminently in accordance with the democratic feeling that had grown in intensity from the time Rousseau first preached the doctrine of equality. All the boroughs with a population of less than 15,000 were disfranchised or merged in their counties, with the result that the inhabitants of the disfranchised boroughs became voters for some single member county constituency ; boroughs with more than 15,000 but less than 50,000 inhabitants were to return one member each, while those of over 100,000 inhabitants were divided into separate constituencies, with additional seats in proportion to their population. At present England and Wales (including Monmouth),

with a population of nearly 39,500,000 and an E. of 25,085,000, return 528 members (Wales and Monmouth returning 36 of these) ; Scotland, with a population of 4,893,000 and an E. of 2,980,000, returns 74 members ; and Northern Ireland, with a population of 1,250,000 and an E. of 785,700, returns 13 members. The net result of the reforms of the nineteenth century was an accession of power to the executive and the E. at the expense of the House of Commons. Prior to the Reform Act of 1832 a defeat of the ministry did not necessarily involve its resignation. Both the ministry and the majority in the House were for the most part in the confidence of the king. But after 1832 a general election became for the first time nothing more nor less than a vote to return a House pledged to support some particular statesman, with the result that a change of ministry necessarily followed. The distribution, prior to 1918, was far from perfect. The progressive shifting of the population and the huge absolute increase in the whole population since 1885 rendered the old distribution in numerous instances peculiarly inequitable and as far removed from the spirit underlying the idea of equal electoral areas as the principle of plural voting from the doctrine of equality of all men. The result of this general inequality of areas and voting power was an agitation of intermittent activity for various reforms, some having for their object the institution of a purely personal for a proprietary qualification, others the representation of the political opinions of the minority. In the years immediately preceding the Great War the movement for adult suffrage, and the consequent abolition of the principle of plural voting, formed one of the principal measures on the programme of the Liberal government. The various aspects of the question of representation of minorities, the case for which was first thoroughly advocated by John Stuart Mill, included (1) an attempt to secure additional power in the representation for the educated, thrifty, and well-to-do (fancy franchise) ; (2) an attempt to secure representation for every opinion which can find supporters equalling in numbers the result of the division of voters by seats ; (3) an attempt to break the power of the majority through the instrumentality of such a machine as the so-called three-cornered constituency of the Act of 1867 ; and (4) an attempt of the advocates of proportional representation to offer a wider choice to the voter and to secure the return of independent members. (*See also* PROPORTIONAL

REPRESENTATION.) On the introduction of adult suffrage by the
Representation of the People Act,
1918, the E. increased from 8,357,000
to 16 million, including 6 million
women. The Representation of the
People (Equal Franchise) Act increased
it to the present figure (*see* ELECTIONS),
the large increase over 1918 being accounted for by reducing the age limit
for women from 30 to 21 years of age
and by giving all women the vote on
equal terms with men. Proportional
representation is applied only to
University constituencies returning
2 or more members : 11 seats were
thereby affected. The principle of
equal electoral areas obtains in Germany, Scandinavia, the United States,
Canada, and S. Africa ; and in Spain
so far as elections to the Senate are
concerned. Other countries, like
Austria and Switzerland, still adhere
to the system of representation of
communes, or territorial divisions for
administrative purposes, like the old
English shires, hundreds, and chartered towns. A system of double
election prevails in the United States
and in France. In the United States
the E. elect the members of the
Electoral College on the Tuesday after
the first Monday in November of
every fourth year, when the presidential election takes place. The Electoral College is thus composed of
states' representatives, who, on the
second Monday of the succeeding
January, elect the president. There
are 531 votes in the Electoral College,
and therefore 266 secure a majority.
As in America so in England, an
election really means that the E.
chooses some one particular statesman, for the Electoral College is no
more than a species of conduit pipe,
and in practice exercises no independent choice. (*See also* CABINET.)

**Electors, The German Imperial** (*Kur-
fürsten*), the great princes in whom
was vested the right of choosing the
emperor or king of the Romans.
Under the Carlovingians the crown
was hereditary, then Germany became an elective monarchy, and
finally by 1257 the number of electors
was fixed at seven—three lay princes,
the Count Palatine of the Rhine
(imperial steward), the Duke of Saxony (marshal), the Margrave of
Brandenburg (chamberlain), and
three spiritual electors, the Archbishops of Mainz, Trèves, and Cologne
(chancellors). As to the seventh
elector there remained considerable
doubt. Bavaria claimed the place,
but in 1289–90 the King of Bohemia
was chosen. During the Thirty Years'
War, Bavaria was added to the electors (1623), the Peace of Westphalia
(1648) finally establishing the elec-

torate. In 1692 the ninth electorate of
Brunswick-Lüneburg (recognised in
1710 as Hanover) was added. Changes
took place during the French ascendency, and the electors' powers really
came to an end (1806) on the dissolution of the Holy Roman empire,
though as late as 1866 the title ' elector of Hesse-Cassel ' was used. *See*
Harnack, *Das Kurfürstenkollegium*,
1883 ; Bryce's *Holy Roman Empire*,
ix. (ed. of 1904) ; Fisher, *The Mediæval Empire*, 1898 ; Henderson's translation of the ' Golden Bull ' issued by
Charles IV., 1356, in *Select Hist. Doc.
of the Middle Ages*, 1892.

**Electra** (Gk. Ἠλέκτρα, the bright or
brilliant one) was the daughter of
Agamemnon and Clytæmnestra, and
sister of Iphigenia and Orestes. She
saved her brother from Ægisthus and
Clytæmnestra, who after the murder
of Agamemnon intended to kill him,
and later assisted him in avenging
Agamemnon's death. She married
her brother's friend, Pylades, and
became by him the mother of Medon
and Strophius. Her tomb was shown
in later times at Mycenæ.

**Electric Batteries,** *see* ACCUMU-
LATOR ; CELL, VOLTAIC.

**Electric Bells and Alarms.** The chief
parts of an ordinary E. B. are the
electro-magnets A, and the armature
C to which the knocker of the bell
is attached. C is connected by a thin
spring to the point D. At P there is a

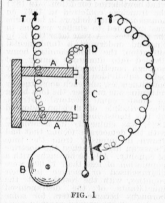

FIG. 1

platinum-pointed screw which makes
contact with a spring attached to C.
B represents the bell itself. The
electro-magnet A is made in the shape
of a U, and the wire is wound around
the arms so that when the current
passes the coils, which are connected
in series, the magnet becomes one of

the horseshoe variety. The two coils are joined together, the other end of the wire being connected to T and to D. The armature is fastened to D by means of the spring. The terminals T are connected to the external circuit. Now consider the action of the mechanism : initially the screw P is in contact with the spring attached to C; a complete circuit is thus formed and immediately the magnet becomes excited and attracts to it the armature C; this effects a break in the circuit at P, the current stops and the magnets then cease to attract C, which flies back under the action of the spring attaching it to D and again making contact at P. In this way the circuit is alternately made and broken at P, thus giving to the armature C an oscillating motion which causes the striker to strike the bell B continuously. The above type is called an *electric trembling bell.* For signalling purposes the *single stroke bell* is more useful. This bell is very similar in construction to the trembling bell ; but the screw P is omitted, the terminal T being connected directly to D. Thus when the current passes, the magnets are excited and the armature is attracted to them, thus causing the striker to strike the bell. So long as the current flows, the magnet continues to be excited, and thus C will not fly back until the current is broken in the outside circuit. It should be noted that the circuit is not broken inside the bell as in the trembler, but by means of a push button (say), which can be manipulated at the will of the operator, the bell being struck once for each contact made at the push. A simple circuit for ordinary household use is shown in Fig. 2. The

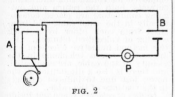

FIG. 2

terminals of the bell A are connected to the poles of the battery, the push P being inserted at any convenient point in the circuit from which the circuit can be completed, thus bringing the battery B into action and causing the current to flow through the bell. Various types of bells are now used, and one further type may be noted. This is the *continuous ringing bell,* which is used mainly in con-

nection with fire or burglar alarms. This bell continues to ring when once started until it is checked by means of a small cord which hangs down the side. In construction it is similar to the trembling bell, but it has in addition a third terminal, a trigger, and another contact pillar. The trigger rests upon the armature, and when this armature is attracted by the magnets, the trigger is released and makes contact with the second pillar, thus completing the circuit and causing the bell to continue ringing. By means of the cord attached to the trigger it can be drawn back to its normal position and the ringing checked.

*Indicators.*—When a number of push-buttons are installed in the same house, it is necessary to know at

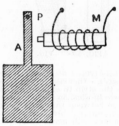

FIG. 3

which push contact was made in order to ring the bell. The indicator is a simple device suited for this purpose. It consists essentially of an electro-magnet M and an armature A pivoted at P, with a flag attached at its lower end. When the current passes the magnet is excited and attracts the armature, causing the armature to rotate about P. When the current stops the armature falls back under the action of gravity and continues to swing like the pendulum of a clock for some time after the current has ceased to flow. One of these is put ' in series ' with the bell for each position of a push button, and thus acts as a signal. These indicators are all collected together on one board called the ' Indicator Board.'

*Fire alarms.*—These usually depend on the expansion of metals when subjected to a rise of temperature. Fig. 4a represents one type where two equal strips of different metals are riveted together at their ends. These metals have different coefficients of expansion. When the temperature rises, one of the metals expands more than the other, but, being riveted together, the metal with the larger coefficient expansion will bend outwards, as in Fig. 4b, making contact with a key as shown and completing the circuit. Another variety used consists of only one strip

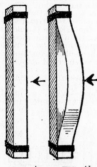

FIG. 4a    FIG. 4b

of metal riveted at A and B to the wall (say). Increase in temperature causes the strip to expand and warp, as shown in Figs. 5a and 5b, since the distance between the rivets A and B will not appreciably alter. Contact with a key will again complete the circuit. A very ingenious alarm is the 'Aero' system. Copper tubing of fine bore is installed through the building and connected up to a closed chamber fitted with a very

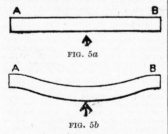

FIG. 5a

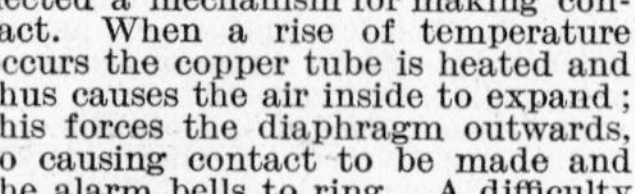

FIG. 5b

flexible diaphragm to which is connected a mechanism for making contact. When a rise of temperature occurs the copper tube is heated and thus causes the air inside to expand; this forces the diaphragm outwards, so causing contact to be made and the alarm bells to ring. A difficulty arises because during the day and night there are changes of temperature; this is overcome by means of

leak valves whereby this ordinary expansion is overcome, the valves being adjusted so that the air will pass out through them except when there is rapid expansion due to a sudden rise in temperature.

*Burglar alarms.*—These generally consist of devices attached to windows, doors, etc. They consist generally of a brass plate attached to the movable part, and a spring to the fixed part of the window. They are so placed that any movement of the window will bring these into contact one with the other, thus completing a circuit and setting the bell ringing.

**Electric Cables.** These are conductors through which electric currents are carried from place to place.

*Manufacture of cables.*—The interior of the cable consists of a bundle of copper wires. These are treated with tin to protect them from the action of sulphur. In the smaller cables these wires are then covered by a layer of tape, but in the larger cables this is generally omitted. The wires are then coated with vulcanised bitumen, and the whole is pressed into one solid mass of uniform thickness by the application of very high pressure. A covering of tape which has been treated with bitumen is then added over the vulcanised bitumen. The number of coatings of this tape varies in different cables. Underground cables are treated further by the addition of a coating of jute yarn, and then one of hemp braid. It may be pointed out that after the addition of each of the above coverings, the cable is pulled through a vessel containing hot compound. The insulation is made more perfect by increasing the thickness of the layer of vulcanised bitumen. When cables are employed for conducting alternating currents, both the return and outgoing conductors are placed concentrically in the same cable and insulated from each other by a thick coating of vulcanised bitumen. By this method inductive effects of any apparatus, *e.g.* a telephone in the vicinity of the cable, are eliminated, and there is also a diminution in the power lost due to induced currents in the coatings of the cable.

*Laying of cables.*—When put inside a building, they must be protected and well insulated. Generally, perhaps the most efficient method is to enclose the wire in iron tubing. There are three important ways of laying underground cables. In the first system the cables are placed in rectangular iron troughs, the dimensions of which depend on the number of cables which they have to contain. The cables are kept as far away as possible from the iron, and are supported inside by wooden bridges, in which slots are cut to fix the cables a sufficient distance apart. The bridges are treated with bitumen before being placed in position. When the cables are laid, the whole trough is filled with bitumen and then covered with a layer of concrete. This is the solid system, but it has the disadvantage that only with difficulty can a cable be withdrawn in the event of a fault occurring. However, because of the good insulation, the occurrence of a fault is very rare in this system. Another system which overcomes this difficulty is by using blocks of bituminous concrete containing circular holes bored longitudinally. Only one cable is placed in each hole. Manholes or draw-boxes are provided at convenient places, and when the concrete blocks are being fitted along in a trench, the cables may be drawn through the hole. If a fault occurs the offending cable can easily be removed without digging up the trench. In a third system, a fibrous material is used as the insulator. This generally consists of layers of tape and fine yarn in the order named, and these are saturated with hot bitumen. Immediately, before the bitumen has had time to cool, a coating of lead is put on by the aid of hydraulic pressure. This has the great advantage of being practically impervious to either air or moisture.

**Electric Circuit.** A circuit consists of any closed network of wiring along which a current will flow. The most important law applied to such a network is that due to Ohm, which states that $C = \dfrac{E}{R}$ (where C represents the current, E the electromotive force, and R the resistance, all these quantities being measured in practical units). The resistance of the wires is the question to consider under this heading. The resistance of a wire depends on its length and cross section; its material chiefly, however, is modified by changes of temperature.

Expressed mathematically $R = \rho \dfrac{l}{s}$, $l =$ length, $s =$ cross section, and $\rho$ is a constant depending on the material. $\rho$ is called the specific resistance of the material, and is measured by the resistance of a piece of the wire 1 cm. long and of 1 sq. cm. cross section. The specific resistance varies with the material of the conductor, the specific resistance of a good conductor being low, whereas that of a bad conducting material is very high. The *effect of temperature* is generally to increase the resistance with a rise of temperature. The resistance of many ma-

terials decreases with rise of temperature. Two important laws, due to Kirchhoff, are often applied to a network. The first states that no electricity can disappear in any part of the circuit. Thus, if a number of wires branch out from a main, the sum of the currents in the branches is equal to the current in the main wire. The second law states that in any network the fall of potential is always equal to the product of the current and the resistance of the wire between the two points considered.

*Resistances in series and in parallel.* —Resistances joined in series are shown in Fig. 1, where the two resistances are joined in the circuit, forming

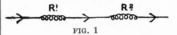

FIG. 1

a continuous path. The symbols used having the same meaning as before, the effective resistance will be the sum of the two resistances, $R = R_1 + R_2$. Fig. 2 shows four resistances

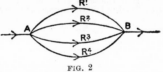

FIG. 2

joined in parallel. If E = fall of pressure between A and B, and $C_1, C_2, C_3, C_4$ be the currents in the wires $R_1, R_2, R_3, R_4$, respectively, also if C be the total current, and R the effective resistance of the four wires, then $C = C_1 + C_2 + C_3 + C_4$. But $C = \dfrac{E}{R}$, also $C_1 = \dfrac{E}{R_1}$, $C_2 = \dfrac{E}{R_2}$, and so on. Thus $\dfrac{E}{R} = \dfrac{E}{R_1} + \dfrac{E}{R_2} + \ldots$, and hence $\dfrac{1}{R} = \dfrac{1}{R_1} + \dfrac{1}{R_2} + \dfrac{1}{R_3} + \dfrac{1}{R_4}$.

*Battery resistance.*—The battery forming part of the circuit offers a resistance to the production of the current. This is termed the internal resistance of the battery in contradistinction to the external resistance. The internal resistance is generally represented by $r$, and the external resistance by R, thus the total resistance is $r + R$. Hence $C = \dfrac{E}{r + R}$, and for large currents a battery of low resistance should be used in order to minimise the resistance.

*Grouping of cells.*—Cells may be grouped in series or in parallel as illustrated in Figs. 3 and 4. In the series grouping the opposite poles are

FIG. 3

joined together, whereas in the parallel grouping poles of the same sign are grouped together. Suppose the number of cells grouped together

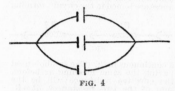

FIG. 4

in either system be $n$. The total E.M.F. in the series grouping will be $n$E, the total battery resistance $nr$, and thus $C = \dfrac{n\text{E}}{\text{R} + nr} = \dfrac{\text{E}}{\dfrac{\text{R}}{n} + r}$.

In the parallel grouping the total battery resistance will be $r$, and the E.M.F. will be equivalent to that of only one cell. Thus $C = \dfrac{\text{E}}{\text{R} + \dfrac{r}{n}}$. Clearly then, for maximum current, when the external resistance is high compared with the battery resistance, the series grouping is the more efficient, whereas when the external resistance is low in comparison, the parallel grouping is more suitable.

*Counter E.M.F.*—When a current is passed through an electrolyte (a liquid conductor), an E.M.F. is set up in the opposite direction and thus decreases the current flowing. The effective E.M.F. is the difference between the driving E.M.F. and this opposing E.M.F. Thus if $e$ represents this opposing E.M.F., then $C = \dfrac{\text{E} - e}{\text{R}}$.

*Alternating current circuit.*—It has been noted under dynamos that in an alternating current, the current moves backwards and forwards, thus showing that the E.M.F. must be a varying quantity; this variation may be shown graphically as it approximates to a sine curve. This curve may easily be described as follows: Take the circle of Fig. 5 and divide its circumference into a number of equal parts, and then divide the line AA in Fig. 6 into the same number of equal

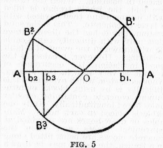

FIG. 5

parts. Let the radius OB of the circle rotate, and when it comes to a marked point, such as B¹, measure off the vertical height B¹$b_1$ above the line AA, and draw this line from the corresponding point B¹ in Fig. 6. When a complete revolution has been made, we have all the points between the points AA; and by joining the ends of the lines drawn from these points we have what is termed a sine curve. The value of the lines, of

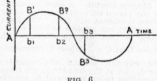

FIG. 6

which B¹$b_1$ is typical, gives the instantaneous value of the current. By comparison of these figures, it is clear that $b_1$B¹ is proportional to the angle through which OB¹ has rotated, and thus $b_1$B¹ is proportional to the sine of the angle represented by OB¹ from the property of the curve, and hence $C = k \sin \theta$ (where $\theta$ is this angle and $k$ is a constant). Now $C = \dfrac{e}{\text{R}}$ (where $e$ is the effective E.M.F.), and hence $C = \dfrac{\text{E}}{\text{R}} \sin \theta$, where E is the maximum E.M.F., the constant $k$ being equal to $\dfrac{\text{E}}{\text{R}}$. Thus $e = \text{E} \sin \theta$. We have neglected the question of self-induction so far. This occurs in most circuits. In this case the current does not rise and fall simultaneously with the E.M.F. and has a certain amount of lag depending upon the self-induction. As a result, the maximum of E.M.F. and that of current do not occur simultaneously, and hence the direction of the E.M.F. reverses before that of the current, and thus for the moment the E.M.F. is acting against the current. This clearly will occur twice in a period, *i.e.* at each alternation. The lag is usually measured in degrees, its magnitude being called the ' angle of lag.' The power developed in the circuit is obtained by multiplying together the virtual voltage and amperes, and also the cosine of the angle of lag. The ratio of this to the product of the number of volts and amperes in a circuit free from induction is called the *power factor.* To explain this self-induction consider a coil of wire ; when a current commences to flow in the circuit there is an increase of lines of force through the coil, and this variation of the number of lines causes a current to flow through the coil in the opposite direction to the initial current, thus retarding its rise. On stopping the current there is again a variation in the number of lines of force through the coils, and this, causing electric induction, sets up a current in the same direction as the original current, thus retarding the fall of the circuit. The magnitude of the induced current will depend on the number of turns in the coil, its shape, and the strength of the current. Thus, the self-inductive effect or ' inductance,' which is measured in units called the *henry,* tends to retard the rise or fall of the current. Thus it is clear that when an alternating current flows, this self-inductive effect is brought into play at each alternation, and so the current will not only lag behind the E.M.F. applied, but its value will be lower than it would be in the absence of self-induction. It is therefore evident that two quantities offer obstruction to the passage of the current, viz., the resistance of the coils and the self-inductive effects, the total obstruction being called the *impedance* of the circuit. Under electro-magnetic induction, it has been pointed out that the current induced depends upon the rate at which the lines of force cut the coils, hence in the case of an alternating current it will depend on the rate of the alternation. Expressed mathematically, the impedance of the circuit = $\sqrt{R^2 + (2\pi n)^2 L^2}$ (where $n$ gives the number of alternations per second, L the coefficient of self-induction, and R the resistance). Hence

$$C = \frac{E}{\sqrt{R^2 + (2\pi n)^2 L^2}}$$ (where C is the

virtual current and E the virtual voltage).

*Measurement of alternating currents.* —The essential parts of the instruments consist of two separate coils, one consisting of a few turns of thick wire and the other of a large number of thin wires ; these coils are joined together by a wire, their other ends leading off to the terminals of the instrument. One of the coils is fixed to the frame of the instrument, while the other coil, which is made large enough to contain the fixed coil, is suspended by a silk thread. When the current passes, the magnetic fields produced tend to turn the suspended coil, and thus afford a mode of measuring the current in terms of the twist of the coil. Since the coils are in series, even if the current is reversed, the deflection will be in the same direction, since the direction of the current will be reversed in *all* the coils. Thus such an instrument can be used for the measurement of an alternating current, since in these the direction of the current is only reversed rapidly.

*Choking coils* in a simple form consist of a coil of wire with iron cores to increase the self-induction. They are used in the alternating current circuit to reduce the current strength, or to reduce the fall of potential or pressure between any two points. Its great advantage is that, since it is designed to possess great self-induction, the current is choked and the energy is not wasted in the production of heat, but the major part is given back to the circuit. Occasionally it is necessary to vary the self-inductive effects. This may be conveniently done by using a core consisting of a bundle of straight iron wires, this core being capable of being withdrawn from the coil to a varying extent, and thus causing a variation in the self-inductive effect. The iron core is made of a bundle of iron wires to reduce eddy currents which would necessitate a waste of power due to the heat so developed.

*The effect on the capacity of a condenser.*—If a condenser is charged by an alternating current, it becomes charged in opposite directions as the current reverses ; thus a current due to the charge on the condenser tends to flow in the opposite direction to that of the primary current. This current from the condenser is of the alternating variety. The E.M.F. of the primary current assumes a zero and a maximum value ; when the value is zero, there is no E.M.F. acting against that of the condenser, and thus the current from it is a maximum. Similarly, when the primary E.M.F. is a maximum, this current will be a minimum. Here we consider practically no resistance in the external circuit, and thus we see in this case the phase difference between the two currents is 90°. This effect is of very great importance on the question of cable circuits. The cable acts like a condenser, and therefore this effect might assume great proportions. This is minimised by making the capacity of the cables as low as possible.

**Electric Coherers,** *see* WIRELESS TELEGRAPHY.

**Electric Condensers,** *see* CONDENSER, ELECTRICAL.

**Electric Conductors,** *see* CONDUCTION; ELECTRICITY.

**Electric Distribution.**—If the area of distribution is very limited, the principle of the constant current is employed, since in this case the current utilised is not very large, and it has practically the same value in all parts of the circuit. This, however, is impracticable in very large areas. In this case the distribution takes place through underground cables, and questions of economy demand that the cost of these should be a minimum. Electric power is the quantity in which the amount of electricity utilised is measured, and it is measured by the product of the voltage and current. Now, the higher the voltage employed the smaller may be the cross section of the cable, and thus, by using high pressure and a low current, the amount of copper utilised may be smaller. There is a limit to the extent of this pressure, as the lamps manufactured cannot use a pressure higher than about 250 volts. As the current passes along the wires there is a loss of pressure due to the resistance, and when power is utilised from the cables to light lamps, etc., at varying distances from the supply, it is clear that the voltage along the wires must decrease as we go further away. In order to keep all the lamps at the same brightness the voltage should be the same at all parts of the circuit. This ideal condition is impossible, but it may be approximated to by making the cables very thick to minimise resistance, and by utilising the *feeder system*. The feeder consists of a separate cable from which no current is taken. It is connected to the middle of the main in order to bring the current into it. Along the main, as has been pointed out, there is a drop in the voltage, and the feeder is joined on at certain points to bring the voltage up to its normal value. The best places to tap the mains by feeders are those in which the demand on the current supply is greatest. The voltage on each feeder is adjusted independently, since it is clear that they

will not always carry the same current, nor be of the same length or resistances ; this is done by the ' boosting dynamos.' It has been pointed out that the only way to save expense on the cables is to make the pressure as high as possible. This difficulty of electric lamps limiting the extent of this pressure led to the introduction of the *three wire system*, which doubles the pressure on the mains, while the pressure on the lamps remains unchanged. Let $M^1$ and $M^2$ represent the mains in the diagram, let P be the

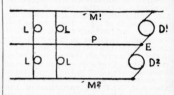

middle wire, and let the mains be joined : $M^1$ to the negative terminal of the dynamo $D^1$, and $M^2$ to the positive terminal of the dynamo $D^2$, and the positive terminal of $D^1$ be joined to the negative terminal of $D^2$. Let the lamps L be joined two by two in series across the mains. Now, when there is the same number of lamps between $M^1$ and P and P and $M^2$, there is a constant potential along P, and thus no current tends to flow along it ; but on removing a lamp from between $M^1$ and P (say), this equilibrium is disturbed; this results in increasing the resistance between $M^1$ and P, and thus there is a greater fall of pressure than between P and $M^2$, which lowers the potential at the point on P where the lamp has been taken out. The potential at the point E is clearly constant, and thus a current flows along P ; thus it may be deduced that the current that P carries is only due to the increase of the number of lamps over that on the other side of it. This by proper adjustment may be made very small, and thus the wire P may be made much smaller than the mains $M^1$ and $M^2$. This explains in brief the action of the system. Now, suppose each dynamo capable of maintaining a potential difference at its terminals of 100 volts : clearly when they are joined in series, as in the diagram, the potential difference between the mains $M^1$ and $M^2$ will be 200 volts, and also the pressure on the lamps will be only 100 volts, thus showing that, while the pressure in the mains is doubled, the pressure on the lamps is unaltered.

Economic considerations determine

the site of the supply station, which in large towns usually lies outside the boundaries. To supply an ordinary voltage of about 500 volts, the feeders would be very long, as well as the mains. It is therefore necessary still further to increase the pressure. This will be higher than can be utilised by lamps, consequently ' sub-stations ' are introduced which re-ceive the high pressure current from the central station and reduce its pressure. The most efficient system, when the supply station lies at a distance from the town area, is to use an alternating current, using preferably a three-phase current, since this requires less copper for its transmission. If the alternating cur-rent itself is used it can be reduced in pressure by means of *transformers* (*q.v.*), which can be enclosed in a very small space on the side of the street. But for house lighting, etc., a continuous current is needed. To obtain this from the alternating current, the current is utilised for driving machines which will generate a continuous current.

**Electric Furnaces,** *see* FURNACES; METALLURGY.

**Electric Fuses,** *see* ELECTRIC LIGHT-ING.

**Electric Generator.** In all dynamo-electric G. the electro-motive force is induced into the conductor or turn by cutting a magnetic field. This varies every revolution, and when the ends of the turn are taken out to slip rings the current is shown to vary from zero to a maximum twice every revolution of the turn. This is alternating current. Direct or uni-directional current is obtained by taking the leads to a device called a commutator, which is fixed on the same shaft as the turn of wire, and reverses the direction of the current once every half-revolution, thus making the alternating current into a pulsating direct current. There are two main types of alternators : (*a*) those with fixed armature and rotating field magnets, and (*b*) those with fixed field magnets and rotating armature. The rotating part is termed the rotor, and the fixed part the stator. All except very small alternators belong to class (*a*). As the E.M.Fs. generated are often of the order of 6000 volts or more, the advantages of having the arma-ture fixed are that the windings can be better mounted and it is easier to insulate and ventilate them ; the leads from the armature are also fixed, since the commutator is done away with. The current supplied to the field magnets is of the order of 100 volts, and is fed into and out of them by means of slip rings on the

shaft. There are three other classi-fications of alternators, grouped according to° the way that their armatures are wound ; they are (i.) single-phase, (ii.) two-phase, and (iii.) three- or poly-phase machines. Direct current Gs. are divided into four types according to the manner in which the field coils are excited ; they are : (*a*) shunt machines, (*b*) series machines, (*c*) separately ex-cited machines, and (*d*) compound wound machines. In the shunt machine the whole of the field circuit is placed across the terminals so that the field is always at full-line voltage. The shunt G. has poor regulation, the voltage greatly decreasing as the load increases. The series machine is one in which the whole of the load current flows through the series field coils ; thus the voltage of the machine is proportional to the load applied. This type is used where the load is constant. Separately excited ma-chines are used in large stations where exciting current is readily obtained from the station bus-bars and a voltage regulator is used. A com-pound-wound machine is essentially a shunt machine with a few series turns added. This has the effect that when the load is applied the drop in voltage due to the shunt field is counterbalanced by the rise in voltage due to the series field. If the winding is such that the voltage on full load and no load is the same, the machine is said to be ' level-compounded ' or ' flat-compounded ' ; when the full load voltage is less, it is ' under-compounded' ; and when more, the machine is said to be ' over-com-pounded.'

**Electric Heaters,** *see* ELECTRIC LIGHTING.

**Electric Indicators,** *see* ELECTRIC BELLS.

**Electric Insulators.** As defined in ELECTRICITY, an insulator is a body which does not allow electricity to pass through it. Metals, solutions of salts, water, and alcohol are not in-sulators. It is found that the best insulators are *dry* ebonite, glass, shellac, sulphur, silk, paraffin, sealing-wax, and many other fats, oils, and resins. All gases are insulators unless they are under the influence of Röntgen rays or great heat. It is found that a little moisture is detri-mental to a substance's insulatory properties. Thus the glass of a Leyden jar is coated with shellac varnish, otherwise it would become covered with a conducting film of moisture. The stands and supports of all electrostatic and electromagnetic machines are insulators. Marble, glass, and porcelain are most com-monly used for this purpose in large instruments. In small machines and laboratory ap liances, ebonite is often used. The insulating supports on telegraph wires are made of porcelain. Cable wires are insulated from each other by surrounding them with gutta-percha. This is then surrounded with tarred hemp, and then with hemp dipped in an insulatory composition. This keeps the cable insulated from the sea-water, which is conducting. On a small scale silk and cotton are used for covering wires and bobbins of electrical apparatus. In electrical heating appliances, where great heat and strain are encountered, mica is the substance usually employed for insulating any material. For insulating purposes in very delicate instruments quartz or silk fibre is used. The latter is quickly affected by the damp, but the former is not.

**Electric Lamps.** The first attempt to apply electric power to lighting purposes resulted from the discovery by Davy in 1810 that when the terminals of a powerful battery are connected to two pieces of carbon, the current continues to flow when the ends of the two carbons are not in contact. A brilliant light is emitted when this takes place, termed the electric arc. The gap between them is filled with an intense glow. Particles of carbon are projected from the positive terminal and float about freely in this space; these become intensely luminous and are thus the chief factor for the emission of the light. A chemical effect also takes place when the carbons are exposed to the air, resulting in the carbons gradually being burnt away. The effect of the positive carbon throwing off these particles is shown in Fig. 1, where the point of the carbon assumes a hollow form like a crater. Due to the combined action of these effects, the distance between the points of the carbons increases, and ultimately the gap will be too great for the current to pass. Modern electric arc lamps attempt in various forms to overcome these difficulties automatically. The general method is to pass the current through an electro-magnet which is connected in series with the lamp; when the magnet is excited it attracts an armature, the motion of which is utilised to adjust the distance between the carbons. The brush lamp, illustrated in Fig. 2, exemplifies these principles. $T_1$ and $T_2$ are the terminals by which the lamp is connected into the main cir-

FIG. 1

cuit. The negative carbon C is fixed, while the carbon $C^1$ is movable, its movement being regulated in a manner to be described, so that as the carbons gradually waste away the arcing distance is adjusted. The current enters at the positive terminal $T_1$. It then travels through the solenoids A and A so as to give very powerful and opposite poles at the lower extremities. The currents then unite and travel through the connection P to the positive carbon C, thence to the negative carbon C which is connected to the negative terminal $T_2$. Now consider the action of the lamp, the carbons being initially in contact:

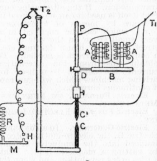

FIG. 2

the current passes through the solenoids A, causing the soft irons B to be drawn upwards, B is connected to the arm holding the positive carbon, and thus the movement is transmitted and the carbon is raised. This results in an increase of resistance in the main circuit, and thus more current travels through the coils A, and the magnetic force is increased. Thus the distance would continually increase until the current ceased. To obviate this, another coil of thick wire, not shown in diagram, is wound around the coils A in opposite directions to the main coils on A, causing a diminution of the intensity of the magnetisation of the irons B, and so B falls a little. In this way the distance between the carbon points is kept at the proper arc distance. This is the main principle of the lamp, but in actual practice the mechanism is far more complex than that described above. When a number of arc lamps are used they are mostly connected up in series. A difficulty arises from the fact that if any one of the lamps fails to act, the whole group is cut off from the current. A device is introduced whereby the lamp on failing to act becomes short-circuited, the current taking up a new path through the lamp.

*Incandescent lighting.*—The principle underlying all phases of lighting is that of heating a body to a very high temperature. It has been noted under ELECTRICITY that one of the effects of passing an electric current through a body is the production of heat. Further, the greater resistance which the body offers the greater the heat produced. Clearly it is necessary to use a substance which has a very high melting-point. Edison introduced the system of using a long car-

FIG. 3

bon filament enclosed in a glass globe which is exhausted of air as completely as possible. This type of lamp is illustrated in Fig. 3. The filament is now generally made by forcing a solution of cellulose through a very fine pipe. When the filament is dried, it is reduced to a uniform thickness by forcing it through jewel dies; it is then transformed into solid form by the process of carbonising. Carbon is an exceptionally good absorbent of gases. As the temperature rises these gases expand and force their way out, thus causing small holes in the carbon. It is necessary to diminish this tendency in the case of filaments and thus the process of carbonisation takes place at a very high temperature. It is then subjected to the process of 'flashing' to correct further this fault. The filament is first cut to the required size and then connected to the terminals of a dynamo. It is then surrounded by coal gas and is traversed by currents sufficient to raise it to white heat. The gas is decomposed to a certain extent and carbon particles are deposited in the filament. If the filament is not of uniform cross section the heat developed in the different parts will vary, and so decomposition of the gas will be greater at the places of highest temperature. A greater quantity of carbon will thus be deposited on the thinner parts of the wire. The process of flashing is continued until the whole filament assumes a uniform temperature. It is then placed in a partial vacuum and a continuous current passed. In this way the filament is hardened, its resistance is decreased, and its absorbent properties practically destroyed. The ends of the filaments are worked into the glass as at L.

The portion shown in Fig. 4 is enclosed in a brass covering; the brass loops, which pass through the rings L (Fig. 3), making the electrical connection, and the spring extends the casing so as to make the connection good. In most modern lamps this arrangement is now altered; the top of the lamp is provided with a brass collar divided into segments, to which the ends of the filament are connected. Contact is made by the apparatus illustrated in Fig. 5, where the two pins make contact with their respective segments; the S-shaped piece of material is made of porcelain to

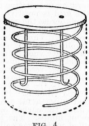

FIG. 4

ensure good insulation. One of the most useful lamps is the tantalum lamp. The filament is made of tantalum, a substance which overcomes the many deficiencies of the carbon filament. It is exceptionally strong and has a very high melting-point, and owing to the fact that its resistance increases with temperature, it is less sensitive to fluctuations of pressure

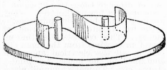

FIG. 5

than the carbon filament, which decreases in resistance as the temperature rises. Another important type of lamp is the mercury vapour lamp. This consists of a long tube of varying length, in which is placed a little mercury which forms the negative terminal of the lamp. The tube is exhausted of air; a high voltage is necessary to start the lamp working in order to break down the internal resistance; when this is done some of the mercury vaporises, giving out when it becomes incandescent a characteristic light.

*Electric Lamp and Valves.*—Owing to the advent of radio, the electric radio tube has become a household article. The discovery by Edison that a heated filament of wire when placed in a vacuum tube emitted small particles of electricity was the first step on the road. Professor Fleming improved on this idea, and invented what is known as the thermionic valve or electron tube. By this device the incoming signals from the aerial of a radio set release quantities of electricity from the filament of the tube to the anode. This electricity is dependent on the voltage applied to the plate and whether the grid is given positive or negative potential. When the grid is positive, the flow of electrons across the gap will be increased ; if it is negative, this flow will be decreased. Thus valves can be used for amplifying very small impulses of electricity such as are received on an aerial from a transmitting station.

During recent years the tungsten filament lamp has become popular, owing to the greater illumination received from it. It is also stronger, and gives a far whiter light than either the carbon or tantalum filament lamps. The lamps used are filled with a gas called argon ; this is an inert gas which enables the filament to burn at a higher temperature than in a vacuum lamp, thus making the light whiter and more efficient. Pearl lamps, which are interior frosted lamps, are the most popular, owing to the fact that the frosting softens the lights and yet does not cut down more than $2\frac{1}{2}$ per cent. of illumination. Argon and neon lamps are discharge tubes in which a current passes through one or other of these two gases at a pressure of a few millimetres. They are useful for advertising purposes.

**Electric Lighting and Wiring of Houses.** This consists of setting up a system of wires from the main circuit to all the electrical apparatus contained in the house, *e.g.* lamps, stoves, etc. To make a circuit along which the current flows, there should be a continuous line of conductors, any break in which will stop the current. These breaks or gaps are a necessary feature of the system, in order that the supply may be controlled. These gaps consist of a mechanism called a *switch*. The rough description of this mechanism is that it consists of two brass blocks insulated from one another, each being the terminal of a wire. A brass lever is so adjusted to make or break contact with both blocks, thus making or breaking the circuit. To minimise sparking when contact is made or broken, the lever is made to work automatically so that its action is practically instantaneous. Fig. 1 gives a rough illustration of a switch. $A^1$ and $A^2$ represent the brass blocks, B the lever fastened to $A^1$, and C a spring. B is pressed down from above to make

contact with $A^2$; when the pressure is released B immediately breaks contact by the action of the spring C.

*Fuses.*—One of the chief properties of a current flowing through a wire is the production of heat. When too great a current is allowed to flow, the heat developed may be enormous, and thus cause damage to the insulating material. The danger of overheating is minimised by using thick wires. Another, and the mostly em-

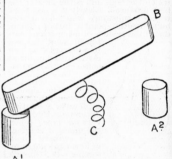

FIG. 1

ployed, contrivance is the *fuse*. This consists of a very thin wire fixed in a box which will not burn. Being so much thinner than the cable, the heat is developed at a faster rate, and the temperature reached is soon high enough to melt the wire ; this causes a break in the circuit and thus any further damage is prevented. This wire is generally three or four in. long ; the best material for its construction is fusible metal (an alloy of tin and lead), owing to its low melting point, and thus the molten metal itself is not so destructive. As a matter of practice all the fuses are located in the same place. The main cable is attached to a brass bar ; the distributing cables are attached to brass blocks opposite, these being insulated from one another on an earthenware base. Thick brass arms effect the junction at this point. Fig. 2

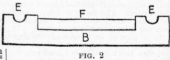

FIG. 2

represents such a bar. B is the brass arm and F the fuse. The ends E fit into the brass blocks. In this way the arm B can be taken out of the circuit and the fuse easily renewed before it is replaced. The system of wiring is practically independent of the voltage of the supply. The function of the system is to afford a complete circuit for the current from the source through the various apparatus back to the source. The wire used generally consists of a core of wire strands, insulated by a covering of rubber (pure and vulcanised) and then a layer of tape which has been soaked in bitumen. A most important feature of the system is to note the occurrence of *leaks and short circuits*. Of two paths a current will choose the one of least resistance, and if the outgoing wire and the return wire *both together* come into contact with earth, the earth being a good conductor, the current will take the earth circuit rather than the various apparatus. Thus the necessity of good insulation. If the leak is great an electric arc may be developed, and a great deal of damage caused. A short circuit is made when the outgoing and return wires make contact with one another. If the voltage is high, this is accompanied by an intense flash and a great evolution of heat, and the current immediately ceases. These short circuits are of very frequent occurrence. The electricity meter is placed on one of the mains which come from the town main, and thus all the electricity utilised passes through it and is measured. Switches are placed near so that the house may be cut off the town mains. One method which was frequently adopted was that of two mains leading from the switchboard and various branches being made off to the lamps. This necessitated a large number of joints, which, to a large extent, spoiled the insulation and also increased the number of fuses, since these must be placed wherever the size of the wire varies. To overcome this, the wire is now made the same thickness all through, and a few lamps are attached to each wire. In this way the number of joins and fuses is greatly decreased. The cables themselves are encased in a lead covering to exclude moisture. They are generally fixed on the walls.

*Fittings* include the various devices for connecting the lamps, etc., to the cables, and for their support. In ceiling fittings, the cables enter at a broad flanged base and pass down to the connecting screws of the lamp. Several lamps are often connected at the end of these cables on the same fitting. The most generally used fitting is the pendant. A small porcelain box is screwed on a piece of wood on the ceiling. This contains two brass terminals insulated from one another by porcelain. The cables which lead in from the base are attached to these terminals. To these terminals a pair of flexible cables are attached, these are twisted together and passed through a hole in the bottom of the porcelain cap. This cap is fixed to the ceiling as shown in Fig. 3. The cords hang downwards, and to the ends the lamp is attached. Another fitting is the bracket which is attached to the wall; it consists of several short arms

FIG. 3

at the end of each of which a lamp is suspended. A very useful contrivance for portable instruments, such as reading lamps, etc., is the wall socket. The socket is similar to the above-described porcelain cap, but it has two holes which contain brass tubes attached to the cables. The plug is also a porcelain cap containing two insulated brass terminals to which two brass pins are attached which fit the brass tubes in the socket. Flexible cords are attached to the terminals, and at the other end to a lamp. The current is supplied to the lamp by pushing the pins into their corresponding sockets.

*Electric heaters.*—The development of heat due to the passage of a current is utilised in these appliances. The wire is generally contained in enamel, against which the body to be heated is placed. They have the advantage that little heat is wasted, and are free from smoke and the various other inconveniences caused by the process of combustion which underlies the numerous other types of heating appliances.

There are five different systems of wiring. They are : (a) Vulcanised india rubber (V.I.R.) in steel conduit ; (b) V.I.R. in lead sheathing ; (c) V.I.R. in wood casing ; (d) V.I.R. on porcelain cleats; (e) rubber-sheathed cables. Of these five methods the first two are those most employed in house wiring; the third method is used chiefly in public buildings, offices and schools; V.I.R. on porcelain cleats is employed in factories and workshops where the wiring is of a temporary nature and has to be fastened on steel girders. Rubber-sheathed cables have a marked advantage over others in that they are not so greatly affected by moisture; thus they are used in public baths, laundries, boiler-houses and other places where there is always a large amount of moisture in the air. Steel conduit may be employed either to screw together or to be connected by spring collars. More skill is required to instal screwed conduit, since it involves the use of taps and dies and the lengths of conduit have to be cut accurately, and also it is hard to bend. One disadvantage of this method is that if there are many cables in the same conduit and one of them catches fire, either by earthing on to the conduit or by a short circuit, all the other cables are also destroyed. Lead-covered cable is the simplest to instal, in that it can be run along woodwork or brickwork on the surface and can be easily painted over to hide it; moreover it bends easily and can be made to conform readily with the contour of a wall or ceiling. This latter point is very important, as it makes the wiring of old houses possible since wires can be bent out of sight. Wood casing is resorted to only where wiring has to be carried out on the surface of walls, and where long lengths of it are to be visible, when wood casing made to resemble picture rails is employed and is painted or distempered to match the walls. This type of wiring needs great skill, as each corner has to be accurately cut in order to avoid unsightly joints. Cable on porcelain cleats has the great advantage that it is easily and rapidly erected, and that when a break occurs in the wiring it is easily seen and repairs quickly effected.

**Electric Meters** are used to measure (1) the strength of an electric current at any time, or (2) the quantity of electricity supplied, or (3) the quantity of electrical energy supplied.

*Ammeters and voltmeters.*—The heating or magnetic effects of an electric current may be used to measure it. In *Siemens'* electro-dynamometer there are two coils, one fixed and one movable, at right angles to each other and in series. The movable coil carries a pointer which moves over a horizontal (limited) scale. When the current passes, the movable coil is displaced, but is

brought back to the original position by twisting it by means of a torsion head. The angle of twist varies as (current)[2]. Thus the current can be found. The expansion of a wire when heated by a current can be used to measure the quantity passing per second. In *Lord Kelvin's current balance* the attraction between coils through which a current is passing in opposite directions is measured against a mechanical force, and thus the current strength is measured. The *Weston ammeter* is essentially a suspended coil galvanometer (*q.v.*). The instrument is usually shunted. If the magnetic field is uniform, the deflecting couple varies as the current. *Lord Kelvin's ampere gauge* consists of a fixed coil and a piece of soft iron wire carrying a pointer which moves over a horizontal scale. When a current passes in the coil, the iron wire is sucked into it, and the motion of the pointer measures the current. The amount of silver or copper deposited from their solutions can be used to measure quantity of electricity. In this case the instrument is called a *voltameter*. Weston's instrument may be used as a *voltmeter* by removing the shunt and adding a high resistance of low heat coefficient in series.

*Wattmeters and supply meters.*—The power supplied is equal to the product of the E.M.F. and the current. The energy supplied is equal to power multiplied by time. A wattmeter measures the power supplied, and is essentially a combination of an ammeter and a voltmeter. The best known form is *Weston's*. A fixed coil of low resistance (the current coil) corresponds to the ammeter. The field due to this coil varies as the current (C). A coil of high resistance (the pressure coil) swings in this field. The current in this coil is proportional to the potential difference (P.D.). Thus the deflection is proportional to C×PD, *i.e.* to the power. If the current is alternating the deflection varies as the mean power. *Supply meters* are of two kinds: *quantity meters* and *energy meters*. If the P.D. in an electrical supply is practically constant, then the power varies as the current, and the energy as the quantity. Thus, any wattmeter used in such a system becomes a quantity meter for measuring energy. If in a meter it is so arranged that the energy supplied is read directly, this would be an energy meter. *Electrolytic meters* can be used to measure quantity of electricity. Edison used silver and copper voltameters. In the *Bastian meter* water is electrolysed by the current. The rate of loss of water measures the quantity of current passing. This rate of loss can be read directly. In the *Wright meter* mercurous nitrate is used as the electrolyte. Here the polarisation is small. Mercury forms the anode, and a platinum cone the cathode. Mercury dissolves at the anode and is formed at the cathode, from which it falls to the bottom of the vessel. The vessel is graduated so that the volume of mercury in the bottom can be read. The mercury automatically siphons off when it reaches a certain height, so that the quantity formed in a given time can be measured, and thus the quantity of electricity passing can be estimated. *Motor meters* are another form of meter. Fig. 1 shows a sketch of *Ferranti's meter.* BB is an electro-magnet with a steel core E. This forms a uniform field inside an iron ring HH. This space is filled with mercury, in contact with

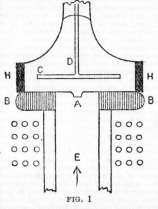

FIG. 1

the electro-magnet only at a point A. A light fan C is suspended in the mercury. The current passes along E, to the mercury through A, and then radially to the ring HH. This causes the mercury to rotate, taking the fan with it. The driving force varies as the (current)². The fluid resistance on the fan varies as the (speed)². Thus, the speed of the fan varies as the current, and the number of revolutions varies as the quantity of electricity. In Chamberlain and Hookham meters a copper disc is placed in the mercury. The current causes it to rotate. A ' brake disc ' is attached to the same spindle. This rotates in a non-uniform field. Eddy currents are set up, giving a retarding couple varying as the speed. Thus speed varies as the current.

*Alternating current meters.*—The Siemens' electro-dynamometer and the wattmeters described can be used for alternating currents as well as direct currents, with a little modification. Alternating *supply meters* fall into two classes : (1) Motor meters, (2) clock meters. Of the second class the *Aron meter* is the best known. It consists of two clocks electrically driven. A coil is suspended below each clock. The current in these coils is in such a direction that the speed of one clock is retarded and that of the other increased, due to the magnetic action on the pendulums. The difference is measured by means of a differential gear. This difference varies directly as the energy supplied to the system, and is read off by the rate of translation of the differential gear. This method can be used for one, two, or three phase currents. *Motor meters* consist of small motors. The field coils carry the whole current, the armature only a shunt current ; a resisting torque varying as the speed of the armature is supplied by a ' brake disc.' The number of revolutions of the armature then measures the energy supplied. Blatby and others used two coils for alternating currents, one of thick wire carrying the whole current, and another of fine wire carrying a current varying as the pressure applied, so designed that the current lags 90° behind the pressure. A rotating field is produced, giving eddy currents in a suspended disc, which then rotates. Speed of rotation varies (after a magnetic brake is applied) as the power. Thus the number of revolutions varies as the energy supplied. For measuring small alternating currents, especially when the frequency is high (as in radio practice), a thermocouple is used to measure the current in conjunction with a resistance. The resistance is put in the main circuit whose current is to be measured ; one junction of the thermocouple is fixed to this resistance, and the leads of it connected to a milliammeter (an ammeter calibrated in thousandths of an ampere) ; the other junction is connected to a point at constant temperature. The heating effect of the resistance sets up a current in the thermocouple circuit which varies with the current passed through the resistance.

There are many types of meters ; they are divided into two main kinds, (*a*) switchboard meters, and (*b*) portable meters. The switchboard meters are themselves divided into two types: the ' flat ' instrument, which is comparable to a flat clock-face ; and the ' edgewise ' instrument, in which the readings are shown on the edge of a rotating drum. Recording instruments are those which in place of the usual pointer have a finger with a small ink pen attached, and this pen is trailed over a continuous chart of paper, which is passed under it by means of clock mechanism. The instrument is made more robust than the usual type, since the pointer has to overcome the friction of the pen on the paper and prevent sticking.

**Electric Motors.** The dynamo is a machine for the conversion of mechanical energy into electrical energy. This suggests the possibility of the reverse action, viz. that by supplying electric power to the armature of the dynamo and also maintaining the magnetic power of the field magnets, it should be possible to obtain mechanical energy from the shaft. In order to do this the speed of the machine must correspond to the frequency of the current, and thus a process of speeding up is necessary. This necessity vitiates its practicability. Later, it was discovered that the motor could be started by the current itself. The alternating current sets up a varying magnetic field; this magnetic field is acted on by the ordinary laws of magnetic attraction and repulsion, and thus a magnetic moment acts on the coils. The armature of the motor is exactly similar to that of the dynamo, therefore, because of the large number of coils, at every instant there is a coil whose magnetic axis is at right angles to that of the field magnets; and the moment of the armature acts continuously, causing it to rotate. But due to its rotation an E.M.F. is set up tending to stop the rotation of the armature; this E.M.F. is due to the action of the machine as a dynamo, as we clearly have coils rotating in a magnetic field. This E.M.F. is called ' the counter E.M.F.' An increased load on the motor obviously results in a slackening of speed, reducing the counter E.M.F., and so more current flows through the coils. Now the moment on the coils increases with the current, and thus a greater power is developed. Further, under DYNAMOS (*q.v.*), it has been pointed out that this counter E.M.F. increases with the magnetic field, so the effect of increasing the magnetic field will be to decrease the speed of rotation and *vice versa*. It is found that the amount of metal required for conduction is least for the three-phase current, and thus a three-phase alternating current is universally used for the purposes of motive power.

*Starting the motor.*—The rotor (technical term for the rotating part) is initially at rest, and gradually gathers speed. Thus the counter E.M.F. being zero, there is a rush of current; this tends to destroy the machinery. To obviate this rush of current a special rotor is used, its terminals being connected to slip rings on the shaft. Brushes connected with a starting resistance are placed on these rings. The action of this device is that as the speed of the motor increases this resistance is gradually short-circuited, and when the maximum speed is attained the resistance is cut out. Alternating current motors can be divided into three groups, depending upon the type of rotor employed in their construction, viz. (*a*) synchronous motors; (*b*) asynchronous or induction motors; (*c*) commutator motors. Synchronous motors are merely alternators used as motors, and their constructions are identical. The number of poles on an alternator is determined by the speed at which it is to be driven, and similarly the speed of a synchronous motor determines the number of poles it shall have. Like alternators, synchronous motors require direct current excitation for their rotor poles, and this is performed in the same way as is done on alternators, *i.e.* by a direct-current generator mounted on the same shaft as the rotor. One serious drawback to the use of synchronous motors is that they are not self-starting, but have to be rotated at their normal speed before they can be started. The induction motor is by far the most common type of a.c. motor, because its construction is very simple. It is reliable, and can be made to start against a very heavy load. The rotor of an induction motor consists of a number of insulated conductors, arranged to form a drum, with the ends fixed together into a ring. The alternating polyphase current supplied to the stator winding sets up rotating fields of a uniform strength. These fields induce currents in the copper bars of the rotor, and repulsion is set up between like poles, and the rotor will rotate in the same direction as the inducing field and try to keep pace with it, but it will never quite succeed. Commutator motors are mostly applied to domestic uses, as they are best used as single-phase motors, polyphase motors being too complicated in structure to be practical. The single phase motor is the same as the d.c. motor except that the poles of the former must be laminated and only series wound motors can be used.

**Electric Potential,** see CONDENSER, ELECTRICAL; ELECTRICITY—*Electrostatics*.

**Electric Power Generation.** The modern power station has grown to dimensions undreamt of many years ago. The development of the steam turbine and the improvement in the methods of steam generation have made large alternators of the capacity of 50,000 K.V.A. possible. The cycle of operations at the generating station is as follows : the coal is fed from hoppers down chutes on to an endless chain grate, which passes slowly into the combustion chamber of the boiler ; the coal fires and heats the water in the tubes above it ; the heat rises, and to dry it and raise it to very high temperatures it is fed back again through super-heaters. The steam is then fed into a separator to remove any impurities which may be in the steam and also any water which may inadvertently be carried along with the superheated steam or which may be stopped in the pipe when the plant is started up from cold. The steam then passes on its way to the turbine through a stop valve and a governor valve ; the steam then enters the turbine and is impinged on to the blades of the wheels, and thus a torque or turning momentum is applied to the turbine shaft and rotates it. The turbine has connected to it the alternator and the exciter for the alternator. The steam, after leaving the turbine at the low pressure end, passes into the condenser. Here the steam is cooled below the temperature of the steam leaving the turbine and is then passed on to the hotwell. From this hotwell the water is pumped back to the boiler tubes, and again passes through the cycle of operations. The alternator has all its controlling equipment on a panel on the main switchboard of the station, and all the leads are taken from the alternators to busbars behind the panel. From the panel the power is fed to switchboards, which in their turn feed the distribution system, by cable ducts, out into the streets. If the current distributed is of high voltage, the switchgear for each section of the distribution scheme is installed in a separate cubicle. The alternators are of two types, *i.e.* the synchronous and the induction types. In the case of the synchronous type, the electrical power is obtained by the rotation of the armature conductors in a constant magnetic field produced by exciting coils in which a direct current flows. The induction type has magnetic fields of the rotating polyphase type, and is produced by polyphase alternating currents flowing in the same windings as the load current. The frequency of this type of machine is us ally ' set ' by a synchronous machine in the external circuit. This ' frequency setter ' is required to supply the necessary exciting current of the induction generator. A few induction generators of a station may be used with advantage, as they cause less damage on a short circuit or very heavy overload.

**Electric Power Transmission.** E.P.T. lines are those which are used for transmitting relatively large amounts of power from one point to another as compared with distribution circuits which convey small amounts of electricity to numerous points. Power is generally transmitted at high voltages to reduce its loss in the lines. At the generating end, the voltage is stepped up by suitable transformers or converters to the line voltage. It is then transmitted. At the load end there are transformers and converters which reduce the voltage down to one suitable for distribution. Most of the E. P. T. lines of the world are used in connection with hydro-electric schemes, where the power generated at the river-falls is transmitted to the large towns ; the manufacturing area being surrounded by hydro-electric plants which supply the power. The converse of this system is where the large power station is situated in the manufacturing area where the costs of generation are least and lines radiate from it to supply the surrounding country. But little E. P. is transmitted by long underground cables because of the cost ; and, in the case of very high voltages, cables have yet to be made to overcome the insulation problem. Hence most transmission lines are overhead, and consist of two main kinds, steel-tower lines and wood-pole lines. The steel-tower lines are used where very high voltages are employed, and therefore are required to give greater ground clearance ; lattice steel towers are also used because of their great strength, and larger size conductors can be carried on them, and therefore heavier current can be transmitted. Wood-pole lines are used for short lines in which the voltage is not as great as in steel-tower work. They are not designed for carrying large currents and will not stand the strain of larger conductors. In steel-tower lines the towers can be much further apart than the poles in wood-pole lines. Thus it will be seen that the greater strength of the one with its heavier cost of erection counterbalances the inferior strength of the other with its relative cheapness of erection. Failure of supply on overhead lines can be brought about by many causes ; lightning striking the lines is very dangerous, but this has been eliminated by the use of choke coils at the line ends; birds settling on the lines and short-circuiting the conductors or earthing them is a common cause of failure; trees falling on the line; very high winds; and snow and ice in winter are all troubles which the overhead-line engineer has to consider when erecting such lines. Telegraph wires, roads, railways and canals all have to be guarded when they are crossed by lines, and the proper clearances must be given by the engineer.

**Electric Railways,** *see* RAILWAYS.

**Electric Supply.**—*Continuous current.* This embraces the methods for the transformation of energy from convenient sources into electrical energy, in which form it is conveyed to other localities for further transformations, light, traction, etc. The place in which the various instruments are placed is called the central station. The sources of energy are generally coal, water power, and wind power. In England the former is used most extensively. The machines for effecting the transformation of this energy into electrical energy are the various types of dynamos. In addition to the dynamo, we find also the *battery*, which consists of a large number of storage cells. This battery acts as a regulator. It is necessary to maintain a constant pressure in the main circuit, and this is not easily possible by the dynamos alone. In order to effect this the battery is connected in parallel with the dynamo, as in Fig. 1, the storage battery being charged by the dynamo itself. Their mutual interactions may be summarised by observing that if the E.M.F. of the battery is less than the potential difference of the terminals of the dynamo, the machine is supplying current to the external circuit and charging the battery, whereas if

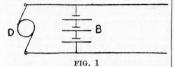

FIG. 1

the E.M.F. of the battery is equal to the potential difference of the terminals of the machine, they are equally active in feeding the external circuit. In actual practice the battery is charged by an auxiliary dynamo when the system consists of a large number of dynamos working together. The switchboard has attached to it all the switches, ammeters and voltmeters by which the whole supply is regulated and the current and pressure are measured. All the cables from the dynamos, accumulators, etc., are brought to the switchboard.

*Small stations for lighting and power.*—In small stations which supply an isolated house (say), a single dynamo is generally sufficient. This is driven by a gas engine as the motive power. The dynamo is employed to charge a storage battery during the day, the battery itself then being used for the various purposes required. It is, however, found to be more economical to use more than one

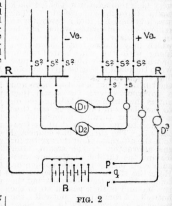

FIG. 2

dynamo, several small ones being less wasteful than one large one. One method, the one most generally used, will suffice to show the way in which they are connected up. The dynamos are connected together in parallel on to two bars called omnibus bars. Fig. 2 shows roughly this method. R represents the bars to which the two dynamos are connected in parallel. In the circuit are the switches S, by which any dynamo can be put into or taken out of the system. To these bars are also connected the outside cables, also containing the switches $S^2$. The regulating battery B is charged by the transformer $D^3$ by joining $qr$, and may be discharged by joining $pq$, its action being that of a regulator, as previously explained. As the cells composing the battery are slowly discharged, their E.M.F. gradually decreases, and it is necessary to correct this by placing more cells of the battery into action by means of switches. The above method is the one generally used in the larger power stations. The immense ad-

vantages which accrue from the use
of the three wire system (*see* ELECTRIC
DISTRIBUTION) has largely displaced
the system previously explained. The
dynamos are connected to omnibus
bars as in the previous case, as also is
the external circuit. The middle wire
is connected to the middle bar M, the
excess of current being supplied to it
by the two balancing dynamos $D^1$,
one placed on each side. As the prime
motive power, various new engines
have been utilised, of which the turbine promises to be most economical.
The previous discussion has mainly
dealt with the problem of lighting.
The principles underlying the supply
for traction purposes are very similar.
Here there is the advantage that the
time of running is known, and further
variations of pressure are not so important as with lighting. Compound
dynamos are used so as to give an increased pressure with an increased
load. This is an important factor,
since the variation occasionally is

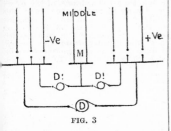

FIG. 3

very sudden. The use of the three
wire system is not so universal as in
the case of lighting. The supplies
for lighting and traction are always
separate, other than in small towns.
Even here the respective systems
are separate owing to the great
variations of the traction supply.
They are connected up to separate
switchboards which have no connection with each other.

*Alternating current.*—The prime
movers in these stations are similar
to those of the continuous current
stations. The alternators are generally connected up in parallel. These
are represented in Fig. 4 by A, connected to the omnibus bars B. The
current clearly depends upon the
number of alternators working, and
thus, owing to the varying demand on
the current, arrangements are made
whereby any number of alternators
may be put into or taken out of the
system. The difficulty arises when
an alternator is put into the circuit.
It is necessary to switch the machine
into the circuit at the exact moment

when it is in step with the other
machines in the circuit, so that the
machine will immediately take up
its share of the load without causing any variation of pressure in
the circuit. An instrument to indicate this is called a ' synchroniser.'

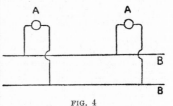

FIG. 4

A simple diagram illustrating the
principle of this instrument is shown
in Fig. 5. The alternators $A^1$ and $A^2$
can be connected to the omnibus
bars B by the switches $S^1$ and $S^2$
respectively. Further, each alternator is connected to the secondary
coils of the transformers $T^1$ and
$T^2$, the primary coils of the transformers being connected in series
with the lamp L; then the current induced in these primaries may travel
in the same direction, when the lamp
will glow brightly, or in the opposite
direction, when the light will be more
feeble. Assume the alternator $A^1$ to
be connected to the omnibus bars.
At the instant of the maximum
brightness the two alternators are
obviously in the same phase, and
thus at this instant the alternator
$A^2$ may be placed in the circuit. Even
if there is a slight difference of phase
the action of the current in the

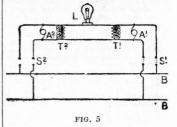

FIG. 5

circuit tends to eliminate this difference. All the alternators work at a
very high pressure, averaging about
70,000 volts; hence the necessity
for great care in manipulating the
current. The switches have long insulating handles, all metallic parts

being enclosed, so that contact with them may be eliminated, and are separated from one another by walls.

Economic considerations determine the site of the station. It is clear that there would be a great deal of energy wasted in conducting a continuous current over a number of miles. This necessitates a continuous current station being placed near the town; an alternating current, on the other hand, may be conducted from a great distance without any relative loss of energy. The objections to the use of alternating currents can easily be overcome by placing commutators in small stations in the town to effect a conversion of alternating current into a continuous current.

During recent years the question of E. S. has become a very important one, owing to the tremendous increase in the use of electricity. The use of alternating current has become almost universal, owing to the facility with which it can be distributed. Direct current needs more costly plant to generate and distribute it: d.c. sub-stations consist of a rotary converter which either converts a.c. to d.c. or high-voltage d.c. to low-voltage d.c., and this converter, being a moving machine, needs careful attention, whereas an a.c. sub-station contains a transformer, which, being static, is less likely to be a cause of trouble, and is cheaper to maintain. In most large towns the system of distribution is as follows: The mains from the generating station are high-voltage a.c., three phase; these mains are run to sub-stations situated at the best distributing points in the town. In the sub-station is a transformer or transformers with their high-tension switchgear, and on the low-tension side there are other fuses and switchgear. The supply to houses is single-phase a.c. with one side earthed to neutral point on the transformer. This system is taken into the houses, and is then split up into two circuits, one for cooking and heating, and the other for lighting. In country districts, where the amount of electricity used is small and the houses are relatively far apart, the laying of underground mains is too dear to be practicable; thus the villages are supplied by overhead transmission, and the distribution is carried in the same way as in towns, except that the houses are served from transmission lines carried on wood poles running down the roads from which each house taps its own power. This method is also used in rapidly growing towns, since the amount of electricity increases so rapidly that the continual replacing of underground cables is too costly. In U.S.A. and Europe the system of supply by overhead lines is fast becoming universal, since by this method electricity can be transmitted from hydro-electric power stations situated in mountains to cities and towns at a minimum of cost.

**Electric Testing,** see ELECTRICITY.

**Electric Traction.** There are three different systems of electric traction in use. They are: (i.) Direct-current systems; (ii.) single-phase systems; (iii.) three-phase systems. In the direct-current systems the voltages used vary from 600 to as much as 3000 volts. In the low-voltage system each motor is designed to take the full voltage of the trolley rail to earth. In most other systems the motors are designed to take half the voltage, motors being arranged in series of pairs. In the single-phase systems the third rail is not used, owing to the high voltages employed; the voltages of the overhead wires range from 3000 to 10,000 volts and over, and low frequencies of the order of 15 to 33¼ cycles per second are used. The motors are not run directly from the supply voltage, and it has therefore to be stepped down to 200 to 600 volts, which is the terminal voltage of the motors. The three-phase traction system requires the use of two overhead wires for each track, the track itself forming the necessary third conductor for the distribution, and the frequency varies from 16⅔ to 45 cycles per second. The voltage ranges from 750 to 15,000 volts; transformers are carried on the trains to step down the voltage to 400 to 600 volts at the motor terminals. There are both advantages and disadvantages in each system, each of which must be considered. The cost of maintenance of a 600 volt d.c. system is low, and the motors used cost less, weigh less, and occupy less space than those of a high voltage d.c. system; on the other hand, a low voltage d.c. system requires the use of frequent sub-stations to convert the power available to the line voltage; also these converters are rotary, while in the case of a.c. systems the sub-stations are static in that they contain only transformers and the necessary switchgear. Rotary converter sub-stations also cost more to instal and maintain than transformer sub-stations. With a.c. systems transformers are required on the locomotives, thereby adding greatly to the cost and weight of the train equipment. Low voltage d.c. systems are used chiefly on inter-urban traffic, whilst the high voltage d.c. and ᴬ.c. systems are used on long distance trains. In Italy and Switzerland, owing to the lack of coal and the abundance of water power, the electric locomotive is all-powerful. In Northern Italy there are several three-phase systems of which the most notable is the Genoa–Milan railway, which employs 3000 volt three-phase current, all of which is obtained from hydro-electric power stations. *See also* TRAMWAYS.

**Electric Units**, *see* AMPERE, BOARD OF TRADE UNIT, COULOMB, DYNE, ERG, FARAD, JOULE, MHO, VOLT, WATT.

**Electric Waves.** When a current in a circuit is a low-frequency alternating current, it radiates waves of energy from it when the current is at a maximum; and these waves return when the current is zero. But when the frequency is high, part of the energy is sent out into space, and never returns. This energy is said to be radiated; and in radio circuits, where the frequency ranges from 10,000 to 20,000,000, this loss forms the main loss of the circuit. The radiated wave is an electro-magnetic wave, and travels with the velocity of light (186,000 m. per second). These waves are propagated in all directions over the earth's surface, and the length of the wave is found by dividing the speed of the wave in metres per second (300,000,000 m.-sec.) by the frequency in cycles per second, the result being the wave-length in metres. As the wave travels outwards from the transmitter the wave tends to increase its height. If the earth is a good conductor, the wave remains upright; if, however, it is a bad conductor, the wave tilts forward in the direction of motion, and the crest of the wave overhangs the base, and if the air is ionised and thus acts as a brake on the wave, the wave tips backwards. Radio waves can be reflected and refracted in the same way as light. A mass of metal will deflect a wave out of its path; a mountain which is highly metalliferous will absorb the wave, and a receiving station in the lee of it will receive no signals. Waves, however, will pass through water, and submarines at the bottom of the ocean can receive messages; also they will pass through land, and receiving sets taken down deep mines have been worked efficiently.

**Electric Welding**, *see* METALLURGY.

**Electric Wiring**, *see* ELECTRIC LIGHTING.

**Electricity, Atmospheric**, the occurrence of thunderstorms shows that the atmosphere is in a state of electrification, similar to that obtained in any laboratory experiment. This was shown by Franklin by the use of an ordinary kite. Later investigation has shown that the state is variable, it being positively electrified during fine weather and generally negatively electrified during wet weather. The most convenient electrical unit to employ in these investigations is that of potential (*see* ELECTRICITY). The principal methods that have been employed are the determination of the potential of the earth's surface at a specified place and time, or to measure the difference of potential between a point in the air and the nearest point on the earth's surface. This is measured by placing a burning match at the end of a long insulated conducting rod placed vertically. While there is a difference of potential between the air and the rod, the products of combustion carry off the induced electricity until this difference of potential is destroyed. A quadrant electrometer is attached to the bottom of the conductor, the readings on which will give the difference of potential between the air near the flame and the earth. Another instrument, the principles underlying which are similar to the above, which can also be used for the above determination, is the Kelvin water dropper. The result of these experiments shows that the difference of potential increases with the height. As a result of these experiments, Sir William Thomson found that the difference of potential for a point 9 ft. from the ground varies between 200 and 400 volts. Various theories have been advanced in explanation of this phenomenon, all of which are very unsatisfactory. Explanation has been sought in assuming that particles of water when leaving the surface of water in lakes, etc., due to evaporation, assume a charge opposite to that of the water which they leave. Condensation of vapour has also been held responsible. Further theory has explained the phenomenon as a result of friction between dry air and moist air, or air passing over the earth's surface. The more frequent occurrence of thunder storms in calm than in windy weather is sufficient refutation of this theory. Thus we see that no adequate explanation of the phenomenon has yet been obtained.

The most usual form of lightning is a discharge from a cloud. This occurs when the cloud is at positive potential, and the lightning consists of clearly defined branches directed away from the cloud towards the earth. Sometimes the positive charge is on the ground, and the lightning flashes from the ground to the cloud. There are also cases when the lightning discharge is from one cloud to another. In these cases the charge eventually is discharged to earth from the cloud which received it. One of the phenomena connected with storms is that of balls of fire which apparently accompany very brilliant flashes of lightning. These take up many varied shapes and sizes, varying from the size of a pea to a foot in diameter; they usually glow, and sometimes disappear quietly, and sometimes they explode with great force. These balls are always connected with lightning, and no satisfactory explanation of their substance and formation has yet been stated.

Owing to the very rapid growth of radio communication, the question of atmospheric electrical disturbances and their elimination has become very important. Space is always agitated by electric disturbances, due to ionisation by the wind or the sun's rays, or by thunder storms, with their electric discharges. In tropical regions these ' atmospherics ' or ' statics,' as they are called, become very prevalent, owing, no doubt, to the great heat of the sun. The disturbance itself is an impulse of electricity of exceedingly short duration, and in a radio receiving set gives rise to an unpleasant crackling and hissing sound. In the case of receiving signals such as trans-Atlantic signals, which have to pass over large expanses of ocean, these static disturbances are very prevalent, sometimes making reception impossible; were it not for these statics, trans-oceanic communication could be carried out on ordinary wave-lengths and on a power of one kilowatt; in actual practice, however, the wave-length is of the order of 8000 metres, and the power required is several hundred kilowatts. Many solutions of the static problem have been proffered, but it has yet to be solved; even very high power stations have to transmit very slowly and repeat. The interference can be eliminated to a certain extent by the proper use of coil antennæ and balanced earth antennæ systems. Lightning used to be a very serious problem to the overhead transmission engineer, but this interference has been overcome by the use of choke coils in series with the line, and also by surge absorbers which are large condensers and, as their name implies, absorb the resultant surge in a line when it is struck by lightning.

**Electricity and Magnetism.** In the following article the science has been subdivided into its usual branches, and dealt with in the following order : (1) Electrostatics ; (2) Magnetism ; (3) Current electricity ; (4) Electromagnetic induction ; (5) Electromagnetic waves and Maxwell's theory of light ; (6) Electrolysis. A short account of its historical development is given at the commencement of each branch. This seems the most consistent and convenient method, since the development of any one branch has proceeded independently of that of the others.

(1) ELECTROSTATICS.—This part of the science deals with electricity in equilibrium. A Greek philosopher, Thales, who lived about 600 B.C., discovered that amber, when rubbed, acquired the property of attracting light substances, such as pieces of pith or cork. Towards the end of the sixteenth century, Gilbert found that this property was also possessed by many other substances, such as sulphur and glass. All such phenomena are studied under the science of electricity, the name being derived from the Greek word for amber. Gilbert's work was followed up by Boyle, who added to the list of electrics. In 1729 Gray discovered the properties of insulators and conductors. If an electrified piece of sulphur is laid on another piece of sulphur it retains its electricity for some time. The same thing occurs if it is suspended by a piece of dry silk thread. If, however, it is rubbed gently with a damp cloth, or with the hand, or touched all over with a piece of metal foil, it loses its charge. The sulphur and dry silk thread are called insulators, whilst the hand, the damp cloth, and the metal foil are conductors. If a metal rod is held in the hand and rubbed with a dry cloth, no electrification apparently takes place, but if the metal rod has an ebonite handle by which it is held, the rod becomes electrified on rubbing. In the first case electricity is produced on the metal, but it is immediately conducted away by the hand. In the second case the ebonite handle, which is an insulator, prevents the electricity escaping. Whilst Gray was pursuing his researches in England, scientists on the continent were busy making and perfecting electrical friction machines and condensers, and about this time the Leyden jar made its appearance. It was during this period also that Dufay discovered that there were two kinds of electrification. This can be established as follows : A wire stirrup is suspended by means of a dry silk thread. In the stirrup a rod of glass or ebonite can be suspended after it has been electrified. Electrify

one end of an ebonite rod by rubbing it with a piece of dry flannel, and suspend it in the stirrup so that it hangs in a horizontal position. Now electrify another rod of ebonite by rubbing it with flannel and bring it near the electrified end of the suspended rod. The latter is repelled. Now electrify a piece of glass by rubbing it with dry silk, and bring it near the suspended ebonite. The latter is attracted. This shows that there are two different kinds of electrification produced on the ebonite and glass. Dufay called the electricity produced on the ebonite ' resinous ' or negative (−), and that produced on the glass ' vitreous ' or positive (+). If the flannel and silk are very dry, it is found that, after rubbing, the former attracts the suspended ebonite rod whilst the latter repels it. This shows that when a piece of ebonite is rubbed with flannel the ebonite becomes negatively electrified whilst the flannel becomes positively electrified. In the case of glass and silk, the glass becomes positively electrified and the silk negatively electrified. These experiments led to the proposition of the two-fluid theory. All unelectrified bodies were supposed to contain vast equal quantities of vitreous and resinous fluids. When a body was electrified, it was supposed to gain an additional quantity of one fluid, and lose an equal quantity of the other, so that the total amount of fluid does not alter. In later years Franklin (1706–90) maintained the existence of one fluid only, which unelectrified bodies possess in a certain normal amount. A positively charged body has more, a negatively charged body less, than this normal amount. Franklin also did much work with the Leyden jar, and succeeded in showing that the seat of the charge is the dielectric (*see* CONDENSERS). On this foundation Faraday and Maxwell have built up the whole theory of electrical science. Canton (1718–72) was the first to discover the phenomenon of electric induction. Coulomb and Cavendish investigated independently the law of electric attraction and repulsion, and Faraday, at the beginning of the nineteenth century, showed that electricity was a measurable quantity.

*Electric induction.*—Suppose C is an insulated conductor and is positively charged (Fig. 1). Suppose AB is an insulated, unelectrified conducting cylinder on which three pith balls are suspended, as shown in the diagram. When C is far from AB the pith balls all hang vertically. When C is brought near to one end of AB (say the end B), the end B becomes charged with electricity of the opposite sign to that of C, whilst the end A is charged with electricity of the same sign as C. There is no charge on the middle parts of AB. This is shown by the fact that whilst the pith balls on the ends are deflected from their stands and away from AB, the middle ball is undeflected. If AB is touched with the finger or otherwise connected to earth, whilst still under C's influence,

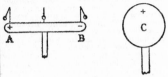

FIG. 1

it loses its charge at the end A. If C is now removed, the body AB becomes uniformly charged with electricity of the opposite kind to that of C. AB is then said to be electrified by induction or influence. It is obvious that these phenomena can be explained from the fact that like charges repel, and unlike charges attract each other. The unelectrified cylinder is considered to have an equal quantity of positive and negative electricity. It will be seen that a more vigorous explanation is possible from considerations of electric potential. Electric induction gives us the best means of obtaining a continuous series of charges and all friction machines are based on this principle.

*The electrophorus* is the simplest of influence machines. This consists of a disc of resin, or some other material easily excited, A (Fig. 2), and a polished metal plate, B, with an insulating handle, CD. The metal plate

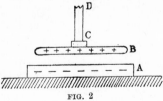

FIG. 2

should be a little less in size than the resin disc. The latter is electrified by striking it with dry flannel or fur. The metal plate is then placed upon it. The plate will not touch the disc except at a few points. Thus between most of the surface of the plate and that of the disc there will be a thin film of air. Thus B will be electrified by induction, that is, positive electricity will appear on the face of B near to A, and negative electricity on the face farther away. If the metal plate is now touched with the finger, the negative charge will be conducted away. Thus on removing the plate it will be found to have a positive charge. B can be charged by this method many times without appreciably altering the charge on A. A is often fitted into a shallow metal vessel, called the sole, which prevents leakage from A, and this increases the utility of the arrangement.

*Variation of electric force with distance.*—It was shown by Æpinus that the electric force between two charged bodies diminishes as the distance increases. Coulomb, who made experiments with a torsion balance of his own invention, was the first to publish proof that the force varied inversely as the square of the distance between the electrified bodies. Coulomb experimented first on the couple required to produce a twist in a wire, and found that for a given twist the couple varied as the fourth power of the diameter of the wire. Coulomb's balance consists of a small gilded pith ball, A (Fig. 3), placed at one extremity of an arm, ABC, of shellac. This arm is sus-

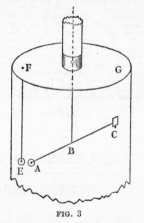

FIG. 3

pended by a very fine silver wire, so that it hangs in a horizontal position. At the top of the silver wire is a graduated screw, so that the wire can be subjected to a known twist. A second ball, E, is suspended by an insulating rod, so that it just touches

A. The whole apparatus is placed within a cylindrical glass case. The ball A is then charged, and E brought up to it. When they touch, the charge is shared between them and they repel each other. E is fixed, so the rod ABC is twisted through an angle. The wire is now given a known twist. The rod ABC takes up another position, making a different angle with its original

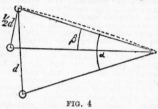

FIG. 4

position. Knowing these two angles, the distance between the balls can be ascertained and the force between them is known from the twist given to the wire thus: Suppose that $\alpha$ is the angle ABC (Fig. 4) first turns through. Then suppose a twist, $\gamma$, is given to the wire, and let the angle of ABC with its original position be now $\beta$. The total twist in the wire is now $(\beta + \gamma)$. The original twist was $\alpha$. Suppose now $\gamma$ be made such that the distance, $d$, between the balls is halved, it will be found that $(\beta + \gamma)$ is four times $\alpha$; if the distance $d$ is reduced to $\frac{1}{3}d$, $(\beta + \gamma)$ will be nine times $\alpha$, and so on. Since the force between the balls varies as the twist in the wire, it must vary inversely as the square of the distance between them. Coulomb was thus able to prove that this law was approximately if not absolutely true. Cavendish employed another method of proving the law of inverse square. It can be shown mathematically that if the law of inverse squares does hold, then there is no force inside a uniformly charged sphere. If the power is anything except the inverse square then there is force within the sphere. Now, whenever an electric force acts on a conductor, we have electric separation of induction, and parts of the conductor become electrified differently from other parts. If then we find that within a charged conductor no separation of electricity occurs, it shows that no electric force exists. Cavendish took a conducting globe and supported it on an insulating stand. He then enclosed the globe in two hemispherical conducting shells, which fitted exactly together to form a spherical shell without anywhere touching the globe. He then made connection between the globe and the shell by means of a wire pushed through a hole in the shell, and charged the shell, afterwards removing the wire by means of a silk thread in such a way that the shell was not discharged. He then removed the hemispherical shells and tested the

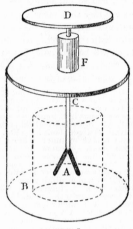

FIG. 5

inner globe for a charge. For this test, he used two pith balls which were suspended side by side. He found that the globe was uncharged, and so proved that there was no force inside a charged sphere, and also that the charge of a conductor resides on the surface. Thus he deduced that the law of inverse squares held.

*Gold leaf electroscope.*—Cavendish, in his experiment, used a pair of pith balls as his electroscope. This is not very sensitive. A very sensitive instrument has been devised by Bennet. It consists of two gold or aluminium leaves, A (Fig. 5), suspended from a brass rod, C. This rod terminates in a disc, D, after having passed through an insulating cork, F. Thus A, C, and D form one conductor, which is well insulated. The leaves, A, are surrounded by a cylinder of wire gauze, B. In some instruments this is replaced by strips of foil placed on the glass vessel surrounding the leaves. When the leaves are electrified, they repel each other to an angle which roughly indicates the intensity of their electrification.

*Electricity as a measurable quantity.*

—The preceding experiments have all been qualitative. But we can speak of giving a conductor a definite amount of electricity just as we can speak of pouring a definite amount or water into a vessel. The following ice-pail experiments, due to Faraday, justify the use of the term ' quantity of electricity.' Faraday placed a pewter ice-pail, A (Fig. 6), on an insulating stand, C, and connected the outside to a gold-leaf electroscope, D. A charged metal ball, B, was then lowered into the pail by means of a silk thread. As it approached, the leaves of the electroscope gradually diverged. The divergence attained a maximum when B was well inside the pail. On moving B about inside the pail, it was found that the divergence of the leaves did not alter. Another uncharged ball was lowered into the pail and allowed to share the charge on B. Still the deflection was unaltered. Finally, the balls were allowed to touch the inside of the pail. The deflection of the leaves did not change. On drawing the balls out again they were found to be uncharged. It is thus concluded that the divergence of the leaves depends on something which remains constant however the ball is moved about inside A. This something we shall call a quantity of electricity, and this quantity remains constant, not depending on the position, nature, or size of the charged body. Having accepted the idea of quantity of electricity we can show that the induced

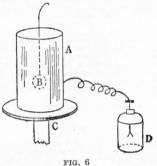

FIG. 6

charge in the inside of the vessel is equal and opposite to the inducing charge, because when the ball touched the inside of the vessel the quantity on the outside did not change. Again, the charge on the inside of the vessel must be equal and opposite to that on the outside, since, if the ball were taken out before touching the inside, the pail would be uncharged.

*Unit of quantity.*—The electrostatic unit of quantity of electricity is defined as that quantity which, when placed on a small particle at unit distance from a similarly charged particle, repels it with unit force, the particles supposed to be separated by air. It can be proved by means of the torsion balance that the force between two charges, $e_1$, $e_2$, is proportional to their product. Thus if $f$ be the force and $r$ the distance between the charges $e_1 e_2$, $f = \dfrac{e_1 e_2}{Kr^2}$ (where K is the specific inductive capacity which has unit value for air). See CONDENSERS.

*Electric intensity.*—The electric intensity at a point in an electric field is the mechanical force which would be exerted on a small particle charged with unit positive quantity of electricity and placed at the point. The electric intensity must not be confused with the mechanical force between two charged bodies.

*Electric potential.*—This can be defined as that which measures the condition of the body on which its power of communicating electricity to, or receiving electricity from, other bodies depends. From this definition it is at once seen that electric potential is analogous to temperature, and to pressure in hydrodynamics. The difference of potential between two points can be defined as the work done against the electric forces in bringing one positive unit of electricity from one point to another, the state of the field supposed to be unaltered by the transference. The potential of any point in space can be defined as the work which must be done in bringing up to the point from an infinite distance a particle charged with unit positive quantity of electricity. Consider the potential at a point P, at a distance $r$ from a charge $e$ at O (Fig. 7). Suppose the

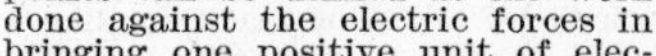

FIG. 7

charge is positive, and concentrated at a point—O. Join OP and produce to a great distance. Let Q, R, S be points on OP, distant $r_1 r_2$, etc., from O. The force at P is $\dfrac{e}{r^2}$, at Q it is $\dfrac{e}{r_1^2}$, at R it is $\dfrac{e}{r_2^2}$, and so on. Suppose Q, R, S are close together, so that $r_1^2$ is almost the same as $r_2^2$ and both can be put as equal to $r_1 r_2$, and so on. Let $v_1$, $v_2$, etc., be potentials at Q, R, S, etc.

Then $v_1 - v_2 = \dfrac{e(r_2 - r_1)}{r_1 r_2}$, because the work done from R to Q on unit positive charge is equal to the difference of potential and also to the product of the force and distance. Also $v_2 - v_3 = \dfrac{e(r_3 - r_2)}{r_2 r_3}$ ∴ $v_1 - v_2 = \dfrac{e}{r_1} - \dfrac{e}{r_2}$, $v_2 - v_3 = \dfrac{e}{r_2} - \dfrac{e}{r_3}$, and so on, adding all such terms together to a point distant $r_n$ from O, we get $v_1 - v_n = \dfrac{e}{r_1} - \dfrac{e}{r_n}$. Let Q coincide with P, and let $r_n$ be infinite. Then $v_n$ will be zero and $\dfrac{e}{r_n}$ will be zero. Therefore the potential at P is $V = \dfrac{e}{r}$. Application of the principle of potential gives a concise explanation of many electrostatic phenomena. Take for example electric induction. It was seen that in bringing up a conductor, AB, of cylindrical shape to a positively charged body, C (Fig. 1), the end of the cylinder nearest the charged body became negatively electrified and the other end positively electrified. Now the charged body, C, sets up an electric field, the potential in which diminishes as the distance from A increases. When AB is brought into this field, the end B near C is at a higher potential than A. Thus since AB is a conductor, electricity will flow from the end B to A until the potential is uniform. Thus B becomes negatively electrified and A positively electrified. It has been shown that the charge resides on the surface of a conductor. The surface density of the charge at any point is that amount of electricity which would cover unit area surrounding that point if the electrification over this area were uniform, and equal to that at the point.

*Capacity of a conductor.*—It is found that the charge of an isolated conductor is proportional to the potential, *i.e.* that there is a constant ratio between them. This ratio is termed the electric capacity of the conductor, or it is the quantity of electricity required to raise the potential of the conductor by unity.

*Gauss' theorem.*—Suppose we have an imaginary surface, S, surrounding a charge, $e$, at O (Fig. 8). Consider a small element of area, $\propto$, at AB (say). Let N be the electric intensity normal to AB. Then the sum of all the products N $\propto$ (or $\Sigma \propto$ N, as it is written) is equal to $4\pi e$. If AB is small, the intensity O over it can be taken as uniform and acts along BO, and is equal to $\dfrac{e}{OB^2}$. With centre O and radius OB draw a sphere cutting OA in R.

The force normal to AB is then $\dfrac{e}{\mathrm{OB}^2}$ $\times \cos \widehat{\mathrm{RBA}}$. The product of the area and this force is (area AB $\times \dfrac{e}{\mathrm{OB}^2} \times \cos$ $\widehat{\mathrm{RBA}}$). This is equal to (area BR $\times$ $\dfrac{e}{\mathrm{OB}^2}$), since area BR is equal to (area AB $\times \cos \widehat{\mathrm{RBA}}$). With centre O describe any sphere cutting OA in P and OB in Q. Then area PQ : area RB = $\mathrm{OQ}^2 : \mathrm{OB}^2$. Therefore area BR $\times \dfrac{e}{\mathrm{OB}^2}$

$= \text{area PQ} \times \dfrac{e}{\mathrm{OP}^2}$. This holds for all such elements, AB. Thus $\Sigma \propto \mathrm{N}$ is the

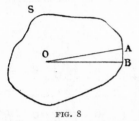

FIG. 8

same for the sphere as for the imaginary area S. But for the sphere N is constant and equal to $\dfrac{e}{\mathrm{OA}^2}$ and $\Sigma \propto$ is equal to $4\pi \mathrm{OA}^2$. Therefore for any surface S surrounding O the product $\Sigma \propto \mathrm{N}$ is equal to $4\pi e$. The proof can be extended to any number of charges. It can similarly be proved that $\Sigma \propto \mathrm{N}$ for surfaces not surrounding the charge is zero.

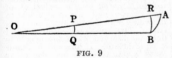

FIG. 9

*Force at a point, P, outside a charged sphere.*—Through P draw a sphere radius OP (Fig. 10). The force normal to this sphere is everywhere the same and equal to that at P ($f$ say). Thus $\Sigma \propto \mathrm{N}$ is equal to $f \times 4\pi \mathrm{OP}^2$, and this is equal to $4\pi e$ $\therefore f = \dfrac{e}{\mathrm{OP}^2}$. If $\sigma$ is the surface density on the sphere, the charge $e$ is $4\pi (\mathrm{OP})^2 \times \sigma$. The force at a point very near the sphere is then $\dfrac{e}{\mathrm{OP}^2} = 4\pi\sigma$. This is Coulomb's law. Thus the sphere acts at external points as if its charge were concentrated at the centre. Therefore the potential,

at a point indefinitely near the sphere, and therefore that of the sphere itself, is $\dfrac{e}{r}$ ($r$ is the radius).

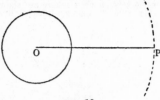

FIG. 10

*Capacity of a sphere.*—The capacity is the ratio $\dfrac{e}{\mathrm{V}}$. Now $\mathrm{V} = \dfrac{e}{r}$. Thus the capacity is $r$.

*Energy of a system.*—Suppose a sphere is initially uncharged and a charge, E, is brought up to it in very small amounts, $e$. Suppose at any time the potential of the sphere were V. The work done in bringing up a charge $e$ would be $e\mathrm{V}$. The potential would be raised to $\mathrm{V}_1$ (say). The work in the next instalment would be $e\mathrm{V}_1$. Represented graphically we get a diagram as shown (Fig. 11). The total

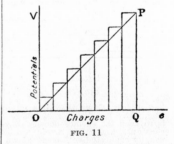

FIG. 11

work done is the sum of all the vertical strips. If $e$ is made very small, the sum of these strips approximates to the area OPQ, *i.e.* it is $\frac{1}{2}\mathrm{EV}$ (where E is the total charge and V the final potential). The energy of a sphere is therefore $\frac{1}{2}\dfrac{\mathrm{E}^2}{r}$.

*Lines and tubes of force.*—A line drawn such that its direction at any point is in the direction of the intensity at that point is called a line of force. If a tubular region of space be imagined as bounded by lines of force it may be called a tube of force or a Faraday tube. The importance of these tubes of force and the dielectric through which they pass will be considered under electromagnetic waves and Maxwell's theory. The lines of force from a positively charged sphere are shown (Fig. 12). The dotted lines are lines

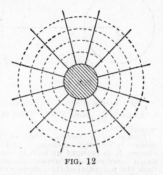

FIG. 12

of equipotential. An equipotential line is one which passes through all points of the same potential.

*Electrometers.*—The attracted disc electrometer (Fig. 13) consists of a metal disc, S, which is supported by three fine springs, so that its surface

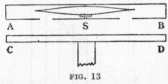

FIG. 13

lies slightly about that of a guard ring, AB. The function of this ring is to keep the surface density on S constant, and thus avoid errors usually connected with edges of conductors. Another metal disc, CD, is placed on an insulating stand and parallel to S. It can be moved nearer to S by means of a micrometer screw. In using the instrument the guard ring and disc are connected to earth, and are thus at zero potential. The disc CD is connected to the conductor whose potential is required. The disc CD is moved until the disc S is in the place of AB. The distance, $d$, between S and CD can be read off on the micrometer screw. The force, $f$, required to bring S into the place of AB is determined, when CD is absent, by placing known weights on S. It can be proved that if V is the potential

of CD, $V = \sqrt{\dfrac{8\pi d^2 f}{S}}$. Thus V can be determined.

*Quadrant electrometer.*—This electrometer was devised by Lord Kelvin and is extremely sensitive. In the simple form a light aluminium disc (called the needle) is supported in a horizontal position by a wire (Fig. 14). Any force tending to displace the needle is opposed by the torsion in this wire. A shallow metal box divided into four quadrants, A, B, C, D, surrounds the needle. Each of the quadrants is supported on an insulating pillar. Opposite quadrants are connected together. When the needle is in equilibrium and the

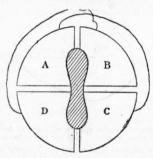

FIG. 14

quadrants uncharged, it lies over the junction line between two quadrants. The needle is charged to a high potential. It still lies over the junction line as before. Any deflection of the needle is noted by the reflection of light from a small mirror attached to it, which reflects the light on to a scale. The position of the spot of light is observed when the needle is in equilibrium. If one pair of quadrants is put to earth and the other connected to the body whose potential is required, the deflection of the spot of light is proportional to the potential. If the opposite pairs of quadrants are connected to two sources of potential, $V_1$ and $V_2$, and if $V_0$ is that of the needle, which must be great compared to $V_1$ and $V_2$, the deflection of the needle is approximately proportional to $V_0(V_1 - V_2)$. Thus if the deflection is noted for a known difference of potential, a difference of potential producing any other deflection can be ascertained.

(2) MAGNETISM.—It was known to the ancients that certain black stones, iron ores, which were found at Magnesia in Asia Minor, possessed

the power of attracting to themselves small pieces of iron. Such stones were called magnets. Several centuries later it was found that if a magnet were suspended freely by a thread, it always tended to set in one definite position. One end pointed N., the other S. Thus the magnet became known as the lodestone or 'leading-stone.' Practical use was made of this magnetic property in the formation of the compass needle. It was found that the needle does not point directly N. and S., but in a magnetic meridian, making an angle, called the declination (q.v.), with the geographical meridian. Burrows discovered that this angle changed during a voyage, and Halley in 1863 proved that the changes in declination at sea were not due to the effect of neighbouring land, but to the magnetic properties of the earth as a whole. In 1544 Hartmann discovered that a needle pivoted to move freely in a vertical plane dips down towards the N. when magnetised by a lode-stone. Gilbert (1540–1603) collected all magnetic phenomena then known into his book, *De Magnete*, and also brought forward the conception of the earth as a huge magnet. Coulomb, with a modified torsion balance, investigated the mutual action of magnets, but it was left to Gauss to prove definitely that the law of inverse squares held for magnetic forces.

*Magnetic phenomena.*—A small piece of watch-spring or steel can be magnetised in the laboratory in three ways : (1) Method of single touch; (2) method of double touch ; (3) electrical method. Fig. 15a illustrates the method (1). The watch-spring is laid

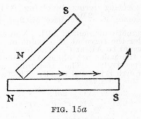

FIG. 15a

on the table, and one pole of a bar magnet drawn along the whole length of the spring. The process is repeated, always starting at the same end. The end at which the process starts has the same polarity as the pole used for magnetisation. Fig. 15b represents method (2). Opposite poles of two equally strong bar magnets are placed close together in contact with the

middle of the spring, and then drawn apart towards opposite ends of the spring. This is repeated several times. The electrical method is of great practical importance. If a wire is wound around a piece of soft iron and a current is passed through the wire, the soft iron becomes highly magnetised. In practice, the soft iron is in the shape of a large horse shoe.

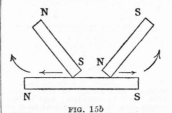

FIG. 15b

To produce a permanent bar magnet a piece of steel is placed across the ends of this large horse shoe and the current is passed through the wire for several short periods. The bar magnet is taken away at right angles to the surface where contact is made. A horse-shoe magnet is made in much the same way. The degree of magnetisation acquired by a piece of steel depends upon the strength of the magnet used in the process. But in every case there is a limit to the magnetisation produced. The steel is then said to be *saturated*. The magnetisation of a piece of steel may be destroyed by strongly heating, or by violent usage. A bar magnet when suspended tends to point N. and S. The end pointing N. is called the north seeking, or simply the north pole, and the other end is called the south seeking or south pole. The line joining the poles is called the *magnetic axis*. It can easily be shown by two suspended magnets that like poles repel and unlike poles attract each other. Thus we have an analogy to electrostatics. A unit pole is defined as that pole which, placed at unit distance in air from a similar pole, repels it with unit force. The pole is positive or negative according as to whether it is north or south seeking. Unlike electrostatic effects, magnetic effects are observed only with iron to any extent, and also the force between two poles is independent of the medium between them, unless it be iron. Just as electric charges produce electric charges on conductors in their neighbourhood, so a magnetic pole produces magnetic poles on pieces of iron in its neighbourhood. Thus iron filings cling to a pole of a magnet because poles are induced on each filing, and opposite poles of neighbouring filings cling together, often producing long chains. A magnetic pole, or a whole magnet, is the centre of a field of force, the intensity at any point of which is defined as the

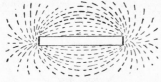

FIG. 16a

force that would be exerted on unit positive pole placed at that point. This force is directive, and a line drawn such that the tangent to it at any point is in the direction of the magnetic force is called a line of magnetic force. The form of these

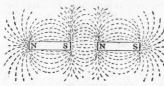

FIG. 16b

can easily be seen for a combination of magnets, by placing the combination under a sheet of glass and sprinkling filings on the glass. On tapping the glass the filings arrange themselves along the lines of force. Figs. 16a and 16b show the shape of these lines for a single bar magnet and two magnets respectively.

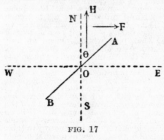

FIG. 17

*Variation of magnetic force with distance.*—Gauss showed that the force due to a magnetic pole varied

as the inverse square of the distance. Suppose a magnetic needle, AB, is placed at O, at which point there is a force, F (Fig. 17), in an east and west direction. Let NS be the magnetic meridian at O, and H the horizontal component of the earth's force at O. Let $\theta$ be the angle which AB makes with NS. If $m$ is the strength of each pole, the horizontal force on it due to the earth is H$m$, and if $2l$ be the distance between the poles, the couple due to the earth is $2ml$H $\sin \theta$. Similarly, the couple due to F is $2$F$ml \cos \theta$. Now $2ml$ is called the *moment*, M, *of the magnet*. Thus we get that H $\tan \theta =$ F. Assume, for the time being, the law of inverse square. Let AB (Fig. 18) be a small

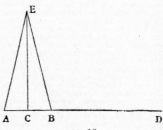

FIG. 18

magnet, of length $2l$ and pole strength $m$. Consider the force at a point D in AB produced at a distance $r$ from C, the centre of AB.

$$F_1 = \frac{m}{(r-l)^2} - \frac{m}{(r+l)^2} = \frac{m[(r+l)^2 - (r-l)^2]}{(r-l)^2(r+l)^2}.$$

Neglecting terms involving $l^2$ this becomes $F_1 = \dfrac{2M}{r^3}$ (where M$=2ml$, the magnetic moment of AB). Now consider the force at E a point on the normal to AB at C. The forces due to the poles act along AE and EB respectively. The resultant acts through E parallel to AB. The value of this force is

$$F_2 = \frac{2m}{(AE)^2} \cdot \frac{AC}{AE} = \frac{2m}{r^2+l^2} \cdot \frac{1}{(r^2+l^2)^{\frac{1}{2}}} = \frac{M}{r^3}$$

neglecting terms in $\dfrac{l^2}{r^2}$.

If we had assumed that the force varied inversely as the $n$th power of the distance, we should have had

$$F_1 = \frac{nM}{r^{(n+1)}} + F_2 = \frac{M}{r^{(n+1)}}, \quad i.e. \quad F_1 = nF_2.$$

On testing the forces at D and E with a magnetised needle, it is found that $F_1 = 2F_2$, and therefore the law of inverse squares holds. This proof is due to Gauss.

*Interaction of magnets.*—It has just been shown that the force at a point, F (Fig. 19), due to a small magnet, AD, is $\dfrac{2M}{r^3}$ where $r = GF$.

Suppose $M^1$ is the moment of a small magnet, CD, whose centre is at F. If

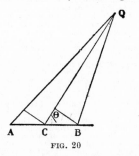

FIG. 19

CD is deflected through an angle $\theta$, the couple acting on it is obviously $C = \dfrac{2MM^1}{r^3}\sin\theta$ (from the above deflection of a needle in Fig. 17). The force which AB exerts on the pole $m^1$ at C is $\dfrac{2Mm^1}{(r-l^1)^3}$. The force on the pole $(-m^1)$ at D is $-\dfrac{2Mm^1}{(r+l^1)^3}$. Thus the total force of translation is

$$F = 2Mm^1\left(\frac{1}{(r-l^1)^3} - \frac{1}{(r+l^1)^3}\right).$$

Neglecting squares and higher powers of $l$, this reduces to $F = \dfrac{6MM^1}{r^4}$. Thus the couples vary inversely as the cube of $r$, whilst the forces of translation vary as the fourth power of $r$. By similar processes other positions of AB and CD may be investigated.

FIG. 20

*Magnetic potential.*—The difference in magnetic potential between two points is defined as the quantity of work required to carry unit positive pole from one point to the other. The potential at a point is the work required to bring a unit pole up from infinity to that point. It can be shown just as in the case of an electric charge that the potential due to a pole $m$ is $\dfrac{m}{r}$.

*Potential due to a magnet.*—Let AB be the magnet with centre C (Fig. 20); Q be the point and $Q\widehat{C}B = \theta$. Thus the potential at Q due to $m$ at A is $\dfrac{m}{AQ}$, that due to $-m$ at D is $-\dfrac{m}{BQ}$. Thus the potential, V, due to the whole magnet is

$$V = m\left(\frac{1}{AQ} - \frac{1}{BQ}\right) = m\left(\frac{1}{r+l\cos\theta}\right.$$
$$\left. - \frac{1}{r - l\cos\theta}\right) = \frac{2ml\cos\theta}{r^2} = \frac{M\cos\theta}{r^2}.$$

*Magnetic induction.*—Magnetic substances like iron become magnetised under the influence of magnetic force. If a north pole were placed near a bar of iron, a south pole would be induced on the end of the bar nearer the pole. Attraction would take place, and the bar of iron would move into a stronger part of the field. If the bar were of bismuth, a north pole would be induced on the end nearer the pole and the bar would tend to move into the weaker parts of the field. Iron is said to be a *paramagnetic* substance and bismuth a *diamagnetic*

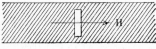

FIG. 21

substance. The magnetisation induced on the bar is measured by the resulting magnetic moment. The *intensity of magnetisation* is the magnetic moment per unit volume. Soft iron becomes more strongly magnetised than steel, *i.e.* it is more *susceptible* to magnetisation than steel. *Susceptibility* is measured by the ratio of the intensity of magnetisation to the magnetic force. This magnetic force is that force actually within the bar. If a narrow crevasse (Fig. 21) were cut in the iron perpendicularly to the magnetising force H, the force on a unit positive pole placed in this crevasse is defined as the magnetic induction, B. It can be proved that $B = H + 4\pi I$, where I is the intensity of magnetisation. Therefore $B = H(1 + 4\pi K)$ (where K is the susceptibility). The ratio of the magnetic induction in the iron to the magnetic force is called the *magnetic permeability*, $\mu$,

$$\therefore \ \mu = 1 + 4\pi K.$$

If a bar of iron is placed in a magnetic field, which is gradually increased in intensity from zero, it is found that the relation between B and H, when plotted, gives a curve such as OA

(Fig. 22). When the magnetic force is reduced, the relation between B and H does not give the curve AO, but another curve such as ADC. In fact, the iron may be taken through a cycle such as ADCEA. The name of hysteresis has been given to this phenomenon. The iron seems to retain its induction.

*Theories of magnetisation.*—Weber suggested that an iron bar consists of a vast number of magnetised molecules. When it is unmagnetised, these molecules have their axes in divers directions. When a magnetic

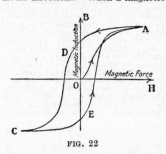

FIG. 22

force is applied, more and more of the molecules set so that their axes point in the same direction. Contiguous poles of the magnets neutralise each other except at the ends. Thus we have magnetic poles at the ends, and obviously the slight elongation which is observed when a bar is magnetised should be expected. Ewing has modified and improved Weber's theory to a large extent. Magnetic saturation is obtained when all the molecules point in the same direction.

*Terrestrial magnetism.*—The declination can be found by suspending a magnet and thus finding the direction of the magnetic meridian. If the direction of the geographical meridian is known at the place of experiment, the declination is easily determined. The dip is found by means of an instrument called the dip circle. This in essence is a magnetised needle suspended so as to revolve freely about a horizontal axis. The angle of dip, *i.e.* the angle the needle makes with the horizontal, is read off on a circular scale. For the corrections to be applied in the use of the dip circle and declinometer, the reader should refer to larger works.

*To find H.*—We known that a bar magnet produces a force $\frac{2M}{r^3}$ at a

point end on to it, and at a distance *r*. Thus a compass needle will be deflected through an angle, $\theta$, where $\frac{2M}{r^3} = H \tan \theta$, if placed at the point. Thus we have one relation between H and M. If now the bar magnet is suspended so as to be in a horizontal position and it is allowed to oscillate, its period can be proved to be $2\pi \sqrt{\dfrac{k}{MH}}$ (where *k* is the moment of inertia of the magnet). Thus we have a second relation between M and H, if the period is accurately determined. Thus we can find M and H. The dip and the declination and H are now known. It is then easy to determine the vertical component of the earth's force and the total force I (say). For $I = \dfrac{H}{\cos i}$ (where *i* is the dip) and $V = I \sin i = H \tan i$.

(3)    CURRENT    ELECTRICITY.— About 1786 Galvani noticed that the leg of a frog contracted under the influence of a discharge from an electrical machine. He thought that it was due to some property of the animal. In 1800 Volta showed that this was not so, and also invented a pile known by his name. It consists of a series of little discs of zinc, copper, and paper moistened with brine, placed one on top of the other, starting with zinc and finishing with copper. This is really a primitive primary battery. Faraday was the first to show that the current got from such a pile is the same as an electrostatic current, save that the former is a huge quantity of electricity driven under a small difference of potential, whilst the latter is generally a small quantity of electricity driven under a very large difference of potential.

*Electric cells.*—*See* CELL, VOLTAIC.

*Magnetic effects of a current.*—In 1820 Œrsted discovered that a compass needle was deflected when brought near to a wire through which a current is passing. This showed that the current gave rise to a magnetic field surrounding the wire. The following rule of Ampère gives the direction of deflection of the compass needle. Imagine yourself swimming in the wire in the direction of the current and with your face *towards* the compass needle. Then the north pole of the needle will be deflected towards your left hand. Ampère and Weber experimented on coils, and showed that they acted like magnets of the same shape and size as the coils, and of suitable strength. Thus, a long helical coil, called a solenoid, when suspended so as to swing freely, sets, when a current is passed through it, like a magnet of the same length and shape. As the length of the solenoid is shortened, the length of the equivalent bar magnet is shortened also Thus, when we have one single turn of wire, the equivalent magnet is a disc magnetised perpendicularly to its plane. Such a disc is called a *magnetic shell*. If this single coil is held so that its face is perpendicular to the line of sight, and if the current appears to pass round the coil in the clockwise direction, then that face will have south-seeking polarity (Fig. 23).

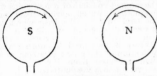

FIG. 23

The opposite face will have north-seeking polarity. This relation between a magnetic shell and a coil carrying a current holds for a coil of any shape and size, the equivalent shell being of the same size and form as the coil and having its edge coincident with the wire carrying the current. It has been seen that the effect of a bar magnet at external points depends on its moment. The strength of a shell is defined as the magnetic moment per unit area. The electro-magnetic unit of current can be defined as that current which is equivalent to a magnetic shell of unit strength. If two circular coils carrying currents are placed parallel to each other it is obvious that they will attract each other if the currents flow in the same direction and repel if they flow in opposite directions. It has been shown that the potential of a magnet of moment, M, is $\frac{M \cos \theta}{r^2}$

(where $\theta$ is the angle which the magnetic axis makes with the line joining the point and the centre of the magnet). Let S be the strength of a shell, *i.e.* magnetic moment, per unit area. Then V, the potential at a point, is equal to $\frac{S \propto \cos \theta}{r^2}$ (where $\propto$ is the area). But $\frac{\propto \cos \theta}{r^2}$ is the solid angle subtended at the point by the shell. Thus $V = S\Omega$ (where $\Omega$ is the solid angle). We defined the unit current as equivalent to a shell of unit strength. Thus the magnetic potential due to a coil carrying a current, $c$, at a point is $V = c\Omega$.

Consider a point, P, very near the plane of the coil on the side which has north-seeking polarity and, Q, a point on the opposite side of the plane. The solid angle subtended at P by the coil, or its equivalent shell, is $2\pi$, and that at Q is $-2\pi$. Therefore the difference of potential between P and Q is $4\pi c$. Thus the work done in taking a unit pole from P to Q by a path around the edge of the shell is $4\pi c$. If there were a shell actually in place of the coil, we should have to finish the circuit by passing from P to Q through a hole in the shell, and the work already done would be reversed, making the total work zero. In the actual case, there is air between P and Q, and thus there is no discontinuity of force. Therefore, since P and Q are very close together, the work from Q to P is negligible. Thus the work done in taking unit positive magnetic pole around a circuit one is $4\pi c$.

*Force inside a solenoid.*—Let a unit positive magnetic pole be taken along PQ parallel to and inside the solenoid. Then let it be brought out perpendicularly to PQ between the

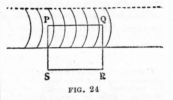

FIG. 24

coils along QR, then along RS parallel to QP, and finally along SP, through the coils, back to P. The work done for each turn of wire is $4\pi c$; thus, if there are $n$ turns in unit length, the work done is $4\pi nlc$ (where $l = $ PQ). The lines of force due to a solenoid are similar to those of a magnet, except that instead of ending at the poles they pass inside the coil. Thus the lines are crowded inside the coil, whereas if the coil is long, the number in the region of RS is small; thus the work done from R to S can be neglected. There is no work done along QR and SP because these lines are normal to the lines of force. Therefore, if H is the force inside the solenoid, H$l$ is the work done along PQ and is equal to $4\pi ncl$. Thus $H = 4\pi nc$.

*Force due to straight current.*—Suppose the current is flowing along an infinitely straight wire of which AB is a portion. Imagine a circle drawn around AB, and a unit positive pole taken around this circle. The lines of force surrounding AB are circles, since the magnetic force of the equivalent shell is perpendicular to the surface. The plane of these circles is perpendicular to AB. The work done in traversing the circle DEF with the unit pole is $4\pi c$. The force H is constant around the path since DEF is a line of force. Thus the work done is also $2\pi r$H. Therefore H = $\dfrac{2c}{r}$ (where $r$ is the radius of the circle). The electro-magnetic unit of current has been defined as that current flowing in a coil which has an equivalent magnetic shell of unit strength. It may also be defined, in a more practical form, as that current which, flowing in unit length of wire bent into an arc of unit radius, exerts unit mechanical force on a unit positive magnetic pole placed at the centre of the arc. Thus the force at the centre of a circular coil of radius, $r$, is $\dfrac{2\pi c}{r}$, and is perpendicular to the plane of the coil. It can be shown that the force at a point P on the normal to the coil, through the centre O, is $2\pi c\dfrac{r^2}{(r^2+x^2)^{\frac{3}{2}}}$ (where $x=$OP).

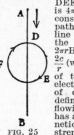

FIG. 25

*Galvanometers.*—The magnetic force produced by currents may be used to measure the intensity of the current. This is most frequently done by means of a tangent galvanometer, which consists of a circular coil of wire placed with its plane in the magnetic meridian. If the magnetic field is not wholly that due to the earth, the plane of the coil must contain the resultant magnetic force. At the centre of the coil there is a short magnet which can turn freely about a vertical axis. When no current is in the coil, the magnet will have its axis in the plane of the coil. A current in the coil produces a force at its centre at right angles to the plane of the coil. Let this force be G$c$ (where $c$ is the current). G is called the *galvanometer constant.* Thus, if H is the magnetic force at the centre of the field when no current is in the coil, the resultant magnetic force has components G$c$ perpendicular to the coil and H parallel to it. We have already proved that in such a case the magnet will be deflected through an angle $\theta$, where $\tan\theta = \dfrac{Gc}{H}$. Thus we see that the current is proportional to $\tan\theta$. Hence the name

tangent galvanometer. A common type of tangent galvanometer has a long thin pointer attached to the magnet and perpendicular to it. This pointer moves over a horizontal circular scale, and thus $\theta$ can be read off at once by reading off the deflection of the pointer. It is obvious that if H is decreased, the galvanometer is more sensitive. Thus a sensitive galvanometer (devised by Lord Kelvin) carries a control magnet above the coil which can be adjusted to make the field of force at the centre of the coil a minimum when no current is passing in the coil. Also the magnet consists of a few strips of magnetised watch spring fixed on the back of a small mirror which is suspended by a fibre of silk so as to hang with its plane vertical. The angle $\theta$ is measured by noting the deflection of the image of a spot of a light reflected from the mirror on to a graduated scale. The sensitiveness of a tangent galvanometer may also be increased by using it in an *astatic* manner. Two small magnets are hung, as shown in Fig. 26, from the same silk fibre so that their axes are in opposite directions. Each magnet is the centre of a coil. These coils are in the same plane, and arranged in series such that the currents in them are in opposite directions. It is obvious that the restoring couple on this system due to H is very small, because the effect on one magnet neutralises that on the other, whilst that due to the force arising from the current is very great.

FIG. 26

*Sine galvanometer.*—This is similar in arrangement to the common tangent galvanometer first described. The coil is first placed in the magnetic meridian. The magnet will also point in this direction. A current is now passed through the coil and the magnet deflected. The plane of the coil is now rotated until it contains the direction of the magnetic axis in its deflected position. If $\phi$ is the angle of deflection of the magnet, it is easy to show that the current $c = \dfrac{H}{G}\sin\phi$. Hence the name sine galvanometer.

*D'Arsonval galvanometer.*—In this galvanometer the coil carrying the current moves whilst the magnet is fixed. The coil consists of a number of turns of fine wire. It is suspended by very fine metal wires which also serve to convey the current to the coil. The coil moves between the poles of a horse-shoe magnet, and the field is intensified by a fixed cylinder of soft iron inside the coil. When a current passes through the coil it tends to place itself so as to include as many tubes of induction as possible, *i.e.* it tends to place itself at right angles to the lines of magnetic induction. The motion of the coil is resisted by the torsion of the wire. Equilibrium is attained when the couple due to torsion just balances that due to the coil's tendency to turn. It can be proved that in such a state the current C is equal to $\dfrac{k\theta}{BA n}$ (where $\theta$ is the deflection, $k$ is a constant, B is the magnetic induction, and A the area of the coil). A mirror is attached to the coil, so that $\theta$ can be determined with accuracy by the method already mentioned for the sensitive tangent galvanometer.

*Ballistic galvanometer.*—A tangent galvanometer may be used to measure the total quantity of electricity passing if the time taken for it to pass is very short. If $\theta$ is the throw of the magnet, *i.e.* the first deflection produced after the electricity has passed, it can be proved mathematically that Q, the quantity of electricity passed through the coil, is equal to $\sin \frac{1}{2}\theta \dfrac{TH}{\pi G}$ (where T is the period of swing of the magnet, H the force at the centre when no current is in the coil, and G the galvanometer constant). It should be noticed that for the simple tangent galvanometer it has been proved that the force at the centre of the coil when unit current passes in it is $\dfrac{2\pi n}{r}$. This is, therefore, equal to G.

*Soft iron instruments.*—Soft iron electro magnetic instruments may be used in cases where a high degree of accuracy is not needed. Many types are in general use, but the general principle on which they are all based is that a piece of soft iron when placed in a magnetic field which is not uniform tends to move from weak to strong portions of the field. In most instruments the piece of iron is flat and is egg-shaped, and is made so that it can be just inside a coil of wire; when a current is passed through the coil, the iron is sucked further into the coil, and when the current is less, the iron tends to fall to its normal state. The moving portion has the pointer of the instrument fixed to it, and it is controlled by small weights; the instrument has to be carefully fixed so that it is exactly upright, otherwise it will not register truly.

*Electromotive force and resistance.*— When an electric current flows along a wire we conceive that electricity is passing, and thus the ends of the wire must be maintained at a permanent difference of potential. This difference of potential is called electromotive force (E.M.F.). The electromotive force between two points is thus defined as the work which must be done in conveying unit quantity of electricity from one point to the other, against the electric force. We have already defined the electro-magnetic unit of current. The electro-magnet quantity is that quantity of electricity conveyed past a point by an electro-magnetic unit of current in unit time. The electro-magnetic unit of electromotive force is thus defined as the difference of potential which must exist between two points when unit work is done in conveying unit electro-magnetic quantity in unit time. The practical unit of E.M.F. is the volt, which is $10^8$ times the electro-magnetic unit. The practical unit of current is the ampere, which is one-tenth of the electro-magnetic unit. In 1827 Dr. Ohm found that the current strength in a wire is proportioned to the applied E.M.F. Ohm verified this by showing that along a homogeneous linear conductor the rate of fall of potential is constant. If C is the current and E the electromotive force, then by Ohm's law $e = kE$ (where $k$ is a constant, and known as the conductivity of the conductor). In other terms $c = \dfrac{E}{R}$ (where R is a constant, called the resistance of the conductor, which only depends on the nature, dimensions, and temperature of the conductor). It became possible at once to measure two resistances by applying the same electromotive force and comparing the currents produced. The unit of resistance must evidently be defined as the resistance in which unit E.M.F. produces unit current. If electromagnetic units of E.M.F. and current are employed, the electro-magnetic unit of resistance follows. If practical units are employed, viz. the volt and ampere, then the practical unit of resistance, called the ohm, follows. The ohm is $10^9$ times the electro-magnetic unit.

*Resistances in series.*—Suppose AB, CD (Fig. 27) are a number of

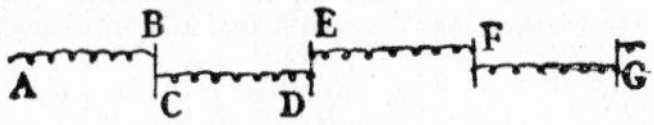

FIG. 27

conductors joined together in series, the potential of the end B will be the same as that of C, that of D the same as that of E, and so on. The conductors must be of the same material.

Let $E_1$, $E_2$, etc., be the potential differences between the ends of the different conductors, $r_1$, $r_2$ their resistances. The current, $c$, must be the same for all, since electricity does not accumulate. Therefore $c = \dfrac{E_1}{r_1} = \dfrac{E_2}{r_2} = \dots$

If R is the effective resistance of the combination, then $c = \dfrac{E}{R}$ where E = $E_1 + E_2 + \dots$ Thus $cR = (r_1 + r_2 + r_3 + \dots)c$, $\therefore R = r_1 + r_2 + r_3 + \dots$

*Resistances in parallel or multiple arc.*—Suppose the beginnings of all the conductors were joined together and all their ends (Fig. 28). They are

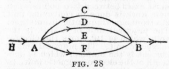

FIG. 28

then said to be in multiple arc. The current, $c$, flowing along HA and in at A, must equal $c_1 + c_2 + \dots$, the sum of the currents in the conductors ACB, ADB, etc. Now $c_1 = \dfrac{E}{r_1}$, $c_2 = \dfrac{E}{r_2}$, and so on, since the potential difference between the ends is the same for all the branches, $\therefore c = E\left(\dfrac{1}{r_1} + \dfrac{1}{r_2} + \dfrac{1}{r_3} \dots\right) = \dfrac{E}{R}$, if R is the effective resistance of the whole combination. Thus $\dfrac{1}{R} = \dfrac{1}{r_1} + \dfrac{1}{r_2} + \dfrac{1}{r_3} + \dots$

*Kirchoff's laws* enable us to apply our results to any complex network of conductors. They are: (1) *The algebraic sum of the currents which meet at any point is zero.* (2) *In any closed circuit the algebraic sum of the products of the current and resistance in each of the conductors in the circuit is equal to the E.M.F. in the circuit.*

*Wheatstone's bridge.*—Wheatstone made use of a combination, which goes by his name, to determine the ratio of resistances. Suppose the circuit of a voltaic cell branches off at A (Fig. 29) into two arms, ABC and ADC, as shown, which rejoin at C. Let the current flow from A to C. Consider a point, B, in the arm of C. Its potential, $V_B$, must be intermediate between the potential $V_A$ at A and $V_C$ at C. The potential in the arm ADC gradually falls from $V_A$ to $V_C$ as we pass from A to C. Thus there must be some point, D, where the potential is the same as that at B. If now B and D were joined to the terminals of a galvanometer, no current would flow in it. When this is the case, let $c_1$ be the current in ABC, and

$c_2$ that in ADC. Let $p$, $q$, $r$, $s$ be the resistances of the parts AB, BC, CD, DA respectively. By Ohm's law, $V_A - V_B = pc_1$, $V_B - V_C = qc_1$, $V_A - V_D = rc_2$, and $V_D - V_C = sc_2$.

$\therefore \dfrac{V_A - V_B}{V_B - V_C} = \dfrac{p}{q}$ and $\dfrac{V_A - V_D}{V_D - V_C} = \dfrac{r}{s}$ but $V_B = V_D$, since there is no current through the galvanometer. Thus $\dfrac{p}{q} = \dfrac{r}{s}$. Thus if the ratio $\dfrac{p}{q}$ and the resistance, $r$, is known, we can find $s$.

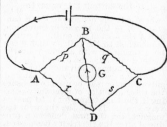

FIG. 29

There are two laboratory instruments based on these principles, the metre-bridge and the post-office box. In the metre-bridge a long, thin, uniform wire, AB, is stretched alongside a scale (Fig. 30). The ends are soldered to thick copper bars, AH and BD, of negligible resistance. GE is another thick copper bar. A known resistance, R, is placed in the gap HG, and the unknown resistance, S, in gap ED. A galvanometer is con-

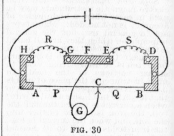

FIG. 30

nected to the copper bar, EG (at F), on the one hand, and to a movable jockey, C, on the other. The bars AH and BD are connected to the terminals of a battery. The movable jockey, C, is moved along the wire until no deflection of the galvanometer is noticed. We have then the relation that $\dfrac{R}{S} = \dfrac{\text{resistance of AC}}{\text{resistance of BC}}.$ If the wire is uniform the ratio of the resistances of AC and BC is equal to the ratio of their lengths, which can be read off. A modification of this bridge has been devised by Carey Foster for accurate work. In the post-office box the resistances $p$, $q$, and $r$ are all arranged in a box. The arrangement is shown in Fig. 31. A

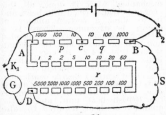

FIG. 31

number of brass blocks are connected together, inside the box, by carefully adjusted resistance coils of various values. By inverting a plug between adjacent brass blocks, the resistance that was connecting those blocks is thus cut out. In the actual arrangement the resistances of the arms AC and CB are such that $p$ may be made 10 or 100 times as great as $q$ and vice versa. The resistance in the arm AD may be made anything from 1 ohm to 10,000 ohms. The unknown resistance is inserted between B and D, the galvanometer between D and C, and the battery between A and B. Both the galvanometer connection and the battery connection can be made or broken by means of the keys $K_1$ and $K_2$ respectively. When no current flows in the galvanometer, when $K_2$ and $K_1$ are pressed down in the order named, the relation $\dfrac{p}{q} = \dfrac{r}{s}$ holds. Thus S can be found with considerable accuracy. The resistance of a galvanometer can be found by inserting it in the arm BD instead of S. When no current flows through this galvanometer (no galvanometer is then required in the arm DC), the usual relation holds, where the unknown resistance, S, is that of the galvanometer. The resistance of a cell also can be found by placing it instead of S in BD and removing the battery in the arm BA.

The *Potentiometer* is one of the best methods of comparing or measuring potential differences or electromotive forces. It possesses three main advantages over any other

method, namely: (*a*) it is a 'zero' method, *i.e.* one in which no deflection has to be observed; (*b*) in measuring the E.M.F. of batteries no current is taken from them; hence the true E.M.F. may be found; and (*c*) as no current passes through the galvo and battery it gives the accurate measurement of current and resistance facilitating the verification of the accuracy of ammeters and voltmeters. In its simplest form the potentiometer (*see* Fig. 32) consists of seven wires of manganin or platino-iridium, each 1 metre in length, the wires being joined in series by thick copper strips. The potentiometer wire is connected in series to indicate any fluctuations in the current during the test. A standard cell (1·434 volts) is connected to the end A; the negative terminal being joined through a galvo (G) a resistance (R) to the sliding contact (K) which is placed 143·4 cm. from A: the difference of potential produced by the battery between A and K tends to send a current through the circuit A G R K while the E.M.F. of the standard cell tends to drive current in the opposite direction, and by adjusting the current in the potentiometer the P. D. between A and K can

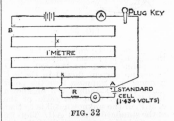

FIG. 32

be made to equal the E.M.F. of the standard cell, and under these conditions no current will flow in the standard cell circuit and no deflection of the galvo will be produced; such a condition is effected by adjusting the jockey X. When this condition of balance is obtained, the resistance (R) is removed to obtain greater selectivity, and X further adjusted to obtain no movement of the galvo. It is clear that the P. D. between A and K is then 1·434 volts, which corresponds to 0·01 volt per cm. length of AK.

*Specific resistance.*—Imagine a cube of the substance whose edge is 1 cm. The resistance between opposite faces of this cube is called the specific resistance of the substance. It is obvious from the relation between resistances in parallel that the resistance of a wire varies inversely as its cross section.

*Comparison of electromotive forces.* —Electromotive forces may be compared electrostatically by means of a quadrant electrometer. A more useful method is the potentiometer method, based on the application of Ohm's law. A long thin wire, AB, of high resistance is stretched by the side of a scale (Fig. 33). A constant current is passed through the wire by means of a battery, $B_1$. The potential falls gradually and evenly along AB if the wire is uniform. Thus if the cell to be tested, whose E.M.F. must be less than that of $B_1$, is connected as shown, a point such as P will be found, which will give with A a difference of potential equal to the E.M.F. of the cell. There will then be

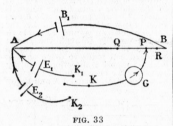

FIG. 33

no current in the galvanometer when the key $K_1$ is pressed. Suppose Q was the point found for the cell $E_1$, at which no current flowed in the galvanometer. Suppose R is the point found for a standard cell of known E.M.F. ($E_2$), then the ratio of the E.M.F. of the unknown cell is to that of the standard as AQ : AR. Thus we can find the unknown E.M.F. By means of a three-way key, $KK_1K_2$, the standard cell can be quickly changed for the unknown. The standard cell used in these experiments is the *Clark cell*. It consists essentially of mercury in contact with a paste of mercury sulphate, on which rests a solution of zinc sulphate, kept saturated by the presence of crystals of the salt. In this solution dips an amalgamated rod of pure zinc. A platinum wire dipping into the mercury forms the positive pole of the cell. A *storage cell*, or accumulator, is usually used for the purpose of obtaining a current. This is described under ELECTROLYSIS.

*Heating effects of electric currents.* The conversion of energy from an electrical form into that of heat takes place when current flows through a conductor, the incandescent lamp

being a particular example, in which case approximately 95 per cent. of the power is dissipated into heat and only 5 per cent. converted to light energy. The power, in watts, absorbed by a circuit is the product of the current in amps, and the voltage in volts. This may be expressed by the expression $W = EI$. The energy, in joules, absorbed by this circuit in $t$ secs. $= EIt_1 = I^2Rt$, since 1 joule $= 0·1$ watt second. If no mechanical work is done, all this energy is transformed into heat, and in so doing a certain amount of energy is expended. There is a relation between energy expended and heat produced, and the relation is such that if $4·2 \times 10^7$ ergs., *i.e.* $4·2$ joules, of work are done, a quantity of heat is developed sufficient to raise 1 grm. of water 1 degree centigrade. This is known as the caloric or metric unit. The British thermal unit is the British heat unit, and is the quantity of heat required to raise 1 lb. of water through $1°$ Fahrenheit, and is equivalent to 778 ft./lb. of work. Now $I^2Rt$ is measured in joules, hence the quantity of heat (H) developed in $t$ secs. in a circuit of which the resistance is R ohms and the current I amps. is given by :

$$H = \frac{I^2Rt}{4·2} = 0·24 \ I^2Rt \text{ calories.} $$

This is known as Joule's law, and the heating effect as Joule's effect. The law may be expressed in words as follows. The heat generated in a simple circuit is proportional to the product of the square of the current into the resistance, and the time in seconds during which the current continues to flow.

*Thermo-electricity.*—Seebeck found in 1821 that if a circuit consisting of two dissimilar metals be taken and the junctions kept at different temperatures, a permanent current will flow in the circuit. In 1834 Peltier found that when a current was passed across a junction of two dissimilar metals reversible heating effects occur. Heat is evolved when the current passes one way across the junction and absorbed when it passes in the opposite way. This is called the Peltier effect. From mathematical reasoning we should expect that if a circuit were made of two dissimilar metals and one junction were kept at a constant temperature, the E.M.F. in the circuit should increase as the temperature of the other junction increased. It is found, however, that as the temperature of the second junction is gradually raised, the E.M.F. increases to a certain limit, then decreases again, and is finally reversed. Lord Kelvin found that when a current flows along a wire of which the temperature varies from point to point, heat is liberated at a given point in the wire when the current is flowing in one direction, and absorbed when the current is in the opposite direction. This reversible heating effect is known as the Thomson effect, and can be applied to explain the discrepancy alluded to above. For a fuller account of the Peltier and Thomson effects and their mathematical treatment, the reader should consult standard works on electricity.

(4) ELECTRO-MAGNETIC INDUCTION.—Faraday was the first to discover the phenomenon of electro-magnetic induction. The following are practically the same experiments that Faraday performed. Take a cylindrical coil consisting of many turns of fine wire wound on a hollow reel (Fig. 34). Connect the ends of the coil to a delicate galvanometer.

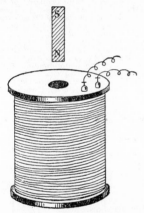

FIG. 34

Bring the N. pole of a magnet rapidly towards one end of the spiral. The needle of the galvanometer will be deflected in one direction. Now suddenly withdraw the magnet again. The needle is deflected in the opposite direction. It can be seen that the deflection is not permanent, but only takes place just as lines of force are being introduced into, or taken away, from the coil. It can be shown that the current induced is also proportional to the rate at which the magnet is introduced. Now, instead of the magnet, use a coil wound on a thin cylinder through which a steady primary current is flowing. It will be seen that when this primary coil is introduced deflection of the galvanometer needle takes place, and when it is withdrawn a deflection in the opposite direction occurs. It can also be noted that a current is induced in the coil, which is called the secondary coil, in the same direction as the primary current whenever the number of tubes of magnetic induction threading the secondary circuit is *diminished*, and in the contrary direction if the number is increased. Thus attraction will occur between the coils when the tubes are diminishing, that is, when the primary coil is being removed, and repulsion when it is being brought nearer the secondary coil. Thus the induced current is such that it tends to stop the motion producing it. This is Lenz's law. Faraday, from the result of his experiments, explained the action of Arago's disc. This consists of a compass needle placed above a horizontal copper disc which is rotating in its own plane. It is found that the needle moves with the disc. Faraday stated that by the motion of the disc relative to the needle, eddy currents were induced in the disc, and these were such that they tended to stop the relative motion of the needle and disc. Thus the needle is dragged around with the disc. It is found that currents are produced in the secondary coil when the current in the primary coil is suddenly stopped or commenced. Faraday showed experimentally with his apparatus that the induced current in the secondary coil is proportional to the *rate of charge* of the number of tubes of force threading the coil. It has been proved mathematically and demonstrated experimentally that the induced E.M.F. *is* the rate of decrease of the tubes of magnetic induction threading the secondary coil.

*Coefficients of induction.*—The number of tubes of magnetic induction which thread a circuit when unit current is flowing round it is called the coefficient of self-induction of the circuit. It is obvious that when the current is stopped, these tubes suddenly diminish. A current is then induced in the primary coil itself such that it tends to prolong the primary current. When the current is started the induced current in the primary coil tends to prevent the current starting. The number of tubes of magnetic induction threading a circuit when unit current passes through another is said to be the coefficient of *mutual* induction of the two coils. We know that the force inside a solenoid when unit current is passing is $4\pi n$, where $n$ is the number of turns per unit length. The area of a single turn is $\pi r^2$, and thus that of $nl$ turns is $\pi r^2 nl$ ($l$ is the length of the solenoid). Thus the self-induction of the solenoid is $4\pi n^2 r^2 l$. This discovery of electro-magnetic induction has led to vast progress in electric machines. Practically all modern electrical machinery depends on the induction of currents.

*The Ruhmkorff induction coil* enables us to obtain an alternating current of high frequency from the direct current of a few cells. *An alternating current* is one which changes its direction a large number of times per minute. The primary coil, P (Fig. 35), consists of a few turns

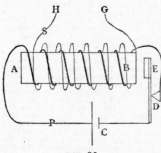

FIG. 35

of *thick* copper wire. The secondary coil, S, is wound over the primary, and consists of a vast number of turns of very fine wire. Both the coils are wound on a bundle of soft iron rods, AB. The primary current, which is supplied by a cell or number of cells, CD, is broken at frequent intervals of time. The method of doing this is as follows : One terminal of the primary coil is connected to a fixed platinum stud, D, the other terminal to a spring which carries a piece of soft iron, E. When the spring is unbent it touches the stud D and a current passes in the primary. The core of soft iron becomes magnetised and attracts the soft iron disc, E, thus breaking contact at D. The current is stopped, and the core immediately becomes unmagnetised, the spring flies back and contact is again made. The process is then repeated. When the contact in the primary is broken, a current flows in one direction in the secondary coil, when it is made the current flows in the opposite direction in the secondary. Thus an alternating current is set up in the secondary current of great frequency.

(5) ELECTRO-MAGNETIC WAVES AND MAXWELL'S THEORY.—Faraday was the first to consider the dielectric as the seat of all electrical processes. Suppose we have an alternating current in one circuit inducing an alternating current in a secondary circuit at some distance away. To originate a current in a conductor means expenditure of energy. We believe in the conservation of energy, so that if energy disappears at one place and reappears at another, it must have passed through the intervening space, and existed there somehow in the meantime. A wave motion of some kind is suggested, and a vehicle is necessary to convey those waves. It is known that the propagation of light is a wave motion, and the vehicle necessary for this propagation is the ether. Maxwell, in his theory, declared that it was not philosophical to fill all space with a new medium for every new wave motion that appears. Thus if it could be shown that some property of the medium necessary to convey electro-magnetic waves is identical with some property of the medium necessary for conveying light waves, we should have strong reason for believing that the medium was identical for both phenomena, and that light is an electro-magnetic phenomenon. Thus, says Maxwell, if we can prove that the velocity of electro-magnetic waves is the same as that of light, we should have strong reason for stating that light was an electro-magnetic phenomenon.

*Mode of propagation of electro-magnetic disturbance.*—Let A and B (Fig. 36) be the two vertical armatures of a plate condenser. Faraday conceived the idea of tubes of force which passed from the positive armature, A, to their negative armature, B. These tubes are horizontal except near the ends, when they are curved as shown. Each tube has a positive charge at one end and a negative charge at the other. Faraday showed that if these tubes were supposed to be in a state of tension and also to exert a lateral force one on the other, then all phenomena of the electric field could be explained. Suppose that A and B were suddenly connected near the top by a wire, the plates would be discharged. There would be a flow of positive electricity up one plate and of negative electricity up the other. As the process

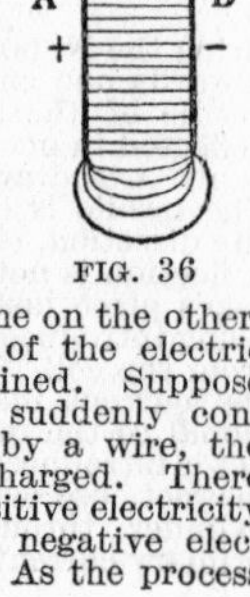

FIG. 36

goes on the tubes move parallel to themselves towards the wire with a definite velocity. They contract into the wire and disappear. The motion of these tubes gives rise to magnetic force and induction in the medium between the plates. From mathematical analysis Maxwell showed that the velocity, $v$, of the tubes of force is equal to $\dfrac{A}{\sqrt{K\mu}}$ (where A is the ratio of an electro-magnetic unit of current to the electrostatic unit, K is the specific inductive capacity of the medium, and $\mu$ its magnetic permeability). Maxwell stated that this velocity is that of an electro-magnetic disturbance in this medium, and obtained the same expression by other modes of analysis. Thus in air for which K and $\mu$ are each unity, the velocity of an electro-magnetic wave should be A. It has been proved by experiment that A is very closely equal to the velocity of light. Thus Maxwell's theory of light is considerably strengthened. Again, the ratio of the refractive indices of two substances (see LIGHT) is the ratio of the velocity of light in the two media. From Maxwell's theory this ratio should be $\dfrac{\sqrt{K_2}}{\sqrt{K_1}}$, i.e. inversely as the square roots of the specific inductive capacity. Experiment has shown that for electro-magnetic waves of frequencies comparable to those of light the ratio $\dfrac{\sqrt{K_2}}{\sqrt{K_1}}$ does approximate to the ratio of the refractive indices. Besides this, Maxwell's theory is the only theory that explains all observed phenomena in light.

*Electric waves.*—About thirteen years after Maxwell published his theory, Hertz made known the fact that he had produced and detected electro-magnetic waves, and also that their velocity was approximately that of light. It can be shown that the discharge of an electrified system of capacity, C, through a circuit of self-induction, L, is oscillatory and of period $2\pi\sqrt{LC}$. The oscillations, however, rapidly die away. It is known that a vibrating tuning fork held near an open pipe will throw the air column into vibration, and elicit a note from the pipe if the length is adjusted so that its period is the same as that of the fork. In a similar way an oscillating discharge in a circuit will produce an electric oscillation in another circuit which possesses the same periodic time. It was on this principle Hertz worked. Fig. 37 shows the simple vibrator used by

him. It consists of two brass plates, A and B, to each of which is attached a stiff wire carrying a brass knob. These are gilt and placed about two or three millimetres apart, so that when A and B are oppositely electrified a spark passes. Electric oscillation is set up, the spark passing back

FIG. 37

and fore from A to B. The time of each oscillation in Hertz's experiment was about $\frac{1}{300000000}$ of a second. At each passage of the charge, induced currents appear in neighbouring conductors, and if the periodic time of oscillation in one of these should happen to be the same as that of the vibrator, the oscillations induced in it will become multiplied, and may attain considerable intensity. The resonator made by Hertz (Fig. 38) consisted simply of a circle of wire, the ends terminating in brass knobs, whose distance apart could be adjusted. The length of the wire was such that its period was the same as that of the vibrator. When the vibrator is in action the induced

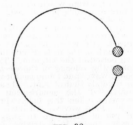

FIG. 38

current swings backwards and forwards in the circle from one knob to the other, and finally attains such a strength that sparking actually occurs between the knobs. For testing the laws of reflection and refraction of waves Hertz used more delicate apparatus. He concentrated the radiation by use of zinc reflectors bent to the shape of parabolic mirrors. By connecting the knobs of the vibrator to an induction coil continuous sparking takes place. There is then no need for the plates

A and B. Figs. 39a and 39b show the vibrator and resonator respectively. With this apparatus he proved that electro-magnetic waves are reflected from the walls of a room. He also had a huge prism made of pitch, and found that the waves were refracted by it. He determined the index of refraction and found it to be 1·69. The index of refraction of pitch for light waves is between 1·5 and 1·6.

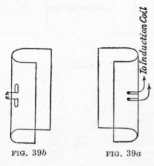

FIG. 39b                FIG. 39a

The discrepancy is due to the fact that the wave length for electromagnetic waves is very great compared to that of light, and an agreement can hardly be expected. Hertz placed the receiver in front of a huge sheet of zinc, from which waves from the vibrator were being reflected. By investigating the field in front of the zinc with his resonator he showed that stationary waves were being produced. He was able to find the wave length of the disturbance for a known period of the vibrator. Thus he found the velocity of the electromagnetic waves and found that it was approximately that of light. He also demonstrated the polarisation of these waves, in fact they behave in all ways like light waves. All these experiments of Hertz go to support Maxwell's theory in a striking way. Practical application of Hertz's results has been made by Marconi and others in wireless telegraphy (q.v.).

(6) ELECTROLYSIS.—In 1800, just after the announcement of the discovery of Volta's pile, Nicholson and Carlisle found that if two brass wires leading from the terminals of the pile were immersed near each other in water, hydrogen gas was evolved from one wire whilst the other was oxidised. If platinum wires were used oxygen gas was evolved from the second wire. Also they noticed that the volume of hydrogen was twice that of oxygen. Thus they said that the phenomenon

was one of decomposition of water. Soon after this, the chlorides of magnesia and soda were decomposed by the passage of an electric current, and also silver and copper were precipitated from their solutions, an observation which led to the process of electroplating (q.v.). In 1807 Davy obtained potassium and sodium from moist potash and soda by passing a strong current through them, thus laying the foundation of the practical method of obtaining these metals (see ELECTRO-CHEMISTRY). The fact that the products of decomposition appear only at the poles was made the basis of a theory of electrolysis by Grotthus in 1806. Suppose we have a solution of a compound which contains the elements AB (Fig. 40). A molecule of the substance near the positive pole is decomposed into its two atoms A and B. The B atom is set free. The A atom attacks the next molecule, annexing the B atom to form a new molecule and liberating the A atom which attacks the next molecule, and so on. The last molecule on the chain is attacked and gives up its B atom to the attacking A atom. The A atom thus set free has not another molecule to attack and thus is set free at the negative pole. Thus it is obvious on this theory that the quantities of the elements evolved at the poles are in the same ratio as they occur in the compound. Faraday called the poles electrodes, and named the electrode by which the current entered the liquid the anode, and that by which it left the liquid the cathode. He called the liquid through which the current passed the electrolyte. Faraday set to work to determine the relation between the amount of chemical de-

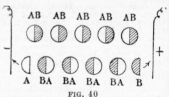

FIG. 40

composition and the strength of the current. He first showed that when several cells of acidulated water were placed in series and a current passed through, the amount of chemical action was the same in each, even if the electrodes in the various cells were of different metals and of different sizes. He also passed the current through one cell, and then through two in parallel. The amount of chemical decomposition in the first cell is equal to the sum of that in the other two. Faraday so framed his first law, which states that ' *the amount of decomposition is proportional to the quantity of electricity which passes.*' Thus an apparatus for the decomposition of water can be used to measure quantity of electricity. Such an apparatus is called a *voltameter.* Faraday then examined the amounts of different metals deposited from their solution by the same current and formed his second law, that ' *the quantity of a substance which separates at an electrode is proportional to the whole amount of electricity which passes and to the chemical equivalent weight of the substance.*' The amount in grammes of a substance which is deposited by a current of one ampere flowing from one second is called the electro-chemical equivalent of the substance. The ratio of the electro-chemical equivalents of two substances is the same as that of their chemical equivalents. It has been proved experimentally that Ohm's law is obeyed by electrolytes. The electrolytic cell is placed in the fourth arm of a Wheatstone's bridge arrangement. Owing to polarisation a direct current cannot be used. But if an alternating current is used the effects of polarisation are overcome, because the gas deposited on an electrode by the passage of electricity in one direction is immediately removed by its passage in the opposite direction. An ordinary galvanometer cannot be used to detect an alternating current. A telephone is used instead. The alternating current produces a buzzing sound in the telephone which is a minimum when the current is a minimum. The alternating current is obtained from a small induction coil. It is found that for very dilute solutions the conductivity (reciprocal of the resistance) is proportional to the concentration.

*Theory of voltaic cell.*—The source of energy of a voltaic cell is the chemical action. For example, in a Daniell cell there is a solution of zinc in sulphuric acid and liberation of copper from copper sulphate. Energy is evolved in the first action and absorbed in the second. The difference goes to provide energy for maintaining the current and doing external work. The work done by a cell giving a current $c$ is $Ect$ where $E$ is the E.M.F. and $t$ the time. If we know the electro-chemical equivalents of zinc and copper we can determine the amount of zinc dissolved and the amount of copper deposited in time, $t$, by a current, $C$. A knowledge of chemistry gives us the data for the amount of energy evolved by the

solution of this amount of zinc and deposition of this amount of copper. Thus it is possible to calculate E. The calculated values agree closely with observed values of E. The exact seat of the potential difference was debated by physicists for years. Volta located it at the junction of dissimilar metals, Faraday at the junction of the metal and electrolyte. It has been shown by experiment that there is a potential difference between the metal and electrolyte. One instrument used is the capillary electrometer (Fig. 41).

It consists of a glass tube, D, drawn out to a fine capillary tube at E. This tube, D, is partially filled with mercury and dips into the electrolyte in a vessel, C. In the bottom of the vessel is placed some mercury, B, which is connected to one terminal of a

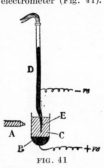

FIG. 41

cell. The mercury in D is connected to the other terminal of the cell. Thus an E.M.F. is applied in the surface between the mercury and the electrolyte. This E.M.F. is adjustable. The surface tension of the area of contact of the mercury and solution at E is affected by its electrical state. There is a certain E.M.F. due to the contact of these liquids. As the applied E.M.F. is gradually increased, having the mercury in D at a lower potential than the electrolyte, the surface tension of this layer increases, and the mercury in D must be raised to keep the level of mercury in E the same. This is viewed through a microscope, A. As the applied E.M.F. is increased the level in D must be raised till it reaches a maximum, and then it has to be lowered again. The value of the applied E.M.F. at the turning point of the level of mercury in D is equal and opposite to the contact E.M.F. between mercury and the electrolyte. The result of experiments with this electrometer favours the view that the E.M.F. of a cell is the sum of the contact differences of potential between its electrodes and the acid. Polarisation can be explained on this contact potential theory. If the electrodes are platinum and the electrolyte sulphuric acid, hydrogen forms a film on the cathode, and oxygen a film on the anode. The difference of potential of the film of hydrogen and the acid is greater than that between the acid and oxygen. Thus a current tends to flow in the other direction to the direct current.

*Accumulators.*—Suppose an E.M.F. greater than the ordinary E.M.F. of a Daniell cell is applied to it in the opposite direction to its natural E.M.F., a current would flow in the reverse direction, and the chemical actions would be reversed. Such a cell is said to be reversible. Any reversible cell can be used as an accumulator. The usual method is to take two grids of lead as electrodes in sulphuric acid, and to pass a current between them. Hydrogen is evolved at one grid, and a layer of insoluble oxide formed at the other. If left to itself now, a reverse current will flow, and lead sulphate will be formed at both the anode and cathode, until the solutions surrounding them are of equal strength. On recharging, the lead sulphate at the cathode is reduced to spongy lead, whilst lead oxide is formed at the anode. The cell is allowed to discharge again. This process is repeated until a large quantity of spongy lead is obtained. The accumulator is then ready for use. It is charged by connecting to a powerful source of potential difference. It will then give a current for some time without appreciable loss of E.M.F. *See* Hadley's *Magnetism and Electricity for Beginners, Magnetism and Electricity for Students;* Maxwell's *Elementary Treatise on Electricity, Electricity and Magnetism;* J. J. Thomson's *Elements of the Mathematical Theory of Electricity and Magnetism;* Whetham's *Experimental Electricity;* Faraday's *Experimental Researches. See also* CELL, VOLTAIC; GALVANOMETERS; ELECTRO-CHEMISTRY.

**Electro-chemistry** deals with chemical changes brought about by the expenditure of electrical energy, and with the production of electricity from the energy transformed during a chemical change. In this short article it will be impossible to deal with the theoretical questions of E.-C. in more than brief outline. The methods of preparation of substances by means of electrolysis of solutions at moderate fusion temperature will be dealt with and also some of the recent applications of electrical methods to chemical analysis and synthesis. For the refining of metals, electro-plating, electro-deposition, and high-temperature furnaces, *see* METALLURGY. (For the production of electricity *see* CELL, VOLTAIC; ACCUMULATOR, etc.) There are three main methods by which

electrical energy can be made to effect chemical changes.

(1) *By electrolysis of electrolytes.*—Solutions of salts, acids, and bases (*e.g.* alkalies) conduct electricity, at the same time undergoing decomposition, into the metal and the acid radical, hydroxyl, or halogen; the metal being produced at the cathode and the acid radical at the anode. Water is the solvent generally employed, but for organic substances, alcohol or benzene, etc., may be used. When hydrochloric acid is electrolysed, we have hydrogen liberated at the cathode and chlorine at the anode. Here the primary products of the action are liberated, *i.e.* H and Cl. Sometimes, however, these products react in the solution. This is the case with potassium hydroxide (KOH). The primary products are potassium and hydroxyl, but unless special methods of prevention are attempted, the products obtained are hydrogen and oxygen, the liberated potassium reacting on the solution at the cathode to give hydrogen according to the equation $K2 + 2H_2O = 2KOH + H_2$, while the hydroxyl decomposes to water and oxygen: $4(OH) = O_2 + 2H_2O$. The oxygen and hydrogen are called secondary products of electrolysis. Grotthus (1805) evolved the theory that the current first decomposes the molecules of the electrolyte before electrolysis occurred, and this theory was universally accepted until 1887, when the results of Van't Hoff's work on osmotic pressure of solutions was published. Van't Hoff showed that for dilute solutions the dissolved material was subject to laws similar to those governing the volume and pressure of gases, and as a result of this the theory of Grotthus lost ground. Arrhenius (1887) advanced the theory of the dissociation of the electrolyte in solution into ions carrying charges of positive and negative electricity. This theory, together with the discovery of the migration of the ions towards the electrodes, forms the basis of the modern explanations of electrolysis (*see* SOLUTIONS). The laws of Faraday state that the amount of decomposition is proportional to the quantity of electricity passed through the solution. Losses by secondary reactions may reduce this theoretical yield and hence the current efficiency of a cell is expressed in terms of the proportion of the actual yield to the theoretical. Again, when an electrolyte is being decomposed by an electric current, a counter E.M.F. is set up in the decomposition cell, and hence the effective E.M.F. is the difference between the total and the counter E.M.F. In order,

therefore, to produce an electrolytic deposit the decomposing current must have a higher E.M.F. than that which is set up in the decomposition cell. Thus $E - e = CR$, where $e$ is the counter E.M.F. and R is the total resistance. Also $R = \dfrac{d}{a} \times$ specific resistance of the electrolyte, where $d$ and $a$ are the distance apart and the area of the electrodes, respectively. For economical working the resistance R must be made as low as possible, therefore the electrodes are set as closely as working conditions permit and are of large area. The specific resistance must also be kept low and this is found to diminish with rise of temperature in the solution, and with increase of the strength of the solution (within certain limits).

*Electrodes and cells.*—The negative electrode at which the metal is liberated may be of iron, lead, or copper, while the positive electrode may be carbon, platinum, or platinum-iridium alloy with 15 per cent. iridium. Cells are made of various materials dependent on the nature of the solution. Wooden cells coated with pitch are used with acid liquors, or lead tanks in the case of $H_2SO_4$, while stoneware is used for alkaline solutions. Some few processes and technical cells will now be described.

*Sodium by Castner's process.*—The method consists in the electrolysis of fused sodium hydroxide, contained in an iron pot. The products of the electrolysis are oxygen, hydrogen, and sodium. The sodium floats on the surface of the molten caustic and is removed from time to time with a perforated ladle which allows the caustic to drain through. The escape of oxygen and hydrogen in this process represents so much waste electrical energy, and attempts have been made to obtain the metal from the fused chloride. Borcher's apparatus is then used, which consists of a U-tube made in two parts, a narrow limb of iron and a broad limb of fireclay. The narrow limb itself is anode, and the sodium produced there flows down a side pipe to a receiver. The chlorine evolved at the anode is led by a pipe to a receiver and used for the manufacture of bleach. The practical difficulties to overcome when using the fused chloride are serious, owing to the higher temperature required and also to the corrosive action of the liberated chlorine.

*Brine cells.*—The first products of the electrolysis of brine are chlorine at the anode, and alkali hydroxide at the cathode. If these products are required, they must not be allowed to mix; while if hypochlorite, chlor-ate, or perchlorate are required, the chlorine and hydroxide must be allowed to react with one another.

*Castner's process.*—A rectangular tank is used, which is divided into three compartments by two non-porous partitions dipping into narrow gutters of mercury which covers the bottom of the tank. The two outside tanks contain brine, in which are gas carbon anodes, while the centre one contains water and an iron grid, which acts as the cathode. The alkali metal is electrolysed into the mercury in the anode compartments, and is electrolysed out in the cathode compartment. In the cathode compartment the mercury amalgam acts as the anode and hydroxide is formed.

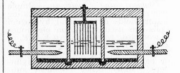

The whole cell is slowly rocked, causing the mercury to flow from one compartment to another, and so the liberated alkali metal is brought into contact with the water. The chlorine is led off by tubes at the top of the anode compartments to bleach chambers. With a 30 per cent. solution at 40° C., and a current density of one ampere per sq. cm., the current yield of hydroxide is 90 per cent.

*Hargreaves-Bird cell.*—This consists of a cast-iron box, divided into three compartments by two asbestos diaphragms made in copper gauze, which forms the cathode. The anode compartment through which brine circulates is the space between the diaphragms, and the anode is a row of gas carbons. No liquid is in the cathode compartment except that which percolates through the diaphragm. Carbon dioxide and steam are blown through the two outer compartments and convert the hydroxide formed on the diaphragm to sodium carbonate.

*Hypochlorite cells.*—Of these the Kellver cell is one of the simplest. It consists of a glazed stoneware vessel divided into compartments by glass plates which fit into grooves on the side of the cell, and around which is wound platinum-iridium wire. These form the cathode on one side of the plate and the anode on the other. The solution enters through holes in the bottom of the cell and the liberated chlorine and hydroxide react to give hypochlorite which flows out at the top of the cell in a cooling vessel. The solution is treated in the same manner several times until the strength is great enough.

*Chlorate cells.*—These do not differ materially from hypochlorite cells. Earlier cells, however, used a diaphragm to prevent reduction of the hypochlorite from which the chlorate is produced. Reduction can be avoided now by the use of potassium chromate without the use of a diaphragm. The solution flows continuously through the cell, the flow being regulated so that the temperature is about 50° C. The percentage of chlorate in the solution is about 3 per cent., and is crystallised out in cooling vats. Similar cells are used for perchlorates ; no description of a special cell has been published.

*Oxygen and hydrogen.*—Simple electrolysis of acidulated or alkaline water yields oxygen and hydrogen. Cells are used with iron electrodes placed close together. An E.M.F. of $2\frac{1}{2}$ volts is generally used, and the gases are drawn off under hoods or bells and compressed into cylinders. Many other chemical substances are now prepared by electrolytic methods, *e.g.* persulphates, sodium, peroxide, and organic compounds. The process of tanning is completed more quickly by the passage of an electric current through the steeping pits.

(2) *By electrical discharges through gases.*—The fixation of nitrogen by means of electricity has claimed much attention during recent years. When an electric spark is passed through air, nitric oxide is the main product. The reaction is a reversible one, but due to the researches of Nernst and Haber the conditions for the reaction $N_2 + O_2 \rightleftharpoons 2NO$ are well known. It was found that the best yield of nitric oxide is obtained by using a cool high tension arc and reduced pressure, so that little decomposition of the gas takes place. Electrical plants have been established in Germany, where the air is treated at the rate of about 75,000 litres per minute, the yield of nitric acid obtained being 57 grams per kilowatt hour.

The production of ozone from oxygen is illustrated in the Siemens-Halske Ozoniser. In this, air is subjected to the action of a silent electrical discharge (actually pressures of over 4000 volts are employed) after being dried with calcium chloride. The ozonised air is then used for the sterilisation of water by forcing it against a stream of water to be treated, as it drops down a tower.

(3) *By the production of high temperatures* (Electrothermal). Various electric furnaces have been designed towards this end (*see* METALLURGY). Carborundum, calcium carbide, graphite (from anthracite), carbon disulphide, and steel (from pig iron) are made by reactions effected by the heat produced in electrothermal reactions.

Other applications of electricity include the settling of dust in gases, and the drying of peat, by using the principle of electro-osmosis (*see* OSMOSIS).

*Electro-chemical analysis.*—Four different methods of quantitative analysis are in use, viz. : (1) Potential measurements for determining the concentrations of ions too dilute for gravimetric calculation ; (2) conductivity measurements for determining concentrations ; (3) titration with a galvanometer in place of an ordinary indicator, and (4) ordinary electro-analysis in which the metal is deposited on a platinum electrode and weighed. These four methods are non-electrolytic and are not used much. The electrolytic method, however, is widely employed, and consists in depositing by electrolysis the substance to be determined on one of the electrodes in a form that can be easily weighed. Metals are deposited in the pure state on the cathode or amalgamated with a mercury cathode. Lead and manganese are deposited as peroxide on the anode. Using a silver anode, chlorine, bromine, and iodine may be obtained and weighed as chloride, bromide, or iodide of silver. *See* Lehfeldt, *Electro-chem.;* Hopkins, *Experimental Electro-chem.;* Thompson, *Applied Electro-Chem.;* *Applied Electro-Chemistry* (Burgess).

**Electro-chronograph,** *see* CHRONOGRAPH.

**Electrocution,** a method of inflicting the death penalty by means of a high voltage current passed through the body. First used in U.S.A. in 1888, it is supposed to be less revolting than any other form of capital punishment (*q.v.*).

**Electro-deposition,** *see* METALLURGY.

**Electrolysis.** Substances behave differently towards the electric current. Some, such as the metals, are conductors of it, while others, like sulphur, are non-conductors. Conductors are divided into two classes. To the first class belong the metals. The passage of an electric current through such conductors is accompanied by a rise in temperature, but no other change is evident. Conductors of the second class are chiefly aqueous solutions of acids, bases, and salts, or substances in a state of fusion. When the current traverses these liquids, simultaneously with the conduction of the current, they undergo chemical change, their components being chemically separated. This phenomenon of decomposition by the electric current is termed ' electrolysis,' and the liquid conductors which show it are called ' electrolytes.' The conduction of the current in an electrolytic solution is accompanied by a mechanical movement of the parts of the dissolved substance. These parts are called ' ions,' those moving in the direction of the positive current being the ' cations,' and those in the opposite direction the ' anions.' The solid conductors by which the current passes into the solution are termed ' electrodes.' The electrode toward which the cation moves is named the ' cathode,' that toward which the anion moves the ' anode.' Thus, suppose some copper sulphate is dissolved in water and placed between copper electrodes in a copper voltameter. The mere act of solution causes the appearance of ions of copper, *i.e.* atoms which are charged with positive electricity, and sulphate ions carrying negative charge. These ions are moving about freely. If a current of electricity is now passed through the solution, the copper ions move towards the cathode, and on arrival there the charge is neutralised by the negative charge at the cathode. They thus become electrically neutral, and are identical with ordinary copper. The metal therefore deposits on the cathode. Similarly the sulphate ions move to the anode, and there neutralisation of charge goes on. Now the sulphate radicle is incapable of separate existence, so the copper of the anode is immediately attacked, giving rise to copper sulphate, which passes into solution. If the same experiment is done, using platinum electrodes, copper is deposited at the cathode as before, but the liberated sulphate radicle immediately attacks the water present to form sulphuric acid and oxygen.

Water is peculiar in that it contains a very small percentage of ions, and is therefore a bad conductor. Faraday, from the investigation of the phenomena, deduced the following laws of E. : (1) The amount of chemical decomposition effected by the passage of the current is proportional to the amount of electricity which flows through the conductor. (2) The amounts of the different elements separated by the same quantity of electricity bear the same relation to each other as the equivalents or combining weights of the elements. If A = amount of material liberated, then $E = C \times t \times e$, where $C$ = current $t$ = time in seconds, and $e$ =

weight of element liberated by one ampere in one second, *i.e.* the electro-chemical equivalent of the element which is proportional to its combining weight. For theory of E., *see* Whetham's *Solution and Electrolysis*, and H. O. Jones' *Elements of Physical Chemistry*.

**Electrolytic Cells,** *see* ELECTRO-CHEMISTRY, ELECTROLYSIS.

**Electro-magnetic Induction,** *see* **Electricity**—ELECTRO-MAGNETIC INDUCTION.

**Electro-magnetic Rotation,** *see* **Electricity**—ELECTRO-MAGNETIC WAVES AND MAXWELL'S THEORY.

**Electro-magnetic Theory of Light,** *see* **Electricity**—ELECTRO-MAGNETIC WAVES AND MAXWELL'S THEORY.

**Electro-magnetic Waves,** *see* **Electricity**—ELECTRO-MAGNETIC WAVES AND MAXWELL'S THEORY.

**Electro-metallurgy,** *see* METALLURGY.

**Electrometer,** *see* **Electricity**—ELECTROSTATICS.

**Electromotive Force (E.M.F.),** *see* ELECTRICITY—*Current*, and VOLT.

**Electron.** The elementary corpuscle or ' atom ' of negative electricity. All matter is built up of Es. and protons (*q.v.*). Plücker (1859) showed that when an electric discharge took place in evacuated tubes, rays were given off from the cathode. Sir J. J. Thomson (1896) proved these cathode rays to be composed of fast-moving particles carrying negative charge. By the application of a magnetic field, they could be deflected, but could be brought back again under the action of an electric field at right angles. The ratio of the mass of an E. to the charge carried by it (*m/e*) was calculated from these experiments, and the actual value of *e* found by Townsend and C. T. R. Wilson by experiments on the condensation of water on charged nuclei when sudden expansion was allowed to take place. The whole of the mass of E. is electrical in origin, and is due to the effects caused by the moving charge.

Es. are also given off from metal surfaces when illuminated by ultra-violet light; from incandescent metals at high temperatures; from certain oxides at red heat, such as lime; during the bombardment of material objects by *X*-rays; and from radioactive materials in the form of *β*-particles. The velocity of an E. varies according to its method of production, but the ratio *m/e* remains appreciably constant.

Atoms are composed of a central nucleus of protons and Es., surrounded by Es. moving in orbits, some circular, some elliptical, according to definite plan.

Mass of E    $9 \times 10^{-28}$ gms.
Charge of E    $1 \cdot 591 \times 10^{-19}$ coulombs.
Radius of E    $1 \cdot 87 \times 10^{-13}$ cms.

**Electrophorus,** see **Electricity—Electrostatics.**

**Electro-plating.** The deposition of metal on prepared surfaces by the passage of electric current through a solution containing the metal. The well-cleaned metal or graphite-coated object to be electro-plated forms the cathode. The solution should possess good conductivity, chemical stability, low price, much dissolved salt, but small concentration of metal ions (often effected by the addition of other substances), whilst the production of even deposits is influenced by current density, temperature, potential difference at the cathode, colloids, etc. For silver-plating, the solution contains silver and potassium cyanides, and potassium carbonate with a trace of carbon disulphide, using silver anodes.

**Electroscope,** see **Electricity—Electrostatics.**

**Electrostatics,** see **Electricity—Electrostatics.**

**Electrostatic Voltmeters,** see **Electricity—Electrostatics.**

**Electro-technical Industries,** see **Electro-chemistry, Metallurgy.**

**Electro-therapy.** Static E. as developed by the Wimshurst machine, galvanic E., usually obtained from about forty Leclanché or bichromate cells yielding about sixty volts, and faradic E. as produced by a simple form of induction coil, are all used in the interests of medicine. Electricity may be used to produce physiological effects, as when it is applied to the skin, and when one electrode is applied to the spine and the other to a muscle. In the first case the sensory surfaces are affected, a pricking and burning sensation being produced and the skin made red, showing increased vascularity. The second action is on the motor apparatus and causes the muscles to contract as the current is made and broken. During the Great War, and subsequently, sinusoidal currents were employed, rapid ones to stimulate relaxed muscles and slow sinusoidal current to restore paralysed muscles. Again, when a broad plate electrode is applied to any part of the body, and the other electrode, consisting of a platinum or steel needle, is inserted into a tumour (say), and a current measured in milliamperes ($\frac{1}{1000}$ of an ampere, this being the unit used in E.) passed, an electrolytic effect will be obtained and the tissue will be decomposed. If the platinum electrode be positive the surrounding tissue will condense and contract round it; if it be negative then the

tissue will break up into a loose frothy material. Some nervous and muscular diseases can be diagnosed with the aid of galvanic and faradic currents. Certain diseases of the spinal cord and the cerebro-spinal nerves alter the normal action of the muscles under the electric current. These abnormal effects are referred to as ' reactions of degeneration.' For the treatment of disease the three forms of current are used : the static for nervous disorders, e.g. neuralgia; the galvanic for acute neuralgia, atrophy of the muscles, diabetes, joints enlarged and stiffened by rheumatism, tonsilitis, etc., and the faradic for nervous exhaustion accompanied by insomnia, functional disorders of the generative organs, acute rheumatism, neurasthenia, and other diseases. By passing a suitable current between electrodes applied to appropriate parts of the body, a heating effect is produced, which may act as a sedative to pain, or may stimulate repair of broken-down tissues. Such diathermic treatment is used also for fibrosis of the limbs, empyema, and tuberculous bones.

Electrically produced rays, ultra-violet and $X$-rays are used separately and in conjunction. (See **Cancer, $X$-Rays, Ultra-violet Rays.**) The body itself produces electric currents, and those of the heart are utilised in the diagnosis of cardiac diseases. In conclusion it might be said that belts, rings, and all other contrivances which are advertised as having an electric or magnetic action, only cure in proportion to the faith of the wearer. They have no electrical effect, and if they had, the irregularity of their action and the lack of control of direction of the current would render them very uncertain. The so-called magnetic belts are worse than useless, since it is not known that even the most powerful magnets have any influence on the bodily functions. Electro-magnets are occasionally used to extract from tissues small pieces of steel, e.g. broken needle points.

**Electrotropism,** a very poorly investigated subject dealing with the sensitiveness of plant organs to the action of electric currents. If a plant be grown so that its roots dip into a liquid through which a current is passing, then some of the roots will incline to the anode and some to the cathode, thus showing the acquirement of polarity.

**Electrotyping,** see **Printing, Metallurgy.**

**Electrum** has two meanings in antiquity : (1) A mixture of gold and silver ; (2) amber. In the former sense it occurs in Antigone, where mention is made of Indian gold and the ' E. of Sardis,' as objects of the highest value. This is the native E., but it was also made artificially, and, according to Pliny, E. contained gold and silver in the proportion 4 : 1. It was used for plate and also for money, and coins are still in existence of this metal struck by the kings of Bosporus, by Syracuse, and by other Greek states.

**Electuary** (from a Greek word signifying ' licking.' The term was also used by Latin authors to designate a thick, honey-like substance). The word is used in medicine in French, but in English is restricted to ' lentive E.,' a popular name for a compound confection of senna, an official preparation of the British Pharmacopœia.

**Elegit,** see EXECUTION.

**Elegy,** the general term in Greek for any poem written in the elegiac metre, a combination of the dactylic hexameter and pentameter in a couplet. The word ἔλεγος means a plaintive melody accompanied by the flute, and how it happened that the word was applied to elegiac poetry, the earliest representatives of which by no means confined it to mournful subjects, is doubtful. It may be that the term was only chosen in reference to the musical setting, the E. having originally been accompanied by the flute. The earliest representatives of the E., Callinus of Ephesus (c. 700 B.C.), and Tyrtæus of Aphidnæ in Attica (c. 600), gave it a warlike and political direction, and so did Solan (640–559) in his earlier poems, and the Es. of Theognis of Megara (c. 540), though erotic, are essentially political. The first typical representative of the erotic E. was Mimnermus of Colophon, a contemporary of Solon; and the E. of mourning or sorrow was brought to perfection by Simonides of Ceos (d. 469 B.C.). After this the emotional element predominated. Antimachus of Colophon (c. 400) gave the E. a learned tinge, and was thus the prototype of the elegiac poets of Alexandria, of whom Callimachus of Cyrene was the best. The subject of the Alexandrian E. is either the passion of love, or the learned narrative of fable and history, from which personal emotion is absent. This type was imitated at Rome towards the end of the republic, and the Es. of Catullus are among the earliest attempts, later elegiac writers being Cornelius Gallus, Propertius, Tibullus, and Ovid, who, in his Fasti, showed how a learned subject could be treated in this metre. From this time onward the elegiac metre was con-

stantly employed and was used for every possible subject, e.g. Rutilius Namantianus used it to describe his journey from Rome to France (416 A.D.). After the Renaissance the word E. was introduced into England, but was used to describe a funeral song or lament, the poem of Gascoigne's The Complaint of Philomene, 1576, being among the first to receive the title. Later, however, the word was further restricted to its present meaning, e.g. a poem of regret pronounced at the obsequies of a particular person, and in this modern sense Spenser's Daphnaida is strictly an E., whereas Gray's celebrated poem, An Elegy in a Country Churchyard, belongs to a class apart, being not addressed to the memory of a particular person. Of the famous Es. in English may be mentioned Milton's Lycidas, Shelley's Adonais, Matthew Arnold's Thyrsis, and Swinburne's Ave atque Vale. Tennyson's In Memoriam is generally excluded on the score of length, and Wordsworth's Lucy is a dirge.

**Element** is any substance which, as far as our knowledge extends, is composed entirely of atoms of identical chemical properties (though not necessarily identical in structure—see ISOTOPES). In other words an E. is a substance which up to the present has not been split up into portions possessing different chemical properties. Es. used to be classified as metals and non-metals, and arsenic, boron, bromine, carbon, chlorine, fluorine, hydrogen, iodine, nitrogen, oxygen, phosphorus, selenium, silicon, sulphur, and tellurium; but this list was increased by the discovery of argon, helium, krypton, etc., and in any case, because of the merging of non-metals into metals by stages which make this classification difficult and arbitrary, the periodic system of Mendeléev, as modified in the light of modern knowledge of atomic structure, has been generally adopted (see CHEMISTRY). Most of the Es., except those of the argon group which are only found free, are usually found as compounds, although carbon, copper, gold, hydrogen, nitrogen, oxygen, silver, and sulphur are found in considerable quantities in their free state. The term E. can only be applied in a tentative manner to any form of matter, because with the advance of science it is always possible that some substance once regarded as an E. may be found to consist of simpler forms, e.g. didymium was found to consist of neodidymium and præseolidymium. Chemical analysis is, however, now so precise that we feel confident in stating that there are altogether 92 elements, of which two only remain (1931) to be discovered. Following is a list of the Es. with their symbols and approximate atomic weights (*q.v.*) :

| Element. | Sym-bol. | Approx. At. Wt. | At. No. |
|---|---|---|---|
| Actinium | Ac | 229 | 89 |
| Aluminium | Al | 27 | 13 |
| Antimony | Sb | 122 | 51 |
| Argon | A | 40 | 18 |
| Arsenic | As | 75 | 33 |
| Barium | Ba | 137·5 | 56 |
| Beryllium | Be | 9 | 4 |
| Bismuth | Bi | 209 | 83 |
| Boron | B | 11 | 5 |
| Bromine | Br | 80 | 35 |
| Cadmium | Cd | 112·5 | 48 |
| Cæsium | Cs | 133 | 55 |
| Calcium | Ca | 40 | 20 |
| Carbon | C | 12 | 6 |
| Cerium | Ce | 140 | 58 |
| Chlorine | Cl | 35·5 | 17 |
| Chromium | Cr | 52 | 24 |
| Cobalt | Co | 59 | 27 |
| Copper | Cu | 63·5 | 29 |
| Dysprosium | Dy | 162·5 | 66 |
| Erbium | Er | 167·5 | 68 |
| Europium | Eu | 152 | 63 |
| Fluorine | F | 19 | 9 |
| Gadolinium | Gd | 157 | 64 |
| Gallium | Ga | 69·5 | 31 |
| Germanium | Ge | 72·5 | 32 |
| Gold | Au | 197 | 79 |
| Hafnium | Ha | 178·5 | 72 |
| Helium | He | 4 | 2 |
| Holmium | Ho | 163·5 | 67 |
| Hydrogen | H | 1 | 1 |
| Illinium | Il | 146 | 61 |
| Indium | In | 115 | 49 |
| Iodine | I | 127 | 53 |
| Iridium | Ir | 193 | 77 |
| Iron | Fe | 56 | 26 |
| Krypton | Kr | 83 | 36 |
| Lanthanum | La | 139 | 57 |
| Lead | Pb | 207 | 82 |
| Lithium | Li | 7 | 3 |
| Lutecium | Lu | 175 | 71 |
| Magnesium | Mg | 24·3 | 12 |
| Manganese | Mn | 55 | 25 |
| Masurium | Ma | 98 | 43 |
| Mercury | Hg | 200·6 | 80 |
| Molybdenum | Mo | 96 | 42 |
| Neodymium | Nd | 144·5 | 60 |
| Neon | Ne | 20 | 10 |
| Nickel | Ni | 58·7 | 28 |
| Niobium | Nb | 93 | 41 |
| Nitrogen | N | 14 | 7 |
| Osmium | Os | 191 | 76 |
| Oxygen | O | 16 | 8 |
| Palladium | Pd | 106·5 | 46 |
| Phosphorus | P | 31 | 15 |
| Platinum | Pt | 195 | 78 |
| Polonium | Po | 210 | 84 |
| Potassium | K | 39 | 19 |
| Praseodymium | Pr | 141 | 59 |
| Protoactinium | Pa | 234 | 91 |
| Radium | Ra | 226 | 88 |
| Radon | Rn | 222 | 86 |
| Rhenium | Re | 187 | 75 |

| Element. | Sym-bol. | Approx. At. Wt. | At. No. |
|---|---|---|---|
| Rhodium | Rh | 103 | 45 |
| Rubidium | Rb | 85·5 | 37 |
| Ruthenium | Ru | 101·5 | 44 |
| Samarium | Sm | 150·5 | 62 |
| Scandium | Sc | 45 | 21 |
| Selenium | Se | 79 | 34 |
| Silicon | Si | 28 | 14 |
| Silver | Ag | 108 | 47 |
| Sodium | Na | 23 | 11 |
| Strontium | Sr | 87·5 | 38 |
| Sulphur | S | 32 | 16 |
| Tantalum | Ta | 181·5 | 73 |
| Tellurium | Te | 127·5 | 52 |
| Terbium | Tb | 159 | 65 |
| Thallium | Tl | 204·5 | 81 |
| Thorium | Th | 232 | 90 |
| Thulium | Tm | 169·5 | 69 |
| Tin | Sn | 118·5 | 50 |
| Titanium | Ti | 48 | 22 |
| Tungsten | W | 184 | 74 |
| Uranium | U | 238 | 92 |
| Vanadium | V | 51 | 23 |
| Xenon | Xe | 130 | 54 |
| Ytterbium | Tb | 173·5 | 70 |
| Yttrium | Y | 89 | 39 |
| Zinc | Zn | 65·5 | 30 |
| Zirconium | Zr | 91 | 40 |

**Elemental Spirits, or Angels of the Elements,** were imaginary beings who were supposed to preside over the four elements, the spirits of fire being called Salamanders, those of water, Undines, those of air, Sylphs, and those of earth, Gnomes. They were supposed to dwell in their respective elements, and the belief in their existence was a very popular one in the Middle Ages. Paracelsus wrote a treatise on them.

**Elementary Education,** *see* EDUCA-TION.

**Elemi,** an oleo-resin obtained from the pitch-tree, a native of Manilla. When pure it is pale yellow in colour and resembles honey in consistency. It has an aromatic odour and is soluble in alcohol and ether.

**Elenchus** (Gk. ἔλεγχος, commonly translated by the Lat. *argumentum*, *inquisitio*, *confutatio*, and *demonstratio*), a term frequently used in the Aristotelian system of logic to denote argument, replication, refutation, or the subject or nature of dispute, or demonstration. Aristotle himself defines E. as ' a syllogism of contradiction.' In the last two books of the *Organon*, he classifies and discusses the different kinds of sophistical elenchi, or modes of argument, used by sophists, *e.g.* the sophism designated *ignoratio elenchi*, or sinister deviation from the point under discussion, consists according to Aristotle, in proving something irrelevant.

**Eleocharis,** a genus of cosmopolitan plants in the order Cyperaceæ. *E. palustris* grows in marshy places, forming sometimes a large proportion of the peat in bogs ; *E. tuberosa*, a native of E. Asia, has edible tubers.

**Elephant** (Lat. *elephantus ;* Gk. ἐλέφαντος, ivory), a representative of the Proboscidea, a sub-order of ungulate mammals. There are two existing species of Elephantidæ, the *Elephas Maximus*, also called *Elephas Indicus* or Indian E., and the *Elephas Africanus* or African E. A number of extinct forms serve to connect the E., to a limited extent, with other ungulates, but as the absolutely intermediate type has not been discovered, the origin of the *Elephantidæ* is conjectural. The young Indian Es. are hairy, thus showing affinity with the mam-

huge and bulky, the head being disproportionately large, the ears large and flapping, the neck very short and thick, and the limbs long and stout. The feet are short and broad, and have five toes each, of which the middle one is the largest. Es. are strictly herbivorous, subsisting chiefly upon roots, twigs, leaves, and young shoots. The *Elephas Indicus* is distinguished by its comparatively flat forehead and small ears, as well as by its smooth and nearly naked skin. The average height of the adult male does not exceed 9 ft., and that of the female 8 ft., but this is often considerably exceeded, and there is an enormous skeleton in the museum at Calcutta

INDIAN ELEPHANT

moth. The most remarkable characteristic of the order, and the one from which they derive their title, is the long, flexible, prehensile proboscis, into which the nose is produced. This trunk, as it is called, is delicately sensitive. It has the nostrils at the extremity, and is used for the purpose of conveying food and water to the mouth. Es. have no canine teeth in either jaw, and their tusks are developed only in the upper jaw ; young Es. have a very minute pair of milk-tusks which are shed at an early age ; the permanent tusks continue growing throughout life, and so remain open at their bases, which are enclosed in sheaths of the premaxillary bones, extending upwards in the skull as far as the nasal cavity. The tusks of young Es. are tipped with enamel, but this soon wears off, and they then consist of ivory alone. The build of the E. is

of an E. that lived about 1850–60, which measures 11 ft. 3 in. from the shoulders. The height of the Indian E. is almost precisely twice the circumference of its forefoot. It is estimated that one of this species may live for a century and a half in the wild state. Herds of Es. consist of from thirty to fifty individuals, all of which belong to a single family, a female being invariably the leader. They are fond of bathing and rolling in wet mud, and when heated they squirt water over their backs by means of the trunk. The *Elephas Africanus* differs chiefly from the Indian species in the enormous size of its ears, which, when in repose, completely cover the animal's shoulders. Its colour is a somewhat darker grey, and its disposition fiercer than that of the Asiatic tribe ; also it is more rapid in its movements and has remarkable powers of getting over precipitous ground. Owing to persecution for the sake of its tusks, the African E. has grown much rarer, and is now only found S. of the Sahara, whereas formerly it was spread over the whole of the wooded districts. The white E. is a pure albino, and is sometimes found in Burma and Siam.

**Elephanta Island** (called by the natives **Gharapuri**), a small island in Bombay harbour, about 5 m. from Bombay. It received its name from the Portuguese on account of a colossal statue of an elephant which once stood on the island, but is now in Bombay. It is celebrated for its cave temples, one of which contains a huge three-faced bust about 18 ft. high, representing Siva in his threefold character of Creator, Preserver, and Destroyer.

**Elephantiasis,** a condition in which the legs become thickened and straight up and down like an elephant's. The disease also affects other parts, as E. of the scrotum. It is due to a blocking of the lymphatic glands and channels, combined with irritation of the skin, generally by an external contamination or inflammation. In the tropics, the blocking of the lymph channels is commonly due to a thread-like worm, known as Filaria, and its eggs. In cold climates the condition is rarely seen, but when it is, the blocking is due to various causes. The treatment consists in removing the irritation of the skin from any condition which may be present, by means of applications suitable for each individual case. The flow of lymph through the channels is aided by massage and elevation of the part.

**Elephantine** (the *Yeziret-ey-Taher*, or flowery isle, of the Arabs), a beautiful island in the Nile opposite Assuan. It was the principal place of worship of Khnum or Khnoum, a ram-headed god, who enjoyed great repute as a creator, and was famous for its pottery, a peculiar pink ware with a brownish-pink face.

**Elephant-seal,** or **Sea-Elephant,** termed technically *Macrorhinus leoninus*, a carnivorous mammal, and is the largest of all the Pinnipedia.

**Elephant's Foot,** or *Testudinaria elephantipes*, a plant of the natural order Dioscoreaceæ. It has a peculiar rootstock, with a rough and indented bark, shaped like an elephant's foot. It contains a great quantity of starch and was used freely by the natives of S. Africa for food; hence it is often called Hottentot's bread.

**Elephant-shrew,** the name given to several insectivorous quadrupeds in the family Macroscelidæ. They somewhat resemble the kangaroo-mice in appearance, and use their long hind-legs in similar fashion when they leap over the plains of Africa. The snout is so long that it looks like a proboscis, whence the name. *Macroscelides typicus* is a common specimen, and is called also the jumping-shrew or proboscis-rat.

**Elets,** a tn. of Russia in the gov. of Orel, 122 m. from Orel. It has a splendid position, and is important for its trade in corn and cattle and as a railway centre with foundries. Pop. 42,492.

**Elettaria,** *see* CARDAMOMS.

**Eleusinia,** a festival and mysteries, celebrated, originally only in Eleusis, in honour of Demeter and Persephone. They were regarded by the ancients as the most venerable and the holiest of all the mysteries celebrated in Greece, and were said to have been instituted by Demeter herself when wandering about in search of her daughter. At first the right of initiation was restricted to inhabitants of Attica, but later all Greeks were admitted and even the Romans, but all barbarians were excluded, as well as all who were guilty of murder. Those who wished to take part in the greater E. were first admitted to the lesser E., which were held every year in the month of Anthesterion, at Agræ on the Ilissus. They were then allowed as μύσται to take some part in the great E. the next autumn, but were not initiated into the greater mysteries until the next year. These were celebrated every year in the month of Bœdromion during nine days, and on the second of these the μύσται were purified. The third was spent in fasting and sacrifice, and on the fourth the καλάθος κάθοδος, a procession with a basket containing pomegranates and poppy seeds, took place. On the fifth day (ἡ τῶν λαμπάδων ἡμέρα) the μύσται went with torches to the temple of Demeter, where they remained all night, and on the sixth, the most solemn of all, a statue of Iacchus, son of Demeter, adorned with a garland of myrtle and bearing a torch in his hand, was carried along the sacred road amidst shouts and songs. During the night the μύσται were initiated into the last mysteries (ἐποπτεία), and confirmed their oath of secrecy, previously taken at the lesser E. On the seventh day the initiated (ἐπόπται) returned to Athens. The eighth day was an additional day for the convenience of those who arrived late, and the ninth day (πλημοχόαι) was occupied by a libation, poured in the direction of E. and W. with mystical formula. The object of the E. was to excite and strengthen in the minds of the initiated, by means of the story of Persephone, the faith in the continuance of life, and a system of rewards and punishments after death.

**Eleusis,** a tn. and demus of Attica, 12 m. distant from Athens. It possessed a magnificent temple of Demeter, and it gave its name to the festival of the Eleusinia (*q.v.*). The town had been from time immemorial a seat of the worship of Demeter, but after its conquest, which took place, according to the story, under King Erechtheus, the Eleusinia became a festival common to both cities, though the superintendence of the festival remained with the descendants of Eumolphus, the king of E.

**Eleuthera,** one of the Bahamas, British West Indies, separated from Abaco by the Providence Channel. The soil is fertile, and pine apples, oranges, and lemons are cultivated. Chief town, Governor's Harbour. Area, 235 sq. m. Pop. 6530.

**Elevation,** in astronomy, is the height above the horizon of an object on the celestial sphere, measured by the arc of a vertical circle passing through it and the horizon.

**Elevators, Grain,** *see* CONVEYORS AND ELEVATORS, LIFTS, HYDRAULIC MACHINERY.

**Elf** (Old Eng. *ælf, ylf*), a supernatural, diminutive being of early Teutonic lore. Es. were believed to be tricksy sprites, much given to interference in human affairs. They stole children and placed changelings in their stead, they visited people in their sleep and gave them nightmares, and sometimes inflicted them with diseases, and with their elf-bolts they struck down human beings and cattle alike. They also elf-locked women's hair, *i.e.* they tangled it into a matted mess, which it was considered unlucky to undo. Es. were dwarfish and generally black in appearance. *See* Nilsson's *Primitive Inhabitants of Scandinavia,* 1868 ; Keightley's *Fairy Mythology,* 1850, and article on FAIRIES.

**El Fasher,** cap. of Darfur, Egyptian Sudan, Africa, and centre of the caravan routes across north-eastern Africa. Pop. about 15,000.

**Elgar, Sir Edward Wm., Bart.** (*b.* 1857), British composer. Practically self-taught, both as conductor, executant, and composer, E. spent his early years at teaching and similar drudgery. His music is deeply imbued with the mysticism, not only of Christianity (he is a Roman Catholic), but also of paganism, as is realised, for instance, in *King Olaf.* E. has devoted most of his attention to choral writing, and, besides *Olaf,* has produced *The Kingdom, Caractacus,* and others, the best being his setting of Newman's *Dream of Gerontius,* 1902. This is one

of the finest works in British choral music, yet was at first received with indifference, but since its eulogism by Richard Strauss it has become widely popular. In *The Apostles,* 1903, E. carries his ideas to a point of originality beyond anything else he previously composed. His orchestral works include the beautiful overture, *In the South,* the fine *Enigma* variations, 1894, and the offspring of this latter work, the two symphonies (1908 and 1911), of which the former —an example of Liszt's method of theme-metamorphosis in a more or less classic form—is worthy to rank with some of the finest symphonists. E.'s songs, chamber-music, and smaller works are often poetic, but add no-

SIR EDWARD ELGAR, BART., O.M.

thing to a reputation founded on *Gerontius,* and the A♭ Symphony. On the whole, the character of his music is deeply psychological and yet broad, *nobilmente,* as he directs again and again in his scores. His orchestration, especially for strings, is superb, and his harmony original and strongly chromatic. His two military marches, *Pomp and Circumstance* and the *Coronation Ode,* were inspired by the coronation of King Edward VII. ; the tune *Land of Hope and Glory,* which occurs in both, has long been so popular in England as to be ranked next to *God Save the King* as a national song. His highly individual art, as exemplified in the tone poem *Falstaff,* 1913, was well sustained in his *Spirit of England* and *For the Fallen,* both composed in 1916 during the dark days of the War. Even if his chamber music, produced after the War, does not reveal him at his best, he is the most widely known of all living Eng. composers. In 1924 he conducted the massed choirs and bands at the Royal opening of the British Empire Exhibition at Wembley in 1924 when his Imperial March and *Land of Hope and Glory* were rendered before the King and a vast audience. He was appointed Master of the King's Musick in 1924.

*Bibliography.*—A *Dict. of Modern Music and Musicians*, 1924 (DENT); R. J. Buckley, *Sir Edward Elgar* 1912; J. F. Porte, *Sir Edward Elgar*, 1921.

**El Ghor,** the Arabic name for the great depression extending from the Sea of Galilee to the Dead Sea, Palestine. Length 65 m., breadth 6 to 12 m.

**Elgin, or Moray,** a maritime co. of N. Scotland on the Moray Firth. It formed the central part of ancient Moray province. The soil is mostly alluvial and fertile, but mountainous towards the S. Cromdale Hills (S.E.) contain Carn Eachie (2328 ft.), the highest peak. There are sand-dunes at Culbin. The Spey, Findhorn, and Lossie are the chief rivers. Lochindorb is a large sheet of water (2 m. long). Whisky is distilled; there are salmon and herring fisheries. There are many interesting antiquities including churches and castles, Sweno's Stone at Forres, and 'The Roman Well' at Burghead. Area, 304,931 acres. Pop. 41,558.

**Elgin,** cap. of Elgin co., royal and parl. bor. of Scotland, on R. Lossie. There are ruins of the fine cathedral, 'Lantern of the North,' founded 1224 (burnt 1390, rebuilt later), in the form of a cross, also of the chapter-house and Grey Friars' monastery. The ruined palace of the bishops of Moray is 2 m. N., on Loch Spynie, and 6 m. S.W. is the Cistercian Pluscardine Priory (1230), restored by Lord Bute. There are brewing and woollen industries, saw-mills and sandstone quarries. Pop. 7776.

**Elgin,** a city of Kane and Cook counties, Illinois, U.S.A., on Fox R., 35 m. from Chicago. It manufactures watches, butter, pipe organs, silverware and condensed milk, and is the seat of two academies, Elgin and St. Mary's, and of the N. Illinois Hospital for the Insane, with 1800 patients, and has a library with 60,000 volumes. Pop. 35,929.

**Elgin, Earls of.** The first earl, whose family was by descent connected with King Robert I. of Scotland, was given his earldom by Charles I. in 1633. He was succeeded in 1663 by Robert Bruce, who was created Earl of Arlesbury in 1664, and became lord chamberlain in 1687. Thomas Bruce, the third earl (c. 1655–1741), was a courtier of James II.,

and, for refusing to take the oath of allegiance to William and Mary, was under suspicion. He was imprisoned as a Jacobite conspirator (1690–96), but was allowed to flee to Brussels in 1696. The ninth Earl of Kincardine (1732–71) succeeded as fifth Earl of E. in 1747. Thomas Bruce, the seventh Earl of E. (1766–1841), sold to the nation, in 1816, the collection of sculptures known as the 'Elgin Marbles' (*q.v.*). He was a soldier and diplomatist, and was British envoy to the Porte (1799–1803), where he gathered together his collection. His son, James Bruce, the eighth earl (1811–63), was also a diplomatist. He displayed great ability as governor of Jamaica (1842–46) and of Canada (1847–54). In 1857 he was sent as an envoy to the Far East, where he concluded the treaty of Tientsin with China (1858), and, on the Chinese refusing to ratify it, he captured Pekin (1860). He was appointed viceroy of India in 1862. Victoria Alexander Bruce, the ninth earl, was born near Montreal in 1849. He became Treasurer of the Household and First Commissioner of Public Works during Gladstone's administration (1886), and Viceroy of India (1894–99). He was chairman of the commission of the Scottish Church case (1904), and was appointed by Campbell-Bannerman Secretary for the Colonies (1905–8). Consult *Letters and Journals* of the eighth earl, 1872; and his Life by Bourinot, 1903, and G. Wrong, 1905.

**Elgin Marbles,** the famous collection of ancient Greek sculptures, brought to England (c. 1812) through the agency of the seventh Earl of Elgin, after whom they are named, and acquired for the British Museum (1816). They are portions from the Parthenon (designed by Phidias) and other buildings on the Athenian Acropolis. Elgin's act was denounced as 'vandalism,' but if left these treasures would probably have been destroyed by the Turks. *See* Michaelis, *Der Parthenon*, 1871; *Anc. Marbles in Great Britain* (translated by Fennell), 1882; Newton, *Elgin Room in the Brit. Mus.*, 1881–82; *Anc. Marbles in the Brit. Mus.*, vi.–ix., 1830–42.

**Elgon, or Ligonyi, Mount,** an extinct volcano (about 14,094 ft. high) of Uganda, British E. Africa, 60 m. N.E. of Victoria Nyanza. See *Proc. Royal Geog. Soc.*, 1891.

**Eli** (Heb. 'elevation'), an Israelite priest who was also one of the judges. He was the son of Aaron and of the family of Ithamar. His name chiefly enters the Biblical narrative in connection with the story of Samuel.

**Elias, Mount St.** (N. America), *see* ST. ELIAS, MOUNT.

**Elie,** a small watering-place of S.E. Fifeshire, Scotland, in the Firth of Forth. It has golf-links.

**Eligius,** *see* ELOI.

**Elijah** (N.T., Elias), the greatest and most picturesque of the prophets of Israel, lived during the reigns of Ahab and Ahaziah. His life was chiefly spent in opposing the worship of Baal, which the former king was encouraging. The story of his life and acts is fully told in 1 Kings xvii.-xix. and xxi., 2 Kings i. and ii., 2 Chron. xxi., 12-15. Like Enoch he was translated to heaven instead of dying a natural death, and for long there remained a tradition among the Jews that he would again come to Israel before the advent of the Messiah. This expectation, expressed in Mal. iv. 5, Jesus declares to have been fulfilled in the preaching of John the Baptist. In the N.T., Elias is also mentioned as appearing with Moses on the mount of Transfiguration. The festival of E. is celebrated by the Greek and Roman Churches on July 20. In Greece he is regarded as the patron saint of mountains, and among Roman Catholics legend once described him as founder of the Carmelite order. The Russians have many legends about the Jewish prophet, chiefly derived from the ancient tales of Perun, their thunder-god. *See* Dr. Milligan's *Elijah, his Life and Times,* 1887, and T. K. Cheyne's *The Hallowing of Criticism : Nine Sermons on Elijah,* 1888.

**Elimination,** in algebra, is a process of solving systems of equations which consists in getting rid of a quantity or letter which is common to the equations, by forming another that does not contain that letter. For example, given (1) $x^2 + y = 1$ (2) $x + y = 1$ $\}$ Eliminate $y$, *i.e.* deduce an equation involving $x$ only.

Equation (2) is equivalent to

$$y = 1 - x$$

∴ Equation (1) is equivalent to

$$x^2 + (1 - x)^2 = 1$$
$$i.e., \ 2x^2 - 2x = 0$$
$$i.e., \ x^2 - x = 0$$

which is an equation in $x$ only, ∴ $y$ has been eliminated.

**Eliot, Sir Charles Norton Edge-cumbe** (*b.* 1864), an English statesman and foreign administrator. E. became commander-in-chief of British E. Africa and consul-general at Zanzibar (1900-4). He was first principal of Hong-Kong University (1912). Appointed Brit. Ambassador to Japan, 1919. Retired in 1926, when he was made a member of the Japanese Imperial Academy. His works include : *Turkey in Europe,* 1900 ; *East Africa Protectorate,* 1905 ; *Letters from the Far East,* 1907.

**Eliot, Charles William** (1834-1926), one of the greatest of American university presidents and authorities on education, *b.* in Boston, Massachusetts, U.S.A., March 20. He was the son of a former mayor of Boston, who had also been treasurer of Harvard University. As a matter of course, the son went to Harvard, from which he graduated in 1853. For some years he was connected with the university as tutor in mathematics, and afterwards as assistant professor of mathematics and chemistry. After a period of study abroad, he returned to his country to become professor of chemistry in the Massachusetts Institute of Technology from 1865 to 1869. To everybody's surprise he was elected President of Harvard University in 1869, and held this great position for forty years, after which he was President Emeritus until his death. It was perhaps the longest period of headship of a great school in the history of his country. He became a sort of universal sage. At Harvard he introduced the elective system of studies. In the country at large he was a motive force in improving primary and secondary schools. In religion he became known as one of the greatest spokesmen for the Unitarian faith. He had outspoken views on the relations between labour and capital. He was an active supporter of President Woodrow Wilson, who offered him the embassy to England, which, however, he declined. His mind marched with Wilson's on the great subjects of disarmament and the League of Nations. The 'four-foot shelf of books' chosen and in part edited by E. did much to spread the love of sound literature among his countrymen. Others of his books are *Four American Leaders,* 1906 ; *The Road Toward Peace,* 1915 ; and *A Late Harvest,* 1924. He *d.* at Northeast Harbour, Maine, Aug. 22, at the advanced age of ninety-two, having retained his brilliant faculties of public speech and writing almost to the last.

**Eliot, George,** was the pseudonym taken by Marian Evans (1819-80), the youngest child of Robert Evans, land-agent to the Newdigate family, by his second wife. She was born on Nov. 22, and the best authority for her early life is the easily-discernible autobiographical portions of her novels. Therein many of the characteristics of her father are reproduced in Adam Bede and Caleb Garth, her brother Isaac figures as Tom Tulliver, and herself is introduced as Maggie Tulliver. Marian Evans was brought up to the strict observances of religion, and possibly influenced by an aunt who was a Methodist preacher, she inclined to evangelicalism. In these days she was most austere, theatres were to her something almost unholy, and her favourite reading was Thomas à Kempis and Bunyan, Young and Whiston, *Rasselas*, and *The Lives of the Poets*. At the age of twenty-two, her father moved from Arbury Park to Coventry, and she went with him. Here began the second phase of her life. She made the acquaintance of Charles Bray (1811–84), the author of *The Philosophy of Necessity* and

GEORGE ELIOT

other works, and of Mrs. Bray, whose brother, Charles Hennell (1809–50), had written *An Inquiry concerning the Origin of Christianity* (1838). In such company, for Bray, as well as his brother-in-law, was a free-thinker, Marian Evans began to doubt, and at last to allow her doubts entirely to conquer her. In 1844 when Miss Brabant (afterwards Mrs. Charles Hennell) had to resign the task of translating Strauss's *Leben Jesu*, she it was who brought it to a successful conclusion. This was published in 1846, but Miss Evans' name did not appear. Robert Evans, who had been greatly distressed by the change in his daughter's religious convictions, died in the spring of 1849, and then, after a short Continental tour with the Brays, she for a while made her home with these devoted friends. In 1851 she was offered the assistant-editorship of the *Westminster Review*, and she filled this laborious post for some years, from time to time contributing to its

pages articles and elaborate reviews. This work, which necessitated her living in London, occupied most of her day, but she contrived to find time to translate Fauerbach's *Essence of Christianity*, which was published in 1854, the only book to appear over her own name. The third phase of the life of Marian Evans—the 'George Eliot' period—dates from the beginning of her acquaintance with George Henry Lewes (1817–78), the author of the *Life of Goethe* and the *Biographical History of Philosophy*, which took place in 1853. In the following year they decided to live together, though they could not get married, because Lewes had a wife living, from whom, however, he was separated. It was not with light hearts that they took this step, but having taken it, they regarded the union as being as binding and as legitimate as if it had had the sanction of the law and the church, and it endured until the death of Lewes twenty-four years later. Miss Evans continued to contribute to the *Westminster Review*, and she wrote many reviews for the *Leader*, of which paper Lewes was editor. Lewes was a great believer in the genius of Miss Evans, and in 1856 he persuaded her to see if her gifts lay in the direction of fiction. She made an attempt, and Lewes, without divulging the name of the writer, sent it to Blackwood, who at once accepted it for his magazine. This was *Amos Barton*, and it was followed by *Mr. Gilfil's Love Story* and *Janet's Repentance*. These stories were collected in 1858 as *Scenes of Clerical Life*, and were received with enthusiasm in literary circles. Dickens was especially appreciative, and he alone among the critics discerned the sex of the author. Encouraged by the success of these short stories, Miss Evans began a full-dress novel, *Adam Bede*, which was finished thirteen months later, and published on Feb. 1, 1859. The qualities that marked *Scenes of Clerical Life* were present in *Adam Bede*, which evoked a further chorus of praise, and placed George E. in the front rank of contemporary novelists. *Adam Bede* was followed by *The Mill on the Floss* (1860), which is generally regarded as her masterpiece. The earlier part, which is largely a transcript from life of the youth of herself and her brother, is one of the most beautiful things in English fiction; but taken as a whole the novel gives undue prominence to the childish scenes, a fault the author, in reply to a criticism of Bulwer Lytton, regretfully acknowledged. *Silas Marner* appeared in 1860; and then George E. accompanied by Lewes went to Florence to get material for a projected historical novel of the time of Savonarola. While Thackeray was editor of the *Cornhill Magazine*, Smith, Elder & Co. offered her the hitherto unprecedented sum of £10,000 for the serial and book rights of the new novel, *Romola*, and eventually she accepted £7000 for its appearance in the *Cornhill*. The first instalment was printed in the magazine in July 1862, the last in August of the following year, the story being written from month to month, the last words not being written until June 1863. The author said that she ' began it a young woman, she finished it an old woman,' and certainly the amount of reading that she did in connection with it was enormous. George E. had said of *Esmond* that there was too much history and too little story. Of *Romola* it may be said that not only was the history of the period ' got up ' for the purpose of writing the novel but that the information she had acquired most disastrously overweighted the book. *Felix Holt* appeared in 1866, *The Spanish Gypsy* two years later, and in 1871–72 was published *Middlemarch*. In spite of the over-elaboration of plot and language, *Middlemarch* will for ever be valuable as a picture of contemporary provincial life, and for the many characters that adorn its vast canvas, albeit it is disfigured by the exaggeration with which Casaubon is portrayed. This book at the time raised the reputation of George E. to the greatest height. *Daniel Deronda* (1874) and *Theophrastus Such* (1878), though successful, did nothing to enhance her fame. Lewes died in the winter of 1878, and George E. lost in him husband, friend, and literary adviser, though it may be doubted whether in this last capacity his influence was entirely for good. She bitterly lamented his loss, and shut herself up from all society for some months. In April 1880, she, to the general surprise, being then in her sixty-first year, married John Walter Cross, whom she had known for many years. She died on Dec. 22 in that year. George E. is one of the great names in the annals of Victorian fiction. Her pictures of lower middle-class life in the Midlands are unsurpassed, and when, as in her earlier novels, she is not unduly didactic, her merits as a painter of character are great. *Adam Bede*, *The Mill on the Floss*, and *Middlemarch* show her at her best, and so good are each of these that critics are undecided as to which is her masterpiece. There is a biography by her husband, 1844, with monographs by Mathilde Blind, 1883, and Sir Leslie Stephen, 1902.

**Eliot, Sir John** (c. 1590–1632), an English statesman, an eloquent debater, and leader of the popular party. He led the Opposition in the parliament of 1626, denounced Buckingham, and was imprisoned for a time. In the third parliament (1628–29), he helped to draw up the Petition of Rights, thus again offending Charles I., who dissolved parliament and imprisoned E. and others. His *Monarchie of Man* (written in the Tower) was not published till 1879–82 with other works of his. *See* Forster's Life, 1864 ; Gardiner's *Hist. of England*, v.–vii., 1603–42 ; ed. of Eliot's *Works* and *Letter-book*, by Grosart, 1827–99.

**Eliot, John** (1604–90), an English missionary to the Indians of Massachusetts, known as ' the Apostle of the Indians.' He attempted to organise the nomadic tribes into a great Christian community, and was minister of Roxbury church, near Boston, U.S.A. E. translated the Bible into the Indian languages (1661–63), wrote an Indian catechism (1653), and grammar (1666) ; *The Christian Commonwealth*, 1659 ; *Harmony of the Gospels*, 1678. *See* Sparks, *Amer. Biog.* v., 1853 ; Walker, *Ten New England Leaders*, 1901.

**Eliot, Sir Thomas**, *see* ELYOT.

**Eliott, General**, *see* HEATHFIELD, GEORGE AUGUSTUS ELIOTT, LORD.

**Elis**, or **Elea**, in ancient Greece an important region of W. Peloponnesus, containing the Olympian valley and watered by the Alpheus and Peneus. It lay between Achaia and Messenia, stretching from Arascus and the R. Larissus (N.) to the R. Neda (S.), and bounded on the W. and E. by the Ionian Sea and Arcadian Mts. It was later incorporated in the Roman province of Achaia. The modern Palæopolis occupies the site of the town of E. Since 1899 it has been a monarchy of Greece, with Pyrgos as the capital. See Strabo, viii. ; Curtius, *Peloponnesus*, 1852 ; Leake, *Morea*, i. and ii., ' Peloponnesiaca.'

**Elisha** (N.T., Eliseus), the son of Shaphat and successor of Elijah, was a great prophet of Israel. He lived during the reigns of Jehoram, Jehu, Jehoahaz, and Jehoash, exercising his ministry over a total period of nearly sixty years. As compared with his predecessor, whose faithful attendant he was, E. shows a mild and beneficent temperament instead of Elijah's fire and austerity. This comparison is fully brought out by a study of their miracles. His story is chiefly told in 2 Kings ii.–ix. E.'s festival is celebrated in the Greek Church on June 14.

**Elixir**, from the Arabic *al-iksir* and ultimately from the Greek *xérion* (a drying powder), is primarily an alchemical term for a supposed agent capable of transforming base metals into gold or silver and of prolonging human life indefinitely. It is therefore approximately equivalent to the philosopher's stone. There were two main Elixirs, viz. the Great Red E. and the White E. The latter turned mercury, etc., into silver, while the former turned silver or any other metal into gold. The term E. is also applied to a drug of syrupy consistency intended to be slowly swallowed to lubricate the throat in cases of cough and irritation. Another meaning of E. is a medicated flavoured syrup.

**Elizabetgrad,** *see* ZINOVIEVSK.

**Elizabeth :** (1) The cap. of Union co., New Jersey, U.S.A., 5 m. from Newark, on the Elizabeth R., Newark Bay, and Staten Island Sound (Elizabethport), forming a residential suburb of New York. There are factories of chemicals, electrical machinery, the Singer Sewing Machine Co.,

princess was brought under this influence also. During the reign of her half-brother Edward VI. she fell under the influence of Lord Seymour, Lord High Admiral of England, for whom she seems to have entertained some affection. He was, however, held to be only exercising his influence for the purpose of attaining his ambition, and was subsequently executed. During Mary's reign, although she had supported the claims of her half-sister in preference to those put forward by Northumberland in favour of Lady Jane Grey, she fell under suspicion. She was accused of complicity in the rising of Sir Thomas Wyatt and was imprisoned in the Tower and later at Woodstock. In 1558 she succeeded to the throne of England without any open opposition. Diplomatic compromise may be taken as the keystone of her reign. She had been educated as a Catholic, but

AUTOGRAPH OF QUEEN ELIZABETH

shipbuilding yards, iron-foundries and railway machine-shops. Settled in 1664 as 'Elizabethtown,' the place has many historical buildings. Pop. 114,589. (2) The cap. of Pasquotank co., North Carolina, U.S.A., on the Pasquotank R., 40 m. from Norfolk, Virginia. It has a fine, deep harbour, cotton-mills, and shipyard. The first General Assembly of Virginia met here in 1665. Pop. 10,037.

**Elizabeth** (1533–1603), Queen of England, daughter of Henry VIII. and Anne Boleyn, *b.* in Greenwich Palace on Sept. 7. After her father's marriage with Jane Seymour, E. and her half-sister Mary were declared illegitimate. Her early childhood was spent under a cloud, as was the greater part of her life until her accession. She was splendidly educated, her tutors had been steeped in the New Learning, and the future queen had the full benefit of this. The influence of the Reformation had by this time been fully felt in England, and the

had imbibed Protestant doctrines, the result being that her religious convictions were somewhat shadowy. She, however, was responsible for the establishment of the Church of England on a basis which she hoped would be acceptable to all, Catholic and Protestant alike, the Thirty-nine Articles and the Book of Common Prayer as we have them at the present time being products of her reign. She, however, became a Protestant, not from religious convictions, but because it was necessary for the salvation of England and the increase of English power that she should be recognised as the Protestant champion of Europe. It is necessary to view the acts of Queen Elizabeth from two standpoints. First, as a queen and therefore the head of the English nation, and secondly as a woman. In her former capacity, ' the days of good Queen Bess ' amply describe the history of the time. By sheer diplomacy she and her ministers teered the ship of state through difficult times. She kept England nominally at peace until it was absolutely essential to strike, and when she struck, she struck with the whole force of a united England behind her. She played off her opponents skilfully one against the other, and in this way saved England from disaster. She kept the peace with Spain and yet at the same time encouraged the attacks made by the privateers of the West upon the Spanish power in America. When the Armada came it cannot be said that England was prepared, save that every Englishman was prepared to face united the efforts of Spain, and the speech of the queen at Tilbury, made when England was face to face with the greatest of her dangers, mirrored the opinion of England excellently. As a queen E. can only be described as popular, brave, courageous, and diplomatic, and perhaps her true greatness lies essentially in the fact that in her and through her England found her own aims and ideals most amply and excellently expressed. She owed her great power and popularity also to the fact that she was able to read the mind of the nation. She had great energy, industry, and physical strength, all essential Tudor qualities. From her mother she inherited great physical attractions, but also a coarseness and boldness which detracted not a little from her physical charms. Her qualities as woman and queen are illustrated by the way in which she made the gift of her hand the centre of the diplomacy of her earlier years. At home her two greatest romances were with the Earl of Leicester and later with the Earl of Essex. Her great passion was, however, for the former. She was inordinately vain, and was also cruel and capricious. Able to make up her mind and to act upon it with a suddenness that confounded her enemies, she also at times seems to have experienced the greatest difficulty in arriving at a decision, as witness her treatment of her cousin, Mary Queen of Scots. Both as a woman and queen she was only too obviously insincere, and the masculinity of her characteristics detracted greatly from what feminine charms she had. The ' Virgin Queen ' passed away at Richmond on March 24. Her reign had seen a great revival in England on practically every side, socially, politically, and in the realm of learning. The English Renaissance came in her reign. Shakespeare, Spenser, Marlowe, Jonson, were all writers during her time, and her reign may be called the golden age of English literature. The revival was experienced not only in letters, but the exploits of the ' pirates of the West ' reflect glory not only upon the reign of E., but also on the history of England for ever. The queen herself was despotic, as had been all the Tudors, but her despotism was based upon the only foundation on which it could be successful, the trust of her subjects. *See* James Anthony Froude, *History of the Reign of Queen Elizabeth* (Everyman's Library); Strickland, *Queen Elizabeth* (Everyman's Library); M. Creighton, *Age of Elizabeth.*

**Elizabeth** (1596–1662), Queen of Bohemia, wife of Frederick V., Elector Palatine, and daughter of James I. of Great Britain and Anne of Denmark, *b.* at Falkland Castle, Fifeshire. From 1603 till her marriage in 1613 she was brought up in England. In 1619 Frederick was chosen to fill the throne of Bohemia, and from that time onwards Elizabeth's life was dogged by misfortune. The king was routed by the Catholic League and the royal family endured sore poverty in Holland. She had thirteen children, among whom were Charles Louis, restored to the electorate in 1648, and Sophia, who afterwards became the mother of George I. of England. See *Five Stuart Princesses* (edited by R. S. Rait), 1902.

**Elizabeth** (Pauline Elizabeth Ottilie Louise) (1843–1916), known under the pseudonym of Carmen Sylva in the literary world, *b.* at Neuwied, Germany, daughter of Prince Hermann of Wied and Princess Maria of Nassau. Married Prince Charles of Rumania in 1869, having previously travelled for five years. In 1881 Rumania was declared a kingdom, and the same year E. was crowned queen. The following year she became a member of the Academy of Sciences of Bucharest, and in 1890 she visited England. She published several volumes of romances, poetry, and philosophical writings— chiefly written in German—including *Bucarest,* 1892; *Das Leben meines Bruders Otto Nicolas, Prinz zu Wied,* 1883 ; *Les Pensées d'une Reine,* 1882 ; *Pilgrim Sorrow* (trans.), 1883 ; *Sparks from the Anvil; or, Thoughts of a Queen,* 1913 ; *A Royal Story Book,* 1911 ; *From Memory's Shrine* (trans. of Reminiscences), 1911 ; *Poems* (trans.) 1912 ; *La Servitude de Pélesch, conte autobiographique,* 1893 ; *Povestile Pelezului,* 1896 ; *In der Lunca,* 1904 ; *Geflüsterte Worte* (essays), 1903, 1906. She wrote in Eng., Fr., Ger., and Rumanian. Became queen-dowager, 1914. Died March 2.

**Elizabeth** (Elisabeth Philippine Marie Hélène of France) (1764–94), commonly known as ' Madame Elizabeth,' sister of Louis XVI., *b.* at

Versailles, guillotined on May 10, 1794.

**Elizabeth, St.,** of Hungary (1207–31), daughter of Andrew II., king of Hungary, *b.* in Pressburg. She married at a very early age Louis IV., landgrave of Thuringia. He was converted by the miracle, much celebrated in Ger. legend, of the changing of the bundle of bread, carried by E. for the poor, into red roses, on his sternly commanding her to display the contents. Louis died in 1227, and E. being persecuted by her brother in-law, Henry Raspe, retired to Marburg, where she eventually died. Four years later she was canonised by Gregory IX. on account of the frequent miracles reported to have been performed at her tomb. *See* Montalembert, *L'Histoire de Sainte Elisabeth de Hongrie,* 1836.

**Elizabeth Petrovna** (1709–62), Empress of Russia and daughter of Peter the Great, *b.* near Moscow. She succeeded to the throne in 1741. The great event of her later years was the Seven Years' War, when the Russians many times defeated Frederick the Great. E. was of a licentious, idle temperament, but inherited some of her father's genius for government. She was also a patroness of art and literature, and was one of the founders of Moscow University. *See* R. N. Bain, *The Daughter of Peter the Great.*

**Elizabethton,** a city, co. seat of Carter co., N.E. Tennessee, U.S.A., making artificial silk, etc. Pop. 8093.

**Elizabeth Tunnel,** 60 m. N. of Los Angeles, California, U.S.A., penetrates the Coast Range Mountains and is five m. long.

**Elizabethville,** a tn., cap. of the Katanga Prov., Belgian Congo, Africa. Founded in 1910. Is 946 m. from Buluwayo, and 1619 from Beira. It has a theatre, park, hospital, public library, an annual agricultural exhibition, and two daily newspapers. Many notable buildings have been erected, including a Rom. Catholic Cathedral; 8 m. away is The Star of the Congo Mine. The smelters of the Union Minière du Haut-Katanga, railway sidings and native compounds, etc., are in the suburb of Lumbumbashi.

**Elizabetpol** (tn. of Russia), *see* YELISAVETPOL.

**Elk,** or **Moose,** *Alces malchis,* the largest living species of forest deer. It is known in the Old World as the E., but in America as the moose, the American 'E.' or wapiti having less resemblance to the European broad-horned deer than to the red deer. The E. is distributed over the forested regions to the N. of Europe and Asiatic Russia, and it is now every-where protected by laws, and carefully preserved. It is easily tamed and has frequently been trained to draw sleighs. The antlers, found in the male alone, have their basal portion, which is in the form of a short cylinder, in the same plane as the forehead. The base expands into a huge, broad 'palm,' at the edge of which are short branches. The height at the shoulders is about 6 ft. In the breeding season, the males fight with great fury, inflicting such wounds with their horns that the combats frequently result in death.

**Elk, Irish,** *Cervus megaceros,* an extinct species of deer closely allied to the fallow-deer of the present day, the bones of which are found among

**SKELETON OF IRISH ELK**

the clays and marls of the Irish bogs and also in certain parts of Great Britain and the continent. It stood 6 ft. in height, and is characterised by the enormous size of its antlers, which sometimes had a spread of close on 11 ft. It became extinct soon after the coming of man to Europe.

**El-Khargeh,** or **The Great Oasis,** a large and fruitful valley in the Libyan desert, the most S. of the Egyptian oases. From 80 to 200 m. long and 10 m. broad.

**Elkhart,** a city of Elkhart co., Indiana, U.S.A., on the St. Joseph R. Important manufacturing centre; has automobile and machine industries, and makes paper, musical instruments and iron bridges. Pop. 32,949.

**Elk-Hound,** a small Norwegian dog which much resembles the Eskimo dog (*q.v.*), but is considerably smaller in size. Its coat is thick, with a full under-coat, and the tail is bushy. The colour is grey, with a darker shade on the back.

**Elkins,** a city of W. Virginia, co. seat of Randoph co., in a lumbering and coal mining region, has various manufactures and a college. Pop. 7,345.

**Ell** (Lat. *ulna*, the forearm), a measure now used to denote length, originally taken in some way from the forearm. The E. varies in different countries, thus the Eng. E. as a measure of cloth is equal to 1¼ yds., the Flemish to ¾ yd., and the Fr. to 1½ yds.

**Ella,** *see* ÆLLA.

**Ellagic Acid,** or **Gallogene** ($C_{14}H_8O_9$), a yellow, odourless powder of agreeable taste only soluble in alkalis. Medicinally it is used as an astringent in cases of tuberculosis and inflammation of the bowels, becoming active only on reaching the alkaline fluids of the intestines.

**Elland,** a tn. in W. Riding of Yorkshire, England. Manufs. woollens and fireclay goods, has iron and dye works. Pop. 10,550.

**Ellenborough, Edward Law,** first **Baron** (1750–1818), was educated at Charterhouse and Cambridge. In 1771 he became a pupil of the special pleader, George Wood (afterwards a Baron of the Exchequer), and four years later began practising on his own account with great success. Called to the Bar in 1780, he was soon in the enjoyment of a large practice. His first great chance came in 1788 when he was retained as leading counsel for the defence of Warren Hastings. His admirable conduct of this case made him famous, and long before it had reached its close he was engaged in many of the most important trials of his day. In 1802 he succeeded Kenyon as Lord Chief Justice, and was raised to the dignity of Baron E. In 1806 he was offered the post of Lord Chancellor in the 'Talents' ministry, but this he declined, though he joined the cabinet without office. Through ill-health he retired from the bench in Nov. 1818. His biography will be found in Campbell's *Lives of the Chief Justices of England*, 1857 (vol. iii.).

**Ellen's Isle,** a small island of Perthshire, Scotland, situated in Loch Katrine. It is celebrated in romance, and immortalised by Sir Walter Scott, who made it the haunt of the Lady of the Lake.

**Ellerman Lines, Ltd.,** a steamship company formed by Sir John Ellerman (formerly chairman of the Leyland Line) in 1901 and registered as the London, Liverpool & Ocean Shipping Co. In the ensuing ten years, it included under the one management the Papayanni Line, the City Line, the Hall Line, the Westcott and Laurence Line, and others. In 1913 it acquired the share capital of Bucknall's Steamship Lines, the name of which was changed in 1914 to Ellerman and Bucknall Steamship Company. Sir J. Ellerman is also chairman of Ellerman's Wilson Line, which was registered in 1891 as Thos. Wilson Sons & Co., the name being changed in 1917 after it was taken over by Sir John Ellerman.

**Ellery, William** (1727–1820), an American politician, *b.* in Newport, Rhode Is. He sat in the Congress of 1776 and was a signatory of the Declaration of Independence.

**Ellesmere :** (1) An urban district in Shropshire, 16 m. N.N.W. of Shrewsbury, on the G.W. and L.M.S. Railways. Pop. 1831. (2) Arctic regions W. of Smith Sound, and opposite N.W. Greenland. They are almost entirely ice and snow-covered wastes.

**Ellesmere, Frances Leveson-Gower Egerton,** first **Earl of** (1800–57), Eng. politician and writer, the second son of the first Duke of Sutherland. From 1828–30 he was Irish Secretary, and Secretary for War in 1830. Amongst his writings are a translation of *Faust*, *History of the War of the Sicilian Vespers*, and *Life of the Duke of Wellington*.

**Ellesmere Canal,** Cheshire, England, belonging to the Manchester Ship Canal, and connecting the Severn and Mersey. Length, 68½ m.

**Ellesmere Port,** an urban dist. and seaport of Cheshire, England, on the Mersey, 6½ m. N. of Chester at the junction of Ellesmere Canal and the Manchester Ship Canal. It is a depôt for iron ore and pig iron and has large docks and warehouses. Pop. 13,075.

**Ellet, Charles** (1810–62), an American engineer, *b.* in Penn's Manor, Bucks co., Pennsylvania. The first wire suspension bridge of the U.S.A., at Fairmount, Philadephia, was his work, and he constructed most of the principal iron and steel bridges in the U.S.A. He is chiefly remembered as the inventor of naval rams, and in the American Civil War equipped nine Mississippi R. steamboats as rams, defeating a fleet of Confederate rams. He met his death during a naval engagement.

**Ellice,** or **Lagoon Islands,** a group of coral islands in the Pacific Ocean to the N. of the Fiji Is., with an area of 14 sq. m. and extending about 350 m. in length. They were annexed by England in 1892, and are administered by the British in conjunction with the Gilbert Is. The principal crops are the pandanus fruit and the coconut, which are the staff of life. Each of the 150 varieties of pandanus bears a distinct name, and most are edible. The one important export is copra. Pop. 3000, all Christianised.

**Ellichpur**, or **Ellichput**, a city in Berar, British India, 100 m. N.W. of Nagpur. It was at one time a great city, but now has little commerce. Contains some interesting ruins. Pop. 23,899.

**Ellicott, Charles John** (1819–1905), an Eng. prelate *b.* at Whitwell, near Stamford, where his father was rector. In 1861 he was made dean of Exeter, and two years later bishop of Gloucester and Bristol. His episcopate lasted forty-two years, and he threw himself vigorously into diocesan work. In 1857 E. was one of the five clergymen who published a revision of the gospel of St. John, followed by revisions of the Romans and Corinthians and other epistles. He also wrote *The Destiny of the Creature, Our Reformed Church and its Present Troubles*, etc.

**Elliot, Sir Gilbert**, *see* MINTO, EARL OF.

**Elliot, Jane** (1727–1805), a Scottish poetess, daughter of Sir Gilbert E., *b.* at Minto House, Teviotdale. The greater part of her life (1756–1804) was passed in Edinburgh. She is remembered for her most exquisite ballad, *The Flowers of the Forest*, a touching lyric on the disaster of Flodden. Sir Gilbert Elliot, her eldest brother, was also a song-writer.

**Elliotson, John** (1791–1868), an Eng. physician, *b.* at Southwark, London. He studied medicine at Edinburgh and Cambridge, and in 1834 became physician to University College Hospital. He was a student of hypnotism and mesmerism, and in 1838 was compelled to resign his offices on this account. He edited a magazine, *The Zoist*, devoted to the subject, and founded a mesmeric hospital in 1849. E. was one of the first British physicians to advocate the use of the stethoscope. Among his publications are : *Lectures on Diseases of the Heart, Human Physiology, Surgical Operations in the Mesmeric State without Pain*. Thackeray dedicated his *Pendennis* to E.

**Elliott, Ebenezer** (1781–1849), an Eng. poet, the 'corn-law rhymer,' *b.* near Rotherham, Yorkshire. He was educated at various schools, and in 1797 entered his father's iron foundry. He had a successful career at Sheffield as a bar-iron merchant, and on his retirement in 1841 settled at Great Houghton. From the age of seventeen he began writing poems, publishing the *Vernal Walk*, in imitation of Thomson, in 1801. He is chiefly remembered, however, for his *Corn-law Rhymes* (3rd ed. 1831), which are vigorous, simple, and full of a vivid description. They are inspired by a fierce hatred of injustice, and by their sincerity and earnestness are saved from the common fate of political poetry. *See* Carlyle's essay, 'Corn-law Rhymes,' in *Miscellanies*, iv.

**Elliott, May Gertrude (Lady Forbes-Robertson)**, an actress, *b.* Dec. 14, 1874, at Rockland, Maine, U.S.A., sister of Maxine E. She made her first appearance on the stage at New York with E. S. Willard in *The Middleman*, and was first seen on the London stage at Daly's Theatre in 1895 as Sylvia in *The Two Gentlemen of Verona*. She married Johnston Forbes-Robertson in 1900, and since played many leading parts with him. Her most successful rôles are those of Desdemona, Ophelia, the 'slavey' in *The Passing of the Third Floor Back*, Little Britain in *Mice and Men*, and Maisie in *The Light that Failed*. Her later parts include Gina Ashling in *The Eyes of Youth*, 1918 ; Sarah Gilman in *Sarah of Soho*, 1922 ; and Maria in *Twelfth Night*, 1927.

**Ellipse.** In general language an E. is a regular oval. In geometry it may be defined in a number of different ways, of which two are given here :

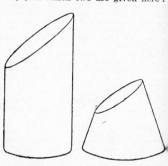

(1) The section of a cone by any plane less inclined to the base of the cone than is the side of the cone. (2) An oblique section of a right cylinder or the oblique projection of a circle. An E. is the orbit of a particle moving under the influence of a central force, which varies inversely as the square of the distance of the particle. This law is the gravitational law of force, and an E. represents the orbit of a planet, if the individual planet and the sun are considered alone (the other planets exert attractions and disturb the orbit).

The *foci* of an E. are the points S and S¹, such that the sum of the distances SP and S¹P of any point on the E. from the foci is the same whatever the position of P. The straight line

AA¹ passing through the foci is the *major axis*, and the line BB¹, perpendicular to AA¹ at its middle point, is the *minor axis*. If AA¹ = 2a and BB¹ = 2b, C² = A²(1 − e), where e is the *eccentricity*. Also SP + S¹P = 2a. If AOA¹ and BOB¹ be taken as the axes, the co-ordinates of the point P (ON and OT) are connected by the equation :

$$\frac{x^2}{a^2} + \frac{y^2}{b^2} = 1$$

(where ON = x and OT = y).

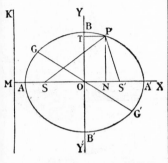

The *diameter* is any straight line through the centre, terminated by the E., such as GOG¹. The *directrix* is the line MK, such that the distance of P from the focus S bears a constant ratio less than unity to the distance of P from MK.

**Ellipsoid**, in geometry, a solid body whose plane sections through one of the axes are ellipses ; all other sections are ellipses or circles. The term is often used to indicate the solid body generated by the rotation of an ellipse about one of its axes ; but it is better to use the term spheroid for this body. The E. is very largely used in the mathematical theories of elasticity, heat and light, *e.g.* the strain E., E. of expansion, or the wave surface in a doubly refracting substance.

**Elliptic Compasses.** The trammel, or E. C., depends on the fact that the sum of the distances of a point on an ellipse from the foci is a constant.

**Elliptic Polarisation.** Elliptically polarised light, when examined with a Nicol's prism, will give an illumination which will vary as the Nicol is rotated. It is thus distinguished from ordinary light, but not from a mixture of ordinary and plane polarised light. It may be distinguished by first passing the light through a quarter wave plate of mica with its axis parallel or perpendicular to the plane of maximum polarisation ; for elliptically polarised light thus becomes plane polarised, and may be extinguished on rotating the Nicol's prism.

**Ellis, Alexander John** (1814–90), an Eng. phonetician, mathematician, and musician. His original name was Sharpe, but he assumed the surname Ellis (1825). He was associated with Sir J. Pitman, founding the system of printing known as ' phonotypy.' His works include *Phonetics* . . ., 1844 ; *Essentials of Phonetics*, 1848 ; *The Hist. of Musical Pitch*, 1880 ; *Pronunciation for Singers*, 1877. See *Proc. Roy. Soc.*, xlix., 1891 ; *Phonetic Journal*, 1890.

**Ellis George** (1753–1815), an author, sprang into notoriety in 1778 with the publication of *Poetical Tales, by Sir Gregory Gander*. He was one of the contributors to the *Rolliad*, and in later years, with Canning, founded the *Anti-Jacobin*. In 1790 he published *Specimens of the Early English Poets*, and fifteen years later, *Specimens of Early English Romances in Metre*.

**Ellis, Sir Henry** (1777–1869), an Eng. antiquarian, assistant librarian at the Bodleian, Oxford, and the British Museum (1800), chief librarian of the British Museum (1827–56). His works include an edition of Brand's *Popular Antiquities*, 1813 ; of Dugdale's *Monasticon* (with others), 1817–33 ; *Introduction to Domesday Book*, 1816 ; *Original Letters Illustrative of Eng. Hist.* (three series), 1823–46 ; *Elgin Marbles of the Classic Ages ;* and *The Townley Gallery of Sculpture*, 1847. E. was director of the Society of Antiquaries for many years.

**Ellis, Henry Havelock** (*b.* 1859), a fellow of the Medico-legal Society of New York, *b.* in Croydon, Surrey. He was educated at St. Thomas's Hospital, and was engaged in teaching in New South Wales (1875–79). Returning to England, he practised as a doctor, but soon abandoned this profession to devote himself to literature. His publications include *Man and Woman : A Study of Human Secondary Sexual Characters*, 1894 and 1904 ; *The Evolution of Modesty*, 1899 and 1910 ; *Sexual Inversion*, 1897 ; *Sex in Relation to Society*, 1910 ; *The Soul of Spain*, 1908 ; *The World of Dreams*, 1911 ; *The Task of Social Hygiene*, 1912 ; *Impressions and Comments*, 1914, 1921, and 1924 ; *Essays in War-Time*, 1916 ; *Kanga Creek*, 1922 ; *Sonnets with Folk Songs from the Spanish*, 1925.

**Ellis, Robinson** (1834–1913), an Eng. philologist and classical scholar, educated at Guernsey, Rugby, and Oxford. He published numerous critical works on Catullus and translations, *Catulli Veronensis Liber*, 1867,

1878; *Fragments of Catullus*, 1871; *Commentary on Catullus*, 1876. Other works are Ovid's *Ibis*, 1881; ' Glossæ in Apollinarem Sidonium' (*Anec. Oxon.*, Classical Series), 1885; ' Orientii Carmina' (*Vienna Corp. Script. Eccles.*, xvi.), 1888; *New Fragments of Juvenal*, 1901; *Appendix Vergiliana*, 1907; *The Annalist Licinianus*, 1908; *The Amores of Ovid*, 1912, and various articles in many journals and classical reviews. Died at Oxford Oct. 9.

**Ellis, William** (1794–1872), an Eng. missionary, sent by the London Missionary Society to the S. Pacific Islands (1816–25). From 1831 to 1841 he was foreign secretary to the London Missionary Society. His visits to Madagascar resulted in *Hist. of Madagascar*, 1838; *Three Visits to Madagascar*, 1858; *Madagascar Revisited*, 1867; *The Martyr Church*, 1870. Other works were *Polynesian Researches*, 1829; *A Tour through Owhyhee*, 1826. *See* Life by J. E. Ellis, 1873.

**Ellis Island**, a small is. in New York harbour, 1 m. from Manhattan Is., used as an immigrant station (since 1892) and a magazine.

**Elliston, Robert William** (1774–1831), an Eng. actor and manager, first appearing (1791) as Tressel in *Richard III.* at Bath. In 1796 he came to the Haymarket, London, and was manager there (1803). E. was considered one of the finest actors of his day, especially in comedy, and was praised by Lamb and Leigh Hunt. *See* Life by Raymond (1848, 1857), Oxberry (1826).

**Ellon**, a par. and vil. of E. Aberdeenshire, Scotland, on the Ythan, 12½ m. from Inverurie. Once the cap. of Buchan, the village belonged to Kinloss Abbey. Pop. of par. 3437.

**Ellora, The caves of**, in the Nizam of Hyderabad's dominions, India, 2 m. from the walled tn. of Ravza or Khuldabad, the holy shrine of the Deccan Mussulmans, and the burialplace of the Emperor Aurangzeb and many other celebrities. Ravza is now in great part deserted, and ruins of mosques and tombs abound in every direction. The E. group of cave temples comprises twelve Buddhist, seventeen Brahman, and five Jain works. They are mentioned by an Arab geographer of the fifteenth century as a celebrated place of pilgrimage. The Buddhist caves date from 350–750 A.D. The Brahman caves were probably constructed in the seventh and eighth centuries A.D. There are sculptures of the slaughter of the Buffalo demon, Siva and Parvati playing chess, three skeleton demon gods, Bhairava with a necklace of skulls, three river goddesses, etc. The five Jain caves date from the eighth to the thirteenth century.

**Ellore**, a tn. of Godavari dist., Madras, British India, 37 m. from Masulipatam, near Lake Kolar. It was once the cap. of the N. Circars. There are carpet manufs. Pop. about 29,500.

**Ellsworth**, a city of Hancock co., Maine, U.S.A., at the mouth of Union R., 27 m. S.E. of Bangor. It has a trade in timber and fish. Pop. 3557.

COMMON ELM

A. leaf; B. flowering branch; C. flower (enlarged); D. fruit (samaras).

**Ellsworth, Oliver** (1745–1807), an American statesman and jurist, *b.* at Windsor, Connecticut; studied at Yale and Princeton, and practised law at Hartford, 1771. Was a member of the General Assembly of Connecticut, and held many legal and political offices in the state. Advised Washington to send Jay to England to negotiate a new treaty. Appointed by Washington Chief Justice of the Supreme Court, 1796, and was sent by Adams to France to negotiate a new treaty.

**Ellwangen**, a tn. of Germany, in Würtemberg, and cap. of Jagst, W. of the Ellwangen mountain crowned by a castle built in 1354, containing a collection of antiquities and the Schönenberg with a pilgrimage church. It possesses many fine churches and owes its origin to a monastery founded in 750 A.D. Pop. 5650.

**Ellwood, Thomas** (1639–1714), an Eng. author and Quaker preacher, intimate friend of and reader to Milton after he became blind. E. first suggested to Milton the idea of his second epic, *Paradise Regained*, after reading the MS. of *Paradise Lost*, 1665. E.'s own works include : *Sacred History of the Old and New Testaments*, 1705–9 ; *Forgery no Christianity*, 1674, and other polemical works ; *Darideis* (a poem), 1712 ; *Autobiography*, 1714.

. **Elm**, the name applied to species of *Ulmus*, four of which occur in Britain, while all the sixteen are to be found in N. lands and on Asiatic mountains. The fruit is characteristic, being a one-seeded samara, and the leaves are curious, the sides being unequal in size. *U. campestris*, the common or small-leaved E., and *U. montana*, the wych-elm, are our best-known species; *U. Americana* is a tall tree and yields a good timber.

**Elman, Mischa**, *b.* 1891, at Talnoi, Russia. Russian violinist of Jewish descent. Trained by Fidelmann and Auer. He first appeared in London in 1904 and in New York, 1906, and is now one of the leading violinists of the world.

**Elmina**, or **St. George del Mina** (native *Odena*), a dist. and fort. tn. of the Gold Coast. British W. Africa formerly (till 1872) capital of the Dutch possessions in Guinea. Close by is the inlet of Baya, with the suburb Garden Town. It was founded about 1471. It exports palm oil, gold and ivory. Pop. 20,000.

**Elmira**, cap. of Chemung co., New York, U.S.A., on Chemung R. (New town Creek), 74 m. from Syracuse. An important railway centre. The more important industries include railroad car shops, steel bridge plants, valve and radiator works, and the manuf. of shoes, fire engines, silk and knitted goods and bicycles. It is the seat of Elmira College for Women, and of the noted Reformatory. Pop. 47,397. See Winter, *The Elmira Reformatory*, 1891.

**El Misti**, or **Arequipa Volcano**, a grand, almost extinct volcanic mountain of the Andes, Peru (*c.* 20,000 ft.), close to Arequipa. Harvard University erected a meteorological observatory near the summit, in use from 1893 to 1901. There are various stations at Mont Blanc (15,700 ft.), Pampa de los Huesos (13,400 ft.), and Mollendo (sea-level). The name is also applied sometimes incorrectly to Huayna Putina volcano, S.E. of Arequipa.

**Elmshorn**, a tn. of Schleswig-Holstein prov., Prussia. It manufs.

textiles, margarine and sausages, and carries on shipbuilding and tanning. Pop. 15,400.

**Elmsley, Peter** (1773–1825), an Eng. philologist, classical scholar, and critic. He assisted Davy in deciphering the papyri found at Herculaneum (1819). E. produced excellent critical editions of several dramas of Sophocles and Euripides. See *Elmsleiana Critica* (Cambridge), 1833.

**El Obeïd**, or **Il-Obeïd**, the cap. of Kordofan, Egyptian Sudan, Africa, 240 m. from Sennaar. There are several mosques and the barracks of the Sudan Camel Corps. An Anglo-Egyptian army, under Hicks Pasha, was annihilated by a Mahdist force close by (1883). It is the terminus of the railway from Cairo and its pop. of 17,000 is rapidly increasing.

**Elocution** (Lat. *elocutio*, from *eloqui*, to speak out), a branch of oratory which teaches the art of effective speaking, especially public speaking, having regard solely to the utterance or delivery. It directs the proper use of gesture, the modulation of the voice, and deals generally with the methods of speaking. In anct. times E. held a prominent place in education, and great attention was paid to the study of it in Greece and Rome. Nowadays it is even more carefully cultivated in the U.S.A. than in Britain, its teaching having diminished in the latter country during the second half of the nineteenth century. See Bell's *Standard Elocutionist* and Ward's *System of Oratory*.

**Eloge** (ϵὐλογία, praise), an encomium or panegyrical oration in honour of a deceased person, describing his merits and services, especially one pronounced by the secretary of the Fr. Academy, or by a newly-elected member on his predecessor. These *éloges académiques* form a considerable branch of Fr. literature. See *Eloges* of Fontenelle (1731), Thomas (1759–70), Alembert (1779–87), Cuvier (1819–27), and Flourens (1833–67).

**Elohim** (Heb. plur. of *Eloāh*, God), one of the chief names by which God is designated in the Hebrew Scriptures. The plural expresses the idea of greatness and supremacy, and is mainly used with a singular verb as a title of the Supreme Being, especially in N. Hebrew literature. It was probably of later date than the title ' Yahweh ' (Jehovah), which was considered as a more personal and intimate name for the Deity. Writers of O.T . passages (especially of the Pentateuch) in which the name E. occurs are called Elohists. (*See* J·HVIST.) See Kautzsch, *History of Old Testament Literature* (Taylor's trans.), 1898 ; Schultz, *Old Testament Theology*, ii. (trans. 1892).

**Elohist,** see HEXA EUCH.

**Eloi (or El gius), Saint** (588–*c.* 659), a Fr. benefactor, founder of many monasteries and hospitals. He was a favourite minister of Clotaire II. and Dagobert I. He is the patron-saint of jewellers and goldsmiths. In 640 he became Bishop of Noyon. *See* St. Ouen (Audœnus), *Vita;* Migne, *Patrol. Lat.*, lxxxvii., 1844–64.

**Elongation,** in astronomy, the angular distance of a heavenly body from some relatively fixed point, such as the angular distance of a planet from the sun or of a satellite from its primary, as seen from the earth. Thus the angular distance of Venus is about 45°.

**Elopement,** the secret departure of a woman from the house or home to which she is bound by ties of law or duty. The word is most commonly applied to the conduct of a daughter who runs away from her father to contract a clandestine marriage with her lover. Thus, from 1754 onward Eng. sweethearts would elope to Gretna Green, where they could easily and quickly become legal man and wife.

**El Paso,** a port and cap. of E. P. co., Texas, U.S.A., on the Rio Grande, opposite Ciudad Juarez (El Paso del Norte), Mexico. The industries include smelting, flour-milling, railway car repairing, box-making and meat packing, and the trade is in copper, silver, lead, wool, hides and live stock, especially with Mexico. Seekers for nearly perennial sunshine find it at E. P., at an elevation of 3800 ft. Pop. (1910) 39,279, (1920) 77,560, (1930) 102,421.

**Elphin,** a tn. of co. Roscommon, Ireland, formerly the seat of a bishop. The see, however, no longer exists, having been united with Kilmore in 1833. Pop. 649.

**Elphinstone, George Keith,** see KEITH, VISCOU T.

**Elphinstone, Mountstuart** (1779–1859), an Eng. historian and statesman, son of the eleventh Baron E. Educated at Edinburgh and Kensington, he entered the Civil Service of the E. India Company (1796), and became one of the founders of the Anglo-Indian empire. E. was aide-de-camp to Wellesley (1803), sharing in his campaign; envoy to Kabul (1808), and resident at Poonah (1810–17). He helped to win the Battle of Kirki against the Mahrattas (1817), and was made Governor of Bombay (1819–27). He ruled wisely in the Deccan, but refused the governor generalship of India owing to ill-health. He wrote : *Account of the Kingdom of Cobool* . . . 1815 ; and *History of India* . . ., 1841. *See* Colebrooke's Life, 1884 ; Heber's *Indian Journal*, 1844 ; Kaye, *Lives of Indian Officers ;* Mill, *History of India*, 1841 ; *Journ. Roy. Asiatic Soc.*, xviii. pt. 2.

**Elphinstone, William** (1431–1514), a Scottish prelate and statesman, Bishop of Aberdeen (1483), and founder of King's College, Aberdeen (1494, completed 1506). He helped to establish the printing-press of Chepman and Millar, 1507. His chief work is the *Breviarium Aberdonense*, 1509–10 (reprinted 1853). *See* Boece's *Memoir* (Moir's trans.), 1894 ; Gardyne, *Lyf of W. Elphinston*, 1878 (Laing's ed.).

**El Reno,** a tn. of Oklahoma, U.S.A., 30 m. from Oklahoma. Has a collection of Indian curios and relics, a remount station for the U.S.A. Army and graded schools for Indian children. It is on the Meridian Auto Highway from Winnipeg to the City of Mexico. Its industries include railroad shops and incubator factories. Pop. 9. 84.

**Elsheimer (or Elzheimer), Adam** (*c.* 1574–1620), a Ger. landscape-painter. He worked largely in Rome, and was called by the Italians ' Adamo Tedesco.' His pictures are mostly small and beautifully finished. He excelled in colour and chiaroscuro, and in imitation of nature, and his scenes by torchlight and moonlight were much admired. E. was founder of the school later represented by Rembrandt and Claude Lorrain. His works include : ' Flight into Egypt ' (Louvre), ' Ceres in Search of Persephone,' ' Tobit and the Angel ' (engraved by Count Goudt), ' Christianity Triumphing over Paganism,' ' Martyrdom of St. Lawrence ' (National Gallery). *See* Passavant, *A. Elsheimer*, 1847.

**Elssler,** the name of two celebrated Austrian dancers. *Thérèse* (1808–78) and *Fanny* (1810–84). They made tours in Europe and America. Beautiful, of kindly disposition, and possessing complete mastery of their art, they were everywhere beloved and admired.

**Elster, Black,** or **Schwarze,** a river of Germany, rising in Upper Lusatia, E. Prussian Saxony. The B. E. flows into the Elbe, 9 m. from Wittenberg. A branch, the Neue Graben, forms an island 19 m. long.

**Elster, White,** flows N. past Greiz, Gera, and Leipzig, finally joining the Saale 3 m. from Halle. A branch, the Luppe, also flows into the Saale. Length about 120 m. Little of either the Black or White river is navigable.

**Elstow,** a par. of Bedfordshire, England, 2 m. from Bedford. John

Bunyan was *b.* in this village (1628). Pop. 412.

**Elswick,** a par. and W. suburb of Newcastle, Northumberland, England. It has rapidly increased in importance since the opening of Armstrong's engineering works (1847). Pop. 12,556.

**Elswick Works.** Founded by Sir Wm. G. Armstrong (*q.v.*) in 1847 as engineering works, and ordnance works were added in 1857. They changed from a private concern to a limited company in 1882, and amalgamated with the Whitworth Company of Manchester in 1897. There are shipyards for mercantile vessels at Walker-on-Tyne, and for warships at Elswick.

**Eltham,** a par., Kent, England, pleasantly situated 3 m. S. of Woolwich. Its royal palace was destroyed during the Commonwealth. Pop. 28,308.

**Elton,** a shallow salt lake in the gov. of Astrakhan, Russia. It receives eight salt-water streams and has no outlet. The Crimean salt fields now supply the salt for which this lake was once worked.

**Elton, Charles Isaac** (1839–1900), an English jurist and ethnologist. His valuable *Origins of English History* deals with the Celtic element in the English race. He wrote also *Custom and Tenant Right.*

**Elutriation** (Lat. *elutriare*, to wash out), the process of separating lighter and heavier pulverised substances by washing out or decanting. The method is employed in the preparation of clay and other materials for pottery manufacture. The material is placed with water in a vat where grinding wheels pulverise the material and keep the water flowing; the finer particles pass with the water into settling vats where they are deposited.

**Elvan,** the name given by Cornish miners to dykes of quartz-porphyry, granite-porphyry or other Plutonic rock found in association with granite and penetrating sedimentary strata. The rock is granular and crystalline and is called by geologists ' quartz-felsite.' It is used for road-mending and for building stone.

**Elvas,** the strongest fortified city of Portugal, near the Spanish frontier, 10 m. W. of Badajoz; trade in wool, wines, fruits, and oil; fine old Roman aqueduct. It has a Roman–Moorish castle, cathedral, theatre, library, etc. Pop. 11,747.

**Elves,** *see* ELF, FAIRIES, etc.

**Elvey, Sir George Job** (1816–93), an English organist and composer, *b.* at Canterbury, where he became a chorister in the cathedral. When only nineteen he was appointed organist at the Chapel Royal,

Windsor. He composed two oratorios, many anthems, etc., and the tune to ' Come, ye thankful people, come.'

**Elwes, Gervase Henry** (1866–1921), Eng. tenor, *b.* Nov. 15, 1866, at Billing, Northants; son of V. D. H. Cary-Elwes. Educated: Oratory School, Edgbaston; Woburn School; and Christ Church, Oxford. Hon. attaché at Munich, 1891; later at Vienna and Brussels. Studied music at Vienna, Brussels, and Paris.

THE WESTERN TOWER OF ELY CATHEDRAL

Abandoned diplomacy, 1895. First public appearance as singer : Westmorland festival, 1903. Sang in 150 performances of *The Dream of Gerontius.* Killed by accidental blow from door of a train in Boston, Mass., Jan. 12, 1921.

**Ely,** a city of Cambridgeshire, 16 m. N.N.E. of Cambridge, situated on rising ground near the R. Ouse in the midst of the fens. It was one of the last strongholds of the Saxons; here Hereward's ' camp of refuge ' held out against the Conqueror. Its cathedral is one of the finest of the Christian churches, and one of the largest in England. It presents examples of Saxon, Norman, and Early English architecture. On its site St. Etheldreda founded, in 673, a monastery, which the Danes burnt down in 870; Ethelwold, Bishop of Winchester, founded a Benedictine abbey about the year 1000; the present cathedral was begun in 1083 and finished in 1534. Its length is 530 ft., breadth across the transepts 180 ft., height 62 ft., the western tower is 225 ft. high. During 1322–42 the central tower fell, and the decorated lantern tower, built by Alan de Walsingham to replace it, is one of the most interesting features of the cathedral as being the only existing specimen of a Gothic dome. The choir exhibits great splendour of carving and sculpture. Among historical personages connected with E. are Bishop Thurston, Canute, and Cromwell, who lived here 1636–40. Market-gardening is carried on, and pottery and clay pipes are manufactured. Pop. (1911) 7917. *See* Clement, *History of Ely :* and Stewart, *Architectural History of Ely Cathedral.*

**Elwood City,** a borough of Lawrence co., Pennsylvania, U.S.A., 36 m. N.W. of Pittsburgh, manufacturing steel, brass, etc. Pop. 12,323.

**Elymais,** a tn. and dist. of Susiana, in Persia. The tn. contains a famous temple which Antiochus the Great wished to despoil in order to pay his tribute to Rome.

**Elymas,** the title of Bar-jesus, who in the presence of Sergius Paulus, Governor of Cyprus, withstood Paul and Barnabas (*Acts,* ch. xiii). E. is explained as *Magos,* 'Sorcerer,' and the word seems akin to the Arabic ' alama,' ' to know,' whence ' alim,' ' learned Man.' E. seems to have been a representative of that system of interpreting Nature and natural powers which in the anct. world took the place now occupied by science. It claimed to be a religion as well, and wonders wrought by means revealed only to the initiated, possibly at times by legerdemain and at others by recondite forces, were relied upon to secure adherents. E. doubtless regarded Paul and Barnabas as rivals competing for the favour of the governor, and employed his black arts against them. Paul replied in kind; and the blindness that fell upon the ' sorcerer ' was demonstration of a power behind the apostle greater than any known to E. The Cypriot, Simon, who assisted Felix against Drusilla, and Simon Magus, probably belonged to the same class. (*Temple Bible Dict.*)

**Elyot, Sir Thomas** (*c.* 1490–1546), an Eng. writer and diplomatist, best known as the author of *The Governour,* the first treatise on education, written and printed (1531) in Eng. In 1511 he was clerk of assize, while his father was judge; Henry VIII. employed him on several diplomatic missions. He was a friend of Sir Thomas More. Among his many works are : *Bibliothecæ Elyotæ,* a Latin-English dictionary still of philological interest; *The Castel of Helth, The Defence of Good Women,* and *The Image of Governance,* an allegorical work in which he attacks the vices of his time.

**Elyria,** a city of N. Ohio, with many manufactures, including laces, heaters, invalid chairs, fishing tackle, chemicals, golf balls, automobiles and engines. Pop. 25,633.

**Elysium, or The Elysian Fields,** in anct. mythology the place where dwell in perfect happiness the departed heroes and virtuous men favoured by Zeus. Homer's Elysium is a beautiful meadow at the W. extremity of the earth, on the banks of the R. Oceanus. Subsequents poets deviate somewhat from Homer's conception.

**Elytra** (Gk. ἔλυτρον), the name given to the horny sheaths which constitute the fore-wings of beetles. They fold over the back, generally meeting in the middle in a straight line, and serve to protect the hindwings and the soft posterior parts of the body. The presence of E. is the distinguishing mark of beetles, but they are also to be met within earwigs.

**Elze, Frederich Karl** (1821–89), a Ger. writer, who became a celebrated Shakespearian scholar. He was *b.* at Dessau and was appointed to the chair of Eng. at Halle in 1875. He wrote *William Shakespeare, Englischer Liederschatz,* a work on the Elizabethan dramatists, and translated *Hamlet.*

**Elzevir,** the name of a family of celebrated Dutch printers and publishers of the sixteenth and first half of the seventeenth centuries. The Es. issued beautiful editions, whose value time has increased. The family is supposed to have come from Liège or Louvain, or possibly even from Spain. The founder of the E. Press was *Louis* (1540–1617), *b.* at Louvain, but who, as a supporter of the Reformation, took refuge in Leyden, where—and subsequently at The Hague—he became a bookseller and publisher. He was succeeded by his five sons, *Matthias, Louis, Gilles, Joost,* who practised in Utrecht, and *Bonaventura* (1583–1652), who carried on the Leyden house in association with his nephew, *Abraham,* for twenty-six years, during which time most of its masterpieces were issued. Many of these were printed for his uncle Bonaventura by *Isaac,* who printed also for his brother *Jacob,* established at The Hague. Isaac was the first printer of the family. Isaac's son, *Louis,* was the founder of the house in Amsterdam. Under him, in association with his cousin *Daniel*, the work reached perhaps its highest standard (1639–55). Of the total number of works (1208) produced by the Es., 968 were Latin, 44 Gk., 22 in Oriental languages, 120 French, 33 Flemish, 11 Ger., and 10 Italian. *See* Willems, *Les Elzéviers*.

**Emæus**, the faithful swineherd in the *Odyssey*, who recognises Odysseus on his return, and aids him in destroying the suitors.

**Emanation** (Lat. *emanatio*, a flowing forth), an anct. system of philosophy according to which all existences have successively flowed or emanated from the Supreme Essence, from God. This doctrine is found in Egyptian and Indian mythology, in Neoplatonism, and in Christian Gnosticism.

**Emancipation**, in the Rom. law, was the act by which a father set his son free from paternal authority. The twelve tables required that the son should be formally sold three times, bought back, and then liberated according to the ceremony for freeing slaves. *See* Abolitionists and Catholic Emancipation.

**Emancipation of Catholics**, *see* Catholic Emancipation.

**Emancipation of Slaves**, *see* Abolitionists; Manumission.

**Emanuel I.** (1469–1521), King of Portugal, surnamed the Great, the Fortunate; became king in 1495. His reign is the most brilliant in the history of Portugal. A code of laws prepared by the king and a court in which chivalry, art, and science were encouraged, greatly improved the internal condition of the country. Externally its possessions were extended by the explorations of Vasco da Gama, Cabral, and Albuquerque, and Portugal became the first naval and commercial power of the world.

**Emba**, a riv. of Asiatic Russia, prov. Uralsk. It rises in the Mugoyar Hills and flows 380 m. into the Caspian.

**Embabane**, or **Mbabane**, a tn. of Swaziland. British S. Africa, 12 m. N.W. of Bremersdorp. It became the seat of gov. in 1905. There are tin mines. White pop. 320.

**Embalming**, the art of preparing and preserving dead bodies from decay, principally by the use of medicaments. It was widely practised by the ancients, more especially in Egypt, where it was carried to a fine art, and the body so preserved there was called a mummy, a word derived from the Arabic for bitumen. It has been suggested that the origin of E. in Egypt was to be traced to a dearth of fuel for cremation purposes, or to the impracticability of burying bodies in a soil that was annually disturbed by the inroads of the Nile. This

explanation, however, seems to be far from satisfactory, and E. doubtless originated in the idea of preserving the body for a future life. The anct. Egyptians embalmed not only human beings, but also sacred animals, such as cats, crocodiles, etc. Modern E. dates from the eighteenth century. Dr. Frederich Ruysch, of Amsterdam, is said to have employed the use of alcohol, while William Hunter used essential oils, camphor, saltpetre, pitch, or resin. Then, again, J. J. Boudet (1778–1849) embalmed with tan, salt, camphor,

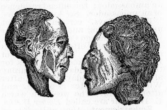

HEADS OF EGYPTIAN MUMMIES

cinnamon, and other aromatics. Later on, fluids were injected, consisting of sodium chloride, alum, potash, glycerine, or composed of alkalis, arsenic, and alcohol. In the Royal College of Surgeons, London, are still to be seen bodies preserved by William and John Hunter, the renowned anatomists.

**Embankments**, mounds, banks, or earthworks raised for the purpose of protecting the land from the inroads of the sea or overflow of rivers; a levee, such as the Thames E. Reservoirs are formed of dams, or E. of earth, or, in hot countries, of cement. E. in engineering, therefore, serve two main classes of utility: they preserve the level of railways, canals, and roads where a piece of low-lying ground has to be crossed, or they confine a body of water by preventing it encroaching on the land. E. are much used for irrigation purposes, *e.g.* the great dam of the Nile at Assouan.

**Embargo** (a Spanish word meaning 'stoppage'), the seizure of a ship or ships, either as a matter of precaution, or in view of hostilities. E. is the most usual form of reprisals, and thus constitutes the temporary or permanent sequestration of the property of individuals by the government in times of peace or war. Es. in anticipation of war, however, have long since fallen into disuse, and it has even become customary for the belligerents to grant a respite to the enemy's trading vessels to leave their ports at the outbreak of war. The Hague Conventions of 1907 confirmed this, and only that power in a state which is authorised to declare war can decree an E., hence, in its hostile sense, it is an act of war. The sequestration by a nation of vessels or goods of its own citizens or subjects for public uses is sometimes called a *civil* E., in contradistinction to a general prohibition from leaving port intended to affect the trade or naval operations of another nation, known as *international* E.

**Embassy**, a mission entrusted to an ambassador ; the official residence of an ambassador. *See* AMBASSADORS.

**Ember Days**, certain days set apart for fasting and special prayer in the Anglican and Catholic churches. The clergy are often ordained on certain E. D. The council of Placentia (1095) fixed these days for the Wednesday, Friday, and Saturday after the first Sunday in Lent, after Whit Sunday, after Sept. 14, and after Dec. 13. The weeks in which E. D. occur are called *Ember Weeks.*

**Embezzlement**, the unlawful or fraudulent appropriation to his own use by a servant or clerk of money or goods received by him for and on account of his master or employer. To convict of this felony (*see* under CRIMINAL LAW) the prosecution must prove that the accused was a clerk or servant of the person robbed, that the money or goods alleged to be embezzled were received for or in the name of or on account of his employer or master, and that the accused intended to appropriate unlawfully such money or goods. The crime of E. is to be distinguished from larceny (*q.v.*) in that the original taking of the property was lawful, while the gist of larceny is the wilfully wrongful taking possession against the will of another from the very beginning. Some specific sum must be proved to have been appropriated, it being settled law that a general deficiency in the accounts of the accused will not suffice to prove the charge. Three separate acts of E. may be charged in the same indictment where committed against the same employer or master, within six months from the first to the last of such acts. If the accused be indicted for E. that will not preclude a conviction for larceny instead, if the facts turn out to be more consistent with the latter crime having been committed. The converse also applies. The punishment for the common law felony of E. is a maximum of fourteen years' penal servitude or imprisonment up to two years. E. by factors, trustees, and directors is a mis-

demeanour, punishable with seven years' and two years' respectively (*see also* FALSIFICATION OF ACCOUNTS ; FRAUD). In U.S.A. the law of E. is founded principally on the Eng. Act of 1799, passed to meet the *casus omissus* of a clerk in Esdaile's bank, who received a note for £100 which he appropriated instead of crediting the bank's customer with it. The statutes of the majority of the states are drafted so as to include E. in larceny, and indeed sometimes call E. by the name of statutory larceny. The punishment varies in the different states. *Authorities :* Harris, *Principles of Criminal Law ;* Archbold's *Criminal Pleading Practice.*

**Emblements**, the produce of land, such as crops, garden, cereal, and vegetable products, which are the annual result of the tenant's labour. These are considered in law as belonging to the tenant and not to the landlord ; they are subject to the same conditions as personal chattels. Trees, grass, etc., are not E. In the U.S.A. the English common law of E. has been very generally adopted, though in some states the tenant is entitled to compensation not only from his landlord, but also from the incoming tenant.

**Embolism**, a plug ; a blocking of a blood vessel by a substance carried by the blood-stream from some other part of the circulation. The importance of this condition depends on the source of the plug and its nature, whether it contains infective bacilli, which will cause infective changes at the seat of the plug, or simply acts as a mechanical blocking of the circulation. Both of these are serious, for when the E. lodges in the brain it may produce paralysis, either with a slow or a sudden onset. Emboli are apt to occur in septic conditions, and are characteristic of pyæmia, a condition in which pus-forming germs are found in the blood. Sudden paralysis of the brain is known as apoplexy. The E. may originate from the heart, even in cases in which the victim is unaware of having any cardiac affection.

**Embossing**, the art of producing raised patterns on the surface of metal, leather, cardboard, or similar substances. Strictly, the term applies only to raised impressions made by means of engraved dies or plates, as opposed to those made by carving, chasing, chiselling, hammering, and the like. Crests, monograms, and addresses are embossed on notepaper. Dies for plain E. are generally cut deeper than those used with colours. In anct. times goldsmiths made much use of this method of decorating cups, vases, bowls, etc., by beating out bosses from the under surface of the metal in ornamental designs. The finishing touches are generally put from the front. E. is largely used in bookbinding. *See* Theophilus, *Christian Art of the Eleventh Century*, 1847; Cellini's *Treatises*, 1898; *Ency. Brit.* ix.; Harrison, *Decoration of Metals*, 1894; Haslope, *Repoussé Work for Amateurs*, 1902.

**Embracery,** the misdemeanour of attempting to influence a juror corruptly to give his verdict in favour of one side or party, by promises, persuasions, entreaties, money, entertainments, or the like. A juryman who corruptly endeavours to influence his fellow-jurymen to take his view is also guilty of E. The juryman who consents to give a corrupt verdict is equally guilty with the person persuading. The punishment is fine, or imprisonment, or both.

**Embrasure,** in military architecture the openings or crenelles between the teeth of a battlement in parapets, flanks of bastions, etc., are called Es. The name is also applied to the openings in a fort or casemate through which cannon are pointed. In domestic architecture an E. is the inward enlargement of the cheeks or jambs of a window or door made by slanting the sides.

**Embroidery** (Fr. *broderie* from *bord*, edge, which gave the verb *border*, and by transposition *broder*, to ornament the edge), the art of ornamenting in relief with needle and thread of silk, wool, linen, metal, etc., various kinds of fabric. The mummy clothes of anct. Egypt show the earliest extant E., and the ' pomegranates' of blue and purple and scarlet' of the book of Exodus were of E. Biblical references to the art abound, and the finest and most elaborate work was for ages destined for church vestments and furniture. The Babylonians were renowned embroiderers, whose work was sought after throughout the East. The Phrygians, too, were such marvellous embroiderers that the Gks. came to call their work *phrugiai*, and the Roms. *opus phrygium*; their name for the beautiful gold-embroidered work, *auriphrygium*, gave the Eng. ecclesiastical word *orphrey*. Homer and other classical writers refer to and describe magnificent embroideries. The art reached its greatest perfection in the early Middle Ages, when also it came to be more widely used for secular purposes. In Greece and Rome laws were made to moderate its use, but without success. The most distinguished artists did not scorn to make the designs from

which the highest ladies in the land executed their embroideries. No workers were more skilled in the craft than the Eng., a fact to which the Bayeux tapestry (which is not tapestry, but E.) and the Syon Cope (now in the S. Kensington Museum) bear testimony. At the times of the Crusades, E. was used for heraldic devices and with this a complicated symbolism of colour and design came into being, and this is still observed in heraldic and ecclesiastical E. Saxony was the first country to produce the white E. worked on muslin and other white fabrics, for which Switzerland and Scotland became noted later. Among

EMBROIDERY ON ROBE OF ASSYRIAN KING

the moderns, the Chinese excel as embroiderers; their best work is done on silk. The Hindoos use thread of silk, gold, and silver, together with spangles, beads, pearls, coins, and precious stones. Other than the needle, the only instrument used in the art of E. is a square frame on which the fabric is stretched when the work is large and elaborate, and a small circular frame of Chinese origin, called a 'tambour,' is sometimes used for small work. The principal E. stitches are: stem, crewel, cross or cushion, satin, knotted, button-hole or blanket, chain or tambour; padded E. requires couching stitch. In *appliqué* E. designs cut out of another material are worked on to the fabric to be decorated. At the present day much E. is made by machinery. Jossué Heilmann, of Mülhausen, was the first to make a successful embroidering machine, and this was patented in England early in the nineteenth century. *See* Day and Buckle, *Art in Needlework* (New York), 1900; Townsend, *Embroidery*, 1899; Caulfield and Saward, *Dictionary of Needlework* ; Dolby, *Church Embroidery* ; and Christie, *Embroidery and Tapestry Weaving.*

**Embrun,** a fort. tn. in the Fr. dept. of Hautes Alpes. It stands on a rock platform on the R. Durance. Pop. 3500.

**Embryology,** the study of the development of the living organism, or of the formation of a new individual or embryo from an ovum. As such it is a branch of the science of biology. For a history of the rise of the science of embryology and for a general view of it, *see* the article on BIOLOGY. In the higher plants and animals the cell (*q.v.*) is a highly complex structure, and the greatest complexity of functions and changes takes place in the *nucleus* of the cell. Within the cell of an animal and of certain plants is the *centrosome,* which is neither part of the protoplasm nor of the nucleus. This centrosome begins the process of cell division by itself dividing into two parts. Afterwards the nucleus does so, and so the whole cell divides. The nucleus breaks up into a number of threads, and the number of these is constant for any given species. In the higher types of animals and plants the individual is composed of myriads of cells united together into tissues and organs and so into the organism. The original cell from which these were formed by successive divisions is described as the ovum or egg, and in the higher animals and plants this must be fertilised to enable it to develop. In the lower plants and animals, particularly in some insects, the natural development of unfertilised ova is not infrequent, and in others a physical stimulus may initiate development (*see* EXPERIMENTAL EMBRYOLOGY). Such development is said to be parthenogenetic (Gk. παρθένος, maiden; γένεσις, birth).

In the higher animals, some of the earliest cells formed by the division of the ovum constitute the germ cells of the new animal. This fact led to the theory of the continuity of the germ plasm (*see* BIOLOGY), but this theory is not applicable to the germ cells of plants or of the lower animals. Germ cells of the female are ova ; those of male animals are spermatozoa, and of plants spermatozoids. Fertilisation is the union of an ovum and sperm, and takes place in the body of the female of higher animals and in the ovules of plants. Many lower aquatic animals and plants, and even some fishes, liberate the ova and sperms in the water, where they unite. The eggs of frogs are fertilised externally, the male adding spermatozoa as the ova appear.

Spermatozoa are usually some of the smallest animal cells, and are very active. Each has a 'head' consisting of the nucleus surrounded by a thin film of cytoplasm and connected by a small tapering cytoplasmic portion with the 'tail,' a fine hair-like part which by its movement propels the sperm along, tail first. The flowering plants, with the exception of some Gymnosperms, have no motile spermatozoids, and the function of these is performed by a nucleus and small amount of cytoplasm formed in the pollen grain. This sends out a tube which penetrates the ovule and conveys the fertilising nucleus to the ovum.

Generally, compared with the sperms, and even with other cells of the organism, the ova are large and laden with food material, the yolk, but some organisms have small ova with the food supply deposited in cells around them.

In the formation of the ovum, the mother cell, or oocyte, divides first into two unequal cells : the smaller of these is the first polar body, and is usually extruded. The other, the secondary oocyte, divides, forming the ovum and the second polar body, and this, too, is usually extruded. During the first division the nuclear material is halved (*see* CELL) and fertilisation restores the full number of chromosomes. In pathenogenetic development, the full complement of chromosomes is sometimes gained by the fusion of an egg with a polar body, or by failure to reduce the number of chromosomes in the division of the oocyte. Very occasionally, individuals with the single number of chromosomes develop and are usually abnormal. Although sometimes several sperms may enter the cytoplasm, the nucleus of only one fuses with that of the ovum. The two nuclei fuse completely, losing their individuality, and in the subsequent divisions each nucleus may be regarded as derived half from the nucleus of the sperm and half from that of the ovum. Soon after fertilisation has taken place the cell begins to subdivide. The methods of division of the fertilised ovum of an animal depend upon the quantity and disposition of the yolk. Where there is only a small amount of yolk, as in mammals, the ovum divides to form a sphere of cells. In those cases where there is a large amount of yolk collected at one pole of the ovum, the cells form more quickly and are much smaller at the other pole, giving an unequal division. If the result of segmentation is a ball of cells, giving a hollow sphere, it is called a blastula; if it is a solid ball of cells, a morula; and if partial, so giving a disc of cells, it is known as a blastoderm. The next stage results in the formation of a gastrula. Usually the blastula becomes invaginated, one hemisphere sinking into the other, giving rise to a two-walled sac with the opening known as a blastopore. In the higher animals a middle layer, the mesoderm, is formed between the outer layer (ectoderm) and the inner one (endoderm). The ectoderm forms the epidermis, the nervous system, the lens of the eye, and certain glands; the endoderm lines the midgut and its outgrowths; and the mesoderm forms the muscle, the skeleton, most of the viscera, blood and lymph vessels, blood, connective tissue, and certain membranes. For the further facts of recapitulation and continuity of germ plasm, see BIOLOGY.

**Emden**, a fort, seaport, the chief tn. of Est-Friesland, Prussia. It is situated near the junction of the Ems with the Dollart, and is surrounded by walls and moats. It has a very Dutch-like appearance, intersected as it is by canals crossed by a great number of bridges. The old tn. is enclosed by well-preserved walls, bastions and moats. The beautiful town hall (1576), the Gothic Great Church of the twelfth century, Gasthaus church, the Natural History, Art, etc. museums are noteworthy. E. is by canal an outlet for the Rhenesh–Westphalian industrial region. There is shipbuilding, shipping trade in corn, cattle, cheese, and smelting. Pop. (1928) 31,740.

'**Emden**,' German raiding cruiser, which had a notable career during the Great War under the command of Captain von Müller. At the outbreak of the war the *Emden* was in Eastern waters, and within a few days joined Admiral von Spee's fleet at Tsingtau. At Müller's request she was given a roving commission. In order to obscure her identity the *Emden*, which had only three funnels, put up a dummy fourth funnel, which made her resemble, at a distance, a British warship. She made towards Indian waters, reaching the Bay of Bengal in the first week of Sept. 1914. Her first capture was a Gk. steamer, *Pontoporros*, carrying Indian coal to a British port: this occurred on

Sept. 10. Other successes came quickly, as many as six vessels being prepared for sinking at the same time. The procedure followed by Müller was to transfer from these ships to his own the articles he required, and to tranship their personnel to the *Pontoporros* and then to sink the vessel. On Sept. 18 the *Emden* bombarded Madras and set fire to the oil tanks. Such a career could not be allowed to continue for long, and soon an organised search was made for the *Emden* by ships of Britain, France, Japan and Russia. On Oct. 28 she sank a Russian cruiser in Penang harbour and also a Fr. ship which attacked her. She was eventually sunk off the Cocos Islands by the Australian cruiser *Sydney* on Nov. 9, 1914. There was nothing particularly brilliant in her career, for she generally hit unarmed ships or those which were no match for her armament, and when she did eventually meet a ship on more equal terms she was outclassed. Her captain and crew, however, behaved chivalrously towards the captured personnel.

**Emerald**, a precious stone belonging to the beryl species, its green colour alone differentiating it from the other beryls. It occurs as six-sided prismatic crystals of the hexagonal system, is transparent or translucent, has an uneven conchoidal fracture, a vitreous lustre, becomes much harder on exposure to air following extraction from the mine, and is rendered electric by friction. Oxide of chromium is supposed to give it its green colour. The E. is cut on a copper wheel with emery. The finest stones are found in Muzo, Colombia, and there are mines also in Siberia, at Henbachthal, and at Canjargum in India. The E. was greatly valued by the ancients, who invested it with talismanic and medicinal properties; it was supposed to be good for the eyes, and Nero, among others, wore E. eye-glasses.

**Emeritus**, a term applied, among the Romans, to a soldier who had served out his time; now extended to designate any one (especially a professor) who has retired from office on account of old age or infirmity.

**Emerson, Ralph Waldo** (1803–82), a lecturer, essayist, and poet, *b.* at Boston, U.S.A., son of a Unitarian minister; educated at Boston Latin School and Harvard University; was ordained in 1829, but resigned three years later as a protest against the administration of the Lord's Supper. In 1833 he first visited Europe, and met Landor, Carlyle, and others. His friendship with Carlyle lasted all his life and resulted in an exchange of notable letters. The following year he began in real earnest his life of lecturer and writer, and at once established his position as a leader of the New England transcendentalists, although he disclaimed sympathy with their school of philosophy at large. He worked side by side with Bronson Alcott, Margaret Fuller, Channing, and Thoreau, but in a broader spirit; and with them he developed transcendentalism, particularly in its theological aspect, as a protest against dogmatic rationalism in religion. His attitude in philosophy was strongly influenced

EMERSON'S HOUSE AT CONCORD

by Platonism, the Ger. idealisms of Hegel, Fichte, and Schelling, and the Fr. idealisms of Cousin and de Staël, resulting finally in an indefinite conception of the God-like nature of the human soul and the correlation of human and divine wisdom, which may be described as a vague but inspiring pantheism. Of his innumerable lectures, the courses delivered at Boston during 1835 and 1836 on *Representative Men* and *The Philosophy of History* were perhaps the most noteworthy. His prose works are for the most part extensions and revisions of his lectures, and show in an even more marked degree his truly transcendental lack of purely logical coherence, as might well be expected when his method of working is considered. E. was wholly an intuitionist, and recorded his impressions and flashes of inspiration as they occurred to him, subsequently

synthesising them under such headings as seemed conveniently comprehensive. As a result of this, it may be observed in his writings that thoughts and criticisms have been too often distorted, merely to fit their expression into an epigram. E. himself confessed that 'I do not know what arguments mean, in reference to any expression of a thought.' His writings betray a complete absence of that symphonic style which is indispensable to a philosophy pure and simple, and they are, moreover, full of self-contradictions. These contradictions are not the result of any systematic evolution within the author's mind; they are rather the spontaneous interpretations, but in different moods, of the same mental experience. Each idea is complete in itself, rather than concatenated with its context. His work thus resolves itself into the expression of a personality which is governed by emotion, not by reason. And it is this predominant characteristic of E. which, however derogatory it may be to his work as pure philosophy, gives to it the charm of geniality, warmth, and confidence which is the secret of his undoubted attraction. As a theorist, devoted to the study of the higher instincts and their spiritual significance, and living out of touch with reality, he was an anomaly. For instance, he praised freedom, yet was slow to lend his support to a specific abolitionist movement against American slavery. And he preached always the 'infinitude of man'; he loved the 'human idea,' but his admiration for the unit, physical man, was by no means excessive. By reason of his singular elevation of character and sentiment, E. was essentially a poet. It is in his poetry that the true E. is most clearly delineated; albeit, in spite of his eloquent pages on rhythm in *Poetry and Imagination*, it must be confessed that his verses are often far from musical. One can quarrel, however, only with his incomplete mastery of form and technique. Whatever the faults of his outward expression—the rough metre and forced simile of his poetry, or the inconsequence of his prose—the inner ideas of his writings are always lofty of conception, and in their own way frequently of rare beauty. E. was a real prose-poet of a high order, and by the beauty of his thoughts, the terse eloquence of their expression, and the broad spirit of optimism in his works, has gained his wide recognition and popularity. E. has been recognised by Americans and by sound European critics as one of the greatest of the writers his country. His essays have become American classics and have had a profound influence in their own country. In spite of some roughness of form, his poems have caused him to be recognised as one of the most original poetic voices of the U.S.A. Unlike Europeanised poets like Longfellow, he turned to is own country, its own fauna and flora, for subjects for his lyrics. His extended stay in England gave him the opportunity to write his *English Traits*, still one of the best books ever written on the subject. *See Life* by Garnett.

**Emerson, William** (1701–82), an eminent mathematician who, failing in an attempt to follow his father's profession of schoolmaster, near Darlington, lived in retirement, pursuing his favourite studies of mathematics and mechanics. He was eccentric, but possessed of rare intelligence and energy. His chief works are : *Method of Increments, Mechanics,* and *Doctrine of Fluxions.*

**Emery,** an impure variety of crystalline corundum ($Al_2O_3$), being mixed with oxides of iron and silica. It was originally obtained from Cape Emeri in the island of Naxos, but is now largely worked in various parts of Asia Minor and near Philadelphia, U.S.A. The very finest particles are obtained by elutriation, *i.e.* the finely powdered material is stirred up with water, and, after standing for some time, the top layer is run off and the very fine particles allowed to settle slowly. E. is a purple-black solid, next in hardness to diamond, and is largely used as an abrading and polishing agent, for cutting and grinding glass, metals, and certain gems. E. wheels are made by mixing the powdered E. with some binding material and subjecting the mixture to heat and pressure. E. paper and cloth are made by dusting the powder over the material which has been coated with glue. Pure corundum and the artificial ' carborundum ' (SiC) are now largely prepared, and have superseded E. to a certain extent.

**Emery, Isabel Winifred Maud (Mrs. Cyril Maude)** (1862–1924), Eng. actress, b. Aug. 1, 1862, in Manchester, the daughter and granddaughter of actors. At fifteen she appeared for the first time in London at the Princess's Theatre. In 1881 she became a member of Henry Irving's Lyceum company, understudying Ellen Terry and playing her own parts ; she toured twice with this company in America. She married Cyril Maude in 1888. From 1896 to 1902 she played at the Haymarket. After an interval of three years, during which ill-health caused her

to be absent from the stage, she reappeared at His Majesty's. She appeared as Beatrice to Tree's Benedick, and she took *Olivia* on tour, and also played in H. A. Vachell's *Her Son.* She appeared in a charity performance in 1915. Died at Little Common, Bexhill, June 15.

**Emesa** (Syria), *see* HEMS, or HOMS.

**Emetic,** an agent that produces vomiting. The origin of the word dates back to antiquity, and in the days of the Roms. not only was it a regular accompaniment of a banquet but it was an intrinsic part of daily life. Es. are often replaced by the stomach tube or hypodermic syringe. The Es. most commonly in use are : copious draughts of warm water, mustard and water, or common salt and water, and are useful in cases of poisoning.

**Emeu,** or **Emu,** a ratite bird in the family Dromæidæ. Like the cassowary, to which it is allied, it is common to Australia, but is being gradually destroyed. It stands about 5 or 6 ft. high and is second in size only to the

EMU

ostrich. It differs from the cassowary in having a broad beak, no helmet, short feathers on the head and neck, and no wattles on the neck, no spines on the wing, and the claws of all three toes are almost equal to one another. The wings are rudimentary, but the powerful legs are well adapted for running, and are capable of giving dangerous kicks when the bird is roused. There are only two living species, *Dromæus Novæ-Hollandiæ,* the common E., and *D. irroratus,* the spotted E. Both are monogamous, and the male wholly or partially incubates the eggs. Their diet is strictly vegetarian, and both their flesh and eggs are eaten by natives.

**Emigrants' Information Office,** a dept. of the Colonial Office now called the Oversea Settlement Department of the Dominions Office (*see* OVERSEA SETTLEMENT DEPARTMENT).

**Emigration,** the act of leaving one country in order to settle in another. In the early ages such a process was carried on by whole nations, who, having exhausted the fertility of their own lands, sought to acquire fresh habitats by conquest. Nowadays it is more of an individual process, and is determined by the greater prospects of material benefit offered by life in the destined country. E., therefore, usually takes place in the older countries, whose sons are lured away to younger lands. It first assumed notable proportions in the nineteenth century, when America was the chief goal. The greatest exodus was from Ireland, and the total number of emigrants from that country between May 1, 1851, and Dec. 31, 1910, was 4,187,443, leaving the country far less thickly populated than heretofore. Usually E. does not alter the social condition of the country of origin, though the loss of the more ambitious units is necessarily felt. In many European countries, however, emigrants have been actuated by a desire to escape from tyrannical political institutions. It was at the close of the Napoleonic wars that E. from Great Britain to the colonies overseas was promoted as a remedy for distress and unemployment. The population was then mainly agricultural, and State-aided E. was advocated as a channel for the redundant labour in these islands, the more so as much of the land in the Colonies was under the control of the home Gov. Opinion was, however, divided over the application of the suggested remedy. William Horton, who was Under-Secretary for War and the Colonies in 1822, advocated state-aided and mass E. of able-bodied workers, who were to be given free passages and free grants of 100 acs. of land in the Colonies, free farming implements and a year's provisions. Edward Gibbon Wakefield (*q.v.*), the more celebrated protagonist, held that the pauper type of emigrant was unsuited to conditions overseas, and he therefore evolved a system of State-aided E., the cardinal features of which were that (1) emigrants should pay a sufficient price for land (about £2 an ac.); (2) the proceeds of sales in the Colonies should be used as an E. fund to assist more labourers to emigrate; (3) emigrants should be judiciously selected; (4) E. should be controlled by a central authority; and (5) the Colonies should become self-governing as

soon as possible. In 1823 and 182 Horton induced Parliament to tr his scheme on a small scale. Late he secured an amendment of th Poor Law Act of 1834 to enab parishes to mortgage their poor rate so as to provide for their able-bodie paupers in the Colonies, and durin the ensuing few years a number emigrants were assisted under the Act. But this plan lacked th vision behind the ideas of Wakefield whose system of colonisation formed the basis of the Gov. policy of settle ment in S. Australia and Ne Zealand and generally thereafte About 1832 the Gov. adopted th policy of assisting the E. of womer mechanics and agricultural labourer and in 1834 an Act was passe embodying Wakefield's principle with the view of settlement of S Australia. In 1845 the Gov. set u the Colonial Land and Emigratio Board, the original purpose of whic was to take over the work of the S Australian Commission appointed i 1835 for carrying out Wakefield' scheme. The Board's functions wer extended to control the whole E movement to the colonies and th sale in Great Britain of colonial land Between 1840 and 1873 the Boar granted free or reduced passage to over 352,000 settlers. But fror 1850 onwards the general view bega to gain ground that Gov. super vision of E. was unnecessary The Colonists became self-governing and assumed the control of thei own lands; the prevalent opinior led by the Manchester School o thought, was that the Home Gov need take no further interest i British persons who left the hom country, and gradually the duties c the Board were absorbed by th Board of Trade, the Colonial Offic and the Colonial Legislatures. Fror 1878 till the Great War the Gov. too little part in E. beyond subsidisin a small office known as the Emi grants' Information Office (*see* OVER SEA SETTLEMENT D PARTMENT), estab lished in 1886, which gave informa tion to those wishing to emigrat whether to the colonies or to foreig countries. The number of Britis Emigrants rose from 227,542 in 1880 to 454,527 in 1911. Their principa destinations were Canada, U.S.A. Australia, New Zealand, and S. Africa in the order named. By 1912, how ever, attention began to be attracte to the importance of Empire develop ment and the need for a better dis tribution of the white populatio within the Empire (*see* EMPIR SETTLEMENT AC ).

**Emigration Societies.** Several or ganisations exist for the purpose o

...iding various classes of persons to migrate to British dominions and colonies. The chief among them are :

*Salvation Army* (Head office : Migration House, 3 Upper Thames Street, London), provides farm training for boys, and finds situations overseas for boys, domesticated women, adult farm-workers and others; arranges nominations by immigrants' friends abroad ; organises personally conducted parties across the ocean; operates reception lodges and temperance hotels overseas; and has a system of ' after-care ' for young people who emigrate.

*Church of England Council of Empire Settlement* (39 Victoria Street, London, S.W.), represents the Church as a whole in all matters relating to Empire Settlement ; secures nominations, arranges for loans in necessitous cases. Has created organisations for reception, placing and after-care of migrants, and for linking them up with the Church oversea.

*Young Men's Christian Association (Migration Department)*, (Kingsway House, 103 Kingsway, London, W.C.), co-operates with the Churches in Canada and Australia in settlement work ; and in cases of necessity gives financial help towards passages, and conducts parties of settlers overseas.

*The Society for the Oversea Settlement of British Women* (Caxton House, Westminster, London, S.W.), acts as the Women's Branch of the Oversea Settlement Department and is an amalgamation of the principal Women's Emigration Societies. It includes on its Council representatives of other Women's Organisations and co-operates with the Immigration Authorities and Voluntary Societies in the Dominions. It has representatives and hostels overseas, finds suitable posts, gives introductions, sends specially conducted parties to Canada, supplies advice and information and in certain cases arranges loans for passages.

Other societies or agencies which are concerned, *inter alia*, with E. are the British Dominions Emigration Society (34 Newark Street, Stepney, London, E.) ; British Legion (*q.v.*); Dr. Barnardo's Homes (*q.v.*); Catholic Emigration Society ; Middlemore Emigration Homes (Birmingham) ; National Association of Boys' Clubs; Scottish Council for Women's Trades ; and the Fellowship of the Maple Leaf (for migrating teachers to the W. provinces of Canada and to Australia) ; and the 1820 Memorial Settlers' Association (for migrants to S. Africa).

**Emigrés**, the name applied to those who, remaining faithful to the royal house, left France on account of the Revolution. On the fall of the Bastille, July 14, 1798, the princes of the royal family, followed by many nobles, officers, monks, and priests, quitted France, the princes with their close adherents forming a court at Coblenz, others settling in Germany, Belgium, Italy, Holland, and Switzerland. Numbers of the E. served in the Prussian army against France. Their estates were forfeited and severe laws were passed against them. Many did not return to France till after Napoleon's downfall, though granted an amnesty when he became First Consul. They were not able to recover their possessions.

**Emilia**, a former compartimento of Italy, bounded by Lombardy, the Adriatic, the Marches and Tuscany, and Piedmont and Liguria. It included the modern provinces of Parma, Piacenza, Modena, Reggio, Ferrara, Forli, and Ravenna. The Via Emilia is a Rom. highway forming, with the Via Flammina, part of the great road from Rome.

**Eminence**, a title conferred on cardinals by Pope Urban VIII. (1631). They had previously been Most Illustrious.

**Eminent Domain**, the *dominium eminens* of the law, a phrase denoting the universal right in the public over property. In accordance with this law the gov. may compel a private individual to give up, on receipt of compensation, property required for the public good.

**Emin Pasha** (1840–92), the name adopted by Edward Schnitzer, scientist and administrator. His parents were Jews of Silesia, where his father was a merchant. He studied medicine at Breslau University and graduated at Berlin. He then went to Turkey and received an appointment on the staff of Hakki Pasha at Scutari, taking a Turkish name and adopting the dress and customs of the Turks in order to identify himself as nearly as possible with those whom he worked. In 1876 he went to Egypt, where he worked under the name of Dr. Emin Effendi. Gordon appointed him in 1878 medical officer and later governor-general of the Equatorial Province. Gordon employed him on many diplomatic missions, his extraordinary power as a linguist, together with his wonderful tact, making his services invaluable. From the abandonment of the Sudan by Egypt until the arrival of Stanley's relief expedition (1889) he held and administered this district singlehanded. He reluctantly left with Stanley, but later returned to Central Africa in the service of Germany. He was killed by Manyema Arabs. He had abolished the slave trade in his province, studied its flora and fauna, made route surveys of over 4000 m., pursued meteorological investigations which resulted in the establishment of Lado as the E. Equatorial standard, and made vocabularies of many African dialects.

**Eminescu, Mihail,** one of the greatest poets of Rumania, was *b.* Jan. 15, 1850, at Ipatesti. His father, a farmer, sent him to schools popular songs of his country, but his own verse was filled with a bitter melancholy. At first his poems made little impression, but gradually he became the main influence on the younger generation. The revolutionary cry of his *Emperor and Proletarian,* the concise beauty of his sad sonnets, the patriotic ardour of *Epigones,* in which he presents a virile fresco of ancient times, and his bitter sentiment toward women

EMMANUEL COLLEGE, CAMBRIDGE

in Cernovitz and Blaj. He soon left the latter, running away with a theatrical troupe in the capacity of prompter. Overtaken by his father, he went to the Universities of Jena and Vienna, and later completed his studies at Berlin, specialising in philosophy. During a short period he was a teacher, and was then appointed to a post in the national library at Jassy. Deprived of this position, he became editor of *Timpul,* the conservative paper of Bucharest. In 1883 symptoms of madness developed. He was discharged as cured, but was returned later, and was killed by a fellow-madman in June 1889. As a poet he devoted himself mainly to two themes— love and the beauties of Nature. He was largely influenced by the in his *Evening Star* have all become famous. He left also some brief sensual poems which remind one of Heine—*Desire, Blue Flower. Oh Remain!* His short story *The Poor Dionise,* is one of the masterpieces of the literature of his country.

**Emir, Ameer, Amir** (Arab *Amir,* chief or lord), a Turkish title instituted A.D. 650 by Fatima, daughter of Mohammed, and bestowed upon the califs, descendants of the Prophet who called themselves Emir-al-Mumenin, 'chief or commander of the faithful.' They alone were allowed to wear the green turban. The title has been assumed by tribal chiefs in the East and in Africa.

**Emmanuel,** see IMMANUEL.

**Emmanuel College, Cambridge.** This was founded in 1584 by Sir

Walter Mildmay as a Puritan institution in connection with Cambridge, on the site of a Dominican friary. The foundation consists of a master, sixteen fellows, and thirty scholars. Extra scholarships on other foundations are awarded by preference to pupils of Uppingham and other midland schools. The greater part of the present building dates from the second half of the eighteenth century. The chapel was designed by Sir Christopher Wren (1677). Richard Holdsworth, Gresham professor, and William Sancroft, Archbishop of Canterbury, were masters of Emmanuel. Bishops Joseph Hall and Thomas Percy, Sir W. Temple, Dr. Samuel Parr, and John Harvard (after whom the college in America was named in 1638, in recognition of his services to American education) all studied at Emmanuel. There is a fine picture-gallery attached to the master's lodge, and the library contains valuable MSS.

**Emmaus,** a vil., Judea, not identical with the present E., but possibly situated in the valley of the Urlas, 7 m. from Jerusalem, where remains of important baths have been discovered. Josephus says that E. means ' warm bath.' Jesus appeared to two disciples (Luke xxiv.).

**Emmenagogues,** *see* MATERIA MEDICA.

**Emmendingen,** a tn. of Baden, Germany, on the Eltz, 9 m. N.N.W. of Freiburg.

**Emmenthal,** the valley of the river Emmen, one of the finest of Switzerland; canton of Bern. Famous for its cheese.

**Emmerich,** a walled tn., Rhenish Prussia, situated on the Rhine, 49 m. N.N.W. of Düsseldorf, and near the Dutch frontier, 94 m. E. of Rotterdam, and of very Dutch appearance with extensive river trade. St. Willibrord, an Eng. missionary, is said to have founded a church here in 697. The Münster church is of the eleventh to twelfth centuries, a golden reliquary of the eighth is preserved in it. Manufactures oils, fats, machines, paper, chemicals, leather and sausages. Pop. 13,600.

**Emmet,** *see* A T.

**Emmet, Robert** (1778–1803), rebel, distinguished himself at Trinity College, Dublin, by his brilliant oratory. As a protest against the visitation of Lord Clare and Dr. Duigenan in 1798 to investigate the political tendencies of the students, he withdrew his name from the books. Like his brother, Thomas Addis E., he was an enthusiastic United Irishman, and after a visit to Paris in 1802, where he interviewed Napoleon and Tallyrand, he engineered a rising in Ireland. The idea was to seize Dublin Castle, and to hold the lord-lieutenant as a hostage; but the insurrection was ill-planned. Only a small body of revolutionaries assembled, and these committed such crimes of violence that E., broken hearted, fled. He was captured, tried, found guilty and hanged.

**Emmet, Thomas Addis** (1764–1829), rebel, practised with success as a barrister in the Irish courts. An active politician, he joined the ranks of the United Irishmen, and in 1795 was elected secretary of that society. He was not in favour of an insurrection, however, unless there was active support from France. He was imprisoned at Fort St. George in 1799, but in three years was transported to Holland. Thence he went to Paris, where he took an active part in organising a battalion of Irish in the pay of France, and in 1804 he sailed for the U.S.A. He was called to the New York Bar, where he became a leading counsel. He was an elder brother of Robert E. There is a biography by Haynes (1829).

**Emmich, Otto A. T. Von** (1848–1915), Ger. general; b. Aug. 4, 1848; was early prominent in the Great War through being in command of the force that besieged Liège in Belgium. He advanced to the frontier on Aug. 4, 1914, and attempted to take the fortress by a coup de main on the night Aug. 4–5; but the last forts held out until Aug. 16. In 1915 he went to the E. Front as a Corps Commander, and took a successful part in the battles of the Dunajec (*q.v.*) and the San. His corps was situated on the right of Mackensen's XI. Army; it distinguished itself particularly during the operations of May 2–5, 1915, when Mackensen broke through the Russian line between Gorlice and Tarnow. Died at Hanover, Dec. 22.

**Emmius, Ubbo** (1547–1625), a Dutch writer on chronology and history, professor of Greek and of history at Liers, E. Frisia. He is best known as the author of the erudite work, *Vetus Grecia Illustrata.*

**Emmons, Ebenezer** (1799–1863), American geologist, b. May 16, 1799, at Middlefield, Mass. Graduated at Williams Coll., 1818; Professor of Natural History there after receiving in 1830 a medical diploma from Berkshire Inst., Pittsfield. Made contributions to botany, geology, and mineralogy of N. states; and report on quadrupeds of Massachusetts. Appointed geologist-in-chief of second dist. of geological survey of N.Y. State. His theory that what he named the ' Taconic ' rocks of the Green Mountains were a system older than the Silurian is now regarded as wrong. In 1838 he became Professor of Chemistry at Albany Medical College. In 1858 he had charge of the geological survey of N. Carolina. Died at Brunswick, N.C., Oct. 1.

Emotions, a term used in philosophy to indicate one of the three groups into which mental phenomena may be divided. Thus we may say that the states of the mind may be classified under *knowing, feeling,* or *willing.* The first term includes such facts as perceiving, remembering, and reasoning, and they may further be said to be *intellectual* operations. The second term would include all pleasurable and painful conditions of the mind, whether simple, such as the distress of hunger, or complex, such as love ; and it is this class of mental states which is indicated by the term *emotions.* The third term covers all active mental operations, *e.g.* walking, speaking, and also efforts to do things, active impulses, and resolutions. To cover all the phenomena of the third class, the term willing must be extended to cover random movements as well as voluntary actions and volitions.

These three states of mind are clearly marked off from each other, and if one of these aspects of mind becomes well marked, it militates against the other aspects. Thus strong feeling opposes calm thinking (knowing) and well-regulated action (willing). While they are thus distinctive, however, they are also in some respects closely connected. They are properties of mind and do not exist in isolation from each other. Thus experience of a bodily pain (feeling) causes us to localise and recognise it (knowing), and to endeavour to alleviate it (volition). Most feelings are embodied in the intellectual states, while intellectual states are usually accompanied by some shade of feeling, agreeable or disagreeable, while they also involve concentration of mind, or voluntary activity. Willing, again, depends upon feeling for its motives, and on knowledge for its guidance. Now, a mind may be predominated by either of these three states, in which case it will be distinguished by special features of the other two states, specially related to the first. Thus men or women who have vivid feelings usually have a rapid imaginative insight into things. So this division of mind under three aspects is according only to the most prominent aspect. We cannot, perhaps, find a pure E., but we can find states of mind in which E. is more marked than the other two states.

Now, feeling marks any state of consciousness which is pleasurable or painful. There are, of course, mixed states of feeling, which are partly pleasurable and partly painful, agreeable and disagreeable, such as grief, anger, etc., and it is difficult often to know which is the preponderating element. Again, feeling covers all pleasures and pains, whether simple mental effects or the more complex effects. Thus those effects which depend merely upon nerve stimulation, such as the pains of hunger and thirst, and their corresponding pleasures, and which are commonly marked as *sensations,* are included under the term E. as well as those effects which depend upon some amount of mental activity, such as fear, hope, regret, etc., which are known as *emotions.*

The correlation between the states of feeling and their physical accompaniments illustrates the close connection between mind and body. Facial movements, gestures, modifications of voice, and even internal organic effects are well known to accompany feeling. Pleasure, pain, anger, fear, love, etc., all evidence this, and each has its characteristic expression, and so close is the connection that often the adoption of the expression will dispose the mind to adopt the appropriate feeling. The experience of actors illustrates this. All feeling involves an excitation of nerve-centres, and diffuses itself over the nervous system in a circle of effects. The development and continuance of a feeling depend upon this cycle of effects. If they are stopped, as when the manifestations are repressed, the E. itself tends to subside. The physical changes have an effect on the E. too, giving it character, as is evidenced by the sense feelings which accompany the disturbed action of the heart in fear, etc. These expressions may be distinguished from the E., and frequently outlast it, while it is also commonly known that giving way to a feeling causes it to subside more rapidly ; this being explained by the idea that the movements carried out then cause a loss of intensity in the sensations accompanying the E.

Expressive movements are partly instinctive—*e.g.* crying, frowning, etc., and appear early in life—and partly acquired. Imitation plays a big part, and it is easy to see how in this way we acquire actions expressive of ennui, moral displeasure, etc. Sometimes the will aids in the acquirement of these movements, as in the adoption of the conventional look, tone of voice, and gesture of the social circle moved in. Several theories have been advanced to explain these movements. It is generally agreed that all feeling tends to produce certain bodily effects which are proportionate in strength and range to the intensity and persistence of the feeling. Spencer showed that, as the feeling becomes more intense, so larger muscles are called into play, e.g. twitching of fingers, then movement of the arms, and so on as agitation increases. Wundt amplified this by saying that the motor centres of attention are involved, and the due regulation of thought disturbed. Violent E. of any kind illustrates this well. To account for the distinctive movements attached to the various feelings, Bain suggested that pleasure is connected with an increase, and pain with a decrease, in the vital energies, and so the expression of pleasure would have greater vigour of action than the expression of pain. But Sully shows that strong and violent feelings, whether pleasurable or painful, have very like results, and that the strong contrast in energy between certain feelings, say anger and fear, does not coincide with a contrast of pleasure and pain. Therefore he suggests that it is connected with the feeling as energetic in character, or depressing and paralysing.

Psychologists have tried to bring the varieties of pleasure and pain under certain laws. One or two of the principles they have formulated may be said to be approximately correct and of some practical import. Thus they have formulated the law of stimulation or of exercise. We may say that all pleasure is connected with the exercise of some capability, faculty, or power of the mind; or that it is the accompaniment of some organ which is connected to the nerve centres, or the seat of conscious life. And, in general, moderate stimulation of an organ or exercise of a capability produces pleasure, and this pleasure increases with the strength of the stimulus to a certain point. Beyond that point the pleasure diminishes and passes into a painful effect, as with the blinding light of the sun, a very loud sound, or very great mental effort. Painful states of feeling may be caused by the absence of stimuli, as in the effect of darkness, the restlessness of a boy repressed, and those mental conditions like ennui, tedium, and dullness. Again, an obstruction to activity will cause painful effects, as when a train of thought is impeded by forgetfulness. Another principle rather less important is that of change or contrast. A pleasurable stimulation continuing to act may become painful, or even if this does not happen it may at least lose its pleasurable effect. Change, therefore, involves pleasure because it limits

the duration of any stimulus, and because it is a necessary condition of that vivid active attention which is necessary—always provided that the change is not so violent that it causes shock.

Now, feelings may be divided into two divisions, those arising directly from a process of nervous stimulation or the excitation of sensory nerves, and those depending on some manner of mental activity. The first, which may be termed bodily feelings, involves processes in the outlying parts of the organism, and may be called *sense feelings*. The second, being connected with central nerve forces (the brain), may be called *emotions*.

Sense-feelings may arise from disturbances of some part of the organism, as in hunger, thirst, heat and cold sensations, etc., and pleasures or pains connected with the excitation of special senses, and the pleasures or pains of muscular sensation, etc. The latter class are much more easy to distinguish and localise than the former. Further, painful feelings are more numerous than pleasurable ones in the case of internal organic sensations, as in digestion, etc., while with the special sense the pleasurable are more prominent, and with the higher senses, hearing and sight, the pleasurable element is the greatest; and of these it may further be stated that they are closely connected with the mental feelings.

E. fall into well-marked varieties of pleasurable feelings, together with the corresponding painful ones, as in the case of love, etc. In most cases the pleasurable feelings are the ones indicated, the corresponding pain being understood. Fear is a notable exception, as in this case the painful feeling is understood, the feeling of restored confidence being regarded as the negative side. Great difficulties confront any effort to classify the E. Popularly, love, anger, fear, etc., are regarded as easily distinguishable, but the feelings thus indicated shade into one another in a perplexing manner. Thus, fear and reverence are two different E., yet a trace of the former is probably present in the latter. One obvious classification would be according to the distinction between pleasure and pain. But the pleasures and pains of love, etc., have very numerous points of similarity. Another method, followed by Spencer, would be to classify them according to the degree of intellectual activity involved. This would give grades of E. corresponding to sensation, perception, imagination, and thought. But the E. of beauty, for instance, may be excited by either of the last three grades, so that this does not fully answer.

The general laws which apply to mental development also apply to the development of the E. They are deepened by exercise, and there is a progress from simple feelings to complex E. The growth of the E. cannot be fully explained as the result of individual experience. They arise uniformly when the appropriate circumstances occur, usually early in life, e.g. the child has a disposition to feel anger when he is annoyed or injured. On the other hand, an instinctive element enters into feelings which may be shown to be largely the result of individual experience. It may be noted that this instinctive capacity for any particular E. is not the same in all cases. Similar experiences and circumstances may not produce the same result in different individuals, so that children are born with unequal amounts of natural tendency to feel in various ways. The sum of these instinctive dispositions makes up the natural emotional temperament, and this is undoubtedly caused by the physical differences, nervous and muscular, which exist at birth. These instinctive emotional tendencies can be explained by referring them to ancestral experience and allowing that there are transmitted associations. The infant will smile at its mother, and has an instinctive fear of strange men and animals; and the charm of the mother's face may be explained as having vaguely called up countless pleasurable feelings of companionship and love in the past development of the race, while the fear may be called up by reminiscences of dangers and evils which the race has had to associate with strangers and wild animals. The laws of heredity also seem to aid in the transmission of E.

The study of the development of the E. enables us to divide them roughly into three groups or orders, giving successive stages in the progress of the emotional life. First we get Individual or Personal E. which are confined to the individual and depend upon a more or less distinct personal reference. These grow up around self and self-activities, the pleasures of hope, success, reputation, etc., or they attach themselves to objects having a special personal relation, as in the child's love of its mother. Secondly, we have Sympathetic E., which involve participation in other people's experiences, and so are purely representative. They presuppose a certain amount of personal emotional experience, and are non-personal and common in direct contrast to individual E.

Thirdly, we have the highly complex E. termed Sentiments, viz. patriotism, love of humanity, etc. These may be subdivided into three classes: (a) Intellectual, or the attachment to truth; (b) Æsthetic, or admiration of the beautiful; and (c) Moral, or reverence for duty, which includes love of humanity and the worship of moral excellence. All these E. involve a higher form of representativeness than sympathy, although they depend upon it to a very large extent, and they are entirely non-personal and common, turning the mind absolutely away from self to a disinterested contemplation of an object. See Bain, The Emotions and the Will; Herbert Spencer, Principles of Psychology; Baldwin, Handbook of Psychology; Sully, Handbook of Psychology; Stout, Manual of Psychology; Darwin, Expression of the Emotions in Man and Animals; Sully, Outlines of Psychology, with Special Reference to Education; Bain, Education as a Science. See also PHILOSOPHY, PSYCHOLOGY, and CHILD STUDY.

**Empecinado, Don Juan Martin Diaz, el** (1775–1825), a Spanish patriot, a famous and redoubtable guerilla chief who harried the Fr. during the Peninsular War. He became field-marshal in the regular army, but, involving himself later in the insurrections of the Constitutionalists, he was hanged. He incorporated his sobriquet el empecinado (' the pitch-coloured ') with his name.

**Empedocles**, a Greek philosopher, law-giver, physician, poet, and high priest of Agrigentum in Sicily, b. about 490 B.C. He analysed the universe into the four elements, fire, air, earth, and water, fire being the essence of life, the other elements forming the basis of matter. His system is founded on this theory together with another which supposes two opposing forces, Love and Hate. The world began when the elements, which had been torn asunder by the force of Hate, tended to come together again under the influence of Love. The different species arose out of the different minglings of the elements. His chief work was a sublime epic on Nature. See Stein, Fragmenta; Baltzer, Empedocles.

**Emperor, Title of.** Among the Romans emperor or imperator was the title borne by the commander of an army, then by the governors of provinces, then by the head of the Roman empire. In modern times it has become the highest title of dignity and is assumed by several European sovereigns who rule over a vast territory where dwell people of more than one nationality. The rulers of Russia, Austria-Hungary and Germany before the Great War were called *emperor*. Queen Victoria assumed the title of *empress* in 1876.

**Emperor Moth,** the name given to *Saturnia carpini*, a species of Coleoptera, and is also applied to the whole family of Saturniidæ. *S. carpini*, which is also called *S. pavonia*, is common in England, though rare in Scotland, and in the heather-districts the bright-green larvæ, studded with red or yellow warts, may often be observed. Their general colour is greyish with purple and orange tinges, and they are remarkable for the eyespot common to both wings of both sexes.

**Empetraceæ,** a small natural order of dicotyledonous plants, containing only four species. The best-known species is E. *nigrum*, the crowberry, which grows wild on mountainous heaths of Britain.

**Emphysema,** an inflation; an abnormal presence of air. Medically, it consists of an enlargement of air vesicles of the lungs, which are the terminations of air passages. It occurs in bronchitis and other conditions where there is excessive coughing. It causes lessening of the aerating surface of the lung and shortness of breathing; in young lads, it may only give trouble on exertion, causing the ' broken wind ' of schoolboys. In older persons with chronic bronchitis, the chest becomes enlarged and barrel-shaped from decreased breathing in the lung requiring increased depth of breathing. Increased work is also thrown on the heart to drive the blood through the inflated lung; in time it fails to drive sufficient blood through, so that the heart's action is embarrassed, and the badly aerated blood causes the sufferer to look blue. The treatment of E. consists in attending to the underlying causes, the bronchitis or asthma, and in maintaining the action of the heart.

*Surgical emphysema* is due to air in the general connective tissues of the body, from injury of some air-passage or wound of the chest-wall, without injury to the lung. Only in severe cases is it necessary to make incisions to allow the air to escape; in ordinary cases respiration is not impeded, nor is the heart's action embarrassed.

**Emphyteusis** (Gk. ἐμφύτευσις, a planting in) or **Jus Emphyteuticarium,** in anct. Rom. law, the right of enjoying all the fruits, and disposing at pleasure, of the *prædium* (estate) of another, subject to the payment of a yearly rent (*pensio* or *canon*) to the owner. Both lands and buildings could be subject to E. Though the *emphyteuta,* or person who enjoyed the right, could dispose of his rights as he pleased, the *dominus,* or owner of the land or building itself, had a right of preemption. The old right relating to *agri vectigales*—leases of lands held of the Rom. people, of municipalities, or of the college of priests, *i.e.* short or long lettings by the state—was, about the time of Justinian, united with that of emphyteusis. The J. E., though based on an institution of the civil law, only assumed its peculiar character in the time of the Lower Empire, whereas other and equally characteristic *servitudes* owed their existence to the praetors.

**Empire Day,** the celebration, throughout the British empire, of the anniversary of Queen Victoria's birthday, May 24. It has been officially recognised since 1902, when the Earl of Meath inaugurated the festival as a means of training school children in good citizenship.

**Empire Marketing Board.** An official executive body formed in 1926, following a recommendation of the Imperial Economic Committee, for the purpose of developing trade with the Empire. The Board is under the chairmanship of the Secretary of State for the Dominion Affairs, is non-political in character, and representative of every part of the British Empire. Its aim is to promote the marketing of Empire produce in the United Kingdom. From the outset it was realised that very little purpose would be served by asking the public to buy Empire produce on patriotic grounds alone. By quality and price and accessibility such produce must justify the choice of the purchaser. The British Empire is known to be able to produce almost any and every commodity of as good quality as any, but in many parts production is still in the early stages. Riper marketing experience is required. Constant experimentation with new products is necessary, a work which is performed unremittingly by the Imperial Institute (*q.v.*). These requirements offered opportunities of which the E. M. B. was not slow to avail itself. Whence the Board has always regarded as part of its duties to help producers to turn to their advantage the resources of science and economic investigation; to show them how to grade produce; how to transport it safely, and how to display it in the retail shops. In scientific research the Board works through existing scientific institutions which it assists financially on the advice of various gov. organisations at home or overseas. In this connection, valuable investigations into the mineral contents of pastures have been carried on, with the support of the Board, at the Rowett Research Institute in Aberdeen, the Cawthron Institute and the Department of Agriculture in Wellington, New Zealand, at the Waite Institute, at Adelaide University, and at centres in S. Rhodesia and Kenya. In economic investigation the Board contributes to schemes directed to improving the efficiency of production and of marketing in its various stages, working, in this latter regard, through the agency of the Ministry of Agriculture, with which it places funds for marketing purposes. One of the most important of the Ministry of Agriculture's activities thus helped by the Board is the ' National Mark ' scheme, the aim of which is the application to certain graded home products of a single mark, the National Mark, carrying with it a guarantee of quality. Home-killed beef is one of the more recent products to be sold under the National Mark, which has already been applied to eggs, flour, malt products, and various fruits. It may, therefore, be readily inferred that one of the chief activities of the E. M. B. is a continuous publicity campaign. In the stimulation of interest in the Empire and its development, the Board has invoked all the paraphernalia of modern advertising. It has advertised not only in the newspapers, but also by means of elaborate and artistic posters in its special poster frames ; it has arranged displays at exhibitions, organised lectures and displays of Empire films, and issued a number of publications dealing with various aspects of Empire marketing. The Board's poster frames number now (1930) some 2000, displayed upon selected sites in about 500 towns in Great Britain and N. Ireland, and sets of posters, showing scenes of production in almost every country of the Empire, at home and oversea, have appeared upon them ; and suitable posters are now reproduced and issued together with explanatory leaflets to over 20,000 schools. The whole work of this Board is an interesting experiment in the application by an official, but not bureaucratic, organisation of the most modern methods of scientific research and publicity to some of the problems of Empire development.

**Empire Music Hall,** formerly one of the chief London music halls, in Leicester Sq., W., established in 1887 and now converted into a cinema theatre. These variety theatres developed out of the ' saloon theatres ' of London, 1830–40, owing to the

restrictive action of the ' patent' theatres at that time, which had the sole right of representing ' legitimate drama.' Later, sketches of short duration were allowed on the music-hall stage. Music halls must be licensed, but there is no censorship as for drama. The Disorderly Houses Act of 1751 still controls the chief halls (*see* Greary, *Law of Theatres and Music Halls*, 1885). The Empire was particularly noted for its ballets and revues.

**Empire Settlement Act.** The Settlement Act of 1922 forms the basis of the present British policy of State-aided Empire Settlement. This Act empowers the British gov. to co-operate in agreed schemes for assisting the migration of suitable persons in the United Kingdom who intend to settle in the oversea Dominions. These schemes may be either development or land settlement schemes, or schemes facilitating settlement by help with passage money, training for life overseas, or otherwise ; the contribution of the British gov. may not exceed half the expenses of the scheme and their liability to contribution is limited to fifteen years as from May 31, 1922. The object of the current policy of settlement is to distribute the white pop. of the British Commonwealth in the most efficient manner, economically speaking, as between all the parts of the Empire. Although at the present moment (1931) the world depression in trade has reacted unfavourably on the policy, the essential need of the oversea Dominions for an increase of pop. to develop their resources, as well, indeed, as the introduction of fresh capital, remains the objective in which both the British and Dominion govs. are agreed. The policy was reconsidered at the Imperial Conference of 1930, and re-endorsed in a resolution which while recognising that the existing economic difficulties were such as to render impracticable any considerable flow of migrants, recommended that the govs. concerned should take such measures as might be best calculated to secure the paramount object— namely, the better distribution of the white population of the Empire, as and when economic conditions might permit.

The genesis of the present policy of State-aided Empire Settlement is to be traced to the Report of the Dominions Royal Commission, appointed to 1909, to inquire into the development of the natural resources of the Empire (*Cmd.* 8462). This Commission urged the need for more effective supervision and direction of migration by co-operation between the

Home and Dominions govs. The sequel was the appointment, at the end of 1918, of the Overseas Settlement Committee to advise the gov. on the subject. This Committee's recommendation led to a scheme in 1919 for state assistance in the form of free passages to ex-service men and women and their dependents who desired to settle elsewhere in the Empire. This scheme was terminated at the end of 1922, by which time free passages had been granted to over 80,000 persons. Opinions differ on the results of the Empire Settlement Act, though for several years after its passage large numbers of persons migrated to Canada, Australia and New Zealand under the various schemes organised under the Act. Up to 1926, some 251,794 persons were assisted to proceed overseas. The gross outward movement to the Dominions in that period was about 130,000 a year, the number of assisted settlers being about 65,000 a year; these totals were below expectation, but were not unsatisfactory in view of the difficulties imposed by modern conditions on a more rapid movement. In succeeding years the flow of assisted migration has fluctuated considerably, but present conditions, which include the temporary suspension of assisted passages except for certain classes of migrants, afford no true criterion of the success or otherwise of the policy formulated under the Act. The Overseas Settlement Committee, through the Overseas Settlement Department, co-operates with a large number of voluntary organisations in sending migrants to the Dominions under approved schemes (see EMIGRATION SOCIETIES).

**Empirical Formula,** in chemistry, the simplest formula for a substance in which the atoms of the various elements in the compound are shown in the correct ratio but not necessarily the correct numbers. Thus the empirical formula for grape-sugar is $CH_2O$ but its true formula is $C_6H_{12}O_6$. In the case of most solids, only the empirical formulæ are known, the true formulæ being indeterminable.

**Empiricism** (Gk. ἐμπειρία, trial, experience), a philosophical term signifying a belief that actual sense-experience is the source of all ideas and excluding all possibility of *a priori* knowledge or conceptions. This view arose out of the system of Heraclitus, rejected by Socrates and Plato. It maintains that the mind at first is a *tabula rasa* (clean slate) upon which experience must write all impressions. The sophists of antiquity were empiricists. The scholastics taught that the mind can attain to true intellectual apprehension not by innate ideas but by concepts derived from sense-experience. Descartes' philosophy established a compromise, one part of knowledge being considered innate, another empirical or derived from outside. (*See* INNATE IDEAS.) Many English thinkers have held empiricist views (Locke, Hume, John Stuart Mill). Locke made experience the basis of all knowledge, sensation, and reflection, while Berkeley and Hume developed this philosophy on different lines. This empiricism formed a strong contrast to the Cartesian 'rationalism' of the Continent. Its chief fault is perhaps that it gives a wrong account of experience, representing it as piece-meal, whereas the two elements of knowledge (*a posteriori* facts of experience, and *a priori* facts) are essentially and inseparably united, as Kant held in his philosophy. In medicine, the term empiric was applied to those who (in opposition to the Dogmatici and Methodici) drew their rules of practice from personal experience, disregarding the more scientific methods of inference and deduction and all philosophical theory. Hence the word came to mean an untrained practitioner, one who prescribed solely on individual observation and experiment, a quack-doctor. Empirical laws are those adopted merely because found (or supposed) to be beneficial and successful in practice, without any reason authorising them (as distinguished from 'causal' laws).

**Employers' Liability,** *see* WORKMEN'S COMPENSATION.

**Employment Exchanges.** These are local offices, at first called Labour Exchanges by the Labour Exchanges Act, 1909, established for the purpose of mobilising labour, gathering information as to employers requiring workpeople, and, conversely, as to workpeople seeking employment, and, generally, enabling applicants for labour to obtain it. They are an antidote to unemployment borrowed from Germany, and in view of the success attending the experiment in that country, it is remarkable that they were not established in England before, though in this connection considerable good had been done by local distress committees under the Unemployed Workmen Act, 1905. The Act of 1909 empowers the Ministry of Labour (to which department the duties were transferred in 1917 from the Board of Trade) to set up and maintain E. E., wherever they think fit, and to assist any E. E. maintained by other authorities. The Act provided that the powers of any central body or distress committee, and of any local council acting through a special committee, to maintain employment registers under the Unemployed Workmen Act, 1905, might, after one year from the passing of the Act, only be exercised under the control and with the sanction of the Local Government Board (now Ministry of Health) and that that sanction should not be given except after consultation with the Board of Trade (now of the Ministry of Labour). The Ministry of Labour is empowered to make general regulations with respect to the management of E. E., and the expenses incidental to administering the Act are payable out of moneys provided by parliament. The Act also provides that any person knowingly making false representations to any officer of an E. E. for the purpose of obtaining employment shall be liable to a fine not exceeding £10. The central office of the E. E. is at Queen Anne's Chambers, Westminster, S.W., the branch exchanges being classified into seven territorial divisions, each with its office and clearing-house, subject to the control of the Central Office. The Ministry of Labour is empowered to advance travelling expenses to applicants for work where work at a distance has actually been found for them, but such power is subject to restrictions in regard to trade union rates of wages and trade disputes. By 1929 there were about 1200 E. E. in the country.

Tables showing the vacancies notified at Employment Exchanges, and the numbers of vacancies filled in the period 1913–1929.

### Number of Vacancies Notified.

| Years. | Men. | Boys. | Women. | Girls. | Total. |
|---|---|---|---|---|---|
| 1913 | 714,270 | 143,715 | 270,325 | 94,518 | 1,222,828 |
| 1916 | 909,721 | 148,091 | 846,196 | 145,010 | 2,049,018 |
| 1917 | 906,627 | 146,103 | 814,785 | 131,927 | 1,999,442 |
| 1918 | 977,999 | 148,158 | 808,490 | 132,570 | 2,067,217 |
| 1919 | 900,970 | 155,978 | 731,320 | 163,096 | 1,951,364 |
| 1920 | 581,406 | 133,662 | 469,068 | 127,997 | 1,312,133 |
| 1921 | 554,781 | 57,077 | 337,560 | 75,184 | 1,024,602 |
| 1922 | 448,219 | 56,371 | 278,756 | 75,994 | 859,340 |
| 1923 | 604,298 | 82,539 | 288,824 | 84,632 | 1,060,293 |
| 1924 | 747,375 | 134,277 | 269,664 | 117,210 | 1,368,526 |
| 1925 | 790,053 | 157·047 | 425,929 | 136,736 | 1,509,765 |
| 1926 | 635,905 | 140,210 | 378,725 | 126,989 | 1,281,829 |
| 1927 | 737,660 | 168,458 | 402,353 | 150,485 | 1,458,956 |
| 1928 | 775,792 | 180,560 | 419,211 | 160,678 | 1,536,241 |
| 1929 | 993,510 | 209,162 | 477,131 | 182,895 | 1,862,698 |

### Number of Vacancies Filled.

| Years. | Men. | Boys. | Women. | Girls. | Total. |
|---|---|---|---|---|---|
| 1913 | 566,150 | 90,387 | 199,395 | 65,921 | 921,853 |
| 1916 | 636,095 | 116,900 | 695,631 | 108,609 | 1,557,235 |
| 1917 | 623,830 | 120,525 | 706,034 | 104,834 | 1,555,223 |
| 1918 | 669,732 | 122,054 | 624,220 | 98,906 | 1,514,712 |
| 1919 | 658,836 | 117,166 | 408,033 | 105,928 | 1,289,963 |
| 1920 | 454,624 | 106,938 | 284,451 | 95,695 | 941,708 |
| 1921 | 515,071 | 49,592 | 216,942 | 61,057 | 842,462 |
| 1922 | 411,123 | 50,334 | 190,126 | 64,154 | 715,737 |
| 1923 | 554,998 | 75,119 | 211,984 | 75,141 | 917,242 |
| 1924 | 678,762 | 112,224 | 277,984 | 95,978 | 1,164,948 |
| 1925 | 729,864 | 127,042 | 338,303 | 110,876 | 1,306,085 |
| 1926 | 588,420 | 115,349 | 305,971 | 105,967 | 1,115,707 |
| 1927 | 683,501 | 140,466 | 324,928 | 124,971 | 1,273,866 |
| 1928 | 729,140 | 149·312 | 339,967 | 133,009 | 1,351,428 |
| 1929 | 930,525 | 169,131 | 382,481 | 148,610 | 1,630,747 |

The duties of E. E. were considerably increased when they were extended to the scheme of unemployment insurance (q.v.) which was instituted in 1912. Ordinarily the payment of benefits is made at E. E., but in some cases trade unions and other associations of workpeople pay out the state benefits together with an additional sum provided out of their own funds. For full information as to statistics see the *Seventy-fourth Abstract of Labour Statistics of the United Kingdom*, issued in 1912 by the Board of Trade ; and for information on unemployment insurance the *Report on National Unemployment Insurance to July 1923*, and subsequent reports.

**Empoli**, a tn., Italy, in Tuscany, on the Arno, in a beautiful and fertile district. Manufs. linen. It was very flourishing in the Middle Ages. Pop. 5800.

**Emporia**, a city of Kansas, U.S.A., the cap. of Lyon co., 53 m. S.S.W. of Topeka. It has railway shops and other industries and is the commercial centre for a large agricultural and stock raising region. It is the seat of the Kansas State Teachers College with an enrolment of 5000 and of the College of Emporia (Presbyterian). Pop. 14,067.

**Empson** (or **Emson**), **Sir Richard,** an English lawyer and statesman, was the son of a wealthy citizen of Towcester, Northamptonshire, and was trained for the Bar. Like Edmund Dudley, he was the unpopular agent of Henry VII., and was employed in exacting taxes and penalties due to the crown. He shared with Dudley a reputation for harshness and tyranny in his exactions. In 1491 he became Speaker of the House of Commons, and in 1504 Chancellor of the Duchy of Lancaster. In the second year of Henry VIII.'s reign, he and Edmund Dudley were both convicted of tyranny and constructive treason, and were beheaded on Tower Hill, Aug. 17, 1510.

**Empyæma** (literally, pus in ; meaning pus in the cavity of the pleura). This occurs in a late stage of pleurisy, pleurisy itself being inflammation of the pleura, which is the lining of the chest-wall and the covering of the lung. The term E. is also used for any collection of fluid in the pleural cavity, before an exploratory operation has been done to learn the nature of the fluid, whether serum, a clear fluid, or pus. Pleurisy and E. commence in the pleura, or extend from the chest-wall, as in growths, injuries, or disease of other parts, as the kidneys, or from the lung, as in tubercle, or the pleura and lung become diseased at the same time, as in

pleuro-pneumonia. When pus is present, it must be removed by aspiration, that is, drawing it off. If the underlying cause remains, pus recollects, and an opening must be made to maintain drainage and to prevent pus accumulating.

**Empyrean** (Gk. πῦο, fire). According to the old metaphysical philosophers the E. was the highest and purest of the four celestial spheres, the region of the most rarefied elements of fire. Poetically it is the source of light and the abode of the blessed.

**Ems,** or **Bad Ems,** a magnificently situated tn. and watering-place of Prussia in Hesse-Nassau on the R. Lahn, 10 m. E.S.E. of Coblenz and 15 m. N. of Wiesbaden. Its alkaline mineral springs are among the most efficacious in Europe for the cure of nervous, respiratory, and liver disorders Pop. 7160. Famous as the place whence William I. of Prussia despatched the telegram to Bismarck which provoked the Franco-Prussian War of 1870.

**Ems,** a river of N.W. Germany. It rises in Westphalia, flows through Hanover, and after a course of 200 m. enters the North Sea, forming an estuary between E. Friesland and the Netherlands and developing an expansion called the Dollart. Three canals connect it with the Lippe, with Jade, and with Dortmund.

**Emsdetten,** a manufacturing com. of Westphalia, Prussia, 15 m. N. of Münster. Pop. 13,320.

**Emu,** see EMEU.

**Emulsin,** or **Synaptase,** a neutral substance contained in almonds with the power of acting as a ferment converting the amygdalin of almonds into oil of bitter almonds, hydrocyanic acid, and a sugar. In its pure form it is an odourless and tasteless white powder, which is soluble in water.

**Emulsion** (a suspension, that is, an even diffusion, which does not separate on standing, of a heavier substance in a lighter medium), a medical preparation in which the drugs neither rise nor fall on standing. Thus, oil, a heavier substance, is suspended by yolk of egg in water, which is lighter. Amongst other drugs, olive oil and petroleum are frequently given as Es.

**Enabling Act,** see CHURCH ASSEMBLY.

**Enamels and Enamelling.** Enamel (formerly 'amel,' through Fr. *amail*, *email*, from a Late Latin word *smaltum*, same root as 'smelt') is, in the strict sense, the hard, vitreous compound which is fused on the surface of metallic objects for purposes of decoration or utility. The base of enamel is a compound called flux; this is clear and vitreous, and is composed of silica, minium, and potash. Whilst in a state of fusion, oxides of metals are added to colour it, which stain the flux throughout its mass. When a high temperature is required to fuse it, the enamel is termed 'hard'; the harder the enamel the greater its durability, and hence value. When hard enamels are used, pure metals must also be used, as an excess of alloy causes the metal to melt before the enamel is fused,

rotating the pestle with as much pressure as possible. The powder thus obtained is washed repeatedly in distilled water until all the floury part is removed. The metal to be enamelled must be cleaned by the application of water and acid; for copper, nitric acid is used; for silver, sulphuric acid, and for gold, hydrochloric acid; all the acid is then removed completely by washing and drying in sawdust. The pulverised enamel is then spread in sufficient thickness to cover the

[*British Museum*

AN ENAMEL PANEL SHOWING ST. ANTHONY AND THE ARCHER, BY LEONARD LIMOUSIN, 1536

The arms shown are those of Jean de Langeac, Bishop of Limoges, 1532–41

or the enamel to part company with the metal after firing. Enamels are either transparent or opaque. The elements have all undergone an equal degree of liquefaction in the former case, whilst all transparent enamels are made opaque by the addition of 'calx,' a mixture of tin and lead calcined. In order that the developments which have occurred in the enamelling art may be understood, a brief résumé of the processes required may be given. After the enamel has been procured in lump form, it must be 'pulverised'; for this it is placed in an agate mortar and covered with water; a pestle is then held vertically over the enamel and struck sharply with a hammer to break it, after which it must be ground into a fine grain by

required parts of the metal, which is then dried in front of the furnace. It is then placed carefully, on an iron or fireclay plate, into the muffle of the furnace, which is heated to a bright pale red. When it shines all over it is removed. The process of firing takes only a few minutes, and generally no annealing process is required. The art of enamelling has been practised since very early times. The earliest examples in Assyria are enamelled on bricks and pottery. The Gks. used the art for articles of personal adornment, and the Roms. for the most part copied the Gks. After the fall of Rome Byzantium was the centre of the enamelling art. The inhabitants of Great Britain are thought to have excelled in the art at an early epoch, the Celtic work of Ireland being of great beauty. The introduction of the ' basse-taille ' process raised enamelling from merely a decorative to a fine art. Of comparatively recent years a revival of interest in both decorative and utilitarian enamelling has taken place, the present extensive use of enamelled plates for advertising purposes is one example among many of the latter. All the examples of enamelling, of whatever period, fall into one of the following classes, according to the method of applying the enamel employed : ' champlevé,' ' cloisonné,' ' basse-taille,' ' plique-à-jour,' and ' painted,' and this order is that in which the varieties became known. In champlevé enamels, cells or troughs are cut away in the plate to be enamelled, leaving a metal line raised between them, which forms the outline of the design. The enamel is laid in these cells and filed, smoothed, and polished after fusion. The cloisonné method differs from the above only in that instead of the cells thin metal strips are bent to the outline of the pattern and fixed to the plate by silver solder or the enamel itself. The Pala d'Oro in St. Mark's, Venice, is the finest example of this class of work. The basse-taille process is a combination of metal work, in the form of engraving, carving, and enamelling. The metal is engraved with the design and carved into a bas-relief below the general surface of the metal, so that the enamel when fused is level with the uncarved parts of the design. Transparent enamel is generally used for this process. Plique-à-jour enamel may be termed translucent cloisonné, as it is similar to cloisonné, save that the ground on which it is fired is removed, rendering it transparent. In painted enamel the colours are laid on to a background of enamel. Miniature-painted enamels do not, properly speaking, come within the category of enamels as the colours applied after the enamel has been fired upon the gold plate used are not vitreous compounds. See *L'art du feu ou de peindre en émail,* 1721 ; Emil Molinier, *Dictionnaire des Emailleurs,* 1885 ; Labarte, *Recherches sur la peinture en émail,* 1856 ; C. Popelin, *L'Email des peintres,* 1866 ; H. Cunynghame, *Art of Enamelling on Metals,* 1906 ; A. Fisher, *Art of Enamelling on Metals,* 1926 ; L. Falize, *Claudius Popelin et la renaissance des émaux peints.*

**Enaré, Lake** (spelt also **Inara, Enari, Indiagher**), a lake of Russian Lapland in the extreme N. of the prov. of Uleaborg.

**Encatnacion,** an important commercial tn. at the terminus of the Paraguay Central Railway, Paraguay, S. America.

**Encaustic Painting.** This term is employed to describe a picture painted by means of heated wax. It is an ancient method of painting, and the final process consisted of an application of heated wax to the picture. This process is now practically obsolete, but some people consider that neither oil nor fresco paintings are so permanent as the E., which is unfortunately one of the lost arts. Emma J. Greenland, at the close of the eighteenth century, did indeed make some experiments in the endeavour to ascertain the ancient methods, but they met with but poor success, the tint and texture being neither as brilliant nor durable as oil painting. We have no important examples of classic Gk. E. painting, but there are some interesting Egyptian remains of the kind, brought to light at the Oasis of Fayum in 1887.

**Encephalitis Lethargica** (sleepy sickness) occurred first in Vienna in 1917. The general symptoms are fever, lassitude, headache, pain in the back, muscular rigidity and paralysis, sensory and gastro-intestinal disturbances. The fever usually ranges between 100° and 103°. The lethargy is the most common characteristic symptom, and varies greatly in degree, from a mere drowsiness to a stupor from which a strong stimulant will arouse but for a few moments. Yet in some cases there is restlessness, excitement, and even maniacal symptoms, instead of lethargy. The stupor varies in duration from a few days to months, when recovery may still occur. The muscular rigidity is characterised by mask-like facial expression with tremors of muscles in hands and arms. E. L. first occurred in Great Britain in 1918. It is believed to be of microbic origin and communicable from one individual to another.

**Encephalocele,** a protusion of a portion of the brain substance through an opening in the skull. It is more commonly a congenital condition ; its importance depending upon its size and situation. It may be described as a visible tumour of the brain, in contradistinction to a cerebral tumour, which is understood as a growth inside the brain.

**Encephaloid Cancer** is so called from a fancied resemblance to brain material. It is a soft cancer as contrasted with scirrhous or hard cancer, and contains a relatively large amount of cells and blood vessels and a less amount of connective tissue.

**Encephalon, or Brain** (*q.v.*), is that enlarged upper portion of the cerebro-spinal axis contained in the cranium.

Q 2

It comprises the *medulla oblongata*, the *cerebellum* with the *Pons Varolii*, and the *cerebrum*, which last part is subdivided into the *mesencephalon*, the *thalamencephalon*, and the *cerebral hemispheres*. The average weight of the entire mass is some 50 ozs. in the male and 5 to 5½ ozs. less in the female. The E. increases rapidly in weight up to the seventh year, then more slowly, and appears to reach a maximum between the ages of twenty and thirty. Its average specific gravity is about 1·036, the white matter being denser than the grey.

**Enchantment**, *see* INCANTATION and MAGIC.

**Enchondroma,** a tumour containing cartilage, which generally develops in connection with the cartilaginous growing portion of a bone. It can be removed by operation, and does not recur.

**Encina (or Enzina), Juan del** (1468–1534), a Spanish poet and founder of the secular drama in Spain, was *b.* at Salamanca. He began writing poetry at a very early age, and *Cancionero*, a collection of odes, lyrics, and dramatic pieces, was printed at Salamanca in 1496. In 1519 he made a pilgrimage to Jerusalem, and wrote a poetical account of this in 1521. His fame, however, does not rest on either of these works, but on his *Representaciones*, fourteen dramatic poems, partly religious, partly secular, the latter of which were acted in Spain in 1492. His most popular work, *La Farsa de Placida y Victoriano*, was condemned by the Inquisition and lost in 1559. E. held three important positions, viz. secretary to the first Duke of Alva; musical director in Pope Leo X.'s chapel at Rome; and, having taken orders in 1519, he became prior of Leone.

**Encke, Johann Franz** (1791–1865), a German astronomer, studied under Gauss at Göttingen. Through Bessel's influence he became secretary of the Academy of Sciences at Berlin (1825), and director of the observatory there. He superintended the execution of the star-maps of Berlin Academy (1830–59) and the erection of the new observatory (1832–35). He is most famous for his discussion of the orbit of the comet discovered by Pons, 1819. It has since been known as E.'s comet, and has the shortest known period of about three and one-third years. E. also wrote *Die Entfernung der Sonne*, 1822–24 (two tracts based on the transits of Venus, 1761 and 1769). He issued four vols. of *Astronomische Beobachtungen auf der Sternwarte zu Berlin*, 1840–56. *See* Life by Bruhus (1869).

**Enclosures,** *see* ALLOTMENTS; COMMONS and ENCLOSURES.

**Encratites** (Gk. 'Εγκρατῖται, self-controlling), a sect of Christian ascetics of the second century (*c.* 172 A.D.) found at Rome and in Asia Minor. Their leader was the Gnostic Tatian, and they practised total abstinence from flesh, wine, and marriage. They substituted water for wine in the Eucharist, and were hence sometimes called ' Hydroparastatæ,' or Aquarians. They existed as late as the fourth century, and the name came to be given to ascetic Gnostics generally.

**Encrinal (Encrinital) Limestones.** This name is given to limestones which abound in the calcareous fragments of crinoids, large masses of the rock being entirely composed of the joints and fragments of their skeletons. Many cylindrical bodies may be found, some flat and coin-shaped, but more often they are elongated and perforated along their long axis by a canal. Hence in some parts these are called ' St. Cuthbert's beads.' Such remains are commonest in limestones of the Silurian, Devonian, and Carboniferous ages. Large beds occur in the Hamilton and Helderberg groups in New York state, and in the mountain limestones of N. England.

**Encrinites, or Crinoidea** (Gk. κρίνον, lily, and εἶδος, form), the name of a class of radiated animals, forming an order in the class Echinodermata. They include many species, mostly fossil (' stone lilies '). They have been obtained from Gotland Is., the Wenlock of England, and the Niagara group of N. America (Silurian system). *See* Zittel and Eastman, *Textbook of Palæontology*, i., 1900; Bather, ' The Crinoidea ' in Lankester's *Treatise on Zoology*, ii., 1900.

**Encyclical Letters** (from Lat. *encyclicus*, circular), an expression indicating in a general sense circular ecclesiastical letters sent on some important occasions by the pope to the bishops. These letters differ from the papal bulls in that the latter generally have some more special object in view. The E. L. is singular (*epistola*), and is issued to the hierarchy, being sealed with the Fisherman's Ring. E. L. generally contain instructions and warnings against dangers which may threaten the church.

**Encyclopaedia,** a derivative from the Gk. ἐνκύκλιος παιδεια, circular or complete education; it originally meant the whole group of studies which every free-born Greek youth was required to complete in preparation for active life; the liberal curriculum. The phrase was adopted by the Roms., and in both the ancient languages came to mean systematic study of, or instruction in, all the branches of learning. With this idea of encyclic education was soon associated the notion of collecting the materials of such instruction into a single work, where the contents and relations of the various arts and sciences should be systematically expounded, There were many early attempts to produce such a work, though the name E. was not used till the sixteenth century. This is now its common application.

The earliest Es. were treatises or groups of connected treatises adapted for continuous study, not merely for reference, and they contained the more or less extensive accumulation of learning made by their authors individually. The first E. is said to have been compiled by Speusippus (d. 339 B.C.), a disciple of Plato, but of this nothing is known. Among the Roms., Marcus Terentius Varro (d. c. 27 B.C.) was the first encyclopaedist, but his Disciplinarum Libri IX., containing treatises on grammar, rhetoric, arithmetic, etc., and another work on Rom. antiquities, have both been lost. The earliest E. we possess is the famous Historia Naturalis of Pliny the Elder (23–79 A.D.), a work on natural science, considered especially with reference to human life, and including geography, medicine, and the history of art. In the fifth century, Martianus Capella, a native of N. Africa, produced an E. of the seven liberal arts, which was used extensively as a school text-book in the Middle Ages. A similar work was compiled by Isidore, Bishop of Seville (c. 570–636), and there were one or two Gk. Es. in the twelfth century. Of these early works the most important is the great Bibliotheca Mundi, or Speculum Maius, or Speculum Triplex, of Vincent of Beauvais, a Dominican friar of the thirteenth century. In 1541 the name cyclopaedia was first used by Ringelberg of Basel, and Paul Scalich used the term E. in 1559. The seventeenth century saw many Es., including Alsted's, 7 vols., in Latin ; the Grand Dictionnaire Historique of Louis Moreri, with an alphabetical arrangement; Hoffmann's Lexicon Universale; and, most famous of all, the Dictionnaire Historique et Critique of Bayle (1697). The ancient type was changing, and the E. was becoming assimilated to the dictionary. The alphabetical arrangement led to a change of purpose and character in the compilation, which became a work of reference, giving, instead of the exposition of the system of human knowledge, only the mechanical arrangement of its contents. This aim and method have been adopted by modern Es. in varying degrees. An

important characteristic of modern methods is the employment of a large body of specialists both as compilers and editors. Some co-operation existed in the earlier productions, but an elaborate system became essential in the nineteenth century, owing to the rapid advance and multiplication of the special sciences. Coronelli planned a vast Bibliotheca Universale, of which only a small portion appeared (Venice, 1701–6). In England the dictionary method was followed by John Harris (c. 1667–1719), who compiled a Lexicon Technicum. A supplement ' by a society of gentlemen ' appeared in 1744, and was long in popular use. Another more important English work is the Cyclopædia of Ephraim Chambers (d. 1740), which contains a systematic use of cross-references. Chambers may be regarded as the father of English encyclopaedic lexicography, and he also exerted a wide influence on continental works of this type. It was a French translation of Chambers's Cyclopædia, by John Mills, which formed the basis of the famous Encyclopédie of Diderot and D'Alembert (1751–72). In their hands it became the organ of the most advanced and revolutionary opinions of the time, and was the object of much violent persecution. So thoroughly was it identified with the philosophic movement of the time, that the term encyclopédiste came to be applied to all who held certain views. It was published in twenty-eight volumes, including eleven of plates, and five supplementary volumes followed (1776–77) with over 200 plates, and an analytical table of contents in two volumes (1780). The Encyclopædia Britannica (Edin. 1768–71) was planned by William Smellie, a printer, Andrew Bell, an engraver, and Colin Macfarquhar. It was a compromise between the alphabetical and the scientific distribution of subjects. There have been many successive editions, and the fourteenth edition (1929) has twenty-four volumes.

Little change has taken place in the theory of E. making since the beginning of the nineteenth century, but there has been a notable growth of the encyclopaedic dictionary and of the special E. The two types meet in the Grand Dictionnaire Universal du XIXième Siècle (1865–78) of Pierre Larousse, which is a complete dictionary of the French language and includes proper names and a vast amount of information. Among special dictionaries may be mentioned the Dictionary of National Biography (1885–1901), ed. by Leslie Stephen and Sidney Lee. Other noteworthy Es. in English are : *The Edinburgh Encyclopædia*, ed. by Sir David Brewster ; *The Penny Cyclopædia* (29 vols.), ed. by Charles Knight ; *The English Cyclopædia* (31 vols.), ed. by Knight ; *Chambers's Encyclopædia* (10 vols.), ed. by Andrew Findlater ; Johnson's *Universal Cyclopædia* (10 vols.) ; *The Cambridge Encyclopædia ; The New International Encyclopædia* (20 vols.) ; *Harmsworth's Encyclopædia* (8 vols.), 1905. Every leading language could furnish a list, and an article on the history of Es. is to be found in vol. cxiii. of the *Quarterly Review*.

**Encyclopédistes.** This was the name given to a group of Fr. thinkers who were connected with the *Encyclopédie*, a celebrated Fr. work published by Diderot and D'Alembert at Paris in 1751–72, embodying the prevailing

JEAN LE R. D'ALEMBERT

tendencies of the time as regards philosophy, religion, and politics. It appeared in twenty-eight volumes, and was doubtless undertaken because of the success of *Chambers's Encyclopædia* in England. Many of the greatest writers of the day figured among the collaborators— Voltaire, Rousseau, Montesquieu, as well as the chief editors.

**Endecott, John** (1589–1665), *b.* at Dorchester. He went to America in 1628, where he became manager of the plantation of Naumkeag (Salem). Two years later he gave place to John Winthrop and headed several expeditions against the Indians. From 1641–44 he held respectively the position of deputy-governor and governor of Massachusetts, and died at Boston, March 15. E., though a brave and benevolent man, was of an austere Puritan disposition.

**Endemic,** a disease affecting a community, which is caused by local conditions. This distinguishes it from an epidemic, which is a disease brought to a community from a distance. An epidemic, such as small-pox, tends to pass on, whereas an E. disease, like malaria, tends to remain.

**Enderby Land,** a large, desolate island or tract in the Antarctic regions, just S. of the Antarctic Circle, visited by Biscoe in 1831, and named after his employers. It was first discovered by Dirk Gerritsz, 1599.

**Endive,** *see* CHICORY.

**Endlicher, Stephen Ladislas** (1804–49), an Hungarian systematic botanist, whose chief work *Genera Plantarum* has largely influenced succeeding botanists.

**Endocardium.** This membrane lines all the cavities of the heart, following the inequalities of the inner surface of the organ and becoming continuous with the inner coats of the attached blood vessels. Beneath a layer of epithelial cells the E. consists of connective tissue with a close network of elastic fibres; occasionally plain muscular fibres are present. The ordinary cardiac muscular fibres in many places are separated from the E. by some amount of areolar tissue, which in certain subjects may contain considerable quantities of fat. The membrane is usually thicker in the auricles than in the ventricles. Endocarditis or inflammation of the E. may be either simple or ulcerative, and may be associated with a variety of diseases.

**Endocarp,** *see* FRUIT.

**Endogamy** (Gk. ἔνδον, within, and γάμος, marriage), the custom of marrying only within the limits of a tribe or clan, as opposed to exogamy (marriage outside of the clan). This is possibly characteristic of the earliest stages of social organisation. In many cases it doubtless arose from racial pride and a contempt for neighbouring peoples. E. prevails in certain parts of Central America, Java, and elsewhere. Since in time E. will impoverish the breed, a restricted form began to be common. Thus the Abors, Kochs, and other Indian peoples forbid marriage between those of the same clan or subdivision of the tribe. *See* McLennan, *Primitive Marriage*, 1865 ; Avebury, *Origin of Civilisation*, 1902 ; Frazer, *Totemism and Exogamy*, 1910 ; Westermarck, *History of Human Marriage*, 1894.

**Endogens,** plants in which secondary wood is developed in bundles which are external to the primary bundles, and by this means growth in thickness of the stem and root takes place. Monocotyledons is the class of plants in which these so-called closed bundles occur, but only such members of the class as arborescent Liliaceæ, and Yucca, etc., are E.

**Endometritis,** see UTERUS.

**Endomorph** (Gk. ἔνδον, within, μορφή, form), the term used when one mineral is enclosed within another, the surrounding one being called the perimorph. Such inclusions of minerals are very common in the constituent minerals of crystalline schistose and igneous rocks, and are due to the successive formation of two minerals in a narrow space.

**Endor,** an ancient vil. of Palestine, mentioned in the O. T., S. of Mt. Tabor, 6½ m. from Nazareth. The present site is called Endur.

**Endorsement,** the act of endorsing, that is, writing one's name on the back of a bill of exchange, cheque, note, etc., signifying one's approval, sanction, or ratification of same. When endorsed in this way, a bill may be freely transferred from hand to hand and is negotiable. This is termed *general* E. A *special* E. is where the document of whatever nature is made payable to the order of the transferee, viz, the person to whom it is transferred. Sometimes the document is made transferable by simple delivery to any person without further E., and this is known as a *blank* E.

**Endosmosis.** When a dilute solution of a substance is placed in a funnel closed at one end by parchment, and the whole immersed in water, the solution in the funnel will rise, due to the fact that water passes in through the membrane faster than the solution passes out. The phenomenon is known as E. *See* OSMOSIS.

**Endowed Schools Acts,** parliamentary Acts made to prevent misapplication of the foundations for the support of secondary education in England. The Acts do not apply to the chief public schools nor to any schools kept up in any way by voluntary subscriptions without monetary endowment. *See* under EDUCATION.

**Endrod,** a tn., Hungary, in co. Békés, situated on the Körös, 20 m. N.W. of Csaba. Pop. 13,850.

**Endymion** (Gk. Ἐνδυμίων), in Gk. legend a beautiful youth beloved by Diana (Selene, the moon-goddess). One story makes him a king of Elis, whose grave is shown at Olympia. He was said to have been granted by Zeus the gift of eternal sleep and perpetual youth. The more general story makes him a hunter on Mt. Latmos. E. is sometimes supposed to be a personification of the sun, or of the setting sun's plunge into the sea. The subject frequently forms the theme of pictures (see those of Watts in modern times), and is found on ancient wall-paintings and Rom. sarcophagi. *See* Keats, *Endymion;* Robert, *Antike Sarkophag-Reliefs,* iii.,1898.

**Enema,** a liquid preparation intended for injection into the rectum, by means of a syringe or other suitable apparatus. It was formerly known as clyster. Es. most commonly in use are water, soap and water, or oil.

**Enemy.** By the principles of international law (*q.v.*) individuals are regarded as Es. only so far as necessary for war. This is a radical modification of the doctrine of Grotius at the close of the Middle Ages, that a 'war declared against him who has the supreme authority in a population is considered to be declared against all his subjects and those who may join themselves to him as his allies.' In the ancient doctrines of E.'s character it was an unquestioned right in any one belligerent state to confiscate for its own profit all property and rights of the subjects of the opposed or E. state which happen to be or subsist within the ambit of its territory or power. But where E. subjects are allowed to remain in a country and enjoy their property it is now deemed inequitable among civilised nations to confiscate the property of those who do not happen to remain or are absent at the outbreak of war, and who as individuals, in fact, are no source of danger. *See* works by Westlake, Hall, Birkenhead; *International Law.*

**Energumen** (Gk. ἐνεργούμενος, demoniac, wrought upon), the name given to one supposed to be possessed by evil spirits. In primitive races mental and nervous afflictions are frequently thus explained, and a cure thought to be effected by means of prayers or incantations. Such persons were sometimes known as 'energici,' or 'χειμαζόμενοι' ('tossed by the waves'; of uncontrollable impulse). They could only occupy the porch with the lepers and the defiled at church services. The order of exorcists in the Church was instituted to free Es. from their obsessions. *See* Harnack, *The Expansion of Christianity,* i. 152–80.

**Energy,** the power of doing work : in physics and theoretical mechanics, that attribute of a body or material system by virtue of which the body or system is enabled to perform work. Simultaneously, work is defined as the overcoming of resistance through distance. The E. of a system, if due to motion, is called E. of motion, or 'kinetic' E.; whilst the E. it possesses on account of its position or its state of strain is called ‘potential’ E. by way of distinction. A steam-hammer when at rest in its highest position is a good type of ‘potential’ E. Again, in the vibrations of a pendulum, the E. is constantly being changed from a kinetic to a potential form. All forms of E. can be classified under one or other of the types, kinetic or potential E. For instance, kinetic E. is visible in mass motion, visible or invisible wave motion (sound, light, etc.) of electric currents, and so on; and potential E. is recognised in raised masses, magnetised bodies, separated electric charges, etc. One characteristic of all E. is its property of transformation, and in all its transformations there is evident the property of *conservation* of E. The physical law that is known by this name asserts that the total amount of E. in any isolated system is absolutely invariable in amount. E. may be added or abstracted from without, but as long as no external influences intervene the total quantity of E. within the system can neither increase nor decrease. It is usual, therefore, to say that the entire E. of the universe is conserved. Galileo seems to have been familiar with the idea that E. cannot be created, a fact which he inferred from a careful study of the machines, all of a simple nature, that were used in his day. However, there appeared to be many cases in which E. is destroyed, and the indications would prove that all mechanical energy is gradually wasted away by frictional and such-like losses. The motions of the celestial bodies are far more easily described by the aid of the principle of conservation of E. than they could be without it.

**Enfantin, Barthélemy Prosper** (1796–1864), the son of a banker in Paris, became one of the chief founders of the Saint-Simon school of Socialism. From 1826 till 1830 he was associated with Bazard in carrying on Saint-Simon's work, but they eventually disagreed on the question of marriage, E. being an advocate of free-love, which led to his prosecution in 1832. He was imprisoned for a year, and on his release became editor of the journal *Le Crédit Public.* His principal works are: *Doctrine de Saint–Simon,* written in conjunction with others; *Traité d'Economie Politique ; La Religion Saint-Simonienne. See* Castille's *Le Père Enfantin,* 1859.

**Enfield,** a tn. and par. of Middlesex, England, 10½ m. N. of London Bridge, situated in the valley of the Lea. It has of late years become a residential suburb of London. The New River flows through it, and Middleton

House, the home of Sir Hugh Middleton, the first director of the New River Company, is here. The perpendicular church contains fifteenth to sixteenth century tombs. There are remains of Enfield Palace at which Princess Elizabeth was staying at the time of her father's death, now the Constitutional Club. There is an anct. British entrenchment in what was the park. Charles Lamb resided at Chase Side, and Isaac Disraeli, father of Lord Beaconsfield, was *b.* here in 1766. The Royal Small Arms Factory is at Enfield Lock. Pop. 60,743.

**Enfield,** a tn. of Connecticut, U.S.A., situated in Hartford co. on Connecticut R. Tobacco is grown and carpets and casket hardware made. Pop. 13,404.

**Enfield, William** (1741–99), an English Nonconformist clergyman, *b.* at Sudbury in England, and author of the well-known *Speaker's, Preacher's Directory,* and *Abridgement of Brucker's History of Philosophy.* Also compiled *Institutes of Natural Philosophy,* theoretical and experimental.

**Enfilade** (Fr. from *enfiler,* to thread, to pass through from end to end), a military term used when the firing is directed along an enemy's line or parapet. It is a most effective form of fire, being extremely difficult to meet, and entrenchments or parapets are useless as cover. The usual form of defence against an E. is a *traverse,* or bank of earth raised at right angles to the lines of defence.

**Enfranchisement,** *see* COPYHOLD.

**Engadine,** the Swiss part of the valley of the Inn in the canton of the Grisons. It is traversed by a carriage road from the Maloja Plateau (5935 ft.) at the S.W. end to Martinsbruck (3406 ft.) at the N.E. end, a distance of 56 m. It is divided into the Upper and Lower E., the capital of the former being Samaden (pop. 967), of the latter, Schuls (pop. 117). The Upper E. is the best known, and is a favourite health resort, the mineral waters of St. Moritz having been known since the sixteenth century. Pontresina is a centre for tourists. The valley is reached by road over the passes, and there is a railway running under the Albula Pass to St. Moritz. The language spoken is Ladin (an old Romance tongue) or German. Total pop. 11,712.

**Engelberg,** a beautifully situated vil. of Switzerland, the terminus of the electric railway from Stansstad on the Lake of Lucerne, a favourite summer resort, and one of the most popular winter sports centres in Switzerland. The Benedictine Abbey was founded in 1120 and the whole valley ruled by the abbot until 1798. No ladies are allowed to inspect the valuable library, but men may.

**Engels, Friedrich** (1820–95), a German Socialist, *b.* at Barmen, the son of a wealthy cotton-spinner. After spending two years in England writing for the organs of the Owenite and Chartist movements, he went to Paris and there visited Karl Marx (*q.v.*). The two became close friends and worked so much together during the remainder of their lives that the works of the one became more or less the works of the other. E. wrote in collaboration with Marx, *Die heilige Familie oder Kritik der Kritischen Kritik* (Frankfort), 1845; and *Manifest der Kommunistischen Partei*, the famous communist manifesto (London, 1848; English ed. 1848 and 1888). After the death of his friend he published the third and last volumes of Marx's great work, *Das Kapital*, 1885. *See* Dr. Fr. Mehring, *Aus dem Literarischen Nachlass von Karl Marx, Friedrich Engels, und Ferdinand Lassalle* (Stuttgart), 1902.

**Enghien** (Flemish *Edingen*), a tn. in prov. Hainault, Belgium. It is famous for its lace, and was once the seat of the Condé family, the dukes of E. The castle was burnt down, but the park still remains, and contains a stone cottage built by an ancestor of the present owner, the Duke of Arenberg, for Jean Jacques Rousseau. Pop. 4600.

**Enghien, Louis Antoine, Henri de Bourbon Condé, Duc d'** (1772–1804), the son of Henri Louis Joseph, Prince of Condé, and Louise Thérèse Mathilde, sister of the Duke of Orleans (Philippe Egalité), *b.* at Chantilly. In 1788 he commenced the military career for which he had been trained, but when the French Revolution broke out he emigrated and tried to raise troops abroad. In 1792 he was given a command in the French royal army of *émigrés*, and served in the Condé army under his father and grandfather. After the peace of Lunéville (Feb. 1801), he retired to Ettenheim in Baden, having married the niece of Cardinal de Rohan, the Princess Charlotte. In 1804 he was falsely accused of being implicated in the Cadoudal-Pichegru conspiracy, and by Napoleon's orders he was seized ? ıd taken to the castle of Vincennes, where after the pretence of a trial he was shot. He was the last of the great house of Condé.

**Enghien-les-Bains**, a tn., dept. Seine-et-Oise, France. It is not far from the forest of Montmorency and only 8 m. from Paris, and is a favourite health resort with sulphurous water. Pop. 5100.

**Engineer, The**, a leading engineering journal, founded in 1856. Its contributors include many of the foremost men in the profession. One of its features is the information obtained from abroad.

**Engineering**, an illustrated weekly paper, founded by an American, Zerah Colbourn, in 1866. The illustrations are one of the chief features, and special prominence is given to naval subjects.

**Engineering and Architectural Societies.** While the leading architectural societies are found mainly in London, several of the important engineering societies are located in other large towns dealing with some specific engineering industry. Some of the societies are : Royal Institute of Brit. Architects (f. 1834), 9 Conduit St., W. 1.; Incorp. Assoc. of Architects and Surveyors, 1 Wilbraham Place, S.W. 1.; The Architecture Club (1922), 229 Strand, W.C. 2 ; Architectural Assoc. (1847), 34–36 Bedford Square, W.C. 1; R. I. of Architects of Ireland (1839), 8 Marrion Sq., Dublin. The Institution of Civil Engineers (1818), Great George St., Westminster, S.W. 1; Inst. of Mechanical Eng. (1847), Storey's Gate, St. James's Park, London; Soc. of Engineers (Incorp. 1910), 17 Victoria St., London; Brit. Engineers' Assoc. (Incorp. 1912), 32 Victoria St., London; Inst. of Marine Engineers, 85–88 The Minories, London; Inst. of Electrical E. (1871), Savoy Place, London; Inst. of Mining Engineers (1889), 225 City Rd., London; Junior Inst. of E. (1884), 39 Victoria St., London; Inst. of Municipal and County Engineers (1873), 84 Eccleston Sq., London; Inst. of Structural Engineers (1908), 10 Upper Belgrave St., London; Inst. of Gas Engineers (1863), 28 Grosvenor Gdns., London; Inst. of Water E. (1896), Parliament Mansions, Westminster, London; Inst. of Heating and Ventilating E., 12 Russel Sq., London; Inst. of Automobile Engineers, Watergate House, London; The Illuminating Engineering Soc., 32 Victoria St., London; Inst. of Engineers and Shipbuilders in Scotland (1857), 39 Elmbank Crescent, Glasgow; Inst. of Civil Engineers of Ireland (1835), 35 Dawson St., Dublin; N.E. Coast Inst. of Engineers and Shipbuilders, Bolbec Hall, Newcastle-upon-Tyne.

**Engineering Drawing** is the chief medium by which the engineer conveys his ideas to others, and the drawing office is the connecting link between the engineering department and the machine shops. The draughtsman's function is to develop the sketches drawn by the engineers into the finished drawing from which the machinist takes all his measurements. It is in the drawing office that the inventions come to life and indeed where many may reveal fatal flaws. From the pencil-drawing an ink tracing is made on tracing paper or cloth; this work is done by junior draughtsmen, and in many works it is done by girls. Photo-prints are taken from these tracings, the commonest of which are the ferro-prussate or 'blue' prints; of these prints several are sent down to the drawing stores in the machine shops and one copy is put in the records. A drawing office is an excellent place for the young engineer to receive his training, for he sees designs of all the pieces of machinery from their earliest stages to completion.

**Engineering Education and Training.** When a boy leaves school there are two courses open to him for gaining his training; they are (i.) A three years' course at a University, at the end of which he sits for his degree; or (ii.) practical training at manufacturing works coupled with evening classes. The deciding factor in the choice is, of course, the amount of capital which can be spent upon the training. The first of these two is by far the better because it enables the student to acquire a thorough acquaintance with theory. The first year at the University is spent mainly in the study of mathematics, physics and chemistry, together with Fr. and Ger., in preparation for the intermediate examination, which is taken at the end of the first year. The second year takes the student further into mathematics, covering differential and integral calculus while continuing physics and modern languages. He now specialises in the branch of engineering which he proposes to take up, whether mechanical, civil, electrical, or one or other of the sub-divisions of these main classes. In the third year mathematics include the problems which the engineer is likely to meet with in the course of his work. At the end of the third year he sits for his degree.

Engineering works take youths at the age of fourteen for training as skilled mechanics and as foremen. Those who show exceptional ability are often encouraged to attend evening classes so as to acquire a better knowledge of their profession with the view of obtaining positions on the technical staff of the works. In large works these boys are under the care of instructors, who put them to and aid them to complete set tasks.

**Engineering, Military.** M. E. is the adaptation of engineering practice to military requirements. As was evident in the Great War, a civilian engineer can readily take his place on the executive side of M. E., but on the administrative side military experience and training are required. A modern army must rely on civilian resources to a very great extent, not only for man-power and material, but also for technical experts, and among the latter the military engineer is of the highest importance. The Great War gave a great impetus to scientific development, notably in chemistry, metallurgy, and electricity, which three branches of scientific study have had a revolutionary effect on the military machine, e.g. in the making of poison gas, high explosives and synthetic oil; in the application of the internal combustion engine to aviation and tanks; and in wire-less telegraphy, respectively. M. E. is directly concerned with all these developments, and at the moment, the greatest problem for military engineers is 'mechanisation,' i.e. the utilisation of mechanically produced power in order to increase mobility and to conserve physical energy. The task of M. E. is to assimilate the tremendous increase of engineering knowledge into the technique of war. The co-operation of the General Staff of a modern army with the military engineer is necessary to effect this process. But as the members of the General Staff of a modern army are not experts in M. E., though they are responsible for policy, the modern military engineer must be able to act in a consultative capacity as well as to carry out the current and ordinary engineering work of an army. In other words, his task is to interpret the policy of the General Staff in terms of the developments of science. Besides the military engineer, there is the engineering specialist, whose duties are restricted to the work of research and design in military maintenance. On the extent to which the distinction between the military engineer and the specialist in design and research is preserved in departmental organisation, efficiency in M. E. will largely depend. Every new device, and every application of a new weapon has its reaction on numerous other devices and weapons, e.g. if a more efficient anti-tank gun is produced, a faster or more highly armoured tank must replace previously existing tanks, and this, in turn, may call for progress in bridge design to carry a heavier tank. Thus, to attain all-round efficiency in an army, the fighting machines must be evolved as a co-ordinated whole; and it is in this sphere that the consultative advice of the military engineer assumes such importance to-day. In the British Army the training of military engineers is effected by the education and theoretical training of personnel of the Corps of Royal Engineers; which training comprises a course of theoretical training at Cambridge University; a course of applied practical training in military *matériel* at the School of Military Engineering; a period of practical apprenticeship with civilian mechanical and electrical manufacturers and consultants; and experience in combatant duties by co-operation with other arms of the army through the R.E. field companies.

**Engineering Review, The,** a monthly publication, founded in 1899. It is mainly scientific, and the chief articles are professional records of research and work carried out by leading men in the profession.

**Engineering Standards Association, British,** a committee formed to fix standards in constructional work, as steel for ships, boilers, rails, etc. It includes representatives from the following bodies : Institutions of Civil, Mechanical, and Electrical Engineers; Institution of Naval Architects, and the Iron and Steel Institute. The societies mentioned above supply the funds, which are augmented by a government grant and contributions from railway companies and engineering firms. Offices : 28 Victoria St., London, S.W.

**Engineers, Corps of Royal.** Before the eighteenth century the technical elements of the British Army, *e.g.* artillery and engineers, were provided by the Board of Ordnance, and both artillery and engineers officers formed part of the early ' Artillery Trains.' The system under which artillery units were raised for a campaign was found to be inadequate and uneconomical, and as a result artillery cos. (now Royal Artillery) were established in 1716, and the ancestor of the R.E. in 1717, both emerging from the Board of Ordnance. Before 1757 the officers of the R.E. did not have military titles, but in that year they were first granted commissions. It was not until 1788, however, that the military officers of the Engineer Department were constituted the ' Corps of Royal Engineers,' the men being still regimented in the Corps of Royal Military Artificers. When Napoleon

invaded Egypt a detachment was sent to Constantinople to train the Turkish army, and other companies performed good service in Egypt, Malta, Italy, Sicily, and the West Indies. In 1813 the title of the Corps of Royal Sappers and Miners displaced that of Mil. Artificers and did effective work under Wellington during the Peninsular and Waterloo campaigns. The Crimean War was the scene of manifold activities by the engineers, and the officers and men were, immediately afterwards, united to form one corps under the title of ' Royal Engineers.' After the Indian Mutiny the Bengal, Madras and Bombay Corps of Engineers were transferred to the R.E.

Being a scientific corps the R.E. has ' nursed ' many important branches of military science, particularly the Royal Flying Corps (now the Royal Air Force), which was evolved from the Air Battalion of the R.E., and the Royal Corps of Signals which was evolved from the Signal Units of the R.E.

The widespread services of this corps are aptly expressed in their mottoes, granted in 1832, ' Ubique ' and ' Quo fas et gloria ducunt.' The King is Colonel-in-Chief of the Corps.

**Engines,** *see* AERO ENGINES, AIR ENGINE, BOILERS, GAS ENGINES, STEAM ENGINES.

**England and Wales.** Topographically England and Wales may be viewed together or as separate units ; administratively, for purpose of local and imperial government, in matters of statistics, etc., they are one. Special geographical features peculiar to Wales will be found in that article, and there are separate articles on the various counties both of England and Wales. Of the group of islands which lie off the W. coast of Europe, and which form the United Kingdom of Great Britain and Ireland, England (including Wales), the most important portion in wealth, population, size, and as possessing the centre of the imperial government and administration, lies between lat. 55° 46′ N. at the mouth of the Tweed, and lat. 49° 57′ 30″ N. at the Lizard, and between long. 1° 46′ E. at Lowestoft, and 5° 43′ W. at Land's End. It is separated from Scotland N. by a line running from Berwick-on-Tweed to the head of Solway Firth ; on the E. by the North Sea, S. by the English Channel ; the Strait of Dover, 21 m. at its narrowest point, divides it from the coast of France, which is 100 m. distant at the Lizard. At the S.W. corner the broad and deeply indented Bristol Channel parts the S.W. coast of England from Wales and opens on the Atlantic; on the W., St. George's Channel divides Wales from Ireland and leads to the Irish Sea and thence to the N. of St. Patrick's Channel between Ireland and Scotland. The coast-line, following broad indentations and including the islands of the Isle of Wight and Anglesea, is about 2350 m. The total area is 58,315 sq. m., of which England contains 50,939 and Wales 7376 sq. m. England is divided into forty territorial counties, and Wales into twelve (see further *Population* and *Local Government*, below). The Cheviot Hills, highest point the Cheviot (2676 ft.), form a considerable portion of the N. boundary; S.W. lie the Cumbrian mountains with Scafell Pike (3210 ft.), the

centred in Bradford, Leeds, and Huddersfield, established before the age of steam and then spreading to the W., now no longer drawing its supplies from the former sheep-farms of Yorkshire and the Continent but from the world. The great iron and steel works are at Middlesbrough, Stockton, centred on the Tees, shipbuilding on the Tyne, the cutlery and armour plates at Sheffield, from early times celebrated for its knives. To the N., the Northumberland coal fields reach the coast at Newcastle, with South Shields and Sunderland on the coast. To the W. the inflow of cotton through Liverpool has changed Lancashire into a vast hive of cotton-spinning and cotton-weav-

ON THE SUSSEX DOWNS

[*Southern Railway*

highest of England's mountains; here, in Cumberland and Westmorland, is the Lake District; E. and running as the central feature of N. England is the Pennine Range, which reaches almost to the Midlands, and E. and W. of which are to be found the great centres of industry, for in close proximity are the great coal fields, which on the E. side supply the iron and steel industries, originally getting all their raw material from the iron ores of this region; it is this close proximity of coal that on the discovery of steam power and of the use of coal for iron-smelting established this part of England as the centre of the world's industries in the early part of the nineteenth century. The high moorlands of the Pennine Range form an anticline, with a few beautiful health resorts, and much picturesque scenery especially round the Peak in Derbyshire. On the E. side are concentrated the wool industries,

ing towns, centring on Manchester, and further S.W. the coal fields supply necessary power to the potteries of Stoke and the surrounding districts. Away from the Pennines, but still in reach of the coal, lies Birmingham, the nucleus of the great metal-working industries of the Midlands, and Coventry, that of motor-cars, bicycles, while on the fringe lie such manufacturing centres as Leicester, Nottingham, working chiefly in leather and lace. The proximity of the sea, never, throughout England, more than 75 m. distant, and the navigable rivers have played an important part in the development. The Tyne, the Tees, the Humber, with its great shipping port of Hull on the E., the Mersey, on the W., with Liverpool and its great artery the Manchester Ship Canal leading to the very centre of the cotton industry and linked by a network of canals, still bearing coal and heavy traffic to the potteries, Birmingham, and the Midlands, all these factors, combined with the rapid development of the railways prior to those of any other country, form an easy explanation of the unchallenged supremacy of England, commercially and industrially, when America was in its infancy and the Continent of Europe was still recovering from the ravages of continual wars and the confusion of political revolutions. Where the Pennine Range ends begins the great Midland plain, reaching from the fenland districts of Lincoln, Huntingdon, and Cambridgeshire, now drained, and the rich agricultural levels of Norfolk to the typical inland country stretching from Leicester and Nottingham to the valley of the Thames to the S. and to Warwickshire, Worcestershire, and Gloucestershire to the W., where the Bristol Channel fed by the Severn and the Avon, and the great industrial city and port of Bristol bring the natural water-way for traffic to its doors. This plain district is the centre of the agricultural industry of England, both tillage and pasture, and the scenery is typical of pastoral England, the chief towns being originally and in many cases still market-towns, though the railway has made Crewe, for example, a great engineering centre, while Reading is a manufacturing town in an agricultural district. London (q.v.) and the Thames stand by themselves, and dominate the home counties, as they are termed, which lie on both banks of the river. One of the greatest of the world's ports, a manufacturing town of the most diverse industries, the centre of the money markets of the world, the business heart of the country, the seat of government of the empire, London spreads the dwelling-places of its workers wider and wider. Along the Thames valley lie a line of residential towns and districts, and the railways bring a daily tide of those who sleep in the country and work in the town. From the white chalk cliffs of Dover through Kent and Surrey in a curving line lie the North Downs overlooking the gardens of Kent and the low Weald, once forest-clad and set with iron-works, now agricultural and attracting residential building; to the W., below and within the Downs, are the healthy pine-wooded and sandy heather of Surrey, falling into Hampshire and rising to the great plateau of Salisbury Plain. Running along the S. coast, from the flat marshes of the old world port of Rye, are the whalebacked bare South Downs looking on a ring of sunny seaside resorts, with Brighton in the centre. Southampton,

with its great docks and shipping trade, and Portsmouth, with its naval docks and arsenals, are made by the inlet of Southampton Water, guarded from the Channel by the Isle of Wight. Cornwall forms a rocky peninsula, connected geologically with the mountain system of Devon; here on the S. coast lie the sunniest and warmest part of the British Isles. W., where Land's End meets the Atlantic, the scenery is bold and rugged and beautiful, and up the Cornish and Devon coast of the Bristol Channel is perhaps the most lovely district in England, where the wild uplands of Exmoor and Dartmoor stretch down in wooded combes to the sea. On the Welsh side of the Bristol Channel lie the great steam coal-fields of S. Wales centring in the ports of Cardiff and Barry Dock, with Newport, Swansea, and Merthyr-Tydvil, seats of iron and copper smelting and tin-plate manufacturing. Wales, mountainous and rugged, finds her industrial life here; the centre is agricultural and thinly populated; the N., though with great slate quarries, chiefly attracts countless visitors to her scenery of mountain (Snowdon, 3560 ft., is the highest point in England and Wales), lake, and sea (see further WALES). On her land side Wales meets the great midland plain in the pastoral and agricultural county of Shropshire, with isolated hill country. The N.W. coast of England stretches from the Mersey estuary, leading to Liverpool and the industrial centres, along the sand-levels where lies Blackpool, the Brighton of the N., to Morecambe Bay and the great shipping and iron-works of Barrow-in-Furness.

*Scenery.*—The Eng. countryside varies from well-wooded hills to cultivated plains. Mountain country is centred in the Lake District, Cumberland and Westmorland, and in Wales, while much of Yorkshire, Devon, and Cornwall is moorland with moss-covered rocks, bogs and streams. The bare downs of Sussex were once covered with forest, but are now treeless grasslands. The downs continue into Kent, which is called the Garden of England. Here are the fruit fields, the orchards and the hop-gardens, with near them the cone-shaped oast houses. The E. plain is flat country, much of which is fenland, drained by the Ouse, smaller rivers, and the Norfolk Broads. Much of the Midlands is spoilt by the smoke and sulphur of the industrial area, but attempts are made to preserve walks from the builders. In the S. also, where Greater London spreads over a vast stretch of land, many parks and commons have been preserved.

One characteristic of Eng. scenery is the division of the land into fields, and the most common barriers between them are hedges of clipped hazel and hawthorn trees. Gaps in the hedges are bridged by wooden stiles, while in some counties the fields are divided by low stone walls. By the side of the hedge grow many wild flowers—primroses, violets, ground ivy, and wild roses. Other common wild flowers are the buttercup, daisy, scabious, pansy, poppy, snowdrop, daffodil, celandine, and dandelion, while in the woods are found bluebells and wood anemones. The most common trees are the oak, hawthorn, elm, ash, horse-chestnut, willow, birch, poplar and beech.

beautiful timbered houses, and in London there are whole streets of that admirably urban eighteenth-century architecture. The university towns of Oxford and Cambridge have buildings of every century, from the fourteenth. Durham University is housed in the old castle. Several famous castles still stand, among them are the Tower of London with its keep, that was begun in 1078, Windsor Castle and Arundel Castle. Of historic ruins there are Bodium Castle in Sussex, with a moat still full of water, and Tintagel in Cornwall, where King Arthur is supposed to have held his court, and many others. Penhurst Castle, in Kent, is the manor

THE BRIDGE OVER THE OUSE AT ST. IVES, HUNTS

This is one of the many interesting old bridges that are scattered all over England. It is a fifteenth-century bridge, but to the chapel in the centre was added the tower-like superstructure after 1689

Different kinds of fir trees also flourish, but the only nut trees are the eating chestnut, walnut and hazel. Blackberries, strawberries, and mushrooms grow wild in fields and hedges, while the grass is everywhere green throughout the year, greenness being a feature of the Eng. countryside.

The Eng. coast is very varied, differing from sandy or shingle shores to granite or chalk cliffs. St. Ives in Cornwall is an attractive fishing village with cobbled streets and white stone cottages. The many rivs. are well stocked with fish, including salmon, roach, dace, and barbel. The Wye in the West is one of the most beautiful rivs. New bridges are mostly plain and of concrete, but there are a number of interesting old ones, such as the fifteenth-century bridge over the Ouse at St. Ives, Huntingdonshire.

In the tns. old houses may still be found. Chester has some very

house in which Sir Philip Sidney lived; its great hall, with grey time-worn oak-raftered roof and minstrel's gallery, is exceptionally well preserved. Humbler dwellings in the villages are the cottages of lath and plaster with skilfully-thatched roofs. Melbourne, near Cambridge, is a typical old-world village. Some timbered cottages still exist, one of which is Milton's Cottage at Chalfont St. Giles. Another famous cottage—of whitewashed brick—is John Wesley's in Swanage.

Parts of the forests—the New Forest, Sherwood and Ashdown Forest—still remain, and some, such as Epping, are state-preserved. At Waltham, near Epping, is an Eleanor Cross, and many other old stone crosses are scattered over England. Since the Great War nearly every village green has its war memorial, while the Cenotaph (q.v.), the British war memorial to all those who fell in the war, is in London at

Whitehall. There are many famous caves, such as the Cheddar caves in Somerset, while probably the oldest monuments are the circles of stones at Avebury and Stonehenge, the latter dating from *c.* 1680 B.C.

There are few wild animals left in E., and those few are hunted. The fox and the otter and semi-wild ponies and deer are the largest that remain. There are many birds, both resident and visitant, but there again the larger ones, such as the buzzard and the peregrine falcon, have all but been killed off, although many counties preserve certain birds by law.

*Geology.—See* GEOLOGY.

*Climate.*—The mean annual temperature ranges from 48° F. in the N. to over 52° F. in the Scilly Isles, off Land's End, but this variation moves diagonally, and the W. coast is warmer throughout its length than the E. The mean coldest temperature is about 40° F., the hottest, 61°. The prevailing winds are southwesterly and westerly, but from April the tendency is towards easterly winds. The rainfall is heaviest in the W., especially in the Lake District, Wales, Cornwall, and Devon, where it exceeds 40 in., and in the first two places as much as 60 in. On the E. coast, especially at the Wash and the Thames estuary, it falls to 25 in. Sunshine reaches about 1600 hours in the year on the S. coast and falls to less than 1300 in Yorkshire.

*Population.*—By the census of June 1921 the total pop. of England and Wales was 37,886,699, of which 18,075,239 were males and 19,811,460 were females. This total comprises visitors and residents, British nationals and aliens, civilians and non-civilians, and is the largest ever recorded, showing an increase of 1,816,207 over the returns by the previous census, April 1911. The decennial increase per cent. in 1881 was 14·4; 1891, 11·6; 1901, 12·2; 1911, 10·9; 1921, 4·9. In 1921 the pop. of England was 35,681,019 and of Wales 2,205,680. The pops. of the counties of England, census, 1921, are: Bedfordshire, 206,462; Berkshire, 294,821; Buckinghamshire, 236,171; Cambridgeshire, 129,602 and Isle of Ely, 73,817; Cheshire, 1,025,724; Cornwall, 320,705; Cumberland, 273,173; Derbyshire, 714,662; Devonshire, 709,614; Dorsetshire, 228,160; Durham, 1,479,033; Essex, 1,470,257; Gloucestershire, 757,651; Hampshire (incl. Isle of Wight), 1,004,918; Herefordshire, 113,189; Hertfordshire, 333,195; Huntingdonshire, 54,741; Kent, 1,141,666; Lancashire, 4,927,484; Leicestershire, 494,469; Lincolnshire, 602,202;

London (administrative county, including the city of London), 4,484,523; Middlesex, 1,253,002; Monmouthshire, 450,794; Norfolk, 504,293; Northamptonshire, 349,363; Northumberland, 746,096; Nottinghamshire, 641,149; Oxfordshire, 189,615; Rutlandshire, 18,376; Shropshire, 243,062; Somersetshire, 465,710; Staffordshire, 1,348,877; Suffolk, 400,058; Surrey, 930,086; Sussex, 727,997; Warwickshire, 1,389,977; Westmorland, 65,746; Wiltshire, 292,208; Worcestershire, 405,842; Yorkshire, 4,182,529. The population of the counties of Wales, 1921: Anglesey, 51,744; Brecknockshire, 61,222; Cardiganshire, 60,881; Carmarthenshire, 175,073; Carnarvonshire, 130,975; Denbighshire, 154,842; Flintshire, 106,617; Glamorganshire, 1,252,481; Merionethshire, 45,087; Montgomeryshire, 51,263; Pembrokeshire, 91,978; Radnorshire, 23,517. The population of towns, exceeding 100,000, in E. and W. (census 1921), are: London (Greater London, the 'outer ring' with the administrative county), 7,480,201; Birmingham, 919,444; Liverpool, 802,940; Manchester, 730,307; Sheffield, 490,639; Leeds, 458,232; Bristol, 376,975; West Ham, 300,860; Kingston upon Hull, 287,150; Bradford, 285,961; Newcastle-upon-Tyne, 275,009; Nottingham, 262,624; Portsmouth, 247,284; Stoke-on-Trent, 240,428; Leicester, 234,143; Salford, 234,045; Plymouth, 210,036; Cardiff, 200,184; Croydon, 190,684; Bolton, 178,683; Willesden, 165,674; Rhondda, 162,717; Southampton, 160,994; Sunderland, 159,055; Swansea, 157,554; Tottenham, 146,711; Birkenhead, 145,577; Oldham 144,983; East Ham, 143,246; Brighton, 142,430; Middlesbrough, 131,070; Derby, 129,796; Walthamstow, 129,395; Leyton, 128,430; Coventry, 128,157; Blackburn, 126,643; Gateshead, 125,142; Stockport, 123,309; Norwich, 120,661; Preston, 117,406; South Shields, 116,635; Huddersfield, 110,102; Southend-on-Sea, 106,010; Burnley, 103,157; St. Helens, 102,640; Wolverhampton, 102,342.

INDUSTRIES.—*Agriculture:* The average acreage under crops and grass in England and Wales for the years 1919–29 was 25,707,443, of which 10,524,678 ac. were arable land (1929 showing a decrease of 160,987 ac. on the previous year), and 4,516,772 ac. were permanent grassland for hay, and 10,665,993 ac. permanent pasture. Wheat, barley, and oats show an acreage under crops of 1,310,115, 1,077,332, and 1,683,542 in England (excluding

Monmouthshire) in 1929, a decrease in the year of 64,827 and 62,499 for wheat and barley and an increase of 87,785 for oats. In Wales (including Monmouthshire) the acreages (1929) for wheat, barley, and oats were 20,094, 42,950, and 170,866 respectively, a decrease of 507 and 2222 ac. for wheat and barley, and an increase of 3907 ac. for oats. Other considerable crops in England and Wales (1929) are : turnips and swedes 699,376 ac., potatoes 518,808 ac., mangold 299,174 ac., and beans 157,050 ac. Sugar-beet is chiefly grown in the E. counties. In 1929–30 229,918 ac. were under cultivation, and eighteen factories absorbed nearly 2,000,000 tons of beet and produced 5,800,000 cwt. of commercial sugar. On an average there are 1,000,000 horses, 6,000,000 cattle, 15,000,000 sheep, and 2,500,000 pigs. The average number of persons employed each year, both permanent and casual labourers, during the years 1921–9 was 784,670, a decrease of nearly 10 per cent. since 1921, and the number of holdings of over 1 ac. has decreased from 420,133 in 1921 to 404,970 in 1929, the average size of a holding being about 66 ac. Counties with over 30,000 ac. under cultivation for wheat (1929) are : Cambridgeshire and Isle of Ely, Essex, Gloucestershire, Hampshire, Hertfordshire, Huntingdonshire, Lincolnshire, Norfolk, Northamptonshire, Nottinghamshire, Oxfordshire, Suffolk, Wiltshire, and Yorkshire ; with over 30,000 ac. for barley : Cambridgeshire, Essex, Lincolnshire, Norfolk, Suffolk, Yorkshire, while Cheshire, Cornwall, Cumberland, Devonshire, Durham, Essex, Hampshire, Kent, Lancashire, Lincolnshire, Norfolk, Northumberland, Nottinghamshire, Shropshire, Staffordshire, Wiltshire, and Yorkshire are the largest oats-producing counties. Devonshire, Gloucestershire, Kent, and Worcestershire have extensive orchards, and Kent is famous for its hops and small-fruit growing. The total value of agricultural produce is £221,370,000, of which 154,320,000 is for livestock and livestock products, 43,120,000 for farm crops, and 23,930,000 for fruit, vegetables, and flowers.

*Fisheries.*—The E. coast, with its fleets of trawlers fishing in the N. Sea, is the most important ; the great port of Grimsby is pre-eminent, but Yarmouth, especially for herrings, and Lowestoft are important. Brixham on the S. coast and the Cornish pilchard-fisheries should be mentioned, and Milford at the head of Milford Haven in Wales transmits large quantities to inland towns.

Oysters are important at Whitstable and the Essex coast. The total quantity of sea fish landed annually is about 700,000 tons, and the value (excluding shell-fish) is about £14,000,000. The annual value of shell-fish is £500,000. Nearly 8000 vessels are engaged in the fishing industry, and half this number are steam-driven. Close on 35,000 persons are employed.

*Mining.*—Far exceeding all other minerals together coal stands easily first ; the largest fields are in Durham, Yorkshire (W. Riding), and Lancashire ; Derbyshire, Staffordshire, and Northumberland are also important, while the Glamorganshire fields are unique in the world for their fine, hard steam coal. Anthracite coal is found in the W. half of the S. Wales coal-fields. The total annual production in England and Wales is over 200,000,000 tons, valued at about £160,000,000. The great iron-ore district is at Cleveland in Yorkshire (N. Riding), nearly 2,000,000 tons being mined annually, and Barrow-in-Furness benefits by the very rich hæmatite of Cumberland and N. Lancashire. The only coal-field which combines considerable workings in iron-ore is N. Staffordshire. The total ironstone mined in England and Wales annually is about 11,000,000 tons, of which the metal content amounts to 30 per cent., the value being £3,000,000, but the large metal works depend chiefly for their raw material on imports, especially from Spain, coming to Middlesbrough. Lead, tin, and copper, once extensively mined in Derbyshire for the first and Cornwall for the last two metals, have now ceased to be of importance. A fine china clay is mined in Cornwall ; slate is quarried especially in the Lake District, but the great centre is Wales. Industrial workers in mines and quarries number over a million, of whom 900,000 are engaged in coal-mining.

*Textiles.*—The great cotton industry, the greatest in the world, is practically confined to S. Lancashire, to which the raw material is brought through Liverpool, connected by the ship canal to Manchester. The moist atmosphere of the district has aided the combination of the most skilled workmen, the machinery for which the acutest inventors are constantly devising improvements, and the ever-ready coal supply for power which established Lancashire as the centre of the world's cotton industry in the early nineteenth century. Oldham and Bolton are the chief spinning towns, the latter being the fine-cotton spinning centre. Preston, Burnley, Blackburn, Bury, and Rochdale are weaving towns, while Rochdale is also a woollen town, being important for flannel manufacture. The woollen industry, however, centres in the W. Riding of Yorkshire round Leeds. Bradford is important for worsted manufacture, and also has silk, velvet, and plush mills. Near Bradford, on the Aire, is the model town of Saltaire, built by Titus Salt in 1853, with its alpaca works. Halifax, in the Calder valley, makes lighter worsteds and baizes, and has a large carpet-making industry. The Colne valley is a busy woollen district, and Huddersfield is noted for fancy cloths. Heavier woollens are manufactured round Dewsbury and Batley, the former being the rag market of the world, where old wool materials are reconditioned. Wakefield, Barnsley, Keighley, Morley, Heckmondwike are all woollen towns. The industry has spread into Lancashire, Rochdale, at Aston, and

*Iron and Steel.*—The iron industry first centred in the Forest of Dean and in the Kentish Weald, where raw material and wood fuel were easily obtainable. When wood was replaced by coal, iron works were set up near the coalfields in the Midlands and S. Wales. With the insufficiency of domestic supplies of raw material, smelting in the Midlands was largely replaced by the manufacture of articles in iron and steel, and two towns—Birmingham and Sheffield—have attained pre-eminence, the former being associated with all kinds of metal ware, the latter more especially with cutlery. With the discovery of the Cleveland deposits, Middlesbrough (N. Yorkshire) became one of the great iron-smelting districts, others being S. Durham, S. Wales, N. Lancashire, and Cumberland, the latter depending largely on Spanish ores. Production of pig-iron is

has entered on a period of depression.

WINDSOR CASTLE

Glossop, while Denton and Stockport specialise in felt hats and velours. The Yorkshire wool industry has almost eclipsed the long-established manufacture of 'West of England cloth,' but this is still made at Stroud (Gloucestershire) and Trowbridge and Bradford (Wiltshire). The silk industry is also of long standing, especially in parts of Derbyshire, Staffordshire, and Cheshire. The artificial-silk industry is mostly run in connection with cotton and wool, but is widely distributed. Jute fabrics and yarns are manufactured at Barnsley. Textiles constitute about 37 per cent. of the value of native products exported from England, the value of cotton and wool yarns and manufactures exported being (1929) £135 and £53 millions respectively. By the Census of Production, 1924, cotton yarn was valued at £187,000,000, piece goods at £157,000,000, and miscellaneous cotton manufactures at £13,000,000, but since that date the industry which employs 500,000 people

valued at £35,000,000 (Census of Production, 1924) and of steel at £150,000,000. The average output of pig-iron per annum is about 6,000,000 tons, of steel 9,000,000 tons.

Allied to the iron industry is that of ship-building. When iron replaced wood as the material for ships, the industry shifted from the Thames to the Clyde, but in England the most active shipyards are on the N.E. coast, especially at Newcastle on the Tyne, Sunderland on the Wear, Stockton and Middlesbrough on the Tees, and Hartlepool. These yards account for some 500,000 tons of shipping a year, while smaller yards are in existence at Hull, Southampton, Barrow-in-Furness, and Liverpool.

Steam engines and rolling-stock are made at Manchester, Birmingham, and Newcastle, while the L.M.S. Railway has works at Crewe, the G.W.R. at Swindon, the S.R. at Eastleigh near Southampton, and the L.N.E.R. at Doncaster and Darlington. The manufacture of agricultural machinery is carried on in the corn districts, especially at Lincoln, Grantham, Norwich, and Ipswich.

*Other Industries.*—The presence of both clay and coal has made Staffordshire the centre of the pottery industry, and the pottery towns of Burslem, Tunstall, Hanley, Fenton, Langton, and Stoke are now incorporated in the county borough of Stoke-on-Trent. The industry is very centralised, but Worcester and Derby have long been famous for porcelain, while Stourbridge makes fireclay. Glass is also made near the coalfields, at Birmingham, S. Lancashire, and Worcestershire. In connection with the salt deposits of Cheshire and S. Durham, alkali and chemical works operate in the valleys of the Weaver and Wenlock, Cheshire, also at St. Helens in Lancashire, and Flint in Wales. Paper-making requires abundance of water, and is carried on in the Thames estuary, especially at Gravesend. The manufacture of dyestuffs is also a Thames industry at Silvertown, and on the Mersey and Manchester Ship Canal. Chair-making is a local industry among the beechwoods on the Chiltern Hills. Leather-work is widespread, more especially at Northampton for shoes, Leicester, Stafford, and Walsall. Lace-making by hand is an old industry, still pursued at Honiton, S. Devonshire.

COMMUNICATIONS.—*Railways:* There are 50,000 single-track miles of English and Welsh railways and 20,000 route miles. During the Great War, 1914–18, the railways were under gov. control, and were decontrolled in 1921. By the Railway Act of that year 120 railway companies were amalgamated into four systems : (1) the Southern Group, (2) the Western Group, (3) the North-Western, Midland, and West Scottish Group, and (4) the North-Eastern, Eastern, and East Scottish Group. The first group, organised as the Southern Railway, has a length of line of 2229 m., and serves the S. coast and S.W. of England from Waterloo, London, and also the S.E., combining the former London, Brighton and South Coast Railway and South Eastern and Chatham Railway, having important channel connections, linking England with the Continent. The Great Western Railway, combined with the Cambrian Railway and local S. Wales lines, constitutes the second group, running from Paddington, London, to Plymouth and Penzance, and through Bristol and the Severn Tunnel to S. Wales and Fishguard; also N.W. through Birmingham to Birkenhead. Its length of line is 3817 m. The third group is the largest, organised as the London, Midland and Scottish Railway, having 7217 m. of line. It serves the industrial Midlands and Scotland, and combines the former London, North-Western and Midland Railways from Euston and St. Pancras, London, together with the provincial Lancashire and Yorkshire Railway, N. Staffordshire Railway, Caledonian Railway, and others, comprising thirty-five companies in all. The fourth group covers the coal, iron, and ship-building areas of the E. part of England, and extends into Scotland. Organised as the London, North-Eastern Railway, it has 6722 m. of line, and includes the six trunk lines of the former Great Northern from King's Cross, London, the Great Eastern from Liverpool Street, and the Great Central from St. Marylebone with the North-Eastern from York and the North British from Edinburgh.

*Canals and Rivers.*—Many of the chief ports of the country are situated on river or on river estuaries. Liverpool on the Mersey estuary; Bristol with its ports at Avonmouth and its harbour up the R. Avon; London, with its network of docks on each bank of the Thames; the Humber, with Hull; and the Tyne, with Newcastle, need only be mentioned. The Manchester Ship Canal was opened in 1894, and is 35½ m. in length, being an artificial arm of the sea, making Manchester the fourth port in the United Kingdom. The canal system, which was highly developed during the latter part of the eighteenth century, receded in importance on the coming of the railways, and has, comparatively speaking, been neglected, a neglect which has been enhanced by the fact that many canal lines are owned by railway companies. The Humber and the Mersey are connected by the Aire and Calder canal from Goole to Leeds, thence by the Leeds and Liverpool canal. Sheffield is connected with the Trent by the Sheffield and S. Yorkshire and thence to the potteries district by the Trent, Mersey, and Bridgewater canals. Birmingham and district is also served by a canal system leading to the Severn and Trent. The Grand Union canal draws traffic from London to the N. and the Midlands. The total length of canals in England and Wales is 3640 m.

*Roads.*—England is suitable geographically for road-making, and good materials are abundant. With the ' Calamity of the Railways ' the upkeep of the roads was neglected, but with the coming of the motor-car and the lorry, improvement of the highways became imperative, and at the present time (1930) the cost of maintaining and rebuilding roads borders on £60,000,000 annually. This cost is borne by the county councils, which by the Local Government Act, 1929, are the Highway Authorities for all county roads, *i.e.* classified roads and rural roads, and by the borough and urban councils, who are responsible for all roads within their areas other than county roads. Large annual grants for road maintenance are made from the Road Fund, administered by the Minister of Transport. (*see also* HIGHWAYS.) Heavy transport by road rather than by rail has increased, and motor-coach routes connect up the main towns, while the motor-omnibus provides a local service in town and country. For these heavier vehicles a speed limit of 30 m.p.h. is fixed, but for cars and motor-cycles the limit has been abolished (Road Traffic Act, 1930). Progress in road construction has been made with the arterial roads such as the Great West Road and the new Dover Road; their main features are width, comparative straightness, and a smooth surface, while their monotony is relieved by the planting of trees. There are now (1930) about 15,400 m. of road in England and Wales, of which 12 per cent. are Class I. 8 per cent. Class II. and 80 per cent. unclassified.

*Local Government and Administration.*—For purposes of local government England and Wales are divided into administrative counties, of which there are sixty-two, following roughly the geographical and territorial counties, but London forms a county by itself, and Yorkshire and some other counties are split up into two or more administrative counties, while some smaller counties are grouped. The counties are divided into rural and urban districts governed by district councils, and the parishes of the rural districts have parish councils or parish meetings. Outside the county authority, except for certain purposes, are the boroughs, some being entirely independent. First are the county boroughs, which have all the powers of a county council and are independent. They are the old 'cities and counties,' such as Bristol, Nottingham, etc., and towns over 50,000 in population which have obtained the rank of a county borough from the Local Government Board. Non-county boroughs are of two classes, both quarter-sessions, boroughs of 10,000 population and over, and of under 10,000 population, with varying independence of county rating, etc.

*Society, Religion, etc.*—Social distinctions in England depend almost entirely on occupation, and there is no homogeneous 'upper' nor 'middle' class. The former land-owning class has been largely dispossessed since the Great War, and big estates have been broken up. The only class with any cohesion is the wage-earning class, which, together with all other employed persons, including salaried and professional, numbers 15,465,000, or 90 per cent. of the total occupied pop., numbered at 17,178,000 in England and Wales (Census of Occupations, 1921). Many distinctions subdivide the wage-earning class, 6,008,000 being engaged in manufactures, 2,349,000 in agriculture, fishing, mining, etc., 2,557,000 in commerce and finance, including clerks and shop assistants, etc., 1,484,000 in transport, etc. In central and local gov. work a million and a half persons are employed. The professional class numbers 667,000, or less than 4 per cent. of the total, and out of this number 42 per cent. are engaged in education and 26 per cent. in medicine. Of the remaining 10 per cent. outside the employed class employers number 637,000 (or 3·7 per cent.) and independent workers 1,076,000 (or 6·3 per cent.).

Occupational organisation—including trades unions, professional associations, scientific bodies, etc.—are a marked feature of social structure. Club-life of a more recreative character is becoming increasingly popular, and there are in England and Wales 11,780 Registered Clubs, political, social, athletic, etc., with an active membership of nearly four million.

The established religion in England and Wales is the Church of England, numbering 2,701,000 communicants. The Welsh Church was disestablished in 1920. Other large denominations are the Wesleyan Methodist and the Congregationalist, counting over 400,000 members each, while the actual Roman Catholic pop., children and adults, is over two million. Of Jews there are nearly 700,000.

*Bibliography.*—Lord Avebury, *Scenery of England*, 1904; C. B. Fawcett, *Provinces of England*, 1919; M. de C. S. Salter, *Rainfall of the British Isles*, 1921; H. J. Fleure, *Races of England and Wales*, 1923; G. A. Greenwood, *England To-day*, 1926; R. Cragg, *Anvil and Loom*, 1926; A. Carr Saunders and C. Jones, *Survey of Social Structure of England and Wales*, 1927; W. R. Inge, *England*, 1927; A. Demangeon, *Les Îles britanniques*, 1927; G. D. Chisholm, *Handbook of Commercial*

*Geography*, revised, 1928; H. C. Kidd, *New Era for British Railways*, 1929; W. Dibelius, *England*, 1930.

*History*.—See ENGLISH HISTORY; GREAT BRITAIN.

**England, Church of**, a title which, as *Ecclesia Anglicana*, first appears in Magna Charta (1215), to denote the body of orthodox Christians in communion with the bishops of the country. The name becomes, however, a particular title of this body, as distinct from the Roman Communion, during the Reformation period, when, acting under Royal pressure through its Convocations, it freed itself from the papal yoke. The Eng. Church was probably founded towards the end of the second century B.C., but was almost entirely swept away by the Saxon invasion. At the end of the sixth century, a mission was sent from Rome by Gregory the Great, which re-established the faith in Britain. This mission was headed by Augustine of Canterbury. The history of the mediæval Eng. Church contains a continuous series of protests against papal extortions and encroachments, and in the reign of Henry VIII. political events brought this general dissatisfaction to a head. Convocation declared Henry to be supreme head of the Church of England (1533), while at the same time the king declared that he claimed no *spiritual* power. The process of limiting the papal power terminated in 1534 when Convocation declared that the Bishop of Rome had no more authority in England than any other foreign bishop. So far traditional doctrine had been preserved, but the Books of Common Prayer successively authorised by Cranmer under Edward VI. introduced the Reformed teaching into the Church of England. Under Mary the realm was reconciled with Rome by Cardinal Reginald Pole, Cranmer's successor as Archbishop of Canterbury. Elizabeth reversed this policy and the severance became final in 1570, when Pius V excommunicated the Queen, and forbade any of his adherents in England to remain in communion with the Eng. Church. In spite of the disorders of the time, the Eng. Church maintains that it succeeded in retaining the anct. ministry and the anct. faith. Rom. Catholics deny both these things, saying that Archbishop Parker at Canterbury was not validly consecrated, and that the Church of England adopted the current Protestant doctrines. Agai ist this, however, Anglicans quote certain great continental historians, such as Bossuet and Döllinger. The doctrine of the Church of England is to be found in the three creeds and the Book of Common Prayer, including the Thirty-Nine Articles. In England and Wales there are forty-three dioceses, administered by seventy-six bishops, assistant bishops and bishops suffragan. Thirty of these dioceses form the province of Canterbury and thirteen the province of York. *See* Wakeman's *Introduction to the History of the Church of England*, 1898; Newbolt and Stone's *Church of England, An Appeal to Facts and Principles*, 1903.

**England, New,** *see* NEW ENGLAND.

**Englewood,** a city of Bergen co., New Jersey, U.S.A., 1 m. W. of the Palisades of the Hudson R. It is a residential suburb of New York, from which it is 14 m. distant. Pop. 17,805.

**English Association,** formed in 1907 to enlist the support of all those interested in Eng. language and literature. Its aims are to promote the recognition of English as an essential element in the national education, and to discuss the various methods of teaching English. Membership is open to all and there are numerous branches in the Empire. London office : 4 Buckingham Gate, S.W.

**English Bazar,** or **Angrezábad,** the prin. tn. of Malda, in the Rajshahi div. of E. Bengal and Assam, India. In 1770 a commercial residency was established here. Pop. 13,667.

**English Channel** (Fr. *La Manche*, the sleeve), the sea between England and France. Its length is about 350 m., and the greatest breadth between Ushant and the Scilly Isles is about 100 m. The average depth is from 20 to 30 fathoms, reaching 60 fathoms at the entrance to the Strait of Dover and as much as 94 fathoms at Hurds Deep. The tides are peculiar, parts of the Eng. coast having a double tide, the effect generally being to cause higher tides on the Fr. coast (42 ft. at St. Germain) than on the Eng. coast (7 ft. at Portland). W. winds are the most prevalent, gales occurring chiefly between Oct. and Jan., and fogs are common throughout the year. *See also* CHANNEL TUNNEL.

**English Church Union,** *see* CHURCH UNION (ENGLISH).

**English History.** The history of England begins with the landing of the Jutes on the island of Thanet, and the settlement of that tribe in the S.E. corner of our island. That the Eng. were unknown to the Britons and were simply called in in order to beat back the attacks of the N. tribes on the weakened and effeminate tribes of the S., is a theory that cannot well at the present time be held. The official Rom. position of the Count of the Saxon shore points definitely to the fact that the Roms. had suffered from the depredations of these tribes, on the outlook continually for land to plunder. Now in 449 they came not to plunder but to settle. From their N. Ger. homes they swooped down upon a Britain which they knew to be defenceless, and determined to make it their home. The Eng. were composed of three tribes, the Angles, and Saxons, and the Jutes, and so thoroughly was the settlement made in Britain, that one at least of these tribes (the Angles) disappears entirely from Germany. Generally speaking, we may say that the Eng. conquest occupied roughly 150 years, was ruthless in its severity, and was to a large extent a conquest of extermination.

dence that the Britons in the W. were able to hold the Saxons at bay for some considerable time. We have little evidence of the intermingling of the races, although certainly a greater intermingling took place than has been commonly recognised. At the end of the sixth century we can divide Britain into the following large divisions: Northumbria, Mercia, E. Anglia, Kent, and Wessex, with the British kingdoms of Strathclyde, N. Wales, and W. Wales. Obviously, a constant struggle went on between Northumbria and Strathclyde, Mercia and N. Wales, and Wessex and W. Wales. Of the actual history of the Eng. conquest we know little. The *Anglo - Saxon Chronicle*, upon which we depend for so much of our information, was not commenced until the end of

HAROLD'S OATH TO WILLIAM (*Bayeux Tapestry*)

The Britons were driven gradually to the mountains of the W., and the Eng., assuming the position of conquerors, called them the foreigners, a name preserved at the present time in the name Welsh. The chief settlements were: the Angles in Northumbria (Bernicia and Deira) and the E. districts of England, N. of the Thames; the Saxons, S. of the Thames and extending for some time, at least, up the valley of the Severn; the Jutes only in Kent, with a small settlement in the Isle of Wight. The theory that the conquest was due to the inability of the Britons to hold their own against the fresh vigour of the Eng. is true only when judged in the light that the Eng. did ultimately conquer the country, but to hold as a corollary of this that the Britons were weak, effeminate, and easily overpowered is not correct. The conquest occupied 150 years; we have records of many battles slowly contested, and we have evi-

the ninth century. The heathen Eng. tribes, before the end of the sixth century, left little evidence of their work in Britain, and it is only after the conversion to Christianity, carried out in the S. principally by Augustine (597), and in the N. by the Celtic Church, whose apostle, St. Aidan, did so much that England's history assumes clearer outlines. England was not easily converted, and the kings of Kent and Northumbria were for a long time opposed by the heathen King of Mercia. Wessex drops out of the struggle for some time, being occupied by internal quarrels. It is impossible to follow here in any detail the constant struggles of Mercia, Northumbria, and later Wessex for supremacy. The heathen king, Penda, made the heaviness of his hand felt in the N., only to be finally overthrown at Winwaed (655). For a time the King of Northumbria became the bretwalda, that is, the overlord of Britain, a title purely nominal and carrying with it little, if any, authority. In 664 was held the Synod of Whitby, which finally settled that the Eng. Church should follow the rule of Rome and not of Iona. Almost immediately afterwards Theodore of Tarsus became Archbishop of Canterbury, and by his judicious organisation of the church as a national church, he did much to pave the way for an ultimate amalgamation of the Eng. tribes into an Eng. nation. In the meantime, the power of Northumbria had waned, the battle of Nechtansmere had led to the annihilation of the Northumbrian armies, and Mercia under her kings, Ethelbald and Offa, sprang into the foremost position. Under Offa England again took some part in the councils of Europe. The Emperor, Charles the Great, recognised Offa as the king of England, and there began to be fairly constant intercourse between England and the Continent. Offa also built the Great Dyke which protected Mercia from the outrages of the Welsh. With the death of Offa, however, came the overthrow of Mercia, and Wessex came to the front. Egbert of Wessex may be regarded practically as the first real overlord of England. In turn he conquered or forced to submission all the great kingdoms, and by 825 we may say that he had at least laid the foundations of a united England. The century which followed was of vast importance to England, since, during the latter half of this century, we get the beginning of the invasions of the Danes. Before the death of Egbert, the Danes had appeared in England. They had been known before; they had been probably a source of danger to the Roms., but now they came in greater numbers, content at first to plunder and retire, but later coming over definitely with a desire to settle in the country. They attacked and conquered Northumbria and E. Anglia before they actually attacked Wessex. The early life of Alfred the Great (q.v.) was taken up in fighting against this enemy, and this was his first task as king. But Alfred realised that it was impossible to drive them out entirely, and after the Treaty of Wedmore (878) he divided England up into Wessex and the Danelagh, and gave that portion of England, N. and W. of Watling Street, to the Danes, on condition of their adopting Christianity. But he also adopted the only real means of preventing fresh incursions by the Danes. He built a fleet which guarded the Channel and the E. coast, and which succeeded in defeating the Danes

before they were able to land. By these means Alfred succeeded in keeping peace in the land during the greater part of his reign, and he was able in that way to carry out a great number of necessary reforms. But before the end of his reign the attacks of the Danes had again commenced and were continued during the reign of Edward the Elder, who succeeded in establishing his supremacy over the Danelagh, and who, in 924, was recognised as the overlord of the whole of England, and was acknowledged by the Scots and the Welsh. The outstanding name in the period which followed is that of Dunstan, who influenced the policy during the succeeding reign. Himself an Englishman, he recognised that it was essential for the two races, Eng. and Dane, to work together, and although he was held by the Eng. to favour the Danes too much, nevertheless, his work was well done and a recognition of the only home policy. In 978 succeeded Ethelred the Redeless (Unready), and during the reign the Danish troubles began again. Time after time the country was invaded, but Ethelred, by means of large levies of Danegeld, bought off the invaders for a time, but the invaders returned only too ready to gain more money so easily, and finally in 1002 Ethelred caused the massacre of the Danes which called down on him the vengeance of Sweyn, and which led to the rule, from 1016 to 1042, of the Danish kings. Ethelred fled into exile in Normandy, an exile which had a great effect upon the ultimate history of England. Cnut, the first and the best of the Danish kings, ruled wisely and well. His great scheme was the foundation of a N. empire which should have England as its centre, and although he did not succeed in establishing a permanent empire, he ruled England sternly but well and as a national king. His two sons, Harold and Harthacnut, are notorious, principally for the evil lives they lived, and in 1042, on the death of Harthacnut, the old Saxon dynasty was restored in the person of Edward the Confessor, the son of Ethelred the Redeless. Edward the Confessor (q.v.) was more fitted to be priest than king, and during his reign the power lay in the hands of Godwin, Earl of Wessex, and later of his son Harold. Edward was largely under Norman influence, and the Normans played a great part in his reign. Finally, William, Duke of Normandy, declared that Edward had promised him the crown, and forced Harold—a chance presence—to swear an oath to help him to obtain it. Harold did so, but on the death of Edward he was elected king by the witan, and took up arms in the defence of the kingdom. His brother, Tostig, deprived of his earldom of Northumbria, invaded England and fought, together with Harold of Norway, against Harold of England, at Stamford Bridge. Harold was victorious, but turned with his men S. to confront the Normans who had landed in the S. In Oct. 1066 was fought the battle of Hastings, and on Dec. 25 of the same year William was crowned King of England, elected by the witan in Westminster Abbey. The Norman Conquest was the beginning of the final process in the welding of the Eng. nation into one compact body. The breadth of the land. Further, by the Oath of Salisbury all tenants had to swear allegiance directly to the king, and finally the Domesday survey gave him the grasp of details never before known, which made his grip on the country firmer and more easily maintained. He ruled with a hand of iron, but the heaviness of his hand was felt by Norman noble and Saxon serf alike. The fusion of Norman and Saxon would have come at a much earlier period but for the possession of Normandy by the Eng. kings. This naturally retarded the process. When William died a dispute arose concerning the succession, but Normandy had been left to Robert (the eldest son), and

THE BATTLE OF HASTINGS
(From the Bayeux Tapestry)

end was still a long way off. William brought in his train numberless Normans, all of whom had to be rewarded by the king with Saxon lands. The Saxons, therefore, sank to the bottom of the social scale, and for long there was no attempt made at the fusion of the races. William was occupied for long with the completion of the conquest of England, and when this had been done he turned his attention to the government of the country. William was not only a great warrior, he was also a great king. He realised the difficulties of a sovereign with a completeness that was only possible in a man who was both king and feudal vassal. He saw also the limitations of feudalism on the Continent, and he determined to remedy, as far as possible, these defects. There were to be no more great earls who could on occasion adopt regal style. The estates of his followers were scattered throughout the length and England to William Rufus. Constant quarrelling took place, and finally Robert handed over Normandy to William as a pledge for a sufficient sum of money to go on crusade, and a promise that whichever of the two died first the survivor should succeed to both dominions (England and Normandy). Unfortunately, during Robert's absence, William died, and the throne was seized by Henry I. (1100). In 1101 Robert returned from crusading and invaded England, but was repulsed, and in 1106 Henry crossed over to Normandy and defeated and took prisoner Robert at the battle of Tenchebrai. During the rest of his life Robert remained the forced guest of his brother. Henry I. was the first of the Norman kings to encourage the fusion of the races, he himself married a Saxon wife, and in this way did much to ensure the popularity of his house. He ruled sternly but wisely, and the wisdom of his policy was seen in the help which he received from his Saxon subjects in putting down the revolt of the barons of the W. In 1120 his only son William was drowned in the wreck of the *White Ship*, and the greater part of the rest of Henry's life was taken up in the attempt to get his daughter Maud recognised as the heir to the throne. Previous to his death in 1135, Henry coerced the barons into promises to recognise Maud, but the barons disliked the idea of being ruled by a woman, and further dreaded the power which such recognition would give to the husband of Maud, Geoffrey of Anjou. Finally, when Henry did die the barons elected as king Stephen of Blois, whose only claims to the throne were that he was the grandson of William I., and that he was a brave but complaisant and easily pleased warrior. With the accession of Stephen, in 1135, we get the beginning of the Civil War, which continued practically during the whole of his reign, was to the barons a period during which they were able to exercise their power unchecked. The people, crushed between the forces of the king and of Queen Maud, also found themselves crushed by the barons even more terribly. But it taught England definitely that the power of a strong if tyrannous king was less to be dreaded than the power of an unchecked baronage. Finally, in 1153, the Treaty of Wallingford was signed by Stephen and Henry FitzEmpress of Anjou. By the terms of this treaty, Stephen was to reign until his death, when he was to be succeeded by Henry II. Henry II. was one of the greatest kings of England. He ruled not only England, but Normandy, Maine, Anjou, Touraine, and Aquitaine. He was acknowledged overlord of Scotland, Ireland, and Wales; he practically ruled Brittany—in fact his dominions may be regarded as stretching from the Pyrenees to the Orkneys. He destroyed the power of the baronage, and by judicious reforms he obtained the support of the people, but he failed when he attacked the church. The point at which he had been aiming, the subordination of ecclesiastical law to the crown, failed when it had almost succeeded, by the murder of Becket in 1170. During his reign, Strongbow crossed over into Ireland and began the conquest of that country, although Henry himself had, at the beginning of his reign, determined on that course. The latter part of Henry II.'s reign was a failure, owing to his constant quarrels with his son. His eldest son had died virtually fighting against him; Richard was a

source of constant trouble, whilst John, the darling of his old age, was untrustworthy and Judas-like. The last days of the king were passed in one long struggle with his arch enemy, Philip Augustus, and his sons, and in 1189, after being compelled to give in, he died. He was succeeded by his son Richard, who, however, spent the greater part of his time out of England, either on crusade or in France. During the greater part of his reign his brother John plotted against him, attempting, finally, to keep Richard in captivity in Austria. Even when the treachery of John was obvious to Richard, it was forgiven. In 1199 Richard died, and was succeeded by his brother John. That the succession question was still in a state of chaos is obvious from an examination of the successions during the Norman and early Angevin dynasties. In only one instance had the heir by right of primogeniture succeeded. John now succeeded to the throne which would have been occupied by Arthur under present-day conditions. His succession was recognised as in no way extraordinary, and was generally accepted. The disappearance of Arthur, and generally expressed belief that he had been murdered by John, however, turned the favour from John's side, nor did his manner of ruling, nor yet his open immorality, tend to make him more popular. He had energy which he did not use and ability and intelligence which he misapplied. The early years of his reign were occupied in a struggle for the Fr. possessions. For a long time it had been the unhidden ambition of Philip Augustus to win back those portions of France which were still held by the Eng. He had struggled against Henry II. and Richard I., but his opportunity came when John, unpopular throughout the whole of his dominions, succeeded. In 1204 the Château-Gaillard was lost, and Normandy passed into the hands of the Fr. John by no means gave up hope, and struggled constantly against the Fr., forming league after league. He, however, soon found himself in difficulties enough at home. In 1205 the barons refused to fight for the recovery of Normandy; in the following year, in spite of the violent opposition of John, Stephen Langton was appointed Archbishop of Canterbury. John refused to recognise him, and in 1208 England was laid under an interdict and later the king excommunicated. During this period John had alienated the sympathies of the barons and of the people. Gradually he saw himself beset on every side by dangers; France threatened, the barons negotiated, the church thundered. He turned for support to the strongest power, and became the vassal of the pope. England was to be held in fee from the papacy. This was the final blow to the barons. Led by the church, they banded themselves together under Stephen Langton, and resolved to force the king to issue a charter which would safeguard their liberties. After a struggle John found that he must surrender, and at Runnymede, in 1215, he signed the Great Charter, intending to keep it as little as he had kept most other oaths. The Great Charter was the work of the barons, supported by the church, de Burgh. The Charter was constantly re-issued and confirmed, and De Burgh's policy was largely that of England for the Eng. In 1232, however, began the personal rule of Henry III., a period which is noted for the domination of foreign favourites. Henry was a pious weakling, who had but little mind of his own, but who could on occasion be extremely obstinate. He was continually exacting money, and many expedients were attempted by the baronage to obtain control of the purse. The most outstanding personage of the reign was Simon de Montfort, who came to England as a favourite of the king and remained

AN EXTRACT FROM THE MAGNA CHARTA

and was thoroughly reactionary. But the signing of it reconciled a number of the barons, and John had more support after it was signed. He attempted to punish the N. barons who had been chiefly responsible for the Charter, and they in turn invited the Dauphin to England as king. War was still raging in 1216 when John died, leaving the throne to his son, Henry III., aged nine. During the early part of the reign the chief difficulty was the Civil War. Through this dangerous period Henry was guided by William Marshall, Earl of Pembroke. The charters were confirmed, the baronage reconciled, and Louis, the Dauphin, finally left the country (1217). From 1217–32 the country was ruled well by William Marshall, and on his death by Hubert to uphold the rights and privileges of the baronage. In 1248 he was appointed governor of Gascony, and shortly afterwards was deprived of this post owing to the representations of the Gascons that he was overstern. He remained out of England until 1253, when he returned to place himself at the head of the baronage. In 1258 the king agreed to the Provisions of Oxford, and these provisions were finally submitted to the arbitration of St. Louis of France, who held that the king was not bound to obey them. In the same year (1264) civil war broke out between the barons, led by Simon de Montfort, and the Royalists, whose principal leader was the Prince Edward. The Royalists were defeated at the battle of Lewes, and the king and prince became prisoners. The Mise of Lewes followed, and in 1265 was held the famous parliament of Simon de Montfort, to which the Commons were summoned. Later in the year Prince Edward escaped, defeated the barons' army, now much weakened by desertion, and killed Simon de Montfort. The death of Simon, however, did not interfere with his policy, since this was carried out by the Prince Edward, who, although an opponent, yet learnt much from his enemy. The remainder of the reign passed quietly, the chief power up to 1270 being in the hands of Prince Edward, who in that year departed to the East on crusade. In 1272 Henry III. died, and although it was two years before Edward returned to this country, there was no dispute over the succession. Edward I. was one of the greatest of our kings, and as a law-maker and organiser ranks with Henry II. and William I. (*see* under EDWARD I.). Part of his great aim was to construct a united Great Britain, and the Scottish war which raged practically from 1294 to 1307 was a result of this policy. He died in 1307, with the Scots in open rebellion, and just after Robert Bruce had been crowned king. Meanwhile Wales had been finally subjugated. Edward II. succeeded his father, but his rule was influenced throughout by his favourites, Gaveston and the Despensers. During his reign the lords ordainers took practically all the power from him, but again there was a reaction in his favour, and for a time he ruled with his favourites and with the support of the people. In 1314 he gathered the largest army which had ever been sent into Scotland, and proceeded to attempt to relieve Stirling, then besieged by Bruce. He fought the battle of Bannockburn and met with the greatest defeat ever inflicted upon the Eng. by the Scots. In 1327 the conspiracy of the queen and her lover, Mortimer, caused him to be deposed, and in the following year he was cruelly murdered in Berkeley Castle. He was succeeded by his son Edward III., one of England's warrior kings. At the beginning of the reign the independence of Scotland was recognised, and the reins of government passed for a short time into the hands of the queen-mother and Mortimer. In 1330, however, Edward III. asserted his position and became sole ruler. The early part of his reign was taken up with a Scottish war, and then finally, in 1337, Edward claimed the throne of France in right of his mother. The claim was obviously but a pretence, since Edward had previously recognised

the King of France and done homage to him for Guienne. It was necessary, however, to conquer France if Scotland was to be conquered, or if the woollen trade with Flanders was to be kept. He attacked France from two points, through Guienne and from the N. In 1346 he won the battle of Crécy, and in the following year besieged and captured Calais. In 1346 also Neville's Cross had been won, and the Scottish king taken prisoner. The Fr. war ceased in 1349 owing to the outbreak of the Black Death, a plague which helped very largely in the social revolution which followed. The condition of the serfs and peasantry of England was helped very largely by the devastation caused by that plague. In 1356 the Black Prince won the battle of Poitiers. This was the last great victory of Edward's reign. The rest of his life was spent in dissoluteness and under the influence of Alice Perrers, his mistress. During his reign, however, great strides were made in the constitutional government of the country, and the power of parliament increased rapidly. This was due to the fact that Edward, in order to wage war, was in constant need of supplies, and was prepared to grant great privileges in order to obtain them. He died in 1377, preceded by his son the Black Prince. He was succeeded by his grandson, Richard II. Richard had ability, which, however, was not always employed in the right direction. He was fearless, and to a certain extent popular, but the period of his personal rule was tyrannical, and Bolingbroke, returning from exile in 1399, was easily able to depose him. He was imprisoned and finally murdered in Pontefract Castle. With him ended the Plantagenet line of kings. During his reign died Wyclif, the great reformer, and just at the end of the reign Chaucer, the first of the great Eng. poets, died also. Henry IV., who succeeded Richard II., was the eldest son of John of Gaunt, the third son of Edward III. He claimed the throne, not by conquest, but by parliamentary election, and was the founder of the House of Lancaster. He ruled the country wisely and prudently, and though it is true that he was never personally popular, he at least kept the country at peace. In 1403 Hotspur rebelled against him, and was supported by Owen Glyndwr, both of whom were overthrown by Henry IV. at the battle of Shrewsbury. Henry also persecuted the Lollards, a name given to those who adopted the new religious teaching of Wyclif. After a long and painful illness Henry IV. died in 1413. He was succeeded by his son, Henry V., concerning whom so many stories are told of the wildness of his youth. He, however, proved himself a strong and capable king, but did not live long enough to enjoy the fruits of his triumphs. He also persecuted the Lollards, and renewed the war with France. In 1415 he achieved a notable victory at Agincourt. France was at this time divided into factions, and taking advantage of this fact, by judicious alliances Henry succeeded, in 1420, in forcing the Fr. king to sign the Treaty of Troyes, which gave Henry the Fr. king's daughter's hand in marriage, the regency of the country, and the ultimate succession to the throne of France. In 1442, just after the birth of an heir to him, he died. He was succeeded on the thrones of both France and England by his young son, Henry VI., for whom the regents, Bedford and Gloucester, administered the country. During the early part of the reign the Eng. still continued to win victories, but finally the Fr. settled the differences amongst themselves, and after the appearance of the Maid of Orleans went from victory to victory, finally, in 1454, driving the Eng. out of everywhere save Calais. At home the war expenses and the constant stream of returning soldiers made social conditions bad, and this found expression in the revolt of Cade in 1450. Meanwhile, the king had had lapses from sanity, and the Yorkists began to claim the throne, alleging, and correctly, that their candidate, Richard, Duke of York, was the more direct descendant of Edward III. The argument was answerable in only one way, and that was that the Lancastrians were on the throne by right of election by parliament. In 1455 war definitely broke out, and lasted up to 1471. The Yorkists were at first successful at St. Albans, and the king fell a prisoner into their hands. In 1460 York was defeated and slain at Wakefield by Margaret of Anjou, but the Earl of March, coming up from the W., entered London, was proclaimed king, and marching up N. defeated Margaret at Towton. For some time the country remained more or less at peace; the king-maker dictated the policy of the country. But the king flouted the great earl on two occasions, and drove him to the camp of the Lancastrians. Warwick landed from France and forced Edward into exile, proclaiming Henry VI. again. Edward, however, returned unexpectedly from exile, defeated and slew Warwick at Barnet, crushed

the last hope of the Lancastrians at Tewkesbury, and again established himself firmly as king. He had great statesmanship and cunning, but was a man of vicious life whose excesses finally killed him. He ruled as a despot, and may be regarded as the first of the new monarchy. The old institutions had broken down, the church was u dermined by we 1th and laxity in high places, the nobility weakened and impotent, the commons desirous only of a king who would keep peace and allow them to trade. The country was on the verge of a new awakening, and Edward was sagacious enough to read the time aright. He kept peace; when he did go to war he withdrew for a sufficient sum of money, and he was a great patron of the new learning and of the art of printing—typically a prince of the Renaissance. He caused great jealousy by the promotion of his wife's (Dame Rivers) relations; he died in 1483. His son, Edward V., succeeded him, only to be murdered in the Tower, after a two months' reign, by his uncle, Richard of Gloucester, who on the death of the prince and his brother caused himself to be proclaimed as Richard III. He was a brave prince and a prince who had good ideas and ability to carry them out, but he was unpopular, and gradually the story of the murder of the princes increased this unpopularity. A conspiracy was made against him by Henry Tudor, Earl of Richmond, who landed in the country from France, met Richard at Bosworth Field, and there defeated and slew him, owing principally to the wholesale desertions of Richard by the nobles. Henry was crowned on the battlefield. Henry Tudor was descended on his father's side from the Tudors, on his mother's (illegitimately) from John of Gaunt, and was therefore hailed by the Lancastrians as the representative of their line. He claimed the throne by descent and by election, and finally put an end to the rival claims by marrying Elizabeth of York, the daughter of Edward IV., thus uniting the two lines. He crushed the remaining power of the baronage, he overthrew what little power remained to the clergy, he ruled despotically, but he restored the industries of the country and raised England again to the rank of a European power. He was miserly, but to him the possession of money meant the possession of power. The attempts of Simnel and Warbeck were defeated, and Henry's position was strengthened by the marriage of his son to Catherine of Aragon, and his daughter to Jame IV. of

Scotland, both marriages of vital importance to England. He died in 1509, leaving Henry VIII. with a secure hold on the throne and the affection of the people. The reign of Henry is notable chiefly for the separation of the Eng. Church from Rome. At the beginning of his reign there was some slight trouble with France and Scotland, the Scottish war being ended in 1513 by the battle of Flodden. Wolsey, Henry's chief minister during the early part of his reign, remained firm to the policy of preserving the Balance of Power (q.v.), the Emperor Charles V. and the Fr. constantly bidding one against the other for the friendship of England. Henry's attitude towards the doctrines of the church may be judged from the fact that he published a book against the doctrines of Luther, and received in gratitude from the papacy the title ' Defender of the Faith.' By 1526, however, he had grown tired of his wife, Catherine of Aragon, and began to have religious scruples as to the validity of the marriage. He demanded, through Wolsey, a dissolution of the marriage and a decree of nullity from the pope, Clɛme t VII. This wɔs rɛf sed an i the fact that the troops of Charles V. (Catherine's nephew) had just captured Rome, and the pope was in their hands is believed by some histori ns to have det rmi ed this pap l deci ion. Finally, the pope appointed two legates, Wolsey and Campeggio, to try the case, but Campeggio received orders that it was to be adjourned to Rome. In the meantime, Henry, who desired to marry Anne Boleyn, accused Wolsey of putting unnecessary obstacles in the way. When the trial was adjourned to Rome he disgraced Wolsey, and taking the advice of Cranmer and Cromwell, he broke away from Rome and forced the Eng. Church to obey him as supreme head of the church. There was no change in doctrine save in a few minor points. The Six Acts forced the doctrines of the Church of Rome even o ɩ rec lcitraɩ ts who hoped to introɑuce the reforme l doctrines curre ɩt on the Co tinent into the English Church; ɴɛv rth l ss Henrɣ was now head of the church and not the pope. In order to obtain full control over the churches, the monasteries were dissolved. In 1536 the smaller ones went; in 1539 the larger monasteries suffered also. These chɑ ges provoɤed sever l aɓortive r b lli ns which were ɾut down with gr at crуelt ɾ. Their lands enriched the king and the nobility. During the later years of the reign a tendency towards

Protestantism became more apparent in the country. The influence of the Ger. Reformation was being felt more and more, but' it is necessary to separate distinctly the so-called Eng. Reformation and the Ger. Reformation. In his old age Henry became merely a brutal tyrant; he died in 1547, having married six times. He had been given authority to settle the succession for himself. By his will he had left the throne to Edward VI., to be followed, if he died without children, by Mary, daughter of Catherine of Aragon; she in turn to be followed by Elizabeth, daughter of Anne Boleyn. Edward VI. was only nine years of age when he succeeded; the country was ruled for him by the protectors, Somerset and Northumberland. During this reign Protestantism first gained a secure footing in the country. The churches were stripped of images, the Catholic service was stopped, and the first Eng. Prayer Book was issued. In many parts of the country this attempt to oust the Catholic religion was deeply resented, but in spite of this Protestantism spread. In 1553 Edward VI. died. He also left a will which set aside that of his father, and gave the throne to the Lady Jane Grey. This plot was due to the influence of Northumberland, who knew that his power was at an end the moment that Mary succeeded to the throne. Mary, however, found no difficulty in obtaining recognition, and Northumberland, Dudley, his son, and the Lady Jane Grey were committed to the Tower, and later beheaded. Mary had always been a fervent Catholic; she now restored the Catholic religion, and for a time England reverted to the papacy. She married Philip II., King of Spain, and this, together with the religious persecutions which took place, did much to make her unpopular. Further, the alliance with Spain involved a war with France, and during that war Eng and lost her last Fr. possession, Calais. Amongst the ' heretics ' burned during this reign were Latimer, Ridley, and Cranmer. Mary died in 1558 ; she was disliked by her subjects, but she was perfectly sincere in her convictions, though she was somewhat of a fanatic. She was succeeded by her half-sister, Elizabeth, who found little difficulty in obtaining the throne and was from her accession regarded by the majority of her subjects with affection. One of the most complex figures in Eng. history, she lived in a period when one false step would have meant ruin, or at least great national danger. She was beset on every side by enemies, and was regarded even by some of her own subjects as a usurper, and yet she managed to sail the ship of state safely for forty-five years. That she was helped by circumstances there is no doubt, that her ministers were clever men cannot be denied, but much must be allowed to her own personality and genius. She tried to provide the Church of England with a 'via media,' a compromise of doctrine which should reconcile Catholic and Calvinist. The upshot was sporadic persecution of the extreme and violent among the Puritan sectaries, and a series of Penal Laws against Recusants, Jesuits and Seminary Priests. Her great danger, politically, lay in Scotland and Spain. France could, for the time being, be disregarded, since internal affairs kept her busy and desirous of peace. Scotland was disturbed by the religious quarrels, and, finally, Mary Queen of Scots, Elizabeth's greatest rival, was driven a fugitive into England, where she remained a prisoner until her execution in 1587. The following year came the great Armada, the blow Elizabeth had long expected, but which had been delayed whilst both sides tried what diplomacy could do. Eng. seamanship and the elements combined to wreck the hopes of Spain, and the shattered Armada returned home defeated. This was the crowning victory of Elizabeth's reign; no longer need she dread the power of Spain; England was at last one of the great powers. But the point to be noticed most during Elizabeth's reign is that series of events which may best be described as the Eng. Renaissance. The sea rovers plundered the Spanish Main, discovered new lands, and made a name for themselves throughout the world. In every department of national life fresh developments were made. She died in 1603 after a reign which will always be remembered as one of the greatest in the history of the English nation. (See under ELIZABETH.) She was succeeded by James VI. of Scotland and I. of England. Thus the united Great Britain of Edward I. was accomplished through the marriage schemes of Henry VII. The early events of the reign were the attempts to reconcile Puritanism and Anglicanism, which failed, and the Gunpowder Plot of 1605. During this reign we find all the essential causes of the civil war which broke out during the next reign : the mistaken foreign policy, the unpopularity of the king, the unjust taxation, and the desire to rule despotically, this time by right divine. The Stuarts tried to carry on the old policy of the Tudors, and

to be despotic monarchs. The essential difference between these two dynasties was that whereas the Tudors were personally popular, the Stuarts were not, whereas the Tudors ruled despotically only because the people supported them, the Stuarts failed because they claimed a divine right to rule in spite of the people. It must be remembered that from this period onward, towards the end of the century, Puritanism played a great part, and Puritanism meant not only a desire for liberty of worship, but also political liberty as well. It was in the struggle against Puritanism that divine right and passive obedience were overthrown. During the reign of James, the Thirty Years' War broke out in Europe, and the king tried to act for a time as the arbiter of Europe. His schemes failed, and he died in 1625 with the reputation of being the wisest fool in Christendom. Charles I. succeeded. His reign may best be described as one long series of blunders. Parliament attacked his favourites, refused him supplies, and, finally, in 1628, forced the Petition of Right upon him. From 1629 to 1640 he ruled without a parliament. During this period occurred the famous ship-money cases, and continual breaches of the law. Finally, it was on the rock of the Church in Scotland that Charles foundered. His attempts to imitate his father and force Episcopacy on the Scots roused anger in Scotland, the introduction of the Prayer Book of Laud led to open rebellion, and the first Bishops' War broke out (see SCOTLAND). The Short Parliament (1640) was summoned and dissolved within three weeks. Then followed the Long Parliament, which undid the work of the eleven years' tyranny, but which at the same time did much that was unconstitutional. Strafford was executed ; Laud met with the same fate later. Ship-money was declared illegal, the Star Chamber abolished, and finally the king was forced to consent to the reading of the Grand Remonstrance. He then made his fatal mistake ; he attempted to arrest five members, and failing, left London. He went N. and tried to enter Hull, but was refused admission, and finally, on Aug. 22, 1642, he raised his standard at Nottingham. At first the Royalists were successful, but this was due chiefly to the fact that the Royalists were more accustomed to arms than the Roundheads ; but finally came the formation of the New Model Army, and the defeats at Marston Moor and Naseby. The king surrendered to the Scots, and was finally handed over to the Eng., by whom, after prolonged nego-tiations and the outbreak of the second Civil War, he was executed (Jan. 1649). For the next eleven years England was a commonwealth —for the first four years a republic, for the remaining seven a protectorate. The execution of the king roused horror throughout Europe; Scotland and Ireland rose in revolt, and Charles II. was crowned in Scotland, but the Scots were routed at Dunbar and Worcester, and the Irish at Wexford and Drogheda. For a short time England, Scotland, and Ireland were united. In 1653 Cromwell be-came Protector, and although he ruled as tyrannously as Charles I., still he was an efficient tyrant, whereas Charles

toleration for the Catholic religion in the interests of national unity, but the influence of the Protestant land-owners and city merchants was too strong for him and Charles was deter-mined never to go on his travels again. It was a period of national disaster and shame; the guns of the Dutch were heard on the Thames from the City of London. In 1665 broke out the Great Plague, and in the following year the Great Fire destroyed London. The Popish Plot, fabricated by Titus Oates, led to the introduction of the Ex-clusion Bill, and the Petitioners and Abhorrers formed the nucleus of the Whigs and Tories of the following century. The country was inflamed by religious quarrels, and through it all

THE SPANISH ARMADA
(From an old print)

was not. Further, his foreign policy was spirited and popular, and placed England high in the councils of Europe. In 1658 Cromwell died, and there was chaos for a time in England. Richard Cromwell was inefficient, and finally Monk, marching down from Scotland with the army, de-clared in favour of a free parliament which restored Charles II. The Restoration was hailed with enthu-siasm by the vast majority of the nation. The sombreness of the Puri-tan era had disgusted them, and was also partly responsible for the ex-cesses of Charles II.'s reign. The Cavalier Parliament went much further than the promises of Charles in the Declaration of Breda would have led one to expect. The reign of Charles is one of the most sordid in Eng. history; to all intents and pur-poses Charles was the headman of Louis XIV. He aimed always at

Charles worked quietly for permanent toleration. Towards the end of his reign, when everything seemed black-est, he appealed to his people, and the latter years of his reign were years of triumph. He died in 1685, witty and cynical to the end. James, Duke of York, who succeeded him, inherited far more of the attributes of his father, Charles I. His obstinacy led him into difficulties which his brother would have avoided, and his open avowal of the Catholic faith, whilst it did not at first alienate his subjects, prepared the way for the Revolution. James openly attempted to restore freedom for the Catholic faith. Catholics were introduced into the army and the universities, the penal laws against them were dispensed with, and the king finally issued a Declaration of Indulgence (1687). Seven bishops petitioned against this, but they were imprisoned and tried for seditious libel. They were acquitted amidst the applause of the people, even the army which James had gathered at Hounslow cheering the acquittal. At the same time an heir was born to James, and this made a speedy action necessary. Hitherto the next heir to the throne had been Mary, the daughter of James II., a Protestant, and the wife of William of Orange. Now it was certain that the heir would be educated in the Catholic faith. Messengers were despatched to William of Orange. William landed at Brixham ; before the end of the year he was in London, and by that time James had fled, had been recaptured, and permitted to escape again. William and Mary signed the Declaration of Right and were declared joint sovereigns, whilst Catholics or any who should marry a Catholic were barred from succession to the Eng. throne. The Revolution had been bloodless. Rebellions broke out in Scotland and Ireland, but were speedily crushed. In 1692 the Massacre of Glencoe took place, and Ireland, after the Treaty of Limerick, gave no more trouble until the end of the century. That the Irish had right on their side when they spoke of betrayal there can be no doubt. England in the meantime engaged with Holland in the war of the Protestant Succession against Louis XIV., and although William was not a successful general, still, in 1697, the Treaty of Ryswick made Louis acknowledge for the first time that he had not been altogether successful. Both sides, however, now prepared for the greater struggle which they saw must come. The question of the Spanish Succession must soon be settled, and both William and Louis were interested in that settlement (see SPAIN—History). The Partition Treaties were drawn up and agreed to, but finally Louis accepted the will of the Spanish king which left Spain to the Fr. king's grandson, and England and France again prepared for war. But even now the Eng. were not prepared to go to war on the point of the Spanish Succession—only when Louis made the second of his great blunders. James II. died, and he acknowledged the Old Pretender as James III. England immediately clamoured for war, and during the preparations William III. died (1702). He had already been preceded by Mary, who died 1694, and since they had no children, was succeeded by Anne, the second daughter of James II. The war of the Spanish Succession broke out at the beginning of the reign. It was fought in order to preserve the Balance of Power in Europe and prevent France from dominating the whole of the Continent. Marlborough, the Eng. commander, won the victories of Blenheim (1704), Ramillies (1706), Malplaquet (1705), Oudenarde (1709). Gibraltar was captured by the allies and Louis was forced to acknowledge defeat, but the allies pressed terms too heavily upon him and he made another desperate effort to free himself, succeeding certainly in mitigating the terms imposed on him. Meanwhile at home the Tories had become powerful and were desirous of peace, and so in 1713 was signed the Treaty of Utrecht, which gave us the beginning of our colonial empire but which ought to have given us more. The Eng. further deserted their allies and made terms only for themselves. In 1707 the Act of Union between England and Scotland had been passed and had come into force (see SCOTLAND—History), and towards the end of the reign the question of succession had to be settled. The last child of Anne had died in 1700, and the Act of Settlement had vested the crown on the nearest Protestant heirs of Sophia, Electress of Hanover, and her descendants. But the Tory ministers, St. John and Harley, plotted the restoration of the Stuarts, and it was well known that the queen favoured the restoration of her half-brother, but the sudden death of the queen and the swift measures adopted by the Whigs prevented any serious steps from being taken, and in 1714, on the death of Anne, George I. was proclaimed without difficulty. The Act of Union of 1707 had made England and Scotland one under the name of Great Britain, and from the accession of George I. the history of both countries is treated under the heading GREAT BRITAIN.

**English Language, The,** a member of the W. Germanic branch of the Teutonic or Germanic division of the great Aryan or Indo-European family of languages, to which family belong also the classical and romance tongues. The Germanic group divides into three smaller groups : the E. Germanic, of which the Gothic is the only literary representative; the N. Germanic, to which belong the Swedish, Norse, and Icelandic; the W. Germanic, to which belong High Ger., Old Saxon, Frisian, and all the dialects of Old Eng. There were originally no great differences of vocabulary and syntax between these groups.

The original inhabs. of England were Celts, but after the conquest of the land by the Roms., the process of Latinising them probably went on in England just as in France or Spain. After the departure of the Roms., the Picts and Scots so harassed the helpless Britons that they are traditionally credited with having called in the aid of heathen tribes from the other side of the North Sea (*see also* under ENGLAND). Bede tells us that they were ' de tribus Germaniæ populis fortioribus,' and he gives us to understand the Anglians settled to the N. of the Humber, the Saxons around the Thames, and the Jutes in the Isle of Wight and the land opposite to it. The accuracy of this statement has been much questioned on account of certain difficulties it presents, but it is now recognised as generally correct, and it will be seen later that the test of language supports it.

On the analogy of the Ger. language, the development of Eng. is divided into three periods. *Old English* (O.E.) from the beginnings, usually placed at the year A.D. 700, until 1200. A subdivision is made about 900, all before that being called Early Old Eng. (e.O.E.), all after, Late Old Eng. (l.O.E.). *Middle English* (M.E.) dates from 1200 to 1500, and *New* or *Modern English* (N.E.) from 1500 to the present day. Old Eng. is also known as Anglo-Saxon, but it is important to notice that its writers themselves claimed to be writing ' Englisc,' and that since the history of the language is perfectly continuous there is little reason to give its early phases an entirely different name from the later ones. There is, of course, no clear division between O.E. and M.E., or between M.E. and N.E. The transition is gradual, and the characteristics of the later form may be found in works earlier than the date of division. Yet, though the development is perfectly continuous, it has been so great that the ' Englisc ' of Alfred would be perfectly unintelligible to a man of the present day.

1. *Old English* is divided into four dialects : (1) *Northumbrian* and (2) *Mercian*, which are grouped together under the name *Anglian*; (3) *W. Saxon*, and (4) *Kentish*. Northumbrian was spoken roughly from the Humber to the Lowlands of Scotland ; Mercian from the Humber southward to Essex and the Thames. W. Saxon from Kent westward. The two Anglian dialects were very similar, and the remains of them which have survived are not sufficient to allow us to differentiate between them. The most valuable remains of the Kentish dialect are some charters made for the disposal of property, and since charters are things which no one would copy, it is certain that we possess them in the original form, showing the exact dialect of the

district where the charter was made. The first dialect to rise into literary prominence was the Northumbrian, and during the e.O.E. period the Northumbrian schools were some of the most learned in Christendom. From them came the learned Alcuin (A.D. 735), confidant and adviser of Charlemagne. There is no reason to doubt that much work was produced in the vernacular both in poetry and in prose. But all, with the exception of a few fragments, such as a riddle, Bede's death-song, some glosses, and the beginning of Cædmon's Hymn, preserved in Bede's *Ecclesiastical History*, have perished. The invasions of the Danes during the eighth and ninth centuries swept away the Northumbrian literature, together with all other monuments of the culture which had been raised. As the Northern literature fell, a new one arose in the S. under the guidance of Alfred, and a large number of the works produced in the period which followed are extant in transcripts. Thus, almost our whole knowledge of O.E. rests upon W. Saxon, and this dialect is regarded as the norm, and all the others as variations from it. O.E. was a synthetic language, that is to say, it expressed variations by inflection rather than by prepositions or auxiliaries. Nouns had four cases, nominative, accusative, genitive, and dative, but nominative and accusative frequently coincided. There were two declensions, the strong and the weak. Much levelling had gone on among the declensions of the strong nouns, so that the separate five strong declensions are hardly distinguishable. The masculine word *dōm* (judgment) will show the typical form : *Sing.*, nom. and acc. *dōm*, gen. *dōmes*, dat. *dōme* ; *plur.*, nom. and acc. *domas*, gen. *domā*, dat. *dōmum* ; neuters of this declension with a short stem vowel add *u* in the nom. and acc. plural. The strong feminine ends in a consonant or *u*, and is declined thus : *Sing.*, nom. and acc. *giefu* (gift), gen. and dat. *giefe* ; *Plur.*, nom. *giefa*, acc. *giefe*, gen. *giefena* or *giefa*, dat. *giefum*. The weak declension nouns make their oblique cases in the singular with *n*, and in the plural thus (of the noun *nama*, a name), nom. and acc. *naman*, gen. *namena*, dat. *namum*. A certain number of nouns, such as *bōc, fader, mann*, are declined in special ways, and are generally grouped together under one head as consonant stems. The grammatical gender of O.E. is not necessarily connected with the natural gender. Thus, as we have seen, the noun *dōm* is masc. and *giefu* is fem., similarly, we have *dœg* (day), masc., and *ār* (honour), fem. As in Modern Ger., the word for child (çild) was neuter, as also was wíf, the word for woman. Adjectives were inflected according to both strong and weak declensions, and had also separate forms for each of the genders. The weak form was used in particular positions, of which the most common is after the definite article. If the noun had the article, therefore, the adjective was weak; if it had none, the adjective was strong. The definite article had also its three genders, masc. se, fem. seo, neut. þæt; it was used as a demonstrative as well as an article. The verbs, as in Modern Eng., were both strong and weak, and broadly speaking, there have since been few changes of verbs from one class to the other. The strong verbs made their past tense by an internal vowel change, and their past participle by the addition of -en and, except in one conjugation, by a vowel change. The vowel in the preterite plural and second sing. differed from that in the rest of the singular. The parts of an O.E. verb given in paradigms are thus the infinitive, the first pers. sing. of the preterite, the first pers. plur. preterite, and the past participle. The following paradigms of a few verbs show the method of variation: drîfan (to drive), drâf, drifon, drifen; biddan (to pray), bœd, bœdon, boden; ceosan (to choose), ceas, curon, coren. Weak verbs did not vary the preterite vowel, and so the plur. pret. is not given. They formed their pret. and past part. either in -ode and -od, or -de and -ed. Thus, we have lufian (to love), lufode, gelufod; hieran (to hear or obey), hierde gehiered. Some few weak verbs have also a change of vowel, thus, ı encan (to think), þohte, ge oht. The O.E. verb had only two proper tenses, the present and the preterite, the former of these being normally used to express future as well as present time. The use of the auxiliaries (wile, hœfde, etc.) is early seen, though it does not become common until towards the end of the O.E. period. The order of words is less fixed than in Modern Eng., on account of the abundance of inflections. The general order closely resembles that of Modern Ger., which has kept the old Teutonic grammar almost intact. Not only was the grammar and syntax of O.E. purely Teutonic, but its vocabulary also was practically pure. Cognates, with most of the words found in our old texts, are also found in Gothic, Old Norse, Icelandic, Old High Ger., Old Saxon, etc., and the development of the science of philology in recent years has made the relations between them comparatively clear.

The regularity of these relations was broken only when Eng. started the introduction of a foreign vocabulary. A certain number of words borrowed from Latin are found in O.E. documents. As would be expected, these occur mostly in relation to ecclesiastical services, ornaments, and practices for which no Germanic word would exist. A few others were brought over by the Saxons from the Continent, having been borrowed in earlier intercourse with the Roms. Such a word is strœt (street).

A word must be said as to the spelling and pronunciation of the early Eng. and their scribes. There are no traces whatever of an original Germanic alphabet, for it is now quite clear that the Runic alphabet, or 'futhorc,' was derived at a date before the fifth century B.C. from the alphabet in use among the Gks. This alphabet was used at an early date in England for inscriptions on (Runic) crosses, etc., but there is no sign of any written Runic literature. The introduction of the Latin alphabet came with the Christianising of the country, being brought in slightly differing forms by the missionaries both from Ireland and from Rome. The Celtic form was generally adopted, with certain modifications, from the Runic alphabet. From this the sign þ was taken to signify the unvoiced th as in ' thin,' and the sign þ replaced the Latin u (v). In order to denote the voiced th as in ' there,' a crossed d was used in the form ð. This character is known as ' thorn.' These two signs came to be confused at an early date, and there is no clear distinction between them in existing MSS. But their origin shows the attempt naturally made to render the spelling phonetic, and this attempt was kept up with a greater or less degree of success until the invention of printing caused the gradual fixing of the spelling. During the O.E. period, however, we may regard the spelling as quite phonetic, except for a few defects, one of which, the lack of distinction between hard and soft th, has been already mentioned. Moreover, f had to do duty for both the voiced and the unvoiced sounds, being pronounced unvoiced except between two vowels. The letter y had the sound of Ger. ü, while initial c was probably pronounced ch. The letter g was often soft when it commenced a word and in certain other cases, so often has i substituted for it. Thus iung and geong are both forms of the word for young. The combination cg as in hrycg (back) is pronounced as gg. Medial h was a guttural sound, similar to the Modern Scotch ch in loch. Double consonants were not slurred as in N.E., but each was given its full value.

2. *Middle English.*—Though it is true that the Norman Conquest accelerated the decay of the O.E. grammar and syntax, yet it was not the cause of this decay. The action had set in a good many years before, and for a long while the Fr. court had very little influence on the native language. Layamon's *Brut* shows surprisingly few borrowings from Norman Fr., and this is indicative of the general state of affairs. The loss of its synthetic character left the language in a very poor state, for the rigid order of an analytic language had not yet been made, and frequent ambiguity results. The best monument of this transition period which may be consulted is the last entry, that for the reign of Stephen, in the Old Eng. Chronicle. In the M.E. period the dialects are found somewhat differently distributed, and so receive different names. (1) The *Northern* corresponds roughly to the old Northumbrian, and still includes Lowland Scotch, of which language in its modern form it is the ancestor. (2) The *Midland*, roughly equivalent to the old Mercian, is divided again into E. and W. Midland, sometimes with further subdivisions into N. and S.E. Midland, N. and S.W. Midland. (3) *Southern*, the descendant of the old W. Saxon, with an admixture of Mercian. The dialects of the W. country, as shown, for example, in Barnes's *Dorsetshire Farmer*, show this dialect at a later stage. (4) *Kentish*, which, from its proximity to London, and the fact that both Chaucer and Caxton were Kentish men, has had a considerable influence on the development of the language. But this division, though it is probably agreeable to the facts in a general way, does not carry us very far when we come to an examination of M.E. manuscripts. Nor is it quite so complete and satisfactory a division as was the O.E. one. In O.E. there was a standard literary W. Saxon dialect, and the MSS. which we possess show agreement in their spelling system and the pronunciation which lies behind it. This is not so in M.E. Almost every village may be said to have developed its own dialect as the old forms died out, and the survival of a literary language was impossible during the period of Fr. dominance. Another difficulty then arose for the scribes. They were most of them educated in the writings of the centuries past, and here they found a system of spelling which did not adequately represent the changed sounds of the new generations. Many of them, by copying the old texts, introduced an arbitrary spelling into Eng. Hence dates the commencement of the decay of the old phonetic spelling. This will, perhaps, be the best place to speak of a curious spelling experiment which was made by a northern writer of the name of Orm or Ormin. He wrought a lengthy metrical version of the Gospel known as the *Ormulum*, in which he employed an elaborate metrical system, the exact meaning of which has yet to be discovered. It relies largely on the doubling of consonants, but there are also other devices, such as two or three strokes over a letter. Orm was very proud of his spelling and charged all his scribes to retain his forms intact; but there is no trace of any other writer having adopted his scheme. It is in this period that we again find the work of the North prominent. The anct. culture had been swept away by the Danes, but these vandals, after having visited the shores of the E. coast as pirates, ultimately settled in our land and became peaceful settlers. In the time of Alfred, as is well known, the N.E. half of the country was Danish, and our annals also register a Danish dynasty. Now the Danish (or Scandinavian) was a language closely related to the Anglian dialects, differing from them chiefly in its inflections. The result of intercourse between Anglians and Danes is, therefore, easy to see. The stems of the words became important, the inflections were useless, and hence the process of getting rid of them went on fastest in the North, where Fr. influence was least strong. Hence the early M.E. pieces in Northern dialect, such as the *Cursor Mundi*, are characterised by a surprising modernity, for not only have the inflections almost all disappeared, but the syntax shows many features characteristic of that of the present day. A northern MS. of the beginning of the thirteenth century would be easier than Chaucer for a modern reader to understand. The Southern dialect is the least advanced of the three, and hence the most difficult to read. The Midland dialect is the ancestor of Modern Eng. This is accounted for by its position, in one or two ways. As lying intermediately between the Northern and Southern dialects it was the means of communication between them, for they were mutually unintelligible. But both Northerners and Southerners would probably have some acquaintance with Midland. Secondly, it is important to note that both the universities of Oxford and Cambridge lay within the Midland area. Most important of all was the fact that it contained London, already

the great metropolis of the kingdom. Here, too, the Midland dialect was found in its least singular forms, for intercourse between people speaking all kinds of dialects led to much levelling. It is this London dialect that forms the source of Chaucer's ' Eng. undefiled.' But though the basis was thus Midland, many words, spellings, and pronunciations were borrowed from the other dialects. The most important borrowings were made from Scandinavian through the Northern. We have already mentioned something of the influence of the Danish invasions on the Northern dialect in hastening its inflectional disintegration. The influence is also seen in vocabulary. Many of the commonest and most useful Eng. words were borrowed at this period. Among pronouns, both *she* and *they* are Scandinavian, the original Eng. forms being *heo* and *hi*. In the South these forms survive almost to the end of the M.E. period. *Egg* is another example of borrowing, for the Eng. form, frequent in M.E., is *ei*. There is much difficulty in discovering the exact dialect in which a M.E. text was written. The chief cause of this is, of course, the frequent copying of MSS. The scribe copied them or wrote them from dictation in the dialect to which he was himself accustomed, and if this dialect was different from that of the original MS., confusion resulted. Since this process of copying occurred not once but many times in the case of popular poems, such as the *Havelok*, the rime is the best test in the case of poetry, but even this is rendered uncertain by the fact that the poet himself might well have used a form from another dialect with which he was acquainted in order to procure a rime.

We have said that the influence of the Norman Conquest on vocabulary worked but slowly. Its influence on the spelling, however, very soon took effect, as all writing soon fell into the hands either of the Normans or of those trained by them. It will be as well to mention one or two of the changes thus brought about: (1) *ou* was written for O.E. *ū*, as, for example, in *mouse* for O.E. *mūs, house* for O.E. *hūs;* (2) *qu* replaced O.E. *cw,* e.g. *queen* for *cwēn;* (3) in many words where confusion was likely to occur in writing on account of the number of down strokes, *o* replaced *u,* e.g. *comen* for O.E. *cuman;* (4) *w* and *th* replaced þ and ð; *k* also became more common; (5) O.E. *y* was written *u,* e.g. *synn(e)* appears as *sunne*. This becomes a characteristic feature of the Southern dialect. In inflection the chief change from O.E. to M.E. is in the direction of simplification.

All the O.E. diphthongs disappeared, and all vowels in unaccented syllables tended to level as *e*. *M* in inflectional syllables also became *n*. Thus *an, on,* and *um* all appear as *en*. There was also a regular series of vowel changes and lengthenings. Only one or two can be mentioned here. O.E. long *ā* became *ō*, pronounced as the *au* in *aught*. Thus *stān* became *stǭn*. In the Northern dialect alone does the original *a* remain, and its pronunciation of *stone* as *stane,* etc., is still one of its characteristics. In all but the South, O.E. *ȳ* (= Ger. *ü*) coalesced with original *ī*. New diphthongs were formed by the union of vowels with the guttural ; (*g*) or *h*. Thus O.E. *dæg* becomes *dai* or *day,* but plural *dages* generally appears as *dawes*. O.E. *weg* becomes *wei* (= way), *fœgn* becomes *fain,* and so on. Initial *g*, probably soft even in O.E., became *y,* as in *yard, young, youth,* from O.E. *geard, geong, gioguð.* Initial *h* followed by another consonant was generally dropped, as in *ring, lauerd* (lord), from *hring* and *hlaford*. In the combination *hw,* however, metathesis takes place, though the original pronunciation generally remains. The verbs simplified considerably, and in M.E. the pres. plur. indicative ending forms a useful dialect test. Here the South had the old -*aþ,* Midland has -*en,* and North -*es* or no inflection at all. Cases almost entirely disappear, the genitive singular being the only one which retains its original inflection. The word order gradually becomes fixed as this process goes on.

3. *New English.*—About a hundred years after the London dialect had first been raised to literary eminence by the poet Chaucer, its orthography was finally cast into a mould by Caxton, who in 1477 introduced printing into England. Some trimming would be needed in the century and a half that was to follow, but in no material point does the grammar of Caxton differ from that of twentieth century Eng., and his spelling is still easily intelligible. The following are the most important of the few grammatical differences : (1) The use of the plural -*eth* ; (2) the infinitive ending -*en,* also found sometimes in the plural ; (3) occasional retention of imperative plural in -*eth* ; (4) gen. sing. in -*es* and -*is*. Spelling was still very variable, but the period of regulating this soon follows, and once again we find the general phonetic principle, though with the revival of learning many men, but slenderly equipped for the task, attempted to re-spell old words not according to the pronunciation, but according to their real or supposed etymology. *Subtle* had the *b* inserted on account

R 2

of its derivation from Latin *subtilis*. The *b*, however, had never been pronounced since the derivation was through the Fr. *sutil*. An example of mistaken etymology is seen in the word *rime* (from O.E. *rīm*), which was misspelt *rhyme* on account of its supposed connection with Gk. ρυθμός, with which is connected the word *rhythm*. But the earlier principle was phonetic, and it was carried out with fair consistency. Thus the spellings *ea* and *ee* denoted different sounds, *ea* as in *sea* represented the open *e* sound (pronounced somewhat as *a* in *mate*), while *ee* denoted the closed *e*. The difference is still shown by an Irishman. The open *ō* (*au* in *aught*) was frequently written *oa*, and in one word, *broad*, the Elizabethan pronunciation is retained. An *e* as in *stone* was added to denote a long vowel, while the doubling of a consonant, e.g. *penny*, showed a preceding short vowel. Thus a standard orthography was attained, and it has never since been revised. Thus the first folio edition of Shakespeare's works (1623) can be read quite easily by one almost destitute of training. But we should comprehend little if their author were to read them to us, for the pronunciation has undergone a series of gradual changes which in sum amounts to a revolution. This revolution has resulted in our vowel system being a European curiosity, while in Shakespearian times it was in accord with that of the Continent. Thus *ā* was pronounced as in *father* and except at court, where it had its present sound, the *ā* was pronounced as in Ger. Long *ē*, usually written *ea*, *ee*, or *ie*, was pronounced as *a* in *mate*. In some cases, such as *head* and *feather*, shortening has since taken place. There has been no considerable change in *ĕ*. Long *ī* was then pronounced as *ee* in *meet*, but has since diphthongised into *œi*, but *ĭ* has remained constant, as has also *ŏ*. Long *ō*, as we have seen, was pronounced as in *broad*, and this sound later became represented by *au* or *aw* as in *saw*. Short *ŭ* was pronounced as in N.E. *put*. Long *ū* was pronounced in the Continental manner, and has since diphthongised into *yu*. Gutturals still proved a fertile source of diversity in pronunciation and spelling, and hence the famous diversity in Modern Eng. between the various pronunciations of *-ough*. In the eighteenth-century drama we frequently find *through* pronounced *thruf*, and dialectical *enew* may still be heard for *enough*. Generally speaking, it may be said that the guttural either disappeared or turned into *f*. This shows briefly the chief changes in the vowel system of N.E., though it is impossible to

show here the steps by which it took place. It is not by any means to be supposed that there was any sudden and conscious change. The greatest point, however, in which the Eng. of our own century differs from that of Caxton is in its vocabulary. Middle Eng. was still comparatively a pure language, but since the invention of printing there has been a steady influx of words borrowed from all parts of the globe. Borrowings from Latin had been made even before the arrival of the Eng. in our land. Fr. borrowings were frequent during the M.E. period, as were also incorporations from the kindred Scandinavian tongue. The Renaissance saw an immense number of borrowings from Gk., and more especially Latin, and vast numbers of these were never incorporated into the language. Many, indeed, of the Elizabethans definitely aimed at the Latinising of their vocabulary. Fr. again gave us many words during the Restoration period, and here again a perusal of such writers as Dryden will show us that only a proportion of the borrowings became naturalised. At other times we have borrowed from Dutch, Italian, Portuguese, Turkish, Chinese, and in fact from almost every language with which we have come in contact. In general, it will be found that the borrowings from these languages can be classified under regular heads. Thus Gk., from its clearness and accuracy of thought, has been called on to supply mathematical and scientific terms. The Dutch, whom we have met principally at sea, supply nautical terms and one or two for painting. Similarly Italy supplies musical terms. It will generally be found that our borrowings from Asiatic languages were for the naming of articles for which we had no Eng. equivalent, such as junk, bungalow, etc. The extent of our borrowings from the classical languages has given the Eng. language a large number of doublets, and these, assuming slightly different meanings, add greatly to the richness of the language, so much so, indeed, that its varying shades and tones can be adequately expressed in no other language.

BIBLIOGRAPHY.—Such great progress has been made in the study of philology during the past century that all books published on the subject before the middle of the nineteenth century are practically useless. For Old Eng., in particular, *see* E. Sievers' *Old English Grammar*, translated by A. S. Cook (last ed. 1903), the principal work on the subject; T. N. Toller's *Anglo-Saxon Dictionary*, 1882–99, based on the late J. Bosworth's MS. Collection, not quite trustworthy, especially in the earlier parts; C. W. M. Grein's *Sprachschatz der Angelsächsichen Dichter*, 1861–64, which, however, deals only with the poetic vocabulary, is excellent; H. Sweet's *Student's Dictionary of Anglo-Saxon*, 1897; H. Sweet's *Anglo-Saxon Reader* (8th ed.), 1908, and *Second Anglo-Saxon Reader*, 1887. Middle Eng.: F. H. Stratmann's *Middle English Dictionary* (revised by H. Bradley), 1891; E. Mätzner's *Altenglische Sprachproben: Wörterbuch*, vol. ii., commenced 1867, has been enlarged to form a complete M.E. dictionary; Mayhew and Skeat's *Concise Dictionary of Middle English*, 1888; B. Ten Brink's *Chaucer's Sprache und Verkunst* (Eng. trans.), 1901; R. Morris and W. Skeat's *Specimens of Early English*, Part I., *1150–1300* (2nd ed., 1887); Part II., *1298–1393* (3rd ed., 1894); W. Skeat's *Specimens of English Literature, 1394–1579*, 1886. New Eng. and General: Abbott's *Shakespearean Grammar*, 1872; A. Schmidt's *Shakspere-Lexicon* (3rd ed.), 1902; F. Koch's *Historische Grammatik der Englischen Sprache* (revised ed), 1878–91; H. Sweet's *New English Grammar, Logical and Historical*, 1892–98; R. Morris's *Historical Outlines of English Accidence* (revised ed.), 1899; *A New English Dictionary on Historical Principles*, known shortly as 'Murray's,' or the 'Oxford,' dictionary (publication commenced 1888, still in progress; for particulars *see* under DICTIONARY); W. Skeat's *Etymological Dictionary of the English Language* (3rd ed.), 1899, and *Concise Etymological Dictionary of the English Language* (revised ed.), 1901; H. Sweet's *History of English Sounds*, 1888; and *Elementarbuch des gesprochenen Englisch* (3rd ed.), 1899.

**English Literature** had no birth within the shores of the British Islands. When the three Low Ger. tribes, Angles, Jutes, and Saxons, of whom Bede tells us in his *Ecclesiastical History*, came to our shores, they brought with them a literature which had already passed through many centuries of development. But whatever may have been its vicissitudes since that time, and under whatever foreign influences it may have come, E. L. throughout its history clearly shows its kinship with these early writings, the unity of its spirit and their spirit.

(1) *Old English.*—It will be well first to deal with the poetry of Old Eng. So few are the remains which have come down to us that we must here deal with particular poems, though when we read of the strange freaks of fortune by which they have survived, we feel that we have so little to base our judgment on that it must be almost worthless. Chief among the Old Eng. poems comes the great epic of *Beowulf*, which deals in simple but stirring fashion with the life-story of an anct. Teutonic hero. It divides into three main parts, the first two of which tell of his encounters with Grendel, a monster of the moors, and with Grendel's mother. These take place in the prime of his life, and the last section tells how he meets his death when attacking a dragon on behalf of his people. But the highly developed state of literature at this time is seen less plainly in the subject than in the treatment. There was in Old Eng. a recognised diction which the poet had to use in addition to the metre. The chief feature of this diction is its parallelism, which it shares in common with the old Hebrew poetry. Below are given a few lines, from 1311–14 :

' Hraðe wæs tö būre. Beowulf fetod
Sigor-ëadig secg. samod ær-dæge
Eode eorla sum. æoele cempa
Self mid gesiðium,'

which may be translated, ' Quickly was Beowulf, victory-blessed man, fetched to the chamber before dawn. The noble champion went one of a company of earls, himself with his companions.' The general construction of the lines will be seen from this example. In each line there are three alliterative syllables, of which two occur in the second half of the line. In each half line there are two stressed, and a variable number of unstressed syllables, all the alliterative syllables being stressed. *Beowulf* probably reached its final form in the seventh century, though the original poem was much older, and contained none of the few Christian elements which appear in the poem as we now have it. Among other early Eng. poems may be named *Widsith*, or ' The Traveller,' certain elegiac lyrics such as *The Seafarer*, *The Wanderer*, and metrical translations of parts of the Bible. Though the poems we have named were not Northumbrian, it was in the N. that the first great literary school arose, associated with the names of Cædmon, Cynewulf, and Bede. To Cynewulf are attributed many extant poems, such as *The Phœnix* and that most marvellous of Old Eng. religious lyrics, *The Dream of the Rood*. Other remains consist of Charms, Runic verses, Gnomic verses, and Riddles. Old Eng. prose is associated principally with the name of King Alfred, and it is thanks to the industry of that monarch that we possess many translations of Northumbrian work which would otherwise have been lost on the destruction of the school by the Danish inroads. His works were of all kinds and should be sought under his own name. The *Anglo-Saxon Chronicle* is also a valuable monument, often showing great vigour and command of language. Reference should also be made to the names of Aelfric and Wulfstan. Generally speaking, however, the prose of the period is entirely inferior to the poetic production.

(2) *Middle English.*—The beginning of the twelfth century was a momentous period for European literature. It saw the rise of that Fr. literature which was to be the standard and model for the whole of Europe during the later Middle Ages and after. The influence was long in taking a thorough hold on England—and its final fruit in the poetry of Gower and Chaucer was late in coming. The poetry of the period from 1200 onwards shows little trace of connection with that which we have just been considering. The older diction has gone, and, except for a set of poems written in the N.W. and N.E. Midlands, the old metre has also gone. Rhyme is now commonly used either instead of alliteration or in conjunction with it. A S.W. work, generally placed between 1100 and 1200, the *Poema Morale*, shows not only the transition state of the language, but also the terrible condition of the verse. All poetic skill has been lost, and the long fourteen-syllable couplets drag mournfully along. The *Ormulum*, which opens thus : 'þiss boc iss nemmnedd Orrmulum, Forrþi þatt Orrm itt wrohhte,' besides being noted for its curious spelling, shows more vigorous versification. It will be noted that the verse here is the common measure which is still so popular. An important northern school of poetry is found during this period, its chief productions being the *Lay of Havelok the Dane*, and the *Cursor Mundi*, a huge attempt to give a history of the world from the creation down to the time of writing. The lyrics and ballads of the time were generally handed about and retouched until the fifteenth century, in which or in even later times they were written down in their final forms. *The Owl and the Nightingale* is the best of the early Middle Eng. lyrics. A great deal of work was also done in the production of *Lives of the Saints*, which forms a distinct section of thirteenth and fourteenth century literature. Even more was done in the translation of the Fr. metrical romances, among which may be named the *Seven Sages, William and the Were-*

*wolf, Sir Tristrem,* etc. Matter for romances was generally considered under three heads which will give a good idea as to what these romances dealt with, viz. (1) the matter of Rome, which included stories of Alexander and all Eastern subjects ; (2) the matter of Britain, which included King Arthur and the Round Table ; (3) the matter of France, which dealt with Charlemagne. Neither poetry nor prose, however, is in a very flourishing condition till we come to the great group of writers who flourished in the middle or later fourteenth century. First among these we must name William Langland, who is generally considered to be the author of *The Vision of William concerning Piers the Plowman*. Except for a few half-jocular allusions in the poem itself, absolutely nothing is known about the author, even his surname being uncertain. The poem itself shows traces of several recensions, probably by different hands. It is a long and confused allegory, dealing with man's quest for truth, and it has a current of satire directed against all classes of the community, not least against the poor, whose cause it champions. Though written but a few years before Chaucer's great works it has a much more archaic tone. The loose alliterative verse emphasises this. These obstacles are sufficient to have deterred many from an attempt to read *Piers Plowman*—a most unfortunate state of affairs, since the intrinsic merit and mystic beauty of the poem would amply have repaid them for the initial difficulty. John Gower, the 'moral Gower,' as Chaucer calls him (c. 1325-1408), was a slightly earlier contemporary of the master of Eng. poetry. He represents the height of the Fr. culture of his time, and his verse shows the highest result of the Fr. influence which could have been achieved without the genius of Chaucer. Were he not overshadowed by this genius, he would be held in much higher repute, for his *Confessio Amantis*, taken in small quantities, is most interesting. He makes almost exclusive use of the Fr. octosyllabic verse. Gower's trilingualism is interesting as a feature of the time. He wrote three long works, of which the *Confessio Amantis*, a long string of tales in Boccaccio fashion to illustrate the seven deadly sins, is in Eng. ; the *Vox Clamantis* is in Latin ; and the *Speculum Meditantis* in Fr. These were the three polite languages of the day in England. But with Geoffrey Chaucer (1340-1400), the later Middle Ages found their fullest expression in almost every way. It has been held that in the *Canterbury Tales* every facet of mediæval life is viewed in turn. Chaucer at first started under the Fr. influence, and he shared in the Fr. inability to work out a plot properly. His *Parlement of Foules* is entirely in the school of the *Romaunt of the Rose*. But two visits to Italy brought him in touch with Boccaccio and the Italians, and it was from the *Teseide* of this writer that he especially profited. The Italians had kept more in touch with the old Latin poets, and had retained the Virgilian art of keeping control of the story. *Troylus and Cressid* was under this influence. But Chaucer never gave up what he had learnt from the Fr., and to the end the enchanted garden of the Rose had its charm for him. But to this knowledge he added what he had learnt from the Italians, and his own genius, working on these two lines and transforming them by his unique knowledge of Eng. life and manners, brought him to the great and final period of the *Canterbury Tales*. So natural and abundant is the humour in these, so good the connection, and so well sustained the interest, that it is generally held that Chaucer would have made a novelist equal to Fielding. Not the least, perhaps, among Chaucer's services to Eng. poetry was his discovery of the decasyllabic line, which he generally wrote in the heroic couplet. Though this measure had been used before in Eng., it was he who gave it its suppleness by a free use of syllabic equivalents, and it was he who made it the most popular of Eng. measures. Hitherto the Fr. octosyllabic measure had occupied this position. It is usual to divide the followers of Chaucer into two schools, the Scottish and the Eng., of which it will be well first to consider the northern one. Scottish poetry was at first indistinguishable from Northern Eng. The same dialect was spoken from the Humber to the Firth of Forth, the ancestor of Lowland Scotch. The Scotch themselves spoke of it as 'Inglis.' Almost contemporary with Chaucer comes John Barbour, Archdeacon of Aberdeen (1316?–95?), whom patriotic ardour stirred up to write the adventures of the Bruce, in a book bearing that title, and from him the beginning of Scottish poetry is dated. The influence of Chaucer upon the poets of the following century in the northern kingdom was most beneficial. They were vigorous and had a true poetic spirit and appreciation of nature. The influence shows least in Henryson (*c.* 1430–*c.* 1506), but appears stronger in William Dunbar, who lived somewhat later, and whom Sir Walter

Scott described as the greatest of Scottish poets. He can hardly have forgotten Burns at the time. Gawain Douglas, Bishop of Dunkeld, also owed much to the southerner. This poet is noted as being the first to use blank verse in Eng. poetry. He used it in the translation of certain books of the *Æneid*, to which his own poetic genius contributed beautiful prologues. King James I. (1394–1437) must be classed with these poets, though almost all his literary work dates from the period of his long captivity in England. The *Kingis Quair* tells the story of his love for Jane Beaufort, whom he afterwards

*The firſt Chapter.*

A
6.d
18.2
o b
9 a
δ+ c

IT ꝭ begyn nynge ⟨God⟩ created hea uen ⁊ earth: and ꝭ earth was voyde and emptie, and darck- nes was v- pon the de- pe,⁊ ꝭ ſpi- te of God moued vp̄ the water.

And God ſayde: let there be light,⁊ there was light. And God ſawe the light that it was good. Then God deuyded ꝭ light from the darckneſ,and called the light, Daye:and the darckneſ, Uight. Then of the euenynge and moinyuge was made the firſt daye.

A PAGE FROM THE FIRST PRINTED ENGLISH BIBLE, COVERDALE'S, 1535

married. It shows the 'aureate language' which was to be characteristic of the later Chaucerians. In England, however, the disciples of Chaucer, in spite of their obvious and frequently expressed devotion for it, did little credit to their master's name. This was partly due to changes in the language. Among other things, the final *e* had now become silent, and they were thus unable to understand Chaucer's versification. They could find no regularity in it, and so themselves aimed at none. Their verse can only be described as sprawling. The two leading names are those of John Lydgate and Thomas Occleve (both *c.* 1370–1450). Lydgate was a monk of Bury St. Edmunds monastery, and his writings are voluminous in the extreme. His principal works are : (1) the *Troy Book*, which tells the old story from Dictys Cretensis and Dares Phrygius ; (2) the

*Story of Thebes,* which, in a happily-written prologue, he joins on as one of the *Canterbury Tales*; (3) the *Falls of Princes,* a long work, of which the plan brings the *Monk's Tale* to our mind. It is a long catalogue of the accidents of illustrious men, taken from a Fr. version of Boccaccio's *De Casibus Illustrium Virorum.* Occleve's chief work was a poem on the duties of kings, *De Regimine Principium,* which he presented to Henry V. Stephen Hawes, who died about the end of the first quarter of the sixteenth century, is often called the last of the Chaucerians. He was a scholar, and was familiar with French and Italian poetry. Somewhat more important, however, is Alexander Barclay (*d.* 1552), who published an extremely lively translation of a Dutch satire, *The Ship of Fools.* With John Skelton (*d.* 1529), we find the entire collapse of the old order of verse. Some of Skelton's verse is on the old plan, but all of it which has any vitality is in ' Skeltonic ' metre, a kind of ragged doggerel with lines of two or three feet rhyming here, there, and everywhere. The time was certainly ripe for a new order of poetry. But before tracing the rise of the new poetry we must go back for a while to the history of the fifteenth century prose. Chaucer, with his translations and prose tales, was the first to write a good middle Eng. prose. Wyclif and his followers are responsible for some Biblical translations and pamphlets. The historian, John of Trevisa (1326–1412), also deserves mention, while the *Travels of Sir John Mandeville* are valuable monuments. Sir John Fortescue (*d.* 1476) was a vigorous writer on law and history, his chief work being a treatise on *The Difference between Absolute and Limited Monarchy* and *De Laudibus Legum Angliæ.* Reginald Pecock, Bishop of Chichester, may in many ways be considered a predecessor of Hooker. His *Repressor of over-much Blaming of the Clergy* (*c.* 1450) was an elaborate prose treatise against the Lollards. Mention must also be made of Malory's *Mort d'Arthur* (*c.* 1470), that glorious crystallisation of the dying spirit of chivalry. In spite of these works, however, Eng. prose cannot yet be said to be really alive.

The new poetry came with the Renaissance. In 1453 the city of Constantinople had fallen into the hands of the Turks, and a rush of Gk. scholars to Italy, bringing with them their MSS. and learning, had taken place. An enormous impulse in the study of Gk. and Latin had followed, and this impulse had passed across Europe in a mighty wave,

bringing new life as it came. The Reformation arose partly from the new learning and partly from deeper causes, but the result of the two was an entire falling away of the old world and a veritable renaissance of all things. The new birth in literature was heralded by two men, Surrey (1514–47), and Wyatt (1503–42). These were the first to make a definite effort to model the literature of their native land on that of Italy. They were both courtiers, and henceforth for at least a century the court is to be the centre of literature, whereas during the Middle Ages each monastery had acted as a small centre for the gathering and diffusion of what learning there was. To Wyatt we especially owe the sonnet, the introduction of which form, with the alterations necessitated by the difficulty of rhyming in Eng., was to bring out such a mass of sonnet sequences during the last ten years of the sixteenth century. Surrey's special work was the introduction of blank verse into England, though his management of it is so stiff and classicalised that one can hardly wonder that it was long before it was taken up. During the next half-century the only name of any importance that emerges is that of Thomas Sackville, Lord Buckhurst, afterwards Earl of Dorset. A composite work called *The Mirror for Magistrates* was put in hand. It was a long work, which we can describe as an enlarged edition of Lydgate's *Falls of Princes,* and the various ' Falls ' were contributed by different authors. All the contributions but those of Sackville are quite negligible. These are the *Induction* and the *Fall of the Duke of Buckingham,* which show a verve and power of imagery that point forward to Spenser. It is to Sackville, in conjunction with Thomas Norton (1528–84), that we also owe the first blank verse tragedy, a cold Senecan creation named *Gorboduc* or *Porrex and Ferrex.* But this will be referred to again when we are considering the drama. Elizabethan literature burst into fullness of bloom with the year 1579. To this year belong the first plays of the university wits, the *Euphues* of John Lyly, and the *Shepherd's Calendar* of Edmund Spenser. Even the least learned in E. L. has heard of the vogue of Euphuism, and this vogue is directly traceable to Lyly's work. The *Calendar* also was hailed by all the poets of the day, and Spenser was universally hailed as the greatest poet since Chaucer. The mention of Chaucer's name may be dismissed as conventional, since it is probable that none but Spenser himself had read this author. In spite of his borrowing from the Italians and the Fr., it is noticeable that Spenser is under particular obligation here to the early poet, thus providing a valuable link between the birth and the new birth of Eng. poetry. Immediately following Spenser came a glorious outburst of song, unparalleled since in any period of our history. There was then no convention to bind or guide a poet, and none could then write without some inspiration. Great as was the volume of work produced, it is true to say that there is no poet in whose work one can find no sparks of the celestial fire. Many names have come down to us, and hundreds more are lost. Spenser himself, in his Irish exile, went on to add to his laurels, and the first three books of the *Faerie Queene* appeared in 1592, and his miscellaneous poems appeared at intervals. In all the writers of the period, the patriotic vein is strongly marked, particularly so in a small group of writers who devote themselves almost entirely to England's glories—William Warner, Michael Drayton, and Daniel. Drayton was the author of *Polyolbion, The Barons' Wars*, and *England's Heroical Epistles*; while Warner wrote the huge but dull *Albion's England*. We must here pause for a while to trace the origins of that drama which was the truest and greatest glory of the Elizabethan period. The degenerate classical drama of the first centuries had been opposed and finally exterminated by the church. The same body ultimately resuscitated a form so useful for instruction. It is doubtless from the dramatic accounts of the Resurrection given in church on Easter Day that the 'miracle' or 'mystery' plays took their rise. They speedily passed outside the church buildings and freed themselves from ecclesiastical control, though they long retained their religious nature. The miracle plays of the Middle Ages (thirteenth century onwards) consisted of a cycle of plays, sometimes nearly fifty, dealing with events in the religious history of the world, from the Creation to the Last Day. Four cycles are generally spoken of: the *York, Chester, Coventry*, and *Towneley* cycles, each of which has certain prevailing characteristics. Pathos, humour, tragedy, comedy, realism, in fact all the qualities of the true drama, are found there in embryo. From the miracle play came the morality, where instead of Biblical, apocryphal, and historical characters, virtues and vices are represented in conflict for the soul of man. Greatest of the moralities is *Everyman*. The moralities generally tended to approximate to the comedy of manners Another development

was the interlude, and to this kind John Heywood particularly devoted himself. This certainly was an attempt at the comedy of manners. The post of honour as the first Eng. comedy is usually given to *Ralph Roister Doister*. From about the same period (1540) dates *Gammer Gurton's Needle*. In 1561, however, was produced Sackville and Norton's *Gorboduc*, the first Eng. tragedy to be written in blank verse. It was avowedly on the Senecan model, and is stiff, cold, and didactic. It was some long time before the example of its versification was taken

WILLIAM SHAKESPEARE

up. The Elizabethan playwrights fall into two groups, of which the first-named is the earlier. The university wits, as they were called, were men of education, members of one or both of the universities. They wrote their dramas with a definite attention to classical models, and expressed great contempt for the second school, that of the players themselves. Among the former class we may name Lyly, Peele, Greene, Nash, and Kyd, while Marlowe, the great predecessor of Shakespeare, though not actually one of the group, belongs to them by nature and training. Shakespeare himself is the great product of the second school, though a follower both of Lyly and Marlowe. Lyly (1554–1606) was the author of a number of prose comedies, almost all of which were played by children. From him Shakespeare learnt the value of prose conversation. Marlowe's work for the drama was much more important. Hitherto the Eng. drama had lacked life and unity of purpose; a good dramatic medium was also needed. All these wants Marlowe supplied. He took up blank verse, and wrought it to a fine temper; he introduced a roaring tragedy in which there was certainly no lack of life. Furthermore, every one of his leading characters has a dominant idea which rules the entire piece. In *Tamburlaine the Great*, his first piece, which is often considered the characteristic example of the Marlowe drama, the dominant idea is the lust of power it breathes through every line. Consuming avarice is the keynote to *The Jew of Malta*, while in *Dr. Faustus* the consuming desire for supernatural knowledge is everywhere. In Shakespeare's earlier plays, such as *Titus Andronicus* and *King John*, the Marlowe influence is extremely strong. The number of playwrights who flourished during the last twenty years of Elizabeth's reign and the years immediately following it is enormous, and the output of each individual was very great. Plays were produced once or twice and then thrown aside to make way for something new, for history, anct. and modern, while all the worlds of the imagination were being ransacked to satisfy the ravenous hunger of the new-born intellect and mind. Then, if time pressed or the theme seemed suitable, the old play would later be used as the basis of a new production. The speed with which this was done, and the carelessness with which old pieces were thrown aside and lost, is shown by the claim that Heywood, author of *The Woman Killed with Kindness*, makes to have been author or part-author of more than two hundred pieces, of which about twenty-five have come down to us. Shakespeare (1564–1616) developed the romantic comedy and out of the current type of 'revenge play' he evolved his magnificent tragedy, while his great contemporary, Ben Jonson (1573–1637), was writing the 'comedy of humours' with rigid adherence to the pseudo-classical unities of time and space. Jonson's influence, combined with that of Fr. models, was considerable on the drama after the Restoration, while in his own day his importance in Eng. as a literary dictator almost equals that of Samuel Johnson. Almost all the great poets of the Caroline and Jacobean periods were in their youth sealed 'of the tribe of Ben.' The two collaborators, Francis Beaumont (1584–1616) and John Fletcher (1575–1625) wrote romantic plays of a sentiment more strained than in Shakespeare. Of the 'revenge school' of writers are Webster (c. 1600), Marston (1575?–1634), Ford (b. 1586?), and Tourneur (d. 1626); while Chapman (1559?–1634?), Massinger (1583–1640), Middleton (1570?–1627), Dekker (b. 1570?), and Rowley (1585?–1642?) were successful in

tragedy and comedy of either style. For further developments of the Eng. theatre *see under* DRAMA. The Elizabethan playwrights frequently wrote in collaboration, groups of two, three or more writers composing one play, and then separating. In the case of Beaumont and Fletcher a permanent collaboration is found of so perfect a nature that it is impossible accurately to estimate the contributions of each to the partnership. James Shirley (1596–1666) is generally spoken of as 'the last of the Elizabethans.' As a dramatist he would not rank high, but in his voice the tone of the great ones who had preceded him is still to be recognised, a spark of their fire can yet be seen. His name carries the history of the Eng. drama down to the time of the Commonwealth, and at the beginning of this period Parliament closed all the theatres and forbade their use. When they reopened with the Restoration, the type of drama was a new one, looking to Fr. masters rather than to native ones. This was but natural, since, in the meanwhile, a high classical drama had developed in France, whilst the latest plays acted in the Eng. theatre, the only tradition available, were of a most degenerate type. But we must now retrace our steps to consider the development of prose during this period.

Mediæval prose, as has been seen, was almost negligible. Latin was the official language of learning and theology, so although the vernacular might be used for poetry there was as yet nothing to develop a native prose style. The first man of mark to make a point of using the vernacular and a definite effort to write well in it was Roger Ascham, who declares his intention in the introduction to *Toxophilus* (1544). It is important to notice that Sir Thomas More's *Utopia* (1516) was originally written not in Eng. but in Latin. The Eng. translation by Ralph Robinson did not appear until forty years later. A more important work of Ascham's was *The Schoolmaster* (1570), the first Eng. educational treatise. Ascham belonged to a small group of classical scholars whose attempt to start an Eng. prose style was not only founded on the model of the classics, but combined a respect for the capabilities of the vernacular which they did not wish to spoil by the wholesale importation of classical words or by twisting it into classical forms. Ascham's prose is straightforward, somewhat heavy and devoid of ornament, but it is perspicuous and pleasant to read even at the present day. The various translations of the

Bible which appeared (Tyndale, 1525, Coverdale, 1536), also gave a great impulse to the development of a good prose style. Prose pamphleteering was common; two important controversies of this nature were: (1) The Martin Marprelate controversy, in which episcopal government was attacked; and (2) the Harvey-Nash controversy, between Nash the playwright and Spenser's friend and mentor, Gabriel Harvey. Nash came the better out of the conflict. A certain number of prose romances were produced by the dramatists, and these are mostly modelled on that marvellous work, the *Euphues* of Lyly, of which mention has already been made. This book, together with the *Arcadia* of Sir Philip Sidney (1590), shows the self-conscious striving after an ornamental style which characterises the period. Nash's *Rosalynde*, from which Shakespeare took the plot of *As You Like It*, is the best-known imitation of the *Euphues*. Nash's *Adventures of Jack Wilton* is a romance which already looks forward to the picaresque novel. A high level of prose is founded in the Eng. *Book of Common Prayer* which appeared in 1549, but this was the work of several hands. The *Ecclesiastical Polity* of Richard Hooker (1553–1600), which appeared in 1593 (Books i.–iv.) and 1597 (Book v.), may be considered to show the high-water mark of the magnificent Latinised style which the Elizabethans affected. Its prevailing features are the long sentences, the rhetorical language, the heavy ornament and occasionally the Latinised syntax and vocabulary. This position might, however, be taken by the A.V. of the Holy Bible, which appeared in 1611. The long survival of the contempt for the vernacular is shown by Francis Bacon, whose *Advancement of Learning* appeared in 1605, and the *History of the Reign of Henry VII.* in 1623. He took particular care that those works which he intended to go down to posterity should be translated into Latin. Whereas, however, the Latin translation is almost unknown, the Eng. originals are now classics of the language. With the reign of Charles I. we come to a group of prose writers who have the use of the magnificent 'Latin' prose in common. These are Bishop Jeremy Taylor (1613–67), whose *Holy Living and Dying* is world famous; John Milton (1608–74), whose 'purple patches' occur most especially in *Areopagitica*; Sir Thomas Browne, whose grand but melancholy music was the delight of the whimsical Charles Lamb; and Robert Burton (1576–1637), whose *Anatomy of Melancholy* was also one of Lamb's favourite

works. All these writers are gorgeous, grand, and, in a sense, unique. In a different place, and somewhat prophetic of the style which was to arise after the Restoration, are Ben Jonson, the philosophical school of Hobbes, and the adherents of the Royal Society of which Bishop Sprat was the spokesman.

The important task now remains of bringing the history of poetry down to the Commonwealth period. It was in this department more than in those of prose and drama that the period from 1600 onwards excelled. It evolved a lyric school of surpassing sweetness and delicacy of touch, whose products have been the despair

JOHN MILTON

and admiration of later lyricists. The genius in the wedding of poetry and song which was handed down from the later Elizabethans (such as Campion) here reaches a much higher level of art. Even if an Elizabethan were fantastic, he was so naturally. Now art began first to be added to inspiration and then to replace it. This is the period of those whom in his *Life of Cowley*, Samuel Johnson so aptly calls the *metaphysical poets*. They aimed at quaint conceits, and sought for farfetched comparisons, though, as the learned doctor says, ' they were often worth the carrying.' And whereas some, as we have said, produced song of the greatest sweetness and delicacy, others deliberately aimed at harsh and irregular versification. It was the over-emphasising of these peculiar qualities of the school which ultimately led after the Restoration to the reaction which culminated in the accurate and polished verse of Alexander Pope. Signs of the approaching change are to be found even among the metaphysicals themselves. But at the time the school was so widespread that it is possible, by subdivision, to bring almost all the poets of James I. and Charles I.'s reigns under it. We should thus subdivide them into Pure Wits, Court Wits, and Religious or Devotional Wits, for in the parlance of the day the word ' wit ' was used to describe the particular excellence of quaint erudition which was particularly sought after. The great master of the school was John Donne (1573–1631), who during the first part of his life wrote a large number of love songs, but in the latter half devoted himself to religion. The Wit school also produced a fine poet in Abraham Cowley (1618–67). Among the court poets, known also as the cavalier poets, the two chief names are those of Richard Lovelace and Sir John Suckling. With these poetry was the recreation of their leisure hours. Others whose names must not be forgotten are, George Wither (1588–1677), who also distinguished himself as a satirist, William Cartwright (1611–43), William Habington (1605–45), and John Cleveland (1613–59). Two of the best lyricists of this period are Andrew Marvell (1621–78) and Henry King (1592–1669); both were touched by the metaphysical style which also infected the devotional writers. Of these the best known is George Herbert (1591–1632), whose entire works are suffused with a delicate spirituality. His best poetical works were published under the title The Temple, to which another of the school, Richard Crashaw (c. 1616–50), wrote an introductory series, Steps to the Temple. Henry Vaughan's chief work is the Silex Scintillans. But the greatest lyricist of the period yet remains to be named. Robert Herrick (1591–1674) has never lost the position he attained in his own time. The delicate flower and love pieces, which form the greater part of his Hesperides, together with the ' pious pieces ' in Noble Numbers, testify not only to his poetic skill but also to his mastery of the technique of versification. His comparisons are often as far-fetched as those of the most pronounced metaphysician, and his vocabulary is far more curiously Latinised, but one forgets these defects in his delicate and Epicurean atmosphere. It is sometimes forgotten that all Milton's shorter pieces, by many considered to be his best work, were produced before 1642. Then came the twenty years during which his conscience compelled him to devote his best energies to politics

and the prose works which dealt with matters of state. Then, under the Restoration, he returned to the Muses and produced the two epics with which his name is popularly associated, Paradise Lost and Paradise Regained. His earlier work includes the Hymn on the Nativity, 1629; L'Allegro and Il Penseroso, 1633; Comus, 1634, and Lycidas, 1637. In these all his particular excellences are found in a more compressed form than in Paradise Lost, where long barren stretches occur between the bursts of glorious rhetoric. Moreover, the early poems do not show the coldness and hardening mannerism of a later work such as Samson Agonistes (1671).

After the death of Charles I., when the court was in exile, France proved a refuge for many of those who were afterwards to return with Charles II. in 1660. Here, at the famous Hôtel de Rambouillet, they came into touch with a new literary movement. Boileau was then coming into prominence as literary dictator, and it is in his Art Po tique that the principles and rules of the classical poetry and drama are laid down. A reaction had set in against the freedom of the preceding century and the extravagance it had led to. A return to primitive simplicity had come, and the classics were now held up as the only models of excellence. Horace and Aristotle, much interpreted, were now become the legislators of Parnassus. Corneille had already lifted the Fr. classical drama to noble heights, and it was under his influence that the Restoration drama began. The entire absence of human beings has been mentioned as the chief feature of the Cornelian drama. Every one is drawn more than life-size, virtues and vices are both thrown into high relief. The leading character is actuated by one motive, and this principle, applied in a slightly lesser degree to all the characters, materially simplifies human life for the purposes of the stage. The Restoration drama had always a striking hero, kept very much in the limelight, as we may say, and his importance has led to its receiving the name of the heroic drama, and to its vehicle, the decasyllabic couplet, being called the heroic couplet. Davenant, in his Siege of Rhodes, opened the series of these plays, but for long their principal exponent was no less a man than Dryden, among whose heroic plays may be named Tyrannic Love, 1669, and the Conquest of Granada, 1670. These plays are characterised by a brilliant rhetoric which commonly degenerates into rant, and by an extravagant emphasis on ' honour.' The best of Dryden's plays in this style is

*All for Love*, written in blank verse, of which Dryden had before been an opponent. It is as Dryden says, the only play he had written for himself, and shows that he had tired of the ranting style before his audiences. The play is an attempt to rival Shakespeare's *Antony and Cleopatra*, dealing as it does with part of the situation of the older play. A comparison of the two will show the main points of difference between the romantic and classical dramatic styles better than would the lengthiest exposition. Following the great tragedy of Corneille in France, came the comedy of Molière, and following the heroic drama in England came the comedy of manners, of which William Congreve (1670–1729) was the most brilliant exponent. Johnson quotes a passage from his *Mourning Bride* as the greatest in Eng. drama. But Congreve's greatest comedies are *Love for Love* and *The Way of the World*. They are pictures of contemporary ' gallant ' life, and depend for their effect upon the dialogue. This is brilliant and sparkling, while the plots are of a most hackneyed type. Great as was the moral licence shown in the plays of Beaumont and Fletcher, it is still greater in the Restoration drama, and it is the unsavoury nature of the subjects and their treatment that have been chiefly instrumental in bringing them into disrepute. Before Congreve, Sir George Etheredge had made an attempt to write comedy on somewhat similar lines, but with little success. Wycherley, Vanbrugh, and Farquhar were also able writers of the comedy of manners, though none have Congreve's sparkling brilliancy.

To trace the development of poetry during this period it is necessary to go back once more to the writers of the first half of the century. A small group of writers during this period had kept alive the Spenserian tradition both in versification and manner of thought. The two Fletchers, Giles (1584–1623) and Phineas (1582?–1665), head this, and the only other important followers are Wither (1588–1667) and Browne (1591–1643). After this the style is completely lost and remains so, except for an occasional flash in the eighteenth century, until the romantic revival. But there are a few poets who are more historically important as the precursors of the correctness which Dryden was to lift high. In the classical age, the names of Fairfax and Edmund Waller are usually linked as the founders of the ' correct ' style, but it is probable that their work was not quite so original as it was then supposed to have been. It was in Dryden that the heroic couplet, the one vehicle of the school's poetry, reached a condition which many consider better than that in which Pope left it. Even Gray, who was not prejudiced in favour of the Popean metre, could speak of his predecessor's—

' Two coursers of ethereal race,
  With necks in thunder clothed and
    long resounding pace.'

His frequent variation of the decasyllabic couplet with the Alexandrine was eschewed by Pope. After the death of Dryden (1700) there is for a short while an extremely barren space in poetic history. There was left no great or even moderate poet, if we except Matthew Prior (1664–1721), who produced some good lyrics. On account of the repute in which she was held by Wordsworth, we may also name Lady Anne Finch, Countess of Winchelsea, who is almost entirely unknown except for the extracts which Wordsworth gives. The next great name is that of Alexander Pope (1688–1744), who first came into prominence in 1711 with the publication of his *Essay on Criticism*. When he had made his first attempt in verse he had received advice which he never forsook. This advice was to strive after correctness, for we had had many great poets, but not a single correct one. His other leading works are the *Dunciad* (1728 and 1742–43), a savage satire on his opponents among the ' Grub Street ' writers; the *Rape of the Lock* (1711 and 1714), considered to be the best occasional poem ever written ; the translations of Homer (*Iliad*, 1715–20 ; *Odyssey*, 1725–26), done purely for financial reasons; and the *Essay on Man*, in which he versified the philosophy of his friend Bolingbroke. The couplet which he used was particularly adapted to epigram, and in this he excelled. His *Essay on Man* in particular has furnished a surprising number of popular quotations. The aim of the Popean school was not so much originality as polish and neatness, the manner of expression was the most important consideration. Its poets aimed at saying ' what oft was thought but ne'er so well expressed.' We have said that at the time when Pope began to write there was no poet of even mediocre powers. Pope perfected a method by which even the mediocre could write accurate and even good verse. He was, therefore, universally followed, and the classical style, with its couplet, dominated Eng. poetry until the end of the eighteenth century. It is true that during the whole of the time we find undercurrents of what we commonly call romanticism. The two

Whartons lodge their protest against the devotion to satiric verse and urge the superiority of the imagination. Thomas Gray (1716–1771) and William Collins (1720–1756) are the two finest of the poets who did not follow the prevailing methods, and in each case the chilling atmosphere had injurious effects. Their output is not sufficiently large to enable either of them to take rank as a great poet, though each shows considerable genius in the little work he did. James Thomson (1700–48) is a more obvious predecessor of the early romantic poets, such as Cowper. He wrote a series of descriptive poems in blank verse, called *The Seasons*, the popularity of which shows how strong the sympathy with Nature really was. Thomson also wrote *The Castle of Indolence* in Spenserian metre. Philips

SAMUEL JOHNSON

and Gay wrote some good lyrics, and the latter also produced the famous *Beggar's Opera* (1727) and its sequel. As the century passes, the signs of a fresh change in verse become more frequent, and a great leader only is needed. Macpherson's *Ossian* and Percy's *Reliques of Ancient English Poetry* are two of these.

The great work, however, of the period we are now considering was its fashioning and perfecting of the modern prose style. Hitherto all the great prose writers had used the magnificent but cumbrous Latin style. But this was only truly suitable to the highest imaginative work, and before prose could become the medium for the expression of every variety of knowledge, its form must undergo a radical transformation. Here it was that the Fr. influence was entirely good, for Fr. prose had already some centuries to look back upon. Its

chief mark was the short sentence, equivalent, one may say, to the couplet in verse. Classic severity led also to the diminution and even the banishment of ornament, and in most cases this was a great advantage. It further rendered the differentiation between prose and poetry more distinct. Henceforth, none could hold with Sir Philip Sidney that prose might well be poetry. Dryden was the first to write the new prose, and anyone reading his critical essays and prefaces will at once perceive its extreme modernity and lucidity. It has been said that the writers of the old school wrote as if they wished merely to unburden their minds, sometimes even delighting in obscurity, while Dryden, first of all, primarily considers his readers. He writes only that he may bring his points home to their minds. The vehicle which Dryden thus introduced was then polished and made more supple and delicate by Sir William Temple and his followers, who formed what is known as ' The Genteel School.' Their services to Eng. prose were very considerable, but the fact that there is little of intrinsic value in their works has led to their being often forgotten. The instrument having thus far been brought into condition it now had to be put to the multiform uses for which it was to be destined. Daniel Defoe was largely instrumental in doing this. Defoe was a typical journalist who in his day put his hand to every variety of literature and journalism, of which latter class of writing Sir Roger L'Estrange is the first exponent. In journalism he anticipated most of the modern devices, the leading article, answers to correspondents, etc., but his news was not remarkable for accuracy. In many ways his position is a difficult one to determine. Was he a pioneer or merely a clever follower? This difficulty arises in the case of his essays. It is certain that he wrote essays before the *Tatler* appeared, but it is probable that these hardly reached the level of literature, and it is equally certain that all his best work in this direction was produced under the influence of Steele. Defoe's other publications were voluminous, and comprise a certain quantity of journeyman rhymes. When he was already past the prime of life Defoe produced the work with which his name is chiefly associated and which was later followed by others of the same kind. Here again it is difficult to say how near to the novels *Robinson Crusoe* may be placed. It is impossible here to trace the long history of the origin of the novel, but this is certainly the last stage of preparation for its coming. The essay reached its brightest level in the *Tatler* (1709), written by Richard Steele with the help of Joseph Addison and others, and in the *Spectator* (1711–14) written by Addison with the help of Steele and other literary men of the day. Steele and Addison attempt to treat learning and experience of humanity in such a way that they will be interesting and comprehensive to all gentle folk, and thus to widen the bounds of education. They were the first writers who addressed themselves to women as forming even the majority of their readers. The influence of these papers was greater, however, on morals than on literature. It is interesting to notice how once again we have an approach to the novel in the Sir Roger de Coverley series. This was, of course, before *Robinson Crusoe*. The work of Swift (1667–1745), with his severely plain style and his savage and sometimes inhuman satire, must not be forgotten. *Gulliver's Travels* is one of the few books that interests all ages, and this very fact shows the author's consummate satiric skill. In this respect, Swift's writings form an interesting comparison with those of Addison. The style of Lord Bolingbroke (1678–1751), though polite, is somewhat superficial, while the exact contrary must be said of that of Bernard de Mandeville (?1670–1733) in his famous *Fable of the Bees*. The work of Samuel Johnson (1709–84), though great in many ways, must be considered rather retrograde in point of style, for it shows much affinity with that of the previous century. As the first lexicographer, and as the writer of the *Lives of the Poets*, a great debt is owing to him, though the Johnson of the *Rambler* might well have been spared. Without Johnson, also, we could not have had Boswell's Life. The middle of the eighteenth century saw the rise of the Eng. novel, which has grown to embrace every department of life. Samuel Richardson inaugurated this great movement with *Pamela* (1740), a psychological novel with a somewhat morbid ' love ' interest, written in letters. Richardson improved on his first attempt in *Clarissa Harlowe*. Anger at Richardson's morbidity led Fielding to commence *Joseph Andrews* as a parody. His interest in it, however, led him to continue it as a serious work. This was followed in 1749 by the epoch-making work, *Tom Jones*, still considered by many the best novel in Eng., on account of the excellence of the plot. Smollett and Laurence Sterne complete the four who formed the Eng. novel. Towards the end of the century Fanny Burney's *Evelina* and *Cecilia*

commenced the type of novel which was continued by Jane Austen and Maria Edgeworth. The drama during this period steadily deteriorated, and has never since recovered. Only *The Good-Natured Man* (1768) and *She Stoops to Conquer* (1772), by Oliver Goldsmith, need be mentioned.

The year 1798, when *Lyrical Ballads* by Wordsworth and Coleridge was published, is an epoch-making date in literature. This work inaugurated the great romantic movement, of which the immediate predecessors had been Cowper (1731–1800), Blake (1757–1827), and Crabbe (1754–1832). In Scotland, Burns (1759–96) had already rekindled the almost expiring flame of Scottish poesy. He had many links in common with the Eng. romantics. During the next century the bounds of literature extend so widely that it is impossible to cover the whole field of thought. The most that can be done is to indicate the main lines of development, and to refer to works which deal with the period in detail. Wordsworth's dogged perseverance and self-confidence led him to continue in the way he had begun, while Coleridge, whose actual production is small, yet had an enormous influence on the movement's development by his critical writings and advice. His *Biographia Literaria* is still the great classic of constructive criticism. Then, with the second generation, poetry expanded to cover the whole of human life. Sir Walter Scott (1771–1832), Byron (1788–1824), Shelley (1792–1822), and Keats (1795–1821), though they had much in common, take each of them a step into some new department and bring fresh contributions to the treasury of genius. The novel began to be cultivated with greater breadth, and the rise of the newspaper and magazine opened fresh fields for literary energy. The Popean poetry, however, did not quite die, but continued as a vehicle for the floods of political satires which were continually issuing from the press. After Gibbon (1737–94) came a great swarm of historians, anxious to found their theories on original research. The greatest achievement in the development of the novel was undoubtedly made by Scott, whose enormous contemporary popularity it is difficult to over-estimate, for the historical novel was then a new departure. After the decline of Scott's powers through over-work, Bulwer Lytton for a while occupied the field. Dickens (1812–70), though deficient in artistic form, brought great vitality and humour to his work. Dickens was animated by a philanthropic idealism which is evident in the work of Mrs. Gaskell (1810–66) and also, though more romantic, in the novels of Charlotte Brontë (1816–55) and of her younger sister, Emily, of Charles Kingsley (1819–75) and of Benjamin Disraeli (1804–81). (*See* BEACONSFIELD.) Something allied to the idealism of these authors came with the Oxford Movement. In poetry, its greatest result was Keble's *Christian Year*, while its greatest product in prose was the beautiful and haunting style of Cardinal Newman, best shown in his *Apologia*. Meanwhile an unalloyed realism was appearing in the novels of Thackeray (1811–63), a clear-sighted, ironic, and penetrating writer, the greatest of the other realistic novelists : Trollope (1815–82) ; Reade (1814–84) ; and George

SIR W. SCOTT

Eliot (1819–80). These were followed by Hardy (1840–1928) and Gissing (1857–1903), both governed by a sombre philosophy, the one of fatalism and the other of despair. In poetry they are allied to James Thomson (1834–82), while Hardy, himself a great poet, has dominated all that is best in twentieth-century endeavour. Samuel Butler's (1835–1902) novel, *The Way of All Flesh*, appeared posthumously ; but Butler, a philosophical writer, shares in the reaction against mechanism of his contemporaries in the novel. So also does Meredith (1828–1909), but with more faith in the kindliness of nature, a faith spiritually expressed in his poetry. As a novelist he is master of psychological analysis. Although the novel figures so largely in nineteenth century achievement, criticism and

the essay also flourished after a dogmatic beginning with Jeffrey (1773–1850) and the Edinburgh reviewers. A sounder theoretic criticism was established by Wordsworth (1770–1850) and Coleridge (1772–1834), followed by the practical criticism of Hazlitt (1778–1830), while the essay achieves permanent distinction through the inimitable Lamb (1775–1834), De Quincey (1785–1859) and Leigh Hunt (1784–1864) ; nor was the great prose of Landor (1775–1864) without lasting influence. Matthew Arnold (1822–88), who is much indebted to the Fr. critic Sainte-Beuve, inaugurated a new school of criticism, and henceforth criticism becomes a true department of art. J. A. Symonds (1840–93) led to Walter Pater (1839–94), in whose writings literature is no longer considered as an art by itself, isolated from the rest, but is fitted into its true place with painting, sculpture, music. In history the great names are those of Hallam, Carlyle, Macaulay, and Froude, but in each of these, except the first, the literary and philosophical elements bulk more largely than the historical. The names of Milman, Grote, Buckle, Freeman, and Green are also well-known to all. The drama, in spite of a flood of imitations of the Ger. plays which came with the early romantics, never rose again into high levels of either tragedy or comedy. The poetry of the Victorian age continues the romanticism of the century's beginning, tending with Tennyson (1809–92) towards a perfecting of form and with Browning (1812–89) towards a preoccupation with psychology. Allied to these great poets are others : Beddoes (1803–49), Elizabeth Browning (1806–61), Clough (1819–56), Patmore (1823–96), and Christina Rossetti (1830–94). With Matthew Arnold's poetry a refined classicism was introduced, while in the middle of the century the Pre-Raphaelite movement in painting spread to literature through the genius of D. G. Rossetti (1828–82) and William Morris (1834–96), although the latter sought his inspiration more in mediævalism. The critic of the artistic revival and the apostle of beauty was Ruskin (1819–1900). Towards the end of the century romantic poetry became imbued with Fr. symbolism, and Swinburne (1837–1909) possessed a unique capacity for verbal music. Swinburne in poetry and Pater in criticism were the patron saints of the æsthetic school of the 'nineties, in which Oscar Wilde (1856–1900) was the most notable. George Moore (*b.* 1852) in his work combined the æsthetic doctrine of art for art's sake with the realism of the Fr. novels of Zola, while having something in common with the Celtic Revival. The Fr. naturalism which Moore imbibed was assiduously avoided by Stevenson (1850–94) in his adventure novels. The typical poet of the Celtic Revival is W. B. Yeats (b. 1865), who is also a playwright, but in the plays of J. M. Synge (1871–1909) Irish mysticism is tempered with a humorous observation of Irish life. Other poets of the Celtic Revival are Lionel Johnson (1867–1902), George Russell (' A.E.') (b. 1867), Padraic Colum (b. 1881), James Stephens (b. 1882), Katharine Tynan, etc. Gerard Manley Hopkins, also an Irish poet, is too individualistic in his poems, 1876–89, to belong to any school, but his rhythmic experiments have influenced a succeeding generation since his poems were first published posthumously in 1918. Tennyson was succeeded as Laureate by Austin (1835–1913) and after him by Robert Bridges (1844–1929), with Tennyson one of the greatest of England's practising Laureates. Symbolism was carried over into the twentieth century by John Davidson (1857–1909) and Arthur Symons (b. 1865), while Francis Thompson (1860–1907) was, like Hopkins, a Rom. Catholic and, like him, an adept in verbal music. Hardy in *The Dynasts* (1904–8) reached epic grandeur, other notable epics of the twentieth century being *The Dawn of Britain* (1906–7), by C. M. Doughty (b. 1843), the author of *Travels in Arabia Deserta*, and *The Torch-Bearers*, an epic by Alfred Noyes (b. 1880), completed in 1930. Kipling (b. 1865) has become the poet of imperialism, combined with a love of Eng. soil; he is also known as a novelist and short-story writer. As an imperialist he is allied to the poets Henley (1849–1903) and Newbolt (b. 1862); but socialism has found its spokesmen in Shaw (b. 1856) and Wells (b. 1868), and also, but of a more mediæval guild variety, in Chesterton (b. 1874) and Belloc (b. 1870). Shaw in the drama and Wells in the novel were dominant, if not in artistic expression, in all sociological thought of the second decade of the twentieth century, and with them, dominant alike in art and thought, is D. H. Lawrence (1885–1930), poet and novelist; while the social novels of Galsworthy (b. 1867) and Arnold Bennett (1867–1931) and the adventure novels of Conrad (1856–1924) are among the finest achievements of the present century. The open-air school of nature writers must also be mentioned : Jefferies (1848–87), W. H. Hudson (1846–1922), and Edward

Thomas (1878–1917), poet and essayist; while a forerunner of these authors is George Borrow (1803–81). Several poets writing about 1910 are classed in the ' Georgian ' group : Sturge Moore (b. 1870); W. H. Davies (b. 1870); Masefield (b. 1874; Laureate, 1930); W. W. Gibson (b. 1880); Lascelles Abercrombie (b. 1881); Margaret Sackville (b. 1882); Flecker (1884–1915); Squire (b. 1884); Brooke (1887–1915), and of the younger poets of this group Edmund Blunden (b. 1896) is perhaps the best, but their note was tragically changed by the war, which bred its own generation of poets; Siegfried Sassoon (b. 1886); Isaac Rosenberg (1890–1918); Wilfrid Owen (1893–

CHARLES LAMB

1918); Robert Nichols (b. 1893); Robert Graves (b. 1895); and Sorley (1895–1915). Contemporary with the Georgians, but professing the definite poetic aim of avoiding abstraction, is the ' Imagists ' group, Eng. and American : Aldington, ' H.D.', Ezra Pound, F. S. Flint, and Aldous Huxley (better known as a novelist). Among the most successful experimenters in post-war poetry are Osbert, Sacheverell and Edith Sitwell, and, in the novel, James Joyce. Other post-war novelists are Hugh Walpole, Somerset Maugham, Stephen Hudson, E. M. Forster, Compton Mackenzie, Virginia Woolf, Martin Armstrong, C. E. Montague, and R. H. Mottram ; while history and fiction have met in a form of biographical writing, exploited by Lytton Strachey, Philip Guedalla, and others. T. S. Eliot's poem, *The Waste Land*, 1922, expresses an intellectual approach to the disillusionment of life after the war, and has established the reputation of its author as one of the best of post-war poets. Other contemporary poets who may be mentioned are Edgell Rickword, Herbert Read,

Laura Riding, Humbert Wolfe, W. J. Turner, L. A. G. Strong, Harold Monro, and Claude Abbott. Most of these authors, like T. S. Eliot, have also established their reputations as literary critics. *See also* under CRITICISM ; DRAMA, etc.

BIBLIOGRAPHY.—*Cambridge History of English Literature* (edited by Ward and Waller), 1905 ff.; Hallam's *Literature of Europe in the Fifteenth, Sixteenth, and Seventeenth Centuries* (4 vols.), 1837–39; Craik's *Compendious History of English Literature and Language*, 1861; Taine's *History of English Literature* (trans. by Van Laun), 1871; W. Minto's *English Prose Literature*, 1872; Ward's *English Poets* (2nd ed. 4 vols), 1883; H. Morley's *First Sketch of English Literature* (enlarged ed.), 1886; Stopford Brooke's *History of English Literature to the Accession of King Alfred*, 1892 (new ed., 1901); Saintsbury's *Short History of English Literature*, 1900 (new ed., 1903); and *Later Nineteenth Century Literature*, 1907; Courthope's *History of English Poetry*, 1895; Morley's *Library of English Literature* (5 vols.), 1876–82; and series of *English Writers;* Chambers's *Cyclopædia of English Literature* (new ed. 3 vols.), 1901; Craik's *English Prose Selections* (4 vols.), 1892–94; Legouis and Cazamian, *A History of English Literature*, 1927; Edwin Muir, *Transition*, 1926.

**English Review, The,** was started by John Murray, the celebrated publisher. It first appeared as an annual register, entitled *The London Mercury.* A 2s. 6d. review of the same name was founded by Chapman & Hall in 1908. Noteworthy for its high literary qualities, and devotes itself to the publication of such articles, essays, belles lettres, short stories, and poems, by whomsoever written, as it deems remarkable for intrinsic merit. Many an obscure or struggling writer has sprung into fame through the medium of its pages.

**English River,** an estuary on Delagoa Bay in S.E. Africa.

**English River,** *see* CHURCHILL RIVER.

**Englishry,** a term used during the Norman rule in England. It was used to show contempt, for if the hundred could prove that a murdered person was English, that is to say, make a ' presentment of E.,' it escaped without punishment. This was abolished in the first half of the fourteenth century.

**Engraving,** primarily the art of drawing on a substance by means of an incised line. The term was early applied to the work produced by that process and later to the impression of the engraved work upon a sheet of paper. This article deals with E. on metals. (For a further knowledge of the art the reader is referred to PROCESS WORK, PHOTOGRAVURE, MEZZOTINT, and ETCHING.) From very early times gems have been engraved with ornaments or signets, and commemorative inscriptions have been cut into metal tablets, but technically the word E. is confined to the incision of a design upon a plate of metal or a wooden block, for the purpose of producing upon paper by the aid of ink a series of reproductions of that design. On metals, Es. are usually in intaglio, that is, the lines are sunk in and possess a positive value in that they actually trace the design. In woodcuts the lines are negative, their object being to leave the true design projecting in relief. Copper and steel are the favourite metals of engravers, but zinc, brass, silver, and iron have also been employed. Steel is much harder to work with than copper, but on the other hand its very toughness makes it possible to take off a greater number of good impressions. By means of electrolysis, it is now open to the engraver to protect his copper plate by a thin coating of steel; the result of this has been almost to do away with steel plates altogether. Copper has always been preferred where the aim of the artist is to produce a highly finished and delicate reproduction of the design.

' Line E.' implies the use of a tool called the graver or burin. This consists of a steel rod some 4 in. long, with a square or lozenge-shaped section, a sharp edge being secured by cutting the section obliquely. The engraver controls the rod by grasping a wooden handle, and in making his strokes varies the pressure in accordance with the thickness of the line desired. When his work is finished he covers the plate with printer's ink, presses it into the incisions by the aid of a dabber, rubs away the superfluous ink with a piece of muslin and then carefully lays a sheet of moistened paper on the engraved surface. The plate, with the paper thus attached, is placed on a board which slides between two rollers in what is called the copperplate press. Blankets soften the contact of paper and roller. ' Etching ' involves the use of a mordant to eat into the plate. An etching-ground is spread over the copper surface and the lines are opened up with an etching needle. ' Dry-point ' is a method of E. akin to the processes already described. The implement used is a steel point stronger and more tapering than the etching needle. When this is firmly drawn across the metal surface, quite a distinct burr—like a miniature thorn —is produced, the effect of which is to leave a semi-luminous ridge of tone at the side of each line, and thus to impart to the whole print an attractive richness of tone. Skilful engravers often blend these three processes in the one plate.

'Tone-processes' aim at achieving a result on the plate similar to that produced by a colour wash in painting. If the artist uses the 'crayon or chalk-manner,' he first perforates his etching-ground with special needles like the mace-head or roulette, his aim being to suggest the rough texture of crayon strokes. If he follows the 'stipple method,' he imitates broad tone surfaces by covering the etching-ground with dots and short strokes, using the curved stipple engraver, the dry-point, or the roulette for the purpose. The essential distinction of the 'mezzotint' process is that the craftsman begins with a dark ground and proceeds to create his lights by a negative and scraping device. With the assistance of a kind of chisel, called the 'cradle' or 'rocker,' he roughens the plate by raising metal points or burrs. At this stage the copper would print a rich black, but the mezzotinter removes the burrs with his 'scraper' in proportion to the tone he wishes to produce. Thus, if he scrapes down to the bottom of the indentation, he will get a smooth surface, which will not be able to hold any ink and will therefore print white. For 'aquatints' the plate is prepared for E. by a porous coating of sand or resinous gum. This method produces Es. not unlike mezzotints.

Not more than twenty-five good mezzotints or dry-points can be obtained from one plate, as the brilliancy of the impression depends on the delicacy of the burr. A steel facing, however, increases the number to a hundred, whilst with this protection as many as three thousand line Es. may safely be taken off. The value of a print depends on the engraver and the fineness of the impression, which decreases, naturally, with the number taken. 'Artist's proofs' are treasured, as they bear the signature of the painter or engraver, or of both. The signature is considered a guarantee of the quality of the print and may imply retouchings by the artist.

*History of line-engraving and etching.—Line-engraving :* E. is an art of comparatively recent development and the earliest known illustration,

with metal as the medium, is the 'Flagellation,' which is dated 1446, and is the work of a German who lived in the neighbourhood of Cologne or Basle. In Italy the art grew side by side with painting, and arose, as some men think, from that of niello, which was a process of incising a pattern on gold or silver and then filling in the groove with a black compound (nigellum). The work of Maso Finiguerra (*d.* 1464) with its plentiful cross-hatchings illustrates the 'Fine Manner,' whilst that remarkably fine achievement of the Florentine Antonio Pollajuolo

AN ENGRAVING BY DÜRER :
'Christ on the Cross'

(*d.* 1498), namely 'The Battle of the Nudes,' exhibits the broad and simple lines of parallel shading which characterises the exponents of the so-called 'Broad Manner.' Somewhat similar in style is 'The Virgin and Child' of Andrea Mantegna (*d.* 1506). Albrecht Dürer, the German (*d.* 1528), Marcantonio Raimondi, the Bolognese (*d. c.* 1530), and Lucas van Leyden, the Netherlander (*d.* 1533) form a conspicuous triumvirate of engravers. Formal dignity, refinement of touch, and unremitting care are a few of the merits of Dürer's portrait of Albrecht of Brandenburg and his 'St. Jerome in the Wilderness.' Marcantonio is famous for his reproductions of Raphael's work. According to Vasari it was the engraver's magnificent

'Death of Lucretia' which was responsible for his long association with that painter. Lucas's skill may well be studied in his 'David playing before Saul.' The first French engraver of note was Jean Duvet (d. 1561), whose 'Apocalypse' series emphasises his mysticism and at the same time his somewhat heavy, overloaded style. In England the same distinction must be reserved for William Rogers (b. c. 1545), who executed several portraits of Queen Elizabeth, all of which, however, are stiff and too ornate. Professional print-sellers, ready to provide portraits for historians and maps for discoverers, first began to flourish in the latter half of the sixteenth century. The pioneers were mostly Netherlanders, like Hieronymus Cock and Philippe Galle, many of whom migrated to Italy and Germany and thus popularised commercial Es. abroad. Robert Nanteuil (d. 1678), who was engraver at the court of Louis XIV., stands easily at the head of all French engravers of portraits, and a similar honour among his own countrymen is with justice claimed for William Faithorne (d. 1691). In this country John Faber (d. 1756) made a name as a mezzotint engraver, and one of the last of the great burinists was the painter and poet, William Blake (d. 1827). There is true inspiration in his 'Illustrations of the Book of Job,' which have, moreover, only rarely been surpassed in purity of line, harmony of composition and independence of stereotyped convention, whether in execution or design. Since Blake's day, etchings and later heliogravures have quite superseded line Es., and the burin, it seems, will soon be a tool of very subsidiary importance.

*Etching :* Albrecht Dürer was a pioneer in this field and etched his 'The Cannon' upon iron. Van Dyck (d. 1641), who was 'the solitary great etcher' of the Rubens school, depended for his splendid effects on the use of the open line and vigorous, dotted work, and aimed always at broad effects. Rembrandt (d. 1669), on the other hand, who is the perfect 'painter-etcher,' relied on close-hatching, and discovered how, by leaving ink on the surface of the copper, he could cope with the difficult task of reproducing the chiaroscuro of his paintings and ensure a rich and liquid surface tone. His etchings embrace portraits, landscapes, and religious themes, 'Christ with the Sick around Him, Receiving little Children,' being widely accepted as his masterpiece. Other and notable painter-etchers of Holland were, Adriæn van Ostade (d. 1685),

Paul Potter (d. 1654), and Nicolæs Berchem (d. 1683). In the eighteenth century the Italian school of etching reached its high-water mark in the delicate 'Capricci' of Giovanni Tiepolo (d. 1770), and the architectural designs of Piranesi (d. 1778). A school of satirical etching developed in England. Hogarth (d. 1764) etched his own paintings, such as the 'Rake's Progress,' whilst Thomas Rowlandson (d. 1827) illustrated the story of Dr. Syntax and the *Vicar of Wakefield*, and proved himself a brilliant caricaturist. Cruikshank (d. 1878) may well be mentioned in connection with Rowlandson, as he has won universal favour by his sympathetic interpretation of Dickens's odd characters. Early in the nineteenth century (1807–19), appeared Turner's *Liber Studiorum*, which contained some excellent plates of his own as well as the etchings of a number of less famous engravers. Francisco Goya (d. 1828) is the finest Spanish etcher; his power to seize upon all hypocrisies and affectations is well exemplified in his 'Caprichos,' whilst his 'Desastres de la Guerra,' are remarkable, if almost repulsive, expositions of the terrors of war. In the last century the work of Delacroix (d. 1863), and of Decamps (d. 1868), did much to revive the art, which in some respects seemed to have grown stagnant. Other notable French etchers were Legros and Meryon (d. 1868). But the greatest etcher of the day was probably the American Whistler (d. 1903), whose charming and exceptionally individualistic work is seen at its best in 'Battersea,' and the 'Venice set.' Modern exponents of the art are, Zorn, the Swede (b. 1860); Thaulow, the Norwegian; the Englishman, Haden (b. 1818); and two Germans, von Menzel (d. 1905) and Max Klinger (b. 1857).

**Engrossing,** the term applied to the practice of buying up any commodity in such large quantities that the buyer then commands the market. It was practically the same sort of system as forestalling, which meant buying cheap to sell at a much larger price. Under the old laws these practices and all others like them were considered as crimes and contrary to justice, and were forbidden by the statutes of the land. But in 1844 all the laws with regard to these practices were finally abolished, and they are now considered quite legal—a fact which is proved by the modern system of forming 'trusts.'

**Enharmonic,** a term used in music to denote an interval which is less than a semitone. On an instrument with keys, however, such as the piano, no difference in sound exists, but merely a difference in name, the same key bearing both names, as for example E♭ and D♯. This change in notation, however, enables the composer to pass easily into another key which is sometimes of great use to him.

**Enid,** a city of Oklahoma, U.S.A., with an air-port. The leading grain market of the state, and the trade centre for a large agricultural district and for gas and oil fields. It is an important railway junction, has railroad shops, oil refineries, flour mills, and meat-packing plants, and makes agricultural implements and wire. Pop. 26,399.

**Enkhuizen,** one of the dead cities of the Zuyder Zee, Holland, and a delight to every visitor. The great Dromedaris Tower (1540), a splendid relic of the old fortifications, stands guardian over a queer little harbour. It takes an hour to walk round the town, but its once busy streets are now gardens and its former pop. of 40,000 has fallen to about 8000. There are many interesting buildings, the chief being the belfry of 1524, called the Zuidertoren, and the orphanage or Weeshuis (1619). The herring fishery was the great wealth of E., but now not one of the 400 smacks remains. Paul Potter was b. here.

**Enlargement of Objects.** An enlarged image of an object can be produced by a lens, a curved mirror, a combination of lenses, or a combination of lenses and mirrors; but not by a convex mirror or a concave lens alone. For concave mirrors the magnification is greatest when the distance of the object from the mirror is nearly equal to the length of the mirror. With a convex lens three cases are possible : (1) if the object is nearer to the lens than the focal length, the image is virtual and magnified ; (2) if the distance between the object and the lens is greater than the focal length, but less than twice the focal length, the image is real and magnified ; (3) in other cases the image is diminished.

**Enlistment,** the method by which the army is recruited in such countries as do not have a form of conscription. Most of the European countries have some form of conscription, but in the case of Great Britain and America E. takes its place. Up to the beginning of the eighteenth century E. took place through an official who had no definite recognition by the army authorities, but who received a commission for every recruit. The period of service for which a soldier enlisted was not determined, in fact he served as long as he was physically fit. At the beginning of the nineteenth century recruiting was taken over by the army authorities, and since that time many changes have been made. A man on enlisting nowadays must make declaration before a magistrate or before the commanding officer. He then takes the oath, signs a declaration, and is then, and only then, held to have enlisted. Punishment for false declarations can be made either in a civil court or by means of a district court-martial. A soldier is at liberty to purchase a discharge under certain conditions, but never when the country is at war. Recently soldiers have enlisted for twelve years, seven with the colours and five with the reserve, but many alterations have been made in this now. In the Artillery, enlistment is for six years with the colours and six with the reserve. Further, it is possible to re-enlist at the end of twelve years' service and do twenty-one, after which a soldier becomes entitled to a pension (or after eighteen years' service if discharged on medical grounds after completing that period). The Special Reserve enlisted under special terms, usually for six years, with the possibility of doing more later if they so desired.

**Enna,** *see* CASTROGIOVANNI.

**Ennis:** (1) A tn. in co. Clare, Ireland. It is the county town, and is situated on the Fergus about 20 m. N.W. of Limerick. In the town are the remains of a Franciscan abbey, and also a Roman Catholic church and college, while close by is a race-course. The port is Clare Castle. Pop 5742. (2) A tn., in Ellis co., Texas, U.S.A. It lies to the S.E. of Dallas, with cotton gins and compresses and cotton seed oil mills. Pop. 7069.

**Enniscorthy,** a tn., co. Wexford, Ireland, situated on the Slaney, about 14 m. N.W. of Wexford. It has a beautiful situation, the land around being very fertile. Below E. the river is navigable for barges. The castle, now partially destroyed, is an interesting old building. Pop. 5472.

**Enniskillen,** the county tn. of Fermanagh, Ireland. Situated on an island between Upper and Lower Lough Erne. One of its chief industries is the manuf. of cutlery, and it is also engaged in tanning. E. was granted its first charter in the seventeenth century. Pop. about 5400.

**Ennistimon,** a tn. in co. Clare, prov. of Munster, Ireland. Pop. 1205.

**Ennius, Quintus** (*c.* 239–*c.* 169 B.C.), one of the first Roman poets, was *b.* at Rudiæ in Calabria. Although little is known of his history, he seems at first to have pursued a military career. At about the age of thirty-eight he became acquainted with M. Porcius Cato and accompanied him to Rome. From that time he seems to have lived chiefly at Rome, and was successful in obtaining the rights of Roman citizenship, a thing which a foreigner very rarely did. He was a man of great learning, having a good knowledge of Gk. as well as Latin, so that he was able to earn his living as a tutor. He was buried in the Scipios' tomb and his monument placed among those of that family. Of his works, which it is believed existed as a whole until the thirteenth century, only fragments now remain, among them being dramas, satires, and annals.

**Enns :** (1) A tn. of Upper Austria, standing on the river of the same name, about 10 m. S.E. of Linz with a museum and local Roman antiquities. Pop. 4190. (2) A river of Austria which rises S. of Radstadt, and flows into the Danube. Chief trib. is the Steier.

**Enoch** (Heb. *Hanōkh*), the name of four persons in the Bible : (1) A son of Cain (Gen. iv. 17) ; (2) a grandson of Abraham (Gen. xxv. 4) ; (3) a son of Reuben (Gen. xlvi. 9) ; (4) the son of Jared and grandson of Enoch (1), with whom he has probably been confused. In Gen. v. 18–24 we read that after a life of 365 years this E., who ' walked with God,' was translated—' he was not, for God took him.' The number 365 hints at certain connections between the Hebrew tradition and a Babylonian sun-god. Later Jewish legend makes E. the inventor of writing, arithmetic, and astronomy, and the apocalyptic books described below were ascribed to him. Among the Arabians he is known as *Idris* (the learned one). The ' St. Enoch ' of Glasgow is a corruption of St. Thenaw, the mother of St. Kentigern.

**Enoch, The Book of,** an apocalyptic work belonging to the two centuries immediately preceding the Christian era, which purports to give an account of the revelations made, both before and after his translation, to the Enoch ' who walked with God.' It gives a history of the introduction of sin into the world and the fall of the angels. It describes the deluge which followed on the intercourse of the fallen angels and the human race, the course of the world after that time until the period of the Messianic kingdom, and the final judgment. It also gives some explanation of astronomy, the seasons and the secrets of nature in general. The B. of E. was originally written in

Hebrew, in the Palestinian region, and was then translated into Greek. It was well known to the early Christians, by many of whom it was held in high esteem. St. Jude in his general epistle quotes from Enoch in v. 14. The work was lost sight of about the seventh century, and only quotations from it could be obtained until 1773, when Bruce, the traveller, brought back from Abyssinia two Ethiopic copies of it, which proved to have been made from the Greek version. A translation was published by Archbishop Lawrence in 1821, and the Ethiopic text followed in 1838. The B. of E. is held to be of composite origin, and Professor Charles divides and dates it thus : (1) ch. i.–xxxvi. before 170 B.C.; (2) ch. lxxxiii.–xc. a few years later ; (3) ch. xci.–civ. between 134 and 95 B.C.; (4) ch. xxxvii.–lxx. between 94 and 64 B.C. The rest of the work consists chiefly of quotations from a lost Book of Noah, etc. The Book of the Secrets of Enoch is a similar mystical work, *See* R. H. Charles's *Book of Enoch*, 1893.

**Enoch, The Book of the Secrets of,** has been also called ' the Slavonic Enoch,' because the MSS. of it, which have only recently been discovered, are in that language. It seems, however, to have been originally written in the Greek language during the first century A.D., and also to have been composed in Egypt. This book, which is entirely independent of the Book of Enoch—sometimes known as the ' Ethiopic Enoch '—gives an account of the way in which Enoch was taken up into the heavens, seven in number, and of his visions there, followed by an account of his subsequent experiences. See *The Book of the Secrets of Enoch*, translated by W. R. Morfill and edited by R. H. Charles, 1896.

**Enock, C. Reginald** (*b.* 1868), an engineer, traveller, and author. He has spent much time abroad in professional work, especially in N. and S. America and the British Empire. He undertook explorations in the Andes, and scientific work for the governments of Peru and Mexico. His works include : *The Andes and the Amazon ; Mexico ; Peru ; Farthest West ; Your Share of Empire ; Pioneering and Map-making . . .*

**Enos,** a seaport of Greece, situated on the Maritsa. It is impossible for any but small vessels to enter the harbour owing to the large amount of sand present there. Pop. 7000.

**Enschede,** a tn. of Holland in the prov. of Overijssel. One of the principal centres of the cotton industry and has parks, people's university and industrial museum. Pop. 46,300.

**Ensign:** (1) Originally the name applied to the lowest rank of commissioned officer in the British army. He obtained this name from the fact that it was his duty to carry the colours or ensign, but as this is not a custom now, the title was changed in 1871 to that of second lieutenant. (2) The national flag used on board ship, and flies from the pole known as the E. staff. The red, white, and blue Es. which are in use now date from some time back, but their present use differs slightly from the former. The red E. is used for merchant vessels. Ships of the Royal Navy fly the white E., and so does the Royal Yacht Squadron, while the Naval Reserve, in common with certain yacht clubs, flies the blue E.

**Ensilage,** see HAY AND ENSILAGE.

**Ensival,** a textile manufacturing commune in the prov. of Liège, Belgium. It stands on the Vesdres, N. of Spa. Pop. 6880.

**Enstatite,** a silicate of magnesium, is translucent and white in colour, or sometimes has a greenish hue. It has been found in Moravia, Prussia, and other parts of Europe.

**Entablature** (Lat. *in,* and *tabula,* a tablet), the architectural term for the crowning part of a structure, carried by the columns in the classic orders. It usually consists of three distinct sections: the architrave, resting directly on the columns; the frieze, the decorative member; and the cornice, the projecting and protective member. There are, in all, seven forms: the Greek Doric, the Roman Doric, the Tuscan, the Gk. Ionic, the Rom. Ionic, the Corinthian, and the Composite, the last two being entirely Rom. The simplest, but also the highest in proportion, of these was the Gk. Doric. The group of three members which the term E. designates was original and constant in Gk. architecture, and was derived from the methods of construction. In certain countries, such as in Provence (France) and Italy (Rom. province), where classic forms survived or were imitated, the E. lasted during the Middle Ages. Occasionally the decorative member, *i.e.* the frieze, is omitted. In all probability it did not exist in the archaic temple of Diana at Ephesus, neither is it found in the Lycian tombs. It is easier to find examples in which the mediæval artists reproduced separate parts of the E. than where the entire group was used.

**Entail.** An entailed estate or estate tail is an estate of inheritance in land settled on several persons successively in a strict line of devolution,

ENTABLATURE (DORIC)

such persons being exclusively the heirs male or female of the grantee or grantees. The word E. is derived from French *tailler,* 'to cut,' because the succession to the estate was cut down to the grantee for his life and then to his issue. Estates tail are either *general, i.e.* are granted 'to A and the heirs of his body' without restriction as to sex or maternity; or *special, i.e.* restricted in one or other of the above ways, *e.g.* 'to A and the heirs *male* of his body,' or 'to A and the heirs *female* of his body,' 'or to A and the heirs of his body by his wife B.' The history of the development of estates tail may be said to be intimately bound up with the traditions and associations of county families; the whole object of their legal creation being to tie up property in strict family settlements so as to ensure that the estates should devolve from father to son for ever. The old common law judges always construed a gift 'to A and the heirs of his body' as a gift of the full disposable estate of inheritance or fee simple (*q.v.*) (*see also* DE DONIS), conditional on issue actually being born to A. Consequently when issue was born A could sell the estate and bar his own issue. Though it is now theoretically impossible to tie up lands in a family for ever, and though the tenant-in-tail can bar the rights of everyone by executing and enrolling a *disentailing deed* within six months of obtaining possession, the custom is for the eldest son of the grantee, on coming of age, to execute a deed with the consent of his father barring the E., and for the father and son then to enter into a deed of re-settlement by which they re-settle the land on the father for life, with *remainder* to the son for life, and then after the death of the son, to the son's eldest son in tail; this process being repeated every time an eldest son reaches twenty-one. The efficacy of this compromise in thus preserving the posthumous pride of ancestors depends entirely on the continuous desire of each father to tie up the lands in the family and on the continuous obedience of each eldest son on attaining twenty-one. If, however, the son prove disobedient, the father can deprive him of all income while he (the father) remains alive, and so it comes about that the son generally abstains from his right to bar *his own issue* (which he can do without the consent of his father) and 'surrenders his birthright for a financial mess of pottage.' In this connection must be noticed the meaning of the term 'protector of the settlement.' A protector is a statutory creation, and denotes the tenant of the first life estate under the deed creating the E. (usually, of course, the eldest surviving ancestor), or some person or persons appointed by the deed itself to act as protectors. The existence of the 'protector' prevents a tenant-in-tail *not yet in possession* from barring the *whole* E. unless he obtains the consent of such protector, though, as seen above, he may bar his own issue.

**Entebbe** (white pop. about 50, of district about 150), the administrative centre of the Uganda Protectorate, British E. Africa on the N.W. of the Victoria Nyanza, with charming views over the is.-studded lake. There are Botanical Gardens and a cotton ginnery, and cotton, cocoa, rubber, etc., are grown in the dist. The sleeping sickness has entirely disappeared. The headquarters of the Commission appointed by the League of Nations for the study of tropical diseases is here, as also the new European Hospital, Government House and Court House.

. **Entellus Monkey, or Hanuman,** the *Semnipithecus Entellus* of India. Its body is from 2 to 4 ft. long, and the non-prehensile tail is longer than the body. The general colour is dirty and yellowish, but the full whiskers and beard are greyish-white. In character it is mischievous, noisy, and quarrelsome.

**Entente Cordiale** (lit. means ' cordial understanding '), the term applied to friendly relations existing between Powers, most often used of England and France. It implies a certain amount of interests in common between the two countries and an active promotion of those interests by both Powers.

**Enteralgia,** *see* COLIC.

**Enteric Fever,** the name given to a fever which mainly affects the intestines. It is also known as *typhoid fever,* and on the Continent as *abdominal typhus.* Typhus was a name formerly used to designate both typhus and typhoid. Typhoid is distinguished from typhus by being due to a different germ, which causes characteristic changes in the bowel, a different rash, and is water-born, from defective sanitary arrangements. The explanation of the methods of contamination of the water supply is one of the most complicated questions of sanitation, and the experience learned from every epidemic must be brought to bear to prevent a similar incident in other localities, where the water supply is apparently free from contamination. The period of incubation, or latency, of E. F. varies considerably in accordance with the number of bacilli swallowed. Consequently, it is often extremely difficult to trace the source and cause of contamination. Many people may have been infected and have travelled to distant parts before symptoms of the disease show themselves. Thus, epidemics may be very widespread, and isolated cases may occur far removed from their original source, and may themselves be the centre of fresh epidemics. The ravages of this disease emphasise the importance of a pure water supply for communities, and of proper sanitary arrangements in every house; of efficient drainage, and sanitary supervision of milk and other articles of food. The disease is recognised by symptoms seen at the patient's bedside, and by blood examinations in the laboratory. Anti-typhoid vaccination yields good results in preventing the disease and rendering its attacks less virulent and dangerous. In the tropics the germ may be dust- or wind-born, and in hot climates the disease is more difficult of recognition where malaria is prevalent, as patients frequently suffer from both malaria and typhoid. Enteric mainly affects the small intestines, causing ulceration, and may lead to hæmorrhage and to perforation, even in mild cases when patients in apparent health are able to walk about. These cases, known as *ambulatory typhoid,* may suddenly without warning have perforation, which in the majority of cases is fatal. So that all cases of suspected typhoid should be put on starvation diet, as even a morsel of bread may bring about the catastrophe, to the lasting regret of well-meaning friends. Relapses are by no means infrequent; it would seem as if the immunity of the patients became exhausted after, say, one or two weeks, starting from the commencement of the disease, and then apparently the patients reinfect themselves and have a return of all their symptoms. In addition to typhoid being sometimes a mild affection and sometimes extremely severe, convalescence is usually prolonged, and patients who have apparently recovered may be infective for a period of years. These are known as 'typhoid carriers,' and may contaminate water supplies over wide areas or in different localities. Their detection is extremely difficult, and in unsuspected cases the source is ascertained only by searching for them with extreme diligence. When suspected, typhoid carriers can be proved by examination of the blood.

**Enteritis,** inflammation of the intestine, *i.e.* of the small intestine. This is practically another name for diarrhœa, which in an ordinary case is the only symptom. In acute cases pain is usual, and is generally worse some little time after food has been taken. The appetite is either lost or capricious; the tongue is coated, and sometimes the abdomen may be inflated and gurgling sounds heard. In a cold climate, the condition, as a rule, passes in a week or so, but when there is some underlying cause beyond errors of diet, as in cases of tuberculosis or advanced liver or kidney disease, the condition may become chronic. In the tropics, the disease may exist for years, requiring for its cure removal to a cold climate. *Prevention* consists in the avoidance of those articles of diet which experience has shown disagree. With regard to wearing a belt, that must be left to individual judgment and discretion, as so much depends on the muscular vigour of the patient and the kind of life that is led. *Treatment* —Nothing relieves pain more satisfactorily, and terminates diarrhœa better, than a teaspoonful of castor oil every two hours, until the solid contents are removed. If there is pain, five drops of laudanum can be added to each dose. Relief is also obtained by fomentations and other forms of heat. In no condition is confinement to bed so beneficial. The diet should consist of boiled milk, barley water, yolk of egg and water, and rice water, the choice depending on the circumstances of the locality. The diarrhœa of children is often due to warmth ; sometimes in cold weather from excessive clothing, and in warm weather to natural heat and the position of the cradle or cot near the floor. Much benefit results from tepid baths, or sponging with tepid water. In artificially fed children, unsuitable milk diet may maintain the condition. In addition to milk, the diet should contain similar articles to that of adults and after a time beef tea, jelly, or other meat preparations may be added.

**Entertainments Duty.** This duty which was introduced in 1916 is charged on payments for admission to any entertainment, the only exemptions allowed being in cases of schools, educational and scientific institutions and charitable purposes. There is no duty when the payment for admission (exclusive of duty) is not over 6*d.* The present (1931) rate is 1*d.* where the payment does not exceed 7*d.*, 2*d.* where it does not exceed 1*s.* 1*d.*; 6*d.* where it does not exceed 3*s.*; and 1*s.* 6*d.* where it does not exceed 10*s.* 6*d.* (with intermediate rates between these). The rate is 2*s.* on prices over 10*s.* 6*d.* and not over 15*s.*; and where the price is over 15*s.* the duty is 2*s.* for the first 15*s.* and 6*d.* for every 5*s.* or part of 5*s.* over 15*s.* The duty yields about £6,000,000 annually to the Exchequer.

**Entomology** (Gk. ἔντομα, insects, λόγος, a discourse), the science that treats of insects. The term is often loosely used to include the study of other small animals, such as centipedes and spiders. The science began with Aristotle, who differentiated a class of animals, *entoma*, and included in it the true insects, arachnids and myriapods. His grouping was followed for 2000 years. Modern E. has several branches, the chief being: (1) Classification; (2) Anatomy and physiology; (3) Bionomics, or the study of habits and life-history; (4) Embryology; (5) Cytology; (6) Ecology; (7) Palæoëntomology, or the study of fossil insects. It had its beginning in the splendid work done in the seventeenth and eighteenth centuries. Mention must be made of Malpighi's work on the silkworm (1669), Swammerdam's *Biblia naturæ,* in which he showed the true nature of the larva of an insect, and of Redi, the Italian, who disproved the theory of the spontaneous generation of maggots. At the same time John Ray was working on the classification of insects, and was the first to reach the modern lines of arrangement. In 1735 Linnæus, working on the lines laid down by Ray, made a new classification of insects, which is the foundation of all modern work. The work of classification has been carried on by workers of all nationalities, and is now very complex and accurate. The anatomical work of Malpighi and Swammerdam has had many followers, the field becoming so large that workers at the present time have to specialise very strictly. The most famous work is perhaps that of Lavigny, who established the homology of the jaws of all insects in 1816. Amongst Eng. workers in insect bionomics should be mentioned W. Kirby, W. Spence, Lord Avebury, and Miall. Much useful work has been done by C. U. Riley of the U.S.A. The embryology, cytology, and ecology of insects and Palæoëntomology are essentially products of the last century, but already great strides have been made in both branches. Most of the recent embryological work has been done in Germany and the U.S.A. British, Colonial, and American entomologists have made considerable contributions to entomological cytology and ecology. Recognition of the economic im-

SIR RONALD ROSS

portance of insects with regard to diseases of plants and animals has led to the appointment of gov entomologists in the U.S.A., Canada, and Great Britain, and applied E. has made rapid progress during the present century.

As a result of the researches of many workers, notably Grassi, Laveran, Manson and Ross, the mosquito was recognised in 1898 as a carrier of the malaria parasite. Subsequently mosquitoes have been proved to carry organisms causing elephantiasis, yellow fever, and Dengue fever. The most effective method of extermination is to render

uninhabitable the swamps which form the breeding-places of the insect. In England, extensive work on mosquito control is being carried out at Hayling Island.

House-flies are other active agents in spreading disease. In feeding on refuse, they collect on their mouth-parts and legs organisms which they deposit, when walking or feeding, on the food of man. In addition to various bacteria causing tuberculosis, typhoid fever and other diseases, flies may carry eggs of the hook-worm and of other worms parasitic in man. The gad-fly and tsetse fly transmit disease directly to horses and cattle.

The irritation and disease caused by flies to the troops in the Great War stimulated efforts to exterminate these pests. The methods used include the exclusion of air from the eggs by closely trapping the larvae; the addition of borax or of powdered hellebore to the breeding-grounds; and the preventive measure of the immediate destruction of all refuse. In America, Africa, and Asia investigations are being made on the habits of insects injurious to cotton and tobacco plants, fruit trees, and forest trees of economic value. In many cases, spraying with appropriate solutions, or the introduction into the district of an animal which preys on the insect pest, is beneficial.

The destructive habits of locusts have been famous for hundreds of years. Uvarov and Zolstarevsky have established three biological species: gregarious species forming swarms, solitary species that never swarm, and transitional species showing all grades between solitary and gregarious forms. In the Old World the most destructive locust, the desert locust of Syria, Palestine, Arabia, and Africa, seems to breed best in dry desert and semi-desert areas. In 1928–2, swarms of these insects devastated Palestine, and knowledge of insect ecology (*see* ECOLOGY) led entomologists to prophesy a continuance of the invasion until 1931, and its subsequent subsidence for twelve or thirteen years. Spraying and fumigation may be effective in the swarming phase, but the most effective treatment is to cover the breeding-grounds, when discovered, with Paris green, or with white arsenic, or to spread them with poisoned bait.

Morgan and Bridges' work on the cytology and genetics of Drosophila, and Goldschmidt's investigations on the gypsy moth, have led to new developments in the relation of cytology to genetics and to the problems of heredity. E., beyond all other sciences, affords an opportunity for the amateur worker. The Société Entomologique de France and the Entomological Society of London admit professional and amateur members. The insects when collected are best killed by prussic acid in some form. When they are relaxed they must be set. *Setting* consists of pinning the insect on to cork, the body of the insect lying in a groove in the cork, the wings and other parts being arranged in the best possible manner by means of needles or *setting bristles*. Paper braces are then put on to keep the whole in position, and the insect is thoroughly dried. It is then ready to be put in the collection. *See* H. G. Fernald, *Applied Entomology* (1921); E. D. Sanderson and L. M. Peairs, *Insect Pests of Farm, Garden and Orchard* (1921); A. T. Gillanders, *Forest Entomology* (1912).

**Entomostraca** (Gk. ἔντομον, insect, ὄστρακον, shell), the name given to a sub-class of Crustaceans, most of whose species are enclosed in a delicate, transparent, bivalve shell which can be opened or closed at the will of the animal. Many of them are very small, and are found in great numbers in stagnant, fresh, and salt water; some are parasitic. The E. comprise many thousand species which fall under four great orders, Phyllopoda, Ostracoda, Copepoda, and Cirripedia.

**Entophytes** (Gk. ἐντός, within, φυτόν, plant), the term applied to certain plants, generally parasitic, which live inside other plants or inside animals. These are frequently harmless, but some have fatal results in animals, as is the case with many bacteria.

**Entozoa,** *see* PARASITES.

**Entraygues,** *see* AVEYRON.

**Entrecasteaux,** *see* D'ENTRECAS-TEAUX.

**Entre-Douro-e-Minho,** was originally a prov. of Portugal, its W. boundary being the Atlantic, with the R. Minho on the N. separating it from Spain, and the Douro on the S. The district is well cultivated and mountainous, and is also one of the most densely populated in Portugal. It is now divided into three parts : Vianna, Braga, and Porto. Pop. 1,304,353.

**Entrenchment,** the general term applied to any earthwork which is thrown up to protect soldiers against an enemy. Es. may be made very hastily and simply, as in the case of the ordinary shelter trenches, or they may be of a much more complicated and permanent nature. In the case of the former the men are provided with implements so that they

can easily and quickly dig up the earth to form a parapet behind which they can take shelter and over which they can fire. They are also so constructed that they do not form any obstruction to the artillery who may want to drive over the ground.

**Entre Rios,** a prov. of the Argentine Republic, and lies between the two rivers Parana and Uruguay. Some parts of this district are low-lying and marshy, but others are well watered and fertile, so that the inhabitants are chiefly engaged in cattle-rearing and agricultural pursuits. Large tracts of the country are also covered with forests. Pop. 425,373.

**Entropion,** a curving in of the eyelids, the opposite of ectropion. It causes constant irritation by the eyelids coming in contact with the eye, with resulting interference with vision. One cause of E. is Traucoma (a contagious eye disease), a condition which, in most countries, precludes the admission of emigrants.

**Entropy,** *see* THERMODYNAMICS.

**Entry :** (1) Taking possession by the legal owner of lands and tenements when another person is wrongfully in possession of them. Formerly E. could be effected by force, but as this self-redress led to great abuses, forcible entries were, by two Acts of Richard II., made punishable by fine and imprisonment. To establish forcible E. it must be proved that the E. was accompanied with some circumstances of actual violence or terror, as *e.g.* by the aid of unusual weapons, a considerable number of persons, or with menace of life. Mere violence without such exceptional circumstances would amount to no more than trespass, giving rise to an action for damages. It is to be noted, however, that where possession has been obtained by a trespasser (as distinct from the position of a person who was rightfully in possession in the first instance but who subsequently became technically a trespasser through some default) the rightful owner, according to one decision, may use reasonable force in ejecting him, and need not appeal to the law for assistance. The remedy for forcible E. is either by an action for damages, by indictment, or by an information before justices of the peace. A forcible E. by more than three persons acting in concert might amount to and be punishable as a riot (*q.v.*). The Conveyancing Act, 1881, gives to a person entitled to any rent charge or other annual sum charged upon or payable out of land, power, if the sum or any part is unpaid for forty days after falling due, to enter into possession of the land and take the income of it until all the arrears due at the time of E. and incidental expenses are paid. If he cannot enter peaceably his appropriate remedy is by action of ejectment (which has taken the place of the old remedy by *writ of entry*) to try the question of title. A valid E. to give possession must be upon some part of the property claimed, and it is safer for the person entering formally to declare that he takes possession of the whole. (2) In leases: Formerly, E. was necessary to complete the tenancy, and till E. a tenant had no more than what was called an *interesse termini* (a right to have the lands), which, however, was a transferable right, though it could be surrendered or released. But the doctrine of *interesse termini* was abolished by the Law of Property Act, 1925, and now all terms of years take effect from the commencement of the term without actual entry. E. is also not necessary to complete a freehold title. As to a sheriff's power of E. *see* under EXECUTION.

**Enver Pasha** (1881–c.1922), Turkish politician and leader of the ' Young Turks.' Early triumphed over Abdul Hamid (*q.v.*) in his agitation for the restoration of the Constitution of 1876, and was then sent to Berlin as military attaché. He was in command of an army corps in the Balkan War, 1913 (*q.v.*), and during the peace negotiations brought about the assassination of the War Minister, which office he then filled himself, and placed his adherents in the other important state offices, his purpose being to override any possibility of interference by the Western Powers. In the Great War he became the virtual ruler of Turkey so far as domestic affairs were concerned, but was a complete failure in war policy, being unable to win the confidence of the Ger. adviser, General Liman von Sanders (*q.v.*). After the collapse of Turkey, he was condemned to death, but having already fled the country, the sentence was nugatory. Always treacherous, he then appeared in Turkestan in 1922, where a rising against the Bolshevists was in progress, and purported to act as mediator. After being imprisoned by the insurgents, he came out as their leader against the Soviet, but only to suffer a series of defeats. It is not improbable that he was trying to play into the hands of the Bolshevists, and though the manner and date of his death are uncertain, it seems that he was killed at Baljiwan in July 1922.

**Environment,** the term applied to all conditions which are not part of the individual self of a person, and which tend to alter each individual, thus forming certain varieties and species. The E. may be physical, including such things as geographical or chemical conditions, the latter including the state of the air, the conditions of food, and many other such influences. There is also a social E. showing the influence of one individual upon another. This leads also to the establishment of new customs and new institutions, thus bringing about a new type of individual.

**Envoy,** *see* DIPLOMATIC SERVICE.

**Enzelli,** a seaport tn. situated on the Caspian Sea in the prov. of Ghilan, Persia. It is about 15 m. N.W. of Resht, and is the port of that town. After the Russian revolution of 1917 the Entente Powers tried to organise unaffected elements in Armenia and Georgia, and with this object Major-General L. C. Dunsterville (*q.v.*) was sent from Mesopotamia with a small force early in 1918. He reached E. only to find the place in the hands of the hostile Bolshevists and the neighbourhood dominated by a band of organised brigands some thousands strong. He therefore withdrew and marched by another route to Baku (*q.v.*). Pop. 3000.

**Enzio** (*c.* 1220–72), King of Sardinia and natural son of Frederick II. About the year 1238 he married Adelasia, an heiress, and the title of King of Sardinia was conferred on him by his father, as well as that of vicar-imperial in Italy. In the year 1241 he was victorious over the Genoese fleet, taking prisoner several church dignitaries. He followed this success by others, but in 1249 was himself conquered and made a prisoner, spending the rest of his life in captivity at Bologna.

**Enzymes,** ferments present in the digestive juices which render food substances soluble and diffusible. This process is termed *digestion,* and consists essentially in changing colloid food substances into crystalloid bodies, as in the latter condition they can dissolve in the fluid contained in the alimentary canal, and then diffuse through the mucous coat into either the blood vessels or lymphatics, and so become available for utilisation. E. are probably colloid bodies themselves, and they act as *catalytic* agents and commence the change in the chemical nature of the food substances. They perform this function in the presence of acids and alkali, but for each E. there is an *optimum temperature* at which the action is most vigorous, and there are high and low critical temperatures at which the action ceases. It is remarkable that the many complicated food materials yield but few compounds after digestion; proteins are changed into peptones, tyrosin, and leucine by the E. (*pepsin* and *trypsin*) of the gastric glands and pancreas; the fats are changed into fatty acids and glycerine, or emulsified and saponified by the *steapsin* of the pancreas; carbohydrates are changed into glucose with or without intermediate stages by the *Ptyalin* of the salivary glands, the *amylopsin* of the pancreas and *invertase*, *maltase*, and *lactase* of the intestinal glands.

**Eocene**, in geology, is the lowest of the three groups into which Lyell divided the Tertiary system. His classification, based on the relative percentages of recent species of mollusca contained, has been modified by Beyrich, who inserted the Oligocene group, to include strata formerly classed as Upper E. and partly Miocene. The E. and Oligocene are sometimes classed together as the Palæogene or Older Tertiary. In Western Europe the E. follows the Cretaceous so abruptly as to suggest that a break existed between the Cretaceous and Tertiary periods. In Europe, and in America and New Zealand, the deposits merge into one another, and no sharp line can be drawn between Cretaceous and E. rocks. During E. and Oligocene times, the floor of the Cretaceous sea was upraised into low lands with lake and estuaries. The colossal disturbances of the earth's crust, by which this upheaval occurred, continued throughout Tertiary time, great mountain chains such as the Alps and Himalayas being formed. The British E. strata are confined to the S.E. of England, where they occupy two synclinal depressions in the chalk, viz. the London and Hampshire Basins. The deposits are marine and estuarine, consisting of clays, sands, and marls, and have been arranged in the sequence shown in the subjoined table:

referred by some geologists to the E., and by others to the Oligocene. In Antrim and the Inner Hebrides occurs a magnificent development of Tertiary volcanic rocks. These consist of basaltic sheets traversed by numerous bands of gabbro and basalt dykes, the date of their emission being fixed by the discovery of intercalated leaf beds of the same age as the Bournemouth beds (*see* table).

Two great E. regions may be distinguished in the European area. The first, termed the Anglo-Gallic province, includes the E. of the Eng. area, of N. France and of Belgium, and the similarity of the deposits points to the fact that this was one great tract of sedimentation. The second, the S. European or Alpine E. area, is much more extensive. It includes the whole of S. Europe, extends southwards into N. Africa, to the Sahara and Egypt, and stretches eastwards to the Himalayas, and through Java and Sumatra to the Philippines. There existed, then, over this great area, a huge sea (of which the Mediterranean is a remnant) connecting the Atlantic and Pacific Oceans, and out of which the Alps, the Pennines, and part of the Carpathians rose as islands. In the waters of this sea, the ' Mittelmeer,' massive systems of limestone were formed by Nummulites, a genus of gigantic disc-shaped Foraminifera, which attained a great development in early E. time. The nummulitic formations of N. Africa and India are very rich in fossils, yielding large corals of the reef-building type. molluscs, and echinoderms. The problematical ' Flysch ' of the Swiss Alps or ' Macigno ' of the Maritime Alps probably represents the littoral deposits of the Older Tertiary period, and consists of thick grey sandstones and shales with scarcely any organic remains. The E. of the Libyan desert, as well as being remarkably fossiliferous, are of special interest, since they show a perfect petrographical

| London Basin. | | Hampshire Basin. |
|---|---|---|
| Upper } Eocene } | Upper Bagshot Sands | Barton Sands<br>Barton Clays |
| Middle { Eocene { | Middle Bagshot Sands<br>Lower Bagshot Sands<br>(upper part) | Bracklesham Series (including the Bournemouth Beds and the Alum Bay Beds) |
| Lower { Eocene { | Lower Bagshot Sands (part)<br>London Clay<br>Oldhaven Beds<br>Woolwich and Reading Beds<br>Thanet Sands | Bognor Series (equivalent of London Clay)<br>Plastic Clays (similar to Woolwich and Reading Beds) |

Outside the typical area the E. rocks occur in patches. The deposits of Bovey Tracy in Devonshire have been and palæontological passage from the Cretaceous into the Tertiary beds in question. In N. America the E.

rocks are mainly of the fresh-water type. The marine deposits are represented by the Alabama beds, and occur in the valley of the Mississippi from the Gulf of Mexico to beyond the mouth of the Ohio. On the Californian coast these marine E. rocks attain a thickness of 3000 ft. Over the Rocky Mountain region, from Mexico to British Columbia, is found the lignite bearing, fresh and brackish water formation known as the Laramie beds. Deposits of a similar type are found between the Rockies and the Wahsatch Mts., *i.e.* in the waste known as the bad lands. In the Rockies these beds attain a thickness of 13,000 ft., and have been subdivided into the following divisions : (1) Wahsatch group, (2)

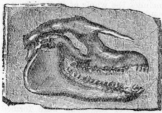

A FOSSIL OF THE EOCENE PERIOD

(*Palæotherium magnum*)

Green R. group, (3) Bridger group, and (4) Uinta group. These rocks are of great geological importance because of their extraordinary richness in vertebrate and mammalian remains. The mammals suddenly developed during E. time, and are chiefly of the placental group, which preponderate at the present day. The hoofed beasts or Ungulates were dominant, and were divided into two groups with paired and unpaired hoofs, as representatives of which we may mention the 'Palæotherium,' and the 'Anthracotherium.' The Dinocerata found in the Rocky Mts. form a special group of Ungulates, which resembled the 'Proboscideans,' except for the fact that they had three pairs of horns and were armed with long sabre-like upper canines. They were also characterised by a diminutive brain in comparison with the size of the skull. The Carnivores were represented by the primitive Creodonta, and Rodents and Insectivores have been found. Regarding the fossils of Invertebrates, we find that the Ammonoidea and Belemnites, which flourished in Cretaceous time, have wholly disappeared, and with them the sponges and the Hippuri-

tidæ. The great reptilian families which flourished from Triassic time onward are practically extinct during E. time. The Molluscoidea are represented by forms which exist at the present day and the Cœlenterata by reef-building corals. The Flora of the E. consisted mainly of Dicotyledons (tropical and subtropical forms), Monocotyledons (such as the Palms), and Conifers.

**Eon de Beaumont, Charles Geneviève Louise Auguste André Timothée d'** (Chevalier d'Eon) (1728–1810), Fr. diplomatist, and trusted agent in Louis XV.'s secret diplomacy, serving him in Russia (1755), and in England (1762–65). In 1759 he fought bravely as captain of the Fr. forces in Germany. He had assumed woman's dress on his first mission to Russia, and was desired by the gov. (1777) to wear it for the rest of his life in France, whence many held that he was really a woman. His political and historical essays appeared (1775) as *Loisirs du Chevalier d'Eon . . . See* Bachaumont, *Mémoires secrets*, 1777 ; Grimm, *Correspondence . . . ,* 1829–31 ; Telfer, *Strange Career of the Chevalier d'Eon*, 1885 ; his *Life and Times* by Homberg and Jousselin, 1911 ; Lang's *Hist. Mysteries*, 1905.

**Eos** (Ἠώς), the Gk. goddess of the dawn (Lat. *Aurora*), daughter of Hyperion and wife of Tithonus.

**Eötvös (or Eoetvoes), József, Baron** (1813–71), a Hungarian statesman and author, leader of the Centralist Liberal party (1844), and a supporter of Kossuth, contributing to his *Pesti Hirlap* numerous articles, collected later as *Reform.* He wrote the comedies *Kritikusok* and *Házasulók*, and the tragedy *Boszú*, 1830–33. Of his novels, *Karthausi* (1842), *A falu jegyzöje* (' The Village Notary,' 1844–46), and *Magyarország 1514—ben* (1847–48) won much fame. He was Minister of Public Instruction in 1867, and did much for elementary education and religious toleration in Hungary.

**Eötvös, Roland, Baron** (1848–1919), Hungarian statesman and physicist ; *b.* July 27, 1848, at Budapest ; son of Baron Joseph E. Educated at Königsberg and Heidelberg. At Budapest: 1871, lecturer ; 1873, professor—of experimental physics. From 1873, connected with Hungarian Academy of Sciences ; president from 1889. He made many curious discoveries with regard to gravitation and capillary attraction. Life member of Hungarian House of Magnates. Minister of Public Worship and Education, 1895–96. Died at Budapest, April 8.

**Eozoon** (ἠώς, dawn, and ζῷον,

animal), peculiar structures of calcite and serpentine, something similar to Stromatopora and other hydroid corals, found among the early crystalline gneisses and schists of the lower St. Lawrence valley and the Archæan limestones of Canada. The researches of Möbius and others go to prove that they are a mineral concretion or segregation of purely inorganic origin. E. has been discovered in rocks of the same age in Bavaria and in limestone blocks thrown from the crater of Vesuvius.

Epacridaceæ, a natural order of dicotyledonous plants closely allied to the Ericaceæ, with the small-leaved genera of which they agree in habit, and from which they are scarcely distinguishable. They are to be found wild in Australia as shrubs with alternate or occasionally opposite leaves, and in British greenhouses are cultivated for their showy flowers. Two of the chief genera are *Epacris* and *Dracophyllum*.

Epacts (Gk. ἐπακταί), intercalary (brought in) days, the excess of a solar over a lunar month or year in days. The E. for any year is the number of days in the moon's age on the first day of the year (Jan. 1, in the Gregorian, Victorian, and early Latin calendars; March 22, in the Dionysian calendar, or old style). The number varies for each year (usually increasing by eleven from one year to the next). E. are used for fixing the dates of movable feasts of the church. See *Philosoph. Trans.*, xlvi., 1750 ; Bonnycastle, *Astron.*, xiv., 1787 ; Delambre, *Astronomie Moderne*, i. See GOLDEN NUMBER.

Epaminondas ('Επαμεινώνδας, or 'Επαμινώνδας) (c. 418–362 B.C.), a brave and upright Theban general and statesman, of a poor but noble family. After the Thebans had recovered the ' Cadmeia ' and expelled the Spartans (379), he speedily became a democratic leader, and was sent to represent Thebes at the Spartan Congress (371). He refused to surrender the Bœotian cities, aiming at a Bœotian confederacy under Thebes. War followed, and the Spartan supremacy was crushed at Leuctra (371). With Pelopidas he invaded the Peloponnesus, restored Messenia's independence, and founded Megalopolis (Arcadia) (369). During a fourth invasion of the Peloponnesus E. was slain in the Theban victory at Mantinea (362). He made great innovations in military tactics. See Cornelius Nepos, *Vita ;* Xen. *Hell*, vii. ; Du Mesnil in *Historische Zeitschrift*, 1863 ; *Leben*, by Bauch, 1834 ; Pomtow, 1870

Epaulement, a part of siege-works or a covering mass in military fortifi-

cations, raised to protect the troops from the enemy's fire. It differs from a parapet in making no provision for firing over it by the defenders. Siege batteries are usually shielded by one so constructed as to form an obtuse angle with the main line of battery, protecting the gunners from flank fire. It is used in general of any screen designed to protect the troops.

Epaulettes, or Epaulets, a fringed shoulder-piece or ornamental badge of rank worn as part of a uniform, especially naval or military, probably a survival of the mediæval metal shoulder-plate (sixteenth century). It was adopted by commissioned officers in the British navy (1795), and is usually of gold bullion with various devices and embroidered designs to mark the degree of rank. Formerly E. were worn by nearly all armies and navies, but after 1855 they were no longer worn in the British army by all ranks, and in U.S.A. only general officers of the army wore them after 1872. See UNIFORMS.

Epée, Charles Michel, Abbé de l' (1712–89), a Fr. Jansenist. One of the founders of the system for instructing deaf-mutes largely by means of the manual alphabet and signs. He founded a school for the purpose (1755). His *Dict. général des signes* was completed by Abbé Sicard. See *Vie* by Valette, 1857 ; Morel, 1833 ; Berthier, 1852.

Epéhy, Battle of, see FRANCE AND FLANDERS GREAT WAR, CAMPAIGNS IN—1918.

Eperies, a tn. in Czechoslovakia on the Tarcza, 21 m. from Kaschau. It is the seat of a Gk. Catholic bishop, has a Lutheran academy of theology and law, and an eighteenth-century cathedral. Linen, woollens, earthenware and beer are manufactured. The only opal mine in Europe is 6 m. N.W. of E. The chalybeate and royal salt springs of Soovar are close by. Pop. 14,590.

Epernay (Aquæ Perennes), tn. of Marne dept., France, on the Marne, 18 m. from Rheims. It is an important entrepôt for Champagne wines, which are stored in vaults in the chalk rock. Spinning, tanning, and brewing are carried on, and corks, casks, and pottery manufactured. It was frequently bombarded during the Great War. Pop. 20,670.

Ephemera (from ἐπί and ἡμέρα), a genus of insects often known as Dayflies or May-flies, somewhat resemble dragon flies, and as adults live only for one day. They have a voracious larval existence in water, sometimes lasting for two or three years. The insect as it emerges from the water is called the ' sub-imago,' and after shedding its delicate covering becomes a full-grown 'imago.' They haunt river-banks and ponds on summer evenings The sub-imago and imago are used as baits by anglers, and called 'green drakes,' and 'grey drakes.' *E. vulgata* is the best-known species. Others are *Palingenia*, *Cloë*, *Cœnis*, and *Heptagenia* or *Bäetis*.

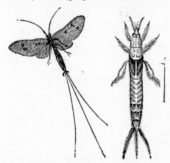

EPHEMERA VULGATA
(Mayfly)

**Ephemeris** (ἐφημερίς, journal, diary), a table stating for successive days the predicted position of and other particulars concerning heavenly bodies. The *Astronomical Ephemeris, or Nautical Almanac* of the United Kingdom, is published annually, containing ephemerides of the chief stars and planets, data of eclipses, etc. France, Germany, Spain, and U.S.A. issue similar almanacs.

**Ephesians, Epistle to the,** a letter bearing the name of St. Paul, addressed to the Christians at Ephesus, one of the chief cities of Asia Minor, at which the Apostle had spent two years (Acts xix. 8 ff.) on an earlier occasion. The tone of the epistle, however, shows no restriction to a local church, and this, coupled with the facts that the words 'at Ephesus' in the first verse are omitted in some MSS., and that there is no reference to individual Ephesians, has led to the hypothesis that the letter is indeed an epistle general. The date of the epistle is usually placed during St. Paul's imprisonment at Rome, about A.D. 60–65, and there is now substantial agreement as to its authenticity. Its Pauline authorship was, however, denied by the Tübingen and Dutch schools. The subject of the letter, the mystic unity of the Church in Christ, closely resembles that of the Epistle to the Colossians, a fact which supports the theory which makes them almost contemporary.

**Ephesus** (Ἔφεσος), a famous ancient city of W. Asia Minor, probably founded about the eleventh century B.C. Its ruins still exist on the banks of the Cayster, near the Gulf of Scala Nova, 35 m. from Smyrna, It was chief of the twelve Ionic colonies from Greece, situated in Lydia. E. was subject in turn to Crœsus (560 B.C.), the Persians (479–387), Athenians, Macedonians, and Romans. It was noted for its temple and worship of Artemis (Diana), the great nature-goddess of Asia Minor. This temple (rebuilt after 356 B.C.) was considered one of the wonders of the world; it was destroyed by the Goths (A.D. 263). Besides its ruins, there are interesting remains of a fine theatre, odeum, and stadium. Excavations have been systematically carried on only since the nineteenth century (*c.* 1874) by the Austrian Archæological Institute, and by Wood and Hogarth for England. E. was the birthplace of Heraclitus, scene of the Legend of the Seven Sleepers, and seat of the Ionian school of painting. St. Paul visited it several times (*see* Acts xviii.–xix.). The railway from Smyrna to Aidin passes the ancient site, and Ayasuluk is the chief village near it. *See* Strabo Γεωγραφικά; Herod, i.; Curtius, *Ephesus*, 1874; Falkner, *Ephesus and the Temple of Diana*, 1862; Wood, *Discoveries at Ephesus*, 1877; Fergusson's *Temple of Diana*, 1883; *Times*, Aug. 1905; Benndorf, Heberdey, and others in *Forschungen in Ephesos*, i., 1906 (for Austr. Arch. Inst.); Hogarth, *Excavations at Ephesus*, 1908.

**Ephesus, Councils of.** The third ecumenical council, convoked by Theodosius II., under the presidency of Cyril of Alexandria, A.D. 431, was notable for the attendance, for the first time, of papal delegates from Rome, who were instructed to adjudicate on the opinions of the Council, but to abstain from debate. This Council condemned the heresy of Nestorius, but did not itself definitely state the prevailing doctrine. Theodosius also convoked the 'Robber' Council of A.D. 449 held under Dioscurus of Alexandria, which restored Eutyches as archimandrite and priest, from which office he had been driven by the Synod of Constantinople, and deposed Flavian, the Patriarch.

**Ephialtes :** (1) The Malian traitor, who showed the Persians the mountain defile of Anopæa. Following this, they came up behind Leonidas and his Spartan band and overcame them at the Pass of Thermopylæ (480 B.C.). (2) An Athenian statesman, political friend of Pericles, and opponent of Cimon. He helped to pass democratic reforms (c. 462 B.C.), and limited the power of the Areopagus. He was probably assassinated at the oligarch's instigation (c. 456). See Plutarch, Pericles; History of Greece, of Grote (1846–56), Thirlwall (1835–47). (3.) A son of Poseidon and Iphimedia, one of the giants who

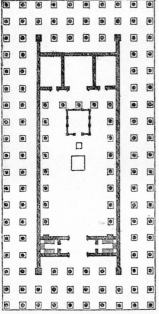

PLAN OF THE TEMPLE AT EPHESUS

revolted against Zeus, piling Pelion and Ossa upon Olympus. See ALOIDÆ.

**Ephod** (perhaps from Heb. *âphad*, to put on, clothe): (1) A Jewish priestly vestment, especially that worn by the high-priest, of blue, purple, scarlet and fine linen (byssus) interwoven with gold thread. Similar garments of plain white linen were apparently worn by any servant of the temple. They were sleeveless, with buckles of onyx stone on the shoulder-straps, the names of the twelve tribes being inscribed, six on each buckle. In front the high priests wore the jewelled breastplate with the oracle-pouch for the Urim and Thummim. See Exod. xxviii.; 1 Sam. ii., xxii.; 2 Sam. vi. (2) Apparently an image, forming part of the equipment of a sanctuary. It was worshipped and perhaps used in connection with the teraphim in divination. See Judges viii., xvii., xviii.; 1 Sam. xxi., xxiii. Consult Hastings, *Dict. Bibl.*; Cheyne and Black, *Ency.*, *Bibl.* ; Benzinger, *Heb. Arch.*, 1894 ; Foote in *Journal of Bibl. Lit.*, x 1902 ; Singer, *Jewish Ency.*, v.; Moore, *Judges*, 1895.

**Ephori**, or **Ephors** (Ἔφοροι, overseers), the chief magistrates of the anct. state of Sparta. They were five in number, and were elected by and from the people (ἐξ ἁπάντων) without any qualification of age or property. Their authority gradually widened until it included a superintendence over the whole commonwealth, including the kings, and they had the right of calling them to account for their actions and of punishing them with fines and reprimands, and even of prosecuting them before the senate.

**Ephorus** (fl. c. 340 B.C.), a Gk. historian, b. in Cymæ, Asia Minor. He was the author of a universal history, which treated the history of the Gk. and barbarian world, during a space of 750 years, ending in 340 B.C. It was much read, and in spite of hostile criticism was admired by many, among them Polybius.

**Ephraem**, or **Ephraim** (fl. A.D. 370), a Syrian writer, b. at Nisibis. He spent the early years of his life in his native city, engaged in study, but after its surrender to the Persians by Javian in 363 went to Edessa. Here he seems to have spent his life as a hermit outside the city, engaged in teaching and writing. He was ordained deacon, but refused to accept any further promotion in the church. At the time of the famine in Edessa he rendered great assistance to the suffering poor by urging the rich to deny themselves for their brethren's good. His writings were in Syriac, for he knew no other language, and consist of treatises on theological subjects, epistles and addresses to monks, apophthegms, homilies on parts of Scripture and characters in the O.T., and hymns. They were held in very high esteem, and most of them were translated both into Latin and Gk. The standard edition of his works is that of Assemani (Rome, 1732–46). An English translation of some of his pieces was published by Henry Burgess in 1853. By the Rom. Catholics he is numbered among the Doctors of the Church.

**Ephraim**, the younger son of Joseph, who was exalted by his father's benediction above his elder brother

Manasseh. He was the ancestor, according to the Jewish tradition, of the tribe of Ephraim, which with the tribe of Manasseh formed the ' house of Joseph ' (Josh. xvii. 14 ; 2 Sam. xix. 20, etc.). The tribe of Benjamin earlier separated from these two. Ephraim, which had within its borders many important places, was the chief of the tribes of the N. kingdom, and its name is often used as synonymous with that of Israel. Chief among these places may be named Shechem, the burial-place of Joseph, and the sanctuary of Shiloh. The tribe was a warlike one (Judges viii. 1, and xii. 1 ff.), and produced Joshua, the conqueror of the land of Canaan.

**Epiblast,** *see* EMBRYOLOGY.

**Epicharmus** (*c.* 540–450 B.C.), a Gk. comedian, *b.* in the is. of Cos. He spent the earlier part of his life in the study of philosophy, and did not begin writing comedies until his removal to Syracuse in 484. Of these thirty-five are extant, written in the Doric dialect, and to him is due the literary form of the Sicilian comedy. He introduced a regular plot and did away with the low buffoonery then current for comedy in Sicily. He took his subjects from the stories of gods and heroes as well as from life, and his plots seem to have been simple and the action rapid. His language was elegant, and he was celebrated for his choice of epithets ; indeed, he was called by Plato, ' the prince of comedy.'

**Epic Poetry** (Gk. ἔπος, a story), the name given to narrative poems of sufficient magnitude which are distinguished by beauty of thought and expression, and whose subjects possess both dignity and interest. Epics have sometimes been classified as sacred, heroic, allegorical, etc., but these divisions often merge into one another. Some again have been styled epics of growth, having been built up of old legends and traditions ; others epics of art, created mainly by the poet's imagination.

Very early poetry consisted mainly of sacred hymns, tribal legends, and popular verses like the *Epigrams* attributed to Homer. The first narrative poems mentioned in history are those of ancient Greece, some of which, dating back before Homer and Hesiod, are now known only by name, every fragment of them being lost. These, composed before writing was invented, were designed for singing and recitation, and for centuries poetry continued to be mainly oral, being carefully memorised by trained singers, who thus carried on from one generation to another the traditions of their race. Now and again some occasion would be marked by the

production of a new poem, many a forgotten bard ' leaving great verse unto a little clan.' The *Iliad* and *Odyssey*, greatest of Greek epics, are ascribed to Homer, but of that poet himself nothing is certainly known, not even his birthplace or the date of his existence. Even his authorship of the poems has been contested, some critics alleging them to be a collection brought together from ancient sources. A doubt whether writing was commonly used, if at all,

HOMER
(Naples Museum)

in Homer's time, has been urged by some who maintain that works of such magnitude as the *Iliad* and *Odyssey* cannot have been the *oral* productions of one man. It is also contended that there are differences in character, manners, and ideas which show the *Odyssey* to be of considerably later date than the *Iliad*. But, waiving these controversies, it is agreed that these poems are not only the oldest but also among the noblest in the world, and they have greatly influenced the subsequent poetry of all Western nations. Hesiod, the second great poet of ancient Greece, though according to one tradition contemporary with Homer, probably lived some time later. His works are a mixture of epic and didactic verse ; the only one which has come down to us fairly complete, *The Works and Days*, being something like Virgil's *Georgics*. Another reputedly his, the *Theogony*, though imperfect and bearing traces of much alteration, is on a grander scale, dealing with Greek stories of the creation and of the early gods and demi-gods. His revolt of the Titans helped to inspire the sixth book of *Paradise Lost*. In the dawn of Rom. literature its writers often looked to Greece for their models. Ennius (239–170 B.C.), when writing his *Annals*, a poetical chronicle of Rom. history, took his metre from Homer instead of adhering to the old Saturnian verse. About 150 years later Virgil wrote, also in hexameters, the *Æneid*, which has ever since been regarded as a type of perfect art; yet its author was so dissatisfied with it that when dying he left word for the MS. to be burned, but this was forbidden by Augustus. No other Latin epic-writer ever approached the excellence of Virgil. As the sagas of Greece were wrought into great poems, so in mediæval Europe legend clustering round the names of historical personages like Alexander, or of national and sometimes mythical heroes such as Siegfried, King Arthur, and Charlemagne, became in many instances moulded into epics. Of the Teutonic lays, the *Nibelungenlied*, telling the story of Siegfried and Kriemhild, and the fatal Nibelung treasure, takes rank as one of the greatest of poetic romances. It has sometimes been paralleled with the *Iliad*, not for beauty of style or pictorial description, but as containing more human interest and development of character, and being more complete as a narrative. An earlier version of some part of the story, wilder and full of Scandinavian magic, is found in the *Volsunga Saga*. In the *Nibelungenlied* the pagan atmosphere is somewhat modified, but the whole is fierce and sad, and the closing scenes terribly tragic. Among old Teutonic epics are some of English origin, the best of these being *Beowulf*; another fine one is *Havelok*, the scene of which is partly laid in Lincolnshire. Among the greatest of Icelandic sagas, which, in unrhymed poetry marked with frequent alliteration, related early Norse histories and legends, were the stories of *Burnt Njal*, *Grettir the Strong*, the *Laxdalasaga*, and *King Olaf*. The authors of many fine sagas are unknown; the last and greatest whose name has survived was Sturla Thordsson (1215–84). French mediæval epics were composed of song-cycles clustering round central figures or groups, the *Geste du Roi*, for example, relating the legends of Charlemagne and his warriors. To this set belong the *Chanson de Roland*, *Ogier the Dane*, and other great lays. The original chansons or gestes, the work of

itinerant jongleurs, already displayed much of the clearness, eloquence, and force so characteristic of French literature. The *Roland* is the finest lay of feudal chivalry. The one great epic of Spain was the *Poem of the Cid*, written in the twelfth century; the Cid Campeador himself died in 1099.

In more modern times epics have gradually been superseded by the drama and the novel, though Italy and England have produced two masterpieces, the *Divina Commedia* of Dante (d. 1321) and Milton's *Paradise Lost*. These are the only modern poems which, for sustained beauty and grandeur both of thought and diction, take rank with the *Iliad* and *Odyssey*. Other Italian epics of note are Tasso's *Jerusalem* (1593), and various romantic and burlesque poems by Pulci, Ariosto, and others. Several distinguished French authors, including Voltaire, have written historical poems, but with no great success. Boileau's mock-heroic *Lutrin*, however, has been much admired. The famous *Lusiad*, so distinguished in the literature of its nation that the Portuguese has been called 'the language of Camoens,' is a spirited and fanciful epic on the adventures of Vasco de Gama. Various mythical and romantic episodes are introduced; Venus, Mars, Bacchus, Neptune, and Tethys taking part with Portuguese leaders and Oriental princes in the development of the plot. Besides *Paradise Lost*, England has one great allegorical success, the *Faerie Queene*, and many ambitious failures. Who now remembers the 'epics' of Davenant, Cowley, and Blackmore, even by name? But of what may be called miniature epics. *Marmion* is a fine specimen, containing as it does one of the finest battle-scenes in all literature. A very curious national poem, the *Kalevala*, consists of a series of Finnish mythical and magical legends, collected and arranged by Dr. Lönnrot, who lived and worked among the Lapps from 1830–50. His translation was made in a metre like that of Hiawatha. The whole poem, however, rather deserves the name of a book of rambling chronicles than an epic.

The most famous of Oriental epics are the Persian *Shah Nameh*, and the Indian *Mahabharata* and *Ramayana*. *See* Murray's *History of Ancient Greek Literature;* Andrew Lang's *Homer and the Epic;* Ker's *Epic and Romance;* Leon Gautier's *Les Epopées françaises;* Professor Saintsbury's *English Prosody*.

**Epictetus** (Gk. 'Επίκτητος), a Gk. philosopher, *b.* at Hierapolis in Phrygia. He lived a long time in Rome as a slave in the house of

Epaphroditus, a favourite of Nero. Receiving his freedom from his master, he became a professor of the Stoical system, which he learned from the lectures of Musonius Rufus. He taught first at Rome, but after the expulsion of the philosophers by Domitian in A.D. 94, went to Nicopolis in Epirus. Here he appears to have spent the rest of his life, for the discourses which Arrian took down in writing were delivered by E. when an old man at Nicopolis. He was favoured by the Emperor Hadrian, but little else is known of his life, except that he was lame and very poor. He formed numerous disciples by free conversations after the manner of Socrates, and one of these, Arrian, compiled the short manual *Enchiridion*, which bears the name of E. He also wrote the philosophical lectures of his master in eight books, from which some account of his doctrine may be gathered. The main point on which he laid stress was the independence of the human mind of all external circumstances, such being not in our power. This freedom is to be attained by patience and renunciation. The duty of man is to find all his happiness within himself, and the power of which he should be most sure is the deity in his own breast.

Epicureanism, a system of philosophy in which human happiness was regarded as the highest good. It was founded by Epicurus, who claimed to be independent of all his predecessors, but he was in reality indebted both to the Cyrenaics and Democritus. His system, however, differed from that of the Cyrenaics in his conception of pleasure. This he regarded as something lasting and imperishable, consisting in pure and noble mental enjoyments, *i.e.* in the freedom from all influences which disturb our peace of mind, and thereby our happiness. His *summum bonum* was peace of mind, and this he based upon φρόνησις, which he described as the beginning of all good and the origin of all virtues. In his physics he followed the materialistic system of Democritus, and his views are set forth in the *De Rerum Natura* of Lucretius. According to him we obtain our knowledge of things from εἴδωλα or images of things which are reflected from them and pass through our senses into our minds. Of the gods, too, he considers we obtain our knowledge in the same way, and he regards them as in the enjoyment of perfect happiness which would be interrupted if they took part in the government of the world, therefore they exercise no influence upon the world of man. Epicurus

had numerous pupils who propagated his doctrines, and yet no system of philosophy has been so much attacked as his. This was probably owing to a great extent to the conduct of the men who called themselves Epicureans, and gave themselves up to the enjoyment of sensual pleasures.

Epicurus (Gk. Ἐπίκουρος) (342–270 B.C.), a Gk. philosopher, founder of the Epicurean school, which was so named after him, born in Samos, where he spent the first eighteen years of his life. He began the study of philosophy at an early age, and in 310 began to teach first in Mytilene and afterwards in Lampracus. In 306 he went to Athens and purchased a garden, the famous Κῆποι Ἐπικούρου, in which he established his philosophical school. Here, surrounded by his friends and pupils, and three brothers Neocles, Charidemus, and Aristobulus, he spent the rest of his life engaged in the study of philosophy. His mode of living was simple and his habits temperate; he was a kind-hearted friend and a patriotic citizen. Of his works only a few are extant, although he appears to have been a prolific writer and, according to Diogenes Laertius, who calls him πολυγραφώτατος, was the author of 300 volumes. All that remains of them are some fragments of his great work Περὶ φύσεως, three letters, besides his will, and a compendium of his doctrine in forty-four short propositions, written for his scholars to learn by heart.

Epicycle (Gk. ἐπί, upon, κύκλος, circle), in anct. astronomy, a small circle, which was supposed to move on the circumference of a larger one called the ' deferent.' It was used for representing the motions of the heavenly bodies, and when the observed motion was so irregular and complicated as not to be resolved with one E., others were added, till a nearer approximation was obtained. This heaping of E. on E. resulted in a complex entanglement, and, as soon as astronomers came to understand and test the Copernican theory, this system sank into oblivion.

Epidaurus (Ἐπίδαυρος), a tn. of ancient Greece, situated in a recess of the Saronic Gulf, on the eastern coast of Peloponnesus in a dist. called Argolis, under the Romans. It was originally inhabited by Ionians and Carians, whence it was called Epicarus, but it was subdued by the Dorians under Deiphontes, who thus became the ruling race. It was the chief seat of the worship of Æsculapius. The temple of this god lay on the highway to Argos, 5 m. W. of E., and was frequented by patients from all parts of the Hellenic world. A few ruins are still extant, and the sacred enclosure is even now called Hieron (ἱερόν), or the Sanctuary.

**Epidemic,** a general term to express common to, or affecting, a whole people, or many people ; prevalent ; general. It is applied to mental, moral, social, and physical phenomena, as an E. of suicide, E. folly. Technically, in sanitary science, it means a contagious disease, or generally a wide-spread disease. The term E. is equally applicable to disease occurring both in men and in animals. It has the advantage of directing attention to the fact that a disease

Other individuals with tissues susceptible to the organisms.

Many secondary factors also operate, and the effect of an infective disease on individuals may depend on age, sex, relative immunity, climate, and other conditions.

The co-operation of doctors, bacteriologists and other pathologists, and of mathematicians, is essential to advancement of E. In clinics, observations on the interaction of host and parasite (*see* PARASITE) are made, and the discovery that healthy people may act as carriers and may distribute organisms causing infectious diseases was one of the most

THE RUINS OF THE THEATRE AT EPIDAURUS

affecting but few individuals in any one locality may have a very wide distribution, as E. meningitis and other diseases, which require great administrative consideration to adopt measures for limiting and eradicating a disease. The term E. is a disease coming *on* a people, and is used in contradistinction to endemic, a disease *in* a community.

**Epidemic Hæmoglobinuria,** *see* BLACKWATER FEVER.

**Epidemiology** is the science of epidemics, and is concerned with the cause, infectivity, epidemic and pandemic manifestations of infective diseases, and their prevention.

Epidemics and pandemics result from the conjunction of three essential factors : (1) An available store of organisms causing the disease. (2) Effective transmission of these organisms in sufficient numbers. (3)

important during the present century. The scientist who observes the life-history and reactions of these organisms contributes facts on which preventive measures can be based, and the statistician analyses such large numbers of results that he can detect, and sometimes correct, possible errors in observations and records. Curves obtained by graphing statistics make it possible to predict the probable course of an epidemic and its probable periods of recrudescence.

Application of the results of E. should eventually lead to the prevention of infective diseases. Bibliography : *The Principles of Epidemiology,* by C. O. Stallybrass.

**Epidermis,** *see* SKIN.

**Epidote,** a mineral of a green or grey colour, which is composed of silica, alumina, lime, oxide of iron, and oxide of manganese. Fine crystals, 3 in. in length, are found at Arendale in Norway, and also in Sweden, and at Franconia, New Hampshire, and some good specimens come from Piedmont.

**Epiglottis** (Gk. ἐπί γλώττη, ' over the glottis '), a leaf-like lid of yellow elastic tissue which covers the larynx during the act of swallowing. A long stalklike ligament (the *thyro-epiglottidean*) connects it inside the larynx with the thyroid cartilages.

**Epigoni** ('Επίγονοι), the descendants of the seven heroes who perished before Thebes. Ten years after their death the E. marched against Thebes to avenge their fathers ; took possession of the city, and razed it to the ground.

**Epigram,** properly an inscription, such as was often written upon a tomb or a work of art to describe its character. Inscriptions of this sort were from early times put into metrical form, and the writer generally tried to put good sense and spirit into them. They were generally, though not always, written in the elegiac metre. The greatest master of E. was Simonides of Cess, the author of almost all the sepulchral inscriptions on the warriors who fell in the Persian wars. The form of the E. was also used to embody in concise and pointed language the clever ideas or the passing moods of the writer, often with a tinge of wit or satire, and it was a very favourite form of composition with the Alexandrian poets, some writers devoting themselves entirely to it. Indeed, some of the choicest gems of Gk. literature are to be found in the Es. ; the Gk. anthology has preserved 4500 Es. The art was also practised in Rome from Ennius till the latest times, and in the second half of the first century A.D. Martial handled it with the power of a master. Among English poets there is no writer whose fame rests solely on his Es. Many practised the art, *e.g.* Ben Jonson in his *Underwoods,* Herrick, Dryden, Waller, Prior, but the best epigrammatical writer in English literature was Pope.

**Epilepsy** (Gk. ἐπι, upon ; λῆψις, violent seizure), a nervous disorder, characterised by sudden loss of consciousness and attended by convulsions. The disorder is specially noticeable as affecting individuals of great mental or physical vigour. Rightly or wrongly there are traditions that Hercules, Cæsar, Mohammed, and Napoleon had E. Epileptic fits are characterised by the nature of the convulsion, the alteration in the expression, the condition of the eyes, and subsequent exhaustion of mind

and body. Sometimes the convulsions do not occur, or are so slight as only to be noticeable by experienced observers who are present at the time of the attack. These cases are known as epileptic vertigo (giddiness), minor E., masked E. In these cases the main characteristics are loss of consciousness and volition, with loss of power to think and move. The onset of these cases is usually abrupt ; their duration is short, lasting but a few seconds. Besides E. (*i.e.* major E., with convulsions and loss of consciousness ; minor E., with loss of consciousness), there is also *partial* E., with convulsions but not loss of consciousness. This partial, otherwise known as Jacksonian, E., is caused by a localised defect in the brain ; and when the locality is determined the defect, *e.g.* a tumour, can be operated on. *Aura,* literally a breath, is the feeling the epileptic has, as of a breath of air on some part of the skin, causing a shudder to reach the brain, and when the shudder reaches the brain, then the convulsions and (or) loss of consciousness occur. From its original meaning, an aura is applied to any warning of E. ; the warning may be noticed by the patient, or sometimes only by others, as a change of habits or mental disposition. The dread of E. is due to the possibility that the mildest case may become grave, resulting in maniacal excitement and insanity. Though epileptics may maintain vigour of body, mental and moral integrity, there is always the possibility that the disease may become more serious, if not in the sufferer, then in a descendant. E. may follow any form of nervous defect, or be followed by nervous defects, in children. Such preceding or succeeding defects may be motor (*i.e.* causing paralysis), mental, or moral. Every epileptic and child of an epileptic should be under the best hygienic conditions conducive to health of both mind and body.

**Epileptic Colonies,** tracts of ground set apart for the care and training of epileptics. The idea was first conceived in 1887, and since that date numerous colonies have been formed in various countries. The first distinct attempt to provide for epileptics was inaugurated by a Lutheran pastor, Friedrich von Bodelschwingh, who founded at Bielefeld in Westphalia, Germany, the Bethel Colony, which has grown to be a village inhabited solely by epileptics. Here everything has been provided to meet their special needs. There are schools and industrial teachers, and physicians to study and treat their cases. Outdoor occupations are provided, special diet is arranged for, and there are all sorts of recreations and amusements. The first colony founded in England was at Chalfont in 1893; there are others at Warford, Liverpool, Godalming, Chelford, and Croydon.

**Epilobium,** a genus of Onagraceæ, consisting of numerous species growing wild in colder climates; the British species are commonly known as willow-herbs.

**Epilogue** (ἐπίλογος), the name given by the Gks. to the peroration of a speech, but is now generally applied to the appendix of any literary work, more particularly of a drama. As a literary form it has mostly been employed by English writers; indeed, Ben Jonson made it a particular feature of his dramas, using it either to apologise for the defects of his play or to assert its merits. Later on the E. became very fashionable, and dealt with other subjects besides the preceding play, e.g. with politics, criticisms, etc., and at the time of the Restoration hardly a play was produced on the Eng. stage which did not finish with one. Dryden even wrote a *Defence of the Epilogue.*

**Epimedium,** *see* Barrenwort.

**Epimenides,** a poet and prophet of Crete, was a native of Phæstus, and appears to have spent most of his life in Cnossus. All sorts of stories are told of his life, and he is said to have lived to a very great age. He visited Athens about 590 B.C., at the invitation of its inhabitants, in order to undertake the purification of the city, which had been visited by a plague in consequence of the crime of Cylon.

**Epimetheus** (the man of afterthought) was the brother of Prometheus (the man of forethought). Zeus, in order to punish mortals, bestowed upon him Pandora, who was the cause of all the diseases and sufferings which befell mankind.

**Epinal,** a tn. at the foot of the Vosges Mts., on the Moselle, cap. of the Fr. dept. Vosges. It is an important fort, and is also the centre of a cotton-spinning region, and manufactures cotton, machinery and iron goods. The water power of the Moselle is utilised for the iron works, the manufacture of the coloured pictures of saints and of textiles. Among its buildings are the Church of St. Maurice, with a twelfth-century tower, the museum, and the library, which contains some very valuable manuscripts. Pop. 30,000.

**Epinay, Louise Florence Pétronille Tardieu des Clavelles d'** (1726–83), a Fr. writer, *b.* at Valenciennes. She was acquainted with the Fr. men of letters of her day, including Voltaire and Diderot, and was on an intimate footing with Rousseau, for whom she furnished a cottage in the valley of Montmorency, and afterwards with Grimm. Her publications include *Mes Moments Heureux,* 1752; *Lettres à mon Fils,* 1758; *Conversations d'Emilie,* 1774, which was crowned by the Fr. Academy; and *Mémoires et Correspondance,* published in 1818, her chief work.

**Epiphanes,** the surname of Antiochus IV., who reigned over Syria from 175 to 164 B.C. Twice he seized Jerusalem, and the revolt of the Maccabees was the outcome of his cruel treatment of the conquered Jews.

**Epiphanius, Saint** (*c.* A.D. 315–402), a father of the church, *b.* in Palestine of Jewish parents, and after founding a monastery near Besanducan, his native village, was in 367 appointed to the see of Constantia (formerly Salamis) in Cyprus. Although Jerome called him the 'Five-tongued,' in allusion to his linguistic powers, others account him ignorant, and all agree in finding his *Panarion* (edited at Paris in 1622)—a history of eighty sects and heresies—the work of a bigot too zealous in condemning his opponents to weigh the justice of his ill-considered accusations. A violent controversialist, he condemned the doctrines of Origen in a Cyprian council of 401.

**Epiphany.** This word, in Gk., means an apparition of a divine being. The feast of the E. is a festival held by the Rom. Catholic and Anglican churches on Jan. 6, to commemorate the manifestation of Christ, and it includes three different events. From an early time in the East the feast was associated with the baptism of Christ, the adoration of the Magi, and the miracle of Cana. Many special observances were connected with the day, which under the name of Twelfth Night, in England, closed the Christmas festivities. The date of Easter for the year was formerly on this day solemnly announced to the faithful in the Rom. Catholic Church. The King of England still observes the day of the E. in the Chapel Royal by offerings of gold, frankincense, and myrrh at the altar. In both East and West the E. has always been a festival of the highest rank.

**Epiphyllum,** a genus of Cactaceæ, is indigenous to Brazil, but the showy flowers of the species make them favourite hothouse plants in Britain. There are only four species, and these are generally epiphytic in habit.

**Epiphytes,** plants which grow on others for support only; they do not absorb nourishment from the host as is the case with parasitic plants. A simple example of an E. is moss growing on the trunk of a tree. In forests, especially in the tropics, E. form quite a feature of the vegetation, and rare orchids are often found growing in the débris collected on the top of a tree; by this means they get more light than if they were growing on the ground. E. often have aerial roots which grow downwards, but never reach the ground; they absorb nourishment and moisture from the air.

**Epirus** (from Gk. Ἤπειρος, mainland), a div. of anct. Greece, corresponding to the S. of modern Albania, bounded by Illyria, Macedonia, and Thessaly, and stretching southward along the Ionian Sea to the Ambracian Gulf. The Greeks regarded the inhabitants as semi-barbaric, but frequented the oracle of Dodona. The chief towns were Ambracia (a colony from Corinth) and Phœnice. For a little over two centuries from 450 B.C. E. was ruled over by the Molossians, the most famous of whom was the redoubtable Pyrrhus, who offered a desperate resistance to the Roms. (295 B.C.), Æmilius Paulus victimised the Epirotes with a most terrible policy of repression, when in 168 B.C. they assisted Macedonia in her bid for independence. Henceforward their history is a blank.

**Episcopacy** (from Late Lat. *episcopatus*, the office of a bishop, *episcopus*), the term applied to the system of church organisation where a bishop possesses the chief ecclesiastical authority within a defined district or diocese. In this way it differs from both Presbyterianism and Congregationalism. The former has a government by elders, and in the latter the community of worshippers is autonomous. E. represents a very special conception of the Christian church. In this system, the bishop, in his own person, sums up the collective powers of the church in his diocese, by divinely bestowed authority. Thus, both individually and collectively, the bishops are the essential ties of Catholic unity. In the judgment of many observers, this is observed in the Rom. Catholic Church by the development of the supreme power of the papacy, which was finally confirmed at the Vatican Council (1870). In the modern Rom. Catholic Church, bishops of the Latin rite exercise their sway in defined territories and in subordination to papal supremacy. In differing degrees the same is true of patriarchs of the Oriental rites in communion with Rome. Since the Reformation, the word is more especially connected with those churches which have preserved the episcopal model, while ceasing to be in communion with Rome. The Church of England is by far the most important of these, and, since the Reformation, has been the chief champion of E. against papal, Presbyterian, and Congregational pretensions. Anglican opinion is considerably divided as to the divine origin of E., but a great modification has taken place in the character of the Eng. episcopate with the constitutional changes of the eighteenth and nineteenth centuries. The episcopal office in its essentials has practically disappeared from the Protestant communities of the Continent, though the Lutheran churches of Denmark, Norway, and Sweden still preserve the episcopal system in something of its historical sense. England is the country where the prerogatives and functions of bishops have remained the least impaired. The Reformation being guided by the king's own hands was effected in a very conservative spirit, and although E. was abolished by law under the Commonwealth, the bishops were restored at the Restoration, and the thought and time of the monarchy were closely connected with them. In the Protestant Episcopal Church of the United States, the functions of the bishops are similar to those of English prelates. The bishops of the Methodist Episcopal Church of America derive their orders from Thomas Colne, a presbyter of the Church of England, who was ordained by John Wesley in 1784 as 'superintendent' of the Methodist Society in America. In all the ancient churches, E. is regarded as of divine origin, and the bishops are looked upon as the guardians of the tradition of apostolic orthodoxy. *See* Hatch, *Organisation of the Early Christian Churches*, 1881; Moberly, *Ministerial Priesthood*, 1898; Reville, *Les Origines de l'Episcopat*, 1894; Lightfoot, *Saint Paul's Epistle to the Philippians*.

**Episcopius, Simon** (1583–1643), a Dutch theologian, *b.* in Amsterdam, his real name being Simon Bischop. It was he who gave form and system to the doctrines of Arminius, and who bravely endured a life of persecution rather than stifle his protest against the excessive dogmatism of the fanatic Calvinists of his day.

**Episode,** an incident in the life of an individual or people which is irrelevant to the broad march of events, that is, a deviation or, to use another metaphor, an excrescence. It is a Gk. word (ἐπείσοδος) meaning 'after-entrance,' and, as Aristotle explains in his *Poetics*, was descriptive in the drama of all that happened between the choric songs. From the nature of their later origin, the scenes between the actors were, theoretically at least, subordinate to the performance of the chorus, and a rift in their continuity.

**Epistaxis,** bleeding from the nose. Apart from injury, this is not infrequent, both in boys and girls, just before or about the age of puberty. In older persons, it may indicate the onset of a fever, or febrile condition, as in a common cold. In all cases it indicates that there is more blood in the system than the veins are capable of containing. It is sometimes due to changes in the blood vessels themselves, or to changes in the heart, lungs or other organs when the circulation of the blood is impeded or when the blood is at high tension. *Treatment.*—Nose-bleeding is often salutary, and tends to subside of itself. When frequent or severe it can be checked by the application of water, cold or iced, to the neck or forehead ; a cold key, or other application, is beneficial. Other useful expedients are : closing the bleeding nostril with the fingers ; drawing off the blood from the head to other parts of the body, as by the application of fomentation or mustard to the abdomen or legs. E. is *avoided* by attention to the alimentary canal, or anything that disturbs the circulation, as violent emotion and violent exercises.

**Epistemology,** a branch of philosophy, denoting inquiry into knowledge, into its source, nature, and limitations. The word is derived from the Gk. ἐπιστήμη, understanding or knowledge, and λόγος, account. The problem of knowledge has tentative beginnings in Heraclitus, who distinguishes between sense knowledge and the higher thought, which is open ' only to philosophers.' With Heraclitus, knowledge is due to the response between ' the inner fire which constitutes our soul or rational nature ' and the ' outer which is the reality of the world.' With Empedocles knowledge is not a spatial and material function, and man can know everything because he is himself compounded of everything ; and Democritus went beyond his predecessors in attempting to found his cosmology on a philosophical doctrine of knowledge. He stressed the difference between our ordinary perception, which sees only the unreal images of things, and thought, which reveals their atomic structure ; but his materialism really drives him to a reliance on sense perceptions as the basis of all knowledge. Epicurus adopted this theory, which demands for both perception and thought an objective cause, and is therefore forced to an acceptance of the real existence of divine forms to explain man's belief in them. Coming to modern times, we find that E. is beginning to assume the foremost place in philosophy. Hobbes denied the reality of universals, and emphasised deduction and mathematical laws, but, as his theory of knowledge denies any objective validity to mathematical deduction, it carries us no farther. Locke, inquiring into the origin of knowledge, finds it to be entirely empirical, and that the innate ideas of the reason have no existence ; and, similarly, he denies the existence of innate practical or moral principles ; in sum, the source of all our knowledge of external objects is Sensation (*see also* INNATE IDEAS). The weakness of this theory is that, if it be true, absolute science and religious dogmas are alike incapable of proof. Spinoza's rationalism denies the existence of anything outside of God, and postulates that the human mind has an adequate knowledge of the eternal and infinite essence of God. Man, in Spinoza's philosophy, is a mere part of the world of phenomena, but can escape from its finiteness through salvation— a theory which illogically purports to reconcile reality and appearance while, at the same time, recognising the existence of the world of appearance. Leibniz's theory of knowledge opposes Locke's position that all our knowledge comes from sense experience, his conception of the human mind taking into account the reaction of the mind itself in knowledge, or, in other words, he does not regard the mind as a mere passive recipient of ideas. Berkeley, developing the empiricism of Locke, asserts the non-existence of unthinking matter, a paradox which had a powerful effect on E. and on philosophy generally He postulates the falsity of all abstract ideas and asserts that all possible ideas must be particular concrete facts of consciousness possessing characteristics or images which we can discover and describe. But he also allows that we have knowledge of other reality than that of our ideas, for we ' may be said to have some knowledge or *notion* of our own minds, of spirits and active beings, whereof, in a strict sense, we have no ideas,'—an admission which led him almost to go back on sensations, in his emphasis on the intellectual apparatus of experience as enabling us to rise to truth and to God. Hume supplemented the empiricism of Locke and Berkeley in his analysis of knowledge, which reduces every positive object of knowledge either to an impression or an idea; the former term comprises sensations and emotions, the latter the faint images of these livelier perceptions in thinking and reasoning. In the idealism of Kant, the world of our knowledge is one which derives its explanation from the unity of the self, or of consciousness; and the self is not merely an individual, but is essentially universal, and this knowledge has a rational validity and significance. In other words, we *create* the world, and the world is the product of our own understanding, which otherwise would be a mere blank tablet. Fichte, going further, regards reality as wholly the construct of the Ego, and he asserts that philosophy teaches man to look for everything in knowledge, or in the Ego. Since Hegel, modern philosophy has divided into two schools, the one holding, the other denying that the way of reconciliation between Matter and Spirit is something we can comprehend by rational insight; the latter comprise the Positivists, scientific and theological agnostics and Kantians, the former the Spiritualists, the theists and the idealists of the philosophy of Hegel and Berkeley.

**Epistle** (from Gk. ἐπιστολή, a letter or despatch), in essence a letter, that is, a communication written to an individual at a distance, because actual conversation is for the time being impossible. An arbitrary though very real distinction, however, has been drawn between the two. Thus E. suggests dignity, not to say pomposity, and literary style, and flavours, moreover, of the archaic and Old World, so that no one would think of describing the wonderfully intimate and vivacious letters of Robert Louis Stevenson as Es. As early, at least, as Rom. times it was the fashion to write and also to preserve letters which were likely to interest future generations. Cicero certainly had some thought of posterity as he penned those E. which his faithful freedman Tiró edited after his death. Historically they are the most valuable collection of letters ever made, and naturally suggest themselves to any one who wishes to furnish proof of the inestimable worth of this species of contemporary record at once personal and full of life. Other classical writers of E. were the younger Pliny, Plutarch, and Seneca, whilst in the imperial days the 'literati' amused themselves by composing Es. purporting to be written by great men like Plato and Demosthenes. The N.T. contains the Pauline Es. and the Es. of James and Jude, whilst in the time of the early fathers Cyprian,

Jerome, and Augustine committed their thoughts and purposes to Es. The Horatian *Epistles* are really highly finished essays, but they have inspired a crowd of skilful imitators, among them Boileau, Scarron, and Voltaire in France, and Ben Jonson and Dryden in this country. The *Epistle to Dr. Arbuthnot* exhibits Pope in his noblest mood.

**Epistolæ Obscurorum Virorum** ('Letters of Unknown Men') appeared in 1516, and were followed the next year by a second part, the work of Ulrich von Hutten. In feeling they were intensely Protestant, and thus spurred on the Reformation. As they were full of vehement denunciations of monks and scholastics, it is natural that fear of persecution should have induced the author to conceal his name. He has been variously identified with Grotus Rubianus, Hutten, Erasmus, and Reuchlin.

**Epistyle** (Lat. *epistylium*), in architecture, the E. is the lowest division of the entablature, consisting of the main beam that rests immediately upon the abacus, *i.e.* the upper member of the capital of a column, supporting the architrave.

**Epitaph** (from Gk. ἐπί, upon, and τάφος, a tomb) is properly an inscription engraved on a tomb, though in its wider meaning it embraces verse written in memory of the dead, which was never carved on any monument. Brevity is the mark which distinguishes Es. from elegies. Four or five thousand years ago the Egyptians inscribed upon their sarcophagi the name, lineage, office, and life dates of their deceased. No nation has excelled the Gks. in the tenderness, grace, epigrammatic finish, and twilight sadness of their literary Es. Such Latin invocations as 'Siste Viator' (Stay, traveller!) were naturally suggested by the position of the burial places close beside the public ways. Until a few centuries ago Latin was the language of Es. in this country, the native English being discarded in favour of what Dr. Johnson called 'classical stability.' But this fashion, which offends some visitors to Poet's Corner in the Abbey, is fortunately dying out.

**Epithalamium** (from Gk. ἐπί, at, and θάλαμος, the bridal chamber) was the song invoking all blessings and happiness which boys and girls of ancient Greece used to sing to the bride and bridegroom on their marriage. Sappho, Anacreon, and Pindar wrote epithalamia, which thus found a worthy niche in literature. The finest nuptial hymns that have survived from the classics are Theocritus's eighteenth idyll, and Catullus's *Marriage of Thetis and Peleus.*

Spenser's *Epithalamium* is one of the gems of English verse.

**Epithelioma**, a new growth occurring on the skin, or growing in connection with the skin. It is usually caused by continued irritation, as on the tongue from an irregular tooth, or on the lip from a pipe. It may occur on the skin from continued irritation, as of soot in chimney sweeps, etc. It may commence as an innocent looking pimple and remain as such for months or years. After a time the growth breaks down and forms a sore or ulcer, which may persist for months and years. All spots and sores, especially when subject to continued irritation, should have immediate attention, or they may be fatal. The word cancer is a lay term, signifying a tumour, which has been fatal, or probably will be, and E., if untreated, is frequently fatal.

**Epithelium, or Epithelial Tissue** is widely distributed. Its most important situations are: (1) On the surface of the skin; (2) on mucous membranes; (3) on the inner or free surface of serous membranes; (4) on the inner surface of the heart, blood vessels, and lymphatics. Every epithelial tissue is formed entirely of cells united together with cohesive matter and the mass thus formed closely invests the surface on which it is situated. It contains no blood-vessels, though plasma may diffuse through the minute channels sometimes existing between the cells. Nervous fibrils are usually abundant. The component cells vary in structure and shape, hence the most convenient classification of epithelial cells is according to shape and arrangement, viz.: (1) Simple epithelia, subdivided into (*a*) pavement or scaly, as in such a serous membrane as the peritoneum; (*b*) columnar, *e.g.* lining the mucous membrane of intestines. 'Chalice or goblet' cells are columnar cells distended with mucus; (*c*) spheroidal or glandular, *e.g.* in the liver; (*d*) ciliated, *i.e.* bearing spontaneously-moving filaments on their basal ends, as in nasal membrane. (2) Stratified E. of various types having cells in layers, the deeper usually columnar and the superficial ones flattened as in the E. of the front of the cornea. (3) Transitional E. of several types, but intermediate in character between (1) and (2), *e.g.* lining the ureters.

**Epoch** (from Gk. ἐποχή, a pause) has a special astronomical meaning. It is impossible to determine the position of a planet or other body in its orbit unless its place at a given point of time is known. This given moment is called the 'epoch,' although this word often implies the mean longitude of the body at that particular moment.

**Epode**, an essential part of the chorus in Gk. drama. It was called ἐπῳδός περίοδος and followed the strophe and antistrophe, being sung when the choir had returned to its original place. The E. was also a form of lyric invented by Archilochus and finely handled by Stesichorus. Horace imitated Archilochus's metre in his fifth book of *Odes*, which he accordingly named *Epodes*. In these, iambic trimeters and dimeters alternate.

**Eponym** (from Gk. ἐπώνυμος, derived from ὄνομα, a name), the mythical individual who has given his name to a people sprung from his descendants. Legend says that Pelops begat the Peloponnesians; Dorus, the Dorians; and Italus, the Italians.

**Epping**, a par. and tn. of Essex, England, situated to the N. of Epping Forest, about 16 m. N.E. by N. of London. It has an elevation of 380 ft. above the level of the sea. The forest was once part of the anct. forest of Waltham, and originally covered the whole of Essex county. What remains of it now is preserved by the City of London, and forms one of the largest and most frequented pleasure grounds of the country. Pop. 4197.

**Epsom** (a corruption of Ebbisham, the local manor), a market town, 14¼ m. S.S.W. of London, in Surrey, England. The Royal Medical College on the Downs was founded in 1851 as a school for doctors' sons. There are sculptures of Flaxman and Chantrey in the Gothic church (rebuilt in 1824). In 1618 the springs containing sulphate of magnesia were discovered, and it seemed likely that E. would become a fashionable inland spa. To-day, however, the waters are forgotten, and E. is famous because the Derby and Oaks are run on the racecourse on the Downs near Tattenham Corner. Pop. 18,803.

**Epsomite, or Sulphate of Magnesia**, used as a fertiliser, also in dyeing cotton goods.

**Epsom Salts** were so called because they were first manufactured by evaporating the water of the mineral springs at Epsom. But they occur also in sea water, in the mineral springs of Pullna and Seidlitz, etc., in the Stassfurt mines (as reichardite), and in America are procurable from limestone beds. The chemical formula is $MgSO_4.7H_2O$, and they are therefore described as hepta-hydrated magnesium sulphate. Their needle-like crystals belong to the orthorhombic system. In medicine E.

S. are commonly used as a purgative : the intensely bitter taste can be disguised.

**Epstein, Jacob,** Russo-Polish sculptor, *b.* in New York, 1880. Educated at the School of Art Students' League, New York. Later, he completed his training at the Ecole des Beaux Arts, Paris. Migrated to London in 1904. Has become the most criticised sculptor of the present day. One of his first works in England was the series of figures on the frieze of the British Medical Association's building in the Strand, London. Still more symbolical, and consequently still more provocative, are his ' Rima ' in Hyde Park, his Oscar

*[Underground-Rly. Co.*
' NIGHT ' BY JACOB EPSTEIN

Wilde Memorial in Paris, and his figures of ' Night ' and ' Day ' on the London Underground Railway premises in Broadway, Westminster. Other famous works are his ' Two Doves ' and ' Marble Venus,' executed in 1913 and 1914 respectively. The figures are striking in their naturalistic treatment, and almost always suggest the embryonic. The cry of ' immoral ' has frequently been raised, notably over the Strand figures and the Wilde memorial in Père-Lachaise. This latter is the figure of a nude man whose sphinx-like face twists in a smile of mingled despair and tragic bitterness. In some beholders it evokes horror and resentment, in others wonder at the strength of realistic suggestion. Probably his loftiest contribution to art is the noble and dignified ' Maternity ' in the Tate Gallery. He

has also executed a large number of bronzes, especially portraits. One of his most recent bronzes was the ' Madonna and Child,' in which there is revealed ' a great emotional and formal suavity ' in the movement of the arms of the two figures, while the general impression of the faces and figures visualised in the group is that of 'intense vexation of soul coupled with a spiritual recognition of the obstacles to be encountered in reaching happiness.' E. has also produced a number of drawings, the most characteristic of which are the neurotic ' The Sisters,' and the ' Mother and Son ' series. E.'s most recent work of importance is his ' Genesis ' (1931), a bold conception which produced the usual ' storm ' of criticism as well as imitations by other sculptors.

**Epworth,** a market tn. and the birthplace of John Wesley (*b.* 1703), 10 m. N.N.W. of Gainsborough in Lincolnshire, England. Pop. 2000.

**Equation** may be broadly defined as the statement in mathematical symbols of the equality existing between any two magnitudes. Thus $x = y$ is a statement of the fact that the magnitude represented by $x$ is equal to that represented by $y$.

*Mathematical equations.* — These consist solely of the type above defined. Simple equations are of the type $2x + 3x + 5x = 100$, where only one symbol, $x$, is employed. This symbol is called the unknown : when the value of this symbol is obtained it is termed the *solution of the equation.* The two sides of the equation are distinguished by the terms right-hand and left-hand side. The general method of solution of a simple equation is to transpose all the terms containing the unknown $x$ on to the left-hand side and the numerical quantities on to the right-hand side. This may be done by using the property of an equation that if any term is taken from one side to the other its sign must be changed. All the $x$'s, then, are added together, and the right hand divided by the coefficient of the $x$, whence the value of $x$ is obtained. It is important to remember that the symbol $x$ stands for a *numerical quantity.* These equations are divided into two classes, *identical* and *conditional.* The equation $x + 2 + 4 = x + 6$ is one which is true for *all* values of $x$, and is called an identical equation or identity. The equation $4x = 12$ is true only for the value $x = 3$, and hence is termed a conditional equation. When an equation contains two or more unknowns, *e.g.* $2x + 3y + 4z = 6$, it is called *indeterminate.* To get a definite solution of this equation two other relations be-

**Equation** 531 **Equation**

tween $xyz$ must be given. The number of equations required to get a definite solution of any equation containing two or more unknowns is the same as the number of unknowns. Such a group of equations are called *simultaneous equations*. All the equations cited above are called equations of the *first degree*. The *degree* of an equation is determined from the highest power of the unknown occurring in the equation. Thus $x^2 - 6 = 9$ is one of the second degree, $x^3 + 3x + 3 = 0$ is one of the third degree, and so on. An equation of the second degree is sometimes called a quadratic, one of the third degree a cubic, and one of the fourth degree a biquadratic. The solution of equations of higher degree than the quadratic equations opens up the large subject of the *Theory of Equations*. This subject embraces all questions connected with the solution of every type of equation. The cubic was first solved in 1505 by Scipio Ferreo, although the general method of solution is known as Cardan's method. This solution is, however, not due to Cardan, but was obtained by him from Tartaglia. The solution of the biquadratic was first obtained by Ferrari, who was a pupil of Cardan. Abel has shown, to the satisfaction of mathematicians, that it is impossible to obtain a general solution of equations higher than those of the fourth degree. It may be pointed out that by means of the relations between the solutions or roots of the equation and the coefficients of the terms of the equation, equations of a higher order may be obtained provided some other relations are also known, *e.g.* a relation between the roots themselves. But this obviously is a particular type of equation, and is not embraced by Abel's demonstration. Approximate values of the roots of equations in which the coefficients are numerical may be found by employing *Horner's method of approximation* to any degree of accuracy. For fuller discussion *see* Chrystal's *Algebra*, and Burnside and Panton's *Theory of Equations*.

*Binomial equation* is an algebraical equation consisting of only two terms. Its most general form is $a_1 x^p \pm a_2 x^r = 0$. This may be reduced to the form $x^r \pm a = 0$, where $p - q = r$ and $\dfrac{a_2}{a_1} = a$. The solution of this would be $x = {}^r\!/\!\pm a$, showing that $x^r + a = 0$ has imaginary roots and $x^r - a$ has real roots.

*Equation to a curve.*—A curve may be viewed as the path traced out by a point moving under a given condition. If the co-ordinate (*q.v.*) (*see also* GRAPHS) of any point on the curve be taken, this condition can be expressed by a relation between the $x$ co-ordinate and the $y$ co-ordinate; this relation is termed the equation to the curve, *e.g.* $x^2 + y^2 = a^2$ is the equation for a circle.

*Astronomical equations.*—All the motions of the astronomical bodies can be reduced approximately to a simple law. In order to get results as accurate as possible, certain corrections have to be applied to the results obtained from the simple law. These corrections are termed astronomical equations. Thus the moon may be considered theoretically to move around the earth according to the law of gravitation, but observation shows deviations from the results of such a movement. The sun affects the motion, as also do the planets, acting directly on the moon itself and indirectly on the earth. These are the simpler effects on the motion of the moon, but those alone do not account for the whole of the deviations obtained by observation. For each of these causes an equation has to be applied to the results obtained by the simple law of gravitation to obtain as accurate a result as possible of the motion of the moon.

*Equation of time.*—Through causes explained in the article on day (*q.v.*), the length of the solar day varies. To get a fixed measure of time astronomers conceive of an imaginary sun which moves uniformly in the celestial equator, completing its circuit in the same time as the real sun. The time given by this means is known as *mean solar time*, and *mean noon* is that time when the imaginary sun is on the meridian, the time when the real sun is on the meridian being known as *apparent noon*. Clocks keep *mean* and sun-dials *apparent* time, and the difference between these is known as the equation of time. On four occasions in the year, about April 15, June 15, Sept. 1, and Dec. 24, these coincide, and then, of course, the equation of time is zero.

**Equation, Chemical.** A C. E. represents both qualitatively and quantitatively the substances which react together and those which are produced. Every reaction must obey the law of the conservation of mass; and, therefore, the masses of each element shown on the left-hand side of the equation must be equal to those shown on the right-hand side. The equation $CaCO_3 + 2HCl = CaCl_2 + H_2O + CO_2$ expresses the fact that 100 grams of calcium carbonate ($CaCO_3$) react with 73 grams of hydrochloric acid (HCl), producing 111 grams of calcium chloride ($CaCl_2$) and 44 grams of carbon dioxide ($CO_2$) (atomic weights $Ca = 40$, $C = 12$

O = 16, H = 1, Cl = 35·5). The equation further shows the relative volumes of the reacting gases and of the products. Since a gram molecule of any gas (*e.g.* HCl = 1 + 35·5 = 36·5 grams) occupies 22·4 litres under standard conditions of temperature and pressure, the equation shows that 44·8 litres of hydrochloric acid gas would produce, from sufficient calcium carbonate, 22·4 litres of carbon dioxide. In these respects a C. E. is very useful, but it has certain defects. As ordinarily written it does not show the physical states of the substances, whether solids, liquids, or gases; it does not deal adequately with the many cases of balanced action, nor show the thermal changes which accompany reactions, though many of these points can be indicated by the use of additional symbols or figures.

**Equator** (from Late Lat. *œquator,* from *œquare,* to equalise), an imaginary great circle drawn on the earth's surface in a plane at right angles to its axis, and equidistant from either pole. It is the dividing line between the N. and S. hemispheres. This E. is often called 'terrestrial' or 'geographical' to distinguish it from the 'celestial equator.' *See* EQUINOCTIAL.

**Equatorial Current,** *see* ATLANTIC OCEAN.

**Equerry,** in royal households, an officer in the department of the master of the horse, who accompanies the king or prince when he goes riding in state. The 'gentleman of the equerry' was originally in charge of the royal stables, the word E. being the Fr. *écurie,* stable.

**Equidae.** The horse family; in zoology a family of solidungulate perissodactyl (hoofed animals). Middle digit and hoof enlarged, and

PALÆOTHERIUM MAGNUM

This primitive ungulate of the Upper Eocene is regarded as being ancestral to the Horse family

alone support the body; lateral more or less reduced in size and functionless. The first and fifth digits and corresponding metapodials, in living genera, are wanting; also the second and fourth, but the metapodials are present, though they are mere splint bones. The shaft of the ulnea is atrophied, its extreme being consolidated with the radius; fibularis rudimentary and ankylosed with the tibia. Skull very elongated; lower jaw deep behind, and bony orbit of the eye is complete. Many fossil genera through the tertiary, as *e.g. Hipparion, Merychippus, Protohippus,* etc.

**Equilibrium,** in mechanics, is the state of rest of a body under the action of two more forces. The E. may be *neutral, stable,* or *unstable.*

*Neutral equilibrium.*—If a body or a material system is balanced by the forces which act upon it in any position in which it may be placed, its E. is *neutral.* This is the case with a sphere or a circular cylinder of uniform material placed on a horizontal plane. Any body whose centre of gravity is at the fixed point of support, or is always at the same height above the point of support, is in neutral E.

*Stable equilibrium.*—But if when the body is displaced very little in any direction from its E. position and left to itself it commences and continues vibrating without ever experiencing more than very small deviation from the position of E., the E. is said to be *stable.* This is the case with a pendulum, or with a sphere loaded in its lowest part.

*Unstable equilibrium.*—If, on the other hand, the system can be displaced in any way from a position of E., so that when left to itself it will not vibrate within very small limits about the position of E., but will move farther and farther away from it, the E. is said to be *unstable.* Thus an egg or a billiard cue standing on end presents a case of unstable E. In many cases the E. varies with the direction of displacement; but if it is unstable for any possible displacement, it is practically unstable on the whole. Thus a coin standing on its edge is in neutral E. for displacements in its plane, but is in unstable E. for those perpendicular to its plane. It is, therefore, practically in unstable E.

The *conditions* required for E. vary according to the number of forces and according as the forces are acting in the same plane or not. Thus *two co-planar forces* can only balance when they are equal in magnitude and directly opposed to each other. *Three co-planar forces* acting at a point will be in E. if they can be represented in magnitude and direction by the three sides of a triangle taken in order.

In the figure the forces of 20 lb. wt., 30 lb. wt., and 13·75 lb. wt. will balance, for they can be represented by the sides of the triangle EFG, EF being 3 in. long, FG being 1·375 in. long, and GE 2 in. long. *Any number of co-planar forces* acting at a point will be in E. if they can be represented in magnitude and direction by the sides of a closed polygon taken in order. If the forces lie in one plane, but do not meet in a point, the conditions for E. are : (1) The sum of all the resolved parts of all the forces in any two directions at right angles must be separately zero ; (2) the sum

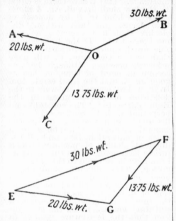

of the moments of all the forces (or of their components) about any point must be zero. The condition (1) must be satisfied if there is to be no translation ; and the condition (2) must be satisfied if there is to be no rotation. If the forces do not act in one plane, we may make use of the Principle of the Virtual Work. If the points of application of the forces receive any very small displacements consistent with the mechanical connections, the total work done will be zero, when the forces are in E.

**Equimultiples** (from Lat. *æquus*, equal, and *multiplex*, manifold), the products obtained by multiplying quantities by the same quantity. Thus 15 and 85 are E. of 3 and 17, and $a^2bc^2$ and $bc^2$ of $a c^2$ and $c$.

**Equinoctial**, another name for the 'celestial equator,' which is the imaginary great circle traced by the points of intersection of the plane of the terrestrial equator and the celestial sphere. The 'equinoctial points' are the points of intersection of the ecliptic and terrestrial equator, this intersection indicating that the sun is

exactly on the equator. Astronomical observers therefore choose this juncture as a convenient season to secure a uniform reckoning of time. *See* EQUINOXES.

**Equinoctial Gales,** a popular superstition to which science lends no support. Winds and storms are not more prevalent at the equinoxes than at other seasons.

**Equinoxes** (from Lat. *æquus*, equal, and *nox*, night) are the two days in the year, March 21 and Sept. 22, when the days are equal to the nights all over the world. Owing to the inclination of the axis, on which the earth rotates, as it journeys round the sun, the portion of its surface which is lightened by the sun's rays, the circle of illumination that is, varies, but at the E. the sun apparently describes the equatorial circle and exactly half of each parallel is illuminated. At the vernal E. (in March) the sun passes from S. to N., which results in the days lengthening in the N. hemisphere, and from N. to S. in the autumnal, when the days shorten.

**Equisetum,** a genus of plants, popularly known as horsetails, belonging to the order Equisetaceæ. Of the twenty species of the genus, about half are British. In general habit they all bear a strong family likeness to each other, all having stiff, upright, jointed stems, with whorls of little-developed leaves, those of each whorl being united to form a sheath around the stem. They have a creeping, much-branched rootstock which penetrates the ground to a great depth. The fructification is in the form of cones, each of which is borne at the end of an upright stem or branch. The commonest wild species is E. *arvense*. The rough stems of some species are used in several occupations for the purpose of giving certain woods a high polish ; while the stems of other species are used for polishing metals.

**Equitable Charge.** An E. C. or mortgage arises either : (1) From the mortgage of an equitable as distinct from a legal interest, *e.g.* where a *cestui que* trust (*i.e.* beneficiary of an estate in real or personal property held by trustees) charges his property as security for a loan ; or (2) by reason of the form of mortgage being recognised by equity and not at common law. A common law mortgage implies the conveyance by deed of the mortgagor's legal interest to the mortgagee ; equity allows the creation of a charge (a) by mere deposit of title deeds, or (b) by an unsealed written agreement to deposit without actual deposit of deeds. Generally speaking, the incidents in

both legal mortgages and E. Cs. are
the same, but where property has
been mortgaged by deed, whether
before or after the creation of an
E. C. on the *same* property, the legal
has priority to the equitable mortgagee.

**Equitable Estates,** *see* ESTATE.

**Equites** (from Lat. *equus*, horse),
horsemen or knights of anct. Rome.
At first they formed part of the
army. Servius Tullius increased the
number of 'centuriæ' (hundreds),
into which they were divided, from
six to eighteen. The first six were
purely patrician; the latter twelve,
plebeian. But beside the 'equites
equo publico,' who received money
for their mount from the state
treasury, there were 'equites equo
privato,' volunteers providing their
own horse. After the second Punic
War the knights exerted a political
influence second only in importance
to that of the senate. They farmed
the provincial taxes and constituted
the capitalist class. The democrat,
Gaius Gracchus, used them as a foil
to the aristocracy, a policy imitated
without intermission up to imperial
times, and guaranteed their support
by granting them control of the jury
courts, as well as the revenues of Asia.
Under Augustus many civil posts of
honour, such as the prefecture of the
corn supply, were open to them after
military service. Once more, however,
they became primarily soldiers instead of financiers.

**Equity.** In England E. is a science
which in a general sense corresponds
to natural justice. But as administered in the courts it has a
narrower meaning as connoting
merely that portion of natural justice
which, crystallised into technical
rules, and operating according to
clear-cut principles, has found a
definite place in the general legal
system. The fundamental notions of
Eng. E. are to be deduced from a
series of leading maxims upon which
the courts act in the administration
of their equitable jurisdiction. These
maxims are as follows : (1) E. follows
the law (*see* below). (2) E. will not
suffer a wrong to be without a remedy
by reason of a merely technical defect. (3) He who seeks E. must do E.
(4) E. looks to intention rather than
form. (5) E. acts *in personam, i.e.*
equitable rights are primarily based
on the assumption that a court of E.
does not, like a common law court,
issue judgments to be executed by
its own officers, if necessary by force,
but grants decrees (*q.v.*) which the
parties themselves are to execute on
pain in default of so doing of being
treated as guilty of contempt of
court. (6) E. imputes an intention to

fulfil an obligation. (7) E. looks on
that as done which ought to have
been done (*see* CHARITABLE USES).
(8) Delay defeats E., *i.e.* a suitor in
E. must not sleep on his rights when
he knows what they are. (9) ' He who
comes into E. must come with clean
hands.' (10) Equality is E. (11)
Where there are equal Es. (equitable
rights) the first in time shall prevail,
*e.g.* a purchaser for value of the E.
of redemption of a house takes subject to the mortgagee's interest, even
though he thought there was no
mortgage. (12) Where there is equal
E. the law shall prevail, *e.g.* A mortgages his land to B by deposit of
title deeds, and then without disclosing that fact executes a legal
mortgage to C. If the proceeds on
sale are insufficient to satisfy more
than one of the loans, C. will have
priority, because, although he was
second in point of time, he has as
good an E. and the legal estate too.
In its widest sense, E. answers to the
definition of justice given in the
Rom. Pandects : ' The constant and
perpetual wish to render every one
his due.' In any system of law the
general meaning corresponds to a
sense of natural justice, and all the
different shades of meaning which
jurists have assigned to this variable
term may be referred to that primary
notion. These different shades have
been enumerated by Austin as
follows : (1) A species of interpretation of statute law, as denoting that
the judges will generally construe a
statutory enactment on the assumption that the legislature desired to
be both uniform and consistent. (2)
Judicial impartiality. (3) The mode
of formation of E. procedure or the
matter whence the judges derive
their equitable principles, whether
natural law, international law, some
standard of ethics, or a sense of
justice, all susceptible of summarisa-
tion in the maxim *summum jus
summa injuria* (Cicero, ' Extreme
justice is often extreme injustice ').
(4) Good principles of judicial legislation. (5) The cheerful performance of
duties not legally enforceable. (6)
Morality, positive or otherwise. (7)
That portion of our law which is administered by a court of E. ; and (8)
rights in the nature of a set-off or
counterclaim. But however variable
the meaning of E. may be, in England
it now connotes a body of technical
principles which have been evolved
in the course of centuries by successive chancellors and other E. judges
(*see* CHANCELLOR). To follow out the
history of the office of Lord High
Chancellor and the Court of Chancery
(*q.v.*) in England is practically to
trace the growth and maturity of

Eng. E. It is hardly possible to define E. as now administered in England, or to make it intelligible otherwise than by a minute enumeration of the matters cognisable in the courts in which it is administered in its more concrete and modified sense. (*See* as to matters assigned to the Chancery Division, under CHANCERY, COURT OF). E. in England is the very antithesis of common law (*q.v.*). The remedies for the redress of civil wrongs and the enforcement of civil rights were formerly always distinguished by division into two classes, those administered in courts of law, and those administered in courts of E. Accordingly, rights may be distinguished into legal and equitable. Courts of common law formerly proceeded by certain highly technical forms of action, *e.g.* trespass (*q.v.*), trover (*q.v.*), detinue (*q.v.*), assumpsit (*q.v.*), and an error in the form of action was fatal; form was more than substance. But there were and must now always be many cases in which a simple judgment for either party will not do entire justice. The ordinary law courts had no machinery for such a purpose, but courts of E. adjudicated by decrees, so framed as to meet all the exigencies of the case, which varied, or qualified, the legal remedy so as to suit it to mutual and adverse claims and the substantial rights of all the parties. A court of E., therefore, always had jurisdiction in cases where a plain, adequate and complete remedy could not be had in the common law courts: and unless the common law remedy was such as to reach the whole mischief and secure the whole right of the party present or future, the courts of E. interposed and gave relief. Before the Judicature Act, 1873, the jurisdiction of a court of E. was sometimes concurrent with that of courts of common law; sometimes auxiliary to it; and sometimes exclusive. The concurrent jurisdiction was exercised in cases where the rights were purely of a legal nature, but where other and more efficient aid was required than a court of common law could vouchsafe. The most common exercise of the concurrent jurisdiction was in cases of account, accident, dower, fraud, mistake, rectification, misrepresentation, partnership, and partition. A court of E. exercised its auxiliary jurisdiction in cases where the courts of law had no like authority. By this assistance it removed legal impediments to the fair decision of a question in issue at law, as by compelling a party to disclose documents which he makes part of his own case, by compelling him to admit material facts on oath where a court of

law was unable to enforce disclosure. The exclusive jurisdiction was exercised mainly in cases involving merely equitable rights, or rights not recognised at common law. Most cases of trust and confidence fell under this head. In particular this jurisdiction was exercised in granting injunction to prevent waste or irreparable injury; in appointing receivers of property which was in danger of being misapplied; in compelling the surrender of securities improperly obtained; in enforcing specific performance of contracts (*i.e.* literal compliance as opposed to damages for breach); and in supplying the defective execution of instruments by correcting them according to the proved intention of the parties. (For the manner in which a suit in the E. side of the old Court of Chancery was commenced, *see* under CHANCELLOR, LORD HIGH, and CHANCERY, COURT OF.) The old method of petitioning by Bill and Answer has fallen into disuse, and the proceedings in the Chancery Division are now, like those of the common law courts, simplified as far as compatible with the circumstances of each particular case.

Since the passing of the Judicature Act, 1873, the distinction between law and E. has lost some of its importance, but the effect of that Act may easily be misunderstood if a literal fusion of the principles of law and E. be assumed. The practical effect of the Judicature Act was this: (1) It assimilated to a great extent the procedure of the Chancery Division and the King's Bench Division. (2) It reconstructed the Chancery Court into a Chancery Division of the High Court of Justice. (3) It fused the rules of law and E. to the extent that they are both now concurrently administered by all courts of law, whether nominally belonging to the King's Bench Division or the Chancery Division. (4) It provided a general principle that where there is any conflict or variance between E. and common law, E. should prevail; and (5) it allocated to the Chancery Division most of the subject-matter formerly peculiar to the old Court of Chancery (*q.v.*). In short, the fusion was a fusion merely of administration, the principles of E. being in no way affected; and even this fusion of administration is only partial when it is recollected that so large a number of causes and matters appropriate to the old Court of Chancery are still automatically assigned for hearing to the Chancery Division. 'The main object,' says Lord Watson in Ind Coope & Co. *v.* Emmerson, 1887, 12 Appeal Cases, at p. 308, 'of the Judicature Act was to enable the parties to a suit to obtain in that suit, and without the necessity of resorting to another court. all remedies to which they are entitled in respect of any legal or equitable claim or defence properly advanced by them so as to avoid a multiplicity of legal proceedings.'

*Eng. and Rom. equity contrasted.*— In England E. in its origin and development was essentially the same as Rom. E., or the system of law administered by the prætors. Both bodies of principles claimed to override the existing and stricter civil law by virtue of a supposed intrinsic superiority. There were differences, however, in material sources. In Rome the equitable jurisdiction of the prætors was referred to a specific source in the *jus gentium*, or law of nations, which the Romans regarded as nothing less than an emanation from the law of nature, a divine law harking back to an ideal past and owing its catholicity to the assumed equality of all men. In England the material source was never avowed. In point of fact the process was a surreptitious one. E. varied, according to Selden's celebrated aphorism, ' with the length of the Chancellor's foot.' Historically it would seem that the Chancellor administered his E. with the tacit approbation of the king, such moral justification as it might have had being the assumption that the defendant in a harsh case was bound ' to purge his conscience ' and do right where the common law could not compel him to do so. But phrase it as we may, both systems owed their efficacy to their expediency, their impartiality, and a natural sense of justice. Moreover, both systems had their authorisation in the royal or imperial prerogative (whether confessedly so in England or not), for in no system of jurisprudence can a judge, theoretically at least, claim to give decisions contrary to the statute law or civil law. Hence the paradox *æquitas seqitur legem* (E. follows the law). Rom. E. did, no doubt, in a far greater degree, meet social exigencies, and the fiction implied in the above maxim was far more transparent. There were differences in form, source and manner of enunciation. Eng. E. was, and in practice now is, largely administered by an exceptional civil tribunal—the Chancery Division. Prætorian E. and the *Jus Civile* were administered by one and the same tribunal. Again, the E. of the Roms was statute law, whereas chancery law is judiciary for the most part; and finally the subjects with which each system is concerned differ widely, *e.g.* the urban

prætor altered root and branch the whole law of intestate succession; but no Eng. chancellor would have ventured on such a revolution. The whole difference between the two systems, however, is unessential and merely historical if we regard E. objectively as a distinct system of law: it is a real difference, on the other hand, if we view it as merely the process of tempering all rigid law by principles of inherently superior fairness.

**Equivalents, Chemical,** *see* ATOMIC HEAT.

**Equuleus,** a constellation, near Aquarius, in the N. hemisphere. The name means ' colt,' and Ptolemy called it Ἵππου προτομης. It contains a remarkable double star (δ Equulei). After Capella it is the most rapid binary known, its period of revolution being 5·7 years. *Equuleus Pictoris* (Painter's Easel) was a new constellation introduced by Nicolas de Lacaille, 1763. It is near Canopus in the S. hemisphere, and is usually called Pictor.

**Era,** *see* CHRONOLOGY.

**Era, The,** a weekly paper which first appeared in 1838. It was intended as an organ of licensed victuallers, and being supplementary to the *Morning Advertiser*, gave considerable attention to sporting intelligence; but to-day it is devoted almost exclusively to theatrical news.

**Erard, Sebastian** (1752–1831), a Fr. maker of musical instruments, constructed his first piano in Paris in 1780. During the Revolution he was in London, and again from 1808–12. He invented the harp with double pedals and the grand piano with double escapement. His instruments won high commendation from the foremost musicians of the day.

**Erasistratus** (*b. c.* 300 B.C.), a famous physician and anatomist, *b.* at Iulis in the island of Ceos. He was the son of Cleombrotus and Cretoxene, and became a pupil of both Metrodorus and Theophrastus. About 294 B.C. he was physician at the court of Nicator, King of Syria, but he later settled in Samos and founded a school of medicine. E. discovered the difference between sensory and motor nerves, and believed the heart to be the origin of veins and arteries. His works only remain in fragments. Consult Hieronymus, *Erasistrati et Erasistrateorum Historia*, Jena, 1790; and Fuchs, ' De Erasistrato Capita Selecta ' in *Hermes*, vol. xxix., Berlin, 1897.

**Erasmus, Desiderius** (1466–1536), a Dutch scholar and theologian, the illegitimate son of Rogerius Gerardus. He styled himself ' Roterodamus,' a native of Rotterdam, though a contemporary document states that he was *b.* in his father's native town of Gouda. He was educated at St. Lebuin's church, Deventer (1475–84), and was a chorister at Utrecht. On the death of his father in 1484, he went to a school at Hertogenbosch, and later joined a religious order in the house of St. Gregory's at Steyn, being ordained a priest in 1492. Shortly afterwards he became secretary to Henry of Bergen, Bishop of Cambrai, and in 1495 entered the college of Montaigu, in the University of Paris, where he won great fame as a scholar. He eked out his living by taking pupils, one of whom, William Blount, Lord Mountjoy, persuaded him to visit England in 1498. At Oxford he discussed theology with John Colet and began his friendship with Linacre, Thomas More, and others, but returned to Paris to his Gk. studies in 1500. In this year he brought out his *Collectanea Adagiorum*, which contained extracts from the Classics and from the Fathers. E. travelled about the Continent considerably, teaching privately and studying wherever he went. In 1506 he went to Italy as the tutor of the two sons of Baptista Boerio, Henry VII.'s physician. There he made new friendships with such men as Aldus Manutius, the Venetian printer, who published for him a new and enlarged edition of his Adagia, entitled *Chiliades Adagiorum*. In Venice, Alexander Stewart, the natural son of James IV. of Scotland, at whose side he fell at Flodden, became his pupil and friend, and in Rome he was honoured by all the members of the papal circle. In 1509 he again came to London and stayed with his friend More. At this time he wrote his brilliant satire called *Encomium Moriæ*, in which kings, popes, bishops, and the like, all came under his lash. He now visited Cambridge, where he finished his work on the Gk. N.T., and on Seneca and St. Jerome, and where he taught Gk. and lectured on divinity. E. had now a large circle of disciples, both on the Continent and in England, who were proud to look up to him as their master and teacher. In 1511 he published *De Duplici Copia Verborum et Rerum*, a text-book of rhetoric, and his N.T. appeared in 1516. From 1516 to 1521 he lived chiefly at Louvain, near the court, though he not infrequently journeyed to Brussels or to Basel, and in 1517 went for the last time to England. At Louvain he took an active interest in the founding of Hieronymus Busleiden's Collegium Trilingue, and there, too, he prepared his edition of the *Christian Fathers*. About this

time he formed a friendship with Johann Froben, a publisher of Basel, and in 1521 E. settled permanently in that town to become Froben's general literary adviser. Between 1516 and 1536 Froben's press issued a remarkable series of the Fathers, including Jerome (1516), Hilarius (1523), Ambrose (1527), Augustine (1528), and Origen (1536), which was largely the work of E., though he had many coadjutors. Froben died in 1527, and two years later E. moved to Freiburg to avoid the religious dissensions that were

DESIDERIUS ERASMUS

disturbing Basel, but he returned to the latter town in 1535, where he *d.* of dysentery in the following year. E. never left the Church of Rome, though he refused again and again to enlist in its service against the Reformers. The Lutherans he ridiculed in his *Diatribe de Libro Arbitrio*, 1526, and Ulrich von Hutten in his *Spongia*, 1523, but the papists suffered equally in his *Colloquia*, published between 1516 and 1536. He was accused of indifference and of wavering, but it was only natural that such a hard and sure hitter should make enemies. E. was a great scholar, and had vast literary acquirements. His letters, numbering about 3000, are of particular interest, and are published by the Oxford University Press (vol. i. 1906, vol. ii. 1910). The complete edition of his works was published by the Froben Press in 9 vols. (Basel, 1540), and by Le Clerc in 11 vols. (Leyden, 1703–6). His autobiography, *Com-*

*pendium Vitæ*, was written in 1524, and is included in the Basel edition. For his life, consult S. Knight, 1726; J. Jortin (2 vols.), 1758–60; R. B. Drummond (2 vols.), 1873; F. Seebohm, in *Oxford Reformers* (3rd ed.), 1887; Froude, 1894; and Emerton, 1899. His early letters (to 1517) have been translated by F. M. Nichols (2 vols.), 1901–4.

**Erastus, Thomas** (1524–83), a Ger.-Swiss theologian, whose surname was Liebler, Lieber, or Liiber, *b.* at Baden, Switzerland, of a poor family. He studied theology at Basel (1540), and later philosophy and medicine at Padua. In 1558 he became Professor of Medicine at Heidelberg and private physician to the Elector Palatine, Otto Heinrich. He was elected privy councillor and a member of the Church Consistory (1559), and occupied the chair of ethics at Basel in the last year of his life. E. was chiefly renowned as a theologian. At the conferences of Heidelberg (1560) and Maulbronn (1564) he upheld the Zwinglian doctrine of the Sacrament of the Lord's Supper, and, through the influence of the Calvinists, he was excommunicated on a charge of Socinianism. His most important work, written in 1568, published posthumously in 1589, was entitled *Explicato gravissimæ quæstionis utrum excommunicatio, quatenus religionem intelligentes et amplexantes, a sacramentorum usu, propter admissum facinus arcet, mandato nitatur divino, an excogitata sit at hominibus*, and upheld the right of the state to punish ecclesiastical offenders. Hence, ' Erastianism ' is used to denote the doctrine of the supremacy of the state in ecclesiastical matters, though this was supported by Grotius rather than by E. E. also published treatises on the theories of Paracelsus and on astrology, alchemy, medicine, etc.

**Erasure,** or **Razure** (Lat. *radere*, to scrape or shave), the alteration or interlineation of a deed, will, or other formal writing. According to British law, an E. is presumed to have been made at or before execution in the case of a deed or other document. In the case of a will, however, the writing stands without the alteration, unless the witnesses have initialled such alteration and have made a note of it at the end of the will. An alteration made in a deed by a stranger without consent of the parties does not prevent its contents from having effect; if altered by a defendant, it may be given in evidence by him, but if by a plaintiff, he cannot enforce any benefit that may thereby accrue to himself. In Scotland, the law presumes that the E. was made after execution. If it is

desired to make any alteration, addition, or deletion in a deed, such E. must be ' noticed in the body of writ ' and must be ' subscribed by the attesting witnesses.'

**Eratosthenes** (*c.* 276–*c.* 194 B.C.), a Gk. mathematician and scientific writer, *b.* at Cyrene. He was a pupil of Callimachus at Alexandria, and subsequently studied philosophy with Ariston and Arcesilaus at Athens. About 235 B.C. he returned to Alexandria and succeeded Callimachus as chief librarian. E. in his Χρονογραφία invented a scientific chronology, fixing the conquest of Troy as the basis of his calculations. He also invented a ' sieve ' (κόσκινον) by means of which prime numbers might be discovered. He measured the earth, and calculated that its circumference measured 252,000 stadia. His book on mathematics is lost, but fragments remain of his astronomical poems, *Hermes* and *Erigone*.

**Erbium** (symbol Er, atomic weight 168, atomic number 68), a metallic element of the rare earths. The rare earth metals are present in the minerals gadolinite, samarskite, euxenite, fergusonite, and cerite. It forms rose-coloured salts and a rose-coloured oxide, the former of which possess a characteristic absorption spectrum.

**Ercildoune, Thomas of** (*fl. c.* 1220–*c.* 97), a Scottish poet and prophet, also called Thomas the Rhymer, to whom the surname Learmont has sometimes been given. From two existing charters of the thirteenth century, it appears he had lands at Ercildoune (now Earlston) in Berwickshire, which were given by his son to the foundation of the Holy Trinity at Soltra in 1294. He had a reputation almost equal to Merlin's as a prophet; and in the *Scotichronicon* he foretells the death of Alexander, and Wyntoun asserts that he prophesied the result of the battle of Kilblane. He also occurs in the works of Barbour, Harry the Minstrel, and Hector Boece. The old romance connected with the name of T. of E. was first attributed to him by Robert Mannyng de Brunne, but modern scholars have shown that its dialect is southern in form and that the text probably dates from the early fourteenth century. It has been suggested that the extant version may be based on one actually written by Thomas, who borrowed freely from Fr. sources. Consult Sir J. A. H. Murray's edition, published by the Early Eng. Text Society, of *The Romance and Prophecies*, 1875; A. Brandl's *Thomas of Ercildoune* (Berlin), 1880; Lumby's *Early Scottish Prophecies* (E.E.T.S.), 1870; *The Whole Prophecie of Scot-*

land, 1603 (reprint by the Bannatyne Club, 1833).

**Ercildoune,** see EARLSTON.

**Ercilla y Tuñiga, Alonso de** (1533–95), a Spanish soldier and poet, b. at Madrid. He was attached to the train of Philip II., with whom he came to England in 1554. Soon afterwards he joined a small company of adventurers who sailed for Chile to crush the revolted Araucanians. Having suffered imprisonment at the hands of his comrades, he was released and returned to Spain in 1562. His fame rests on his epic poem, *La Araucana,* which has been highly praised by Cervantes and Voltaire.

**Erckmann - Chatrian,** the literary signature of two famous Fr. writers who collaborated in their work. Emile Erckmann (1822–99) was b. at Phalsbourg and d. at Lunéville. He practised law from 1842–58. Louis Gratien Charles Alexandre Chatrian (1826–90) was b. at Soldatenthal, in Lorraine. He was first a teacher and afterwards a clerk in a railway office. The partnership dates from 1847, and continued till 1889. Their best known works are : *Histoires et contes fantastiques,* 1849 ; *L'Illustre Docteur Mathéus,* 1859 ; *Madame Thérèse,* 1863 ; *Histoire d'un conscrit de 1813* (1864) ; *Waterloo,* 1865 ; *Le Blocus,* 1867 ; *Le Grandpère Lebigue,* 1886. They also wrote dramas : *Le Juif polonais,* 1869 ; *Les Rantzau,* 1882, etc. Consult J. Claretie, *Erckmann-Chatrian,* 1883, in the Célébrités Contemporaines series.

**Erdelyi, Joseph,** b. in 1896 at Nagyvarad, is one of the greatest of the latter-day lyric poets of Hungary Not much is known of his life and education. His father was a labourer on one of the great Magyar landed estates. In a period when the Budapest cafés were filled with poets who wrote in artificial and, so to speak, perfumed verse, E. burst upon them, bringing a fresh breath of air from the country. His memory was filled with the wild songs of the peasantry and the wailing music of the Hungarian gipsies. He was not ashamed of his origin. He gloried in it. He wrote poems which for the first time threw the light on the condition of the men who toil for small wages on the great farms. He quickly published two volumes—*Violet Leaf* in 1922 and *At the End of the World* in 1924. He tired of the capital and its artificialities, married and returned to the country. In 1928 he published *The Last Royal Eagle.* His poems are full of good humour. He illustrates his points with anecdotes from the country hamlets. When he lived in Budapest, the famous primas, first violin and leader of a gipsy band, tried in vain to please him. He preferred the ruder gipsies of his place of origin. They were the only ones who could speak to him in music that he understood and that he has transposed into his verses.

**Erdmann, Johann Eduard** (1805–92), a Ger. philosopher, b. at Wolmar in Livonia. He published sermons and treatises, his chief works being : *Leib und Seele,* 1837 ; *Grundriss der Psychologie,* 1840 ; *Darstellung der Geschichte der neuern Philosophie,* 1834–53 ; *Grundriss der Logic und Metaphysik,* 1841 ; and *Ernste Spiele* (4th ed.), 1890.

**Erdmann, Otto Linn** (1804–1869), Ger. chemist, b. at Dresden ; Professor of Chemistry at Leipzig University from 1830. Devoted much time to the chemical analysis of indigo and other dyestuffs. His *Manual of Chemistry* and *Principles of Drugs* went through several editions. In 1827 he published an instructive treatise on nickel and in 1861 a brochure on the study of chemistry, which was translated into several languages. In collaboration with Werther, he directed the Ger. Journal of Practical Chemistry.

**Erebus,** in Gk. mythology, the son of Chaos, and the father of Æther (upper air) and Hemera (day) by his sister Nyx (night). The word denotes utter darkness, and is used by poets with regard to the gloomy subterranean region through which the departed shades must pass on their way to Hades.

**Erebus, Mount,** a volcano in Victoria Land, Antarctica, discovered by Captain (afterwards Sir James) Ross in 1841, and named after one of the vessels in the expedition. The volcano is active, and is 12,500 ft. in height. See ANTARCTIC OCEAN.

**Erechtheum,** a temple dedicated to the worship of Erechtheus (*q.v.*) on the Acropolis at Athens. The present remains, which are of great beauty, date from about 400 B.C.

**Erechtheus, or Erichthonius :** (1) An Athenian hero, the son of Hephæstus (Vulcan) and of Atthis, the daughter of Cranaus. As a child he was secretly brought up by Athena (Minerva), who concealed him in a chest which she entrusted to Agraulos, Pandrosos, and Herse. They opened the chest, though they had been forbidden to do so, and saw a large serpent twined round the body of a child. They were filled with fear and committed suicide by hurling themselves from the rock of the Acropolis. E. became King of Athens, and is said to have first introduced to Athens the worship of Athena, to whom he erected a temple on the Acropolis. He settled the dispute between Athena and Poseidon (Neptune) as to the possession of Attica in favour of the former. On his death he was placed among the stars, and his worship was celebrated in a temple called the Erechtheum on the Acropolis. (2) The grandson of the above and the son of Pandion, whom he succeeded as King of Athens. He waged war against Eleusis, and killed Eumolpus, Poseidon's son; whereupon he was slain by a thunderbolt by Zeus, at Poseidon's request. In anct. myth these two heroes were regarded as one person, but they were distinguished as two by later writers.

about 15 m. S.E. of Chalcis. It was of great commercial importance, and had many colonies, including the Cyclades. In 490 B.C. it was destroyed by the Persians before the battle of Marathon, for its interference in the Ionic revolt (498). During the fifth century B.C. it was subject to Athens, but regained its independence of Philip of Macedonia through its leader Phocion (354). It was the birthplace of Achæus and Menedemus. At the modern village, sometimes known as Nea Psará, the American School of Athens carried out important archæological investigations from 1890 to 1895.

Erfurt, a tn. in Prussian Saxony, situated on the Gera. The beautiful

THE ERECHTHEUM, SHOWING THE CARYATIDES

Eregli : (1) A tn. (anct. *Cybistra*) of Asiatic Turkey, situated midway between Konieh and Adana. In the neighbourhood are hot springs. It exports corn, wool, nuts, skins. Pop. 7200. (2) Also called Benderegli (anct. *Heraclea Pontica*), a seaport in Asia Minor, on the Black Sea, about 128 m. E. of Constantinople. There are fine coal mines in the neighbourhood, and it has a good port. Here Xenophon embarked with 10,000 Gks. on his return to Greece. Pop. 7000.

Eremecausis, the gradual combination of the combustible elements of a body with the oxygen of the air. This process of slow combustion continually takes place when animal and vegetable substances become decomposed through exposure to the atmosphere. It differs from fermentation and putrefaction in that it cannot take place without the access of atmospheric air. The term was first used by Liebig, but is now seldom encountered.

Eretria (modern *Aletria*), an anct. seaport of Eubœa, on the Euripus,

cathedral, Beatæ Mariæ Virginis, dates from the twelfth century. Other churches of interest are the Predigerkirche (twelfth century); the Reglerkirche, a fine example of the Romanesque style (twelfth century); the Barfüsserkirche, in the Gothic style. The old monastery of St. Augustine, in which Luther lived as a friar from 1505 to 1508, has been converted into an orphanage. The university, at which he studied, was suppressed in 1816 and its funds devoted to the endowment of the Academy of Sciences and to the maintaining of its fine library. There are a municipal theatre, museum, and library with 130,000 volumes. E. is a flourishing industrial centre, its chief manufactures being boots and shoes, machinery, dress materials, furniture, musical instruments, chemicals, tobacco, malt, etc. During the Thirty Years' War, E. was held by the Swedes ; in 1648 it was ceded to the Elector of Mainz, but, refusing to submit, was forcibly taken in 1664.

The city was incorporated with Prussia in 1802. Pop. (1925) 136,578.

**Erg** (abbreviated from Gk. ἔργον, work), in dynamics, is the unit of energy or work necessary to overcome the force of one dyne as it acts through a distance of one centimetre. Thus the power of machinery may be measured by the number of Es. per second of which it is capable. It is also applied to the energy of two grams moving with a unit speed. *See* MECHANICS.

**Ergasteria**, or **Laurion**, a mining tn. in Greece, 25 m. S.E. of Athens. It has anct. lead and silver mines, reopened in 1864, and cadmium and manganese are exported. Pop. 3800.

**Ergeri**, or **Argyro-Castro**, a vilayet of Janina, Albania, situated on a trib. of the Viosa, 47 m. from the tn. of Janina. It is a picturesque tn. with many mosques, and manufs. tuli, a kind of snuff. Pop. 9000.

**Ergot**, or **Spurred Rye**, a diseased condition or fermentation of rye and of other cereals. A sweet yellowish mucus exudes from the ears of the corn on its first appearance. The ears then lose their starch and the ovaries show a whitish tissue of the mycelium of the fungus. Bread that has been made of such infected rye often gives rise to certain nervous complaints, known as ergotism. The drug *ergota* or *Secale cornutum* is used medicinally. *See* MATERIA MEDICA.

**Eric**, the name of several Danish and Swedish kings : *Eric VII.* (1412–59), the son of Duke Wratislaw of Pomerania, was *b.* in 1382. He succeeded Queen Margaret of Denmark, thus uniting the kingdoms of Denmark, Norway, and Sweden. The last named he lost in 1437 during the revolt of the peasants of Dalecarlia, and he was deposed from the throne of Denmark two years later. *Eric VIII.* (1155–60), called ' the Saint,' a pious Christian, fell in battle against the Danes. *Eric XIV.* (1560–68), the son of Gustavus Vasa, was *b.* in 1533. He was a cruel and capricious ruler, and brought much suffering upon his subjects. He limited the power of the dukes at the Arboga Riksdag in 1561, and extended his rule into Esthonia. His matrimonial ambitions reached to Christina of Hesse, Mary Queen of Scots, and Queen Elizabeth of England, but he finally married Katrina Månsdotter, a Swedish peasant girl, who alone appears to have been able to control him in his fits of temper. He murdered the three Stures in 1567, thus causing the revolt of the nobles, who completely threw off his yoke in 1568, and elected his brother John to the throne. He *d.* in 1571 from poison, said to have been administered

by his brother. *See* Kruse's version of his story, *König Erich*, 1871.

**Erica**, the typical genus of Ericaceæ, includes more than 400 beautiful species, all of which occur in Europe, S. Africa, and the Mediterranean. The majority of these frequent the Cape of Good Hope, and are often cultivated in British hot-houses; in their native land they form scraggy

ERICA FILAMENTOSA

(Cape Heath)

shrubs with little beauty, but when cultivated become extremely handsome. The plants have pendulous, bell-shaped flowers, which vary in colour from red, pink, and purple to white. There are only five British species, and all require sandy peat earth and a moderately-shaded situation before they will grow. *E. cinerea* is a common plant found extensively on moors of Great Britain, while *E. tetralix*, the cross-leaved heath, is also well known. The other British species, including *E. vagans*, occur only in Cornwall and in Ireland.

In France the commonest heath is *E. scoparia*, a plant from which briar-wood pipes are made.

**Ericaceæ**, a large order of dicotyledonous plants of varied characters growing in nearly every part of the world, but avoiding tropical climates and showing a distinct preference for peaty soils. Four representative genera of the fifty are *Rhododendron*, *Arbutus*, *Vaccinium*, and *Erica*.

**Ericht, Loch**, a lake situated partly in Inverness-shire and partly in Perthshire, Scotland, in the districts of Badenoch on the N., and Rannoch on the S. It lies 1153 ft. above sea-level. Its area is about 7¼ sq. m., its length being 14 m., and its breadth varying from ⅛ m. to 1 m.; its greatest depth is about 512 ft. The lake is drained by the R. Ericht into Loch Rannoch. The neighbouring scenery is wild and rugged; the overhanging mountain on the W. side of the lake is Ben Alder (3757 ft.). There is good salmon and trout fishing.

**Ericson, Leif**, son of Eric the Red, is said to have furthered the explorations made by his father in Greenland by discovering Helluland (Labrador?), Markland or Woodland (Nova Scotia?), and Vinland or New England about A.D. 1000. Consult Archibald Williams's *Romance of Early Exploration* (Seeley); Justin Winsor's *History of America, Arctic Exploration and Greenland*.

**Ericsson, John** (1803–89), a Swedish naval engineer, *b.* at Langban-shyttan, Wermland, Sweden. He was first employed as a draughtsman by the Swedish Canal Company (1815), but entered the army in 1820 and served for six years. From 1826 to 1839 he lived in England, where, in conjunction with John Braithwaite, he constructed a locomotive engine for the Liverpool and Manchester Railway (1829). He also invented the caloric engine (1833), a screw propeller (1836), and improved appliances for naval steam engines. In 1839 he sailed for the United States, where he became a naturalised citizen in 1848. He built the first American armoured turret ship, the *Monitor*, which was launched in 1862, and fought a month later, with the Confederate ram, the *Merrimac*. E. also studied torpedo boats and sun motors, and published *Solar Investigations*, 1875; and *Contributions to the Centennial Exhibition*, 1877. He *d.* in New York, but was buried in Filipstad, Wermland. See *Life* by W. C. Church (2 vols.), 1890.

**Erie Canal**, in New York, U.S.A., connects Lake Erie at Buffalo with the Hudson River at Albany and Troy. It was begun in 1817 and completed in 1825, at a cost of over seven million dollars, the construction being superintended by De Witt Clinton. The length is about 350 m. and there are thirty-four locks. The original width and depth were 70 feet by an average of about 9 feet, but recently much money has been expended upon improvement, in order to allow a shipping-way for vessels of 1000 tons and upwards, and it is now 150 feet broad and has an average depth of 12 feet. Together with the Champlain, Oswego and Caynga–Seneca Canals, it constitutes the New York State Barge Canal System, which is the main route by which grain is brought to New York.

**Erie City**, the co. seat of Erie co., Pennsylvania, U.S.A., on Lake Erie, 148 m. N. of Pittsburg. It is situated on many railway lines. It has an excellent harbour, and is a well-built city. Its chief products are lumber, coal, iron-ore, petroleum, fish and the city's varied manufactures—foundry and machine shop products, engines, silk goods and washing machines are shipped. One of its parks is the site of a Fr. fort erected in 1749. Pop. 115,967.

**Erie, Lake**, the most southerly of the Great Lakes, forming the St. Lawrence system in N. America, lying between Canada and the United States. It is bounded on the N. by Ontario, on the S. and S.E. by Ohio, Pennsylvania, and New York, and on the W. by Michigan. It is connected with Lake Ontario by the Niagara R., and with Lake Huron by the Detroit and St. Clair Rs. It is 241 m. long by 30 to 60 m. broad, its area being 9940 sq. m. It is 573 ft. above mean sea-level. Its waters are shallow, the greatest depth being 210 feet.

**Erie Railroad Company** operates a railway between New York City and Chicago, Ill. It holds the capital stock of a number of subsidiary railway companies and of four coal companies. The latter are the source of much of its fuel supply, and their output forms a large portion of the coal carrying trade.

**Eries**, an Iroquoian tribe of N. America, now extinct, who formerly occupied the eastern and southern shores of Lake Erie. Their language resembled that of the Hurons. They were nearly exterminated by the Iroquois league in 1656, the survivors of the struggle afterwards joining the Senecas.

**Erigena, Johannes Scotus** (c. 800–c. 877), a mediæval philosopher and divine, probably a native of Ireland. His real name was Johannes Scotus, E. or Ierugena being an adopted surname, apparently connected with the word Erin (q.v.), and signifying Irishman. Nothing definite is known about his early life. About 843 he visited the court of Charles the Bald, where he became the head of the schola palatina. His earliest work that has come down to us is De divina prædestinatione, which was vehemently attacked on account of its unorthodoxy, and was censured at the councils of Valence (855) and Langres (859). At the request of Charles the Bald, he then translated the pantheistic writings of Dionysius Areopagiticus. His greatest work was De divisione naturæ, which was described by Honorius III. (1225) as ' swarming with worms of heretical perversity.' E. argues that Universe or God is the ultimate unity of all things, and that all things are worked out through the divine processes. Revelation or religion forms a prominent part in the divine process, while reason or intellectualis visio is the prime faculty of man. Haméau fixes E.'s death at about 877, the date of the death of Charles the Bald. There is a story, however, that about 882 he visited Oxford at the request of Alfred the Great and became the abbot of a monastic school at Malmesbury, where he was stabbed to death by his pupils. The complete edition of his works was published by Migne in 1853 in Patrologiæ cursus completus, vol. cxxii. De divisione naturæ has been edited by Thomas Gale (Oxford, 1861) and C. B. Schlüter (Münster, 1838). The De divina prædestinatione was published in Mauguin's Veterum auctorum . . . opera et fragmenta (Paris), 1650 ; and his poems in Traube's Poëtæ Latini aevi Carolini (vol. ii.), 1896. Consult St. René Taillandier, Scot. Erigène et la philosophie scholastique, 1843 ; Christlieb, Leben und Lehre des Johannes Scotus, 1860 ; the article in Dictionary of National Biography ; and Alice Gardiner, Studies in John the Scot, 1900.

Erigeron, a large genus of the Compositæ ; the majority of the species are indigenous to N. America. E. Philadelphicum is found in the United States, where it is used as a medicine, possessing stimulant and diuretic properties. E. acris occurs in Great Britain, and with several other plants is known as flea-bane ; it has a strong scent which is said to keep away these insects.

Erin, an ancient name for Ireland. The form was originally Eriu, of which Erinn was the dative case. Eriu later became a dissyllable, Eire. It has been suggested that the word originated from Eire, the wife of MacCool, one of the kings reigning in Ireland at the time of the coming of the Milesians. The name gained popularity through the writings of Moore.

Erinaceus, see HEDGEHOG.

Erinite (arseniate of copper), occurring in concentric and mammillated layers, is bright green in colour, with a specific gravity of 4·0 to 4·1. It is found near Limerick.

Erinna (fl. c. 600 B.C.), a Lesbian poetess, supposed to have been a contemporary and friend of Sappho. Only fragments of her poems remain, but these were held by the Gks. to rank with those of Homer. See the editions published by J. Pellegrino, 1894, and by Bergk in Poetæ Lyrici Græci (new ed.), 1900. Her best-known poem is the Distaff ('Ηλακάτη), which is written in a mixture of the Æolic and Doric dialects and of which only four lines remain. E. died at the age of nineteen.

Erinyes, see EUMENIDES.

Eriophorum, a genus of Cyperaceæ, grows in Northern lands of temperate climate. The British species are called wild cotton, cotton-grass or cotton-sedge, and have a sedge-like appearance. They are to be found in marshy and sedgy heaths, and the long cottony tufts of hair are sometimes used for stuffing cushions.

Eriostemon, a genus of Rutaceæ which flourishes chiefly in Australia. The species are evergreen shrubs and are cultivated in greenhouses for their pretty pink and white blossoms.

Eriphia, a genus of brachyurous crustaceans classed sometimes with the Xanthidæ, sometimes with the Cancridæ, and is closely related to Cancer, the edible crab. The species are found on tropical shores.

Eriphyle, the daughter of Talaus, and the wife of Amphiaraus the seer, who tried to escape from joining the expedition of the Argives against Thebes. E., bribed by Polynices with Hermonia's golden necklace, betrayed her husband, and was murdered by her son Alcmæon on his father's death in battle.

Eris (Lat. Discordia), the Gk. goddess of strife, the friend and sister of Ares (Mars), and like him she delighted in war. She sowed dissensions among the gods and was expelled from heaven by Zeus. It was she who, not having been invited to the nuptials of Peleus and Thetis, threw the golden apple, detur pulchriori, in the midst of the assembly and thus caused the jealous rivalry between Hera (Juno), Aphrodite (Venus), and Athena (Minerva). Thus she indirectly was the cause of the rape of Helen by Paris and of the Trojan War.

Erith, an urban dist. of N.W. Kent, England, situated on the Thames, 12 m. E. of London. It was formerly an important naval station until the end of the seventeenth century. There are wharves, gun factories, and engineering works, also flour mills, brickyards, ballast works, and manufs. of oil, glue, gunpowder, etc. Pop. 31,370.

**Eritrea** (from ἐριθεία, red, part of the Gk. name for the Red Sea), the official name of the Italian colony on the African coast of the Red Sea. It extends from Ras Kasar, a cape in 18° 2′ N., to Ras Demoira in 12° 42′ N., a distance of about 650 m. To the inland the Anglo-Egyptian Sudan, Abyssinia, and French Somaliland form the boundaries; the boundaries towards Egypt were determined by a protocol in 1891, and towards Abyssinia by the treaties of 1889 and 1891. Three distinct climatic zones are found in the colony : that of the coastlands, that of the escarpments and valleys, and that of the high plateau and Alpine summits. The first zone is characterised by great heat and humidity; the second has a more temperate climate, but considerable variation of temperature occurs owing to nocturnal radiation; a moderately cool climate prevails in the third zone. The flora in the zones is what would be expected from the climate, ranging from a tropical nature in the low country to temperate on the plateau. The lion, panther, elephant, camel, and numerous species of antelope are found. There are no navigable rivers in the colony; the chief streams are the Setit, the Mareb, the Baraka, the Anseba, and the Hadas. Semi-nomadic shepherds form the population of the plains and foothills; Afars and Somalis are found chiefly in the S.; whilst the plateau is inhabited by Abyssinians. The nomadic tribes are largely of Arab or Hamitic stock, but include several tribes of negro origin. The principal towns on the coast are Massawa, Assab, and Zula; those of the interior, Asmara, Mogolo, Saganeiti, and Arrasa. The low country is suitable for pastoral purposes only, but the intermediate zone and the high plateau are well adapted for the cultivation of crops. Massawa is connected with Asmara by railway, to Perim by cable, and with Adis Ababa by telegraph. E. is governed by a civil governor who is responsible to the Ministry of Foreign Affairs at Rome. The area is about 60,000 sq. m. and the pop about 500,000.

**Erivan,** cap. of the Soviet republic of Armenia since the conquest of the short-lived independent republic of Armenia by the Bolsheviks. Situated 234 m. S.S.W. of Tiflis by rail on the edge of a hot dry plain, and dominated by Mt. Ararat. Wine is made, and

fruit and tobacco are grown in the vicinity. Some manufacturing is carried on, and there is a hydro-electric station. There is an old Persian quarter and a Russian quarter, and the ruins of a sixteenth century fortress stand on a steep rock. Pop. is 62,000, of whom 56,000 are Armenians and 5000 Turks and Tartars. (2) A dist. of the Socialist Soviet republic of Armenia with a pop. (1926) of 175,816. It is noted for its wines and fruits.

**Erlangen,** a tn. of Bavaria in Franconia, situated on the Regnitz at its junction with the Schwabach, 11½ m. N.W. of Nuremberg. A Protestant university, the only one in Bavaria, is in the New Town, which is regarded as one of the best built towns of Germany. The manufactures are hosiery, tobacco, leather, plate-glass, and there are important breweries. After the Edict of Nantes was revoked in 1685, many of the French Huguenots settled here, and it is to this that the town owes the foundation of its success. Pop. 29,600.

**Erlanger, Camille** (1863–1919), Fr. composer; b. May 25, 1863, in Paris. At the Conservatoire, he was pupil of Decombes and Mathias for the piano, and of Durand and Tandou for harmony. He was in Léo Delibes' class for composition. In 1888 he won the Prix de Rome with the cantata *Velléda.* During residence in Italy he sketched out *Saint Julien l'Hospitalier* (a dramatic legend founded on a story by Flaubert), which came to be reckoned among his principal works—composed by 1893, and performed 1896 at the Conservatoire. Operas : *Kermaria,* 1897; *Le Juif Polonaise,* 1900 ; *Le Fils de l'Étoile,* 1904 ; *Aphrodite,* 1906; *Hannele Mattern,* 1908 ; *Noël,* 1911 ; *La Sorcière,* 1912 ; *Gioconda,* 1914. Died in Paris, April 24.

**Erlau,** or **Eger,** a tn. of Czechoslovakia. It is strongly fortified, having six gates. Vineyards cover the surrounding hills, and the manufacture of red wine occupies the greater number of the people. E. has at times suffered very considerably at the hands of the Turks. A fine minaret, remains of a mosque, is a reminder of those times. Pop. 25,000.

**Erlkönig, Dɘr,** or **Erl-King,** a mythical character that appeared in Ger. literature towards the end of the eighteenth century. He is represented as a bearded giant with a golden crown, who lures little children and others to the unknown land of death. Goethe's ballad on the legend has been translated into English by Sir Walter Scott.

**Ermelo,** a small tn. of the Netherlands, in the prov. of Gelderland, situated 4 m. S. of Harderwijk. Pop. 6700.

**Ermenonville, a** vil. of France in the dept. of Oise, about 7 m. S.E. of Senlis. It is noted as the place where Rousseau died. Pop. 500.

**Ermine, a** name given to the stoat (*Putorius ermineus*) when it puts on its white winter coat. During the summer months the fur is a reddish-brown shading into white underneath, but in the winter turns to pure white. The tail is black. *See* STOAT.

**Ernakulam, a** tn. of India, in the Madras Presidency. It is the cap. of the native state of Cochin, and is situated on an inlet on the W. coast, opposite the town of Cochin, and 2 m. from it. Pop. 23,192.

**Erne,** or **Sea-eagle** (*Haliaëtus albicilla*), a species of Falconidæ widely distributed over the Old World. Its diet consists chiefly of fish, but it will also play much havoc

ERNE

with young lambs. In general character and habit it is much like *Aquila chrysaëtus*, the golden eagle, but it is smaller, has a longer beak and fewer leg-feathers. The eyrie is built on sea-cliffs difficult of ascent, and in the early spring contains two or three white eggs.

**Erne, Loch** and **River,** situated in Ireland. The river rises in Lough Gowna, in the co. Longford, and flows generally northward, through Lough Oughter until it enters Upper Lough E., which is a shallow piece of water about 13 m. long, containing numerous islands. The river passes Enniskillen, and flows through Lough E., finally emptying itself in Donegal Bay. Lough E. is 18 m. long, is noted for its beauty, and contains trout and pike.

**Ernest I.** (the Pious) (1601–75), the founder of the Dukes of Saxe-Gotha, was the son of John, Duke of Weimar. He served with distinction in the Thirty Years' War, and in 1640 came into possession of the duchy of Saxe-Gotha.

**Ernest II., Augustus Charles John** (1818–93), Duke of Saxe-Coburg-Gotha, eldest son of Duke Ernest I., was *b.* at Coburg. He succeeded his father in 1844. He was the first German prince to visit Napoleon III. Almost every European court received him, his position being strengthened by the fact that he was brother-in-law to Queen Victoria and the nephew of Leopold, King of the Belgians. Several musical works and books of travel were written by him.

**Ernesti, Johann August** (1707–81), a German philologist and Biblical critic, was *b.* at Tennstädt, Thuringia, and educated at the Saxon cloister school of Pforta and the universities of Wittenberg and Leipzig. He was made professor extra-ordinary of ancient literature at the university of Leipzig in 1742, professor of rhetoric in 1756, and doctor of theology. By his erudition and manner of work he paved the way for a revolution in theology. He was the founder of the grammatico-historical school; his best work was in hermeneutics. By his influence and example he inspired men who were to be greater than himself; his numerous works include translations of the classics, criticisms and translations of the Bible, etc.

**Ernesti, John Christian Theophilus** (1756–1802), a Ger. scholar, *b.* at Armstadt. He published editions of Silius Italicus and Æsop, and a Ger. version of the principal works of Cicero. His *Lexicon Technologiæ Græcæ Rhetoricæ* (1795) and *Lexicon Technologiæ Romanorum Rhetoricorum* (1797) are very good works of their kind.

**Ernestine Line,** a branch of the house of Saxe, which was founded by Ernest (1441–88), the eldest son of Frederick II., the Elector of Saxony. John Frederick, called the Charitable, lost the electorate and many of the possessions. In 1572 two sons of John Frederick II. divided the estates and formed the houses of Weimar and of Coburg. The former was divided into the houses of Weimar and Altenburg in 1603, the latter in 1592 into the houses of Coburg and Eisenach, which became extinct in 1633 and 1638 respectively. The chief of the line of Weimar died in 1605, leaving three sons; the eldest founded four branches of the family, which were re-united in 1748 under Ernest Augustine, Duke of Weimar, to form the duchy of Saxe-Weimar-Eisenach. His youngest son, Ernest, Duke of Gotha, *d.* in 1675, and left seven sons, but most of the branches are extinct and the E. L. now survives only in the houses of Weimar, Saxe-Meiningen, Coburg-Gotha, and Altenburg.

**Ernle, Rowland Edmund Prothero,** 1st Baron, English man of letters, *b.* Sept. 6, 1852, at Clifton-on-Teme; third son of Rev. Geo. Prothero, afterwards canon of Westminster. Educ. : Marlborough ; and Balliol College, Oxford. 1st Class mod. history, 1875 ; Fellow of All Souls, 1875–91 ; proctor, 1883–84. He was editor of the *Quarterly Review,* 1894–99 ; M.P. (Cons.), Oxford Univ., 1914–19. Member royal commission on railways, 1913 ; on commercial and industrial reconstruction, 1916. President Board of Agriculture, 1916–19. Ennobled Feb. 4, 1919. Fellow of Royal Historical Soc. Has published : *Pioneers and Progress of English Farming,* 1887 ; *Life and Correspondence of Dean Stanley,* 1893 ; *Letters and Verses of Dean Stanley,* 1895 ; *Letters of Edward Gibbon,* 1896 ; *H.R.H. Prince Henry of Battenberg : a Memoir,* 1897 ; *Letters and Journals of Lord Byron,* 1898–1901 ; *The Psalms in Human Life,* 1903 ; *Letters of Richard Ford,* 1905 ; *The Pleasant Land of France,* 1908 ; *English Farming, Past and Present,* 1912 ; *The Land and its People,* 1925 ; *The Light Reading of our Ancestors,* 1927 ; and reprints of magazine articles.

**Ernst, Oswald Herbert** (1842–1926), an American soldier, studied at Harvard and West Point. Assistant-engineer of the army in the Civil War, he went as astronomer (1870) on the expedition to observe the total solar eclipse in Spain. He became instructor at West Point (1870–78), and had charge of the river and harbour improvements in the West (1878–86), including the deepening of Galveston Harbour. He superintended public buildings and grounds in Washington (1889–93), and the military academy (1893–98). E. served in the Porto Rico campaign, and was a member of the Isthmian Canal Commission (1899, 1901, 1905). He retired as colonel (1906). His *Manual of Practical Military Engineering* appeared in 1873.

**Ernst, Paul Carl Friedrich,** Ger. author and playwright : *b.* March 7, 1866, at Elbingerode, Harz ; son of Wilhelm E., foreman ore-dresser. Descended on mother's side from the composer Heinrich Schütze. Educated : gymnasiums of Tübingen, Berlin, and Berne. At first professed socialism ; turned strongly against it. Published 2 vols. translations of old Italian novels in 1902, and an autobiographical novel, *Der Schmale Weg zum Glück,* in 1903. In 1905 left Berlin and became playwright at Düsseldorf. Plays include three comedies and four tragedies, *Demetrios, Canossa, Brunhild,* and *Ninon von Lenclos. Ein Credo* (essays) appeared 1912. Then several novels, and the following critical works : *Zusammenbruch des Marxismus,* 1918 ; *Zusammenbruch des deutschen Idealismus,* 1919 ; and *Zusammenbruch und Glaube,* 1922.

**Ernulphus, or Arnulf** (1040–1124), a Fr. Benedictine monk, was made prior of Canterbury by Anselm, Abbot of Peterborough in 1107, and Bishop of Rochester in 1114. He was noted alike for his legal knowledge and his virtuous life. His mention in *Tristram Shandy* as a master of cursing is because of a curse which he mentions in his most famous work, a collection of documents concerning canonical law, etc., known as *Textus Roffensis.*

**Erode, or Erroad,** a tn. of India, in the presidency of Madras, situated about 54 m. N.E. of Coimbatore and 36 m. S.W. by W. of Salem. Pop. 22,911.

**Erodium,** a genus of plants belonging to the Geraniaceæ which grows in temperate lands. The two British species are known as stork's-bill or heron's-bill.

EROS

**Eros,** the god of love in the Gk. mythology. Hesiod is the first to mention him, as one of the oldest gods, and one of the most powerful. He it is who brings harmony from chaos by uniting the elements. Chronos laid a world-egg in the bosom of Chaos, according to Orphic mythology, and from this egg sprang E. This conception of E. is an early one, and in later times he represents the god of sexual passion, and is said to be the son of Aphrodite by Zeus, Ares, or Hermes. He is a wanton child, tormenting gods and men by his arrows, and is often represented as blind. In art E. is always shown as a beautiful winged boy; his attributes are the bow and arrows, and a burning torch. For the Rom. version of E. *see* CUPID, and for the legend of Cupid and Psyche *see* PSYCHE.

**Eros,** the name of a minor planet which was discovered by Witt at Berlin on Aug. 14, 1898. It is remarkable for the fact that it has an orbit between the earth and Mars, while every one of the other five or six hundred known asteroids lie between Mars and Jupiter. Its mean distance from the sun is 1·46 times that of the earth; but as the eccentricity of its orbit is large on those rare occasions when in opposition near perihelion, it could approach the earth to a distance of 0·16. It was therefore used for a series of experiments for determining the sun's parallax in 1900, which has taken ten years to work out. The results arrived at confirm those of Sir D. Gill, but add thereto a little more accuracy.

**Erosion,** *see* DENUDATION.

**Erotic Literature** (Gk. ἔρως, love), the name given to that literature which has for its principal subject the passion of love. Human love is, of course, meant, as otherwise practically all literature would come under this heading, being inspired by love of nature, art, etc. Among the erotic poets of Greece the names of Alcæus, Sappho, Mimnermus, and Anacreon stand out as singers of passionate lyrics, whilst Callimachus and Philetas sang in a more scholastic strain. Nor must the delightful idylls of Theocritus be omitted. In Rom. times Petronius was the founder of E. L.; the poets Horace, Ovid, Tibullus, Propertius, and Catullus have all written much beautiful verse which come into this class. In France in the Middle Ages we have Conon de Bethune, Gâce Brulé, Bodie, etc., in the twelfth and thirteenth centuries; they were troubadours, and the form of their songs was by no means fixed. In the following century ballads, rondeaux, etc., were introduced, but there is not much talent until the time of the Renaissance. Then we have the voluptu-

ously melancholy songs of Marot, the passionate lyrics of Ronsard, the spiritual strains of Louis Labé, the tender sensuality of J. du Bellay and Jean the Second. The eighteenth century was the golden age of French E. L., with such men as Gentil-Bernard, Dorat, Bernes, Bertin Conward, A. Chénier, etc. The poetry of the succeeding century embraced too many elements to come under the head of 'erotic' work, though elements of eroticism were in it. In England the time of the Civil War and the Commonwealth produced some of our best E. L.; the lyrics of Herrick, Waller, Carew, Suckling, Lovelace, Cowley, etc., all belong to this class. Since then the same may be said as in the case of Fr. literature, though many of Shelley's lyrics might be termed erotic, and of later years much of Swinburne.

**Erotomania** (Gk. ἔρως, love; and μανία, madness), a form of insanity arising from love. It differs from nymphomania and satyriasis in that the imagination only is affected, and the grosser symptoms of these diseases are absent.

**Erpenius** (a Latinised form of Thomas van Erpen) (1584–1624), a Dutch Orientalist, who was professor of Oriental languages at Leyden. Here he set up an Arabic printing press at his residence, and was made Oriental interpreter to the government. His *Rudiments of Arabic*, 1620, is still one of the best books on the subject, and his *Arabic Grammar*, 1613, was for long the supreme authority. Among his translations may be mentioned his edition of *El Meken*, 1623, and *Two Centuries of Arabic Proverbs*, 1614.

**Erpetology,** or **Herpetology,** *see* REPTILES.

**Erpeton,** or properly **Herpeton** (Gk. ἑρπετόν, a reptile), the name given to a genus of non-venomous serpents native to S. Asia.

**Erratics,** or **Erratic Boulders** (Ger. *Findlinge*), scattered blocks of rock which are found on the continent of Europe, and have evidently been removed by some agency from their original site. What this agency was for a long time employed the minds of scientists, and several theories were evolved. The earliest theory was that they had been dislodged from their original positions and transported by the agency of a flood; this is known as the diluvial hypothesis. This theory is now generally discredited. The next theory was brought forward by Sir C. Lyell, who thought that the transport and distribution had been effected by floating icebergs. A widespread submergence of the land of the European continent must have been necessary before this could have occurred. This, the drift hypothesis, still finds some supporters. The third theory, that of glacial action, is now generally held as the result of the investigations which were carried out among the Alps, where such erratics abound. According to this theory E. B. are isolated masses of ore which have been borne along by ice-sheets for some distance from their original position; the ground moraine which accompanied them has been washed away in course of time. E. B., or perched blocks, as they are sometimes called, are very familiar objects in Alpine glacier districts, but are also easily recognised in regions where there is now no ice. They bear all the characteristic marks of the action of ice, such as erosion, striation, and smoothness of outline. Not only are boulders of

AN ERRATIC BOULDER

hard rock transported by ice, but huge masses of stratified rock have been torn from their beds by the same agency. Thus large blocks of Scandinavian rocks are scattered over the plains of Denmark, Prussia, and N. Germany; the masses of chalk in the cliffs near Cromer are well known, and a mass of chalk of about 2,000,000 cubic ft. in bulk has been transported a distance of about 9 m. at Firkenwald. The statue of Peter the Great at St. Petersburg (Leningrad) had for its pedestal an erratic boulder hewn into shape. The boulder at Mouthey in the canton of Valais contains 7063 cubic ft., and is large enough to support a small house on the top; it is known as the 'Pierre de Marmettes.' This huge mass has been transported by the action of ice for a distance of over 30 m. down the valley. Erratic boulders are very numerous on the shores of the Firth of Forth.

**Erromanga,** an island of the New Hebrides, about 35 m. long and 25 broad. It is well watered and extremely fertile. It has been called 'the Martyr's isle' on account of the

many missionaries who have laid down their lives there, including John Williams and James Harris, killed in 1839, Geo. and Ellen Gordon, killed in 1861, and James Gordon, killed in 1872. Pop. about 1800.

**Error,** in law, is any mistake in fact, in law, or in the form of process which needs to be rectified either by the court before which the action was tried or by a Court of Appeal. Since 1875 all appeals in civil suits must be made to the Court of Appeal. In criminal procedure, an E. in the indictment may be cured by the Court which tries the case, or recourse may be had to the Court of Criminal Appeal.

**Errors of Observation.** The results of any determination of a physical or chemical quantity are always affected by errors due to the inaccuracy of the observation. The sources of error may be classified broadly as:—(1) Inaccurate methods; (2) defective instruments or impure materials; (3) influence of conditions; (4) defects of the observer. Errors due to the first cause can only be detected by special investigations, but may and can be removed by a modification of the method. Instrumental defects can be detected by special tests and a correction can be applied. Thus a balance may not be correct; but a careful investigation will show how far it is inaccurate, and what correction should be applied, provided the error is not due to a lack of sensitiveness, for which no allowance can be made. Fluctuations of the weather and of the temperature may cause temporary alterations of the value of the quantities measured. In astronomy the changes of the weather will disturb the amount of refraction; and in the processes of weighing and measuring, alterations of temperature will have a very marked effect. If it is possible to do so, the conditions should be reduced to the standard value, or the conditions should be noted and the necessary corrections calculated from a knowledge of the numerical relation between the quantity required and the conditions. The errors due to the observer are of two classes: (1) Mistakes which consist in a wrong registration of the value measured. Such errors are preventable and can be detected by repetition or checking by another observer. The second class are due to the imperfections of the senses, such as defective vision, lack of ability to seize the exact instant of an occurrence, etc. The errors of an observation are usually very numerous, but they differ in their influence on the final result. Some always affect the result in the same direction (though not to the same extent) and are called *constant errors*. Others sometimes increase and sometimes diminish the result, and are called *accidental errors*. Mistakes and constant errors can be removed ; and it is therefore more advantageous to give time and attention to their removal than to make an effort to allow for these errors by calculation. Constant errors can be detected by change of material, of method, of instruments, or of the observer. When the presence of a constant error has been detected, its cause must be found and steps must be taken to remove it. Accidental errors are often subdued by making a large number of observations and taking the arithmetical mean or average of the results obtained ; the assumption being made that the number and magnitude of the errors in one direction are probably equal to the number and magnitude of the errors in the other direction. But this method of subduing accidental errors is not applicable to all cases ; and recourse must sometimes be had to the method of least squares (*see* PROBABILITY). Many determinations of physical and chemical quantities involve subsidiary measurements. It is important that the subsidiary measurements should be made in such a way that the errors of those measurements have the least effect on the final result. Thus in experiments involving the use of a tangent compass or galvanometer the error in making a reading will have the least influence on the result if the deflection is about 45°.

**Ersch, Johann Samuel** (1766–1828), the founder of Ger. bibliography, born at Grossglogau. He entered the university of Halle as a theological student, but worked more on bibliographical and geographical lines. After going with J. E. Fabri to Jena, he went to Hamburg and edited the *Hamburger Zeitung*. In 1800 he returned to Jena, where he was made librarian of the university and, in 1802, professor of philosophy. In 1803 he moved to Halle, where he was professor of geography and statistics, and in 1808 principal librarian ; he died at Halle.

**Erse**, a corrupted form of ' Irish ' which was applied to the Gaelic dialect of the Highlanders by the Scottish Lowlanders. In the eighteenth century E. was used to signify the Gaelic of the Scots, now it is used more for the Irish Gaelic.

**Erskine, Ebenezer** (1680–1756), the founder of the Secession Church in Scotland, *b.* in Berwickshire. He was preacher at Portmoak in Kinrossshire from 1703. After taking part in the Marrow Controversy on the evangelical side, he was transferred to Stirling in 1731. With three others he was suspended in the patronage dispute for upholding the right of the people to choose their own pastor. He was deposed in 1734, and although the sentence was recalled, he would not return, and was finally deposed in 1740. Before this he had formed the Associate Presbytery, the origin of the Secession Church, in 1733. The latter was split up in 1747 into Burghers and Anti-Burghers, of which E. headed the former.

**Erskine, Henry** (1746–1817), a famous Scottish lawyer, was the second son of the Earl of Buchan, and was *b.* at Edinburgh. After a distinguished career at the Bar he became Lord Advocate. In politics he was a very earnest Whig, and it was owing to his influence that many useful legal reforms were brought about. He was noted both for his wit and his oratorical powers.

**Erskine, John, of Dun** (1509–91), a Scottish reformer, son of the laird of Dun, Sir John E. ; was educated at King's College, Aberdeen. He was obliged to go abroad in 1530, having accidentally caused the death of a priest, and there he came under the influence of the Reformation. The reformers Wishart and Knox were his personal friends, and all through the reign of Mary Queen of Scots, and part of the following, E. was a leading man and a reconciling influence in the religious quarrels of the time. He held the office of superintendent of the Reformed Church of Scotland for Angus and Mearns from 1560 to 1589, and was several times elected moderator of the General Assembly, although a layman. He was a member of the King's Council from 1579, and aided in the compilation of *The Second Book of Discipline* in 1578.

**Erskine, John** (1695–1768) an eminent Scottish jurist, was called to the Bar in 1719. After a distinguished career there he was made professor of Scots law at the University of Edinburgh in 1757, and held this post till 1763, when he resigned. His two principal works were very famous, and are still amongst the authorities on Scots law ; they are the *Principles of the Law of Scotland*, 1754, and the *Institutes of the Law of Scotland*, 1773. He *d.* at Cardross, near Dumbarton.

**Erskine, Thomas, first Baron Erskine** (1750–1823), Lord Chancellor, served at sea, first as midshipman and then as lieutenant, from 1764 to 1767, when he retired from the senior service and purchased a commission in the 1st Royal Regiment of Foot. Returning to England in 1772, he, at Lord Mansfield's suggestion, studied law. Six years later he was called to the Bar, and at once achieved a great success. So high was his reputation that within eighteen months of his donning wig and gown he was selected to represent Admiral Lord Keppel on his trial by court-martial, when the sailor was acquitted on all counts. In 1783 he took silk, and within eight years was earning £10,000 a year, the greatest income hitherto made by any lawyer. He it was who first refused to go on circuit except for a special fee—a practice since followed by all leading men at the Bar. He entered parliament in 1783, but lost his seat in the following year. He was, however, again returned to Westminster in 1790, but was too much occupied with

LORD ERSKINE

his professional duties to take an active part in the proceedings of the House. In the Grenville administration (1806) he became Lord Chancellor, and he was one of the commissioners appointed to inquire into the charges brought against the Princess of Wales. He retired with the ministry in the next year, and did not again hold office. As Lord Chancellor his ignorance of the law of equity militated effectively against his success in that great office. In 1820 he took an active part in securing a fair trial for the queen. For his biography, see Campbell's Lives of the Chancellors.

**Eruptive Rocks,** see IGNEOUS ROCKS

**Erymanthus,** a high mountain of Greece, situated in Arcadia, 20 m. S.S.E. of Patras. It is now named Olonos, and is about 7320 ft. in alt.

**Eryngium,** a genus of umbelliferous plants, occurs in tropical and temperate lands, and consists principally of perennial spiny herbs with flowers in dense heads. *E. maritimum,* the sea-holly or Eryngo, is a native of sandy sea-shores of Europe, and is found in Great Britain; in England it bears the additional names of sea hulver and sea holme. The root is candied as a sweetmeat, and has been used in medicine as a tonic and diuretic.

**Erysimum,** a genus of cruciferous plants, contains herbs with many-flowered racemes, all of which flourish in Europe, Asia, and round the Mediterranean. *E. cheiranthoides,* the worm-seed or treacle-mustard, occurs in Britain, and bears numerous small yellow flowers. Formerly used as a remedy for intestinal worms.

**Erysipelas,** see SKIN—*Diseases.*

**Erythema,** a superficial, non-infective inflammation of the skin, with characteristic redness, disappearing when pressure is made by the finger or a piece of glass, and promptly reappearing on removal of pressure. The first cause of E. is dilatation and accumulation of blood in the minute vessels of the skin. It may be due to local causes, as heat or cold, friction, accumulation of sweat, or other local irritants; the result of changes in the blood vessels themselves; to substances absorbed through the alimentary canal, such as special articles of diet, and other causes of alimentary toxæmia. After the condition has lasted for some time, pigment is deposited in the skin, and the colour due to this does not disappear on pressure. E. is seen as an accidental complication in fevers, particularly smallpox, measles, scarlet fever, typhus, typhoid, and cholera. The *treatment* of E. itself consists in the application of spirits, or other cooling lotions, powders, or a bland ointment. The appearance of E. is so variable, both in different individuals and in different parts of the body at the same time, that it is known as *E. multiforme,* and special technical terms are used to describe the extent and elevation of the spots and the shape of their margins.

*Erythema nodosum* is a special condition, with red, oval, raised spots, from the size of a pea to that of a hen's egg, chiefly on the lower extremities. The tint varies, is first pale red, then dark red, and finally livid, being very similar to the changes gone through in a bruise. The lumps are painful, and run their course in from two to four weeks. Although painful, they do not suppurate or burst, and are most common in young persons of delicate physique. They are usually accompanied by fever and constitutional disturbance, so that rest in bed is generally appreciated.

**Erythræa**, a genus of Gentianaceæ, inhabits dry sandy places of temperate lands. *E. centaurium*, the lesser or common centaury, is found in Britain by the waysides and edges of fields.

**Erythrina**, a leguminous genus of tropical trees and herbs, with bright red flowers and frequently with prickly stems. *E. Caffra*, the Kaffir-boom, produces a good timber.

**Erythronium**, *see* DOG'S TOOTH VIOLET.

**Eryx**, a genus of oviparous snakes, is closely allied to the genus *Boa* in the family Boidæ, but the species of E. differ from those of *Boa* in having a very short obtuse tail and narrower ventral plates. They occur in Asia and Africa.

**Eryx**, the name of a high mountain of N.W. Sicily, and now named Mont St. Giuliano. A temple of Venus once was on the summit, whence the goddess was called Erycina.

**Erzberger, Matthias** (1875–1921), Ger. politician, who came into prominence during the Great War. In his earlier years he took up teaching and journalism. Entered Reichstag 1903. During the Great War worked for peace and as Secretary of State conducted the Armistice negotiations on Germany's behalf with the Entente, the terms of which he signed. In 1919 became Finance Minister in new republican gov. He brought an action for slander against Dr. Helfferich, and during the course of the trial he was wounded by an assassin. Erzberger's power in politics was based upon his being the mouthpiece of the Catholic working class. His articles in the Press aroused great animosity against him in his political opponents and this led to his assassination on Aug. 26, 1921.

**Erzerum, Erz-Rum,** or **Arzerum,** a vilayet and tn. of Asiatic Turkey, 110 m. S.E. of Trebizond, occupying the centre of the Armenian plateau. The country (pop. 270,380) is mainly agricultural, though salt and coal are found; there are iron, saline, and sulphur springs. An extensive trade in cattle, horses, mules, furs, wheat, etc., is carried on. The tn. has a citadel, founded about A.D. 415 by the Emperor Theodosius the Younger, many mosques and former Dervish monasteries; the former industries have declined; there is petroleum in the vicinity. The chief industries are iron and copper working. In 1517 it was acquired by the Turks, and the Russians took it in 1829 and 1878 respectively, but by the Treaty of Berlin it was restored to Turkey. During the Great War E. was seized by the Russians in Feb. 1916 in their campaign against the Turks. After the Russian revolution the Turks recaptured the place in March 1917. In June 1919 a provisional gov. was set up at E. by the Nationalist party, headed by General Mustafa Kemal Pasha. Pop. 48,500.

**Erzgebirge** (meaning ore mountains), a chain of mountains, which separates the kingdoms of Bohemia and Saxony. It extends about 120 m., at length meeting the Riesengebirge range. On the northern slopes there are fertile valleys; the central part of the chain forms a plateau, while the southern slopes are very steep, in some places almost perpendicular. The highest summits are the Fichtelberg, nearly 4000 ft., situated in the N.E., and the Keilberg, over 4000 ft., in the S.E. Between these stands Gottesgab, the most elevated town in Bohemia. The geological formation of the chain is gneiss, granite, and clay slate. It is specially rich in ores; lead, silver, copper, tin, mercury, gold, and iron abound, also quantities of sulphur, bismuth, cobalt, arsenic, coal, etc. There are several holiday resorts among the heights, such as Barenfels, Kipsdorf.

**Erzingan, Erzinjan,** or **Eriza,** a tn. of Turkish Armenia, situated on the Kara Su, or the western upper branch of the Euphrates, about 80 m. W.S.W. of Erzerum, exports fruit, sheep, oxen, and horses. There are frequent earthquakes. It was taken by the Russians on July 26, 1916. Pop. 23,000.

**Esau,** son of Isaac and Rebecca, and elder twin brother of Jacob. His name signifies ' hairy ' (Hebrew), and he was so called because he was red and hairy at birth. In Gen. xxv. is given the story of how he sold his birthright to his brother Jacob for a ' mess of red pottage,' and Gen. xxvi. relates the story of how Jacob impersonated the hairiness of his brother and succeeded in deceiving his blind father, thus gaining the blessing intended for the first-born. E. became a hunter, and eventually the leader of a tribe inhabiting Mt. Seir, S. of the Dead Sea.

**Esbjerg,** a seaport in Denmark on the N. Sea, on the W. coast of Jutland. A harbour was constructed here in 1868 to give Jutland an export haven in place of Schleswig-Holstein, lost in 1864, and to this it owes its rapid rise. It has valuable fisheries, and is an important export centre, chiefly for fish, eggs, bacon, and cattle. Pop. (1925) 24,131.

**Escalators,** moving stairways for transport of passengers. Owing to the fact that stairways can carry more passengers an hour than lifts,

Es. are rapidly taking the place of lifts on underground railways. The E. consists of a number of steps fastened to an endless belt which follows the incline of the stairway. Each step consists of a separate small trolley running on four rollers, which are staggered at the angle of the stairs; the top of the trolley consists of an inverted L-shaped step, which

One of the most recent types of escalators in use on London's Underground system, showing three staircases.

sinks to level at the top and bottom of the stairway. A hand-rail travels round at the same speed as the stairs and is of flexible composition. Powerful electric motors work the moving stairways and self-operating brakes are fitted to meet the possibility of a sudden breaking of a coupling or of a gear wheel.

**Escallonia,** a genus of Saxifragaceæ, consists of about fifty shrubs with alternate evergreen leaves and red or white flowers. All the species inhabit S. America, on the high grounds especially in Alpine regions, while a few, e.g. *E. rubra*, are cultivated in Britain.

**Escanaba,** co. seat of Delta co., Michigan, U.S.A. It is situated on a promontory at the mouth of the R. Escanaba, on the little bay de Noquette, 60 m. S. of Marquette. It has an exhilarating climate and is a summer resort and touring centre. It possesses a good harbour and commodious docks, and ships 6 million tons of iron ore annually. The fisheries and manufactures are important.

Lumber and furniture are exported. Pop. 14,524.

**Escapement,** *see* HOROLOGY.

**Escar,** or **Esker,** *see* ASAR.

**Escarpment,** *see* GEOLOGY.

**Esch,** or **Eschan der Alzette,** a tn. situated in the grand duchy of Luxemburg, with coal and iron mines. Pop. 21,208.

**Eschatology,** derived from two Gk. words, meaning 'last' and 'a discourse.' This is the term under which the doctrines of Christian theology are grouped, concerning the existence of man after death, and the final destiny of the world. E. was in existence among all the great nations of antiquity, dark and ill-defined, as in the Greek, and elaborate as in the Egyptian religion, and with it grew up, more or less definitely, the idea of retribution. Protestant E., however, is generally confined in practical discourses to a consideration of the four 'last things': the Return of Christ, Resurrection of the Dead, the Last Judgment, and the Final Recompense. Speculations regarding the after-life were prevalent among the ancient peoples, but the Christian teaching has its roots in the O.T. and the apocryphal and apocalyptic literature. The chief religious parties who do not recognise eternal punishment as a scriptural doctrine are treated at UNIVERSALISTS (*q.v.*) and CONDITIONAL IMMORTALITY (*q.v.*), and the question of an intermediate state at PURGATORY (*q.v.*). The trend of recent theology is towards an attitude of reserve on the subject, and some schools prefer to speak of the 'Christian hope' rather than of E. (*See* Salmond's *Christian Doctrine of Immortality*.) Eschatological speculations are to be found in More's *Utopia* and Plato's *Republic*, and in the effort to realise the eschatological dreams of human society many have found compensation for the silence of science concerning a survival of the individual.

**Escheat** (Fr. *echoir*, from Lat. *cadere*, to fall or happen). This term is applied to an incident of feudal tenure whereby, when there was no tenant qualified to perform the services, land reverted or fell back to the lord. In theory, at all events, there is no such thing as absolute ownership of real property, the most extensive estate one can possess being looked upon as a subordinate estate, held of a superior landlord, to whom it will eventually return. Up till 1870 E. took place in England when the tenant was convicted of a capital felony, but after that date this kind of E. was abolished. E. still takes place for want of heirs when the owner of land dies intestate.

**Eschenbach,** *see* WOLFRAM VON ESCHENBACH.

**Eschscholtz,** or **Escholtz Bay,** the name of an inlet of Kotzebue Sound, situated in Behring Strait, Alaska. Through this passes the parallel of lat. 67° N., which is the Arctic circle boundary.

**Eschscholtzia,** a genus of beautiful yellow-flowered plants, belongs to the order Papaveraceæ. The species are natives of N. America, but they are frequently cultivated as border plants in Britain; two of these are *E. crocea* and *E. californica.* The fruit has an explosive mechanism.

**Eschwege,** a tn. in Prussia, in the prov. of Hesse-Nassau. It has active industries, including coal, iron and zinc mining, rolling mills, cable works, etc. Pop. 26,000.

**Eschweiler,** a tn. in Rhenish Prussia, situated 8 m. to the N.E. of Aix-la-Chapelle. It possesses valuable coal-mines, and is an important manufacturing town, being the seat of large iron-works, tanneries, breweries, etc. Pop. 26,100.

**Escobar y Mendoza, Antonio** (1589–1669), a Spanish churchman and writer. Educated by the Jesuits, at the early age of fifteen he took the habit of that order. He was famous as a preacher. His writings, which fill forty folio volumes, belong to the field of moral theology, and were not popular with Catholics, who considered they tended to inculcate a loose system of morality. His statement that purity of intention may be a justification of actions which are contrary to the moral code and to human laws was much ridiculed in France by Molière, Boileau, La Fontaine and Pascal.

**Escorial** (Sp. from *escoria,* slag; from Lat. *scoria,* slag), the place of ashes, a celebrated monastery and palace in Spain erected by King Philip II. in gratitude to St. Lawrence, on whose day (Aug. 10, 1557) the victory of St. Quentin was gained. The E. stands 2700 ft. above sea-level, and is built of solid granite. It is designed to resemble the famous gridiron on which St. Lawrence was martyred. It was begun in 1563 and finished by the famous architect Herrera in 1584. It has numerous rooms and passages, mostly gloomy and small, but the chief attractions are the magnificent church, royal palace and tomb, monastery, and college. There is also a valuable library. In 1808 the E. was plundered by the French, and it has been frequently visited by fire and lightning, so that it has been many times repaired and added to, but it still stands as a monument to its original builder.

**Escosura, Patricio de la** (1807–78), a Spanish novelist and poet, *b.* in Madrid. He wrote several plays of very unequal merit, amongst which may be mentioned : *Barbara de Blomberg, Las Flores de Don Juan,* and *El Tio Marcelo.* His best known novel is a tale of Philip II., entitled *Ni Rey ni Roque.*

**Escrow,** *see* DEED.

**Escuage,** or **Scutage** (Lat. *scutum,* shield), in feudal times, was a tax of a pecuniary nature, frequently levied by the crown as a substitute for the personal service of a knight or vassal. This tax was first exacted in 1159 and was restricted by Magna Charta. It was quite usual for a knight to pay this fee by way of compensation for his personal service.

**Escuintla,** a tn. of Guatemala, situated 30 m. S.W. of the city of Guatemala, with which it has railway communication. It is the cap. of the dept. of the same name, carries on a considerable trade, and is a popular winter resort. Pop. 14,000.

**Esculapius,** *see* ÆSCULAPIUS.

**Esculic** (Æsculic) Acid, an acid obtained from the bark of the horse chestnut (*Æsculus Hippocastanum*) and similar trees.

**Escutcheon** (Fr. *écusson,* in contradistinction to *écu,* an ordinary shell), this term, in heraldry, signifies the shield on which arms are painted. In modern heraldry, the name *inescutcheon,* or E. of pretence, is commonly used where there is more than one such charge, and it is also sometimes employed as an honourable amendment or augmentation. The E. *en surtout* is distinct from the E. in charge, as being charged with some particular coat and placed in the centre of a heraldic shield.

**Esdraelon,** or **The Plain of Jezreel,** a noted plain of Palestine, lying to the S.E. of Acre. It is bounded by Mt. Carmel on the W., Gilboa on the S.E., and the Galilean highlands on the N., and stretches across central Palestine with an average width of ten or twelve miles, forming a break between the mountains of Galilee on the N. and those of Samaria on the S.; it is exceedingly fertile and capable of a high state of cultivation. The river Kishon waters the plain, which in the spring is clad in a mass of verdure. Many battles have been fought here, both in ancient and modern times, including Lord Allenby's victories over the Turks in the Great War in 1918.

**Esdras, The Books of.** There is considerable confusion as to the nomenclature of the various Ezra books. According to the A.V., the First and Second Books of Esdras appear

T 2

among the apocryphal books. According to the Septuagint Version, the First Book of Esdras appears as Esdras A, while under the heading Esdras B appear the canonical books of Ezra and Nehemiah. Through the influence of Jerome, this arrangement was not followed in the Vulgate. Here the Book of Ezra is styled Esdras I.; Esdras II. is the Book of Nehemiah, while Esdras I. and II. are re-named Esdras III. and IV. The date of Esdras I. is probably the second century B.C. It is a compilation consisting of : (1) Translation of part of Ezra, (2) part of Nehemiah, (3) part of Chronicles, and (4) an original portion giving the discussion of Darius and the three young men. The translation is free and in superior Gk. to that of Esdras B in the Septuagint. The Second Book of Esdras, the most pathetic of the Jewish apocalypses, dates from the last years of the first century A.D. It contains sixteen chapters, of which ch. i., ii., xv., xvi. are later additions, the first two chapters certainly being by a Christian author. The rest of the book tells of seven visions shown to the prophet Ezra, the whole being in the extreme pessimistic tone of the school of Shammai. It is not yet settled in what language Esdras II. was originally written. It now survives only in versions Latin, Syriac, Ethiopic, etc.

**Esh,** a vil., Durham, England, situated on a height 4 m. N.W. by W. of that city. There is a famous college of St. Cuthbert for the training of Rom. Catholic priests, which contains a fine library and museum. E. colliery is in the vicinity. Pop. (1911) 10,175.

**Esher,** a village and urban district in co. Surrey, England, about 15 m. S.W. of London. A 300 year-old clock is keeping good time in the church. To the east of the village is Claremont, built by Lord Clive, the conqueror. It was purchased in 1816 as a residence for the Princess Charlotte on her marriage with Prince Leopold of Saxe-Coburg, and she died there on Nov. 6, 1817. Her husband, who became King of the Belgians in 1831, transferred his rights to the Crown. Louis Philippe, the exiled King of the Fr., died there in 1850, and his queen in 1866. Cardinal Wolsey once lived in a mansion built here by William of Waynflete, Bishop of Winchester (1447-1486), of which the gateway remains. The Sandown Park race course adjoins the station. Pop. 14,309.

**Esher, Reginald Baliol Brett,** second Viscount (1852-1930), son of first viscount, to whose title he succeeded in 1899 In 1903 he became Chairman of the War Office Reconstitution Commission. He acquired some distinction as a writer, having published *Footprints of Statesmen*, 1892 ; *The Correspondence of Queen Victoria*, 1907 ; *The Tragedy of Lord Kitchener*, 1921. Died suddenly in London, Jan. 22.

**Esher, William Baliol Brett, Viscount** (1815-99), *b.* in London, son of the Rev. Joseph Brett of Chelsea. Educated at Westminster and Caius College, Cambridge. Called to the Bar in 1840 ; became a Q.C. in 1861 ; appointed Master of the Rolls, 1883. Retired from the bench in 1897, when he was created a viscount.

**Eshowe,** or **Ekowe,** or **Echowe,** a small tn. of Natal, S. Africa, situated about 30 m. N. of the estuary of the R. Tugela, overlooking the Indian Ocean. There are several hotels and the remains of the old fort where Col. Pearson was shut up by the Zulus. Pop. (white) 675, (coloured) 357.

**Esk,** the name of numerous Scottish and English rivers. Among the chief are : (1) The N. Esk flowing through Kincardineshire and Forfarshire, Scotland, rising near Edzell, and flowing into the North Sea, 4 m. from Montrose ; length about 30 m. (2) S. Esk, rising in the Grampians, flowing through Strathmore to Montrose harbour, with Brechin and Montrose on its banks ; length about 50 m. (3) A river of Dumfriesshire, formed by the confluence of the Black and the White E. in Eskdalemuir, flowing 35 m. to the Solway Firth, near Sarkfoot. (4) Two small streams, N. and S. Esk, rising in Peeblesshire, and flowing through Midlothian. They unite at Dalkeith, flowing into the Firth of Forth at Musselburgh. The N. branch passes Roslin Castle, Hawthornden, Habbie's Howe, Melville Castle ; the S. branch, Dalhousie Castle and Newbattle Abbey.

**Eskdalemuir,** a par., Dumfriesshire, Scotland, about 12 m. from Langholm. There is a National Magnetic Observatory to replace the one which was formerly at Kew. Pop. about 400.

**Eski-Djumna,** a town in Bulgaria. It lies 18 miles W. of Shumla. The inhabitants breed silkworms and make pottery. Pop. 10,540.

**Eskilstuna,** a tn. in Sweden, 57 m. W. of Stockholm. Sometimes called the Sheffield of Sweden on account of its iron, steel, and copper works. Pop. 13,500.

**Eskimo,** or **Eskimaun Indians** (commonly called **Eskimos** or **Usquemonds**), a race dwelling in the northern coasts of America, from Labrador to Mount St. Elias, and also occupying Baffin Land and the shores of Greenland. They are known as Innuits, a word signifying ' man ' in their own tongue; the word ' Es.' being said to be a term of reproach meaning ' eaters of raw meat,' applied to them by some Indian neighbours, the Algonquins, living S. of them. The Es. are a race of the yellow type, but of a lighter colour than the Algonquins and rather smaller in stature. Their sustenance is chiefly derived from the capture of seals, which are their staple food and very valuable to them in numerous other ways, supplying them with dog-food, boots, clothing, tents, light, heat, and harpoon lines. They also procure food by pursuing the chase on land and by fishing. The *kayak*, a small slim boat for one man, is their most interesting and best-known invention for hunting. Its

crawling on hands and knees; indeed in some parts, N. Alaska for example, the huts are half under ground. Some of these winter dwellings shelter as many as forty or fifty persons. The E. men and women are clad alike in trousers of seal or deer skin, according to the season, and in a loose-fitting shirt, surmounted by a hood, which is enlarged for women and children. The Es. are very ingenious in their manufactures, and during the long winter days indoors the men make carvings of walrus ivory, horn and wood, for use as well as ornament. The women spend most of their time in making the clothing and tents. As to the religion of the E., he believes all things to be ensouled, and spirits innumerable to abound everywhere.

[*Canadian Pacific*

ESKIMOS IN *KAYAKS*

framework is covered with skin, and with the waterproof jacket worn by the man, completely protects him from the waves, so that even if he capsizes he is able to rise unhurt by means of his paddle. The dog-sledge is in use everywhere amongst the Es., except by those in South-Western Greenland, and the E. dog is admirably adapted for transport by sledge, being strong and powerful. The Es. are a cheerful and generous race, and are friendly and hospitable to strangers. Their pastimes are athletic sports and dramatic entertainments, and their children mimic the elders on a small scale. Their dwellings are of two kinds, tents for summer, and houses or huts for winter use. The tents are generally made of sealskin; but the winter dwellings are usually built of stone, covered with moss and banked up with snow, the entrance consisting of a long passage, only high enough to admit a man

**Eskimo Dog,** a sledge-dog used in the Arctic regions. It is broad chested, with a stout, thick neck, erect ears, and long, sharp muzzle, not unlike the grey wolf of the prairie. It is only half domesticated, and does not bark, but howls like a wolf. E. Ds. have a great deal of staying power; they are rarely fed by their Eskimo masters, which perhaps accounts for their sharp uncertain tempers. There are two breeds, the ' Ostiaks ' and the ' Samoyeds.' The former is wolf-like, but the latter is entirely white and resembles a large Pomeranian.

**Eski Shehr,** a tn. in Asiatic Turkey, Asia Minor, connected by rail with Scutari, and the centre of the Anatolian Railway system. It has celebrated warm springs and valuable deposits of meerschaum in its immediate vicinity, pipes of the material being manufactured in the town. The Gks. were defeated here by the

Turkish Nationalists in April 1921. The Moslems were defeated near here by Godfrey de Bouillon in 1097.

**Eski Zagra,** or **Eski Sagra,** *see* STARA-ZAGORA.

**Esmarch, Friedrich von** (1823–1908) a Ger. military surgeon, *b.* in Schleswig-Holstein. He was educated at the universities of Kiel and Göttingen, and was nominated professor and director of the Kiel University in 1860. In 1866 he became superintendent of surgical work in the Berlin hospitals, and was considered one of the greatest authorities on hospital management and military surgery.

**Esmeraldas,** a tn. in Ecuador, S. America, bordering on Colombia. Vessels anchor outside the bar (depth, high tide, 10 ft.) and load and discharge by means of launches. It is the centre of a rich agricultural district, and the headquarters for a number of merchants and mining companies. Straw hats are manufactured and gold is mined. Pop. about 5000.

name of the pike, which belongs to the family *Esocidæ.* It is characterised by the absence of scales on the head, by a long narrow body terminating in a forked caudal fin, and by a long, broad, depressed snout in which the upper jaw exceeds the lower in length. The pike inhabits the fresh waters of Europe, America, and Asia, and not uncommonly attains a length of 45 or 46 in., with a weight of 35 or 36 lb. It is the most voracious and greedy of all fresh-water fish, and will devour all kinds of smaller fish, even the young of its own kind.

**Espalier** (Fr. railing for fruit-trees ; Lat. *spatula,* broad piece, blade). Signifies a railing on which fruit trees are trained. The term E. is also applied to the system of training plants to grow as Es. on a trellis (espalier). Es. may be constructed of wood, iron, or, more cheaply, by means of strong wire, supported by upright wooden or iron posts. Es. have the advantage of protecting the

ESOX (PIKE)

**Esna,** a tn. of Upper Egypt, 25 to 30 m. S. of the ruins of Thebes, on the l. b. of the Nile. It is celebrated for the ruins of a vast ancient temple to the ram-headed god Khnum, built in the time of the Rom. emperors Claudius and Vespasian and others, and also possesses a Coptic monastery. Its chief manufs. are pottery, shawls, and cotton, in which commodities it carries on an active trade. A barrage was built and opened in 1909 to hold up the Nile water in low floods. Pop. about 20,000.

**Esop,** *see* ÆSOPUS.

**Esoteric** and **Exoteric** (Gk. ἐσωτερικός, inner, and ἐξωτερικός, outer), terms originally derived from the ancient ' mysteries,' the first designating doctrines intended only for the initiated, the second those intended for the uninitiated or general public. By analogy these words have been used to mark distinctions thought to exist between certain classes of the writings of Aristotle and other philosophers. Aristotle himself only uses the term ' exoteric,' which Grote takes to refer to the ' dialectic ' as opposed to the ' didactic ' method.

**Esox,** or *Esox lucins,* the generic

fruits to a great extent from the wind, and thus preventing a large quantity being shaken off before they are properly ripened. The most suitable fruit trees for Es., commonly grown in Great Britain, are apple and pear trees. Their treatment is usually similar to that of wall trees, but they are generally trained to form horizontal branches. For the raising of Es., plants of one year should be chosen and planted at distances that will allow of each one covering a surface of about 20 sq. yds. The stem should be cut about 12 in. from ground-level in about a year from planting, immediately above three buds. Lateral branches will then be formed by two of these buds, while the highest one will form the extension of the stem, and these three stems must be kept in an equal condition of vigour during the summer. During the second year no more lateral branches must be allowed to grow, but after this a fresh pair of lateral branches can be allowed to grow each year. The wood of the tree will be fully established in about sixteen years.

**Espartero, Baldomero** (1792–1879),

*b.* at Granatula, La Mancha, was the son of a cartwright. He was originally intended for the priesthood, but volunteered into the ' Sacred Battalion ' of students on the French invasion of Spain, and fought in S. America in 1816 after the War of Independence. He played an important part in the Carlist wars, and as commander-in-chief concluded the Carlist Convention in 1839, which brought the war to an end. In 1841 he became regent, from which position he was driven two years later by a counter-revolution. In 1854, however, he was recalled to save Isabel II.'s throne, and for a time he became dictator and able to conciliate all progressive parties. He retired from public life in 1856. *See* Life by Florez.

**Esparto Grass,** or *Stipa tenacissima,* a species of Gramineæ closely allied to the feather-grass and occurs in N. Africa. It is a graceful plant often cultivated in Britain for its beauty, and is largely used in the manufacture of paper. Two other species of grass, *Lygeum Spartum* and *Ampelodesma tenax,* both of which are to be found in Africa and round the Mediterranean, serve the same purpose as E. G.

**Esperanto,** the international auxiliary language invented by Dr. L. L. Zamenhof, an oculist of Warsaw, and first published in 1887. The first journal in the language, *La Esperantisto,* which was issued in 1889 from a press in Nuremberg, was suppressed, as the Russian government forbade its entry into Russia on the ground that the journal contained contributions by Tolstoy. The language, which in 1895 had spread to France, began an era of rapid progress from the first international congress, held in Boulogne in 1905. In construction, E. differs fundamentally from its predecessor, Volapük. Every word, before incorporated into Volapük, underwent a process of mutilation, and the author (Abbé Schleyer) did not even hesitate to create words arbitrarily. (' Volapük,' *e.g.,* is a corruption of two English words, ' world ' and ' speech.') On the other hand, E. is based, broadly speaking, on the principle : *that, with a view to attaining the maximum of internationality, the vocabulary of the international language should consist of root-words which are found to be common to several languages of Romance and Germanic origin, due attention being paid to other factors.* International words (e.g. *theatre, nature, park, character, centre, form, telephone*) are incorporated into the language without change, beyond conformity with the orthography.

E., too, is strictly phonetic, its twenty-eight letters representing distinct sounds, and there are no digraphs. Each part of speech has a distinct termination, *e.g.* nouns end in *o,* adjectives in *a,* derived adverbs in *e* : there is only one conjugation to the verb, which has twelve terminations; the prepositions have a clearly defined meaning and by the aid of some thirty prefixes and suffixes the language assumes a wonderful flexibility. Its protagonists guard the language from arbitrary or capricious changes, while at the same time they allow great latitude in the adaptation of new words to the international setting. The author of E. (*vide* the ' Declaration ' of Boulogne, etc.) disclaims any rights of ownership or control of the language. This attitude is of vital importance, as it was on the question of ownership that Volapük came to grief. The headquarters of E. in England is the British Esperanto Association, 142 High Holborn, London, W.C. The Universala Esperanto-Asocio is an association founded to utilise the auxiliary language for tourist and commercial purposes. The following is the Lord's Prayer in E. : ' Patro nia, kiu estas en la ĉielo : Sankta estu Via nomo : Venu regeco Via : Estu volo Via, kiel en la ĉielo, tiel ankaŭ sur la tero : Panon nian ĉiutagan donu al ni hodiaŭ : Kaj pardonu al ni ŝuldojn niajn, kiel ni ankaŭ pardonas al niaj ŝuldantoj : Kaj ne konduku nin en tenton : sed liberigu nin de malbono : ĉar Via estas la regado, la forto, kaj la gloro, eterne. Amen.' *See also* Ido (Revised Esperanto).

**Espinal,** a tn. in Colombia, S. America, 75 m. S.W. of Bogota. It has pottery works and tobacco plantations. Pop. 10,000.

**Espionage.** The organised employment of secret agents by govs. to obtain information concerning other countries which cannot be obtained by open methods. It also includes the dissemination of false information intended to deceive other countries. As the essence of espionage is secrecy, it follows that any treatise upon the subject, purporting to give details of the inner workings of any particular current system, must be regarded with doubt. The value of secret information is immense, because it gives the receiver a definite advantage over the opposite party, and by no one is this appreciated more than by military commanders. An early example of spying is to be found in the Old Testament, where Moses sent men to ' spy out the land of Canaan.'

One novel method of conveying information to the authority concerned is that employed by Istiæus when at the Court of Darius, King of Persia. He was watched so minutely that he hit upon the idea of shaving his servant's head, writing a message on the head, and then, when the hair had grown again, sending him to the person concerned.

Before the Great War Germany had a well-developed secret service, and it is estimated that over 20,000 of her agents were in France in various occupations. There is always a note of picturesqueness connected with spying, mainly due to the fact that it appeals only to the more adventurous spirits who have the dual gift of caution and boldness. Among the Great War spies Colonel T. E. Lawrence and Mata Hari will be remembered. The former was British and operated in Egypt and Palestine ; whilst the latter was a Javanese woman, who operated in France on behalf of Germany. She was caught and executed.

Spying during peace is usually confined to the collection of information on behalf of the diplomatic service.

**Espirito** or **Espiritu Santo**, a maritime state of Brazil, first occupied by the Portuguese in 1535. It is bounded N. by Bahia, W. by Minas Geraes, S. by Rio de Janeiro, E. by the Atlantic. There are tropical forests on the slopes of the Serras dos Aimorés and Negra. It is swampy near the coast. Rio Doce, the chief river, divides it into two ; the Parahiba do Sul is on the S. boundary. The area is about 17,310 sq. m. The cap., Victoria, on Espirito Santo Bay, is the best harbour. It is well watered and very fertile and produces coffee, sugar, corn, and timber. There are 30,000 German colonists with their own schools and churches, and also many Italians. Pop. 640,000.

**Espiritu Santo**, the largest of the New Hebrides, 75 m. by 45, is heavily wooded and well watered. The highest point is Santo Peak, 5520 ft. There are a number of British and Fr. settlers. Coconuts, cotton, cocoa and maize are grown. Santo, as it is usually called, has a numerous native population, but of late the death-rate has been very great. Cannibalism is still occasionally practised.

**Esplanade** (from Lat. *explanare*, to level), in fortification, the glacis of the counterscarp, or sloping of the parapet of the covered way towards the country. Also the open space separating the citadel of a fortress from the town. It is especially used of a level terrace, intended as a

public promenade, such as the open walks along the ' front ' at seaside places.

**Esprit, St.**, *see* BAYONNE.

**Espronceda, José de** (1810–42), a Spanish poet and revolutionary politician. He was early imprisoned by the gov. for his radical views (c. 1825), and banished shortly afterwards. E. wrote the historical romance, *Don Sancho Saldaña ó el Castellano de Cuéllar* (1834). Returning to Madrid, he took part in the revolutionary contests (1835–36). Byron's influence in his writings is very marked. His best work was lyrical poetry, such as *El Diablo-Mundo, El Estudiante de Salamanca, El Verdugo, A la Patria, Hymn to the Sun*, and *El Mendigo*. His ambitious *Dona Blanca de Borbon* was not so successful. *See* Kennedy, *Modern Poets and Poetry of Spain*.

**Espy, James Pollard** (1785–1860), a meteorologist, *b.* in Pennsylvania. In 1843 he was appointed to the Washington observatory, where he laid the basis of the western bureau. He published *Philosophy of Storms* in 1841.

**Esquimalt**, or **Esquimault**, a seaport tn. of Vancouver Is., Canada, important as a naval station on the Pacific. It contains a naval yard, dry dock, arsenal, and hospital. There are a salmon cannery and a ship-building yard and an extensive harbour on the Juan de Fuca Strait. Pop. 6484.

**Esquimaux**, *see* ESKIMO.

**Esquire** (Old Fr. *escuyer*, from Lat. *scutarius*, shield-bearer), originally the attendant on a knight and bearer of his shield or armour. He ranked below the knight bachelor, and his office served as the apprentice-stage of knighthood. The title was one of function, not birth, and was not hereditary. It came to be a title of honour, implying a rank between that of knight and valet. According to Coke (2 *Institutes*, 688), any one may be called E. (usually written Esq.) who has a legal right to call himself a ' gentleman,' *i.e.* one who lawfully bears a coat-of-arms. The title is widely used now by courtesy for men of all ranks, excluding manual labourers and small shopkeepers. Those legally entitled to bear it include sons of peers or knights and their eldest sons, officers of the army and navy, and members of the Bar. E. has followed much the same course as the word ' gentleman.' *See* Selden, *Titles of Honour*, 1672 ; *New English Dict.*, iii. *See also* SQUIRE.

**Esquirol, Jean Etienne Dominique** (1772–1840), a French physician, *b.* at Toulouse. In 1817 he became a lecturer on the diseases of the brain, and in 1825 first physician to the Maison des Aliénés, but after being deprived of his appointments during the Revolution, retired from the profession. He wrote *Des Illusions chez les Aliénés,* 1832, and *Des Maladies Mentales,* 1838.

**Esquiros, Henri François Alphonse** (c. 1812–76), a French poet, politician, and historian. He wrote both poems and novels of a strong socialistic tendency, and was imprisoned for his *L'évangile du peuple,* 1840. E. went to Holland and then to England, sending studies to the *Revue des deux Mondes,* afterwards known as *L'Angleterre et la vie anglaise,* 1859–70. Other works are : *Les Hirondelles,* 1834 ; *Charlotte Corday,* 1840 (a novel) ; *Songs of a Prisoner,* 1841 ; *Les Vierges martyres, les Vierges folles, les Vierges sages,* 1841–42 ; *Histoire des Montagnards,* 1847 ; *La Morale universelle ; L'Emile du XIX^e Siècle,* 1870.

**Essad Pasha** (c. 1875–1920), an Albanian chieftain who, during the Balkan War (1912–13), defended Scutari against the combined Montenegrin and Servian forces, and who, at the conclusion of that siege, proclaimed himself prince of an autonomous Albania owning the suzerainty of Turkey. The family of Essad, the Toptanis, came from Tirana, near Durázzo, and was of considerable wealth and power—Essad's brother, Gani, being the special friend of, and executioner to, the Sultan Abdul Hamid. Gani, losing the sultan's high favour, was done to death—a deed which made Essad the sworn foe of the Hamidean régime. He joined the Young Turk revolution in 1908, and from then till 1912 represented Durázzo in the Turkish parliament. His support of the Young Turks was of a very qualified nature, and he even tried to negotiate a British protectorate. When Prince Wilhelm of Wied became Mpret in March 1914, E. became his Minister of War and of the Interior ; but was exiled for disaffection—returning to become President of the Albanian Provisional gov. Oct. 5, 1914 : which he accomplished by terrifying the senate. When enemy forces drove him from Albania, he retired to Salonika. He afterwards presided over the Albanian delegation in Paris. At the close of the war he managed to overthrow the Italianised gov. established at Durázzo. He was murdered in a Paris street, June 13, 1920, by an Albanian named Aveni Rustam.

**Essay** (Fr. *essai,* attempt). What is now generally understood by an E. is a literary composition of moderate length on any given subject other than purely scientific. It should treat of life in general, and not of any specialised subject. It originally implied a want of finish, and Dr. Johnson defined it as ' an irregular, undigested piece.' An E. is strictly rather a series of personal comments than a finished argument or conclusive examination of any matter. As a separate form of English literature, it dates from the close of the sixteenth century. The name appears to have become common on the publication of Montaigne's *Essais,* 1580. The first great name connected with the history of the English E. is that of Bacon (1561–1626). Abraham Cowley may, however, perhaps be more

**W. HAZLITT**
One of the great essayists of the nineteenth century

truly regarded as the father of the English E. His E. *Of Myself* may be taken as a typical example of what such compositions should be. Other essayists of the seventeenth century were Sir Thomas Browne, Sir William Temple, and Dryden. The eighteenth century was the great age of essay-writing. In 1711 Addison and Steele founded the *Spectator,* thus popularising the E. as a form of literature in England. The *Tatler* and the *Guardian* also contained numerous examples of typical Es., mostly the work of Steele and Addison. Fielding's Es. appeared in the *Covent Garden Journal,* 1752, Dr. Johnson's in the *Rambler,* 1750, the *Adventurer,* 1752, and the *Idler,* 1759. Other essayists of this period were Swift, Goldsmith (in the *Bee* and the *Citizen of the World*), and Sydney Smith. (*See* Chalmer's *British Essayists,* 1817,

45 vols.) Such terms as review, memoir, or treatise, apply better to more exhaustive studies, such as Locke's *Essay Concerning Human Understanding*, or Burke's *Essay* on *the Sublime and Beautiful*, while the journalistic ' article ' may be used for slighter sketches than those entitled to be called Es. A great revival of the E took place early in the nineteenth century, and with this movement Lamb's name is always closely connected. His *Essays of Elia* appeared 1823, the *Last Essays of Elia*, 1833. Other essayists of note of this century are Hazlitt, Leigh Hunt, Carlyle, Macaulay, Thackeray, Walter Bagehot, Walter Pater, and Robert Louis Stevenson. Names of the earlier period that deserve mention as writers of works closely approaching the E. in style are those of Sir Thomas More, Sir Philip Sidney, Burton, Sir Thomas Overbury, Samuel Pepys, Bernard Mandeville, Laurence Sterne, Defoe, and others. De Quincey, Southey, and Shelley all belong to the nineteenth century. The E. in modern times has not been quite so popular. Men are less often essayists first and foremost, but poets, historians, or novelists, who write Es. occasionally in leisure hours. Some of the chief names are Augustine Birrell, A. C. Benson, E. V. Lucas, Andrew Lang, G. K. Chesterton, Austin Dobson, George Saintsbury, Max Beerbohm, Hilaire Belloc. Pope alone in the eighteenth century conceived an E. in heroic verse. His Es. *On Criticism* and *On Man* are really treatises, but the *Moral Essays*, if in prose, might have appeared in the *Spectator*. Apart from this all Es. are understood to be prose writings. In America the chief essayists include W. Irving, N. Hawthorne, J. R. Lowell, and Emerson. In Germany, Lessing, Schlegel, and Hermann Grimm are among the best. The E. took firm root in France at a comparatively late period, the chief representatives being Voltaire, Cousin, Rousseau, Sainte-Beuve, Michelet, Gautier, Lamartine, Anatole France, and E. Faguet.

**Essays and Reviews.** In 1860 a remarkable volume was published under this title. All the contributors, excepting one, were clergymen of the Church of England, and the book was severely censured for heterodox views by nearly all the bishops and formally condemned by convocation in 1864. Bishop Thomson (afterwards Archbishop of York) and Bishop Wilberforce replied to the *Essays and Reviews* in their works *Aids to Faith*, and *Replies to Essays and Reviews*. The volume contained the following seven papers: (1) 'The Educa-

tion of the World'; (2) 'Bunsen's Biblical Researches'; (3) ' On the Study of the Evidences of Christianity'; (4) ' The National Church '; (5) ' The Mosaic Cosmogony '; (6) ' Tendencies of Religious Thought in England '; (7) ' The Interpretation of Scripture.'

**Essen,** an old tn. a few miles to the N. of the Ruhr, in the centre of the Rhenish-Westphalian Coal Measures, Germany, which are among the most prolific in the world. Its famous Krupp works are the largest steel works in Europe; they manufacture locomotives, goods-trucks, electric cranes, machinery, cash registers, cinematographic apparatus, surgical instruments, etc., but no war material. The welfare arrangements for the 35,000 employees are unsurpassed; they include 12,000 workers' dwellings, a dental clinic, maternity home, and a library of 100,000 volumes. Besides these works there are numerous machine-shops, foundries, chemical factories, and coal mines. The Münster Kirche is one of the most anct. churches in Germany, the W. choir, with its tower, dates from the tenth century. The Protestant Market Kirche was probably completed in 1066. E. had 3480 inhabitants in 1803 and 466,130 in 1930.

**Essen, Hans Hendrik von, Count** (1755–1824), a Swedish field-marshal and statesman. He was a favourite of Gustavus III., fighting under him (1788–90). He warned the king against his assassination, but was unable to prevent it (1792). E. was governor of Stockholm (1796), becoming grand equerry in 1800. Charles III. made him councillor of state, with the title Count, and sent him as ambassador to Paris, where he negotiated peace (1810). *See* Thiers, *Histoire de l'Empire;* Wieselgren, *Essen,* 1855.

**Essence** (Lat. *essentia*, from *esse*, to be) : 1. In philosophy, the equivalent of Gk. οὐσία, and was originally used in the same sense as ' substance.' Later ' substance ' came to be used for the undetermined substratum of a thing, E. for the qualities expressed in the definition of a thing. Locke neatly defines it by saying : ' Essence may be taken for the very being of a thing, whereby it is what it is.' 2. In pharmacy, Es. are solutions of essential oils in alcohol, and are capable of being prepared in two ways : (1) By adding refined spirit to the odoriferous parts of plants or to the essential oils, and distilling. (2) By adding the essential oil to the refined spirit and agitating till a uniform mixture is obtained. Thus E. of lemons is merely a solution of volatile oil in rectified spirit. The term E., however, has received a more comprehensive significance and is applied to a liquid possessing the properties of the substance of which it professes to be the E. *Quintessence* (Lat. *quinta essentia*, fifth E.), the pure E. of anything, a solution of an essential oil in alcohol. The name applies to the purest essence obtained after five distillations, and was originally used to denote ether.

**Essendon**, a tn. of Victoria, Australia, situated in Bourke co., on the Moonee Ponds, at a distance of 5 m. from Melbourne. Pop. 18,744.

**Essenes**, a Jewish religious brotherhood of the time of Christ. Though it played a somewhat important part in the history of Jerusalem, very little is accurately known about the E. The Roman historian, Pliny, the Jewish Josephus, and Philo the Alexandrian are the authorities who speak of them from personal knowledge. They are nowhere mentioned either in the Bible or in the Talmud, though it has been commonly held that the Nazirim referred to in the Talmud are the E. under another name. On the one hand, the E. were highly-developed Pharisees, laying exceedingly great stress on the maintenance of ceremonial purity. Ceremonial washings formed an important part of their practice, and white garments were worn. Their food was specially prepared by the priests, and the common meal was eaten with great solemnity. Asceticism was the keynote of their system ; every form of sensual enjoyment was held to be sinful. Marriage and intercourse with women were entirely forbidden. The E. were communists, mostly engaged in agriculture. The proceeds of all labour went into the common purse, from which all expenses were paid. Entrance to the order could be obtained only by a three years' novitiate. The E. objected to animal slaughter, and this fact prevented many of them from joining in the temple service. Moreover, it is said that they engaged in sun-worship. The sect came to an end in the second century A.D. Owing to resemblances to the E. in life and teaching, John the Baptist has been regarded as one of them, but there are important facts against this theory. *See* Lightfoot's *Epistles to Colossians and to Philemon*.

**Essential Oils**, the oils which possess the odours in a concentrated form of the plants or vegetable substances from which they are obtained. These oils are generally contained in a special gland or cell within the plant. The E. O. are generally insoluble in water, but they dissolve freely in alcohol, ether, or fatty oils. They contain a large proportion of carbon which causes them to ignite easily, but as a rule they leave no permanent grease spot. They possess an aromatic smell, a hot burning taste, and can be distilled unchanged.

**Essequibo**, a riv., British Guiana, which has its source in the Acarai Mts., about 45 m. N. of the Equator. It is a river of many rapids, and therefore very difficult to navigate. The most noted falls of the E. itself are the Aretaka cataracts. There are several tributaries, the Cuyuni with the Mazaruni, the Rupununi, and the Potaro. After flowing for a distance of 620 m. the E. enters the Atlantic, and at its mouth it measures a width of 20 m. Among the natural wonders of the Essequibo River region are the Kaieteur Falls (the old man's fall) on the Potaro river. These have a clear drop of 741 ft., or nearly five times the height of Niagara Falls. Owing to the difficulty of the journey, but few people from other parts of the world have visited this spot, and its remoteness and seclusion greatly enhance its impressiveness. The Potaro river here has a width of 400 ft. and a depth of 35 ft., plunging down a valley of nearly 800 ft., whence it flows away amid ravines of thickly wooded sandstone cliffs on a winding course, broken in places by falls and rapids, which have to be circumvented by portages, until eventually it reaches the Essequibo. The district round the falls has now been proclaimed by the gov. of British Guiana as the Kaieteur National Park and steps have been taken to prevent destruction of birds and animals. The altitude of the setting, which is worthy of the passing of an Arthur, is from 1200 to 2000 ft. and hopes are entertained of making it a health resort for British Guiana.

**Essex** (A.-S. East-Seaxe), a maritime co., S.E. England, bounded by Cambridge and Suffolk on the N., E. by North Sea, S. by R. Thames, W. by Middlesex and Hertfordshire. The surface is flat and marshy near the coast, but richly wooded in the centre and N. Among the chief rivers are the Thames, Stour, Lee, Colne, Crouch, and Blackwater. Farming is good, and splendid wheat-crops flourish in E. Cereals, teazels, saffron ; hops are largely grown, and livestock raised. The manufactures include silk, lace, and strawplaits. There is a government powder-factory at Waltham Abbey. Oyster-fisheries and breweries are important. The Tilbury and Victoria and Albert Docks of the Port of London are on E. coast. Harwich is the port for continental

562

traffic, and the capital is Chelmsford. Pop. 1,468,341. *See* Wright, *History and Topography of Essex*, 1831; *Victoria County History, Essex;* Kelway's edition of *Memorials of Old Essex*, 1908.

**Essex, Earl of.** This title was conferred in 1572 on Walter Devereux, the scion of an old Herefordshire house, but was originally borne by Devereux's ancestors (the Mandevilles, Bohuns, Bouchiers), and by Thomas Cromwell. In 1139, King Stephen created Geoffrey Mandeville Earl of Essex, and the family of Bohun was the next to bear the title, but on the death of Humphrey Bohun, the peerage seems to have reverted to the crown. In 1461 Edward IV. created Henry Bouchier Earl of Essex, but on the death of his successor, the earldom became extinct, and in 1540 it descended upon the Cromwell family in the person of Thomas Cromwell. The family of Parr obtained the earldom after the execution of Cromwell, but forfeited it in 1553. Thus the title was borne by six different families in English history. Two members of the Devereux family had the honour conferred upon them, viz. Robert earl marshal of England and one of Queen Elizabeth's favourites; and Robert Devereux, commander-in-chief of the parliamentary forces in the Civil War. The earldom expired in 1646 at his death, but Charles II. conferred the title on the Capel family in 1661, and the present earl is a representative of this family.

**Essex, James** (*c.* 1723–84), an English architect, son of a carpenter, *b.* at Cambridge; he was educated there at King's College. He showed great skill in Gothic architecture, and restored and altered many public buildings. These include King's College Chapel; Ely and Lincoln Cathedrals. He also designed the Ramsden building at St. Catherine's College (1757), the stone bridge at Trinity College (1766), and the Sidney Sussex College Chapel (1784).

**Essex Regiment,** formerly the 44th and 56th regiments, which were linked in 1881 to form the present regiment. The 44th was raised in 1741. Served in N. America under General Braddock, and remained in Canada until 1765. Returned to America 1775 and served against the Fr. also in West Indies. Fought under Abercromby in Egypt in 1801. Joined Wellington's army in Peninsula in 1811; and captured a French ' Eagle ' at Salamanca; fought at Waterloo; thence in Burma and Afghanistan, Crimean and China Campaigns. The 56th was raised in 1755, served at Havana in 1762,

and was in the defence of Gibraltar, 1779–83. Served again in W. Indies : then went to India (1805). Served in Crimea and then in Egypt. Fought in S. African Campaign, 1899–1902. Raised thirty-one battalions during Great War and served in France, Flanders, Gallipoli, Egypt, Palestine. This is one of the few regiments which bears an ' Eagle ' on its colours, which commemorates that captured at Salamanca.

**Essex, Robert Devereux,** second **Earl of** (1567–1601), an English nobleman and favourite of Elizabeth, son of Walter (*d.* 1576). He was educated at Cambridge, and accompanied Leicester's expedition to Holland in 1585. E. became Master of the Horse (1587) and took part in Drake's expedition to Portugal (1589). In 1591 he commanded an expedition to Normandy, and the land-forces at Cadiz in 1596. He married Sidney's widow in 1590, became Privy Councillor, 1593 ; earl marshal of England, 1597 ; and chancellor of Cambridge University, 1598. E. was also commander on ' the islands voyage,' an expedition to the Azores. In 1599 he was appointed lord-deputy of Ireland, but fell into disgrace for the failure of his operations against the Irish rebels (see note on Shakespeare's *Henry V.*, prol. to Act. v.). He tried to force a hearing from the Queen, and failing in that formed a plot to compel her to dismiss his enemies from power. For this he was accused of treason and executed, Bacon being his prosecutor. Elizabeth was said to have been inconsolable for his loss. *See* Clarendon (Edward Hyde), *The Characters of Robert, Earl of Essex, and George, Duke of Buckingham,* 1700 ; *Edinburgh Review,* July, 1853 ; Hume, *History of England.*

**Essex, Robert Devereux,** third **Earl of** (*c.* 1591–1646), an English general, son of Robert (executed in 1601), *b.* in London. James I. restored to him his father's rank and titles (1604). He was a companion of the Prince of Wales (later Charles I.), but by 1626 had joined the parliamentary party. E. was lieutenant-general in the army sent against the Scottish Covenanters (1639). He refused to accompany Charles in his flight from London, and became leader of the Presbyterian party. In 1642 he commanded the parliamentarian army, and fought at Edgehill; captured Reading, and relieved Gloucester (1643). E. won the first battle of Newbury in 1643. His invasion of Cornwall (1644) proved unsuccessful, and his army capitulated at Lostwithiel. E. resigned his commission (1645) on the passing of the 'Self-denying Ordinance.' He was the last of his family to bear the title. *See* Codrington,

ROBERT DEVEREUX, THIRD EARL OF ESSEX

*Life of Robert, Earl of Essex*, 1646; Cust, *Lives of the Warriors of the Civil Wars of France and England*, 1867.

**Essex, Walter Devereux,** first **Earl of** (c. 1541–76), an English nobleman and statesman, son of Sir Richard Devereux. In 1569 he raised troops to suppress the northern rebellion under the earls of Westmorland and Northumberland, and was created Earl of E. in 1572 for this service. A favourite of Elizabeth, he was sent as commander (1573) to conquer the Ulster rebels. His attempts to subdue and colonise Ulster were not very successful. E. resigned his command in 1575, but returned as earl marshal of Ireland, and *d.* at Dublin. *See* Hume, *History of England;* Devereux, *Lives of the Earls of Essex*, 1853.

**Essington Port,** a bay of N. Australia on the N. side of Coburg peninsula. The shores of the bay are low and destitute of vegetation. The climate is unhealthy. On the W. side, 17 m. from its entrance, the British settlement of Victoria was founded in 1839. It was abandoned in consequence of its insalubrity in 1845.

**Esslingen,** an anct. tn. of Würtemberg, Germany, with 40,560 inhabs., dominated by a castle. It has three churches of the thirteenth and fourteenth centuries and a fine late Gothic town hall of 1430, the Katherine hospital founded in the thirteenth century, and the remains of the town walls. The industrial quarters are outside the old tn., there are machine, textile (especially

gloves), leather, toys and furniture industries. It is celebrated for its wines. Pop. 40,560.

**Essonnes,** a French tn. in Seine-et-Oise, on the Essonne, half a mile S.W. of Corbeil. Pop. 9630.

**Est,** a canal in the N.E. of France, starting from the Meuse near Givet, and traversing the valley of the Meuse to Port-sur-Saône. It includes canalised portions of the Rs. Meuse and Moselle. The total length is 285 m.

**Established Church,** *see* ENGLAND, CHURCH OF; SCOTLAND, CHURCH OF; STATE CHURCH.

**Estaing, Charles Hector Théodat, Comte d'** (1729–94), a French admiral, was a native of Auvergne. In 1778 he went to help the U.S.A. against Britain, and in the following year took St. Vincent and Grenada. He was, however, wounded in a subsequent engagement and returned to France, where he was eventually put to death for supporting Marie Antoinette.

**Estaires,** a French tn. in Nord, on the Lys, 12 m. W. of Lille. In the Great War, captured by the Gers. in their final effort of 1918 on April 10; two days later General Haig issued his fateful Order of the Day containing the sentence ' every position must be held to the last man; there must be no retirement.' Pop. 6610.

**Estancia,** Brazil, 25 m. S.W. of Sergipe on the Piauky. It exports cotton and tobacco. Pop. about 12,000.

**Estate.** An E. signifies that title or interest which a person has in lands, tenements, hereditaments, or other property. It is either real E., which comprises freehold lands, tenements, or hereditaments, and copyhold lands; or personal E., which comprises all other kinds of property or rights in or over property, including leasehold interests in lands, tenements, and hereditaments (*see also* ENTAIL, FEE, FEE SIMPLE, and FEE TAIL). This is the modern legal connotation of the term, and it signifies not the subject of ownership itself, but the proprietary interest subsist ing in it. Es. are either in possession or in expectancy. Es. in expectancy are divided into Es. in remainder or reversion (*see* CONTINGENT REMAINDER, REVERSION (in law)). An E. in reversion arises either expressly, or by mere implication of law, as where a tenant in fee simple grants a life E. to another, and thereby impliedly reserves to himself the E. ownership in reversion. Es. may be enjoyed by one person only, or by more than one either severally (*see* COMMON, TENANCY IN) or jointly. Es. are also either legal or equitable. A legal E. subsists in the owner when he is in actual possession, and is also either entitled to the beneficial interest himself or holds in trust for some other person. A mortgagee by deed is the legal owner of land, the subject of the mortgage, but holds the residue of proceeds where a sale takes place for the realisation of his debt in trust for the mortgagor, or equitable owner. An equitable E. subsists in a person who, though not the actual and legal owner, is entitled to the beneficial interest of the property of which some other person is in possession as legal owner. Es. in popular language have come by a process of metonymy or extension to mean the actual lands and premises of a landowner of some territorial pretensions. The word

personally or by his elected representatives. Originally the phrase denoted the nobles, the clergy, and the commons, but the growth of parliament and the consequent elimination of the clergy as a separate political body gradually tended to stereotype the phrase in the above and narrower meaning. Analogous estates are, of course, to be found in most countries with an established polity. The term Fourth Estate of the Realm has often been applied to the public Press, on account of the enormous influence exerted by it in regard to public matters.

**Estaunié, (Louis-Marie-) Edouard,** Fr. novelist; *b.* Feb. 4, 1862, at Dijon; son of a mining engineer. Educated at Jesuit Coll. of Dijon, and Lycée St. Louis; old pupil of

THE TOMB OF BEATRICE D'ESTE AND HER HUSBAND

Although this lady lived only twenty-two years (1475–97), she is one of the most celebrated members of the House of Este.

was also used formerly as a synonym for status, or a man's condition in life. It is still used with a somewhat similar connotation in respect of the hierarchy of political classes, which in Great Britain are the three Es. of Lords Spiritual. Lords Temporal, and Commons. *See* ESTATES OF THE REALM.

**Estate Duty,** *see* DEATH DUTIES.

**Estate Tail,** *see* ENTAIL.

**Estates of the Realm** means the classes or orders of men invested with political rights in a nation or state. In Great Britain, for example, the three E. of the R. are the Lords Spiritual (or bishops), the Lords Temporal (peers entitled to vote in the House of Lords), and the Commons. The sovereign and these three estates together form the corporation or body politic of the kingdom. The Commons or third estate comprises not only the members of any given House of Commons, but the whole of the electorate, *i.e.* every one who has a voice in parliament whether

Ecole Polytechnique. After science-teaching in Paris, employed in engineering section of department of posts and telegraphs, became director of construction, and finished as inspector-general of telegraphs. Began novel-writing with *Un Simple*, 1891, followed same year by *Bonne Dame*. Became celebrated with *L'Empreinte*, 1895, suggested by his Jesuit education. There followed :— *L'Epavé*, 1902; *La Vie Secrète*, 1908; *Les Choses Voient*, 1913; *Solitudes*, 1917; *L'Ascension de M. Baslèvre*, 1921; *L'Appel de la Route*, 1923; *L'Infirme aux Mains de Lumière; Le Labyrinthe*, 1924; *Tels qu'ils furent*, 1927. He was elected member of the Academy, 1924.

**Estcourt** (3833 ft. high), the seat of magistracy for Weenen co., Natal, S. Africa, has large bacon and cheese factories. The climate is one of the finest in Natal and the scenery charming. Stock-breeding is carried on on a large scale. (White) Pop. 971.

**Este**, a tn. of Italy, in Lombardy. It gave name to a noble family, very prominent in Italian history, of the fifteenth and sixteenth centuries, from whom the present royal family of England is descended. The tn. has picturesque battlements and walls from the Venetian period. Pop. 12,660.

**Este, House of,** one of the most ancient and famous princely families of Italy, founded by Oberto II. (*d. c.* 1015), Margrave of Casal Maggiore. To Azzo II., his grandson, the Emperor Henry III. granted Este and other Italian fiefs. Azzo was created Duke of Milan, and assumed the name of Este. His two sons Welf (Guelph) IV. and Fulco I. founded respectively a German and an Italian branch of the H. of E. The Italian branch furnished the leaders of the Guelphs in the thirteenth and fourteenth centuries. The male Italian line became extinct on the death of Hercules III., 1803. The Estensi were mostly good and enlightened rulers, and founded the universities of Padua and Ferrara. *See* Muratori, *Annali d'Italia;* Pompeo Litta, *Famiglie celebri Italiane;* Crawfurd, *History of the House of Este,* 1681.

**Estella**, a tn. in the prov. of Navarra, Spain. It figured largely in the Carlist wars of 1833. Pop. 5658.

**Estepa**, a tn. in the prov. of Seville, Spain, which figured in Roman times under the name of Astapa. Pop. 8234.

**Estepona**, a seaport tn. in the prov. of Malaga, Spain. It produces large quantities of fruit and vegetables. Pop. 9673.

**Esterhazy de Galantha,** the name of an ancient Hungarian family dating from the thirteenth century, at which time it was divided into two branches, one of which died out in 1838. The three existing branches into which one of the original ones was divided are the Csesznek, Altsohl, and Forchtenstein. The chief members of the family are : *Paul IV.* (1635–1713), who became a field-marshal at the age of thirty, and was made a prince of the empire. *Nicholas IV.* (1765–1833), a great promoter of art, and the man to whom Napoleon is said to have offered the throne of Italy. *Paul Anthony* (1786–1866), a diplomat, who was Austrian ambassador in London until 1842, and in 1848 became Minister for Foreign Affairs under Batthyani. *Moritz* (1807–90), who was also a diplomat and statesman.

**Esters, Ethereal Salts, or Acidic Ethers,** are compounds formed by the replacing of the hydrogen in acids by alkyl groups; they occupy the same position in organic chemistry as the metallic salts do in inorganic. They are formed by the action of an acid or acid chloride on an alcohol, and are, as a rule, pleasant, fruity-smelling liquids, non-miscible with water, which are hydrolysed on heating with alkalis, an alcohol and the salt of an acid being formed. The fats consist of the palmitic, stearic, and oleic E. of glycerin, and on boiling with soda, the sodium salt of the acid (soap) and glycerin are formed. The process is known as ' saponification.' Many E. are used for flavouring purposes, *e.g.* amyl acetate (jargonelle pear), ethyl butyrate (pineapple), etc., the former also being used as a solvent for celluloid.

**Esther, Book of,** tells how in the reign of the Persian king Ahasuerus, Haman, the king's minister, was at last bringing to a successful end his intrigues for the extermination of the Jews. But Ahasuerus had just married Esther, a Jewess, though her nationality is kept secret from her husband. She and her uncle, Mordecai, make a counterplot, which is ultimately successful. Mordecai is made minister and raised to great honour; Haman is hanged on the gallows 50 cubits high, which he has prepared for Mordecai, and instead of the massacre of the Jews, a massacre of the Persians takes place by royal edict. The book then tells of the institution of the feast of Purim to commemorate this great deliverance. Ahasuerus is the Gk. Xerxes, and Mordecai is represented as becoming minister in the twelfth year of his reign, *i.e.* in 474 B.C. The date of composition, however, is the third or second century B.C., and the historical setting is so untrustworthy that many critics regard it as entirely the invention of the writer, a romance intended to further the observance of the feast of Purim. The work was in much favour among the Jews, and later became incorporated into the Christian canon of the O.T. Luther, in later years, did not scruple to express the small account in which he held the work. The tone is, indeed, violent and secular. It is noteworthy that the name of God does not appear once, while the name of the Great King appears about two hundred times.

**Estienne, or Etienne,** a family of Fr. printers, *see* STEPHENS.

**Eston,** an urban dist., 4 m. S.E. of Middlesbrough, with extensive blast furnaces, iron foundries, and steam sawing mills. The Cleveland ironstone was first discovered here. Pop. 30,635.

**Estonia, Estland, Eesi-Maa, or Eesti-Wabariik.** The most N. Baltic province. During the thirteenth century was under the sway of Denmark but in 1346 was handed over to the Teutonic knights. In 1561 it came under the rule of Sweden, and in 1781, by the Treaty of Nystadt, Russia became its ruler, until, on the outbreak of the Soviet revolution, it became a Republic. It has an area of about 18,600 sq. m., and is bounded on the N. by the Gulf of Finland, on the S. by Latvia (q.v.), on the W. by the Baltic Sea, and on the E. by Lake Peipus and Soviet Russia. The pop. is about 1,150,000 persons, of whom about 90 per cent. are Estonians and the remainder Russians, with a small sprinkling of Gers. and others. The surface of the land is generally low and flat, and it is subject to great extremes of temperature. The chief industry is agriculture which employs over half the workers, but, in addition, there are some important manufactures, such as cotton, woollens, paper, matches and distilling, and the Kreenholm cotton mills near Narva are the largest in Europe. Estonia is governed by a single chamber under a President-Premier and his ministers. The 100 members of the Parliament are elected triennially by adult suffrage. The head of the state is both Prime Minister and President of the Republic. Since the rising on Dec. 1, 1924, all Communist organisations have been prohibited. The ratio of university students is the highest in the world : 20 per cent. of the budget is devoted to education. The revenue and expenditure of the Estonian Budget balance at about £5,100,000. The annual exports are £6,000,000, and the imports £6,300,000. The capital city Tallin or Reval, with a pop. of 122,000, is an important Baltic port connected with the interior and with Russia by railway. There is a university at Dorpat (q.v.).

**Estoppel,** the legal term which is applied to anything which prevents a person from denying or confirming a fact on account of his own actions. The three kinds of E. are : (1) Those of record, which prevent either of the parties from offering any statements contrary to the recorded judgment ; (2) E. by deed, which prevents a man from denying any statement made by him in a written deed ; (3) E. in pais or by conduct, which includes such instances as a tenant's inability to deny his landlord's title, once the tenant is in possession.

**Estovers,** a term applied to the supplies of wood which a tenant has the right to take for purposes of fuel or repair from the estate on which he lives.

**Estrays,** animals which are not wild but are found wandering without an owner in any public place or on some one else's property. They become the temporary property of the lord of the manor if found within the confines of a manor, or if in any other place they become subject to the crown. Should they not be claimed within a year and a day this proprietorship becomes permanent.

**Estreat,** a term in Eng. law applied to a true copy of some writing, particularly a fine or amercement entered in the records of a court of law. It is also applied to recognisances when the conditions of the latter are not kept. Under these circumstances only are recognisances estreated, and the parties are considered as debtors to the crown.

**Estrées, Gabrielle d'** (1573–99), the daughter of the Marquis Antoine d'E., and mistress of Henry IV. of France. She married Nicolas d'Amerval, Seigneur de Liancourt, but she left him on account of her preference for Henry. The latter, it is said, wished to divorce Marguerite de Valois and to marry Gabrielle, but her sudden death prevented the carrying out of his plans.

**Estrella, Serra da,** a mountain range of Portugal, stretching from the S.W. to the N.E. for about 75 m. through the old province of Beira. It is a granite range and culminates in Malhão, 6540 ft. high.

**Estremadura :** (1) Originally a prov. of Portugal, now the dists. of Santarem, Leira, and Lisbon. The Tagus divides the district into two parts, the N. one being mountainous. The chief products are wheat and wine. The chief towns are Lisbon and Setubal. Area about 6937 sq. m. Pop. 1,544,704. (2) An anct. dist. of S.W. Spain, now occupied by the two provs. of Badajos and Caceres. Area about 16,000 sq. m. Agriculture is very little attended to, but the people are engaged in breeding domestic animals. There are also copper, silver, and lead mines. Pop. 1,258,600.

**Estremoz,** a tn. in the prov. of Alemtejo, Portugal, situated to the N.E. of Evora. Pop. 4870.

**Estuary** (Lat. æstuarium, from æstus, the tide), the name given to an inlet of the sea at the mouth of a river, where the water of the river and the sea meet, and the fresh and salt are mingled. The river seeks an exit in the sea, and the tide flows in towards the river, so that some estuaries are subject to tidal waves of great force.

**Eszek** (Oslek), a tn. of Jugo-Slavia, situated on the R. Drave, about 13 m. from its junction with the Danube. It is an important trading centre and manufactures silk and flour. It is built on the site of the Rom. town of Mursia. Pop. about 23,000.

**Etah** : (1) A dist. of India, in the United Provinces. Area about 1740 sq. m. Pop. 827,760. (2) An Eskimo settlement, situated on Smith Sound, Greenland.

**Etampes,** a tn. in the dept. Seine-et-Oise, France. It is interesting on account of its old churches, town-hall, and castle ruins. Pop. 10,070.

**Etaples,** a watering-place and fishing port in the dept. of Pas-de-Calais, France, situated near the mouth of the Canche R., about 15 m. S. of Boulogne. Its antiquities bear testimony to its importance in Rom. times, while in the Middle Ages it was noteworthy. A treaty was signed here in 1492 between Henry VI. of England and Charles VIII. of France. Base for Brit. Army in the Great War 1914–18. Pop. 6530.

**Etawah,** the cap. of the dist. of Etawah, United Provinces, India, situated on the left bank of the Jumna in a picturesque locality. This town, which is an important trading centre, contains many fine streets, Hindu temples, and steps or *ghats* leading down to the river, affording facilities for the pilgrim's ablution. Pop. (town) 41,558.

**Etching,** the art of engraving by eating into the metal with a mordant. The so-called ' Dutch bath ' (hydrochloric acid and potassium chlorate), dilute nitric acid or a solution of perchloride of iron is the mordant commonly used. A thin layer composed of gums, waxes, and resins is spread over the metal plate to form the 'etching-ground.' One method of applying the ground is as follows. The gums, etc., are squeezed into a ball covered with silk. If the heated copper is brought into contact with the ball, the composition oozes through the silk, and as it melts, may be spread over the plate with a silk pad or dabber. Usually the etcher holds the ground over a flame so as to blacken it with smoke. The object of this is to show up the lines he opens. If he wants to transfer a design, all he need do is to cover a thin sheet of paper with chalk and then trace over the design on the paper, when it is laid upon the copper plate. When the drawing is indicated on the ground, the plate is immersed in the acid bath, and the mordant ' bites ' into the lines. After the most delicate strokes are sufficiently etched, the plate is taken out and these strokes are filled up with a stopping-out varnish, like Brunswick black. This process of immersion in the bath and stopping-out the lighter gradations is continued until the acid has bitten

in sufficiently to make the blackest lines. If he likes, the etcher can proceed in a different way. At first he uses his need [?] only the darkest lines an [?] dips his plate into the mordant so as to get these partly bitten. He next draws in the parts, which are to be a shade lighter, and allows the acid to corrode these. This process is persisted in till he comes to the lightest parts. It will be seen that the corrosion is in proportion to the depth of tone required. If a soft ground E. is required, that is one imitating the texture of a crayon drawing, tallow is mixed with the E. ground and the design is firmly traced through a sheet of paper, when the grain of the latter and the kind of pencil used will leave their mark. *See* Engraving for the history of E.

**Etching of Crystals** is achieved artificially by subjecting crystals to the action of such solvents as caustic alkalis or acids, although rock salt often becomes etched by a natural process. This salt, being deliquescent, becomes coated, after crystallisation, with a layer of water. In course of time tiny rectangular depressions are formed all over the surface. When a crystal is immersed in some solvent ' etch figures ' are formed. The crystallographer frequently uses the etching marks to assist him in his classification of a certain piece of crystal; for they are found to be closely related to its crystallographic form.

**Eteocles,** in Gk. mythology, was the son of Œdipus and Jocaste. He, with his brother Polynices, succeeded to the throne of Thebes on the flight of their father. They undertook to rule in turns, but could not agree over this arrangement, which led to the flight of Polynices to the court of Adrastus to obtain vengeance. The result of this was a war known as the Seven against Thebes, which figures largely in Gk. literature. In this war E. and Polynices met in combat and killed each other. This story is told in *The Seven against Thebes* by Æschylus.

**Eternal Punishment,** *see* Hell.

**Etesian Winds** are those which are

ETCHING
NEEDLES

prevalent, during summer, over the S. part of Europe. Their direction is N. across the Mediterranean Sea to N. Africa, and seem to be caused by the rising of ted air over the Sahara and the consequent influx of cooler air to replace it.

**Etex, Antoine** (1808–88), celebrated Fr. sculptor, architect and painter, *b.* in Paris. Studied sculpture under Dupaty and Pradier, painting at the Ingres School, and later, architecture under Duban. In 1829 he took the second prize for sculpture at the School of Fine Arts, with his ' Hyacinthe mourant.' He also won in the same period prizes for a painting of a nude bather shown in the Lebrun Gallery, and other awards. His chief work is that which he was commissioned by the Fr. Gov. to do for the Arc de Triomphe and the colossal groups on the rear face of the Arc. These groups represent the *Resistance* of France to the coalition of 1814, and *Paix*, 1815, but though impressive, suffer to some extent by such close juxtaposition with *La Marseillaise*, the masterpiece of Rude, which is to be seen on the opposite side. Other fine pieces of E. include a marble figure, ' Olympia,' inspired by Aristo and now at Trianon, and a marble group of ' Hero and Leander,' now in London. His work was, however, criticised by G. Planche, is lacking in simplicity, though revealing all the secrets of the art. Publications include, *Etude sur la vie et les ouvrages de J. Pradièr* (1859) ; *L'Institut et L'Académie des Beaux-arts* (1860).

**Ethal,** also called **Cetyl Alcohol,** for it seems to be the hydroxide of a radical called cetyl. It is a solid, transparent, white crystalline mass, which melts at about 50° C., and is contained in spermacetti.

**Ethane** ($C_2H_6$), a gas composed of hydrogen and carbon, is contained in the gas which rises from the earth. It is colourless, without smell, and will burn in air with a luminous though pale flame, and is insoluble in water. E. is the second number of the paraffin series, the first being methane or marsh-gas (*q.v.*).

**Ethelbald** (856–860), King of Wessex, second son of Ethelwulf. He rebelled against his father and took the kingdom, leaving him only Kent. E. ruled well, putting Danes to flight. He married (858) Judith, his father's widow, and at the instigation, it is said, of St. Swithun, he left her.

**Ethelbert** (*c.* 552–616), fourth King of Kent, succeeded his father Ermeric in 560. His marriage with Bertha, daughter of Charibert, King of the Franks, led indirectly to St. Augustine's mission, and by him E. was converted to Christianity in 597, and he in his turn influenced thousands of his subjects to turn Christian. He destroyed pagan temples and built churches, and also established the first written Saxon set of laws. This brought about a rebellion under Rædwald which was successful.

**Ethelbert** (860–866), third son of Ethelwulf. By his father's will he was to have Kent as under-king. On the death of Ethelbald he took the whole realm, contrary to his father's will, which had named Æthelred.

**Ethelbert, or Albert, Saint** (*d.* 794), a king of E. Anglia during the Mercian supremacy under the rule of Offa. Offa's wife was afraid that E. would marry their daughter Alfrida, and possibly supplant her husband, so she prevailed upon Offa to have E. put to death.

**Etheldreda, Saint** (*c.* 630–*c.* 679), abbess and founder of the religious house of Ely. She was married twice, but preferred the religious life, and so withdrew from married life into a convent. She was also known by the name of St. Audrey, the origin of the present word *tawdry*, originally applied to a cheap kind of lace purchasable at St. Audrey's Fair.

**Ethelfleda** (*d. c.* 919), was the daughter of King Alfred, and the wife of the earldorman of Mercia. She was successful in helping to subdue the Danes, and on the death of her husband (*c.* 912) assumed the rule over his lands. She had the title ' The Lady of the Mercians.'

**Ethelfrid, or Ethelfrith,** King of Northumbria (593–617), the son of Æthelric. He gained a victory over the Britons of the N. at Dawstone in 603. In 617, however, he was defeated and slain in a battle against Rædwald of E. Anglia.

**Ethelred I.** (*d.* 871), King of the W. Saxons. He was the son of Ethelwulf and elder brother of Ælfred. It was in his reign that the Danes first attempted to make settlements in England. He conquered them at Reading and Ashdown, and was conquered by them at Merton, where he was wounded fatally.

**Ethelred II.** (968–1016), surnamed ' the Unready ' (lacking in ' rede ' or counsel). He succeeded his half-brother, Eadward the Martyr (978). At first he tried to repulse the Norsemen by bribery, but finally he massacred the Danes (1002) in time of peace in a brutal manner, which led Sveyn to gather a large force to avenge the slaughter, when E. was conquered and obliged to flee to Normandy, his father-in-law being the duke. He was recalled by his former subjects in 1014, which was the year of the death of Sveyn.

**Ethelwold, St.**, Bishop of Winchester (963–984), *b.* during the first quarter of the tenth century. He was the companion and helper of St. Dunstan, and these two together, with the king's authority, helped to reform the monasteries, replacing the canons by monks, and enforcing the rule of celibacy.

**Ethelwulf**, a ruler of Wessex and Kent (839–858), the son of Egbert. His reign was occupied with constant incursions of the Danes, by whom he was defeated at Charmouth about 842, and over whom he was successful a few years later at Ockley.

**Ether**, in physics, *see* ÆTHER.

**Ether**, **Ethyl Ether**, or as it is sometimes called, **Sulphuric Ether** (($C_2H_5)_2O$), is prepared by the so-called ' continuous process,' by the action of sulphuric acid. on ordinary alcohol; 9 parts of concentrated sulphuric acid and 5 parts of alcohol are heated to 140° C. in a retort, whereby ethyl hydrogen sulphate is formed ($C_2H_5.$ $OH + H_2SO_4 = C_2H_5.HSO_4 + H_2O$). A slow stream of alcohol is then run in, which reacts with the ethyl hydrogen sulphate to form E. ($C_2H_5.HSO_4 +$ $C_2H_5.OH = (C_2H_5)_2O + H_2SO_4$. The sulphuric acid which is regenerated reacts with more alcohol according to the first equation, and so the process may be regarded as ' continuous,' at least, until the water formed dilutes the sulphuric acid to such an extent as to render it ineffective. The crude E. which distils over is washed with caustic soda solution, the top layer containing the E. being dried over lime and redistilled. E. is a colourless, mobile and volatile liquid, with a peculiar smell, it is lighter than water (sp. gr. 0·72) and boils at 35° C. It is somewhat soluble in water, and readily dissolves fats, resins, and oils, for which purpose it is largely used in the arts. E. is very inflammable, burning with a somewhat luminous flame, and forming an explosive mixture if its vapour is mixed with air. Chemically it is stable and not readily reactive. Owing to its low boiling point (below blood heat) it vaporises so rapidly in the air as to produce intense cold. Use is made of this in some freezing machines, and also in producing local anæsthesia by freezing. Medicinally it is also used as a heart stimulant, in small quantities; and more generally as an anæsthetic when inhaled, for which purpose it is safer than chloroform.

**Etheredge, Sir George** (*c.* 1635–91), a dramatist, was a man in easy circumstances, who wrote plays merely to amuse himself in those hours that he could snatch from the pleasant saunterings of a man about town. He wrote three comedies : *The Comical Revenge, or Love in a Tub,* 1664 ; *She Would if She Could,* 1667 ; and *The Man of Mode, or Sir Fopling Flutter,* 1676. These plays had wit, but their indecency was such as to bring upon them the censure of Steele, though in this respect they were no whit worse than those of many of his contemporaries. Shortly after the production of his last comedy he was knighted, though why this honour was bestowed upon him has not transpired. He was sent as minister to The Hague by Charles II., and by James II. in 1685 to Ratisbon, where his private conduct was disgraceful and his diplomatic value nothing. His works were collected and edited by Verity (1888).

**Ethers**, or **Alkyl Oxides**, are a class of compounds of which ordinary or Ethyl E. (*q.v.*) is the best known. They are related to the metallic oxides in the same way as the alcohols are to the hydroxides. Their formulæ may be represented by $ROR^1$, where R and $R^1$ are two hydrocarbon radicals. They are prepared by the action of the alkyl halides on silver oxide, or of the alkyl hydrogen sulphate on the alcohol. Chemically the Es. are neutral, inert bodies varying from volatile liquids to wax-like solids. The term E. is often applied to esters, which may be regarded as Es. in which one of the radicles is of an acidic character.

**Ethical Societies.** In America seven flourishing societies exist for the discussion of social and moral questions. These are the New York, Philadelphia, Brooklyn, and Westchester Societies for Ethical Culture, and the Chicago, St. Louis, and Boston Ethical Societies. In London the Ethical Church in Queen's Road, Bayswater, W. 2, and South Place Ethical S., Conway Hall, Red Lion Square, W.C. 1, are the leading meeting places; while the Hampstead E. Institute, 59 Finchley Road, N.W., S. London E. S., Oliver Goldsmith School, Peckham Rd., S.E. 15, Wimbledon E. S., 138 Grande Drive, Raynes Park, and the Société de Morale fondée sur les Lois de la Nature, Emerson Club, 1 Little George St., Westminster, are the lesser branches. The Women's Group and Young People's Group meet at the headquarters of the E. Union in 12 Palmer St., S.W. 1., and the Forest Group arranges for rambles. The *E. S. Chronicle* is published at 12 Palmer St., and the Hon. Sec. of the Ethical Union is Miss N. Freeman. The Presidents have included Profs. Gilbert Murray, Graham Wallas, Felix Adler, L. T. Hobhouse, Frederick Soddy, J. H. Muirhead, Dr. J. S. Mackenzie, and J. A. Hobson. The object of the Union is 'to advocate the supreme importance of the knowledge, love and practice of the Right.

Ethics, the science which deals with human character and conduct, not considering them in the light of their own nature, but in respect of the moral judgment which have been diversely passed upon them. Like logic, therefore, it is a universal and practical science, dealing with elements common to the whole of the human race. This definition will at once show its intimate relations both with psychology and sociology, though it is noteworthy that the anct. philosophers all regarded ethical questions from the individual rather than the social standpoint. But although E. and psychology are closely related there is a clear distinction between them which may be shortly expressed by saying that while psychology deals with the explanation and analysis of mental processes, and with the world as it is, E. concerns itself with the judgments, either condemnatory or laudatory, passes on these processes and their resultant actions, with the world, not only as it is, but also as it ought to be. An ethical bearing is thus pre-supposed for the many psychological questions which come under discussion in E. Thus we have the question of the nature of volition itself, and the relation of will and character, which is considered substantially apart from the various acts of will which go to form it and which result from it. Character has been defined, indeed, as 'the habit of the will.' Then come the questions of Hedonism, conscience, and the freedom of the will, and among modern writers the question of the relation of the social life to E. E., as we have seen, deals with two subjects which are inseparably related : (1) Character, in relation to which it investigates the nature of duty and virtue ; (2) conduct, in relation to which it attempts to differentiate between the various virtues and vices, and to discover the extent and range of obligation. Thus E. is seen to deal not only with the problems of action as they exist, but also the more critical question of the principle or principles by which conduct should be regulated. The basis of E. is, indeed, the search for the *summum bonum*, the quest of man's highest good. It is by their varying conceptions of this highest good that the various schools are chiefly differentiated. Thus, broadly classifying, we may make two great schools, the hedonistic and the rationalistic, to be found among both anct. and modern thinkers. The Cynics and Stoics were rationalists, that is to say,

that they held the life of virtue or reason to be the sought-for end, beside which nothing is to be considered. But Socrates, before this, when attempting to define virtue, had found himself compelled to do so in terms of pleasure. The chief good must also be the greatest happiness. Emphasis is laid on this by the hedonistic schools of Cyrenaics and Epicureans (*see* EPICUREANISM), where virtue is considered as leading to the highest pleasure, or, to use the Aristotelian term, εὐδαιμονία, somewhat misleadingly translated happiness by modern ethicists. With Plato and Aristotle the Socratic view is kept in its entirety and explained in a still deeper sense, and it is thus found that hedonism takes a lower place. Plato, indeed, in certain of his dialogues, explicitly condemns it. Aristotle taught that the highest good for any being is the perfect development and full exercise of its function ; and since man is differentiated from the lower animals by reason, it is in the development of his moral and intellectual abilities that his end consists, the life of virtue and knowledge. The life of virtuous activity is subordinate and inferior to the life of the philosopher. It will be seen from this explanation that the Gks. treated of E. mainly from the individualistic standpoints, though the relation of E. to politics is not ignored. The scholastic philosophy, based as it was on Aristotle and his commentators, did not materially alter this view, save that the contemplation of the Deity was not explicitly propounded as man's final end and *summum bonum*. E. was brought into close union with religion and the conception of duty was that of obedience to the commands of God. Later, however, attention was chiefly devoted to casuistry, and instead of new theories on the subject being broached, energy was chiefly expended in the application of the principles and recognised laws to conduct under all possible variations of circumstances. E. shared, however, in the new birth of the Renaissance, and the doctrine of Utilitarianism took its rise. Utilitarianism, called also Universal Hedonism, in contrast to the Egoistic Hedonism of the Epicurean schools, is essentially social in its attitude. We have already remarked on the development of the doctrine of pleasure by Epicurus, and this conception had not been wanting from the scholastic system, for here the consideration of reward and punishment went always side by side with the consideration of obedience and disobedience to duty, of virtue and of vice. The Utilitarian philosophers frankly took up again this view, but with them it was the pleasure of the greatest number, rather than of the individual, that was to be sought. Now, too, a definite attempt was made to establish E. on some basis other than the theological, but the idea of rewards and punishments still survives to a large extent. Hobbes and the naturalistic school founded their E. on the natural results of human action. E. to them was the codification of the results of actions according as they finally gave pleasure or pain. As this conception becomes more and more altruistic, we see that virtue becomes equivalent to utility, and so the successors of Hobbes are commonly known as the Utilitarian school. A somewhat similar view, though expressed in the language of rationalism, was that of Cumberland, who, in his *De legibus Naturæ* (1672), gives ' the common good of all ' as the final end, though he expresses ' good ' in terms of perfection as well as of happiness. Many ethicists of the following period, such as Shaftesbury and Butler, make use of similar phraseology. But it was in David Hume (1711–76) that the Utilitarian school found its first capable exponent, almost, one might say, its founder. Virtue he defined as the quality which an onlooker approves, and vice as that which the onlooker blames. With this as his basis, he proceeds to examine the virtues and vices, showing that in every case that quality is approved which is useful or directly agreeable. Thus utility becomes the sole criterion of virtue. Paley, in his *Moral Philosophy* (1785), though taking his stand on the basis of Christianity, was a notable exponent at a later period of the utilitarian principle. The period of the Fr. Revolution was one of considerable activity in this department of thought, and here again Utilitarianism is the main principle. Bentham widely extended the sphere of its operation, and caused the complete reunion of E. and politics, by applying it to the latter of these. The names of Ricardo and J. S. Mill are even more important. The latter was principally occupied in the defence of his theory, rather than in its exposition, for Bentham's works had evoked a large number of attacks. All these writers regarded man as a social being, and insisted on the fact that the most necessary virtue was benevolence or unselfishness, but it was objected that no reason was ever given why the advancement of the general happiness should be the duty of the individual. Paley, as we have seen, met this objection by theological motives, while Bentham did so by regarding the community as the unit. But no

truly satisfactory proof of the principle has yet been adduced. Meanwhile, though Utilitarianism was the more prominent, Rationalism also appeared in various forms, as interpreted by the Cambridge Platonists and the eighteenth century Intuitional school, of which Butler may be regarded as the founder. This school regards conscience as the final judge of actions, but its weakness lies in the failure to give a complete definition of conscience. The ethical system of Emanuel Kant, given to the world chiefly in his *Groundwork of the Metaphysics of Morals* (1785) and the *Critique of Practical Reason* (1788),

DAVID HUME

was an attempt to clear away the many difficulties of the intuitional system. Thus, through the transcendentalism of Germany, came into England the ethical idealism which has exercised so powerful an influence on the development of Eng. thought in every department of philosophy during the past century. See the works of the ethicists referred to in the text, and also Sidgwick's *Outlines of the Hist. of Ethics*, 1888 ; T. H. Green's *Prolegomena to Ethics*, 1883 ; Spenser's *Principles of Ethics*, 1893. *See also* COMPARATIVE ETHICS.

**Ethicus**, or **Æthicus**, the reputed author of a cosmography, and also perhaps of a fuller, though less ambitious, work, entitled *Alia Totius Orbis Descriptio*. Internal evidence, such as the mention of the gate of St. Peter in Rome, and of other signs of Christian supremacy, assigns the cosmography to the latter part of the fourth century. It is mentioned by Isidorus of Seville (seventh century) and other writers, and an abridged form of the second book is found in *Orosius*. The compendium is an abstract of anct. geographical lore, and may well have been put together from the results of the survey undertaken, at the instance of Julius Cæsar, by the three geometers, Polycleitus, Zenodoxus, and Theodotus.

**Ethiopia** (Gk. Αἰθιοπία, the ' Kush ' of the Bible), the classical name for a part of N.E. Africa, confined on the E. by the Red Sea, and to the N. by Egypt. The provs. of Abyssinia, Kordofan, Sennaar, and Nubia roughly cover the anct. E. The etymology of the word is unknown, although it may well be Egyptian, but the Gks., with their passion for derivations, referred it to two words ' aitho ' and ' ops,' and said it meant ' swarthy-faced.' Homer refers to the ' blameless Ethiopians,' whom he thought of as the men dwelling far away on the furthest borders, and tells how the gods went to their banquets. Herodotus recounts with evident delight a number of fairy tales about E., which he gathered from Egyptian priests. Thus, he divides the country E. and W. into the lands of the straight-haired and woolly-haired races, and discourses at some length on the elephant- and fish-eaters, the tortoise- and serpent-eaters, the Troglodytes (' dwellers in caves '), and the Blemmyes (' hideous men '), etc. Originally occupied by independent tribes, it became an Egyptian province under the eighteenth dynasty, and paid tribute in negroes, ivory, gold, etc. During the eleventh century B.C., E. was formed into an independent kingdom with the capital at Napata. In 750 B.C. she was so strong that Egypt was obliged to acknowledge her yoke. When Egypt successfully rebelled in 660, the Ethiopians continued free till the Persian conqueror, Cambyses, forced them in 530 to recognise his rule. The island of Meroë, famous for the oracle of Jupiter Ammon, now became the capital. In the course of the third century B.C. Ergamenes destroyed the theocratic government and established a military domination in its stead. Meroë fell before the armies of Augustus when Queen Candace was counted among his victims. The great city of Meroë was a ruin in Nero's day, and in the sixth century its kingdom was supplanted by Christian Nubia. From the first century A.D. up to about 1000 the so-called Axumite dynasty reigned at Axum, and this was succeeded by another Christian power, that of the Zagues. From about 1300 the history of modern Abyssinia (q.v.) begins. Scanty Egyptian stelæ and records, and a few Ethiopic, trilingual, and Sabæan inscriptions, are almost the only sources of Ethiopian history.

**Ethiopian Languages, The,** were spoken by the Ethiopians who from very early times inhabited parts of N. Africa. The language which they used up to the fourteenth century, and which remained the language of writing and the church, was the ' Lesana Ge 'ëz.' The word ' Ge 'ëz,' which means ' free,' or perhaps ' migration,' itself suggests the truth, namely that this tongue is a development of a foreign one—in this case Arabic—the actual alphabet of twenty-six letters being directly borrowed from Sabæan or S. Arabic. There are seven vowels, represented by hooks, which cannot be written without their consonants. Two dots separate adjoining words, and all the letters are disconnected. No other Semitic dialect has so flexible or elaborate a syntax. It was written from left to right and contains a number of words in common with Aramaic, Hebrew, Gk., and the African dialects. For speech the Ge 'ëz was superseded by the Amharic.

**Ethmoid Bone** (' sieve-like ') is somewhat spongy in texture and cubical in form. It lies at the root of of the nose between the two orbits of the eye sockets, and is one of the constituent bones of the cranial box, the orbital plate of it being situated immediately behind the lachrymal bone.

**Ethnography.** See ANTHROPOLOGY —Ethnography; ETHNOLOGY — Descriptive Ethnology or Ethnography.

**Ethnology,** defined by Huxley as ' that science which determines the distinctive characters of the persistent modifications of mankind ; which ascertains the distribution of those modifications in present and past times, and seeks to discover the causes, or conditions of existence, both of the modifications and of their distribution.' It is, therefore, as he points out, a branch of Anthropology (q.v.), which in its turn is a branch of Zoology (q.v.), one of the natural subdivisions of Biology. As will be seen from a study of the subject, it also touches Philology, Psychology, and Sociology. E. again may be said to ' treat of the various large and small groups of human beings distributed over the face of the earth, and describe their mental, moral, and physical characteristics ' (Haberlandt). All communities which have existed, whether still existing, or having become absorbed in conquering or neighbouring tribes, or, having lost one of their most distinguishing features—their language—for that of another people, are considered under Historical or Palæo-Ethnology. Beyond this period of tradition, however, there are evidences of human groups, and this gives rise to the study of *Primitive History*. (*See* Dr. M. Hoernes' *Primitive Man*, published by Dent & Sons, Ltd.) It is possible to classify races according to languages, physical features, or according to culture. By classifying according to physical marks, like the colour and quality of skin and hair, we arrive at an anthropological division. Classifying according to culture gave rise to an obsolete method of classifying according to civilisation. By this method the races were divided into hunters, breeders of cattle, and agriculturists. All these methods, however, while possessing their own particular advantages and disadvantages, commonly suffer from the fact that they often separate related classes and *vice versa*. *Ethnography*, or *Descriptive Ethnology*, however, uses the divisions of the earth and its natural configuration, and these are found to correspond in general to the fundamental divisions of the human race. So we may proceed along this line studying the various historical and other connections of the race, while using any distinctions that language, structure, or culture may give us.

*History*.—The science of E. is comparatively modern, because, although a vague knowledge of foreign lands and races has always been possessed, it is of comparatively recent date that the discovery of lands has been practically completed, so enabling us to take a survey of the whole earth. In the Middle Ages the science was not expanded greatly, although men like Marco Polo and Mendez Pinto, gained a knowledge of the Far East. Then dawned that period during which Columbus discovered the New World, so giving us access to a knowledge of the Peruvian and Mexican civilisations. This, which is sometimes known as the *First Period of Ethnology*, it is interesting to note, was passed amid such fierce fighting occasioned by the hunting of gold and animals and the exploiting of the new countries for their stored up wealth, that the natives of these countries became looked upon as possessing no feeling or intelligence. In fact a Papal Bull was required to decide that they were rational beings. The discovery of the islands of the South Sea and of Australia by Captain Cook marks the *Second Period of Ethnology*. The state of Europe at that time induced a desire for knowledge of other races, and their customs and culture. Rousseau, Forster, and Voltaire stand out as leaders of this movement. As time passed China and India be-

came more familiar, and the colonising efforts of the various European countries led to the discovery and study of the peoples of the S. Seas and of S. and Mid-Africa. It is possible now to give a fairly complete description of the human inhabitants of the earth, with their mental, moral, and physical characteristics.

*Data used in Ethnology*.—It used to be considered that savage tribes were retrogressive from more highly evolved societies, and although this is now known to be by no means generally true, it is not easy always to distinguish between cases of retrogression, incomplete development, and standstill. There are examples of retrogression, although the law of development is undoubtedly maintained throughout the lives of nations. This principle of development is founded on the idea that all races evolve along the same lines, from states of barbarism to those of high culture, and that the height of culture attained marks the stage which has been reached in the development of the people. As a general principle this is correct, but the course of development of all living peoples has not always been identically the same. Although E. is able to study traces and remnants of very anct. conditions, yet gaps remain in the grades of man's development. Primitive groups are encountered which have completed their growth in their limited sphere, while the cultured nations have only slowly but surely reached a long period of prosperity owing to a series of favourable circumstances and a fortunate union of their developing forces.

*Developing forces in the life of nations :* (*a*) *General*.—The nature of these forces may now be briefly considered. Natural history elucidates the fact that the life of any organism depends upon its equipment and suitability for its environment. Man, of course, is an organism, and as he is the highest his relations with the outer world are more numerous than are those of any other. Plant organisms have to contend with atmospheric and soil conditions, and with attacks and competition of other plant and animal organisms. Most animal organisms also depend upon the suitability to their environment and other external forces, but when we reach animals that herd together, notably mammals, a new condition arises, viz. that the struggle for existence is carried on socially and not individually. With man this condition has attained vast importance, and has led not only to the permanent superiority of the human over all other species, but has also led to the development of human civilisation. In this development, the forces acting may be divided into external, internal, and social forces. The first class would include the physical requirements of life, and the conditions of nourishment and competition; the second, the cultivation and development of organic and mental feature; the third, the influences arising from family, tribal, and national life, such as the number of the society, the division of labour, and the conditions of barter and exchange.

(b) *Exterior factors.*—Natural influences, such as climate and the configuration of land, affect the lives of human groups through the domestic and social relations. This is clearly understood with regard to the animal and plant worlds, but in the case of man, a difficulty arises from the fact that nations merely remain in their primitive home. But in the life of nations, comparatively short periods of time will cause drastic changes in social life if the habitation is changed. The effect of climate and latitude on human society is well understood. As a typical example we may take the cases of dwellers in polar and tropical zones. In the first case, the conditions are such that the people are held in poverty, and consequently their social and intellectual life is cramped, while in the second case the energies are dulled by the heat and rendered superfluous by the ease with which life can be maintained in those regions. Again, the character of the land occupied plays a great part in the destiny of a people. Its insular or continental position, the distance from the sea, the formation of the soil, the amount of navigable water, the extent of mountains and rocky surfaces, the richness of the soil, the extent of the woods, its vegetation, and its mineral wealth, all bear obvious relation to the development of the people.

(c) *Inner factors.*—It used to be understood that the physical and mental capacity of nations was everywhere the same, excepting, perhaps, the degenerate peoples, such as the Weddas and the African dwarfs. This induced the idea that development depended only on the exterior forces. Now, however, it is more usual to believe that the varied forms of life not only exhibit nature's influence, but also indicate the net balance of a nation's forces, which are consequently not all equal.

(d) *Social forces.*—One of the great factors in human development is the numerical strength of the group. The efforts of the individual must be taken up by succeeding generations and distributed by neighbours if it is to be of use. The social principle involved in the division of labour is an obvious factor, and the connection and intercourse between people, whether in war, commerce, or marriage, are of immense importance. Migrations, changes of settlements, forcible seizure or friendly exchange of wives among inter-related or strange tribes, and the theft of children and slaves, are all factors which exercise influence upon a nation's development. In the study of E. we may treat it from either of four aspects, viz. biology, technology, society, and intellectual culture.

(1) *Biology.*—The developing forces described above have created an immense variety of groups of people, extending from the nomad hunting tribes, like the bushmen of S. Africa, to the great states of the Far East, and ethnography or descriptive E. teaches us how to recognise the most varied representative of nations, notwithstanding the great differences which do exist in external, mental, and moral characteristics, they all, nevertheless, possess certain features in common. It is in biology that the identity of the form of life shows itself. If we take the life among peasants, even in modern civilised conditions, we approach as nearly as possible to the primitive peoples. Hunting and fishing in common are social institutions for the provision of food. In the primitive stages man derived his food direct from Nature. First, we have trees like the palm, the fruit-bearing trees of Brazil, the bread-fruit, and the date trees, then come the seeds of plants, berries, and edible roots. The former gives rise to arboriculture and the latter to agriculture. Superior to both these, however, is animal food, for the eating and digesting of which man has suitable organs. Man has always been, as far as we know, a pantophagist, and has, of course, in some regions developed into a cannibal. Drink is the next great necessity to food for man. It is a menace to the nations of the coral island of Oceania, and determines the social and political composition of the life of nations inhabiting the waterless portions of Central Asia and E. Africa. Again, sugar and salt are physiologically necessary to all races. All animals sleep at night, and man is no exception, and since the senses are then dormant, the birds retire to their nests, the animals to their various lairs, and likewise does man to some kind of abode. Primitive man prepared his shelter almost exclusively for sleep. Even advanced tribes enact their family and social life

almost wholly outside and between the tents. Thus, the abode shows the development and reacts upon it. It represents protection from the vagaries of climate, and we may further trace the development of a people by the length of their sleep. Cultured people are able to dominate and restrict the need of sleep according to the requirements of work or pleasure, while savage man has a great and compelling need of sleep. Even now the Papuans, Andamans, etc., are conspicuous 'long sleepers,' just as our forefathers were, according to Tacitus. In the lower tribes, again, posture during sleep bears a relation to the conditions of life. Primitive man slept in a cowering position, rolled up, so to speak, so as to expose the smallest portion possible to attack, and the bushman sleeps so to-day. Bedrooms arise from easily understood moral considerations. So low a type as the Bubis showed distinct proofs of considerate feeling in erecting special sleeping huts for all girls and boys, each only big enough for one. Although primitive history traces man back to caves, it is to be doubted whether man ever was housed in caves or trees. Even the Weddas are above this. Migratory tribes, of course, improvised their sleeping place wherever darkness overtook them, of a weatherboard of branches and underwood laced together and placed in a slanting position in the direction of the wind. Permanently settled people would stick branches in a circle in the ground and bind the tops together, and cover the whole with skins. Then would come beehive dwellings, wooden houses, huts of clay with straw roofs, clay-brick dwellings, and stone buildings. Again, with ornament and clothing, it is ethnologically regarded as correct to say that man first thought of ornamenting himself and afterwards of covering his nakedness, although it is difficult to separate ornament from clothing with some groups. The question of clothing does not always depend upon the question of shame. The inclemency of the weather and illness make clothes a necessity, and examples can be given to show that the covering of the bones was not the only consideration which

PILE-DWELLINGS OF THE NICOBAR ISLANDERS
(One of the earliest types of dwellings evolved by Man)

led to the use of clothing. The material used for clothing is intimately connected with the economic condition of the nation, and it therefore furnishes valuable data to E. Taking weapons again and considering the protection of life, it is obvious that the first would be a quickly raised stone or a broken branch, which may even be used by monkeys. The development of weapons then depended on the geographical surroundings. Stone and wood would be the materials used in pre-metal days. Armour for the head and upper part of the body is the next development. After the safeguarding of the individual, the next thought is to safeguard the settlement by means of palisades, thorn hedges, etc., which gradually lead to moats and ramparts, and so to properly fortified places.

(2) *Technology* involves all those ways and means by which all groups of mankind have attained their respective degrees of culture. Primitive history does this for prehistoric ages, and from thence on the history of culture continues the task, using ethnographical results and historic archæological evidences. We may pass over the preparation of food and the obtaining of fire by remarking that they were communistic or social not individual efforts. With the development of implements and industry, we may divide primitive history into the Early and Later Stone, a Bronze, and an Iron Age. E., however, goes further and can enumerate tribes which are still in the age of unperforated and unsharpened stone implements, whilst others belong to a later Stone Age, since they use neatly polished stone vessels. E., indeed, might speak of a Shell Age.

(3) *Society*.—Man being of a preeminently social disposition, he has family ties which develop to produce the tribe and from thence the state. The family and tribal life is, of course, founded on relationship, and the state on political right. In the course of this social life, the social function of morality, justice, ownership, etc., are produced and are based originally on relationship, then taken over by the tribe and finally by the state. The basis of the tribal life is the family, but the form of the family is not always the same. The family, as we know it, based upon marriage, and consisting of parents and children, is believed to be of late origin, and has evolved from much larger groups. Defenders of this opinion hold that the foundation of the human family was promiscuous sexual intercourse within the group, and this is based upon, among other things, the existence of the maternal line of descent. It is conceived that, wherever the descent from the mother is the accepted origin, and gives the name, position, etc., the inference is that the parental origin is unknown. The predominance at present of the rule of paternal descent, however, may be used to prove that this view is wrong. Two groupings of families thus are seen to exist or have existed—mother-right and father-right. Descent, according to motherhood, shows great antiquity. This organisation of families, according to maternal line of descent and that of patriarchal grouping, can be met with to-day among Indian tribes and in the Malay Archipelago, etc. The contrary theory would maintain promiscuity

and mother-right to be corruptions and not the primitive organisation of the family or tribe. The members of the tribe link up to form a state ruled by joint labour, with common aims, work, and objects. The state grows out of the tribe, but it derives a lot of its power from the development of the priesthood, since nearly all primitive states are theocratic. So also the idea of property and right can be seen to develop and lead to law and order.

(4) *Intellectual Culture*.—Man is by birth placed in an environment which decides the form of his life, and so he assumes a national intellectual habit. Language is one of the possessions we come into unconsciously in childhood. The districts poorest in culture have a large abundance of languages and dialects, sometimes even as in some Brazilian tribes the language of men and women is different. Then, again, art in all its forms is a good sign of the degree of culture, although not so good as language. The dancing of the savages may be shown to bear distinct traces of the drama. The mask is used in both, and the mask is a sign of deep drama. Both drama and dancing originate in worship and song, so chief priests work themselves to a frenzy by their aid. No people in the world, again, is devoid of religion, and a study of the religion of a people, in fact, furnishes excellent material for E. Perhaps the best sign of development of culture is the amount of knowledge of science and writing. The beginnings of both can be sought among primitive nations. The principle of the art of writing was attained, of course, through the transferring of pictorial characters into phonetic signs, giving the world-historic creation of the alphabet.

*Descriptive ethnology or ethnography*.—According to an approximate calculation, the population of the earth is over 1,500,000,000, six-sevenths being civilised and one-seventh belonging to the lower orders. This divides man into races possessing history and those with none, and almost entirely agrees with the contrast between light and dark coloured races. Man is identical, of course, all over the world, but in the same way that the subdivisions of the earth point to geographical connection, the natural families are related to one another and appear connected in the same zones. All the highest stages of form and culture appear in the N. hemisphere, which is the most favoured by nature and where man is most widely distributed. It might further be stated that in the N. hemisphere dwell the white race and the related Mongolians, while in the S. dwell the dark-coloured races. Anthropology (q.v.) divides man according to his physical qualities, such as colour of skin, quality of hair, and shape of skull. The hair is distinguished as ivory, smooth, woolly, curly, corrugated, and spiral, while the forms of skull are evolved from the comparison of height with length ; in this manner three types of head are noticed : (1) Dolichocephaloi, or long ; (2) mesocephaloi, or average ; and (3) brachycephaloi, or short. The subdivisions of the races are continually changing according to the signs observed in them. According to the monogenetic view, mankind sprang from one primary form, which has since developed into species according to the influences of climatic and other forces. This view is far more generally held than the polygenetic theories. Neither the limits nor the distinguishing features of species can be regarded as fixed. Blumenbach, the founder of scientific anthropology and E., recognised five races : Caucasian, Mongolian, Ethiopian, American, and Malay, and of these the Malay is now regarded as being the result of a comparatively recent mixture in which the Mongolian element predominates, while the American may also be regarded as a remote branch of the same group. Thus we may reduce these divisions to the first three. Quatrefages, the Fr. anthropologist, attaches most importance to the colour of skin and form of the skull, and divides men into three races : white, yellow, and black, with two mixed races, viz. American and Oceanic. Modern ethnologists would seek to eliminate the word race and classify either according to civilisations or according to domestic conditions. For fuller information and a classification of the races, beginners should read Ethnology by Haberlandt (Temple Primers, Dent). For other books on the same subject, see A. H. Keane, Ethnology ; J. G. Frazer, The Golden Bough ; G. L. Gomme, Ethnology in Folk-lore ; Ratzel, History of Mankind ; E. B. Tylor, Primitive Culture ; J. L. de Quatrefages, Histoire des races humaines ; Annual Reports of American Bureau of Ethnology, Smithsonian Institute, Washington, and the publications of the Folk-lore Society.

**Ethyl,** an alkyl, or organic radical, having the formula $C_2H_5$ ; which, although it does not exist by itself, forms part of many compounds, such as alcohol, ether, etc., in which certain properties of radicals persist.

**Ethylamine** ($C_2H_5.NH_2$), a substance resembling ammonia in its odour and many of its properties. It may be obtained from coal tar, but is best prepared in a pure state by the reduction of methyl cyanide (acetonitrile). It is also formed, along with diethylamine ( $(C_2H_5)_2NH$), and triethylamine ( $(C_2H_5)_3N$), by the action of ethyl bromide or iodide on alcoholic ammonia. E. is a colourless, volatile liquid, boiling at 18° C. It has a strong ammoniacal odour, and when in a dilute state is reminiscent of stale fish. It is very soluble in water to an alkaline solution, and with hydrochloric acid forms a salt which is deliquescent and soluble in alcohol, thus differing from the corresponding salt of ammonia.

**Ethyl Chloride** ($C_2H_5Cl$) is obtained by passing hydrogen chloride into alcohol, in the presence of anhydrous zinc chloride, and condensing the product which passes over in a cooled receiver. E. C. is a colourless, ethereal liquid, boiling at 12° C., which is soluble in alcohol, and only sparingly so in water. It is used as a local or refrigerating anæsthetic in dentistry and minor operations, and also as a general anæsthetic in place of nitrous oxide.

**Ethylene,** or **Olefiant Gas** ($C_2H_4$), a hydrocarbon prepared by heating alcohol with excess of sulphuric acid, whereby the ethylhydrogen sulphate, which is first formed, is broken up into E. and sulphuric acid. A better method is to pass the vapour of ethyl alcohol over heated alumina, the latter acting as a catalyst : $C_2H_5OH = C_2H_4 + H_2O$. E. is a colourless gas with a faint ethereal odour, and is insoluble in water. It burns with a very luminous flame, forming carbon dioxide and water. Chemically E. is an ' unsaturated ' substance, uniting directly with an equal volume of chlorine to form ethylene dichloride or ' Dutch liquid,' and also with bromine, hydrogen, chloride, sulphuric acid, etc. It is present in small quantities in coal-gas. E. is used to some extent as an anæsthetic, but more largely as an artificial ripening agent for oranges, grape-fruit, etc.

**Ethyl Ether,** see ETHER.

**Etienne,** or **Estienne,** a family of Fr. printers, see STEPHENS

**Etienne, St.,** is one of the finest of the old churches of Paris. It was founded in 1220 for the people who lived in the parish on the hill of St. Guinevere, whence the dedication to St. Etienne du Mont. Formerly the abbey church, it was completely rebuilt during the years 1517-1626. Here Pascal, Racine, and Tournefort lie buried, whilst the building itself, with its unique gallery, nineteen apsidal and lateral chapels and graceful vaultings, is a delight to all art lovers.

**Etienne-de-Baigorry,** chief tn. of

the valley of Baigorry, in the Basses-Pyrénées, France. There are copper and iron mines in the district.

**Etiolation,** *see* BLANCHING.

**Etiology,** the consideration of the causes of disease. These are divided into : (1) Predisposing or remote, (2) exciting or proximate, (3) determining. The various causes act in different ways, sometimes as remote, proximate, or determining : (*a*) *Age.* It is common knowledge that certain diseases are always regarded as children's ailments. (*b*) *Heredity.* The importance of this factor is apt to be confounded with the habits and customs acquired by children from their parents. (*c*) *Intermarriage.* This cause is so remote that it is more closely related to statistical investigations than to practical medicine. (*d*) *Sex.* As anæmia and hysteria, more common in females than males. (*e*) *Temperament.* Some individuals are described as sanguine, others as phlegmatic, many, however, have the nervous temperament. (*f*) *Climate and locality, town and country life.* (*g*) *Hygienic conditions.* Under this head, importance must be attached to occupation, air, previous disease, mental and moral states, physical conditions, temperature, diet, etc. All these factors must be borne in mind when considering the causation and prevention of disease.

**Etiquette** is derived from the Old Fr. *estiquette,* 'a label,' another and closer Eng. derivative being 'ticket.' The *estiquette* seems to have been a kind of card of introduction, a meaning which offers some explanation of its later sense. The behaviour dictated by good breeding, the formal ceremonies prescribed by authority as appropriate to various social, court, and other official functions, and especially the observance of the rules of precedence, and to the other proprieties of rank and office, are all part of E., which may briefly be described as ' conventional decorum.'

**Etiquette, Madame,** *see* NOAILLES.

**Etive,** a salmon riv. and sea-loch of Argyllshire, Scotland. The river rises on Rannoch Muir and finally is merged in the Firth of Lorne. The loch into which it flows is some 20 m. long, and is a submerged valley noteworthy for its natural beauty.

**Etna,** a flourishing industrial bor. of Allegheny co., Pennsylvania, U.S.A. It is a suburb of Pittsburg, 2 m. to the S., and lies on the W. bank of the Allegheny river and produces iron, steel, brass, and enamelled ware. Pop. 7493.

**Etna,** or **Monte Gibello** (from Gk. Αἴτνη, which comes from αἴφω, I burn), a volcano, 10,758 ft., in the prov. of Catania on the E. coast of Sicily. By rail the circumference of its base measures 86 m., and it is estimated to cover over 450 sq. m. In shape it is a truncated cone, and has as many as 200 craters. On the W. side the symmetry of its slope is interrupted by a deep gully, 3 m. wide, known as Valle del Bove. The anct. geographer, Strabo, mentions the three distinct zones of vegetation. Most of the highest region, down to a level of 7000 ft., is barren except for some stunted Alpine shrub, and is usually covered in snow, besides scoriæ and ashes. The next zone is the zone of forests, the upper part of which is covered with birch trees, whilst the lower reaches (up to 6000 ft.) are dense with evergreen pines and chestnuts. The lowest region, which extends up to about 3000 ft., has the splendid fertility natural to volcanic soil. Here olives, vines, and all kinds of vegetables flourish, and the slopes are dotted everywhere with populous cities and villas. From 476 B.C. there have been repeated and serious eruptions. Catania was overwhelmed by the eruption of 1169, and in 1669 a great abyss, 12 m. long, was opened up in the side of the mountain.

**Eton,** a tn. on the l. b. of the Thames, opposite Windsor, in Buckinghamshire, England. Pop. 3500.

**Eton College,** one of the most notable of Eng. public schools, was founded in 1440 by Henry VI. under the title of ' The College of the Blessed Mary of Eton beside Windsor,' but, in consequence of the political chaos, it was not completed till 1523. The first headmaster was Bishop Waynflete. The original foundation consisted of a provost, ten priests, four clerks, six choristers, a schoolmaster, twenty-five poor scholars, and twenty-five infirm bedesmen, but, by the Public Schools Act of 1868, this was altered to a provost, ten fellows, who form the governing body, two chaplains, and seventy king's scholars or collegers. The number of pupils averages 1100. The ' Oppidans,' *i.e.* boys not on the foundation, form the great body of students. There are twelve vacancies a year for collegers, filled by selection. Until 1851 the education was purely classical, but in that year mathematics was introduced, and physical science was added in 1869. The Gothic stone chapel, with its rich and varied stained glass and its fine carving, is the chief architectural beauty of the college. Collegers live within the walls, but most of the boys live in masters' houses, which are built of brick and picturesquely grouped about the older buildings and quadrangles. There is a special chapel for the younger school, a museum, and a fine library with a good collection of Oriental manuscripts. In 1908 King Edward VII. opened the much-needed school hall, and a domed octagonal library in memory of the Etonians who fought in the Boer War. There are also science schools, a school of mechanics and an observatory. Speech Day is celebrated on George III.'s birthday, June 4; there is an annual cricket match at Lord's between the school and Harrow, and on St. Andrew's Day the oppidans play the collegers at football. Twenty-four foundation scholarships at King's College, Cambridge, are reserved for E. boys, and there are, besides, several exhibitions and scholarships at both Oxford and Cambridge. Both Oxford and Cambridge rely much on Etonian oarsmen in their boat races. The eccentric custom known as 'Montem' was abolished in 1846.

*Bibliography.*—R. A. Austin-Leigh, *Guide to the Buildings of Eton College,* 1921.

**Etretat,** a favourite seaside resort in the dept. of Seine-Inférieure, France. The church of Notre Dame is interesting for its fine Norman work, and there are Rom. remains. Pop. 2020.

**Etruria,** the name of the country of the Etruscans. Etruria Propria, through which the Arno flowed, lay W. of the Apennines and the Tiber; Etruria Campaniana lay S. of the Tiber; and Etruria Circumpadana embraced the valley of the Po. The famous confederation of twelve cities in Etruria Propria included Veii, Tarquinii, Clusium, Cære, Cortona, Volaterræ, Vulci, Volsinii, and Perusium; in the N. province were Felsina (Bologna), Mantua, Ravenna, and Hatria, which gave its name to the Adriatic; and in the S. was Capua.

Varro dates the Etruscan era back to 1044 B.C., so that the Etruscans are of far greater antiquity than the Roms. They called themselves Rasena, whilst their Gk. name was Tyrrheni. Most Gk. historians agree in regarding them as emigrants from Lydia—a belief supported by the structural similarity of the tombs found in Tarquinii and elsewhere in E. and near Sardis in Lydia. Yet Dionysius of Halicarnassus is right in emphasising the difference between the Etruscan and Lydian civilisations, and it seems difficult to believe that at such an early period a whole people should have sailed so many miles across the seas in search of a new home. It might naturally be thought that their language would solve the problem, but the only remains of this are some thousands of inscriptions, mostly sepulchral. These consist chiefly of proper names and so afford no solution. Analogies have been suggested between Etruscan and languages so different as Basque and Armenian, but the truth seems to be that Etruscan is quite independent of all Semitic and Aryan dialects. *See also* EUGUBINE TABLES.

But if the Etruscans did not voyage W. all the way from S. Asia Minor, it is almost certain that they settled in Italy as conquerors—a conjecture which many facts combine to support. Thus even in the days of Herodotus the cities of Cortona and Cære had what was called a ' Pelasgic ' stamp, that is to say, they bore traces of a more primitive settlement than the Tuscan, and were still inhabited by aborigines. Moreover, Livy notes that the country folk spoke a different dialect from that of the townsmen, which may well have been if the cultivation of the soil were left to an

FIGURES FROM AN ETRUSCAN TOMB

autochthonous and servile population. But above all the recognition of the Etruscans as an intrusive and victorious nobility offers a simple explanation of the speedy collapse of their power and the rapid disappearance of both their language and civilisation. As a type the Etruscans were thick-set and small, with black hair and dark complexion. The characteristic Tuscan skull differs from that of any other Italic tribe, and the one people with whom ethnologists have compared them are the Kheta or Hittites of the Bible, who, curiously enough, have left sculptural records in Sardis, the chief town of Lydia.

E. was an empire when Rome was still an insignificant city among hundreds in her dominion. Thus the Tarquin kings and the famous Lars Porsena of Clusium were probably Tuscan officials or magistrates sent to Rome in token of her subjection, and the Servian wall, the Capitoline temple, and the Cloaca Maxima still bear testimony to the reality of the Etruscan occupation. It was, moreover, to their conquerors that the Roms. owed their colleges of augurs, their triumphs, their gladiatorial shows, their twelve lictors, their purple-bordered toga prætexta, their curule chair, and above all their regard and respect for women. The Etruscans attained their highest glory in the sixth century B.C., when they figure in Gk. history as the allies of the Carthaginians, who, in 538, expelled the Gk. colonists from Corsica, and again when they (the Etruscans) were defeated in a famous naval battle against the tyrant Hiero I. of Syracuse (474), and once

ETRUSCAN AMPHORA

more when they sent ships to help the Athenians during the siege of Syracuse (414). Indeed they were celebrated in anct. times, like the Phœnicians, as a great sea power. But as early as 423, when the Samnites seized the stronghold of Capua, Etruscan supremacy had begun to decline. The inroads of the Gallic hordes affected E. even more than Rome, and in 396, after a ten years' siege, the veteran Camillus finally captured and destroyed the populous and splendid city of Veii in spite of its cyclopean walls. The S. province swore allegiance to Rome in 351, and, after a series of crushing defeats, the fate of the Etruscans was finally sealed by the decisive Rom. victory at the Vadimonian Lake (283), when Tarquinii was obliged to put an end to her stubborn resistance. Hence-

forwards, as with Greece after Chæronea, E. has no history. See also ETRUSCAN ARCHITECTURE.

**Etruria,** a dist. of Hanley in the co. bor. of Stoke-on-Trent. In 1769 Josiah Wedgwood and Thomas Bentley opened here their famous E. potteries; there are also large iron works.

**Etruscan Architecture.** Archæological evidence, derived chiefly from burial urns and tombs, goes to prove that the Etruscans (see ETRURIA) were quite devoid of any artistic sense. To judge from the so-called hut-urns, their most primitive dwellings were one-roomed, rectangular structures with thatched roofs and wattled walls. These were replaced by wooden cottages with sloping roofs of planks running longitudinally and also transversely. Their temples were usually square, with the 'cella' divided into three compartments, the decorations, like acroteria and friezes, being of terra-cotta nailed to wooden walls. Underground sepulchral monuments, like 'la Cucumella' in Volsci, were clearly imitations of similar 'tumuli' in Lydia, whilst most Etruscan ornament, such as capitals, mouldings, and metopes, was but a crude and almost barbaric transcription of Gk. originals. The Roms. would speak of colonnades with the pillars far apart as in the 'Etruscan style,' which shows that the Tuscan architects had reproduced their borrowed models not in stone but wood, which permits of a greater span for the architrave. There are still ample remains of the massive cyclopean walls which surrounded the chief towns, sometimes for 6 or 7 m.

**Etsch,** see ADIGE.

**Etterbeck,** a suburb of Brussels, Belgium. Pop. 23,100.

**Ettlingen,** a tn. 4½ m. S. of Karlsruhe, on the Alb, in the free state of Baden, Germany. The town, which is on the Mannheim–Basel Railway, is both quaint and attractive. Pop. 9440.

**Ettmüller, Ernest Moritz Ludwig** (1802–77), a Ger. philologist. His great work was his patient research into Middle, High, and Low Ger., and into the anct. Norse literature. From 1829 to 1852 he published scholarly editions of old texts, including *Beowulf*, 1840, and he also brought out a *Lexicon Anglo-Saxonicum*, and translated the old Norse songs from the Niebelungen saga, 1837.

**Ettrick :** (1) A river which waters part of Selkirkshire, Scotland. It rises in Capel Fell (2223 ft.) in the S.W., and flows almost due N.E. for over 30 m., receiving the waters of the Yarrow only before joining the Tweed, 3½ m. below Selkirk. It passes through a country full of literary associations, for the 'E. Shepherd,' James Hogg, lived in the parish of E., and Deloraine, which brings back the hero of Scott's *Lay of the Last Minstrel*, lies below Buccleuch. E. Water, upon which E. stands, is part of the river. (2) A forest, once covered all Selkirkshire and parts of the shires of Edinburgh and Peebles. It was once a favourite hunting ground for kings. Trees have long since given place to green pastures.

**Etty, William** (1787–1849), an Eng. painter, was the son of a miller. After seven years in a printer's works, he at last (1806) realised his ambition and attended the Royal Academy Schools in London, having for one year the advantage of Sir Thomas Lawrence's tuition. ' Sappho ' (1811), which was hung at the Royal Institution, was his first success, but the delicacy of his flesh tints and the graceful tenderness of his women soon procured him a wide recognition. One consequence of his study of the Venetian masters during his Italian tour of 1821 was that he became famous as a colourist, and especially for the rich glow of his draperies and for the skill with which he harmonised his backgrounds with his centra figures or subjects. His masterpieces, including ' Youth on the Prow and Folly at the Helm,' 1832 ; ' Cleopatra's Arrival in Cilicia ' ; and ' The Sirens,' may be seen in the Manchester, Edinburgh, Glasgow, Liverpool, and London art galleries.

**Etymologicum Magnum,** a Byzantine Gk. lexicon. In 1848 Dr. Gaisford published his edition as the result of many years' arduous research.

**Etymology** (Gk. ἔτυμον, and λόγος), an investigation into the origin and original significance of words. It forms a subsidiary part of the science of comparative philology, but has only been scientifically studied within the nineteenth century. False Es. have been often suggested through ignorance and half-knowledge. Folk-E. has played an important part in the development of languages. Words that people have known from their childhood are taken for granted, but it is quite different with the new terms they meet. These arrest their interest and, believing that every word has its signification, they seek for this, guided by resemblances of sounds with words already known, thus reaching false conclusions through false analogies. Various examples of the same illogical process are found in the O.T., in the Homeric tales, in quaint Es. of mediæval writers, and even in some of the present-day dictionaries. Scientific E. was made possible by the birth of

philology and study of the languages of the East. It no longer sought the relation between the words of a single language, exclusively within itself, but extended its view to a whole group of cognate tongues, or, wider still, to a whole family. Thus a new science arose under the title of Comparative Grammar. The evidence that the group of languages known as the Aryan languages forms a family, *i.e.* are all sister-dialects of one common tongue, consists in their grammatical forms being the same, and in their having a great many words in common. In judging whether an individual word in one of these tongues is really the same as a word in another of these tongues, one is no longer guided by similarity of sound. Words are constantly undergoing changes, and each language follows its own fashion in making these changes. Corresponding words, therefore, in the several languages, must have, in the long course of ages, come to differ greatly ; and these differences follow certain laws which it is possible to ascertain. Of the laws of interchange of sound, Grimm's Law, named after the great Ger. philologist, is the most important. It exhibits the relations found to exist between the consonant sounds in the three groups of the Aryan languages. Followers of this theory were Curtius and Fick. The Teutonic revival in the nineteenth century in England commenced a history of Eng. upon an historical method from which has grown a really scientific Eng. E., as seen in the dictionaries of Professor Skeat and Dr. Murray.

**Etzel** (or **Attila**), King of the Huns, *see* ATTILA.

**Eu** (the Rom ' Augusta '), a tn. on the l. b. of the Bresle, 64 m. N.N.E. of Rouen, on the Western Railway, in the dept. of Seine-Inférieure, N.W. France. It is noted for the fine Gothic church of St. Laurent (twelfth century), and for its château (begun in 1578) of the Prince of Orleans, destroyed by a fire in 1902. Pop. 5740.

**Eua,** or **Eoa,** one of the Tonga Islands, S.E. of Tongatabu, in the Pacific. It was discovered by Tasman in 1643.

**Eubœa,** also called **Negropont** and **Egripos,** the largest island of the Grecian archipelago, having a length of some 90 m., and a breadth varying from 4 to 30 m. It lies in a direction N.W. to S.E., is separated from the mainland by the narrow strait Euripus, and protects the coasts of Attica, Bœotia, and S. Thessaly. The promontory of Artemisium, where the Gks. gained a great victory at sea over the Persians (480 B.C.) forms a

N.E. extremity. Part of the same mountain range, which guards the E. of Thessaly, traverses the island from end to end, Mt. Dirphys, now Delphi (5725 ft.), in the centre being the highest peak. Chalcis and Eretria, the chief towns, were both Ionic settlements from Attica, which in their turn founded Cumæ and Rhegium, etc., in Magna Græcia. Eretria was destroyed and its inhabitants carried off to Persia during the great invasion of 490 B.C. In 506 B.C. the Athenians established a hated cleruchy in Chalcis because that city had joined the Spartan league. After an ineffectual revolt, Pericles reduced the island to submission to Athens in 446. After some years of independence E. fell successively under Macedonian, Rom., and, during the Middle Ages, Venetian rule. From 1470 onwards it was subject to Turkish domination, but in 1830 it was incorporated with independent Greece. All the conquerors have found E. useful for its corn and cattle. Pop. 115,000.

**Eubulus** (*fl.* 350 B.C.), an Athenian politician, was an orator and a man of some force, but it is impossible accurately to gauge his merits, as the pages of Demosthenes, his arch-enemy, are the most reliable source of our information concerning him. E. was largely influential in securing the acquittal of Æschines, and further advocated peace at any price, a policy hateful to Demosthenes.

**Eucaine,** a synthetic drug, comparable to cocaine in many of its actions, which is used as a local anæsthetic in place of the latter, since it is less poisonous. Two Es., the *a* and the *β*, are prepared, the latter being preferable ; they are both derivatives of oxymethylpiperidine, and are prepared originally from acetone. E. is most frequently used in operations on the eye and nose, where it is applied to the surface in solution.

**Eucalyptus,** a genus of Myrtaceæ, contains about two hundred lofty trees occurring in Australia and the Malayan Archipelago. Many reach a height of 150 ft. and a girth of 25 ft., and they frequently become hollow ; *E. amygdalia* attains a height of 300 ft. The species are of great economic value, yielding oils, kinos, and useful timber, while the well-known oil of E. is obtained from *E. globulus,* the blue-gum tree.

**Eucharist.** The Christian offering of praise and thanksgiving is known by many titles, though that which we are now considering seems to have been the most used in early times. In the Book of Common Prayer, the terms used are the ' Lord's Supper ' and the ' Holy Communion ' ; among Rom. Catholics and some Anglicans, the term ' Mass ' is generally used, while members of the Eastern Orthodox Churches would speak of the ' Liturgy ' or the ' Holy Sacrifice.' From the beginning of the Christian church, the Holy E. has been regarded as the greatest of all the sacraments, and round it has gathered the richest ceremonial of the church. But as we trace through the ages the history of Eucharistic doctrine, we are faced with the sad fact that the sacrament of unity has been turned by men, generally over-anxious to dogmatise, into a source of controversy and discord. There are, in the N. T., two distinct narratives of the institution of the E., each appearing in two forms. The first is that of Mark (xiv. 22 ff.) and Matthew (xxvi. 26 ff.), the second is that of Luke (xxii. 17 ff.) and Paul (1 Cor. xi. 23 ff.). A reference to the institution occurs in the fourth gospel and this reference dates the Last Supper on the day before the Passover, whereas the Synoptic narratives state that it took place on the ' first day of unleavened bread, when they killed the passover.' No solution of this discrepancy is known. The word *Eucharist* is connected with two parts of speech in Gk., a noun and a verb. The verb εὐχαριστεῖν means ' to feel thankful ' and ' to give thanks.' It is the very word used of the thanksgiving of our Lord at the Last Supper. St. Matthew says λαβὼν ποτήριον εὐχαριστήσας εἶπεν (xxvi. 27), and St. Paul εὐχαριστήσας ἔκλασεν (1 Cor. xi. 24). As Justin Martyr tells us, the disciples of the second century continued to give thanks over the bread and the cup, and hence the term εὐχαριστεῖν came to mean to consecrate, and the term εὐχαριστια was employed to denote the consecrated elements themselves. Thus St. Irenæus says that after the consecration the bread is no longer common bread but *eucharistia,* consisting of two parts, an earthly and a heavenly. At a very early date the liturgical nature of the E. developed considerably, and it has even been held that St. Paul's account of the institution was taken from a previously existing order of service. From N. T. times onward, however, we do find liturgies in an advanced stage of development. The extent of the earliest fixed order can be seen by a comparison of the distinct groups of liturgies. It is impossible here even to touch on the development of liturgiology, but these groups may be mentioned : the Rom., the Gallican, the Alexandrine, and the Antiochene, containing the liturgies of St. Basil and St. Chrysostom. There is no doubt that the E. was at first celebrated in the evening after supper in imitation of Christ's own procedure. But it is equally certain that the change from evening to morning was universally made at a very early date. It is sometimes held that this change was made by St. Paul in the Corinthian Church. St. Augustine (ad. Januar) makes no reference to the occasion of the alteration, but says, 'It has seemed good to the Holy Spirit that, for the honour of so great a sacrament, the Lord's Body and Blood should enter the Christian's mouth before other food. It is for this reason that the custom is observed throughout the world.' Fasting communion made a morning celebration the ordinary procedure, though it is probable that on fast days, when the faithful were fasting till 3 p.m., it would take place later. In all the earliest references to the Holy E., it is considered that those who are present at the Consecration will all communicate. All those who had been present at the early part of the service but were unable to communicate had already departed at a given signal before the central act of the service began. Those who had departed would include the insane, the catechumens, and certain classes of penitents. The faithful all remained and all communicated with the priest. The first falling away from this standard is shown in the second canon of the Council of Antioch (A.D. 344) when it is ordered that those who attended the service as far as the lections, but refused to communicate, should be cast out of the church until they repent and confess. The separation being effected by the exorcist. Until the twelfth century, it is admitted by all writers that the laity received the sacrament under both kinds in all solemn public administrations, though the species of bread alone was used under special circumstances. In certain parts, the custom of receiving the species of wine through a tube sprang up on account of the great fear which was felt lest any of the sacred element should be spilt. The greatest care was taken that no portion of the consecrated bread should fall to the ground. In the East the custom of receiving the Blood of Christ by the method known as *intinction* early began. Here the particles of the consecrated bread were placed in the chalice, the two elements being given together into the communicant's mouth by a spoon. This practice was condemned in the West as schismatical and against apostolic tradition. It is generally agreed that the early Christians received the sacrament standing, this being the usual posture for all prayer on the Lord's Day and during Eastertide. It was necessary that all communicants should be baptised persons and that they should not be undergoing ecclesiastical censure. It is noteworthy that the importance of private confession to a priest is insisted on in several places before the end of the eighth century. An Eng. example occurs in the *Penitential* of Archbishop Theodore (c. A.D. 700), where a profession is made for dispensation from the rule if necessary. After special cases of excommunication and penance, reconciliation by the bishop or his deputy was, of course, necessary. As for the days on which the E. was celebrated, our starting point is the celebrated passage in the Acts (ii. 46) which is sometimes held to imply *daily* celebration. Particular mention, however, is later made only of the Lord's Day (xx. 7), and later allusions in the early writers make it comparatively clear that the Lord's Day was long regarded as the special day for ' the breaking of bread,' even as it now is. The days next fixed for communion were the ' Station Days,' *i.e.* Wednesdays and Fridays. Daily celebrations were, however, in use by the time of Chrysostom. We may infer from a canon of the Council of Eliberis (c. A.D. 300) that at that time weekly communion was the regular rule of the church universal, and such it continued to be in the East until the end of the seventh century. Bede, when writing to Egbert, says that even the more devout amongst the Eng. laity do not communicate except at Easter, Christmas, and Epiphany, but advises insistence on daily communion, which he speaks of as the custom among many of the continental churches. At the present time the Chuch of England insists on communion ' three times a year of which Easter shall be one.' The Rom. Catholic Church, while encouraging frequent communion requires under pain of sin only once a year ' at Easter or thereabouts.'

**Euchlorine,** an explosive, yellowish-green coloured gas, first prepared by Davy by heating hydrochloric acid with chlorate of potash. It has an extremely irritating odour, and is a powerful oxidising agent. It consists of a mixture of chlorine and chlorine peroxide, $ClO_2$.

**Euchre,** a game of cards, popular in America, but not played until the end of the nineteenth century. Thirty-two cards are used, all cards below seven being rejected. The cards rank as at whist with the exception of the ' Bowers.' The knave of trump suit (right bower) is the best trump; the knave of the same colour (left bower) is the next best, that card belonging to the trump suit. Each player receives five cards from the dealer by two or three at a time, the top card turned up being trumps. When two play the non-dealer either 'orders up' the trumps or passes. If he passes then the dealer either takes up the trump or passes. If both pass, the non-dealer may call other trumps or may pass again when the dealer makes. If both pass again the hand is thrown in and the cards are dealt again. If the hand is played the non-dealer leads and the dealer plays and must follow suit if possible. The game then continues as at whist, a player 'ordering up,' or taking up, or making the trump wins five tricks (a march) and scores two points ; if three tricks (the point) he scores one. If he fails to make three tricks he is euchred, and his opponent scores two. Game is five up. Four-handed E. is generally played. Then the players cut for partners. If the first hand passes, the second may assist, when his partner the dealer takes up the trump and the hand is played. If a player has a very good hand he may play alone against the other three. But he can only play alone when his partner 'orders up,' or when his partner assists, or when he takes up the trump, or when he orders up the trump. The scores are reckoned as before, except that a player playing alone scores four points if he wins five tricks.

**Euchroite,** a basic arsenate of copper occurring as a distinct mineral. It is related to clinoclase, cornwallite, and tyrolite, all of which are generally isomorphous with the corresponding phosphates of copper.

RUDOLF EUCKEN

**Eucken, Rudolf** (1846–1926), a doctor of philosophy, educated at Göttingen. His works deal chiefly with the history of philosophy. In 1903 he was elected D.D. of the University of Giessen and in 1910 of the University of Glasgow. In 1908 he won the Nobel prize for literature. He wrote many works, amongst which may be mentioned the following: *Grundbegriffe der Gegenwert,* 1878 ; *Die Einheit des Geisteslebens,* 1888 ; *Der Sune und Wert des Lebens,* 1908 ; and *Können wir noch Christen sein ?* 1911.

**Euclase** (' easily fracture '), a very rare mineral bearing some relation to beryl, and found in Brazil and the S. Urals.

**Euclid** (*fl c.* 300 B.C.), a Gk. mathematician, lived, according to Proclus (A.D. 412–485), in the days of Ptolemy I. of Egypt, was older than Archimedes (*b.* 287 B.C.) and Eratosthenes (*b.* 276 B.C.) and younger than Plato. His life is practically a blank, but many of his treatises, including the famous *Elements* (Στοιχεῖα), have come down to us. This work, which includes five books on plane geometry, one on proportion, three on the properties of numbers, one on incommensurable magnitudes, and finally three on solid geometry, was for centuries the text-book on geometry in all schools, and has only in comparatively recent years been superseded on the Continent and in the United States. His *Data* (Δεδομένα) contains ninety-five theorems, in which it is shown that, given certain hypotheses, other things are deducible. The *Phænomena* deals with the appearances produced by celestial motions. The musical treatises, entitled *Introduction to Harmony,* and *Section of the Scale,* and the *Optics* and *Katoptrics,* etc., are of doubtful authenticity. (*See also* GEOVE RV.)

**Euclid,** or **Eucleides of Megara** (*c.* 450–374 B.C.), was one of the most zealous disciples of Socrates, and also the founder of that school of philosophy variously called the Megarian, dialectic, or eristic. His philosophy prepared the way for the sceptics, for he delighted in proving contradictory propositions and so encouraged doubt. His writings have all perished.

**Eucratides,** King of Bactria, who lived in the second century B.C. Demetrius, son of Euthydemus, having disputed with E. the succession to the throne and besieged him for five months, was at length completely defeated by E., who, thereafter had several victorious campaigns in Asia over the Indi. But, unwisely attacking Mithridates, King of the Parthians, he was defeated and perished at the hand of his own son, who was associated with him in the government of Bactria.

**Eudæmonism** (from Gk. εὐδαιμονία, which describes the condition of a man under the care of a kindly spirit or genius), a much abused term in philosophy in the sense that every writer has contorted or enlarged its meaning to express his own ideas. As a system of philosophy E. upholds happiness as the chief goal of man, the confusion arising from the diverse conceptions of what is essential to that state. According to Aristotle the truly εὐδαίμονες are those who enjoy a contemplative existence without material anxieties, and without an impediment to the full and complete realisation of their highest self. Plato conceived a magnificent social ' eudæmonia,' to which every member of the state contributed, and in which everyone shared. For the Epicureans E. was equivalent to hedonism (see ETHICS).

**Eudemus of Rhodes** (*fl.* 330 B.C.) is associated with Theophrastus as an earnest follower of Aristotle. His *Eudemian Ethics* (seven books) are still extant.

**Eudialyte,** or **Eudyalite** (from Gk. εὐδιάλυτς, easily dissolved), a vitreous bisilicate of calcium, sodium, iron, zirconium, and other elements found in Greenland in the form of pink rhombohedral crystals.

**Eudiometer** (from Gk. εὖ, well, and δῖος, the root of Zeus), was primarily an apparatus to determine the purity of air, that is the amount of oxygen in it, but it is now generally used for the analysis of gases and especially of gaseous mixtures. A E. consists essentially of a graduated glass tubular vessel fitted at the top with platinum electrodes for the introduction of the electric spark. As a measure it depends on the observation of the amount of shrinkage after one or more chemical reactions in the volume or volumes of the gas or gases under consideration. In the case of air the reaction is set up by the explosion caused by the introduction of an electric spark. A known volume of the atmosphere is confined with about half its volume of hydrogen. After an electric current has been passed through the mixture, all the oxygen of the air unites with some of the hydrogen to form aqueous vapour, which soon condenses. The shrinkage therefore measures three times the volume of the oxygen, this gas combining with twice its own volume of hydrogen to form water.

**Eudocia,** or **Athenais** (*c.* 401–*c.* 460), wife of Theodosius II., Byzantine emperor, was the daughter of an Athenian sophist. When her brothers denied her a share in her father's inheritance, she sought and won the protection of Pulcheria, sister to the Emperor Theodosius, whom she (E.) eventually married (421). She repaired to Jerusalem, and became implicated in the Monophysite controversy (453), but Euthymius, the saint, finally reconciled her to the ' true faith.' Among her works were a paraphrase of the Book of Daniel and a poem on her husband's Persian conquests. E. is sometimes wrongly referred to as Eudoxia.

**Eudocia** (*d.* 462), the younger, the daughter of the above and of Theodosius II. When her first husband, Valentinianus III., was murdered by Petronius Maximus, she fell an unwilling victim to the usurper, and, in revenge, invited Genseric, King of the Vandals, to Italy. The barbarian sacked Rome, and took E. to Africa.

**Eudocia** (*c.* 1021–96), widow of the Byzantine emperor, Constantine X.

**Eudoxus,** a Gk. navigator, was dispatched in 125 B.C. by Ptolemy Euergetes, King of Egypt, to explore India and the Arabian Sea. His adventures are recounted by Strabo, who included E.'s discoveries in his great geographical work.

**Eudoxus of Cnidus** (*c.* 407–*c.* 355 B.C.), a Gk. astronomer, studied under Plato for some time, spent many years in Egypt, learning from the priests, and later opened a school in Athens which rivalled that of Plato. According to Pliny and Strabo he first fixed the length of the year as 365¼ days, whilst Vitruvius ascribes to him the invention of the sun-dial. He was also a mathematician and philosopher, and won golden opinions from Cicero.

**Euganean Hills,** in N. Italy. They are a low volcanic range forming a small group extending for about 10 m. from the neighbourhood of Padua to Este. They are covered with wood, and contain many hot springs. The culminating point is the Mount Venda, 1890 ft. high.

**Eugene,** a city of Oregon on the Willamette R. The chief industries are iron works, machine shops, flour mills, manufs. of waggons, furniture, and woollens. It is the seat of the University of Oregon. Pop. 18,901.

**Eugène, François, Prince de Savoie** (1663–1736), a renowned Fr. general, was *b.* at Paris. He was the youngest son of the Count of Soissons, grandson of Duke of Savoy. Originally intended for the church, but his tastes were more for military renown. After his father's death, and on the refusal of Louis XIV. to give him a commission, he left France and served under Emperor Leopold as a volunteer against the Turks. He displayed great courage and tactical talent and rapidly rose. In the Coalition War in Italy against France, he

U 2

covered himself with glory, became a field-marshal in 1693, and put an end to Turkish power in Hungary by winning the famous battle of Zenta in 1697. He commanded the Italian army in the War of Succession in 1701, but effected little of importance, owing to the smallness of his forces. In 1703 he became president of the council of war, took over command of the Ger. army, and assisted Marlborough to win the battle of Blenheim, 1704. After being checked by the Fr. general, Vendôme, and twice wounded, he defeated the Fr. and drove them out of Italy. He shared with Marlborough the victories of Oudenarde and Malplaquet. After the retirement of England and Holland from the struggle, Prince E. was unable to withstand the enemy on the Rhine, and was defeated by Villars in 1712. In 1716 war with the Turks recommenced, and the prince was everywhere successful. He defeated an army twice the size of his own at Peterwerdein, took Temesvar, and after a desperate battle took Belgrade by assault. After the Peace of Passarowitz, he laboured with unwearied energy in the cabinet. He *d.* at Vienna.

EUGENIA PIMENTAN
(Allspice)

**Eugenia,** a genus of Myrtaceæ, contains numerous species, all of which grow in the tropics, and many bear edible fruits. The best-known plant in the genus is *E. caryophyllata,* which produces the cloves of commerce; they are the dried flower-buds of the tree. *E. Malaccensis* is known as the Malay apple, or rose apple.

**Eugenics** is that science which has for its aim the perpetuation of those inherent and hereditary qualities which aid in the development of the human race. (*See* BIOLOGY—*Practical Value of Biology.*) Sir F. Galton, by his valuable research work and his many publications, added considerably to the importance and value of the science. Not only this, but in his will he left sufficient money to found the Galton Chair of Eugenics at the London University, which is occupied by Prof. Karl Pearson (1930). Attached to the chair is a valuable library and laboratory. He also directs the Galton Laboratory for National Eugenics, which publishes the *Annals of E.,* the *E. Laboratory Memoirs, The E. Lab. Lecture Series,* and the important *Treasury of Human Inheritance,* an extensive collection of family pedigrees, illustrating the inheritance of physical, mental, and pathological characters in man. Besides the works of Galton, there is an extensive literature on Eugenics, of which a few recent books may be mentioned: Karl Pearson's *Grammar of Science,* 1911; C. W. Saleeby's *The E. Prospect,* 1921; L. Doncaster's *Heredity,* 1921; S. J Homes' *Studies in Evolution and E.,* 1923; L. Darwin's *Need for E. Reform,* 1926; J. A. Thomson's *Heredity,* 1926; also G. K. Chesterton's counterblast, *E. and Other Evils,* 1922.

**Eugenics Education Society,** a society in connection with which the Galton Chair of Eugenics was inaugurated on the death of Sir F. Galton (1911), with the large sum of money bequeathed by him for that purpose. He first coined the word eugenics (Gk. εὖ, well, good, and γένος, race) in his work on *Human Faculty,* 1883. The aim of the society is to further the study and progress of national eugenics, and to spread a knowledge of the subject by publications and lectures. Its chief organ is *The Eugenics Review,* a quarterly magazine. The society is now known simply as the Eugenics Society and holds monthly meetings at which papers are read by leading doctors and eugenists. Sir Bernard Mallet succeeded Major Leonard Darwin in the presidency which the latter held 1911 to 1928. The present offices are at 20, Grosvenor Gardens, London.

**Eugénie, Marie Ignace Augustine de Montijo** (1826–1920), daughter of the Count of Montijo, Empress of the

Fr., was *b.* May 5, at Granada, Spain, In 1853, at Notre Dame, Paris, she was married to Napoleon III., and three years later she became the mother of the Prince Imperial. In 1870, on the fall of the empire, came to England and took up her residence at Chislehurst, afterwards removing to Farnborough. Three years after her coming to England, Napoleon died, and in the Zulu War of 1879 she lost her son. *See* Edward Legge, *The Empress Eugénie*, 1910. While on a visit to her nephew the Duke of Alva, she *d.* in Madrid, July 11.

**Eugenin** (C₁₀H₁₂O₃), a substance which is obtained from oil of cloves.

**Eugenius**, the name of four popes: Eugenius (St.) I., pope from 654–8, festival, Aug. 27; Eugenius II., pope from 824–7; Eugenius III., pope from 1145–53; and Eugenius IV., pope from 1431–47. The latter's pontificate was marked by a schism created by proceedings in the council of Basel towards the reform of the church and the limitation of papal authority. He excommunicated the council and the council deposed him, but he succeeded in re-uniting the Church round his own person and office. Holding a council at Florence, he concluded a re-union with the Greek Church (1439), and later with Armenians (1439), Jacobites (1443), Nestorians (1445).

**Eugubine, or Iguvine Tables,** the name given to seven bronze tablets, the inscriptions on which form a very remarkable memorial of the Umbrian language. They were discovered at Gubbio in 1444, where they are still preserved. The characters on four of them are Etruscan, on two Rom., and on one partly Rom. and partly Etruscan. The language used somewhat resembles the older forms of Latin and also the Oscan dialects. The subjects of the inscriptions are directions concerning sacrificial customs and forms of prayer. The first publication of these was in Dempster's *Etruria Regalis*, but the first judicious attempt was that of Lanza in his *Saggio di Lingua Etrusca*. *See:* Aufrecht and Kirchoff's *Die Umbrischen Denkmäler*.

**Euhemerus and Euhemerism,** the latter is the name applied to the historical theory of the origin of mythology, from its founder Euhemerus, a native of Messene about the fourth century B.C. While voyaging to the Indian Ocean he professed to have discovered a new island called Panchaia. Here he is supposed to have found a number of inscriptions representing the principal gods of Greece as mere earthborn beings, deified after death for their superior strength and abilities.

His work *Hiera Anagraphe* was lost, but for it he was accused of Atheism and his name became a byword for mendacity. Many eminent men, among them Polybius, Lactantius, and St. Augustine, adopted its theory. Later Gk. writers simplified the theory, eliminating extravagant things and leaving a list of commonplace and credible stories. Thus Æolus became an anct. mariner, the Cyclopes, a race of savages inhabiting Sicily; Atlas, an astronomer; and Scylla and Pegasus, fast-sailing pirates. The system still exists in some current handbooks of mythology. Euhemerism was the favourite theory of the so-called philosophical historians of the eighteenth century in France. It was extended to England by a translation of Abbé Bauer's great work, *The Mythology and Fables of Antiquity Explained from History*. Vossius, Bochart, and Huet belong to this school; Mr. Gladstone was the latest and ablest exponent of sacred Euhemerism. Herbert Spencer also embraced the theory in his explanation of the origin of religion.

**Eulenspiegel** (Ger. ' owl-glass '), the prototype of all knavish fools of later times, *b.* at the end of the thirteenth century, near Schöppen-stadt, in Brunswick. He was three times baptised, once in the font, secondly in the mud, and the third time in hot water. He wandered over Europe, experienced many wonderful and comical adventures, and perpetrated many knavish tricks. His place of burial is not certain, as two places claim to have his bones in their respective churchyards. One stone stands to his memory at Mölln, near Lübeck, where he is supposed to have *d.* in 1350. His bones are also at Damme in Belgium, where his death is placed about 1307. In modern times his story is embodied in one of the masterpieces of Belgian literature—*La Légende d'Ulenspiegel*, by Charles de Coster. The first edition appeared in 1868. It is really a kind of epic which celebrates the struggles of the people to secure freedom from Spanish tyranny. Gerhard Hauptmann, the great German poet and dramatist, published a vast poem called *Eulenspiegel* which in parts was so mystic that it puzzled his critics.

**Euler, Leonhard** (1707–83), a Swiss mathematician, *b.* at Basel, and studied under John Bernouilli. He went to St. Petersburg, where he became Professor of Physics, and in 1733 of mathematics in the Academy. In 1741 he was invited to Berlin by Frederick the Great, and he published many valuable papers during this period. His later years were spent in St. Petersburg in total blindness, but his servant wrote at his master's dictation. The *Introduction to Algebra* was completed in this way. His chief works are : *Theory of Planetary Motion, Institution of Differential and Integral Calculus, Introduction to Analysis of Infinities.*

LEONHARD EULER

**Eulerian Numbers.** Named after Euler (1707–1783), a Swiss mathematician of international repute. The expansion of $\cos x$ is $\cos x = 1 - \dfrac{x^2}{2!} + \dfrac{x^4}{4!} - \ldots$, and the expansion of $\sec x = \dfrac{1}{\cos x}$, may be written $1 + \dfrac{A_1 x^2}{2!} + \dfrac{A_2 x^4}{4!} + \dfrac{A_3 x^6}{6!} + \ldots$ where $A_1$, $A_2$, $A_3$, etc., are known as E. Ns., the first nine of which were first computed by Euler. The first five are 1, 5, 61, 1385, 50521, and the 50th contains 127 figures. Some of the properties of these numbers may be noted here, viz., every E. N. is a positive odd integer ; the sum of any two successive E. Ns. is divisible by 3. The chief usefulness of E. Ns. is in the summation of certain series.

**Eumenes** (*c.* 360–316 B.C.), a Macedonian general, and a native of Cardia in the Thracian Chersonesus. At a very early age he was employed as private secretary by Philip II. of Macedon, and, on the death of that prince, by Alexander. When Alexander died, Cappadocia and Paphlagonia were assigned to E. He was put to death by Antigonus.

**Eumenes I.,** the King of Pergamus.

He succeeded his uncle, Philetærus, in 263 B.C. The only event of importance in his reign was his victory near Sardis over Antiochus Soter, which enabled him to secure possession of the districts round his capital.

**Eumenides** (the ' well-wisher '), a euphemistical name for the Erinyes, the Rom. Furiæ, or Diræ, three fearful maidens who dwelt in the depths of Tartarus. Their function is to punish men for crimes such as perjury, murder, inhospitality, and violation of filial duty. Their names are Alecto, Megæra, and Tisiphone. In the poets they sometimes appear as one, and one finds, in the tragedies of Æschylus, a whole chorus of Erinyes. Later, they were considered as goddesses and sacrifices of sheep and libations of nephalia (honey and water) were offered to them. Later poets and sculptors represented them as winged virgins, dressed in the garbs of huntresses, with serpents encircling their heads. Milton confuses them in some of his works with the three Fates, Clotho, Lachesis, and Atropos.

**Eumenius :** (1) A Trojan killed by Camilla in Italy (*see* Virgil, *Æneid*, ii.). (2) A Gallic rhetorician, *b.* at Autun about A.D. 280. He was grandson of Glaucus, the Athenian rhetorician who had settled in Gaul. E. practised rhetoric successfully both at Autun and at Rome, and was appointed to the court of Constantius Chlorus, and put at the head of a new college in Autun. Of the panegyrics attributed to him, one was made before the Emperor on the occasion of the retaking of Britain : another on the foundation of colleges, and a panegyric on Constantina Augustina, spoken at Treves and full of hyperbole. These speeches have frequently been reprinted, especially in the collection known as the *Duodecim panegyrici veteres.*

**Eumolpus** (' sweet singer '), in Gk. mythology the son of Poseidon and Chione, a legendary priest, poet, and warrior. The Eleusinian mysteries were generally considered to have been founded by E. As priest E. purified Heracles from the murder of the centaurs ; as musician he instructed him in the playing of the lyre. He is said to have been the first priest of Dionysus, and to have introduced the cultivation of the vine and fruit trees.

**Eunapius** (*b. c.* A.D. 347), a Greek anti-Christian historian and a native of Sardis. He is the author of *Lives of the Philosophers and Sophists*, edited by J. F. Boissonade, 1849 ; and also of a history from *c.* A.D. 268 to *c.* A.D. 404.

**Eunomius,** a leader of an extreme

sect of Arians who were called after him Eunomians. His confession of faith to Theodosius in 383 was rejected. His theory was that of Arius carried to an extreme. After his death his followers disbanded through internal quarrelling.

**Eunuch** (Gk. εὐνοῦχος, 'one who has charge of a bed), etymologically, one who has charge of women's apartments in the Eastern countries. The term, however, applies particularly to a person who has been castrated in order to serve as attendant in a harem. Sometimes Es. occupied high official places in the state, so that the word E. was applied to a high official, the chamberlain. The barbarous custom of castration was probably earliest practised in Africa, but it was also a custom among the Roms. Many Es. formerly employed in choral work in Italy as youths were often castrated to prevent their voices from breaking, and thus preserved the pure, clear 'timbre' of the boy's voice. In the eighteenth century 4000 boys were yearly castrated for musical purposes.

**Eunus** (d. 133 B.C.), a Syrian slave and leader of a revolt of slaves in Sicily in 135 B.C. While working at Enna he lead the slaves of a slave-owner, Damophilus, in a successful attack on the town, and before the revolt was crushed it had spread all over the island.

**Euonymus**, a genus of shrubby and arborescent plants in the order Celastraceæ, is indigenous to Europe and Asia. The species are used in the manufacture of spindles.

**Eupatoria (Tewpatoria),** a Russian seaport and health resort, on the W. coast of the Crimea. There are a great many Jewish inhabitants, and it contains the residence of the spiritual head of the Karaite sect. Trades are carried on in cereals, skins, cowhair, felt, tallow, and salt. Formerly, in 1736, it belonged to the Turkish territory, but the Russians are now in possession. Pop. 12,000.

**Eupatorium** (Gk. εὐπατόριον), a genus of Compositæ, which takes its name from Mithridates Eupator, king of Pontus, who first recognised its medicinal properties. There is only one British species, *E. cannabinum,* the hemp-agrimony, which grows in marshy soil. Formerly it was highly valued as a medicine. It is very abundant in America. *E. perfoliatum,* or cross-wort, is used as a substitute for Peruvian bark.

**Eupatridæ,** literally translated means 'sons of noble fathers,' the anct. nobility of Athens, the autochthonous population, the dwellers in the city, the descendants of royal stock. The E. represent the only nobility that had any political recognition in early times. They were at the height of their power in the period during the limitation of the monarchy.

**Eupen,** an industrial town with a hydropathic establishment, Belgium, 9 m. S. of Aix-la-Chapelle. By the Treaty of Versailles (1919) it was stipulated that the districts of Eupen and Malmedy should be transferred from Germany to Belgium, if the inhabitants wished it, as a subsequent plebiscite indicated. Pop. 12,417. The district ceded has an area of 380 sq. m. and a pop. of 62,000.

EUONYMUS EUROPÆUS

(Spindle Tree)

A, Flowering branch. B, Fruit.

**Euphorbia,** the principal genus of Euphorbiaceæ (*q.v.*), contains over 700 species, widely distributed in the warmer parts of the globe, and a few in Britain. Both herbs and shrubs are common, while some of the plants occurring in the hotter and drier countries have succulent stems and greatly resemble the cacti. These, however, may be distinguished from cacti by their emitting a milky latex when punctured, and by the fact that the spines, when present, never form clusters. The inflorescence is most curious and forms a *cyathium* resembling a single flower; five bracts surround a number of male flowers, each reduced to a solitary stamen, and in the centre is a single female flower which forms an ovary of three carpels. *E. lathyris,* the caper spurge, is a common weed in cottage gardens, and *E. amygdaloides*, the wood spurge, is also well known in Britain.

**Euphorbiaceæ**, an order of Dicotyledons, contains over 4000 species of trees, shrubs, and herbs, and is distributed over the whole globe. Many contain dangerously poisonous substances, while some are used as purgatives, others have a farinaceous substance used as food, *e.g.* cassara, and rubber, castor-oil and cascarilla bark are well-known products. Few of the characteristics are common, but the flowers are always unisexual and regular. There are generally five perianth leaves, the stamens may be

heroes slain by Menelaus (*Iliad*, xvii. 1–60). In support of his theory of the transmigration of souls, Pythagoras declared he had once been E., whose shield hung up on the temple of Argos. Pythagoras claimed this shield as his own.

**Euphrasia**, a genus of Scrophulariaceæ, contains about fifty species of semi-parasitic plants. *E. officinalis* is the common euphrasy, or eyebright.

**Euphrates** (Babylon. *Puratta*; Hebrew *Perath*; Arabian *Frat*; Gk. Εὐφράτης), the largest riv. of W. Asia. It rises in Armenia in two branches, the Kara Su and the Murad; the for-

ON THE RIVER EUPHRATES

united or free, one to many in number, and the ovary is superior usually with three united carpels, is trilocular, and there are always one to two ovules in each loculus. Some of the chief genera are *Euphorbia, Ricinus, Croton, Manihot.*

**Euphorbium**, derived from the *Euphorbia officinarum* growing in N.W. Africa, a violent, irritant, and acrid substance, formerly much used in medicine, especially as a remedy for angina pectoris, as it acts on the nerve-centres for breathing and for the heart. It is dangerous to use E. except in minute doses. The term is sometimes inaccurately applied to the various species of gum-resin.

**Euphorbus**, the son of Panthous, one of the bravest of the Trojan

mer rises about 20 m. N.E. of Erzeroum, in the Tcheldis Mts., the latter 45 m. N.E. from the nearest point of Lake Van. Both these rivs. flow in a S.W. direction till they unite near Kebban in about 39° N. lat. and 39° 25′ E. long. The united stream flows S.W. then to Sunaysat, having forced a passage through the main range of the Taurus Mts. and formed a succession of rapids and cataracts. For a considerable distance it forms the boundary between Mesopotamia and Syria; thence it flows S.E. to its junction with the Tigris, and the joint riv., now called Shat-el-Arab, empties itself by several arms into the Persian Gulf, after a course of about 1700 m. The present place of junction with the Tigris has been shown by Sir W.

Willcocks to be at Garnat Ali, 30 m. higher up than Kurna, the former place of confluence. Formerly the Tigris and the E. preserved each a separate course to the sea. The distance between the two rivers varies from 18 to 19 m. The principal tributaries of the E. after it emerges from the mountains are, on the right, the Sagar; on the left the Balik Su and the Khabur. The principal towns on the banks are now Sunaysat, Bir, Ana, Hit, and Hilla, but the greater part is inhabited only by roving tribes of Bedouins. The river is navigable for small craft as far as Bir, a distance of 1200 m., whilst larger vessels can ascend as far as the confluence with the Tigris. The E. has played a conspicuous part in the history of the world, as the many ruins of great cities on its banks bear witness; besides Babylon, ' the glory of kingdoms,' Ur, Zarsa, Nippar, and Sippara were situated there. The canal system of the river was very complete in early times, and contributed not a little to the amazing fertility of the region. Our information on the E. has of necessity increased greatly by reason of the British occupation and administration of Iraq. Characteristic floods have often occurred during this period; that of 1929 was probably the highest for nearly forty years, and illustrated the effect that river floods have had on the life of Iraq since the dawn of history. Warning is now given by wireless from Syria of the daily rise and fall of levels at Dair-al-Zor, so that at least all available labour for the defence of the dykes can be secured. The provision of labourers for the dykes is decreed by law to be the duty of the agricultural community. Whirlpools, as in 1929, caused severe erosion and undermined the embankments. One counteractive measure is to divert the river as, e.g. into the Habbaniya depression, but the experience of the British authorities is that this depression may soon be filled. The damage by floods to crops may be severe, and if the floods are very high, the river becomes indistinguishable from the sheets of water spread over the land; while, as in 1929, a small quantity of E. water may travel some 40 kilometres across country and flow into the Tigris. Owing to the fact that the prevailing N.W. wind acts with the current of rivers in Iraq, sailing craft have to be towed up-stream; the E., like the other rivers, is very shallow in autumn, so that the draught of ships has to be limited to 3½ feet, and this is so even on the Tigris which is deeper than the E. No steamers ply on the E., owing to its shallowness, which is particularly marked in the Hammar Lake; but sailing craft carry local freight; and motor boats can be hired on the Middle E. See also BAGHDAD RAILWAY; and for further details of the Tigris, see TIGRIS.

**Euphrosyne,** one of the Graces, ' The Joyous One,' see CHARITIES.

**Euphuism,** the florid mode of speaking and writing towards the end of the reign of Queen Elizabeth. It was brought into fashion by the romance *Euphues,* written in 1578 by John Lyly, who in addressing his writings chiefly to women said he would rather see his works ' lie shut in a lady's casket, than open in a scholar's study.' His idea was not to improve, but to amuse. E. did not attempt to render the simplicity of nature, but to be artificial and affected in its desire for refinement.

**Eupion,** a highly inflammable liquid of the paraffin series, discovered by K. Reichenbach. It is formed from many substances, such as wood, coal, caoutchouc, bones, resin, and the fixed oils.

**Eupoda** (Gk. εὐποδία, goodness of foot), the name given to a section of Coleoptera noted for the thickness of their hind legs. The genus *Sagra* especially is so developed, and is therefore known as the kangaroo beetle.

**Eupolis** (c. 446–411 B.C.), an Athenian poet of Old Comedy who flourished in the time of the Peloponnesian War. He is ranked by Horace as one of the greatest writers of his school. In the elegance and purity of his diction he was reputed to be equal to Aristophanes, and in command of irony and sarcasm to rival Cratinus. His plays are *Kolakes, Maricas, The Baptae, The Demoi,* and *Poleis.* He was erroneously supposed to have been drowned by Alcibiades, who threw him into the sea for having attacked him in one of his plays.

**Eurasian,** a term used to denote children b. of a Hindu mother and a European father. For more than half a century it was confined to India, but is now descriptive of any half-caste.

**Eure,** a dept. of north-western France, formed in 1907 from a portion of the old prov. of Normandy. The territory of Eure is broken up by its rivers into well-wooded plateaus. The climate is mild, but most variable. Chief products, wheat, flax, and beetroot, cattle, and horses of pure Norman breed, for which the district is famous. Fruit is abundant; the minerals are marl and brick-clay. Pop. 323,650.

**Eure-et-Loir,** a dept. of N. France,

situated to the S.E. of the dept. of Eure, is divided into the four arrondissements of Chartres, Chateaudun, Dreux, and Nogent-le-Rotrou. The eastern portion is a gently undulating plain, called the Beauce, the western, called the Perche, is of a more diversified nature, with hills, forests, and numerous rivers. The chief river in the N. is the Eure, in the S. are the Loire and the Huisne. None of the rivers is navigable save the Eure for a short distance. The Perche district has a slightly colder and healthier climate than the Beauce, where fever sometimes occurs, caused by the pools of rain water which form the only water supply in summer for many villages. Wheat and oats are the principal crops, and apples are largely grown. Textile goods and boots are manufactured and there are foundries. Area of province 2293 sq. m. Pop. 330,000.

**Eureka,** a city of California, U.S.A., on Humboldt Bay, co. seat of Humboldt co., and the most westerly city in the U.S.A. Great quantities of redwood lumber are shipped. Pop. 15,752.

**Eureka Springs,** a city of N.E. Arkansas, U.S.A., in the Ozark Mountains, a health resort, with radio-active springs. Resident pop. 2276.

**Eurhythmics** (Gk. εὖ, well ; ῥυθμός, flow) is a method, developed by M. Jaques-Dalcroze, of teaching music through its realisation and interpretation by movements of the body. By a succession of exercises carefully graded and directed, an intellectual appreciation of rhythm is attained, based on the natural perception of rhythm illustrated by the movements of many people in response to a barrel organ playing a march or dance music. Later exercises develop the imagination and encourage its expression by free descriptive movements.

Attention and concentration, in addition to physical control, are exacted by all the exercises, by means of which the sense of hearing and the judgment of direction and intensity of sound are trained. Concentration is essential, for even momentary wandering causes the movements of the body to be out of time with the music. Moreover, without concentration, the high degree of physical control that can be gained would be impossible, for the more difficult exercises demand separate control of each arm, the legs, and head, so that each can move at a different rate from the other and simultaneously express four different rhythms.

The Eurhythmic method of teach-ing music incorporates the development of mental and physical control, thereby increasing efficiency.

*Bibliography*—*The Eurhythmics of Jaques-Dalcroze.*

**Euripides** (Εὐριπίδης) (c. 480–406 B.C.), the last of the great trio of Gk. tragedians (Æschylus, Sophocles, Euripides). The Parian marble gives the date of his birth as 485. He was probably born in the is. of Salamis, on the day of the famous battle according to tradition, of humble parents. (*See* Aristoph., *Acharnœ*, 478 ; *Equit* 17 ; *Ranœ*, 840.) He received a good education, and

EURIPIDES

became the friend of Protagoras, Anaxagoras, Socrates, and others. He acquired great oratorical skill under Prodicus, beginning his career as a writer, about 455, winning third place with the *Pleiades.* Not till 441 did he secure the first prize, and only about five times in all. The scientific and philosophic thought expounded in his plays, often approaching religious scepticism, did not find favour with his contemporaries. He represented the new moral and social influences that were affecting Athens, and in the next century his popularity increased ten-fold, and many considered his dramas superior to those of Æschylus and Sophocles. He is noted pre-eminently as a master of pathos and for his delineation of female character. He is interested in the experiences of the ordinary individual, rather than in that of legendary beings, drawing his characters with a fine realistic touch. E. has been called the most modern of the three great Athenian dramatists, and 'the forerunner of Rationalism.' The ancient criticisms of Aristophanes and others are very prejudiced, but Quintilian and Cicero both admired E. Unfortunate in both his first and second marriages he finally left Athens, about 409, and *d.* at the court of Archelaus of Macedonia. A noble cenotaph erected to him at Athens declared that 'all Greece was his monument.' About eighteen of his plays only are extant, but titles of many more are known. Among the best are : *Hippolytus, Medea, Alcestis* (438 B.C.), freely translated in Browning's *Balaustion* 1871 ; *Ion, The Bacchæ, Iphigenia in Aulis.* Others are : *Orestes, Hecuba, Electra, The Suppliants,* and *Troades.* The one extant satiric drama, *The Cyclops,* is also his. In more modern times great homage has been paid to the genius of E., Milton, Browning, Schiller, and Alfieri were all ardent admirers. Among numerous editions may be mentioned those of Lascaris (1496, four plays), Musurus (Aldine ed., 1503), Nauck (3rd ed. 1871), Dindorf (5th ed. 1870), Kirchhoff (1867), Paley (1877), and Sandys (1880), have also produced complete editions. Consult Mahaffy, *Introduction to the Study of Euripides,* 1879 ; Symonds, *Greek Poets,* 1893 ; Verrall, *Euripides the Rationalist,* 1895 ; Haigh, *Tragic Drama of the Greeks,* 1896 ; Norwood, *Riddle of the Bacchæ,* 1908 ; Nestle, *Euripides, der Dichter der griechischen Aufklärung,* 1901 ; and Gilbert Murray's *Euripides* (translations), and *Athenian Drama,* iii.

**Euripus,** or **Euripos,** *see* EUBŒA.

**Euroclydon,** a N.E. wind in the Mediterranean now called Gregalia. It is mentioned in Acts. xxvii as being the cause of the shipwreck of the vessel in which St. Paul was sailing.

EUROPA AND THE BULL

**Europa** (Εὐρώπη), daughter of Agenor, or of Phœnix, King of Phœnicia, and sister of Cadmus. The Gk. legend was that she was beloved by Zeus, who assumed the form of a white bull and carried her away to Crete, where she became mother of Minos, Rhadamanthus, and Sarpedon. After death she was worshipped at Crete as 'Hellotis.' There is considerable discussion as to the etymology of her name. *Cf.* the myth of Persephone. *See* Horace, *Odes,* iii. 27; Ovid, *Metam.* ii. 833 ; Roscher's *Lexicon der Mythologie.*

**Europa Point,** the most S. point of the Straits of Gibraltar.

**Europe** is situated in the North Temperate Zone. It is, except Australia, the smallest of the continents, but is both historically and politically the most important. Its area is 3,800,000 sq. m., about one-fourteenth of the total land area of the globe, the greatest length being 3400 m., and the greatest breadth 2400 m. Geographically, E. should be regarded as forming with Asia one great division of the land surface of the globe. Its eastern boundaries are the Caspian Sea, Ural R., and Ural Mts. These boundaries do not, however, mark a distinct difference either in flora, fauna, or political divisions, as Russia in E. and Siberia are now united in the Union of Soviet Socialist Republics. The other boundaries are : on the N. the Arctic Ocean, on the W. the Atlantic Ocean, on the S. the Mediterranean Sea, Black Sea, and Caucasus Mts. The boundaries of the U.S.S.R., however, extend beyond the Caucasus to include the Transcaucasian Republics of Georgia, Azerbaijan, and Armenia. The coast line of E. is greater in proportion to its size than that of the other continents, being some 50,000 m. The land is penetrated by large seas and gulfs, and its coast-line contains several large peninsulas, conditions which greatly favour its trade. The surface is divided into two parts, the great central plain, occupying two-thirds of its surface, stretching from the Ural Mts. to the Atlantic, and the highlands in the centre and the S. Apart from these two divisions is the mountainous district of Scandinavia, including the British Isles. The southern system consists of the Alps, Pyrenees, Sierra Nevada, Apennines, Balkans, and Carpathians. The great transverse watershed runs from N.E. to S.W., and the rivers therefore flow generally N.W. and S.E. The two chief centres of this watershed are the Valdain uplands and the Alps. From the Valdain plateau flow the Volga (2100 m.) into the Caspian Sea, the Don into the Sea of Azov, the Dnieper into the Black Sea, the Northern Dwina into the White Sea, and the Western Dwina into the Baltic.

From the Alps flow the Danube (1700 m.) into the Black Sea, the Rhine into the North Sea, the Rhone, Po, and Adige, into the Mediterranean. There are three principal groups of lakes, viz. the Alpine lakes with Geneva, Constance, Lucerne, Neuchâtel in Switzerland, Maggiore, Garda and Como in Italy, and Balaton in Austria, the Scandinavian group with Wiener, Wetter, and Mälar in Sweden, Miosen and Randsfjord in Norway, and the lakes of the central plain, Ladoga, Onega, Peipus, Ilmen in Russia, and Saima and others in Finland. The islands, with the exception of Iceland, lie near the mainland, the principal being Great Britain and Ireland, Sardinia, Corsica, Sicily, Iceland, Nova Zembla, and Crete.

*Geology.*—In earliest geological times the coast of E. appears to have had a greater extension towards the N. and N.W., whilst the southern and eastern districts were under the sea. The oldest rocks, those of the Archæan and Palæozoic periods, are most continuous in the northern part of the continent, and extend over a large part of N. Russia, Finland, the Scandinavian Peninsula, and the northern and western parts of the British Isles. They also occur in Brittany, Central France, and Spain. In the rest of E. they form isolated clusters, but appear to be the foundation of the Alps, Pyrenees, Caucasian, and Ural ranges. The newer rocks of the Mesozoic and Cainozoic periods are generally found on the lower lying lands, but occur, nevertheless, in the Pyrenees, Alps, Caucasus, Carpathians, and Apennines. Their most continuous belt is in the central plain from the North Sea into Russia. During the Cambrian period the southern part of E. was covered by a shallow sea, with a few isles of Archæan formation, while a large inland sea existed in the N. of Scotland, and apparently also in Wales. In the following, Silurian, period the continent was further submerged, the British Isles disappearing almost entirely. This was apparently a period of great volcanic activity. Next came the Devonian and Old Red Sandstone periods. The latter was deposited in lakes and inland seas, while the former is of marine origin. Between the Silurian and Devonian periods the sea had receded and left great masses of land uncovered. The Atlantic Ocean, however, still stretched over the S. of England and the centre of E., while submarine volcanic eruption was frequent in Germany. The Carboniferous period marked a further extension of the sea, which covered Ireland and England, the low grounds of Central E. and a great part of Russia. Volcanic disturbance was frequent, and eventually the sea receded, leaving vast tracts of newly exposed lands. At the beginning of the Mesozoic era, large inland seas appear to have covered parts of E., including the southern portions of the British Isles, and the lower course of the Rhine. Towards the close of the Triassic period, however, the land subsided, and allowed these lakes to become connected with the open sea. During the Jurassic period the British Isles seem to have risen above sea-level, with the exception of S.E. England. Similarly Southern France and Eastern Spain were submerged, and the lower parts of N. Germany and Russia, Italy, Austria-Hungary, and the Balkans were also partly under water. This submergence appears to have lasted for a very lengthy period, but towards the close of the Jurassic period the land again rose, and in the early Cretaceous period Middle E. was generally dry. Later on, however, the land again subsided, leaving a vast sea over Central E., while the Mediterranean Sea was of far greater extent than at present, and covered part of France, Spain, Italy, and Greece, and was probably connected directly with the Indian Ocean. At the beginning of the Cainozoic period the land had again risen and left the centre of E. above sea-level. The southern lands were, however, represented only by islands and narrow peninsulas, a condition which persisted until the late Miocene period. During the Eocene period, the Alps, Pyrenees, and Carpathians were thrown up, and a further elevation of the same ranges was effected in the Miocene period. During the Pliocene period the bed of the Mediterranean was elevated, uncovering the lands of Southern Europe. Violent changes of surface do not seem to have taken place in the Pleistocene period, but there were successive elevations and depressions. During this period the British Isles appear at one time to have formed part of the continent, while at a later period large tracts of them again lay under water.

*Climate.*—The climate of E. is very favourable. The major portion of the continent lies within the N. temperate zone, only parts of Norway, Sweden, and Russia being within the Arctic Circle. Owing to the fact that there is a long coast-line facing the Atlantic, and also to the presence of big inland seas, the climate is to some extent of an insular character. The Gulf Stream washes the western shores and keeps their ports open all the year round. The prevailing winds come from the S.W., and are genial in character. In spring, however, cold E. winds blow from Siberia and lower the temperature considerably even in Western E. On the other hand hot winds blow across the Mediterranean from the sandy regions of N. Africa and impart to the southern shores of E. a sub-tropical climate. There are four regions of climate which may be distinguished : the southern, along the shores of the Mediterranean, where there is seldom frost except in the mountains ; the western, along the shores of the Atlantic and inward as far as the Oder, in which frost is not of long duration, and is not intense in degree ; the eastern or continental region, where the frost is more prolonged and the extremes of temperature are greater ; and the northern region, along the northern coasts, where the climate is sub-Arctic. The rainfall diminishes from W. to E. Ireland has an average of 208 rainy days, Scotland 170, and the region of the Volga 90.

*Population and language.*—The population of E. is some 480,000,000, or an average of 126 to the square mile. The inhabitants are divisible into three main types. The Teutonic or Nordic type—long-headed, blond, tall, eyes blue, and nose aquiline—is spread over N.W. Europe, disseminating from Scandinavia and, in prehistoric times, from Russia. The virile Nordic people have unfortunately been much reduced through the ages by wars. Other long-headed men who in early times migrated into S. Europe now form the Mediterranean or Iberian type— long-headed, dark hair and eyes, medium height, slender, and broad of nose. The Pyrenean Basques are a sub-type of the Mediterranean stock. These two races of Europe are separated by the intermediate Alpine type of Central Europe— round-headed, broad-faced, light hair, grey eyes, medium height, rather stocky. This type prevails in N. Italy, Auvergne, Savoy, Switzerland, the Tyrol, Alsace-Lorraine, Würtemberg, S. Germany, and Bavaria. Of the same stock as the Alpine race are the Slav-speaking peoples of Eastern E., divisible into two branches—the N. Slavs (Russians, Slovaks, Czechs, and Wends) and the S. Slavs (Serbs, Croatians, Slovenes, and Bulgarians). Both are broad-headed, but the Southern Slavs are taller and darker. The Slavs originally penetrated Russia from the S.W., overlaying the primitive, indigenous types, now represented by the long-headed Nordic Esths and Finns, to whom the Magyars and Letto-Lithuanians are racially related. The other primitive elements among the Eastern European peoples are either of Mongolian or Tartar-Turkish origin. The former are represented by the Lapps and Samoyeds in the N. and the Kalmuk and Kirghez peoples of the Caspian steppes in the S. Tartar-Turk is the name given to the scattered Turkish-speaking peoples found in Russia and the Crimea.

The principal languages of E. belong to the Aryan family. Celtic is spoken in the extreme W., its branches being Cymric in Wales, Manx in the Isle of Man, Gaelic in the Highlands of Scotland, Erse in Ireland, and Armorican in Brittany. Teutonic is spoken in the centre, N., and W. Its main divisions are High German in Germany proper, Low in the plains, including English, Dutch, and Flemish ; Scandinavian in Iceland, Denmark, Norway, and Sweden. Slavonic is spoken in the eastern countries by Russians, Poles, Lithuanians, Letts, Wends, Czechs, etc., and the Romanic languages in France, Spain, Portugal, Italy, Wallachia, Greece, and Rumania. Non-Aryan tongues are Magyar in Hungary, Basque in the Pyrenees, and Turkish in the peninsula.

*Religion.*—All the European nations, except the Turks, are Christians. The three branches of Christianity are the Roman Catholic, prevalent in Southern E., the Orthodox, known lo sely as the ' Greek Church ' in the eastern countries, and the Protestant Church in the northern and central countries. Soviet Russia has no official religion. There are some 10,000,000 Jews in E. and 5,000,000 Mohammedans (Turks, Russian Tartars, Albanians, and some of the Slavs). The Kalmuks in S. Russia are Buddhists, while the Samoyedes and some of the Lapps and Finns are idolaters.

*Vegetation.*—Vegetation is generally very rich in the southern and central countries, but is not so plentiful in the N. E. may be divided into three zones in this respect : the southern, central, and northern. In the southern countries, S. of the Alps, the trees are chiefly evergreens ; among the cereals, rice, maize, millet, and wheat are grown, as well as the olive, grapes, oranges, lemons, figs, and chestnuts, and to some extent the cotton shrub, date palm, and sugar cane. The majority of these plants appear to have been introduced from Africa and Asia, while maize and the American aloe have been brought from America. In the central countries the chief cereals are wheat, barley, oats, and rye. Here are found the richest wheat areas of the world, notably in the valley of the Danube and the blacklands of S.W. Russia. The chief fruits are the apple, plum, pear, and cherry, while the vine is cultivated to 50° N. The trees are deciduous, being chiefly oak, beech, birch, elm, and alder. In the northern countries the chief trees are pines, larches, firs, birches, and willows, during the winter, are covered with snow. In the early summer, however, the Steppes are covered with grasses, which afford a rich supply of hay.

*Animals.*—There are very few species of wild animals now left in Europe, and those that still remain are few in number. The bison exists

| Country. | Area in sq. m. | Census. | Population. | Density of pop. per sq. m. |
|---|---|---|---|---|
| Albania . . . . | 17,374 | 1921 | 831,877 | 48 |
| Andorra . . . . | 191 | 1921 | 5,231 | 27 |
| Austria . . . . | 32,369 | 1923 | 6,526,661 | 201 |
| Belgium . . . . | 11,752 | 1928 | 7,923,077 | 675 |
| Bulgaria . . . . | 39,824 | 1927 | 5,596,800 | 140 |
| Czechoslovakia . . | 54,195 | 1928* | 14,523,186 | 267 |
| Danzig . . . . | 754 | 1924 | 386,000 | 512 |
| Denmark (inc. Faroe Is.) . | 17,110 | 1925 | 3,434,555 | 201 |
| Estonia . . . . | 18,355 | 1929 | 1,116,474 | 61 |
| Finland . . . . | 149,641 | 1927* | 3,582,406 | 23 |
| France (inc. Corsica) . | 212,659 | 1926 | 40,745,874 | 191 |
| Germany (exc. Saar) . | 185,889 | 1925 | 62,348,782 | 335 |
| Greece (inc. Crete) . | 49,022 | 1928* | 6,204,684 | 126 |
| Hungary . . . | 35,911 | 1926* | 8,457,852 | 236 |
| Iceland . . . . | 39,709 | 1927 | 103,317 | 3 |
| Irish Free State . . | 26,592 | 1926 | 2,972,802 | 112 |
| Italy . . . . | 119,744 | 1927* | 40,796,000 | 341 |
| Yugo-Slavia . . . | 96,134 | 1921 | 12,017,323 | 125 |
| Latvia . . . . | 40,856 | 1927 | 1,870,520 | 46 |
| Liechtenstein . . | 65 | 1921 | 11,500 | 177 |
| Lithuania (exc. Memel) . | 20,550 | 1923 | 2,011,173 | 98 |
| Luxembourg . . . | 999 | 1927 | 285,524 | 285 |
| Monaco . . . | 8 | 1928 | 24,927 | 3116 |
| Netherlands (inc. inland water) . . . . | 13,205 | 1927* | 7,625,938 | 577 |
| Norway (exc. Spitzbergen). | 124,964 | 1925* | 2,772,000 | 21 |
| Poland . . . . | 149,140 | 1928* | 30,212,962 | 202 |
| Portugal (exc. Azores) . | 34,254 | 1920 | 5,628,610 | 164 |
| Rumania . . . | 122,282 | 1926 | 17,153,932 | 140 |
| Russia-in-Europe (U.S.S.R.) | 1,492,000 | 1926 | 108,100,000 | 73 |
| Saar . . . | 738 | 1925* | 770,000 | 1043 |
| San Marino . . . | 38 | 1928 | 13,013 | 342 |
| Spain (inc. Balearic Is.) . | 191,910 | 1923 | 21,289,650 | 116 |
| Spitzbergen . . . | 30,880 | 1921 | 1,503 | — |
| Sweden (inc. inland water). | 173,157 | 1927* | 6,087,923 | 35 |
| Switzerland . . | 15,976 | 1927* | 3,987,000 | 249 |
| Turkey-in-Europe . . | 8,819 | 1927* | 2,000,000 | 227 |
| United Kingdom . . | 94,284 | 1921 | 44,173,704 | 469 |

* Official estimate.

which become more stunted in size as the N. is reached, and give place to mosses, lichens, and dwarf shrubs. Barley, rye, oats, and potatoes are the principal objects of cultivation. In the N. of Russia exists the region of the Tundras, dreary wastes of ice and rock, where only stunted shrubs, lichens, and mosses are found. In the S.E. of the same country is another well-marked region, the Steppes, broad treeless plains, which, in Lithuania and the Caucasus; the brown bear, wolf, and wild boar are found in the larger forests. The reindeer and elk dwell in the northern countries, while the stag, fallow deer, and roebuck exist in Central E. The chamois is hunted in the Alps and the Carpathians, and the ibex in Sardinia. The fox and lynx are also found. The Barbary ape exists only on the Rock of Gibraltar, and the beaver is sometimes seen in

E. **Russia.** Of domestic animals the chief are the horse, donkey, cow, sheep, pig, goat, dog, cat, and reindeer. Silkworms are also reared in Italy and France. Web-footed birds, such as the wild duck and the goose, abound in the northern seas, while the vulture and the eagle may be seen in the Alps and southern ranges. The seas contain numerous kinds of fish, which are of great value as food. In the north-western seas the herring, mackerel, cod, haddock, sole, and pilchard are caught; in the Mediterranean the tunny, sardine, and anchovy. Salmon is abundant in northern and western rivers. In the Arctic seas the whale, seal, porpoise, and walrus are obtained. Oysters are specially cultivated round the coast, and other shell-fish, such as the lobster and crab, are caught in large numbers.

*Minerals.*—E. possesses vast deposits of minerals, but is very poor in precious stones. Coal is abundant in Great Britain, Germany, France, Belgium, Austria, and Russia. Iron is found chiefly in Great Britain, Germany, France, Belgium, Sweden, Austria, Russia, and Spain. Copper is found in Spain, Portugal, and Germany, and lead in Germany, Spain, and England. Zinc is chiefly found in Germany, Belgium, the United Kingdom, and France. Gold is mined in the Ural Mts., and silver in Germany and Austria. Platinum comes from the Ural Mts., quicksilver from Spain. Salt is produced in the United Kingdom, Germany, Russia, France, Spain, and Italy. Sulphur is obtained from Sicily, and graphite from Bavaria and Austria. Transcaucasia is rich in oil, copper, and manganese.

*Political Divisions and Constitutions.*—The countries of E. with their areas and populations are shown in the table on p. 596. The Great War, 1914–18, resulted in the creation of seven ' succession ' states out of the former Tsarist and Habsburg empires :—in N.E. Europe the four Baltic Republics of Finland, Estonia, Latvia, and Lithuania, and in Central Europe Poland, Czecho-Slovakia, and Yugo-Slavia. Russia-in-E. now consists of six federated republics—Russia proper, White Russia, the Ukraine, Georgia, Armenia, and Azerbaijan. In the Balkans the Serbs, Croats, and Slovenes have been united in the kingdom of Yugo-Slavia, while Rumania and Greece have been enlarged, Bulgaria reduced, and the small kingdom of Albania (*q.v.*) created. Austria and Hungary make two small independent republics, and an enlarged Italy now borders on Yugo-Slavia. Alsace-

Lorraine has been restored to France. The dominant factor in the reconstruction of E. has been racial nationality, but Memel and Danzig are Free Cities, and the demilitarised straits of Constantinople are under international control.

Government in E. is mostly popular with a responsible parliament. In the Ger. Republic the President is elected by the people, and has legislative powers, but no veto. In Poland the President has neither legislative powers nor veto. The powers of the Austrian President are also curtailed. In local Ger. states and in Estonia the Swiss method of ' collegial executive ' prevails. Of the new constitutions Yugo-Slavia alone provides for a king, while the forty hereditary rulers in E. in 1910 have been reduced to fourteen. The legislatures of E. mostly consist of two houses, of which the lower is of primary importance. Finland, Estonia, and Yugo-Slavia have only one house. All the new constitutions (*see also* CONSTITUTION) provide for the protection of minorities by proportional representation. In general, the states of E. submit to parliamentary government and the decision of majorities.

*History.*—The history of E. begins with the Greek communities, and its subsequent culture has been to an incalculable extent indebted to Grecian standards. When in the fifth century B.C. E. was threatened by the Asiatic hordes of the King of Persia, the Greek communities united against the common foe and averted the danger by their signal victories at Marathon (490 B.C.), Salamis (480), and Platæa (479). Though capable of joint action in times of great peril, Greece was not a corporate whole, but a collection of small independent cities, each striving for supremacy over the others. This supremacy was at first obtained by Athens. Her power was, however, envied by the other Grecian cities, and at the end of the Peloponnesian War, which lasted twenty-eight years, Athens was taken by Lysander, the Spartan general, and its democratic government destroyed (404 B.C.). The Spartans, owing to the rigid military training of their citizens, managed to remain supreme for some thirty years, when Epaminondas, the Theban general, inflicted a series of defeats upon them. The internal struggles of the peninsula made it an easy prey for the rising power of Macedonia, and when Philip was succeeded by his son, Alexander, the latter was master of almost the whole of Greece. His marvellous victories in Asia (334–

323 B.C.) led to no decisive result, and his empire was upon his death speedily broken up by the contending generals. With the fall of Greece we are brought face to face with the growing might of Rome, which, in the fourth and third centuries B.C., had conducted a series of successful wars against the neighbouring Latin and Samnian tribes, and thereby made itself the leading state in Italy. Its expansion brought it into conflict with the Grecian cities in the foot of Italy, and they sought help from Pyrrhus, King of Epirus, the most renowned general of his time (281 B.C.). Even Pyrrhus's ability was, however, no match for the tenacity of the Romans, and when he left Italy (274 B.C.), the remaining states soon acknowledged Rome's supremacy. The latter's triumph only brought her into conflict with Carthage, which, situated upon the African coast near the modern Tunis, was at that time mistress of the Eastern Mediterranean. The contest that ensued was one between the two rival civilisations of the Semites and the Aryans, and determined the future history of the world. The first Punic War lasted from 264 to 241 B.C. Success at first fluctuated, owing to the superiority of the Carthaginians upon the sea. The Romans, however, with undaunted energy, built fleet after fleet, utterly defeated their opponents upon their own element, and obtained as their reward the adjacent island of Sicily. Carthage, however, again returned to the attack, and the military genius of Hannibal, during the second Punic War (218–201 B.C.), shook the power of Rome to its foundations. But in spite of awful disasters at Trasimene and Cannæ, the Romans never yielded, and when Hannibal's brother, Hasdrubal, was defeated and slain with a second invading army at the battle of the Metaurus (207 B.C.), the tide turned steadily against the Carthaginians. A third war saw the total destruction of Carthage (156 B.C.). Its greatest rival vanquished, Rome went from conquest to conquest; Greece, Spain, Macedonia, Asia Minor, and N. Africa fell under her sway. Her political institutions were introduced throughout S. Europe. Her conquests, however, only aggravated the cleavage between the aristocratic and democratic portion of her populace, while her huge armies prepared the way for a military dictatorship. Julius Cæsar's ambition and the astuteness of Augustus established the Roman empire.

The transfer of the capital to Constantinople in A.D. 323 led subsequently (A.D. 395) to the division of the Roman dominions into the empires of the E. and W., and both portions were soon to suffer the irruptions of the savage hordes from the N. The direct cause of these irruptions was the invasion of E. by the Asiatic tribes of the Huns under Attila (A.D. 451), which set the tribes of Central E. in motion and flung them upon the Roman frontier. In the general upheaval, Britain fell to the Angles and the Saxons, Gaul to the Visigoths, Burgundians, and Franks (the latter of whom also conquered W. Germany), Italy to the Ostrogoths, and N. Africa to the Vandals. These barbarians, though they overthrew the Roman power, nevertheless had respect for Roman institutions, and kept up the fiction of the Roman empire long after the reality had passed away. In the midst of the disruption the Christian church maintained its unity, and the Pope finally claimed the right of disposing of the imperial crown. During the sixth century Italy was perturbed by the invasion of the Lombards, while in the eighth century the Mohammedans swarmed into Spain and Gaul, to be checked ultimately at Tours by Charles Martel (732). The latter's triumphs were continued by his grandson Charlemagne, who succeeded in establishing a powerful empire throughout Central E. from the Ebro to the Danube, and was crowned Emperor of the West by Pope Leo III.

Charlemagne's vast empire was divided by his grandsons into France, Lotharingia, and Germany, Lotharingia ultimately being parcelled out between France and Germany. The next centuries were occupied by struggles between the monarchs and their feudal lords, the latter increasing their power at the expense of the former. During the ninth and tenth centuries occurred the raids of the Northmen, who, sailing from Scandinavia, established themselves in Normandy and S. Italy and harassed Great Britain, which, during the following century, was destined to fall to one of their descendants, William of Normandy. From the end of the eleventh century till the latter half of the thirteenth, E. was agitated by the organisations of the crusades, which had the effect of bringing the warriors of various nations into touch with one another, and thereby did much to promote mediæval culture. The fourth crusade (1202–4) was especially remarkable, because the crusaders were diverted from their true goal to the capture of Constantinople, and established a French empire in the Balkans which lasted some sixty years. The German kings still claimed for themselves the title of Emperors of the West, but their power was very unsubstantial and their influence greatly weakened by the conflict with the popes over the question of investiture. In Spain a succession of small states was formed as the country gradually freed itself from the Moorish yoke, while in the E. of Europe the knights of the Teutonic order, whom the failure of the Crusades had left without occupation, turned their attention to the neighbouring country of Prussia and converted the Wends to Christianity.

The Hundred Years' War (1337–1453), which the English kings waged against France in prosecution of their claim to the French throne left that country far more unified than it had been before, and the crafty policy of Louis XI. broke down the power of the big feudal lords. His successors were therefore free to devote themselves to foreign conquests. Their attacks on Italy, however, brought them into conflict with Charles V., who had inherited the Netherlands, Spain, Naples, and Austria, and was elected Emperor of Germany in 1519. His son, Philip II., succeeded to the hereditary dominions, but the imperial crown passed to the Habsburg family. During the fifteenth century the Ottoman Turks captured Constantinople (1453), and spreading northward, conquered the whole of the country up to the walls of Vienna. By severing the connection of E. with the east, they were the cause of the great oversea discoveries which ensued, while Greek fugitives carried to Western E. the accumulated treasures of learning of the eastern empire, and so brought about the Renaissance and later the Reformation. Spain, the most ardent defender of Catholicism, was weakened by the loss of the Netherlands and by English attacks upon her colonies, while in the seventeenth century the Portuguese reasserted their independence. In France the religious wars led to the establishment of the Bourbon dynasty and paved the way for the reign of Louis XIV. In Germany the Protestant states were for a time ·in serious jeopardy, but were rescued by the military genius of their Swedish ally, Gustavus Adolphus. The treaty of Westphalia (1648) left the land in a most exhausted condition. Sweden, however, gained Upper Pomerania, Wismar, Stettin, and Bremen. By the defeat of Denmark in 1643 it had also increased its dominions and was now the leading Protestant power in E. In a later war (1657–58) Denmark was forced to surrender all its remaining Swedish provinces, and a further war stripped Poland of Esthonia and Livonia. Sweden's power was, however, broken by its king, Charles XII., who, after successfully defeating a coalition of Russia, Saxony, and Denmark, led his army into Southern Russia, where he was utterly defeated by Peter the Great at Pultowa (1709). France, which by the treaty of Westphalia had received the province of Alsace, was the strongest power in E., and shortly afterwards defeated Spain, forcing her to the disadvantageous peace of the Pyrenees (1659). Shortly afterwards Louis XIV. married the Spanish Infanta Maria Theresa, who became the heiress of the Spanish throne upon the extinction of the male line. The French invasion of Flanders had, however, already raised the jealousy of the other Powers and led to a triple alliance between England, Sweden, and Holland. When Louis's grandson, the Duke of Anjou, was proclaimed heir to the Spanish throne, a new coalition was formed (1701) between England, Holland, and Austria. In the campaign which ensued, the military genius of the Duke of Marlborough proved superior to that of the French generals, and after defeats at Blenheim, Ramillies, Oudenarde, and Malplaquet, Louis made peace. The King of Spain renounced his right of succession to the French throne, and surrendered the Netherlands, Naples, and Milan to Austria.

While Louis's wars were exhausting France, Prussia was gradually growing in strength. This duchy fell by inheritance to the Elector of Brandenburg in 1618, and its independence of Poland was established by the great elector Frederick William in 1656. In 1700 Frederick III. took the title of King of Prussia. Later on, in 1740, Frederick the Great suddenly invaded Silesia, and brought on the Seven Years' War (1756–63), in which he successfully defended his capture against Austria, France, and Russia. The latter country had steadily risen in importance since the battle of Pultowa had overthrown Swedish supremacy. Peter the Great had extended his dominion to the Baltic, founded St. Petersburg, and introduced the methods of Western civilisation. In 1772 Frederick the Great agreed with Austria and Russia to divide Poland among their three kingdoms. During the Seven Years' War mentioned above, England had taken the side of Prussia, and had captured Canada and India from France. The reign of Louis XV. was marked by misfortune and extravagance, and brought France into a state of impoverishment and bankruptcy from which it only emerged by the convulsion of revolution.

It is impossible to appraise accurately the importance of the French Revolution. For France itself it meant a complete rupture with the monarchic tyranny of the past. With the monarchy succumbed the aristocracy and the clergy. The intensity of the convulsion was so great that the rest of E. thought that the country must be prostrate, and was surprised and alarmed to find it arise to a career of conquest. The enthusiasm of the people created a succession of victorious armies with capable generals to lead them. Hoche, Pichegru, and Moreau were only eclipsed by the far greater genius of Napoleon, whose military daring changed the map of E. He extended his rule over all Germany W. of the Rhine, a considerable part of N. Germany, and the major part of Italy; made his brother-in-law Murat King of Naples, his brother Joseph King of Spain, and another brother, Louis, King of Holland. He also placed one of his marshals, Bernadotte, upon the throne of Sweden. Happily, England remained free from attack owing to the naval victories of the Nile (1798) and Trafalgar (1805), and was able to keep Napoleon's ablest marshals well occupied in Spain during the Peninsular War. Prussia and Austria suffered terribly, however, and the lesser states were formed into a Confederation of the Rhine under Napoleon's patronage. The attempt to ruin England, by the so-called Continental system of refusing to allow her to trade, was quite unsuccessful and only galling to Napoleon's unwilling confederates. Upon the weakening of his power by the disastrous Russian campaign of 1812, the vanquished nations again rose into revolt, and the campaigns of 1813 and 1814 determined the issue in their favour. Napoleon's escape from Elba and his brief return to imperial power but culminated in the disaster of Waterloo, and cost Ney and Murat their lives. At the Congress of Vienna, France was reduced to the limits of 1790 and the map of E. redistributed. The Netherlands became a separate kingdom which lasted until 1830, when the Belgians threw off the alliance and established a kingdom for themselves. The German states formed a loose confederacy under the presidency of Austria, while Italy was partitioned under princes, the Venetian provinces remaining under Austrian control. The Holy Alliance formed between Russia, Austria, and Prussia for the administration of their respective kingdoms according to the principles of Christianity became the greatest factor in furthering reactionary measures and impeding the growth of constitutional liberty. In 1827 Greece recovered its freedom by the intervention of France and England, whose fleets defeated the Turks at Navarino. In 1830 the French rose against the reactionary rule of Charles X. and chose Louis Philippe, the son of Philip Egalité, as their ruler. In spite of attempts at liberal administration, the reign of the citizen king became increasingly unpopular, and he was forced into exile in 1848. This was the signal for which E. was waiting. The whole period from 1815 to 1848 was one in which the nations had endeavoured unsuccessfully to wrest constitutional liberty from their despotic rulers. With the formation of the second French republic, the symptoms of unrest became too ominous to be stifled. The smaller German states wisely gave way, and in 1850 the King of Prussia granted a constitution, the King of Denmark having already done so in 1848. The desire for German national unity, though thwarted by the jealousy of Austria, found expression in the Vor-Parliament of Frankfort and in the formation of the German National Assembly. In 1849 the Hungarians revolted from Austria and waged a successful conflict until Russian troops reduced them to surrender. In France a wave of enthusiasm had resulted in the nephew of the great Napoleon being elected president, and by the end of 1852 he had succeeded in becoming emperor. To retain his position he kept the nation's thoughts fixed upon foreign affairs. In 1854 he joined with England to prevent Russia from aggrandising itself at the expense of Turkey, and so brought about the Crimean War. In 1859 he helped the King of Sardinia, who had become the champion of the movement for a united Italy, in his war against Austria, and received Nice and Savoy as his reward. The Italian national movement, fostered by Mazzini, was powerfully helped by Cavour, the Sardinian statesman, who earned the gratitude of France and England by his help during the Crimean War. The victories of France and Sardinia in 1859 at Magenta and Solferino added Parma, Modena, and Tuscany to Sardinia, while Garibaldi's expedition of 1860 led to the further addition of Naples and Sicily. Austria, however, was still left in possession of the Venetian dominions, and the Pope held the papal states. In 1863 Napoleon was induced to set up Archduke Maxi-milian of Austria as Emperor of Mexico under French protection, and the latter's capture and execution by the rebels greatly injured the French emperor's prestige. In the meantime, Prussia had gradually ousted Austria from supremacy in German affairs. The attempt of Denmark to incor-porate the German duchy of Schles-wig into the kingdom led to the de-claration of war by Prussia and Austria, and to the capture of Schleswig-Holstein. The administra-tion of the latter soon provided Prussia with an excuse for war, which was declared in 1866. The Austrians were completely defeated, and the Italians, who sided with Prussia, captured Venice. Hanover, who had supported Austria, was annexed to Prussia. The question of the Spanish Succession in 1870 led to the Franco-Prussian War. The peace of 1871 added Alsace-Lorraine to the German empire, which was formed during the course of the war under the headship of Prussia, Austria having hence-forth no voice in German affairs. The withdrawal of the French garrison from Rome enabled the Italian state to make that ancient city her capital and seat of government. By the Lateran Treaty (1929) the Pope acquiesced in this arrangement.

During the latter years of last century, the principal readjustment of European territory was in the Balkan peninsula. In 1859 the duchies of Moldavia and Wallachia were united into the kingdom of Rumania. The independence of Rumania and Serbia was recognised by the Treaty of Berlin in 1878, after the Russo-Turkish War, when Bul-garia was made a principality under the suzerainty of Turkey. In 1885 Bulgaria annexed E. Rumelia, and in 1908, taking advantage of the annexation of Bosnia and Herze-govina by Austria, formally asserted her independence of Turkish rule. During the autumn of 1912 an alliance was formed between Bul-garia, Greece, Serbia, and Monte-negro against Turkey, and the whole of the Turkish dominion in E. cap-tured, with the exception of a small territory around Constantinople and the Sea of Marmora. The question of apportioning the captured territory led to a quarrel in which Bulgaria attacked Greece and Serbia and after a month of fierce fighting (July, 1913) was compelled to come to terms by the Treaty of Bucharest (see BALKAN WAR-). Austria, sup-ported by a Conference of Nations, prevented Serbia from gaining access to the Adriatic through Albania, and thus further stimulating the

anti-Austrian propaganda already strong in Serbia (see also FRANCIS FERDINAND OF AUSTRIA). Turkey-in-E. was restricted practically to Constantinople, but Turkey was befriended diplomatically by the Central Powers, Germany and Aus-tria, while England's former support of Turkey as against Russia was withdrawn after the Armenian atro-cities of 1895. The division of sympathy in the Balkans was the epitome of the state of affairs through-out E. Germany and Austria had formed a Dual Alliance since 1879, and in 1882 this had been extended to include Italy, forming a Triple Alliance (q.v.) of which the terms were secret. On the other side there was the Entente Cordiale (q.v.) between France and England, an agreement (1904) which settled old quarrels, leaving France a free hand in Morocco and England in Egypt. England had sought this agreement with France as a reply to the Ger. naval policy, which was to challenge England's supremacy on the seas. Germany came forward as the champion of Morocco against Fr. intervention, and in the inde-cisive diplomatic struggle which ensued at the Conference of Algeciras (q.v.) (1906) Eng. sympathy was with France. England, however, by the terms of the Entente, was not bound, except morally, to undertake con-certed action with France against Germany or any other country. A more definite agreement assuring mutual aid in the event of Ger. aggression had existed between France and Russia since 1894, and this was followed in 1907 by an Anglo-Russian treaty, somewhat counterbalanced by the Anglo-Japanese Treaty (q.v.) contracted in 1902. England formed these alliances, as Germany had already refused a rapprochement at the beginning of the century, and for the first decade there was such growing distrust between the Powers that this period is known as being one of 'Armed Peace.' Although no actual approach to war was made in diplomatic circles, the General Staffs of the various Powers were preparing for all eventualities, and military ' conversations ' took place between France and England. It was explicit, however, that these conversations in no way bound the govs. of either country, and Eng-land's attitude was impartial, while remaining loyal to France.

The mistake of diplomacy at this period was a short-sightedness over the fact that an enhanced com-petition in armaments must lead inevitably to their use in war. The only gov. which viewed the prospect of war with complacency was that of Count Berchtold (*q.v.*) in Austria-Hungary. These belligerent intentions were directed against Serbia, and were as vigorously met by an intense Serbian hatred of Austria. Serbia had been cheated by Austria of the full fruits of victory in the Balkan Wars, and one of several Serbian plots resulted in the assassination of the Archduke Francis Ferdinand, heir apparent to the Austrian monarchy, and his wife on June 28, 1914, at Sarajevo in Bosnia. The complicity of the Serbian gov. was not in question, but on July 23 Austria delivered an ultimatum to Serbia, with an order of compliance within forty-eight hours. To the impossible terms dictated Serbia was extremely conciliatory, but despite Eng., Fr., and Italian mediation and half-hearted pacification by Germany, Austria declared war on Serbia on July 28. Russia mobilised, and on July 31 Germany's protestations about localising the Serbian conflict being of no avail, war was declared between Germany and Russia. France determined to stand by her Russian alliance, and Germany declared war on France on Aug. 1. The same day the Ger. ambassador in London attempted to obtain British neutrality on the promise of respecting Belgian territory, but England gave no guarantees, and the Ger. Chancellor came to regard the treaties assuring Belgian neutrality as a 'scrap of paper' for which England ought not to go to war. However, when Germany invaded Belgium, public feeling was sufficiently aroused in England to justify the declaration of war with Germany on Aug. 4, 1914. The Belgian route was only one direction of the Ger. march on Paris; a second division of the Ger. army advanced through Luxembourg, and a third through Lorraine towards Nancy. Belgium offered a stout resistance, but was speedily overcome, and the Ger. advance continued until checked within 52 kil. of Paris. On Sept. 6 began the Battle of the Marne (*q.v.*, and *see also* under FRANCE AND FLANDERS, GREAT WAR CAMPAIGNS IN, 1914–18). Meanwhile the Pact of London was signed on Sept. 5 between England, France, and Russia, whereby each country engaged not to make a separate peace. Japan, which had come into the war on Aug. 15 by the terms of the Anglo-Japanese Alliance, acceded to the Pact a year later, some limitations being made by the Allies as to Japan's intentions in the Pacific.

Germany was relying on the Sultan of Turkey, who was bound by a treaty of Aug. 2, 1914. This treaty was secret, and Allied diplomacy was directed towards securing Turkish neutrality. That this was to be a vain effort was shown by the incident of the *Goeben* and *Breslau* (*q.v.*), two Ger. cruisers stationed at Constantinople, which the Turkish gov. pretended to have bought, but which remained manned by Ger. crews. England, however, was not anxious to declare war on Turkey, for fear of embroiling the Mohammedans of India and Egypt; but attacks on Russian Black Sea towns caused Russia to declare war on Turkey, and France and England followed suit. Turkey was by this time fully mobilised. Bulgaria, although Ger. in sympathy, remained neutral with the avowed intention of seeing which way the war was going before deciding which side to join. Greece and Rumania also wavered.

In Feb. 1915 the Allies attempted to win the Balkans by an attack on Constantinople. In March the naval effort to force the Narrows proved disastrous, over 2000 men and three first-class battleships of the Anglo-Fr. fleet being sacrificed in vain (*see* under DARDANELLES). It was then hoped to succeed by land, but not until the end of April did the expeditionary force arrive (*see* GALLIPOLI CAMPAIGN). Meanwhile the Allies sought help from Greece and Bulgaria, but these nations drove contrary bargains, which were not helped forward by the Allied failure in the Dardanelles. Italy, however, after prolonged diplomatic interchange with Vienna, decided to join the Allies, and concluded the secret Treaty of London, April 26, 1915. Trentino and Cisalpine Tyrol, Trieste, and part of the Dalmatian coast were promised to Italy, among other concessions, and these terms, together with the Allied obligations to Serbia, made it impossible to make a satisfactory offer to Bulgaria and Greece as the price of their intervention. Italy declared war on Austria-Hungary on May 23, 1915, but by this time the Russian advance was being checked by the Ger. counter-offensive, and there was no hope of Austria collapsing between a combined Russian and Italian invasion. The Allies had had great hopes of Russia since the beginning of the war, hopes which had been somewhat fulfilled by the Russian successes in Galicia (*q.v.*) during the winter, 1914–5 (*see also* RUSSIAN FRONT IN GREAT WAR). Hindenburg's two Ger. invasions of Russian Poland, although the second was partially successful, both failed to take Warsaw, and all three countries, Germany, Austria, and Russia, made overtures to win Polish loyalty. Meanwhile on the Western Front a position of stalemate had been reached. The Battle of the Marne (q.v.) had been succeeded by that of the Aisne (q.v.), where the Gers. were strongly entrenched and the Allies handicapped by a shortage of ammunition. Battle succeeded battle with no decisive result—Neuve Chapelle in March and Ypres (q.v.) in April, when poison gas was first used—but the Gers. were able to hold their positions on the Western Front while concentrating an attack on the Eastern. In May and June 1915, coincident with the Italian mobilisation, the Austro-Ger. army under Mackensen retook Lemberg and drove the Russians out of Galicia. Hindenburg met with equal success in Poland, and by Oct. all Poland and part of Courland and Lithuania were in German hands. The Russian retreat continued throughout Oct., while in Aug. the Allies made one more attempt to capture Gallipoli as an offset to the Ger. occupation of Warsaw, but the expedition proved a terrible failure.

Allied prestige was so low in 1915 that Germany was easily able to outbid the Allies in the effort to secure Bulgarian aid (see BULGARIA). A secret convention was signed between Bulgaria and the Central Powers on Sept. 6, 1915. On Oct. 14, when Bulgaria was mobilised, war was declared on Serbia, and the Allies then declared war on Bulgaria. The Allies counted on Greece fulfilling her treaty obligations by aiding Serbia, but the Gk. Premier, Venizelos, whose sympathy was with the Allies, was forced out of office by King Constantine, who was a more cautious patriot, and Greece retained an armed neutrality which became a distinct menace. Serbia was encompassed on all sides and rapidly overcome. A small Allied expeditionary force failed to be of material aid (see MACEDONIAN FRONT), and by the end of Dec. the Allied troops abandoned their foothold in Gallipoli in order to reinforce the garrison at Salonika. In Jan. 1916 Montenegro was overrun by an Austrian army, and in Feb. the Italians were forced to evacuate Albania. Simultaneously the Ger. army was attempting a decisive blow on the Western Front, and from Feb. to June terrific and costly assaults were made against the Fr. fortress of Verdun (q.v.). On March 27, 1916, the first general war council of the Allied Powers was held in Paris, followed in April by an Allied Inter-parliamentary Conference, and in June by an Economic Conference. The report of serious food shortages among the populations of Central Europe decided the Allies to plan simultaneous drives on the Fr., Russian, and Italian fronts. A recuperated Russian army under Brussilov (q.v.) made successful advances into Galicia during June, July and Aug., and captured the province of Bukowina (q.v.). At the same time, Cadorna (q.v.), the Italian general, was driving back the weakened Austrian army on the Trentino front, while reserving the major effort to be made on the Isonzo front. By Aug. the heights W. of Isonzo (q.v.) were carried and the province of Gorizia (q.v.) was won. These successes decided Rumania to enter the war on the side of the Allies. A treaty between Rumania and the Entente was signed on Aug. 17, 1916. Rumania, assured of support from the Russian army in Bukowina and the Anglo-Fr. army in Salonika, threw the whole of its army into Transylvania (see RUMANIAN FRONT). A supreme and unexpected effort by the Ger. General Staff under Hindenburg succeeded in crushing Rumania, with the help of a Bulgarian and Ger. army under Mackensen, who attacked Rumania from the S. and entered Bucharest on Dec. 6. The Allied offensive failed in Macedonia, while a virtual Allied occupation of Greece rendered the Venizelist faction unpopular, and thus strengthened the position of King Constantine. In Palestine British troops were supporting the Arab revolt against the Turks, and in May 1916 the Sykes-Picot agreement between Great Britain, France, and Russia was concluded, regarding the partition of the Ottoman empire in the event of an Allied victory. Meanwhile the Allied effort towards forcing a military decision was being made on the Western Front, and the Battles of the Somme (see SOMME, BATTLES OF THE) were waged from June to Nov., battles which proved terribly costly and indecisive, although part of the Ger. army was deflected from Verdun, thus relieving the Fr. garrison. On the sea Germany was endeavouring to overcome British supremacy by the use of submarines, but became embroiled with neutral countries. Portugal joined the Allies in March 1916, and the U.S.A., already angered by the sinking of the Lusitania (q.v.) in May 1915, issued further warnings to Germany to respect merchantmen. The Grand Fleets of England and

Germany only encountered each other once during the war, on May 31, 1916 (*see* JUTLAND, BATTLE OF). The British advance guard suffered at the hands of the Ger. fleet which, however, on the arrival of the main British fleet, succeeded after a conflict in returning to their bases, not to emerge again during the war. Admiral Jellicoe wisely refused an engagement within the Ger. mine area, and the British fleet remained in control of the seas.

The year 1916 ended in a position of stalemate, with widespread depression among the Entente Powers. There was a general political reshuffle. In England during Dec. Asquith was succeeded as Premier by Lloyd George, and Grey as Foreign Secretary by Balfour. Lloyd George formed a Coalition War Cabinet, and in France Briand, while remaining Premier, formed a new French War Cabinet on much the same lines. Joffre retired from the command of the Fr. army, and was succeeded by Nivelle, whose counter-attack at Verdun in Oct. and Nov. was the only Allied victory of 1916 which could offset the defeat of Rumania. In Russia the corrupt and ineffective gov. was beginning to meet openly with the opposition it merited. In contrast to the pessimistic criticism of the war govs. prevailing in the Entente, the Central Powers were consolidated in an optimism which proved to be unfounded. The German gov., in which Von Jagow, Foreign Secretary since 1912, was succeeded in Dec. 1916 by Zimmermann, believed itself in a strong position which would make possible a successful diplomatic peace. The trend towards peace had gathered strength in Austria since the death of Francis Joseph (*q.v.*) and the accession of the Emperor Karl on Nov. 21, 1916. Berchtold had been succeeded as Foreign Minister by Burian early in 1915, but Karl, in his efforts to hold the Dual Monarchy together by means of peace, was seconded by Czernin, who had displaced Burian. On Dec. 12, 1916, a proposal to hold peace negotiations was submitted by Bethmann-Hollweg (*q.v.*), the Ger. Chancellor, on behalf of the Central Powers. No terms were stated, and the offer was rejected by the Entente, who also made no terms beyond indicating the necessity for reparations and guarantees. The Allied refusal was represented in Germany as showing an aggressive militarist spirit, and allowed General Ludendorff and the Emperor Wilhelm once more to stimulate the Ger. armies to resistance. Wilson, the President of the U.S.A., however, encouraged by Bernstorff (*q.v.*), the German Ambassador, endeavoured, on the strength of the German peace proposals, to act as mediator and secure a ' peace without victory.' Both sides submitted their terms privately to President Wilson, but they clearly conflicted, *e.g.* over the possession of Alsace-Lorraine. The Allies, however, on Jan. 10, 1917, assured the President of their adherence to his ideal of a League of Nations. Meanwhile Bethmann-Hollweg was overridden by Ludendorff (*q.v.*), who became in effect a military dictator. The immediate issue was the unrestricted use of submarines. Falkenhayn (*q.v.*), Ludendorff's predecessor, had protested against their restriction in 1915, and, the Admiralty now promising to subdue England within five months, Ludendorff launched on Feb. 1, 1917, the unrestricted U-boat campaign. This decision annulled Bernstorff's effort to secure American mediation, and on April 6, 1917, America declared war on Germany. Ludendorff and Hindenburg calculated on winning the war before the intervention of America became effective, and in the first half of 1917 the submarine warfare was proving a serious menace. Two and a quarter million tons of British and one and a half million tons of Allied and neutral shipping were destroyed between Jan. and June. Moreover, the Allied offensive on the Western Front during 1917 proved the practical impossibility of piercing the Ger. lines, while Germany was relieved of a powerful enemy by the collapse of the Russian monarchy in the March Revolution (*see* RUSSIAN REVOLUTION, THE). The Tsar Nicholas II. was deposed, and a provisional democratic gov. was organised on March 15, and the U.S.A. were first among the Allied states to accord official recognition. The Revolution had been supported by the military leaders, and it seemed that Russia would prosecute the war with renewed vigour. The Foreign Minister, Milyukov, issued a note to this effect, but Prince Lvov's Provisional gov. was rapidly breaking up under the opposition of the Soviet Party, which represented the war-weariness of the Russian people. A reconstruction was attempted by Tcheidze and Kerensky (*q.v.*) on May 16, 1917, and a manifesto, disavowing all thought of a separate peace, appealed to the Allied democracies for a revision of war aims in accordance with the ideals of the Russian Revolution. Kerensky made a great effort to discipline the army, and with Brussilov as Chief of Staff organised a campaign in Galicia in June 1917. This was at first successful, but misfortune developed into complete rout, and the Russians threw down their arms, refusing to fight. Russia was further disrupted by the movement towards autonomy among the Poles and Finns, the Letts of Courland, the Ruthenians in the Ukraine, the Esthonians, the Lithuanians, and the Georgians of the Caucasus. The Provisional gov. was also severely attacked by the Bolsheviki (q.v.) (majority), the extremist section of the Soviet Democratic Party. After the failure of the military offensive, Prince Lvov, head of the Provisional gov., resigned on July 17, but an attempt by Lenin (q.v.) and Trotsky (q.v.), the leaders of the Bolsheviki, to seize the power was thwarted by Kerensky, who became head of the Provisional gov. and virtual dictator. Kerensky, with the aid of General Kornilov (q.v.), who had superseded Brussilov, then set up a military dictatorship, but later arrested Kornilov, and vainly tried to save his gov. by sympathising with the extremist faction. The Allied Paris Conference refused to revise war aims, thus disappointing the hopes of the Kerensky gov., which was finally put out of power by a Bolshevist coup d'état on Nov. 7. Lenin established a dictatorship of the proletariat, and repudiated political democracy as it is understood in Western E. (see SOVIET, UNION OF SOCIALIST REPUBLICS). Peace offers were at once made to Germany on a basis of 'no annexations and no indemnities,' and a conference was opened at Brest-Litovsk on Dec. 22, 1917. The Ruthenians (Little Russians) were represented, having formed the Ukrainian People's Republic on Nov. 20, and after the breakdown of negotiations between Germany and the Soviet, Ukrainia signed a separate treaty with Germany on Feb. 9, 1918. Meanwhile Finland had become an independent republic on Dec. 4, 1917, and Lithuania on Dec. 11. On Jan. 14, 1918, the conference of Brest-Litovsk came to an end, and in spite of the Russian attitude of 'neither peace nor war,' hostilities were resumed, and a military thrust into Russia during Feb. resulted in the Soviet submitting to the Ger. terms, March 13, 1918 (see BREST-LITOVSK, TREATY OF). Rumania, being isolated, had signed a peace treaty with the Central Powers on March 7 (see BUCHAREST, TREATY OF). Rumania and Russia being out of the war, General Sarrail, commanding the Allied garrison in Salonika, was unable to take the

offensive. Meanwhile the Allied support to the revolt which Venizelos had raised against the King reached the pitch of an armed occupation of Athens, followed by the forced abdication of Constantine, who retired in favour of his second son, Alexander, on June 12, 1917. This move served to alienate Gk. sympathy, but by the end of June Venizelos was installed as Prime Minister, the Allied army of occupation was withdrawn, and the Gk. army put at the disposal of Sarrail and his successor, Guillaumat.

The break-up of Russia into its constituent peoples was not without effect in Central Europe, especially in Austria-Hungary. The Emperor Karl had intrigued with the Entente to secure a separate peace during 1917, but in April of the following year Germany compelled him to dismiss Czernin from the post of Foreign Minister and to reinstate Burian, who was more in sympathy with pan-Germanism (see under AUSTRIA-HUNGARY). The Russian example stimulated the Socialists of all countries in their efforts towards peace, but there was strong animosity between the Socialists of the Entente and those of Germany and Austria, and the International Conference at Stockholm (1917) proved a failure. In Aug. 1917 the Pope put forward a plea for peace, which was welcomed by Austria, but President Wilson replied that the action of the Ger. gov. rendered a compromise useless. The defeatist movement was strong in the Allied countries, and in France Briand was put out of office, but by Nov. a reactionary Cabinet was formed under Clemenceau, who prosecuted the pacifists. In Oct. and Nov. the Gers. took advantage of pacifist propaganda in Italy, and Ludendorff planned to break through the Italian line on the Upper Isonzo at Caporetto, where a crushing defeat was inflicted on the Italian army (see CAPORETTO, BATTLE OF). It was hoped by putting Italy out of the war to save the integrity of Austria, and at one time, until the arrival of reinforcements, Venice itself was threatened. In this crisis a reorganisation of the Italian ministry made Orlando Premier, and the Italians, together with the other Allied peoples, became convinced that a peace by compromise was futile. By Dec. the first drafts of American troops were arriving to stiffen the resistance on the Western Front, where the Third Battle of Ypres and the Battle of Passchendaele had been waged, sanguinary and indecisive. On Jan.

8, 1918, President Wilson enunciated the celebrated 'Fourteen Points' (q.v.), which were accepted as embodying the Allied war aims, and in one clause advocating the autonomy of the constituent peoples of the Dual Monarchy was spelt the doom of the Habsburgs. Following on this came the Congress of Oppressed Nationalities, held in Rome in March 1918, and the Pact of Rome was concluded between Italy and the Yugo-Slav peoples.

Germany, all but decisively victorious in Italy, and despite the partial failure of the submarine campaign, was to make one more supreme effort. With commanding strategy, Ludendorff and Hindenburg planned a colossal offensive at an unexpected point on the Western Front where the British and Fr. armies joined. The attack was launched on March 21, 1918, against the central sector of the Allied lines between Arras and the R. Oise. The British armies were rolled back, but the Gers. failed in their purpose of taking Amiens (q.v.). An order for conscription was passed by Parliament in London, and the result was further to antagonise the various Irish factions. One important result of the Ger. advance was the decision, at long last, to unify the Allied command under Marshal Foch. This had for long been advised by President Wilson, but beyond a conference at Rapallo on Nov. 9, 1917, between the Prime Ministers and Chiefs of Staff of France, Great Britain, and Italy, the formation of a Supreme War Council and a subsequent Allied Conference at Paris on Nov. 29, little had been done. In May 1918 the Gers. launched a second offensive against the Fr. lines on the Aisne and the Oise. Ludendorff succeeded in driving a 30 m. salient to the Marne, but in accomplishing this, and also in making the Amiens salient in the British lines in March, he had lost very nearly the million and a half men which he was prepared to sacrifice to win the war by this final military drive. Meanwhile American reinforcements were arriving in numbers, and the Italians were checking the Austrian drive on the Piave R. On July 15, 1918, the Gers. began their third and final offensive in the Second Battle of the Marne. Foch's counter-attack with Fr. and American troops proved successful, and by Aug. the Ger. armies were in retreat.

In the near East Foch planned a simultaneous offensive in Macedonia under Franchet d'Esperey (q.v.) and in Syria under Allenby (q.v.). Bulgaria was put out of the war, an armistice being signed at Salonika on Sept. 30. A month later, following Allenby's successes in Syria, Turkey also signed an armistice. This defection of Germany's allies weakened the strong position Germany had gained among the former Russian dependencies. Italian successes against Austria forced an armistice on Nov. 3, and the Dual Monarchy split up into its constituent states. Czechoslovakia emerged as a republic and Yugo-Slavia as a kingdom, while on Nov. 13 Ger. Austria was proclaimed a republic and the well-intentioned Emperor Karl (see Charles) abdicated. Three days later Hungary also became an independent republic. In Germany events moved even more quickly. Ludendorff resigned on Oct. 27, and on the following day a naval mutiny at Kiel was the beginning of a widespread socialist revolution. On Nov. 7 Bavaria became a republic and the king fled, while two days later Wilhelm II. also abdicated and a republic was established in Berlin. The Provisional gov. under President Ebert hastened to accept the Allied terms, and the Armistice was signed on Nov. 11.

On Jan. 18, 1919, the Peace Conference formally opened at Paris, but the huge plenary sessions came to no decisions not already reached by the Council of Ten, which council was superseded in March by the still smaller Council of Four, consisting of President Wilson, Clemenceau, Lloyd George, and Orlando. On April 30 the Ger. delegation arrived in Paris to receive the terms of the treaty. Ger. criticism and protest led to a partial revision, mainly through fear of throwing Germany into anarchy, and the main concession to Ger. opinion was the grant of a plebiscite in Upper Silesia, which, together with E. Prussia, eventually decided for Germany (March, 1921). After a reorganisation of gov. Germany signed the treaty, together with all the Allied and Associated Powers, at Versailles on June 28, 1919 (see VERSAILLES, TREATY OF). In the forefront of the treaty was set the League Covenant (see COVENANT OF THE LEAGUE OF NATIONS). Although this was the result of President Wilson's idealistic purpose, he was no longer supported by the American Senate, which refused to ratify the treaty. America accordingly concluded a separate peace with Germany and Austria. The Treaty of Versailles was followed by the Treaty of Saint-Germain, concluded with Austria on Sept. 10, 1919; of Neuilly with Bulgaria on

Nov. 27, 1919; of the Trianon with Hungary on June 4, 1920; and of Sèvres with Turkey on Aug. 10, 1920. The treaty with Hungary was delayed owing to the establishment on March 21, 1920, of a Soviet gov. under Bela Kun, who was only overthrown by the advance of Rumanian troops (*see* HUNGARY). He was succeeded by the Archduke Joseph, who formed a Prov. gov. The Treaty of Sèvres was never ratified by Turkey, owing to the opposition of the Nationalists under Mustapha Kemal, who took advantage of the dissensions between France and England over Syria and Palestine to strengthen his position. Turkey resisted the attempts which Greece made to take over the new possessions awarded at the 1919–20 Peace Conference, and a Græco-Turkish war was only terminated by the revision in Turkey's favour of the Treaty of Sèvres by the terms of the Lausanne Treaty, July 24, 1923. The unratified Treaty of Sèvres had been designed to reduce the Transcaucasian territory which Turkey had gained from Russia by the Treaty of Brest-Litovsk, but the newly-created Federal Republic of Transcaucasia could not resist the Turks, and in 1918 became disintegrated into the three Republics of Georgia, Armenia, and Azerbaijan. In 1919 the Caucasus became a sphere of British influence and the Ukraine of Fr. influence. With the withdrawal of the British troops the same year, Soviet Russia took over the country by force, and added the three Transcaucasian Republics to the U.S.S.R., at the same time concluding an agreement with Turkey (the Treaty of Kars, Oct. 13, 1921), whereby the boundaries were fixed and the Autonomous Soviet Socialist Republic of Ajaria was created to include the Free Port of Batum. Turkey on Oct. 29, 1923, became a republic, and the Sultan, Mohammed VI., fled from the country. In Greece, Venizelos failed to establish order and retired. On April 23, 1924, a republic was established by the Gk. electorate, but the following year General Pangalos set up a dictatorship.

The principal results of the peace treaties were in geographical reconstruction. The Treaty of Versailles confirmed the creation of the 'succession' states of Poland. Czechoslovakia, and Yugo-Slavia, and of the Baltic States, Esthonia, Latvia, and Lithuania, while Danzig was made a Free City under the League of Nations. Rumania became enlarged by the possession of Bessarabia, Bukowina, and part of the

Banat of Temesvar, while the Ukrainian Republic on Dec. 30, 1922 concluded an alliance whereby it became one of the federated states of Soviet Russia. The boundary between Italy and Yugo-Slavia on the Eastern coast of the Adriatic presented one of the most difficult problems of post-war E. The Ital. premier Orlando demanded the cession of Dalmatia and Fiume to Italy, the first-named transference being in accordance with the secret treaties of 1915 and 1917; but he was succeeded in July 1919 by Francesco Nitti. The unauthorised *coup d'état* of D'Annunzio (*q.v.*), who won a plebiscite in Fiume and raided Zara, upset the conciliatory attitude of the Nitti Cabinet; but although in Nov. 1920 Fiume (*q.v.*) was proclaimed a Free City under the League of Nations, it was not until Jan. 1924 that the problem was settled by an agreement made at Rome, whereby Fiume, although governed by Italy, should remain a free port to Yugo-Slavia. Italy immediately after the war had been upset by internal discord, the Socialists and the Fascists vying with each other in revolutionary ardour. The Fascist Party had come into being in March 1919, and professed an ideal similar to that which had inspired the Bolshevik movement in Russia and elsewhere. The Fascist leader, Benito Mussolini, organised an armed force of irregulars, known as Black Shirts, and these took an active part in furthering the revolutionary strikes of 1919 and 1920. In May 1921 a General Election showed the country to be ready to return to constitutional normality, but an unreasoning fear of anti-nationalist Bolshevism still prevailed among the middle classes, and Mussolini, emphasising the nationalism of Fascist ideals, posed as the deliverer of Italy from Bolshevism. Meanwhile the Fascist movement was assuming the proportions of an armed revolt, and his position being strengthened by a succession of parliamentary crises, Mussolini renounced his republican ideals, and his band of irregulars, armed with cudgels and castor-oil bottles, commenced their march on Rome. On Oct. 21, 1922, Mussolini entered Rome in triumph, and was invited by the King to form a ministry, thus legalising his position (*see* FASCISM).

In the United Kingdom the Coalition gov. was attempting to bring civil war in Ireland to an end by a compromise treaty (Dec. 1921) between England and the Republican gov. under President de Valera. The Irish Free State, thus created, was granted dominion status, and in 1922 a gov. was organised under Michael Collins; but the compromise remained unacceptable to the extreme Republicans and also to the Ulster Unionists. Ulster remained part of the United Kingdom but with legislative autonomy.

On the Continent of E. a series of international conferences was attempting to adjust the Treaty of Versailles. The first meeting of the League of Nations was held at Paris on Jan. 16, 1920, with Léon Bourgeois, Fr. representative, as chairman (*see* under LEAGUE OF NATIONS). European diplomacy, however, was conducted by conferences outside the sphere of the League. On Feb. 12, 1920, a London Conference was held between the Premiers of Great Britain, France, and Belgium, and the Foreign Minister of Yugo-Slavia. Millerand had succeeded Clemenceau as Premier of France. The principal decision of this conference was that Constantinople should remain Turkish. The next Allied Conference, held at San Remo in April 1920, was occasioned by military events in Germany. The militarist party in Germany had had a temporary success over the Republic in the ' Kapp Putsch ' of March 14–17, and a subsequent Spartacist (Communist) outbreak in the Ruhr was suppressed by the Reichswehr (Regular Ger. Army), which, by entering the demilitarised zone on the r. b. of the Rhine, contravened Art. 42 of the Treaty of Versailles. Fr. troops therefore occupied Frankfort and Darmstadt (April 6, 1920). Disarmament was discussed at the San Remo Conference, and Germany was notified of the necessity of fulfilling all treaty obligations, but was invited to a conference at a future date. This conference was to take place at Spa, but previous to it a succession of inter-Allied conferences took place, concerned with economic problems, with the war (1920) between Poland and Soviet Russia, and the Near Eastern question. On July 5, 1920, the Spa Conference opened, but although the Gers. had great hopes that the hardships of their country would be relieved, the reparations question was aggravated by the hostile attitude of certain Ger. industrial magnates. A compromise was reached over the delivery of coal, and Germany agreed to deliver 2 million tons per month for six months, and the Allies to make Germany a loan dependent on the price of coal. By Dec. 1922, however, deliveries of coal were in arrears, and Germany was declared in

default by the Reparations Commission, which had been set up to assess the amount of reparations, an exact figure not having been stated by the Allies at the Peace Conference. A conference between France and England in Aug. 1920 led to a decision to give military support to the Poles, who accordingly won a victory against the Russians at the Battle of the Vistula on Aug. 14. The Entente had already lent active support to the free-lance and anti-Bolshevist armies under Generals Kolchak, Denikin, Judenitch, and Wrangel, but Lloyd George was now in favour of an agreement with the Soviet, whereas France recognised the Crimean gov. of General Wrangel.

The first Inter-Allied Conference of 1921, held at Paris on Jan. 24–30, was concerned with reparations and disarmament (*see* REPARATIONS). Briand was now Premier of France. The Paris Conference at which figures for monthly deliveries of coal after the Spa Agreement had expired were drawn up, was preparatory to the London Conference, Feb. 21 to March 14. At London Germany made counter-proposals to the Paris terms, but failing the unconditional acceptance of these terms Dusseldorf, Duisburg, and Ruhrort were occupied by Allied military forces on March 7. At a second Conference of London, April 29 to May 5, the Supreme Council of the Allied Powers delivered an ultimatum to Germany, threatening the occupation of the Ruhr unless Germany undertook fulfilment of all treaty obligations. The Ger. gov. resigned, but a Cabinet was formed by Wirth in time to accept the ultimatum on May 11, a day after the expiry of the time limit. Deliveries of coal were maintained, while in May and Aug. Germany paid two instalments of £50,000,000, which greatly strained her resources and caused the mark to depreciate. The Reparations Commission had fixed Germany's liability at £6,600,000,000, for which sum Germany issued bonds according to the ultimatum of May 6. The subject of Ger. disarmament was discussed at a meeting of the Supreme Council at Paris Aug. 8–13, 1921. The chief business of the Paris Conference was the question of the partition of Upper Silesia. The plebiscite of March 20, 1921, had been in Germany's favour, but as France and England could not agree as to the boundary line to be drawn between Germany and Poland, the matter was referred to the League of Nations. The decision of the Council, issued on Oct. 20, 1921, prevented a rupture in the Entente, and in compromising between the Fr. and Eng. views the Council recommended that for fifteen years no customs barrier should exist at the new frontier with regard to the natural products of the country.

On Nov. 12, 1921, the Washington Conference opened its first session for the discussion of disarmament and the problems of the Pacific. England was represented by Balfour, and Briand, the French Premier, was present at the opening. The conference continued into 1922, and the principal achievement was the Five-Power Pact between the U.S.A., the British Empire, France, Italy, and Japan with regard to the limitation of capital ships and aircraft carriers for a period of fifteen years. The limitation of cruisers was discussed five years later at Geneva, but inconclusively. In 1929, however, naval disarmament was carried a stage further at the London Conference, opened on Jan. 21, when a Three-Power Pact was concluded between Great Britain, the U.S.A., and Japan with regard to limitation of cruisers, destroyers, and submarines. Unfortunately France and Italy were not in sufficient agreement to justify their adherence to a similar Five-Power Pact.

To return to the reparations question of 1921, Briand on Dec. 18 conferred with Lloyd George, the immediate occasion being the Ger. admission of inability to pay the reparation instalments due in Jan. and Feb. On Jan. 6 a larger conference of all the Allied Powers, with an American 'observer,' was held at Cannes. Besides reparations, the business of the Conference was to project a European Economic Conference to be held at Genoa. An Anglo-French treaty guaranteeing British aid in the event of Ger. aggression against France was put forward by Lloyd George, but rejected by Briand as humiliating, there being no mention of a reciprocal obligation of France to support England. In 1919 similar guarantee treaties had been drawn up by France with Great Britain and the U.S.A., but they were never ratified. Briand was recalled to Paris on Jan. 11, 1922, on the false assumption that he was not protecting Fr. interests, and, being deposed from power, he was succeeded by Poincaré, whose party had come forward through the growing conviction in France that Germany should be made to fulfil her treaty obligations to the letter. Poincaré, who also acted as Foreign Minister, met the

Foreign Ministers of Great Britain and Italy at Paris on March 22 in an attempt to bring the Graeco-Turkish war to an end by negotiation. The attempt failed, and the war continued until Aug., when Turkey forced Greece to accept the Armistice of Mudania. The Treaty of Lausanne followed in July 1923. The final act took place seven years later, in 1930, when a commercial convention and a pact of conciliation and arbitration were signed by Greece and Turkey.

The European Economic Conference was opened at Genoa on April 10, 1922, and was attended by representatives of twenty-nine European states, including Russia, but excepting Turkey. The U.S.A. were invited, but declined. The main business of the Conference was to explore the possibilities of renewing economic relations between Russia and the other countries of Europe. A draft treaty to this effect was put forward, but was rejected first by France and Belgium, then by the Soviet gov. itself. The only tangible result of the Genoa Conference was a separate agreement between Germany and Russia, signed at Rapallo on April 18, for the mutual renunciation of reparations and the resumption of diplomatic and economic relations. The result of this treaty, although in the spirit of the Conference, served to prejudice the other members. The Conference ended on May 22, matters being referred to a meeting of economic experts to be held at The Hague on June 26. Meanwhile a temporary pact of non-aggression was signed, and possibly prevented war between Russia and Poland. The Hague Conference, however, failed to bring about any settlement between Russia and the rest of Europe.

With regard to reparations, the issue became clearly defined as a conflict between the Eng. contention that only an economically stable Europe could enable Germany to pay her debts, and the Fr. point of view, which regarded Germany as already able to fulfil her obligations. Anglo-Fr. conferences were held in London on Aug. 7 and Dec. 9, 1922, and again in Paris on Jan. 2, 1923, when Bonar Law put forward a British scheme of payments involving a four years' moratorium, which was rejected. The Reparations Commission had granted a moratorium, which had elapsed on Aug. 31, 1922, and Germany became liable to pay 500 million gold marks on Jan. 15, 1923. On Jan. 11 Fr. and Belgium troops were moved from Dusseldorf (occupied as a 'sanction' since

March 1921) to Essen (see FRANCE; RUHR). The M.I.C.U.M. (Mission Inter-alliée de Controle des Usines et des Mines) was set up to supervise the production of coal in the Ruhr, but the Ger. Coal Syndicate, which was to take its orders from the M.I.C.U.M., moved its headquarters from Essen to Hamburg. This was the first step in the policy of passive resistance initiated by the gov. of Chancellor Cuno. Ger. officials refused to co-operate with the Fr., and by Jan. 30 a state of siege was declared by the Fr. commander-in-chief, General Degoutte. Martial law was proclaimed, and the Fr. occupation of the Ruhr, which has been described as ' a state of war without military front,' was effected. Some bloodshed was inevitable, especially in connection with the Separatist Movement under Dorten and Smeets, who aimed at establishing a Rhineland Republic, unofficially supported by the Fr. The Separatists were also strong in Bavaria, but an impartial report by the British ambassador showed that Separatism would cease as soon as Fr. influence was withdrawn. Nearly all towns in the Ruhr were deprived of their burgomasters, some of whom were court-martialled for obstructing the Army of Occupation. The most sensational trial was that of the directors of Krupp's steel works, who received sentences varying from heavy fines to imprisonment for fifteen years. By May 5764 Ger. railwaymen with their dependents were deported, and during the whole occupation (from Jan. to Nov.) it was estimated that 147,020 Ger. citizens were expelled, of whom 46,292 were State officials. The railways were reorganised and staffed by the Fr., and Fr. engineers took over the coal mines. Great Britain gave no diplomatic support to Poincaré's policy, and indeed British protests only fell short of breaking the Entente relationship. From the Fr. point of view the pressure on the Ruhr was successful, and displayed the superiority of Fr. industrial ability. It is disputed, however, whether the receipts of coal in 1923 were adequate compensation for the expense involved, and they did not exceed the reparation deliveries for the previous year. The Fr. victory remained a moral one, for the economic stability of Europe was much shaken. The value of the mark stood at several billions to the pound sterling, and the Fr. franc had become halved in value during the Poincaré administration. Germany seemed about to disintegrate, and after the order for passive resistance

in the Ruhr was withdrawn by the Ger. gov. on Sept. 26, martial law was proclaimed throughout the country. Stresemann, who had succeeded Cuno as Chancellor on Aug. 12, held Germany together, and by the efforts of Luther, the Finance Minister, the currency was stabilised on the basis of the *rentenmark*. In Nov. Marx became Chancellor, but Stresemann remained in the gov. as Minister of Foreign Affairs.

On Nov. 30 the Reparations Commission met and inaugurated two Committees of Experts. This step had been suggested by Lord Curzon, British Foreign Minister, in his note to France of Aug. 11, but had been rejected. The first Committee held its inaugural meeting at Paris on Jan. 14, 1924, under the chairmanship of General Dawes (*q.v.*), U.S. representative. The purpose of the Dawes Committee was to draw up a scheme of reparations and to provide for the economic recovery of Germany. The second Committee, under the chairmanship of McKenna, the British representative, had the subsidiary purpose of inquiring into the value of Ger. capital placed abroad during the ' flight from the mark.' Both Committees submitted their reports to the Reparations Commission on April 9. The finding of the McKenna Committee was that about 7 milliards of gold marks represented Ger. capital in foreign investment. The Dawes Committee drew up a detailed plan for the stabilisation of Ger. currency and a scheme of reparation payments on the basis of a two years' moratorium, followed by two years' transition, the full payment to begin in the fifth year (*see* DAWES PLAN). The Ger. gov. expressed its readiness to co-operate under these conditions, and all the Allied countries with the exception of France accepted the Dawes Plan. M. Poincaré's objection that the evacuation of the Ruhr could not begin until the scheme was in operation was removed by his defeat in the May elections. M. Poincaré's retirement rendered M. Millerand's position of President untenable. On June 11 he resigned, and was succeeded by M. Gaston Doumergue, while on June 14 M. Edouard Herriot became Premier. He found it possible to co-operate closely with Mr. Ramsay MacDonald, who had succeeded Mr. Baldwin as Prime Minister of England in Jan. 1924. At the important Conference of London, which opened on July 16, Mr. MacDonald presided, and the proceedings were marked by the cordial co-operation of the U.S.A. through the

American representative, Mr. Frank B. Kellogg. It was agreed that America should also be represented on the Reparations Commission, thus diminishing the domination of specifically Fr. interests, and this made possible the loan to Germany proposed in the Dawes Plan. By Aug. 2 an agreement was reached which satisfied the doubts of Eng. and American bankers as to Germany's security. On Aug. 9 a ministerial crisis was averted in France. M. Herriot gained the consent of the Minister of War and of Marshal Foch to a military evacuation of the Ruhr within twelve months. The negotiations at the London Conference were admirably conducted by Mr. MacDonald, and on Aug. 16 the London Protocol recording acceptance of the Dawes Plan without modification was signed by all parties concerned. The plan was immediately put into operation. On Oct. 10 the Loan Agreement between British, Fr., Belgian, and American bankers and Ger. financial delegates, providing for a loan to Germany of 800,000,000 gold marks (£40,000,000), was signed at the Bank of England. On Oct. 28 the M.I.C.U.M. was dissolved, and the Reparations Commission formally anounced that the fiscal and economic unity of Germany was restored. In the new year a Conference of Allied Finance Ministers was held at Paris, and an agreement was signed on Jan. 14, 1925, with regard to the division of reparations received from Germany. In May the Reparations Commission replied to the Conference of Ambassadors that Germany was fulfilling her obligations under the Dawes Plan, and by July 31 the evacuation of the Ruhr was completed.

While the reparations problem which had been troubling E. for five years was thus for the moment being settled, affairs in Eastern E. centred during the years 1920-3 partly on Hungary and partly on the W. boundaries of Soviet Russia. The fear of Hungary, where, until 1921, the possibility of a Habsburg restoration remained, and also the lesser fear of Bulgaria, were countered by the formation of the Little Entente by treaties signed on April 23 and June 7, 1921, between Czechoslovakia, Yugo-Slavia, and Rumania. Rumania concluded a further defensive treaty with Poland on March 3, 1921, as Rumania could obtain no recognition from Soviet Russia for her possession of Bessarabia. Three years later, March 1924, a Russo-Rumanian Conference at Vienna failed to settle the Bess-

arabian question, and a Moldavian Autonomous Republic on the l. b. of the Dniester came into being on Oct. 11, thus increasing Rumanian apprehension. In this year (1924) the Little Entente looked for alliances with France and Italy. An Italo-Yugo-Slav Pact was concluded on Jan. 27; a Franco-Czech Treaty on Jan. 25; and an Italo-Czech Pact on July 5. No agreements were made, however, between France and Rumania, and the Czecho-Polish agreement was not made until the following year. Rumania was one of the fifteen countries which by 1924 had not accorded a de jure recognition of the Soviet gov. Preliminary negotiations between Great Britain and the U.S.S.R. had resulted in a Trade Agreement, concluded on March 16, 1921. Subsequent disputes, concerned especially with anti-British propaganda in the East, threatened to break this agreement, but on Feb. 1, 1924, the British gov. accorded official recognition to the Soviet gov., and in the same year the govs. of France, the Scandinavian States, Austria, Czechoslovakia, Hungary, and Greece did likewise.

The frontier problems in Eastern E. were settled largely through the Permanent Court of International Justice, inaugurated in Dec. 1920. There were boundary disputes and local conflicts between Germany and Lithuania over Memel; between Lithuania and Poland over Vilna; between Poland and Czechoslovakia over the Javorzina district; between Austria and Hungary over the Burgenland; and between Albania and Yugo-Slavia over the delimitation of the Albanian frontier. The boundaries of Poland were not fixed at every point until March 15, 1923, when the seizure of the Vilna district in 1921 by Zeligowski, an independent Polish general, was recognised in the demarcation of the frontier by the Conference of Ambassadors. The Javorzina district between Czechoslovakia and Poland had been divided by a Delimitation Commission on Sept. 25, 1922, but the frontier line was not finally accepted by the Council of the League of Nations until March 12, 1924. The other European problem closely allied to the boundary question was the protection of minority peoples within the states newly-created or enlarged by the peace treaties. Under the auspices of the League of Nations a number of Minority Treaties were concluded.

With regard to Finland, Latvia, and Estonia a succession of conferences between the years 1921 and 1925 provided for the economic policy of the Baltic. At these conferences Poland was represented according as the sympathy of the Baltic States fluctuated over the Polish-Lithuanian dispute. On Nov. 1, 1923, Estonia and Latvia concluded a Defensive Alliance.

Although the boundary problems of Central E. and the Baltic were at length settled by negotiation, the delimitation of the Albanian frontier led to a serious political murder. On Aug. 27, 1923, General Tellini, head of an Italian commission, was murdered with his companions while investigating the Graeco-Albanian frontier near Janina. An Italian ultimatum was delivered to Greece and accepted with reservations. On Aug. 31 the Italians occupied the island of Corfu. Greece placed the Italian ultimatum before the League of Nations, but at the same time was forced to submit to the Conference of Ambassadors, who demanded an inquiry into the murder of their agents. The Italian action, however, was condemned by the Assembly of the League, then in its Fourth Session. The Italian gov. held that the League should not take action at the request of Greece, but the unofficial settlement drawn up by the Council was adopted by the Conference of Ambassadors, and the evacuation of Corfu was effected by the payment of a heavy Gk. indemnity to Italy.

At the settlement of the reparations problem by the adoption of the Dawes Plan by the London Conference, the cognate questions of security and disarmament had been advisedly excluded. The problem of security remained for the Fifth Assembly of the League, Sept. 1924. The draft agreement was accepted, entitled the Geneva Protocol (q.v.), for the Pacific Settlement of International Disputes, which had already come up for consideration at the Fourth Assembly. The Geneva Protocol condemned all war save in self-defence or at the instigation of the League. The Fr. and British govs. of Herriot and MacDonald respectively had been active in sponsoring the Protocol, although the latter had emphasised the difficulty of defining aggression. Also it was evident that the Protocol, in ruling the compulsory acceptance of arbitration, would arouse the British objection to anything in the nature of a super-state. Moreover, Great Britain was influenced by the opposition of the Dominions, and when on Oct. 8 the MacDonald gov. was replaced by the Conservative Government of Stanley Baldwin,

Great Britain rejected the Protocol. This decision was communicated by Mr. (soon afterwards Sir) Austen Chamberlain, the British Foreign Minister, to the Council of the League of Nations during the session in March 1925.

The British gov. preferred a regional pact, and it remained with England to suggest an alternative to the rejected Protocol. A Three-Power Pact between Great Britain, France and Belgium was proposed, its main purpose being to guarantee the ' present territorial status on the Rhine.' Correspondence between Mr. Austen Chamberlain and M. Briand, the Fr. Foreign Minister, revealed that France regarded the pact as protecting the frontier from Ger. attack, while England wished to make the frontier inviolate from both Ger. and Fr. invasion. The Fr. unilateral was opposed to the British bilateral interpretation, but the difference was to some extent solved by an offer from the Ger. gov. voluntarily to guarantee the permanence of the W. frontiers as fixed by the Treaty of Versailles. Discussions on extending the pact to include Germany were embittered by the Allied decision, communicated on Jan. 5, 1925, to postpone the evacuation of Cologne in view of the Ger. failure to carry out the disarmament clauses of the Peace Treaty. Negotiations proceeded, however, and it was at length decided to restrict the pact to the Rhineland area. Germany, despite the wishes of France, could not guarantee the permanence of her E. frontier as she had done with regard to her W. France was therefore left free to assist Poland, should there be a breach of the Ger.-Polish Arbitration Treaty. In Sept. 1925 a committee of jurists met in London for the purpose of finding formulae which would bridge the opposing points of view. Three draft texts of the Rhineland Pact were drawn up. A month later, on Oct. 5, the Conference of European statesmen opened at Locarno in Switzerland. Austen Chamberlain, chairman, and Briand represented Great Britain and France respectively, while Chancellor Luther and Foreign Minister Stresemann represented Germany, and Foreign Minister Scialoja Italy. Belgium, Czechoslovakia, and Poland were also represented. The success of the Conference depended on a resolution of the difficulties which might prevent Germany's eventual admission to the League of Nations. When this was reached, the Treaty of Mutual Guarantee went forward, and was hastened to a successful conclusion by Italy's decision to join with France and Great Britain in guaranteeing the Rhineland. Signor Mussolini arrived on Oct. 15. The next day the Locarno Pact was initialled by the delegates, and the date of signature was fixed for Dec. 1, to take place at London. The Pact comprised (1) a Treaty of Mutual Guarantee between Germany, Belgium, France, Great Britain, and Italy, (2) an Arbitration Convention between Germany and Belgium and between Germany and France, and (3) an Arbitration Treaty between Germany and Poland and between Germany and Czechoslovakia. Treaties between France and Poland and between France and Czechoslovakia were also concluded (*see* LOCARNOCONFERENCE AND TREATIES). Similar arbitration and conciliation treaties were concluded in this year between Poland and Czechoslovakia, and between Poland and Estonia, Finland, and Latvia, and Switzerland also signed similar treaties with the majority of continental European states. In Germany the struggle to secure parliamentary ratification of the Locarno Pact was successful, Ger. liberal opinion being aided by the evacuation of Cologne by the Allies in Nov. 1925. A Ger.-Russian Commercial Treaty, designed to placate Russia's mistrust of Germany's foreign policy at Locarno, was signed on Oct. 12.

Art. 16 of the Covenant of the League of Nations, which provided for military co-operation with the League against an aggressor, was modified under the Locarno Treaties and interpreted so as to allow of Germany's entry into the League. The Assembly was convened in March 1926, to discuss the Ger. request, but Germany's admission to a permanent seat on the Council was frustrated by the similar counter-claim made by Spain, Poland, and Brazil. This affront to Germany's prestige was somewhat amended by Germany's formal admission at the Seventh Assembly in Sept. 1926; but although Poland was conciliated, Spain and Brazil threatened to withdraw, and Brazil did indeed withdraw in 1928. The other major problem which confronted the League in 1926 was that of disarmament. The Temporary Mixed Commission on Disarmament had been dissolved in 1924, and from 1926 to 1927 a Preparatory Commission worked at preparing a Draft Convention. At a Preliminary Disarmament Conference held at Geneva in March 1927, the Soviet delegate, Litvinov, proposed universal disarmament, but this the other nations could not

accept as limiting their sovereign powers of defence (*see* ARMAMENTS, LIMITATION OF). The U.S.A. were co-operating with E. over disarmament, and on April 6, 1927, Briand, now Foreign Minister in the Poincaré gov., suggested a bilateral treaty with the U.S.A. for the renunciation of war, and the draft was submitted to America in June. On Dec. 28 Mr. Kellogg, Secretary of State for America, suggested a multilateral treaty to which other states should be invited to adhere. This, however, would have annulled France's defensive alliances, and it was decided to limit the pact to aggressive wars, a ban on which had already been passed at the Eighth Assembly of the League on Sept. 24. On April 7, 1928, the American draft treaty was submitted to Great Britain, Germany, Italy, and Japan. After protracted negotiations the Briand–Kellogg Pact for the outlawry of war was signed by fifteen nations at Paris on Aug. 27, 1928 (*see* KELLOGG PACT). Of the thirty-three states which subsequently adhered to the Pact, sixteen were European. The Kellogg Pact initiated a system of arbitration treaties, of which the first was that between France and the U.S.A., signed on Feb. 6, 1928. A similar treaty was concluded between France and the Netherlands on March 10, and between Greece and Rumania on March 12, while a Treaty of Neutrality, Conciliation, and Judicial Settlement was signed between Italy and Turkey on May 30 and between Italy and Greece on Sept. 23.

In Eastern E. the peace was threatened by the dispute between Poland and Lithuania over the possession of Vilna. A technical state of war had existed since Zeligowski's *coup de main* in 1921, and was brought to a technical end in 1927 by the Conference at Geneva to which Pilsudski (*q.v.*), Marshal of Poland, and Waldemaras, Prime Minister of Lithuania, were invited by the League of Nations. No settlement, however, was reached throughout 1928, and it was feared Russia would intervene in favour of Lithuania; but on Dec. 29, 1928, Litvinov, the Soviet Foreign Commissary, proposed an Eastern Peace Pact between Poland, Rumania, Estonia, Latvia, and the U.S.S.R., and this was signed on Feb. 9, 1929. Lithuania, Persia, and Danzig adhered in April, while Finland refused. Soviet relations with Great Britain improved in 1929, when diplomatic negotiations were resumed with the Labour gov. in London. Between the U.S.S.R. and

Germany a Treaty of Conciliation was signed on Jan. 24, 1929.

A step forward in the policy of liquidating the War, initiated at Geneva in 1928, was the formation of a Committee of Experts to make a definitive settlement of reparations. The Committee, representing seven Powers, met at Paris on Feb. 11, 1929, under the chairmanship of Owen D. Young, the American representative. The report of the Young Committee was completed by June 7; it was proposed to establish an International Bank, and reparations were fixed at 38 milliard gold marks, payable between Sept. 1929 and March 1966. The Spa percentages, settled by the Financial Agreement of Jan. 1925, were altered, and this caused some discontent with the Young Plan in England, but at the International Conference which met at The Hague on Aug. 6, 1929, Mr. Philip Snowden, representing Great Britain, secured some modification of the Young Plan in England's favour. Simultaneously with the reparations discussions, the Political Commission at The Hague Conference, under the chairmanship of Mr. Arthur Henderson, completed and signed an agreement whereby the evacuation of the British, French, and Belgian forces from the First and Second Zones of the Rhineland should begin from Sept. 1929, and of the Fr. forces from the Third Zone immediately after the ratification of the Young Plan by the Fr. and Ger. govs. Total evacuation was completed by June 1930.

The problem of security which has engrossed post-war E. is an economic one as well as military. As nations protect themselves by armies, so do they by economic barriers. Some advance, however, towards economic co-operation in E. has been made by the creation of international cartels in industry. In May 1927 a World Economic Conference was held, and efforts were made at securing the removal of trade restrictions and the unification of customs nomenclature. On such basic products as wood, cement, leather, and iron it was agreed to reduce tariffs. An Economic Consultative Committee came into being in 1928 to supervise the carrying into effect of the recommendations of the Conference. Inquiries into coal, sugar, and agriculture were undertaken in 1929. The result of a Tariff Conference, opened at Geneva on Feb. 17, 1930, was a Commercial Convention, but not a tariff truce, which was signed on March 25, whereby eleven nations waived their right to denounce the various commercial treaties then existing. Customs reform in E. can be effected only by an economic reorganisation of the kind advocated by Briand on Sept. 5, 1929. His speech to the Tenth Assembly of the League of Nations endeavoured to bring the long-held pan-European ideal into the sphere of practical politics, and his proposition of a United States of E., later embodied in a memorandum to the various governments of E., has been under active discussion. From an economic union E. would proceed to a closer union politically, but the proposed federation would remain within the League of Nations—regional agreements being permitted by the Covenant—and would not affect the sovereignty of the individual states (*see* Briand).

Bibliography.—J. Geikie, *Prehistoric Europe*, 1880; Himly, *Histoire de la Formation Territoriale des Etats de l'Europe Centrale* (2nd ed.), 1894; Munro, *Lake Dwellings of Europe*, 1890; Ripley, *Races of Europe*, 1899; Freeman, *Historical Geography of Europe* (3rd ed.), 1903; Black, *L'Europe politique et sociale* (2nd ed.), 1892; T. L. Stoddard, *Racial Realities in Europe*, 1924; K. H. F. Guenther, *The Racial Elements in European History*, 1927; I. Bowman, *The New World*, 1928; *Europa Year Book;* also the annual *Statesman's Year Book* and *Almanach de Gotha.* On history: Gibbon, *Decline and Fall of the Roman Empire;* Hallam, *Europe in the Middle Ages*, 1872; Freeman, *General Sketch of European History* (2nd ed.), 1876, *The Chief Points of European History*, 1886; C. A. Fyffe, *A History of Modern Europe, 1792–1878* (6 vols.), 1901–7; G. B. Adam, *European History: an Outline of its Development*, 1899; *The Cambridge Modern History*, 1902–11; *The Cambridge Medieval History*, 1911 *et seq.*; Lodge, *Modern Europe*, 1897; Bryce, *Holy Roman Empire*, 1904; T. H. Dyer, *History of Modern Europe, 1453–1871*, 1901–7; C. Oman, *The Outbreak of the War*, 1919; C. J. H. Hayes, *Brief History of the Great War*, 1920; H. M. V. Temperley, *History of the Peace Conference*, 1920–4; A. J. Toynbee and others, *Survey of International Affairs*, 1920–5, 1925–7; R. Muir, *Expansion of Europe*, 1925; J. H. Rose, *Development of European Nations*, 1926; D. B. Horn, *History of Europe*, 1927; R. B. Mowat, *History of European Diplomacy*, 1927; F. Alexander, *From Paris to Locarno and After*, 1928; R. L. Buell, *Europe: A History of Ten Years*, 1928; M. W. Graham, *New Governments of Eastern Europe*, 1928; E. Grey, *Twenty-five Years*, 1928;

A. H. Morley, *New Democratic Constitutions of Europe*, 1928; J. W. Wheeler-Bennett, *Information on the Renunciation of War*, 1928, and *Documents on International Affairs*, 1929; I. A. L. Plunkett, *History of Europe*, 1929; G. P. Gooch, *Recent Revelations in European Diplomacy*, 1930; E. Herriot, *The United States of Europe*, 1930.

**European Corn Borer** (*Pyrausta nubilatis*), a moth, comparatively harmless to crops in Europe, where it has long been known, but regarded as a serious menace in the U.S.A. It made its first appearance on the E. coast of America in 1917, having been carried in presumably on English vessels, and since then has penetrated further W. It has chiefly attacked Indian corn, where its ravages have threatened the future of the whole crop. The alarm of agriculturists during 1926 led to the sum of ten million dollars being granted by Congress to fight the invader, and two lines of defence have since been adopted with some promise of success. One of these is the importation of parasites that prey upon the moth, and the other consists in thoroughly cleaning up the fields after an Indian corn harvest, and destroying all stalks and vegetable refuse with fire, in order to prevent further breeding of the moths.

**Europium**, a chemical element discovered by Demarçay in 1896. It belongs to the group of rare earths. Its symbol is Eu, its atomic weight 152 and its atomic number 63. Europium oxide is a pale pink powder.

**Eurotas**, one of the chief rivers of the ancient Peloponnesus, in Greece, now named Morea. Its course is not more than 50 m., flowing through Laconia to the Gulf of Gythion.

**Euryale ferox**, a species and genus of Nymphaceæ, is an elegant aquatic plant which inhabits the lakes of the E. Indies and China.

**Eurydice :** (1) In Gk. legend, the wife of Orpheus. She was bitten by a serpent while fleeing from Aristæus. Orpheus descended to Hades after her, and by his exquisite music persuaded Pluto to allow her to return with him to the upper world. The condition that Orpheus should not once look behind him being broken, his 'half-regained Eurydice' was snatched from him again. This legend has been the subject of many pictures, including one by Watts. Copies of a Gk. relief (end of fifth century B.C.) are at Rome, Naples, and Paris. *See* Virgil, *Georgics*, iv.; Ovid, *Metam*, x. 1. (2) An Illyrian princess wife of Amyntas II. of Macedonia, mother of Philip II. of Macedon (359–336 B.C.) and Perdiccas III. *See* Justin, vii.

4, 5. (3) A relative of Philip, round whom numerous political intrigues centred as to the succession after the death of Alexander the Great (323 B.C.).

**Eurymedon**, in ancient geography, a riv. of Pamphylia, Asia Minor. At its mouth the Athenian commander Cimon signally defeated the Persians in 466 B.C. Its modern name is Koprü-Su.

**Eurynome**, a genus of decapod brachyurous crustaceans, belongs to the family Maiidæ, and the species are known as spider-crabs. *E. aspera* inhabits the Mediterranean.

**Eurypharynx**, *see* PELICAN FISH.

**Eurystheus**, *see* HERCULES.

**Eusebius of Emesa**, a Gk. ecclesiastic, *b.* at Edessa. He refused the offer of the see of Alexandria, being averse from all theological disputes; but he accepted the small bishropic of Emesa, in Phœnicia, instead. He was, however, driven from this, as his powers as mathematician and philosopher resulted in his flock accusing him of sorcery. Only a few fragments of his works are extant. Died A.D. 360.

**Eusebius of Nicomedia** (*d.* 342), a Gk. bishop and theologian, related through the maternal side to the Emperor Julian, whose early tutor he was. Like Eusebius of Cæsarea, he was a defender of Arius, and placed himself at the head of the Arian party after the Council of Nice. The Emperor Constantine was baptised by him in 337, and two years later he was promoted to the see of Constantinople.

**Eusebius Pamphili of Cæsarea** (*c.* 264–*c.* 349 A.D.), the 'father' of ecclesiastical history, probably *b.* in Palestine. His name, Pamphili, was assumed after the martyrdom of his instructor, Saint Pamphilus. About 313 he became Bishop of Cæsarea and took a prominent part in the Council of Nicæa, where he was the leader of the temporising party. He has the reputation of being the most learned father of the church, after Origen and Jerome, and Constantine, who appreciated his moderation and other good qualities, said that he was fit to be the bishop of practically all the world. He wrote two treatises which have come down to our time, the *Preparation* and the *Demonstration* of the Gospel, two apologetic works, and many other writings of the highest value, the chief of which are : *The History of the Church, from the Time of its Founder to the Year 323*, and the *Chronicon*, a history of the world down to 328, valuable as containing extracts from many ancient writers whose works are no longer extant.

Some of the most informative passages in his *History* are those on the written liturgy and primitive ritual; on the Ignatian Epistles; on the persecutions of Diocletian and Trajan, and on the Thundering Legion. Writings of less importance are: *The Martyrs of Palestine*, and a panegyrical *Life of Constantine*. The first edition of all E.'s works was published in 1542 at Basle.

**Euskirchen,** a Ger. tn. in the Prussian Rhine prov., at the junction of railways from Cologne and Bonn. Its industries include cloth, and metalware factories, iron foundries. The church of St. Martin dates from the thirteenth and the Town Hall from the fourteenth century. Pop. 14,550.

**Eustachian Tube** (after Bartolommeo Eustachio), a cylindrical tube lined with mucous membrane, dilated at both ends and connecting the cavity of the middle ear with the pharynx, to which it passes downwards, forwards, and inwards, for a distance of about 1½ in. It is partly osseous, but chiefly cartilaginous. Sound vibrations acting on the *tympanic membrane* and the *fenestra ovalis* cause constant changes of pressure in the middle ear, which changes are equalised by means of this tube. It is open during rest, but closed during deglutition. Permanent occlusion of this tube is one of the most common forms of deafness. *See* EAR.

**Eustachian Valve,** after Eustachio, the attachment which in the fœtus directs the blood from the inferior vena cava through the foramen ovale into the left auricle. Its remains will be found attached to the right and lower margins of the opening of the inferior vena cava.

**Eustachio, Bartolommeo** (c. 1500–74), an Italian physician and anatomist, b. at San Severino. He is celebrated for his discovery of the Eustachian tube (*q.v.*). Anatomical science was greatly enriched by his researches. He also discovered the rudimentary valve of the heart. E. was physician-in-ordinary to the popes and professor of medicine in Rome, where he died. His chief works are the *Opuscula Anatomica*, 1564; and *Tabulæ Anatomicæ*, edited in 1714.

**Eustathius** (d. c. 1193), a celebrated Gk. scholar, b. at Constantinople. He first became a monk and afterwards a deacon and teacher of rhetoric in his native city. In 1160 he became Archbishop of Thessalonica and subsequently of Myra. E. was a man of great learning, and was deeply versed in the ancient classic authors. His commentary on Homer (1st ed. Rome, 1542–50) is his

principal work. Some letters and theological and historical treatises were first published by Tafel in 1832.

**Eustatius, St.,** or **St. Eustatia,** an island of the Dutch West Indies, situated in 17° 50′ N. lat., and 62° 40′ W. long., 12 m. N.W. of St. Kitts. The surface is uneven, several of the hills being volcanic in character. The chief town is Orangetown. The area of the island is 8 sq. m. and the population about 1500. It was first occupied by the Dutch West India Company in 1634. In 1781 it was captured by Rodney, but was afterwards restored to the Dutch. The island comes under the government of Curaçao.

EUTERPE

**Eutaw Springs,** near Eutawville, in S. Carolina, U.S.A. The springs originate at the foot of a hill, and spread into a large stream which disappears underground to appear again further on. The last battle of the War of Independence was fought here 1781.

**Eutectic,** the name which was given by Guthrie to those mixtures in which the components are in such proportions as to solidify on cooling, after melting, at one temperature like a pure substance. This temperature, which is called the E. point, is the lowest freezing temperature of any mixture of the components. E. mixtures play an important part in the constitution of alloys, the heterogeneous structure of which may be demonstrated by the uneven action of etching agents.

**Euterpe,** a genus of tropical spineless palm, is found largely in the forests of S. America. There are several species; *E. edulis,* the Assai or cabbage palm, produces a bud which is eaten as food, a fruit from which oil is obtained, and wood used for building purposes.

**Euterpe,** in ancient Gk. mythology, is one of the nine goddesses who presided over the different departments of literature. E. was the muse of lyrical poetry, and is represented with the double flute.

**Euthanasia,** *see* DEATH.

**Eutheria** (Gk. εὖ, well, and θηρίον, an animal), a term given to a sub-order of mammals (*q.v.*) comprising all but the marsupials and monotremes, and was first applied by Gill in 1872. It is a synonym of Monodelphia and Placentalia.

**Eutocius** (Εὐτόκιος) (*c.* A.D. 550), a Gk. mathematician and geometer of Ascalon, in Palestine, and pupil of the architect, Isidorus. He is noted for his *Commentaries on Apollonius of Perga and Archimedes,* four of which are extant, including comments on Archimedes' *Treatise on the Sphere and Cylinder.* E. discusses the problem of the duplication of the cube and gives several solutions.

**Eutropius, Flavius** (*d. c.* A.D. 370), a Rom. historian of the fourth century. He was secretary to the emperors Constantine and Julian, accompanying the latter on his Parthian expedition. He probably rose to high office in the state, possibly that of senator or consul. He wrote *Breviarium Rerum Romanorum ab urbe condita,* a concise history down to the death of Jovian, A.D. 364. The best editions are those of Grosse, 1813 ; Hartel, 1872 ; and Droysen, 1879. *See* Suidas, *Eutropius ;* Moller, *Dissertatio de Eutropio,* 1685 ; Duncker, *De Pœanio Eutropii Interpreta,* 1880 ; Germadius, *De Viris Illustribus.*

**Eutyches,** founder of the Eutychian heresy, which said that after the Incarnation Christ had but *one* nature, the human nature being absorbed in the divine nature. The cause of E., however, was somewhat favoured at Alexandria, where Cyril had taught a less-developed form of the same doctrine, and owing to the influence of Dioscurus of Alexandria, a fresh council was held at Ephesus. To this period belongs Pope Leo's famous treatise on the two natures of Christ in the Incarnation. E. was restored by the ' Robber Council ' of Ephesus (449), but this decree was reversed at Chalcedon (451). After this, the heretic disappears from history, and the sect was put under penal laws.

**Euxine, or Black Sea,** a sheet of water bounded N. by Bulgaria, and S. and E. by Asia Minor. The early Gk. navigators gave it the epithet of ' Axenus,' *i.e.* ' unfriendly to strangers,' but as Gk. colonies sprang up on the shores, the name was changed to ' Euxinus,' or ' friendly to strangers.'

**Evagoras** (Εὐαγόρας), King of Salamis in Cyprus from *c.* 410–374 B.C., a descendant of Teucer, Telamon's son. The Athenians and Egyptians aided him in his long wars with the Persians, ending with a peace in 376 (*see* Xen., *Hell.* ii. 1). He was assassinated, and succeeded by his son, Nicocles. An oration of Isocrates praising E. is still extant. Evagoras II. succeeded Nicocles, and was dethroned by Protagoras.

**Evagrius** (Εὐάγριος) (*c.* 536–94), surnamed ' Scholasticus ' of Antioch, a Syrian church historian, who wrote a *Church History* (from A.D. 431–594), a continuation of the work of Eusebius (*see* ed. of Bidez and Parmentier, 1898). He also translated Athanasius' *Life of St. Anthony* into Latin.

**Evald Johannes** (1743–81), a Danish poet, *see* EWALD, JOHANNES.

**Evander** (Εὔανδρος), in classic legend, a Gk. hero, son of Hermes. About sixty years before the Trojan War he led an Arcadian colony to Latium, founding Pallantium (later the Palatine Hill). He was supposed to have taught the inhabitants various arts and the worship of several Arcadian gods, particularly of Pan (Faunus). He was worshipped among the heroes of Rome on the Aventine. E. was father of Pallas, and ally of Æneas against Turnus in Virgil's story (see *Æneid,* viii., x., xi). Consult Nettleship, *Lectures and Essays.*

**Evangelical** (εὐαγγελικός, of good tidings, for the Gospel). This term was originally claimed as a right by all Protestants, in that their beliefs were derived entirely from the evangel or Bible. In the course of time, however, its use and meaning have varied greatly. The term has been especially applied to the school which insists on the utter depravity of unregenerate human nature, necessity for conversion, justification of sinners by faith, free offer of the Gospel to all mankind, and the divine inspiration, authority, and sufficiency of Holy Scripture (reserving the right of individual believers to interpret scriptural passages according to their judgment). In the Anglican communion, holders of such beliefs are usually known as ' Low Church.' In Germany the word applies to the United Church as opposed to the Lutheran and Reformed churches, but it is also sometimes assumed by the pietistic party within the Protestant Church. *See* CHURCH HISTORY.

**Evangelical Alliance,** a voluntary association of Christians of various countries and denominations, first formed in London, 1846, at a conference of 921 clergymen and laymen, representing some fifty sections of the Protestant Church. The idea started in Scotland, as a protest against Popery and Puseyism. Nine points were agreed upon as a basis of the alliance formed by members holding ' the views commonly called evangelical.' Its aims include maintaining religious liberty throughout the world and succouring the persecuted. It held many international meetings. Its chief publication is *Evangelical Christendom. See* Arnold *History of the Evangelical Alliance,* 1897 ; Bonnet, *Lettres sur l'Alliance Evangélique,* 1847.

**Evangelical Church** This religious body of N. America was founded in E. Pennsylvania by Jacob Albright (Albrecht) in 1800. The rules of government and beliefs adopted were very similar to those of the Methodists. Albright was leader of the association till his death, 1808. In 1816 the first annual conference was called, and in 1818 the present title was first adopted. A general conference was instituted, 1843. Internal controversy in 1891 caused a division and the branch which met at Philadelphia took the name of ' United Evangelical Church.' But by an Enabling Act the two churches were reunited, and the new organisation being officially established at Detroit, 1922. The church now has a total membership of over a quarter of a million, more than 30,000 of whom are in Europe, chiefly in Germany and Poland. There are foreign missions in China and Japan. The principal colleges of the E. C. are the North Central College and Evangelical School of Theology, Naperville, Illinois ; the Western Union College, Le Mars, Iowa ; Albright College, Myerstown, Pa. ; and Schuylkill College and School of Theology, Reading, Pa. It also has homes for orphans and old people and a number of hospitals. The church has seven bishops, one residing in Europe. Publications : *Evangelical Messenger* ; *Christliche Botschafter. See* Plitt, *Die Albrechtsleute,* 1877.

**Evangelical Synod of North America.** A religious communion established in 1840 at Gravois Settlement, Missouri.

It is strictly evangelical in principle, and its members accept the Reformed and Lutheran doctrinal statements so far as they are in agreement. When not in agreement, the Synod follows the Scriptures and assumes the liberty of conscience prevailing in the Evangelical Church (*q.v.*). A new constitution was adopted at a great conference in 1927. The organisation has over 1200 pastors, over 350,000 communicants, and over 1200 Sunday schools. It owns property of the value of nearly 40 million dollars, and has missionaries in India and Honduras besides the U.S.A. Publications : *The Evangelical Herald; The Light Bearer.*

**Evangelical Union, The,** the name of a religious body (also called Morisonians) formed in Scotland, 1843, by the Rev. J. Morison of Kilmarnock and other ministers who had left the United Secession Church. They were joined by ministers from the Congregational Union who held similar views. The chief article of their faith was belief in the universality of the Saviour's atonement. They also believed in the freedom of the human will. By 1896 the Congregational Union absorbed nearly all the churches. See *Doctrinal Declaration* of the union, 1856 ; Ferguson, *The History of the Evangelical Union,* 1876 ; *The Worthies of the Evangelical Union,* 1883.

**Evangelist** (the bringer of good tidings, preacher of the Gospel), a term used in the New Testament, signifying an official of the Christian Church, whose chief duties seem to have been those of a missionary and pioneer, carrying the Gospel message to new places and preparing the way for organising work which was to follow. The E. is not permanently connected with any local field of work, nor is he devoted to the usual service of the pastorate, his work is of an itinerary rather than a local nature. Thus Philip of Cæsarea and Timothy of Ephesus are called Es. The term was also used in post-apostolic times for those who read and explained the written Gospels in public worship, but though this has continued to be its distinctive meaning, the official name is more often used to-day in its earlier sense and has been transferred to the writers of the four Gospels.

**Evans, Sir Arthur John** (*b.* 1851), an English archæologist, keeper of the Ashmolean Museum, at Oxford. Extensive archæological researches were made by him in the Balkans and also in Crete, where he discovered the pre-Phœnician script. His works include *Illyrian Letters, Through Bosnia, Cretan Pictographs and Pre-Phœnician Script,* etc., etc.

**Evans, George Essex** (1863–1909), Australian poet; *b.* June 18, in London; youngest son of John Evans, Q.C. Educated at Haverfordwest Grammar School and in Guernsey; emigrated in 1881. Accompanied a survey party in the Australian bush; worked on his brother's farm near Allora, Queensland. Became journalist, contributing to papers throughout Australia. Appointed, by Queensland gov., district registrar at Toowoomba, 1888. Edited the *Antipodean* annual, 1892, 1893, and 1897, with assistance from R. L. Stevenson. Compiled a Guide to Darling Downs, 1899. Compiled report on resources of Queensland. Poetry : *The Repentance of Magdalenè Despar*, and other verses, London, 1891 ; *Loraine*, and other verses, Melbourne, 1898 ; the fifty-guinea-prize poem on inauguration of the Commonwealth, 1901 ; *The Sword of Pain*, Toowoomba, 1905 ; *The Secret Key*, etc., Sydney, 1906. Died at Toowoomba, Nov. 11.

**Evans, Sir George de Lacy** (1787–1870), a British general, *b.* in Ireland. In 1815 he fought at Waterloo. He also distinguished himself at the siege of Sebastopol and the battle of Inkerman in the Crimean War, for which services he received the thanks of the House of Commons in 1855 and was created G.C.B.

**Evans, Marian,** *see* ELIOT, GEORGE.

**Evans, Oliver** (1755–1819), an American mechanist and inventor, *b.* at Newport, Delaware. He invented a machine for making wire card teeth (1777) used in carding cotton and wool, and is also noted for his improved machinery for flour-mills. E. is said to have invented the first steam engine constructed on the high-pressure system, sending his drawings and specifications to England, 1795. He also made the first steam dredging machine of U.S.A. His project of a railway between New York and Philadelphia failed through lack of funds. E. has been called the ' Watt of America.' He wrote *Young Millwright's and Miller's Guide*, 1795. See Thurston, *Growth of the Steam Engine*, 1878.

**Evans, Robley Dunglison** (1846–1912), an American naval officer; appointed to the Naval Academy from Utah in 1860. He was in command of the *Iowa* at the naval battle of Santiago in the Spanish-American War, and was commander of the *Yorktown* at Valparaiso in 1891, where he earned the name of ' Fighting Bob Evans.' In 1901 he was made rear-admiral, and in 1902 commander of the Asiatic fleet. He became commander of the Atlantic fleet in 1905, and in 1907 commander-in-

chief of that fleet on tour of the world. *A Sailor's Log*, published in 1891, is his work. He retired from public life in 1908.

**Evans, Sir Samuel** (1859–1918), British judge; *b.* May, at Skewen, Glam. He took LL.B. at London University, and practised as solicitor at Neath from 1883. He sat in parliament for Mid Glamorgan from 1890 till his elevation to the Bench. Called to the Bar in 1891, he took silk in 1901, and was Solicitor-General 1908-10. He was made president of the Probate, Divorce, and Admiralty Division, 1910. Almost totally inexperienced, at the time of his appointment, in the business done in his court, he qualified by constant study, and during the Great War delivered sound judgments in prize cases—in which he relaxed the traditional rule against ' alien enemies ' being allowed to appear. Died Sept. 13.

**Evans, William** (1811–58), a landscape painter in water-colours, is usually known as ' Evans of Bristol.' A painter of Welsh scenery, one of his finest works is ' Troth Mawr.'

**Evanston**, a beautiful residential city of Cook co., Illinois, U.S.A., 12 m. N.W. of Chicago. It is the seat of the North-Western University of the Methodist Episcopal Church and of the Dearborn Observatory, and of three theological colleges and the headquarters of the Women's Christian Temperance Union. Pop. 63,338.

**Evansville,** a city in Indiana, U.S.A., a manufacturing and commercial city, on the high bank of the Ohio River with fine parks and drives. There are many coal mines near and a trade in coal, hardwood lumber, and agricultural products ; flour, furniture and cigars are manufactured. Pop. 102,249. Water power is supplied by a dam in the Ohio R.

**Evaporation, or Vaporisation,** is the process by which a substance changes into the state of vapour. Some solids, such as snow, camphor, iodine, etc., readily disappear in the state of vapour at temperatures well below their melting points. The E. of a liquid may go on at all temperatures, but the rate of change is greater the higher the temperature, until the boiling-point (*q.v.*) is reached, when ' free E.' occurs. The rate at which E. takes place depends (1) on the area of the surface exposed ; (2) on the freedom from vapour of the space above the liquid ; and (3) on the nearness of the vapour pressure to the external pressure. Thus, taking a quantity of liquid, it will evaporate most rapidly if placed (1) in a shallow vessel ; (2) in a draught, so as to remove the vapour as soon as formed ;

and (3) if heated, or placed under an exhausted receiver, the vapour pressure being increased in the former case, and in the latter the external pressure reduced. If a quantity of liquid is placed in an evacuated vessel, some of it will evaporate until the space above the liquid is 'saturated' with the vapour; equilibrium is then maintained, or in other words, E. and condensation take place at equal rates. For every temperature there is a maximum vapour pressure, which becomes equal to atmospheric pressure at the boiling-point of the liquid. The presence of another gas or vapour, such as air, has no effect upon the magnitude of the vapour pressure, but merely increases the time taken to arrive at the state of equilibrium. A large amount of heat is absorbed in the process of E., the remaining liquid and its surroundings being cooled, sometimes to a considerable extent. Thus, by placing a dish of water under the receiver of an air-pump, together with some sulphuric acid to absorb the vapour, the water may be frozen by rapidly exhausting the receiver. Again, by directing a spray of ether upon animal or vegetable tissue, the latter is soon frozen by the cold produced by the rapid E. of the former, use being made of this for producing local anæsthesia in the case of small operations.

*Evaporation in nature.*—E. is constantly taking place all over the surface of the globe, but is most rapid in tropical regions, where the hot air is able to take up a large amount of moisture from the sea, lakes, and rivers. This water-laden atmosphere, when it condenses with a cooler climate, is chilled and gives up some of its moisture in the form of rain, snow, or hail, according to the surrounding temperature. Thus the water on the earth is undergoing a constant cycle of E. and condensation which may be represented as follows :—

$$Sea \nearrow \begin{matrix} vapour \rightarrow cloud \\ \\ river \leftarrow rain \end{matrix} \swarrow \nwarrow$$

Taking the West of Europe, E. is rapid in spring and still more so in summer, and on the other hand, from November to February it is almost at a standstill, due to the falling temperature and consequent moisture-laden state of the atmosphere. Measurements of the annual E. have been made at various places, the following being a selection. Interior basin of the United States in lat. 36° N., 150 in.; Cumana, S. America, 136 in.; Madras, 91 in.; County Cavanagh, Ireland, 13 in.; and over a very large area in Europe less than 20 in. It has been found that in general the annual E. and rainfall are approximately proportional.

*Commercial applications of evaporation.*—E. plays an important part in most manufacturing processes, and various means have been devised to facilitate the removal of moisture from solutions and substances. Thus brine is concentrated by being made to trickle down piles of brushwood, placed in a current of air, a large surface being thereby exposed for E. The same principle is applied to the coolers used in breweries and elsewhere, a stream of water being made to trickle over the pipes containing the warm liquid. Liquids like sugar, syrups, and various extracts are evaporated in vacuum pans, in which the external pressure is reduced as far as possible by suction pumps, so that E. will proceed fairly rapidly, even at a low temperature. The same principle is made use of in the multiple effect evaporator, which consists of a series of vacuum pans in which the vapour produced by the E. of the liquid in the first pan is used to heat the liquid in the second pan, and so on. In freezing machines of the liquid ammonia type, the low temperature is produced by the rapid E. of the liquefied ammonia under reduced pressure.

**Evarts, William Maxwell** (1818–1901), an American statesman and lawyer, *b.* in Boston. He was principal counsel for Andrew Johnson in the president's trial for impeachment, and afterwards became Attorney-General for Johnson's cabinet, 1868.

**Eve,** *see* ADAM.

**Evection** (Lat. *evectio*, carrying upward, forth), in astronomy, a lunar perturbation or inequality, first discovered by Ptolemy. This inequality or eccentricity of the moon's orbit (alternately increasing and decreasing) is produced by the sun's action. E. may alter the moon's place by a maximum amount of 1° 15′ in either direction, and the time of occurrence of an eclipse by six hours. These variations take place almost semi-annually, and depend partly on the position of the perigee. *See* LUNAR THEORY, MOON.

**Eveleth,** a city of St. Louis co., Minnesota, U.S.A., lying in the midst of the great red and brown hematite iron ore deposits of the Mesali Range. Mining and shipping are the principal industries. Pop. 7484.

**Evelyn, John** (1620–1706), a diarist, was educated at Southover free school, and went, in 1637, to Balliol, but came down in two years without a degree. He had some time before been admitted as a law student, and in 1640 he took up his residence in the Temple, though he never, apparently, thought of practising as a barrister. He was interested in horticulture, and improved the grounds of his father's estate of Wotton. From 1641 he travelled much on the Continent, but settled in England in 1652 at Sayes Court, Deptford, where he devoted much of his time to the gardens, which he brought to a state of high perfection. After the Restoration he held many minor offices and

*History of the Grand Visiers*, 1677. He contributed some Gk. hexameters to his father's *Sylva* (3rd ed.), 1678. Examples of his verse are in Dryden's *Miscellanies*, and Nichols' *Collection of Poems*.

**Evening Primrose**, *see* ŒNOTHERA.

**Evening Standard**, a penny London evening paper formed, by an amalgamation in 1905, of two evening papers, the *Evening Standard*, founded in 1827 as the *Standard*, and the *St. James's Gazette*, founded in 1880. The

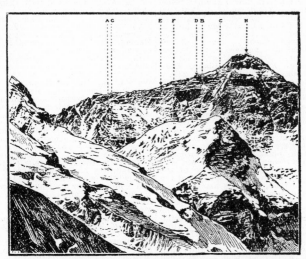

[*Courtesy of 'The Alpine Journal'*

MOUNT EVEREST

A, Camp. VI.: 26,700 feet.    B, Point reached by Somervell in 1924.    C, Point reached by Norton in 1924.    D, 'The Second Step,' where Mallory and Irvine were last seen alive.    E, 'The First Step.'    F, Point reached by Finch and Bruce in 1922.    G, Point reached by Mallory, Norton and Somervell in 1922.    H, The Summit.

sat on various commissions. For a while he was secretary of the Royal Society, but twice declined the presidency. A friend of many notable people, including Pepys, he was *au courant* with most of the events of the day, which were duly recorded in his interesting *Diary*, which was first published in 1818 (new editions by Wheatley, 1879, and Austin Dobson, 1906).

**Evelyn, John, the Younger** (*c.* 1655–98), an English translator and scholar, son of the diarist (*d.* 1706). E. translated Plutarch's *Life of Alexander the Great*, 1683–86; Rapin's poem, *Of Gardens*, 1673; Chassepol's

*St. James's Gazette* was from the first distinguished for its strongly literary character, and belonged rather to the category of reviews, like the *Spectator*. There were three other penny Conservative evening papers in the field against it, with the result that the 'news' element was increased, and it fell into line with particular movements by becoming an ardent supporter of Imperialism (*q.v.*). In 1903 it became the property of C. Arthur Pearson, who, in 1905, amalgamated it with the *Evening Standard*, which had also become his property. It is now controlled by Lord Beaverbrook (*q.v.*) and makes a prominent feature of politics.

**Everdingen, Aldert (Allart) van** (1621–75), a Dutch landscape painter and engraver; studied under R. Savery and P. Molyn, surpassing both. He excelled in sketches of rugged scenery, marine views, and storms. Among his best pictures are : 'Landscape with River,' *c.* 1648 (Louvre); 'Landscape with Waterfall,' 1650 (Munich); 'Wooded Slope,' 'Castle by River,' and 'Norwegian Waterfall' (Berlin Museum); 'Norwegian Landscapes' (National Museum, Amsterdam); 'Storm at Sea' (Munich). His most famous etchings are the series illustrating 'Reineke Fuchs.' Some of his original drawings are in the British Museum. *See* Descamps, *Vies des Peintres Flamands ;* Blanc, *Ecole Hollondaise ;* Förster, iii. 207, 241.

**Everest Mount, or Chomokankar,** a summit of the Himalayas, situated in Nepal. The height has been ascertained as over 29,000 ft., and it is the highest mountain in the world. Its name is derived from Sir George Everest, a surveyor-general of India. Recent attempts to reach the highest peak have formed an epic story of British pluck and endurance. In 1921 a reconnaissance party was sent out by the joint enterprise of the Royal Geographical Society and the Alpine Club, and this made a most helpful survey of the mountain. In the following year a climbing party approached the mountain by the Rongbuk Glacier on the Thibetan side, and in this attempt Norton, Somervell, and Mallory reached the height of 26,800 feet without making use of oxygen ; while Bruce and Finch, with a Gurkha who accompanied them, reached 27,200 feet with oxygen. In 1924 a carefully organised expedition under General Bruce set out from Darjeeling in the last week of March, forming themselves into two parties as they crossed Thibet in order not to overcrowd the rest-houses. In April the command was taken over by Col. Norton, owing to the ill-health of Gen. Bruce. Camps were established at different heights in the mountain; terrible snowstorms and blizzards were encountered, and at one time the temperature recorded 56° of frost. On May 15 a visit was paid to the Holy Lama in the Rongbuk Monastery, and his blessing was bestowed upon the native carriers. Early in June came the final stages. Setting out from North Col Camp, Norton and Somervell climbed to the height of 28,130 feet without oxygen. Later, with five porters to carry provisions and reserve oxygen cylinders, Mallory

and Irvine established a still higher camp. It is unknown whether they actually reached the summit, for when last seen they had achieved the height of 28,230 feet, but the attempt cost them their lives, and their bodies have not been recovered. An illustrated account of this expedition, with a contribution by each of the survivors, is in the *Geographical Journal* for December 1924. *See* also *Mt. Everest, the Reconnaissance,* by C. K. H. Bury, 1921 ; *The Assault on Mt. E.,* by the Hon. C. G. Bruce, 1922 ; *The Fight for E.* by E. F. Norton, 1924 ; and *The Epic of Mt. E.,* by Sir F. Younghusband, 1926.

**Everett,** (1) until 1870 part of Malden, 3 m. N. of Boston, U.S.A., now a city with a pop. of 48,424, with important manufactures, including coke, chemicals, leather goods, tools, trunks, etc. (2) A city of Washington, U.S.A. 28 m. N. of Seattle on Puget Sound, with a fine harbour and beautiful mountain scenery, many lumber mills, iron works, and factories and salmon canneries. Pop. 30,567.

**Everett, Alexander Hill** (1792–1847), an American scholar and diplomatist, brother of the orator, Edward (*d.* 1865). E. was *chargé d'affaires* in the Netherlands (1818–24), minister at Madrid (1825–29), confidential agent to Cuba (1840), and commissioner to China (1846). He published *Europe, or a General Survey . . .,* 1821 ; *New Idea.. on Population,* 1822 ; *America,* 1827. From 1829–35 he owned and edited the *North American Review.* E. belonged to the Democratic party; he contributed to the *Monthly Anthology,* 1803–11 ; wrote *Critical and Miscellaneous Essays,* 1845–47, and a volume of poems in 1845. He also published the orations *The French Revolution* and *The Battle of Bunker Hill. See* Griswold, *Prose Writers of America ;* Allibone, *Dict. of Authors.*

**Everett, Edward** (1794–1865), an American orator and statesman, *b.* in Mass., brother of A. H. Everett, the diplomatist. He graduated from Harvard in 1811, studied divinity, and became a Unitarian minister in 1813. Two years later he was appointed Eliot professor of Gk. at Harvard. In 1820 he became editor of the *North American Review.* In politics he was a Whig, and was appointed minister to Great Britain in 1840. He *d.* at Boston.

**Everett-Green, Evelyn** (*b.* 1856), an English author, studied music, and for two years was nurse in a London hospital. Since 1883 she has followed a literary career, writing historical fiction and novels for young people. Her numerous works include : *The*

*Last of the Dacres*, 1886; *Monica*, 1900; *Married in Haste*, 1907; *Miss Mallory of Mote*, 1912; *Confirmed Bachelor*, 1915; *Eyes of Eternity*, 1918; *Ghost Hall*, 1925; *Claud the Charmer*, 1927; *Miss Goshawk of Goshawk*, 1929.

**Everghem,** a small tn. of E. Flanders, Belgium, situated 4 m. N. of Ghent. Makes lace, linen and cotton goods. Pop. 8100.

**Everglades,** a lake in S. Florida, U.S.A. It is large but shallow, and contains a great number of small islands which are covered with dense overgrowth and are frequented by numerous alligators. Florida is sometimes called ' Everglade State.' after this swampy district. Considerable information about the E. is to be obtained from books by Willoughby and Whitehead.

**Evergreens,** are those plants, shrubs and trees which keep their leaves and do not shed them annually. The leaves sometimes live as long as four or five years on E. trees, but they are constantly shedding and making new ones, so that the trees are never left bare. In tropical climates certain trees that are decidu-ous when grown in temperate regions are E. ; as an example of this the *Robinia pseud-acacia*, popularly known as acacia, may be quoted. All conifers except the larch are E., and many shrubs and creepers, *e.g.* box, laurel, ivy, etc., are cultivated be-cause they do not shed their leaves in autumn.

**Everlasting Flowers,** or **Immortelles,** are flowers which retain their form and colour for a long time after they have been picked and dried. A few genera of the order Compositæ are among the best known, and several are cultivated in gardens for decora-tive purposes, they are often dyed bright colours, and some are bleached white. *Antennaria dioica*, mountain everlasting, or cat's foot, is the only British species growing wild, but *Anaphalis margaritacea* is naturalised in S. Wales, Scotland, and the Channel Islands. Species of *Helichry-sum* are the ones best suited for culti-vation in gardens. They should be gathered on a dry day before the flowers are fully opened.

**Eversley,** a vil. of N.E. Hampshire, England. There is in the neighbour-hood a fine old Jacobean residence, Bramshill House, which was built for the son of James I. Pop. 864.

**Evertsen,** a Dutch naval family which produced several distinguished officers, of whom five were brothers. Two of them were killed in action, viz. Vice-Admiral Cornelius in 1666 in the second battle off the N. Fore-land; and Admiral Jan in the same

year in ' St. James's Fight,' Cornelius. the son of Jan. attained the rank of vice-admiral and *d.* in 1679. No fewer than nine members of the E. family fell in action at sea.

**Everyman,** an independent weekly literary journal, was first published on Oct. 18, 1912, by J. M. Dent and Sons, Ltd. During the War it ceased publication but was revived in Jan. 1929. It reviews literature, old and new, and also discusses the vital questions of the times from an un-biassed platform, either political or sectarian. Leaders of every form of thought are amongst the contributors to the journal, which enjoys a unique position in British journalism. The present editor is C. B. Purdom.

**Everyman's Library.** The title of a universal library of the representa-tive works of all time, initiated in 1906 and published at popular prices by Joseph Malaby Dent (*q.v.*), and continued by the firm J. M. Dent and Sons, Ltd., in London, and E. P. Dutton & Co., Inc., in New York. The name was suggested by Ernest Rhys, the general editor, whose cue was the line in the old morality play of that name : ' Everyman, I will go with thee, and be thy guide.' It now comprises (1931) nearly 900 volumes, and from a dozen to two dozen new volumes are issued every year, so that the founder's purpose of producing one thousand volumes in all is well on the way to fulfilment. There existed in Eng. previously to its inauguration a number of inexpensive series of classics, but nothing on a large enough scale to ensure the universality essential to complete success. Among these earlier attempts were Henry Morley's *Universal Library*; the *Camelot* Series; Grant Richards' *The World's Classics*, now continued by the Oxford University Press; and J. M. Dent's own edition of the *Temple Classics*. There were also two very notable continental exemplars, the *Réclame* library of Germany and the *Bibliothèque Nationale* of France. The principle of the democratisation of knowledge was the fundamental purpose of E. L., and it was in no small measure a spur to the enthusi-astic co-operation of editors, printers, paper-makers, binders and other collaborators of the publisher. The essentials of inexpensive production, coupled with reasonable quality of materials and workmanship and an attractive format, having been settled, some 10,000 copies of nearly every book in the first one hundred and fifty of the series were printed and issued in three batches; and the price of each volume was fixed at one shilling (increased since the Great

War to two shillings). The success of E. L. necessitated the establishment of Dent's own works, The Temple Press, Letchworth, Herts, the firm's City binding works not being large enough to cope with the enormous binding requirements of E. L. volumes. Binding at Letchworth accordingly commenced at the end of 1906, and two years later the factory was enlarged by the installation of a printing plant. To-day all the volumes are bound at Letchworth; most of them are also printed there, but some are still printed by the outside printers who played a generous part in the inauguration of the library, among whom R. Clay &

THE EVERYMAN'S LIBRARY DEVICE

Sons, Ltd., of Bungay, Suffolk, are outstanding. A feature of the standard of production of E. L. is that practically all the volumes are newly set and moulded on inclusion in the library, and that the stereo-plates from the moulds are constantly renewed when reprinting, so that a clean type impression is effective y obtained. In addition to the ordinary cloth binding, there is a special library binding in which all the volumes are obtainable, and about a quarter of the most popular volumes are issued in a leather binding. The E. L. consists of thirteen sections; Biography; Classics; Essays and Belles Lettres; Fiction (which with over 250 volumes is naturally the largest section); History; Oratory; Poetry and Drama; Reference (in which section *Everyman's Encyclopaedia* was originally issued); Romance; Science; Theology and Philosophy; Travel and Topography; and books for Young People; and included in every section is a large number of translations from famous foreign works. 'A cosmic convulsion,' wrote the late Sir Edmund Gosse, 'might utterly destroy all the other printed works in the world, and still, if a complete set of E. L. floated upon the waters, enough would be preserved to carry on the unbroken tradition of literature.' Although most of the volumes have a wide appeal, the publishers have boldly included many lesser-known works of great importance to students, and such classics as Grote's *History of Greece*, in 12 volumes, Gibbon's *Decline and Fall of the Roman Empire*, in 6 volumes, Mommsen's *History of Rome*, in 4 volumes, and *Hakluyt's Voyages*, in 8 volumes, besides many others which, in the ordinary way, are either not accessible to the general public or only available at prohibitive prices.

**Evesham**, a municipal bor. and market tn. of Worcestershire, England. It is situated on the r. b. of the Avon, 15 m. S.E. of Worcester. The extreme fertility of the soil renders the neighbourhood most suitable for market gardening, which is the chief industry. There is a fine bridge over the river, here navigable, also a library, technical college, hospital, etc. A battle fought here in 1265, by which Henry III. regained the throne and the barons were crushed for a time: the Prince of Wales defeated Simon de Montfort, Earl of Leicester. E. is noted for its abbey founded in 701, a magnificent detached tower, rebuilt in the fifteenth century, 110 feet high, and containing a clock with chimes and ten bells, which still remain, also a mutilated gateway of the twelfth century, a fine arch and the abbot's stables. Pop. 8688.

**Eviction**, in law, means the ejectment of a person from possession of lands or tenements. E. may be total or partial, an instance of the latter being where some other person sets up a claim to a right of way or other easement over the land. Entry by a landlord to view the state of repair, or to effect alterations, is not E. or trespass if the tenant agreed to allow the landlord to enter for such purposes. To maintain an action for damages for E. physical expulsion need not be proved, any act tending to prejudice the quiet enjoyment or comfort of the tenant being an E. or *constructive* E. The remedy for E. is generally by an action of damages for breach of a covenant (*q.v.*), for quiet enjoyment, and an action of ejectment to recover the land (*see* ENTRY); but when there is no contractual relationship between the tenant and the person evicting him, an action of damages for trespass would be the appropriate remedy, and if the evictor acted without colour of right, the tenant would recover heavy damages. *See also* RECOVERY OF LAND.

**Evidence.** Legal evidence denotes the means by which facts are ascertained for judicial purposes. It is a branch of the law of procedure, but there exists no general or codifying Act, and indeed it is probably undesirable that judicial discretion in the matter of reception of E. should be so fettered. James Fitzjames Stephen was employed in 1872 to draw a code for England, but the code drawn never passed into law, although its model, drafted by the same judge, subsequently became the Indian Evidence Act of 1872. The whole of our law of E. as it exists now, is a system of restriction upon the admission of testimony, and based as it is upon the formal rules of inductive logic, reveals a strong tendency to narrow the freedom which formerly characterised, especially in state trials, the conduct of judicial proceedings. The bulk of the rules of E. is negative in character, that part of the law of E. which relates to *relevancy* of facts as distinct from *mode of proof* of a fact deemed to be relevant being dominated by four primary rules of exclusion or rules which, subject to certain important exceptions, exclude the admission as E. of facts which outside legal circles might well be regarded as affording excellent testimony. These rules include the following four classes of facts : (1) Facts similar to, but not specially connected with, each other, *e.g.* if the issue is whether A forged B's signature to a cheque, the fact that he forged C's signature on some former occasion is irrelevant. But if there is a question whether an act was done intentionally or accidentally by A, the fact, if so, that such act formed part of a systematic course of conduct would be relevant, *e.g.* if A is suing on a policy of fire insurance, the fact that he had sustained fires in other houses insured by him would be relevant to the issue whether the fire was accidental or not. (2) The fact that a person not called as a witness has asserted the existence of any fact. This is the fundamental principle which is more popularly expressed in the maxim that hearsay is no E. The most striking exceptions to this rule are afforded by the various rules of convenience which allow of the admission of statements by deceased persons (as to which *see* DE-CLARATIONS OF DECEASED PERSONS), and statements which amount to admissions. Admissions may be E. against a party to an action when made in his behalf by any person who has a substantial interest in the event

of the proceedings, or who is an agent expressly or impliedly authorised by that party to make such admissions. But admissions made ' without prejudice ' can under no circumstances be adduced in E. The rule against hearsay renders irrelevant statements in books or documents not made by parties to the proceedings or their authorised agents. Exceptions to this rule, excluding documentary E., include, *inter alia*, entries in public records, official books, or registers ; recitals of public facts in statutes and proclamations, and statements in works of history. Final judgments, orders or decrees of any court are always E. as against all persons of all facts stated or decided by such judgments, etc., or upon which they are based, but not of facts which may only be inferred as probable from their existence. (3) The fact that any person is of opinion that a fact exists. Fact not opinion is what a witness is in general required to state. But the opinions of experts on points of science or art are admissible in E., subject to the judge's decision on their competence as experts. As a matter of law judges have full power on all technical matters to call in the aid of judicial assessors, but except in Admiralty cases they seldom avail themselves of their statutory powers. (4) The fact that any person's character is such as to render conduct imputed to him probable or improbable. E. of character, may, however, be given in criminal trials in certain circumstances stated in the Criminal Evidence Act, 1898. That Act allows the prosecution to give E. of a prisoner's bad character if the prisoner has himself or by his counsel given E. to establish his own good character, or has at the trial cast imputation on that of the prosecutor or the witnesses for the prosecution. E. of previous convictions may be given before the verdict (*a*) if proof of such former offences is admissible on other grounds, *e.g.* as showing a systematic course of conduct (*see* above) ; (*b*) to rebut E. of good character.

E. is said to be either oral or documentary. Documentary or written E. consists of records, documents under seal, such as charters and deeds, and writings not under seal. Bentham used the term real E. to denote such E. as was neither oral nor documentary in the above special sense ; but E. which is not oral is generally classified, even if unscientifically, as documentary. Acts of Parliament are records of the highest nature, from their quality as the memorials of the legislation ; but a distinction is made with respect to E. between public and private statutes. A public statute requires no proof in courts of justice; but private Acts must be proved by copies compared with the original roll of parliament. Records of the proceedings of courts of justice are proved by exemplifications, sworn copies and office copies. Exemplifications are transcripts of the records of different courts, accredited by having the seals of such courts attached to them. Sworn copies are transcripts made by individuals who authenticate them upon oath when they are produced in E. Office copies are copies certified to be true and accurate by an officer expressly entrusted with that business. The reception of various certificates, official and public documents, is regulated by various statutes, especially the 8 and 9 Vict. c. 113. Charters and deeds are proved by the production of the instrument and proof of the execution by the party to be charged with it; but where the document is more than thirty years old the execution need not be proved. The general rule is that the original deed must be produced. Deeds attested must, in general, be proved by one at least of the attesting witnesses; but if the witnesses be dead, or cannot be found, the execution may be proved by proof of the handwriting of the party. The method adopted to prove handwriting in general is to secure the testimony of some person acquainted with the handwriting of the individual in question, or who has seen him write, or who has had written correspondence with him; but otherwise the testimony of persons skilled in caligraphy as 'experts' is wholly excluded. Practically all persons are competent to give evidence at the present day. Formerly plaintiffs and defendants were not allowed to give evidence on the ground that they were interested parties, the result being that probably the best possible E. was excluded. Where the judge decides that any witness is too young or mentally infirm to testify, the witness is incompetent to give E. In certain cases witnesses may claim a privilege (see CONFIDENTIALITY IN LAW). Since the passing of the Criminal Evidence Act, 1898, both the accused and the husband or the wife of the accused are competent witnesses; but the principle that the accused is not compelled to incriminate himself is preserved by the provision that such witnesses are not compelled to give E. except that the wife or husband of accused may be called either for the prosecution or the defence, and without the consent of the accused, if he (or she) is charged with any offence under the Vagrancy

Act, 1824 (neglect to maintain wife and family), offences against the Person Act, 1861 (relating to rape, indecent assault and the like offences), the Married Women's Property Act, 1882 (offences by a married man or woman against the other spouse's property), and the Criminal Law Amendment Act, 1885 (sexual offences). E. must be given on oath unless the witness objects to being sworn, upon the ground that he has no religious beliefs, when he may instead solemnly affirm in the Scottish fashion. Children of tender years who do not understand the nature of an oath may give E. without being sworn if the judge thinks the child sufficiently intelligent to give E. and to understand the moral obligation of speaking the truth. Stephen, *Digest of Evidence*; Taylor, *Evidence*; Roscoe, *Nisi Prius*.

*United States.*—The rules in the Courts of the U.S.A. are closely assimilated to the Eng. In American procedure E. is authoritatively defined as ' any knowable fact or group of facts, not a legal or a logical principle, considered with a view to its being offered before a legal tribunal for the purpose of producing a conviction, positive or negative, on the part of the tribunal, as to the truth of a proposition, not of law or of logic, on which the determination of the tribunal is to be asked ' (Wigmore). The orthodox proposition always was and has continued to be that the rules of E. at common law trials obtained also at Chancery; but the practice of chancery shows important qualifications of this. The variances in Chancery practice may be classed as follows : (a) the required mode of taking testimony in writing, instead of orally. This was, of course, in itself a totally contrary rule to that of common law. It had several effects on other rules—in particular, as to the mode of taking objections to E. (by motion to strike out an answer to an interrogatory); as to the rule of impeachment (by forbidding it after publication of the depositions); and as to the mode of cross-examination (by requiring the cross-interrogatories to be framed before the answers to the direct interrogatories were known—thus depriving the cross-examination of its sting. (b) The Chancery Court enforced the tradition of the Canon law, requiring two witnesses to every material allegation. This not only gave rise to the general rule on overcoming the defendant's oath, but also led to rules for such characteristic Chancery issues as divorce bills and bills of personalty. It also perpetuated the Canon law rule concerning confessions in divorce suits. (c) The Court of Chancery radically parted from the Common law courts in granting discovery before and during trial, i.e. in denying the common law privilege of a party-opponent to refuse to testify personally or to disclose any of his evidence at any time. In this important rule lay the chief characteristic contribution of Chancery to the American law of E. In a few respects, also, it adopted an admittedly different rule—as when it required the summoning of all the attesting witnesses to a will of land, or when it occasionally admitted a deposition without cross-examination. (d) Finally, there were a few variant rules often spoken of as rules of E., but really rules of procedure or of substantive law—as when in Chancery parol E. was admitted to reform a deed.

Reverting to common law rules of E.: the rules of admissibility are in general the same for the trial of civil and of criminal cases. It is true that certain rules of admissibility are applicable in criminal cases only—such as the rule of corroboration in perjury; but this is because the issues thereby evidenced arise in criminal cases only; also certain rules are modified or created for certain kinds of criminal issues, such, e.g. as the rules for admitting and corroborating an accused's confession, the rule for bigamous marriage, and the rule for a party's character; but these are few and are due to special considerations affecting a particular issue or a particular sort of evidence. When E. is offered to a judge in establishing the grounds of a motion and heard ex parte only, the usual system of rules of E. is not applied, partly because there is no opponent to invoke them, partly because the judge's determination is usually discretionary, and partly because it is seldom final. Generally, in a case of conflict of laws, the Courts will not look to any foreign law for the rules of admissibility and this general principle has received uniform recognition in U.S.A. as well as in Eng. But in the case of a conflict of Federal and State laws of the U.S.A., the application of this principle is: (1) that in the Federal Courts their own rules of E. would ordinarily have prevailed, for Federal jurisdictions rest on a sovereignty separate from that of the States. Legislation has, however, had effect as follows (i.) In Chancery proceedings (since the Statute of 1862), the local State rules are applicable to the 'competency' of witnesses. This

provision, however, is ignored or narrowly construed in the Federal decisions. (ii.) In Admiralty proceedings the Federal Courts originally had their own rules of E., but the Statute of 1862 directs the adoption of the local State rules. (iii.) Common law trials, being expressly named in the Statute of 1789, were from the beginning subject to the rule; so that in the Federal Courts a Federal statute prevails over the State rule upon the same subject, but in the absence of a Federal statute the State rule is followed. But criminal cases are held not to be included under the term 'trials at common law,' in consequence of which irregular construction the Federal rules for criminal trials are determinable by an artificial test which, though reformed in the past two decades, is still somewhat obscure and complicated. (2) In the State Courts the legislation of each jurisdiction is supreme, except so far as limited by the Federal Constitution.

The rules of E. which have been expressly sanctioned by the various constitutions are comparatively few. They include usually the privilege against self-crimination, with occasional limitations of its scope; the accused's right to confrontation or cross-examination of witnesses; the rule for two witnesses in treason; the accused's right to process for compelling the attendance of witnesses; and the right of testifying without regard to defects of theological belief. Apart from these rules, however, the Legislature has the power to alter or create any rule of E. (Consult Wigmore on Evidence, 1904–8).

**Evil.** A general definition of this term might be that of frustrated desire, or, one of the causes of frustrated desire, since if a being had no aspirations or wishes, nothing could be an E. It is the existence of desires of a wrong nature that cause E. The existence of E. is one of the everlasting problems both of theology and philosophy—how to account for it, and what to infer from it: and in accordance with the significance attached to it, philosophy inclines to an optimistic or pessimistic view of the world, or, further, an attempt to compromise between the two. The last theory would explain E. as being due to the presence of some definite E. principle warring against the triumph of good, and is thus of a dualistic character. J. S. Mill, in his Essays on Religion, regards this as a plausible explanation of the mixture of good and E. in the world. The difficulty of explaining E. is theological rather than scientific, it being often stated that for science there is no E. in the universe. The teachings of Freud and the psychoanalysts on the origin of the 'sense of guilt' are of interest in this connection.

**Evil Eye.** From the earliest times there has existed the superstition that certain people possess the power of injuring, bewitching, and even killing by a glance from the eye; hence the expression Evil Eye. Children and young people were supposed to be particularly susceptible, and in the East any unexpected calamity befalling a child was accounted for by its having been 'overlooked.' The glance of a person suffering from any physical calamity, such as a cast in the eye or a squint, is regarded as particularly dangerous. The power was supposed to be involuntary in many cases and not cultivated with evil intent. Few of the old classic writers fail to refer to it, and the wearing of amulets or charms against it was universal. Envy was supposed by many to be the impulse of the E. E., and it was therefore looked upon as unfortunate to have one's possessions praised unduly, the prosperous in particular having reason to fear it. The power of the E. E. over animals as well as children was dreaded, and in the Scottish Highlands as late as the eighteenth century the belief as affecting cattle was universal. It is still feared for horses in India, China, and Turkey.

**Evil-Merodach, Avel, or Amel-Marduk** (' man of Marduk '), King of Babylon (c. 561–559 B.C.), son and successor of Nebuchadnezzar. He released Jehoiachin, King of Judah, from prison in the thirty-seventh year of his captivity (see 2 Kings xxv, 27). He was killed in a rebellion led by his brother-in-law, Neriglissar (Nergalsharezer), who seized the crown in his stead. Berosus (third century B.C.) speaks of him as an arbitrary and unwise ruler.

**Evolute,** see CURVE.

**Evolution** (Lat. *evolutio*, an unrolling), literally, the process of opening out, or unfolding what is wrapped up. In biology it is applied to the unfolding of successive phases of development in the growth of animal and vegetable organisms. Spencer's definition is as follows : ' E. is an integration of matter and concomitant dissipation of motion; during which the matter passes from an indefinite, incoherent homogeneity to a definite, coherent heterogeneity, and during which the retained motion undergoes a parallel transformation' (*First Principles*, pt. ii. chap. xvii.). The theory of E., first started by C. Bonnet in 1762, is the hypothesis that the germ (instead of being

brought into existence by the process of fecundation) is developed from a pre-existing form which contains the rudiments of all parts of the future organism. This theory (also called the theory of Preformation) is directly opposed to that of 'epigenesis.' This latter view, which originated with Aristotle, was supported in the eighteenth century by C. F. Wolff, who believed that development came about through a series of new formations and transformations, and 'epigenesis' entirely superseded the old evolutionist theories of Bonnet, until they were revived in a more refined form in the 'germ-plasm' theory of Weismann. It is shown

A. RUSSEL WALLACE

that the ovum cannot be entirely undifferentiated, as parts of the adult organism may be traced back to corresponding parts in the embryo. E., however, in this sense is only a branch of embryology (*q.v.*). The word is more generally applied to the development of matter from its simple unorganised condition—or even from the electron-systems called atoms from which matter itself evolved—to the present structure of the physical universe. This is called Inorganic E. and its main direction is towards the 'degradation' of energy, for in every transformation of inorganic matter some energy is wasted. Living matter is a more complex form of inorganic matter, and the living may be said to have originated from the non-living. Setting aside the possibility of spontaneous generation, matter gradually assumed the properties of living matter through the medium of colloidal compounds of carbon which form the proteid, common only to plant and animal life. Organic E. traces the development of simple unicellular forms of protoplasm, called protista by Haeckel (*q.v.*), to more complex multicellular forms, from aquatic forms to terrestrial, from invertebrates to vertebrates, and from mammals to man (*see* BIOLOGY). The theory of E. is especially associated with the name of Charles Darwin (*see* DARWINISM), but it had been foreshadowed by Aristotle among the Gks., and by Linnæus and Buffon, Erasmus Darwin and Lamarck in the eighteenth and nineteenth centuries. A group of Catholic Darwinists also appeal to St. Augustine's teaching of "rationes seminales." Apart from the fact of E., various theories as to its method have been propounded—the theory of descent by Lamarck and that of natural selection by Darwin and Russel Wallace. In addition, there is the theory of orthogenesis that evolutionary change follows definite and predetermined directions, and also Cope's theory of kinetogenesis or 'mechanical genesis.' In so far as Orthogenic E. tends towards the development of the 'highest' type, it has not been a straight ladder-like process, but one of slow experiment and frustration, as is shown by the study of palæontology. In fact, E. does not show any tendency to produce a high type, only a number of types, and it is only to the E. of Mind that Orthogenesis in the sense of evolving 'upwards' can be applied strictly. We must assume, however, that something of the same nature as Mind is inherent in all living organisms, but in the course of E. new properties arise. Such E. Bergson calls 'creative' and Lloyd-Morgan 'emergent.' It *must* be borne in mind that E. as a theory cannot adequately explain the cause of such emergences; it only professes to show their relation to preceding and succeeding emergences. Before the emergence of Mind in man E. was operated by the blind purpose of adapting types to their environment and of insuring the survival of those best adapted, but with the beginning of what is called the 'psychozoic period' Mind became dominant, and, with Mind, values, and subsequently ethical values, came into being. Man is the agent of a self-conscious E., which, as Huxley points out in *Evolution and Ethics*, is at variance with the non-moral cosmic process from which he himself has evolved. We may hold, however, that a self-conscious ethical E. will be the central fact of future development. Whereas before Mind the direction of E. was decided by environment, Mind enables man to control this and, in the words of L. T. Hobhouse, 'to grasp the conditions of its development that it may master and make use of them in its further growth.'

BIBLIOGRAPHY.—C. Darwin, *On the Origin of Species*, 1859; *The Descent of Man*, 1871; St. G. Mivart, *On the Genesis of Species*, 1871; E. Haeckel, *The History of Creation*, 1876, also *The Evolution of Man*, 1905; H. Spencer, *Factors of Organic Evolution*, 1887, also *First Principles*, 1900; G. J. Romanes, *Mental Evolution in Man*, 1888, also *Darwin and after Darwin*, 1892; A. R. Wallace, *Darwinism*, 1889; A. Weismann, *The Germ-Plasm*, 1889, also *The Evolution Theory*, 1904; Geddes and Thompson, *Evolution of Sex*, 1889; G. H. Eimer, *Organic Evolution*, 1890; T. H. Huxley, *Evolution and Ethics*, 1893, also *Collected Essays*, 1894; W. Bateson, *Materials for the Study of Variation*, 1894; E. D. Cope, *Primary Factors of Organic Evolution*, 1896; L. T. Hobhouse, *Mind in Evolution*, 1901, also *Morals in Evolution*, 1906, *Development and Purpose*, 1913; E. Westermarck, *The Origin and Development of the Moral Ideas*, 1917; H. Bergson, *Creative Evolution*, 1911; R. S. Lull, *Organic Evolution*, 1917; J. S. Huxley, *Essays of a Biologist*, 1923; C. Lloyd-Morgan, *Emergent Evolution*, 1923; A. Dendy, *Outlines of Evolutionary Biology*, 1923; E. S. Goodrich, *Living Organisms*, 1924.

**Evolutions, Military,** the movements by which bodies of troops are enabled to change the position, order, and direction of their primary formation. Changes of front, formations of line, square, or column come under the term, and it also embraces such movements as marching, counter-marching, facing, defiling, wheeling, etc.

**Evora** (**Ebora**, or **Liberalitas Juliæ**): (1) Dist. of Portugal, extending W. from R. Guadiana and the Spanish frontier. Pop. 155,918. (2) Tn. and archiepiscopal see, cap. of above, Alemtejo prov., 70 m. from Lisbon. It has ramparts and a citadel, a fine Gothic cathedral (1186), narrow, picturesque streets and places, a theatre, library, and an archæological museum, in the building of the former Jesuit university. There are also the lyceum, archiepiscopal seminary, and orphanage. It manufactures textiles and leather and has a trade in wine. The aqueduct and ruined temple of Diana are attributed to Sertorius, who captured E. about 80 B.C. E. is bounded by the Serra d'Ossa on N. and E. Pop. 16,150.

**Evremond, Saint-, Charles Marguetel de Saint-Denis** (1613–1703), *b.* at St. Denis in Normandy, and educated at Clermont, Caen, and later at the Collège d'Harcourt in Paris. He afterwards entered the army, and fought with distinction in the Thirty Years' War, seeing much service in the Netherlands. He had to flee, however, in 1661, first to Holland and thence to Eng., where he received a cordial welcome from Charles II. and became the chief figure of the salon of the Duchess of Mazarin in London. His fame as a Fr. writer and wit is notably illustrated in his *Conversation avec le Père Canaye*, and *Lettre sur la Paix des Pyrénées*, and his writings include various essays and comedies and the charming letters to Ninon de l'Enclos. For good volumes of selections, *see* C. Giraud (1865) and Lescure (1881). Although he lived for the best part of forty years in Eng., E. never learned Eng., and was unacquainted with Shakespeare. He was buried in Westminster Abbey. E. figures in Dickens's *Tale of Two Cities* under the assumed name of Charles Darnay.

**Evreux,** a tn. in France, cap. of the dept. of Eure. The cathedral (eleventh century) is its most interesting building. The church of St. Taurin is noted for its belfry, 144 ft. high. It manufs. hosiery and textiles, and has iron and copper works. Pop. 18,840.

**Ewald, Georg Heinrich August von** (1803–75), a famous Ger. Orientalist and biblical critic of Göttingen. He was professor of philosophy and Oriental languages at Göttingen, 1827–37; professor of theology at Tübingen, 1838–48; and again at Göttingen, 1848–67. He lost his position for a time for political reasons, both in 1837 and 1867. His first book on *Genesis* appeared in 1823. E.'s greatest work was *Geschichte des Volkes Israel*, 1843–59, translated into Eng., 1867–86. Other works are a *Hebrew Grammar*, 1827–35; *Die Poetischen Bücher des alten Bundes*, 1835–9; *Die Propheten des alten Bundes*, 1840; *Alterthümer des Volkes Israel*, 1848; *Die Lehre der Bibel von Gott*, 1871–76. Many of his works have been translated into Eng. *See* Cheyne's ' Lectures ' in the *Expositor*, 1886; Davies, *Heinrich Ewald*, 1903; Renan in *Revue des Deux Mondes*, Nov. 15, 1855; Wex, *Professor Ewald als Punier gewürdigt*, 1843.

**Ewald, Johannes** (1743–81), a Danish poet, son of a pastor. In 1764 he wrote an allegorical poem entitled *Lykkens Tempel*, which was well received, but his lyrical power is best shown in the biblical drama, *Adam og Eva*, 1769, and in the lyrics *Til Sjaelen* and *Til min Molkte*. His most beautiful work, the opera *Fiskerne*, was written in 1778, containing a song called 'Kong Christian stod ved höjen Mast,' which has become the national song of Denmark.

**Ewart, James Cossar** (*b.* 1851), a Scottish zoologist, educated at Penicuik and Edinburgh. He has held numerous educational positions, becoming professor of natural history of Aberdeen in 1878, and regius professor of natural history at Edinburgh University, 1882. Started a marine station near Aberdeen in 1879, and became a member of the Fishery Board for Scotland in 1882. His works include : *The Locomotor System of the Echinoderms* (with Romanes), 1881; *On the Preservation of Fish*, 1887; *Guide to Zebras, Hybrids,* etc., 1900; *On a Prejvalsky Hybrid*, 1907; *The Development of the Horse*, 1915; *Moulting of the King Penguin*, 1917; *The Nestling Feathers of the Mallard*, 1921.

**Ewe,** a group of Negro people in W. Africa, living off the Slave Coast, in a country which they style ' Ewe-me ' (Land of the Ewe). Their family consists of five groups : the Anlo, the Krepi, the Jeji, the Dahomeyans, and the Mahi, all speaking different dialects of E. They are a pagan tribe and noted for their human sacrifices in honour of the dead.

**Ewell, Richard Stoddert (Stoddard)** (1817–72), an American soldier on the Confederate side in the Civil War. He graduated at West Point in 1840. In the Mexican War (1847) he was present at Contreras (*q.v.*) and Churubusco (*q.v.*). He helped to suppress the outbreak of the Apache Indians in 1857, and resigning his commission on the outbreak of the Civil War, 1861, served under ' Stonewall ' Jackson. E. commanded a division near Richmond (1862) and a corps of Lee's army at Gettysburg (1863). He was badly wounded at the battle of Bull Run (1861), and at Warrenton Turnpike. He was also present at Winchester, the Wilderness, and Spottsylvania Court-house (1864). Captured by Sheridan at Sailor's Creek, near Appomattox R. in 1865, he lived in retirement after the war.

**Ewing, Sir James Alfred,** Scottish civil engineer, *b.* March 27, 1855, at Dundee ; in 1881 he pointed out the phenomenon of *hysteresis*, or the lagging of magnetic effects behind their causes. He was professor of mechanical engineering at the Imperial University, Tokyo, Japan, 1878–83 ; at Dundee University College, 1883–90 ; at Cambridge University, 1890–1903—Rede lecturer there, 1904. He was director of naval education, 1903–16 ; a member of the Ordnance Research Board, 1906–8. Made K.C.B., 1911. During the Great War he was in charge of the cipher department of the Admiralty. He was awarded the Albert medal, 1929. His publications include: *Treatise on Earthquake Measurement*, 1883; *Magnetic Induction in Iron and other Metals*, 1891; *The Steam Engine and other Heat Engines*, 1894; *The Strength of Materials*, 1899; *The Mechanical Production of Cold*, 1908; *Thermodynamics for Engineers*, 1920; *The Physicist in Engineering Practice*, 1923.

**Ewing, Juliana Horatia Orr** (1841–85), an Eng. writer for young people, *b.* in Yorkshire, daughter of Margaret Gatty, author of *Parables of Nature*, to whose publication, *Aunt Judy's Magazine*, she largely contributed. She married Major E. in 1867, and to this connection may be attributed her interest in soldiers, as exemplified in many of her tales. Amongst her delightful stories of child-life may be mentioned: *The Brownies*, *Jan of the Windmill*, *Mrs. Over-the-Way's Remembrances*, *Old-fashioned Fairy Tales*, *Our Garden*, *A Soldier's Children*, *The Land of Lost Toys*, etc. Her biography was published by her sister in 1885.

**Ewing, Thomas** (1789–1871), an American politician. He supported Harrison for the presidency, 1840, becoming Secretary to the Treasury, 1841, of the Interior, 1849–50. E. strongly advocated the passing of a Bill for a national bank, vetoed by Tyler. He was a delegate to the Washington Peace Congress, 1861, but throughout the Civil War upheld the Lincoln administration.

**Examination**, in evidence, denotes the interrogation upon oath of witnesses. E.-in-chief means the interrogation of one's own witnesses; cross-examination, that of the opposing witnesses; and re-examination, that of one's own witnesses after they have been cross-examined. In E.-in-chief counsel is not entitled to put leading questions, that is to say, questions which suggest the answer expected. In cross-examination there is no such limitation, or, indeed, any other limitation than that imposed by the discretion of counsel himself or the presiding judge. Questions in re-examinations can only be put upon matters arising out of the cross-examination; the object of re-examination is to rehabilitate a witness whose testimony has been shaken in cross-examination, but leading questions may not be put any more than in E.-in-chief. On application to a judge in chambers, leave may be obtained to examine witnesses abroad, by the process called taking evidence on commission. *See also* EVIDENCE.

**Examinations.** Educational Es. as now held have evolved from those of the mediæval universities. Since the function of the universities then was only to teach, their tests were directed towards ascertaining fitness to lecture —successful candidates obtaining the Doctor's or Master's degree. Among the earliest university tests of which we know details were those held at Bologna in the thirteenth and fourteenth centuries, which consisted of a private *viva voce* E. and a public 'conventus' or delivery of a speech and maintenance of a thesis against opponents. The same principle obtained in the rather more complicated system in vogue at Paris. In both cases the questions included both 'set books' and 'unseens,' and heavy fees were required of the candidates, who were placed in order of merit. The Bachelor's degree, which of course preceded the Doctor's, was sometimes awarded without E. on the completion of a course of study, and what test was prescribed in other cases was usually more or less formal. Written answers to set questions, and practical, *i.e.* other than oral tests, in subjects such as medicine, were later innovations, while the competitive element and the number of subjects required for E. have also largely increased in the course of years. But on the whole the present system of university education is a recognisable development of the mediæval system, with the difference that the Bachelor's degree has become more important. Thus at Oxford the stages are Responsions or 'Smalls,' Moderations, and Finals (Pass and Honours) for B.A., three years, after which M.A. is awarded on payment of a fee without E. At Cambridge they are the Previous E. of 'Little-Go,' and the Tripos E., in two parts. London has a Matriculation, an Intermediate, and a Final E. for the Bachelor's degree, and it and other modern universities have largely increased the number of 'faculties' in which degrees are awarded. Numerous other classes of educational E. are now in vogue. Open competition is usually adopted for civil service and other public appointments, while numerous tests are held by various professional and technical bodies in different branches of knowledge. E. are also recognised to have a distinct educational value, and are largely used in schools. The question of the actual value of E., especially those conducted on a competitive basis, for getting the best man for the position or honour, is a very vexed one, involving as it does the fact that the nervous strain of such tests has an adverse influence upon many people. The standard of marking to be adopted is also a point of considerable difficulty, since it is obviously unfair to expect the same percentage on a memory as on a capacity test.

*Examinations (U.S.A.).* Excepting as a means of entry to the higher professions, Es. are regarded rather differently in America from what they are in Great Britain. Entry into most of the universities has depended more on evidence of reasonably sound preparation in a good grounding school than upon any set tests. But in some cases this method is being modified. The American mind attaches importance to gradu ation, for which an examination is a usual condition, but in many cases the diploma gained is rather evidence that the student has been an attentive and satisfactory scholar than that a severe test has been passed. In America, examinations of a semi-psychological nature are becoming increasingly popular, especially for entry into business houses and for selecting men and women for promotion. While many of these tests are exceedingly clever and very ably conceived, they often appeal rather to the swift superficial mind than to the slower and more profound. As a critic remarked of a selected set of test papers, ' A city newsboy would certainly pass : but a banker would be plucked.' It is probable, however, that for certain commercial purposes such tests may be useful in eliciting information about a candidate that a set E. would miss. In these tests a candidate may be given a purposely faulty picture and be asked to point out the mistakes. He may be asked to make a sentence from a number of jumbled words, and to find the natural opposites in a group of related ideas. This kind of E. is also used in schools as part of the educational course rather than as the test of knowledge at the end of a term. *See* C. Russell's *Class Room Tests;* B. D. Wood's *Measurements in Higher Education;* D. A. Laird's *Psychology of Selecting Men;* H. A. Toops' *Test for Vocational Guidance of Children.*

**Examiner of Stage Plays,** *see* CENSORSHIP OF THE DRAMA.

**Exanthema** (a blossoming out), fever accompanied by an eruption. The commonest are : Measles, German Measles, Smallpox, Chickenpox, Typhus, Typhoid, Scarlatina, and Erysipelas. In most countries these are compulsory notifiable diseases.

**Exarch,** a word of Gk. derivation, signifying chief person, or leader. In the Rom. empire the viceroy of the Byzantine emperor in Italy bore this title, and it has been conferred at different times on governors and chief officers, both in secular and ecclesiastical matters. In the Christian church E. was originally a title of the bishops, but afterwards came to be applied to a primate only. The spiritual head of the modern Bulgarian church bears the title of E.

**Excalibur,** the mystic sword of the legendary King Arthur, which, according to the promise of Merlin, he received from the Lady of the Lake. At his death it was hurled into the lake by Sir Bedivere, where it was received by a hand which rose from the waters.

**Excambion,** in Scots law, the term applied to the exchange of heritable subjects. Writing is not essential to the legality of an E., word of mouth, supported by subsequent possessions, being accepted in a Scots court of law.

**Excavation,** in an engineering sense, is an open cutting of greater or less dimensions, as opposed to a tunnel, which is roofed in. The various types of machines that have been invented to accelerate and facilitate E. are known as excavators. These machines, which are sometimes known as ' steam navvies,' combine the properties of a digger and a crane, and are very useful in dock works and for cutting canals. The kind that generally comes into operation first has the appearance of an ordinary steam crane, save that it is mounted on wheels and rails. It is fitted with an iron bucket or scoop with a heavy handle to which a second chain is fastened. The machine that is used to widen the cutting made by the other class is stationed on a temporary line of rails a few feet from the edge of the cutting. The jib of the machine is lowered until the row of buckets cut into the earth ; they then scrape up the side of the bank and passing over the excavator empty themselves into waggons beyond. The machine and the waggons which receive the excavated material are moved along together. Another class of excavator is known as the ' ladder excavator '; this comprises a ladder pivoted at the upper end which can be raised or dropped at the lower end to any required angle. The ladder is constructed of two channel irons braced together, a trolley running in the middle and forming the back of the bucket. The resistance of the excavated material is met directly by a chain which is attached to the bucket. A small independent engine controls the movements of the ladder. The operation of filling, emptying, and lowering a bucket of half a cubic yard capacity takes about forty seconds. Generally speaking, the first type of excavator is capable of more varieties of work, but the second is more powerful. The most economic method of working is for double track roads for waggons to be cut on the flank, a central gullet having first been cut for the machine's own passage. These machines are a modification of the dredgers which are used so extensively for dock works, etc.; in America they are called 'dredgers,' as are the other variety, a practice which is confusing. 'Grabs' are sometimes called 'excavators,' but this use is illegitimate, as grabs can work in both water and on land, and the term 'excavator' is properly applied only to land machines.

**Excellency,** a title of honour, now borne in Great Britain by the viceroy of India, the lord-lieutenant of Ireland, the governors of colonies, and ambassadors.

**Excelsior Springs,** a city of Clay co., Missouri, U.S.A., 939 ft. high, the most popular spa in the Middle West, with 200,000 visitors annually and twenty mineral springs, and an annual fox hunt. Pop. 4565.

**Excentric,** *see* ECCENTRIC.

**Excess Profits Duty.** A special war tax imposed in 1915, which was not ultimately repealed until 1921. Previous profits over a series of years were taken as a basis, and the gov. claimed from 40 to 80 per cent. of the amounts made over and above this allowance. The tax had certain simple advantages during the years that private firms were manufacturing munitions, for though there were checks upon the charges such firms might make, in case of overcharge four-fifths of the amount thus gained naturally returned to the public Exchequer. Some of the extra profit of ordinary traders during this time resulted from rises in the values of stocks, and this reacted against them when prices fell, as the amounts that should have been a reserve for this loss had been swept away in taxation, and under the three-years average system the trader had no adequate means of making good his deficiencies.

**Exchange** (Fr. *changer*; It. *cangiare, cambiare, cambire*, to barter or exchange), a term applied to many transactions and to the circumstances connected with them, all of which have, however, the basal idea of the giving of one thing—material, labour, or rights—for another. The *Exchange of Lands*, in law, is a mutual or reciprocal grant of equal interests in land, the one in consideration of the other, as a grant of a fee simple in return for a fee simple. Facilities for E. by parties under disability or tenants for life are now provided under the Inclosure Acts and the Settled Land Acts. In ecclesiastical procedure, the *Exchange of Livings* is conditioned by the consent of the bishops and patrons of both the benefices concerned. It is effected by resignation, and no monetary compensation for inequality in the value of the livings may be offered or accepted. *Exchange in Commerce* is used in various senses of the giving or receiving of money or of one currency in return for an equivalent sum in another currency (*see* EXCHANGES, FOREIGN); the giving or receiving of money in one place for a bill providing the payment of an equivalent sum in another place; the rate at which this documentary transfer of money may be made, etc. *The Exchange* is applied to the assemblage of merchants, bankers, and brokers for the transaction of business in commodities, stocks, bonds, bills, etc., and also to the place in which they meet for such purpose, *e.g.* the Royal E. in London, the Bourse in Paris, and the Stock E. in New York. A *Deed of Exchange* is a legal document recording the transfer of lands, etc., and is provided for by the Real Property Act of 1845.

**Exchange, Bill of,** *see* BILL OF EXCHANGE.

**Exchanges, Foreign,** the term applied to the settlement of the balance of indebtedness arising out of the carrying on of trade between different countries. This settlement involves much complicated business, since the balances are continually changing both in amount and direction, and, in order to effect the remittance of money in the most economical manner, it is necessary to ascertain the relative values of the currencies of many different countries. The basic theory of exchange is that only the balance into which the financial transactions resolve themselves shall be liquidated, this being done when possible by a transfer of credit, or, failing that, of gold. The subject of F. E. has an important bearing upon the choice of a monetary system, since if, in a given case, this is based upon an enforced depreciated currency, the exchange operations of that country with others are bound to be prejudicially affected. F. E. is at its simplest when 'at par,' *i.e.* when a sum of currency in one country is able to buy a bill for a sum of currency in another country, the two sums being equivalent to the same amount of bullion of a given standard. The discharge of international liabilities may be performed in three ways : (1) By means of the actual remittance of bullion or cash in coin. This method is little used owing to its costliness, since the expense of conveyance and the premium for insurance materially increase the amount of the remittance. (2) By means of the remittance of international securities, *i.e.* certain well-known government bonds and other securities or stocks and shares, the certificates of which are accepted in payment of international debts. This method is also expensive since brokerage charges have to be added to the cost, and the margin between the buying and selling price is also a loss. (3) By the remittance of bills of exchange. This is the cheapest and easiest method of F. E. and consequently the most common. These bills, which may be of various currencies, need not be drawn upon the country to which they are remitted, *e.g.* it may be most profitable to effect a remittance from London to Paris by means of a Berlin bill drawn upon Paris. The principle upon which this business is transacted may be roughly illustrated thus : A, a merchant in London, has to make a remittance to Paris to a merchant, B, in that city. B, in order to save A the risk and expense of transmitting cash, draws a bill for the amount due upon him. B sells this bill to C, another Paris merchant, who sends it in place of cash to settle his account with D, in Eng. At the expiry of the time the bill has to run, D takes it to A, and receives cash in exchange for it, while the possession of the bill marks A's discharge from B's debt. The bills, which are any first-class ones on the market, are commonly drawn at three months' date.

F. E. and the market price of bills of exchange are affected by two main causes, viz., the relative indebtedness of the two countries involved, and the rate of discount ruling in each. The first cause is dependent upon the law of supply and demand, since if one country is considerably in debt to the other, the price of bills upon the creditor rises in the debtor's market owing to the competition of merchants who are trying to buy bills to remit, while in the creditor's market the absence of demand for bills upon the debtor tends to lower their price. The second factor is really the value or price of money in the two countries, since a high rate of interest in one country will tend to make foreign merchants buy bills upon it, and the increasing demand again leads to an increase in price. When the price of bills upon a country goes beyond a certain height, known as the specie, or gold point, *i.e.* the point at which the buyer pays to the seller a premium equal to the amount of the cost of transport, gold begins to flow in, as the debtor then prefers to make payments in cash. The turning of F. E. in favour of a country is marked by the approach of this point. The inverse position is produced by the fall of the price below par. So far as F. E. in England are concerned, where the rates of exchange are quoted in foreign money, high rates are favourable to England ; but when the rates are quoted in English money, low rates are in England's favour. The Great War played havoc with the ratio of F. E. This was only natural when it is realised that the trade and commerce of the whole world were affected, and that the greatest commercial nations in the globe were active belligerents. The natural flow of trade and consequently of bills of exchange between the nations was severely impeded, and in the case of the enemy countries stopped altogether. The inflation of the currencies of Germany and Austria by means of the free use of the printing press contributed to the fact that the currencies of these countries had for some time not even an external nominal value. With regard to internal value, it is worthy of record that when the new Reichsbank was formed in Germany, it called in all its previous circulation and converted it into Reichsmarks at the rate of one trillion Marks for one Reichsmark. The following is a typical daily report of the F. E. market. The figures quoted are the numbers of dollars, francs, pesetas, reichsmarks, etc., that will be exchanged against the pound sterling on the particular day.

| | |
|---|---|
| New York | $4{\cdot}85\tfrac{15}{32}$—$4{\cdot}85\tfrac{17}{32}$ |
| Montreal | $4{\cdot}86\tfrac{1}{2}$—$4{\cdot}86\tfrac{5}{8}$ |
| Paris | 123·79—123·84 |
| Brussels | 34·83—34·85 |
| Berlin | 20·42—20·43 |
| Oslo | $18{\cdot}16\tfrac{3}{8}$—$18{\cdot}16\tfrac{5}{8}$ |
| Stockholm | 18·13—18·14 |
| Copenhagen | $18{\cdot}16\tfrac{5}{8}$—$18{\cdot}16\tfrac{7}{8}$ |
| Switzerland | 25·06—25·07 |
| Amsterdam | $12{\cdot}06\tfrac{5}{8}$—$12{\cdot}06\tfrac{3}{4}$ |
| Finland | 192·85—193·00 |
| Italy | 92·70—92·75 |
| Madrid | 46·95—47·05 |
| Lisbon | 108·22—108·26 |
| Rio T. T. | $4\tfrac{19}{32}$—$4\tfrac{21}{32}$d |
| Valparaiso 90 days | 39 95 |
| Calcutta T. T. | $1/5\tfrac{3}{4}$—$1/5\tfrac{25}{32}$d |
| Yokohama | $2/0\tfrac{7}{16}$—$2/0\tfrac{15}{32}$d |
| Buenos Aires | $33\tfrac{5}{16}$—$33\tfrac{7}{16}$d |
| Vienna | 34·51—34·54 |
| Prague | 163·94—163·97 |
| Warsaw | 43·31—43·35 |
| Greece | 375·00—375·15 |
| Sofia | 668—673 |
| Rumania | 818—$818\tfrac{1}{2}$ |
| Constantinople | 1,025 |
| Hungary | 27·78—27·81 |
| Riga | 25·17—25·27 |
| Estonia | 18·21—18·26 |

**Exchequer** (Norman-Fr. *eschequier*). The name of the king's court of revenue is taken from the fact that in early times the accounts were reckoned upon a chequered cloth, re-sembling a large chess-board, round which the officers sat. The English and French words are allied to the Latin root *scac*, which appears in *scaccum*, a chess-board, and *scac-carium*, the Court of E., and also the chequered cloth used there. It appears that the sums of money received by the treasurer were scored upon the squares of this cloth with counters, the process being suggestive of a game of chess. The name only began to be used about the time of Henry I., and previous to the use of the chequered cloth as an aid to cal-culation business was transacted by means of ' tallies,' or notched sticks.

**Exchequer, Chancellor of the,** the head of the Treasury Department, being one of the most important members of the cabinet in the British government. He must be a member of the House of Commons, and acts as the first finance minister of the crown, having the duty of preparing the annual budget, *i.e.* the estimates of revenue and expenditure, and the imposition or removal of taxes in order to meet deficit or surplus, and the management of all matters relat-ing to public money. With the excep-tion of certain times, when his place is taken by the Lord Chief Justice of the King's Bench, the Chancellor acts as one of the Lords of the Treasury. The office of C. of the E. may be held by the Prime Minister, if the latter is a member of the House of Commons, and the combined office has been held by William Pitt (1804–6), George Canning (1827), Sir Robert Peel (1834–35), and William Ewart Gladstone (1873–74 and 1880–82). The Chancellor was originally an under-treasurer, who checked the proceedings of the Lord High Treasurer. He also had important judicial functions, sitting on the ' equity side ' of the Court of Ex-chequer. These disappeared in the eighteenth century, the last C. of the E. who sat as a judge being Sir Robert Walpole, who gave a decision in this capacity in 1735.

**Exchequer Bills,** instruments of credit issued, mainly under Acts of Parliament passed *ad hoc*, by the Treasury Commissioners, for the purpose of raising money for the necessities of the Exchequer. It con-tains an engagement by the govern-ment for the repayment of the prin-cipal advanced, with interest in the meantime. The bill runs for five years, and payment may be claimed at the end of any year, while interest, the rate of which is fixed at the beginning of each year, is paid half-yearly. *See* PUBLIC DEBT.

**Exchequer Bonds,** *see* PUBLIC DEBT.

**Exchequer Court,** one of the three great courts of the realm, having the functions of a court of revenue and a court of common law. In its latter capacity it is now merged in the King's Bench Division, but in its former it deals with all matters relat-ing to the revenue of the kingdom. It is connected with the Treasury, and its operations are supervised by the Audit Office.

**Excise and Customs Duties** are two forms of raising revenue by taxation of commodities. The excise duty is levied upon articles produced within the country, and includes licences for carrying on certain trades, while the customs duty is levied upon articles imported from abroad and sometimes upon articles exported. The term ' cus-tom ' dates from the conflict between the crown and parliament as to the latter's right to control taxation, it being urged that certain taxes on im-ports and exports were the preroga-tive of the crown owing to long-stand-ing custom. Customs dues were, how-ever, levied in England before the Norman Conquest, and were regulated by Magna Charta (1215). The excise duty originated during the Civil War in the year 1643. The method of levying both forms of duty is a very difficult problem. Due regard must be had to the selection of proper articles for taxation, not only from the nature of the commodity itself, but from the ease with which the duty can be levied, the avoidance of undue discouragement of industry, or of incentive to smuggling. In the British Isles the taxation is devised for revenue purposes only, but in other countries the question is com-plicated by the attempts to stimu-late home production by taxing im-ported articles. It is evident, how-ever, that the more effectively such a tax checks competition the less customs duty accrues to the revenue.

Customs duties were originally a payment for protection against possible robbery, and were levied not only upon goods entering the king-dom, but upon goods transferred from one place to another. In Scot-land the duty on imported goods was termed the great custom, that on goods entering the towns from rural districts, the small custom. In 1707 the duties were made the same as in England. The customs in Eng-land were originally farmed out, the right to levy being sold for an annual sum. The system was put an end to in 1671, and a board of commis-sioners appointed, to whom the

Excise Department (formerly under the Inland Revenue Department) was transferred on April 1, 1909. The board consists of a chairman, deputy-chairman, and three commissioners. Before the Great War it had been the British policy to reduce the number of articles on which duty was levied, and in 1913–14 these were only about twenty. To meet the necessities of war and of changes in policy during the peace, additional duties were levied. The present duties (1931) may be classified roughly under three headings: (1) Taxes on goods which are taxed for Revenue raising purposes; (2) Key Industry Duties; and (3) Taxes on goods levied for the protection of certain important industries. Within the first of these are certain commodities considered as luxuries and semi-luxuries, which yield convenient and substantial returns, such as wine, sugar, tobacco of foreign manufacture, and on such commodities as beer, spirits, and playing cards, which are subject to excise when manufactured internally. Key Industry duties are levied to maintain in peace times certain trades which are essential under war conditions. These include the manufacture of optical glasses, arc lamps, magnetos, valves, and carbon electrodes. The total revenue from this source in 1929 was £1,648,000 gross, of which over a million was the cost of collection. In the industries protected by the levy of taxes in class (3) are the manufacture of motor cars, gramophones, artificial silk and lace. During 1929, the revenue from Customs was £122,710,000 and from Excise £129,460,000. The largest amounts were from beer (£71,254,674) spirits (£36,651,631), entertainments (£6,695,847), sugar (£11,753,395), tobacco (£62,909,000), and wine (£5,947,899).

**Excitants,** see STIMULANTS.

**Exclusion Bill** (1679–80), a measure brought forward by Shaftesbury to prevent the Duke of York (afterwards James II.) from coming to the throne, owing to his adherence to the Rom. Catholic faith. It was three times passed by the Commons, but on each occasion Charles II. dissolved parliament.

**Excommunication** (Lat. *ex,* out of, from ; *communis,* common), exclusion by formal sentence of offenders from the rights and privileges of the religious community to which they belong. The history of the practice of E. may be traced through pagan analogues, Hebrew customs, primitive Christian practice, mediæval and monastic usage, and modern survivals in existing Christian churches. That

the Christian church has always laid claim to the powers of E. is shown by such early writers as Irenæus, Cyprian, Basil, Ambrose, etc., who give proof of the existence of two degrees of E.; the first involving exclusion from the participation in eucharistic service, and the second involving ' exclusion from all church privileges.' The former was the usual punishment for light offences, the latter the penalty for graver scandals. The necessity for church discipline did not cease to be recognised at the Reformation, though its administration would seem to have passed through a period of some confusion. In some cases, the old episcopal power passed into the hands of the civil magistrate, in others it was conceded to the presbyterial courts. In the Anglican Church the right of excommunication is in the hands of the bishops, though it is never exercised. The reformers claimed the power of E., and Luther insisted on the right as inherent in the ministers of the church. Calvin, too, asserted that it was of the very essence of the ministry. At first civil disabilities followed E., but later this ceased to be the practice. In England, until 1813, persons excommunicated were debarred from bringing or maintaining actions, from serving as jurymen, or from practising as attorneys in the courts of the realm; but all these disabilities were finally removed by statute. E. censures a culprit and punishes his conduct, and by thus warning, endeavours to recalls him to salvation. Whether the power of E. rests in the church or the clergy has been an important question in the history of English and American churches. Archbishops, while exercising visitatorial jurisdiction, bishops within their sees, and heads of religious orders within their own communities possess the power to issue E. (subject to appeal to the sovereign), but the power can never be delegated to laymen. In contemporary English Free Churches the purity of the church is commonly secured by the removal of persons unsuitable for membership by a vote of the responsible authority. In the Rom. Church E. is either *ferendel sententiæ,* when the intervention of judicial process is required to attach it to a given person; or *latæ sententiæ,* when a crime carries E. with it automatically. An excommunicated person may be *tolerandus,* who is cut off from the spiritual benefits of the Church only; or *non-tolerandus,* against whom the faithful are warned. These may not participate in any Church functions or exercise any juridical or teaching office. E. in certain cases is reserved in varying degrees of stricture to the Pope.

*See* Schilling, *Der Kirchenbann nach canonischen Recht*, and Von Kober, *Der Kirchenbann.*

**Excretions,** the eliminatory products of such organs as the skin (*q.v.*), kidneys (*q.v.*), intestines (*q.v.*), etc., viz. sweat, urine, fæces, etc. *See also* RESPIRATION.

**Exe,** a riv., England, which rises in Exmoor. It flows through the counties of Somerset and Devonshire in a southerly direction, its chief tributaries being the Barle, Loman, Batham, Culm, and Creedy. Its course of 54 m. is through beautifully wooded and picturesque country. The towns passed are Dulverton, Topsham, Exeter, etc. Its estuary is navigable for 8 m., and as it is a mile in width, vessels of large size can enter. A canal connects it with Exeter.

**Execution** means the enforcement of judgments and other proceedings analogous to judgments of courts of law in civil actions. The term denotes the process by which a party is put into possession of that to which the judgment declares him to be entitled. It is generally effected by a writ directed to the sheriff or other proper officer, commanding him to seize goods or take other compulsory proceedings to carry out the judgment. In the simplest form of judgment the defendant is ordered to pay the judgment creditor *forthwith*, and the latter may at once proceed to E. Under a writ of *fi. fa.*, which is the most ordinary form of E., the sheriff is directed to ' cause to be made ' (*fieri facias*) out of the goods and chattels of the debtor the sum recovered by the judgment, together with interest at 4 per cent., and to bring the sum into court for payment to the judgment creditor. Armed with this writ the sheriff may enter the premises of the debtor and seize what property of the debtor he can find, with the exception of wearing apparel and bedding, tools and implements of trade to the maximum value of £5. He may then sell the goods seized, including leases of land, but not freehold estates of inheritance (*see* ESTATE, FEE, FEE SIMPLE, FEE TAIL), for these latter go to the heir of the debtor. Where goods seized are claimed by a third person the sheriff must take out an interpleader summons upon which an issue to try the title to the goods will be directed. For the application of a writ of elegit to enforce E. against the debtor's lands, *see* ELEGIT. In many cases the ordinary processes of the common law will not avail to enforce a judgment, *e.g.* against a share of the proceeds of land to be, but not yet sold, or against rents. In such cases the court may in its discretion appoint a receiver by way of what is called equitable E. Another mode of equitable E. is to obtain a charging order against a partnership interest. Execution against debts owing to the judgment debtor is enforced by process of attachment of the debts (*see* GARNISHEE). Other writs of E. are of *attachment* (*q.v.*), of *possession*, or to put the plaintiff into possession of land recovered in an action, and of *delivery* to enable the plaintiff to get possession of property other than land or money. E. is also used to denote the giving effect to the sentence of a court of criminal jurisdiction, and in this sense usually means the E. of sentence of death (*see* CAPITAL PUNISHMENT). For the meaning of E. in relation to deeds and wills, *see* DEED, WILL.

**Executive.** In every sovereign political society, or state, there must exist some person, group of persons, or body independent of all external control, with power to maintain the independence of the state against aggression from without and to preserve order within. Such person or body is known as the E. Non-sovereign political societies may also possess an E., but in all such cases, as *e.g.* in the case of colonies and protectorates, that E. acts under the active or latent control of the E. of some other state or suzerain power. E. powers are to be distinguished from legislative, although both may be vested in one person or group of persons. The function of a legislature is to make laws, but the functions of the E. are (1) to give those laws legal effect, and to enforce them where necessary, and (2) to determine the policy of the state in its foreign relations. In the case of an absolute and despotic monarchy, all the executive powers reside in one person who may or may not be assisted by a council of chosen advisers. In a limited constitutional monarchy, the E. power resides collectively in the crown and its responsible ministers or cabinet (*see* CABINET and CROWN). In federal states the E. powers reside in some central body composed of representatives of the various federated bodies. In the English Crown Colonies a nominated governor or governor and council wield the E. powers (*see* COLONIAL LAW, CROWN COLONIES).

It is to be observed that the interdependence of the legislature and E. of those representative governments of the present day which possess what may be termed a ' parliamentary E.' is such that the E., far from being distinct from the legislature, is, in reality, chosen from among the members of the latter, and not only appointed but dismissed by the elective portion of the legislature. In the case of those representative governments where the E. power is in an emperor and his ministers, or a president and his cabinet, the E. is not appointed by the legislature, and is therefore a ' non-parliamentary E.' Under the constitutions of England, Belgium, Italy, and the French republic there exist parliamentary Es., while examples of non-parliamentary Es. are to be found in the United States and the German empire. For an exposition of the various prerogatives of the E. in England, *see* CROWN ; and for the relationship between the E. and parliament, *see* CABINET. *See also* CONSTITUTION.

**Executor.** The person or persons to whom another person commits by his last will the carrying out of his testamentary wishes is or are his E. or Es. An E. can only be appointed by will or by codicil. But he need not be termed an E. in the will if it can be inferred from the powers and duties vested in him by the testator that he was to be E. A person appointed E. may accept or refuse office, but he will be taken to have accepted if he performs acts of authority over the estate or property from which it may reasonably be implied that he meant to accept, and similarly his refusal may be implied from his abstaining from intermeddling in the administration. The authority of an E. dates from the moment of the testator's death. The will is the only source of his title to act, but probate of the will is the only evidence of that title. Before probate an E. may validly perform any of his executorial functions, such as receiving debts or paying legacies, but he can maintain no action at law until he takes out probate. Where there are several Es. they are not bound to act jointly, and most executorial acts are valid even if done by one E. separately. The duties of an E. are to bury the deceased in a fitting manner, but without incurring unreasonable expense ; then he should prove the will and take out administration. The other duties are, within a convenient time after the testator's death, to collect the goods comprised in the estate, make an inventory of the personalty, advertise for creditors and debtors, and deal with the personal effects as directed by the will. He has a year in which to pay or transfer the legacies ; but if the solvency of the estate is beyond question, he should pay or transfer them before the end of the year, and may be sued if he does not do so. At the end of his year he must submit an account of his dealings to the proper authorities. These dealings will, in general,

be the payment of debts and legacies in the order laid down by the rules of equity. Since the Land Transfer Act, 1897, real property also vests, in the first instance, in the Es. or other personal representatives of the deceased, whether the deceased died intestate or not ; and an E. may sell the real estate if necessary for the purpose of paying debts, but where not required for debts the E. must transfer the real estate to the devisee, or, if not devised, to the heir. An E. should be careful not to mix the moneys belonging to the estate with his own, as he may be charged interest on it. Interest is charged on all moneys received by an E. and not properly applied, or which have been allowed by him to lie idle. If a stranger, *i.e.* one not constituted E. by the will, assumes the functions of an E. by intermeddling in the administration, he is called in law an E. *de son tort, i.e.* an E. of his own wrong. Such acts of intermeddling do not include the burial of the deceased, or the preservation of the goods, or payment of funeral expenses, or other acts which may appropriately be termed acts of salvage or charity. An E. *de son tort* is liable for such assets as come into his hands, and may be sued as if he were the rightful E. There is no remuneration allowed to an E. save as expressly provided for by the will.

**Executory.** In the English law of real property an E. interest is a future estate or title to land, which is said to arise of its own strength when the contingency on which it rests is fulfilled, and to put an end to prior estates or interest ; *e.g.* in an ordinary marriage settlement of land, the settlor, a day or two before the marriage, conveys land to trustees to hold for him until the marriage takes place, and after that to such other uses or trusts as may have been agreed upon between the spouses or their parents. In the law of contract, an E. consideration (*q.v.*) means a future as opposed to a present consideration, or a promise as opposed to an act.

**Exedra,** in architecture, a term applied to an open recess, such as a niche containing a seat, the space within an oriel window, or the spaces between the buttresses of a cathedral.

**Exegesis,** a term meaning exposition or explanation applied by the Gks. to the interpretation of the Holy Scriptures. Hermeneutics is the term frequently used as applying to the discovery of the meaning of the Bible, but E. is distinguished from it as more properly covering the exposition and application of Holy Scripture to faith and conduct.

In a general sense, however, the

term has now come to be applied to the science and art of the elucidation of Scripture. E. includes both the study of the text and the doctrinal bearing of same, with the conclusions that may be deduced from it. Thus, it may be seen that E. requires a wide and accurate learning as well as a certain amount of intuition of an intellectual and spiritual nature. Amongst the great exegetes may be mentioned Calvin, Origen, Meyer, and Augustine, and all of these have been distinguished for their scholarly attributes and spiritual insight. The materials for the critical study of the O.T. are scanty as compared with the New, and the difficulty of attaining definite conclusions is therefore greater. MSS., versions and quotations are the different kinds of critical materials ready to the hand, and here again the student of O.T. history is very slenderly equipped.

The two main currents discovered in the history of E. are the literal and allegorical. The tendency to seek an underlying sense in writings of venerable age come to be looked upon as authentic and weighty, if not inspired, gave rise to the allegorical method, of which the attractiveness is very great, as it gives full scope for the penetrating of original minds, and is thus more popular than the literal method. Nevertheless, the old theory of verbal inspiration is no longer held by the intelligent scholar, and the nineteenth-century exegetes were the first to establish a satisfactory critical *modus vivendi* by insisting on the human as well as the divine element in the Scriptures. The Jewish E. of the O.T. is seen in the Talmudical writings, and the Hellenic Jews were responsible for seeking to make a reconciliation by means of allegorical interpretation, between the traditions of Hebraism and the results of Gk. philosophical thought. Philo was the greatest master of this art, and he formulated the twofold teaching in the Pentateuch—the verbal and the figurative. The Alexandrian school also adopted this system, and the same influences show themselves, though to a lesser extent, in the writings of Hippolytus and Augustine. As opposed to these, the Antiochene school, represented by Theodorus, Lucian, Diodorus, and Chrysostom, shows a marked contrast. These writers aimed at a grammatical and historical criticism, which at times, however, degenerated into an unspiritual and bare interpretation. Exegetical work was practically at a standstill during the Middle Ages, except for some collections and views of the fathers; but Nicholaus of Lyra made a transition to the modern period in his *Postillæ*, emphasising the literal sense, and the humanists, as personified in Erasmus, began to make serious and systematic philological investigations. The names of contemporary exegetes are too numerous to mention, since a continuous chain has laboured at the elucidation of the Scriptures on sound scientific lines. Alford, Lightfoot, De Wette, Perowne, Hitzig, Oehler, Keil, Lagrange, etc., are among the number. For E., *see* Hatch's *Hibbert Lecture*, 1888; and Cave's *Introduction to Theology*, 1896. For fullest and latest information, also see *The Cambridge Bible for Schools and Colleges*, and the *International Critical Commentary*.

**Exelmans, Remy Joseph Isidore, Comte** (1775–1852), a marshal of France, who fought under Murat in the Spanish campaign, during which he was taken prisoner and sent to England. He escaped in 1811 and joined Napoleon's army in Russia in 1812, being made a general of division for his bravery. He was exiled from France at the fall of Napoleon, but allowed to return in 1823.

**Exempla, or Exemplar,** a short story with a moral, a kind of fable (*q.v.*).

**Exequatur,** in international law, the term applied to the document issued by the state to which a consul is accredited, confirming his appointment. This appointment has, of course, previously been made by commission or patent issued by the consul's own state. The foreign state is at liberty to decline an E., or to withdraw it when issued.

**Exeter,** the co. tn. of Devonshire, in England, 172 m. from London, a great railway centre and a principal centre of the S.W. The chief object of interest in the city is its cathedral, which most people consider unsurpassed in the beauty of architecture. The general character is Decorated (1280–1369). The massive Norman transeptal towers were opened below in the thirteenth century and the main structure subsequently transformed into the Decorated style. The most noteworthy features within are the unbroken roof, with no central tower, beautiful sculpture, minstrels' gallery, and window tracery. The library contains a famous collection of Anglo-Saxon poems and the original copy of the Domesday Book relating to Devonshire. The great bell, on which the clock strikes the hours, is said to weigh 6 tons. There are considerable remains of the old city walls, and eight or nine ancient churches, and many quaint old houses, especially in the picturesque High Street. The Guildhall has a timbered roof of 1464 and an Elizabethan portico projecting over the pavement. The Bishop's Palace contains a magnificent mantelpiece of about 1486. The fifteenth-century Tuckers' Hall was the home of the Guild of Merchant Adventurers, and the Norman House contains original Norman work. St. Nicholas Priory has a thirteenth-century kitchen and a Guest Hall. The Norman gateway of Rougemont Castle, mentioned by Shakespeare, is still almost intact. The Northernhay laid out in 1612 is said to be the oldest public park in England. University College comprises an Art Gallery and a Museum. The surrounding country is very beautiful, commanding extensive and picturesque views, and with high stretches of moorland. Its chief manufs. are flour mills, tanneries, breweries, paper mills, and iron and brass foundries. The manuf. of woollen goods was at one period very important, but has now become extinct. One member is returned to the House of Commons by E., which is probably the oldest of the ancient cities of England. It has been besieged more often than any. An historical event of importance that took place in E. was the landing of William of Orange in 1688. Pop. 59,582.

**Exeter,** a tn. of New Hampshire, U.S.A., cap. of Rockingham co., 12 m. from Portsmouth, at which many eminent men were educated, there are some fine colonial homes. It was at Exeter that the first independent state Government was formed. It contains the Phillips Exeter Academy. Pop. 4872.

**Exeter, Peerage of.** The titles Earl, Marquess, and Duke of E. have been borne by members of the families of Holand (Holland), Beaufort, Courtenay, and Cecil. The first Duke of E. was John Holand, son of Thomas (d. 1360). He was created Duke by Richard II. in 1397, and as the king's half-brother held a high position at court, but was degraded from his rank by the parliament of Henry IV. After plotting against Henry's life, he was beheaded in 1400. The second duke, Thomas Beaufort, was created in 1416. He was the youngest son of John of Gaunt by Katharine Swynford. The title expired on his death (c. 1426). In 1443 John Holand, son of the first duke, was created Duke of E. under Henry VI. His son, Henry, also held the title, but died without sons (c. 1473). He supported Henry VI. in the Wars of the Roses, and was attainted (1461). In 1525 the Earl of Devon, Henry Courtenay, was created Marquess of E., the title becoming extinct on his execution (c. 1538), though sometimes given to his son Edward. The earldom of E. was

bestowed on Thomas Cecil, second Lord Burghley, 1605, son of William (d. 1598), by James I. His direct descendants carried on the title, Henry, the tenth earl, becoming Marquess of E. in 1801. (Tennyson's *Lord Burleigh* is founded on an incident in the life of Henry, 1754–1804.) The present (fifth) marquess is a lineal descendant (William Thomas Brownlow Cecil). *See* Cockayne, *Complete Peerage*, new ed., 1910.

THOMAS CECIL, 1ST EARL OF
EXETER

**Exeter Book,** or *Codex Exoniensis,* a unique manuscript of Anglo-Saxon poetry, in the possession of the dean and chapter of Exeter Cathedral. It was presented to the library of the cathedral by Leofric, who was Bishop of Exeter, 1050–71, and probably dates from the first half of the eleventh century. It contains 246 pages of vellum, upon which, besides some legal documents, are the original of the following poems : ' Crist ' and ' Guthlac,' probably both by Cynewulf ; ' Azarias,' an independent text of the Song of Azarias in the Junian Cædmon, *Daniel ;* ' Phœnix,' probably by Cynewulf ; Cynewulf's ' Juliana ' ; ' The Wanderer,' a beautiful dramatic lyric ; ' The Gifts of Men ' ; ' The Father's Teaching ' ; ' The Seafarer,' a haunting description of the painful and yet voluntary exile of the seaman ; ' The Spirit of Men ' ; ' Widsith,' probably the oldest poem in the book ; ' The Fates of Men ' ; ' Gnomic Verses,' containing rather trite philosophy ; ' Wonders of Creation ' ; ' The Rime Song ' ; ' The Panther,' ' The Whale,' and ' The Partridge,' all three fragments of an old English ' Bestiary ' ; ' Address of the Soul to the Body'; 'Deor'; 'Riddles,' fifty in number, of which many are probably by Cynewulf; 'The Wife's Complaint'; 'The Last Judgment'; 'A Prayer'; 'The Descent into Hell'; 'Alms'; 'Pharaoh', an incomplete 'Paternoster'; a didactic fragment and some different forms of two 'Riddles'; 'The Husband's Message'; 'Ruin,' and about forty more 'Riddles.' The MS. has been described by Humphrey Wanley in his *Catalogue* (1705), and by J. J. Conybeare in 'Account of a Saxon MS.,' read 1812 and printed in *Archæologia*, 1814. It was transcribed by Robert Chambers in 1831 (Brit. Mus. Addit. MS. 9067), and first printed by Benjamin Thorpe in 1842. The poems are now printed in Grein's *Bibliothek* (vol. iii.); Pfeiffer's *Germania* (vol. xix.); and Professor Gollancz's edition for the Early English Text Society.

**Exeter College, Oxford,** founded in 1314 by Walter de Stapledon, Bishop of Exeter. Twelve scholars studying philosophy were supported at Oxford by the income of the rectory of Gwinear, Cornwall, which he had conveyed for this purpose to the dean and chapter of Exeter, Stapledon housed them in Hart Hall and Arthur Hall, in the parish of St. Peter in the E., but in 1315 removed them to buildings on the present site, known as Stapledon Hall. In 1404 Edmund Stafford, Bishop of Exeter, added two fellowships and gave the college its present name, and the endowment was further increased by Sir William Petre in 1565, and Mrs. Shiers in 1770.

**Exeter or Exon Domesday,** a part of the great survey of England ordered by William the Conqueror. The *Exeter Domesday*, which is preserved at Exeter, contains the original returns made by the twelve local jurors sent from each hundred in the counties of Wiltshire, Dorsetshire, Somersetshire, Devonshire, and Cornwall. It includes the details, omitted from the great *Domesday Book*, of the tally of live stock. It was published in 'record type' in 1816, in a supplementary volume to the government reprint of *Domesday Book*. See DOMESDAY BOOK.

**Exeter Hall,** a large building which formerly stood on the N. side of the Strand, London, originally built in 1831 as a proprietary establishment to be used for the meetings of religious and charitable societies. It was purchased by the Young Men's Christian Association in 1880.

**Exhibit,** in law, a document shown to a witness while giving evidence and sworn to by him, or shown to a deponent while being sworn previous to making an affidavit in which it is referred to.

**Exhibitions.** This term has come to be applied to the display of goods to the public for promoting trade and denotes in a general sense a public show. The first E. of any national importance was that credited to the Marquis d'Avèze at Paris in 1798, consisting of a collective display of the art factories of France, including those of Sèvres and the Gobelins. In 1801, a second E. of the same kind was held, and a third of a greatly improved kind in 1803. A fourth was held in 1806 and attracted 1422 exhibitors. This concluded the number of E. held in France till after the fall of the empire ; but a fifth was held in Louis XVIII.'s reign, and others at various intervals. The impetus given by the Paris display was felt all over Europe, and E. began to be held in all the chief cities between 1820 and 1850, including the United Kingdom and Ireland. These E., however, were all of a smaller nature—more or less confined to the products of the particular country in which they took place ; and the first great International E., promoted by the Society of Arts, was held in London in Hyde Park, where a site was obtained for the erection of the Crystal Palace, designed by Sir Joseph Paxton, at a cost of £193,168, under the presidency of Prince Albert. This E. was opened by Queen Victoria in 1851. The building was composed entirely of glass and iron, and was afterwards removed to Sydenham, where it stands at the present day. It remained open for over five months, and attracted 6,170,000 people, the money drawn amounting to £505,000, of which sum £150,000 was profit, and was invested in the purchase of an estate at S. Kensington on which numerous institutions have been placed. In 1862 the second great International E. was held in London, in a building at S. Kensington, but the outlay of this one was so great that the receipts did not cover it, and it resulted in a deficit of about £10,000.

Vienna held an international E. in 1863, but was surpassed by the Paris E. of 1878, which made an advance in magnificence and size upon all previous displays. Paris again excelled all its predecessors from this point of view in 1889 with its Universal E., the Eiffel Tower being one of its chief attractions, and again in 1905 the Paris E. was on a scale vast enough to mark worthily the completion of the century, nearly every civilised nation in the world being represented.

In later years, important Es. have been held in Glasgow, New York, and St. Louis, and the Franco-British E.

held at Shepherd's Bush in London in 1908 was a great success. In the artistic taste and magnificence of the buildings and the interest of their exhibits, this E. may be said to have vied with, if not gone beyond, the great Paris E.

The Japanese-British E. was held in the same place in 1910, and also proved a success. An E. was also held at Brussels in the same year; but the success of this was unfortunately marred by a large fire, in which the British section especially suffered.

the presidency of the Prince of Wales, and opened by the King on April 23, 1924. It covered a vast area of 216 acs., and the various buildings housed treasures amounting in value to many millions of pounds. Among the royal visitors were the King of Denmark, the Kings and Queens of Italy and Rumania. There was an average attendance of over 3,000,000 people during each of the summer months, and the closing of the E. was postponed until 1925. The most notable buildings were the Palaces of Art, Industry, and Engineering, the

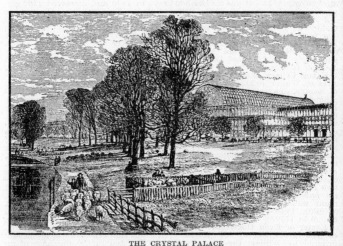

THE CRYSTAL PALACE

in its original position in Hyde Park for the Great Exhibition of 1851

Practically the whole year round there is held somewhere in London an exhibition of a specialised nature, e.g. there are Rose, Chrysanthemum, and other Shows at the Horticultural Hall, Cattle, Horse and Dog Shows at the Agricultural Hall—where also may be seen the annual Drapers' Exhibition, in addition to bakery, confectionery, brewery and other trade exhibitions. Olympia is the setting for many interesting exhibitions organised by the great London dailies, as well as for motor shows, advertising exhibitions, international horse shows, and the magnificent spectacle of the Royal Tournament. During the Christmas holidays a Schoolboys' Exhibition is held in London. But the greatest E. Great Britain ever undertook was the British Empire Exhibition held at Wembley, under

last-named being six times the size of Trafalgar Square. In this was a display of electrical, marine, transport, motor, and other engineering appliances, with rolling-stock from the great railways; here a power station generated and supplied all the electric light and power used throughout the Exhibition. Vast and beautiful Pavilions represented the Dominions and Colonies—Australia, Burma, Canada, Ceylon, India, East, West, and South Africa—as well as the Home Government. Many visitors were attracted by the model coal-mine, cigarette factory, printing works, and other displays, while the Amusement Park and the Tattoo were immensely popular; in the first six months the Queen's Doll's House gained £20,000 for charity. In 1929 Spain, considered a backward country, had two Es., one at Barcelona and the other at Seville. The Barcelona E. was notable for the most beautiful electrically illuminated fountains the world ever saw.

The British Empire Exhibition held in Buenos Aires in 1931 showed a very modern tendency in its display of films, featuring many phases of industry. In 1931, from May to Nov., the French held an exceedingly beautiful colonial Exposition at Paris to show the progress of the French colonial empire. One of the many notable buildings was a reproduction of the famous temple of Ang-Kor.

*United States.*—There have been many notable E. in U.S.A. commercial history. In 1876 was held at Fairmount Park, Philadelphia, the Centennial E. to celebrate the 100th anniversary of American independence. The visitors numbered nearly 10,000,000, and the total receipts amounted to about £800,000. The most remarkable feature was the display of U.S. machinery. A World's Industrial Fair was held at New Orleans in 1884–85, but it did not meet with the same degree of success as the Centennial E. Then followed the great Chicago E. of 1893, held at Jackson Park, Lake Michigan, to celebrate the 400th anniversary of the discovery of America. A company with a capital of £2,000,000 undertook the financial arrangements, and the central government at Washington allotted large sums for the purposes of foreign exhibits. The total receipts from admissions were £3,000,000, while the expenses were over £5,000,000, the difference, however, being made up by subscriptions and government grants. There have also been important international E. at New York, Buffalo, Jamestown, San Francisco, and St. Louis in recent years, that at St. Louis being held to commemorate the Louisiana purchase. In 1933 Chicago is to open a great world's fair to celebrate a centenary of progress. It is promised that it will excel those previously held at Chicago and St. Louis, which were the biggest the world has known.

**Exhumation.** Under the English law it is a misdemeanour as well as sacrilege to disinter or interfere with a human body in any way without lawful authority for so doing, when the corpse is buried in consecrated ground. The ecclesiastical courts have power to grant faculties for removing interred remains, but only that they may be re-interred in other consecrated grounds. In cases of suspected foul play, the coroner may order disinterment for medical inspection, and E. may also be ordered by the Home Office, but otherwise no body may be disinterred without licence.

**Ex Libris,** *see* BOOKPLATES.

**Exmoor,** a dist. on the borders of Somerset and Devon, England, near the Bristol Channel, mainly moorland and marsh, the hills rising to 1100–1700 ft. The chief heights are Dunkery Beacon and Exe Head. Sheep and ponies are largely raised, and the Exmoor breed is famous, while the red deer is still found and carefully preserved. The R. Exe rises among the uplands. There are many prehistoric barrows.

**Exmouth,** a seaport, Devonshire, England, at mouth of R. Exe, on the English Channel, 9 m. S.E. of Exeter. It is a noted watering-place, having beautiful surroundings and a sheltered climate. There are good docks, which are 530 ft. long and were opened in 1869. E. is worth visiting for its matchless sunsets. A fifteenth-century mill-wheel called Marpool Mill is still in motion. There is a wealth of pleasure grounds and shaded walks and a spacious esplanade 2 m. long. Pop. 13,614.

**Exmouth, Sir Edward Pellew,** first Viscount (1757–1833), British admiral, entered the navy at the age of thir-

EDWARD PELLEW, VISCOUNT
EXMOUTH

teen, and very early in his career proved himself capable and gallant. He rose rapidly in the service and in 1816 he won world-wide recognition by his bombardment of Algiers when the Bey refused to abolish Christian slavery. For this service he was made viscount. There is a biography by Edward Osler (1835).

**Exocetus,** *see* FLYING-FISH.

**Exodus, The Book of,** the second book of the Pentateuch, was generally attributed by tradition to the authorship of Moses, to whom, indeed, the Jews attribute the authorship of all these five books. It continues the history of the family of Israel after the death of Joseph, though now it is less the record of a family than that of a nation. It tells of the birth and training of Moses, the departure from Egypt, and the events in the wilderness. It is a composite narrative, the various sources being much the same as those of Genesis. The book ends with the account of the construction of the tabernacle and its fittings according to the divinely-ordained pattern, and with the entry of the glory of Yahweh into his dwelling-place. *See* Estlin Carpenter and Harford-Battersby's *Hexateuch* (1900) and various introductions to the study of the O.T.

**Exogamy,** a term applied to tribal custom compelling marriage outside the tribe, clan, or 'totem,' thus the converse of endogamy (*q.v.*). E. holds good among the aborigines of Australia; the Somalis and Bakalaharis of Eastern Africa; the tribes of Western and Equatorial Africa; the Khasias, Iuangs, Waralis, Cracons, and Hos of India; the Kalmucks, Circassians, Samoyedes, Ostiaks, and Yakuts, and the N. American Indians.

**Exogens,** *see* DICOTYLEDONS.

**Exorcism** (from a Gk. word meaning ' to conjure out '), the act of conjuring evil spirits to depart out of the person possessed, the term being specially applied to the freeing of an individual from a possessing spirit. There are numerous examples of the exercise of E. in the early church, Tertullian and Origen speaking of it as an ordinary occurrence. The professional exorcist was known among the Jews, and the art was practised by women in Greece. The ancient rite of E. in connection with baptism is still retained in the Rom. ritual, which contains also a form of special service for the E. of possessed persons.

**Exoteric,** *see* ESOTERIC.

**Exotic Plants** are those introduced from a foreign country, as opposed to indigenous or native ones. Popularly speaking E. P. are those which have come from tropical or sub-tropical climates, and so have to be grown with heat under glass. For the hardier ones a greenhouse is sufficient which keeps out frost and cold winds, but to which air is daily admitted; but the more tender ones require much more heat, no direct outside air, and a great deal of moisture.

**Expansion.** An E. or increase of bulk due to the action of forces from within is a notable effect produced by heat on matter. It has been found by experiment that in general all bodies expand by heat or rise of temperature. The length of a metallic bar varies with every change of temperature, and is always the same at the same temperature. This mere increase of length is more correctly called ' elongation ' or ' dilatation.' The tire of a cartwheel is thus fixed by enlarging the iron hoop by heat. When cold it subsequently contracts, and clings closely to the wooden framework. In structures such as bridges and arches E. and contraction likely to ensue from changes of temperature must be taken into account. Watches and clocks are liable to go faster in cold weather, and slower in hot, as a result of the E. or contraction of their balance-wheels and pendulums. Exceptions to the ordinary rule of E. under heat are vulcanised rubber, oxide of copper, and the diamond at low temperatures, iodide of silver and iron beyond red-heat. Water begins to expand when lowered to 40° F.; otherwise most bodies begin to contract when the temperature is lowered. Among solids metals are the most expansible by heat. The observed E. of a liquid or gas within a containing vessel is called its ' apparent E.,' the ' true E.' being found by correcting for the changed E. of the vessel. When homogeneous bodies are uniformly heated E. takes place equally in all directions, resulting in change of volume but not of form. In all bodies or systems that are not homogeneous, E. is not equal in all directions, and change of form results from the changes of temperature. *See also* BAROMETER, HEAT, THERMOMETER.

**Expansion,** in mathematics, the detailed working out of a contracted expression contained in a short statement; the writing out in full of its meaning, or the result thus obtained. Thus the E. of $(a+b)^2$ is $a^2+2ab+b^2$. Among theorems for E. may be mentioned Taylor's and Fourier's. *See* Todhunter, *Algebra*, xxxvi., Fourier series.

**Expectation of Life** is the technical term used to indicate the number of years which any one from any group of persons (males, females, sailors, plumbers, etc.) may live, the attendant circumstances being normal. In other words, it is the mean time which a number of persons at any moment of age will live after that moment. The same idea is expressed by the Fr.

*vie moyenne,* average life—or by the Eng. expression *after life-time,* meaning the duration of life after any particular moment of life. Tables showing E. of L. have been compiled and issued at intervals from 1843, when A. W. Farr, the Deputy Registrar-General published English Life Table No. 1. This was followed in 1853 by English Life Table No. 2, and in 1864 by English Life Table No. 3. These publications are also known as Farr's Life Tables, and comprise a large number of tables of annuities and anniversary tables for the estimation of different kinds of life contingencies. Tables showing the E. of L. are used by Insurance Companies in fixing their premium terms for policies payable at death or at a stipulated age and also their terms for annuities.

**Expectorant,** a drug which aids expectoration and facilitates the removal of secretions from the air passages. The simplest ways of aiding expectoration are : The local application of heat, by means of inhaling steam, medicated sprays containing ammonia, creosote, iodine, carbolic acid, eucalyptus, etc. The drugs taken internally are : ipecacuanha, iodides, and chlorides of potassium, sodium, and ammonium Es. are used for colds, bronchitis, and other affections of the air passages.

**Expeditionary Force, British,** *see* BRITISH EXPEDITIONARY FORCE.

**Expenditure, National.** The gross expenditure of Great Britain in recent years (each ending March 31) is shown in the following list :—

| Year. | Expenditure. |
|---|---|
| | £ |
| 1904–5 | 151,769,000 |
| 1913–14 | 197,493,000 |
| 1914–15 (Great War) | 560,474,000 |
| 1915–16 ( ,, ) | 1,559,158,000 |
| 1916–17 ( ,, ) | 2,198,113,000 |
| 1917–18 ( ,, ) | 2,696,221,000 |
| 1918–19 ( ,, ) | 2,579,301,000 |
| 1919–20 | 1,665,773,000 |
| 1920–21 | 1,195,428,000 |
| 1921–22 | 1,079,187,000 |
| 1922–23 | 812,497,000 |
| 1923–24 | 788,840,000 |
| 1924–25 | 795,777,000 |
| 1925–26 | 826,100,000 |
| 1926–27 | 842,395,000 |
| 1927–28 | 838,585,000 |
| 1928–29 | 818,141,000 |
| 1929–30 | 748,712,000 |
| 1930–31 | 824,575,000 |
| 1931–32 | 803,500,000 |
| (Budget Estimate) | |

**Experience,** really a philosophical term, but a very ambiguous word, and often used in an historical sense

referring to the process in the past by means of which we have gained present knowledge. It is a continuous process, widening and extending the knowledge of an individual, and embraces both present and future. Pain, sorrow, pleasure, good and evil, and any change of sentiments and views all come under the heading of E. It is employed in a religious sense also ; thus people talk of ' experiencing ' religion, that is, becoming converted. The work of the mind, by means of which knowledge grows, is a work of discovery ; and actual E., whether it be wide or narrow, is not mere data only, but concrete, definite knowledge. The widest conception of the term is when the whole race is substituted for the individual. Then we obtain a collective E. embracing life as a whole and the knowledge gained by living it. From this all-comprehensive meaning, all other meanings in which the term is used are more or less legitimate abstractions. Primary E. may be reduced to the barest minimum of sensation and feeling, that is to say, a distinction is drawn between what is directly perceived and what is only inferred, and E. can be explained as manufactured out of these immediate or primary data of sense. When regarded in this way, controversy arises between false empiricism and its counterpart, rationalism.

**Experiment** (from Lat. *experiri,* to try), literally the action of trying anything, putting it to the proof or test. A great method of scientific inquiry, as opposed to observation. An operation, in science, undertaken either to discover something unknown, or to test an hypothesis and illustrate truths already proved and known. It consists in the arrangement of the elements or essential features of some process, so as to allow observation at will. Laboratory Es. serve to distinguish purely accidental circumstances from the really essential conditions of any phenomenon. In meteorology, biology, and even astronomy, Es. play an important part. Newton's law of gravitation was founded on experiment. *See* J. S. Mill, *Logic,* iii.

**Experimental Embryology** is that branch of Embryology concerned with the conditions necessary for the development of ova into new individuals, the mode of development, the functions of the various cells formed by the division of the ovum, and the relative importance of the nucleus and the cytoplasm, both in development and heredity.

Although fertilisation is generally essential for the formation of embryos, there are several animals and plants in which the unfertilised ovum develops. Fertilised ova of the honey-bee produce females; unfertilised ova develop into males. Aphides produce two kinds of ova, one parthenogenetic (*see* EMBRYOLOGY) the other requiring fertilisation, and many other Invertebrata are frequently reproduced by parthenogenetic ova. Experimentally the unfertilised eggs of sea-urchins have been activated by chemical methods. Starfish eggs exposed for a time to a comparatively high temperature develop without fertilisation, and a frog's egg, pricked with a needle, will develop parthenogenetically. Such experiments have led to the conclusion that the egg in itself contains all that is necessary for actual development, and sperms, or physical or chemical stimuli, merely enable the reactions to begin. An additional rôle of the sperm is to carry hereditary factors (*see* CELL and HEREDITY) and hence the inheritance of the embryo formed by a fertilised ovum is biparental.

The relative parts played by ova and spermatozoa in heredity have been investigated mainly by experimental hybridisation and by inducing sperms to enter enucleated eggs. The general results of such experiments, carried out mainly with various Echinodermata, show that some characters are transmitted through the nucleus, and therefore inherited from both parents. Characters distinctive of the group to which the animal belongs may be transmitted through the cytoplasm of the ovum, but experiments on the development of enucleated ova activated by the sperm are not yet conclusive, especially since such ova do not usually develop beyond the larval stage. The small amount of cytoplasm provided by the sperm is negligible as an agent in inheritance.

The cortex, *i.e.* the cytoplasm at the periphery of the egg, secretes a substance, 'fertilisin,' that enables spermatozoa of the same species to enter, while it inactivates those of other species. Removal of the cortex renders the egg incapable of fertilisation. Immediately the sperm enters, a membrane is formed, excluding other sperms, but in large yolky eggs the membrane forms slowly, and several sperms may enter; only one fuses with the ovum.

By centrifuging eggs it has been shown that some, *e.g.* Ascaris, are of the 'mosaic' type, having their materials arranged in a definite pattern, which is destroyed by the experiment, and consequently the egg develops abnormally. Eggs of frogs and sea-urchins are not damaged by centrifuging, and in such eggs differentiation of the cells may not take place until after the fifth division of the ovum.

The stage at which cells become differentiated has been determined by interchanging cells from various parts of the embryo at different stages of development. Undifferentiated cells produce tissue normally formed in the region to which they are transplanted, but differentiated cells, even though the differentiation be invisible, will develop into the kind of tissue they would have produced before transplantation. Since some parts of the embryo induce in the area to which they are transplanted the development of structures which do not normally arise there, they are regarded as 'organisers.'

Prof. C. M. Child has shown the existence of definite metabolic axes generally approximately coincident with the axes of symmetry in the egg and the embryo. An axial gradient, *i.e.* a fall in metabolic rate, extends from the anterior to the posterior pole, and from this primary gradient secondary gradients extend laterally, particularly in limb-forming regions. The existence of metabolic gradients has an important bearing on development.

The action of external environment upon the growth of embryonic cells is studied by growing them in culture media.

Experimental E. shows that stages of development are conditioned each by the preceding one. The functions are not irrevocably fixed from the initiation of the cells, but are determined mainly by the relations between the cells themselves and by other environmental factors.

**Experimental Psychology** is virtually a new science, since much that was studied as such up to a few years ago is now regarded as physiology. It has not been found possible to submit all the questions of psychology to the test of laboratory experiment, but the method may nevertheless be applied to a considerable number. Experimental studies of the processes of remembering and forgetting have been carried out, whilst hearing, seeing, feeling, tasting and smelling have been investigated experimentally.

In the last few years attention has been concentrated upon experimental studies of abilities of various kinds. Typically, these studies have proceeded from the devising of tests of various kinds, which have then been applied to large groups of individuals. The wide applications of the tests, and the study of the individuals tested, have enabled the experimenter to know something of the implications of the various scores given for success with the tests. He may then apply them to new individuals, and, from the scores they make in connection with the tests, predict with some confidence the extent to which the individual will show the ability which the test is designed to discover. The application of statistical methods to the interpretation and standardisation of the tests has resulted on the one hand in the formulation of the tests of proven reliability; and, on the other, in the development of new views regarding ability.

The formulation of tests has had important results in the educational field, since the ' intelligence tests ' of Binet, Terman and Burt appear to be tests of educability. In the industrial field, certain tests have been devised which show whether the person tested possesses the necessary ability to follow callings which demand proficiency in certain operations. In industry, not only have tasks been analysed and shown to consist of combinations of simple operations, but the ability for performing such operations has been experimentally investigated, and the conditions under which such operations may be best carried out by persons with the ability to perform them have also been studied. As a result, the industrial psychologist is finding himself increasingly in possession of reliable information which enables him to advise employers as to whom to engage or reject, and further to inform them as to the conditions in which their output may be raised to an optimum and their works maintained at a constant standard of maximum efficiency. Interesting studies have been made of the effect of temperature, ventilation, noise, lighting and other factors on the general behaviour and output of workers, and others are still being made. The increasing importance of this department of psychology led to the foundation by Sir Charles S. Myers, M.D., Sc.D., F.R.S., of the National Institute of Industrial Psychology.

The Foundations of Experimental Psychology, edited by Carl Murchison, U.S.A., 1929 ; Industrial Psychology, edited by Charles S. Myers, London, 1929 ; Industrial Psychology in Great Britain, London, 1925 ; Experimental Psychology, Mary Collins and James Drever, London, 1926 ; Fatigue Study, Gilbreth, London, 1919 ; The Nature of Intelligence, C. Spearman, London, 1923 ; The Abilities of Man, London, 1927.

Expert Witness, see under EVIDENCE.

Exploration, see GEOGRAPHY.

Explosion, the sudden and forcible expansion of certain substances through the action of heat or other cause. This expansion may either take the form of the conversion of solids or liquids into gases, or the increase in bulk of gases themselves through chemical changes.

Explosives, compounds or mixtures of an unstable character which can readily undergo chemical changes of an explosive nature.

According to the official British list of authorised explosives, the classes recognised are : gunpowder, nitrate mixture, nitro-compound, chlorate mixture, fulminate, ammunition, firework. Some of the best known E. are :

Gunpowder, an intimate mixture of potassium nitrate, charcoal and sulphur in the proportions 75 : 15 : 10, mainly used for blasting.

Gun-cotton, or trinitrocellulose, is a typical high E. discovered by Schönbein (1845), by the action of a mixture of nitric and sulphuric acids on cotton. Other forms of cellulose besides cotton, when nitrated, give nitrocelluloses.

Nitroglycerin, discovered by Sobrero (1846), made by the action of nitric and sulphuric acids on glycerin. Kieselguhr, a siliceous earth absorbs it (see DYNAMITE). Chemically it is glycerin trinitrate.

Cordite is made by making a paste of nitroglycerin, gun-cotton, and vaseline (30 : 65 : 5) with acetone, and after forcing through dies, allowing the excess of acetone to evaporate. The result is a horny brown substance. Cordite is used largely for sporting rifles.

Blasting gelatine is a mixture of nitrocellulose and nitroglycerin.

Picric acid (trinitrophenol), used largely for high explosive shells.

Trinitrotoluene is safer to handle than picric acid. It is a high E. and gives rise to clouds of undecomposed carbon.

Amatol, composed of trinitrotoluene (20) and ammonium nitrate (80).

Ammonal, like amatol, but with powdered aluminium.

Cheddite contains potassium chlorate, castor oil, and a nitro-body.

Sprengel mixtures contain an oxidising agent such as nitric acid or potassium chlorate, together with a combustible substance like nitrobenzene, petroleum, etc.

Schultze smokeless powders are made from nitrated wood and potassium and barium nitrates.

Oxyliquit is liquid oxygen in a suitable absorbent such as kieselguhr.

Fulminates of silver, mercury, etc., suitable for use in percussion caps. (See also BLASTING, BULLET, DYNA-

MITE, FIREARMS and INFERNAL MACHINES.)

**Explosives Committee,** a body under the organisation of the War Office for the purpose of advising on subjects connected with explosives.

**Exponent, or Indices.** In algebra, the E. or index is a symbol placed just above and to the right of another (termed the base) in order to indicate the power to which that base is to be raised. Indices may be positive, negative, or fractional. Thus, with a positive index, $a^2$ indicates $a \times a$, i.e. $a$ raised to the second power; with a negative index, $a^{-2}$ indicates $\frac{1}{a^2}$, or the reciprocal of $a$ to the second power; while with a fractional index $a^{\frac{1}{2}}$ indicates $\sqrt{a}$, or the square root of $a$.

**Exports,** see IMPORTS and EXPORTS.

**Express.** The word E. in the British Postal Department signifies immediate delivery of letters or packets by a special messenger at a higher rate, on the system introduced in 1891. Express train was the name given in 1845 to one running ' expressly' to take passengers to one particular place and not stopping elsewhere (what would now rather be a 'special'). To-day it means a train travelling at a high speed stopping only at a few important intermediate stations. In the United States the express system is an institution for the rapid and safe delivery of light goods and parcels, the idea having first originated in 1839 with W. F. Harnden. The present Adams Express Co. was formed (1849) as 'Adams and Co.'s California Express,' and the Wells Fargo Co. started 1852. The American-European Co. was the first trans-Atlantic E., founded in 1855. A feature of the American system is the 'Collect on Delivery' business, goods being marked C.O.D. The companies aim at saving their clients all trouble, taking entire responsibility from the time of collection to that of delivery. The parcel post (1883), post office, and railways undertake most of such duties in the United Kingdom. See F. J. Stimson, *History of the Express Business,* 1883.

**Expressionism in Art,** a form of Art which endeavours to express the inner life of the artist, in which process the objective content is but a means to that end, wherein the subjectivity of the artist engrosses the interest so much that the external object may not dispute its supremacy, and either disappears or becomes unrecognisable. In brief, subjective presentation accompanied by total or almost total distortion of nature to the point of unrecognis-

ability, or by suppression of all external reality. According to Max Raphael 'Art should merely reproduce the artist.' For a proper appreciation, or perhaps interpretation, of a picture, the critic will require to translate the detail of the picture as symbolic of some experience, whether physical, intellectual or spiritual, of the artist, much as psycho-analysts interpret the recollected incidents of dreams. Among prominent expressionist painters are Severini, Nolde, Boccioni, Schafler, Casper, Münch and Max Raphael. Bibliography: *Expressionism in Art,* Pfister.

**Extension,** in logic, a term used of any given term to describe the total number of objects to which it may be applied, being practically synonymous with ' Denotation,' and opposed to ' Intension ' or ' Connotation,' which are used of the attributes essential to the conception of the term.

**Extenuating Circumstances,** a legal term used in reference to crimes, describing cases in which the gravity of the act is mitigated or excused, from the point of view of punishment, because of the causes leading up to the commission of the act.

**Extortion,** in Eng. law, the term applied to the improper, premature, or excessive exaction of money or money's worth by public officers; also to such exaction by means of threats of personal violence or blackmail. E. is regarded as a misdemeanour by the common law. *See* THREATS.

**Extracts** are solutions or syrups containing one or more substances that have been removed from admixture with others by means of a solvent. The methods of extraction depend on the particular case, but as a rule, the solvent, which may be water, alcohol, ether, acetic acid, etc., is poured over the crushed or powdered substance, and, after standing, is strained off. The substance is said to be macerated if the solvent is cold and digested if warm. When the substance is boiled with the solvent, a decoction results. Many forms of apparatus for performing extractions have been devised, with a view to minimising the amount of solvent used, and thus rendering the subsequent concentration of the E. a less tedious process.

**Extradition** (Lat. *ex,* out, and *traditio,* handing over), the giving up of a person accused of crime to the gov. in whose territory the offence was committed by the gov. in whose territory he has taken refuge. Great Britain has entered into E. treaties with practically all civilised nations; the offences for which E. is permissible are naturally all of a serious nature, including arson, murder, piracy, embezzlement, etc. In most states offences of a political nature do not allow of E.; such offences are not those with a political motive, but those which ' are incidental to and form part of political disturbances.' Criminals are not given up unless some specific treaty is in existence with the gov. requiring them, and in Eng. law the gov. has no power to surrender a fugitive criminal without express statutory authority. It is necessary to show the offence enumerated and the specific treaty, and also that the acts with which the fugitive is charged amount to the alleged offence according to the laws of both the govs. concerned. The authority in Great Britain is contained in the Extradition Acts of 1870–73. The fugitive can be tried only on the specific charge for which he was given up. Whether a state is called upon to give up its own subjects varies with different nations; the procedure in relation to Great Britain and other nations is briefly as follows: With France and Germany neither gov. surrenders its own subjects; with Spain and Switzerland Great Britain only surrenders them; with Austria, Russia, Belgium, and the Netherlands it is optional. If a Spanish subject committed a crime in Austria and took refuge in England, the Eng. gov. would surrender him to Austria only after the consent of Spain had been obtained. A fugitive is committed on the same evidence as for an ordinary crime, but is not surrendered until a diplomatic representation of the gov. demanding him has been addressed to the Secretary of State. In the U.S.A. foreign E. is not regulated by the individual states but by the Federal gov. When a demand is made for E., the accused is handed over if his probable guilt is established at a preliminary examination before a commissioner or judge. An E. treaty embraces all previous crimes committed by the same person. Inter-state E. is provided for by Act of Congress under the Constitution. The fact that an act may be no crime in one state does not debar another where such act is a crime from demanding surrender. Release by writ of *Habeas Corpus* is the procedure on an improper surrender.

**Extra - Territoriality, or Exterritoriality,** a term of international law, which denotes the exclusion of certain individuals from the rule that everybody within the boundaries of a state is subject to the laws of that state. It is also used to describe the quasi-exterritoriality of the dwelling-place of an accredited diplomatic agent, and of public ships of one state when cruising in other waters than their own. Generally speaking, all cases where a state refrains from enforcing its laws within its own territory are cases of the operation of the principle of extra-territoriality. The persons who come under this rule are those of foreign sovereigns, whether travelling under an incognito or not, ambassadors, ministers, plenipotentiary and other accredited diplomatic agents. Not only are the persons of these included, but their suites also, and their belongings. Public ships in foreign waters also enjoy the rights of exterritoriality. Consuls are not as a rule included, save in some non-Christian countries. In certain non-Christian states also extra-territoriality has been granted by treaty to the subjects of contracting Christian states who are resident therein (*see*, however, CAPITULATIONS). Eng. settlements in the Far East are subject to the conditions of the treaties by which they came into being. The limits of consular jurisdiction show a tendency to contract; and, at the Washington Conference, 1921, a resolution was passed in favour of taking steps to relinquish consular jurisdiction in China; but the subsequent very disturbed condition of that country delayed the implementing of the resolution. In May 1931, after some nineteen months' negotiation, the Chinese National Gov. announced the abolition, as from 1932, of extra-territorial rights of foreigners resident in China. This announcement followed China's refusal to accept the Powers' demands that foreign jurisdiction should continue at Shanghai, Canton, Tientsin, Peking and Hankow. Previously, in Dec. 1929, a mandate had been promulgated ordering that all foreign nationals should abide by the laws and ordinances of the central and local govs. It was further announced that courts for the trial of criminal and civil cases involving foreigners were to be established in special areas, including Shanghai, Tientsin, Mukden and Canton. Outside the jurisdiction of these courts, foreign defendants might petition to have their cases tried in special courts, and it was stated that advisers would be attached to these courts who would not necessarily be Chinese. So far, the Chinese have adhered to their decision of Dec. 1929 and, failing a solution to their taste, extra-territorial privileges will disappear. At the outset, the British Gov. required to be satisfied as to the safeguards which the Chinese Goverment would provide in this special judicial and administrative system to protect foreign residents against miscarriage of justice, and if these were forthcoming they were prepared to agree, in concert with the other Powers, to the abolition of extra-territorial rights. But from the beginning of the negotiations they have insisted that Shanghai and the other three treaty ports should be outside the scope of the negotiations, their opinion being that the municipal councils in these settlements could hardly function if extra-territorial rights were abolished. An exceptional case of exterritoriality was that granted to the residence of the pope by an Italian law. When armies are allowed by another gov. to cross the borders of their own state, they thereby come into possession of exterritorial rights. It was laid down in the arbitration of the *Alabama* case that the extension of exterritoriality to ships was not the law of nations or an absolute right, but simply an act of courtesy; such a view is not in accord with the universal practice of civilised nations. The extension of immunity to vessels owned by States and engaged in trade was an issue before the English courts in *The Porto Alexandre* (1920), in which case the Court of Appeal in spite of the commercial difficulties that might arise, felt bound in view of the prevailing fashion of internationalisation to follow the decision in *The Parlement Belge* (1878) where the fact that a ship had been declared by a foreign sovereign to be in his possession as sovereign was held to be conclusive and to confer immunity from the local jurisdiction.

**Extravasation,** the passage of fluid from a vessel. The term is also applied to the passage of fluid into an unusual position by bursting or perforation. E. of blood is the most commonly seen, as in a bruise, the size of which depends upon the amount of blood that leaves the damaged vessels, and the changes that a bruise goes through are caused by the alteration in the blood. The extravasated blood is either absorbed or remains fluid, and has to be removed, or else gangrene of the skin or damage of deeper parts results. The *treatment* of a bruise consists in applying cold to check the bleeding, and when the bleeding has been arrested and there is no longer an increase of swelling, heat is applied to dilate the neighbouring vessels and enable them to drain off the extravasated blood.

**Extreme and Mean Ratio,** in geometry, a phrase used of the proportional division of straight lines. Thus if AB is a straight line, and the point of division is at C, the line will be divided in extreme and mean ratio,

or medial section, if the ratio AB : AC = AC : CB. The term is used by Euclid, who states the problem in Book II. prop. 2.

**Extreme Unction,** a sacrament of the Rom. Catholic Church, reserved to those at the point of death. It is believed to give spiritual aid to the person receiving it and also, when God so wills, to restore bodily health. The custom of anointing the sick with oil doubtless had its origin in the counsel of St. James (James v. 14), but it is noteworthy that this passage makes the cure of the sick person the object of the act. There are still traces of this primitive view in the Rom. rite of unction. In the Gk. Church the ceremony is known as 'The Holy Oil,' or 'The Oil of Prayer,' and the primitive view has remained more fully. In the 1549 Book of Common Prayer, a form of unction was given, but this has since been omitted. The practice of unction of the sick with the primitive intention has lately been revived in the Eng. Church with episcopal consent.

**Exuma, Great and Little,** two of the Bahama Is. These two, together with the smaller Exuma Keys, are about 150 sq. m. in area, and support a pop. of 2300. The chief tn. is Georgetown.

**Eyalet** (Arabian *wālī*, a governor; *wilāyer*, a province), originally the term applied to a pashalic, or one of the largest administrative divisions of the Turkish empire; now to a prov. under the administration of a governor-general. 'Vilayet' is an analogous term.

**Eyam,** a vil. of W. Derbyshire, England, 10½ m. N.E. of Buxton. It stands in a romantic vale in a dist. noted for its beauty, geological interest, and anct. British and Saxon remains. Barytes mining is carried on. In E. churchyard is a fine ninth or tenth century Runic cross, restored by John Howard in 1788. The vil. was ravaged by plague in 1665–6. Pop. 1175.

**Eyck, Hubert Van** (*c.* 1370–1426), an early Flemish painter, probably *b.* at Maaseyck on the R. Maas, and lived at Bruges and later at Ghent. He usually worked in conjunction with his brother John, being appointed together with him by Philip of Charolais as court painter at The Hague in 1422. They are said to have invented painting in oils, and certainly perfected the art of colour mixing, their work being famous for transparency and brilliance of colouring. To Hubert is attributed the major part of 'The Adoration of the Lamb,' of which four panels, up to the Great War, still in the church of St. Bavo at Ghent, and the other six in the Berlin Museum, were, under the Treaty of Versailles, returned from Berlin. Two lesser works by van E. are at Madrid and Naples. He had great intellectual power, and represented scriptural scenes and characters through the medium of such life as he himself had observed.

**Eyck, John Van** (c. 1390–1440), an early Flemish painter, brother and pupil of Hubert (q.v.), and like him b. at Maaseyck. During Hubert's lifetime he worked with him, and after his death completed ' The Adoration of the Lamb.' He also became court painter to the Duke of Burgundy in Lille. He d. at Bruges. His work, while lacking the power of conception of Hubert's, shows more attention to detail and delicate finish. His works, mainly portraits, historical subjects, and landscapes, include : ' The Consecration of Thomas à Becket '; ' St. Francis receiving the Stigmata '; ' The Virgin and Child '; the ' Madonna di Lucca,' the ' Portrait of Himself and Wife ' (in the National Gallery, London); ' Portrait of Jan de Leeuw '; ' Head of Christ as Salvator Mundi.'

**Eyck, Margaret Van,** a painter, sister of Hubert and John. She lived a retired life as a member of the order of Our Lady of Ghent, and d. before 1431, being buried in the cathedral of Ghent. She is believed to have executed some miniatures in the missal of the Duke of Bedford.

**Eye.** The E. is one of the higher sense organs, and like those of hearing and smell, it consists of an essential part and an accessory part. The organ of vision, strictly speaking, consists only of the eyeball, but it is also necessary to discuss its many important appendages. The eyelids, fringed by the eyelashes (cilia), consist of integument with a thin layer of dense fibrous tissue strengthening their margins. They are closed by the orbicularis muscles, and the upper is raised by the levator. The meiobomian glands, which secrete sebum, open on the free margin of the eyelids. A layer of mucous membrane (conjunctiva) lines their inner surface and is continued over the front of the eyeball. The upper lid is the larger and more movable, and joins the lower at the inner and outer canthi. Near the inner canthus, on each lid, will be seen the slight elevation (papilla lachrymalis) pierced by the lachrymal canal, which is the drainage channel for the fluid from the conjunctiva ; this fluid is continuously secreted by the lachrymal gland, which is lodged in the orbit on the outer side of the ball. The reflex action of winking the lids about once in every two minutes distributes the fluid

over the ball and thereby washes it. The lachrymal canals from above and below converge and open into the lachrymal sac, the upper slightly dilated end of a duct about ⅓ in. in length descending to the fore-part of the lower meatus of the nose. Stimulus of the lachrymal gland by pungent vapours or the stress of strong emotions may result in an excessive secretion of the fluid exceeding the capacity of the lachrymal duct and tears result. The conjunctival mucous membrane becomes continuous with the nasal mucous membrane by means of this system of canals. The

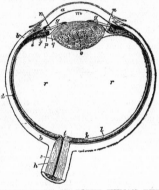

LOWER HALF OF RIGHT HUMAN EYE

a, cornea; b, sclerotic; c, sheath of h, optic nerve; d, choroid; e, f, p, ciliary body ; g, iris; i, blind spot; k, yellow spot; l, retina; m, anterior chamber, o, lens; h, suspensory ligament of lens; r, posterior chamber.

globe of the E. is not perfectly spherical, its anterio-posterior diameter being about ⅞ of an inch, as also is its vertical, but the transverse diameter is usually a little longer, about 1 in. The eyeball consists of three concentric coats and of certain fluid and solid parts enclosed by them, viz. (a) the tough, firm, fibrous external coat, the sclerotic and cornea; (b) a middle vascular pigmented and in part muscular membrane, the choroid and iris; (c) an internal nervous and epithelial layer, the retina. The corneo-sclerotic case is kept in shape by (i.) the aqueous humour which distends the cornea ; (ii.) the vitreous humour which fills the less convex sclerotic chamber ; these two humours are separated by the crystalline lens. The whole may be represented as a 'water-camera' of the highest degree of perfection and adaptability. A brief description of each of the above parts follows. The sclerotic coat is a strong, opaque, fibrous structure extending over about $\frac{5}{6}$ of the eyeball. Its outer surface is pearly white; its inner is of a light brown colour. The remaining $\frac{1}{6}$, although not changed essentially in character, is transparent, and is termed the cornea. The cornea is normally from $\frac{1}{2\sqrt{}}$ to $\frac{1}{2\sqrt{}}$ inch in thickness. The choroid coat is a thin membrane, and supports in its outer layers the larger arteries and veins of the E. Its inner stratum is covered by hexagonal pigmented cells; these, which were formerly considered as part of the choroid, belong in reality to the retina. Near the corneosclerotic junction the choroid becomes raised up into a number of longitudinal ridges or puckers (*ciliary processes*) arranged meridionally and forming a circle. The *iris* at its circumferential border is continuous with the choroid. It is a curtain with a round hole (pupil), and is provided with circular and radiating unstriped muscular fibres which adjust the size of the pupil. (Though unstriped, these fibres contract with extreme rapidity.) The pigment cells of the iris vary in different individuals, and the different colours of Es. are partly dependent on the amount and distribution of the contained pigment. The retina is the delicate membrane containing the expanded termination of the *optic nerve*. It varies in thickness from $\frac{1}{3\sqrt{}}$ to $\frac{1}{2\sqrt{0}\sqrt{}}$ of an inch, and forms the lining between the choroid and the vitreous humour extending nearly to the outer edge of the ciliary processes; its indented border is termed the *ora serrata*. It, for the most part, is of even texture and smooth surface, but almost exactly opposite the middle of the posterior wall is a slight circular depression (*yellow spot*), and not far from this, towards the nasal side of the eyeball, is a radiating appearance produced by the spreading of the optic nerve at its point of entrance.

It is impossible within the limits of this account to deal with the microscopic structure of this wonderful membrane. No less than eight distinct strata build it up, of which only four are here mentioned. The innermost layer is one of nerve fibres, and lying next to this is the layer of nerve cells; the outermost layer consists of the pigment cells previously mentioned, and immediately within is the layer of *rods* and *cones*, the former far exceeding the latter, except in the yellow spot. These bodies are closely packed, and it is suggested that each rod or cone conveys but one impression, so that any image, even microscopic in size, must be the result of combined impressions from a number of rods and cones. The *aqueous humour* is a watery solution of saline and organic material, while the *vitreous humour* is of a soft gelatinous consistency, and serves as a support for the delicate retina from which, in most parts, it may be readily separated. The crystalline lens, about $\frac{1}{2}$ inch across and $\frac{1}{4}$ inch thick, is a transparent solid body, double convex in shape and enclosed by an elastic capsule with attached suspensory ligaments subject to varying tensions. Its posterior convexity is the greater. It is composed of a number of concentric laminæ, resembling the coats of an onion, and each lamina is composed of ribbon-shaped fibres built together in a peculiarly curved manner. The lens, which is practically spherical in the fœtus, becomes more and more flattened with advancing age. The action of the E. is roughly as follows : Diverging beams of light from any one point in an object strike all over the surface of the cornea, this gathers them slightly together, refraction follows in the aqueous humour, and the lens brings them to a focus, in normal vision, on the retina. The rods and cones are affected by the image, and in consequence cause disturbances and stimuli in the nerve fibres and an impulse is transmitted via the optic nerve to the brain. There are special adjustments for the varying distances of objects. This *accommodation* is brought about by (1) a compression of the ball of the E. by its muscles which cause a change in the form of the cornea; (2) a shifting of the lens bodily ; (3) a pressure of the iris upon the front of the lens. The muscles which move the eyeballs are six in number, four *recti* and two *obliqui* ; and by means of the contractions of these several muscles the eyeballs may be moved in any desired direction. The diseases of the E. are many and various. Inflammation of the cornea (*keratitis*) usually results in loss of transparency of this part. Inflammation of the iris (*iritis*) may cause *photophobia*. A clouding of the crystalline lens is known as *cataract* (*q.v.*). *Glaucoma* is caused by inflammation of the retina, and various forms of *conjunctivitis* are known as *acute catarrhal conjunctivitis*, *e.g.* hay fever; *granular conjunctivitis*, or *trachoma*; *epidemic muco-purulent conjunctivitis*, or *school ophthalmia*.

**Eye,** a tn., Suffolk, England, on a trib. of the R. Waveney, 20 m. N. of Ipswich. Formerly a centre of the pillow-lace industry. Pop. 1781.

**Eyebright**, *see* EUPHRASIA.

**Eyemouth**, a tn., Berwickshire, Scotland, at the mouth of the R. Eye, 8 m. N.W. of Berwick. Has large fishing industry. Pop. 2573.

**Eyes, Propagation by**, consists in carefully cutting out the eye, as it is called, and planting it afresh; this soon shoots out and becomes a new plant. The best known example of this form of propagation is the potato.

**Eylau, Preussisch**, a tn. of E. Prussia, Germany, 23 m. S.E. of Königsberg. A famous battle was fought here on Feb. 7–8, 1807, between the Fr., under Napoleon, and the Russians and Prussians.

**Eyra**, the native S. American name for a species of wild cat, *Felis eyra*, which ranges through the W. hemisphere from Mexico to Paraguay. It is reddish-yellow, with white spots on the face, and is about the size of the domestic cat.

**Eyre, Edward John** (1815–1901), a British colonial governor and Australian explorer, son of a Yorkshire vicar. He emigrated to Australia, becoming a squatter on the Lower Murray R., a stipendiary magistrate and protector of the aborigines. He undertook difficult journeys to prove the possibility of an overland route between S. and W. Australia. Starting in 1841, he reached Albany in about five weeks, publishing an account of his journey in England, as *Discoveries in Central Australia*, 1845. In 1846 Grey appointed him lieutenant-governor of New Zealand. He was transferred to the W. Indies in 1854, governing St. Vincent and Antigua, and finally became governor of Jamaica in 1862. E. took stern measures to suppress the negro rising there (1865). For this he was superseded by Grant, and prosecuted by a committee of which J. S. Mill was president. Carlyle and Kingsley were on the committee for his defence. He was acquitted in 1867, and retired with a pension.

**Eyre, Sir Vincent** (1811–81), an Eng. general, who served in Afghanistan (1841–42). His *Military Operations at Cabul . . . with a Journal of Imprisonment in Afghanistan*, published in 1843, gave an account of his eight months of captivity with Akbar Khan. He fought in the Indian Mutiny, being with Havelock and Outram at the relief of Lucknow. *See* Memoir by Malleson (*Recreations of an Indian Official*, 1872).

**Eyres Peninsula**, a triangular piece of land on the S. coast of S. Australia, lying between Spencer Gulf and Anxious Bay, its base being formed by the Gawler range.

**Eyre-Todd, George**, Scottish author,

*b.* June 2, 1862, at Glasgow; son of Henry Todd. Educ. at Glasgow, one time lecturer on Eng. literature and Scottish history at Glasgow Athenæum. Later, editor of *The Scottish Field*. His works include: *Ossian*, 1888; *Byways of the Scottish Border*, 1892; Abbotsford Series of Scottish Poets, 1891–96; *Ancient Scots Ballads, with their Traditional Airs*, 1894; *The Glasgow Poets*, 1902; translation of Barbour's *Bruce*, 1907; *Works of Macrae*, 1909; *The Angel of Robert Burns*, 1917; *The Legend of Languoreth*, 1922; *The Highland Clans of Scotland*, 1923; *L.M. & S. Rly.*, 1925; *History of Glasgow*, Vol. II., 1929.

**Ezekiel** ('El (God) will make strong'), one of the four greater prophets, is spoken of in ch. i. 3, as 'the priest, the son of Buzi,' and this description by the editor of his pro-

RAPHAEL'S *THE VISION OF EZEKIEL*

phecies is the only extant reference of another writer to him. On the capture of Jerusalem by Nebuchadnezzar, he was carried into Mesopotamia with Jehoiachin, King of Judah, and settled at Tel-abib on the R. Chebar. Here in the fifth year of the captivity (592 B.C.), the call to the prophetic office came to him. He continued it for twenty-two years. It is noteworthy, then, that E. was both prophet and priest, and it is this unique blending of the two which makes his work remarkable. The influence of Jeremiah is particularly strong in his writings. The book of

E. has never had its authenticity severely questioned, though a Talmudic tradition ascribes the authorship to the great synagogue, to which E. did not belong. It may be divided into two great parts, the division coming at the end of either ch. 32 or ch. 39. Chapters 1–39 fall into three divisions : (1) before the siege of Jerusalem, threatening the complete overthrow of the kingdom of Judah on account of its alienation from God ; (2) during the siege, threatening the surrounding nations with divine punishment for their scorn of Judah ; (3) after the siege, an exultant prophecy of the future.

Ezra, the Scribe, is said to be one of the descendants of Sheraiah the high-priest who had been put to death after the taking of Jerusalem by Nebuchadnezzar. He first appears in the Biblical narrative as a Jewish exile, living in Babylon during the reign of Artaxerxes Longimanus, by which monarch he was held in great favour. After the thirty-third year of the reign of Artaxerxes, he was permitted to lead a band of from 1400 to 1600 men with women and children out of Babylon to Jerusalem. In Ezra vii. is given the decree by which Artaxerxes makes the arrangement for this journey, but advanced critics are agreed in declaring it to be spurious. On his arrival at Jerusalem, E. found that the Jews had intermarried with the surrounding nations, and on the authority of the law he called upon them to sever this connection. The result was the institution of a special ' congregation ' devoted to the temple and the law. E. is noted as a restorer of the text of the law, and was held in high repute by later Jews.

Ezra and Nehemiah, the Books of, naturally form one work, both being continuations of the books of Chronicles. It is impossible to consider them apart, as both are constructed from the same sources, and both have undergone the same revision. The book of Ezra falls into two parts, of which the first, chs. i.–vi., tells the history of the Palestinian Jews from the first year of Cyrus down to the sixth year of Darius Hystaspis. Of this section, the portion from iv. 8 to vi. 18 is written not in Hebrew but in Aramaic, the common tongue of the Semitic peoples at this time. The second division of the books, chs. vii.–x., describes the return of Ezra and his company in the seventh year of Artaxerxes, and his action with reference to the mixed marriages. In the original ch. vii. 12–26 is in Aramaic. The book of Nehemiah tells how that Jewish leader was sent by the Persian king as governor of Jerusalem to restore the walls of the city, and describes the manner in which he carried out his work in face of the opposition of Sanballat. The whole work is of a piece with the Chronicles, and was written in close connection with them. There are some difficulties in regard to the chronology of the two books which have not yet been cleared up.

Ez Zebdani, a prosperous' tn. of Syria, about 20 m. N.W. of Damascus, surrounded by celebrated apple orchards and vineyards. Not far off is a remarkable rock-pinnacle, resembling an uplifted finger, which appears to have been a sacred pillar worshipped as a Symbol of Baal Moloch. Even to-day it is venerated by the Moslem peasantry, and is visited by processions of Dervishes. Once every year at Zebdani a Moslem sheik of approved sanctity rides on horseback over the prostrate bodies of fanatics who voluntarily permit themselves to be trampled upon.

Ezzelino da Romano (1194–1259), an Italian Ghibelline leader, was descended from Eccelin, a knight, who had received the fief of Romano, near Padua, in Italy. E. had such a reputation for cruelty that he was called ' the tyrant,' and we find him pictured in Dante's *Inferno*. He has also been made the subject both of a drama and of a novel.

# F

**F,** the sixth letter and fourth consonant of the Græco-Rom. alphabet, representing ' waw,' sixth letter of the Semitic alphabet, which expressed the sounds of *w* and *u*. It is a ' voiceless labio-dental spirant,' originally taking its form from the old Gk. digamma, F. Etymologically it corresponds in general to the Gk. π. *Cf.* Eng. ' father,' Gk. πατήρ; foal and πῶλος; five and πέντε ; fire and πῦρ. In Old Eng., if between two vowels *f* was pronounced like *v*. In modern Eng. the word ' of ' is the only example of this sound for *f*. The letter ' F ' is used in various abbreviations, *e.g.* for fellow (F.R.S.), Fahrenheit, Fluorine (in chemistry).

**F,** in music, is the fourth note in the ascending diatonic scale of C, major and minor, the sub-dominant of the scale. The bass or F clef is on the fourth line of the staff, the note on that line being F, and the other notes above and below being named accordingly (*g, a, b,* etc.). The scale having the note F as its tonic is the scale or key of F. It represents ' forte ' (loudly) in music, being usually written *f*; *ff* stands for ' fortissimo ' or 'piu forte.'

**F., Fahr.** (abbr. for **Fahrenheit**), the name applied to a thermometer, so called from its inventor, Gabriel Daniel Fahrenheit, who substituted mercury for spirits of wine, thereby greatly improving the instrument.

**Fabaceæ** (in botany), *see* LEGUMINOSÆ.

**Fabbroni, A.,** *see* FABRONI, A.

**Faber, Cecilia Francisca Josefa Böhl von** (1797–1877), a Spanish novelist, who used the pseudonym of ' Fernan Caballero.' She was *b.* at Morges, in Switzerland, and in 1813 her father, a Ger. merchant who had married a Spanish lady, settled in Spain with his family. Her first novel, *La Gaviota,* was published in 1849. She also published *Cuentos y Poesias populares Andaluces,* 1859, the earliest collection of Spanish folk-tales and songs.

**Faber, Frederick William** (1814–63), an Eng. Oratorian and hymn-writer, nephew of G. S. Faber (*d.* 1854), *b.*

at Calverley, Yorkshire. Till 1845 he remained a clergyman of the Anglican Church, and then became converted to Catholicism, and was ordained priest. He founded a religious community at Birmingham, later merged in the oratory of St. Philip Neri, with Newman at the head. In 1849 a branch was formed in London, with F. as president. His *Collected Hymns* were published in 1861, including ' O Gift of Gifts, O Grace of Faith,' and ' Paradise, O Paradise.' *See* Bowden, *Life of F. W. Faber,* 1869.

**Faber, George Stanley** (1773–1854), a celebrated Anglican divine, uncle of F. W. Faber (*d.* 1863), *b.* in Yorkshire. He graduated from University College, Oxford, became fellow and tutor of Lincoln College, Oxford, 1793; Bampton lecturer, 1801; rector of Stockton-on-Tees, Durham, 1803. In 1832 F. became master of Sherburn Hospital. Among his works are : *Horæ Mosaicæ,* 1801 ; *On the Mysteries of the Cabyri . . .,* 1803 ; *Difficulties of Infidelity,* 1824 ; *Difficulties of Romanism,* 1826 ; *View of the Prophecies Relating to Judah and Israel*; and *The Sacred Calendar of Prophecy,* 1828 ; *The Primitive Doctrine of Justification,* 1837 ; *Eight Dissertations upon the Prophetical Promises of a Mighty Deliverer,* 1845. Consult *Gent. Mag.,* May 1854 ; Allibone, *Dict. of Authors*; Faber's Memoir in *Many Mansions in the House of the Father,* 1854.

**Faber** or **Fabri, Jacques** (*c.* 1455–1536 or '37), Fr. humanist and precursor of Protestantism ; properly, **J. Lefèvre d'Etaples,** latinised into J. Stapulensis ; *b.* at Etaples. Went early to Paris to study ; in 1486 to Italy, where he remained several years. On return, propagated Aristotelian principles, by translations and paraphrases. Met an old pupil, Guillaume Briçonnet, who had become Bishop of Lodève, and who accommodated him in the abbey of St. Germain-en-Laye. Made Fr. translation of New Testament, and his biblical commentaries aroused antagonism of the Sorbonne. Removed to Meaux (of which Briçonnet had become bishop), and was protected by Francis I. Later accompanied Marguerite of Valois to Blois, where he finished translation of Bible. In 1531, Marguerite removed him for greater safety to Nérac, where he died.

**Faber** or **Fabri, Johannes** (1478–1541), Ger. theologian; *b.* at Leutkirch in Swabia. Real name, Heigerlin. Studied theology and canon law at Tübingen and at Freiburg in Breisgau, became doctor in canon law. In 1518 he was appointed vicar-general of the diocese of Constance. He was friendly with Erasmus, Melancthon, and Zwingli; but, when the breach came, he chose the orthodox side, and became known as the Hammer of the Heretics—from his work, *Malleus . . . in Nœresim Lutheranan* (Cologne, 1524). He was prominent in many disputations, and in 1531 became bishop of Vienna. Died there, May 21, 1541.

**Faber, John** (1684–1756), *see* ENGRAVING.

**Faber, John (Johan), the Elder** (*c.* 1660–1721), a Dutch mezzotint engraver and draughtsman, *b.* at The Hague. One of the first artists to work in mezzotint, he came to London about 1687, and *d.* at Bristol. His pen-portrait of ' Simon Episcopius ' on vellum is in the British Museum. Among his other best works are ' Portraits of Founders of Colleges at Oxford and Cambridge ' (begun 1712); ' The Heads of the Philosophers ' (after Rubens); ' Humphrey Lloyd of Denbigh, Antiquary,' 1717 ; ' Dr. Wallis, Mathematician ' (after Kneller); and portraits of Bishops Atterbury and Hough, of John Caspar and Dr. Sacheverell.

**Fabia Gens,** one of the oldest and most distinguished patrician clans or houses of anct. Rome, probably of Sabine origin, claiming descent from Hercules and a daughter of the Arcadian Evander. It was one of the two gentes entrusted with the management of the ' Lupercalia ' (Ovid, *Fasti,* ii. 375). The chief family names under the republic were Ambustus, Buteo, Labeo, Licinus, Dorso, Vibulanus, Pictor, and Maximus. Among its most famous members were :

(1) *Cæso Fabius Vibulanus,* a Rom. general, who with his brothers, Quintus and Marcus, held the consulship for seven years (485–479 B.C.), being consul himself 484, 481, and 479. He was popular with the plebeians, and won victories over the Veientes and Æqui. In his third consulship, the Fabian family made a campaign against Veii alone. Cæso led out 307 of them, and they settled on the Cremera. After gaining some successes they were trapped in an ambush and all slain by the Veientes, except one youth (477 B.C.). (*See* Mommsen, *Römische Forschungen,* vol. ii.)

(2) *Q. F. Max. Rullianus,* a famous general, consul five times between 322 and 295 B.C. He was twice dictator of Rome, fought in the second Samnite War, gaining victories (325, 322), and at Sentinum, over united Gauls and Samnites (295). (*See* Livy, viii., ix.)

(3) *Q. F. Maximus* (nicknamed Verrucosus and Ovicula), known to fame as ' Cunctator ' (delayer), described by Ennius as ' unus qui nobis cunctando restituit rem,' was repeatedly consul, censor, and dictator of Rome (221, 217 B.C.). As consul (233) he conquered the Ligurians and was granted a ' triumph.' Sent as ambassador to Carthage, he became leader and dictator in the war with Hannibal. His slow, defensive policy, known ever after as ' Fabian policy ' (*cf.* FABIAN SOCIETY), did not at first find favour with his contemporaries, but after the crushing defeat at Cannæ (216), it was at once resumed. In 215 Maximus ravaged Campania, was consul for the fifth time (209), and recaptured Tarentum. He opposed Scipio's aggressive policy, and *d.* in 203 B.C.

(4) *Q. F. Pictor* (*b. c.* 254 B.C.), first Rom. prose historian, the ' father of Latin history,' lived at the time of the Second Punic War. He served in the Gallic War (225), and *d.* after 216. His works (written in Gk.), were known as *Annals of F. Pictor.* Only fragments of his history (from the time of Æneas to the Hannibalic War) are left. Consult : *Histories of Rome,* by Livy, Niebuhr, Valerius Maximus; Aurelius Victor, *Viri illustres* ; Polybius III., *Nouvelle Biographie Générale* ; Whiste, *De F. Pictore Cæterisque Fabiis Historicis,* 1832.

**Fabian Society,** an association founded in London (1883) for the advancement of Socialism. Similar organisations now exist in many other cities. Its rise was due to private discussions on literature and the social duties of the times, started by an American, Thomas Davidson. Meetings were first publicly held in 1888. The name is adopted from that of the famous Rom. Fabius ' Cunctator,' in token that the Society desires to fulfil its aims gradually, by educational and legislative methods, and not by any sudden violent upheaval. Mr. (now Lord Passfield) and Mrs. Sidney Webb and Mr. G. B. Shaw are among its many distinguished members.

**Fable** (Lat. *fabula,* story). The term F., at one time applied to any fictitious narrative, is now more often restricted to a particular kind of literary composition, in prose or in verse, of a more or less humorous nature, in which beasts or even inanimate objects are the actors and speakers, and a moral truth is brought home to the reader by their means. According to Dr. Johnson, ' a " F." or " apologue " seems to be, in its genuine state, a narrative in which beings irrational and sometimes inanimate (*abores loquuntur, non tantum feræ*) are, for the purpose of moral instruction, feigned to act and speak with human interests and passions.' The definition of La Fontaine is a poetic rendering of this. His name is pre-eminent in this connection, and while other Fr. writers of Fs. (Marie de France, Corrozet, Florian, Taine) are only classed as ' fabulistes,' he is known as ' le fablier.' Fs. differ from myths in that they are intentionally made or invented, whereas the latter merely grow and develop out of existing legend. Parables and Fs. are very much akin, their use being strictly parallel to the use of metaphor. Neander's distinction was that in Fs. human passions and actions are attributed to beasts, but in parables the lower creation are only employed to illustrate the higher life, and the bounds of probability and possibility are never exceeded. There is often a close affinity between Fs. and proverbs. The origin and diffusion of Fs. is a much-discussed subject, but it seems probable that their earliest home was Hindustan. They arose out of the beast Fs. of savages, and the moral element appears to be a later development, essential to the F. as we understand it at the present day. La Fontaine, who describes his Fs. as ' une ample comédie à cent actes divers,' says that an apologue has two parts, body and soul (the story and the moral).

Among the earliest known examples are *Pancha Tantra, or Fables of the Brahma Vishnu Sarman* (second century B.C.); *Kalilah;* and *Dimna*, or fables of Bidpai (Pilpai), of which *Hitopadésa*, a modernised form, has three Eng. translations. These passed from India through Persia and Arabia, finally to W. Europe. Other Eastern collections were those of the Arabian Lokman, and Buddhaghosha's Parables. Æsop, famous among the Gks. (*c.* sixth century B.C., Herod., ii. 134), doubtless derived many of his fables from such Eastern sources. (*See* versified version of Babrius, third century A.D., and Jacob's edition of *Æsop's Fables*, 1889.) Phædrus was the Rom. imitator of Æsop. Horace's fable of *The Town Mouse and the*

*Country Mouse* seems to have a purely Rom. origin, unlike any others. The names of Aphthonius (*c.* A.D. 400) and F. Avianus form a link between classical and mediæval writers of Fs. The oldest known Ger. writer is Stricker (thirteenth century), but the mediæval *Reineke Fuchs* goes much further back. Other names deserving of mention are Gellert (1746), Lessing (1759), Hagedorn, Pignotti, Kryloff (translation by Ralston), Prior, Gay, Andersen, Yriarte (*Blackwood's Magazine*, 1839). Kipling's *Jungle Book*, Rostand's *Chante-*

LA FONTAINE

*cler*, and Maeterlinck's *L'Oiseau Bleu* may be considered as modern revivals of the fable-form in literature. J. C. Harris's *Uncle Remus* (Brer Rabbit) tales are not merely fables, but records of the folk-lore of the African-Americans. Beufey (1809–81), Cosquin (*b.* 1841), and Jacobs (*b.* 1854) are all modern writers on folk-lore. Consult, Tylor, *Primitive Culture*, vol. i.; *Pantschatantrum* (ed. Kosegarten), 1848; *Hitopadésa* (ed. Müller), 1864; Keller, *Untersuchungen über die Geschichte der griechischen Fabel*, 1862; Grimm, *Reinhart Fuchs*, 1834; Robert, *Fables inédites des XIIe, XIIIe et XIVe siècles . . .*, 1825; Lessing, *Ueber das Wesen der Fabel*, 1760; Weddigen, *Das Wesen und die Theorie der Fabel*, 1893.

**Fabliaux**, a group of entertaining compositions, in the form of tales in eight-syllable rhymed verse, numbering over 100, and forming a marked section of Fr. mediæval literature. The word ' fabliau ' is really a diminutive of ' fable.' A fabliau always had reference to some event and was usually satirical and comic in quality.

F. seem to have existed as early as the eighth century; but all the early examples are lost. The oldest preserved appears to be *Richeut*, about 1156, and the most modern are those of Jean de Conde and Watriquet at the beginning of the fourteenth century.

**Fabre D'Eglantine, Philippe François Nazaire** (1755–1794), Fr. dramatic poet, *b*. Limoux, and beheaded in Paris. In spite of the hostility of his many enemies, he was successful with his *Le Collatéral* and was thereby encouraged to follow it up with his *Philinté de Molière ou la Suite de Misanthrope*, which remains his masterpiece. *L'Apothicaire* followed in 1790, but in 1794 he was arrested by the Committee of Public Safety on the charge of forging a decree of the National Convention relating to the company of Invalides. Robespierre, who prosecuted, had no real belief in the substance of the accusation, but later he was charged with enriching himself in the course of his public duties for the revolutionaries, though in fact he was an ardent supporter of the Revolution. His verse is somewhat difficult, but his comedy is well conceived if inappropriate in expression.

**Fabre, Jean Henri** (1823–1915), a Fr. entomologist; was *b*. Dec. 21, at Sainte-Léone in Aveyron. In middle life was professor at the Natural Philosophy College of Ajaccio and the Lycée of Avignon. An opponent of evolutionary theory. Wrote: *Life and Love of the Insect*, 1911; and *Social Life in the Insect World*, 1912. Died at Sérignan in Provence (where he had lived in retirement since 1871). Oct. 11. F. wrote some of the most fascinating books on insects ever produced. They are filled with acute observations on the life and death of the creatures and are of deep interest to laymen. They have been translated into all modern languages.

**Fabriano**, a city of Italy in the prov. of Ancona, 44 m. S.W. of the city of Ancona. It is situated at the base of the Apennines, and possesses a cathedral and the Rossenti Museum. The manufs. are paper and parchment. Pop. 8679.

**Fabriano, Francesco di Gentile Da**, an It. painter, *b*. some time between 1348 and 1370 at Fabriano, and called after his birthplace. He belongs to the early Umbrian and Sienese schools, and painted chiefly in Florence, one of his finest extant pictures being the 'Adoration of the Kings' painted for the church of the Holy Trinity in Florence. A 'Madonna with Saints,' now in the Berlin Museum, belongs to the same period.

In 1426 he executed paintings for Pope Martin V. in the church of San Giovanni, Rome, but this, together with other works, has been destroyed. His pictures indicate, for the most part, a joyful and cheerful disposition, and he had a great love of splendour and rich colouring. F. belongs to the transition period of the fifteenth century. He *d*. about 1428.

GENTILE DA FABRIANO

**Fabricius Caius,** surnamed **Luscinus** (*i.e.* 'the one-eyed '), a Rom. general and statesman of the fourth and third centuries B.C., in later ages renowned as a model of incorruptibility. He was the first member of the Fabrician gens to settle in Rome. After the defeat of the Roms. by Pyrrhus in 280 at Heraclea, F. was sent to treat for ransom, and though Pyrrhus attempted to bribe him, all attempts were vain. During his second consulship, F. was successful in negotiating terms of peace with Pyrrhus. He gained a series of victories over the Samnites, Lucanians, and Brutians, and on his return to Rome received a triumph. In 276 F. was censor, and carried out with great vigour the old Rom. sumptuary laws.

**Fabricius Giorlamo** (1537–1619), an It. anatomist and surgeon, educated at the university of Padua. He studied medicine under Fallopius. Harvey, the discoverer of the circulation of the blood, was amongst his students. His chief work is his *Opera Chirurgica.*

**Fabricius, Johannes Albertus** (1668–1736), a Ger. classical scholar and bibliographer, *b*. at Leipzig. His great reputation is founded on his two literary synopses, the *Bibliothecæ.* At different times of his life he studied both medicine and theology, and he is known among theologians for his collections of apocryphal and pseud-epigraphical literature.

**Fabrics, Textile,** the name applied to those F. produced by weaving, and embraces the production from various raw materials of cotton, wool, silk, flax, hemp, and jute. The most simple form of T. F. is the primitive method in which the threads cross at right angles, regularly passing over and under one another, and a great variety of goods can be made in this way. The checks and stripes in the Scottish clan tartans are thus produced, and the thick corded effect, obtained in materials of the *repp* nature. The production of pile F. is one of the most important developments of plain weaving. They are woven with two warps, one being looped over crossed wires, and the other standing out above the main body of the cloth. The loops are either cut, or remain uncut. An instance of the former treatment is shown in the *Wilton* carpet, and of the latter in the *Brussels* carpet. Chenille, used with such good results in tapestry and carpets, is another example of the plain 'weave.' Historically, T. F. are of ancient date. Homer and other early writers speak of the weaving of the Gks. who used to work (principally in wool) designs and patterns of mythological subjects on their tapestries. The Egyptians also were celebrated from quite early times for their T. F. The supply of raw material and the adaptability of the people to a manufacturing life are the chief influences which control the establishment of the textile industry in any particular country. The earliest forms of machinery used were the hand-loom and spinning-wheel, and the manufacture of homespuns from wool was one of the first of textile industries to spring up among the people. It has now secured a foothold in nearly all countries in which wool F. are required for clothing. The fabrication of cotton had its greatest growth in India, and the industry has developed to a considerable extent of recent years in China, Japan, the E. Indies and Mexico. It is in the S. U.S.A., however, that the most wonderful growth of this industry has taken place, the agricultural labour of the negro having made available the raw material; and its steady advance is evidenced by the fact that more and larger mills are being built, and the old ones developed and enlarged.

To China and Japan we owe our fine and beautiful F. of silks. The silkworm flourishes in these countries and labour is cheap and plentiful. These nations produce F. of a costly and beautiful nature, which cannot be equalled by the more highly-civilised nations; though the introduction of the silkworm into Central and W. Europe caused a wonderful increase and advance in the manufacture of silks in France, Italy, Switzerland, and Austria. The Gers., too, and the U.S.A. have made a great success of the industry during recent years. In Eng. alone the industry seems to have declined a good deal during the last half-century, though the cotton industry, during the same period, has developed to an extraordinary degree. The silk industry was developed in the U.S.A. in 1870, and since then has made exceedingly rapid growth. Although statistics are not available, it is probable that the E. nations, China and Japan, lead the way in the manufacture of this particular F. The growth of the textile industry in Europe is made difficult by the rapid changes of fashion, largely brought about by the desire of big manufacturers to produce the material and effect attractive to buyers, and their unwillingness to keep in stock F. that are out of fashion, principally because it costs too much to sell goods that are not in constant demand. It is, unfortunately, a common experience to be unable to purchase the exact material one bought only a few years back. Most of the books on this subject are merely collections of plates, more often than not in colour and beautifully printed; but these give merely the design, and the nature of the F. has to be guessed at. The *Ornamente der Gwebe* of Fischbach is the best of these books. *See also* W. Morris's lecture on Textiles in *Arts and Crafts Essays*, 1899; T. R. Ashenhurst's *Weaving and Designing of Textile Fabrics*, 1893; Robert Beaumont's *Woollen and Worsted Cloth Manufacture*, 1899; E. A. Posselt's *Technology of Textile Design*, 1896; and Alfred Barker's *Analysis and Reproduction of Textile Fabrics*, 1894.

**Fabrizi, Nicola** (1804–85), an It. patriot, was *b.* at Modena. He established himself at Malta and aided Crispi in the revolutions of 1848 and 1860. Landing at Pizzolo, he joined Garibaldi at Palermo, and was Governor of Messina and Minister of War under the Garibaldi dictatorship. In 1866 he was Chief of Staff to Garibaldi. His political aims were to secure the return of Crispi to power and to obtain concord among the chiefs of the Left party. F. was whole-hearted in his passion for liberty, to which he devoted his whole life,

**Fabroni (Fabbroni), Angelo** (1732–1803), a famous It. biographer, sometimes called ' the Plutarch of modern Italy.' Educated at Faenza and Rome, he was a good Latin scholar, and appointed tutor to the sons of Leopold of Tuscany (1773). His chief work is *Vitæ Italorum Doctrina excellentium qui Sæculis XVII. et XVIII. floruerunt*, 1778–1805. F. became prior of the church of San Lorenzo, Florence, 1767. He also wrote *Laurenti Medicei Vita*, 1784, and *Vita Magni Cosmi Medicei*, 1788–89. *See* Tipaldo, *Biografia degli Italiani illustri*.

**Façade** (from the It. *facciata, faccia*, the face), the front exterior of a building. It is generally used in referring to the front elevation of more important buildings of considerable magnitude, though the term is not necessarily restricted to these. It is usual, however, to speak of the ' front ' of a house, and the F. of a palace, cathedral, etc. The back elevation is spoken of, as the ' rear ' F., and the side, as the ' lateral' F. The sides of a court are also called Fs., and distinguished as the E. or W. Fs., etc. The term originally was used to describe the outline of the aisle terminations, but it later was adopted as a design complete in itself, and used in secular as well as ecclesiastical building.

**Facatativa**, a tn. of Colombia, in the dept. of Cundinamarca, 20 m. N.W. of Bogota. Elevation about 8500 ft. It was formerly a fortress of the Chibcha Indians, whose last chief was killed here in 1538. Pop. about 8000.

**Facciolate, Jacopo** (1682–1769), an It. lexicographer and philologist, b. at Torreglia, near Padua. The revival of the study of anct. literature was the chief subject to which F. gave his attention, and with the assistance of his pupil, Egidio Forcellini, he brought out a new edition of the *Lexicon septum Linguarum*. F.'s mastery of Latin style, as displayed in his epistles, has been much admired for its purity and grace. He was known throughout Europe as one of the most enlightened and zealous teachers of the time.

**Facial Angle** is formed between a line drawn from the nostrils to the ear and another line from the nostrils to the forehead. It is an important feature of anthropometry, or the method of measurement used in anthropology. A protruding jaw indicates an animal type, and, therefore, the highest, most intellectual type of face indicates almost a right angle. Camper (1722–89) was among the first to define the F. A., his followers including Cloquet, Jacquart,

Cuvier, and Kollmann. *See* ANTHROPOLOGY.

**Facility**, in Scottish law, a word applied to mental deficiency to differentiate it from idiocy. If a person voluntarily places himself and his property under the care of one or more trustees, the case is called one of *voluntary interdiction*. The persons so engaged are called interdictors, and a facile person may not transact business—or, if he does, it is null—without the consent of the interdictors. If the court of session appoint interdictors for a facile person, the case is called one of *judicial interdiction*. Even in cases where there has been no interdiction, a contract signed by a facile person is null if it can be proved that such a person was imposed upon contrary to his own interests.

**Factor**, a mercantile agent employed to transact business for another. He is entrusted with the management and disposal of goods, his remuneration for which is called factorage or commission. Unlike a broker, a F. buys and sells in his own name. The first Factors Act was passed in 1825, in the reign of George IV. It enacted that a F., entrusted with the goods of another should be recognised as the legal owner of those goods, so far as to give validity to any contracts made by them with any persons dealing on the faith of that ownership.

**Factor** (Lat. *facere*, to make), in mathematics, is a number which, when multiplied by other numbers, makes up the product. Each of the numbers so multiplied is called a F. Thus 3 and 2 are Fs. of 6, $\therefore 3 \times 2 = 6$. A F. may also be called a *divisor*, because a product can be divided by any of its Fs. without remainder. The Fs. of 12 are 2, 3, 4, and 6, $\therefore 12 = 3 \times 4$, or $2 \times 6$, or $2 \times 2 \times 3$. When a number cannot be divided without remainder by any number except itself and unity, it is called a *prime* number. Thus 2, 3, 5, 7, etc., are prime numbers.

**Factor, Judicial** (from Lat. *facere*, to do), in Scotland is an officer appointed by the Sheriff Court for the purpose of managing property on behalf of one who is for some cause or other incapable of managing it himself.

**Factory Legislation—Great Britain.** The Factory and Workshop Acts have for their object the amelioration of the conditions under which the various classes of workers conduct their operations. The foremost provisions of these Acts are those which regulate the sanitary or hygienic condition of the workplaces, and those which relate to the safety of workpeople, with especial reference to industrial injury, the limitation and control of working hours, particularly of children workers, the protection of child labour, and the more efficient administration of the Acts by means of factory inspectors. These Acts mark an epoch in the social development of civilisation and the state of things effected by them at the present day contrasts so vividly with the industrial Eng. of a century ago as to make it incredible that the social regeneration did not come sooner than it did. In the middle of the eighteenth century the country still reposed on the ruins of the mediæval hierarchy of classes, with its taint of serfdom and bondage. The rise of the towns was slowly dissolving the ties of inborn status, but 'the movement from Status to Contract' was only complete with the industrial revolution brought about by the almost synchronous invention of labour-saving devices by Arkwright, Crompton, and others. With these came the beginning of a new horror— the utter anarchy of private enterprise. Gone was the domestic workshop, and in its place came the factory with single rooms crowded with workers specialising on one single process (see also DIVISION OF LABOUR). The doctrine of laisser faire and freedom of contract was soon to reap its consequences in the picture of 'women working half naked in the coal mines ; infants bound to the loom for fifteen hours in the heated air of the cotton mill and kept awake only by the overlooker's lash ; hours of labour for all, young and old, limited only by the utmost capabilities of physical endurance ; and complete absence of the sanitary provisions necessary to a rapidly growing population.' Small wonder that profits were reckoned at hundreds, and even thousands per cent. where 'white slavery' was carried to such a pitch that medical observation reported the 'rapid spread of malformation of the bones, curvature of the spine, heart disease, rupture, stunted growth, asthma, and premature old age among children and young persons.' Even the serf of feudal times or, later, agricultural labourer, had some sort of personal relationship with his master; the worker, however, being 'free' to contract, took all the incidents of the contract he had chosen to make, the ultimate expression of which was that he was in no better position than the handle or particular part of the machinery it was his duty to manipulate. First Carlyle, and then Mill, Darwin, Spencer, Ruskin, chiefly ruthlessly analysed the individualist view of life, either directly or indirectly,

by searching accounts of the evolution of the conception of the social organism, and parallel with the development of the lessons derivable from this, public opinion was soon expressing itself in practical legislative measures, antithetical to the dogmas of current political economy ; e.g. in Drainage Acts, Local Improvement Acts, Public Health Acts, and the forerunners of the modern Factory Acts.

The first piece of factory legislation to the credit of Eng. statesmen was the Morals and Health Act, 1802, which provided for the ventilation and cleansing of cotton mills and factories, and for the clothing, hours of labour, and religious education of apprentices employed therein. The exciting cause of this Act was, no doubt, the epidemic of fever in 1784 in the Manchester cotton mills which directed public opinion to the dangerous and unhealthy conditions to which the child workers were subjected. The Act, however, did little more than remedy the more glaring abuses of the apprenticeship system, and it was not until after the application of steam power to manufacture that the wholesale employment of children called for the next Act, the Cotton Mills Act, passed in 1819. This Act, which the celebrated Robert Owen was partly instrumental in passing, limited the age at which children might work in factories, and the time of their labour to seventy-two hours per week. From that year to 1856 a series of Acts such as the Act of 1844, limiting the labour of children in calico print works to six and a half hours a day ; and Ashley's Act of 1845, forbidding night work to women, were passed, containing regulations respecting the safety, hours, meal times, and holidays of childern, young persons, and women. But so far legislation only affected the textile and allied industries. Another great fault in the early Acts was that they were almost totally deficient in provisions for enforcing the law, this matter being left entirely to the individual bias of the local magistracy. In 1825, however, the efforts of Lord Ashley were successful in securing the appointment of the first skilled inspectors, a body of persons whose wide judicial and ministerial powers were in strange contrast to the merely inquisitorial functions of the modern factory inspector. From 1860 to 1864 Acts were passed to include in the existing factory legislation a number of non-textile industries. The Act of 1864 was remarkable for a departure in two directions : (1) it included by the generality of its enactment provisions that benefited all classes of labour irrespective of sex or age, *e.g.* by providing for more effective ventilation so as to remove injurious gases, dust, or other impurities; and (2) it assimilated its provisions in some respects to those of the Coal Mines Regulation Acts, by adopting the special rules system of these Acts, especially in regard to 'safety' precautions. By the combined operation of the Sanitary Act, 1866, and the Workshops Regulation Act, 1867, local authorities were invested with powers of administration to secure the general sanitation not only of factories but of all places where manual labour was employed in the manufacture or finishing of articles of sale. As may be gathered, the whole course of the legislation up to the great consolidating Act of 1878 was unsystematic and unscientific. Acts of Parliament were passed purely *ad hoc* to deal with evils the existence of which was only occasionally brought home by the inquiries of successive Commissions or the representations of men like Robert Owen. The net result was that there were up to 1878 a score of more or less unrelated statutes with a mass of regulations framed by inspectors or others avowedly in pursuance of the provisions of these statutes. In 1878, as the result of another Royal Commission, the Consolidating Act of 1878 appeared Like all Consolidating Acts (*q.v.*), this Act made some changes; it increased the minimum age of child labour in textile factories to ten; it made provision for holidays and pauses in the continuous hours of the fixed working-day. Into the detailed provisions of this Act it is not necessary to enter, because the additional legislation of 1883, 1889, 1891, 1895, and 1897 soon made it incumbent on the legislature to pass a second Consolidating Act in 1901. The Acts from 1878 to 1895 were directed mainly to : (1) The development of a specialised hygiene in factory life; (2) the more efficient application of the ordinary Public Health Acts to factories and workshops by successive transference of powers from the factory inspectors to local sanitary authorities; (3) the development of provisions for securing a greater measure of safety against accidents, *e.g.* by the adequate fencing of machinery in factories; (4) the development of the system of regulating by special requirements the conditions under which certain occupations scheduled by the Home Office as unhealthy and dangerous might be carried on; (5) the restriction of the employment of women shortly after childbirth; (6) control of overtime work; and (7) the reduction of the hours of labour for children.

A striking modern feature in 1893 was the first appointment of women inspectors, a principle which has been extended with beneficial results in a number of other directions since that time. There were encroachments in 1891 in the hitherto unfettered power of the employer of exclusively adult male labour to conduct his operations without legislative interference other than in the details of sanitation. Even now the only parts of the F. and W. A. which apply to men are those respecting sanitation and safety, such as cleanliness and ventilation, means of escape in case of an outbreak of fire, and fencing of machinery, and regulations in regard to dangerous trades. None the less the enhanced stringency in these latter respects of the provisions of the Factory and Workshop Act, 1895, is a considerable concession to the moral obligations towards male adult workers, and finds still more adequate expression in the codifying Act of 1901. Speaking generally, it may be said there is no legal limitation of the hours of labour of male adult workers; this matter is indeed one of the primary purposes for which a trade union exists. But the Factory and Workshop Act of 1891 contained an important latent innovation in section 8, under which power was given to the Secretary of State to schedule dangerous and unhealthy incidents or processes in any industry, the power given being in terms comprehensive enough to permit of a limitation of the hours of labour of all classes of workers. This section, though repealed, is in substance re-enacted by sections 79 to 82 of the Act of 1901. The new departures of the Act of 1895 in the requirements as to the sanitary condition of premises in which outworkers are employed and the maintenance of a proper temperature in workplaces of great humidity, and annual returns of persons employed, the investigation of accidents, and the particulars of wages due to piece-workers are all re-enacted and strengthened in the Act of 1901. Further powers to make regulations for the protection of health in cotton cloth factories were given to the Secretary of State by the Cotton Cloth Factories Act, 1897, but with that exception there was no direct legislation on the subject of factories and workshops until the Act of 1901. The Act of 1901 was a much more ambitious piece of legislation than its predecessors. It repealed and re-enacted with new features all the pre-existing Acts. Notable additions were made in the direction of more efficient means for securing sanitation, and for ensuring safety in dangerous trades. The minimum age of child employees was raised to twelve (since further amended by the Education Act, 1918, and the Employment of Women, Young Persons and Children Act, 1920, *see infra*), and numerous regulations were made for establishing a strong administrative control over the industries included directly or indirectly in the Act.

The Act of 1901 applies to textile and non-textile factories, and to ' workshops,' the difference, generally speaking, being that if mechanical power is used in the particular manufacturing process the place is a factory; if not, and only hand-power is used, it is a workshop. Textile industries being as a rule more deleterious to health than non-textile, the provisions affecting them are more stringent than in the case of non-textile factories and workshops. Among textile factories are included those in which is carried on the preparing, manufacture, and finishing of cotton, wool, hair, silk, flax, hemp, jute, tow, china grass, and cocoa-nut fibre. Non-textile factories include the following, whether mechanical power is used or not : print bleaching and dyeing, earthenware, lucifer-match, percussion-cap, cartridge, paper-staining, fustian-cutting, glass, metal, and india-rubber, letterpress printing and book-binding works ; copper mills, iron mills, blast-furnaces and foundries ; paper mills ; flax scutch mills ; and electrical stations. There are special regulations for (1) men's workshops or workshops where male adults alone are employed ; (2) women's workshops where neither children nor young persons are employed ; and (3) domestic workshops, *i.e.* private houses used by members of a family as a workshop. In (3) the hours for women are unrestricted. It is to be noted that such of the provisions of the Act as relate to dangerous machines, accidents, and regulations for dangerous trades are also applicable *inter alia* to docks, wharves, quays, and private railway lines or sidings used in connection with factories.

*Persons to whom the Act applies.*— These comprise: (1) young persons, *i.e.* boys and girls between the ages of fourteen and eighteen, or, where an educational certificate has been obtained, between thirteen and eighteen ; and (2) women, *i.e.* females above eighteen. Men are contemplated no less by this Act than by its predecessors as being able to look to their own interests, and, generally speaking, the only provisions that apply to them are those which are designed to secure efficient sanitation and safety, *i.e.* those sections

which relate to cleanliness, ventilation, fencing of machinery, regulations for dangerous trades, and means of escape in case of fire. In the case of women and young persons, there are not only special regulations as to sanitation and safety, but meticulous provisions as to working hours, meal times, holidays, and overtime. Children (*i.e.* persons between the ages of twelve and fourteen) were also included in the Act, which contained, for their protection, stringent provisions as to safety and health ; and this Act also contained an unconditional prohibition of employment of any child under twelve years of age— in which latter respect the Act supplemented the Elementary Education Amendment Act, 1899, which made it unlawful to employ any child under twelve so as to prevent full time attendance at school. But these and the like provisions (such as those of the Employment of Children Act, 1903, which absolutely forbade the employment of children in any occupation likely to be injurious to life, limb, health or education, regard being had to his physical condition) are now unnecessary, for the Education Act, 1918, prohibits altogether the employment of children in factories, workshops, mines and quarries ; and a ' child ' in this context is defined (by reference to the Education Act, 1921) to be a person of any age ' up to that at which his parents cease to be under the obligation to cause him to receive efficient elementary instruction or to attend school under the enactments relating to elementary education ; and a child will, for this purpose, cease to be of school age at the end of the school term in which he attains the age of fourteen (or fifteen if this age is fixed by byelaw). Finally, under the Employment of Women, Young Persons and Children Act, 1920, the general prohibition of the employment of children under fourteen is extended to *any industrial undertaking.* (*See* further under CHILD WELFARE ; and for the legislation in regard to children generally, *see* under Children Act, 1908, which Act amended the Employment of Children Act, 1903, in particulars other than those noticed above.) It may also be observed that the first factory Acts prescribed the minimum age of children allowed to be employed as eight.

*Health and safety.*—The provisions in the Act for ensuring the sanitary condition of factories and workshops, are designed to keep them free from effluvia, secure proper ventilation and periodical lime-washing of staircases, ceilings, and inside walls, and also to prevent overcrowding; and ensure the maintenance of a reasonable temperature. As to 'safety,' the Act provides that dangerous parts of machinery, like mill gearing and wheel races, must be fenced, means of escape in case of fire provided, and steam boilers kept in proper condition. It regulates the use of self-acting machines by, *inter alia*, disallowing any woman or young person to work between the fixed and traversing part of any such machines; and provides that the doors of a factory or workshop must open from the inside. A court of summary jurisdiction is empowered to prohibit the use of dangerous machines or premises. As to accidents, the Act, as amended by the Notice of Accidents Act, 1906, provides that all serious accidents must be notified to the inspector of the district, and in certain cases to the certifying surgeon of the district. Power is also given to the Home Secretary to direct a formal investigation of any accident occurring in a factory.

The 'Employment' provisions cover hours and holidays, overtime, night work, and fitness for employment. The hours of employment in textile factories for young persons and women are fixed at a twelve-hour day, of which not less than two hours must be allowed for meal-times. Half-holidays must be allowed on Saturdays. There are exceptions to the above general provisions, especially in the case of five hours' spells in certain textile factories provided the employment begins at 7 a.m., and the whole time between that hour and 8 a.m. is allowed for meals. Then follow analogous provisions as to hours in non-textile factories and workshops. There are restrictions on employment inside and outside a workplace on the same day, and a prohibition of employment on Sunday, or during meal times. There are certain special exceptions as to hours and holidays allowable in the case of such non-textile factories and workshops as may be authorised by a Special Order from a Secretary of State. Letterpress factories and laundries in the county of London, and various urban and rural districts around London, were the subject of an Order in 1907. There are also variations, as to the ordinary period of employment in the case of male young persons, above sixteen, in lace factories and bakehouses. Fish and fruit preserving industries and creameries are also specially excepted by reason of the perishable nature of the article dealt in. In newspaper printing offices another day may be substituted for Saturday so as to give the employee a half-holiday, and in the same connection there may be variations so as to permit of Sunday instead of Saturday employment in Jewish factories or workshops.

Under this part of the Act the employment of females within four weeks after childbirth is prohibited. Employers are also compelled to obtain medical certificates of the fitness for employment of young persons under sixteen.

The Act also throws on the employer the duty of seeing that child employees attend school during part of the day. Children of thirteen who obtain from the Board of Education a certificate of having attained a certain standard of proficiency are exempt from school attendance, and may be classed as young persons for the purposes of the Factory Acts.

The Act also compels the employers in the case of dangerous and unhealthy industries to notify certain industrial diseases contracted in a factory or workshop, such as lead-poisoning, arsenical poisoning, and anthrax. The Secretary of State has power to make regulations for the safety of persons employed in dangerous trades, and breach of which renders the occupier, owner, or manager of a workplace liable to a fine not exceeding £10, and in the case of a continuing offence to a fine not exceeding £2 a day.

There are also provisions enjoining the keeping of lists of outworkers in certain trades, showing the names and addresses of such workers whether directly employed as workers or as contractors. This part of the Act also lays down the conditions of labour in domestic factories and workshops, which conditions, however, are by no means onerous.

That part of the Act which relates to administration provides for the appointment, duties, and powers of factory inspectors and certifying surgeons. Local authorities have concurrent powers of entry, inspection, and taking legal proceedings with inspectors. It also lays down the procedure applicable to the making of Special Orders by the Secretary of State for extending or varying the provisions of the Act to certain industries. Occupiers of factories and workshops must notify inspectors of their occupation, fix up in their premises abstracts and notices of the Act, keep general registers showing the children and young persons employed, the accidents that occur, and other matters prescribed and make periodical returns of persons employed to the chief inspector of factories.

Since the Act of 1901 the principal amending or additional Acts passed are the Notice of Accidents Act, 1906 ; the Census of Production Act, 1906 ; the Factory and Workshop Act, 1907 ; the Employment of Women Act, 1907 ; the White Phosphorus Matches Prohibition Act, 1908. The Shops Acts, 1912 and 1913 ; the Education Act, 1918 (noticed *supra*); the Employment of Women, Young Persons and Children Act, 1920 (noticed *supra*); the Women and Young Persons (Employment in Lead Processes) Act, 1920 ; the Factory (Workmen's Compensation) Act, 1923 ; the Lead Paint (Protection against Poisoning) Act, 1926 ; the Shops (Hours of Closing) Act, 1928 ; and the Factories and Workshops (Cotton Cloth Factories) Act, 1929. The Notice of Accidents Act requires notice of ' dangerous ' occurrences, even though bodily injury has not been caused thereby,' and in other respects strengthens the procedure as to notifying accidents. The Census of Production Act amends the Act of 1901 by allowing slight modifications in certain cases of the intervals of time for sending in returns of persons employed. The Factory and Workshop Act of 1907 brings under the general provisions of the Act of 1901 all laundries that are not private house laundries. It also prescribes special regulations in regard to the use of stoves for heating irons, and fans for regulating temperature in laundries. The Act is applied with necessary modifications to charitable or reformatory institutions, not already subject to gov. inspection, where any manual labour is exercised in making, repairing, ornamenting, washing, or adapting for sale articles not intended for use in the institution itself. The Employment of Women Act, 1907, takes away the exemption given by the Act of 1901 in respect of the period of time for employment of women in flax scutch mills, and thus brings that industry into conformity with the general provisions as to periods of employment. The White Phosphorus Matches Prohibition Act, 1908, prohibits the use of white or yellow phosphorus in the making of matches, and the sale or importation of matches so made. The provisions of the Truck Acts as to payment of wages in current coin will be found under Truck Act. The Lead Processes Act of 1920 is an important measure for the protection of persons engaged in certain dangerous occupations where poisonous lead is used.

Previous legislation dealing with this commodity had been limited to safeguarding the health of workers in lead-making factories and no provision was made for the safety of those who dealt with it as a completed article. The fact that lead is so widely used in manufacturing processes made further precautions necessary. The Act provides that all women and young persons employed in any processes where it is used shall be medically examined at periodical intervals, and also that there shall be proper hygienic rules for its handling. The Factory (Workmen's Compensation) Act passed in 1923 placed the onus of responsibility for the workman's welfare more fully upon the employer than had hitherto been the case, and increased the amounts of compensation. The question as to what constituted a notifiable accident was decided by the rule that one which caused more than three days' absence from work came within that category. The Factories and Workshops (Cotton Cloth Factories) Act, 1929, empowers the Secretary of State to strengthen the existing statutory regulations governing the use of artificial humidity, in accordance with the report of Jan. 23, 1928, of the Committee appointed by the Home Office in 1924 to inquire into the question. The Shops Act, 1913, makes special provision for the application of the principles of the Act of 1912 to refreshment houses and hotels, etc., which latter Act provides that no assistant may be employed for more than sixty-five hours a week exclusive of meal times, with provision for annual holidays and twenty-six holidays on Sunday in every year. The Shops Act, 1928, provides the exact hours of Saturday employment with special exceptions in the case of holiday resorts, the sale of tobacco and perishable or urgently needed goods, such as medicines. (*See also* Labour Legislation.) There are also a number of other Acts incidentally affecting factory workers, such as the Shop Clubs Act, which makes it an offence in an employer to include under the conditions of employment a term that any workman shall discontinue his membership of any friendly society. *See* Redgrave, *On Factory and Workshop Acts*, 1909 ; E. Austin, *Law Relating to Factories and Workshops*, 1902 ; H. Evans Austin, *Law Relating to Laundries, Charitable, Reformatory, and Public Institutions*, 1907 ; Ruegg and Mossop, *Law of Factories and Workshops*, 1902.

Labour problems received careful attention during the peace discussions at Versailles, and an International Labour Organisation was created by the Peace Treaty. This organisation was passed on to the League of Nations, under which it does much useful work for the protection of operatives whose tasks involve special or unusual perils such as those from fumes, infection, dust, poisoning, strain or accident. It also makes provision for instruction to be given on such medical and scientific points as should reduce or avoid risks.

*United States of America.* Labour movements in the U.S.A. during and since the Great War period have not been as much influenced by legislation as by internal adjustments in business firms, and by friendly arrangements between masters and men. The experiment of paying high wages which has had hitherto a remarkable record of success has led to a new kind of rivalry between employers, and a more general willingness to regard the well-being of employees as essential to the success of the business. The slogan ' Safety First ' is one of many indications of carefully planned arrangements to eliminate risks and prevent accidents where possible; and joint committees of men and masters have been so successful in this connection, and especially through the publication of methods and results, that legislative action has been little needed. However, much of the impulse to provision for safety devices grew out of the fact that every state in the U.S.A. adopted some form of law providing for workmen's compensation for industrial injuries in lieu of the rule of the employer's liability for injuries due to his employee. The workers were thus given a right to relief which was automatic and certain. The U.S.A. Gov. led the way by an Act of Congress in 1908, which applied this rule to designated classes of employers of the U.S.A.. The States of Maryland and Montana were the first to follow this example. The movement in the U.S.A. towards reforming business from within has had a great influence upon Canadian industries, and, in consequence, Canadian employers and workmen have been more disposed to explore avenues of mutual welfare than to appeal for new legislation. The recommendations of the International Labour Organisation set up by the Treaty of Versailles have also been adopted in Canada.

**Factory Inspectors,** *see* FACTORY LEGISLATION.

**Faculty :** (1) A term formerly applied in philosophy to a fundamental function of the mind. Modern psychologists, however, regard the mind as a unity, not possessing faculties, but different activities. (2) In ecclesiastical law, a F. is a dispensation or licence. *The Court of Faculties* is the court of the Archbishop of Canterbury for granting certain dispensations, such as marrying without publication of banns. This authority rested in the pope till the reign of Henry VIII. The sittings are held at 23 Knightrider Street, Doctors' Commons. Its chief officer is called the master of faculties, and attached to the court are a registrar, deputy registrars, a record keeper, and a seal keeper. *A Grant of Faculty by the Ordinary* is given by the consistory court of the bishop of the diocese, and is necessary in order to effect any alterations in or additions to a church or parsonage. Consult Phillimore's *Ecclesiastical Law,* 1895. (3) The word is also applied to a branch of learning. In this sense it is derived from Latin *facultas,* which was used in mediæval times to translate Gk. δύναμις. Thus, the faculties of mediæval universities were art, theology, medicine, and law. This use has since been further extended to include the body of members of a profession. Thus, in Scotland, certain groups of professors are called ' faculties.'

**Faed, Thomas** (1826–1900), a Scottish painter, brother of John F., *b.* at Burley Mill. He was best as a painter of domestic genre, his pictures of this kind being ' Reading the Bible,' ' Mitherless Bairn,' ' The First Break in the Family,' ' Baith Faither and Mither,' etc. Consult William D. McKay, *The Scottish School of Painting,* 1906.

**Faenza,** a tn., Italy, in the prov. of Ravenna, situated on the Lamone (ancient Anemo), 31 m. S.W. of Bologna. It is a beautiful city enclosed by old walls. In the Vittorio Emanuele Square, which is surrounded by arcades and ornamented with a beautiful marble fountain, is the cathedral of San Costanza, the church of San Michele, and the city hall, once the palace of Manfredi. The cathedral dates back to 1474, and contains some beautiful work by Benedetto de Majana, Innocenzo da Imola, and others. Majolica is manufactured, and there are silk spinning and weaving works and sulphur refineries. Pop. 36,000.

**Faero Islands,** *see* FAROE ISLANDS.

**Faesi, K. Robert,** Ger.-Swiss poet, playwright, etc.; *b.* April 10, 1883, at Zürich; son of Friedrich F., merchant. Professor in Zürich university, lives at Zollikon by Zürich. His tragedy *Odysseus und Nausikaa* (1911), his drama *Opferspiel* (1925), and his comedies *Die offenen Türen* and *Die Fassade* (1918) are of a quality unusual in the Swiss theatre. As literary historian, he has written on A. E. Fröhlich, Paul Ernst, Carl Spitteler, Rainer Maria Rilke, and K. F. Meyer; also *Gestalten und Wandlungen der Schweitzer Dichtung* (1922). In 1928, received Swiss Schiller Prize for his collection of poems, *Der Brennende Busch*.

**Fagan, James Bernard** (*b.* 1873), a dramatist; attended Trinity College, Oxford, and afterwards was on the stage (till 1899). He wrote: *The Prayer of the Sword*, 1904, and *The Earth*, 1909; translated *False Gods* and adapted *Bella Donna*, 1911.

**Fagging** (possibly derived from the Gk. φαγεῖν, to eat, as the fags had often to prepare food), a system prevalent in English public schools by which a junior boy performs certain duties for a senior, such as running errands, stopping balls at cricket, tidying his study. The system was fully established at Eton and Winchester during the sixteenth century. The system usually has the full approval of the authorities. The arguments in its favour are that it gives a certain amount of autonomy to the boys, and that it prevents bullying. It tends to make the younger boys helpful and willing, and involves responsibility upon the elder boys, who are accountable for the good conduct of their fags and to protect them against bullying. A similar system known as *Pennalism* was introduced into the German universities during the seventeenth century, and is established in American colleges, where it is known as *hazing*. School fagging was discussed at the Annual Conference of Educational Associations in January 1931, when the subject was brought forward by the Society for Experiment and Research in Education. The gravamen of criticism of the system was that there were better ways of teaching discipline and self-sacrifice, and that unless very carefully controlled and supervised, the system lent itself to cruelty and taught servility rather than service.

**Faggot Votes,** votes artificially created for party purposes, chiefly at county elections, by transferring sufficient property to give a bare qualification for the franchise to persons who would otherwise be unable to vote. The transfer was made by nominal sale of property merely under mortgage. This practice was checked by Lord Somer's Act of 1696, and by the Representation of the People Act of 1884.

**Faguet, Emile** (1847–1916), Fr. critic and man of letters, *b.* at La

Roche-sur-Yon. He was a master in schools at La Rochelle and Bordeaux, and in 1897 became a professor at the university of Paris. Appointed a member of the French Academy in 1900. He was dramatic critic to the *Soleil*, and literary critic to the *Revue bleue;* and he wrote : *Histoire*

EMILE FAGUET

*de la littérature française depuis le XVIIᵉ siècle jusqu'à nos jours*, 1900 ; and monographs on Flaubert, 1899 ; Zola, 1903; etc. Died in Paris, June 7. *See* A. Séché, *Emile Faguet*, 1904; also A. Belis, *La Critique à la fin du XIXᵉ siècle*, 1926.

**Fagus,** a genus of Fagaceæ to which also belong the sweet chestnut and the oak. In addition to *F. sylvatica*, or beech, the species native to Great Britain, there are about fifteen others, some of which have beautifully-tinted or sharply-toothed leaves and are well known in cultivation.

**Fahlore,** a grey copper ore of two varieties, *arsenical* and *antimonal*. The former occurs crystallised and massive, and consists chiefly of arsenic, copper, iron, and sulphur. The latter occurs crystallised in modified tetrahedrons, and consists chiefly of antimony, copper, iron, sulphur, and zinc.

**Fahlunite, or Tricklasite,** a hydrous silicate of aluminium and iron, being an alteration product of the mineral iolite, due chiefly to its hydration. It usually occurs in regular hexagonal prisms, though its primary form is a right rhombic prism. Its colour is yellowish, greenish, and blackish-brown.

**Fahrenheit, Gabriel Daniel** (1686–1736), a Ger. physicist, *b.* at Dantzic. He lived in England and Holland, studying natural physics, and the manufacture of meteorological instruments. He invented certain improvements in the construction of thermometers, notably the use of quicksilver for alcohol, and devised the scale with freezing-point at 32°, boiling-point at 212°. He was elected a Fellow of the Royal Society of London (1724), and contributed papers to the *Philosophical Transactions*.

**Faidherbe, Louis Léon César** (1818–89), a Fr. general, *b.* at Lille. In 1852 went to Senegal, of which he was appointed governor. In the Franco-German War, he commanded the Northern Army. He withstood the attack near the R. Hallue, but was severely beaten at St. Quentin in 1871. When peace was signed, F. was sent by the French government to Egypt to study the monuments and inscriptions. His archæological works include *Collection des inscriptions numidiques*, 1870; *Epigraphie phénicienne*, 1873; *Essai sur la langue poul*, 1875. Consult his Life by Fulcrand, 1890, and by Brunel, 1897.

**Faidit, Gaucelm** (*c.* 1160–*c.* 1215), a celebrated Provençal troubadour, *b.* at Uzerche, Limousin. He was at first a *jongleur*, and wandered about with his wife, Guilhelma Monja, to the different European courts. In 1202 he accompanied Boniface III. of Montserrat to the crusades. Several of his songs are exhortations to the young and the strong to take part in the Holy War. Among his masters were Richard Cœur de Lion, whose death he lamented in a beautiful *planh*, Raymond d'Agoult, and Geoffrey of Brittany. Several songs and fragments of love lyrics are extant and are of great beauty. Consult R. Meyer, *Das Leben des Troub. G. Faidit*, 1876.

**Faience, or Fayence**, a general term applied to glazed earthenware, porcelain, and other kinds of pottery, and derived from the town Faenza.

**Failsworth**, a tn. of Lancashire, England, 4 m. N.E. of Manchester. Its chief industry is cotton manuf. Pop. 16,972.

**Fain, Agathon Jean François, Baron** (1778–1837); Fr. historian, and secretary to Napoleon I., *b.* in Paris. A member of the Committee of Public Safety on the outbreak of the Revolution; then of the Directory and of the Consulate. Later he became archivist and secretary to Napoleon, whom he thereafter accompanied on all his campaigns, until the Emperor's abdication in 1814. Resumed his functions in 1815, but retired into private life on the return of Louis XVIII. In 1830 Louis Philippe made him first secretary of the Cabinet. His works on the military and diplomatic events of his time, including those of the Empire, are marked by accuracy and

conscientious treatment, the years 1812, 1813, and 1814 being particularly well covered.

**Fainéant Rois**, the 'Do-nothing Kings' of the later Merovingians of France, namely Thierry III., Clovis III., Childebert III., Dagobert III., Childeric II., Thierry IV. and Childeric III. They were so called because during their reigns the rule of the country virtually lay in the hands of the mayors of the palace.

**Fainting, or Syncope**, a sudden loss of sensibility due to arrested circulation. The term is particularly applied to minor cases of shock where the condition of insensibility is transitory. The observable symptoms of F. are a sudden pallor of the face and loss of control over the muscles. The patient falls more or less suddenly and remains inert without any movement whatever. The eyes are half-closed or shut, the limbs are limp, the pulse is very weak or disappears altogether. It may be distinguished from epilepsy by the lack of movement and from catalepsy by the characteristic pallor. A feeling of faintness may not proceed as far as collapse; the patient feels dizzy, staggers for a moment, and suddenly recovers. The immediate cause of F. is an insufficient supply of blood in the brain. This may be brought about by actual loss of blood due to injury, or by poverty of blood due to a weakened condition, or may be preceded by a nervous disturbance. When F. is due to mental emotion, the medulla oblongata is over-stimulated to a condition of partial paralysis; the respiratory functions are sluggishly performed, the heart contracts feebly, and the circulation fails.

*Treatment.*—When assailed by a feeling of faintness, the patient should sit down and press the head downwards between the knees, when the flow of blood to the brain should be re-established. If the patient has already collapsed, he should be laid down with the head as low as possible and the respiratory functions stimulated by cold water on the face, by pungent aromatic vapours in the nostrils, by compressing and relaxing the ribs, etc.

**Fair** (Lat. *feriæ*, holidays), a large market, held periodically. A fair was usually held on a holiday or a saint's feast to take advantage of the concourse of people. According to Cicero, the Greeks utilised the religious games for trading purposes, and the Romans, too, traded during the annual feast at the temple of Voltumna in Etruria. During the reign of Edward I. of England it was felt that the churchyards or immediate precincts of the churches and abbeys were being desecrated by Fs., and a law, embodied in the Statute of Winton was passed to check the custom of holding Fs. near a place of worship. Courts of summary jurisdiction were formed to deal with any disputes or questions that might arise during a F., the date and duration of which had to be publicly made known beforehand. The traders who managed the F. were usually itinerant merchants, who went from place to place with their wares. At the time when means of communication were few, the F. was of great importance, but with the advance of civilisation is passing away. St. Bartholomew F. was held in London at Smithfield till 1855. Other famous Fs. were Stourbridge F. near Cambridge, which lasted for three weeks, Glasgow F. and Greenwich F. In England the F. has in many cases developed into a market for live stock. One of the largest horse Fs. is held annually at Horncastle, in Lincolnshire; Exeter has a F. in December for horses and cattle; Ipswich has one for lambs in August; and Nottingham has an October goose F. Some Fs., such as that of Gloucester, are famous for the agricultural produce sold. In some country towns, such as Witney, the old-fashioned F. still remains. Fs. are still common on the Continent. Leipzig has three annual Fs., each lasting three weeks, where leather, cloth, and furs are the chief commodities sold. Other Fs. of note are those of Frankfort-on-Maine and Frankfort-on-the-Oder, Beaucaire in France, Bergamo in Italy, Debreczin in Hungary, and Nijni-Novgorod in Russia. Siberia has Fs. at Kiakhta and Irbit, and Arabia at Mecca. The F. has many points of similarity with the *mela* of India. Consult Henry Morley's *History of the Fair of St. Bartholomew*, 1859; Cornelius Walford's *Fairs, Past and Present*, 1883; and *The Law relating to Markets and Fairs*, by Pease and Chitty, 1899. This term in the U.S.A. applies now solely to industrial exhibitions and what are known in England as fancy bazaars. In the former are included the 'state' and 'county fairs,' one of the first of which was the New York World's Fair opened in 1853 by a company formed in 1851 (*see also* under EXHIBITIONS).

**Fairbairn, Andrew Martin** (1838–1912), a Scottish theologian, *b.* near Edinburgh, and educated at the Edinburgh and Berlin Universities. In 1877 he was appointed principal of the Airedale Congregational College, Bradford, a post which he gave up in 1886 on receiving a similar appointment at Mansfield College, Oxford.

Author of *Studies in the Philosophy of Religion and History*, 1876; *Studies in the Life of Christ*, 1881; *Christianity in the First and Nineteenth Centuries*, 1883; *The City of God*, 1883; *Religion in History and in Modern Life*, 1884; *Christ in Modern Theology*, 1893; *Philosophy of the Christian Religion*, 1902, and *Studies in Religion and Theology*, 1909.

**Fairbairn, Sir William** (1798–1874), a Scottish civil engineer, *b.* at Kelso, in Roxburghshire. In 1804 he began his apprenticeship at the Percy Main Colliery, N. Shields, where he became a friend of George Stephenson. In 1817 he began a business of his own in Manchester, entering into a partnership with James Lillie, which lasted till 1832. He introduced improvements in mill works and water wheels, substituting iron for wood in the shafting. He was one of the first to build iron ships, which he floated on the Forth and Clyde Canal. In 1835 he established shipbuilding works at Millwall, London, and was consulted by the British Association on the supposed defects in iron caused by hot-blast furnaces. He carried out the construction of the tubular bridge across the Menai Strait, designed by Robert Stephenson, and himself invented the rectangular structures of the Britannia and Conway bridges. He wrote extensively on engineering subjects. Consult his Life by W. Pole (1877), and *Lives of the Engineers* by Smiles.

**Fairbanks, Charles Warren** (1852–1918), an American republican statesman, was admitted to the Bar in 1874. Twice chairman of the Indiana Republican state conventions, he sat for eight years (1897–1905) in the United States Senate, and was three times a delegate at large to Republican national conventions (at St. Louis, Philadelphia, and Chicago). From 1905 to 1909 he was vice-president of the United States; and he was republican candidate for vice-presidency 1916. Died at Indianapolis, June 4.

**Fairbanks, Douglas,** American cinema actor; *b.* May 23, 1883, at Denver, Colorado; son of John F. Attended: Jarvis Military Academy, Denver; E. Denver High School; Colorado School of Mines; and Harvard University. He then took to the stage, under the tragedian Frederick Warde—his first part being François the lackey in *Richelieu*. After a period of Shakespeare, in whose plays F. did not shine, he joined the company of Herbert Kelcey and Effie Shannon. He next became a clerk in a broker's office in Wall Street. After that, he and two acquaintances went as 'hay-stewards' in a cattle-boat to Liverpool— tramped through England, France, and Belgium, working at odd jobs, for three months—then returned to America. For a little while he was in a machine-shop; next, rambling in Cuba and Yucatan. When he returned to the States, he took up acting again. His first appearance on the New York stage was in 1901. He starred in *Man of the Hour* and *The Gentleman from Mississippi*. Married Anna Beth Sully, of Providence, R.I., July 11, 1907. Since 1915, has confined himself to 'the films': such plays as: *The Half-Breed*; *The Habit of Happiness*; *The Good Bad Man*; *Reggie Mixes in*; *The Mystery of the Leaping Fish*; and *Manhattan Madness*. In 1917 he became possessed of his own producing company. Divorced, 1918. Married, secondly, March 28, 1920, the film-actress Mary Pickford.

**Fairbury**, the co. seat of Jefferson co., Nebraska, U.S.A., 57 m. S.W. of Lincoln, and centre of a farming county with various industries. Pop. 6192.

**Fairfax, Edward** (c. 1580–1635), an English writer, b. at Denton in Yorkshire. His reputation rests on his translation of Tasso's *Gerusalemme Liberata*, published in 1600 under the title of *Godfrey of Bulloigne*, or *The Recoverie of Jerusalem, done into English Heroicall Verse*. His poem has great beauty; Dryden compared him as a poet with Spenser, and Waller acknowledged that he owed to him the harmony of his numbers. He also wrote eclogues, one of which appeared in Mrs. Cooper's *Muses Library*, 1737; and a *Discourse on Witchcraft*, published by Monckton Miles in the *Miscellanies* of the Philobiblon Society.

**Fairfax, Sir Henry** (1837–1900), a British admiral. He distinguished himself as a lieutenant on the *Ariel* in suppressing the slave traffic of the eastern coast of Africa, and in 1872 acted as naval attaché to Sir Bartle Frere in an expedition to the sultan of Zanzibar. In 1877 he was appointed to the command of the *Britannia*, when he personally superintended the studies of Prince Albert Victor and King George V. He was in command of the *Monarch* at the bombardment of Alexandria (1882).

**Fairfax, of Cameron, Ferdinando, second Baron** (1584–1648), Eng. general of the Parliamentary forces. His name is associated chiefly with the conflict in Yorkshire. When the king left the Parliament and established his quarters at York, the Commons sent F. to report on the king's movements, and F., by protesting against the presentment of the grand jury of Yorkshire, received the thanks of Parliament. He commanded the forces in Yorkshire, but was severely defeated at Adwalton Moor; later he turned the tables on the Royalists at Selby and again at Pontefract. *See* Markham, *Life of the Great Lord Fairfax* (i.e. the third Lord F.) 1870.

**Fairfax, Thomas, third Baron Fairfax of Cameron**, son of Ferdinando (1612–71), a soldier, fought in the siege of Bois-de-duc (1629), and later in the first Scottish War, but it is as a general for the parliament during the Civil War that he is best remembered. He captured Leeds and Wakefield in 1643, and in the following year had a command at Marston Moor. In 1645 he was appointed commander-in-chief of the parliamentary army, and in that year defeated Charles I. at the battle of Naseby. He was one of the king's judges in 1649, and was opposed to his execution. He was a man of great courage and a brilliant general. There is a biography by Markham (1870).

**Fairfield**, a par. and vil. of Derbyshire, England, adjoining Buxton. Pop. (1911) 4114.

**Fairfield**, a city of Jefferson, co. Alabama, U.S.A., 5 m. W. of Birmingham, an industrial suburb of B. founded in 1910 to provide for the employees of the U.S.A. Steel Corporation. Pop. 11,059.

**Fairfield**, a city of S.E. Iowa, with important manufactures, the site of Parson's College (Presbyterian). An annual Chautauqua assembly is held here. Pop. 6619.

**Fairford**, a vil. of Gloucestershire, England, on the Colne at the foot of the Cotswold Hills, 9 m. E. of Cirencester. It is noted for its old church in the Perpendicular style, built by John Tame in the fifteenth century. It has fine stained-glass windows of Flemish workmanship. Consult J. G. Joyce, *The Fairford Windows*, 1872. Pop. 1347.

**Fairhaven**, a tn. of Bristol co., Mass., U.S.A., situated at the mouth of the Acushnet R., on Buzzard's Bay, opposite New Bedford. It has manufs., a good harbour, some fine public buildings and is a summer resort. Pop. 10,951.

**Fairhead**, or **Benmore Head**, a promontory on the N. coast of Ireland, co. Antrim, 5 m. N.E. of Ballycastle. It is of columnar basaltic rock, 636 ft. high. *See* BENMORE HEAD.

**Fairies, Elves** (Fr. *fée*; Low Lat. *fata*, from *fatare*, to enchant; Lat. *fatum*, fate; Old Eng. *ælf*; Dan. *alf*;

Icelandic, *alfr*), supernatural beings existing in the mythology and folk-lore of all nations. They have often been represented as tiny, winged sprites, sometimes malignant, some-times benign, who possess a mysteri-ous power over human destinies. They need not, however, be diminu-tive beings, and have often appeared in the shape of humans. The fairies of Teutonic and Celtic lore pro-bably owe much to the sirens, nymphs, and fauns of classical mythology.

They have often taken the form of a beautiful woman who has beguiled men by her charms. Such were the Sicilian Sirens, whose singing on the rock near Cape Pelorus had such a fatal attraction for all seafarers until Ulysses, by an artifice, sailed safely past them, whereupon they drowned themselves in the sea. There are fairy lemans in Homer, elf-maids in Scandinavian literature, and R. L. Stevenson, in *Island Nights' Enter-tainments*, says that they are not un-common in Samoa. A most beautiful description of the elf-woman, who has pale kings and princes and warriors in thrall, occurs in Keats' ballad, *La Belle Dame sans Merci*. Fairies are soulless beings, but by marriage with a man may attain immortality. Fouqué made use of this superstition in his story of the water-nymph, Undine. When fairies have left their own country to marry and live with men, they have generally been bound by some restriction, which, when disregarded, brought great misery. Melusine built a great castle for her husband, and lived for many years in happiness. Once a week, however, she became a serpent from waist to feet, and the condition was that her husband should never see her when she was thus transformed. But he surprised her one day in her bath, and with a shriek she vanished for ever from his side, only appearing from time to time as a warning of approaching death in his family. According to another superstition, fairies have to pay a yearly tribute to the powers of hell, and for this purpose they are always trying to steal little children, leaving change-lings in their place. The peasants of Ireland still fear for their children, and never dare to speak of the little people as otherwise than 'good,' lest they should take offence and revenge themselves by robbing the cradles. Adults, too, have sometimes been allured to fairyland. They are then undone, and can seldom return from that country. Kirk (*d.* 1692), the author of *The Secret Commonwealth of Elves, Fauns, and Fairies*, it is said, was carried off by fairies. He ap-

peared, however, to a friend, and said that on his next visit, if the friend threw a dagger over his shoulder, the enchantment would be broken. The friend failed him, and Kirk has never again been seen by mortal men. In the old ballad, Janet really effected the escape of Tamlane from fairyland. A human being is undone if he eats fairy food, and Falstaff, it will be remembered, dared not speak to fairies or be a witness of their deeds: 'He that speaks to them shall die; I'll wink and couch: no man their works must eye.' Fairies can be very malicious, Fal-staff was pinched by his friends dis-guised as fairies and hobgoblins. This is the ordinary practice of elfish creatures, and thus Lyly in his *Endymion* has Corsites pinched black and blue by fairies. There always have been good and bad fairies. As in the old nursery fairy tale of the *Sleeping Beauty*, so at the birth of Ogier le Danois six fairies were present, five of whom gave good gifts, but the sixth was a bad fairy. In England, the fairy has been, in general, a domestic spirit, who visits houses at nights, sweeps the floor, threshes the corn, or skims the milk; but 'cropful out of doors he flings, ere the first cock his matin rings.' The German fairy is equally help-ful, and is called *Kobold*, a goblin. Belief in fairies has, however, diminished in England, but the country people of Cornwall are still persuaded of the existence of pixies, who, they say, are really the lost souls of babies who have died before baptism. Considerable interest has been aroused of late years in Celtic fairy legends through the writings of Andrew Lang, W. B. Yeats, Ernest Rhys, and others. Irish fairies dwell in crevasses and underneath old tumuli, in some ways the Irish leprechaun thus resembling the black earth elves of Scandinavia, who burrowed underground dwellings, where they retreated with stolen treasure. Scottish fairies, brownies, kelpies, and the like are supposed to be more malignant than their Irish brethren, and are creatures of storms and tempests.

Consult Keightley, *Fairy Mytho-logy*, 1850 (new ed. 1910); Schreiber, *Die Feen in Europa*, 1842; Maury, *Les Fées du Moyen Age*, 1843; Wirt Sikes, *British Goblins*, 1879; Grimm, *Deutsche Mythologie* (English trans-lation), 1880–88; Croker, *Fairy Legends of Ireland*, 1882; MacRitchie, *Fians, Fairies, and Picts*, 1893; Craigie, *Scandinavian Folk-lore*, 1896; W. B. Yeats, *Celtic Twilight*, 1883 (new ed. 1902); and *Fairy and Folk-Tales of the Irish Peasantry*,

1888; and Rhys, *Celtic Folk-lore*, 1901.

**Fair Isle** (Norse faar, a shire), a small is. of the Shetlands, Scotland, situated between the latter group and the Orkneys, 24 m. S.W. of Sumburgh Head. It has an area of 3 sq. m., and its cliffs are high and rocky. The industries are fishing and knitted articles. The Moorish patterns of the hosiery made here are believed to have come through the wrecked crew of one of the Armada vessels in 1588. Pop. 250.

**Fairlie**, a vil., N. Ayrshire, Scotland, situated on the eastern shore of the Firth of Clyde, and 2½ m. from Largs. It is noted for yacht-building. Pop. 1392.

**Fairlie, Robert Francis** (1831–85), a Scottish civil engineer. He was trained in practical locomotive work at Swindon and Crewe. In 1853 he was appointed superintendent and general manager of the Londonderry and Coleraine Railway, and later of the Bombay and Baroda Railway. In 1864, in Gracechurch Street, London, he patented the 'double-bogie' engine.

**Fairmont**, a tn. of W. Virginia, U.S.A., and the cap. of Marion co. It is situated on the Monongahela, 55 m. S.E. of Wheeling, at an important railway junction. It ships great quantities of coal and manufactures glass, textiles, etc. Pop. 23,159.

**Fair Oaks**, or **Seven Pines**, a railway station of Virginia, U.S.A., situated 7 m. E. of Richmond. It is noted as the scene of a battle, in 1862, of the Civil War, when the Union forces under McClellan gained a victory over the Confederates under Johnston. The former lost 5031 men, while the latter lost 6134.

**Fairy Rings**, bare or green circles in pastures or meadow lands which were once thought to be the scene of the midnight revels of fairies. But sceptics in fairy lore have long been armed with a rational and scientific explanation of the phenomenon. The rings are caused by the growth of the subterranean mycelium of fungi, which radiate outward to find fresh soil and nourishment. The circles are bare because the *Agaricus campestris* (common mushroom), or *Marasimus oreades* (the F. R. champignon), has exhausted the fertility of the earth, so that grass cannot grow, but as soon as the fungi begin to decay the ground becomes re-fertilised by the rich nitrogenous products of putrefaction and the grass grows greener than ever.

**Faisans, Ile des,** or **l'Isle de la Conférence**, an island with many historical associations in the R. Bidassoa, which is on the frontier between France and Spain. Here in 1659 was concluded the 'Peace of the Pyrenees' between Mazarin and D. Luis de Haro.

**Faith** is the acceptance of truth on the authority of another who reveals it (actual F.) or that quality or spiritual vision of the soul which enables it to transcend the confines of the visible and actual and to realise the eternal truth of all the unfathomable mysteries of God. In the Epistle to the Hebrews, it is defined as 'the substance of things hoped for, the evidence of things not seen,' and in Christian theology is regarded as the gift of the Almighty, without which there can be no salvation.

But though the meaning of F. is clear in the abstract, and F. is a force of universal recognition, yet it cannot be expressed or comprised in any formal definition, so that the varying interpretations given to it from time to time must be regarded as diverse, but not conflicting, manifestations of a single and fundamental spiritual vision or capacity. Some regard faith as that divine strength in a man's soul, which wins for him the essential gift of God's grace, whilst others conceive of it as that instinctive and unwavering conviction that the supreme goodness of the Saviour is strong enough to wash away all his impurity and sin. Sometimes, as in the works of Thomas Aquinas, an antithesis is implied between F. and reason, that is between knowledge accepted or credible (divine) authority or deduced from sensible evidence. In not a few Calvinistic churches and stern religious brotherhoods, such as that of the Plymouth Brethren, divine law is deemed an arbitrary expression of God's will, the observance of which is demanded from all believers, even though it appeal to their blind but passionate F. rather than to their reason. A gentler conception is that the reasonableness of the Divine Will is inscrutable, and that a Christian must never lose F. in its ultimate justice in spite of the calamities which overtake many a Job of this world, and in spite of the many other anomalies which seem to belie this belief.

A classification of the different forms or aspects of F. is sometimes attempted. F. is called human or divine according as it is based on man's or God's authority. Habitual F. adheres permanently to the soul; actual F. is the inception or exercise of habitual F. F. is explicit if its object is clearly perceived by the believer's mind; implicit, if it is only known generically and *in globo*.

**Faithfull, Emily** (1835–96), a philanthropist, devoted her life to the improvement of the status, remuneration, and sphere of labour of working women. In 1860 she started the Victoria Press, in which the printing was in the hands of women, and from 1863 to 1881 she continued to publish the *Victoria Magazine*, and to plead in its columns for greater equality between the sexes. Her lectures, both in Great Britain and the States, revealed to the public her noble aims and the disinterested nature of her work.

**Faith-healing** is a mind cure, resting on the firm conviction that, as suggested in James v. 14, pain and disease may be dispelled without medical aid, a lively faith in Divine Power being the one *sine quâ non*. The miraculous recoveries which took place in the temples of the Greek god, Æsculapius, no less than those effected by the king's touch all through the Middle Ages, must be regarded as instances of F. So also may be regarded some of the cures brought about by belief in the efficacy of relics, shrines and holy places such as Lourdes, the tombs of the saints and St. Winifred's Well in Flintshire, and perhaps even some of the miraculous cures worked by Christ and His apostles. The Waldenses, Moravians, and the Peculiar People of a later date all trusted to prayer and anointment with oil for the relief of sickness, whilst faith cures were an integral part of the beliefs of Pietists, and many sects of Puritans and Methodists, as well as afterwards of the Irvingites and Mormons. Professor Blumhardt and Dorothy Trudel conceived of healing rather in the sense of the medicine men of savage tribes, that is, as the expulsion from the body of an evil and tormenting spirit, whilst modern Christian Scientists go so far as altogether to deny the existence of physical suffering and disease. (*See* CHRISTIAN SCIENCE.) Psychologists attribute so-called cures by faith to powers of suggestion, which are peculiarly developed in any assemblage where the nervous and emotional activity is high. In Jan. 1931 the Lower House of Convocation of Canterbury passed a resolution in favour of Spiritual healing. This resolution petitioned the Archbishop of Canterbury to appoint a joint committee to draw up a provisional service for Unction (anointing the sick with oil) and Imposition of Hands for temporary use until a permanent and fully authorised form could be issued under Synodical sanction.

**Faithorne, William** (1626–91), English painter and engraver, born in London. Imprisoned as a Royalist in the Civil War. He was released and went to France. Returned to England about 1650 and carried on work as an engraver and printseller. His

[*Canadian Pacific*

AN INDIAN FAKIR

engraved portraits include those of Oliver Cromwell and Charles I. F. wrote *The Art of Graving and Etching* (1662).

**Faizabad,** or **Fyzabad**: (1) The cap. of the prov. of Badakshan, on the Koksha R., 87 m. E.N.E. of Kunduz, and N. of the Hindu Kush. Murad Beg deported all its citizens to Kunduz in 1821 and razed the town, but it is now once more a flourishing entrepôt for Eastern Afghanistan and the Pamir. *See also* BADAKSHAN (2) The name of a city in the United Provs. of British India. Ajodhya, once a city of great native splendour, is now a suburb. The Mausoleum of the Bahu Begum is the finest in Oude. It is 140 ft. high. Bahu Begum was one of the two Begums of Oude whose alleged ill-treatment was a subject of indictment of Warren Hastings. Ajodhya is one of the seven sacred Hindu shrines. The Janam St. han Temple is 200 by 150 ft., with walls 45 ft. high; ¼ m. to the N. is Ram Ghat, where Rama was cremated. F. is the headquarters of a dist. and of a div. Once the cap. of Oude, it has fallen into decay since the death in 1816 of Bahu Begam, who resided here for many years. Pop. 51,342.

**Fajardo,** a tn. and dist. on the E. coast of Porto Rico. There are sugar plantations and orange groves in the fertile ' environs,' whilst the town itself is a busy entrepôt. Pop. (1920) of town, 6571 ; of district, 14,302.

**Fakenham,** a tn. 20 m. W.S.W. of Cromer, Norfolk. It has an impor-

hundred lives. Indignation in America was widespread over this outrage, which, however, was eclipsed on May 7, 1915, by the sinking of the S.S. *Lusitania.* Both incidents were direct contributory causes to the entry of the U.S.A. in the War.

**Falaise,** a tn. 22 m. S.S.E. of Caen, in the dept. of Calvados, north-western France. It is on the Ante, and is the cap of an arron. There are cotton yarn and hosiery manufs., and tanning is carried on, but the town is famous for its castle, where William the Conqueror was born. It is a square structure crowning a high rock, and dates mostly from the twelfth century A famous fair is held annually in the suburb of Guibray, which lies due E. Pop. 6850.

[D. McLeish

FALAISE

tant corn market and a fourteenth-century church. Pop. 3181.

**Fakirs** (from Arabic *faqîr,* poor), are usually called dervishes in Persia, Turkey, and Egypt, dervish meaning ' a religious Mussulman beggar.' The Fs. of India are properly Hindu ascetics, who belong to strict religious orders, but the term F. is also applied to wandering charlatans, who profit by the villagers' superstitions to gain nefarious livelihoods. *See* DERVISHES.

' **Falaba,' S.S.,** a liner of over 4000 tons belonging to the Elder Dempster Company. During the Great War, when on her way to Sierra Leone, she was torpedoed by a Ger. submarine off the S. coast of Ireland on March 27, 1915. She received only the briefest warning, and sank within a few minutes, with the loss of over one

**Falashes** (from Ethiopic *falas,* a stranger), a tribe of Hamitic stock and Jewish religion, who are subject to the kingdom of Tigré in Abyssinia. They speak Ethiopic (or Geez), and their O. T. and other sacred books are written in this language, not in Hebrew. Though their religion is infected with pagan beliefs, such as faith in the potency of the evil eye, they practise a higher morality than their Christian rulers. Unlike their co-religionists, they live by agriculture, not by commerce. Until 1800 they had their own king, and are remarkable for their voluntary segregation from other tribes or sects.

**Falcon,** the most northerly state in Venezuela, bounded N. and W. respectively by the Caribbean Sea and the Gulf of Venezuela (also by Zulia), and southward by the state of Lara. Tropical bogs and sandy levels line the coast. Inland trade passes through Coro, the capital, the one seaport being La Vela de Coro. Pop. 178,642.

**Falcon** (Lat. *falco*, Teut. *valken*), a name given to certain members of the Falconidæ (*q.v.*), a family of birds of prey which catch their quarry on the wing. They have short curved beaks with one notch in the upper mandible; the wings are long and pointed, and the toes elongated. *Falco candicans*, the Greenland F., is white in colour, and is sometimes called the white gerfalcon; *Hierofalco*, the gerfalcon, is singular in having plumage of a slaty grey; *F. gyrfalco*, the Scandinavian F., and *F. islandicus*, the Iceland F., migrate southward in winter, the latter occasionally reaching Britain; *F. peregrinus*, which, together with the northern F. and other species, is used in falconry, ranges over Europe, China, Japan, N.E. Africa, and N.W. India. This species is known in England as a migrant, and is found nesting on lofty cliffs; it is amazingly swift in flight and devours game and birds of all kinds.

**Falcone, Aniello** (1600–65), an Italian battle painter, is the most famous of Riberia's pupils, and himself the founder of a school. In his battle-scenes, taken both from biblical and secular stories, he shows himself a careful painter, capable of suggesting some of nature's animation. During Masaniello's revolt (1647), he organised his pupils into the 'Compagnia della Morte' (company of death), and paraded the streets by night to murder Spaniards. F. wisely went into exile on the restoration of peace.

**Falconer, Hugh** (1808–65), a British botanist and palæontologist. During his first stay in India (1830–42), he was superintendent of the botanic garden at Saháranpur, and during his second (1847–55), held a similar post at Calcutta. He discovered the *asafœtida* medicinal plant in India, and urged the cultivation there of tea and the cinchona bark. During his invaluable geological researches in the tertiary deposits of the Siwálik hills he made a splendid find of fossils including the Mastodon and an enormous prehistoric tortoise. His *Fauna Antiqua Sivalensis* (1846–9) was never finished. He is justly regarded as a martyr to science, for overwork undoubtedly undermined his health.

**Falconer, William** (1732–69), a Scottish poet, belonged to a large family, all of whom were deaf and dumb except himself. His famous *Shipwreck*, first published in 1762, was based on a personal experience, for he was one of the few survivors of a merchant vessel which foundered off Cape Colonna, Greece. In spite of the somewhat offensive mixture of the artificial, elegant style of Pope with the breezy, technical dialect of a sailor, the life and vivid descriptive passages of the poem are ample excuse for its popularity. In 1764 he directed a rhymed lampoon, 'The Demagogue,' against Wilkes and Churchill, and in 1769 published his *Marine Dictionary*.

**Falconet**, the name given to a small field gun introduced in the fifteenth century. With culverins, sakers, and demi-cannons, etc., falcons formed the lighter ordnance up to the eighteenth century.

**Falconet, Etienne Maria** (1716–79), a Fr. sculptor, spent twelve years in St. Petersburg (1766–78), where he executed for Catherine II. a colossal statue in bronze of Peter the Great, which stands in the square of the senate. He held the ancient sculptors in small esteem, which perhaps accounts for the somewhat meretricious taste apparent in even his fine 'Milo of Crotona.'

**Falconidæ**, a family of diurnal birds of prey, comprising the falcons, hawks, kites, buzzards, eagles, etc., and constituting, with the vultures, the typical Accipitrines. The head is crowned with feathers, and the female is larger than the male; the two sexes associate in pairs and mate for life.

**Falconry** (from Old Fr. *faulconnerie*), the art of training falcons and hawks for the chase. Hawking is commonly regarded as a synonym, but is properly restricted to the practice of F. in the field. Its antiquity is an established fact, but no one knows where or when this 'aerial warfare' was first introduced. There are records proving its early popularity in Asia Minor, Turkey, Persia, Tartary, and China, and it is interesting to read Marco Polo's almost incredible yet undoubtedly veracious account of how Kublai Khan, the great Emperor of Tartary and China, went hawking in the thirteenth century. Pennant has suggested Scythia as the birthplace of F., arguing that thence it spread all over Northern Europe and especially to Norway, where falconers attained such remarkable proficiency. In India the art seems to have been practised from time immemorial, the hawks being trained to the boldest flights, to stoop at the antelope and wild boar, besides at the gazelle and the stag. Here, moreover, as in the East generally, these birds are still used for hunting, and the native Indian gentry still train their largest falcons ' to kill deer by pitching on their heads and picking out their eyes.' To turn to Europe, it is written how even in the eighth century the 'grand fauconnier' in France was 'an officer of great eminence,' with an annual salary of 4000 florins, and as many as 300 hawks. In England, the early Britons of the days of the Roman occupation were skilled in F., whilst among the Saxons there is mention of it in the reign of Ethelbert (760). King Alfred is commended as a falconer, and from the Norman Con-

WANDERING FALCON

quest till the seventeenth century, kings, princes, barons, lords, and even ladies were affected with the hawking mania, William I., Stephen, Edward III., Henry VIII., and Queen Elizabeth being the most enthusiastic of its royal devotees. Change in fashion, but above all the introduction everywhere of the fowling-piece, which so vastly increased the quarry, whilst at the same time doing away with the difficulty and expense of breeding, training, and keeping the hawks, led to the rapid decrease of the sport after the Commonwealth, so that, by the end of the seventeenth century, F. had fallen into general decay. The last owner of heron-hawks died in 1871, yet the foundation of the Old Hawking Club about the same time served to prevent the art becoming entirely obsolete.

Stringent and oppressive laws were early made respecting F., as of all other forms of field sport. Thus, under the Normans the privilege of keeping hawks was reserved only for persons of the highest rank, and it was not till the Carta de Foresta had been wrested from King John that the privilege was extended to all freemen. In Edward III.'s reign, every person finding any species of hawk was instructed by statute to take the same to the sheriff of the county, or to suffer two years' imprisonment; moreover, the stealing of a hawk was made a felony. According to a decree of Henry VII., the stealing or destruction of falcons' eggs brought on the offender a penalty of imprisonment for a year and a day, the term being reduced under Elizabeth to three months. A sixteenth-century ordinance, which forbade hawking from Easter till after the harvest, is of interest as indicating a consideration for agriculture and a smaller regard for the falconers' interests. Further regulations assigned the sort of hawk proper to persons of different ranks.

Thus the eagle, vulture, and merloun were for an emperor; the gerfalcon and tiercel of the gerfalcon, for a king; the falcon gentle and the tiercel gentle, for a prince; the falcon of the rock, for a duke; the falcon peregrine, for an earl; the bastard, for a baron; the sacre and sacret, for a knight; the lanner and lanneret, for an esquire; the marlyon or merlin, for a lady; the hobby, for a young man; the goshawk, for a yeoman; the tiercel, for a poor man; the sparrow-hawk, for a priest; and the kestrel, for a knave or servant.

'Eyasses,' or ' eyesses,' are birds taken from the nest and reared wholly or partially in confinement. These may be flown at pigeons, blackbirds, grouse, partridges, wild duck, pheasants, and indeed all minor quarry. ' Passage,' or wild-caught, falcons are entrapped during the migration or passage from N. to S. in the autumn by means of a decoy-pigeon and a bownet. They are usually better-tempered, swifter, and higher-couraged than the eyas, and are especially used for rooks, herons, and sea-gulls. The training of the eyas differs from that of the passage-hawk, as it has everything to learn, including the way to catch and kill its own prey. The nestling is put on a straw-covered platform in an out-house, and is fed three times a day on lean beef. If it receives insufficient food, ' hunger-traces ' will appear like knife-marks across the point where a feather joins the flesh, and should these break the bird becomes useless. Before the young hawk is allowed to fly, ' jesses,' that is, leather straps are set round its legs, and above them bells are attached with thongs called 'bewits.' It is then allowed some weeks of liberty, when it is said to be 'flying at hack,' the object being to instil in it a little native wildness; for desire for food brings the bird, at intervals, back to its home.

The training for eyasses is practically the same as that for wild-caught falcons. 'Hooding,' that is, obscuring the light by means of a leathern cap, is the first operation as a 'hooded' bird will sit quite quietly, and will not damage her feathers, or otherwise get out of hand by 'bating,' that is, fluttering from the fist or perch. Feeding is only once a day, and always upon the gloved hand. Soon the hawk is 'called off' 'to the 'lure.' The most common kind of 'lure' consists of a flat leather-covered piece of lead, to which pigeon's wings are attached, and also on either side a piece of raw meat. This is later used for luring the falcon back to its owner after a fruitless flight, and this is why the bird is made acquainted with it from the very first. During the training, the hooded hawk is perched on an assistant's hand, being fastened thereto by a leash, whilst the falconer, at a distance of 20 yds. or more, flourishes the lure. When the bird is unhooded, it flies to the flesh on the lure, which is her reward for the flight. After a time she can be trusted to do this without being held by the line or leash. Finally, she is 'entered' at the 'quarry,' that is, she is allowed to go off from the fist to kill a live fowl dangled at the end of a long line. She is then ready to be flown at wild game.

The elaborate processes which belong to the management of a hawk are responsible for the development of a whole technical language to describe them. A few have already been mentioned; whilst as regards the behaviour of the hawk, 'to mount' means to wait on high; 'to bind,' to fasten on the quarry in the air; 'to stoop,' rapidly to descend on her prey from a height; and 'to tower,' to soar high above it.

Hawking has an extensive bibliography, including Lady Juliana Berner's *Boke of St. Albans*, 1486; Turberville's *Booke of Falconry*, 1575–1611; Schlegl and Wulverhorst, *Traité de Fauconnerie*, 1844–53; and the standard English work entitled *Falconry in the British Isles*, by Salvin and Brodrick, 1855.

**Faldstool**, was originally a folding seat, which a bishop in the Romish church would use when not installed in his cathedral throne. The word was later applied to the small desk at which, in English churches, it is

customary for the clergyman to read or chant the litany.

**Falémé, or Tenne,** an important trib. of the Senegal in Senegambia, W. Africa. Rising in Futa-Jallon, it flows northward to the confluence above Bakel. Cascades and rapids impede all navigation 120 m. from the mouth.

**Falerii** (mod. *Civita Castellana*), one of the twelve chief cities of Etruria, lying 32 m. N. of Rome. It was finally reduced to Roman rule

A GATE AT FALERII

in 241 B.C. The fine walls with towers and gates are the sole remnant of Roman days, the site having been abandoned after A.D. 1033.

**Falernian Wine,** a noted and favourite wine of the Romans. Its name was derived from Falernus Ager, a dist. of Campania, Italy, about 20 m. N. of Naples. Horace described it as 'surpassing all wines.' Later, the quality of the wine decreased, on account of the lack of careful cultivation. *See* Petronius Arbiter, *passim*.

**Falguière, Jean Alexandre Joseph** (1831–1900), a Fr. sculptor and painter, studied at the Ecole des Beaux-Arts. His statues are superior to his work in oils, but in these latter he displayed a fine appreciation for the most delicate gradations of light and shade, an appreciation which plastic art almost invariably develops. Of his oil paintings 'Acis and Galatea' deserves mention, whilst his 'Wrestlers' and 'Fan and Dagger' hang in the Luxembourg. Splendid and arresting vitality animates all his sculpture, one of the most impressive illustrations of which is his 'Triumph of the Republic' (1881–86), a quadriga for the Arc de Triomphe in Paris. 'Joan of Arc,' 'Balzac,' and 'Lamartine' exhibit his skill in historical portraiture.

**Faliero, Marino** (c. 1274–1355), a doge of Venice, gained an illustrious victory in 1346 over the Hungarians who were trying to storm Zara, but after his election as doge in his native city in 1354 all his good fortune deserted him. Petrarch describes F. as wise and clear-headed, a description which does not tally with his behaviour as doge, for he suddenly developed an overweening ambition, and weary of the insolence of the nobles, entered into a conspiracy with the common people to destroy them. But the plot failed, F. was executed, and the Council of Ten became stronger than ever. *See* Byron's *Marino Faliero*.

**Falk, Paul Ludwig Adalbert** (1827–1900), a Prussian statesman. Bismarck, having determined on an anti-Catholic policy in 1872, welcomed F. as minister for education. It was F. who drafted the four measures known as 'Kulturkampf,' by which the state arrogated to itself direct control over ecclesiastical matters. A reaction in governmental policy coupled with the death of Pius IX. obliged F. to resign his office in 1879.

**Falkenhayn, General Von,** Prussian general. Ger. Minister of War in 1914. Chief of the Ger. Headquarters Staff and successor to General Von Moltke; the frustration of whose plans at the first Battle of the Marne and in E. Prussia called for a reconstruction of the Staff. His staff work was undeniably good, and though aided by such generals as Von Mackensen, not to speak of the popular idol Hindenburg, it is not too much to say that credit is mainly due to him for the Battle of Tannenberg on the E. Front, the repulse of the Allies at Loos, Neuve Chapelle, and elsewhere on the W. Front, and the failure on the Gallipoli peninsula. In 1916, however, the Ger. armies met with disaster at Verdun, where Pétain repulsed probably the heaviest blows delivered in the war, and on the Somme, where the great retreat to the Hindenburg Line had to be organised. These Ger. failures were capped by the sudden entry of Rumania into the war; but Falkenhayn proved equal to this new belligerent, and gradually reduced its army to a negligible quantity. In these operations he was Commander of the 10th Army. The Ger. Press, however, were disappointed over the general results of 1916, and Falkenhayn was accordingly shelved for Hindenburg, going on a mission

to Turkey. After this he dropped out of public notice, and was put on half-pay at his own request in 1919.

**Falkirk,** a municipal burgh and market tn., 11 m. S.E. of Stirling, in Stirlingshire, Scotland. It stands high and overlooks the fertile Carse of F. To the N. and S. respectively pass the Forth and Clyde and Union Canals, whilst its port, Grangemouth, is 2½ m. to the N.E. Within 3 m. of the town are the Carron iron works and some extensive coal-fields, which account for the supremacy of F. in the light casting trade of Scotland. Local market days have reduced the importance of its three annual trysts or fairs. Historically F. is noteworthy as the scene of two battles, one in 1298, when Edward I. defeated Wallace, and the second in 1746, when the miserable performance of the British dragoons under General Hawley secured an easy victory for Prince Charles. The remains of Sir John de Graehame, a friend of Sir Wm. Wallace, and those of Sir John Stuart, who were slain at the battle in 1298, lie in the churchyard. F. with Stirling and Grangemouth send a member to Parliament. Pop. 33,308.

**Falkland,** a royal burgh, 9 m. E.N.E. of Kinross, in the E. of Fifeshire, Scotland. Brewing of ale and linen-weaving are still carried on, but the old-world village is noted for its ancient palace of the Stuarts. James III. converted Thane's Tower into a royal palace in 1538, and two round towers in the western wing were added by James V., who *d.* here in 1512. As a child Queen Mary loved to stray in its woods, and the castle is full of historic association. It was restored in 1888, but before that day Carlyle had likened it to 'a protrusive shin-bone striking through the soil of the dead past.' Pop. 781.

**Falkland, Lucius Carey,** second Viscount (c. 1610–43), was educated at St. John's College, Cambridge, made a happy marriage, which his father regarded as a mésalliance, and settled down at his country-seat to study Gk., which he soon mastered. F. was a man of lofty ideals, unflinching integrity, and true intellectual vision, whose whole life was rendered a despair and tragedy, because he was obliged to live through the bitter and hopeless struggle between Charles and his parliament. As a member of the latter he in vain lifted up his voice to secure some semblance of a trial for Strafford, and it was the violence and illegality of the Puritan party which forced him over to the side of the king, whose empty promises he at first believed. Clarendon, his friend, who writes that 'mankind could not but admire and love him,' persuaded him to accept the secretaryship of state. The duplicities of the Royalists broke his heart, and realising that the hour of compromise had passed and that his was a completely isolated

LUCIUS CAREY, VISCOUNT FALKLAND

position, splendid though it was, he voluntarily ended a brief but unhappy existence by courting and winning death at the battle of Newbury.

**Falkland Islands** (Fr. *Malouines*, Sp. *Malvinas*), a group, forming a crown colony of Great Britain in the S. Atlantic Ocean, 250 m. to the E. of the nearest shores of S. America. There are more than 100 altogether, but E. and W. Falkland, separated by Falkland Sound, are the only two of any size, having an area of 3000 and 2300 sq. m., respectively. Mt. Adam, the highest peak of the group, attains an elevation of 2315 ft., and W. is more hilly than E. Falkland. Drizzling rain falls on 250 days of the year, and the mean difference in temperature between midsummer and winter is only 10° F., the average for midwinter being 37° F. Sheep farming is the staple industry, the shepherds being mostly of Scottish origin. In 1928 wool worth £280,770 and whole products worth £3,686,521 were exported. The pop. is 2087, of whom 988 live in Stanley, the cap.

**Falkland Islands, Battle of.** Naval battle of the Great War, fought on Dec. 8, 1914, in which the British Admiral Sturdee, completely avenged the defeat of Rear-Admiral Cradock off Coronel (*q.v.*). The Ger. squadron comprised the armoured cruisers *Scharnhorst* (flagship) and *Gneisenau*, light cruisers *Leipzig*, *Dresden* and *Nürnberg*, under the command of Admiral Graf von Spee. The British

squadron consisted of the two battle cruisers *Invincible* and *Inflexible* (17,250 tons, 25 knots, carrying eight 12-inch and sixteen 4-inch guns), the armoured cruisers *Cornwall* and *Kent* (each 9800 tons and carrying fourteen 6-inch guns) and the light cruisers *Glasgow* and *Bristol* (4800 tons, two 6-inch and ten 4-inch guns). The *Scharnhorst* and *Gneisenau* carried twelve 8-inch guns. The intention of the Ger. squadron (betrayed, it was alleged by the Gers., from Chilean sources), was to bombard the Falkland Islands, and Von Spee reached the vicinity of this British colony on Dec. 8. The appearance of the British squadron was a complete surprise and the Ger. ships promptly took to flight. Their speed, however, was inadequate, and they were brought to bay, the Gers. being out-manœuvred for position and out-ranged in gunfire. All the Ger. ships, with the exception of the *Dresden* (*q.v.*), were sunk. The *Scharnhorst* was sunk three hours after the first shot was fired, the *Gneisenau* two hours later. The *Leipzig* was sunk by the *Cornwall* and the *Nürnberg* was sunk in flight by the *Kent*. The Ger. casualties were 2000 officers and men, the British seven killed and four wounded. There were no survivors of the *Scharnhorst*, while of the *Gneisenau's* complement of 700, fewer than 100 were rescued. Von Spee himself perished. The secrecy of the Admiralty's move against Von Spee's raiding squadron was signal proof of efficiency. Admiral Sturdee was awarded a baronetcy for his victory. The vital importance of this victory lay in the fact that it prevented Von Spee from establishing himself in the W. Indies and thereby raiding 20 million tons of sea-borne grain and meat supplies intended for Great Britain. On the defeat of Cradock's squadron at Coronel, the British Admiralty at once prepared this counterstroke, and Admiral Sturdee, on Nov. 11, steamed away with the cruisers *Inflexible* and *Invincible*, reaching the Falklands with almost unprecedented speed. By Dec. 7, when anchored in Port Stanley, he had been reinforced by Admiral Stoddart in the *Carnarvon* and by the cruisers *Cornwall*, *Kent* and *Glasgow*. The British squadron coaled all night, and was still coaling when the look-out station reported that the Ger. squadron was approaching, it being then nearly 8 a.m. By 10 a.m. all the British ships were under way, and the first shots were fired just before one o'clock. In 6½ hours from that time the battle was over; the Ger. squadron having no reasonable chance against the attacking squadron. The whole campaign of these waters is of importance in that it illustrates Great Britain's essential vulnerability. There was no parallel in British maritime history to the dangerous economic consequences that threatened Coronel. British national security was actually in danger through a more or less obscure defeat in a remote corner of the Pacific at the hands of a detached raiding squadron and only the prompt extinction of the raiders could have restored confidence to merchant shipping.

**Fall, The,** an expression used in Christian theology for the spiritual change engendered in Adam and Eve after their temptation by Satan in the Garden of Eden, a change due to their knowledge of, and contamination with, sin. This account of the entrance of sin into the world is responsible for some of the fundamental doctrines of the theology professed by orthodox Christians, Catholics and Protestants alike. By sin, Adam lost the divine life of supernatural grace which was his heritage. Inasmuch as Adam is the supreme head or source of humanity, all mankind must bear the taint transmitted for all time from Adam as the penalty for his (Adam's) unique transgression of God's will. But the burden of this ' original sin ' has been lifted from mankind because Jesus was crucified to restore divine life to mankind and to avert from all who believe in Him the punishment which would otherwise be meted out after death for their share in Adam's fall. Thus the merits of the Saviour give to the Faithful eternal life.

**Fallacy** (from Lat. *fallax*, deceptive) is false reasoning or argument. In spite of the countless varieties of confused thought and ambiguity, it is customary to adopt some classification of F. Thus Bacon in his *Novum Organum* divides them into four *Eidōla* (False Appearances), whilst Mill regards all Fs. as belonging to one of the five following categories : (1) Fallacies of Simple Inspection, which embrace all Natural Prejudices ; (2) Fallacies of Observation ; (3) of Generalisation, including Induction ; (4) of Syllogism or Ratiocination ; and (5) of Confusion, under which come all cases of ambiguous language. But by far the most famous subdivisions of F. are those based on Aristotle. According to him all Fs. are either material, that is misstatements of facts, said therefore to be *extra dictionem*, or *in re* ; verbal, that is arising from the misuse of words ; or formal or logical, that is arguments which transgress the laws of true demonstration, technically called the Syllogism.

Fallacies of the second and third species are said to be *in dictione*, or *in voce*. Under the first heading come *Petitio principii*, or *Circulus in probando* (arguing in a circle) ; *Non sequitur*, or the F. of false cause ; *Ignoratio Elenchi*, or irrelevant conclusion ; and Fallacy of Accident, that is an erroneous argument from the general to the particular.

**Fallières, Armand** 1841–1931), Fr. statesman, *b.* near Agen, S. France, son of a blacksmith. Practised as an advocate at Nerac. Entered Chamber of Deputies in 1876, and was Under-Secretary of State to Jules Ferry at the Fr. Home Office in 1880, and then, successively, Minister of the Interior and Prime Minister. President of the Fr. Republic 1906 to 1913 and president of the Senate eight times.

**Falling or Shooting Stars** are small extra-terrestrial planetary bodies which travel through space in countless numbers and with an illimitable variety of orbit. It is estimated that the smallest, in spite of their flame due to momentary combustion, are no bigger than large grains of sand, and further that their velocity, which is deduced from the length of its fall and the duration of its flight—rarely a second—varies from 60 to 400 m. per minute. The services of photography have now been enlisted for the more accurate investigation of these meteoric bodies, but it has long been observed that star showers appear to diverge from one point, there being innumerable points or ' radiants,' as they are called, for the different showers. Thus those that proceed from Perseus are called Perseids and other meteor swarms, such as the Leonids, Taurids, Pegasids, and Lyraïds are similarly named after the constellations from which they seem to shoot. But their apparent radiation and diversity of flight are an illusion of perspective, their tracks being really parallel and subject to fixed orbital movements. On a clear but moonless night, a watcher of the heavens may see as many as ten an hour with his naked eye, whereas with a good telescope he would see at least twenty times that number. Indeed astronomers compute the number of falling stars through which the earth daily passes as some twenty millions. When they first become visible in the atmosphere they are usually from 40 to 75 m. above the earth's surface, whilst the fiery particles are on an average 250 m. apart, though in heavy showers they may be as near as 20 m. *See* METEORS.

**Fallopian Tubes, The,** so called because they were discovered by a Pisan professor, Fallopius, form the utero-peritoneal canal and carry the ova through a small opening, the ostium abdominale, among the fimbriæ or fringes at the end, into the womb cavity. *See* UTERUS.

**Falloppio** (or **Fallopius**), **Gabrielle** (*c.* 1523–62), an Italian anatomist. His chief physiological discovery was the function of the tubes, now called Fallopian after him, whilst in the anatomical field he made careful studies of the sphenoid and ethmoid bones and the internal structure of the ear. His collected works appeared posthumously (1600).

**Falloux, Frédéric Alfred Pierre, Comte de** (1811–86), a Fr. politician, first revealed to the public his enthusiasm for the old order of things under the Bourbons in his *Histoire de Louis XVI.*, 1840. His love of education and liberty was rather peculiar to his own personality, and met with small sympathy among the legitimists to whom he belonged. As a reward for his support during the Revolution of 1848, Louis Napoleon made him Minister of Education, and he was able to pass the ultra-Catholic ' Loi Falloux ' (1850).

**Fallow** (probably derived from the Old Eng. *fealga*, a harrow), land ploughed and tilled but not sown for a certain period, usually a year. It was early discovered—witness the Mosaic injunction that every seven years the land must have a ' Sabbath rest,' *i.e.* ' lie fallow '—that the soil decreases in fertility if continually sown with grain. Thus farmers resorted to the practice of ' fallowing,' a practice which may well be as old as agriculture itself, the object being to destroy the weeds, such as couch grass (*Triticum repens*), to disintegrate the soil and to give it a thorough aeration. The Roms. left their cultivated fields F. every alternate year, but improved crop rotations have well-nigh done away with the need of ' bare fallow,' except, perhaps, for extremely clayey soils which cannot, otherwise, be adequately cleansed. The succession of green after wheat crops is found sufficient to refresh the earth and is, of course, much more economical than to leave it quite cropless. Land submitted to this process, the green crops being potato, turnips, etc., is called ' green fallow.' Perhaps the most serious drawback to true or bare Fs. is that the nitrates are washed out, as there are no plant roots to retain them, so that the soil must be dressed with guano or manure before re-cultivation in order to restore the needful organic matter.

**Fallow Chat,** *see* WHEATEAR.

**Fallow-deer,** the name given to several genera of Cervidæ, a family of ruminant ungulate mammals; they are characterised by the expansion of the upper part of their antlers into palmate form. Usually they stand about 3 ft. high, and have small heads, large ears, and rather long tails. In colour they are fawn, with a number of large white spots, or they may be yellowish-brown, or, more rarely, dark brown. *Dama vulgaris*, the commonest species, is a native of N. Africa and the countries bordering the Mediterranean, but was introduced into Britain at an early period ; *Cervus mesopotamicus* is a native of the mountains of Laristan ; *C. giganteus*, erroneously called the Irish Elk, is a fossil deer of enormous size, the antlers having in some cases a span of 11 ft.

**Fall River,** a city and port of entry, on Mt. Hope Bay, at the mouth of the Taunton R., in the Bristol co. of Massachusetts, U.S.A. It is one of the chief centres for the manufacture of cotton goods in the U.S.A. Other industries include the dyeing and finishing of textiles and the manufacture of fur goods, cordage, pianos and men's hats. The Fall R., a small affluent of the Taunton, which here makes a descent of about 130 ft. in half a mile, furnishes water power for the city's industries. Many of the buildings of F.R. are of red granite, quarried in the vicinity. There are several parks, Notre Dame College, a textile school, and a conservatory of music. Pop. 119,295.

**Falmouth :** (1) A seaport and market tn. in Cornwall, England. It lies 7 m. S. by W. of Truro, and its harbour is probably the finest in England. There are two graving docks, and foundries, engineering works and ship repairing yards. Granite, china-clay, copper ore, rope and fish are exported. F. has a wonderful climate, and nowhere in the S. of England do tropical plants flourish more luxuriantly. It has become a popular holiday centre. Pendennis Castle was built in 1543 for the defence of the harbour, which is now a favourite yachting water, and the permanent anchorage of the once-famous tea clipper, the *Cutty Sark*. Millions of oysters are dredged from the harbour every year. Pop. 13,322. (2) A tn. 18 m. E. of Montego Bay in Cornwall co., Jamaica. Pop. 2136.

**False Bay,** lies 25 m. S. of Table Bay, in the S.W. of the prov. of the Cape of Good Hope, Africa.

**False Imprisonment,** the incarceration or the detention anywhere of any person against his will and without lawful authority. In Scots law the abuse is called ' wrongous imprisonment.' The injured individual may either apply for a writ of habeas

z 2

corpus, or may make an indictment against his unlawful detainers, and he is further at liberty to enter into an action for damages. *See* MALICIOUS PROSECUTION.

**False Money,** *see* COINING.

**False Point,** the name of a harbour, cape, and lighthouse in the Cuttack dist. of British India, so called because it is often mistaken by sailors for Point Palmyras, which lies 1° further N. Although the port was not opened till 1860, it is the best between Bombay and the Hugli, its commercial value being largely increased by the cutting of the Orissa canals.

omit to make a full and true entry of properties received by him in the proper books or accounts, his purpose being to practise fraud; or if he falsify, mutilate, or destroy any book or valuable security belonging to his company or corporation; or if he make a false entry or omit to set down an important particular, or if he concur with others in doing either of these two things; or, again, if he make, circulate, or publish any written statement of account which he knows to be untrue in any important particular, or if he concur in doing any of these three things. By the Falsification of Accounts Act of 1875 the

[*G.W.R. Photo*

FALMOUTH

The docks and Pendennis Head, and the *Cutty Sark* in the foreground

**False Position,** in arithmetic, a former method of solving a problem by one or two suppositions (also called the ' rule of trial and error '), now largely replaced by the direct method of equations.

**False Pretences,** *see* FRAUD.

**False Swearing,** *see* PERJURY.

**Falsetto,** an expression used in singing to denote the highest register of a male voice. A F.-singer can so blend his top notes with his chest register that there is no perceptible break in passing from one to the other. As to how the larynx is affected in the production of F. tones, there is still great diversity of opinion.

**Falsification of Accounts** was made a misdemeanour, punishable with penal servitude for seven years, under the Larceny Act of 1861, and in Scotland is an offence under the Debtors Act of 1880. By the terms of the former Act every director or officer of a public company or body corporate is liable to the above penalty if he

terms of the above Act, with the penalties attaching thereto, were extended to clerks, officers, or servants who may try in any of the above ways to defraud their employers.

**Falstaff, Sir John,** a famous comic character in Shakespeare's *Henry IV.* (Parts I. and II.) and the *Merry Wives of Windsor.* His prototype, than whom he could hardly be more unlike, was a Lollard martyr, Sir John Oldcastle, who appears in *The Famous Victories of Henry V.,* an old play which Shakespeare adapted. Oldcastle was altered to Fastolfe so as not to shock Protestants, a Sir John Fastolfe (*c.* 1378–1459) having actually existed. Indeed, this Fastolfe, like the inimitable F. of the plays, earned a reputation—undeserved it seems—for arrant poltroonery in the Fr. wars.

**Falster,** a Danish island, 30 m. long, and varying from 2 to 13 m. in breadth, off the S. coast of Seeland in the Baltic. Malaria is endemic in the marshes, but the soil is well watered and yields good crops. Pop. 30,000.

**Falticeni, or Folticeni,** a tn. 9 m. S. by E. of Czernowitz, on an affluent of the Sereth, and cap. of the dept. of Suceava, Rumania. Pop. about 10,000, one half Jews.

**Falun, or Fahlun,** a tn. and cap. of the dist. (län) of Kopparberg, 50 m. W. of Gefle in Sweden. The Kopparberg Mining Company, which has been in existence since 1284, controls the oldest copper mines of Europe. Up to the year 1900 there had been mined some 35 million tons of copper ore. Its present copper output is insignificant, but the company owns many iron-ore mines and large sulphate and sulphite and paper mills. F. has two mediæval churches, and a seventeenth century town hall and a fine industrial museum. The welfare work of the Falun Copper Co. is remarkably efficient. Pop. (1928) 13,611.

**Fama** (in Gk. φήμη), in classical mythology, is the personification of Rumour, and finally came to be identified with Evil Report. The Gks. erected temples to her at Athens and Smyrna, but the Roms. did not follow their example. Sophocles conceived of her as the daughter of Hope.

**Famagusta, or Famagosta,** a seaport tn. on the E. coast of Cyprus, 2½ m. S. of the anct. Salamis. Arsinoe was founded by Ptolemy Philadelphus in 247 B.C. The Christian refugees from Constantia in the reign of Mu'awiyah settled in Arsinoe, which soon became an archbishopric of the Orthodox Church, the name being changed to F. It is now famous for its walls and the fine cathedral of St. Nicholas. The Christians live in the suburb of Varosia, the Moslems, within the walls. F. is the port at which many travellers land in Cyprus, a special train conveying them thence to Nicosia, the capital. Pop. of F. 6980.

**Familiar** (from Lat. *familiaris*, to do with the family), a demon or supernatural spirit, who is the slave of wizards, magicians, and all necromancers, and who responds to his master's call and carries out his wishes. The idea of such an attendant spirit is world-wide. Thus the Arabs used to believe in their Aladdins or genii of the lamp, whilst Eskimos are still superstitious about their ' torn gaks,' and the Hindus and Persians had faith, like the Roms., who set great store by their ' Lares ' and ' Penates,' in presiding household deities. In the Dark Ages all Europe recognised the power of the magicians of Salamanca to imprison evil Fs., and the Christian conception of guardian angels may be connected with belief in such spirits. Agrippa's dying anathema pronounced on his black dog, who embodied his F., is worthy of quotation : ' Abi, perdita Bestia, quæ me totum perdisti.'

**Familiars of the Holy Office** were lay officers of the Court of Inquisition whose chief duties were to apprehend and imprison the accused. They were so called because they were admitted to the secrets of the body they served.

**Family, The,** means in modern times the social group consisting in the narrower sense of the man, his wife, and his children, and in the wider sense of all those who, in varying degree, can claim kinship with that F. whether from the father's or the mother's side. As with all primal origins, the nearer the historian approaches to its final source, the greater is his difficulty in securing reliable data. But from the welter of confusion and doubt there arises this fact, namely, that the most primitive type of F. was matriarchal, that is one in which kinship was counted only on the mother's side. Such is the case with the Nairs of Malabar, whose social organisation is of the rudest kind, and also among all tribes with whom ' beenah ' marriages prevail. Among the Nairs the true F. comprises the woman with her children, mother, and brothers. The husband as a necessary constituent of the group is unknown, the procreation of children being dependent on the casual visits to the woman's house of men who come there for that purpose and then depart. Under these circumstances the uncles, her brothers, become the guardians of the younger generation, and eventually make its members their heirs. The term ' beenah ' is taken from Ceylon and describes all marriages which result in the man going to live with his wife's folk and forsaking his own tribe in order to secure adoption into the woman's. Such a practice was popular among the Semites of Arabia until comparatively recent times. Moreover, the Book of Genesis offers indubitable evidence that it was the custom among the Hebrews in some remoter period. The ' beenah ' husband came to live with the woman in her tribe and among her kinsmen, his offspring being invariably counted among his wife's and not his own F.

A slight advance on the Nair F. is that found among certain savages in Tibet and constantly referred to, on that account, as ' Tibetan polyandry.' Here the wife goes to live with a number of brothers belonging to some other tribe, who are all by turns her husband. The head of the F. is the eldest brother, who can lay lawful claim to all the woman's children : when he dies, the next brother succeeds, and when all the brothers are deceased their privileges pass to the brotherhood's eldest son. The marriage custom of the Britons, as described by Cæsar, bears some resemblance to this, whilst in Strabo there is recorded a similar polyandry among the Arabs, and from the Mahabharata it is clear that an identical custom once prevailed among the Hindus. Such is the evidence of Ethnology prescinding from Revelation as a possible source of knowledge.

Polyandry certainly seems quite at variance with all preconceived notions of the relative position of man and wife in bygone ages, hence many investigators regard it as a corruption of a more primitive family institution, induced by economic pressure or sloth. Polyandry has, indeed, a purely practical and economic basis. Mankind in early days had a tremendous struggle for existence, and found it necessary to restrict the number of women by infanticide, as well as by polyandry. It was not till the food supplies became more assured and until such developments as the domestication of cattle came about that men found they could afford to have a wife each, and began moreover to attach a value to the field as to the household work of the other sex. The matriarchal character of the F. was a natural result of the uncertainty of fatherhood and the practical impossibility, in many cases, of discovering it. Exogamy—that is, marriage outside of the tribe—has been the fashion among all races for all known time, and it is this, coupled with female kinship, which accounts for the diffusion of the totem Fs. throughout numerous tribes—a fact for which Maine, with his patriarchal theory of the development of the F., could offer no satisfactory explanation. Totem Fs. must have been isolated at first. Afterwards, when exogamy was introduced, the children of the woman would naturally adopt her totem—that is, worship the plant or animal which she regarded as sacred, and after they had grown up and married, would carry her totem with them to a strange group or tribe. This hypothesis satisfactorily explains the existence of distinct clans within the same tribe.

The male kinship, which was the rule in the polyandry of Tibet, contains the germ of the modern patriarchal, as also of the monandrous, F., and it is obvious that the purchase system was a further step in that direction. Thus Isaac gave a bride's price or bridal gifts for the privilege of taking Rebecca away to his own people, and purchase marriages were from early periods common among Arabs and Hindus. There was no doubt a long struggle between the Nair and ' beenah ' Fs. on the one hand, and the purchase system on the other, but in spite of the sacred and valid nature of a kinship established in a totem group, the latter tended everywhere to survive and finally to oust the other. The ' Levirate ' was another aid to the establishment of the man's supremacy over his wife and children. For by this process, which was adopted by both Hindus and Hebrews, he might allow his brother or a friend, for a sum of money or else for love, to borrow his wife, and might then appropriate to his own family any offspring from their promiscuous association. This was a favourite means for a wealthy man to strengthen his kindred or F., for he was legally the parent of all his wife's children, no matter to whom she bore them. When, with the growth of true paternal and other higher feelings, the idea took root that actual procreation was essential to the claim of fatherhood, then the patriarchal F. may be said to have been firmly established. Monandry became the rule, and with the decline in the status and importance of women, and likewise with the growth of what is now called conjugal infidelity, polygamy became a recognised and even lawful licence, as indeed it still is among the Ashantis and most of the aboriginal tribes in Australia to-day. Rome offers the most perfect example of a rigidly patriarchal family. Indeed the Eng. word is derived from the Latin *familia*, which meant primarily a ' household of slaves.' That this same word came to include his wife and F., with the rest of his domestic property, may not unfairly be taken to illustrate the small esteem in which the *pater familias* regarded them. Indeed the *patria potestas*, or ' power of the father,' was absolute, including even the power of life and death over all his immediate dependents and relatives. But it is a hopeless error to argue, as has not infrequently been done, that the Rom. system is the type of the group or F. from which have sprung all tribes and nations, even though the legendary growth of Israel from Jacob and his twelve descendants, and the Genesis story of the peopling of the world from the posterity of Noah lend support to such a theory.

**Family Allowances.** A system, which prevails in Canada and the U.S.A., under which the state makes an allowance to mothers on widowhood or incapacitation of the husband. In Canada, mothers' allowances are granted, under Acts of Parliament, in all those provinces which have adopted such legislation, viz. Alberta, British Columbia, Manitoba, Ontario and Saskatchewan. The conditions governing the grant of the allowance vary, however, as between the different provinces, e.g. incarceration of or desertion by the husband is not admissible in some provinces, but, subject to qualifications, is in others. The maximum amount varies from $42·50 a month for the mother and first child in British Columbia, with $7·50 for each additional child, to $30 for a family in Saskatchewan. There has been some attempt to introduce the F.A. system into Great Britain. Opponents to it argue that it would tend to encourage an imprudent increase in the size of families; but this does not appear to be borne out by facts in America.

**Family Compact**, the name given to various treaties between the reigning Bourbon dynasties of France and Spain, also including Naples and Parma, during the eighteenth century. These treaties were made in 1733, 1743, and 1763. They aimed at establishing the Bourbon dynasties in Italy, and also at checking the expansion of England in the colonies of the American continent at the expense of France and Spain. They are an important feature in the great eighteenth century wars of the Polish and Austrian succession.

**Family of Love**, or **Familists**, a religious sect founded by David Joris at Delft in Holland (1501–56). They taught that religion was nothing but love which united man with God, and that there was no need for any doctrine or ceremony. Blunt in his *Dictionary of Sects* (1874) avers that they also denied the reality of sin, and were Antinomians; he divides them into two congregations, known as the ' Family of the Mount ' and the ' Essentialists.' The teaching was brought to England by Henry Nicolai, and in 1575, having been attacked by the Puritans, they petitioned Parliament for toleration. This was, however, not granted, and five years later we find Elizabeth ordering them to be put down as a ' damnable sect.' They are mentioned in the writings of George Fox and Henry Moore, but seem to have disappeared during the seventeenth century.

**Famine**, a scarcity of food-products of such a nature that the population of a district or country is reduced to actual starvation, or the serious danger or probability thereof. The causes of such a scarcity are principally meteorological, i.e. prolonged drought, or sometimes excessive rainfall and storms, leading to floods and the destruction of crops and stores. Crop diseases, the ravages of locusts and other pests, are among other causes ; and the decimation of an agricultural population by war, plague, etc., and economic causes which deprive a population of means of purchasing food-stuffs have also contributed to a state of F. The opening up of the world's food products to all nations by the development of rapid mechanical transport has been the main reason why the risk of F. has materially declined, and transport facilities are the principal object in combating a F. when it occurs to-day. Though serious Fs. occurred in Russia in 1892 and 1905, it is chiefly in the E., in such a vast and unorganised country as China, that F. on a large scale is dreaded. Still more marked is the ever-present threat of Fs. in India, where the people are to a large extent dependent on agriculture, and where a failure of the monsoon for a single year may result in a total failure of the crop. It is not so much the actual want of food-supplies that is the serious factor to be combated, as the immediate want of purchasing power resulting from cessation of the only money-producing labour. Thus the great Indian schemes of famine fighting include not only constant development of irrigation and transport, but elaborate relief works, loans, etc.

**Famund**, or **Faemund**, a lake of Norway, situated 85 m. S.E. of Throndhjem. It is about 38 m. in length, and its greatest width is 5½ m. The Oster Dal flows from it.

**Fan.** This term, derived from Lat. *vannus*, the F. used for winnowing chaff from grain, is used for various devices for creating a current of air, and thus cooling the atmosphere of a room, as in the propeller-shaped electric F. or in other elaborate devices for regulating the temperature, driving fresh air into or otherwise ventilating a room or building. The ' punkah ' of the E., attached to a rope which is steadily pulled by a servant, is familiar to all travellers and residents in India. It is, however, as the light implement, carried in the hand and used for cooling the face, that the F. has historical and artistic interest. Of these Fs., there are two main types, the rigid and the folding F. ; the first consisting of a circle or segment of a circle of light material fixed to a handle by radiating plats of wood, etc. ; the second in which these radiating plats fold together and bring the flexible leaf into a small flat compass. The folding F. came originally from Japan, and was thence brought to China and so to Europe. In the E., Fs. were used by both sexes, and were the central feature in many elaborate ceremonies. The Japanese had war-Fs., coloured bright red, and there are some fans which possess a small poniard concealed in the handle. The Chinese devoted much marvellous art in carving the ivory, tortoise-shell, etc., sticks of the handle. The fixed F. dates from very anct. times. A wooden handle, which once held ostrich feathers, is in the museum at Cairo; it belonged to Amenhotep, the Pharaoh of Egypt of the seven-

tions and scenes to be painted on Fs., and Fr. Fs. of this period, painted on fine vellum, called 'chicken skin,' silk, etc., are highly prized. Charles Conder (d. 1909) painted many exquisite silk Fs. There is a fine collection of Fs. of every age and country in the Victoria and Albert Museum, S. Kensington, London. The design of a F. depends mainly upon the amount of air which it is required to move and the pressure against which it has to move it. Fs. for moving large volumes of air against very little pressure, such as ventilating Fs., have either large

[*After Lepsius*

THE PHARAOH HAREMHÊL CARRIED BY SOLDIERS PRE-
CEDED AND FOLLOWED BY FAN BEARERS

teenth century B.C., and feather-Fs. borne by slaves and servants are found on monuments of all ages. They were used in the mediæval Church to keep flies from the chalice; large feather Fs., *flabella*, are borne behind the pope in processions and in many E. and other countries; the state-Fs. are attributes of royalty and power. The folding-F. was used in England in the reign of Henry VIII. They were introduced from Italy to France by Catherine de' Medici. Spain was the centre for the decoration of Fs., while the carved and decorated framework was made in France and sent to Spain. In the eighteenth century many of the first artists, Boucher, Watteau, Lanceat, etc., designed the decora-

blades (about 3 ft. long) and revolve slowly, or small blades and revolve quickly. Fs. which have to com-press or exhaust air against a pressure of two-inch water gauge or more are usually centrifugal and are con-structed on much the same principle as the centrifugal pump. These Fs. are used for drying apparatus, forcing draughts for boilers, dust exhausting and the conveying of grain and other similar materials. The horse power of the motor required to drive the F. depends on its use; a small domestic F. only requires a motor of $\frac{1}{8}$ h.p., but large forced draught blowers, such as are used in power-houses, require anything up to 50 h.p. To secure economy of power, the right type of F. must be chosen.

For ventilation purposes a propeller F. should be used; where the air is sucked down a duct the duct should be at least of the same diameter as the F. blades, and sharp bends should be avoided in the ducts; but where sharp bends and small ducts have to be used, a centrifugal F. is the best.

**Fandango,** a Spanish dance, of Moorish origin. It is a mixture of the *sequidalla* and *bolero*, and is danced by two people, a male and female, to the accompaniment of the guitar and castanets, and sometimes the tambourine, the music being quick and lively, and played in triple time.

**Fanfare** (Sp. *fanfarria*), a blast of trumpets, used at public ceremonies to announce the approach of a sovereign. It is used in Beethoven's *Fidelio*, in Wagner's *Lohengrin*, and in Schumann's F♭ symphony.

**Fanning,** a coral is. belonging to Britain, situated in the N. Pacific Ocean, and forming part of a group. It lies in lat. 3° 30′ N., and long. 159° 13′ W., and has an area of 15 sq. m. The name is derived from Capt. Fanning, an American, who discovered the group; the is. was annexed by Great Britain in 1888. Pop. about 150.

**Fano,** a tn. and seaport of Italy in the prov. of Pesaro e Urbino. It is situated on the Adriatic coast, 8 m. S.E. of Pesaro, and 29 m. N.W. of Ancona. There are the ruins of a white marble triumphal arch to Augustus, also a cathedral, which possesses valuable paintings. The manufs. are silk goods, bricks, etc., and a trade is carried on in corn and oil. Pop. 11,689.

**Fanö,** an is. of the N. Frisian group, situated in the N. Sea, off the W. coast of Jutland. It belongs to Denmark, and has an area of 20 sq. m. The cap., Nordby, is a summer watering place, and contains a school of navigation. The inhabitants are engaged in fishing and boating. Pop. 3300.

**Fans, Fangs,** or **Ba-Fan,** a race of Aborigines, occupying the district between the Gabun and Ogowé rivs. in Fr. Congo, W. Africa. They are a cannibal race, with fine physique, woolly hair, and a chocolate complexion, lighter than that of the negroes. They wear practically no clothing, but tattoo their bodies and deck themselves in jewellery. The men are warlike, and good hunters; they are skilled in iron, brass, and copper work. They are believed to be moving westwards in large numbers. Cannibalism has diminished since their contact with civilisation, but their morals have deteriorated. *See* Mary Kingsley, *Travels in West Africa,*

1897, and Sir R. Burton, 'A Day with the Fans,' in *Transactions of the Ethnological Society* (vols. iii. and iv.).

**Fanshawe, Sir Richard** (1608–66), an Eng. ambassador and poet, *b.* at Ware Park, Hertfordshire, and educated at Jesus College, Cambridge. He entered the Inner Temple in 1626, and afterwards travelled in France and Spain. Until 1638 he was secretary to the British embassy at Madrid, and on the outbreak of the Civil War fought on the Royalist side. He became secretary to the Prince of Wales, and in 1648 naval treasurer under Prince Rupert. At the Battle of Worcester (1651) he was taken prisoner, but was released, and took refuge on the continent, returning to England at the Restoration. He *d.* in Madrid, where he had been sent as ambassador in 1664. He translated Guarini's *Pastor Fido,* 1647; Camoens' *The Lusiad,* 1655; and some original verse. *See* Lady F.'s *Memoir,* 1676 (pub. 1829).

**Fantasia** (It. signifying fancy, caprice) is the name applied to musical compositions in which the composer follows his fancy, and is not bound down by fixed forms. A F., however, is not without form; it generally consists of several sections, each being independent of the others in form. It is frequently the case that one section interrupts a previous one, and often a brilliant cadenza is used; but the whole is united. An example of this is to be seen in Mozart's F. in D minor. The student of music should examine variations in the Fs. by Mendelssohn, Mozart, and Schumann.

**Fanti,** the name of a negro tribe of the Ishi group, inhabiting the Gold Coast, W. Africa. In the early nineteenth century the Fs. were subjugated by the Ashantis, a race belonging to the same stock as themselves, and have since accepted British protection. Missionaries have been sent out to them by Wesleyan Methodist and Swiss societies. *See* A. B. Ellis, *The Tshi-speaking People of the Gold Coast,* 1887; and Brackenbury and Huyshé, *Fanti and Ashanti,* 1873.

**Fantin-Latour, Ignace Henri Jean Théodore** (1836–1904), a Fr. artist, *b.* at Grenoble, the son of a pastel painter. He studied under Couture, and first exhibited in the Salon in 1861. He moved in the artistic circles of Paris and London, and numbered among his friends Corot, Delacroix, Courbet, and Whistler. His 'Hommage à Delacroix' is a portrait group containing Whistler, Beaudelaire, Legros, Champfleury, and himself. His other notable portrait groups are 'Un Atelier à Batignolles,' 1870; 'Un coin de table,' 1872 ; and ' Autour du Piano ' 1885. He also exhibited some fine lithographs, and some beautiful paintings of still life. Consult A. Jullien, *Fantin-Latour sa vie et ses amitiés*, 1909.

**Fantoccini,** *see* MARIONETTES.

**Fan-tracery Vaulting,** in architecture, a method of vaulting employed in the Perpendicular style, and so called on account of its resemblance to a fan. The ribs radiate from one point in the same curve, and are

FAN-TRACERY IN VAULTED CEILING OF ST. GEORGE'S CHAPEL, WINDSOR

equidistant, terminating at the apex of the ceiling. The intermediate spaces between the ribs are generally filled in with smaller ribs and with decorative ornaments which give it the name of *fan-tracery*. The ceiling of Henry VII.'s chapel in Westminster Abbey is one of the most wonderful achievements of architecture. Other fine examples of this kind of vaulting may be seen over the staircase of Christ Church, Oxford, and in the cloisters at Gloucester and Canterbury.

**Fantuzzi,** an ancient Italian family the members of which were natives of Bologna :

*Jean Fantuzzi,* called the Elder (*d.* 1391), a lawyer ; held several important posts in Bologa.

*Jean Baptiste Fantuzzi,* a doctor of philosophy, wrote a book on peripatetic philosophy, 1536.

*Gaspard Fantuzzi* (*d.* 1532), a Latin scholar.

*Jean Fantuzzi,* the Younger (*d.* 1646), was professor of philosophy in the University of Bologna, and a

member of the corporation called ' Les Anciens.'

*Paul Emile Fantuzzi* (*d.* 1661), a poet and senator. A collection of his lyric poems appeared in 1647.

*Jean Fantuzzi,* a scholar of the eighteenth century ; published an important work on the literary history of Italy (1781–94).

**Farad,** a name derived from Michael Faraday, given to the unit of electrical capacity, *i.e.* the capacity of a body which, when raised to a potential of one volt, has a charge of one coulomb or unit quantity of electricity. It is divided into a million *microfarads*, one microfarad being equal to $10^{-15}$ of a C.G.S. unit.

**Faraday, Michael** (1791–1867), a distinguished Eng. natural philosopher, chemist, and electrician, *b.* at Newington Butts, near London, his father being a blacksmith. He was early apprenticed to a bookbinder, but all his spare time was devoted to scientific reading and experiment to the best of his opportunities. He managed to attend some lectures by Sir Humphry Davy, and in 1813 the great scientist took his case in hand, and made him an assistant in the laboratory of the Royal Institution. He then travelled for some time with Davy on the Continent, and on his return devoted himself to chemistry, in which study he greatly assisted Davy in many ways. In 1827 he succeeded his benefactor as professor of chemistry in the Royal Institution, and in 1832 he was made D.C.L. From this period he continued

MICHAEL FARADAY

his work not only on chemistry, but also on the manufacture of glass for optical purposes, and the study of electricity and magnetism. Among his extremely numerous discoveries may be named those of the condensation of gases into liquids by pressure (1823), the decomposition of hydrocarbons by expansion (1827), electrochemical decomposition (1834), magnetic rotary polarisation (1845), and various later researches in connection with diamagnetism. In 1829 he commenced a series of Christmas lectures at the Royal Institution, which were primarily addressed to young people. They found, however, a much wider audience. F.'s publications are numerous, the most important being: *Experimental Researches in Electricity*, 1839–55; *Chemical Manipulation*, 1827 (2nd ed. 1842); *Lectures on the Non-metallic Elements*, and *Lectures on the Chemical History of a Candle*, 1861. See his *Life and Letters* by Bence Jones, 1870; *Faraday as a Discoverer* (5th ed.), 1894; and Lives by J. H. Gladstone, 1872; W. Jerrold, 1891; and S. P. Thompson, 1898.

**Faraday's Law,** see ELECTRICITY.

**Faradisation,** the application for medical purposes of a faradic current of electricity. Whereas a galvanic current is continuous, a faradic current is interrupted, the interruptions occurring regularly, Both kinds are used diagnostically and therapeutically; in the former case faradism being used for the diagnosis of nervous and muscular disorders, in the latter in cases of general nervous exhaustion, acute articular rheumatism, etc.

**Farāizī,** a Mohammedan sect formed in Bengal during the nineteenth century to check the abuses into which the Mohammedan Church had fallen. Its adherents base their doctrines and rules of life solely on the Koran.

**Farazdaq** (nickname; real name, **Abu Firas Hammām ibn Ghālib**) (*c.* 642–*c.* 732) Arabian poet, *b.* at Basra. His nickname means The Fat. His writings are chiefly satirical—written against people in Basra. He had to flee—first to Kufa, then to Medina, whence he was expelled by the Khalif for licentiousness. He was permitted to return to Basra, where he died. See *Das Leben des Farazdak*, etc., by Joseph Hell, Leipzig, 1903.

**Farce** (It. *farsa*, from Lat. *farcire*, to stuff), a form of dramatic art which makes no pretence of holding the mirror up to nature, aiming at exciting laughter by means of absurd situations and extravagant buffoonery. While the province of comedy is to reveal the humorous interplay of character upon character, and that of burlesque is to caricature some particular fashion, style, or human type, the object of F. is solely to amuse. Rude pantomimes and Fs. prevailed in very early times among the Gks. and Roms. It exists in the primitive drama of all nations. *Gammer Gurton's Needle* is an early form of Eng. F., which, in the hands of Shakespeare, developed into true comedy.

**Farcy,** an outward manifestation of glanders, a contagious disease that attacks horses. It takes the form of ulcers or F. buds which appear on the limbs. *See* HORSES: Diseases.

**Fareham,** a market tn. of Hampshire, England, 5 m. N.W. of Portsmouth. The industries include the manuf. of bricks, earthenware, leather, and ropes. There is a flourishing trade in corn and timber, but F. owes its prosperity largely to its proximity to Portsmouth. Pop. about 10,000.

**Farel, Guillaume** (1489–1565), a Fr. reformer, *b.* near Gap in Dauphiné, France. He studied in Paris, where he was converted from being an ardent Rom. Catholic into an equally ardent Protestant and promoter of the Reformation. He preached with vehement fervour throughout France and Switzerland and made many converts. His friend Calvin was the organiser, while he was the preacher, of the Genevan Church (1835–38) until the two reformers were expelled from the city. He wrote some polemical works on purgatory (1534) and the Lord's Supper (1555). *See* Lives by Ancillon (1691) and F. Bevan (1893).

**Farewell Cape,** the S. extremity of Greenland, situated by the E. entrance to Davis Strait. It is seldom visited on account of the dangerous currents.

**Fargo,** the largest city of N. Dakota, U.S.A., cap. of Cass co., on the Red R. of the N. It is the seat of the N. Dakota Agricultural College, a busy grain-trading centre and distributing point for farm implements. There are a number of fine parks. Pop. 28,619.

**Faria y Sousa, Manuel de** (1590-1649), a Portuguese historian and poet. The work of his life was a compilation of a history of the Portuguese in all parts of the world, but it was never completed, although several volumes appeared after his death. *Europa Portugueza* (3 vols.), *Asia Portugueza* (3 vols.), *Africa Portugueza*. His sonnets and eclogues are mostly contained in *Noches claras* (Madrid), 1624–26, and the *Fuente de Aganipe*.

**Faribault,** co. seat of Rice co., Minnesota, U.S.A., on the Cannon R., 52 m. from St. Paul by rail. It is the seat of the state schools for the deaf, the blind and the mentally defective. It lies to the south of the beautiful S. Minnesota lakes and has various manufactures. Pop. 12,767.

**Faridkot,** a tn. and native state of India in the Punjab. The town has a railway station and is 84 m. from Lahore. During the Sikh wars in 1845, the Raja of F. exerted himself in the British cause, as did also his son in 1857 in the Mutiny. Pop. (dist.) 130,400.

**Faridpur,** a tn. and district of British India in E. Bengal. The town stands on the Ganges, and has a railway station and a government high school. The district has an area of 2300 sq. m., and is flat and uninteresting, and the climate is damp. Rice is the principal crop. Most of the trade is conducted by river, although the Eastern Bengal Railway to Goalanda crosses the district. Pop. (town) 11,700 ; (district) 1,939,000.

**Faridu'd-Din ˌ'Attár,** Persian poet of last half of twelfth and beginning of thirteenth century A.D. There is no certainty as to the precise period of his life. He wrote *Manṭiqu'ṭ, Tayr : i.e.* Speech or Parliament of Birds— a long mystical and allegorical poem. His *Madharu'l-'Ajá'ib* (Manifestation of Wonders) caused his expulsion from Nishápúr. He afterwards lived chiefly in Mecca, where he produced inferior work.

**Faridun, or Feridoun,** in Persian legend, an Iranian king, one of the chief heroes of the Shahnamah. He was the son of Abtin and Firanak, and the story goes that on his birth he was sought out by Tohak, whom he was destined to dethrone. Abtin was killed, but Firanak escaped with Faridun and reared him in Mt. Albury, and when he grew up he overthrew Tohak, captured his capital on the Tigris, and ruled long and prosperously.

**Farina, Johann Maria,** the inventor of the celebrated perfume, Eau de Cologne (*q.v.*).

**Farina, Salvatore** (1846–1918), an Italian novelist, *b.* Jan. 10 in Sardinia. He began by studying law, but afterwards devoted himself to literary work and settled at Milan. His books, which are written in a simple style, are remarkable for their sentimenta humour (in this F. has been compared with Dickens) and their cunning irony. His masterpiece is *Il Signor Jo,* 1880, a charming story of an egoist. Other works are : *Il Tesoro di Donnina ; Amore a cent occhi ; Mio figlio ; Il numero 13 ; Don Chisciottino Amore bendato ; Capelli biondi ; Oro nascosta.* Died at Milan, Dec. 15.

**Farinaceous Foods,** are those which contain starch. The word 'farina' means literally meal or flour formed from grain, when ground, and consists, therefore, of starch, gluten, etc., but it is generally now applied to the farinaceous matter contained in other vegetable products, such as the potato, when it consists almost entirely of starch or fecula, or beans and peas, etc. Among the many F. F., sago, arrowroot, and tapioca are types of the large class of dried foods which are imported into the country, and these consist practically of pure starch and are very nutritious when cooked with milk. Maize, too, though not yet regarded as a food for human beings, has very considerable nutritive qualities, since it contains more carbon and nitrogen than is found in an equal weight of wheaten flour, besides a considerable quantity of free hydrogen, which is found in the fat, a substance in which the grain is somewhat rich. Besides this, it exceeds all other grains in point of economy, but the great objection to its use is its rough taste. It has, however, been used by the poor of Ireland since the potato famine, and in the W. part of America. F. F. give heat and energy to the body, but are not flesh formers although very often an excess of such foods is stored up as fat.

**Farinati, Paolo** (*c.* 1522–1606), Italian painter of the family of the Uberti, *b.* at Verona. He was a pupil of Niccolo Giolfino and A. Badile, but studied also the works of Parmigiano, and soon surpassed his instructors. He formed his style partly on Titian and Giorgione, although in colouring he is inferior to both, but in form he learned more from the works of Giulio Romano. Of his pictures ' The Multiplication of the Loaves ' is generally considered his best, and this was painted in his seventy-ninth year. His other notable works are : ' A Presentation in the Temple,' ' The Marriage of St. Catherine,' ' The Murder of the Innocents.'

**Farinelli** (1705–82), a Neapolitan singer of great eminence, whose real name was Carlo Broschi, *b.* at Naples. He studied under Porpora, and went from Rome to Vienna, where the Emperor Charles VI., who delighted in accompanying him on the harpsichord, loaded him with presents. In 1734 he came to England, and so delighted his audiences with his singing that Handel was obliged to dismiss a rival company over which he presided. From England he went to Spain, where he remained twenty-five years, and was much appreciated by Philip V. and his son Ferdinand VI., both of whom suffered from chronic melancholia. He was a favourite with both father and son, and was endowed with a pension of £2000 a year. He returned to Italy and spent his last days at Bologna. Many extraordinary tales have been told of his vocal skill and of his command over the feelings and sympathies of his audience.

**Faringdon** (' fern hill '), or **Great Faringdon,** a market tn. in the Abingdon parl. div. of Berkshire, England. It has trade in corn, sheep, and cattle, and is interesting for its church of All Saints, a large cruciform building of the Early English period, and for Faringdon House, built by Henry James Pye (1745–1813), the poet. Pop. 3079.

**Farini, Luigi Carlo** (1812–66), an Italian statesman and historian, *b.* at Russi, near Ravenna. He studied medicine at Bologna, and practised in his native state until in 1847 he had to leave the papal states owing to his political opinions. In 1846 he was recalled to Rome and was Under-Secretary for Home Affairs under the new pope, Pius IX. In 1851 he became Minister of Instruction; in 1859 provisional governor of Modena; in 1861 Minister of the Interior in the last ministry of Cavour, whom he succeeded as Premier, 1862–63. His chief publication was *Il Stato Romano* (4 vols.), 1850, partly trans. by Gladstone. *See* his letters to Gladstone in *Mémoires sur les Affaires d'Italie,* 1859; *Lettres sur les Affaires d'Italie* (Paris), 1860; and E. Parri, *Luigi Carlo Farini* (Rome), 1878.

**Farley, Cardinal John Murphy** (1842–1918), American Roman Catholic prelate; *b.* April 20, at Newtown Hamilton, co. Armagh, Ireland. Emigrated, 1859. Was educated at St. John's College and St. Joseph's Seminary in New York state, and later at the North American College in Rome. Ordained priest in 1870, he served Cardinal M'Closkey as secretary for twelve years (1872–84), and in 1900 published his Life. He was created fourth archbishop of New York in 1902, and received his cardinal's hat in 1911. Died at New York, Sept. 17.

**Farm** (A.-S. *feorm,* goods, from Lat. *firma, firmus,* durable), the term used to denote a piece of land let or rented for cultivation or pasturage, together with the necessary buildings. The term ' farmer ' is often used to denote a man who owns as well as cultivates land. In America the farmer generally owns the land he cultivates. *Farm holdings* consist of the residence for the farmer and his family, cottages for the F. labourers, and the F. steading. The dwelling-house varies to some extent with the size and character of the holding, the ' rules of the estate,' the fashion of the district, and the taste and social standing of the tenant. Modern F.

dwelling-houses upon holdings of about 200 acs. and upwards are both commodious and comfortable, substantial in construction, if not ornate in external appearance, usually surrounded by simply but tastefully laid-out grounds and a moderately sized garden. The dwelling-house should be 50 to 200 yds. from the steading, and preferably upon higher ground, and so situated that from the farmer's parlour and bedroom windows the whole homestead can be seen. *Servants' cottages* should be near the homestead at the opposite end from the farmer's dwelling-house. They should be plain, substantial, and roomy. They are often built in one continuous row, and sometimes in pairs but rarely singly. Each family should have three or four compartments, with a separate door and a separate garden for garden produce. At the present time they are more fully provided than they were before 1870. It is usually found that where there is good accommodation for the labourers, the supply of agricultural labour is abundant and of good quality. *The farm steading* is the term used to denote the buildings, etc., used for storing crops, stock, F. implements, and machines. The cost, character, and capacity of the steading depend on the size of the holding, the system of farming pursued, and also with the tastes of the landowner, and sometimes with the fancies of the tenant. They often are determined by the ' rules of the estate.' The greatest steading accommodation is wanted on mixed husbandry Fs., and also where a large quantity of home-grown produce is consumed by cattle in winter. Unfortunately on such a F. the maximum expenditure falls where the land is least able to bear it, viz., in cold districts such as N. of Scotland, where substantial houses have to be built for harbouring the stock in winter. The F. steading should be situated as near as possible to the centre of the holding, on dry and airy elevation. There should be an abundant water supply, and proximity to stagnant water should be avoided. The open part should be exposed to the S. The most common and convenient plan for a F. steading is in the form of three sides of a square, with a wing down the centre. In most modern farmsteads the spacing between centre and side wings is devoted to courts for cattle, and most of the season's dung is placed in one of these courts. Straw barns should be near the centre of the steading and the classes of stock receiving most straw accommodated nearest to the straw barn. Root store should be easily accessible from the cattle compartments; hay store from the stable; dairy from the cow-house, and stock-yard from the threshing mill and straw barn. *Ventilation.*— Careful attention is needed in ventilating the whole of the steading. A sufficient current of air is needed overhead to keep the atmosphere pure without draughts upon the animals. Concrete is largely used in the construction of F. buildings, while galvanised corrugated sheet-iron is largely used in roofing courts for cattle. In America F. buildings are generally of wood. It is common there for all compartments of the steading to be under one roof of great dimensions. *See also* AGRICULTURE, GARDENING—*Intensive Cultivation* or *French Market-gardening.*

**Farm Management.** In the U.S.A., where farms and ranches attain a vast size unknown in Great Britain, the study of F. M. has become of such importance that chairs in this subject were established in various universities during the early part of the twentieth century. It was realised that the old methods of farming were wasteful; generations of agriculturists had run their farms on individual lines without leaving any permanent record of their methods and results, allowing their successors to re-learn by personal experience what had been done before them. Experience and research have now furnished data for instruction in F. M. Farming is regarded as a business which should be run on a thoroughly commercialised basis with the application of established principles to its practical side. In the Universities are taught the best and most profitable methods of producing field crops and live-stock; soil and climatic conditions are studied; the relative merits of various forms of farm implements and equipment are analysed; the problems of labour are discussed; a certain amount of accountancy is taught in order that farm accounts may be properly kept; and the marketing of produce is a feature of the student's course. Sound text-books on this subject are written by various professors of agriculture; notably *Farm Management,* by R. L. Adams, 1921; *The Management of the Farm,* by Llewellyn A. Moorhouse, 1925; and *Farm Economics, Management and Distribution,* by Frank App, 1928.

**Farman, Henry,** Anglo-French aviator, *b.* 1874 at Cambrai. One of the pioneers in aviation. In Oct. 1907 he flew 820 yds. in 52½ secs., and in the same month of the following year journeyed in the air from Châlons to Rheims, covering a distance of 16 m.

in 20 mins. This was the first cross-country flight, and was accomplished in a Voisin biplane, improved after the pilot's own designs. The speed attained was 78 kilometres per hour. During the Great War, his works at Billancourt supplied aeroplanes to allied forces.

**Farmer, Richard** (1735–97), an English scholar and critic, *b.* at Leicester and educated there, and at Emmanuel College, Cambridge, of which he became classical tutor and master in 1775. In 1778 he became chief librarian to the university; in 1780 he was appointed to a prebendal stall at Lichfield, and two years later to one at Canterbury, which he exchanged in 1788 for that of a canon residentiary of St. Paul's. He called himself the 'pioneer of commentators' and in his *Essay of the Learning of Shakespeare,* 1767, proved that the dramatist derived his knowledge of classical and foreign literature from translations.

**Farmers' Clubs** exist for the two-fold purpose of furthering agricultural interests and promoting social intercourse among men who are following the same agricultural occupation. Meetings take place usually on market days, in most of the big agricultural centres throughout the country. The Farmers' Club established at 2 Whitehall Court, London, S.W.1, has a membership of over 1280 farmers, stockbreeders, landowners, and other persons interested in agriculture. It was established at the instance of several members of the Royal Agricultural Society of England and the Smithfield Club, and the Club was formally opened at the York Hotel, Bridge Street, Blackfriars, on June 28, 1843; there it remained for more than twenty years, when the premises were acquired by the railway for Ludgate Hill Station. Meetings are held annually from Nov. to May, when papers are read on current agricultural subjects and on legislation affecting agriculture, and these are subsequently printed and circulated among the members. The National Association of Young Farmers' Clubs has its headquarters in 26 Bedford Square, W.C. 1, where is published the monthly paper *The Young Farmer.* The first of the Young Farmers' Clubs was established by the United Dairies in Jan. 1921, at Hemyock, Devon, and attracted the interest of Lord Northcliffe, who set aside a section of the Ideal Homes Exhibition at Olympia for their show in 1922, and offered a gold cup for competition among the young farmers of America and of Britain. Later the Ministry of Agriculture interested itself in his clubs, in which each young farmer personally rears his own stock. F. Cs. are a feature in the U.S.A., and of Canada, especially in the three prairie provinces of the Dominion. There are also in the U.S.A. a number of boys' and girls' clubs in connection with agricultural extension work. In America, experimentation, improvement in marketing, discussion of anti-pest methods, and the organisation of co-operative marketing are all prominent activities in F. Cs., while demonstrations in educational work and agricultural competitions are periodically organised for the common benefit of members.

**Farmers' Co-operative Unions in America.** The co-operative movement has established a firm hold on the farming industry in the U.S.A. The producers' difficulties in the marketing of the goods naturally tend to increase the cost of food to the consumer, and co-operation has a wholesome effect in the way of lowering prices. The co-operative movement helps to supply ready markets for goods, especially those which are perishable, before there is any likelihood of their deterioration, and it helps to solve the difficult problem of distribution. There are various co-operative unions in America which affect different branches of farming, such as the National Wool Marketing Association, the American Cotton Growers' Exchange, the Farmers' National Grain Corporation, and the Florida United Growers.

**Farmers-General,** those individuals who sought from the state or controller of taxes the privilege of collecting the taxes in return for a certain fixed sum paid into the treasury, such as the ' publicani ' of classical and N.T. times. The system of *fermiers-généraux* was very prevalent in France before the Revolution of 1789. It was largely responsible for the Revolution, and was swept away in it. *See Camb, Modern History,* viii. 3, 1907.

**Farmers' National Congress,** a delegate body representing over 3,000,000 U.S.A. farmers. Its objects are to obtain liberal federal assistance for good roads and inland waterways, the teaching of agriculture in the public schools, a general parcels post, a federal pure seed law, a head tax on illiteracy, and differential duties in favour of American merchant marine.

**Farm-servants,** *see* LABOURERS.

**Farnaby, or Farnabie, Thomas** (c. 1575–1647), an Eng. grammarian and schoolmaster, the son of a London carpenter. He was educated at Merton College, Oxford, and at a Jesuit College in Spain. He was for some time a follower of Drake and Hawkins

and fought in the Low Countries. On his return to England he opened a school in Goldsmith's Rent, London, which became famous all over Europe, He prepared a new Latin grammar and an annotated edition of most of the great classical authors.

**Farnborough,** an urban dist. and par. of Hampshire, England, situated in the Basingstoke parl. div., 2½ m. N. of Aldershot, and 32 m. S.W. of London. A part of the Aldershot camp is in the parish and also an aerodrome. The remains of Napoleon III. and the Prince Imperial are buried in a mausoleum built by the ex-Empress Eugénie at F. Hill. Pop. 14,199.

**Farnborough, Baron,** *see* MAY, SIR THOMAS ERSKINE.

**Farne, Fearne,** or **Fern Isles,** or **The Staples,** a group of small islands, situated in the North Sea, in lat. 55° 38′ N., and long. 1° 37′ W. They belong to Northumberland, England, and are from 1½ to 7 m. off the coast, 20 m. S.E. of Berwick, and 8 m. S.E. of Holy Island. There are altogether seventeen of them. It was here that Grace Darling's heroic rescue took place in 1838, and in 1843 sixty people from the *Pegasus* were drowned. Two lighthouses stand upon the largest of the islands, and upon this also is St. Cuthbert's tower, the remains of a Benedictine priory.

**Farnese Family, The,** an illustrious and powerful Italian family whose early history is obscure. Its importance dates from 1534, when Cardinal Alessandro Farnese was elected pope as Paul III. He alienated the Duchy of Parma and Piacenza for his natural son Pierluigi Farnese. Piacenza was occupied by Charles V. in 1547, but the Duchy of Parma was ruled by the Farnese for over two centuries. *Alessandro Farnese* (1545–92), the third Duke of Parma, was a famous statesman and general, and became governor-general of the Netherlands under Philip II. of Spain. His son and successor, *Ranuccio I.* (1569–1622), instituted the savage persecutions against supposed ' witches ' and ' heretics.' He was succeeded by his second son, *Odoardo* (1612–46), who quarrelled with Pope Urban VIII. about the possession of Castro, which was eventually razed to the ground during the reign of his son *Ranuccio II.* (1630–94), Ranuccio's two sons *Francesco Maria* (1678–1727), and *Antonio* (1679–1731) both died childless and were the last of the male line of the Farnese. The Duchy of Parma passed to Don Carlos of Bourbon, son of Philip V. of Spain and Elizabeth Farnese (1692–1766).

**Farnese Palace,** in Rome, one of the finest specimens of Rom. Renaissance architecture. It was begun under Paul III. when he was Cardinal Alessandro Farnese, and completed by his nephew in 1526 under the direction of Michelangelo. It was inherited by Don Carlos, afterwards King of Naples and Spain, and most of the pictures and antique sculpture were removed to Naples. It now houses the Fr. embassy to Italy.

**Farnham**, a market tn. of Surrey, England, situated on the R. Wey, 38 m. S.W. of London. It is the centre of a hop district. William Cobbett was *b.* here in 1762, and is buried in the parish churchyard. F. is historically interesting. Its castle was built by Henry of Blois, brother of King Stephen, destroyed by Henry III. and

**Farnworth**, a tn. of Lancashire, England, situated on the R. Irwell, in the Radcliff-cum-Farnworth parl. div., 2½ m. S.E. of Bolton and adjoining it; it is also 12 m. S.E. of Liverpool. There are collieries, iron works, tile and brick fields in the district, and the manuf. of cotton goods and sail canvas is carried on. Pop. 27,901.

**Faro** (from 'Pharaoh,' a picture of an ancient Egyptian king on one of the cards of the old Fr. pack), a game of hazard with a full pack of cards, popular in France in the reign of Louis XIV. and still in the U.S.A. The 'bank' is held against an indefinite number of players.

**Faro**, a seaport tn., cap. of the dis-

THE FARNESE GARDENS, ROME

rebuilt and garrisoned by Charles I. It was restored in 1684 by Dr. Morley, Bishop of Winchester. The ruined keep was repaired in 1913–14. Moor Park was the last retreat of Sir Wm. Temple, who *d.* here on Jan. 27, 1699, and it was here that Dean Swift wrote many of his works. The cottage in which Miss Johnson lived is still called Stella's Cottage. Mother Ludlam's and Foot's caves are near by, also the remains of earth-works called Cæsar's Camp. Many Rom. coins have been found. Pop. 12,133.

**Farnol, John Jeffery** (*b.* 1878), English novelist. Studied engineering, but, after a course of art study, began writing fiction for Eng. and American magazines. For two years he worked as a scene-painter at the Astor Theatre, New York. His great success was 'The Broad Highway,' a study of Eng. rural characters in the heroic vein of the old-time workers. Other novels of the same picaresque genre : *The Money Moon, The Amateur Gentleman, Beltane the Smith, Chronicles of the Imp, The Loring Mystery.*

trict of the same name. (1) The town is situated at the mouth of the Rio Fermoso, at the back of three islands, which help to form a fine roadstead. It is the chief port of S. Portugal, and exports fruits, wine, anchovies, cork, etc. A wall surrounds the town, built probably by the Moors, and there is a cathedral, which is supposed to have been a Rom. basilica. There is an arsenal and military hospital, with several educational establishments and convents. F. was almost destroyed in 1755 by an earthquake. Pop. 12,000. (2) The district has an area of 1936 sq. m. Its climate is extremely fine, and almonds, dates, figs, wheat, olives, etc., are grown. Pop. (dist.) 268,294, (town) 13,000.

**Faroe Islands** (Danish *Faar-Öer*, sheep islands), a group of islands belonging to Denmark, and situated in the N. Atlantic between the Shetland Islands and Iceland, 200 m. N.W. of the former. They number twenty-two, of which seventeen are inhabited. They almost all present a steep and precipitous coast seaward, the cliffs being 1000 to 2000 ft. high. The harbours do not afford a very safe anchorage, but they are washed by warm currents, and are always free from ice; the currents which run through the sounds are swift and dangerous, and storms and whirlwinds are very frequent. The surface is almost everywhere hilly, attaining to the height of 2502 ft. in Strömö and 2756 ft. in Österö. All timber for building purposes is imported from Norway, as there are no trees in the islands, but the rocks are covered with moss and ferns and the soil is rich in peat and coal. The chief sources of wealth are wool, sea-bird feathers (especially loons), fish (both fresh and dried), fish oil, and skins. The largest islands are Strömö (28 m. by 8 m.), Österö, Vaagö. Sandö, and Süderö. The capital and chief port of the group is Thorshaven in Strömö; Kirkebö on the same island was formerly the seat of a bishop. The inhabitants are almost exclusively of Norwegian descent, and speak an old Norse dialect, although Danish is the language used in the law courts, churches, and schools. Since 1854 they have enjoyed a certain amount of self-government, electing a local assembly, but they send representatives to the Copenhagen chambers. Their religion is Lutheran. The Faroe Islands were first colonised in the ninth century, and belonged to Norway until 1380, when they passed to Denmark. Area 513 sq. m. Pop. (1921) 21,364.

**Farquhar, George** (1678–1707), dramatist, went on the stage after leaving Trinity College, Dublin, and in that city, about 1695, made his début as Othello. In a subsequent appearance he accidentally stabbed a fellow-actor, and was so distressed that he retired from the stage. He now turned his thoughts to playwriting, and his *Love and a Bottle* was successfully produced at Drury Lane in 1699. In the following year *The Constant Couple* was performed, and was an even greater success. This was followed by *Sir Harry Wildair*, and in this play at his own benefit at Dublin he played the title-rôle. His last plays were *The Recruiting Officer* (1706) and *The Beaux' Stratagem* (1707). He belonged to the Congreve school of dramatists, and had some wit and gaiety in abundance, but no higher sense of morality than the majority of his contemporary playwrights.

**Farr, William** (1807–83), an Eng. statistician, *b.* at Kenley in Shropshire. He studied medicine in Paris and London, but gave up the practice of his profession to accept the post of compiler of abstracts in the registrar-general's office. In 1851 and 1861 he was assistant-commis-

sioner, and in 1871 head commissioner for the census. His chief publications are: *Tables of Lifetimes, Annuities, and Premiums,* 1864; *English Re-production Table,* 1880; and *Vital Statistics,* 1885.

**Farragut, David Glasgow** (1801–70), first admiral of the United States navy, *b.* at Knoxville in Tennesee. He entered the navy in 1810, became lieutenant in 1825, commander in 1841, and captain in 1855. Although a Southerner by birth, on the outbreak of the Civil War in 1861, he adhered to his allegiance to the government at Washington, and in 1862 was appointed as Rear-Admiral to the command of the Western Gulf Blockading Squadron, with which he forced the passage of the Mississippi and captured New Orleans. In 1864 he captured Mobile and in the same year was invested with the newly created rank of vice-admiral, on which he retired from active service. He was made admiral in 1866.

**Farrand, Livingston,** American anthropologist and psychologist; *b.* June 14, 1867, at Newark, N. J.; son of Samuel A. Farrand. He graduated from Princeton in 1888; and from the College of Physicians and Surgeons (Columbia), 1891. Studied in Cambridge, England, 1891–2; Berlin, 1892–3. From 1893 till 1901 he was instructor in psychology at Columbia University; in 1897 accompanied Jessup North Pacific expedition, which visited British Columbia, to study the aborigines. He was from 1901 till 1903 adjunct Professor of Psychology at Columbia; and then, until 1914, Professor of Anthropology at same university. From 1905 till 1914, executive secretary of the National Association for Study and Prevention of Tuberculosis; also for last two years of that term treasurer of the American Health Association and editor of the *American Journal of Public Health.* He was President of the University of Colorado 1914–19. Appointed by Rockefeller Foundation to direct work in France against tuberculosis. From March 1919 till Oct. 1921 was chairman of central committee of the American Red Cross. In 1921, elected President of Cornell University. Wrote: *Basis of American History,* 1904.

**Farrant, Richard** (*fl.* 1564–80), an English composer of church music. He became a gentleman of the Chapel Royal under Edward VI.; became organist of St. George's Chapel in 1564, and returned to the Chapel Royal in 1569. His name is best remembered in connection with the anthem, 'Lord, for Thy Tender Mercy's Sake,' and a chant based on it, but the authorship has not been satisfactorily established, being claimed for John Hilton.

**Farrar, Frederic William** (1831–1903), an English divine, b. at Bombay, and educated at London University and Trinity College, Cambridge. From 1855–70 he was assistant master at Harrow, and from 1871–76 headmaster of Marlborough College. He was elected fellow of the Royal Society in 1864, university preacher in 1868, honorary chaplain to the queen in 1869, and Hulsean lecturer in 1870. He became canon of Westminster and rector of St. Margaret's in 1876, archdeacon in 1883, and Dean of Canterbury in 1895. In 1858 he began his literary work with the schoolboy story, *Eric, or Little by Little*, followed by *Julian Home*, and *St. Winifred's*. He published a number of books on classical and modern philology, but it was by his theological writings that he attained his greatest popularity. *The Witness of History to Christ* (Hulsean Lectures) appeared in 1870; *The Life of Christ*, 1874 (12th ed. 1875); *Life of St. Paul*, 1879; *Early Days of Christianity*, 1882; *Lives of the Fathers*, 1888; *Darkness and Dawn*, 1889; *The Bible, its Meaning and Supremacy*, 1896.

**Farrar, Geraldine**, American operatic soprano; b. Feb. 28, 1882, at Melrose, Mass.; daughter of Sydney F., storekeeper. She received musical education from Mrs. J. H. Long in Boston, Mme. Thursby in New York, Trabadello in Paris, and Lilli Lehmann in Berlin. On Oct. 15, 1901, she made her début at the Royal Opera, Berlin, as Marguerite in Gounod's *Faust*, with such success that she immediately had a three years' contract. From 1906 till her retirement from the stage on April 22, 1922, she was a leading soprano at the Metropolitan Opera House, New York. She appeared on a concert platform in 1927.

**Farrell**, a borough in Mercer co., Pa., U.S.A., on the Shenango R., close to Sharon city, with which it is industrially conjoined. Steel, castings, tin-plate manufactures. Pop. 14,359. The name has been changed from Sharon since 1910.

**Farrell, James Augustine**, American steel-magnate; b. Feb. 15, 1863, at New Haven, Conn.; son of John G. Farrell. Began work at sixteen in a steel-wire mill at New Haven; labourer, 1888, in mills of Pittsburgh Wire Co; rose to superintendent, then to manager. Subsequently, general superintendent of the Olive Steel Wire Co., he organised a wire company at Braddock, Pa.; absorbed 1899, by the American Steel and Wire Co. of N. J., which retained F. as foreign-sales agent. In 1903 he

was made president of the United States Steel Products Co.; in 1911, president of the United States Steel Corporation. Director of other companies in coal and iron business, and chairman of the National Foreign Trade Council.

**Farren, Elizabeth, Countess of Derby** (c. 1759–1829), an English actress, and daughter of George F., an actor. She made her first appearance in London at the Haymarket in 1777, as Miss Hardcastle, in *She Stoops to Conquer*. This success was followed by Rosina in Colman's adaptation of *The Spanish Barber*, and many others. In 1782 she succeeded Mrs. Abingdon at Drury Lane. She played Hermione, Olivia, Portia, and Juliet, but her most successful rôles were Lady Betty Modiste, Lady Teazle, Lady Townley, and Lady Fanciful. In 1797 she married Edward, twelfth Earl of Derby.

**Farren, Ellen**, commonly known as **Nellie Farren** (1848–1904), actress, came of an old theatrical stock, and made her first appearance on the stage at the age of five. She played many parts at Sadler's Wells, the Victoria, and the Olympic theatres, and earned the reputation of being both clever and versatile. It was only after she went to the Gaiety in 1868 and played principal boy parts in burlesque that she became famous. She remained there, a great 'draw' in London, until 1891, when ill-health compelled her retirement from the stage.

**Farrer, Sir Thomas Henry**, first **Baron** (1819–99), an English statistician and civil servant, b. in London, and educated at Eton and Balliol College, Oxford. He was called to the Bar in 1844, but ceased to practise on entering the Civil Service as Secretary to the Marine Department of the Board of Trade in 1850, a post which he held until 1886. He was an advanced Liberal in politics, and a strict free-trader. His theories on trade and finance are embodied in his writings : *Free Trade versus Fair Trade*, 1886 ; *The State in its Relation to Trade*, 1883 ; and his letters and essays in *The Times* and *Contemporary Review*. He published *Study in Currency* in 1898. He was created a baronet in 1883 and a peer in 1893.

**Farriery**, the art of horse-shoeing. It is of anct. origin, and there is evidence that the art was practised by the Celts. It does not seem to have been in use among the Gks. or Roms. The art probably began to grow common after the overthrow of the Western empire towards the close of the fifth century. It has only recently been introduced into Japan, where the former practice was to attach slippers of straw to the horse's feet, these slippers being renewed when necessary. In modern times the art has undergone many changes and improvements, as the methods formerly adopted were considered injurious to the animal and a considerable loss to the owner. The following are some of the chief causes of these evils : (1) Paring the sole and frog; (2) applying shoes, which were too heavy and of the wrong shape; (3) using too many and large nails; (4) applying shoes too small and removing the wall of the foot to make the feet fit the shoes; (5) rasping the front of the hoof. These were often caused by unskilled workmen, who combined the duties of blacksmith and shoe-smith in one trade, although they were not qualified. According to modern principles, shoes should be : (1) As light as compatible with the wear required of them ; (2) the ground face of the shoe should be concave, and the face applied to the foot plain ; (3) heavy draught horses alone should have toe and heel calks on their shoes to increase the foothold ; (4) any excess of growth of the wall or outer portion of horny matter should only be removed in re-shoeing. Care is to be taken in keeping both sides of the hoof of equal height ; (5) the shoes should fit accurately to the circumference of the hoof and project slightly beyond the heel ; (6) as few nails as possible should be used ; (7) the nails should take a short, thick hold of the wall so that the old nail holes may be removed in the natural growth and paring of the horny substance. The need for shoeing a horse's feet is generally well known. The foot is composed of a horny substance which becomes very brittle and breaks away, especially under the influence of moist weather, or of extra strenuous work. In order to prevent this, the rim of iron is placed on the foot and can be renewed from time to time. The shoes and nails are now manufactured with great economy by machinery. The advent of modern methods of locomotion and means of transit have greatly impeded the art of F. In the eighteenth and nineteenth centuries every village had its shoesmith, who, as mentioned above, combined his art with that of the blacksmith, thus causing evils which were only stamped out by modern systems of F.

**Farrukhabad, or Farukhabad,** a dist. and city of British India, in the Agra div. of the N.W. Provinces. The dist. has an area of 1718 sq. m., traversed by the Agra–Cawnpore branch railway. The chief products are indigo, sugar-cane, and potatoes. The capital is Fategarh. The city of Farrukhabad is situated near the Ganges, 86 m. N.W. of Cawnpore, and has a gov. gun-carriage factory. Pop. of dist. 930,000, and of tn. 65,000.

**Fars,** or **Farsistan,** one of the five great provinces of Persia, extending along the N. shore of the Persian Gulf. The name is the same as the Gk. ' Persis,' which, originally the name of the province now called ' Iran,' has come to be the name by which the whole empire is called. The province is traversed by mountain chains running parallel with the coast, intersected by fertile valleys, rich in pasturage, vines, and fruits, and studded with lakes, the chief of which is Lake Bakhtegan. The rivers are small and seldom flow into the sea. The climate varies greatly according to the altitude. The principal products are dates, rice, olives, cereals, cotton, and wine. The capital is Shiraz. Pop. 32,000 in 1884. The area of Fars is about 53,000 sq. m. and the estimated pop. 750,000.

**Farshut,** or **Farshiout,** a tn. of Upper Egypt, situated near the river Nile, 20 m. S.E. of Girgeh in a picturesque country of astonishing fertility. Pop. 17,000.

**Farsley,** a manufacturing tn. of West Riding, Yorkshire, England, situated 3½ m. from Bradford. It has scribbling, spinning and cloth manuf. mills. Samuel Marsden, who first introduced Australian wool into England, and passed his life as a missionary in Australia and New Zealand was born here. Pop. 6119.

**Farthing** (A.-S. feortha, a fourth, and ing, a diminutive) is the smallest Eng. bronze coin, and is equal in value to the fourth of a penny. It was instituted as a silver coin in the reign of Edward I., in which form it continued until the time of Mary. James I. granted a patent to Lord Harrington of Exton in 1613 for the manufacture of copper Fs., but it was not until 1672 that they came into circulation in any number. In the reign of Charles II. tin Fs. were also in circulation for a short time. In 1860 copper Fs. gave place to bronze, in which form they have continued. The experiment of issuing half Fs. was tried in 1842, but not proving successful, the coins were demetalised in 1869. In 1897 the practice was adopted of darkening them before issue, that they might not be mistaken for half-sovereigns.

**Farthingale** (Old Fr. verdagalle, a corruption of Spanish verdagado, from verdago, a stick), a case or hoop upon which were hung voluminous skirts.

The material of the F. was originally wood and later whalebone. It was of Spanish origin, and reached its most exaggerated form in the seventeenth century, when it consisted of a flat circular surface, projecting from the bodice. It was the forerunner of the crinoline (*q.v.*) of the eighteenth and nineteenth centuries.

**Farwell, Sir George** (1845–1915), lord justice; *b.* Dec. 22, second son of Fredk. Cooper F., of Tettenhall, Staffs; graduated from Balliol College, Oxford, and was called to the Bar in 1871. Decided the crucial point in the Taff Vale Rly. case, 1900, concerning the liability of trade union funds to attachment for damages. In 1906, after being for seven years judge of the High Court, he was made lord justice. Died at Timberscombe, Somerset, Sept. 30.

**Fasces** were bundles of rods carried in ancient times by the lictors before the chief magistrates of Rome, symbolising their supreme power over the lives of the people. These rods were made generally of birch-wood or elm, and an axe protruded from the centre. Besides being borne before the magistrates they were also carried before kings and emperors, and in republican times before consuls and prætors. The number of F. was not the same in all cases, but varied according to the dignity of the magistrate. Twelve was the number allotted to a consul, and six to a prætor. In 508 B.C. Valerius Publicola set forth a mandate that in the city the axe should not be carried, since the consuls no longer had the power of life and death in Rome. The axe was present in the case of a dictator, who was preceded by twenty-four lictors, bearing the same number of fasces.

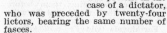

FASCES

**Fascia, or Facia,** an architectural term denoting the bands into which the architrave of the Ionic and Corinthian orders is subdivided. In the Rom. Corinthian order the fasciæ are often divided into small mouldings. The bands are known as the first or upper F., the second or middle F., and the third or lower.

**Fasciation,** a form of monstrosity in plants, often found in buttercups caused by the lateral union of the stems. It is generally caused by the action of gall mites and is hereditary in the garden cockscomb.

**Fascines** are brush-wood faggots used for military purposes. They are generally about 18 ft. in length, not quite a foot in thickness, and are bound tightly together by means of wire or withes. They are used for roofing magazines, for bridge and road making, and also for riveting the steps and slopes of field-works. When cut up into one-third of the length, they can be utilised in filling up a ditch, trench, etc.

**Fasciola,** a parasite which causes liver rot in sheep, *see* LIVER-FLUKE and TREMATODES.

**Fascism.** The name given to the political movement which arose in Italy soon after the Great War to deliver the country from Bolshevism, restore its economic equilibrium, and raise it to its rightful place in the family of nations. The movement was led by Benito Mussolini (*q.v.*), and has successfully dominated administration for the past eight years. The symbol of F. (*Fascismo*) is the same as that of the lictors of Imperial Rome —a bundle of rods (*fasces*) with an axe in the centre, and the *Fascista* salute is that of the ancient Rom.— by outstretched arm. The military organisation of the National Fascista Party—as it is officially constituted, with its Great National Council—is entirely on Rom. lines, with Rom. names like 'legion,' 'consul,' 'centurion,' 'triari,' 'senior' and so forth. The coins bear on one side the Rom. *fascio*, and special gold coins were issued to celebrate the anniversary of the famous 'March to Rome' of Oct. 21, 1922, which carried F. triumphantly into power. Discipline is most rigorous; and the motto of F., 'No discussion, only obedience,' serves to explain the rapidity of the sudden mobilisations and demobilisations carried out by the organisation. F. also possesses a large and powerful Press and a publishing house in Milan. But the decisive factor in the victory of F. was, and is, over and above all, the personality of its leader, the so-called *Duce,* Mussolini, the very soul of the movement.

F. does not, however, present an absolutely new political phenomenon, but is really part of the general historical development of nations. It has been compared to the ' krypteia ' of Sparta, and the ' eterie ' of Athens, or other similar expressions of self-defence of strong active groups or classes, uniting and forming centres of resistance. Other illustrations may be found in the history of the Church in Italy, in the Italian Communes, in England, in Germany and in the Clubs of the Fr. Revolution. It came as a reaction to the complete apathy and disorder in parliamentary State functions in Italy and to the hypnotism of the Italian working classes under the gospel of Lenin following the Great War, conditions which in 1920 were rendering the country an easy prey to the Communist peril. It was a time when the economic chaos was complete ; foreign exchanges were disorganised ; the police impotent ; the Carabineers insulted and even killed by the Communists. Resistance came from the patriots of the Trentino, the Carso and other battlefields of the War, and the first encounter between them and the Communists was in 1921 at Bologna, which date marks the wane of Bolshevism and the rise of F. Progress was at first slow ; for the State was impotent and the only practical policy was force. But masses of the working classes were soon enrolled among the Fascist syndicates scattered all over Italy, and these began activities by settling many important economic disputes and strikes. The army was secretly or openly in favour of F., and, contrary to the hopes of the Communists, would never have marched against the Fascisti. The very generals of the regular army wore the black shirts of the organisation, and themselves directed the march to Rome. In the closing months of 1922 the members of F. increased by leaps and reached even to the Alps and S. Sicily. Finally, in 1922, after a great meeting at Naples and after the March to Rome, Mussolini and his famous quadrumvirate, formed by General de Bono, Cesare de Vecchio, Italo Balbo, and Michele Bianchi, the Secretary-General of the party, was summoned by the King to form the first Fascista Cabinet. In his opening speech before the reconstituted Chamber, Mussolini declared the foreign policy of F. in these words : ' No imperialism, no aggressions, but an attitude which shall do away with the policy of humility which has made Italy more like the Cinderella and humble servant of other nations. Respect for international treaties at no matter what cost. Fidelity and friendship towards the nations that give Italy serious proofs of reciprocating it. Maintenance of Eastern

equilibrium, on which depends the tranquillity of the Balkan States and therefore European and world peace.' At Trieste, on Feb. 6, 1921, Mussolini made it clear that F. did not believe in the principles of the League of Nations, nor in those of the Red Internationals, nor in the possibility of general disarmament ; and he formulated the positive demands of F. as follows : revision of the treaties of peace where these might prove the cause of new wars ; economic annexation of Fiume ; emancipation of Italy by the development of her productive forces ; renewal of relations with the ex-enemy countries, but subject to the maintenance of the existing Italian N. and E. frontiers ;

[*Topical Press*
BENITO MUSSOLINI

vindication of the rights of Italy as regards its colonies ; replacement of the old diplomatic representatives by others from the special university faculties ; and the furtherance of the Italian colonies in the Mediterranean and beyond the Atlantic by economic and educational means and by rapid communication.

F., now (1931) in its ninth year, has certainly transformed the whole material, moral and political structure of Italy. Its achievements include, apart from the successful assertion of Italian foreign policy in the Adriatic and Mediterranean, many great enterprises within the country itself. The more important of these are the reorganisation of the mercantile marine and the improvement of harbours ; city planning ; afforestation schemes which have clothed bare mountains with verdure ; the reservation of special roads for motor traffic and the improvement of roads generally ; and the creation of a network of air lines. One of the most beneficial schemes is that of land reclamation, begun in 1928, under which over 24 million acs. have already been reclaimed, an undertaking which, together with irrigation schemes, has given work to tens of thousands of men, besides increasing cereal production by some 20 million quintals, and thereby conducing to the emancipation of Italy from that dependence on foreign food which, as shown above, is one of the declared objects of F. from its inception.

It has been objected to F. that, like other institutions founded on dictatorships, it must be for ever providing spectacular benefits in order to retain popularity; and undoubtedly the Fascist State, in carrying out its ideals, has and continues to assume heavy financial burdens. Many have entertained the gravest misgivings over the stabilisation of the lire at 92 to the pound. Yet the material benefit to the country has so far outweighed the disadvantages inherent in all dictatorships, and continues to operate as a powerful influence on the imagination of the Italian people as a whole. F. has welded the country together, and, by a remarkable re-awakening of patriotism, tended to obliterate the old distinctions between the N. and S. and remove the traditional antipathies between city and city. It has further strengthened national unity by effecting a conciliation between Church and State and by the settlement of the Rom. question. This latter, crystallised in the Lateran Treaties, has been Mussolini's most remarkable achievement; for the definite recognition by the Vatican of the House of Savoy as the legitimate rulers of Italy and of Rome as the capital of the kingdom has revitalised Italian patriotism as perhaps nothing else could have done. It is clear that the establishment of F. has entailed the abrogation of many fundamental rights of man, hitherto regarded as sacrosanct. This is exemplified in the Law of Dec. 24, 1925, defining the attributes and prerogative of the Prime Minister. Under this law Ministers are responsible to the King for the administration of their departments, but only to the Premier for their policy; and the Premier, with the Royal consent, can abolish or create new Ministries, and he alone can determine Cabinet policy as a whole or discuss policy with the King. But it is equally clear that only a dictatorship could have saved the country after the War.

Membership of the Fascist Party is about one million, but, including the university student groups and other affiliated organisations, is twice that number. Over and above this, however, the plebiscite taken in March 1929 showed that 90 per cent. of the nation were still warmly in favour of the institution. Consult: *Mussolini's Political Speeches*, trans. by Barone di San Sererino (1923) (DENT); G. Salvemini, *The Fascist Dictatorship of Italy*.

**Fashion** (adapted from Fr. *façon*; Lat. *factio*, making, *facere*, to do, or make), used in the sense of the pattern or mode in which a thing is done, particularly employed in the sense of the customary or usual way in which a thing is done, and hence applied to the manner or custom prevalent or characteristic of a particular period, more especially as regards dress or costume. (*See* FRENCH MODES.) The terms fashion and fashionable are also applied to occupations, pursuits, education, etc., as well as to the necessities of dress, though it is in the latter sense it is chiefly used. The invention of weaving may be said to be responsible for the greater variety in the matter of garments; prior to this skins were, of course, the earliest form of clothing. Variations of costume were unknown to most matrons of the anct. world, and in the E. they are as unchanging in this respect as in everything else, the word F. not having the same sgnificance there as it has in the W. The Roms. spread their dress, together with their civilisation, over Europe, and in the fifth century it was gradually modified by the close-fitting garments of the races of the N. It may be said that in the W. the history of conquest is the history of F. Thus the anct. Briton made his garments of skins, which in Rom. times developed into the skin coat or tunic, and later, doublet, and this in time became the prototype of the modern coat and waistcoat. F. in its modern sense may be said to have begun in the fourteenth century; for it is then that complaints seem to have first arisen of clothes being cast aside for others of newer style. Prior to the nineteenth century men's clothes were as sumptuous and delicate in texture as women's, and Pepys, in his *Diary*, records how he had his wife's gowns cut up into waistcoats for himself. A marked feature in men's dress in the fourteenth century was the change from close-fitting tunic and hose to long, loose garments. Dress was originally a symbol of rank, strictly prescribed for the various classes of society, as clearly shown by the sumptuary laws prevailing from the thirteenth to the seventeenth century; but in modern days this state of things has fallen into disuse except in the case of uniforms in the army and navy, law, church, etc. Nowadays everyone can clothe himself as he pleases irrespective of station and rank. Political and religious opinions have been at times symbolised by dress, as in the case of the Puritans and Quakers, but nowadays the clergy are practically the only class of the community who mark themselves off from other men. Dress attained its highest point of significance in France during the latter half of the eighteenth century, when it marked the various stages of the Revolution. Fashionable attire grew more and more eccentric and various with the increase of political turmoil; the women of France began to clothe themselves in the styles of Greece and Rome, the gorgeous and stately dresses of the courts of Louis XIV. and Louis XV. having disappeared with the old régime. At the present day Paris and Vienna may be said to set the fashion in women's dress, while London is rapidly gaining in popularity, and Savile Row tailoring is still regarded as the criterion of a well-dressed man. The development of athletics among women, coupled with the masculine work which they performed during the Great War, has had a far-reaching effect upon their mode of dress. Utility and serviceability have attained a wider recognition than ever before, and women have even defied attempts to impose upon them fashions which they felt would interfere with their freedom of movement and action. The abbreviated skirt, at one time carried to an undignified extreme, is favourably regarded by women for day wear in place of the long, hampering and unhygienic skirts of former days; sleeveless and low-necked frocks, formerly seen only in ballrooms, have become common on the river and the tennis court. The kit of the present day ski-ing enthusiast or of the woman aviator would excite the envy of the old-time 'emancipated' cycling woman whose attempt to introduce the 'bloomer' costume was frustrated by public opinion. In contrast to her more 'sensible' mode of dress is woman's growing love of daintiness in matters of silken underwear and of silk stockings; while outdoor garments of utility, such as mackintoshes, are now made in gay instead of drab and dreary colourings. See *The Cyclopædia of Costume*, by J. R. Planché, 1879; *Costume in England*, by F. W. Fairholt, 1896; *Ancient Egyptian, Assyrian, and Persian Costumes*, by M. G. Houston and F. S. Hornblower, 1920; *Historic Costume in Western Europe*, by F. M. Kelly and R. Schwabe, 1925; *Four Hundred Years of Children's Costumes*, by Percy Macquoid, 1925; *Costumes of Eastern Europe*, by M. Tilke, 1926;

*Costume and Fashion*, by H. Norris, 1927; *Modes and Manners of the 19th Century*, by Max von Boehn, 1927–30; *English Costume of the 19th Century*, by Iris Brook and James Laver, 1929.

**Fashoda** (renamed **Kodok** in 1904), a post on the W. bank of the Upper Nile, Egyptian Sudan, 459 m. S., by river, of Khartum. It is the cap. of the *mudiria* (province) of the Upper Nile. The station is built on a flat peninsula, separated, when the Nile is high, from a low-lying island in the river, with which it runs parallel, by a narrow strip of swampy ground. The climate is most unhealthy. F. is the residence of the 'Mek,' or King of the Shilluk tribe. The Egyptian military post was established at F. in 1865, which was also an important trading station. In 1883–84 the post fell into the hands of the Mahdists. In 1898 the French commandant, Marchand, with a force from the Congo, hoisted the French flag there. Sir Herbert Kitchener, having just captured Khartum, re-hoisted the British and Egyptian flags at F., and invited Marchand to withdraw. The latter refused, and the matter was referred to London and Paris. The French protested that the Egyptian occupation of the Sudan had been suspended by the Mahdist domination and that it was open to them to make a settlement on the Nile. For a while the tension between the two countries was extreme, but in Dec. of the same year France, uncertain of the support of Russia, ordered the withdrawal of the Marchand expedition.

**Fast and Loose,** also called **Pricking at the Belt,** a cheating game much practised by sharpers at the fairs, especially by gypsies in the time of Shakespeare. A leathern strap is rolled or doubled up with a loop in the centre, and placed edgewise on the table. The sharper then seeks for some one to bet that he can catch the loop with a skewer, which looks easy; he then unrolls the belt in such a way that the catching of the loop is an impossibility. From this game comes the expression, 'to play fast and loose'; the modern name of the game is 'Prick the Garter.'

**Fasti** (Lat. *fastus*, lawful), the days on which it was lawful to do business. In early Rom. days such days were declared by the priests and later set up in the Forum on tables called F., which were practically the equivalent of calendar. They were of two kinds, the 'F. sacri,' or 'kalendares,' strictly the calendars of the year, containing the list of lawful and unlawful days, the days for festivals and courts, etc., and the 'F. annales,' or 'historici,' which contained the names of the consuls and other magistrates, and such historical events as were considered worthy to be noted. *See* Ovid's *Fasti*.

**Fasting** (Gk. νηστεύειν) is strictly abstinence from all food and drink for a given period, but it is much more commonly used for abstinence from certain kinds of food only. (1) *Religious.*—It is an accompanying feature of nearly every known form of religion ; its motives and modes of practice varying, of course, according to race, climate, and civilisation. The origin of the practice is buried in obscurity ; some authorities suggest that it arose from the custom of providing food for the dead, others that it was a preparation for the receiving of sacramental food, and others that it is the subjection of the lower nature in order to exalt the higher for the seeing of visions. Whatever the motive, partial or complete abstinence from food at stated periods was practised at a very early date by Parsees, Hindus, Egyptians, Assyrians, Greeks, and Romans. It was a prominent and inseparable feature of the Jewish ritual. The solemn national fast on the tenth day of every seventh month (the Day of Atonement), the penalty for the non-observance of which was death, was the only public fast ordained in the Books of Moses (Lev. xvi. 29–34 ; xxiii.), but the practice of private and occasional public fasts, at periods of national calamity, is frequently recorded (Judges xx. 26 ; 1 Sam. vii. 6 ; 2 Sam. xii. 16). During the captivity the fasts of the fourth, fifth, seventh, and tenth months were instituted to commemorate certain incidents in the downfall of the nation. The number of special fasts mentioned in the N.T. and practised by the Pharisees and the disciples of St. John the Baptist (Luke xviii. 12 ; Mark ii. 18), although insisted upon by the Pharisees, were really voluntary, and were probably never practised by the sect of the Sadducees and others. There is no reason to doubt that our Lord observed the one great national fast, but He neither upheld nor practised the fasts ordained by the Pharisees. The apostles and the fathers of the early Christian Church, however, influenced probably by such passages as Matt. ix. 15, not only practised it themselves, but instituted F. as an obligatory practice for all the members of the church. In the Rom. Catholic Church there are the great forty days' fast of Lent, the quatember fasts of three days in one week of each of the four seasons, while every Friday there is total abstinence from all flesh foods, and the eves of certain feasts. In the Gk. Church

the practice is followed with much greater severity, and the fast days cover about three-quarters of the year. In the Anglican Church F. is regarded only as a useful exercise, praiseworthy, but never obligatory, and not in itself a means of grace ; the Prayer Book, however, enumerates the forty days of Lent, all the Fridays in the year with some exceptions, Ember days, Rogation days, and the eves or vigils of certain festivals. In Scotland the sacramental fast days so long observed have almost entirely fallen into disuse. The Mohammedans, as an offshoot of the Jewish and Christian communities, adopted the practice of F. with many others ; they regard it as an efficacious means of averting the wrath of Allah in national calamities, and of mitigating the penalties of sin. The month of Ramadan, in which Mohammed brought the Koran from Heaven, is strictly observed as a complete fast for all the faithful, eating, drinking, and smoking being forbidden from sunrise to sunset, and voluntary fasts are common. *See* R. Nelson's *Festivals and Fasts of the Church ;* Liesmayr, *Die Entwickelung der Christlichen Fastendisziplin*, 1877 ; Lane, *Modern Egyptians*. *See also* JEWS and MOHAMMEDANISM. (2) *Medical.*—It is more especially to the abstinence from solid food that the term F. is applied. By experiments it has been proved that water is a great prolonger of life, so that whereas the human body cannot survive total abstinence for more than eight days, by taking water freely it is possible to sustain life for thirty or forty days. A Welsh girl, in 1859, who pretended that she had lived for two years without food, was put under the observation of doctors and deprived of food and water, but she died within eight days ; whereas, in 1888, a Frenchman named Jacques, fasted from solid food for thirty days, but took water freely, and the same experiment was successfully tried for forty days by an Italian, named Lucci, in 1890. Some entombed miners survived for ten days in 1876, being kept alive by the aqueous vapour in the mine. Observations have proved that the body wastes less rapidly when kept warm and at rest ; the external application of salt water has sometimes kept shipwrecked sailors alive, but they seem especially liable to delirium. The process of starvation is observed in the waste of the various tissues of the body, first the fatty tissues, and then the proteids of the muscles ; emaciation is, of course, invariable, and a lowered temperature, while apoplexy and intestinal ulceration are frequently accompanying features. A craving for food is insistent in the first days of a total fast, but diminishes, and torpor succeeds it. See DIET and DIGESTION.

**Fastnet Rock,** a rock in lat. 51° 23′ N. and long. 9° 36′ W., situated about 4 m. S.W. of Cape Clear, off co. Cork, Ireland. A lighthouse stands on the rock, and the light, which is revolving and 148 ft. above high-water mark, is visible for more than 18 m.

**Fastolf,** or **Fastolfe, Sir John** (c. 1378–1459), an English soldier probably b. at Caister, near Yarmouth. He served as a soldier in Ireland (1405–6), in Gascony (1413), and the campaigns of Henry V., and distinguished himself at Agincourt (1415) and 'the battle of the herrings' (1429). In 1423 he was appointed governor of Maine and Anjou, and created Knight of the Garter in 1423. The cause of the English defeat at Patay (1429) was long a matter of dispute, and F. was deprived of the Garter by Bedford on a charge of cowardice, but was reinstated. He served with honour in France until 1440, but never completely cleared himself of the popular charges against him. He was reputed to have favoured Lollardry, which may account for Shakespeare's use of his name in Henry IV. when he dropped that of Oldcastle (q.v.). See Chronicles of Monstrelet and Paston Letters. See FALSTAFF, SIR JOHN.

**Fat,** in chemistry, a mixture of glycerides. When the suet of beef or mutton is heated in a muslin bag in water, and kneaded so that the membranes of the F. globules are broken, the melted F. may be collected in the form of a liquid which rapidly cools to tallow. If this tallow be heated to about 200° C. under pressure, it decomposes into glycerol or glycerin, a sweet syrup used in toilet preparations, and certain acids known as fatty acids. All the Fs., butter, lard, bone-fats, etc., and the liquid known as olive-oil, linseed-oil, palm-oil, etc., behave in this way. Glycerol is a trihydric alcohol, and, like the alcohols generally, reacts with acids to form ethereal salts, or esters. The esters of glycerol are termed glycerides, and are distinguished, according to the acids with which they are associated, as triacetin, tripalmitin, tristearin, triolëin, etc. The chief glycerides present in Fs. are the solids tripalmitin and tristearin, and the liquid triolëin. The relative proportions of solid and liquid glycerides determine whether the substance is a F. or an oil at ordinary temperatures. Tallow, for instance, contains a preponderating proportion of tripalmitin and tristearin; lard, which is

much softer, contains more triolëin, while olive-oil contains a preponderance of triolëin. At moderately high temperatures the glycerides are decomposed by water into glycerol and their corresponding acid; thus, tristearin yields glycerol and stearic acid, triolëin yields glycerol and oleïc acid, and so on. The chief uses of Fs. are in the manufacture of soaps, as ingredients in articles of food, as lubricants, and as media for colouring matter, etc. Fs. constitute an important item in an ordinary diet. They contain a relatively higher proportion of carbon than protein, which is the chief constituent of lean meat; and as carbon is discharged in large amounts from the body, it is desirable to replace it by a corresponding preponderance of Fs. and carbohydrates in the diet. In Arctic regions, where the heat of the body has to be kept up by a plentiful supply of combustive material, human beings crave for F. to an extent incomprehensible to dwellers in temperate climates. For F. in the digestive process, see DIGESTION. See also ADIPOSE TISSUE.

**Fatalism,** the philosophic doctrine of the futility of human struggles against destiny, and is the basis of such different systems as those of Hegel and Herbert Spencer. The Stoics associated it with the idea of necessity, and contended that as such it was a power unalterable even by God. Theologically, it is the belief that life is governed by inevitable laws which depend on the arbitrary decrees of an Almighty, and also by the laws of nature; it is exemplified in Spinozism and in the later ideas of predestination. F. is essentially an Oriental conception, and is the predominating spirit of E. philosophy, literature, and religion, finding its strongest expression in the Mohammedan idea of Kismet.

**Fata Morgana,** the Italian name for a curious kind of mirage frequently observed in the Straits of Messina, and so called because it is supposed to be caused by the fairy (fata) Morgana of the Arthurian legends. An observer on the shore frequently sees men, ships, or houses, sometimes in the air, sometimes in the water, the same object frequently having two images, one inverted. The cause is the same as that of the desert mirage. See MIRAGE.

**Fatehgarh,** or **Futtigarh,** a tn. of British India, and the administrative headquarters of the dist. of Farrukhabad, situated on the Ganges in the Agra div. of the United Provinces. A British military station since 1802, and there is a government gun-carriage factory. Scene of a European massacre (Indian mutiny, 1857). An

American Presbyterian mission settlement is here. Pop. 20,000.

**Fatehpur (Futtehpur).** (1) Cap. of a dist. of the same name in the Allahabad div. of the United Provinces, 73 m. N.W. of Allahabad. It has two fine mosques, and a trade in grain and leather, especially ornamental whips. The district lies in the S.E. corner of the Doab (*q.v.*), between the Ganges and the Jumna, with an area of 1618 sq. m., most of which is highly cultivated. Pop. of dist., 686,000 ; of tn., 20,000. (2) A fort. tn. of Rajputana, 145 m. N.W. of Jaipur. Pop. 16,000.

**Fatehpur Sikri,** a former cap. of the Mogul empire, 23 m. W. of Agra, founded in 1569 by Akbar as a thankoffering for the birth of his son, Selim. The magnificent architectural ruins, enclosed by a high wall 7 m. in circumference, include a splendid mosque and several palaces, including that of Akbar. It was deserted within fifty years of its foundation owing to lack of water. Pop. about 6000.

**Fates, The,** *see* MOIRÆ.

**Father,** *see* FAMILY, PARENT, and CHILD.

**Fatherhood, The Divine,** the metaphor of Fatherhood is used in most branches of the Christian Church to show the distinctive feature in the Christian idea of the relation of God to man. In ethnic religions the idea is foreshadowed, but before the coming of Christ it hardly went beyond the idea of God as the progenitor of all things. The idea of the personal and individual relationship between God and each of His creatures is an inherent part of the Christian faith. The Jews called Jehovah 'Father' (Isa. lxiii. 16), and called their own nation His 'Son' (Hos. xi. 1), but they only acknowledged Him as the 'Father of Israel'; the Gentiles were excluded. Christ included all men (Luke vi. 35) as 'children' of God, although undoubtedly the phrase 'your Father' which occurs so frequently in the 'Sermon on the Mount' refers more particularly to His own immediate followers (Matt. v. vi. vii.). In this sense it is used by St. John (I. iii. 1–2), and still more clearly so by St. Paul in his use of the figures of 'adoption' (Roms. viii. 14–15), where he clearly shows his belief that it is only those who 'knowingly' are led by the Spirit of God who are His 'Sons.' As Christ Himself draws the distinction between 'My Father' and 'your Father' (N.B.—He never speaks of 'Our Father') so does St. Paul amplify it (Roms. viii. 15–17). Some few sects of the Christian Church, notably the Calvinists, have denied the 'Fatherhood' of God, regarding Him only as the 'Judge,' which would account for the unbending sternness of their teaching. *See* C. H. Wright's *The Fatherhood of God,* 1867 ; Candlish, *The Fatherhood of God,* 1866 ; Wendt's *Teaching of Jesus* (trans. Wilson), 1892 ; Bruce's *Kingdom of God,* 1889 ; and A. M. Fairbairn's *Christian Modern Theology* (new ed.), 1907.

**Father of the Chapel,** the name bestowed on a person in any printers' trade society who is held responsible for seeing to the faithful performance of the duties and regulations by the members of that society.

**Fathers, Apostolic,** *see* APOSTOLIC FATHERS.

**Fathers of the Church.** The patriarchs are described in the O.T. as the 'Fathers of Israel,' and the early Christians, who looked upon themselves as spiritual Israelites, kept up the use of this title. But for long the Christians abstained from giving the name 'father' to their own spiritual heads, for they remembered our Lord's warning, 'Call no man your father upon the earth ' (Matt. xxiii. 8). However, we read that the mob of Jews and pagans at the martyrdom of Polycarp cried out, 'This is the Christians' father.' In the fourth century we find that Athanasius defends the term ὁμοούσιος as having been earlier used by certain 'fathers,' and after this the word frequently occurs in councils, such as those of Constantinople and Chalcedon. In the stricter sense of the term, the Fathers of the Church are those writers of the early centuries who were remarkable for their perfect orthodoxy and great sanctity, and their writings have ever been regarded as, after the Bible, the most valuable portions of Christian literature. The term is, however, also used to include Tertullian and Origen, and other writers either slightly or entirely heterodox. In the great *Patrologia* of the Abbé Migne, writers such as Theodore of Mopsuestia and Pelagius are included, but these come under the last head of the sub-title, which runs: *Sive Bibliotheca omnium Patrum, Doctorum, Scriptorumque ecclesiasticorum.* Those tainted with heresy or of very slight importance are, indeed, generally spoken of not as 'fathers' but as ecclesiastical writers (*scriptores ecclesiastici*), though they are sometimes included under the former title. Thus the study of patristics or patrology is not restricted to orthodox writers. Almost invariably the fathers of the first century are considered apart from the rest under the title 'Apostolic Fathers,' and so we have here a good starting-point. It is far more difficult to decide up to what date writers shall be included.

Migne, in his *cursus completus*, carries his patrology down to about 1200 for the Latins and to the Fall of Constantinople for the Gks., but for ordinary purposes this range is too extensive. A more common boundary is the time of Gregory the Great (*d.* 604) in the West and that of John of Damascus (756) in the East. After this time the freshness and spontaneity of thought which mark the early writers almost entirely disappears. Two groups of the fathers stand out pre-eminent above the rest, and receive the title ' Doctors of the Church.' The Western or Latin Doctors are Ambrose, Augustine, Jerome, and Gregory the Great; the Eastern or Greek Doctors are Athanasius, Basil the Great, Gregory of Nazianzus, and John Chrysostom. The chief division between the Apostolic Fathers and the limits named above come with the Council of Nicæa and the Conversion of the Empire. Chief among the Ante-Nicene fathers may be named : Justin Martyr, Clement of Alexandria, Origen and Dionysius, Gregory Thaumaturgus, Methodius, Tertullian, and Cyprian. Chief among the Post-Nicene fathers we may mention Eusebius of Cæsarea, Athanasius, Cyril of Jerusalem, Basil, Gregory of Nazianzus, Gregory of Nyssa, John Chrysostom, Theodoret, Cyril of Alexandria, Photius, Hilary of Poitiers, Ambrose, Augustine, Jerome, Rufinus, Leo the Great, John Cassian, Hilary of Arles, Vincentius, and the English Bede. *See* Dowling's *Notitia Scriptorum ss. Patrum,* 1839 ; Krüger's *History of Early Christian Literature in the First Three Centuries,* trans. 1897 ; Hort's *Six Lectures on the Ante-Nicene Fathers,* 1895, and various editions of the fathers.

**Fathom,** a measure of 6 ft. chiefly serviceable for taking marine soundings such as regulating cable lines; also used for mines. This metre is the standard for most European nations. The word fathom comes from the Anglo-Saxon *faëom,* the measurement of the width to which the two outstretched arms extended.

**Fathometer.** An instrument for measuring the depth of the ocean, by measuring the interval of time that elapses between the production of a sound at the surface of the sea and the arrival of the echo from the bottom. Great strides have been made in recent years in the development of these instruments, first suggested in 1912 after the disaster to the *Titanic.* To-day every important ship is equipped with a F., and the reader is referred to *Wood's Sound Waves and their Uses* (Blackie 1930)

for an excellent account of the various types now used.

**Fatigue :** (1) In physiology, ' Muscular F.' is the diminishing of the contractions brought about by stimuli. The muscle is a machine for utilising the energy contained in its own chemical compounds ; if the excitations of the muscles are continued beyond a certain point the muscle cells are poisoned by the excreta of their own waste chemical products. The muscle recovers if allowed to rest unstimulated for a time, or more quickly if washed with an innocuous but unnutritious solution such as 6 per cent. NaCl in water. The same waste-products of the muscles produce ' F.' in the unsheathed ends of the nerve-plates, and the central sensor and motor nerve cells exhibit the same phenomena and a general irresponsiveness to ordinary stimuli. (2) In materials, F. is the term used to denote the weakening of a metal bar by a repeated succession of the strain of loads considerably less than the breaking weight of the bar, as when a car-axle breaks from the continued strains and blows which it experiences, or a member of machinery, such as a piston-rod, which is constantly in alternate tension or compression. F. of metals is due to a molecular change in the metal due to vibration or the constant application of a varying strain.

**Fatigue-duty** is that part of a soldier's work which is distinct from the use of arms and military drill, such as loading stores. ' Fatigue call ' is the bugle note which calls to such duty, and ' fatigue dress ' the uniform worn while engaged in it.

**Fatima** (600–632), the daughter of Mohammed and Khedija. She was considered by her father to be one of the four perfect women of Islam, and was espoused to Ali when only fifteen years of age.

**Fatimides,** the name given to a dynasty of Arabia, which reigned for nearly two centuries over Egypt. Its founder, Obaidallah, claimed to be descended from Fatima, the daughter of the prophet Mohammed, and Ismael, a great-grandson of Ali. But later on a difference of opinion crept in regarding the validity of the claims set forth by the F. Suggestions were thrown out that the founder of the dynasty had no right to the sovereignty, and that he was in reality descended from a family of heretics known as the Carmathian sect. When Obaidallah came into power, he assumed the title of Al-Mahdi-Commander of the Faithful, and reigned supreme over the whole Moslem world. But he became unpopular through his assassination of Al Shii and his brother; his reign was one long series of hostilities against surrounding powers. He *d*. in 933, and was succeeded by Al Qua'im, who was much pestered by the conspiracies of Abu-Yazid and his sons. He was defeated by them at Kairawan in 943, and in 944 was imprisoned in his own capital. He *d*. in 945 during the Siege of Susa, and was succeeded by his son Al Mansur Isma'il. Abu-Yazid was finally quelled by this sovereign. The centre of the F. power became ultimately transferred to Egypt in the reign of Mo'izz liden Allah, who expelled the reigning family and, assuming the title of caliph, founded the city of Cairo (970). But after his death the power of the F. gradually

cereals, roots, etc., and less than 65 per cent. in the case of bulky feeding stuffs such as hay and straw. As a source of manure the value of fattening foods is greater the more nitrogen they contain. Practically speaking, the whole of the mineral constituents and about nine-tenths of the nitrogen of food are recovered in the dung and urine. For the same weight of dry substance consumed, oxen void more manure than sheep, and sheep more than pigs. The composition of the different foods given to fattening animals being well known, it is easy to calculate the amounts of nitrogen, phosphoric acid, and potash of the food which will be recovered in the manure. Each constituent having its

ONE OF THE FEW REMAINS OF THE FORMER GLORIES CREATED BY THE
FATIMIDES IN CAIRO—THE MOSQUE OF EL-HAKIM

waned, and they were content to allow the government to fall into the hands of the viziers. The sovereignty of the F. was at last only recognised in certain external ceremonies and observances, such as the mention of them in public prayer, the impression coins, and the paying of tribute to the vizier of Cairo. The last F. caliph to reside in Egypt was Al-Adid. After his death in 1171, the founder of the dynasty of the Ayubides, Saladin, reigned over Egypt.

**Fattening Foods, Fodder,** and **Forage Crops,** a term used to denote those foods which are mainly used for 'feeding up' cattle. Investigation has shown that in estimating the value of animal manure (feeding stuff for plants) 90 per cent. of the nitrogen of food may be reckoned to be recovered in the case of feeding cakes, pulse, and other highly nitrogenous foods, 85 per cent. in case of foods comparatively poor in hydrogen. .*g*.

market value as a manuring constituent, the money value of the manure obtained from the consumption of a ton of any ordinary food of which the composition is known can be easily determined. Assuming ammonia to be worth 8*d*. per lb., potash 2*d*. per lb., and phosphate of lime 1*d*. per lb., the money value of the manure produced by the consumption of a ton of various foods can be deduced.

*Fodder crops,* or *forage crops,* are grown for consumption by live stock in the green or succulent state, and include numerous leguminous plants, a few cruciferous plants, any of the cereal crops in a green condition, and other grasses, including the ordinary hay crop if eaten fresh, or if stored as silage. Fodders have the important advantages of requiring a minimum of labour, and in some cases of growing so rapidly that they can be produced as catch crops in the intervals between the crops of ordinary rotation, while leguminous fodders actually improve and renovate the soil. Cabbages and thousand-headed kale are very nutritious fodders, and given a fair rainfall grow anywhere, resisting frost well and liking transplanting; they need a heavily manured soil, and can be consumed on the land by sheep or cut and eaten in the yards by cattle. Rape grows in any soil, and follows early potatoes or an early corn crop, or provides a succession of green food for sheep after two or three months. White mustard grows rapidly, providing a good sheep food in six weeks or less. Of leguminous fodders the varieties of clover are the most important. Crimson or Italian clover, commonly called Trifolium, is grown as a catch crop after corn, the other needing usually a full year to provide sufficient growth. They are therefore sown with corn crops, commonly being broadcasted just before or after the first hoeing of the cereals. Lucerne is very valuable on dry calcareous loams and in dry seasons, owing to its deep rooting habit, yields an abundance of rich green food. In clean ground it can stand a number of years and be frequently cut. Sainfoin requires similar culture, and on limestone soils is of great importance in sheep farming. Vetches and tares are grown to provide a long succession of green food for sheep and also for cattle and horses. Lupins make a rich sheep food on poor sandy soils, and the young shoots of gorse are eaten readily and are utilised on otherwise barren land. Other important fodders are rye, grass, maize, and prickly comfrey.

**Fatty Acids**, a group of organic compounds so called because the higher members are found combined with glycerol in fats (*q.v.*). They have the general formula $C_nH_{2n+1}CO \cdot OH$, and may be regarded as derivatives of the paraffins, the alcohols, or the aldehydes. The principal members of the series are formic acid, acetic acid, propionic acid, butyric acid, valeric acid, heptylic acid, lauric acid, myristic acid, palmitic acid, and stearic acid. The first six, except acetic acid, are liquid at ordinary temperatures, possess a pungent smell, and are readily miscible in water and alcohol. The higher members are solids of a waxy or fatty nature, have little smell, are insoluble in water, but are dissolved by alcohol and ether. They are very stable compounds, and, with the exception of formic acid, they are only oxidised with difficulty.

**Fatty Compounds**, one of the two great divisions into which the substances studied in organic chemistry are divided. The word ' fatty ' was originally applied to the acids derived from the paraffins, but is now extended to denote all compounds regarded as derivatives of methane.

**Fatty Degeneration**, a derangement of metabolism by which the protein matter of the tissues, is replaced by fat. Under normal conditions, globules of fat pass from the digestive tract into the tissues, where they are either oxidised to keep up the heat of the body, or are stored in the cells of adipose tissue. Under certain morbid conditions, however, the oxidising capability of the cells seems to be interfered with. The cytoplasm is invaded by granules of fat which can be recognised by the usual fat-staining reagents. The manner in which the change is brought about is somewhat obscure, but it is always associated with some toxic agent. All dead and decaying matter in the body undergoes F. D.

**Faucher, Léon** (1803–54), a celebrated statesman and writer on political economy. He both edited and contributed to the political journals the *Constitutionnel* and the *Courier Français*. In 1842 he visited England in order to study the industrial conditions of that country, and afterwards compiled his *Etudes sur l'Angleterre* (1845). At the close of the Revolution of 1848 appointed Minister of Public Works for the department of Marne, and later on Minister of the Interior. Served under Louis Napoleon, but resigned his office when the emperor advocated universal suffrage. Was a firm upholder of free trade.

**Fauchet, Claude** (1744–93), a French bishop ; also a noted orator and politician. Was appointed Abbé of Montfort Lacarre in Brittany. Elected in 1791 deputy to the legislative assembly and member of convocation. Alarmed by the numerous excesses of the Jacobins, he veered towards the Girondist party. He became suspect in consequence, was arrested in 1793 and executed.

**Faucit, Helena Saville** (1817–98), a celebrated English actress, daughter of John Saville F. She took the Shakespearian parts of Juliet, Imogen, and Hermione, and made such an impression on Macready that he engaged her to take the leading characters in Lytton's *Duchesse de la Vallière*, *Lady of Lyons*, and in Browning's *Strafford*. She married Theodore Martin, who was knighted in 1851.

**Faults** is the name given to any displacement of strata or veins in the earth's crust. They occur in the group of rocks known as sedimentary or stratified rocks. These consist of regular layers of rock of various kinds. Many railway cuttings form examples of rocks formed by sedimentary deposit, and the regular layers which the solid rocks thus exposed to view exhibit can easily be seen. Every running brook which carries down particles of sand, earth, or gravel and deposits them in the lower portions of the bed shows the agency which must have produced the various sedimentary formations. All such strata must have been formed in like manner during long periods of time, and what is now dry land must formerly have been under water. The highest parts of what is now the dry land of the globe were once covered by the ocean. It seldom happens that the sedi-

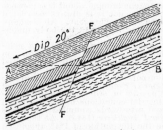

DIAGRAM OF FAULT (FF)

The angle made by the slope of the strata with the horizontal line AB is the angle of dip of the strata

mentary strata exhibit a horizontal arrangement through any great distance. More frequently they have been upheaved and displaced after they were first deposited. Sometimes the land has subsided so that the strata are displaced along a ridge, while another ridge remains quite firm. Thus, what is known as a F. results. The strata are inclined at various angles to the horizon, and sometimes the successive layers of deposit are bent and distorted, giving evidence of pressure exerted upon them. Earthquakes often cause F. in the strata. In many cases sedimentary strata are broken through by masses of igneous rocks, which, by their intrusion in a melted form, have often caused an upheaval of strata. F. are also caused by subsidence of the inner portions of the earth.

**Faun, Faunus,** a rural deity in Roman legend and regarded as the god and protector of shepherds. Later on the name became identified with the Gk. god Pan. F. was supposed to have been the third sovereign of the Laurentines; his predecessors were Saturnus, the god of seed-time and harvest, and Picus, the deity symbolical of storm and lightning.

**Fauna,** a term used by naturalists in reference to the collective animal life of any district or of any period in history. Thus we have the F. of the British Isles, or the F. of the Antediluvian age. F. is derived from the F. of mythology, creatures who were regarded as the protectors of wild animals.

**Faure, François Félix** (1841–99), *b.* in Paris, a son of a furniture maker; became a tanner and merchant at Havre, where he was very successful financially; was elected member of the National Assembly in 1881, and took a keen interest in economics and politics. Appointed Under-Secretary for the Colonies in M. Férrier's ministry in 1888; vice-president of the Chamber in 1893; appointed president of the Republic in 1895 upon resignation of Casimir-Périer. It was through his diplomacy and tact that the Franco-Russian alliance was accomplished in 1897. Died of apoplexy.

**Faure, Gabriel Urbain** (1845–1924), French musical composer, *b.* May 13 at Pamiers. He studied at the School of Sacred Music, directed by Medermeyer, under Dietsch and Saint-Saëns. He became *maître de chapelle* at the church of the Madeleine in 1877, and organist in 1896. Director of the Conservatoire, 1905–20. His music includes pieces for the piano, pieces for the strings, orchestral music, cantatas, and opera— *Prométhée; Pénélope.* His *Birth of Venus* was performed at the Leeds Festival in 1898. Died Nov. 4.

**Fauresmith,** a tn. in the Orange Free State, cap. of the div. of the same name, about 65 m. from Kimberley. The Jagersfontein diamond mines lie a few miles to the S.E.

**Fauriel, Claude Charles** (1772–1844), a French historian and philologist, *b.* at St. Etienne. He was a student of Sanskrit and Arabic, as well as of Latin and Gk., and was appointed a professor in the Paris Faculté des Lettres. His lectures as professor appear in *Histoire de la Poésie Provençale,* in which he attempts to prove that the old Spanish and Ger. poetry originated in France. He was a member of the literary circle of Auteuil, and turned his attention to the study of philosophy. Among his friends were Madame de Staël, Cabanis the physiologist, the poet Manzoni, Benjamin Constant, and Guizot. His works include: A translation of Baggesen's *Parthenais,* 1810; Manzoni's tragedies, 1823; Modern Gk.

folk songs, 1824; *Sur l'Origine de l'Epopée du Moyen Age*, 1833; and *Histoire de la Gaule Méridionale sous la Domination des Conquérants Germains*, 1836, which is his greatest work.

**Faust.** The legend of F. is held by many historians to be of Eastern origin, but its European interest devolves on a sixteenth century magician, F., or Faustus, of Suabia, reputed to have studied necromancy in Krakow and to have exploited Germany in the rôles of astrologer, diviner, medium, alchemist, and swindler, a veritable ally of Mephistopheles. The earliest history of F. appeared at Frankfort in 1587, and was speedily followed by numerous and varied versions, each more embellished than the previous one, the chief of these being G. R. Widmann's (1599). From this, J. N. Pfitzer compiled an encyclopædic version, of which six editions appeared between 1674 and 1726. The chief German edition of the period was published in 1712, under the authorship of ' Christlich Meynenden ' (A Christian Believer). Meanwhile, due to the intolerant bigotry and narrow Protestant sympathies of the 1587 edition, which were strongly in keeping with contemporary religious prejudices, it appeared very rapidly in foreign translations, Danish being the first (1588), English, French, Dutch, and Flemish following during the next six years, and Czech in 1612. The English translation was the basis of Marlowe's *Tragical History of Doctor Faustus* (performed in 1594, published 1604), the finest of the early F. dramas. In Germany every little puppet-show had its own version of the legend, right up to the middle of the eighteenth century. In 1759 Lessing's dramatised version was written, but has since been destroyed save for a few sheets of MS.; it was in his hands that the legend first assumed the shape which has become definitive, a more modern and tolerant spirit superseding the stern uncompromising attitude of the earlier editions. Goethe was the first to introduce the Gretchen incident into his magnificent work (1798). This violation of the legend had no apparent reason, beyond broadening the secular dramatic interest to meet modern demands; and the innovation was condemned by purists as unjustifiable. However, it is Goethe's version—well called the ' divine comedy ' of eighteenth century humanism—that has become recognised as the greatest literary achievement of the vast number that have been attempted on the same subject, and round it has arisen an important and extensive musical literature. Music was written for a production at Stuttgart (1832) by Lindpainter, and a score by Prince Radziwill was published in 1846. A choral dramatic legend by Berlioz, *La Damnation de Faust*, was performed at Paris in 1846, the text being derived by the composer and Gaudonnières from De Nerval's adaptation. The most famous setting is Gounod's *Faust*, performed at Paris in 1859—a very beautiful five-act opera to a libretto by Barbier and Carré. Boito's *Mefistofele* (Milan, 1868) is also from the same source as those of Gounod and Berlioz. On a lower plane altogether, and quite estranged from Goethe's masterpiece, is the *Faust* of Spohr, a romantic two-act opera to a wretched and vulgar text by Bernhard, produced at Frankfort in 1818. Goethe's work has also inspired some ' absolute ' music, notably the *Faust Symphony* of Liszt, and Wagner's *Faust Overture*.

**Faust, Johann** (a printer), *see* FUST.

**Faustina, Annia Galeria,** usually called **Faustina the Elder** (A.D. 104–141), the wife of Antoninus Pius and mother of Faustina the Younger.

**Faustina, Annia, the Younger** (*c.* A.D. 130–175), was the wife of Marcus Aurelius Antoninus and daughter of Faustina the Elder (*supra*). Both were accused of gross profligacy, but there is some doubt of this, for they were both honoured after death by their husbands, who founded ' Puellæ Alimentariæ Faustinæ,' institutions for the relief of poor girls.

**Favara,** a tn. in the prov. of Girgenti, Sicily, about 4 m. E. of Girgenti. Its chief products are sulphur and marble. Pop. about 20,500.

**Favart, Charles Simon** (1710–92), a Fr. dramatist, *b.* in Paris. He was educated at the college of Louis-le-Grand, and his poem, *La France Délivrée par la Pucelle d'Orleans*, obtained a prize at the Académie des Yeux Floraux. He became director of the Opéra Comique, which, under him, rose to a height of success. In 1746 he went with Maurice de Saxe to Flanders with a troupe of comedians, where he became very popular. In 1750 he returned to Paris and resumed his writing. Some of his works are : *L'Anglais à Bordeaux*, *Les Trois Sultanes, Ninette à la Cour*, and *Mémoires et Correspondance Littéraire*, which gives valuable information of the literary and theatrical world of the eighteenth century.

**Faversham,** a municipal bor. and river-port of Kent, about 10 m. from Canterbury. It dates back to about 811, and was a seat of the Saxon kings. It contains the remains of a

Cluniac abbey, founded by King Stephen, in which he is buried, and has a grammar school which was started in 1527. It has a quarter sessions court and a separate commission of the peace. It is important for its oyster fisheries, which are under the direction of an ancient guild, as well as for its shipping trade in coal, timber, and agricultural produce, including especially hops and cherries. There are also powder-mills in the vicinity; brewing, cement, and brick-making are carried on. Pop. 10,865.

**Favonius** is mentioned for the first time in 61 B.C., during the transactions against Publius Clodius for having violated the rites of the Bona Dea. On this occasion he joined Cato, whose sternness he imitated throughout his life, and went so far as to receive the nickname of the ape of Cato. He was a man of weak character, and the motives of his actions were passion and personal animosity, and not the consideration of the public good. His only honourable action is the conduct he showed towards Pompey after his defeat.

**Favonius,** the name given in Roman mythology to a wind which blew from the W. or S.W., and usually prevailed in spring. It is the same as the Greek *zephyrus.*

**Favre, Jules Claude Gabriel** (1809–80), a Fr. statesman, *b.* at Lyons, and studied for the Bar at Paris. He took part in the Revolution of 1830, and openly declared himself a republican. He made himself conspicuous when Louis Napoleon was elected President of France, and tried to organise an armed resistance in the streets of Paris. He established his reputation by his defence of Orsini, 1858, and in 1870, after the defeat at Sedan, proposed the deposition of the Emperor Napoleon III. He was Minister of Foreign Affairs under the Republic, and told Bismarck (1870) that he ' would not yield to Germany an inch of territory nor a single stone of fortresses.' He made several mistakes during the war, and on its conclusion withdrew from the ministry.

**Favularia,** a species of fossil plants, found first in the Devonian period, but most prolific in the Carboniferous. It belongs to the genus *Sigillaria.* The stem branched dichotomously, the leaves were large, and the venation was parallel.

**Favus,** a contagious skin disease, caused by a fungus parasite. It usually affects the scalp in man, but is occasionally found on other parts of the body. It also affects cats, dogs, cattle, mice, rabbits, and other animals. The growth consists of a number of yellow, circular, saucer-shaped scabs, each surrounding a single hair. The scabs grow and become encrusted; ultimately they break off, leaving a bare patch without a trace of hair. The characteristic scab may then develop again, as it is extremely difficult to get rid of all traces of the parasite. The fungus was first described by J. L. Schönlein in 1839, and from the name of its discoverer is called *Acherion Schönleinii.* It is more common in the eastern parts of Europe than the western, and is often associated with uncleanly habits. Contagion may take place from animal to man. The treatment involves removing the crusts with every consideration for cleanliness. The parts should then be dressed with an efficient parasiticide.

**Fawcett, Henry** (1833–84), English economist and politician, was *b.* at Salisbury. He was educated at King's College, London, Peterhouse, Cambridge, and Trinity Hall, where he became seventh wrangler in 1856, and was elected to a fellowship. He entered at Lincoln's Inn with the intention of becoming a member of parliament through a career at the Bar, but was unfortunate to lose his eyesight in 1858. He, however, kept up all his recreations, fishing, rowing, skating, as well as his studies. He was a disciple of Mill, and published in 1863 a *Manual of Political Economy,* the result of which was the election of Fawcett to the chair of political economy at Cambridge. In 1865 he was elected member for Brighton, and re-elected in 1868–74, and is spoken of as being a thorough Radical. In 1873 he took a prominent part in opposing Gladstone's scheme for university education in Ireland. He was a great advocate for the preservation of commons, especially those near large towns, and showed a marked interest in Indian affairs. In 1880 he was offered the place of postmaster-general by Mr. Gladstone, and established in 1882 the parcels post. He is also responsible for the introduction of postal orders, sixpenny telegrams, stamp slip deposits, and the increased facilities for life insurance and annuities. His publications include *Free Trade and Protection, Indian Finance, The Economic Position of the British Labourer, Pauperism, Free Trade and Protection.*

**Fawcett, Millicent Garrett, Dame** (1847–1930), *b.* at Aldeburgh, Suffolk. She was the daughter of Mr. Newson Garrett, and famous for her social and literary work, especially as an advocate of women's suffrage and the higher education and employment of women. In 1867 she married Henry F., the politician. She held the degree of LL.D. (Hon.), St. Andrews, and was president of the National Union of Women's Suffrage Societies. Publications: *Political Economy for Beginners*, 1870; *Tales in Political Economy*, 1875; *Essays and Lectures* (jointly with Henry F.), 1872; *Some Eminent Women of our Time*, 1889; *Life of Sir William Molesworth*, 1901; *Five Famous French Women*, 1906; *Women's Suffrage*, 1912.

DAME MILLICENT FAWCETT

**Fawkes, Guy** (1570–1606), an Eng. conspirator, was *b*. at York. He was a zealous Roman Catholic before he was of age, and served in the Spanish army in the Netherlands from 1593–1604. He came to England at the invitation of Catesby and was initiated into the gunpowder plot. He was entrusted with the actual accomplishment of the design owing to his exceptional courage and coolness. *See* GUNPOWDER PLOT.

**Fawn,** *see* DEER.

**Fay, András** (1786–1864), a Hungarian poet and author, was *b*. at Kohány in the county of Zemplén. He was educated for the law, but settled at Pest, and devoted himself to literature. The publication of his satirical fables (*Mesék*) in 1820 established his reputation, and he became one of the most popular authors of his time. He was also a writer of plays, romances, and novels. Of his novels the most famous are *The House of the Beltekis*, and *Doctor Jávor;* both are humorous. He was founder of the first savings bank at Pest, and one of the founders of the Hungarian national theatre.

**Fay, Morgue de,** *see* MORGAIN LE FAY.

**Fayal,** one of the Azores Islands. It has a fine bay, on which Horta, the chief town, stands. Area about 37 sq. m. Pop. about 27,000. *See* AZORES.

**Fayette, Comtesse de la,** *see* LAFAYETTE, MARIE MADELEINE, COMTESSE DE.

**Fayette, Gilbert Mottier, Marquis de la,** *see* LAFAYETTE, MARIE JOSEPH, MARQUIS DE.

**Fayetteville :** (1) city in Arkansas, U.S.A., cap. of Washington co. It is the seat of the University of Arkansas, and has been a city of the first class since 1906. There are deposits of coal in the vicinity, and the region round is noted for its fruit, especially apples. The chief manufs. are lumber, spokes, handles, waggons, evaporated fruit, and flour. Pop. 7394. (2) A city in N. Carolina, U.S.A., cap. of Cumberland co., situated on Cape Fear R., which has been rendered navigable as far as the coal mines of Chatham co. The former name of F. was Campbelltown, the change being made in memory of Lafayette. The town is a shipping centre for small fruits and vegetables, especially lettuce, melons, and berries, and manufs. cotton goods, silk, lumber, wooden-ware, turpentine, carriages, edge tools, and flour. It was chartered as a city in 1893. It was the scene of a terrible flood in 1908. Pop. 13,049.

**Fayolle, Marie Emile** (1852–1928), marshal of France; *b*. May 14, at Le Puy. Entered the Ecole Polytechnique in 1873, and afterwards joined the artillery. Instructor at Ecole de Guerre, 1897. Brigadier-general on retired list when Great War broke out. On mobilisation, was given command of 70th Reserve div. Succeeded Pétain in command of 6th Army, Feb. 1916. Transferred to 1st Army in Dec. In May 1917 was in command of group of armies in centre, and in autumn was in Italy to assist after Caporetto. Soon recalled, did excellent work until armistice; was retained as general of div. on Gen. Staff, and made marshal Feb. 21, 1921. Died in Paris, Aug. 27.

**Fayrer, Sir Joseph, Bart.** (1824–1907), a surgeon-general and author. In 1850 he became assistant-surgeon in Bengal, and his connection with the Indian medical service lasted for forty-five years. He was a prolific writer on subjects connected with the practice of medicine in India, and above all on the venomous snakes of that country. His great work on *The Thanatophidia of India* is the best book on the subject.

**Fayum,** a prov. of Upper Egypt to the W. of the Nile, a little above the head of the delta, the cultivated area of which is fed with water by the Bahr-Yusuf. Over 400 sq. m. are under cultivation, the chief crops being cereals and cotton, but the province is also noted for its figs and grapes. Olives, too, and rose trees, from which the inhabitants manufacture attar of roses, are grown. Other productions are sugar, flax, hemp, oranges, peaches, and pomegranates, and F. also possesses an excellent breed of sheep. The capital is Medinet-el-Fayum, which is a great agricultural centre. Important explorations have been made by Flinders Petrie at the sites of ancient cities in this province. Dr. Johnson, Librarian of Oxford University, has made interesting discoveries of papyrus rolls in excavated tombs in this region in the years immediately preceding the Great War. Area 669 sq. m. Pop. 517,600. F., the prin. tn., has a pop. of 44,400.

**Fazogli,** a mountainous dist. of Sudan, which is traversed by the Blue Nile. It produces gold, senna, gum, tamarinds, and ivory. Pop. about 499,000 (Funj negroes).

**Fazy, Jean James** (1796–1878), a Swiss economist and statesman, *b.* in Geneva. In 1830, as editor of *La Revolution*, he signed the protest of the journalists against the ' ordonnances ' of Charles X., opposed the candidature of Louis Philippe, and, when the latter ascended the throne of France, joined the Radical opposition, and was the real ruler of Geneva until 1861. He was the author of a *History of Geneva*, 1838–40, and a tragedy in three acts, *La Mort de Leorier*.

**Fealty,** was the service or duty served by a tenant to his superior lord in feudal times. Lands were granted on the conditions of F., suit of court, and rent, it being stipulated that tenants and their heirs should take the oath of F. or fidelity to their lord, which was the feudal bond between lord and tenant; should attend the lord's courts and give assistance by serving on juries, etc. ; and should pay certain annual returns in military attendance, provisions, money, or whatever was required of them. The right of F. is still exacted from copyholders in England, and was in existence in the United States after the Revolution.

**Fear.** The emotion of F. arises in apprehending evil to come. Its characteristics are misery or depression, the prostration of the active energies, except in the form of running away from danger, and the excessive hold of the related ideas. The pain from some actual infliction, such as a blow, a deranged organ, a bitter taste, a discord, a loss, may be severe, but mere pain is not terror. Only when the mind apprehends some painful infliction still in the future, are we liable to the emotion. Although F. is one of the most elemen-

tary emotions, it is one of the most complicated. It presupposes the following mental laws and conditions : (1) For its explanation it is necessary to render a complete account of present pain, both physical and mental. On the mental side we must remember the stimulus of the will, on the physical side the manifestation of present pain, the spasmodic violence of the early stage and the prostration of the functions at all stages. (2) We need to understand the revival of pain in idea, and the subsistence of the state by purely mental forces. (3) Attention must be given to the state of expectation, or belief, as opposed to mere idea or fancy unconnected with any real occurrence. (4) The most characteristic feature in the situation of terror is uncertainty, ignorance, and darkness. In the case of a great but certain and understood evil, the ideal pain may be simply a measure of the reality of the case. The irregular, disproportionate, and eccentric courses connected with terror are brought into relief under future evil of unknown amount or character.

*Characters of fear.—Physical.* The usual and obvious signs of fear imply organic derangement and muscular relaxation, accompanied with strong efforts in particular directions. The result of the whole is a loss of power, and a vehement exertion to escape danger. *Mental.* The general description of the mental state of fear is massive pain or general depression of tone. The strongest figures for massive pain are applied to it, viz. melancholy, gloom, darkness, despair. The excited gaze is part of the voluntary strain. Intense watchfulness must accompany any efforts to avoid an evil agency. The shriek of terror would be in accordance with Darwin's view, of the original employment of the voice, viz. to call for help from companions. In fear we see the extreme case of the ' fixed idea,' or the influence of the feelings upon the conduct through the medium of the intellectual trains.

**Fear, Cape,** a promontory on the Atlantic coast, forming the southern point of Smith's Island, in the S. of N. Carolina. This island stands at the mouth of Cape Fear R. and has a lighthouse on its W. end. The river is 250 m. long, and is navigable to Fayetteville (120 m.). Its entrances were blockaded during the Civil War.

**Feast,** or **Festival,** a day on which the ordinary labour of life is laid aside and enjoyment of a more or less religious nature is indulged in. Throughout the whole world, wherever the general religion of the country has been dear to the whole of the nation, the fixed state festivals have been associated with religion. Probably the Persians are alone among the world's nations in having no regular feasts, and this condition of theirs is artificial rather than natural. Egypt had many festivals, days consecrated to the Nile, Osiris, Ptah, and all her countless deities. The Hindu still observes his ancient festival in the ancient way, except that he must no longer offer human sacrifice. The earliest account of Greek festivals—that in the *Iliad*—speaks of two alone, but in later times these increased greatly in The Hebrews, however, kept their feasts, described in the O. T., with the greatest strictness. The Christian Church (*see* under SPECIAL DAYS) associated some of her festivals with the Jewish and some with the old pagan festivals, calling special attention to the religious significance.

**Feather River,** in California, U.S.A., tributary of the Sacramento, which it joins about 18 m. above the city of Sacramento. It has a length of 250 m., and is navigable for steamers to Marysville. Gold is found on its banks.

**Feathers,** a horny outgrowth of the skin which is peculiar to birds, and

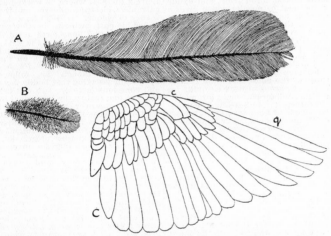

A, Quill of Pigeon; B, Contour feather of Pigeon; C, Left wing of Thrush; *c*, Contour feathers; *q*, Quill feathers

number. The expenses of the festivals were met from the public purse. In the later days of the Roman empire, the city revelled in innumerable feasts, those not only of her own ancient gods, but also those of the deities imported from the E. Different feasts became important at different times, but we may name the *Sementinæ*, the festival of the seed-time in January; the *Lupercalia*, in honour of the god Pan; and the *Saturnalia*. Almost all of these festivals were celebrated by the pagan world with disgusting accompaniments. The Egyptian sensuality was surpassed by the Eastern debauchery introduced into Rome, and the excesses committed at the Hindu festival of Shiva are utterly unspeakable. which corresponds to the scales of fishes and reptiles and the hair of mammals. Feathers as a rule consist of two main parts, axis and barbs, the former of which is divided into the quill, which is bare and hollow, and the shaft which bears the barbs. The quill is embedded in the skin, and has at its base a small hole through which the nutritive sap passes during the growth of the F. The barbs which constitute the vane are lath-shaped and taper to a point, and each one supports a series of outgrowths known as barbules, so that each barb is like a tiny F. As a rule the barbs are linked to each other by means of the barbules, but in the running birds, *e.g.* the ostrich, they are free, hence the familiar loose plume. Many F.,

A A 2

too, have an 'aftershaft' or second shaft springing from the under side near where the quill passes into the true stem. This is as a rule small, but in some birds, viz. the cassowary and emu, the aftershaft is as large as the mainshaft. There are several kinds of F.: Contour F., which form the general outline of the body and of which the 'flight F.' are most developed; down F., which are hidden by the contour F., and often form a very thick covering, as in gulls and ducks; filo-plumes, which are found in all birds in clusters at the bases of the contour F.; and powder-down F., which occur in patches, especially in birds of the heron tribe, and exude a fine dust or powder which gives a peculiar bloom to the plumage. As regards the colour of F., it is usually most prominent in the male birds. F. have been put to various uses. Of these perhaps the chief is their employment for stuffing beds, cushions, and quilts, and for this the F. of the eider-duck are most highly esteemed, those of the goose and swan coming next. F. are also used as quills for writing, and for personal adornment.

**Feather-Star**, or Sea-Lily, the popular name of Crinoidea (*q.v.*), a class of Echinodermata. The commonest species is *Antedon rosacea*.

**Featherstone**, an urban dist. in the Osgoldcross parl. div. of the West Riding of Yorkshire, about 2½ m. from Pontefract. Large collieries are in the neighbourhood, and these afford employment for the inhabitants. Some miners were shot dead during a riot in 1893. Pop. 14,839.

**Febronianism**, a powerful movement which was propounded in 1763 in Germany by John Nikolaus von Hontheim under the pseudonym of 'Justinus Febronius' with the object of restricting the papal power, and of giving independence to the national churches.

**February**, the second month of the year, containing twenty-eight days in ordinary years, but twenty-nine in leap years. It was introduced into the Roman calendar by Numa as the last month of the year, and continued in this position until 452 B.C., when it was placed after January. The name comes from the Latin *Februarius*, from *februare*, to purify, and was originally the month in which the 'Februa,' or great Roman festival of purification, was held.

**Fécamp**, a seaport tn. of France at the mouth of the R. Fécamp, in the dept. of Seine-Inférieure, about 22 m. N.E. of Havre. It has a tidal harbour and dock taking vessels of 20 ft. at neap tide, and of 26 ft. at spring tide. There are cotton, wool, and oil mills, as well as sugar refineries, tan-

neries, and a benedictine liqueur distillery. The chief imports are coal, timber, tar, and hemp, and the exports oil-cake, flint, cod, and benedictine liqueur, which is said to have been manufactured by the Benedictine monks of the abbey as far back as 1510. The town contains a sixteenth century church (St. Etienne) and the abbey church of La Trinité (*c.* 1190). Pop. 16,700.

**Fechner, Gustav Theodor** (1801–87), a Ger. psychologist, *b.* at Gross-Sarchen, near Muskau, in Lower Lusatia. He was educated at Dresden and Leipzig, and became professor of physics at the University of Leipzig in 1834, where he worked at galvanism, electro-chemistry, and the theory of colour. In 1839 he abandoned his post, owing to an affection of the eyes, and henceforth devoted himself to philosophy and the study of the relations of physiology and psychology. His chief work on the subject was *Elemente der Psychophysik*, and though he follows Spinoza in asserting that bodily facts and conscious facts are two distinct sides of one reality, he is original in trying to discover a mathematical relation between them. F.'s law put into words is as follows: 'In order that the intensity of a sensation may increase in arithmetical progression, the stimulus must increase in egometrical progression.' This gave rise to much controversy, and fundamental errors were discovered in F.'s reasoning, but be this as it may, he was in the main the originator of that species of psychology which investigates human faculties with the aid of exact scientific apparatus. Besides the work already mentioned, he wrote: *Das Büchlein vom Leben nach dem Tode*, 1856, 1903 (5th ed., which has been translated into English); *Nanna, oder über das Seelenleben der Pflanzen*, 1848, 1903 (3rd ed.); *Zendavesta, oder über die Dinge des Himmels und des Genseits*, 1851; *Über die physikalische und philosophische Atomenlehre*; *Voschule der Asthetik*, 1876; *Die Tagesansicht gegenüber der Nachtansicht*, 1879; and *Vergleichende Anatomie der Engel*, 1825, a collection of poems and humorous pieces. *See* Life by Kuntze, and for his psychophysical law, *see* Ward in *Mind* for 1876.

**Fechter, Charles Albert** (1824–79), a Fr. actor, *b.* in London. He made his début at the Comédie Française as Seide in Voltaire's *Mahomet*, after which he went to Berlin, where he achieved great fame by playing the part of Armand Duval in *La Dame aux Camélias*. In London his impersonation of Hamlet and Othello was an extraordinary triumph.

**Feciales, or Fetiales** (etymology uncertain), were Roman priests, whose duty it was to determine the circumstances under which hostilities might be commenced, and to demand satisfaction from a hostile state. Four F. generally crossed the borders and launched a spear with appropriate ceremonies, to denote the proclamation of hostilities (*clarigatio*). See Livy, xxxvi. 3, ix. 5 *et al.*; Pliny, *Hist. Nat.*, xxii. 85, etc.

**Fecundation,** see FERTILISATION.

**Federal Council of Evangelical Free Churches.** An organisation, whose members represent the majority of the churches of Protestant denomination in the U.S.A., which was formed in 1908 for the general purpose of acting in matters of common interest to the constituent churches. The Council carries out a number of particular objects through commissions. These particular objects include social service, research and education, the improvement of industrial relations, the promotion of international justice, the improvement of relations with the negro pop. of the country, etc. The Council also acts as the liaison between the church and such national social agencies as the Red Cross, and the Child Welfare (*q.v.*) Movement. About 140,000 local churches are represented by the Council and the communicant membership is over 20 millions.

**Federalist, The,** was a collection of essays published in 1787–88 in New York at the instigation of Hamilton, to defend the new government. They appeared in the semi-weekly *Independent Journal* of New York under the above title, and were written by Alexander Hamilton, James Madison, and John Jay. There were in all eighty-five essays, which were all collected and subsequently published in book form. The collection is still regarded as a classic text-book of political science. (Everyman's Library.)

**Federalist Party, The,** was a political party which was in power in the United States, 1789–1801, and which practically died about 1820. Its chief leaders were Alexander Hamilton and John Adams, and Washington himself was also closely identified with the Federalists. The party reorganised the executive departments, created the federal judiciary and the territorial system, and introduced excise laws, a U.S.A. bank, a protective tariff and bounty system to develop manufactures and agriculture, and a postal system. They also began a new navy, but were prevented by the Democrats from going on with it. This was really the death-b ow to the Federal party, since they were no longer able to

protect their commerce by force, but had to do so by humiliating concessions to England.

**Federal Reserve System, U.S.A.** For a long time the U.S.A. had felt the need of some organisation which would fill the unique place that is so satisfactorily occupied by the Bank of England, in England : that is, not only a corporation that should act as a banker's bank, but should also maintain the gold reserves of the land in a reasonable ratio with its paper money. The American system, which made it easy for great numbers of purely local banks to come into existence, necessitated some rather stringent banking laws, and these, in turn, brought on the gov. the responsibility of being itself a kind of bank for bankers. Naturally this proved unsatisfactory, and in 1913 Congress, upon the insistence of President Wilson, passed the Federal Reserve Act (*q.v.*). This brought about a long-needed reform of American finances and removed the Wall Street grip. Twelve Federal Reserve Banks were armed with powers and charged with responsibilities to act, each in its assigned area, somewhat in the same way as the Bank of England does in England. The Federal Reserve Banking system is under the control of seven directors, including the Secretary of the Treasury, the Comptroller of the Currency, and five others named by the President. Each of the twelve regional Reserve banks is under the control of nine directors. Every national bank is required to join the system and to subscribe for stock in the regional bank of the district to the amount of 6 per cent. of its own capital stock and surplus. Each regional bank is supplied with large government deposits. It is prepared to supply member banks with money as needed. They also issue paper currency. The difference, however, between the English and the American method is that whereas the bank-rate in Great Britain responds easily and naturally to the laws of supply and demand, as the Bank is now responsible for the integrity of the paper currency, these Federal Banks of America have the larger liberty of regulating a currency in conditions of greater freedom and less responsibility. Undoubtedly these powers are used wisely, but the fact remains that the system gives opportunities for inflation which do not now exist in England.

**Federal Trade Commission.** An organisation set up by the American gov. in 1914 to check the growing menace of trusts and monopolies (see TRUST—*Commercial*). The struggle between the gov. and the huge trade combine ever since 1890, when the Sherman Act was passed, has been a record of legal victories for the gov. that have proved practically futile almost as soon as they were obtained. The action of 1914 was apparently an endeavour to control and influence powers that could not be broken, and to what extent it would have been successful is a question complicated by the outbreak of the Great War and the many changes in commercial life that followed swiftly upon its close. The subsequent Wells-Pomerane Act mitigates some of the older restrictions of anti-trust legislation by legalising the alliance of great firms with each other for the purpose of marketing their goods in foreign lands.

**Federated Malay States,** *see* MALAY STATES.

**Federation** and **Federal States.** A federation (Lat. *fœdus*, a league) is a union between two or more states, in which each retains its autonomy, while a central representative government controls matters of general concern. The Amphictyonic League of ancient Greece, the earliest on record, seems to have been religious rather than political. Among other Greek leagues were : the Thessalian, very powerful about 370 B.C. ; the Ætolian, a well-organised federation composed of a number of tribes living N. of the Gulf of Corinth, having a general assembly (παναιτωλικόν) which met yearly, and a permanent committee acting as an executive government ; the Achæan, which became a great political force about 251 B.C., originally comprising ten cities of Achaia, it ultimately included Athens, Megara, Ægina, and almost all the Peloponnesus ; this, too, was a real federation. Coming now to modern history, a remarkable and important league, the Hanseatic, was first formed by the cities of Hamburg and Lübeck about 1247 A.D. to protect their commerce against pirates and robber-barons. Gradually, over eighty towns joined them, and the Hansa Federation (Old Teut. *hansa*, a defensive league), though never formally recognised by the empire, was for centuries a great power. It held its own courts of justice, enforced obedience among its members, and bargained and fought with kings and princes, on one occasion equipping a fleet of 248 ships, with 12,000 men. The Hanseatic Diet, held triennially at Lübeck, was not dissolved until 1630. Modern civilisation, with its improved means of communication and transport, and with many highly organised communities capable of political combination on equitable terms, has facilities for more extensive federa-

tions than were possible in ancient times. Bavaria and Saxony can federate with Prussia, but no power of old could federate with Rome, and the holding together by mutual agreement of immense territories, like those of the U.S.A., would have been beyond human conception. Still, though conditions have altered, principles remain the same. A federation is not a mere alliance from which either of the contracting parties can withdraw at will, nor is it a union in which one predominant power can assume control in local as well as general affairs. Safety and efficiency require a strong central government, which must be fully representative, and must have command of foreign relations and of those internal matters which are of general concern, such as postal and telegraphic services, coinage and national defence. But this central government cannot administer innumerable local details over immense areas or among thickly populated territories with varying interests ; therefore each federal country or state must have a large share of autonomy. The adjustment of relations between principal and subordinate legislatures requires skilful statesmanship, and even when once arranged altering conditions and the growth of new ideas will sometimes raise fresh controversies.

The republic of Switzerland was first founded in 1307 by the men of Schwyz, Uri, and Unterwalden, and in about a century attained its present size, but remained communal rather than federal until 1848, when it was reorganised somewhat on its present lines. As the benefits of a solid government were realised, the powers of the federal parliament were strengthened in 1874, 1898, and again in 1907.

The mediæval German empire was a bulky and loose combination of states, sadly lacking in unity. It was broken up by Napoleon, but reestablished with alterations in 1815. After the war of 1866 Austria was excluded, and in 1871 a federal empire was inaugurated at Versailles, with the King of Prussia as hereditary German Emperor. The abdication of the Kaiser and the monarchs of the other Ger. states in 1918 led to the formation of the new Republics of Prussia, Bavaria, Saxony, Würtemberg, and others. But the Federation of the Ger. states remained in being, under a President (Field-Marshal Paul von Hindenburg, who assumed office in May 1925), a Reichstag representing the whole nation and a Reichsrat which represents the separate states. Manhood and womanhood suffrage with proportional representation are the basis of election.

Among the many national and geographical consequences of the Great War was the establishment of three new European countries which have many of the characteristics of Federated States. These are: (1) Poland, consisting largely of the territory divided between Prussia, Russia, and Austria in 1772, and reconstituted as a nation after 1918; (2) Czechoslovakia, a number of states or parts of states, of which the old kingdom of Bohemia is the chief, including roughly the Slav populations that lie between Germany and Poland on the N. and Austria on the S.; and (3) Yugo-Slavia, consisting of the old kingdoms of Serbia and Montenegro, Croatia, Slavonia, and parts of the Banat, Bosnia, Herzegovina, Carniola, and Styria. Syria and Lebanon, consisting of the four states of Damascus, and Aleppo (*q.v.*), the Alaouites, and Lebanon are federated for certain purposes, but the constitution in each part is still in a rather unsettled condition. The Federated Malay States are dealt with in a separate article (*see* MALAY STATES).

The U.S.A. originally consisted of the thirteen colonies which united in 1775 to free themselves from British rule; to these, others have gradually been added. The struggle between centralisation and local autonomy has led to several great crises in their history. Excessive claims of state sovereignty put forward by Kentucky and Virginia in 1798 and by S. Carolina in 1832 almost led to fighting, and in 1861 the great Civil War broke out over the same question, the Southern States refusing to obey the federal government, and claiming the right to secede.

Included in the British empire are three great federated colonies. The Dominion of Canada was the first example in history of a free F. within an empire, free and autonomous, yet acknowledging the supremacy of the crown. The Commonwealth of Australia was constituted in 1901, the Union of S. Africa in 1909.

Brazil and Argentina are both federal republics, with constitutions resembling that of the U.S.A. *See* Freeman's *Hist. of Federal Government*, 1893; Bryce's *Holy Roman Empire* (new edition), 1904; McCrackan's *Rise of the Swiss Republic* (New York,) 1901; and Woodrow Wilson's *Hist. of the American People*.

**Federation of British Industries.** Established in 1916, and granted a Royal Charter of Incorporation in 1924, the F.B.I. is 'a voluntary association of Manufacturers and Producers for the promotion of their several and mutual interests, governed by an annually elected Grand Council.' It exists in order to encourage and develop British manufactures, and to safeguard the interests of British producers both at home and abroad. It is entirely non-political. The F.B.I. is actively engaged in collating the views of manufacturers on many points, *e.g.* taxation, factory legislation, shipping freights, smoke abatement and river pollution; these it presents in the proper quarter with the weight of organised industry behind it. It also assists its members by giving expert advice on numerous trade points, such as advertising, contracts, customs, exhibitions, fuel economy, insurance, oversea market. It issues four publications—the *F.B.I. Register*, the official list of members and also a comprehensive list of British manufacturers, with a list of products, under 5000 headings; *British Industries*, its monthly organ, with a *Taxation Supplement* and an *Economic Supplement;* the annual *Fuel Economy Review;* and the quarterly *F.B.I. Business Barometer*. The F.B.I. maintains a staff of experts on all points at its London headquarters in Tothill St., Westminster, London, S.W.; and it has representatives in nearly one hundred centres throughout the world. The President for 1930 was Col. Sir James Lithgow, and the Director, Sir Roland Nugent.

**Federici Camillo** (1749–1802), an Italian dramatist, whose real name was Giovanni Battista Viassolo, *b.* at Garessio in Piedmont. He was educated at Turin, and spent the early part of his life on the stage, but in 1778 settled at Padua and devoted himself to literature. He acquired a great reputation by his comedies, most of which were melodramatic in character. His complete works were published in 1816, and another edition in 26 vols. at Florence in 1826.

**Federzoni, Luigi,** Italian journalist and statesman; *b.* Sept. 27, 1878, at Bologna; son of Giovanni F. Edited *Resto del Carlino*, 1903–4; moved to Rome; directed foreign department of *Giornale d'Italia* from 1905; from 1913 edited *Idea Nazionale*. In Great War, an artillery officer. Founder of Italian nationalist movement, led its merger into Fascismo in 1922. Deputy, 1913. In 1922, first Colonial Minister under Mussolini; in 1924, Minister of Interior; in 1926, Colonial Minister again; in 1928, Minister of Interior again, and senator. In 1929, elected President of the Senate. Wrote *L'Africa Romana*, 1929.

**Fedor, Alexiewich,** or **Feodor III.** (1657–82), a Russian czar, was the eldest brother of Peter the Great, and son of Czar Alexis, whom he succeeded in 1676. He fought success-fully against the Turks, forcing the sultan in 1681 to give up his preten-sions over Ukraine.

**Fedor,** or **Feodor, Ivanovich,** or **Feodor I.** (1557–96), a Russian czar, was the son of Ivan the Terrible, whom he succeeded in 1584. His father, knowing his monastic habits, had appointed a regency for carrying on the government, and when F. came to the throne he spent his time in the palace occupied in devotion, while his brother-in-law, Boris Godunoff (the most important member of the council of regency), acted as czar.

**Fee, Fee Simple,** and **Fee Tail.** F. (from Lat. *feodum*) is the same as fief or feud, and means an estate (*q.v.*) or interest in land which can descend to the heir, or, in other words, a freehold estate of inheritance. In the feudal system of land tenure, under which there was a gradation of tenants in fee simple up to the supreme landowner, the king, the word was used in oppo-sition to ' allodial.' Allodial land was land granted absolutely in perpetuity by book or charter (*boc land*). Feudal land, on the other hand, was theo-retically ' property lent,' and was held subject to the performance of the various feudal incidents, such as knight service and the payment of aids. An estate in fee simple means an interest in land descendible at the common law to the heirs general of the preceding tenant. Generally speaking the tenant in fee simple is the absolute owner in perpetuity. A tenant in fee simple can dispose of his land by deed or will for any interest and to whom he pleases. An estate in fee tail is a F. which is limited in its descent to the issue of the tenant. A qualified or *base* F. is created where a tenant in tail, not yet in possession, bars the entail by deed without first obtaining the consent of the protector. *See also* ENTAIL.

**Feeble-minded,** *see* MENTAL DE-FICIENCY ACTS.

**Feeling** comprises all our pleasures and pains, together with states that are indifferent as regards pleasure or pain, and are characterised simply as excitement. Under the muscular Fs. and the sensations are detailed all the susceptibilities of a primary character, due, on the one hand, to the putting forth of muscular energy, and on the other to the operation of the outer world on the organs of sense. There remains a large depart-ment of secondary, derived, or com-plicated Fs. termed the emotions. F. proper may be divided into (1) Formal and (2) Qualitative. The for-mer comprises oppressions, relief, har-mony, and contrast, and the more elementary formal Fs., and also the

more complicated Fs., *e.g.* hope, apprehension, doubt, tedium. The second division includes the lower Fs., or those of sense-pleasures and pains of colours and sounds, and the higher or intellectual Fs., the æsthetic, the moral, and the religious. The modes of derivation or composition of the emotions depend on contiguous growth or the associating process. Association operates in uniting to-gether a number of separate Fs. into one whole, which is then connected with a special object, as in sexual love.

**Fees** : *Architects' fees.*—These will, in general, be fixed by express agree-ment. Where there is no express agreement an architect is entitled to reasonable remuneration, depending on the nature of the work to be exe-cuted. It is usual in express agree-ments to pay a commission varying according to the cost of the expendi-ture. The customary rates are well recognised, and will usually govern cases where there is no express agree-ment. This rate is six per cent. on work costing £2000 rising on a gradu-ated scale to ten per cent. on £100. This covers the preparation of plans and specifications, certificates for the builder, and measurements, etc. But where the work requires more than ordinary skill, such as in the case of alterations to existing buildings, de-signs of high-class fittings and furni-ture for a mansion, an architect is entitled to charge a higher rate. Where the plans are not used, it is customary to charge one quarter of full fees, if the work is only approxim-ate and without plans. But where drawings sufficient for quantities to be estimated and a tender to be invested have been prepared, it is usual to charge two-thirds of full fees. In addition, the architect is entitled to his travelling expenses. Where the architect prepares bills of quantities, *i.e.* estimates of the labour and material required, he may claim an additional commission. Where no works are carried out the remunera-tion is generally by the day, varying with the reputation of the particular architect. Three guineas a day is con-sidered the minimum F. for a man of fair standing, and is generally allowed by taxing masters. The pro-fessional charges of architects are dealt with in rules issued by the Royal Institute of British Architects. *See* Macassey and Strahan, *The Law relating to Civil Engineers and Archi-tects,* etc., and Ernest Todd, *Building and Dilapidations.*

*Clerical fees.*—These are due prin-cipally in respect of marriages and burials. Where the marriage is by banns, the F. for the publication of the banns is about 12s. 6d. in most parishes. In the case of a marriage by licence the F. varies according to the kind of licence. Banns are not necessary where the marriage is by bishop's licence. Such licence is to be obtained at the Vicar-General's office, 3 Creed Lane, Ludgate Hill, London, E.C., or at 1 Dean's Court, Doctors' Commons, E.C., at a cost of between £2 and £3. In country districts a bishop's licence may be obtained at the offices of the bishop's registrars, or through his surrogates or deputies. When the marriage is by special licence of the Archbishop of Canterbury, the F. is between £30 and £40. Such licence can be had on application, through a proctor of the Faculty Office, Doctors' Commons, and enables the marriage to take place anywhere and at any time. The cost of a registrar's certificate, where the marriage is to be so authorised, is 7s.; the F. for a registrar's licence is £2 14s. 6d. where the parties desire to be married by licence. There are also F. payable to the incumbent on the solemnisation of the marriage itself when the marriage takes place in a church. There is no fixed scale, the rate being according to the custom of the particular church. The minimum F. are generally one guinea to the clergyman and 5s. to his clerk or verger. In poor districts the charges are lower. A copy certificate of the marriage may be obtained at Somerset House for 2s. 7d. The marriage register may always be inspected on payment of 1s. Burial F. are by custom due to the incumbent, but they can only be recovered in an ecclesiastical court, for the common law does not recognise such F. Statutory burial F. are, however, recoverable in the ordinary courts, where no express enactment provides for their recovery in the ecclesiastical courts. A customary burial F., to be recoverable, must be of a fixed amount and reasonable. There may also be F. payable by custom for monuments and vaults. Tables of F. for burials may be fixed for any parish by the ecclesiastical commissioners (q.v.) with the consent of the bishop of the diocese. A minister and his sexton are also entitled to F. for services rendered in connection with a burial, the rate of such F. being in accordance with tables approved by a Secretary of State. F. are not ordinarily payable for baptisms; but both on those occasions and on the ceremony of 'churching of women' it is usual to make a gift or offering. See Phillimore's *Ecclesiastical Law*, and Little's *Law of Burial*.

*Legal fees.*—In a wide sense legal F. means any F. provided for by law. In a narrower or technical sense it is practically equivalent to costs. Costs for legal work done may relate either to non-contentious or to contentious work. As in the medical profession, there is a recognised scale for a solicitor's remuneration, but a solicitor and his client may make a special agreement as to costs. In the case of contentious business the solicitor is not entitled to his costs until the bill has been submitted to the Taxing Master's office for approval (*see* COSTS). The items to be seen on a solicitor's bill of costs usually make a formidable total, but the greater part is incurred for counsel's F., witnesses' expenses, and the preparation of documents for the hearing; so that in reality the profit of the solicitor is far below what is commonly supposed, especially when the time spent in the incidental work of preparing a case is borne in mind. The customary F. for a solicitor's attendance is from 6s. 8d. to one guinea a visit, according to the nature of the business and the time taken. Included in the bill of costs which a litigant (whom the court has ordered to pay the costs of legal proceedings) will have to meet, will be court F. (the F. and percentages will be found in either the *Annual Practice* or the *Yearly Practice* in the schedule to the *Order as to Court Fees*). These include, *inter alia*, F. on a writ of summons (10s.), writ of execution (5s.), on entering appearance to a summons (2s.), on taking an affidavit (1s. 6d.), on filing a petition of right (£1) (*see* CROWN), and on drawing up a judgment order or decree (from 5s. to £1). All these F. are payable ultimately to the Inland Revenue authorities in the form of stamps. A solicitor must submit his bill to the client before he is entitled to sue for his costs, and this whether it relates to contentious or non-contentious work. Conveyancing (*q.v.* and CONVEYANCE) F. form one of the most remunerative sources of a solicitor's profits. There are two recognised scales of conveyancing F., under one of which a solicitor charges for all the work he does in connection with the transaction, while under the other he charges a percentage on the amount involved in the transaction. The second scale applies in the absence of a written notice to the contrary from the solicitor to the client before the work was begun. In an ordinary vendor and purchaser transaction the vendor's solicitor's scale for negotiating a sale by private treaty is 1 per cent. on the first £3000, ½ per cent. on the fourth thousand and each thousand up to £10,000, and thereafter ¼ per cent. Where a title is absolutely clear the work involved is almost purely a matter of drawing and engrossing according to precedent. In these cases a client will be well advised to make some special arrangement. There is also a fixed commission scale for building leases. There are also scales of F. for drawing and perusing deeds, wills, or other documents. Generally these F. are 2s. per folio for drawing up the document, 8d. per folio for engrossing (*i.e.* copying out in a clear hand for preservation) and 1s. per folio for perusing. The F. for drawing each sheet of eight folios of an abstract of title (*i.e.* the history of the title to the particular land) is 6s. 8d. A solicitor is also entitled to a F. of 5 guineas daily for every day of not less than seven hours employed on the business of or in travelling for his client. All the above fees are now subject to an increase of 33½ per cent. Barristers' F. are fixed entirely according to the arrangement between themselves and the solicitors who employ them. It is customary to include in counsel's F. an amount for his clerk according to a sliding scale varying from 2s. 6d. on a brief F. under 5 guineas to £2 10s. on a F. of 50 guineas or upwards. The clerk is entitled to sue the barrister for his F., but a barrister may not bring an action against anyone to recover his F., which are legally regarded as being in the nature of *honoraria*. The allowance for counsel's F. is entirely in the discretion of the taxing master. Separate F. are in general allowed for conducting a suit (the 'brief F.'), advising, settling pleadings, consultations, conferences, commissions to take evidence abroad. Where a case extends over a day a refresher may be allowed by the taxing master. A junior counsel customarily receives a F. equal to two-thirds of that of the leader. *See* Scott on *Costs, Annual Practice, Yearly Practice of the Supreme Court. See also* COSTS.

*Medical fees.*—These may be conveniently considered according as they are in respect of attendance on private patients, or by way of remuneration for attendance at the request of the police or to give evidence in a court of law. *Fees for attendance on private patients.*—The F. of a general practitioner are by the etiquette of the profession fixed on a sliding scale based on the income of the patient as indicated by the rental of his house. 'Special' visits are charged for at the rate of a visit and a half, a special visit being where notice to attend has not been given to the practitioner before starting on his daily round. In the case of houses of £10 to £25 rentals the F. for ordinary visits is from 5s. to 7s. 6d. ; £25 to £50, from 5s. to 10s. 6d. ; £50 to £100, from

7s. 6d. to 15s., and similarly where the patient visits the practitioner. Night visits are charged at double the rate of ordinary visits. The scale for detention per half hour is at the same rate as for ordinary visits. There is also a mileage charge varying from 2s. 6d. to 4s. The minimum F. for a consultation is 21s. in every case, but the F. generally charged by a consulting physician or surgeon is 3 guineas a consultation, or 2 guineas for the first and 1 guinea for each subsequent consultation. If the consulting physician or specialist calls upon the ordinary medical practitioner to meet him in consultation, the practitioner is entitled to charge double his ordinary F. as given above. The F. for a certificate of health is at the same rate as for an ordinary visit. The charge for attendance on a servant is the same as that for the master, if the attendance was at the latter's request. The Insurance Acts deprive this convention of most of its force, as servants are entitled to medical benefits under the Act, and to be attended by a 'panel' doctor. The above customary rates apply in the absence of any express agreement between the patient and the doctor. A specialist, consulting physician, or practitioner can, of course, charge what he chooses if the patient agrees beforehand to pay such charge. No doctor on a hospital staff may receive a F. for work done at the hospital, any F. paid by hospital patients are payable to the hospital itself. Medical men may now sue for the F. by virtue of the Medical Act, but they must prove registration as a medical practitioner and possession of a diploma from a recognised examining body. The bye-laws of the Royal Colleges of Physicians and Surgeons prohibit a *fellow* from bringing an action, but such prohibition extends to no one else. Under the National Insurance Act, 1923, insured persons entitled to medical benefits escape all liability for F. and cost of drugs. The medical practitioner on the panel for a specified area looks for his remuneration to the Insurance Committees out of the Panel Fund, and the amount, which will be payable quarterly, will include a rate fixed by the commissioners in respect of each insured person on the practitioner's list, and other rates for various services rendered, to be fixed in agreements between the committee for the particular county or county borough. These other rates will be payable in accordance with the method of remuneration adopted by each committee, whether by capitation, attendance, mileage, or otherwise. *Fees of medical witnesses.* — The following fees remain in operation, but since 1919 they have been regarded as a basis only, as increases varying from 33½ per cent. upwards are now permitted in many courts. A medical practitioner, when called in by the police to attend any one between 8 a.m. and 10 p.m., is entitled, on obtaining a certificate of such attendance from the police inspector on duty, to a F. of 3s. 6d.; if between 10 p.m. and 8 a.m., a F. of 7s. 6d. A medical witness summoned to give evidence in a police court is, where the accused is committed for trial, entitled to a F. of 10s. 6d. for each day if he lives within two miles of the court, and to £1 1s. if beyond two miles; where the accused is not committed for trial he is entitled to F. on the same scale, but should ask the magistrate for a certificate of attendance. The procedure in regard to police court F. is set out in section 2 of the Criminal Law Prosecution Expenses Act, 1866, which provides for the signing by the magistrates of certificates and forwarding the same to clerks of the peace, to be laid before Quarter Sessions, which courts may, on being satisfied by the certificate of its own officer of the correctness of the amount, according to the scale made in pursuance of section 5 of the Expenses of Prosecutions Act, 1851, make an order for payment. In courts of summary jurisdiction justices have power to compel medical witnesses to attend by subpœna, and the witness must attend, whether he is tendered his expenses or not. Apparently a solicitor ought to tender expenses where the witness has to travel from a considerable distance. Again, medical witnesses may be compelled to attend before courts of Quarter Sessions and the Central Criminal Court without tender, but where summoned from another part of the kingdom sufficient tender must be made. Under the Act of 1851, above alluded to, the Secretary of State has, however, fixed the following scale for these courts : £1 1s. a day and 2s. a night, with travelling expenses 3d. a mile each way. But in no case may a medical witness be summoned to the High Court or the Assizes without a tender of reasonable and sufficient expenses, including cost of travelling and residence. The scale in the King's Bench and Chancery Divisions is 1 guinea a day where the witness resides in the place where the case is tried; if not, 2 guineas for his time and 3 guineas for daily expenses exclusive of travelling expenses. The scale of F. in county courts, where witnesses may refuse to give evidence unless paid their expenses, is 15s. for time and 1 guinea a day for hotel

expenses, for ordinary evidence as distinct from expert evidence; in the latter case the F. are from 1 guinea to 3 guineas for time given, and 1 guinea to 5 guineas a day for expenses. According to the 'Rules of the Supreme Court,' an expert medical witness in the High Court is entitled to 7 guineas a day for reading up a case in order to give evidence. In most cases, of course, the remuneration is fixed by the parties calling the witness before the case comes on. In regard to coroners' inquests, the Coroners Act, 1887, authorises coroners to summon medical witnesses to make a *post-mortem* examination of dead bodies over which an inquest is to be held, and such summons the witness must obey or be liable to a penalty not exceeding £5. An expert F. can be demanded where a summons is in proper form. Wood Renton, in Tuke's *Psychological Medicine*, cites cases which throw doubt on the question whether a medical witness subpœnaed to give *expert* evidence is liable to any process for contempt of court if he fails to attend. But apparently it is an unwritten law in the medical world to obey the subpœna and to insist at the trial and before giving evidence on the party who has called him to give a personal undertaking for remuneration. In Scotland a medical witness is entitled to 1 guinea a day for his attendance in court, together with first-class return railway fare; 2 guineas is the F. for a *post-mortem* examination and report, and from 2 guineas to 4 guineas for an analysis of blood stains, according to the amount of work to be done. Under the Workmen's Compensation Act, 1925, there is a statutory scale of F. payable to the medical practitioners acting as medical referees in cases of accidents to workmen. *See* Mann, *Forensic Medicine and Toxicology*, 1908; Prof. Glaister, *Medical Jurisprudence and Toxicology*, 1910; Tuke, *Dictionary of Psychological Medicine;* Taylor, *Law of Evidence*, 1906.

*Stock-Brokers' Charges.*—Stockbrokers' charges are fixed by the committee of the Stock Exchange, and vary considerably for different classes of stocks and shares. The usual charge on the most important securities is ¼ per cent., rising to one half per cent., in a few instances, with a minimum fee of ten shillings on less than £100 and twenty shillings on over a £100. The charges on buying and selling shares also vary, being mostly based on a fee of one penny on each ten shillings, with the same minimum as above.

*Auctioneers.*—For freehold and other leased property : on the first

£300, 5 per cent.; on the next £4700, 2½ per cent.; on the residue 1½ per cent. The charges for selling chattels, stock, and effects are 5 per cent. on the first £500, and 2½ per cent. on the residue. Special arrangements are usually made in relation to non-sales or subsequent sales. The charge for selling furniture, stock-in-trade and other goods on the vendor's own premises is 5 per cent. on the amount realised, plus agreed costs for printing and advertising. The charge for selling horses and pedigree live stock is 5 per cent. Other live stock is 2½ per cent., dead stock 5 per cent.

*Estate Agency.*—Sales by private treaty : First £300 5 per cent., next £4700, 2½ per cent.; on the residue 1½ per cent. Purchases : one half the scale for selling. If no purchase is effected the usual scale for valuation is charged, which is : £1 10s. per cent. on the first £1000, 10s. 6d. per cent. on the next £9000, and 5s. 3d. on the remainder, with a minimum fee of £5 5s.

**Fehling's Solution,** a solution which is used for the detection and estimation of glucose and certain other sugars. It consists of a solution of cupric sulphate mixed with alkali and potassium-sodium tartrate. For use a small quantity of the solution is placed in a test tube and diluted with water. It is then boiled for a few seconds, after which the fluid to be tested is added drop by drop until its bulk is equal to that of the diluted fluid. If sugar is present a yellow precipitate of hydrated cuprous oxide is thrown down, which subsequently loses its water of hydration, and becomes reduced to ordinary red cuprous oxide.

**Fehmarn,** or **Femern,** an island in the Baltic Sea, which belongs to the Prussian prov. of Schleswig-Holstein, and is separated from the north-east corner of Holstein by a channel one mile in breadth. It has an area of 73 sq. m., and is very fertile. Though bare of forest, corn is extensively grown and cattle are reared in the pastures. The fisheries form the chief industry. Burg is the capital. Pop. 9800. (Burg, 3,255.)

**Fehmic Courts** (O.H. Ger. *feme,* court of justice), tribunals, often, but not always, secret, which became renowned in Westphalia about the twelfth century, and afterwards spread throughout Germany. They were composed of free citizens leagued together against feudal tyranny, and acknowledging no jurisdiction but their own. Important cases were tried in secret, when none but initiated members might attend, and the only permissible sentence, *death,* if pronounced, was certainly carried out,

no culprit, however powerful, being secure. Implicit obedience was exacted from all members, who were known to each other by secret signs. *See* Wigand's *Das Fehmgericht Westfulens* (Halle), 1893; Lindner's *Die Feme* (Münster), 1888 ; and Scott's *Anne of Geierstein.*

**Fehrbellin,** a tn. of Prussia, in Brandenburg, situated 33 m. N.W. of Berlin. It was the scene of a battle in 1675, when the Prussians, under the Great Elector, gained a victory over the Swedes under Wrangel. Pop. 1700.

**Fehrenbach, Konstantin** (1852–1926), Ger. statesman; *b.* Jan. 11, at Wellendingen, Baden. In 1882, a lawyer in Freiburg. Sat, 1885–87 and 1901–13, as member of centre, in second chamber of Baden, over which he presided 1907–9. From 1903, in Reichstag of which he became President in June 1918. Presided over National Assembly, Weimar, Feb. 1919. Became Chancellor at head of minority gov., June 1920. Took part in conferences at Spa (July 1920) and London (March 1921). As refusal of reparations-demand led to ' sanctions,' F.'s cabinet gave place to Wirth's. In March 1924, F. became chairman of his party. Worked amicably with socialists. Died at Freiburg-im-Breisgau, March 26.

**Feijoo y Montenegro, Benito Jeronimo** (1676–1764), a Spanish scholar. Became a Benedictine monk at the age of twelve. He is regarded as the initiator of educational reform in Spain. He boldly attacked the dialectics and metaphysics then taught everywhere in his native country ; maintained Bacon's system of induction in the physical sciences. He published *Teatro critico universal* and *Cartas eruditas y curiosas.*

**Feilding, Robert** (1651–1712), known as ' Beau Feilding,' was a member of the Denbigh family, and attached to the court of Charles II. He was noted for his numberless amours, his extravagance, and his profligacy. According to Swift, he married Mary, daughter of Barnham Swift, and wasted her fortune. He was given a regiment by James II., and later became a Roman Catholic and followed James to Ireland.

**Feis,** the name given to various assemblies in Ireland. The F. of Tara, which originated seven centuries before Christ, was mainly a national and political assembly, and was due to meet every third year for the purpose of ' preserving the laws and rules,' but might be called at other times. It was presided over by the Ard-Rig, and consisted of the provincial kings and other distinguished men of Ireland, *e.g.* poets, historians, etc. After the proclamation of the laws the proceedings were festive in character. The last regular F. was held at Tara in 560 A.D.

**Feisal, King of Iraq,** *b. c.* 1884, either at Mecca or at Taif to the E. of Mecca; son (third to grow up) of Husain ibn Ali—afterwards Grand Sherif and Emir of Mecca, and, later, King of the Hedjaz; descended from Hasan, eldest son of Mohammed's daughter Fatima. F. is thirty-seventh in descent from the Prophet. In 1893 he left the Rahab Palace—the country seat of his family—and accompanied his father to Constantinople. He married a cousin in 1905, and returned in 1909 to the Hedjaz, of which his father had become ruler. F. was next engaged in subduing a rebellious sect. In 1913 he became deputy for Jiddah in the Turkish parliament, and began to take part in the Arab national movement. He was at Mecca when the Great War broke out. He is said to have been with the Turkish Governor of Syria in 1915, but to have escaped to the Hedjaz early in 1916. With one of his brothers, he raised the flag of revolt near Medina, June 13; and, having failed in an attack on that city, he became chief of his father's N. army. His forces, co-operating with Allenby, marched from Medina to the E. bank of the Jordan. He met Allenby Oct. 3, 1918, and the same day rode into Damascus in celebration of the overthrow of Turkish power in Syria. Soon afterwards he came W., through France to England in Dec. He attended the Peace Conference in Paris, Feb. 1919; and visited Rome on his way home. In Sept. he was again in Paris in answer to summons, and again visited London. In March 1920 he was back in Damascus; where his appointment as King, and the independence of Syria, were proclaimed. But, next month, Syria was 'mandated' to France; and either F.'s appointment was unpopular, or opponents contrived to make it seem so (he had publicly expressed sympathy with Zionism); and French troops entered Damascus July 25. F., deposed, left for Haifa, and began to turn his attention to Mesopotamia, otherwise Iraq; for the throne of which his brother Abdullah had hitherto been a somewhat passive candidate. F. came W. again in the latter part of the year, and stayed in England—where, as a racing man, he was popular—till March 1921. Passing through Egypt, he was at Bagdad June 29. A referendum of Iraq notables re-sulted in a huge majority for his election: he was enthroned King, Aug. 23, 1921. He has since visited W. Europe several times. For his treaties with Britain and further particulars, see IRAQ.

**Feith, Rhijnvis** (1753–1824), a Dutch poet and writer, *b.* at Zwolle in the Netherlands. He was educated at Harderwijk and at the University of Leyden, and became mayor of Zwolle in 1780. He wrote novels, which have been very much criticised for their morbid melancholy, as well as tragedies, didactic poems, and lyrics. Of his novels may be mentioned *Julia,* 1783, and *Ferdinand and Constantia,* 1785, both of which are written in emulation of *Werther,* and his best tragedies are: *Thirza,* 1784; *The Patriots,* 1784; *Lady Jane Grey,* 1791; and *Ines de Castro,* 1793. Among his poems are: *Old Age,* 1802; *The Grave,* 1792, a didactic poem; and *Odes and Miscellaneous Poems,* 1796–1814.

**Felaniche,** or **Felanitx,** a tn. in Majorca, Balearic Isles, Spain, situated 27½ m. S.E. of Palma. Fruit is extensively cultivated and wine is manufactured. There is also a trade in cattle. Pop. 11,300.

**Feldkirch,** a tn. of Austria and the cap. of the Vorarlberg dist. It is situated about 6 m. above the junction of the Rhine with the Ill. It has considerable transit trade, and there are engineering works, bell foundries, and cotton mills; Kirschwasser is manufactured. F. occupies a strong military position, and is the seat of several administrative offices. Pop. 5000.

**Félegyháza,** or **Kiskunfelegyháza,** a tn. of Hungary, situated 65 m. S.E. of Pesth, on the railway between that city and Szegedin. It is a centre of a vine growing district, and there are extensive orchards. Corn and tobacco are cultivated, and there is a noted cattle market. Several Roman relics have been unearthed in the neighbourhood. In the seventeenth century the town was destroyed by the Turks, and rebuilt in 1743. Pop. 34,000.

**Félibien, André** (1619–1695), French architect and historiographer, *b.* at Chartres. Went to Rome as Secretary to the French Ambassador and, while there, came upon a life of Pius V. in the library of Cardinal Barberini, which he translated. This seems to have started him in his career as a writer on artistic subjects. With the patronage of Colbert and Fouquet, he was successively historiographer of buildings, secretary of the Académie d'Architecture, and keeper of antiquities; but he devoted most of his life to writing. His

*Entretiens sur les vies et sur les ouvrages des plus excellents peintres anciens et modernes* (Paris 1686) won the praise of Voltaire. Another notable work was his *Description de l'Abbaye de la Trappe*, transl. into English in 1871.

**Felidæ,** the name given to an extensive family of carnivorous mammals, of which nearly all the existing members may be included in the genus *Felis*. They are characterised by a lithe body, soft and often beautifully marked fur, feet provided with cushion-like pads and retractile claws, and short, strong jaws with formidable teeth. *F. domesticus*, the domestic cat, and *F. leo*, the lion, are typical and widely contrasted species; others are *F. tigris*, the tiger; *F. pardus*, the leopard; *F. onca*, the jaguar; *F. concolor*, the puma; *F. catus*, the European wild-cat, and *F. maniculata*, also termed *F. caffra*, the Egyptian cat, which is regarded as the parent of our own domestic species. *Lynx*, sometimes termed *F. lynx*, is more frequently regarded as a distinct genus of Felidæ, with *L. pardinus*, the pardini lynx, and *L. canadensis*, the Canadian lynx, as the most familiar species.

FELIS DOMESTICUS ANGORENSIS

(Angora cat)

**Felis** (the cat genus), *see* CARNIVORA, CAT, LEOPARD, and TIGER.

**Felix,** the name of five popes: *Felix I.*, Bishop of Rome, who reigned from 269 to 274. He is said to have suffered martyrdom in the persecutions under Aurelius. *Felix II.*, anti-pope, was raised to the papal chair in 356 on the banishment of Liberius, who refused to condemn Athanasius, but was expelled from Rome on his return in 357. He was regarded as a saint and martyr, and *d.* in 365. *Felix III.*, pope, ancestor of Gregory the Great, succeeded to the papal chair in 483 and held it until his death in 492. He excommunicated the Patriarch of Constantinople, and so produced the first schism between the Eastern and the Western Church. *Felix IV.*,

pope (526–530), was elevated to the papal see by Theodoric, contrary to the wishes of the clergy and people. *Felix V.* was the name assumed by Amadeus VIII. (1383–1451), when he was elected pope in 1439. He succeeded as Count of Savoy in 1391, and was created duke in 1416, but retired to a hermitage by the Lake of Geneva in 1434, and three years later became pope, reigning as Felix V. (1439–49). He *d.* at Geneva in 1451.

**Felix, Antonius,** a Roman procurator of Judæa, was a freedman of Antonia, mother of the Emperor Claudius I., or of the emperor himself. He married Drusilla, daughter of Agrippa I., and wife of Azizus, King of Emesa, whom he induced her to desert, and procured the assassination of the high priest Jonathan, who had offended him by unpalatable advice. St. Paul was sent to be judged before Felix at Cæsarea, and was kept in custody for two years.

**Felix, St.,** the patron saint of Zurich, whose day is celebrated on Sept. 11. He flourished at the beginning of the third century, and was the brother of Regula, who was also regarded as a saint. Both brother and sister suffered for their religion, and the former was beheaded on the site of the great cathedral.

**Felixstowe,** a seaside resort of Suffolk, England. It is situated on the estuary of the Orwell, 12 m. S.E. of Ipswich, and adjoins Walton and it is connected by L. and N.E.R. ferry with Harwich. It is much frequented by visitors on account of its fine beach, pier, and bathing facilities. There are splendid golf links also. F. derives its name from a priory which was dedicated to St. Felix, Bishop of Dunwich. There are an R.A.F. seaplane station and a naval wireless station. It is the headquarters of the Orwell Corinthian Yacht Club. Pop. (1921) 11,655.

**Fell, John** (1625–86), an English divine, son of Samuel F., dean of Christ Church, Oxford. He was *b.* at Longworth, Berkshire. In 1636 he gained a studentship at Christ Church and took orders; deacon, 1647; priest, 1649. During the Civil War he held a commission as ensign for the king, and at the restoration was made canon of Christ Church and chaplain to the king. In 1676 he was consecrated bishop of Oxford, also holding the deanery of Christ Church *in commendam*. He was an extraordinary disciplinarian, encouraged learning and proved himself a capable administrator, but refused all interference. It was written of him that ' He was the most zealous man of his time, for the Church of England,' also ' that he was very rude, and most pedantic and pedagogical, yet still aimed at the public good.' His stern discipline of the undergraduates led to one 'Tom Browne' being threatened with expulsion unless he could translate extempore the 33rd epigram from Martial, to which he replied with the lines :

'I do not love thee, Dr. Fell,
The reason why I cannot tell ;
But this I know, and know full well,
I do not love thee, Dr. Fell.'

He spent large sums of his own money on the building of Christ Church (*q.v.*). He wrote many learned and religious works.

**Fellah**, plural **Fellahin** (Arabic for ploughman), the name applied to the peasantry of Egypt. They preserve to some extent the blood of the ancient Egyptians, but the mixture of race due to long ages of intermarrying with the various peoples who have occupied the country shows in the wide differences to be seen in their colouring, ranging from a deep bronze to almost white. Physically the F. are a fine race ; the men are powerfully built with well-shaped skulls, oval faces, and large, clearly-cut features ; the women when young are often very graceful and beautiful. The majority are Mohammedan in religion. Their huts are of mud, roofed with straw, and only a few of the wealthier of them have brick houses. As a class they are poor, but the growing prosperity of the country is lifting their condition, and the advantages of education, hitherto entirely denied them, may do much for them. They are a cheerful, good-natured, and most industrious people, and under discipline of British officers are becoming sound soldiers. *See* EGYPT.

**Fellata**, *see* FULAHS.

**Fellenburg, Philip Emmanuel von** (1771–1844), a Swiss educationist ; *b.* at Bern. After distinguishing himself at the university of Tübingen he studied the life of the peasants and workmen of Switzerland, and was influenced by Pestalozzi. Later he went to Paris and for a brief period tried a political life. But in 1799 he bought the estate of Hofwyl, near Bern, and started an agricultural college in conjunction with Pestalozzi, from whom he later separated. It was based on a new system of bringing all ranks of society close together by education ; and in spite of the ridicule it first encountered, proved a success.

**Fellhammer**, a vil. of the Prussian prov. of Silesia, near Schleswig, Gottesberg dist., 48 m. S.W. of Breslau. Pop. about 6000.

**Felling**, a tn. in Durham, England. It forms a suburb of Gateshead, and is in the Jarrow parliamentary division. Paper, glass, and chemicals are manufactured there. Pop. 26,152.

**Fellows, Sir Charles** (1799–1860), an English archæologist, *b.* at Nottingham. In 1820 he became a member of the British Association. In 1838 he went on the first of his four expeditions to Asia Minor. His second expedition resulted in the discovery of thirteen ancient cities in Lycia. The fourth expedition was the most famous and satisfactory ; it resulted in twenty-seven cases of marbles, chiefly from Xanthus, being presented to the British Museum. This pioneer of archæologists penetrated to districts unknown by Europeans, entirely at his own expense. In 1845 he was knighted, receiving no other public acknowledgment of the work he had accomplished. William James Muller (*d.* 1845), the English painter, accompanied F. to Lycia, and made many beautiful and interesting sketches of the ancient works of art.

**Fellowship** (Oxford, Cambridge, and Trinity College, Dublin, Universities), the term applied to a member of the foundation of an incorporated college, sharing in the government, and receiving an income from the college revenues. Fs. are conferred generally through open examination, on Bachelors of Arts, whose careers have been distinguished. There are prize Fs. involving no collegiate duties, and official Fs. which are attached to the teaching and tutorial staff. Honorary Fs. are conferred on distinguished persons. The Dublin University fellows hold their office for life. At first fellows were restricted to persons who took holy orders and were celibates ; this was abolished in 1858.

**Felo de se** (literally a felon on himself, *i.e.* a murderer of himself), the technical law term for a suicide, hence used in verdicts where juries do not find evidence of temporary insanity. *See* SUICIDE.

**Felon** and **Felony**, in English law, a legal term for a special but ill-defined group of criminal offences. Whether a particular crime is a felony, a misdemeanour, or a summary offence, must be determined by reference to the common law and to various statutes. Roughly, felonies are the more serious forms of crime, such as were once capital crimes punishable by death, and involving attainder and forfeiture of estates. Treason has been classified as a special form, but is usually grouped as a felony. The principal difference between a felony and a misdemeanour is that a private person may arrest a F. without warrant, that costs of prosecution are paid from public funds ; there are also several differences in procedure and in drawing indictments.

**Felsite**, a term used by geologists for fine-grained igneous rocks of acid composition. They are composed chiefly of felspar and quartz in very minute particles. In colour, the rocks are usually of a reddish-yellow, and are hard and sometimes nodular. They occasionally contain porphyritic crystals of clear quartz, and are then known as quartz-Fs. The variety of formation of these rocks has led to considerable discussion, and it cannot always be determined whether F. is an original substance, or the result of devitrification of primary glass. They are divided up into granite porphyries, orthophyres, felsitic rhyolites, etc. The term soda-Fs. is used of fine grained rocks containing large quantities of soda-felspar.

**Felspar** (from Ger. *feldspath*), an important group of mineral silicates, forming principal components of various plutonic and volcanic rocks. For example, Lyell gives the minerals essential to granite (plutonic) in their order of importance as F., quartz, and mica, and the trachytic rocks (volcanic) are largely felspathic. The chief constituent of all Fs. (sometimes over 60 per cent.) is silica; alumina sometimes reaches 30 per cent., and there are varying proportions of lime and soda. Fs. are classified according to their cleavage as monoclinic (including orthoclase, adularia, and sanidine) and triclinic (albite, anorthite, etc.). The subdivisions are based on chemical composition and crystallography. Fs. decompose when exposed to weather, forming various soils, among others china-clay. Kaolin, from which fine porcelain is made, consists of decomposed orthoclase. The Fs. have a specific gravity of from 2·55 to 2·75, and their hardness, 6 to 6·5, is less than that of quartz. Pure F. is colourless, but many varieties are finely tinted owing to the presence of various minerals. Among these are: Amazon stone, a green F. found in Russia and U.S.A., this is often cut and polished; moonstone, a translucent variety known as adularia (hence its sheen is called adularescence), found in Ceylon; Labradorite, generally dull, but sometimes playing with brilliant blue, purple, and other tints, then very handsome when polished; sunstone, called aventurine from its golden spangled lustre, like that of aventurine glass, found in Russia, Queensland, and U.S.A. The colouring of red and grey granites is due to the Fs. they contain.

**Felstead**, or **Felsted**, a vil. in Essex, England; famous for its public school,

which dates back to its foundation as a grammar school by Richard, first Baron Rich, 1564. It was a well-known Puritan school in the seventeenth century, and four sons of Oliver Cromwell were educated there. Since 1856 extensive new buildings have been erected and playing fields added, and the numbers have greatly increased. Pop. 2089.

**Felt**, a fabric produced by the 'felting' or 'matting' together of fibrous materials, such as wools, furs, and some hairs. The hairs from wool are covered with serrations or minute hooks which can easily be forced together, so as to become 'matted.' Fibre Fs. are interesting as the art of felting preceded the art of weaving in the ancient civilisations of Asia. There are two classes of Fs., the woven F. and the fibre F. In the former, selected wools are used, such as Saxony wool, and woven into a cloth that will endure the subsequent shrinking or felting; to obtain the heavier Fs., two or three woven cloths are stitched together before they are subjected to the process of shrinking. The material is passed between hollow steam-heated rollers which are kept moist and warm, and the fabric, thus treated, tends to shrink and thicken and become dense enough to resist water. Fibre F. is divided into the F. used for hats, impregnated F., and the ordinary F. For the manufacture of F. hats, vegetable fibres, silk, hairs, furs, and wool are used; hair and wool being the most usual. The F. made for hats goes through the same process as other F.; for fur hat Fs., an air blast is used to carry the fibres on to the required shape, and the F. is impregnated with stiffening agents. The principal use for F. is for the linings of furniture, rubber shoes, under-carpets, slippers, steam engine packing, etc. The impregnated iron felt is a later development, used in the construction of bridges, etc., in the place of rubber. Asphalted F. is used for roofing, especially for wooden structures.

**Feltham**, a vil. in the co. of Middlesex, England, situated about 4 m. E. of Staines. It possesses a number of nurseries and market gardens. Pop. 6329.

**Feltham**, or **Felltham**, **Owen** (*c.* 1602–68), an English author, *b.* at Mutford, Suffolk. Noted for a volume of essays entitled *Resolves, Divine, Moral and Political*, 1620. His writing was modelled on that of Bacon, and has a certain charm. The later editions of *Resolves* include a collection of poems entitled *Lusoria*.

**Felton, Cornelius Conway** (1807–62), an American classical scholar, *b.*

at W. Newbury, Mass., U.S.A. He graduated at Harvard College in 1827. In 1829 returned to Harvard as tutor, and three years later was appointed university professor of Greek, and in 1834 Eliot Professor of Greek literature. He became president of Harvard in 1860, and held the post until his death. He edited many classical works and made some valuable annotations to Wolf's text of the *Iliad*, 1833. He published forty-nine lectures entitled *Greece, Ancient and Modern*, an American edition of Sir William Smith's *History of Greece*, and several translations.

**Felton, John** (1595–1628), a mem-

**Felucca,** the name of a particular kind of sailing boat used on the Mediterranean. It is a large boat built with a high bow and raking sternpost, and rigged with three masts, with lateen sails and a jib. It rides low on the water and moves very swiftly, being the fastest sailing boat on the Mediterranean.

**Female Suffrage,** *see* WOMEN'S SUFFRAGE.

**Feme** an old French word, the modern being *femme*, used in English phraseology for 'woman'; *feme covert*, a married woman, *i.e.* protected by a husband, and *feme sole*, a widow or spinster.

[*Canadian Pacific*

A FELUCCA ON THE NILE

ber of an old Suffolk family established at Playford. He served as a lieutenant in the army, and his repeated applications to the first Duke of Buckingham, George Villiers, for promotion being refused, on account of some personal enmity, bred a deep hatred. He went to Portsmouth and, mixing with the crowd of applicants who waited on the duke, stabbed Buckingham dead. Felton was hung; on his way to the gallows the crowd blessed him publicly for delivering them from the hated duke.

**Feltre,** a tn. and episcopal see of Venetia, Italy, in the prov. of Belluno. It possesses a fine cathedral with a sixteenth century polygonal apse. The theatre, once the Palazzo del Consiglio, is attributed to Palladio. Pop. (town) 6506, (commune) 20,000.

**Femur** (thigh), *see* LEG.

**Fences** are made for various purposes, such as enclosing animals on pasture-ground, protecting crops from straying cattle, affording shelter from wind, and marking off boundaries. The ordinary hedge and ditch of an English farm makes excellent fencing, but is expensive in the matter of room, and where there are trees in the hedgerow they impoverish the ground. The hedge itself must be thickly set, and when new requires protection for the growing plants; afterwards it must be cut and trimmed regularly or it will run to top, and gaps must be quickly stopped. Park F. are often constructed of posts and rails with feather-edge boards nailed on the latter, making a strong and neat enclosure. A sunken F., or

' ha-ha,' is one made along the bottom of a hollow which is invisible until one reaches its edge. In parts where stone is plentiful dry-walls are often constructed, in Aberdeenshire of granite boulders, in some English counties of pieces of limestone, the top and bottom layers being sometimes fastened with mortar. On moorlands earthen banks topped with gorse make capital F. Where wood is scarce enclosures are often made of stout wire set up on straining-posts, with minor standards between.

**Fen-chou-fu,** a city in Shan-si, China, situated close to the r. b. of the R. Fen.

**Fencibles,** forces raised for local defence only, or on an emergency, *e.g.* the English volunteers of 1804, at the time of Napoleon's threatened invasion.

**Fencing,** the art of using a sword, foil, or similar weapon, for attack and defence. In mediæval times steel-clad knights fought with lances, axes, and heavy swords, but when armour was gradually abolished by the introduction of fire-arms personal encounters came to be fought most frequently on foot, and success in the *duello* depended mainly on good sword-play. Skilled instructors were required, and were found among the plebeian foot-soldiers, who had for generations ' trusted to their hands to keep their heads.' Schools of swordsmanship were established in Germany, Italy, and Spain, and at length, under Henry VIII., a Corporation of Masters of Defence was formed in England. The teaching, however, was not by any means like that of to-day, as it included the wielding of the huge two-handed sword, sword and dagger, sword and buckler, and other weapons now obsolete. Rapier practice, the commencement of modern F., seems to have originated among the Italians, who discovered that the use of a light swiftly-handled blade was not only prettier but also more deadly than the cut and slash of a heavier weapon. Light and swift must here be understood as comparative terms, for the early rapier was often four to five feet long and fairly weighty. For many years the new system was looked upon with disfavour in England; in Elizabeth's time we constantly find it referred to in opprobrious terms, both gentlemen and professionals speaking of it as a murderous and (of course) ' un-English ' innovation. But the handiness and efficiency of the rapier gradually made it popular, as it could be worn on occasions and in places where a heavy sword and buckler would have been cumbersome and decidedly not ornamental. For the new school Italian teachers were indispensable, and towards the end of the sixteenth century several established themselves in London, the most noted being Salvio and Rocco. The former left a treatise on *The Use of the Rapier and Dagger,* which may remind us of the duel described in *Romeo and Juliet,* Act iii. scene 1, fought with these same weapons. Though excellent for cutting and thrusting, the rapier was still unsuitable for quick parrying, which was done with the dagger, so that in a duel or fencing-match both hands were employed. Sometimes instead of a dagger a second rapier was used, slightly shorter than the first; the pair were known as ' a case of rapiers.' Several well-defined movements of the body (such as the *incartata,* a spring to one side to avoid a thrust), prescribed by the Italian school, gave rise to the frequent jeers about ' skipping ' indulged in by English fencers.

Tricks were then sedulously taught and practised which would now be condemned; in fact, in that age of chivalry our modern ideas of fair-play would have found little favour. Many a teacher professed to have the secret of some infallible stroke by which an opponent could be slain, blinded, or crippled, and these strokes were often mercilessly put into practice. The famous, or infamous, ' coup de Jarnac,' by which Chabot de Jarnac hamstrung Vivonne de Chataigneraie in 1547, was an Italian device taught him by Captain Caizo, and was highly commended by Marozzo of Bologna, one of the most celebrated fencers of the time. Wearing concealed armour was so frequent that it became customary to search the combatants before a duel. One Millaud gained renown by defeating even this precaution when fighting the Baron de Vitaud. He opened his shirt politely and showed his chest; the searcher was satisfied, but Millaud was wearing a very fine steel corslet, painted to look exactly like flesh. He killed his opponent. These instances show the spirit in which combats were often carried on in those days, and no doubt stories of this kind helped to intensify English prejudice. Sword and buckler play went on flourishing in this country long after it had died out among the upper classes, lasting in fact down to the time of Queen Anne. It seems to have been specially popular in the Western counties, forming a principal item at the ' Dover's meetings ' at Wootton-under-Edge (Glos.) and other country revels. Its place was afterwards taken by single-stick bouts, like those described in *Tom Brown's School*

*Days* and *The Scouring of the White Horse*. These contests were varied with boxing matches, and eventually led to the institution of the prize-ring.

The sword had a literature of its own in Italy and Germany even before the invention of printing, and by the end of the sixteenth century many works had been published on the subject, some of them dealing with the gentle art of quarrelling. Saviolo, in his treatise, *Of Honour and Honourable Quarrels*, maintains that looking hard at a man in the street is a fair matter of challenge, and gives a case from Trieste, where this slight cause led to one man being killed, two others wounded, and a fourth beheaded. As to 'giving the lie,' Touchstone's discourse in *As You Like It* is elementary compared with the niceties of the duelling-book.

There were several distinct schools of fencing, the Italian, swift and crafty; the Spanish, elaborate even to pedantry; and the German, which favoured not only the rapier but also heavier weapons. The two former were in turn popular in England and France until in the latter country, under Louis XIV., the invention of the court-sword, with its light three-sided blade adapted only for thrusting, did away with the rapier, and brought in small-sword F. The lead in this was naturally kept by France, and the French style of play has been adopted everywhere except in Italy, which country has a traditional method of its own for this as for other F. The small-sword has a slight tapering blade, bayonet-shaped, and about 34 in. long, of which the half near the guard is the *forte*, the other half the *foible*. The foil used for practice has a steel blade, quadrangular in section, and tipped with a round button, from which it takes its French name, *fleuret* (It. *fioretto*). Foil play was greatly affected by the introduction of the fencing-mask, invented by La Boëssière in 1780, and became quite different in style from actual fighting. With a sharp point every hit must tell, and sword practice was therefore cautious and comparatively deliberate, but with the foil and mask there grew up a convention that no hits were reckoned except those on the body, and even then only according to certain rules. This encouraged a much quicker style of play, and a turn with the foils is now one of the finest of athletic exercises, every muscle in the body and limbs being called into action. The Italian school still keeps to the 'effaced' position, *i.e.* the fencer stands sideways with his right to the front so that the heart is not exposed, but the French have abandoned this for a more

natural attitude, which gives greater freedom and does not tire the muscles so readily. Their grip on the handle is also much lighter than that of the Italians. Many practical swordsmen have objected that conventional foil-play is entirely artificial; a hit for example in the fore-arm which ' does not count ' might disable a man in actual fight. For this and other reasons foil-fencing has not been so popular in England as abroad. But a newer style has arisen in which the rules and conditions are such as to prepare for real combat. This is épée-fencing, in which an ordinary small-sword is used, tipped with a button, sometimes furnished with tiny points to mark a hit; every hit counts. This system was introduced into England in 1900; the London Epée Club was soon established, and has held many open tournaments.

Modern sabre-fencing is descended from the broadsword fighting of the Middle Ages, but with great modifications. The Italian sabre of to-day is very light compared with ancient weapons, and is used for thrusting as well as cutting. One variety, the *sciabola*, is especially dangerous; besides the usual edge, it has also a ' false edge ' on the back of the blade for about eight inches from the tip. In Germany the basket-handled sabres used in university duels are somewhat like the heavy swords carried by old German *Reiters*, having flat curved blades about 32 in. long and 1 in. broad; they are not used for thrusting. Another favourite weapon with German students is the rapier or Schläger; this also is used for cutting only.

*Bibliography.*—Sir R. F. Burton, *The Sentiment of the Sword*, 1911; Egerton Castle, *Schools and Masters of Fence*, 1892; Capt. Hutton, *The Sword and the Centuries* (Grant Richards), 1901; Camille Prévost, article on ' Fencing ' in the *Encyclopædia of Sport* (Lawrence & Bullen), 1897; *Fencing, etc.* (Badminton Library); Lieut. Betts, *The Sword and how to use it* (Gale and Polden), 1908; *Les joueurs d'épée à travers les âges* (Flammarion, Paris); J. J. Renand, *Méthode d'escrime à l'épée* (Paris), 1909; L. C. Roux, *L'escrime dans les universités allemandes* (Paris), 1885.

**Fénelon, François de Salignac de la Mothe** (1651–1715), *b.* of good family at the Château de Fénelon in the province of Périgord. He came to Paris in 1666, and after a term at the Plessis College he entered the famous theological college of St. Sulpice, then recently founded. He took holy orders there in 1675, and in 1678 became director of the Nouvelles Catholiques, a Parisian institution for female converts from Protestantism. On the revocation of the Edict of Nantes in 1685, he accompanied a mission to the Protestants of Poitou and Saintonge. About this time he wrote *Traité de l'Education des Filles*, 1687, and *Traité du Ministère des Pasteurs*, 1688. In 1689 Louis XIV. appointed him preceptor to his grandson, the Duke of Burgundy, and this appointment led to the writing of his *Fables, Adventures of Telemachus, Dialogues of the Dead*, and *History of the Ancient Philosophers*. His services in this direction led to his advancement, and he was presented to the abbey of St. Valéry in 1694, and in 1695 became Archbishop of Cambrai. About this

FRANÇOIS FÉNELON

time arose the controversy concerning the Quietism of Madame Guyon, who, accused of sharing the more extreme views of Molinos, was twice imprisoned. F. defended her so far as the attacks against her were personal, and this led to a long and acrimonious controversy with Bossuet, with whom he had previously been on the best of terms. Bossuet issued his *Instruction sur les Etats d'Oraison*, and F. took up the cudgels on behalf of Madame Guyon, and defended some of her teachings in his *Explication des Maximes des Saints sur la Vie Intérieure*. The latter was published first, in violation of an understanding between the two prelates, apparently without the knowledge of the author and this led to their final estrangement. After some delay, during

which the controversy grew more embittered, the Pope, pressed by Louis XIV., condemned the *Maximes des Saints* in 1699, and F. honourably accepted the decision in accordance with his own declared views on papal authority. Pope Innocent summed up the matter in the words, 'F. erred by loving God too much, and Bossuet by loving his neighbour too little.' Ordered by the king to retire to Cambrai, F. spent his last years in doing good pastoral work within the confines of his diocese. He was buried in Cambrai Cathedral. The only controversy of his later years had reference to the Jansenists, whom he opposed to the point of persecution. It is generally conceded that F. was in many ways a model archbishop, but for the rest his character has been the subject of much speculation and controversy. He carried on a voluminous correspondence, and his many interests included politics, literature, and philosophy. *See* editions of his works by Bossuet, 1821–24 ; Lebel and Leclère, 1820–30 ; Gosselin, 1851 ; Bossuet's *Histoire de Fénelon*, 1850 ; De Broglie's *Fénelon à Cambrai*, 1884 ; biography by Viscount St. Cyres, 1901 ; and Masson's *Fénelon and Madame Guyon*, 1907.

**Feng Kuo Chang** (*d.* 1920), President of the Chinese republic, July 1917–Oct. 1918 ; one of the generals of President Yuan Shih-kai, on whose retirement he became Vice-President under Li Yuan Hung. On deposition of Li and immediate collapse of Manchu restoration, he became President. Secession of southern provinces left him president of N. China only. Schemed to conciliate the S., while his ministers were of the pro-Japanese faction.

**Fêng Yü-hsiang**, the Chinese 'Christian general' ; *b.* 1880, at Chao-hsien, Nganhwei prov. Educated as a Baptist. Began fighting in Tibet, 1909. Brigade commander, 1913 ; military governor of Shensi and commander of eleventh div., 1921. Military governor., Honan, May 1922 ; commandant, Peking garrison, Oct. 1922. Chief of defence, N.W. frontier, 1923. Seized Peking, deposed President Tsao Kun Oct. 22, 1924. Joined Kuomintang, March 1925. Evacuated Peking, April 1926. Won back Shensi, Nov. 1926 ; Honan, May 1927. Memb. council of state, Nanking, gov. Oct. 1928. Expelled from Kuomintang May 23, 1929.

**Feng-tien, Shen-king** (or **Liao-Tung**, but this latter name is generally used now to denote the peninsula alone), a prov. in the Chinese empire. It is situated in Southern Manchuria and occupies about 56,000 sq. m., with a population of about 5,830,000 (estimated). The capital of Shen-king is Mukden (*q.v.*); the province includes the Liao-Tung Peninsula, stretching between the Gulfs of Korea and Liao-Tung; in the southern part of the peninsula lies Port Arthur (*q.v.*). A large part of the province forms a level plain which is extremely fertile, the rest consists of mountains and forests. The chief rivers are the Yalu and the Liao-ho. Among the important towns are Liao-yang, Dalny, or Talianwan, and Niu-chwang. The province is now well served with railways, the Mukden-Peking Railway being one of the most important. The chief products of the province are : barley, wheat, millet, maize, cotton, and indigo.

Fên-ho, the largest river in Shansi, China. It flows in a S.S.W. direction, and is a trib. of the Yellow R. The lower course of the river is the only part navigable, and this only part of the year, as in winter it is frozen over.

Fenians, or Fenian Society, the name of a modern Irish-American movement for the overthrow of British rule in Ireland and the establishment of a republic. The name was derived from the ancient *fiann* or *féinne*, a legendary band of warriors in the heroic age of Ireland. The modern movement originated in America, where the Irish population had been largely increased by emigrants after the famine of 1846-47, and it was there that the first Fenian organisation was founded by John O'Mahony in 1858. The F. were particularly active in the western states, but the movement soon had many ramifications, and agents were sent to Ireland and to the centres of Irish population in England. The result in Ireland was the ' Phœnix Conspiracy,' which was put down with little difficulty by the government. James Stephens, one of the ' rebels of 1848,' and other prominent leaders were arrested, and *The Irish People*, edited by Jeremiah O'Donovan (O'Donovan Rossa), a prominent member of the Phœnix National and Literary Society, was suppressed. Many prisoners were convicted of treason and sentenced to penal servitude. Stephens escaped from prison, and renewed the agitation in America. A raid into Canada occurred in 1866, but it proved a complete failure. The collapse of the movement dates from 1867, when an attempt at insurrection in Ireland proved utterly abortive. The Catholic priesthood never countenanced the movement, and the peasantry were lukewarm. Several outrages took place in England. A raid was made

on the castle and military stores at Chester, but the raiders were betrayed. In the same year (1867) a police van, containing suspected F., was attacked at Manchester, and an attempt was made to blow up the wall of Clerkenwell Prison in London. The energetic measures of the government, and the subsequent Irish reforms, inaugurated by Gladstone, restored tranquillity in Ireland. Fenianism, however, continued to smoulder, particularly in the United States, where another raid on Canada was frustrated by the U.S.A. government. The ' Clan-na-Gael,' and ' United Irish Brotherhood ' were then the two great F. societies, and at the instigation of Michael Davitt they made the new departure which resulted in the Land League and the National League. The Phœnix Park assassination (1882) was connected with the extreme party. *See* J. O'Leary's *Recollections of Fenians and Fenianism*, 1896 ; William O'Connor Morris, *Ireland from 1798 to 1898 ;* and Justin M'Carthy's *History of our own Times*, 1880.

Fenn, George Manville (1831-1909), an English novelist, the author of nearly 200 books of adventure for boys and girls. In some of his books he collaborated with other writers, such as G. A. Henty. Among his best known books, and perhaps the most appreciated by boys, were : *In Freedom's Cause*, *Dick o' the Fens*, and *Quicksilver*.

Fennec, the Moorish name for *Canis zerda*, also called *Vulpes zerda*, a species of fox native to N. Africa and ranging over the whole of the Sahara Desert. It has a coat of a pale fawn colour, which harmonises with its surroundings, black markings on the tip of the tail, and white round the eyes and on the forehead. The ears are huge compared with the size of the head, and give the animal a grotesque appearance. The body and head measure 15½ in. in length, and the tail 6¾ in. The F. is a burrowing animal, and lines its habitation with feathers, hair, and other soft materials.

Fennel, the name given to various species of Umbelliferæ. *F. dulce*, or sweet F., is cultivated in kitchen gardens and used for culinary purposes, especially in fish sauces and with salmon. Sometimes it is boiled and eaten as a vegetable. The seeds contain oil ; they are also infused, and fennel-water, which has carminative properties, is obtained. In a natural state the seeds are very bitter, but under cultivation they become sweet and aromatic and are used to flavour more disagreeable medicines. *F. vulgare*, the common F., occurs on the cliffs near the sea in Britain. Giant F., or *Ferula communis*, grows three or four feet high, and the fibre of its stems is used as tinder.

**Fennell, John Greville** (1807–85), an English artist, naturalist, and angler. He was a member of the staff of the *Field* and the *Fishing Gazette*. In 1866 he wrote the *Curiosities of Angling Literature*, which he added to his *Fishing Gossip*. F. was a friend of Dickens and Thackeray.

**Fenny-Stratford**, a market tn. in Buckinghamshire, England, situated in a valley on the l. b. of the R. Ouzel. There is a church of St. Martin, built in 1730, on the site of an older one, and it is the custom to celebrate St. Martin's Day, Nov. 11, by a service in the church, and the firing of small canon called the 'Fenny Poppers.' Pop. 4305.

isolated spots rising above the surrounding levels were occupied by many monasteries as early as the seventh century, such as Peterborough, Ely, Crowland, Ramsey, and Thorney, from which spread cultivation and a certain amount of drainage in their immediate neighbourhood till the dissolution of the monasteries. In the reign of Charles I. another attempt was made to drain Deeping and Holland F., and the initial efforts were made on the great scheme of the Nene and Ouse F., known as the Bedford Level (*q.v.*). The drainage of the other F. continued through the eighteenth and nineteenth centuries, and now the only part of the original wild, undrained Fenland is Wicken F., S.E. of Ely, now vested in the National Trust and preserved as a unique

IN THE FEN COUNTRY

In the background is Crowland Abbey

**Fens,** a low-lying dist. in the E. of England, situated W. and S. of the Wash, in Lincolnshire, Huntingdon, Cambridge, and Norfolk. The district covers about 70 m. in length, and roughly 35 m. in breadth. It represents a bay of the North Sea now silted up, of which the Wash is the last remnant. It is intersected with many water-courses, and the rivers Witham, Welland, Nene, and Great Ouse. Before the present system of drainage was developed, the whole district was water-logged and consisted of marshy swamps, wide pools, and lagoons. The Romans made the first attempt to drain the F.; they dug the Caer or Car Dykes from Lincoln to Ramsey and constructed earthen embankments along the Welland and the sea-shore, some miles of which can still be seen. An unsuccessful attempt was made in the reign of William the Conqueror to drain Deeping F. After this the district was abandoned, although the forest portions were preserved for the hunting of the Plantagenet kings, and the

natural 'monument,' of wild plant and animal life. The soil of the F. is extraordinarily fertile and affords splendid pastures for cattle. The inhabitants have always been noted for their love of liberty. Boadicea ruled part of the district. Hereward the Wake was a fenman, and Cromwell came from the district, and this spirit showed itself in the steady, though unreasonable opposition displayed to the various drainage schemes, the draining of enclosures always bringing trouble with the people who regarded the land as their own, and were tenacious of their rights. In the more isolated portions of the F. they remained primitive in their habits. Their life was spent in fishing and fowling, both wild fowl and fish swarming in the rivers and marshes. In severe winter good skating can be had in the F., and many famous speed skaters have come from the district. It is interesting to know that the old British dye-plant, woad, is still grown in a few of the F. parishes; another but vanishing feature are the little wind-mills that are dotted about the lonely flats, now no longer used.

**Fenton, or Great Fenton,** a tn. of Staffordshire, England. It is close to Stoke-upon-Trent, and is part of the same parl. and municipal bor., and also one of the big pottery centres, most of the people being employed in the manuf. of earthenware and china. It comprises Fenton Culvert and Fenton Vivian, or Little Fenton. Pop. 26,714.

**Fenton, Elijah** (1683–1730), an English poet, b. at Shelton, near Newcastle-under-Lyme, Staffordshire. He became private secretary to the Earl of Orrery, with whom he went to Flanders, but later he came back to England and was appointed headmaster of the free grammar school at Sevenoaks. He resigned in 1710, and became tutor to Lord Broghill, the son of his former employer. He worked with Pope at the translation of the *Odyssey*, the 1st, 4th, 19th and 20th books being translated by him. He also edited Milton and Waller (1725 and 1729) and wrote a tragedy entitled *Marianne* (1723) and many poems. *See* W. W. Lloyd, *Elijah Fenton, his Poetry and Friends.*

**Fenton, Sir Geoffrey** (c. 1539–1608), an English writer and politician, son of Henry F. of Nottingham, and brother of Edward F. the navigator. He seems to have travelled a good deal in his early days and wrote *Certaine tragicall discourses written out of Frenche and Latin* while in Paris(1567). He also wrote *Monophylo* (1572), and the *Historie of Guicciardine translated out of French* (1579), which he dedicated to Elizabeth. In 1580 he was made secretary to the lord deputy of Ireland, and succeeded in so ingratiating himself with the queen that he kept the post until his death.

**Fenwick, Charles** (1850–1918), Eng. politician, b. at Cramlington, Northumberland. He started life as a collier, but in 1885 he was invited to become Liberal-Labour parliamentary candidate for Wansbeck, Northumberland, which he represented in parliament from that time until the month in which he died. He moved a resolution (July 5, 1888) suggesting the advisability ' of reverting to the ancient custom of paying members of parliament for their services in parliament.' He was a member of the Northumberland Miners' Trade Union from its formation in 1862 and also of its Wages Board. He was parliamentary secretary to the Trades Union Congress, 1890–94; and he served on the three royal commissions —on coal dust, secondary education, and railway accidents—and was a member of the Home Office Depart-

mental Committee on the use of electricity in mines. He refused to subscribe to the constitution of the Independent Labour Party. In 1911 he was made a Privy Councillor.

**Fenwick, Ethel Gordon,** British nurse; b. Jan. 26, 1857 ; daughter of David Davidson Manson, of Spynie House, Morayshire. Educated privately at Middlethorp Hall, York. Became a nurse in : Children's Hospital, Nottingham, 1878 ; Royal Infirmary, Manchester, 1879. London Hospital sister, 1879–81 ; St. Bartholomew's matron, 1881–87. Married Dr. Bedford Fenwick, gynæcologist, 1887. Gordon House Home Hospital, managing directress, 1889–96. From 1893, hon. editor of *Journal of Nursing.* Founder and first member of British Nurses' Assoc. Largely through her efforts, nursing was made a registered profession in 1919. Founder and hon. president, Internat. Council of Nurses, 1900. Has presided over many congresses of nurses, and over Society of Women Journalists.

**Fenwick, Sir John** (1645–97), eldest son of Sir William F. He entered the army and became a major-general in 1688. He was a strong partisan of King James II., conspired against William III., and in 1691 publicly insulted Queen Mary. He was arrested in 1696 for a plot to assassinate the king, and was beheaded.

**Feodor I. (Theodore)** (b. 1557), Tsar of Russia (1584–98), son of Ivan the Terrible ; he was of weak intellect and practically governed by his wife, Irene, and his brother-in-law, Boris Godunov. On his death he left the throne to Irene, who retired to a convent in favour of her brother Boris.

**Feodor II. (Theodore)** (b. 1589), Tsar of Russia (1605), son of Boris Godunov ; a prince of remarkable intelligence. The first map of Russia by a native of the country was drawn by him. The boy prince was foully murdered by the Usurper Demetrius I.

**Feodor III. (Theodore)** (b. 1661), Tsar of Russia (1676–89), eldest son of the Tsar Alexius ; an intellectual and noble prince, a man of advanced ideas, his life's work was to reform his country. Suffered from an incurable disease which half paralysed him. His consort, Agatha, is said to have been the first to advocate shaving of the beard in Russia.

**Feoffment,** in feudal times, was the usual mode of conveying a freehold estate in England, and for a long period it was the only mode. This method of conveying required to be accompanied by *livery of seisin*, either *in deed*, or *in law*. In the case of *livery in deed* the feoffer handed a twig or clod of turf to the feoffee on the land to be conveyed; in *livery in law* the feoffer formally gave possession to the feoffee in sight of the land. A F. was usually evidenced by charter or deed, but writing was not necessary before the Statute of Frauds. The Real Property Act of 1845 rendered F. superfluous, and its use is now very rare.

**Feræ Naturæ,** a term given in Roman law to wild animals and birds, including game, such as rabbits and pheasants. In English, as was the case in Roman law, they become the property of the first person who takes possession of them, subject, of course, to the game laws. A person keeping wild animals is responsible for any damage they may do.

**Ferdausi,** or **Ferdusi,** *see* FIRDAUSI.

**Ferdinand I. of Castile** (*c.* 1000–65) was the second son of Sancho the Great of Navarre. He acquired possession of Castile in 1028, and was recognised first King of Castile in 1033. In 1037 he claimed Leon by right of his wife, who was a sister of Bermudo III. of Leon, and enforced his claim with the sword. He drove back the Moors, extended his frontiers from the Duero to the Mondego, and took the title of Emperor of Spain in 1056. He left a reputation for piety.

**Ferdinand I. of Aragon** (*c.* 1373–1416), surnamed 'The Just,' was the son of John I. of Castile, but was elected King of Aragon in 1412. He proved a strong ruler, and carried on the war against the Moors. Though at first a supporter of the anti-pope, Benedict XIII., an Aragonese, he afterwards agreed to his deposition in order to end the Great Schism.

**Ferdinand V. of Aragon** (1452–1516), son of John II., *b.* at Sos in Aragon. At sixteen he married (1469) Isabella of Castile, and on the death of her brother, Henry IV., in 1474, F. and Isabella were proclaimed joint sovereigns, though Isabella did not allow her husband much share in the government. F. succeeded to Aragon in 1479 on the death of his father, and the union of these two kingdoms marked the beginnings of Spanish ascendancy in Europe. F., who, on his accession, found faction and disorder rife, reorganised the Santa hermandad, or military police, and suppressed the banditti. The menacing power of the nobles was broken down, and vigorous reforms were carried out, the king and queen being ably seconded in all their undertakings by the celebrated Cardinal Ximenes. In the memorable year of 1492, Granada, the last kingdom of the Moors in Spain, was finally conquered, after ten years of strenuous conflict. In that year also Columbus, supported by the queen,

set out on his great voyage of discovery, which made F. and Isabella sovereigns of a new world. A less creditable episode of that period was the spoliation and expulsion of the Jews in 1490–92. The Moors, too, were treacherously treated, a promise of toleration by the 'Catholic kings' being violated. The Court of Inquisition had already been instituted at Seville (1480). In 1500 F. took part in the Conquest of Naples, and, outwitting his allies, made himself master of it in 1503. By arranging politic marriages for his children, he gained for himself allies on all sides of France, and in 1512 he seized a favourable opportunity to add the southern part of the coveted kingdom of Navarre to his dominions, which thus stretched from the Pyrenees to Gibraltar. Isabella had died in 1504, and F. married Germaine de Foix. He *d.* at Madrigalejo, and was succeeded by his grandson, the Emperor Charles V., who was already master of Burgundy, Flanders, Holland, and part of Italy. F. and Isabella were able rulers, but the brilliance of their reign was marred by acts of gross cruelty and bigotry. F. was a shrewd and clever diplomatist, but was deceitful and despotic. For his expulsion of the Moors, the pope conferred on him the title of 'The Catholic.' *See* Prescott's *History of the Reign of Ferdinand and Isabella.*

**Ferdinand I.,** a Ger. emperor (1556–64), *b.* at Alcala, Spain, in 1503, son of Philip I. and brother of Charles V. He married a sister of Louis, King of Bohemia and Hungary, and he claimed the two kingdoms on the death of Louis, in battle, in 1526. His claim to Hungary was contested by John Zapolya, supported by the Turks, but, after buying off the Turks, F. gained the day. When he succeeded Charles V. as emperor in 1556, Pope Paul IV. refused to acknowledge him, and thenceforward the electors resolved not to ask the consent of the pope. F. tried to conciliate Roman Catholics and Protestants, and his reign was marked by wise and enlightened government.

**Ferdinand II.,** a Ger. emperor (1619–37), *b.* at Gratz in 1578. His early training and his education by the Jesuits imbued him with a deep hatred against Protestantism, and he began early to try to put down Protestantism by force, first in his own duchy of Styria, and then in Bohemia and Hungary. When the Bohemians saw that F. intended to deprive them of the privileges they had gained under Rudolf, they declared that he had forfeited the throne and elected Frederick Count Palatine in his stead. This led to the outbreak of the Thirty Years' War, which had already begun when F. succeeded Matthias as emperor in 1619. F., supported by the Catholic League, was at first successful, and gained a firm hold of the Bohemian throne. His general, Tilly, defeated Christian IV. of Denmark and the Protestant confederacy in 1626, but two years later, after Wallenstein was checked before Stralsund, the Catholic cause began to decline. The successes of the Protestant champion, Gustavus Adolphus, and the assassination of Wallenstein, at which F. connived, combined with other causes to bring his fortunes to a very low ebb at the time of his death in 1637. *See* Hurter's *Geschichte Kaiser Ferdinands II.*, 1850–64.

**Ferdinand III.**, a Ger. emperor (1637–57), *b.* in 1608, the son of Ferdinand II. He took part in the

FERDINAND III.

Thirty Years' War before his accession to the throne, and, though more inclined towards peace than his father, was compelled to continue the war for the first eleven years of his reign. A series of disasters in the summer of 1648 forced him to make peace, and the Peace of Westphalia was concluded in October of that year. In the Diet of 1653–54, the last over which an emperor presided in person, important changes were made in the administration of justice.

**Ferdinand I.** (1751–1825), King of the Two Sicilies, was the son of Charles III. of Spain. He succeeded his father on the Neapolitan throne in 1759, ruling over Naples, 1759–1806 and 1815–25, and over Sicily, 1759–1825. He consolidated his dominions as the Two Sicilies in 1816. From 1806 to 1815 Naples was under the domination of Napoleon. F. was a weak ruler, and the government was largely controlled by his wife, Marie Caroline of Austria.

**Ferdinand II.**, King of the Two Sicilies (1830–59), grandson of the preceding, was *b.* at Palermo in 1810. His reign opened with fair promises, but they were unfulfilled, and his despotic rule culminated in insurrection in Sicily (1848). His ferocious bombardment of the chief cities in 1849, which brought the rising to an end, earned for him the nickname of 'Bomba.' His treatment of political suspects was the subject of two notable letters of Gladstone in 1850.

**Ferdinand I.**, first Czar of Bulgaria, *b.* Feb. 26, 1861, in Vienna, the youngest son of Prince Augustus of Saxe-Coburg and Princess Clementine of Bourbon-Orléans. He married : (1) 1893, Princess Maria Louisa, daughter of the Duke of Parma, who died in 1899 ; and (2) 1908, Princess Eleanore of Reuss, who died 1916. On the deposition of Prince Alexander of Bulgaria, F. accepted the offer of the succession. He was elected by the Bulgarian parliament on July 7, 1887, but his sovereignty was not recognised by the Great Powers until 1896. In 1908 he declared the complete independence of Bulgaria and assumed the title of Czar. Though at first thwarted at every turn by Russia, F. set himself very successfully to the task of building up and consolidating his kingdom, and the results were seen on the outbreak of the Balkan War in 1912 ; the result of which was to enlarge the territory of Bulgaria enormously. But his former allies, Greece and Serbia, dissatisfied with this result, turned against him, and, with the assistance of Rumania, in a war that began at the end of June 1913 (in which Turkey took a hand on its own account), greatly reduced Bulgaria's share of the conquests at their final settlement by the Treaty of Bucharest on Aug 10. This left F. bitter and revengeful against the other Balkan States. He remained neutral in the Great War until Oct. 14, 1915, when he entered it on the side of the Central Powers. He was victorious in Macedonia, Thrace, and Rumania ; but his army was defeated by Allied troops at Dobropole, Sept. 1918, and an armistice was signed. On Oct. 4 he abdicated in favour of his son Boris. *See* BORIS III.

**Ferdinand II. of Leon** (1157–88), b. 1136, younger son of Alfonso of Castile and Leon. He was constantly at war, coming in conflict with the Moors, Castile, and Portugal. His repudiation of his wife led to war with his father-in-law, Alfonso I. of Portugal, whom he defeated and captured at Badajoz. The military order of Alcantara was chartered by the pope during his reign.

**Ferdinand III.** (c. 1200–52), ' The Saint,' son of Alfonso IX. of Leon and Berengaria of Castile; became King of Castile on the death of his wife's brother, Henry I., in 1217, and succeeded his father as King of Leon in 1230. Thenceforward the kingdoms were never separated. F. fought with success against the Moors, capturing Ubeda (1234), Cordova (1236), Jaen (1246), and Seville (1248). He subdued Granada and made Seville his capital. He was responsible for the collection and codification of the Latin and Gothic laws known as the *Forum Judicum*. He was canonised in 1671 by Clement X., and is commemorated on May 30.

**Ferdinand III.** (1769–1824), grand duke of Tuscany (1790–99 and 1814–24), younger son of the Emperor Leopold II., b. and d. at Florence. He succeeded his father as grand duke, and continued his father's reforming policy. He was the first sovereign to acknowledge the French republic, but nevertheless became involved in a quarrel with France, and Florence was occupied by the French in March 1799. He was restored later in the year, but in 1801, by the Treaty of Lunéville, Tuscany was formed into the kingdom of Etruria. F. was finally restored in 1814 by the Congress of Vienna. In the meantime F. had been successively elector of Salzburg and grand duke of Würzburg.

**Ferdinand VI. of Spain** (1746–59), b. at Madrid in 1713, the second son of Philip V. He helped to terminate the war of the Austrian Succession, and pursued a steady policy of neutrality in the Seven Years' War, in spite of overtures from England and France. He did much to revive literature and the arts in Spain. He was of weak constitution and retiring disposition, and on the death in 1758 of his wife, Barbara, who was greatly attached to him, he fell into deep melancholy, from which he never recovered.

**Ferdinand VII. of Spain** (1784–1833), eldest son of Charles IV. Discontent with the government and the favourite Godoy led to a popular rising in 1808, which forced Charles to abdicate and placed F. on the throne. F. was almost immediately led by Napoleon to abdicate in turn, and was enticed across the frontier and kept prisoner at Valençay. After the Peninsular War he was reinstated (1814), and promised to maintain the democratic constitution adopted by the government of National Defence at Cadiz in 1812. He twice broke a promise of this character, but receiving French support was able to maintain despotic government. He was succeeded by his daughter, Isabel II., for whose sake he had repealed the Salic law.

**Ferdinand, King of Rumania** (1865–1927); b. Aug. 24, at Sigmaringen; second son of Prince Leopold of Hohenzollern-Sigmaringen; who was brother to Charles, first King of Rumania. Charles had no son. As F.'s elder brother was to succeed his father in Germany, F. was adopted heir to Charles in March 1889. On Jan. 10, 1893 he married Marie, eldest daughter of the Duke of Edinburgh. In 1897 he nearly died of typhoid fever. Troops of the Central Powers overran Rumania on the outbreak of war in 1914 : F. and his family retired to Jassy. He succeeded to the throne on Oct. 11, 1914, and immediately sided with the Liberal gov. against the Central Powers. He was obliged to sign an armistice, Dec. 7, 1917 ; but refused to sign Treaty of Bucharest, May 7, 1918, and denied its validity. In Nov. F. proclaimed expulsion of enemy troops ; he re-entered Bucharest, Dec. 1. In Aug. 1919 he sent into Hungary an expedition which led to the downfall of Bela Kun. F. and Marie were crowned king and queen of Greater Rumania, Oct. 15, 1922, at Alba Julia. Much of his estate was given up to peasants. In 1925 he caused his son Carol (q.v.) to be disinherited in favour of Carol's son Michael ; and his last political act was to instal Carol's opponents in power. F. d. of a malignant growth, at Sinaia, July 20.

**Ferentino,** a tn. and episcopal see, Italy, 55 m. S.E. of Rome by rail, has remains of ancient limestone walls in the cyclopean style. It is a market for oil and wine. Pop. 12,300.

**Fergana,** or **Ferghanah,** a prov. of Soviet Central Asia. All the eastern part of F. was added to the autonomous Kirghiz Soviet Republic (alternatively called Kaizakistan) in 1920. Western F. is now included in the Uzbek Socialist Republic (or Uzbekistan), was formerly the khanate of Khokand. Nearly the whole of the province belongs to the fertile basin of the Syr Daria, the outlying parts being mountainous. To the E. are the Tien-Shan ranges ; to the N. are the Ala-tau Mts., while the Trans-Ala-tau chain encloses the plain on the S. with the Tien-Shan. Minerals, such as iron, coal, etc., are plentiful, and rice, maize, grapes, and melons are produced. The population is mixed, the Tajiks, with the nomad Uzbegs and Kara-Kirghiz being the principal races. In addition to Russian colonists, there are also Kipchaks, Sarts, Persians, Afghans, Hindus, Jews, etc. The chief towns are Khokand, the capital, and Marghilan, the former capital. Area, 35,446 sq. m.; pop. about 2,000,000.

**Fergus Falls**, co. tn. of Otter Tail co., Minnesota, U.S.A., on the Red River; has woollen factories and flour mills. Pop. (largely of Scandinavian origin), 9389.

**Ferguson, Adam** (1723–1816), Scottish philosopher, b. at Logierait, Perthshire, was for a time chaplain to the Black Watch, and is said to have fought at Fontenoy. He succeeded Hume as keeper of the Advocates' Library, Edinburgh, in 1757; became professor of natural philosophy in 1759, and moral philosophy in 1764, at Edinburgh University, and afterwards travelled extensively. It was at his house that Scott, when a boy, had his memorable meeting with Burns. Chief works: *Essay on Civil Society*, 1766; *Institutes of Moral Philosophy*, 1772; and *History of the Progress and Termination of the Roman Republic*, 1782.

**Ferguson, Robert** (c. 1637–1714), 'The Plotter,' a Scotsman by birth, who spent most of his life in political intrigues. At first a Presbyterian minister, he became vicar of Godmersham, Kent, but was ousted in 1662 by the Act of Uniformity. He took a foremost part in the conspiracies against the last two Stuart kings, accompanied Monmouth's futile invasion, and supported the cause of William of Orange. Chagrined at the scant recognition he received under William, he finally transferred his services to the Jacobites. He was a busy pamphleteer, and published a *History of the Revolution*, 1706.

**Ferguson, Sir Samuel** (1810–86), an Irish poet and antiquary, b. in Belfast, was educated at Trinity College, Dublin, and was called to the bar in 1838. He gave up his legal practice in 1867, when he was appointed deputy-keeper of the Irish Records. He was conspicuously successful in that capacity, and was knighted for his services in 1878. His antiquarian works include the *Ogham Inscriptions*, published in the year after his death, and various papers contained in the *Transactions of the Royal Irish Academy*, of which he was a notable president. Much of his leisure was devoted to poetry, and the charm of his lyrics and ballads anticipates the modern Celtic Revival. *The Forging of the Anchor* is generally regarded as his masterpiece. His other publications in verse include *Lays of the Western Gael*, 1865, and *Congal*, 1872.

**Fergusson, James** (1808–86), 'the historian of architecture,' b. at Ayr. His studies in Bengal resulted in the publication of *Rock Temples of India*, 1843; *Ancient Buddhist Architecture of India*, 1848, and *Tree and Serpent Worship*, 1869. Also studied the archæological remains of Palestine and surrounding countries. His monumental work, *A History of Architecture*, was published in the years 1865–76.

**Fergusson, Robert** (1750–74), a Scottish poet, b. at Edinburgh, his father being a clerk in the British Linen Company. He obtained a good education at Dundee Grammar School and St. Andrews University, but, declining to enter the church or to study medicine, he spent his few brief years as a copying-clerk in the commissary clerk's office, Edinburgh. He contributed poems to Ruddiman's *Weekly Magazine*, and the reputation of these drew him into a convivial society in which he ruined his health. A meeting with John Brown of Haddington turned him to serious thoughts, but an injury to his head turned religious melancholy into insanity, and he d. in the city asylum. Robert Burns was greatly influenced by his poems, which were first published in 1773.

**Fergusson, Sir William** (1808–77), an eminent Scottish surgeon, b. at Prestonpans, the inventor of many surgical instruments, and professor of surgery at King's College, London, 1840–70. He was elected president of the Royal College of Surgeons in 1870. *A System of Practical Surgery*, 1842, was his most important work. He was elected a fellow of the Royal Society in 1843. *See* H. Smith, *Biographical Sketch*.

**Feriæ**, the name given to the holy days, or sacred festivals, of the ancient Romans. They were the *dies nefasti*, in contradistinction to the *dies fasti*. They corresponded in some respects to the modern Sunday; political and legal business was suspended, and slaves were given a respite from labour. There were forty-five fixed festivals during the year, in addition to such festivals as the *feriæ Latinæ*, the dates of which were fixed annually, and special festivals at times of danger or victory. In addition to the *feriæ publicæ*, or public festivals, there were *feriæ privatæ*, observed by many single families in celebration of some particular event in the family history.

**Feringhi,** or **Feringhee,** a name for Europeans, common in the East, and dating from the Crusades, the word being a corruption of Frank. In India it is specially applied to the native-born Portuguese of Bengal. It has come to have a contemptuous implication, and was so used in the Indian Mutiny.

**Ferishta, Mohammed Kasim** (c. 1550–1612), a Persian historian, b. at Astrabad. While still young he went to India and became captain in the bodyguard of the Prince of Ahmednagar. In 1589 he removed to Bijapur, and was commissioned by Ibrahim Adil Shah (1585–1628) to write a history of the Mohammedan dynasties of India. He is one of the most trustworthy of Oriental historians, and his work still maintains a high place as an authority. It has been translated by General J. Briggs under the title of *The History of the Rise of the Mohammedan Power in India,* 1829.

**Fermanagh,** a co. of Ireland in the prov. of Ulster, with an area of 715 sq. m. The surface is hilly, the highest points being Cuilcagh, and Belmore, but the chief feature of the county is Lough Erne, which, with the R. Erne joining its lower and upper parts, bisects the county throughout its entire length. The salmon fisheries of the Erne are important, and pike and trout are also caught in most of the loughs. There is an abundance of sandstone and limestone, and iron also occurs. Manufactures are few, the chief being pottery and coarse linen, for the people are chiefly engaged in agriculture. The only tn. of importance is Enniskillen. F. is in the two dioceses of Clogher and Kilmore. By the Government of Ireland Act, 1920, F. was united with Tyrone as a constituency for the return to the N. Ireland Parliament of 2 members. For administrative purposes F. is divided into the urban dist. of Enniskillen and the rural dists. of Enniskillen, Irvinestown and Lisnaskea; Belleek and Clones were merged in the foregoing rural districts in 1921. Pop. (1926) 57,985 (a decline of nearly 50 per cent. through emigration).

**Fermat, Pierre de** (1601–65), a Fr. mathematician, b. at Beaumont-de-Lomagne, near Montauban. He made many discoveries in the properties of numbers, probabilities, and geometry, and is said to have been the first to hit upon the principle of the differential calculus. His writings include: *Arithmetic of Diophantus;*

*Method for the Quadrature of Parabolas;* a treatise on *Maxima and Minima, on Tangents, and on Centres of Gravity;* treatises on *Geometric Loci, or Spherical Tangencies,* and on the *Rectification of Curves.* His collected works were published at Toulouse in 2 vols., 1670–79, and have been re-edited by Tannery and Henry (Paris), 1891–94. F. was also an accomplished general scholar and linguist, and was for a time councillor for the parliament of Toulouse.

**Fermentation,** a process by which a change is effected in the chemical constitution of many organic substances. It is well known that liquids formed from the juice of fruits gradually alter in character with the evolution of bubbles of gas, that milk cannot be preserved from becoming sour without special treatment, and that all dead organic matter putrefies or changes its chemical composition in course of time. These changes are brought about by the activity of various minute organisms, or by the presence of substances which are elaborated by such organisms. Certain Fs. are brought about in the actual presence of living organisms, as in the production of alcohol from sugar solutions, the formation of acetic, lactic, and butyric acids in various organic substances, and the putrefaction of nitrogenous animal and vegetable matter. Other Fs. are due to the presence of non-living substances called *enzymes,* which induce chemical changes in somewhat the same manner as catalysts hasten certain inorganic reactions. F. by the aid of living organisms takes place when the temperature is suitable for their multiplication, where there is abundance of moisture and suitable food, and where there are no substances with a poisonous action on the organism. Perhaps the most important of fermentative processes is that by which the alcoholic liquors of commerce are prepared. This process is due to a member of the fungus group, yeast, which consists of rounded cells about ·01 mm. in diameter, usually grouped in chain-like clusters. When introduced into solutions of sugars containing other organic substances which the yeast uses as food, the cells bud and multiply. The temperature must be maintained between 5° and 30°, otherwise the cells are unable to multiply, and may eventually be killed. The yeast cells contain enzymes which produce characteristic chemical changes, and the action of each enzyme appears to be restricted to a few media. The chief enzymes present in yeast are *zymase,* which causes the breaking-up of glucose (grape-sugar) and fructose (fruit-sugar); *invertase*, which converts cane-sugar into invert-sugar, a mixture of glucose and fructose; and *maltase*, which converts maltose into glucose. In the manufacture of beer, the action is commenced by another enzyme, *diastase*, which is formed in the grains of barley during malting. The diastase converts the starch in the malt into dextrin and maltose. After the introduction of yeast into the wort, the maltose is converted into glucose by the enzyme maltase, and the enzyme zymase proceeds to set up alcoholic F. The effect of this F. is to break up the sugar into alcohol and carbon dioxide, thus: $C_8H_{12}O_6$ (glucose) $= 2C_2H_6O$ (alcohol) $+ 2CO_2$. It is uncertain whether the chemical action accomplished is due *entirely* to the enzymes. The living cells produce a far greater effect than do the enzyme-containing juices obtained by breaking up and pressing the cells, indicating that a 'vital action' operates during F. But possibly harmful enzymes are isolated inside the cells.

*Acetic fermentation* is brought about by a living ferment, *Mycoderma aceti*, which finds its way into weak alcoholic solutions from the air, and, living upon the nitrogenous matter in the solution, causes the alcohol to combine with the oxygen of the air, thus: $C_2H_6O + O_2 = C_2H_4O_2$ (acetic acid) $+ H_2O$. The formation of acetic acid in this way accounts for the souring of beer and light wines when exposed to the air, and is the basis of the manufacture of vinegar.

*Lactic fermentation* is caused by a living organism, the lactic ferment, which has the power of causing milk-sugar, or lactose, to combine with water to form lactic acid, thus: $C_{12}H_{22}O_{11}$ (lactose) $+ H_2O = 4C_3H_6O_3$ (lactic acid). This acid accounts for the sour taste of milk which has been exposed to the air.

*Butyric fermentation* is caused by a living organism, the butyric ferment, which is present in decomposing cheese. It often accompanies the lactic ferment, in which case the lactic acid is broken up with the production of the foul-smelling butyric acid, thus: $2C_3H_6O_3$ (lactic acid) $= C_4H_8O_2$ (butyric acid) $+ CO_2 + 2H_2$.

*Gylcerin by F.* If normal sodium sulphite is added to a sugar solution which is then fermented, the main products are acetaldehyde and glycerin, with little alcohol. Glycerin was manufactured in Germany during the Great War on this principle.

*Fermentation in digestion.*—The higher animals are also capable of producing enzymes. Thus the cells of the salivary glands produce *ptyalin*, which converts starch into sugar, and the gastric tubules produce *pepsin*, which transforms proteins into peptones. *See* DIGESTION.

**Fermo,** a tn. of the Marches in the prov. of Ascoli Piceno, Italy, 34 m. from Ancona. It is the ancient Fermum Picenum, which was founded as a Latin colony in 264 B.C. after the conquest of the Picentes, and remnants of a Roman wall still exist. F. is the seat of an archbishop, and contains a cathedral which dates back to 1227. Pop. 21,000.

**Fermoy,** a market tn. in co. Cork, Ireland, about 20 m. from Cork, on the R. Blackwater. It is an important military station, and the barracks on the N. bank of the river are one of the most prominent buildings of the town, the others being the Protestant church, the Roman Catholic cathedral, and St. Colman's Roman Catholic College. It is also the centre for salmon and trout fishing on the Blackwater, and has large flour mills. Pop. 7352.

**Fern, Male,** or *Aspidium filix mas,* one of the commonest wild British species, and grows in woods and hedgerows. The stem is short and rises but little above the ground, but the leaves or fronds, which are pinnate, are from one to three feet long. The sori are kidney-shaped.

**Fern, Sweet,** or *Myrica Comptonia,* a species of Myricaceæ which has fern-like foliage. It is a shrub with small diclinous flowers and occurs in N. America.

**Fernandez, John,** Portuguese navigator, and reputed to be the first European to visit the interior of Africa. In 1446 he went with an expedition under Antonio Gonzala to Africa, where, being anxious to glean information for his patron, Prince Henry, he remained in the country for seven months after the departure of his companions. His account of his travels among the Desert tribes and West Africa bears a remarkable resemblance to that of Mungo Park. The dates of his birth and death are not known.

**Fernandez, Juan,** a group of two islands and an islet, belonging to Chile, prov. Aconcagua, which are named Mas a tierra (landward), Mas a fuera (outer), and Santa Clara, or Goat Island, respectively. They were discovered in 1572 by J. F., who introduced goats and European plants on them. On the N. side of the inner island is Cumberland Bay, where Alexander Selkirk lived in solitude for four years, which incident is supposed to be the basis for Defoe's *Robinson Crusoe.*

**Fernandez, Juan,** Spanish navigator, who in 1572, while sailing from Peru to Chile, came upon a small group of islands in the Pacific which now bear his name. In 1574, he left Chile, sailing in a south-westerly direction and came upon an island which so greatly attracted him and his companions that he formed the intention (apparently never carried out) of revisiting it with a larger expedition. It has been conjectured that this island was New Zealand.

**Fernandez de Avellaneda, Alonso,** the pseudonym of a writer who anticipated Cervantes in publishing *Segundo tomo del ingenioso hidalgo don Quixote de la Mancha* in 1614, as a sequel to *Don Quixote*. It is a work of some merit, and was probably undertaken under the supposition that Cervantes would leave his masterpiece unfinished, but it is marred by an insolent preface, in which Avellaneda taunts Cervantes with his physical defects and his moral infirmities.

**Fernandina,** a city and port of entry of Florida, U.S.A., in Nassau co. It is situated on Amelia Is., at the mouth of St. Mary's R.; its harbour opens on the N. to Cumberland Sound, and may be entered at high tide by vessels drawing 20 ft. of water. The chief manufs. are cotton, cigars, lumber, and palmetto fibres. Pop. 3023.

**Fernando de Noronha,** an island in the S. Atlantic belonging to Brazil. It takes its name from its Portuguese discoverer (1503), the Count of Noronha. It has a rugged surface and healthy climate, and is the seat of a Brazilian penal station. Pop. 2500, all males, consisting mainly of criminals and soldiers.

**Fernando Po,** an island in the Bight of Biafra, W. Africa, which belongs to Spain and is considered to be one of the most fertile spots on the West African coast. Its surface is mountainous, and a great portion of the island is covered with dense forests of valuable timber. The climate is very hot, and a pestilential wind, the 'harmattan,' frequently prevails, but is healthy after the rainy season. The chief products are cotton, cocoa, coffee, sugar, tobacco, vanilla, and palm oil. There is regular communication with Liverpool and with the northern country. The principal settlement is Port Clarence (1500 inhabitants) on the N. coast, and the capital is Sta. Isabel (pop. 8300). The island's affairs are administered by a Governor-General and council subject to control of the Colonial Department in Madrid. Much is now being done to develop the resources of the island and to improve all the social services. Pop. 17,000.

**Fernan-Nuñez,** a tn. of Spain in the prov. of Cordova, 15 m. S.E. of that city. Pop. 6000.

**Ferne Islands,** *see* FARNE ISLANDS.

**Ferney,** the ancient name for a tn. of France, which in 1788 was officially called Ferney-Voltaire. It is situated at the base of the Juras, 4 m. N.W. of Geneva, in the department of Ain. The village was founded by Voltaire, who resided there from 1758 until his death in 1778. Pop. 1270.

**Fernie,** a city of British Columbia, in the E. Kootenay dist., situated at the junction of Coal Creek with the Elk R. There are extensive coalmines in the neighbourhood, and about 480 coke ovens, which supply fuel for the smelting works in southern British Columbia. Almost destroyed by bush fire in 1908. Pop. 4500.

**Ferns,** in the narrower sense of the word, comprise a large number of genera with numerous species, being widely distributed in all parts of the

CARBONIFEROUS TREE-FERNS

world. They attain their highest development in the tropics. The tree F., characterising the family Cyatheaceæ are the largest representatives; they have a woody, unbranched stem, which bears at the apex a rosette of pinnately compound fronds, which are produced in succession from the terminal bud, and leave, when dead, a large leaf scar on the trunk. The majority of F. are, however, herbaceous and possess a creeping underground stem or rhizome, terminating usually in a rosette of pinnate or deeply divided leaves. A peculiarity common to F. is the coiled position of the young leaves, giving them at the tip the appearance of a crozier, whence their vernation is said to be circinnate, and the leaves continue to grow at the apex until their full size is attained. Peculiar brownish scales, known as paleæ or ramenta, often fringed, invest the stems, petioles, and sometimes also the leaves of most F. Ferns vary very much as regards their branching; in some, as in the bracken F. (*Pteris aquilina*), the stem forks at the apex; in a few, as in some filmy F., the branching is axillary, like that of flowering plants, while in others, as in some of the tree F., the stem does not branch at all. The roots which are found on a full-grown plant are all adventitious, for the original main root of the embryo dies away very early. The reproductive organs are spores which are produced in cases called sporangia. Each group of sporangia is known as a sorus which may or may not have a protective covering, the indusium. In most cases the sori are borne on the under surface of the leaves. When ripe the sporangia burst and liberate the spores, which on germination give rise to what is known as a prothallus. The prothallus is a flat, heart-shaped, green body, which leads quite an independent existence, and which produces sexual organs. The male organs (antheridia) and female organs (archegonia) are borne on the under surface of the prothalli. In the antheridia are produced the spermatozoids, which are free-swimming male gametes, and out of these enters an archegonium and fertilises the female gamete contained therein. This process cannot be observed by the naked eye. The fertilised ovum becomes the embryo of the F. plant. Thus the life history of a F. presents a true alternation of generations: the F. plant, or sporophyte generation, produces asexual spores, which grow into the gametophyte (prothallus) or sexual generation. This in its turn produces male and female gametes, which after fertilisation grow again into the sporophyte. Occasionally asexual reproduction is effected by budding, as in *Asplenium bulbiferum*.

The form and position of the sori and the presence or absence of an indusium are characters upon which are based the classification of F. Most of the British F. belong to the order Polypodiaceæ, which includes *Pteris* (the bracken), *Adiantum* (the maiden-hair), *Asplenium ruta muraria* (the wall rue), *Scolopendrium* (the hart's-tongue), which has entire leaves, *Aspidium*, *Polypodium*, etc., etc. *Osmunda regalis*, the royal fern, belongs to another family; it is peculiar in that the upper pinnæ of the leaves are fertile and develop little or no green, so that there is all the appearance of a flower. There are many species of fossil F., which proves them to have formed part of the flora of the geological ages; tree F. are met with in the Devonian

period, and many forms were abundant in Carboniferous times.

F. are largely cultivated in gardens and greenhouses for decorative purposes on account of their graceful foliage. Bracken, when dried, can be used for stable purposes and thatching, and its root stock contains starch, which, however, is only used when there is a scarcity of food. The only medicinal F. products are the oil from the male F. and a syrup extracted from the rhizome of an American maiden-hair.

In cultivating F. let it be remembered they are shade-loving plants, and like plenty of moisture and soil containing leaf mould. They should be transplanted in early spring or late autumn, and are divided by their rhizomes. This applies to the hardier forms. The more tender F. require glass, with uniform temperature and moisture. The soil must be light and well drained, so that the abundance of water which they require will not rot them. They should be repotted before the roots become pot-bound.

**Ferrabosco, Alfonso** (*fl.* 1544–87), the Elder, an Italian musical composer, appears to have settled in England before 1567, but afterwards returned to Italy. He published two books of madrigals in 1542 and 1587 respectively, and one of motets in 1544. He was the most important of the Italian musicians who lived in England in the sixteenth century, and was held in high esteem by his contemporaries. He had several friendly contests with W. Byrd as to the best setting of madrigals, and also competed with him in the plain song *Miserere*.

**Ferragus, Ferracute, Ferragut, Fernguf,** or **Vernagu,** was a celebrated giant of mediæval romance, in which he appears with various attributes. In *Valentine and Orson* he is described as a giant of Portugal who took Bellisant under his care after she had been divorced by Alexander, Emperor of Constantinople, and as being in the possession of a brazen head which could answer any question put to it. In Turpin's *Chronicle of Charlemagne* he is a giant 36 ft. high, with the strength of forty men, and invulnerable as regards his skin; while in *Orlando Furioso* he is described as a Saracen, son of Lanfusa. He dropped his helmet in the river, and vowed he would never wear another till he had won that worn by Orlando. Orlando slew him with a wound in the navel, his only vulnerable part.

**Ferrandina,** a tn. of Italy, in Basilicata, situated in the prov. of Potenza, 36 m. S.E. by E. of that place. Pop. 8000.

**Ferrar, Nicholas** (1592–1637), a theologian, *b.* in London. He was elected for parliament in 1624, and took part in the impeachment of the Earl of Middlesex. But, foreseeing the outbreak of the struggle between Charles I. and parliament, retired to Little Gidding in Huntingdonshire in 1625, where he organised a small religious community. He was visited by Charles I. in 1633, but his 'Arminian nunnery' was broken up by the parliament in 1647. He left in MS. a harmony of the Gospels, and also of the books of Kings and Chronicles.

residence of the house of Este, and contains the castle which was built about 1385. There is also the cathedral of St. Giorgio, consecrated in 1135; the Gothic Palazzo della Ragione (1315–26), now the law courts; the hospital of St. Anne, where Tasso was confined during his attack of insanity (1579–86); the handsome Renaissance church of St. Cristoforo. The town was also the asylum of Calvin, Marot, and other reformers, and the birthplace of Guarini, Savonarola, and Bentivoglio. Pop. 65,000.

THE CATHEDRAL, FERRARA

**Ferrara :** (1) A prov. of Italy, situated S. of the Po, and W. of the Adriatic. Area, 1019 sq. m. It has a flat surface, and was formerly the main portion of the duchy of F. (formed 1471), and under the house of Este. It was annexed to the Papal States in 1598, and to Sardinia in 1860. Pop. 346,000 (1921), commune 114,300. (2) A city of Italy on the Po di Volano, 28 m. from Bologna, cap. of the prov. of F., and see of an archbishop. It contains a free university (200 students) and was noted for its school of painting in the fifteenth century and as a literary centre in the sixteenth. Besides this, it is interesting as being the former ducal

**Ferrara, Andrea,** a broadsword-maker of the sixteenth century, was probably a native of Ferrara. He worked with his brother, and in 1585 had acquired a great reputation as an armourer at Belluno. Many of his swords have been found in Scotland, as well as in the S. and W. of Europe. He is said to have tempered his sword blades by the method employed by the smiths at Damascus.

**Ferrari, Gaudenzio** (1484–1549), a painter and sculptor of the Lombard School, *b.* at Valduggia, near Novara. He was a pupil of Stefana Scotto at Milan, but made his greatest advance by a minute study of the pictures of Leonardo da Vinci. His works are remarkable for the elevation of their style as well as for the display of difficult and uncommon attitudes. His best are at Varallo, ' The Crucifixion,' a fresco which contains twenty-six life-size figures ; ' Scenes in the Life of Christ,' consisting of twenty-one pictures ; ' A Glory of Angels,' at Saronno, near Milan ; ' The Martyrdom of St. Catharine,' in the Brera Gallery, Milan ; ' Pieta,' in the Royal Gallery, Turin.

**Ferrari, Paolo** (1822–99), an Italian dramatist, b. at Modena ; he began his literary career at an early age. His works are characterised by their vivacious dialogue and good construction. Among his chief are : *Goldoni e le sue Sedici Commedie*, 1852 ; *La Satira e Parini*, 1858 ; *Il Duello*, 1868 ; *Gli Uomini Sey*, 1869. His works have been collected under the title *Opere Drammatiche* (Milan), 1877.

**Ferraria** (in honour of J. B. Ferrari, an Italian botanist), the name given to a genus of Iridaceæ ; they are dwarf plants indigenous to the Cape of Good Hope, and they have glaucous leaves of a dull but sometimes beautiful colour.

**Ferrates,** salts of ferric acid, $H_2FeO_4$. Barium ferrate is obtained as a reddish powder, and is soluble in acetic acid.

**Ferreira, Antonio** (1528–1569). One of the classic poets of Portugal, b. at Lisbon, d. of the plague. He was judge of the supreme court at Lisbon, composing in his leisure the poetry which earned for him the sobriquet of ' the Portuguese Horace,' and gave him a reputation equal to that of Camoëns. Wrote numerous striking sonnets, elegies and odes, but his poetic fame rests mainly on his epistles. Also wrote dramas, such as *Sophonisba* and *Inez de Castro*, in which he invested with the forms of Greek tragedy the most poignant and popular events of Portuguese chronicles ; and a comedy, *Cioso*. Collected works published in Lisbon, 1771.

**Ferrel's Law** is that everything moving on the earth's surface is subject to a deflecting force owing to the rotation of the earth—in the northern hemisphere the force deflects to the right, and in the southern hemisphere to the left. This is especially applicable to the air when in motion—the winds of the northern hemisphere being deflected to the right and those of the southern to the left.

**Ferrer, Francisco** (1859–1909), Spanish revolutionary and teacher, b. at Aleila, near Barcelona. After taking part in an insurrection in Spain, he earned a precarious living in Paris for a time as a teacher. In 1901 he opened a school, the Escuela Moderna, in Barcelona. This school was really a propagandist centre, though it did much for educational reform in Spain. After the attempt in 1906 by Mateo Morral on the lives of the king and queen of Spain, F. was arrested and the school closed. F. was, however, acquitted, only to be again arrested, in 1909, for taking part in riots in Barcelona. Convicted on hearsay evidence, he was condemned to death by the Council of War and executed. *See* Life by William Archer, 1911.

**Ferrers, Lawrence Shirley, Earl** (1720–60), was the last member of the peerage who was put to death as a criminal in England. In the year 1760, while in a fit of temper, he shot his steward, for which crime he was convicted of murder by his peers and hanged at Tyburn.

**Ferret,** an animal belonging to the family Mustelidæ, other species being the badger, weasel, otter, and polecat. The F. is the domesticated albino variety of the latter animal, both of them belonging to the genus *Putorius*. It is very similar to the wild polecat, but a little smaller, being about 14 in. long, has yellowish-white fur and pink eyes. Sometimes, however, Fs. breed with polecats, and the result is a cross-breed having fur tinged with brown. The F. is not altogether tame, and occasionally becomes quite ferocious, exhibiting no affection whatever. The female F. breeds twice during the year, producing from six to nine young ones each time, and she has been known to devour them. This animal was known among the Romans, who employed it, and it is said that it was brought from Africa to the southern parts of Europe. It is used especially to hunt rabbits, and to kill rats. *See* Nicholas Everett, *Ferrets*, 1897.

**Ferri, Ciro** (1634–89), an Italian painter and architect, b. at Rome. He studied under Pietro da Cartona, with whom he executed many paintings ; indeed his style is so similar to his master's that it is often difficult to distinguish the works of the pupil from those of the instructor. Among his best pictures are : ' St. Ambrose healing a sick person,' in the church of St. Ambrogio della Massima at Rome, and a series of frescoes, ' Scenes from the Bible,' in the church of St. Maria Maggiore in Bergamo.

**Ferricyanogen, Ferricyanides, Ferrocyanogen,** and **Ferrocyanides.** *Ferricyanogen* and *Ferrocyanogen* are two isomeric compound radicles containing cyanogen and iron, whose exact chemical composition is not yet understood ; they are often indicated by the symbols Cfy and Cfdy. The ferrocyanogen compounds are either prepared from the potassium salt or from the cyanogen compounds obtained as by-products in the coal-gas manufacture. *Potassium Ferrocyanide* is produced by heating crude potashes in an iron pot closed by a lid having an aperture through which iron filings and certain animal matter, as feathers, horns, and leather, are introduced. The reaction is not well understood, but when the fused mass is lixiviated potassium ferrocyanide ($K_4Fe(CN)_6$) is contained in the solution. It forms quadratic pyramidal crystals of lemon-yellow colour soluble in warm water. It is used in calico-printing and in the preparation of Prussian blue, etc. The *ferrocyanides* of sodium, calcium, zinc, barium, strontium, and many other metals have also been prepared, several insoluble ferrocyanides are made by double decomposition. Thus copper sulphate and potassium ferrocyanide solutions mixed give soluble potassium sulphate and a brown coloured precipitate of cupric ferrocyanide ($Cu_2Fe(CN)_6$). This is used in the preparation of semi-permeable membranes (see Osmosis). *Ferrocyanic Acid* is obtained by adding pure hydrochloric acid to an equal volume of a saturated solution of potassium ferrocyanide, excluding air as far as possible. It is a white powder crystallising in small needles, is soluble in water and alcohol, and readily oxidises on exposure to air. *Potassium Ferricyanide*, or red prussiate of potash, $K_3Fe(CN)_6$, is formed when potassium ferrocyanide is oxidised, *e.g.* by bromine water. It crystallises in dark red prisms and is a powerful oxidising agent. Many insoluble ferricyanides can be made from a soluble ferricyanide and a soluble metallic salt. *Hydroferricyanic Acid* or *ferricyanic acid* ($H_3Fe(CN)_6$), made by adding three volumes of very strong hydrochloric acid to one of strong potassium ferricyanide, is a brown-green crystalline body. *Hydrogen Ferrous Ferrocyanide* is a white powder obtained by boiling an aqueous solution of ferrocyanic acid. The potassium salt, when heated with dilute nitric acid, forms *Williamson's Blue* (probably soluble Prussian blue). Ferrous potassium ferricyanide is known as *Soluble Prussian Blue ;* when precipitated with a ferrous salt, ferrous ferricyanide, or *Turnbull's Blue*, is obtained. Ferric ferrocyanide, or *Insoluble Prussian Blue*, is obtained by oxidising Turnbull's blue with nitric acid or chlorine water ; it is a deep blue powder much used in the

preparation of various colouring matters.

**Ferric** and **Ferrus Salts,** *see* IRON.

**Ferrier, Sir David** (1843–1928). Scottish physician, *b.* Jan. 13, at Woodside, Aberdeen, and educated at the university there and also at Heidelberg. He became F.R.S., 1876 ; and was appointed professor of neuropathology in King's College, London, 1889. He made experimental researches on the functions and diseases of the brain and wrote many medical works—including *Functions of the Brain,* 1876 ; and *Localisation of Cerebral Disease,* 1878, 1890. He was a founder, and for a time editor, of *Brain : a Journal of Neurology.* President of the Medical Soc. of London, 1913. Died at Kensington, March 19.

**Ferrier, James Frederick** (1808–64), a Scottish metaphysician, *b.* in Edinburgh, and the nephew of Susan F. and of John Wilson (' Christopher North '). Educated at Edinburgh High School and University and at Magdalen College, Oxford, he was called to the Scottish Bar (1832), and appointed professor of civil history at Edinburgh (1842), and professor of moral philosophy and political economy at St. Andrews (1845). After having contributed various metaphysical essays to the *Blackwood*, he published : *The Crisis of Modern Speculation,* 1841 ; *Berkeley and Idealism,* 1842 ; and *Institute of Metaphysics,* 1854. His *Lectures on Greek Philosophy* were edited in 1866 by Sir A. Grant, who also wrote a Life.

**Ferrier, Paul** (1843–1920). Fr. playwright, *b.* March 29, at Montpellier. His plays include : *La Revanche d'Iris,* 1868 ; *Chez l' Avocat* and *Les Incendies de Moussolard,* 1873 ; *Les Compensations,* 1876 ; *Les Mousquetaires au Couvent,* 1880 ; *Babolin,* 1884 ; *Tabarin,* 1885 ; *Joséphine rendue par ses Sœurs,* a famous opéra-bouffe with music by Victor Roger, 1886 ; *Le Fétiche,* 1890 ; *Calendra,* 1894 ; *Le Carillon,* 1896 ; *La Belle-Mère,* 1898 ; and certain opéra-libretti, including a collaboration with Sardou, *La Fille du Tabarin,* 1901. Died at Nouan-le-Fuzelière.

**Ferrier, Susan Edmonstone** (1782–1854), a Scottish novelist, *b.* in Edinburgh, the daughter of James F., a clerk of the Court of Session with Sir Walter Scott. Her first work, in which Miss Clavering collaborated for a short time, was *Marriage,* which appeared in 1818, and was followed by *Inheritance* (1824) and *Destiny* (1831). These novels are very lively presentations of Scottish society, and show a rare gift of observation. They were all published anonymously, and many conjectures were made as to their authorship; some people attributed them to Scott, who greatly admired her writings and of whom she wrote in her *Recollections of Visits to Ashiestiel and Abbotsford*, published with a memoir in Bentley's edition of her works (6 vols.), 1881.

SUSAN FERRIER

**Ferro-concrete,** another name for 'reinforced concrete,' was first used for building purposes in America, and has since been introduced to England. Consult Warren's *Handbook on Reinforced Concrete* (New York), 1906.

**Ferrol,** a seaport of Spain in the prov. of Corunna, on the N.W. coast of the Bay of Belanzos, 12 m. N.E. of the town of Corunna. It is strongly fortified, and possesses a naval arsenal, dockyard, wharves, quays, etc. A British syndicate operates the dockyard, employing local workmen. There is a wireless station at F. There is a large, safe harbour, but its entrance is narrow and defended by a couple of forts. The manufs. are leather, linen, and cotton goods, naval stores, rope, and sail-cloth; the exports are brandy, vinegar, corn, and fish, old iron and copper. There are several fine public buildings, including naval barracks, town hall, two hospitals, jail, monastery, and churches. Pop. 30,000.

**Ferro-manganese,** a commercial alloy consisting of: iron, 4 to 6 per cent.; manganese, 50 to 80 per cent.; carbon, 5 to 6 per cent.; and silicon in small and varying amounts. It is used commercially in the manufacture of other alloys, and chemically as a reducing agent.

**Ferro-silicon,** an alloy consisting of: silicon, 10 to 12 per cent.; manganese, 2 to 3 per cent.; carbon, 6 per cent.; and iron 80 per cent. It is used in the formation of other alloys of iron or silicon, and also as a reducing agent.

**Ferrotype,** or **Energiatype,** a photographic process of developing negatives by means of a solution of protosulphate of iron and mucilage of gum-arabic. It was discovered by Robert Hunt in 1844.

**Ferry** (passage by boat across river). This word has the same root as the word 'fare,' and is allied to the German *fahren*, to travel, and to the Latin *fero*, I bear. F. is the term applied to the place where passengers can be conveyed across either an arm of the sea, as at the Haven to Studland Bay, near Parkeston Quay, or across a river as at Twickenham. It is also the name given to the boat which holds the passengers. The right to F. is a franchise or royal grant, and has the same legal significance as the right to hold a fair or market. It has nothing to do with the ownership of land or water. The possessor of the F. is not entitled to ownership of the stretch of water across which his passengers are ferried. He merely has the right to exact reasonable toll for the service he has rendered in supplying boats for the landing of passengers on the other side. He is, moreover, responsible for the condition of his boats and for the ferrymen he employs. No one is allowed to set up an opposition F. unless authorised by Act of Parliament. Car-ferries or train-ferries are vessels used for trains, and have railway-lines thrown across their decks, enabling the cars to run on and off the vessels on their own wheels. There are many varieties of F. boat, such as rafts, flat-bottomed barges with inclined planes for horses. The flying-bridge is worked by means of a long rope or chain attached to a fixed buoy in the middle of the river, and is useful in military operations. There is also the motor F. propelled by steam or electricity.

**Ferry, Jules François Camille** (1832–93), a Fr. statesman, *b.* at Saint Dié. He studied for a barrister, but gave up this profession and devoted himself to politics instead. Elected Republican deputy for Paris in 1869, he strongly urged that peaceful relations should be maintained between France and Germany, but without avail. Created prefect of the Seine in 1870, he had the full responsibility of the Siege of Paris, and was forced to resign his prefectship in 1871. He became a member of the Republican ministry formed in 1879, and eventually became Minister of Education and then Minister of

Foreign Affairs. He was elected Premier on two occasions, and it was due to his administration that two important measures were carried out, the organisation of public education free from clerical interference, and the colonial expansion of the French empire. A French protectorate was formed in Tunis (1881), and the conquest of Indo-China, as well as the exploration of the Congo and Niger districts, were planned. Unfortunately he fell into disgrace on the reverses suffered by the French at Lang-son in 1885. He performed another service for his country in preparing the terms of the peace with China. He fell a victim to the violence of a madman, who attacked him with a revolver, and he died from the wound in 1893.

**Fersen, Fredrik Axel, Count** (1719-94), a Swedish politician, b. in Stockholm. During the Seven Years' War he distinguished himself in skirmishes round Usedom and Wollin (1759), and in the Diet of 1755-56 he was elected a marshal, and subsequently became a leader of the Hat party. At the accession of Gustavus III. in 1772, he made some show of bringing about a reconciliation between the Caps and the Hats, but was never very friendly towards the king, whom he openly opposed in the Diets of 1786 and 1789. He was arrested in 1789, and on his release retired from public life. His *Historiska Skrifter* is a personal document of great interest but not very reliable as history.

**Fersen, Hans Axel, Count** (1755-1810), Swedish marshal; b. Sept. 4 at Stockholm: son of Fredrik Axel, Count F., of Scottish descent, from McPhersons. Colonel in Royal Swedish reg. of Louis XVI. of France, served in American War of Independence. In flight of Louis and Marie Antoinette to Varennes, June 1791, F. made the preparations and accompanied them. Made marshal of Sweden in 1793, and Chancellor of Upsala University in 1799. Murdered by populace in Stockholm town-hall. June 20, on account of a false belief that he had poisoned the crown-prince Charles Augustus.

**Ferte-sous-Jouarre, La,** a tn. and river-port of France in the dept. of Seine-et-Marne. It is situated on the Marne, in the arron. of, and 12 m. E. of the tn. of, Meaux. Pop. 5000.

**Fertilisation,** the fusion of sexual elements in the reproductive processes of animals and plants. The essential fact of F. is that a gamete or sexual cell from the reproductive tissues of one parent becomes so intimately associated with a gamete from the reproductive tissues of the other parent as to form one cell called a zygote, which becomes the starting point of a new living individual. Where there is no F. in the process of reproduction, the development of the new organism is called *partheno-genesis*. In some of the lower plants and animals the fusing gametes are indistinguishable in form, size, and other characteristics. Such sexual processes are called isogamous, and the term conjugation is to be preferred to F. The term F. now becomes restricted to that process by which a cell derived from the specialised tissues of a parent known as male is united to a cell derived from corresponding specialised tissues in the female parent. It is therefore a process characteristic of the higher animals and plants where sexual organs are differentiated into male and female. In animals the organs from which the gametes are derived are the testes in the male and the ovaries in the female. The male gamete is the spermatozoon, a small cell of elongated form. The nucleus is situated in the ' head ' or thickened part, and the remainder consists of a vibratile tail by which the cell moves freely in a liquid medium. The female gamete is the ovum, a cell usually much larger than the spermatozoon. It is quiescent or non-motile, contains a large nucleus and a large amount of nutritive material enclosed in a protecting membrane. Ova are produced in small quantities, while spermatozoa are relatively far more numerous. The ovum and spermatozoon come into conjunction by the admixture of the seminal fluid in the sexual act. The actual fact of F. consists of the penetration of the envelope of the ovum by the spermatozoon. This is probably brought about by *chemiotaxis*, or attraction of a chemical nature exerted mutually by the male and female elements. What happens is that the nucleus of the spermatozoon enters the ovum and sometimes the centrosome does so. With the formation of the zygote by this fusion of cells, the embryonic history of the new organism commences. In plants there are many modes of the sexual process. In certain algæ, similar gametes furnished with cilia move about in the water and eventually fuse; this process is isogamous. In other plants the male cell is a spermatozoid which visits the female cell. In the mosses, for example, the spermatozoids are developod in large numbers in the *antheridium*, and are set free to move in the water by means of two vibratile cilia. The *archegonium* contains the ovum at the bottom of its flask-shaped structure. When the ovum is ready for F., a passage is opened through the archegonium, through which the spermatozoid reaches the ovum. In the phanerogams, or flowering plants, the male element is contained in the pollen of the stamen, which has to be conveyed in some manner to the female element, the ovule of the stigma. F. in flowers is therefore necessarily preceded by pollination, and the special structure of the flower is adapted to that end. Wind is often an active agent in pollination; in this case the pollen is produced in enormous quantity and the stigmas are often feathery so as to catch the pollen. Insects are, however, the great carriers of pollen, and the colour and scent of the flower serve to guide the appropriate insects to their favourite flowers. When the pollination is effected, the male cell passes from the pollen-tube into the female cell, and a zygote is the result of the fusion. It has been shown that cross F. is the rule even when male and female organs are found on the same individual. In many cases this is ensured by the male and female elements in the same plant ripening at different times. The chemical attraction which effects the fusion is only operative between cells of a certain degree of affinity, that is, it generally means that F. can only take place between cells of individuals of the same species. In that one phenomenon the potential characteristics of both parents are fused, and may reappear in the new organism when developed. See MENDELISM. See also Wilson, The Cell in Development and Inheritance, 1902; D. M. Mottier, Fecundation in Plants.

**Fertility of Soil,** see SOIL.

**Fertit, Dar** (region of Central Sudan), see DAR-FUR.

**Fescennine Verses** (Fescennina carmina), an early form of popular poetry in Italy. They took the form of a dialogue, usually in the Saturnian metre, and were composed extempore at weddings and other private festivals. They became so licentious that the practice had to be suppressed by law. See Horace, Epistles, ii. 1, and Virgil, Georgics, ii.

**Fesch, Joseph** (1763–1839), cardinal and archbishop of Lyons, b. of Swiss parents at Ajaccio. He was halfbrother to Napoleon's mother, and was instrumental in bringing about the concordat with the Holy See (1801). He was appointed successively archbishop of Lyons (1802), cardinal (1803), and French ambassador to Rome (1804), but lost favour with Napoleon on account of his ultramontane views. He fled from France in 1814, and lived the rest of his life in Rome.

**Fescue grass,** the name given to a genus of grasses (q.v.); Festuca pratensis, the meadow fescue, and F. rubra, the red fescue, are common species.

**Fess,** in heraldry, one of the honourable ordinaries containing a third of the field. It is regarded by some authorities as having been a belt of honour, given as a reward by kings for service in the army. 'Per Fess' is when the field is equally divided by a horizontal line. 'Per Fess and Pale' means that the field is to be divided into thirds, by the F. line and the Pale line, from the F. point to the middle base point.

**Fessenden, William Pitt** (1806–69), American statesman; b. Oct. 16, at Boscawen, N. H., son of Samuel F., lawyer, of Maine. Graduated at Bowdoin, 1823; admitted to Bar, 1827. Practised at Bridgeton, Bangor, and finally at Portland, Me. Elected to Legislature, 1832 and 1840; became chairman of statute revising committee. Entered Congress as a Whig, 1840, and again in 1845. U.S. senator, 1854 and 1859. Persistent advocate of abolition of slavery. Succeeded Chase as Secretary of the Treasury, June 1864. Resigned March 1865, to go back to Senate. Died Sept. 8 at Portland, Me.

**Fessler, Ignaz Aurelius** (1756–1839), Hungarian historian, b. May 18, at Zurmy. Educated at Pressburg and Raab. Became a Capuchin monk in 1773. In 1774 made revelations to the Emperor Joseph concerning the life of the monks. Called to chair of Oriental languages and hermeneutics of Old Testament at Lemberg, renounced monkhood and became a Freemason. Became Protestant; lived in Berlin, from 1809 in St. Petersburg—where he lost his professorate because charged with atheism. In 1820 became superintendent of evangelical community at Saratov. In 1833 was made gen. supt. of Lutherans of St. Petersburg. Wrote: Die Geschichte der Ungarn und deren Landsassen, 1815–25; some historical novels, and an autobiography, Rückblicke auf meine Siebzigjährige Pilgerschaft, 1824. Died in St. Petersburg, Dec. 15.

**Festa, Constantine** (d. 1545), a famous Italian composer of madrigals and motets. In 1517 he was appointed singer in the Vatican. F. is chiefly remembered for his very popular madrigal Down in a Flowery Vale, which was translated by Thomas Oliphant.

**Festival,** see FEAST.

**Festoon,** in architecture, a sculptural wreath or garland, formed of conventional flowers, fruit, and leaves, suspended by ribbons from a knob or an animal's head. It was used by the Gks. and Roms. probably in imitation of the garlands of flowers that were hung about a sacrificial victim or altar. It may be found as a decorative feature in many Renaissance buildings.

**Festubert, Battle of** (N. France, 20 m. S.W. Lille). A famous battle in the Great War. On May 9, 1915, Sir Douglas Haig opened an attack on the Gers. just N. of Fromelles and also between Neuve Chapelle and Givenchy, F. being in the latter sector. This attack was undertaken in pursuance of a promise made by Sir J. French to Marshal Joffre to keep the enemy occupied on his front as long as possible. Some ground was gained about Fromelles, but the Ger. machine gunners on the Aubers Ridge held up the advance in that area. Progress was arrested for the next few days by dull and misty weather, rendering artillery observation difficult. On May 15 the attack was resumed between Richebourg-L'Avoué and F., in which the Canadian Div. distinguished itself. On May 16 the 7th Div. made good progress immediately due E. of F., having for its objective the line Rue d'Ouvert–Canteleux.

By the capture of the orchard at F. on May 20 the Canadians again distinguished themselves. This position had been strongly fortified by the Gers. The preliminary bombardment drove most of the Gers. to cover, and this enabled the 16th Canadian Scottish to clear the wire entanglement at the edge of the orchard by going through a ditch up to their necks in mud and water. When the bombardment lifted to permit the assault to take place, the Gers. streamed back to their trenches, which had only been manned by machine-gun crews during the shelling, but the Canadians were prepared for them and forced them to retreat. The lack of shells generally was a serious handicap to the British commander, as these were necessary to destroy the Ger. machine gunners who worked great havoc among the attackers. It was this circumstance which mainly decided Sir J. French to cease further attacks and to strengthen and consolidate the ground that had been gained. The result of the battle of F. was to deprive the Gers. of a highly entrenched and fortified area on a four-mile front. Their losses in personnel and material also were heavy. The lack of shells, known politically as the 'shell scandal,' led to the creation of the Ministry of Munitions.

**Festus, Porcius**, flourished during the reign of Claudius, and succeeded Felix as procurator in Judæa, A.D. 62. In the following year, when St. Paul was brought before him, he admitted the innocence of the apostle.

**Festus, Sextus Pompeius**, a Rom. grammarian who flourished during the third or fourth century A.D. He compiled a glossary of Latin words and phrases, *De Verborum Significatione*, part of which is extant. Consult the edition of C. O. Müller (new ed. 1880).

**Feth, Afanasi**, one of the prominent lyrical poets of Russia, was *b.* in the province of Orel, Nov. 23, 1820. His father, Captain Chenchine, was married at Darmstadt, according to the Lutheran church rites. This marriage, being null and void in Russian law, and the son being born before there had been a Russian Orthodox wedding ceremony, prevented the child from bearing his father's name. So he took the name of Feth, which was that of the first husband of his mother. It was as Feth that he entered the University of Moscow. From 1844 to 1856 he served in the army, finally retiring with the rank of captain in the cavalry of the guard. From 1860 to the day of his death, Nov. 21, 1892, he lived as a country gentleman on his estates. He was a great favourite in the circle of the illustrious Turgeniev and, encouraged by him, published a book of poems in 1856. A new edition was issued in 1863, which was sharply attacked, not because of its contents, but because Feth had taken a prominent position as a reactionary who opposed the freedom of the serfs. An impressionist in verse, he deals largely with little etchings of his native land and in love poems. At the age of 63 he surprised Russia with one of his best books—*Evening Fires*.

**Fetiales** (Lat. *fari*, to speak), Rom. priests who acted on behalf of Rome in international affairs and at time of foreign wars. They made diplomatic negotiations with other countries, decided when it was necessary to declare war, and offered thanksgiving sacrifices when peace was made.

**Fétis, François Joseph** (1784–1871), a Belgian musical critic and composer, *b.* at Mons, and trained by his father and at Paris. He was appointed organist and professor of music at Douai (1813); professor at the Conservatoire, Paris (1821); director of the Conservatoire, Brussels, and chapel-master to Leopold I. (1833). In 1827 he founded the *Revue Musicale*, and wrote a *Biographie universelle des Musiciens*, 1834; *Histoire générale de la Musique*, 1869–76; *Esquisse de l'Histoire de l'Harmonie*, 1840; and, in collaboration with Moscheles, *Méthode des Méthodes de Piano*, 1837. He also composed several operas and oratorios.

**Fetishism, or Fetichism,** the worship of inanimate objects which are believed to be possessed with spirits ; the word is also used to indicate the use of charms, which, though not the habitation of spirits, are supposed to have a magical influence derived from spirits of warding off danger

A NIGER FETISH

and bad luck. This cult is prevalent among many uncivilised or semi-civilised races, and flourishes especially among W. African tribes. The word is derived from Portuguese *fetico*, a charm, and was first used in its present sense by fifteenth century Portuguese explorers of the stones, wooden figures, beads, etc., worshipped by negroes. Consult Baudin, *Fétichisme et Féticheurs*, 1884 ; A. B. Ellis, *Tshi-speaking Peoples of the Gold Coast*, 1887 ; and R. H. Nassau, *Fetichism in West Africa*, 1904.

**Fettes College, Edinburgh,** was founded by Sir William Fettes

(*d.* 1836), who left a large endowment for the purpose of educating orphans and children in unfortunate circumstances. The trust funds were allowed to accumulate till 1864, when the buildings were begun. The college was opened in 1876, and the administration is similar to that of an ordinary public school. The headmaster is Rev. W. A. Heard, LL.D.

**Feu and Feu-duty.** In Scottish law, F. is a mode of land tenure which gives the tenant the right of holding certain property, in return for which he makes an annual payment in money, cattle, grain, or in kind, called feu-duty. The land is held from the crown, but the *crown vassals* may give out their land in F. to their vassals, who in turn may F. the land. This process of subinfeudation was prohibited in England by the statute of Quia Emptores in 1290. Consult Rankine's *Law of Landownership in Scotland*.

**Feuchtersleben, Ernst, Baron** (1806-49), Austrian poet and physician ; *b.* April 29, in Vienna, of an old Saxon family. Secretary to the Society of Physicians. From 1844, delivered lectures on training of psychic physicians. From 1847, vice-director of medico-surgical studies ; in 1848 for a little while under-secretary of state for education. Works include : *Die Lehre von den Heilanzeigen* (in Latin), 1833 ; *Uber das Hippokratische erste Buch von der Diät*, 1835 ; *Gedichte* (containing ' Es ist bestimmt in Gottes Rat', 1836 ; *Zur Diätetik der Seele*, 1838 ; *Uber die Gewissheit und Würde der Heilkunst*, 1839—new ed., entitled *Physician and Public*, 1848 ; *Beiträge zur Litteratur-, Kunst-, und Lebenstheorie*, 1837–41 ; *Lehrbuch der ärztlichen Seelenkunde*, 1845. Died in Vienna, Sept. 3.

**Feuchtwanger, Lion,** Ger. author ; *b.* July 7, 1884, at Munich, of a Jewish family. Studied philosophy in Berlin and Munich. Lives in Berlin. In 1907 he pub. a widely-noticed dissertation on Heine's fragment *Der Rabbi von Bacherach* ; also a play, *Der Fetisch*. In 1910 appeared his first novel, *Der tönerne Gott*. In 1916 came a tragedy, *Julia Farnese* ; also a refurbishing of the old Ger. play *Vasantasena*. He adapted *Perser* from Æschylus in 1917 ; and the Ἀχαρνῆς and Εἰρήνη of Aristophanes in the burlesque *Friede*, 1918. Of his dramas, *Warren Hastings* appeared in 1916, and *Jud Süss* and *König und Tänzerin* in 1917. He published the novel *Die hässliche Herzogin* in 1923, and the famous one *Jud Süss* in 1925. The latter was translated into English as *Jew Süss* in 1926. It is a story of Germany in the eighteenth century, a wonderful combination of Teutonic thoroughness of workmanship and Hebrew imagination. Later plays : *Die Petroleuminseln*, with *Kalkutta*, 4 *Mai* and *Wird Hill amnestiert?* 1927. His *Success* (1930) bears a close resemblance to Zweig's famous novel, *The Case of Sergeant Grischa*, being founded on the theme of the unavailing attempts of a determined woman to secure the freedom of a man wrongly condemned to prison. The setting is pre-war Bavaria and the picture presented of political, social and moral chaos is, as it is intended to be, profoundly disturbing. Like *Jew Süss* it is sketched on a great canvas, comprising scores of characters and all of them intensely vital.

**Feud** (M.E. *fede*, through the French, from Old High Ger. *fehida*. *Cf.* O.E. *fāh*, foe), a lasting quarrel, often resulting in warfare, between two families, clans, or tribes. *See* VENDETTA.

**Feudalism** (Late Lat. *feodum*, or *feudum*, a fee or fief), one of the most influential of mediæval institutions, gave rise to legal principles and social ideas which are not by any means extinct at the present time. The question of the origin of F. is one of the most difficult in institutional history ; the main points are now generally settled, though differences of opinion still exist as to points of detail, etc. Institutions have existed in Japan, Africa, and many other places, to which the term 'feudal' might with justice be applied, but when the term F. or 'feudal system' is used without any qualification, the system of mediæval Western Europe is always meant. This system came into existence in the eighth and ninth centuries, owing to the inability of the central government to cope with the disorders of the period. Within the limits of this article any detail is impossible, but a few broad principles and tendencies may be pointed out. The two main features of F. are of Rom. origin ; one related to land and the tenure by which it is held, and the other to the personal relationship of individuals. The latter was known in the time of the Rom. empire as 'patrocinium' ; a poor and landless freeman goes to the rich landowner who can afford him protection, states his need, and offers such services as a freeman may perform in exchange for shelter and support. The other institution was the 'precarium' ; under this form the owner granted the use of a piece of land to another. The object of this practice was not to obtain income, but to serve a friend, to reward a dependent, or to secure a debt, etc. Its chief characteristic from a legal point of view was that the lessee had no right of any kind against the grantor, as the land was revocable at the will of the owner with no penalty. When a small landowner was in trouble, he made over his land as a gift to a rich landowner near, and received it back as a 'precarium' ; this process was known as 'patrocinium fundorum.' These two practices were the foundation of the later feudal system, but they were in their early stages entirely distinct ; the personal relation did not connote the 'precarium,' nor did the holding of land involve any obligation of the 'patrocinium.' When the Franks entered Gaul and found these customs in prevalence, together with many other Rom. institutions, they not only permitted their continuance, but legalised them. In this they were in all probability influenced by the pre-existence of the institution of the 'comitatus,' which had much in common with the 'patrocinium.' The latter had held no stigma for either of the parties entering into it, but in the case of the 'comitatus,' not only was there no disgrace, but the transaction was considered to confer honour on both the chief and the dependent. All these ideas and customs, such as special ceremonies and oaths of allegiance, etc., passed from the 'comitatus' into the feudal system. The idea of the 'precarium' also would not be totally opposed to Frankish ideas, though the practice was mostly carried on by the great landowners until the beginning of the Carolingian period. The church was the chief agent in carrying over the 'precarium' from the Rom. to the Ger. state ; frequently grants of land were made by the church on this system. The Merovingian period was not distinguished by any great change in the character of feudal institutions ; the legalisation of the Rom. practices was the great achievement of that age. The most necessary steps to the formation of the historical feudal system were taken in the Carolingian period ; those are the steps by which the two institutions of the 'patrocinium' and 'precarium' became two sides of a single system. Military service had not previously been connected with the Rom. or Merovingian institutions, and the Carolingian age is remarkable as the period during which military service was established as a necessary corollary of F. Such a step was not made in a short time, and the whole epoch is occupied with the development of the change. Charles Martel made use of very extensive church lands to be given to his followers in order that being thus relieved of some expense, they might be able to furnish cavalry to repulse the

Arabian attack on Gaul; the method used was called ' precariæ verbo regis.' This was the first step towards the unification of the two institutions; about this time the word ' benefice ' displaced ' precarium,' and ' commendation ' was used instead of ' patrocinium.' The judicial functions of the state also passed into private hands during this period. As a result of the extension of the military service principle the duty of defending the state changed from a public obligation to a private agreement. So full sovereignty was exercised by the great lords over all residing within their ' fief,' as ' benefice ' was called at this later period. The process by which this change came about is obscure, and many differing views are held on the subject; in the majority of cases the view of M. E. Beaudouin is probably correct, that such power was usurped, owing to the strong local power of the landowner. In the ideal feudal system the ' fief ' and the ' vassal ' are always connected; the vassal always receives a ' fief,' and a ' fief ' is held by none other than a vassal. Estates of allodial land, that is land which the original owner had held in fee-simple, not as a benefice, frequently formed little states of their own; if the pretensions of the owner were made good, they were distinctly recognised by the general government as independent states. F. was prevalent over Western Europe from the tenth to the thirteenth century; even where allodial lands were numerous, the real government was completely local. At the same time it is noteworthy that the theory of the state, with an almost absolute king at its head, was never totally allowed to lapse even in the palmiest days of the feudal system. The kings themselves never allowed the barons' claim to independence, and thus the decline of F. was simply the conversion of theories into facts once more. The ideal feudal system may be seen in the legal theory (see Blackstone's *Commentaries* for this), and this theory corresponds generally to the actual facts prevailing. But it must be remembered that such a regular organisation as outlined in the legal theory nowhere existed in practice. A rough system of organisation was what obtained in most places, and no satisfactory idea of wages or details can here be given. The national feudal systems of the different countries of Europe presented many constitutional points of difference, and so exercised a different influence on the history of each country. *See* ENGLISH LAW and HISTORY, FRANCE, SCOTLAND, GERMANY, etc., for details of these systems. *See also* articles on

FIEF, VILLEINAGE, SCUTAGE, KNIGHT SERVICE, HIDE, VASSAL, etc, *See* J. T. Abdy, *Feudalism*, 1896; E. de Laveleye, *De la propriété et de ses formes primitives*, 1891; Stubbs, *Constitutional History*, 1866; Leon Gautier, *La Chevalerie*, 1884 (trans. by H. Frith, 1889); J. H. Round, *Feudal England*, 1895, and *Domesday Book and Beyond*, 1897; Vinogradoff's *English Society in 11th Century*, 1908; Henri Sée, *Les Classes rurales et le régime domanial*, and *L'Histoire des institutions politiques de l'ancienne France;* V. Manzel, *Die Entstehung des Lebenswesens*, 1890; H. Brunner, *Grundzuge der deutschen Rechtsgeschichte*, 1901, etc.

**Feu de joie,** a discharge of musketry given as a salute on occasions of public rejoicings. The guns are let off one after another at quick but regular intervals, thus producing a running fire.

**Feuerbach,** a tn. of Würtemberg, Germany, 2½ m. N.W. of Stuttgart. Pop. about 17,600.

**Feuerbach, Anselm** (1829–80), a Ger. painter, *b.* at Spires. His first work of great merit was ' Hafiz at the Fountain,' 1852. After a visit to Italy, his subjects were drawn largely from ancient history and mythology, and before long he was recognised as the leading painter of the Ger. classic school. His chief works are : ' Iphigenia in Tauris,' ' Orpheus and Eurydice,' ' Pietà,' and ' Dante at Ravenna.' *See* Life by Allgeyer-Neumann (2nd. ed., 1904).

**Feuerbach, Ludwig Andreas** (1804–72), a Ger. philosopher, fourth son of Paul J. A. Feuerbach, *b.* at Landshut in Bavaria, and educated at Heidelberg, Berlin, and Erlangen. His first work, *Gedanken über Tod und Unsterblichkeit*, 1830, an attack on the doctrine of personal immortality, was followed by *Abälard und Heloïse*, 1834. In 1837 he married a woman of some means, and was thus enabled to devote his time to study and reading, which resulted in the publication of *Das Wesen des Christentums*, 1841, translated into English by George Eliot under the title of *The Essence of Religion*, 1853. This work is an interesting attempt to prove that God, or the Absolute, is an outward projection of man's inner self, only existing in the human consciousness of the infinite. F. thus denies the existence of God apart from man, and that the highest good is created in man's consciousness as an expression of his human needs. He was made much of by the revolutionary party, who degraded his philosophy into atheism. His complete works appeared in ten volumes (1846–66). Consult M. Meyer, *L. Feuerbach's Moralphilosophie,*

1899; A. Lévy, *La Philosophie de Feuerbach*, 1904; and Karl Grün's Biography, 1874.

**Feuerbach, Paul Johann Anselm Ritter von** (1775–1833), a celebrated Ger. writer on criminal law, *b.* at Frankfort-on-Main, and educated at the university of Jena. His *Kritik des natürlichen Rechts*, 1796, followed by *Anti-Hobbes*, 1798, attracted much attention, and in 1801 he was appointed professor at Jena, and in 1802 accepted a similar position at Kiel. He became second president of the Court of Appeal at Bamberg (1814), and first president of the Court of Appeal at Anspach (1817). His works include *Merkwürdige Criminal-rechts-fälle*, 1808–11; *Betrachtungen über das Geschworenengericht*, 1811, and *Kaspar Hauser*, 1832. A collection of his *Kleine Schriften* was published in 1833. The *Leben und Wirken* were edited by his son Ludwig (2 vols.), 1852.

**Feuillans, Congregation of,** a reformed branch of the Cistercians, instituted during the sixteenth century by Jean de la Barrière, the abbot of a Cistercian monastery in Feuillans. The stricter rules laid down by La Barrière were ultimately confirmed by Pope Sixtus V., and a convent for the new congregation was founded in the Rue St. Honoré, Paris, by Henry III.

**Feuillet, Octave** (1821–90), a Fr. novelist and playwright, *b.* at Saint-Lô in La Manche. He was intended for a diplomatic career, and was for a while cut off by his father on declaring his resolution of adopting a literary career. He contributed to the *Revue Nouvelle* and *Revue des Deux Mondes*, but made his first definite success with his novel *Bellah* (1852), reprinted from the latter paper. This was followed by *La Petite Comtesse*, 1857; *Dalila*, 1857; and *Le Roman d'un Jeune Homme Pauvre*, 1858. He also wrote many comedies, which had long runs, but have not retained their popularity. His best work in fiction was done during his later years, and include *Sibylle*, 1862, his masterpiece; *Monsieur de Camors*, 1867; *Julia de Trécœur*, 1872; and *La Morte*, 1886. He was elected to the Academy in 1863.

**Feuilleton** (a diminutive of Fr. *feuillet*, leaf of a book), a supplement of a political newspaper devoted to literary and art criticism, gossip about the fashions, epigrams, and *bons mots*. It was not usually printed on separate paper, but divided from the political part of the newspaper by a line or by smaller print. It was first adopted in the *Journal des Débats* under the editorship of Bertin, and was so popular as treated by the Abbé Geoffroy that it became a permanent feature in Fr. journalism. The same kind of *causerie* may be found in Eng. papers, but the name F. is used in England exclusively to denote an instalment of a serial story.

**Féval, Paul Henri Corentin** (1817–87), a French novelist and dramatist, *b.* at Rennes. Educated for the Bar, he abandoned a legal profession for literature. His chief novels are: *Le Fils du Diable*, 1846; *Le Bossu*, 1858; *Le Poisson d'Or*, 1863; and *Les Compagnons du Trésor*, 1872.

**Fever** (Lat. *febris*, from *fervere*, to burn), a condition of the body characterised by a temperature above the normal, and accompanied by disturbances of normal functions. The feverish condition is symptomatic of a large number of diseases, but the term is particularly applied to those morbid conditions where high temperature is the predominating symptom; that is, where the rise of temperature is practically a measure of the severity of the disease. The normal temperature of the body is between 98° and 99° F. (about 37° C.); when the temperature is above 103° F. the febrile condition (*pyrexia*) is established; at 106° the condition is known as *hyperpyrexia;* if the temperature rises above 107°, a fatal termination to the disease may be expected. The cause of rise of temperature may be increase of heat-production owing to stimulated oxidation or a decrease in heat-elimination owing to disturbance of the functional activity of the heat-eliminating organs, notably the skin. The greater factor is probably the latter, as in cases of F. due to the action of micro-organisms it has been found that the increase of combustion due to the struggle between the white corpuscles and the bacteria does not produce much rise of temperature. On the other hand, the destructive action of the bacteria and the consequent disintegration of protoplasm are accompanied by a proportionate disability of the cutaneous vessels to effect adequate elimination of heat. The febrile condition is usually ushered in by shivering and alternate phases of cold and heat. Although during the cold fits the skin is clammy and the patient complains of lack of heat, the internal temperature is usually as high as in the hot fits, the sensations felt by the patient being due to nervous disturbance. The pulse is generally rapid and weak, and the secretions are generally disturbed. The digestive secretions are abnormal, leading to loss of appetite and disturbed excretions. There is often constipation, unless diarrhœa is characteristic of the disease, as in dysentery, and the urine is scanty and loaded with sediment. The liver also fails in its functions, and the bile secretion is altered, if not suppressed. The general failure of the nutritive functions leads to wasting and feebleness, the nervous structures are modified and the patient may suffer from delirium. Diseases in which F. occurs may be classified as idiopathic Fs., where the rise of temperature is a predominating factor; and secondary Fs., where other symptoms predominate. The diseases more strictly called Fs. are usually associated with the presence of specific micro-organisms, and are generally infectious. Inflammation of certain organs and tissues is often accompanied by general F., and is called by that name as a secondary or popular title. Thus acute rheumatism is known as rheumatic F., meningitis as brain F. The treatment of F. is usually determined by the cause. As a temporary or soothing measure, the administration of such febrifuges as antipyrin and antifebrin is useful, unless contra-indicated by other symptoms. The application of cold in any form is often resorted to, particularly in the way of sponging, or the application of the cold pack, which consists of wrapping the patient in blankets wrung out of cold water. These measures must, however, be administered with care.

**Feydeau, Ernest Aimé** (1821–73), a Fr. author, *b.* in Paris. His first publication was a volume of poetry, *Les Nationales* (1844), but he was far more successful in writing fiction, for which he showed a genuine talent. In *Fanny* (1858), *Sylvie* (1861), and *Le Roman d'une jeune Mariée* (1857) he depicts the corrupt manners of an immoral age. His other works include: *Du Luxe des Femmes, des Mœurs, de la Littérature et de la Vertu,* 1866; *Histoire générale des usages funèbres et des sépultures des peuples anciens* (1857–61); and *L'Allemagne en 1871* (1872), a caricature of contemporary German life.

**Fez, or Faz,** a sacred city of Morocco, about 85 m. S. of the Mediterranean Sea, and 100 m. E. of the Atlantic Ocean; it lies in a valley, shaped like a pear, and surrounded by orange groves, olive plantations and fruit orchards. The R. Wad-el-Jubor flows through the neighbourhood, and enters the Wad-el-Sebu, about 6 m. northward of the city. The former stream divides the town into two parts, the old part, Fas-el-bali, being on the right bank, and the modern, Fas-el-djedid, on the left bank. Viewed from a distance, Fez has a strikingly handsome appearance, and is celebrated as a 'holy city' of Islam, and a seat of learning. The mosque of

Karueen is said to be the largest in Africa and is used as a kind of university by over a thousand students. The mosque of Muley Edris, built nearly 1100 years ago by the reputed founder of F., is held to be so sacred that any approach by Christian or Jew is forbidden. The interior of the city is not so pleasing. The walls are decayed, and ruined buildings are to be seen on every hand. The streets are narrow and scarcely ever penetrated by the sun. Commercially, Fez is one of the busiest centres of N.W. Africa. The exports are olives, fruits, caraway seeds, citrons, honey, olive oil, hides and leather, tallow, ostrich feathers, ivory, gold, silk scarves, sashes, etc. The fez is also manufactured. There is a regular caravan trade with the interior cities of Africa. The native industries are morocco leather goods, pottery, and gold and silver ware. Fez was founded in 808 by Muley Edris, and it became the capital of the W. African Mohammedan states. In the tenth century, pilgrimages were made to Fez, instead of to Mecca. It was incorporated with Morocco in 1548. In 1911 the city was besieged by hostile tribesmen, but relieved by the Fr. general Moinier. Pop. about 81,000, of whom 70,000 are Moslems, 7500 Jews, and 3500 Europeans, mostly French.

**Fez,** a crimson skull-cap, forming the national head-dress of the Turks. It was so called, because the place of its sole manufacture was formerly Fez in Morocco. France, Germany, and Switzerland also make fezes now. They are brimless and are ornamented with a tassel on the centre of the crown. The dye used for them is obtained from small berries which grow in profusion in the neighbourhood of Fez.

**Fezzan,** a country situated S. of Tripoli, N. Africa, and transferred to Italy, with the rest of Tripolitania, under the Treaty of Ouchy (Oct. 1912). It extends 390 m. from N. to S., and 420 m. from E. to W., and has an area of 156,000 sq. m. It consists of a desert, enclosing numerous oases, and bordered by low ranges of hills. The Jebel-es-Soda or Black Mountains and the Haruj-el-Aswad cross the country on the N. The climate is even and healthy on the whole, as it does not lie within the tropical rain zone; rain is not frequent. Water, however, is found plentifully near the surface of the ground. There are five grain harvests annually; wheat, barley, melons, turnips, and cotton are cultivated, while figs, dates, olives, almonds, henna, alfa, oranges, and grapes form the chief wealth of the country. The principal towns are Murzuk, the capital, and Sokna,

Germa, Gatron, Tejerri, etc. Pop. at least 50,000.

**Ffestiniog** (place of hastening), a par. and tn. of Merionethshire, Wales, situated about 20 m. N.W. of Bala, and 8 m. from Portmadoc. It is the centre of a slate-quarrying district. Pop. 9674.

**Fiacre**, or **Fiacrach, Saint** (Celtic *Fiachra*), (*d. c.* A.D. 670), an Irish anchorite, who was allowed by the Bishop of Meaux (in France) to build a little monastery at Breuil. During life he was famed for his miracles, and after death they were long wrought near his shrine. In 1568 his remains were carried for safety to the cathedral of Meaux, where they still rest. The Hôtel St. Fiacre of Paris, which was named after him, gave its name to a kind of cab (*fiacre*).

**Fians,** an anglicised form of *Fiann,* or *Feinne,* of which the English Fenians is a variation. It is rather uncertain exactly what the Fiann were; what is certain is that the name is derived from Finn MacCool, or Finn MacCumaill, who is the central figure of the later heroic or Ossianic cycle of Irish legend. In Scotland Finn MacCool is called Fingal. Finn was a posthumous child, and was at first called Demni. He was the leader of the F., concerning whom the general opinion is that they were a kind of militia or standing army, which was drawn from all quarters of Ireland to assist in the repulsion of enemies, particularly those from over the sea. The headquarters of the F. was at Almu (Allen) in co. Kildare, where Finn himself usually resided, with several contingents of his followers; the rest were posted at various places throughout the country. The adventures of the F. in war, love, and hunting are the subject of many tales and legends. The admission to this band of warriors was only gained after peculiar and trying ceremonies of initiation. Dr. Skene considers the F. to have been a distinct race, which preceded the Irish and Scottish Gaels and the Germanic people of 'Lochlan' (Scandinavia). The chief figures of the F. were Ossian, the son of Finn MacCumaill, Oscar, the grandson, and Diarmait O'Duibue; the latter eloped with the destined bride of Finn, Granme, the daughter of Cormac MacArt (*q.v.*); the story of this is a well-known legend. The process whereby Finn became associated with the reign of Cormac MacArt is by no means clear; by the year 1000 he was so associated and has been a popular hero for more than 800 years; primarily he is regarded as one with magical powers, and as a great poet. Finn can be shown to have been originally a figure in the traditions of

Leinster and Munster previous to the Viking age; it is impossible that such a band as the F. existed in the second and third centuries, as a number of sages of much earlier date than those which state so have no mention of them. See J. F. Campbell, *Leabhar na Feinne,* 1872; W. F. Skene, *The Dean of Lismore's Book,* 1862, with introduction; D. MacRitchie, *Fians, Fairies and Picts,* 1893; J. G. Campbell, *The Fians,* 1891.

**Fiasco** (an Italian word meaning 'bottle') has long been used in connection with the Italian stage to draw attention to faults in either singing or acting. Perhaps the modern sense of failure is a metaphorical transference from the bursting of a bottle. The word was early borrowed by other nations of Europe, and in this country it is used indifferently of any event which comes utterly to grief.

**Fiat,** a decree, order, or warrant of a judge, or the Attorney-General, or a Secretary of State, ending with *fiat ut petetur. i.e.* let it be done as is asked. One of the commonest instances of its application is in the case of a petition of right for redress of an injury at the hands of the crown (*q.v.*); where a subject suffers such injury he may not sue the crown in the ordinary way, by reason of the maxim that the 'king can do no wrong'; he therefore presents a 'Petition of Right' to the Home Secretary setting out the facts and asking that right be done him in the matter. If the Home Secretary grants his F. the question is decided by proceedings not dissimilar to those of an ordinary action.

**Fiber Zibethicus,** *see* MUSK-RAT.

**Fibre** and **Fibrous Substances** (from Lat. *fibra*), the slender filaments which compose other bodies, which may be either animal, vegetable, or mineral, and are utilised in manufactures. Those used in the arts are either of animal or vegetable origin, with the exception of asbestos, which is mineral. An animal F. of great importance is that of the camel, which is made into excellent cloth, while the hair of the cow makes an inferior woollen cloth. A F. of a silky quality is derived from the byssus of a large shell-fish found in the Mediterranean, and which is used for the making of shawls and gloves. The dicotyledonous plants yield the most important textile F. of vegetable origin, of which flax, hemp, rhea, and jute are good examples. The most valuable is the cotton plant, consisting of hairs all round its seeds. Coir F. is obtained from the husk of the nut of the coconut palm.

**Fibrin,** a protein derived from blood. It is thought that it arises from the action of a ferment upon fibrinogen. F. is only a constituent of blood after it has left the arteries, being formed during the process of coagulation or clotting. Analysis reveals that in 100 parts there are 52·6 parts of carbon, 21·8 oxygen, 17·4 nitrogen, 7 hydrogen, and 1·2 sulphur. It reacts like other proteids, is insoluble in water, highly elastic, tough, and jelly-like. If the blood-plasma of the horse is heated to 55° C., a purer F. is obtained than by beating a blood-clot with twigs. In this latter case globulin and hæmoglobin are mixed with the F. which adheres to the wood.

**Fibroline,** a yarn made from flax, jute, and hemp waste. It is used with linen or cotton yarn for the backs of carpets and similar purposes.

**Fibula,** the splint-bone of the leg, being situated behind the 'tibia,' and extending from the knee to the ankle. It is composed of a slender four-sided shaft and two larger extremities. Ligaments fastened to a roughened surface bind this bone to the tibia. The projecting ankle is formed by the 'external malleolus,' which is a downward projection of the lower end. This extremity articulates with the astragalus, and the upper or head with the upper portion of the tibia. The bone at the back of the astragalus, known as 'os trigonum,' is the lower of the two pressure epiphyses.

ANGLO-SAXON
FIBULA
Silver set with garnets

**Fibula** (a Latin word from *figere*, to fasten), a clasp, buckle, or brooch. Fibulæ or safety-pin brooches were known to the Mycenean age, which is pre-Homeric.

**Fichte, Immanuel Hermann von** (1797–1879), a German philosopher; lectured on philosophy at the University of Bonn from 1836 to 1842, and afterwards was appointed to a chair in Tübingen. In his *System der Ethik*, 1850–53, and his *Psychologie*, 1864–73, etc., he tries to reconcile Herbart and Hegel. Disliking the pantheism of the latter, he was drawn rather towards the theism of Leibnitz and strove to realise philosophically the personality of God.

**Fichte, Johann Gottlieb** (1762–1814), a German philosopher of Swedish descent, *b.* in Upper Lusatia. His early precocity aroused the interest of a local dignitary, Baron von Miltitz, who gave him an excellent education; and after passing through Pforta, where he read Lessing and Goethe, he entered Jena University to study theology. He was now self-dependent, and the next few years found him occupied in private teaching and writing. In 1788 he became a tutor at Zürich, but this relief was short-lived, and settling at Leipzig he was compelled to turn again to literary hack-work for a livelihood. About this time he first studied Kant—an important event in his mental development, which thoroughly reversed the fatalistic tendencies shown in his early *Aphorisms on Religion*, 1790, the result of reading Wolff and Spinoza at Jena. He even commenced a 'popular version' of Kant's *Critique*, but this was left unfinished. Shortly after this, he made Kant's personal acquaintance and submitted a treatise. *A Critique of Revelation*, which Kant approved so highly that he secured its publication in 1792; and F. was at once acclaimed as a significant philosophical force. This success enabled him, in 1793, to marry Johanna Maria Rahn, to whom he had become engaged at Zürich three or four years before; and for the next few months he remained in Switzerland, studying and developing Kantian ideas and principles. In 1794 he secured the chair of philosophy at Jena, and won immediate recognition and renown for his brilliant lectures. These early lectures formed the nucleus of the Fichtean system, and in the same year he published three volumes on the *Theory of Knowledge*. His practical philosophy was given in the *Foundation of the Laws of Nature*, 1796, and the *System of Moral Philosophy*, 1798, his most important work. Meanwhile, from 1795–8 he had been joint editor of the *Philosophical Journal*, and had incidentally become the friend of Goethe, Schiller, Schelling, the Schlegels, Tieck, and Novalis. But in 1798 trouble arose through a paper published in that journal, and the following year F. had to resign from Jena, charged with atheism and disowned by Kant. The rest of his life was practically passed in Berlin with the Schlegels and Schleiermacher; the chief literary results being the *Vocation of Man*, 1800, the *Exclusive Commercial State*, 1800—a socialistic thesis—and *The Way to a Blessed Life*, 1806. In 1810 he was appointed rector at the new Berlin University. With the exception of his lectures on transcendental logic (1812), none of his subsequent work covers any important fresh ground; but during the struggle for national independence he earned some distinction as a patriotic lecturer (1813). F.'s philosophy, known as subjective idealism, aimed at a complete exposition of the fundamental laws and principles which govern cognition. He contends that subject and object are absolutely identical and that the individual ego, the human mind, is non-existent apart from the absolute ego, the divine and infinite spirit of all things, God. ' Knowledge is not merely knowledge of itself, but of being, and of the One Being, God, that really is.' All realities, animate and inanimate, are but sensuous phenomena, material expressions of their essential divine idea, and they have no separate existence, but are the product of the human soul, divinely inspired. The majority of men live in relation to the superficial appearances of things, ignorant of their divine essence ; it is for the philosopher and the man of letters to discover and interpret the fundamental spiritual ideas, of which the appearance is merely a vesture. F.'s influence on philosophy and literature has been enormous ; Hegelian idealism and Emersonian transcendentalism are considerably indebted to him, both for idea and for idiom of expression, whilst Schopenhauer's writings are almost wholly evolved from F.'s later works. *See* HEGEL, IDEALISM, etc.

**Fichtelgebirge** (pine mountains), a mountain system of Bavaria, Germany ; it forms the nucleus of three mountain ranges, the Erzegebirge, Frankenwald, and Böhmerwald. The highest summits are the Schneeberg, 3461 ft., and the Ochsenkopf, 3334 ft. The mountains were once covered with pines. The geological formation is chiefly granite, slate, gneiss, and basalt ; the minerals obtained are iron, sulphur, lead, copper and vitriol. Marble and stone are quarried and the inhabitants are engaged in charcoal burning, forges, and blast furnaces. There are extensive tracts of forest land. Alexanderstad is a noted holiday resort.

**Ficino, Marsilio** (1433–99), an Italian philosopher, was a true son of the Renaissance. Fortunate in the patronage of Cosmo de' Medici, he secured, in 1463, the presidency of a Florentine college. F. fanned the awakening interest in Gk. philosophy by his translation of Plato, and unlike the scholars of the succeeding generation was first a Christian and afterwards a Platonist. The incomplete fusion of ecclesiastical doctrine and pagan thought gave a curious flavour to his sermons, when in 1473 he entered the church.

**Ficksburg**, a tn. of S. Africa, in the Orange Free State, near the Caledon R. In the vicinity are diamond mines and petroleum wells. Petrified fish are found in the fossilised ooze of the Wonderkop. Pop. 3000.

**Fiction, Legal,** some fact, state of things, or proposition assumed to be true by the law avowedly for the purposes of justice or convenience. Fs. in law, though often ridiculous enough, have generally had their origin in some defect in the existing laws or course of procedure, and have in a measure exemplified the desire of judges or other interpreters of law to make the law, in particular cases where some change was necessary, conform to the general and progressive opinion of society. Many Fs. have, far from being injurious, been highly beneficial, and have paved the way to legislative remedy. Social necessities, says Maine (*Ancient Law*), and social opinion are always in advance of law. Law is static, most societies progressive, and Maine thinks that legal Fs. were historically the first agency by which law was brought into harmony with society. But in this sense of the relation of F. to the evolution of law, Maine uses the term to signify any ' assumption which conceals or affects to conceal the fact that a rule of law has undergone alteration, its letter remaining unchanged, its operation being modified.' In this wider signification the term embraces not only Fs. in English law, and Roman law, but the whole of English case-law (Bentham's ' judge-made law '), and the Roman *responsa prudentum* (answers or opinions of jurists of repute) as resting on a fictitious basis. It is a jurisprudential commonplace that the law is constantly and more or less imperceptibly changed by judicial decisions, although all decisions profess to do no more than apply settled principles to new facts ; and similarly with the authoritative answers of the ancient Roman jurisconsults. A good instance of the utility of a legal F. in Roman law was that of adoption which overcame the narrow caste nature of a legal *familia*, by permitting the family tie to be artificially created by adoption or arrogation. Some instances of Fs. in English law are : the proposition that husband and wife are one ; the assumptions in such ancient writs as those of *quo minus* by which the Court of Exchequer (*q.v.*) obtained its common law jurisdiction, and *vi et armis* by which the King's Bench court usurped much of its jurisdiction (*see* KING'S BENCH DIVISION) ; the suppositions involved in *fines* and *recoveries* (*q.v.*) ; and the assumption of the existence of the two legendary and much ridiculed litigants ' John Doe ' and

'Richard Roe,' with the object of applying the readier process of an action of ejectment to the trial of questions relating to title to land.

**Ficus,** a genus of Moraceæ, chiefly indigenous to tropical forests, and containing species with widely diverse characteristics. *F. carica,* the fig-tree of commerce, a native of Asia Minor and Syria, is now found in a wild state in the countries bordering on the Mediterranean. The fruit of the wild variety has not the succulence of the cultivated kinds. *F. elastica* is the indiarubber tree, and is frequently cultivated in small pots ; *F. religiosa,* the peepul, or sacred tree of the Brahmans and Buddhists, yields a gum resembling caoutchouc ; *F. indica,* also called *F. bengalensis,* is the banyan, and yields an inferior rubber, the bark and roots also furnishing a coarse rope-fibre.

**Fidanæ,** an ancient tn. of Italy, situated on the Tiber, 5 m. from Rome. In the reign of Tiberius a gladiatorial show took place here, during which the amphitheatre collapsed and destroyed nearly 50,000 people. No ruins of F. now exist, but it is identified with the modern Costello Giubileo.

**Fiddle,** see VIOLIN.

**Fidei-commissum,** in civil law (*q.v.*), denotes a trust. Scots legal writers generally refer the origin of their law of trusts and trustees to the Roman conception of a F. In Roman law a F. was an informal bequest or devise made to the heir or legatee (who in such a case was called the *fiduciarius*), with a request attached to it that the fiduciarius or trustee should deliver the property to some named person who was incapable of taking directly under the will (the fidei-commissarius or beneficiary). At first the rights of the beneficiary were unenforceable and could only be made good by entreaty. The Emperor Augustus, probably under the inspiration of Christianity, established a system which made fidei-commissa obligatory on the trustee, and appointed a special magistrate, the prætor fidei-commissarius, to compel the trustee to carry out his obligations. For the most part fidei-commissa were created by means of codicils (*q.v.*). English legal historians, generally, are of the opinion that the lord chancellors (*q.v.*) borrowed the doctrine of the English use from the Roman law of trusts.

**Fidei Defensor** (Latin for ' Defender of the Faith '), a title conferred upon Henry VIII. by Pope Leo X. in gratitude for a pamphlet in which that sovereign had roundly abused the heretic, Martin Luther. It was granted in 1521, and was subsequently confirmed by parliament. Like the Spanish appellation, 'Most Catholic,' it is now naturally accorded to every king.

**Fidelity Guarantee,** a form of insurance for the benefit of employers, by which they are guaranteed against fraud, etc., of their employees. The rate of insurance varies, being sometimes 5*s.* per cent. and sometimes 40*s.* Generally, all the employees of a firm are guaranteed under one policy, and length of service, position, etc., are taken into consideration in fixing the premiums. The F. G. companies are : The Bankers' Guarantee and Trust, General Accident Guarantee Society, Law Accident, Ocean Accident, Provident Clerks' Guarantee and Accident, etc.

**Fides,** a goddess of ancient Rome, the personification of fidelity. Numa Pompitius is said to have instituted the festival of F., and to have built a temple to her on the Capitol. She was represented as a matron wearing a wreath of olive or laurel leaves, and carrying in her hand a basket of fruit.

**Fiduciary Issue.** In banking language, a fiduciary issue is that part of an issue of bank notes that is not backed by gold actually held by the bank. As the word fiduciary implies, it is an issue made on the ' faith ' of people in the reputation of the bank. In this sense all bills of exchange, cheques and promissory notes are ' fiduciary ' in so far as the assets behind them are undisclosed. From the time when the Bank of England lent its original Capital to the nation, thus commencing the National Debt, the extent of its fiduciary issue has been regulated by the government.

**Fief,** or **Fee Law,** first meant an estate held in trust, on condition that the person holding it rendered personal or other service to the lord who granted it. There were three varieties of tenures, free, base, and religious. The first consisted in following the lord of the land to battle ; the second were held in virtue of those services which more menial vassals did for their immediate superiors ; and the last were held by virtue of masses said by the priests to whom the land was granted. *See* ENTAIL and FEUDALISM.

**Field,** a term in heraldry for the ground, which is of a special colour, on which armorial bearings are displayed. *See* HERALDRY.

**Field, The,** ' the country gentleman's newspaper,' ranks first in the list of sporting papers. It was started about 1843, and was one of the many with which Bradbury and Evans were connected, both as printers and proprietors. Its earliest editor was

Field

758

Field

Mark Lemon, and Leech supplied
illustrations of hunting adventure.
One of its owners was Benjamin
Webster, the actor, who in time
acquired the whole property and sold
it to Serjeant Cox.

**Field, Cyrus West** (1819–92), founder
of the Atlantic cable, b. at Stockbridge, Massachusetts. At fifteen he
was a clerk in the store of A. T.
Stewart & Co., New York, and in
1840 started a paper business for
himself at Westfield, in which he was
so successful that he was able to
retire in 1853. He then began to
think about a trans-Atlantic telegraphic cable, and having enlisted
the sympathy of Peter Cooper and
other American capitalists, organised
the New York, Newfoundland, and
London Telegraph Company in
1854, and the Atlantic Company in
1856. The cable was completed by
1858 and was hailed with delight,
but it was not in proper working
order until 1866. He also interested
himself in the New York Elevated
Railroad.

**Field, David Dudley** (1805–94), an
American lawyer, b. in Haddam,
Connecticut. He took his degree at
Williams College in 1825, and was
admitted to the Bar in 1828. His
chief aim was the reform of the
judicial system of New York, and
with this in view he visited Europe
in 1836 and thoroughly investigated
the codes in England and the other
countries. In 1847 he was appointed
as the head of a state commission
to revise the practice and procedure of
law in New York. His publications
were: *The Reorganisation of the
Judiciary*, 1846; *Draft Outlines of an
International Code*, 1872.

**Field, Eugene** (1850–95), an American journalist and poet, b. at St.
Louis, Missouri. He studied at
Williams and Knox Colleges, and the
University of Missouri. He wrote for
various papers, but made his reputa-
tion when he became connected with
the *Chicago News* in 1883. He is,
however, chiefly known by his poems
of childhood, of which *Little Boy
Blue* is, perhaps, the general favourite.
His principal works are: *A Little
Book of Western Verse*, 1889; *A Second
Book of Verse*, 1892; *With Trumpet
and Drum*, 1892; *Love Songs of
Childhood*, 1894.

**Field, Frederick** (1801–85), an English divine, b. in London, and was
a direct descendant of Oliver Cromwell, of which he was very proud. He
was educated at Christ's Hospital
and Trinity College, Cambridge, and
became a fellow of his college in 1824.
In 1839 he edited Chrysostom's
*Homilies on St. Matthew*, and in 1842
he was presented by his college to

the rectory of Reepham, in Norfolk.
It was here he executed Chrysostom's
*Homilies on St. Paul's Epistles* between 1849 and 1862. In 1863 he
resigned his living and devoted his
time to Origen's *Hexapla*, which was
published in 1874.

**Field, John** (1782–1837), an English
musician, b. at Dublin. He made
his first appearance in 1794 at a London public concert, and in 1799 performed a concerto of his own composition. He gave concerts with
Clementi, and was received with
great favour. Chopin's 'nocturnes'
owe much, both in form and spirit,
to Field's.

**Field, Marshall** (1835–1906), American merchant, b. at Conway, Mass.
Was a clerk in a dry-goods firm, and
became partner; in 1865 was a
member of a firm which later, in 1881,
became Marshall Field and Co. This
was the largest dry-goods firm in the
U.S.A., and had branches in Europe.
He gave large gifts to Chicago University, and founded the Field
Columbia Museum.

**Field, Nathaniel** (1587–1633), actor
and dramatist, b. in Cripplegate.
In 1600 he acted in Ben Jonson's
*Cynthia's Revels*, in 1601 in the *Poet-
aster*, and in 1606 played the title
rôle in Chapman's *Bussy d'Ambois*.
He was the author of two plays: *A
Woman is a Weathercock*, which deals
with the inconstancy of woman, and
*Amends for Ladies*, which retracts
the charge. He also collaborated with
Massinger in the *Fatal Dowry*, and
prefixed verses to Fletcher's *Faithful
Shepherdess*.

**Field, Stephen Johnson** (1816–99),
an American jurist, b. at Haddam,
Connecticut, and was the brother of
David Dudley F. He was for some
time a partner in Dudley's firm, but
in 1850 went to California, where he
became judge of the Supreme Court
in 1857. In 1859 he was made chief-
justice, and in 1863 was appointed a
justice of the United States Supreme
Court. In 1880 he received sixty-five
votes on the first ballot for the presidential nomination. He retired from
the Supreme Court in 1897.

**Field, William Ventris Field, Baron**
(1813–1907), of Bakeham, English
judge; b. Aug. 21; son of Thos.
Flint Field, of Fielden, Bedfordshire. Educated at King's School,
Bruton, Somerset. From 1830 to
1840, member of the firm of Thompson, Debenham, and Field, solicitors,
Salter's-hall-court. Then entered
himself for Bar at Inner Temple.
Called, 1850; went Western circuit,
afterwards Midland. Took silk, 1864,
was made Bencher, 1865. In Feb.
1875, appointed judge of the Queen's
Bench. On Supreme Court rules

coming into force in 1883. F. was appointed by the Lord Chancellor to sit in chambers continuously for nearly a year, to establish a uniform practice. Decided some very important cases—notably Sharp *v.* Wakefield, which laid down the principle of unfettered magisterial discretion in renewal of drink-licences. Resigned, 1890 ; and on April 10 was given his peerage. Thereafter acted as judge in House of Lords and Privy Council. Died at Bognor, Jan. 23.

**Field Allowance,** a sum of money paid daily to officers of the British Army when they are on active service or at manœuvres, ' in aid of the expenses caused by their being placed under canvas.' The ' extraordinary ' F. A. which is given when troops are engaged in war ranges from £2 10*s.* to 1*s.* 6*d.,* according to the rank of the officer, while the ' ordinary ' F. A. which is given when troops are encamped at home ranges from £1 10*s.* to 1*s.*

**Field Artillery,** see ARTILLERY.

**Fielden, John** (1784–1849), English politician, *b.* at Todmorden, Lancashire. As a boy he worked in his father's factory, and in after years remembered the exhaustion caused by his daily toil, and was a keen supporter of the Ten Hours Bill which became law in 1847. He also took an active part in the agitation for parliamentary reform, and was, like Cobbett, very much against paper money. He published *The Curse of the Factory System,* 1836 ; *The Mischiefs and Iniquities of Paper Money,* 1832 ; *A Selection of Facts and Arguments in favour of the Ten Hours Bill,* 1845.

**Fieldfare,** or *Turdus pilaris,* belonging to Turdidæ, the thrush family, is a familiar winter visitor to the British Isles and Central Europe. It is gregarious in habit, and finds its summer home in the birch forests of Norway, Sweden, and Russia. The nest of the F. is of long fine grass with an intervening layer of mud ; it may be built in birch or fir trees at an elevation of 15 ft., has occasionally been seen quite near to the ground. This bird feeds on berries in hard weather, but also travels in flocks over the fields in search of slugs and other animal food. The plumage varies from ashy-grey to chestnut-brown, the underparts being a rich ochre, spotted with black.

**Field-glass,** an instrument used for viewing objects at a distance, composed of two telescopes, which are identical in construction, placed parallel to one another. It is easy to use and does not strain the eyes like some telescopes, indeed it has the advantage over that instrument in that it allows the use of both eyes. It is of great value to travellers, soldiers, and sailors, and is almost universally employed by the Navy in place of the long telescope used in Nelson's time. There are two kinds of Fs., the Galilean type and the prismatic. The Galilean, which is the ordinary F., consists of two lenses, an object lens and an eye-lens, the object-lens is convex, and the eye-lens concave. It was Porro, an Italian engineer, who discovered that the usual reversing lenses in a telescope could be replaced by a combination of prisms, but these could not be used until a suitable medium was found, owing to the great absorption of light. The prismatic F. was introduced in 1898, and is now in general use. Of this there are several varieties, the special one used by the field naturalists has extending arms which place the object glasses above the head, thus enabling the person using them to keep out of sight ; the object lenses, too, can be placed at any angle. The modern glass is made of magnalium with mountings of horn for the eye-pieces, and each eye-piece can be adjusted to suit each eye, and there must be two prisms in each tube. It is made in four different powers, magnifying three, six, or twelve diameters. The first is used for objects at a short distance, while the last, which does not cover such an area of view, is of great service to soldiers and naturalists.

**Fielding, Anthony Vandyke Copley** (1787–1855), an English water-colour landscape painter, was the pupil of John Varley. In 1810 he became an associate of  the Water-Colour Society and contributed largely to its exhibitions. In 1813 he was a full member, and was made president in 1831. His works are clever, but slight, his best pictures being his sea-pieces and aerial effects. There is a collection of his drawings in South Kensington Museum.

**Fielding, Henry** (1707–54), English novelist, *b.* at Sharpham Park in Somerset. He was educated at Melcombe and Eton, and also studied for a short time at Leyden. He returned to London in 1728, and began a long dramatic career by the publication of *Love in Several Masques,* which was played at Drury Lane. Several comedies and farces followed, and his burlesque, *Tom Thumb the Great,* is said to have evoked a laugh from Swift, who only laughed twice in his life. In 1735 F. married, and bought the little French theatre in the Haymarket, where he produced *Pasquin* and *The Historical Register,* but the Licensing Act of 1737 put an end to his dramatic labours. In 1742 *The History of the Adventures of Joseph*

*Andrews and of his friend W. Abraham Adams* was published. This was a parody on Richardson's *Pamela*, and was prompted probably by a feeling of reaction against the morbid tendencies of Richardson's work. The chief character in the book is Parson Adams, who is a ' noble example of primitive goodness and childlike Christian altruism,' and is perhaps F.'s finest and most original conception. In 1743 appeared three volumes of his *Miscellanies*, the third of which contained his strange *History of the Life of the late Mr. Jonathan Wild the*

HENRY FIELDING

*Great,* a satirical work which places F. second to Swift in ironic power. In 1749 his greatest novel, *The History of Tom Jones,* appeared ; this was popular from the very first, and has been praised by Hazlitt, Coleridge, and Byron, who calls its author ' our prose Homer.' In 1751 *Amelia* was published ; the plot in this is inferior to that of *Tom Jones,* but the descriptions and characters are very fine. His last work was his contribution to *The Covent Garden Journal,* 1752. After his death his *Journal of a Voyage to Lisbon* was published. *See* Lives by Scott and Dobson.

**Fielding, William Stevens** (1848–1929), originally a journalist, *b.* Nov. 24 in Halifax, Nova Scotia ; son of Chas. F. He was educated at Halifax, and was for twenty years connected with the Halifax *Morning Chronicle.* He resigned his position of managing editor of that paper to engage in the active duties of public

life and rose to be Prime Minister in 1884. In 1896 he resigned and was appointed Minister of Finance in the cabinet of Sir Wilfrid Laurier. As Minister of Finance he was charged with the readjustment of the Canadian tariff, and submitted to parliament the British preferential tariff, and the measures imposing a surtax on the products of Germany. In 1902 he was a representative of the Colonial Conference in London, and in 1907 was one of the king's plenipotentiaries for the negotiation of the Franco-Canadian Commercial Treaty in Paris. He was a member of the British Royal Commission on trade between Canada and the West Indies, 1909–10, and a governor of Dalhousie University. A Canadian delegate to League of Nations Assembly, 1922. P.C., 1923. Died at Ottawa, June 23.

**Field-marshal,** the highest rank in the British Army, was introduced by King George II. in 1736, although the title ' marshal ' was in existence much earlier, for Matthew Paris says that in 1214 King John constituted William Earl of Salisbury ' marescalcus ' of his forces. The ' marescalcus campi ' was originally one of a number of officials to whom the name of marshal was given. The marshal was responsible for order in court and camp, and on military expeditions it was the custom for two marshals to precede the army to select a site for the camp, and in time of peace they arranged for the king's lodging. In 1931 the Fs. were : Duke of Connaught, Viscount Plumer, Viscount Allenby, Sir William P. Robertson, the King of the Belgians, Sir W. R. Birdwood, Sir Claud W. Jacob, Sir George F. Milne, Lord Methuen, the Emperor of Japan, and His Majesty King Alfonso (the words "XIII of Spain " have now been omitted in the Army List.

**Field-mouse,** the name given to several species of rodents, which are allied to the ordinary mouse, the vole (*q.v.*), etc. *Mus sylvaticus,* the wood-mouse, is a great pest in fields and gardens, and hoards large quantities of grain ; *M. minutus,* the smallest of British mammals, makes a curious globular nest among reeds and grasses.

**Field-officers,** in the army, are those which rank above a captain, but below a general, viz. majors, lieutenant-colonels, and colonels. The captains, lieutenants, and sub-lieutenants are called company officers. F. are always mounted. *See* OFFICERS.

**Field of the Cloth of Gold** was the name given to the place between Guines and Ardres where King Henry VIII. met Francis I. in 1520. Henry meant to make a great impression in

Europe, and spared no pains to make the scene as magnificent as possible. He succeeded in his purpose, but the meeting was of little avail politically.

**Fields, James Thomas** (1817–81), an American publisher, author, and lecturer, *b.* in Portsmouth, New Hampshire, and was a partner in the publishing firm of Ticknor, Reed & Fields in Boston from 1839 to 1870. He was friendly with the chief writers of his time, both American and British, and the first collected edition of De Quincey's works (1850–55) was published by his firm. In 1862 he succeeded James Russell Lowell as editor to the *Atlantic Monthly*, but in 1871 he retired from business and devoted himself to lecturing and writing. His chief works were, *Underbrush*, 1877, and *Yesterdays with Authors*, in which he mentions his friendship with Thackeray, Dickens, Wordsworth, and others.

**Fierabras,** the name of a prose romance which was very popular in the fifteenth and sixteenth centuries. It was taken from a 'chanson de geste' relating to the Emir Balan, who was conquered by Charlemagne.

**Fieri facias,** *see* EXECUTION.

**Fiery Cross,** an ancient summons to arms which was used in Scotland and sent by messengers from place to place. The token was made of wood, generally in the form of a cross, which was first set on fire and then dipped in the blood of a goat. It was employed by the Highland chiefs on special occasions, especially in time of war, to summon the clan as quickly as possible. Roderick Dhu, in Scott's *Lady of the Lake*, used the F. C. to summon his clan to battle.

**Fieschi** (or **Fiesco**), **Giovanni Luigi, Count of Lavagna** (*c.* 1523–47), a Genoese nobleman who opposed the Republican government which Andrea Doria had restored. He formed a plot to establish an oligarchy, and was encouraged by Pope Paul III., the Duke of Parma, Francis I. of France, as well as by his brothers in Genoa. His object was to seize the fleet and hold the gates of the city. This was successfully accomplished and Andrea put to flight when it was discovered that F. was missing. He had accidentally fallen into the water and was drowned. *See* DORIA, ANDREA.

**Fieschi, Joseph Marco** (1790–1836), conspirator, *b.* at Murato, Corsica. He served as a soldier in Russia in 1812. In 1830 he obtained a government appointment, but was dismissed for fraud. He then began to prepare an 'infernal machine' to revenge himself on society. When this was ready he hid it in his lodgings in the Boulevard du Temple, Paris, and when Louis Philippe was passing along to the Bastille exploded it. Louis escaped unhurt, but several others were injured, and amongst them F. himself. His life, however, was saved for the stroke of justice, and he was executed with his accomplices Morey and Pépin.

**Fiesole,** a small tn. in the prov. of Florence, Italy, and 4 m. from the city of Florence. It is of great historic interest, and contains Etruscan and Roman remains. It was the ancient Fæsulæ, and from 63–62 B.C. was the headquarters of Catiline. There is a well-preserved Roman theatre, with stairways and entrance arches. The chief building is the cathedral, commenced in 1028. The episcopal palace and the palazzo del pretorio, or town hall, date from the thirteenth century. Its decay began in the Middle Ages, with the rise of Florence, and it has now only about 3000 inhabitants, whose chief occupation is straw-plaiting. The pop. of the commune of F. is over 10,000.

**Fiesole, Giovanni,** *see* ANGELICO, FRA.

**Fife,** a musical instrument similar to a flute, but which generally has only one key. It has a compass of about two octaves, and is usually pitched in B♭ or C. Only simple melodies can be executed on it, and it is generally played with the drum. The Army Drum and Fife Bands are still popular. *See* FLAGEOLET, PICCOLO, FLUTE.

**Fife, Alexander William George Duff, Duke of** (1849–1912), son-in-law of King Edward VII. and Queen Alexandra, descended from Alexander Duff of Keithmore, who was *b.* in 1624. From 1874–79 he represented Elgin and Nairnshire in parliament, and from 1908 was president of the County of London Territorial Force Association. He succeeded his father as sixth Earl of Fife in 1879, and was created Duke of Fife in 1889 on his marriage to the Princess Royal, Princess Louise Victoria Alexandra Dagmar, eldest daughter of the late King Edward. He had two daughters: Princess Alexandra, now Duchess of Fife, to whom Queen Victoria stood sponsor, *b.* in 1891, and Princess Maud, Queen Alexandra's god-child. On Dec. 13, 1911, he was wrecked in the *Delhi* off the Moroccan coast and rescued only with difficulty. He appears to have caught a chill and *d.* at Assuan, Jan. 29. His body was brought to England and interred at Mar Lodge, Braemar, the seat of the Fife family.

**Fifeshire,** a maritime co. of Scotland, forming a peninsula on its E. coast, between the Firth of Tay and the Firth of Forth. The R. Eden flows through the length of the county into St. Andrew's Bay, and its highest hills are E. Lomond, 1471 ft., and W. Lomond, 1713 ft. The agriculture of the county is in an advanced state, and coal is mined to the value of about £1,000,000 annually, the mines being at Dysart, W. Wemyss, Leven, Markinch, Dunfermline, Kelty, Lochgelly, Cowdenbeath, and Kirkcaldy; limestone, sandstone, ironstone, and shale are also worked. The chief manuf. is linen, which is carried on chiefly at Kirkcaldy and Dunfermline, but Kirkcaldy is also famous for its oilcloth and linoleum. The county is also noted for its breweries and tanneries as well as for its iron foundries and engineering works; shipbuilding, too, is extensively carried on, and most of the coast towns take part in fishing. The chief towns are Cupar, the county town, Dunfermline, St. Andrews, Kirkcaldy, etc. For purposes of government the county is divided into two divisions, E. Fife and W. Fife, both of which send a member to parliament. Area 504 sq. m. Pop. 22,925.

**Fifteen, The,** the year 1715, which is famous for the first Jacobite rebellion. The Earl of Mar raised the standard of King James, the Old Pretender, but was defeated by Argyll at Sheriffmuir.

**Fifth Monarchy Men,** a religious sect in England in the time of Cromwell, who thought his government was a preparation for the ' fifth monarchy,' during which Christ should reign on earth. They advocated a code of law based on that of Moses, and when they saw their hopes not likely to be fulfilled, turned against Cromwell. Their leaders were arrested, but after the Restoration the sect again gave trouble; the insurrection was suppressed, and Venner and ten others were executed for high treason.

**Fig** (Lat. *ficus*), the name given to the members of a genus of shrubs and trees which belong to the sub-order Urticaceæ, included in the natural order Moraceæ. Fs. are characterised by their pear-shaped receptacles which, by curving inward, form an almost perfect cavity, on the surface of which grow countless flowers, the sterile and fertile being intermingled. They abound in tropical and subtropical regions, occur in about 300 varieties, and range in size from small trailing shrubs to huge trees, one of which is known to have afforded shelter for 7000 men. The *F. Rumphii* and the *F. religiosa* are deemed sacred by both Buddhists and Brahmans. The latter, called also the ' peepul ' or ' bo,' is a large tree with heart-shaped leaves, and is cul-

tivated in Southern Asia. Caoutchouc is obtained in large quantities from the *F. elastica*, or India-rubber tree of the E. Indies—a tree remarkable for its pink buds and its great, shiny, oblong leaves, but, above all, for its gigantic roots, which group themselves snake-wise round the base. All over India the *F. bengalensis*, popularly known as the banyan, flourishes and covers yearly an ever-increasing area with its vast canopy of foliage and branches. For each branch sends down its own root, which, growing to the surface, becomes in its turn

FIG (*FICUS CARICA*)
Leaf and fruit (green Fig)

the parent to new growths, and so both roots and branches multiply apace. The dessert fruit of commerce is grown from the *F. Carica*, so called because, according to legend, the famous F. trees of Attica were originally imported from Caria in Asia Minor. In this species the leaves are deeply lobed in the cultivated tree, though often almost entire in the wild they grow alternate and are rough and deciduous. Single receptacles spring from the axils of the leaves, the numberless single-seeded pericarps being packed close together inside. In colour the fruit varies from pale yellow to purple and bluish-black. ' Caprification' was long since introduced as an artificial aid to fertilisation. Probably the F. is indigenous only in Asia Minor and Syria, spreading thence all along the Mediterranean. Cardinal

Pole introduced it into England, where with southern walls it can be cultivated with success, and in the United States it is grown profitably as far N. as Pennsylvania. The S. of France, the Spanish peninsula, and Asia Minor supply most of the Fs. for Great Britain, the best kinds being shipped from Smyrna. In the warmer climates there are two crops, one from the buds of last summer and the other and more plentiful crop from the spring shoots, which ripen in the autumn. In Southern Europe and Western Asia Fs. form an important article of food, being eaten fresh and also in the form of a mashed cake, whilst medicinally they are used for chronic constipation and also for gumboils. Fig wine is also brewed. Before being shipped abroad the Fs. are usually dried in the sun, or in ovens, being pulled and extended by hand during the process, after which they are compressed in wooden cases.

**Figaro**, a famous character of dramatic fiction, who made his first appearance in the *Barbier de Séville*, 1785, and the *Mariage de Figaro* of Beaumarchais. The word ' figaro ' seems to have meant ' wigmaker ' and to have been common to Spanish and Italian. Since Beaumarchais' time F. has become the type of ingenious roguery, intrigue, and cunning, who displays the utmost sang-froid in all his daring deceptions. He appears conspicuously in Mozart's opera, *Marriage of Figaro*, and Rossini's *Barber of Séville*, 1816, and is sometimes represented as a barber, sometimes as a valet de chambre.

**Figaro, Le**, a popular Fr. newspaper, which was started in 1854 by M. de Villemessant and his colleagues. In the early days its ready sale depended not a little on its light, chatty ' paragraphs,' which were introduced instead of the literary, but often rather ponderous, articles in vogue before. It was not until 1866 that the paper appeared daily. The first journal of the name, which, of course, was borrowed from Beaumarchais' well-known opera, was published in 1826, and was in circulation till 1833. During its short life it counted George Sand, Paul Lecroix, and Jules Janin among its contributors. The present paper in the early days was aggressive, and at one time was almost wrecked by the revolutionary articles of Rochefort. After the death (1879) of Villemessant, who had given *Le Figaro* a distinctly monarchical bias, the management passed into the hands of Francis Magnard, Périvier, and De Rodays. Its quieter tone, compared with the earlier issues, was largely due to the

good offices of Magnard, who *d.* in 1894. In politics the paper is Conservative, and in general it may be said to reflect the prejudices and ideas of the normal man in the street.

**Figeac**, the cap. of an arron. in the dept. of Lot, South-western France. Situated on the banks of the Célé, in a deep valley surrounded by vine-clad, rocky hills, it lies 32 m. E.N.E. of Cahors on the Orléans Railway. Brewing, cloth-weaving, dyeing, and tanning are the chief industries, but the town is notable for its picturesque old houses. Pop. 5860.

**Fighig**, or **Figig**, a walled oasis in the Sahara, 165 m. E.S.E. of Fez, near the frontier of Algeria in South-eastern Morocco. It is an entrepôt for the Timbuktu and Mecca caravans. Pop. about 15,000.

**Figueira da Foz**, a seaport, at the mouth of the Mondego, in the dist. of Coimbra. It is the terminus of the Guarda–Figueira and Lisbon–Figueira railways, and was formerly in the province of Beira. The exports are wine, olive oil, grain, and fruit. Pop. about 8000.

**Figueras**, a tn. and fortress on the Barcelona–Perpignan Railway, 14 m. S. of the French frontier, in Catalonia, Spain. F. is on the fertile plain of El Ampurdan. Ferdinand VI. (1746–59) built its citadel. Pop. 13,000.

**Figueroa, Francisco de** (1540–1620), Spanish poet, reveals in his pastorals and his blank verse, which he introduced into native literature, the influence of Italian literature. It was for his pastorals especially that his contemporary admirers gave him the ambitious title of ' Divine poet.'

**Figurate Numbers**, a succession of series derived from any arithmetical series. The series derived from the natural numbers is obtained as in the following table :

$$1, 2, 3, \quad 4, \quad 5, \quad 6, \text{etc.}$$
$$\text{1st order} \quad 1, 3, 6, \quad 10, 15, 21$$
$$\text{2nd order} \quad 1, 4, 10, 20, 35, 56$$

Here it is seen that the first order is obtained by adding 1, 2, 3, etc., terms of the natural numbers, the second order is obtained by adding 1, 2, 3, etc., terms of the first order, and so on. The numbers of the first order in the above case are called triangular, as equilateral triangles are formed with such numbers of points placed equal distances apart, thus : . . .

etc. Square F. N. are the first order obtained from the series 1, 3, 5, 7, 9 ... The first order is 1, 4, 9, 16 . . ., and

may be represented by

and so on. From the series 1, 4, 7,

764

10 . . . are obtained pentagonal numbers, 1, 5, 12, 22 . . .

**Figure,** in geometry, a diagram drawn to illustrate the truth of a proposition, whether a problem or theorem.

**Figured Bass,** *see* THOROUGH BASS.

**Figurehead,** the figure, statue, bust, or other device attached to a ship's prow immediately under the bowsprit. Merchant vessels used to have timber volutes or scrolls in place of figures, but the fashion of figureheads had gone out before the introduction of steamers, whose bows, therefore, are usually plain. The huge figurehead of the ' fighting *Téméraire* ' and many belonging to other ancient battleships may still be seen at Millwall.

**Figwort,** the name applied to the British species of *Scrophularia*. *S. nodosa* and *S. aquatica* are perennial herbs with brown flowers visited almost exclusively by wasps. They are used medicinally in treatment of the disease ficus.

**Fiji Islands** (formerly **Feejee** or **Fidji**), an island group to the N. of New Zealand, mainly extending between 16° and 19° S. They are mainly volcanic in origin. Generally speaking, on the south-eastern side of the islands are forest and jungle, whilst on the other, or lee-side, is grass land with a less proportion of timber. The climate is cool for the tropics, and though the rainfall varies greatly in the different islands, there are no months when some rain does not fall. Meteorological stations have been established at Mbau and Delanasan. The chief crops are sugar, maize, coconut, tobacco, coffee, arrowroot, a little tea, and cotton, of which the quantity has increased of late years. The natives of the island are most of them engaged in the plantations, but in addition, Indian coolies and labourers from other islands are introduced to work for a period of years ; these labourers and the conditions of work are wholly under the control of the government. Horses and sheep are reared, and there are a few wild cattle. The chief exports are sugar, fruit, copra, cotton, maize, tortoise shell, etc. ; the imports total about £1,500,000 annually, and the exports over £1,700,000. Most of the trade is done with New Zealand, New South Wales, and Victoria. The trade returns for 1927 showed 72,752 tons of sugar exports, valued at £1,125,215 ; £157,819 worth of bananas ; and 26,560 tons of copra, valued at £534,416. The cotton industry has again recently received attention and about a quarter of a million lb. of cotton and 500 tons of cotton seed are now exported. The total shipping tonnage entered and cleared at Fijian ports in 1927 was 1,278,757 of which 918,107 was British. The seaports of the islands possess good harbours, protected by coral reefs. The capital is Suva, on the south-eastern shore is Viti Levu ; the chief islands are Viti Levu (4250 sq. m.), Vanua Levu, Kandavu, Mango, Vulanga, Yathata, Vatuvara, Mothe, Mbau, and Mbalevu. They were discovered in 1643 by Tasman, and in 1874 were ceded by their king to Great Britain, and are now a British crown colony. The constitution of F. is regulated by letters patent of Feb. 9, 1929. There is an Executive Council, consisting of the Governor, the Colonial Secretary, and other high officials, together with two unofficial members nominated by the Governor ; and a legislative council consisting of the Governor and not more than twelve nominated members, seven elected members, and two native members. The natives retain a large share of self-government, and their system of village and district councils has been recognised, and improved, and supplemented by a triennial meeting of chiefs, over whom the Governor presides. The Education Ordinance, 1916, aims at the establishment of a system suitable to the needs of the colony as a whole and of the various races ; and a board of education has been created under a director of education. This board has power to establish government schools both secondary and primary, and to assist undenominational schools. There are two grammar schools at Suva for Europeans, one for boys and one for girls. There are 68 government and assisted schools, 22 for Indians, 33 for Fijians, and 8 for Europeans, other races and half-castes. The total number of pupils was about 5700 in 1929. There are also numerous primary schools conducted by Methodist and Roman Catholic missions, and village schools supervised by native teachers. The natives are a dark-coloured race of a Polynesian type ; they were formerly notorious cannibals, but have reformed in this respect. The total area of the islands is 7435 sq. m., and pop. over 170,000, of which the native Fijians number 89,500, Indians, 69,000, and Europeans, 4200, the remainder being Chinese, half-castes and Polynesians. The spelling of Fijian names varies considerably owing to the peculiar pronunciation.

**Filadelfia,** a tn., 13 m. S. of Nicastro, in the prov. of Catanzaro, Italy. Pop. 6200.

**Filament,** in botany, is the stalk of the stamen, at the apex of which is borne the anther or pollen case. F.

is also used to describe a combination of cells which are connected only by their contiguous ends, as in many algæ, hairs, etc.

**Filangieri, Gaetano** (1752–88), Neapolitan jurist and writer, was a barrister of note and a leader of the Liberal cause. For one year before his death he acted as financial minister to Ferdinand IV., but his *Science of Legislation* (1780–85) will ever be the solid basis of his fame. In this work he discusses the principles of justice both in theory and practice in such a way as to prove himself an historian of learning and true philosophical insight. The influence of the *Contrat Social* is traceable throughout.

**Filariasis,** a diseased condition due to the presence of the parasite *Filaria sanguinis hominis*, or allied forms. The adult Filaria was discovered by Bancroft of Brisbane, and its embryo was discovered in the blood by Dr. Timothy Lewis. The embryo is known as *microfilaria sanguinis hominis nocturna*; it inhabits the lymphatic vessels and makes its appearance in great numbers in the blood at night time. They are about ·35 mm. long. Other species are *microfilaria perstans*, which is found in the blood both day and night, and *microfilaria diurna*, which is found in the peripheral circulation only in the day-time. The larvæ inhabit certain species of gnats or mosquitoes. The larvæ are sucked from the blood by the mosquito and enter the stomach. They afterwards make their way to the base of the piercing apparatus, so that they can once more enter the body of a man when the mosquito bites. The alternative theory to this is that the filaria lives in the body of the mosquito until the death of its host, when it may be conveyed by wind to drinking water, by which it again enters the body of man. It has been observed that the blood of men may contain swarms of these parasites without any symptoms of disease being apparent. Under certain circumstances, however, they lead to dilatation of the lymphatics and a general disturbance of their function. The characteristic symptom of F. is the appearance of chyle in the urine. Chyle is the product of the digestion of fat; it is a liquid of milky appearance owing to the presence of small globules of fat, and under ordinary circumstances makes its way to the thoracic duct, ultimately appearing in the blood stream, where it undergoes combustion or is stored up as adipose tissue. When the lymphatics are obstructed by masses of filaria, the chyle is diverted from its normal course, and, besides causing hypertrophy of neighbouring tissues, ap-

pears in great quantity in the urine. The effect on the general organism is one of malnutrition and inflammation of the lymphatic vessels. In connection with the history of the parasite in its second host, the mosquito, it may be noted that the larvæ are not ejected when the mosquito is fed on banana pulp.

**Filberts** are the fruit of the cultivated *Corylus* or hazel ; they are oval, elongated nuts that have a mild, oily taste, which makes them pleasant food. In England they are extensively grown in Kent, some farmers having 100 acres under cultivation, which in a good year yield as much as 100 tons of fruit. As they weigh heavier unripe they are usually picked in September, whilst still green. Compared with the common hazels (*C. Avellana*), which yield cob-nuts, F. trees have a longer, less open cup or involucre and are more lacerated. The F. is enclosed in the laciniated leafy cups of the female flowers, which look like clusters of coloured styles at the extremities of buds ; their kernels are in some varieties surrounded by deep red pellicles. A F. tree, the stem of which rarely exceeds 2 ft., the tree itself being kept from 5 to 7 ft. high, is closely pruned each year, only the finest young wood, and the likeliest to bear blossom, being left.

**Fildes, Sir Luke** (1844–1927), Eng. painter, *b.* Oct. 18, at Liverpool ; son of Jas. Fildes of Chester. Studied art at the South Kensington and Royal Academy schools. He began his artistic life as an illustrator, and became a popular contributor to the *Cornhill* and *Graphic* ; and also executed woodcuts for Dickens's last novel, *Edwin Drood.* The subjects of his earliest paintings were often sad, not to say depressing—an effect emphasised by the grey coldness of his colour schemes. His ' Applicants for Admission to a Casual Ward ' (1874), and his pathetic ' Widower ' (1876) are the most powerful of this period. ' The Village Wedding ' (1883) and ' An Alfresco Toilette ' (1889), on the other hand, and likewise his more recent and warmer pictures of Venetian men and women, represent the happier side of life. His later work was portraiture. Thus in 1902 he painted King Edward VII., and in 1912 King George V. ' The Doctor ' (1892), which hangs now in the Tate Gallery, is exceptionally good. He became R.A., in 1887, and was knighted in 1906. He was made K.C.V.O. in 1918. Died at Kensington, Feb. 27.

**File,** a steel implement, with teeth or serratures on its surface, much used for abrading and shaping metals and other hard surfaces. The art of filing is known to most savage tribes, hard stone or fishes' teeth being generally employed. 'Single-cut files,' which are suitable for soft metals, have only one set of parallel ridges, whilst 'double-cut files' have two 'courses' or series of chisel cuts, the second, which is usually finer, being at an angle with the first. In shape they are various : ' flat ' files have a parallelogram for their section ; rat-tail files, a circle frequently tapered ; three-square files, an equiangular triangle. Most are 'bellied,' that is thicker in the centre, and in length they vary from ⅜ in. (a watchmaker's) to over 3 ft. (engineer's). Blanks are forged from bars of the best crucible steel and after being annealed and straightened are cut either by hand or by machine. The teeth are incised by a small stout chisel inclined at an angle of about 13° from the perpendicular, the chisel being hit sharply for each cut by a hammer. A skilled craftsman can strike as many as eighty blows an hour. The hardening and tempering of a file is a delicate operation, as excess of heat renders the steel brittle, and too little causes the teeth to wear down very rapidly, whilst hasty cooling often warps the metal and so spoils the tool. The chief difficulty in the way of making thoroughly reliable machinery for file-cutting is that of adjusting the force of the blow to the hardness of the steel.

**File** (from Lat. *filum*, a thread, through Fr. *fil*), used in the military sense as the opposite of a 'rank,' that is to say, it refers to an alignment from front to rear, one man being behind another, whilst 'rank' is an alignment abreast or from right to left. Two men now form a F., the Fs. being 'doubled' or 'trebled' if a denser formation is required : the number has been gradually reduced from sixteen, as it was in 1600. The 'rank and F.' of a regiment properly includes non-commissioned officers and corporals (rank), besides the private soldiers.

**Filelfo, Francesco** (1398–1481), Italian humanist; *b.* July 25, at Tolentino ; son of a working man. Educated at Padua. In 1417, called to teach eloquence and moral philosophy at Venice. Known as expositor of Virgil and Cicero. Secretary to Venetian consul-general, Constantinople, 1419. Taught Latin and Greek at Bologna from 1427, from 1440 at Milan—where Duke Filippo Visconti became his patron ; to the honour of whose successor, Francesco Sforza, F. dedicated an epic, the *Sforziad*. Went to Rome, 1475 ; became professor of Gk. at Florence, 1481, and *d.* there, July 31 of that year.

**Filey,** a fishing tn. and fashionable summer resort of East Riding, Yorkshire, situated 8 m. S.E. of Scarborough. The tn. is divided into two parts. The old town is just a fishing village, while the new, which has developed since 1840, consists of two tiers, with pleasure gardens between. F. contains the remains of a Roman harbour, which proves it to have been a Roman station of some importance. Pop. 4549.

END OF VOL. V.